D0410055

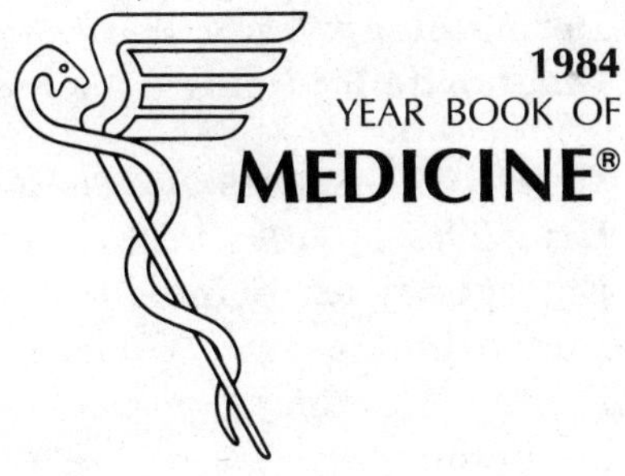
1984
YEAR BOOK OF
MEDICINE®

THE 1984 YEAR BOOKS

The YEAR BOOK series provides in condensed form the essence of the best of the recent international medical literature. The material is selected by distinguished editors who critically review more than 500,000 journal articles each year.

Anesthesia: *Drs. Kirby, Miller, Ostheimer, Saidman, and Stoelting.*

Cancer: *Drs. Clark, Cumley, and Hickey.*

Cardiology: *Drs. Harvey, Kirkendall, Kirklin, Nadas, Resnekov, and Sonnenblick.*

Critical Care Medicine: *Drs. Rogers, Booth, Dean, Gioia, McPherson, Michael, and Traystman.*

Dentistry: *Drs. Cohen, Hendler, Johnson, Jordan, Moyers, Robinson, and Silverman.*

Dermatology: *Drs. Sober and Fitzpatrick.*

Diagnostic Radiology: *Drs. Bragg, Keats, Kieffer, Kirkpatrick, Koehler, Sorenson, and White.*

Digestive Diseases: *Drs. Greenberger and Moody.*

Drug Therapy: *Drs. Hollister and Lasagna.*

Emergency Medicine: *Dr. Wagner.*

Endocrinology: *Drs. Schwartz and Ryan.*

Family Practice: *Dr. Rakel.*

Medicine: *Drs. Rogers, Des Prez, Cline, Braunwald, Greenberger, Bondy, Epstein, and Malawista.*

Neurology and Neurosurgery: *Drs. De Jong, Sugar, and Currier.*

Nuclear Medicine: *Drs. Hoffer, Gottschalk, and Zaret.*

Obstetrics and Gynecology: *Drs. Pitkin and Zlatnik.*

Ophthalmology: *Dr. Ernest.*

Orthopedics: *Dr. Coventry.*

Otolaryngology: *Drs. Paparella and Bailey.*

Pathology and Clinical Pathology: *Dr. Brinkhous.*

Pediatrics: *Drs. Oski and Stockman.*

Plastic and Reconstructive Surgery: *Drs. McCoy, Brauer, Haynes, Hoehn, Miller, and Whitaker.*

Psychiatry and Applied Mental Health: *Drs. Freedman, Lourie, Meltzer, Nemiah, Talbott, and Weiner.*

Sports Medicine: *Drs. Krakauer, Shephard, and Torg, Col. Anderson, and Mr. George.*

Surgery: *Drs. Schwartz, Najarian, Peacock, Shires, Silen, and Spencer.*

Urology: *Drs. Gillenwater and Howards.*

The YEAR BOOK of

Medicine®

1984

Edited by

DAVID E. ROGERS, M.D.
ROGER M. DES PREZ, M.D.
MARTIN J. CLINE, M.D.
EUGENE BRAUNWALD, M.D.
NORTON J. GREENBERGER, M.D.
PHILIP K. BONDY, M.D.
FRANKLIN H. EPSTEIN, M.D.
STEPHEN E. MALAWISTA, M.D.

YEAR BOOK MEDICAL PUBLISHERS, INC.
CHICAGO

Printed in U.S.A.

International Standard Book Number: 0–8151–7314–8

International Standard Serial Number–0084–3873

The editor for this book was Joan David, and the production manager was H. E. Nielsen

Table of Contents

The material covered in this volume represents literature reviewed up to August 1983.

Journals Represented

Acta Endocrinologica
American Heart Journal
American Journal of Cardiology
American Journal of Medicine
American Journal of Nephrology
American Review of Respiratory Diseases
Angiology
Annals of Internal Medicine
Annals of Otology, Rhinology and Laryngology
Annals of Rheumatic Diseases
Annals of Surgery
Antimicrobial Agents and Chemotherapy
Archives of Internal Medicine
Arthritis and Rheumatism
Blood
British Heart Journal
British Journal of Diseases of the Chest
British Medical Journal
Bulletin of the World Health Organization
Cancer
Chest
Circulation
Clinical Endocrinology
Clinical Nephrology
Clinical Pharmacology and Therapeutics
Clinical Radiology
Critical Care Medicine
Diabetes
Digestive Diseases and Sciences
European Heart Journal
Fertility and Sterility
Gastroenterology
Gut
Hepatology
International Journal of Cardiology
Journal of Allergy & Clinical Immunology
Journal of the American College of Cardiology
Journal of the American Medical Association
Journal of Applied Physiology: Respiratory, Environmental and Exercise Physiology
Journal of Clinical Endocrinology and Metabolism
Journal of Clinical Investigation
Journal of Infectious Diseases
Journal of Rheumatology
Journal of Thoracic and Cardiovascular Surgery
Kidney International
Lancet

Mayo Clinic Proceedings
Medicine
Nature
Nephron
Neurosurgery
New England Journal of Medicine
New Zealand Medical Journal
Pediatrics
Pfluger's Archiv: European Journal of Physiology
Postgraduate Medical Journal
Proceedings of the National Academy of Sciences
Quarterly Journal of Medicine
Radiology
Reviews of Infectious Diseases
Science
South African Medical Journal
Stroke
Surgery
Surgery, Gynecology and Obstetrics
Surgical Neurology
Thorax
Transplantation
Western Journal of Medicine

PART ONE

INFECTIONS

DAVID E. ROGERS, M.D.

Introduction

It's hard to believe that I've been at this task—that of editing this section of the YEAR BOOK—for 17 years. And how remarkable are the changes in the nature and patterns of infection during this period! Early on, I was mightily impressed by how profoundly each advance in medical technology altered the kinds of infections creating problems for patients and their doctors. That continues apace. Each improvement in cancer chemotherapy or surgery or invasive procedure has as its unwanted companion a new set of infections produced by microbes previously thought to be benign. You'll see evidence of that throughout this section.

In recent years, I've been similarly impressed by the fact that changes in our society—the way we live, our social mores, our speed of travel, the ways we eat or bathe or what have you—create equally impressive shifts in the patterns of disease seen by infection watchers.

Dr. Walsh McDermott used to say (and often demonstrate) that one could swiftly diagnose the technologic sophistication of any nation or region by a quick look at the kinds of infections that killed its inhabitants. I would now add that one can learn a lot more about their attitudes and culture from watching the infections that make them sick.

So this year we've tried a brief new section which we've called "Social Change and Infection." You'll see what I mean by the above statement as you go through the section.

My joy—and the education I obtain—in working through this section with my colleagues, Drs. William Schaffner and Allen Kaiser, continues unabated. Obvious to any of you who know me well: my erudition in expounding on many new aspects of infectious diseases—therapy, plasmid fingerprinting, prostaglandins, or suppressor cells—stems from their coaching. A fantastic amount of information changes heads during our last cooperative "city desk" effort. Most of what's new moves from them to me. I contribute the "this is the way it was" war stories. We enjoy it thoroughly. We hope you will too.

DAVID E. ROGERS, M.D.

1. Social Change and Infection

1-1 **Acute Rheumatic Fever: A Vanishing Disease in Suburbia.** There is no doubt that the incidence of acute rheumatic fever and the prevalence of rheumatic heart disease have declined considerably in North America and Western Europe during the past 50 years. Mack A. Land and Alan L. Bisno (Univ. of Tennessee Center for the Health Sciences, Memphis) retrospectively analyzed the incidence of acute rheumatic fever (ARF) in Memphis-Shelby County during the 5-year period from 1977 through 1981. Cases were identified by a review of the records of 12 of the 13 general medical-surgical hospitals in the area and by mail and telephone communication with 327 primary care physicians and neurologists.

Fifty-six patients with conditions diagnosed as ARF were identified. Of these, 15 failed to meet the modified Jones criteria. Sixteen of the 41 patients who met these criteria were diagnosed in Memphis,

INCIDENCE OF ACUTE RHEUMATIC FEVER BY RACE AND LOCATION OF RESIDENCE, MEMPHIS-SHELBY COUNTY, 1977–1981

	Inner City	Suburban and Rural
	BLACK	
All ages		
No. of cases	14	6
Incidence*	1.63	0.79
5-17 yr		
No. of cases	9	3
Incidence*	3.74	1.40
	WHITE	
All ages		
No. of cases	1	3
Incidence*	0.34	0.15
5-17 yr		
No. of cases	1	2
Incidence*	1.63	0.49

*Cases per 100,000 population each year.

(Courtesy of Land, M. A. and Bisno, A. L.: JAMA 249:895–898, Feb. 18, 1983; copyright 1983, American Medical Association.)

(1–1) JAMA 249:895–898, Feb. 18, 1983.

but resided elsewhere. The overall incidence of ARF in Memphis-Shelby County for the 5-year period was 0.64 cases per 100,000 population per year. The patients ranged in age from 3 to 57 years (mean, 19 years; median, 16 years), and the peak age incidence (1.88 cases per 100,000 population per year) occurred in patients 5–17 years of age. Blacks were affected by the disease considerably more often than were whites. Among blacks, the incidence of ARF was more than twice as great for those living in the inner city than for those living in the suburbs; a similar trend was seen among whites, but the incidence was considerably lower (table). The most prominent major signs of disease in all 41 patients were carditis and polyarthritis, occurring in 22 and 25 patients, respectively. An unusual finding was the occurrence of chorea in more than 25% of the cases. Seven (17%) of the 41 cases were recurrences; these 7 patients ranged in age from 10 to 58 years (mean age, of 28 years).

In Memphis, ARF remains primarily a disease of socioeconomically deprived black schoolchildren. In contrast, the disease is nearing extinction in the middle-class, predominantly white suburbs of Memphis-Shelby County. The extremely low incidence of ARF demonstrated in this study necessitates reevaluation of current strategies of prevention and diagnosis of this disease, as such strategies were developed in an era when ARF posed a much greater threat to the public health in the United States.

▶ [This is a fine contribution and a most satisfying change. Rheumatic fever has dramatically dropped in incidence in recent years. Data obtained in New York City during 1963–1965 suggested an incidence of 61/100,000 in 5–14-year-olds.[1] In the current study in Memphis it was 1.88/100,000 in the 5–17 year age group. Thus, the authors suggest that we need to reevaluate our current recommendations regarding prevention and diagnosis of this dreadful disease.

But may we not be jumping the gun and underestimating the role that modern medical care may have played in affecting this splendid change? Let me climb on my soap box here.

First, this study (as have all previous studies) showed a much greater incidence of disease in poor inner city black children. (Here, actually a fivefold greater incidence.) While poverty, poor housing, and overcrowding are cited as well known contributions to streptococcal disease and subsequent rheumatic fever, how about differentials in the speed and adequacy of treatment of the poor vs. the affluent?

Second, although the authors cite the studies of Gordis in Baltimore during the 1960s—which showed a then much higher incidence of rheumatic fever (15.6/100,000 overall but a 40.2/100,000 incidence in low-income, predominantly black central city areas)—they fail to mention what I thought was the niftiest finding of the Gordis study.[2] Namely, that introducing a good and responsive system of primary medical care into that area rapidly and profoundly reduced the incidence of rheumatic fever.

Third, in trying to develop some crude indications of the adequacy of community care, we recently tried to approach this problem from the reverse direction. The methodology employed will not satisfy the purists, but the findings were so impressive that I tend to think they are on target.

Both streptococcal infection and acute rheumatic fever are reportable diseases. When we went through the simpleminded exercise of simply running the ratios of *reported* cases of rheumatic fever to *reported* streptococcal infection, I was startled to find that as late as 1960 there were 30 cases of acute rheumatic fever per 1,000 reported streptococcal infections—an incidence very close to that reported in the 1940s by Rammelkamp and his colleagues for *untreated* streptococcal disease. This despite the fact that effective treatment had been around for 15 years! But there followed a dramatic drop: to 13/1,000 in 1965, 7/1,000 in 1975, and 0.1/1,000 in 1980. This, bear in mind, corresponds nicely with the advent of Medicaid and clear evidence that poor black children began to receive physician care at rates that equaled those of their white contemporaries.

That the disappearance of highly rheumatogenic strains, the availability of better housing, etc., all may contribute to the falling incidence of rheumatic fever seems probable. However, let's not put down doctoring. Sometimes it may actually improve health! Take a look at the graphics we were able to construct which tend to support this thesis.[3]] ◀

1-2 **Opportunistic Infection in Previously Healthy Women: Initial Manifestations of a Community-Acquired Cellular Immunodeficiency.** Nearly all patients with the new acquired immunodeficiency syndrome (AIDS) have been male homosexuals and intravenous drug abusers. Henry Masur, Mary Ann Michelis, Gary P. Wormser, Sharon Lewin, Jon Gold, Michael L. Tapper, Jose Giron, Chester W. Lerner, Donald Armstrong, Usha Setia, Joel A. Sender, Robert S. Siebken, Peter Nicholas, Zelman Arlen, Shlomo Maayan, Jerome A. Ernst, Frederick P. Siegal, and Susanna Cunningham-Rundles studied 5 women who appear to have the syndrome (table). Immunologic studies were done in the patients and in healthy controls matched for age, race, and sex.

Clinical Features of Patients With Acquired Immunodeficiency Syndrome

Clinical Feature	Patient 1	Patient 2	Patient 3	Patient 4	Patient 5
Age, *yrs*	31	25	26	37	27
Race	Black	Hispanic	Hispanic	Hispanic	White
Sexual preference	Bisexual	Heterosexual	Heterosexual	Heterosexual	Heterosexual
Drugs used	Cocaine, mescaline	None (sexual partner is heroin addict)	Heroin, cocaine	Heroin, cocaine	Heroin, cocaine
Initial opportunistic infection	*Pneumocystis carinii* pneumonia	*P. carinii* pneumonia	*P. carinii* pneumonia	Esophageal candidiasis	Perianal herpes simplex
Duration of symptoms before diagnosis of opportunistic infection	2.5 months	3 weeks	34 months	2 weeks	3 months
Documentation of initial opportunistic infection	November 1981	October 1981	August 1981	November 1981	April 1981
Outcome of initial opportunistic infection	Survived	Survived	Survived	Died	Survived
Other opportunistic infections	Oral candidiasis	Oral candidiasis	*Candida* esophagitis, perirectal herpes simplex, disseminated *Mycobacterium avium-intracellulare* infection	*P. carinii* pneumonia	Disseminated *M. avium-intracellulare* infection, disseminated cytomegalovirus infection, *P. carinii* pneumonia, pulmonary aspergillosis, pseudomonas bacteremia
Follow-up after biopsy	6 months	7 months	9 months	1 month	7 months
Current status	Alive	Alive	Dead	Dead	Dead
Evaluation for underlying disease	Liver biopsy, bone marrow biopsy, abdominal computed tomography (CT) scan, gallium scan: no apparent disease	Abdominal CT scan, abdominal sonogram, gallium scan, bone scan, bone marrow biopsy, liver biopsy: no apparent disease	Lymph node biopsy, liver biopsy, bone marrow biopsy, splenectomy: no apparent disease	Autopsy: no apparent disease	Autopsy: no apparent disease

(Courtesy of Masur, H., et al.: Ann. Intern. Med. 97:533–539, October 1982.)

(1–2) Ann. Intern. Med. 97:533–539, October 1982.

The women were residents of metropolitan New York City. Four abused drugs, and 1 had close sexual contact with a drug abuser. One patient was bisexual. All the women developed *Pneumocystis carinii* pneumonia and other opportunistic infections, including oral candidiasis, disseminated mycobacterial infection, and ulcerative herpes simplex infection. Three of the women died. All 5 had severely depressed cellular immune function. Lymphopenia was marked in all.

Drug abuse appears to have a role in predisposing to the development of AIDS in women. Community-acquired immunodeficiency should be considered in patient populations other than homosexual men and drug abusers. These 5 cases raise the possibility that the syndrome can be acquired by intimate heterosexul contact. A transmissible infectious agent may be involved, although it appears that multiple factors besides exposure determine development of this disorder.

▶ ↓ The epidemic of the acquired immunodeficiency syndrome (AIDS) continues unabated. As of this writing, the Centers for Disease Control has tallied close to 3,000 cases in the United States, and reports from abroad are starting to appear. We know much more about the syndrome clinically than we did last year. Early diagnosis and treatment of Kaposi's sarcoma now offers a somewhat improved short-term prognosis, especially if the patients have not had complicating opportunistic infections. However, such infections remain a major problem, and those due to *Mycobacterium avium-intracellulare*[4] are perhaps the worst. This microbe produces a progressive unrelenting disseminated infection and is often the ultimate cause of death.

The underlying cause of this syndrome remains elusive. Although numerous hypotheses have been proposed, the current favorite remains an infectious agent, probably a virus which is spread, in the manner of hepatitis B, by intimate contact with blood or body secretions containing the agent.

The vast majority of cases have occurred in men (93%), but AIDS sometimes affects women. The following article described this syndrome in women who were intravenous drug users, had sexual contact with a drug user, or were bisexual. ◀

1-3 ***Pseudomonas* Folliculitis: An Outbreak and Review.** Most outbreaks of *Pseudomonas* folliculitis in the United States have been related to the use of heated whirlpool baths. Tracy L. Gustafson, Jeffrey D. Band, Robert H. Hutcheson, Jr., and William Schaffner report an outbreak of *Pseudomonas* folliculitis occurring in members of a health spa in Tennessee.

The source of the infection was traced to a recently built, heated indoor swimming pool, which had not been chlorinated for 2 days because of failure of an automatic chlorinator system. Forty-seven of 60 members who had used the swimming pool during this 2-day period developed a papulopustular rash or an earache; 10 had an earache only, and 13 had both a rash and an earache. The extent of the rash varied considerably. Of the 37 patients with the rash, 11 had papulopustules. Another 5 had numerous large pustules covering the trunk and extremities, as well as malaise and low-grade fever. The rash resolved within 1–2 weeks in all cases and left no scars except a few hyperpigmented macules. Recurrence of isolated pustules and boils at the site of the original rash occurred for as long as 2 months in several cases. The 23 cases of earache were mild and self-limiting. Cultures were obtained from the pustules of 9 patients, 6 of which

---

(1–3) Rev. Infect. Dis. 5:1–8, Jan./Feb. 1983.

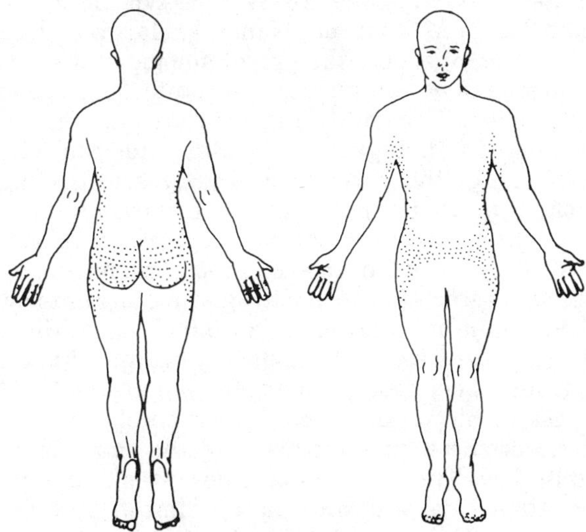

Fig. 1–1.—Distribution of *Pseudomonas* folliculitis. The rash can occur on any hair-bearing skin, but it is characteristically concentrated in the areas shown. (Courtesy of Gustafson, T. L., et al.: Rev. Infect. Dis. 5:1–8, Jan./Feb. 1983.)

yielded *Pseudomonas aeruginosa* serogroup 0-11. A swab of debris from the edge of the pool also grew *P. aeruginosa* serogroup 0-11.

The rash is not unique in appearance and may, at first, be confused with insect bites, scabies, contact dermatitis, bromoderma, staphylococcal folliculitis, varicella, or herpes zoster. However, the rash does have a characteristic distribution (Fig. 1–1), which is shared by few other dermatitides. As it is a folliculitis, it does not involve the palms, soles, or mucous membranes. On hair-bearing skin, it has a marked predilection for the buttocks, hips, axillae, and lateral aspects of the trunk. Large papules in the axillae are quite common and may be the presenting complaint. Many affected individuals will also have systemic complaints of headache, malaise, fatigue, and low-grade fever. Otitis externa and mastitis may also be seen, both of which are usually mild and self-limited. As the popularity of home whirlpools and hot tubs increases, the physician may expect to encounter this disease with increasing frequency.

▶ [Ah, the hazards of our hedonistic pleasure-seeking society! There have now been at least 13 reported outbreaks of folliculitis caused by *Pseudomonas aeruginosa*. In recent years, most cases have followed the use of home whirlpools or redwood tubs or the use of pools in health spas. The distribution of the rash should give the physician a clue as to its etiology. The simultaneous occurrence of otitis or mastitis should heighten suspicion.

Our intrepid author-sleuths report almost everything one would want to know about this annoying cutaneous infection except one thing. How should you treat it? The answer: It goes away by itself.] ◀

1–4 **Hemorrhagic Colitis Associated With a Rare *Escherichia coli* Serotype.** Lee W. Riley, Robert S. Remis, Steven D. Helgerson,

(1–4) N. Engl. J. Med. 308:681–685, Mar. 24, 1983.

Harry B. McGee, Joy G. Wells, Betty R. Davis, Richard J. Hebert, Ellen S. Olcott, Linda M. Johnson, Nancy T. Hargrett, Paul A. Blake, and Mitchell L. Cohen report the epidemiologic and laboratory findings in two outbreaks of an unusual gastrointestinal illness affecting at least 25 persons in Oregon during February and March 1982 and at least 21 persons in Michigan during May and June 1982.

The median age of the patients was 28 years in Oregon and 17 years in Michigan. All patients presented with crampy abdominal pain, initially watery diarrhea followed by grossly bloody diarrhea, and little or no fever; only 3 from each group had fever exceeding 38.5 C. The illness was associated with eating at restaurants owned by the same fast-food chain in Oregon ($P < 0.005$) and Michigan ($P = 0.0005$) and with eating any of 3 sandwiches containing 3 ingredients in common: ground beef patty, rehydrated onions, and pickles. There was only 1 case of bloody diarrhea among employees of the restaurants and none of the family members of the cases in either group had bloody diarrhea. The duration of illness was 2–9 days in Oregon and 3 to more than 7 days in Michigan. A similar percentage in each group required hospitalization (73% and 67%, respectively). Stool cultures did not grow already recognized pathogens. However, a rare *Escherichia coli* serotype, 0157:H7, was isolated from 9 of 12 stool specimens obtained within 4 days of the onset of symptoms in both outbreaks combined and from a retained specimen of hamburger patty from a suspected lot in the Michigan outbreak. The organism did not produce either heat-labile or heat-stable enterotoxin and was not invasive on Serèny testing or tissue-culture assays. However, it did produce nonbloody diarrhea in infant rabbits. The only previous isolation by the Centers for Disease Control laboratory of *E. Coli* 0157:H7 since 1973 was in one patient with hemorrhagic colitis in 1975.

In these two outbreaks, it is suspected that *E. coli* 0157:H7 contaminated the meat before it was made into hamburger patties, survived the cooking procedures, and caused illness among some people who ate the meat. The epidemiology, clinical spectrum, and pathogenesis of this unusual gastrointestinal illness remain unknown or poorly understood and require continued study.

▶ [Here's a fairly dramatic illness, again a probably predictable but unwanted accompaniment of our fast-paced society. Fast foods—fast diarrhea!

It sounds as though the syndrome can be tentatively distinguished from the bloody diarrhea that can accompany shigellosis, amebiasis, campylobacteriosis, or invasive *E. Coli* gastroenteritis by the absence of fever

The evidence implicating *E. Coli* 0157:H7 seems quite convincing. This appears to be a rare serotype that is neither invasive nor enterotoxigenic on standard tests. It has not been previously recognized as an enteropathogenic strain.

My curiosity has been tweaked. Was it McDonald's? Wendy's? Roy Rogers? Gino's? Burger King? Jack-in-the-Box? Make your own list.] ◀

Chapter 1 References

1. Brownell K. D., Bailen-Rose F.: Acute rheumatic fever in children: Incidence in a borough of New York City. *JAMA* 224:1593–1597, 1973.
2. Gordis L., Lilienfeld H., Rodriguez R.: Studies on the epidemiology and

preventability of rheumatic fever. *J. Chronic Dis.* 21:645–654, 1969.

3. Blendon R., Rogers D. E.: Cutting medical care costs: *Primum non nocere* *JAMA* 250:1880–1885, 1983.
4. Zakowski P., Fligiel S., Berlin O. G. W., Johnson B. L., Jr.: Disseminated *Mycobacterium avium-intracellulare* infection in homosexual men dying of acquired immunodeficiency. *JAMA* 248:2980, 1982.

2. Pneumococcal Infections

▶ ↓ The following two articles discuss pneumococcal disease. The first makes the point that the clinical presentation of this classic infection actually is considerably more diverse than the standard texts would have you believe. The diagnosis, especially in the elderly patient, is by no means always a snap. The second article makes a gloomy assessment of the contribution of intensive-care technology to the survival of patients with pneumococcal bacteremia. Note the following facts about pneumococcal infection: it is a sometimes elusive diagnosis; we have only limited success in treating the most severe form of the disease; and pneumococci are slowly developing relative resistance to penicillin. Now you will understand why, once again, I shall attempt to persuade you to be more enthusiastic in your use of pneumococcal vaccine. ◀

2–1 **Pneumococcal Pneumonia in Hospitalized Patients: Clinical and Radiologic Presentations.** The incidence of pneumococcal pneumonia is difficult to assess because of the difficulty in defining bacteriologic criteria that are diagnostic. Another problem in the recognition of this disease is that many physicians are unaware of its diverse radiologic presentation. Sharon Ort, John L. Ryan, Gertrude Barden, and Nicholas D'Esopo report the clinical, bacteriologic, and radiologic features in 94 hospitalized patients with a diagnosis of pneumococcal pneumonia.

Of the 94 patients, 57 (61%) had a radiologic classification of bronchopneumonia and 37 (39%) were classified as having lobar pneumonia. Pneumococcal bacteremia was present in 25 patients (27%). Pretreatment blood cultures were performed in 33 and were positive in 20 (61%) of the patients with a lobar pattern, but blood cultures were positive in only 5 (11%) of 47 of the patients with a bronchopneumonia pattern ($P < .001$). All patients with bacteremia and a roentgenographic pattern of bronchopneumonia had an underlying malignancy. At presentation, a single chill was relatively rare and was seen only in patients with lobar disease; pleural effusion was also rare, but the frequency was much higher in the lobar group. Three of the 4 patients with pleural effusion and lobar disease were bacteremic. Pneumococcal empyema was not encountered. One or more underlying diseases were present in 82 (87%) of the patients, but there were no differences between groups in the incidence of heart disease, diabetes, chronic pulmonary disease, or malignancy. Intubation appeared to be a predisposing factor for the development of a bronchopneumonic pattern of pneumococcal pneumonia, because it had been performed in 18% of the patients with bronchopneumonia but in none of those with a lobar pattern. Ten patients with bronchopneumonia were receiving immunosuppressive therapy compared with only 2 patients with lobar involvement. Gram staining of sputum specimens

(2–1) JAMA 249:214–218, Jan. 14, 1983.

showed no significant differences between groups. Sputum cultures were often "mixed" in both the bronchopneumonic (52%) and lobar (70%) groups.

Although the presence of a lobar pattern on roentgenograms is usually emphasized in the diagnosis of pneumococcal pneumonia, the majority of patients in this study had a roentgenographic bronchopneumonic pattern rather than the classic lobar pattern, which suggests that pneumococcal pneumonia may be underdiagnosed in patients with the bronchopneumonic pattern. The implications of this are important both for treatment and for epidemiologic data used in selecting pneumococcal types for vaccines.

2–2 **Failure of Intensive Care Unit Support to Influence Mortality From Pneumococcal Bacteremia.** In addition to penicillin, other therapeutic and supportive measures have come into widespread use in patients with pneumococcal disease. These include mechanical ventilation, pharmacologic vasopressor therapy, dialysis, and electronic monitoring of cardiac rhythms. To assess the influence of intensive care unit (ICU) support on early mortality, Edward W. Hook III, Christy A. Horton (Harborview Med. Center, Seattle), and Dennis R. Schaberg (Univ. of Michigan) reviewed the records of 134 consecutive patients with pneumococcal bacteremia seen during a 6-year period.

There were 41 (30.5%) hospital deaths among the 134 patients, of which 11 (27%) occurred within 24 hours after admission. Most patients with pneumococcal bacteremia had risk factors that have been investigated previously for their effect on mortality (Table 1). Although almost 70% of the patients were reportedly alcohol abusers, mortality did not differ significantly between alcohol abusers and nonabusers ($P = .43$). Two patients admitted with delirium tremens died. Other factors apparently influencing mortality were age greater than 60 years ($P = .1$), a total leukocyte count of less than 5000/cu mm on admission ($P < .001$), and preexisting malignancy ($P = .16$). Of the 45 patients admitted to the ICU, 34 (76%) died, compared with only 7 deaths (8%) among the 89 patients not admitted to the ICU (Table 2). Only 8 of the 34 patients who died after admission to the

TABLE 1.—Factors Influencing Outcome of Pneumococcal Bacteremia

	No. (%) of Total (N = 134)	No. (%) Mortality
Alcohol abuse	94 (70)	28 (30)
Cardiac disease	14 (10)	5 (36)
Chronic obstructive pulmonary disease	25 (19)	8 (32)
Malignant disease	14 (10)	6 (43)
Diabetes	5 (4)	2 (40)
Age >60 yr.	46 (34)	18 (39)
Total WBC count <5,000/cu. mm.	24 (18)	15 (63)
Pneumonia involving >2 lobes	61 (46)	24 (39)

(Courtesy of Hook, E. W. III, et al.: JAMA 249:1055–1057, Feb. 25, 1983; copyright 1983, American Medical Association.)

(2–2) JAMA 249:1055–1057, Feb. 25, 1983.

TABLE 2.—RELATIONSHIP OF INTENSIVE CARE INTERVENTION TO MORTALITY IN PATIENTS WITH PNEUMOCOCCAL BACTEREMIA

	All Cases	No. (%) of Fatal Cases
Admitted to intensive care unit	45	34 (76)
Intubation	42	34 (81)
Positive end-expiratory pressure	20	18 (90)
Pharmacologic BP support	15	14 (93)

(Courtesy of Hook, E. W. III, et al.: JAMA 249:1055–1057, Feb. 25, 1983, copyright 1983, American Medical Association.)

ICU died within 24 hours. Patients who received positive end-expiratory pressure (PEEP) ventilation, pharmacologic blood pressure support, or both, as well as endotracheal intubation, tended to have even higher mortality (see Table 2). Roentgenographic evidence of involvement of 2 or more lobes was associated with a higher mortality than was involvement of 1 lobe. Thirteen patients (10%) had pneumococcal bacteremia without roentgenographic evidence of pneumonia. The mortality in these patients was 31%, which did not differ significantly from that in patients with pneumonia. Of the 6 patients who had bacteremia without pneumonia and who were admitted to the ICU, 4 died.

In this series, admission to the ICU did not appear to have an influence on the overall mortality in patients with pneumococcal bacteremia. It is concluded that pneumococcal bacteremia continues to be an important cause of morbidity and mortality, despite the application of modern supportive care and antimicrobial therapy.

▶ [The authors of the first paper make a solid clinical point. The textbook description of classic lobar pneumococcal pneumonia does not represent the entire spectrum of pneumonic pneumococcal disease. Indeed, a picture of bronchopneumonia on the chest roentgenogram was the most common presentation (61%) in their series. The two forms of the disease, bronchopneumonic and lobar, had overlapping clinical presentations. The single chill ushering in the disease was rare; it occurred only in a few patients with lobar pneumonia. Bacteremia occurred much more commonly in lobar disease (54%) than in patients with bronchopneumonia (9%). Mixed flora were a common finding in sputum cultures in both groups (bronchopneumonia 52%, lobar 70%). In addition to pneumococci, *Hemophilus influenzae* also was frequently recovered. Gram stains also often showed both these organisms in abundance. The patient population studied was largely an older male group, and the authors wonder whether these mixed results represent true mixed infections, rather than mere sputum contamination. In any event, I was impressed that, of the 80 patients in the entire group that had blood cultures drawn, 25 (31%) had pneumococci recovered from the bloodstream. Rates of that order of magnitude have been reported for years among patients hospitalized with pneumococcal pneumonia.

Patients with pneumococcal bacteremia who are profoundly ill are provided the array of life-support technology available in intensive care units. Even discounting those patients who died within the first 24 hours of admission, the authors of the second paper found that mortality remained high despite intensive care. I am sure the authors hoped to publish more optimistic findings. (What authors do not?) But their review of the data—and my reading of their paper—led to pessimistic conclusions. The more intensive the care, the less likely the patient was to survive. As shown in the second table, having to use positive end-expiratory pressure (PEEP) is a very ominous sign—as anyone who has worked in an intensive care unit (ICU) knows.

These are grim facts. They should spur a more basic look at the problem. I urge stepping back from the tumult at the bedside in order to take a longer view. Much of that sophisticated equipment in the ICU represents what Lewis Thomas would call "half-way technology": elaborate, expensive, and of uncertain benefit. It is humbling to recognize what damage the pneumococcus still can do. This recognition should spur further investigation into the pathophysiology of pneumococcal bacteremia and pulmonary failure. Only when we know a great deal more about these basic events can we hope to design regimens that will successfully turn these events around.

This brings me to pneumococcal immunization, currently our best means of preventing pneumococcal pneumonia. The latest formulation of the vaccine contains antigens of the 23 pneumococcal serotypes most often associated with bacteremia. Fedson and Chiarello[1] have shown that about 65% of patients with pneumococcal bacteremia had been in the hospital, usually for another reason, during the five years prior to the bacteremic event. They suggest that we ought to screen all our hospitalized patients for indications for pneumococcal immunization (splenectomy, pulmonary or cardiac disease, diabetes, age over 65 years)—and that we ought to immunize them. Of course, I think you ought to do this in your office or clinic practice too. Fedson's emphasis on hospitalized patients as a group at special future risk of pneumococcal bacteremia and thus a special target group for immunization is a good idea. Do it.] ◀

Chapter 2 Reference

1. Fedson D. S., Chiarello L. A.: Previous hospital care and pneumococcal bacteremia: importance for pneumococcal immunization. *Arch. Intern. Med.* 143:885, 1983.

3. Staphylococcal Infections

▶ ↓ Epidemic investigation can be fascinating, not only for what we learn of host-parasite interactions, but also for what we learn of human behavior. In the following two articles, methicillin resistance served as a readily identifiable (and clinically important) marker for the epidemic strain of *Staphylococcus aureus*. In the first article by Hailey et al., we are again reminded that hospitals, especially the large teaching hospitals, become terribly busy environments with patients and health care personnel coming and going. The two groups meet just long enough, it would seem, to transfer pathogenic organisms from one to another. In the second paper by Saravolatz et al., the hospital is seen as an innocent bystander, caught in the spin-off of a massive community epidemic among persons whose commonality was intravenous drug abuse. ◀

3–1 **Emergence of Methicillin-Resistant *Staphylococcus aureus* Infections in United States Hospitals: Possible Role of the House Staff-Patient Transfer Circuit** is discussed by Robert W. Haley, Allen W. Hightower, Rima F. Khabbaz, Clyde Thornsberry, William J. Martone, James R. Allen, and James M. Hughes (Centers for Disease Control, Atlanta). Infections caused by methicillin-resistant strains of *Staphylococcus aureus* appear to be increasing in frequency in some U.S. hospitals about a decade after a similar increase was observed in Britain and elsewhere. Clusters of infections reported in journals and in three hospital surveys in the United States have occurred almost exclusively in large, tertiary referral hospitals affiliated with medical schools. In the National Nosocomial Infections Study, in which 63 hospitals regularly reported infections between 1974 and 1981, the increase in methicillin-resistant *S. aureus* infections was accounted for entirely by substantial increases in four hospitals, all large referral centers affiliated with medical schools. Just over a third of all hospitals in the study were so affiliated. Laboratory methods of detecting the bacterial strains in question are probably about as adequate in smaller as in large hospitals.

The predominance of methicillin-resistant *S. aureus* infections in large hospitals may result from the presence of many patients at high risk of infection and from interhospital spread of the organism through the transfer of infected patients and house staff from similar hospitals or nursing homes. Once introduced, a resistant organism spreads among highly susceptible patients. Transfer of patients between burn or trauma units may be an important factor. House staff-patient transfer may also be responsible for the periodic introduction of resistant *S. aureus* into smaller community hospitals. The first step in control is accurate, timely identification of resistant *S. aureus* infections. Employees who have dermatitis or who are associated epidemiologically with spread of an infection should be temporarily as-

(3–1) Ann. Intern. Med. 97:297–308, September 1982.

signed to nonclinical duties. Infected or colonized patients should be discharged home as soon as is medically feasible. It may be best to avoid moving patients who are colonized or infected to other hospitals if possible. If transfer is necessary, infection control personnel at the receiving center can be notified in advance.

3–2 **Community-Acquired Methicillin-Resistant *Staphylococcus aureus* Infections: New Source for Nosocomial Outbreaks.** A recent epidemic of methicillin-resistant *S. aureus* infection occured in Detroit among parenteral drug abusers in the community and resulted in the dissemination of infection among the general population. Louis D. Saravolatz, Donald J. Pohlod, and Lucille M. Arking reviewed the epidemiologic findings during a 19-month period in which 165 patients with 183 infections due to community-acquired methicillin-resistant *S. aureus* were seen. The proportion of community-acquired staphylococcal infections resistant to methicillin increased from 3% to 38% during a period of 1½ years. Factors associated with infection included drug abuse, serious underlying illness, previous antimicrobial therapy, and previous hospitalization. Several different brands of heroin were used by infected drug abusers. A concurrent nosocomial epidemic of methicillin-resistant *S. aureus* infection accounted for about 30% of all nosocomial staphylococcal infections at the height of the epidemic.

Control measures included regular rounds by infection-control nurse practitioners, isolation of all infected patients, and routine culture of suspected and proved drug abusers. Further, clusters of nosocomial methicillin-resistant *S. aureus* infections in inpatient services and wards were reviewed and attack rates calculated. A significant rise led to culture of employees assigned to the areas in question to identify carriers. A precipitous fall in the proportion of nosocomial methicillin-resistant staphylococcal infections was observed. The rate of nosocomial infection was maintained at a significantly lower level than that of community-acquired infections. The community-acquired strains were susceptible to vancomycin, rifampin, and sulfamethoxazole-trimethoprim.

Methicillin-resistant *S. aureus* stains can arise in the community as well as in the hospital, and they present a threat to persons in both settings. Control measures imposed in the hospital will have little effect on the community reservoir. Isolation of infected patients will reduce transmission, but this may be inadequate to control an outbreak. Control measures are best assessed in a surveillance program.

▶ [Methicillin-resistant *S. aureus* strains are not to be regarded as attenuated mutants. Full virulence is illustrated by the occurrence of sepsis, endocarditis, and pneumonia in infected persons. Cephalosporins, even the third-generation cephalosporins, are not adequate substitutes for methicillin and other semisynthetic penicillins. Vancomycin, an antimicrobial agent with potential for renal and ototoxicity, is the drug of choice for such infections.

I was delighted to learn that surveillance cultures of the anterior nares of patients, physicians, and hospital employees were instrumental in limiting the intrahospital

(3–2) Ann. Intern. Med. 97:325–329, September 1982.

spread of methicillin-resistant staphylococci in the Henry Ford Hospital in Detroit. Such surveillance cultures have been crucial in defining the extent of previously reported epidemics due to methicillin-sensitive staphylococci and streptococci. I think all would agree, however, that apart from the epidemic situation, there are no indications for routine surveillance cultures of the noses of patients or personnel.

As carefully documented by Hailey et al., the extent of this epidemic could not be accurately determined from the level of activity of the medical literature. Academic physicians in medical school–affiliated hospitals are more likely to publish than are private physicians in smaller hospitals. Dr. Hailey and his colleagues at the Centers for Disease Control had to rely upon an existing network of reporting hospitals (the National Nosocomial Infections Survey) to verify that the epidemic was, indeed, concentrated in large, tertiary referral hospitals affiliated with medical school. It is the converse of this finding that bothers me. Are small communities and their hospitals also vulnerable to epidemics of illness, and, for lack of academic minded physicians, do they go without definition or response? There is a current trend among hospitals in the United States to organize or "network" under large management systems. This may provide a vehicle for a systematic review of disease trends in the most common type of hospital in our country, the 100-bed community hospital.] ◀

▶ ↓ Although retrospective in design, the following study is an important review of the problems encountered in the therapy of prosthetic valve endocarditis secondary to *Staphylococcus epidermidis.* ◀

3–3 ***Staphylococcus epidermidis* Causing Prosthetic Valve Endocarditis: Microbiologic and Clinical Observations as Guides to Therapy.** *Staphylococcus epidermidis* is a common cause of prosthetic valve endocarditis in the United States. Adolf W. Karchmer, Gordon L. Archer, and William E. Dismukes reviewed data on 75 episodes of prosthetic valve endocarditis due to *S. epidermidis* in patients seen between 1975 and 1980. Five of the 70 patients relapsed. Outcome could be evaluated in 68 episodes. The median patient age was 55 years. A single prosthetic valve was present in 56 patients; 30 had mechanical bioprostheses and 26 had leaflet bioprostheses.

Cures were achieved in 57% of the evaluable episodes of prosthetic valve endocarditis. Twenty-eight of 48 patients treated with antibiotics plus replacement of the valve during active endocarditis were cured, as were 11 of the 20 treated with antibiotics alone. Several patients from whom viable organisms were recovered at operation

OUTCOME OF PROSTHETIC VALVE ENDOCARDITIS DUE TO *STAPHYLOCOCCUS EPIDERMIDIS*

Therapy	All Episodes*			Episodes with Complications†		
	Cured	Failed	Total	Cured	Failed	Total
Medical	11	9	20	5	6	11
Medical and surgical	28	20	48	27	19	46

*In all episodes, patients were treated for at least 6 days.

†Complications included prosthesis dysfunction, temperature of more than 37.9 C for more than 9 days with appropriate antibiotic therapy, and congestive heart failure caused by prosthesis dysfunction.

(Courtesy of Karchmer, A. W., et al.: Ann. Intern. Med. 98:447–455, April 1983.)

(3–3) Ann. Intern. Med. 98:447–455, April 1983.

were cured. Methicillin-resistant organisms were responsible for 53 of 61 infections occurring within a year of operation and for 2 of 9 diagnosed later. Resistance extended to the cephalosporins. All isolates were susceptible to vancomycin and rifampin. Endocarditis was cured in 21 of 26 patients treated with vancomycin for methicillin-resistant infection and in 10 of 20 treated with β-lactam antibiotics. The cure rate in patients given vancomycin was increased by adding rifampin or gentamicin to the regimen.

Prosthetic valve endocarditis due to methicillin-resistant *S. epidermidis* should be treated with vancomycin plus rifampin or an aminoglycoside. In addition to administration of optimal antibiotic therapy, aggressive surgical intervention is needed to debride the site of infection. Further knowledge of the epidemiology and mode of acquisition of prosthetic valve endocarditis to *S. epidermidis* may aid the development of methods to prevent this largely nosocomial infection.

▶ [Endocarditis due to methicillin-resistant *S. epidermidis* probably represents the newest indication for cotherapy with rifampin. Vancomycin remains the first drug of choice. Although the comparisons are not prospectively controlled in this study, there was a clear trend for improved results when rifampin was added to vancomycin therapy. Also of note was the fact that serum bactericidal titers were increased 8-fold or more by the addition of rifampin to the therapy of patients receiving vancomycin. The other finding of note was, unexpected by me, the destructive nature of these infections. Although *S. epidermidis* has been viewed for years as a low-virulence skin contaminant, it is clear that this organism is capable of irreversible destruction of the annulus or myocardial tissue. Bulky vegetations partially obstructed flow in four patients, and myocardial abscesses were noted in one fourth of patients. Most patients required surgical debridement and valve replacement at some point during the course of successful therapy. For further comments on the use of rifampin see abstract 9–7.] ◀

4. Urinary Tract Infections

▶ ↓ Urinary tract infections complicating indwelling catheters continue to be the most common nosocomial (hospital-acquired) infections. A tremendous amount of study has gone into attempts to reduce this infection risk—with considerable success. About 25 years ago, urinary drainage systems still were "open." In other words, catheters drained into open receptacles, or if the catheter entered a bag, the system was disconnected frequently in order to empty the bags, irrigate the catheter, or obtain urine specimens.

In those days, virtually all catheters were complicated by infection within 48–72 hours. At the time, it was noted that bacteria entering the system usually first contaminated the urine in the bag and then ascended along the catheter to reach the bladder where they established an infection. The response to this knowledge was the "closed" system. As every ward nurse knows, these systems require that the catheter-bag junction not be disturbed once the connection has been made. And this worked (along with attention to meticulous aseptic practices in catheter care); infection could be postponed so that now many catheters can be removed before infection occurs.

This was a shared triumph. Academic investigations provided the epidemiologic data; industry responded by devising various closed systems; the investigators evaluated them; and industry then marketed them and provided instruction for ward personnel.

However, for the past decade our ability to reduce catheter-associated infection has been stalled. There have been no new ideas. So, some have gone back to an old notion: If urine in the bag becomes contaminated first, perhaps one can avert bladder infection by instilling antiseptics regularly into the catheter bag. But there is a flaw in this logic: The data incriminating contaminated bag urine are out of date. Contemporary studies overwhelmingly indicate that, when closed drainage systems are used, the entering bacteria gain access at the catheter-urethral junction, above the bag.

Nevertheless, the old-new idea gained some currency and was investigated by a group in Bristol, England. ◀

4–1 **Does Addition of Disinfectant to Urine Drainage Bags Prevent Infection in Catheterized Patients?** Urinary tract infection induced by indwelling catheters is one of the most common forms of nosocomial infection. The addition of chlorhexidine to urine drainage bags has been recommended, but its efficacy is not established. William A. Gillespie, Rosemary A. Simpson, Judith E. Jones, Lina Nashef, Colin Teasdale, and David C. E. Speller (Bristol, England) evaluated the effect of adding chlorhexidine to drainage bags in men with indwelling catheters that were placed after prostatectomy or other transurethral procedures; none of the 58 patients had bacteriuria preoperatively. Sterile 5% chlorhexidine digluconate solution (10-ml) was added to the drainage bag of each study patient through a sterile funnel inserted in the outlet tap each time the bag was emptied. No addition was made to the bags of control patients.

The rate of infection was 51% in the study group and 45% in the control group, not a significant difference. There were no significant group differences in number with preoperative catheterization, dura-

(4–1) Lancet 1:1037–1039, May 7, 1983.

DAY OF ONSET OF INFECTION

Days of catheterisation*

Group	0–2 N	0–2 I	2–4 N	2–4 I	4–6 N	4–6 I	6–8 N	6–8 I	Total N	Total I
Chlorhexidine	8(1)	5(1)	14(2)	7(1)	6(1)	3(1)	1	0	29(4)	15(3)
Control	8(3)	5(3)	9(2)	4(2)	10(4)	3(2)	2	1	29 (9)	13(7)

N = number of patients catheterized; I = number infected.

*Figures in parentheses = number of patients already catheterized before operation.

(Courtesy of Gillespie, W. A., et al.: Lancet 1:1037–1039, May 7, 1983.)

tion of postoperative catheterization (table), age, or type of operation. The bacteria causing infection also were similar in the two groups, gram-positive cocci being most frequent. Urine from the drainage bags of study patients was always sterile, whether or not the catheter urine was infected. In controls, similar organisms were present in specimens from the catheter and the bag. Organisms were never found in the bag before being found in the catheter tube.

The addition of chlorhexidine to catheter drainage bags did not reduce the occurrence of acquired infection after transurethral urologic procedures in this series. There is no reason to believe that another disinfectant would have been more effective, because chlorhexidine kept the bag contents sterile. Studies should be performed in other types of catheterized patients. Disinfectant instillation should not be practiced routinely unless it is shown in prospective controlled studies to be effective.

▶ [It did not work. Infections were just as frequent in the group in which the catheter bags had chlorhexidine instillations as in the control group. Indeed, although the difference was not statistically different, a few more infections occurred in the experimental group. Perhaps the repeated instillations facilitated bacterial entry in some fashion. Two further observations: The catheter bag urine was always sterile in the experimental group; also, although the infecting organisms in the control group were identical to those recovered from bag urine, they were never found first in the bag urine. These last two observations offer strong confirmation of the notion that, today, bacteria gain entrance above the drainage bag.

A team of American investigators has performed a similar but larger study, but their work has, as yet, been published only as an abstract.[1] The disinfectant they employed was hydrogen peroxide. Again, they could demonstrate no benefits by instilling H_2O_2 into the catheter bag.

Back to the drawing boards.] ◀

▶ ↓ The following is an important paper and extends earlier observations by Stamm et al. in which 10^2 or more bacteria per ml of midstream urine were found to be predictive of bladder infection (1983 YEAR BOOK OF MEDICINE, p. 37). In the current study, 10 leukocytes per cu mm of uncentrifuged urine, as measured in a counting chamber, was virtually diagnostic of urinary tract infection. ◀

4–2 **Measurement of Pyuria and Its Relation to Bacteriuria** are reviewed by Walter E. Stamm (Univ. of Washington). Apart from contamination of specimens, bacteriuria indicates either colonization of the urine or urinary tract infection. Assessment of pyuria is the most

(4–2) Am. J. Med. 75:53–58, July 28, 1983.

ASSOCIATION OF PYURIA (LESS THAN 10 WHITE BLOOD CELLS PER CU MM) WITH BACTERIURIA AND URINARY TRACT SYMPTOMS IN STUDIES USING COUNTING CHAMBERS

Symptomatic, Bacteriuric Patients	Asymptomatic, Abacteriuric Patients
45/45	3/53
144/152	0/42
8/8	0/103
44/45	2/64
40/41	0/51

Bacteriuria = more than 10^5 cfu/m.
WBC = white blood cells.
(Courtesy of Stamm, W. E.: Am. J. Med. 75:53–58, July 28, 1983.)

readily available means of establishing the presence of host injury in order to distinguish infection from colonization. The nonpathologic limit of pyuria appears to be 10 leukocytes per cu mm of uncentrifuged urine. The determination of cells per high-power field in centrifuged urine is not a reproducible method, and the results do not correlate with either the leukocyte excretion rate or cells per cu mm counted in a chamber. Pyuria should be measured in the same way that white blood cell concentrations are measured in other body fluids, i.e., as cells per cu mm or cells per ml.

More than 10 white blood cells per cu mm are found in fewer than 1% of asymptomatic, nonbacteriuric patients but in more than 96% of symptomatic men and women with significant bacteriuria (table). Most symptomatic women with pyuria, but not significant bacteriuria, have urinary tract infection caused by uropathogens present in colony counts of less than 10^5/ml or by *Chlamydia trachomatis*. Women with asymptomatic bacteriuria may be classified as having either true asymptomatic infection, associated with pyuria, or transient, self-limited bladder colonization. Most patients with catheter-associated bacteriuria also have pyuria and therefore infection.

The presence of pyuria, accurately measured and expressed as cells per cu mm of uncentrifuged urine, is a useful clinical and microbiologic parameter. Its proper application helps to distinguish between colonization of the urine by bacteria and clinical infection.

▶ [The challenge of this study is not in believing its results and conclusions, but in restructuring the approach of several generations of physicians to the evaluation of urine. Although Dr. Stamm might argue that the logistics of providing a chamber cell count in all patients with suspected urinary tract infection is no greater than that of providing quantitative assessment of bacteriuria (as is routinely performed in every hospital in the United States), there is currently no widespread precedent for this approach. In addition, because physicians are often interested in information regarding other formed structures within urine, urine specimens would need to be examined both in a counting chamber (unspun) and under a cover slip (centrifuged). It is far too much to assume that physicians will ever provide enough clinical information so that the laboratory personnel can decide which of these two time-consuming procedures must be done and whether one, both, or neither is necessary. Follow-up studies, numerous Continuing Medical Education updates, and a threat of accreditation denial by the Joint Commission on the Accreditation of Hospitals will probably be required before quantitative determination of pyuria becomes standard practice in the management of dysuria.] ◀

4-3 **Effects of 10 Milligrams of Ampicillin per Day on Urinary Tract Infections.** Urinary tract infections caused by *Escherichia coli* are closely related to the binding capacity of the organism to periurethral epithelial cells. Gram-negative bacilli, when exposed to β-lactam antibiotics in concentrations less than the minimal inhibitory concentration (MIC), become elongated and produce filaments. Sub-MICs of ampicillin have been shown to inhibit significantly the adherence of *E. coli* to epithelial cells of urine sediment and to increase the survival rate in rabbits infected with *E. coli.* S. Ben Redjeb, A. Slim, A. Horchani, S. Zmerilli, A. Boujnah (Hosp. Charles Nicolle, Tunis, Tunisia), and V. Lorian (Bronx Lebanon Hosp. Center, Bronx, N.Y.) evaluated the effects of ampicillin (10 mg dissolved in water) on urinary tract infection in 38 symptomatic patients, 18 of whom served as controls. All had more than 10^5 colony-forming units (CFUs) of *E. coli* per ml of urine, as well as pyuria. None showed evidence of an upper urinary tract infection. All patients received 2 liters of liquids per day for 3 days.

The concentrations of ampicillin in urine ranged from 0.5 to 4 μg/ml. Most of these concentrations represented 20%–50% of the MIC of the *E. coli* strain of the patient (Fig 4–1). After 24 hours of treatment, 8 of the 20 patients treated with ampicillin showed a CFU of less than 10^5 per milliliter urine. At 2, 3, and 7 days after treatment, 16 of the 20 patients had negative urine cultures (less than 10^4 CFU/ml) (Fig 4–2). Filaments 10–50 μm in length were seen on 8 occasions in the urine sediment after 24 hours of ampicillin treatment. The reduc-

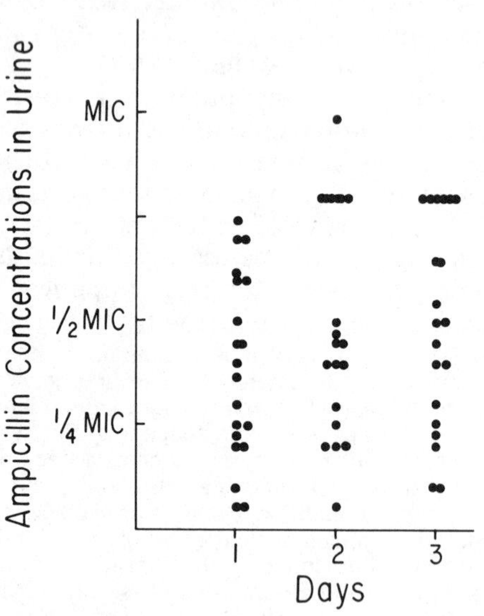

Fig 4–1.—Ratio of ampicillin concentration in urine to the minimum inhibitory concentration *(MIC)* of the *Escherichia coli* strain isolated from each patient. (Courtesy of Redjeb, S. B., et al.: Antimicrob. Agents Chemother. 22:1084–1086, December 1982.)

(4–3) Antimicrob. Agents Chemother. 22:1084–1086, December 1982.

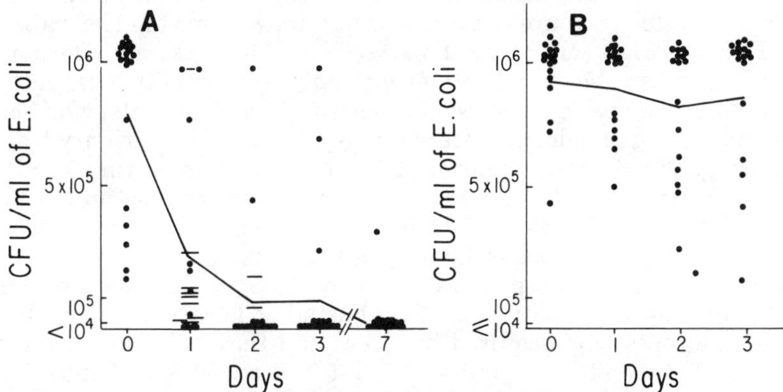

Fig 4–2.—Number of colony-forming units *(CFU)* in the urine of treated patients *(A)* and untreated (control) patients *(B)*. Dashes represent urine samples in which filaments were observed. (Courtesy of Redjeb, S. B., et al.: Antimicrob. Agents Chemother. 22:1084–1086, December 1982.)

tion in the number of *E. coli* organisms in urine was closely followed by a decrease in the number of leukocytes in urine, with virtually normal urinary leukocyte levels on days 3 and 7 after treatment. Patients who served as controls and did not receive ampicillin showed little or no change in the number of leukocytes in urine. The 4 treatment failures were due to a tumor, cystitis secondary to a neurologic bladder, cystitis secondary to calculi, and cystitis in a woman 7 months pregnant.

The prompt decrease in the number of *E. coli* organisms in urine following treatment with 10 mg of ampicillin per day indicates that this dosage produces significant antibacterial activity in urine. Because the urine cultures remained negative as long as 4 days after ampicillin was withdrawn, the activity of this dosage is confirmed.

▶ [For years we've debated just when, for how long, and with how much antimicrobial, should acute urinary tract infections be treated. Although low-dose therapy has intermittantly been advocated, it has never been critically evaluated.

Well, here's a tantalizer. Miniscule doses of ampicillin—10 mg per day—given for three days with lots of fluid resulted in "cures" in 16 of 20 patients. This, despite the fact that urinary concentrations of the drug were well below the MIC of the strains of *E. Coli* producing the infections. Not definitive, but it sure sounds interesting. We will keep you posted.] ◀

▶ ↓ The following paper by Dr. Richard Platt and his colleagues is a meticulous retrospective study of *mortality* associated with nosocomial urinary tract infections. By using a large data base, he was able to contol for other variables which have an influence on the risk of dying, such as the type and severity of underlying illnesses, the age of the patient, and the like. After all was said and done, he observed that urinary tract infection complicating bladder catheterization was associated with an almost 3-fold increased risk of death compared with patients whose catheters did not get infected. ◀

4–4 **Mortality Associated With Nosocomial Urinary Tract Infection.** About half a million patients each year acquire urinary tract

(4–4) N. Engl. J. Med. 307:637–642, Sept. 9, 1982.

infection in acute-care hospitals in the United States, and nearly all nosocomial infections are associated with indwelling bladder catheters. Richard Platt, B. Frank Polk, Bridget Murdock, and Bernard Rosner (Harvard Med. School) examined the mortality associated with such infections in a prospective series of 1,458 patients, who had 1,474 indwelling bladder catheterizations. A total of 136 urinary tract infections, defined as the presence of 10^5 or more colony-forming units per ml, occurred in 131 patients. Gram-negative rods accounted for 74 episodes, yeasts for 35, and gram-positive cocci for 24. In 15 cases, two bacterial species were isolated simultaneously.

Mortalities during hospitalization were 19% in infected patients and 4% in uninfected patients. The adjusted odds ratio for mortality between patients who acquired infection and those who did not was 2.8, with 95% confidence limits of 1.5–5.1. Acquisition of infection was not associated with severity of the underlying disease. Twelve deaths may have been due to acquired urinary tract infection. Two patients had urinary tract pathogens in premortem blood cultures; another 10 died with a clinical picture consistent with serious infection, without diagnostic culture being done. These 12 patients accounted for 16% of all deaths among catheterized patients.

Acquisition of urinary tract infection during bladder catheterization appears to be associated with a nearly 3-fold increase in mortality in hospital patients. The reasons for the association are unclear, but the strength of the relationship and the large number of people at risk require studies to learn whether prevention and treatment of these infections can reduce mortality.

▶ [This report has generated a great deal of interest and discussion among those involved in hospital infection control. Infection complicating bladder catheterization has long been recognized as a risk to life because it occasionally produces bacteremia. This happens once for every 200 catheters inserted (only 0.5%). Therefore, it came as something of a shock when this study purported to show that catheter-associated infections conferred an almost 3-fold increased risk of dying.

Quite appropriately, the authors presented their conclusions cautiously. Because of the limitations of a retrospective study, they were unable to document why many of the patients died. Some had bacteremia with the same organism that had produced a catheter-associated infection. Those are easy to understand. However, others had unexplained episodes of shock, fever, and the like, whereas others just seemed to develop an advanced case of the dwindles. The question of what caused these deaths cannot be answered by the retrospectoscope. I am concerned that increased mortality in this study may be simply a marker for increased severity of underlying disease—despite the authors' best attempts to account for this.

There is no doubt that this paper has dusted the cobwebs off the thinking in this area. That is the beauty of a new idea!] ◀

Chapter 4 Reference

1. Thompson R. L., Haley C. E., Groschel J. Y., et al.: Effect of periodic instillation of hydrogen peroxide (H_2O_2) into urinary drainage systems in the prevention of catheter-associated bacteriuria [abstract no. 769]. *In* Program and abstracts of the 22nd Interscience Conference on Antimicrobial Agents and Chemotherapy. American Society for Microbiology, Washington, D.C., 1982.

5. Nosocomial Infections

▶ ↓ The progressive unfolding of the story of Legionnaires' disease is a remarkable medical detective story. In 1976 it exploded on the scene as a rare, apparently brand new, and terrifying epidemic disease of unknown etiology and high mortality. One historic old Philadelphia hotel, which had the misfortune to house those legionnaires, bit the dust in the ensuing months.

Since then we have yearly reported from the barrage of new information that continues to fill in the picture. First, the microbial etiology of Legionnaires' disease was determined. Second, it was shown to be a disease that had been with us, but unrecognized, for many years. Third, what appeared to be its distinguishing clinical features were detailed, and its response to erythromycin documented. Fourth, methods were developed for its diagnosis, first serologically, then by culture, then by direct immunofluorescent staining of the microbe in respiratory secretions.

That the organism was frequently present in air-conditioning or heat-rejection systems or potable water supplies was also speedily determined, but the relationship of these findings to clinical disease was tough to pin down. Thus, until recently the advice has been: "Don't worry about the presence of *Legionella pneumophila* in these systems unless you are seeing clinical disease."

This year the picture becomes more troublesome. In the first article abstracted here, it seems clear that immunosuppressed leukopenic patients receiving high doses of corticosteroids were infected via respiratory devices aerolizing contaminated tap water. The mortality rate was unknown, but two of six patients who developed pneumonia died.

Two other articles on the same subject with the same findings lend additional weight to the hazards of *L. pneumophila* in the water supply of sick patients. In Iowa City, 24 cases of Legionnaires' disease occurred among immunosuppressed patients, most of them admitted to a brand new hematology-oncology unit, and 11 of them died despite therapy. Again the evidence linking the infection to the water supply—particularly the *hot* water supply—was impressive.[1]

In Pittsburgh the same problem occurred. In an experience with more than 100 cases of nosocomial Legionnaires' disease acquired since 1979, Dr. Yu and his associates postulated early on that the potable water was the source of the problem. When *L. pneumophila* was isolated from more than 30% of selected water sites in an institution, nosocomial legionellosis occurred. In 1981 Dr. Yu and his colleagues began vigorous efforts to reduce the contamination—again paying particular attention to the hot water supply. A decline in the level of contamination was definitely paralleled by a drop in cases of legionellosis.[2]

To make matters yet more troublesome, it now appears that Legionnaires' disease is vastly more common than previously recognized. In a prospective study, the Pittsburgh group cited above found that *L. pneumophila* was the most common single cause of pneumonia in their hospital—22.5 percent![3]

Further, and as one might anticipate, all of the clinical clues that we have touted as suggestive of Legionnaires'—abdominal pain, diarrhea, neurologic signs, abnormal liver function studies, hypophosphotemia, hematuria—did *not* occur more often in patients with *L. pneumophila* pneumonia when prospective methodologies were employed. Yu et al. also make the point that they were not seeing an unusual incidence of pneumonias and that they would have missed the etiology if they hadn't been looking for it.

In the second article abstracted here, the same group nail this down even more definitively. They extended their studies to a community hospital where Legionnaires' disease had never been documented. Here their findings were the same. Eight, or 14% of the nosocomial infections were due to *L. pneumophila.* Alas, and again, the microbe was found in about two thirds of the test sites in the water supply.

There's clearly a lot more work to be done in hospitals, particularly those caring for immunologically altered patients, if we are to prevent this serious infection. ◀

5–1 **Nosocomial Legionnaires' Disease Caused by Aerosolized Tap Water From Respiratory Devices.** Paul M. Arnow, Teresa Chou, Diane Weil, Elizabeth N. Shapiro, and Claudia Kretzschmar (Univ. of Chicago) reviewed 5 cases of nosocomial Legionnaire's disease occurring in 5 months at the University of Chicago Hospitals. The diagnostic criteria included a compatible clinical picture and either isolation of *Legionella pneumophila* from sputum or lung, direct fluorescent antibody staining of lung tissue, or seroconversion. A case-control study was done that used controls who were hospitalized on the same ward and service as patients for at least a week in the 2 weeks before clinical onset of illness.

The 5 patients with hospital-acquired Legionnaires' disease were dissimilar in many respects. All, however, had received high doses of corticosteroids or ACTH and had been treated with respiratory devices aerosolizing tap water about a week before clinical onset of infection. A jet nebulizer unit generally had been used by the same patient for 3 days before being replaced. The findings in the case-control study are given in the table. Analysis of the findings supported a causal role for aerosolized tap water. The attack rate of Legionnaire's disease in corticosteroid-treated patients could have been as high as 38% if 2 patients with fatal pneumonia of unknown cause had the disease. *L. pneumophila* was isolated from tap water and from reservoirs of tap water–filled respiratory devices. The free chlorine concentration of the tap water was less than 0.05 ppm.

Host Factors and In-Hospital Exposures of Case and Control Patients During Risk Period for Nosocomial Legionnaires' Disease

Parameter	No. of patients (%) Case	Control
Total	5	69
Cigarette smoking	1 (20)	24 (35)
Granulocyte count of <1,000/mm³	0	8 (12)
Corticosteroid therapy	5 (100)	23 (33)
Other immunosuppresive therapy	1 (20)	14 (20)
Tap water aerosol from respiratory devices	5 (100)	4 (6)
Sterile water aerosol from respiratory devices	2 (40)	9 (13)
Corticosteroid therapy and tap water aerosol from respiratory devices	5 (100)	0
Corticosteroid therapy and sterile water from respiratory devices	2 (40)	3 (4)

(Courtesy of Arnow, P. M., et al.: J. Infect. Dis. 146:460–467, October 1982; by permission of the University of Chicago Press.)

(5–1) J. Infect. Dis. 146:460–467, October 1982.

Nosocomial Legionnaires' disease may be caused by aerosolized tap water from respiratory devices. Corticosteroid-treated patients may be at particular risk when exposed to such devices. There is evidence from many locales that routine chlorination of tap water does not protect against contamination by *L. pneumophila.*

5–2 **Nosocomial Legionnaires' Disease Uncovered in a Prospective Pneumonia Study: Implications for Underdiagnosis.** *Legionella pneumophila* may be responsible for up to 29% of nosocomial pneumonias in a single institution, and autopsy studies have indicated that up to 6% of fatal nosocomial pneumonias are due to the organism. Robert R. Muder, Victor L. Yu, Jonathan K. McClure, Frank J. Kroboth, Spryos D. Kominos, and Robert M. Lumish (Pittsburgh) undertook a prospective study of pneumonias at a veterans hospital where Legionnaires' disease was known to be endemic and at a community teaching hospital where the disease had never been documented. All pneumonias occurring in adults in 3 nonconsecutive months at both hospitals were investigated. Serologic tests for *Legionella* were done on all patients with pneumonia. Selective culture mediums and direct fluorescent antibody testing for *Legionella* were readily available.

Thirty-two of 57 cases of pneumonia at the veterans hospital were nosocomial; 12 of them were caused by *L. pneumophila* serogroup 1, and 1 by Pittsburgh pneumonia agent (PPA, *Legionella micdadei, Taklockia micdadei*). In 2 other patients both *L. pneumophila* and PPA were demonstrated by direct fluorescent antibody testing, culture, or both. *L. pneumophila* accounted for 32% of the community-acquired cases. Fourteen percent of nosocomial pneumonias were due to *L. pneumophila.* The organism was obtained from 64% of test sites in the water distribution system.

The Legionellaceae can be significant pathogens in a community hospital setting. If nosocomial *Legionella* infection is found and an environmental reservoir of the organism is identified, attempts to eliminate the suspected source seem reasonable. If environmental contamination is discovered in the absence of known disease, an attempt should be made to determine the incidence of Legionnaires' disease at the institution.

▶ ↓ Despite the accumulation of considerable data, the chicken vs. egg argument continues: is the hospital environment an important source of bacteria that cause nosocomial infections or is the environment (walls, floors, sinks, etc.) like a trashbasket, just the passive receptacle for bacteria shed by patients and staff? During the 1950s the inanimate environment was considered an important reservoir for pathogens, and this dated notion is reflected in the numerous cultures of environmental surfaces that still are performed in many hospitals in the name of infection control. Contemporary hospital epidemiologists dispute this view and point to the animate inhabitants of the hospital—patients, nurses, doctors, etc.—as the major reservoirs and transmitters of hospital pathogens. The following study provides persuasive data on this question. ◀

5–3 **Relation of the Inanimate Hospital Environment to Endemic Nosocomial Infection.** Many epidemics of nosocomial infection have arisen from reservoirs of pathogens in the inanimate hospital envi-

(5–2) JAMA 249:3184–3188, June 17, 1983.
(5–3) N. Engl. J. Med. 307:1562–1566, Dec. 16, 1982.

NOSOCOMIAL INFECTION IN TWO HOSPITALS

	OLD HOSPITAL	NEW HOSPITAL	
	LAST 2 MO	AFTER 2 MO	AFTER 12 MO
No. of patients at risk	1631	1730	1816
No. of nosocomial infections	113	120	136
Rate (per 100 discharges) *	6.9	6.9	7.5

*Differences between rates of infection are not significant.
(Courtesy of Maki, D. G., et al.: N. Engl. J. Med. 307:1562–1566, Dec. 16, 1982. Reprinted by permission of The New England Journal of Medicine.)

ronment, but the contribution of the environment to the acquisition and spread of endemic nosocomial infection is unclear. Dennis G. Maki, Carla J. Alvarado, Carol A. Hassemer, and Mary Ann Zilz (Univ. of Wisconsin, Madison) examined the relation between environmental contamination and endemic nosocomial infection in the course of a move of a hospital from a 56-year-old building to a new, more spacious facility. It was hypothesized that the new hospital would initially show considerably less contamination by common nosocomial pathogens than the old one. If surveillance for 6–12 months showed an increase in contamination, its effect on the rate of infection should be detectable.

Common nosocomial pathogens were isolated from 17% of specimens from the old hospital and 4.5% of specimens from the new one just before occupancy. After 6–12 months of occupancy, 11.3% of cultures from the new hospital yielded common pathogens. *Acinetobacter* was recovered most often from the old hospital but was infrequent at the new. Pseudomonads were also recovered frequently from cultures in the old hospital. After 6–12 months of occupancy, the floors of the new hospital showed levels of contamination comparable with those of the old. Nosocomial infection rates are given in the table. The incidence of postoperative surgical wound infection was low throughout the study.

Organisms in the inanimate hospital environment, especially on surfaces and in the air, make a negligible contribution to nosocomial infections occurring endemically in hospitalized patients. Cleaning of the hospital environment is important, especially in the care of immunologically compromised patients and surgical patients. Routine microbiologic surveillance of the inanimate environment, however, is not recommended in the absence of an identified problem with nosocomial infection. Considerable savings in health care costs could result.

▶ [The situation could not have been clearer. A hospital was moving from an antiquated facility into a bright, shining, spacious new building. Dr. Maki and his team of infection-control nurses cultured the environment (surfaces, air, and water) of the old hospital while it was still occupied, and they cultured the environment of the new hospital before any patients moved in and again 6–12 months after the first patients arrived. The team also conducted standardized surveillance for nosocomial infections among patients before and after the move.

In a nutshell, they found environmental contamination with recognized hospital pathogens in the old building. Before occupancy, the new structure was largely free of this flora. However, after 6–12 months of exposure to patients and staff, the new environment had acquired a flora entirely similar to that of the old hospital. Now look at the table: the rate of nosocomial infections did not change significantly. If the hospital environment had been an important source of pathogens, one would have expected a fall in the nosocomial infection rate during the period following the move into the new facility. Q.E.D. As a rule, the environment is not an important source of pathogens in a well-maintained hospital in the United States today. Doubting Thomases (and Thomasinas), please read this short paper in its entirety. Then, please persuade your hospital to discontinue its environmental culturing program.] ◀

5–4 ***Pseudomonas aeruginosa* Peritonitis Associated With Contaminated Poloxamer-Iodine Solution.** Patricia L. Parrott, Pamela M. Terry, Elizabeth N. Whitworth, Loretta W. Frawley, and Rebecca S. Coble (Grady Mem'l. Hosp., Atlanta), I. Kaye Wachsmuth (Centers for Disease Control, Atlanta), and John E. McGowan, Jr., (Emory Univ.) encountered 3 cases of peritonitis due to *P. aeruginosa* in a 3-week period in patients at an outpatient dialysis clinic. Positive cultures were obtained from the first-pass dialysis fluid. Subsequently a fourth patient with peritonitis and a fifth patient with local infection at the site of peritoneal catheter insertion were encountered. All 5 patients recovered after antibiotic therapy.

The *P. aeruginosa* isolates from the 5 patients had identical susceptibility patterns. All the patients had permanent indwelling peritoneal catheters for dialysis. The catheter and machine tubing were wiped with gauze soaked with poloxamer-iodine solution whenever catheters were connected and disconnected. Positive cultures were obtained from an unopened bottle of poloxamer-iodine solution used in the dialysis room and from samples of large containers of the solution. The antimicrobial susceptibility pattern of these isolates was identical to that of the patient isolates.

This is the second instance of contamination of iodophor solution to be reported. Studies are needed to determine the factors that permit bacteria to survive in these solutions. Guidelines for using iodophors as disinfectants and antiseptics need to be reassessed.

▶ [Alas, we continue to find that many antiseptic solutions are not all they are cracked up to be. Over the last five years there seems to have been a decline in reported infections due to contaminated antiseptic solutions. In the main, this has seemed related to the reduction in the use of aqueous quaternary ammonium disinfectants. However, as hospitalized patients get sicker—and as we do more invasive things to them—the need to develop very rigorous sterility standards for the solutions we use on the tubes or catheters we stick into and leave in patients grows ever more important.

In this instance, iodophor solutions were the culprit, and the authors point out the problems of assaying the levels of free and total iodine in these solutions. Another hospital in Haifa reported a marked increase in *Pseudomonas cepacia* isolates from wounds, vaginas, and the urine of catheterized patients, which was traced to dilute chlorhexidine solutions in common use. Although there isolates were initially believed to be nonpathogenic commensals, this view changed when two immunocompromised patients developed fulminant sepsis with *P. cepacia*. Both patients died.[4] We need to set some tough standards for antiseptic solutions and monitor them carefully.] ◀

(5–4) Lancet 2:683–685, Sept. 25, 1982.

▶ ↓ In the highly technological environment of American hospitals, frequent venapunctures and around-the-clock intravenous administration of "miracle drugs" are crucial for the care of our sicker patients. For those of us who have participated in the process as recipients (i.e., patients), the daily blood drawing and constant care of intravenous sites are remembered as a most unpleasant experience. On occasion, particularly in the chronically ill patient, venous access procedures may become intolerable.

The following is a careful documentation of the risk of indwelling subcutaneous catheters in immunosuppressed patients. It offers reasonable proof that the prolonged venous access provided by the Hickman and Broviac catheters are not only a humane but a reasonably safe method of continuous venous access. ◀

5–5 **Prospective Study of Prolonged Central Venous Access in Leukemia.** Maintenance of venous access is a problem in adults with acute leukemia. Janet L. Abrahm and James L. Mullen (Univ. of Pennsylvania) undertook a 3-year prospective study to evaluate 71 right atrial silicone elastomer catheters for long-term venous access in 57 patients scheduled to receive intensive chemotherapy for leukemia. Most had acute nonlymphocytic leukemia. Hickman catheters were used in most cases. Catheters were placed using the same method as for parenteral hyperalimentation. Cephalosporin therapy was given prophylactically, and platelets were transfused if indicated. The catheters were used both to draw blood and to administer drugs, electrolyte solutions, blood products, and parenteral hyperalimentation.

The catheters were in place for a median of 45 days. A total of 19 catheter-related complications developed. Excessive bleeding occurred at 3 catheter insertion sites. There were 8 catheter-related infections (Fig 5–1), all occurring in the 38 patients with systemic infection verified during life. Catheters were left in place in 2 patients with catheter-related bacteremia and in 34 of 36 with non-catheter-related bac-

Fig 5–1.—Septicemia during life was diagnosed in 38 patients, in 34 of whom the catheter was left in place during the septicemic episode. In 20 of these 34 patients, the septicemia eventually cleared. (Courtesy of Abrahm, J., and Mullen, J. L.: JAMA 248:2868–2873, Dec. 3, 1982; copyright 1982, American Medical Association.)

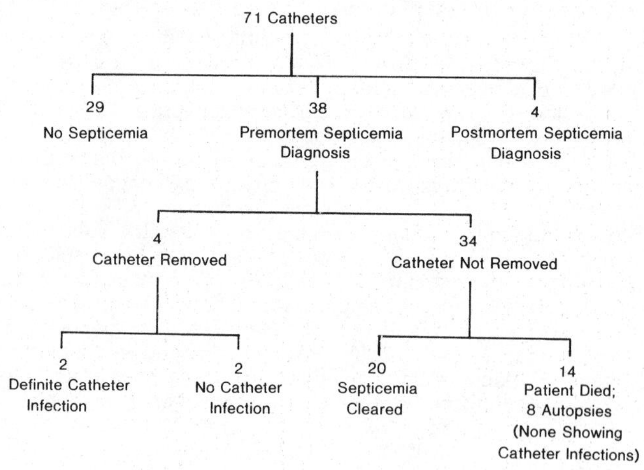

(5–5) JAMA 248:2868–2873, Dec. 3, 1982.

teremia; the bacteremia cleared in 20 patients. Eight autopsies yielded no evidence of catheter-related mortality. Leaks developed in the subcutaneous parts of 3 catheters, which were removed. Complications were infrequent in 35 patients who maintained catheters at home for a median of nearly 10 weeks.

Few serious complications and no deaths resulted from the use of silicone elastomer right atrial catheters for long-term venous access in these adults with acute leukemia. Catheters can be maintained safely even in septicemic, granulocytopenic patients and in those with thrombocytopenia. These catheters may also prove useful for prolonged venous access in patients with such disorders as aplastic anemia and sickle cell anemia and in those requiring chemotherapy for solid tumors or treatment for fungal infection, endocarditis, or osteomyelitis.

▶ [Particularly encouraging was the fact that the indwelling catheter, if colonized, could frequently be sterilized without removal. Most importantly, no related deaths or severe morbidity were noted in this large series of patients or in a series of 27 pediatric patients reported by Shapiro et al.[5] My colleagues in Nashville tell me that indwelling catheters have been placed in selected patients kept at home with potentially curable diseases that require weeks of intravenous therapy (e.g., cryptococcal meningitis, bacterial endocarditis). Insurance companies have recently supported that portion of a course of therapy administered on an outpatient basis, an important consideration in an age of cost containment.] ◀

▶ ↓ Do prophylactic antimicrobials cost less than the infections they prevent? A qualified "yes" according to my colleagues in Nashville. Qualified because of the wide variations in the three principal determinants of cost-effectivenss: cost of prophylaxis, infection rate, and cost of infection. ◀

5–6 **The Cost-Effectiveness of Antimicrobial Prophylaxis in Clean Vascular Surgery** is discussed by A. B. Kaiser, A. C. Roach, J. L.

Fig 5–2.—Effect of infection severity and rate on excess cost of infection in vascular surgery patients. Wound infections were considered class I if only the skin was involved; class II if soft tissues were involved; and class II (most severe) if the implanted graft was involved. Open circles = observed infection rate and excess cost of infection per 100 operative procedures. Solid black lines define the relationship between infection rate and excess costs of infection. Dotted line = cost of cefazolin prophylaxis per 100 operations. (Courtesy of Kaiser, A. B., et al.: J. Infect. Dis. 147:1103, June 1983.)

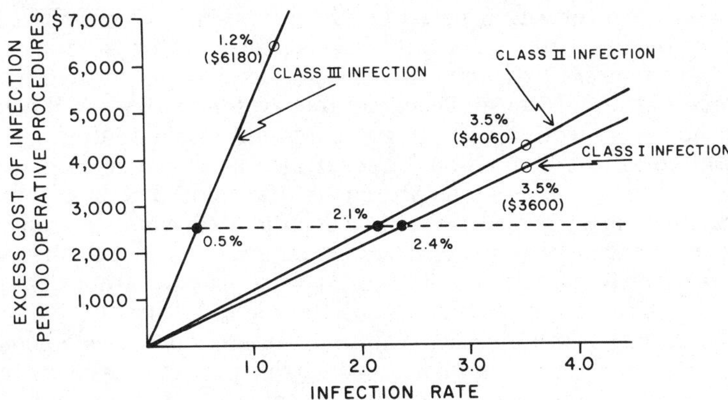

(5–6) J. Infect. Dis. 147:1103, June 1983.

Mulherin, Jr., K. R. Clayson, T. R. Allen, W. H. Edwards, and W. A. Dale (Vanderbilt Univ.). A previous double-blind study of cefazolin prophylaxis in patients undergoing elective vascular surgery showed that infections due to cefazolin-sensitive organisms were prevented. Such infections occurred in 13 of 237 placebo patients and in none of 225 cefazolin recipients. Prophylaxis consisted of 5 doses of cefazolin, 1 gm/dose. A cost analysis showed that the median hospital cost for patients with preventable wound infection was significantly higher than that for all other patients. Excess costs rose markedly with the severity of wound infection. The observations in patients having surgery involving the abdominal aorta are shown in Figure 5–2. The observed infection rate exceeded the "break-even" rate for all classes of infection.

The use of cefazolin perioperatively appears warranted on a cost-effectiveness basis in patients undergoing elective vascular surgery. This will not necessarily be the case at other centers in which the infection rate or excess cost of infection is lower or the cost of prophylaxis is higher. When implantable materials are at risk of infection, however, the cost of infection is so great that antimicrobial prophylaxis can nearly always be justified.

▶ [A more expensive prophylactic antimicrobial (e.g., a third-generation cephalosporin), a lower infection rate (e.g., carotid artery surgery), or a lower cost of infection (e.g., infection following breast biopsy) would render the prevention of infection more costly than the infections themselves. In operations involving implantable materials, the cost of infection is exorbitant, and prophylaxis should be assumed to be cost-effective. However, for all other types of surgery, the variables must be assessed before prophylaxis can be assumed to be cost-effective.

The analysis used by Kaiser et al. is reminiscent of the approach our public health officials have used for years to formulate recommendations for vaccine production and utilization. As cost for inhospital care comes under closer scrutiny, look for additional studies designed to focus our attention on activities that are cost-effective as well as beneficial to our patients.] ◀

5–7 **Recurrent Cellulitis After Saphenous Venectomy for Coronary Bypass Surgery.** Cellulitis is known to develop recurrently at sites of old surgical trauma where the lymph drainage has been compromised. Larry M. Baddour and Alan L. Bisno (Univ. of Tennessee) report data concerning 5 patients who had recurrent cellulitis after coronary bypass grafting. A total of 20 episodes of acute cellulitis occurred in the lower extremity at the site of saphenous venectomy. The patients had high fever and considerable systemic toxicity. Blood cultures, however, were sterile in the 2 patients studied during 3 episodes of cellulitis. The clinical appearance is shown in Figure 5–3. Associated lymphangitis was present in 1 patient. The precise bacterial cause of most episodes was not documented, but the prompt response of 3 patients to penicillin alone suggested group A streptococcal infection. β-Hemolytic streptococci were isolated from the lesion surface in 1 case. The strain was susceptible to bacitracin.

A static pool of protein-rich lymph presumably provides a good medium for bacterial growth and impedes transport of cutaneous microbial invaders to reticuloendothelial elements in draining lymph nodes.

(5–7) Ann. Intern. Med. 97:493–496, October 1982.

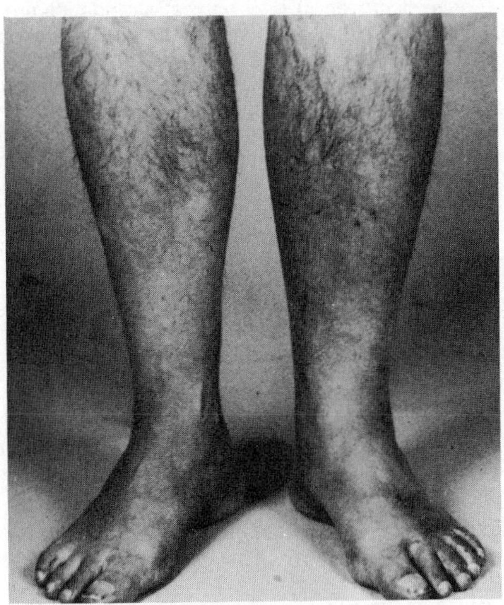

Fig 5–3.—Swelling of left leg with acute inflammation along course of saphenous vein. There is associated *Trichophyton* infection of toes of left foot. (Courtesy of Baddour, L. M., and Bisno, A. L.: Ann. Intern. Med. 97:493–496, October 1982.)

The potential for compromise of lymphatic drainage exists in coronary bypass grafting, especially in the area of the femoral triangle when saphenous venectomy is carried out. Once cellulitis occurs, the inflammation may cause local destruction of lymph channels and further impair lymph flow. How the infecting organism gains entry is unclear. The exact pathophysiologic mechanism of this disorder is not understood, but the inflammatory response may be due in part to immunologically mediated reactions. Human and animal studies suggest that recurrent cellulitis usually results from streptococcal infection mediated, at least partly, by reactions to streptococcal toxins in hypersensitive hosts.

Continuous antimicrobial prophylaxis may be indicated for coronary bypass patients who have multiple, closely spaced recurrences of cellulitis. Regimens similar to those used to prevent acute rheumatic fever could be used.

▶ [The severe constitutional symptomatology, "erysipeloid" appearance of the lower extremity, cellulitis, and the tendency to relapse as described in these five patients is perfectly mimicked by streptococcal cellulitis in patients who have experienced traumatic injury to the lower extremity. Greenberg et al. have described an identical syndrome of cellulitis after coronary artery bypass surgery in 9 patients.[6] Drs. Baddour and Bisno suggest that damaged lymphatic drainage is the predisposing lesion for this illness. I agree—but it is then surprising that, given the magnitude of bypass surgery in this country, additional reports have not previously appeared in the literature. My Nashville colleague, Dr. Allen Kaiser, informs me that he could identify only two patients with similar infections during a 10-year period at Saint Thomas Hospital where almost 10,000 coronary artery bypass procedures and 8,000 abdominal aortic and peripheral vascular procedures have been performed. However, as noted by Greenberg et al., most patients are referred for surgery, many from far away, and additional cases may have occurred. It may be that lymphatics are only occasionally disrupted when the saphenous vein is harvested at the time of surgery. Dr. Kaiser informs me that he has had modest success in managing recurrent episodes of post-traumatic recurrent cellulitis of the lower extremity by instructing patients to keep a bottle of penicillin or erythromycin tablets filled and in the medicine cabinet at home. A 5-day course of therapy begun without hesitation at the first sign of fever and discomfort in the extremity has apparently reduced the frequency of hospitalizations in these patients. Perhaps what is needed is a double-blind, prospective . . .] ◄

Chapter 5 References

1. Helms C. M., Massanari R. M., Zeitler R., et al.: Legionnaires disease associated with a hospital water system: a cluster of 24 nosocomial infections. *Ann. Intern. Med.* 99:172–178, 1983.
2. Best M., Yu V. L., Stout J., et al.: Legionellaceae in the hospital water-supply. *Lancet* 2:307–310, 1983.
3. Yu V. L., Kroboth F. J., Shonnard J., et al.: Legionnaires' disease: new clinical perspective from a prospective pneumonia study. *Am. J. Med.* 73:357–361, 1983.
4. Sobel J. D., Hashman N., Reinherz G., et al.: Nosocomial *Pseudomonas cepacia* infection associated with chlorhexidine contamination. *Am. J. Med.* 73:183–186, 1982.
5. Shapiro E. D., Wald E. R., Nelson K. A., et al.: Broviac catheter-related bacteremia in oncology patients. *Am. J. Dis. Child.* 136:679–781, 1982.
6. Greenberg J., DeSanctis R. W., Mills R. M., Jr.: Vein-donor-leg cellulitis after coronary artery bypass surgery. *Ann. Intern. Med.* 97:565–569, 1982.

6. Sexually Transmitted Infections

6–1 **Nonspecific Vaginitis: Diagnostic Criteria and Microbial and Epidemiologic Associations.** Because of a lack of uniform case definition and laboratory methods, studies of nonspecific vaginitis have given contradictory results. To evaluate possible diagnostic criteria among a population of college students and to investigate the microbiologic and epidemiologic characteristics of nonspecific vaginitis in relation to the diagnostic criteria, Richard Amsel, Patricia A. Totten, Carl A. Spiegel, Kirk C. S. Chen, David Eschenbach, and King K. Holmes (Univ. of Washington, Seattle) retrospectively studied a consecutive series of 397 unselected female university students using sets of well-defined criteria to distinguish nonspecific vaginitis from other forms of vaginitis.

The presenting gynecologic complaints were vaginitis symptoms (140 patients, 35.3%), contraception consultation (93 patients, 23.4%), annual examination (51 patients, 12.9%), pelvic pain (29 patients, 7.3%), menstrual disorder (24 patients, 6%), pregnancy (15 patients, 3.8%), and other reasons (45 patients, 11.3%). Depending on the various sets of criteria applied, the prevalence of nonspecific vaginitis ranged from 12% to 25%, with most sets of criteria giving a prevalence of more than 20%. The proportion of women with nonspecific vaginitis increased almost progressively with increasing vaginal pH. Only 19% of women with nonspecific vaginitis had a vaginal pH of 4.5 or less, compared with 67% of normal women. *Gardnerella vaginalis (Hemophilus vaginalis)* was significantly more prevalent among women with nonspecific vaginitis than among those without nonspecific vaginitis ($P < .05$). The prevalence of clue cells in patients with a diagnosis of nonspecific vaginitis on the basis of other criteria was 85%–97%, compared with 5%–14% in patients without nonspecific vaginitis. Although only 38% of women with positive culture results for *G. vaginalis* had clue cells, the presence of clue cells correlated significantly ($P < .001$) with the concentration of *G. vaginalis* in cultures. More than 50% of the women with nonspecific vaginitis were asymptomatic. The presence of nonspecific vaginitis also correlated with a history of sexual activity, a history of previous trichomoniasis, current use of nonbarrier contraceptive methods, and, especially, use of an intrauterine device.

The following criteria are proposed for the diagnosis of nonspecific vaginitis: the presence of 3 of 4 of (1) a vaginal pH greater than 4.5; (2) a thin and homogeneous-appearing vaginal discharge; (3) positive potassium hydroxide odor findings; and (4) the presence of clue cells

(6–1) Am. J. Med. 74:14–22, January 1983.

on saline wet mount. The application of these criteria should assist in the clinical management of nonspecific vaginitis and in future study of the microbiologic and biochemical correlates and pathogenesis of nonspecific vaginitis.

▶ [After reading about all the specific sexually-transmitted pathogens, those who work in gynecology or sexually transmitted disease clinics are often discouraged with how frequently they are left with a diagnosis of "nonspecific vaginitis." This is a common, troublesome illness, and as Dr. Amsel and his colleagues describe in their article, not much progress has been made since Gardner and Dukes presented their meticulous clinical observations on vaginitis in 1955. They suggested an etiologic role for a small pleomorphic gram-negative organism, *Hemophilus vaginalis.* To digress and to keep you confused, it has also been called *Corynebacterium vaginale* and now is referred to as *Gardnerella vaginalis.* Authors of subsequent studies have debated its etiologic role and whether the illness is sexually transmitted. Recent work by the group in Seattle and others has provided a guarded "yes" in answer to both questions. In a research setting they have provided the criteria for diagnosis of *G. vaginalis* vaginitis as listed in the abstract. The criteria seem a bit elaborate for a busy clinic or office practice, but the presence of clue cells (vaginal epithelial cells heavily coated with bacilli) on a microscopic wet mount seems a useful criterion. It correlates well with isolation of *G. vaginalis.* The patients respond promptly to metronidazole.] ◀

6–2 **Spread of Penicillinase-Producing and Transfer Plasmids From the Gonococcus to *Neisseria meningitidis.*** Meningococci differ from gonococci by the absence of plasmids; only two reports of plasmids in strains of *N. meningitidis* have appeared. J. R. Dillon, M. Pauzé, and K-H. Yeung (Ottawa) characterized a strain of *N. meningitidis* harboring the 4.5-megadalton, β-lactamase-producing plasmid and the transfer plasmid isolated in penicillinase-producing *N. gonorrhoeae* (PPNG). The plasmids in *N. meningitidis* strain M1-221 were identical in size to the plasmids found in PPNG isolates. Restriction endonuclease digestion of the 4.5-megadalton plasmids of meningococcal and gonococcal origin showed them to be identical.

This isolate probably originated in the genitourinary tract. It demonstrates the spread of antibiotic-resistant plasmids from *N. gonorrhoeae* to *N. meningitidis.* Clinically important meningococci have been isolated from genitourinary sites. The occurrence of double infections with *N. meningitidis* and *N. gonorrhoeae* increases the possibility that PPNG isolates may transfer their plasmids to the meningococcus. Because of the variety of symptoms produced by genitourinary strains of *N. meningitidis,* differentiation of meningococcal and PPNG isolates is important.

▶ [Don't panic; penicillin resistance among meningococci is not a problem, yet. When the gonococcus acquired a plasmid that gave it the capacity to produce β-lactamase (a penicillinase), many of us crossed our fingers and hoped that this plasmid would not find its way into the meningococcus. Well, it has happened once. Using the molecular techniques described elsewhere in this section, the authors have convincingly demonstrated that this penicillin-resistant meningococcal strain has acquired two plasmids previously found in gonococci: one that confers the ability to produce β-lactamase and another, a "transfer plasmid," that provides the genetic information that permits the plasmid to be transferred to other bacteria. So it can move and make mischief, if it cares to!

Because both gonococci and meningococci may coinhabit all the major orifices, it is possible that we'll see more penicillin-resistant meningococci, the results of plasmid promiscuity.] ◀

(6–2) Lancet 1:779–781, Apr. 9, 1983.

7. Fungal Infections

7–1 **Treatment of Disseminated and Progressive Cavitary Histoplasmosis With Ketoconazole.** Thomas G. Slama (Indianapolis) evaluated the effect of ketoconazole, an imidazole derivative having a wide spectrum of antifungal activity, in 17 patients seen during a massive outbreak of histoplasmosis in Indianapolis in 1978–1979. Disseminated or progressive cavitary disease was present in 10 and 7 patients, respectively. One patient had failed to respond to amphotericin B therapy. Ketoconazole was given in 16 patients in a single oral daily dose of 200 mg. One patient, because of his weight, received 100 mg initially. Treatment was continued until clinical or mycologic cure was achieved or failure was documented.

Among the 10 patients with disseminated histoplasmosis, all 7 who were not compromised were cured clinically and mycologically with ketoconazole therapy (table); the 3 others who had underlying malignancy, failed to respond. Six of the 7 patients with progressive cavitary histoplasmosis had preexisting chronic obstructive lung disease;

PATIENTS WITH DISSEMINATED HISTOPLASMOSIS

Patient	Age	Race	Sex	Underlying Disease	FID	Complement Fixation	Tissue	Clinical Response	Mycologic Response	Duration of Therapy (days)
1	27	W	M	None	M	Y 1:64 M 1:16	Liver*	Cure	Cure	180
2	28	B	F	None	M	Y 1:256 M 1:16	Liver, abdominal lymph nodes*	Cure	Cure	90
3	54	W	M	Non-Hodgkin's lymphoma	M	Y 1:8 M 1:8	Abdominal lymph nodes, bone marrow	Failure	Unknown	14
4	73	B	F	None	H&M	Y —NR M —NR	Subcutaneous nodule,* bone marrow,* peripheral blood*	Cure	Cure	180
5	56	W	M	Bronchogenic carcinoma	H&M	Y 1:8 M —NR	Bone marrow,* liver*	Failure	Failure	63
6	72	W	F	Chronic lymphocytic leukemia	M	Y 1:64 M 1:32	Cervical lymph mode,* bone marrow*	Cure	Failure	180
7	31	B	F	None	M	Y :64 M 1:8	Bone marrow, liver biopsy	Cure	Cure	180
8	28	W	M	None	M	Y 1:256 M 1:16	Bone marrow*	Cure	Cure	180
9	34	B	F	None	M	Y 1:32 M 1:8	Bone marrow, liver*	Cure	Cure	180
10	83	W	F	None	H&M	Y 1:64 M 1:32	Bone marrow*	Cure	Cure	180

Note: FID = fungal immune diffusion; Y = yeast phase; M = mycelial phase; NR = not reactive.
*Culture positive.
(Courtesy of Slama, T. G.: Am. J. Med. 74:70–73, Jan. 24, 1983.)

(7–1) Am. J. Med. 74:70–73, Jan. 24, 1983.

6 of the 7 responded favorably to ketoconazole therapy. Reactive fungal immunodiffusion test results did not change during treatment, but most complement fixation titers declined. No serious adverse reactions to ketoconazole occurred, and no abnormal laboratory values were found.

Ketoconazole appears to be effective and well tolerated when used to treat progressive cavitary histoplasmosis and disseminated disease in noncompromised hosts. It does not seem to be effective in treating disseminated disease in the immunocompromised host. Further studies are needed in patients with disseminated and progressive cavitary histoplasmosis before ketoconazole can replace amphotericin B.

▶ [The new antifungal agent—the orally absorbed imidazole, ketoconazole—is clearly a helpful new therapeutic agent. This year a whole flurry of articles have appeared that help define its efficacy (or lack of it) and its side effects.

That the drug works in the management of life-threatening histoplasmosis in otherwise healthy hosts is well demonstrated here. Indeed others (see Graybill[1]) feel that even in immunocompromised hosts with histoplasmosis it may deserve further study—the doses used by Slama were low.

Let me summarize how ketoconazole is now assessed by clinicians with the most experience.

(1) It looks like it compares well with amphotericin B in histoplasmosis, and blastomycosis in immunologically intact and compliant hosts.
(2) It is not very effective in sporotrichosis.
(3) The jury is still out on candidal sepsis or urinary tract infections. It has some effect on mucosal candidiasis and is probably the drug of choice here, but the results are not so hot.
(4) It is not quite as nontoxic as initially believed. It can produce hepatitis, particularly in elderly women who have had reactions to other antifungal agents. It now appears to have some endocrinologic effects: gynecomastia, depression of serum testosterone levels, and perhaps, blocking adrenal response to ACTH. The endocrine effects appear to be dose related.

In sum, it's a good addition in a field (fungal infections) where the drugs available all have significant drawbacks.

For further discussion of this agent see references 1–3.] ◀

7–2 **Amphotericin B Nephrotoxicity in Humans Decreased by Salt Repletion.** It has been suggested that tubuloglomerular feedback may be involved in the renal dysfunction induced by amphotericin B. The responsiveness of the tubuloglomerular feedback reflex is influenced by sodium status; salt depletion enhances the vasoconstrictor response. Hugo T. Heidemann, John F. Gerkens, W. Anderson Spickard, Edwin K. Jackson, and Robert A. Branch (Vanderbilt Univ.) describe findings in 5 consecutive patients with renal dysfunction occurring early in the course of systemic amphotericin B therapy; all 5 had improved renal function when their sodium intake was increased, and all 5 were able to complete treatment.

Man, 67, with malaise and a papular palatal lesion of several weeks' duration, had been taking cortisone for Addison's disease for 3 years. The inflamed palatal lesion prevented his eating solid foods and he sustained a weight loss of 28 lb; also, choroidoretinitis and hepatomegaly were present. Fungi were found on palatal biopsy, and *Histoplasma capsulatum* was cultured. Amphotericin B was given intravenously in increased daily dosage, but sharp rises in the blood urea nitrogen, serum creatinine, and potassium

---

(7–2) Am. J. Med. 75:476–481, September 1983.

levels occurred. Treatment was stopped after 9 days. The patient had inadvertently received a 2-gm sodium diet since being hospitalized, while his cortisone treatment was continued. These 2 factors led to a modest sodium depletion. Physiologic saline and fludrocortisone were then given, in addition to a 300-mEq sodium diet; the creatinine, potassium, and blood urea nitrogen levels declined within 2 days. Amphotericin B was reinstituted and continued for 11 weeks. The palatal and ocular lesions resolved with no impairment of renal function.

Four of the 5 patients had evidence of sodium depletion from low sodium intake, diuretic therapy, or vomiting. Sodium loading led to improved renal function in all 5. Amphotericin B treatment was continued in fully effective doses without further evidence of impaired renal function. These findings support a critical role for sodium balance during amphotericin B therapy and are consistent with the hypothesis that tubuloglomerular feedback is involved in mediating impaired renal function in this setting.

▶ [This is a fine contribution. The major limitation of systemic amphotericin B therapy has been nephrotoxicity. Evidence of altered renal function is seen in almost 80% of patients receiving this drug, and it is often the problem that most complicates lifesaving treatment.

The results here were most impressive. Sodium loading resulted in swift drops in blood urea nitrogen and serum creatinine levels and permitted completion of treatment in all 5 patients. Although some patients got fairly waterlogged, this was tolerable and rapidly reversed after the completion of amphotericin B therapy. Clearly this continues to keep amphotericin in the therapeutic ballgame vs. ketoconazole.] ◀

Chapter 7 References

1. Graybill J. R.: Summary: potential and problems with ketoconazole. *Am. J. Med.* 74:86–90, 1983.
2. Hughes W. T., Bartley D. L., Patterson G. G., et al.: Ketoconazole and candidiasis: a controlled study. *J. Infect. Dis.* 147:1060–1069, 1983.
3. Dismukes W. E., Stamm A. M., Graybill J. R., et al.: Treatment of systemic mycoses with ketoconazole: emphasis on toxicity and clinical response in 552 patients. *Ann. Intern. Med.* 98:13–20, 1983.

ruses circulate in the community. These outbreaks do not seem to be necessarily limited to a specific viral type. Football players may be more vulnerable because of the time of year when they assemble to play, the close physical contact among them, unhygienic sharing of team water bottles during practice, and physical exertion. Cases might be reduced by improving team hygienic practices.

▶ [Here's another recently recognized hazard of high school football.

National enterovirus surveillance consistently shows an annual peak of activity during the late summer and fall. Meningitis occurs in only a small number of individuals with enteroviral infections—it's the tip of the iceberg.

Why overt meningeal symptoms are seen more frequently in the football player is not known. However, the authors suggest that perhaps heavy physical activity can enhance the severity of the infection. In the past, the severity of paralytic polio was noted to be greater in those who continued physical activity after the onset of symptoms than in those who did not. Mice infected with coxsackieviruses and then made to swim to exhaustion have greater mortality and higher myocardial titers of virus.

The authors suggest that perhaps the incidence could be lessened by "improvement of team hygiene," for example, using paper cups or not dipping hands into the team water bucket. Well, macho boys will be macho boys. I doubt that such revolutionary changes in high school team mores will sweep the nation!] ◀

▶ ↓ Following on the heels of the successful reports of the treatment of primary genital herpes infections with topical acyclovir, numerous investigators have pursued other uses of this antiviral agent. The new intravenous and oral formulations have fueled this investigative intensity. No sooner was the efficacy of intravenous acyclovir demonstrated in the treatment of primary genital herpes[1] than it was shown that the oral drug also was effective in primary as well as recurrent disease.[2, 3]

Barring any last-minute problems, oral acyclovir should be available for general use in mid-1984. Now, that is good news!

The topical ointment also has been shown to offer relief in a common herpes infection which is not sexually transmitted, fever blisters. ◀

8–3 **Successful Treatment of Herpes Labialis With Topical Acyclovir.** Up to 20% of young adults have recurrent herpes simplex infections about the mouth. No treatment thus far has been effective. A. Paul Fiddian, Jane M. Yeo, Ronald Stubbings, and Donald Dean undertook a double-blind trial of acyclovir cream in 49 adults aged at least 18 who had a minimum of 2 documented recurrences of herpes labialis yearly and who were treated within 24 hours of onset of an episode. The outcome of 74 episodes was analyzed. A 5% acyclovir cream was applied topically 5 times daily for 5 days in 34 episodes, whereas 40 episodes were treated with a placebo cream.

Significantly more lesions in first episodes were aborted in acyclovir-treated patients. Acyclovir treatment did not influence the development of new lesions, but this was low in both groups. The time to first formation of an ulcer or crust and the time to complete healing both were significantly reduced by acyclovir treatment in first episodes and in all episodes (Fig 8–1). Fewer acyclovir-treated patients reported pruritus, and the duration of all symptoms was reduced in first episodes treated with acyclovir. No serious side effects developed.

Acyclovir cream appears to offer an effective treatment of recurrent herpes labialis that is superior to the unproved home remedies currently used. Studies evaluating prophylactic oral acyclovir in the

(8–3) Br. Med. J. 286:1699–1701, May 28, 1983.

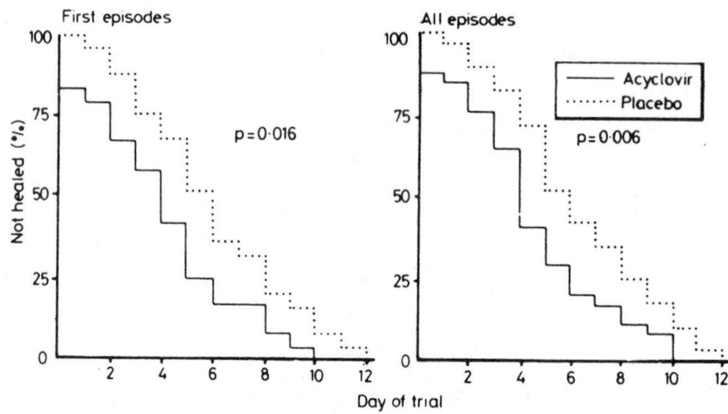

Fig 8–1.—Survival curves showing time to complete healing of first and all subsequent episodes of herpes labialis treated with acyclovir-containing cream or placebo. (In the diagram, the initial separation of curves results from the occurrence of completely aborted lesions in the acyclovir-treated group.) (Courtesy of Fiddian, A. P., et al.: Br. Med. J. 286:1699–1701, May 28, 1983.)

treatment of frequent recurrences of herpes labialis and of genital herpes are in progress.

► [I'm glad this paper with its positive result appeared, because I understand that many people are using topical acyclovir for treating herpes labialis. A sales representative speculated to one of my colleagues that most of the topical medication sold was being used in this circumstance, even though it was not an approved use. The generally favorable clinical impression was borne out by this double-blind study.] ◄

8–4 **Acyclovir Halts Progression of Herpes Zoster in Immunocompromised Patients.** Acute herpes zoster is a common cause of morbidity in immunocompromised patients and carries a risk of visceral dissemination in these hosts. Henry H. Balfour, Jr., Bonnie Bean, Oscar L. Laskin, Richard F. Ambinder, Joel D. Meyers, James C. Wade, John A. Zaia, Dorothee Aeppli, L. Edward Kirk, Anthony C. Segreti, Ronald E. Keeney, and the Burroughs Wellcome Collaborative Acyclovir Study Group report a double-blind study of acyclovir in 94 immunocompromised patients with acute zoster. None was pregnant or had renal dysfunction. The most common reasons for immune suppression were lymphoproliferative cancer, other cancers, and marrow transplantation. Fifty-two patients had localized skin lesions, and 42 had disseminated cutaneous zoster. Acyclovir was given intravenously in a dose of 1,500 mg/sq m of body surface daily for 1 week. Patients given placebo usually received 5% aqueous dextrose solution. Acyclovir was given to 28 patients with localized zoster and to 24 with disseminated disease.

Disease progression was significantly less frequent in acyclovir-treated patients in both groups. Two patients with visceral zoster initially did well with acyclovir treatment. In 4 patients given placebo, visceral disease developed during the study. The effects of acyclovir therapy on the development of new lesions and on symptoms are shown in Figure 8–2. Negative results on viral culture were obtained sooner for acyclovir recipients than for those given placebo. Three acy-

---

(8–4) N. Engl. J. Med. 308:1448–1453, June 16, 1983.

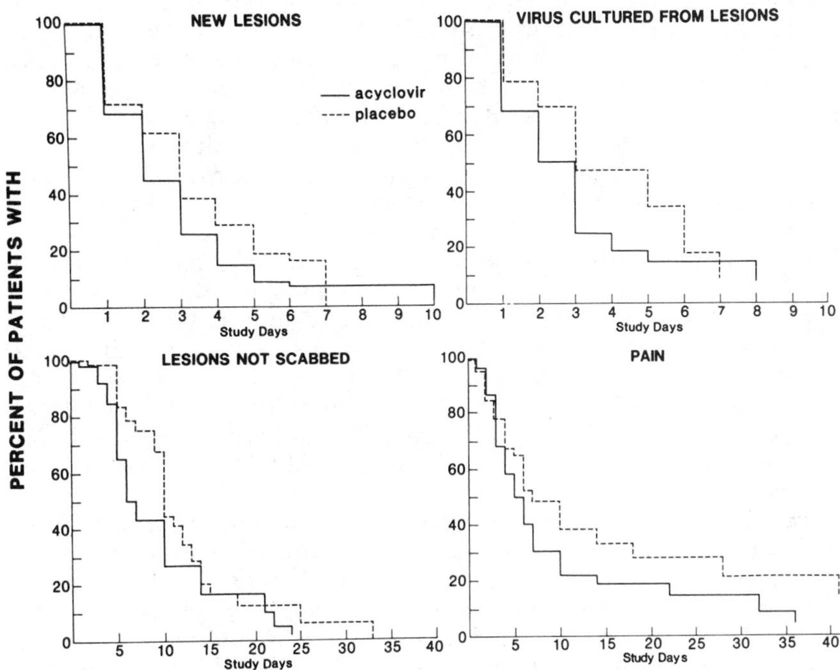

Fig 8–2.—Kaplan-Meier time-to-event graphs for 52 acyclovir-treated patients and for 42 given placebo. None of the differences is significant by the Breslow test. (Courtesy of Balfour, H. H., Jr., et al.: N. Engl. J. Med. 308:1448–1453, June 16, 1983. Reprinted by permission of the New England Journal of Medicine.)

clovir recipients had decreased renal function, as did 1 given placebo.

Acyclovir prevented the progression of zoster in these immunocompromised patients with localized or disseminated cutaneous involvement, and the drug was well tolerated. Further studies are needed to establish optimal therapeutic regimens.

▶ [Just before this paper appeared, one of my colleagues was consulted regarding a young woman with lupus treated with steroids who had developed herpes zoster. Conservative fellow that he is, he elected to watch and treat symptomatically. After two days with increasing pain and new lesions developing daily, he feared dissemination and recommended intravenous acyclovir, recognizing that there were not yet data to support this course. The results were dramatic: the pain abated, there were no new lesions, and the patient's smile returned. The copy of the journal with this article was in the next day's mail; his experience had certainly prepared him to believe the results of the study, and he wished he had started acyclovir a day or two earlier!

Intravenous acyclovir also has been used successfully in prophylaxis of oropharyngeal and esophageal herpes infections in marrow transplant recipients as well as in patients receiving remission-induction chemotherapy for leukemia.[4] But caution! A report has just appeared describing transient neurologic symptoms (lethargy, agitation, tremor, disorientation, and paresthesia) in marrow transplant recipients receiving this drug.[5]] ◀

▶ ↓ The newspapers have been full of articles describing the results of interferon in cancer chemotherapy—with largely negative results. I thought you would like to see the nice results of a controlled trial of interferon-alpha used prophylactically to prevent cytomegalovirus infections in renal transplant recipients. ◀

8–5 **Effects of Interferon-Alpha on Cytomegalovirus Reactivation Syndromes in Renal Transplant Recipients.** In a 6-week preliminary study, prophylactic interferon was shown to delay urinary shedding of cytomegalovirus and to reduce the occurrence of viremia in renal transplant recipients. Martin S. Hirsch, Robert T. Schooley, A. Benedict Cosimi, Paul S. Russell, Francis L. Delmonico, Nina E. Tolkoff-Rubin, John T. Herrin, Kari Cantell, Mary-Lin Farrell, Teresa R. Rota, and Robert H. Rubin undertook a double-blind 14-week trial of interferon-alpha in renal transplant recipients at Massachusetts General Hospital. All of the patients had preoperative cytomegalovirus titers exceeding 1:8 by indirect immunofluorescence. Immunosuppression was with azathioprine and prednisone, and in some cases, equine antithymocyte globulin. Study patients received 3×10^6 units of partially purified interferon-alpha before operation, 3 times weekly for 6 weeks thereafter, and then twice weekly for 8 weeks for a total postoperative dose of 102×10^6 units. The 20 interferon and 22 placebo recipients were well-matched with regard to clinical factors and kidney source.

Cytomegalovirus syndromes were markedly reduced in interferon recipients. Only 1 study patient had a syndrome, compared with 7 placebo patients. Five placebo recipients had fever with leukopenia, 3 had pneumonia, and 2 had fever with atypical lymphocytosis. The affected study patient had had several doses of interferon withheld because of thrombocytopenia. Opportunistic superinfections occurred only in placebo recipients with cytomegalovirus infection during the treatment period. One patient had disseminated aspergillosis and 1 had *Pneumocystis carinii* pneumonia. Cytomegalovirus-associated glomerulopathy occurred in 3 placebo recipients and 1 interferon recipient. One placebo recipient died of cytomegalovirus pneumonia and another of combined cytomegalovirus and *P. carinii* pneumonia. Two study patients died, 1 of cardiomyopathy and 1 of a perforated intestinal diverticulum with gastrointestinal bleeding. Graft function was comparable in the two groups at completion of the 14-week drug treatment period. Cytomegalovirus viremia was infrequent in both groups. Acute reactions to interferon were rare. An average of 5 doses of interferon were withheld because of thrombocytopenia or granulocytopenia, but nearly as many doses of placebo were missed for these reasons. Severe bone marrow suppression occurred in 4 study and 3 control patients.

Interferon-alpha appears to be useful in reducing the risk of serious cytomegalovirus infection in seropositive renal transplant recipients. Recombinant DNA techniques may provide relatively pure, inexpensive interferon preparations in the near future.

▶ [Don't reach for the order sheet just yet; interferon-alpha is still an investigational drug. The results of this well-designed study certainly are encouraging. Only one interferon recipient developed cytomegalovirus infection. That patient, however, had had one third of the scheduled interferon doses withheld because he was thrombocytopenic, and it was during this interval that the infection developed. It is thought that cytomegalovirus infection predisposes transplant patients to other superinfec-

---

(8–5) N. Engl. J. Med. 308:1489–1493, June 23, 1983.

tions. In this study, only placebo recipients who had cytomegalovirus infections developed superinfections. So there was a double preventive impact of the interferon prophylaxis. This clearly is an area to watch!] ◀

8–6 **"Alice in Wonderland" Syndrome in a Patient With Infectious Mononucleosis** is described by Giorgio Sanguineti (Milan) Franco Crovato, Roberto De Marchi, and Giovanni Desirello (Genoa).

Man, 32, previously healthy, suddenly experienced fatigue and intermittent visual disturbances. He perceived objects rapidly moving backward and forward. The disorder progressed and was complicated by blurred vision, distortion of images, and miscalculation of the position of objects. The patient reported feeling "detached," and illusional symptoms were described. Neurologic examination, an EEG, and a computed tomographic study yielded normal findings. Benzodiazepine therapy was begun. A maculopapular rash developed the month after onset of symptoms, with slight fever, pharyngitis, generalized lymphadenopathy, and splenomegaly. There were 20% atypical lymphocytes in a blood smear, and the heterophil antibody test for infectious mononucleosis was strongly positive.

Todd first described the "Alice in Wonderland" syndrome, or metamorphopsia, as a state of visual aberrations occurring in patients with migraine, epilepsy, cerebral lesions, hallucinogenic drug intoxication, hypnagogic states, and schizophrenia. An association with infectious mononucleosis has also been described. An association of the perceptual disturbances with lesions of the parietal lobe has been suggested. Patients with metamorphopsia should be studied for mononucleosis before being classified as psychiatric cases.

▶ [I don't know why the hell we included this article except that the title is captivating and you might be able to wow your colleagues on rounds by casually referring to the "Alice in Wonderland" syndrome as an occasional accompaniment of infectious mononucleosis. If you are asked what that means simply indicate that it's more commonly known as metamorphopsia—then duck and leave quickly!] ◀

Chapter 8 References

1. Corey L., Fife K.H., Benedetti J.K., et al.: Intravenous acyclovir for the treatment of primary genital herpes. *Ann. Intern. Med.* 98:914, 1983.
2. Bryson Y.J., Dillon M., Lovett M., et al.: Treatment of first episodes of genital herpes simplex virus infection with oral acyclovir: a randomized double-blind controlled trial in normal subjects. *N. Engl. J. Med.* 308:916, 1983.
3. Nilsen A.E., Aasen T., Halsos A.M., et al.: Efficacy of oral acyclovir in the treatment on initial and recurrent genital herpes. *Lancet* 2:571, 1983.
4. Hann I.M., Prentice H.G., Blacklock H.A., et al.: Acyclovir prophylaxis against herpes virus infections in severely immunocompromised patients; randomized double blind trial. *Br. Med. J.* 287:384, 1983.
5. Wade J.C., Meyers J.D.: Neurologic symptoms associated with parenteral acyclovir treatment after marrow transplantation. *Ann. Intern. Med.* 98:921, 1983.

(8–6) J. Infect. Dis. 147:782, April 1983.

9. Therapy

▶ Much of the infectious disease literature this past year has been dominated by testimonials to the effectiveness of the new β-lactam antibiotics. Indications for use were focused and limitations explored. And, as has happened with each new drug, side effects unnoticed during investigative trials are now being reported and quantitated. ◀

9–1 **Prolonged Bleeding Times and Bleeding Diathesis Associated With Moxalactam Administration.** Moxalactam disodium (Moxam) is a new, recently approved, broad-spectrum antibiotic. Adverse reactions to the drug reportedly occur in less than 10% of patients, and the reactions are similar to those seen with any of the cephalosporin class of antibiotics. Occasional bleeding secondary to hypoprothrombinemia, usually in debilitated or malnourished patients, has been reported. Michael R. Weitekamp and Robert C. Aber (Milton S. Hershey Med. Center, Hershey, Pa.) describe a reversible bleeding diathesis discovered among 12 consecutive patients who received moxalactam during the period from March 1982 through July 1982 and present 3 illustrative case reports.

Three of the 12 patients were neonates being treated for enteric gram-negative meningitis and were excluded from the study because bleeding-time studies could not be performed. However, no major bleeding diatheses were evident in these patients. Another 3 patients were excluded from the study because they had received moxalactam for less than 3 days. Of the remaining 6 patients, all of whom had received moxalactam for at least 3 days, 5 had prolonged bleeding times. In 4 of these patients, bleeding time exceeded 25 minutes. A bleeding diathesis was evident in all 5 patients with a prolonged bleeding time. Bleeding times returned to normal within 4–8 days after withdrawal of moxalactam. No patient exhibited a prolongation of prothrombin or partial thromboplastin times during diasthesis.

The results suggest that platelet dysfunction secondary to the use of moxalactam is clinically significant and that this adverse reaction may occur more commonly than previously thought.

▶ [The moxalactam molecule is an oxa-β-lactam in which oxygen has been substituted for the sulfa in the β-lactam nucleus, a modification associated with enhanced antibacterial activity. The molecule also incorporates substitutions found in other antibiotics. The α-carboxyl substitution (of carbenicillin) probably accounts for its antipseudomonal activity, and the 7-methoxy group (of cefoxitin) confers increased resistance to aerobic and anaerobic β-lactamases. Unfortunately, although moxalactam incorporates the best antibacterial functions of a number of older β-lactam antibiotics, the undesirable side effects of these older antimicrobials have also found their way into the moxalactam molecule. As noted in this article by Weitekamp and Aber, the platelet defect and prolonged bleeding time noted with carbenicillin has now been documented to occur with moxalactam. Bang and his colleagues have identified

(9–1) JAMA 249:69–71, Jan. 7, 1983.

the platelet defect to be a carbenicillin or moxalactam suppression of ADP-induced platelet aggregation.[1] Moxalactam's other hemostatic defect—prolongation of the prothrombin time—is probably related to its cefoxitin-like resistance to aerobic and anaerobic β-lactamases, plus some degree of biliary excretion. This results in suppression of intestinal flora and decreased production of vitamin K. Thus two different mechanisms have now been demonstrated to account for the occasional patient who develops clinically significant bleeding while receiving moxalactam therapy.

But don't count this drug out yet. Supplementary therapy with vitamin K prevents or treats the moxalactam-induced prolongation of the protime. The extent to which the other third generation cephalosporins suppress the ADP-activation of platelets has not yet been quantitated.

Although these side effects still leave us short of Ehrlich's "magic bullet," the next few papers demonstrate that, whether measured *in vitro* or *in vivo,* the third generation cephalosporins have an important place in our antimicrobial armamentarium.] ◀

9–2 **Cefotaxime: Review of In Vitro Antimicrobial Properties and Spectrum of Activity.** Ronald N. Jones and Clyde Thornsberry discuss the use of cefotaxime sodium, a cephalosporin antibiotic of high potency having a broad spectrum of activity. The drug has remarkable potency against all Enterobacteriaceae, including *Enterobacter* species, *Serratia marcescens,* and *Proteus vulgaris,* all resistant to earlier cephalosporins. Cefotaxime generally inhibits more than 90% of enteric bacilli at concentrations of 0.5 μg/ml or below. It is inactive against *Streptococcus faecalis* and most other serogroup D streptococci. It is moderately active against *Pseudomonas aeruginosa.* Its activity against other pseudomonads and nonfermentative gram-negative bacilli varies, and in vitro susceptibility testing must be used as a guide to treatment. Cefotaxime is active against *Hemophilus influ-*

TABLE 1.—Comparison of the In Vitro Activity of Cefotaxime With That of 6 Other Broad-Spectrum Antibiotics Against Cephalothin-Resistant and Cefamandole-Resistant Organisms

	Result (μg/ml)*		
Antibiotic	MIC_{25}	MIC_{50}	MIC_{80}
Cefotaxime	0.25	16	128
Cefoperazone	4.0	8.0	32
Moxalactam	0.25	8.0	>256
Cefsulodin	16	>64	>64
Cefoxitin	8.0	>64	>64
Amoxicillin	8.0	>64	>64
Gentamicin	1.0	2.0	8.0

Note: Cephalothin-resistant and cefamandole-resistant strains (minimal inhibitory concentrations [MICs] equal to or greater than 32 μg/ml) were frequency-adjusted to simulate the endemic prevalence of resistance in current clinical material. The results are from Fuchs, P. C.: Cefmenoxime (SCE-1365), a new cephalosporin: in vitro activity, comparison with other antimicrobial agents, β-lactamase stability, and disk diffusion testing with tentative interpretive criteria. Antimicrob. Agents Chemother. 20:747–759, 1981.

*The MIC_{25}, MIC_{50}, and MIC_{80} are the lowest concentrations inhibiting 25%, 50%, and 80% of tested strains, respectively.

(Courtesy of Jones, R. N., and Thornsberry, C.: Rev. Infect. Dis. 4(Suppl.):S300–S314, Sept./Oct. 1982.)

(9–2) Rev. Infect. Dis. 4(Suppl.):S300–S314, Sept./Oct. 1982.

TABLE 2.—COMPARISON OF THE IN VITRO ACTIVITY OF CEFOTAXIME WITH THAT OF 7 OTHER DRUGS AGAINST A POPULATION OF AMINOGLYCOSIDE-RESISTANT GRAM-NEGATIVE AND GRAM-POSITIVE BACTERIA WITH KNOWN RESISTANCE MECHANISMS

Antibiotic	Result (μg/ml)*		
	MIC_{25}	MIC_{50}	MIC_{80}
Cefotaxime	0.5	2.0	16
Cefoperazone	2.0	4.0	8.0
Moxalactam	1.0	4.0	16
Cefsulodin	2.0	8.0	>64
Cefamandole	0.5	>64	>64
Cefoxitin	2.0	64	>64
Cephalothin	1.0	>64	>64
Amoxicillin	4.0	>32	>32

Note: The organisms were resistant to kanamycin (minimal inhibitory concentration [MIC], equal to or greater than 64 μg/ml) gentamicin (MIC equal to or greater than 16 μg/ml), tobramycin (MIC equal to or greater than 16 μg/ml), and amikacin (MIC equal to or greater than 64 μg/ml).

*The MIC_{25}, MIC_{50}, MIC_{80} are the lowest concentrations inhibiting 25%, 50%, and 80% of tested strains, respectively.

(Courtesy of Jones, R. N., and Thornsberry, C.: Rev. Infect. Dis. (Suppl.):S300–S314, Sept./Oct. 1982.)

enzae and *Neisseria* species. Most anaerobes are highly susceptible to the drug. The in vitro activity of cefotaxime is compared with that of other agents against antibiotic-resistant organisms in Tables 1 and 2.

The potent antimicrobial activity of cefotaxime against a wide spectrum of organisms appears to result from a number of factors including β-lactamase stability, good ability to pass through cell membranes, strong affinity for lethal penicillin-binding proteins, minimal limitation by the inoculum effect, and bactericidal action at or close to the inhibitory concentration. Clinically useful methods of susceptibility testing have been developed. Susceptibility testing with cefotaxime presents no special problems in the application of agar or broth dilution procedures and the disk-diffusion method.

▶ [As illustrated in this article, the three currently available third-generation cephalosporins, cefotaxime, cefoperazone, and moxalactam, demonstrate remarkable in vitro activity against cephalothin-resistant and cefamandole-resistant organisms (Table 1) and against aminoglycoside-resistant organisms (Table 2). However, little advantage over older cephalosporins and semisynthetic penicillins is to be expected in treating gram-positive coccal infections. Although cefotaxime is clearly superior in vitro against penicillin-resistant *Streptococcus pneumoniae,* it is comparable to ampicillin against penicillin-sensitive strains.[2] Moxalactam's primary therapeutic weakness (in comparison with the other third-generation cephalosporins) is its inferior activity against the pneumococcus.

As with the older cephalosporins, the currently available third-generation cephalosporins remain ineffective against the enterococcus. Activity against *Pseudomonas aeruginosa* is variable. Thus susceptibility testing must be relied upon to determine whether any of these agents can be used in treatment of pseudomonas infections. Perhaps most important, methacillin-resistant staphylococci should also be considered as resistant to the third-generation cephalosporins (see Chapter 3—Staphylococcal Infections.] ◀

▶ ↓ *Bacteroides fragilis* proved to be beyond the range of the first-generation cephalosporins. Second-generation cephalosporins, namely cefoxitin, aided considerably in combating *B. fragilis* infection, particularly in intraabdominal sites of infection where mixed aerobic-anaerobic pathogens are likely. The two following papers explore the utility of the third-generation cephalosporins in therapy of intraabdominal infections. ◀

9–3 **Relative Efficacy of β-Lactam Antimicrobial Agents in Two Animal Models of Infections Involving *Bacteroides fragilis.*** There is increasing concern about the role of anaerobic bacteria in a variety of infections. John G. Bartlett, George J. R. Marien, Manouchehr Dezfulian, and Keith A. Joiner examined β-lactam antimicrobial agents for their efficacy against *B. fragilis* in a rat model of intraabdominal sepsis and in a mouse model of subcutaneous abscess. The rats were challenged with pooled cecal contents to produce intraabdominal sepsis involving a polymicrobial aerobic-anaerobic flora. The antimicrobial agents were given intramuscularly, starting 4 hours after challenge, every 8 hours for 10 days. The mouse model involved subcutaneous abscesses and intraperitoneal antibiotic administration, starting 1 hour after challenge and repeated at 8-hour intervals for 5 days.

In rats with intraabdominal sepsis, optimal results were obtained with carbenicillin, moxalactam, cefoxitin, and cefotaxime. The incidence of abscesses was reduced more by these agents than by cefazolin, cephalothin, or cefamandole. The results obtained with the mouse subcutaneous abscess model are given in the table. The best results were obtained with clindamycin, moxalactam, and cefoxitin. The efficacy of the antibiotics correlated reasonably well with the peak

RESULTS WITH SUBCUTANEOUS ABSCESS MODEL

Agent	Dose (mg/kg)	Mean peak serum level (μg/ml ± 1 SEM)	Median MIC of test strains (μg/ml)*	Decrease in counts ($\log_{10}$ ± 1 SEM)†
Clindamycin	85	16 ± 2	0.25	5.0 ± 0.6
Moxalactam	200	197 ± 23	2	3.8 ± 0.6
Cefoxitin	400	93 ± 6	4	3.5 ± 0.5
Thienamycin	150	65 ± 19	2	2.6 ± 0.5
Cefoperazone	200	176 ± 11	16	
plus CP 45,899	200			2.6 ± 0.2
Cefotaxime	200	142 ± 14	16	1.9 ± 0.4
Carbenicillin	750	712 ± 120	32	1.0 ± 0.3
Ceftizoxime	200	119 ± 5	32	0.9 ± 0.3
Cefoperazone	250	176 ± 11	16	0.6 ± 0.1
Ceforanide	200	264 ± 39	128	0.6 ± 0.1
Cephalothin	200	61 ± 12	64	0.4 ± 0.2
Ampicillin	200	200 ± 61	32	0.3 ± 0.1

*Median MIC with 15 test strains of *Bacteriodes* species.

†Mean decrease in counts with 15 test strains for antimicrobial agent examined, compared with counts without treatment.

(Courtesy of Bartlett, J. G., et al.: Rev. Infect. Dis. 5(Suppl. 2):S338–S344, May/June, 1983.)

(9–3) Rev. Infect. Dis. 5(Suppl. 2):S338–S344, May/June 1983.

serum drug concentrations and the median minimal inhibitory concentrations (MICs).

The relative efficacy of β-lactam antibiotics against *B. fragilis* is a function of several interrelated factors, including in vitro activity, pharmacokinetics, and stability to the β-lactamase of *B. fragilis*. Correlation was relatively good in this study between the reduction in numbers of bacteria per lesion and the therapeutic index based on peak serum concentrations relative to MICs.

9–4 **Multicentered Study of Cefoperazone for Treatment of Intraabdominal Infections and Comparison of Cefoperazone With Cefamandole and Clindamycin Plus Gentamicin for Treatment of Appendicitis and Peritonitis.** Cefoperazone is a semisynthetic injectable cephalosporin antibiotic having greater in vitro and in vivo antibacterial activity than the earlier cephalosporins. It reportedly is highly effective against enteric gram-negative bacilli, *Pseudomonas aeruginosa,* staphylococci, *Hemophilus influenzae,* and most anaerobes. Ian M. Baird (Columbus, Ohio) reviewed the results of cefoperazone therapy for known or suspected intraabdominal infections in 59 patients in an open, noncomparative study; 35 of these patients were evaluable with respect to efficacy. Cefoperazone was given intravenously in daily doses of 4–8 gm.

All but 3 of the 35 evaluable patients had a satisfactory clinical response to cefoperazone. Of 71 pathogens, 62 were eliminated by the drug. The most common isolates were *Escherichia coli, P. aeruginosa,* group D streptococci, *Bacteroides fragilis,* and *Klebsiella pneumoniae.* Adverse reactions occurred in 9 of 59 patients. A comparative study was made of 144 patients, 57 of whom received cefoperazone in doses of 1–4 gm every 12 hours. Satisfactory clinical responses occurred in 90% of 20 evaluable patients given cefoperazone, in 80% of 20 patients given cefamandole, and in 100% of 16 patients given clindamycin and gentamicin. Satisfactory bacteriologic responses were obtained in 100%, 95%, and 100% of these groups, respectively. Adverse

MINIMAL INHIBITORY CONCENTRATIONS OF CEFOPERAZONE, CEFAMANDOLE, AND CLINDAMYCIN PLUS GENTAMICIN FOR CLINICAL ISOLATES IN A COMPARATIVE STUDY OF PATIENTS WITH INTRAABDOMINAL INFECTIONS

	MIC of indicated drug(s) (μg/ml)*		
Organism	Cefoperazone	Cefamandole	Clindamycin-gentamicin†
Escherichia coli	1.16/4.0	2.89/8.0	0.86/2.0
Pseudomonas aeruginosa	2.83/4.0	181/512	2.0/2.0
Bacteroides fragilis	47/64	75/128	0.79/2.0
Other	5.66/16	8/512	0.91/2.0

*Results are expressed as the minimal inhibitory concentration (MIC)/MIC_{90} (concentration required to inhibit growth of 90% of isolates). The MICs were determined only for the agent used in each patient.

†Values shown represent the MICs of gentamicin for aerobic organisms and the MICs of clindamycin for anaerobic organisms.

(Courtesy of Baird, I. M.: Rev. Infect. Dis. 5(Suppl.):S165–S172, Mar./Apr. 1983.)

(9–4) Rev. Infect. Dis. 5(Suppl.):S165–S172, Mar./Apr. 1983.

effects occurred in 5% of cefoperazone-treated patients, 11% of those given cefamandole, and 11.5% of those given clindamycin and gentamicin. Minimal inhibitory concentrations of the various antimicrobial agents for clinical isolates are shown in the table.

Cefoperazone is an effective, safe antimicrobial agent when used in conjunction with surgical drainage to treat bacterial intraabdominal infections. It should be especially useful for empiric therapy in clinically stable patients before bacteriologic findings are available.

▶ [The primary importance of these two studies is to reassure the clinician that a third-generation cephalosporin is adequate for empiric broad-spectrum coverage when anaerobes may be present. As noted in the paper by Baird, even cefoperazone, which has less activity against *Bacteroides fragilis* than the other third-generation cephalosporins, proved effective when compared with clindamycin and gentamicin in intraabdominal infections. I would strongly urge, however, that when *B. fragilis* is proved or suspected to be a predominant pathogen, metronidazole or clindamycin or even cefoxitin be used. They have superior activity against *B. fragilis.* This organism regularly creates an insulating abscess for itself excluding all but a fraction of the administered antimicrobial. Optimal therapy requires maximal dosing with our most effective drugs.] ◀

▶ ↓ In the 1983 YEAR BOOK (p. 48) Drs. Landesman, Corrado, Cherubin, and colleagues were congratulated for an excellent review of cephalosporin therapy of gram-negative bacillary meningitis. The importance of establishing killing levels of antibiotics in the CSF was emphasized by these authors. After therapy based on those guidelines, 96% of 77 patients treated with cefotaxime had a good response. In a follow-up article, these three authors and their colleagues update the accumulated experience with cefotaxime and focus upon the possible explanations of the occasional treatment failure. ◀

9–5 **Treatment of Gram-Negative Bacillary Meningitis: Role of the New Cephalosporin Antibiotics** is outlined by Charles E. Cherubin, Michael L. Corrado, S. Ramachandran Nair, Myles E. Gombert, Sheldon Landesman, and Guy Humbert. Chloramphenicol therapy has not proved very successful in the treatment of gram-negative bacillary meningitis (GNBM). The high failure rate is thought to be related to the wide gap between the minimal inhibitory concentrations (MICs) and minimal bactericidal concentrations (MBCs) of chloramphenicol for *Escherichia coli, Klebsiella,* and other Enterobacteriaceae. The new cephalosporins exhibit little difference between the MIC and MBC against most organisms and should prove more effective than chloramphenicol in treatment of GNBM. The effects of increasing inoculum size of *Pseudomonas aeruginosa* on the activity of the new β-lactam antimicrobial agents are shown in Figure 9–1. This "inoculum effect" should preclude single drug therapy of *Pseudomonas aeruginosa* meningitis. Cefotaxime also is active against gram-positive cocci. Studies in patients with normal meninges indicate that the concentration of cefotaxime in the CSF is about 0.5% of that in the serum 1–2 hours after infusion.

By late 1981, cefotaxime had been used to treat 129 patients with bacterial meningitis with over 90% experiencing a satisfactory outcome. The bacteriologic cure rate of diseases caused by the major meningeal pathogens was 98%, and for those caused by *E. coli* and *Klebsiella,* 96%. Failure was most evident in meningitis caused by

(9–5) Rev. Infect. Dis. 4(Suppl.):S453–S464, Sept./Oct. 1982.

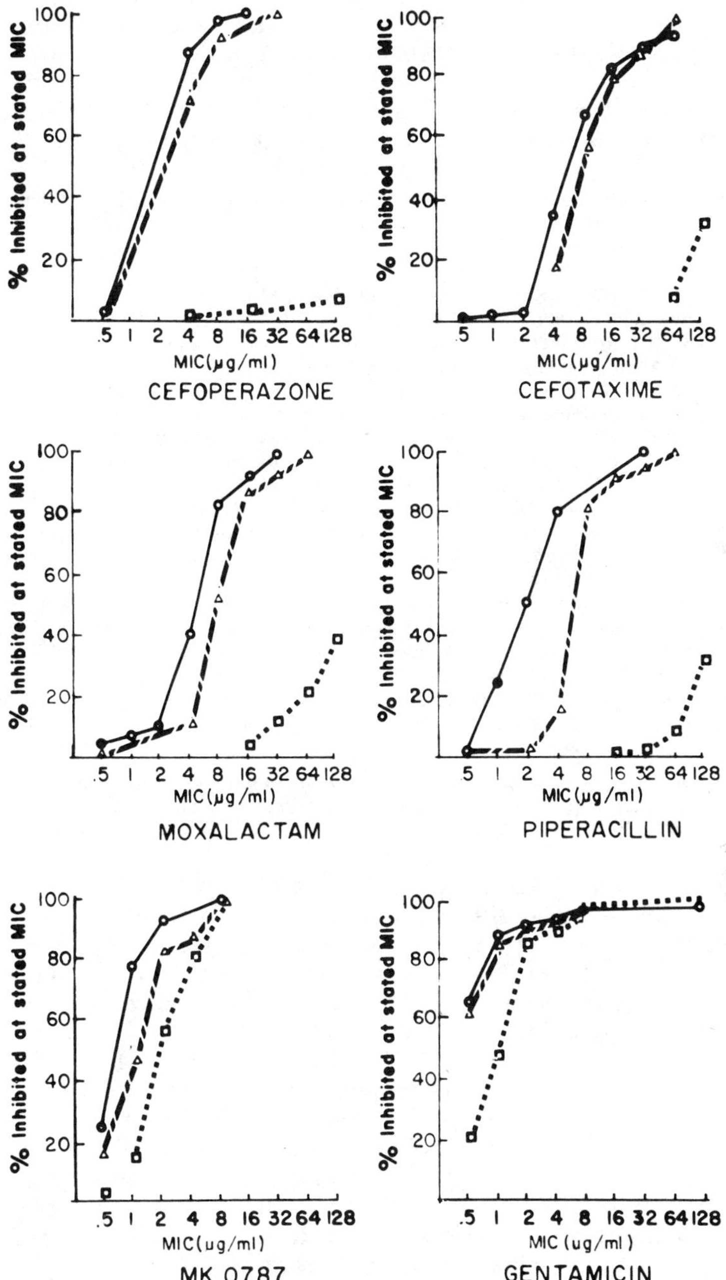

Fig 9–1.—Effects of inoculum size of 40 clinical isolates of *Pseudomonas aeruginosa* on the minimal inhibitory concentrations of cefoperazone, cefotaxime, moxalactam, piperacillin, thienamycin (MK 0787), and gentamicin. Size of the inocula: ○——○ = 10^4 CFU; △—·—△ 10^6 CFU; and □---□ = 10^8 CFU. (Courtesy of Cherubin, C. E., et al.: Rev. Infect. Dis. 4(Suppl.):S453–S464, Sept./Oct. 1982.)

Enterobacter cloacae (2 of 4 patients) and *Pseudomonas aeruginosa* (2 of 7 patients). The applicability of cefotaxime to infections caused by *Streptococcus pneumoniae, Hemophilus influenzae,* and *N. meningitidis* must be assessed by comparative drug studies. Cefotaxime may prove to be effective alternative therapy in patients who are allergic to penicillin. It may be a drug of first choice for treating GNBM where previous treatment was inadequate.

▶ [As data have accumulated, the third-generation cephalosporins, especially cefotaxime, continue to offer predictable efficacy for the treatment of both gram-positive and gram-negative meningitis. Infection due to the major meningeal pathogens, pneumococci, *H. influenzae,* and meningococci, respond with a 98% success rate. Therapy of *Klebsiella* and *E. coli* meningitis has been equally effective.

However, failures have occurred and appear to be species-specific: two of four patients with *Enterobacter cloacae* and two of seven patients with *Pseudomonas aeruginosa* meningitis failed cefotaxime therapy. These four patients constituted the only unqualified failures among patients with gram-negative meningitis. In evaluating these failures, the authors have explored the "inoculum effect" (see Figure 9–1). As the number of viable organisms approaches the high concentrations frequently seen in bacterial meningitis (10^7 organisms per ml), the minimal inhibitory concentrations of the β-lactam antibiotics become inaccessibly high for *Pseudomonas aeruginosa,* rendering therapy ineffective. Another mechanism of failure may be related to the development of resistance during therapy.[3] Certain bacteria, namely *Enterobacter, Serratia,* and *Pseudomonas,* possess inducible β-lactamases that may bind or destroy the newer cephalosporins in vivo.

Our current recommendation in the therapy of *Pseudomonas, Serratia,* or *Enterobacter* meningitis is to combine a third-generation cephalosporin with intraventricular or intralumbar aminoglycoside. Cefotaxime can be used alone with a high expectation of successful therapy when sensitive *E. coli* or Klebsiella are involved. Cefotaxime may also prove to be acceptable alternate therapy of common organism meningitis when conventional therapy (ampicillin, chloramphenicol) cannot be used for one reason or another.] ◀

▶ ↓ Occasionally, major improvements in the management or understanding of infectious processes arise, not from implementation of new products, but from a reappraisal of what is already at hand. The following articles offer new insights into old problems. ◀

9–6 **Endobronchial pH: Relevance to Aminoglycoside Activity in Gram-Negative Bacillary Pneumonia.** Gram-negative bacillary pneumonias (GNBPs) respond notoriously slowly to treatment and are subject to relapse. The penetrance of aminoglycosides into the respiratory tract is variable and often poor. The in vitro bioactivity of these agents is strikingly influenced by pH. Charles R. Bodem, Lawrence M. Lampton, Donald P. Miller, Eugene F. Tarka, and E. Dale Everett (Univ. of Missouri, Columbia) measured endobronchial pH to determine whether it could be a factor adversely affecting the response of GNBP to antimicrobial therapy. Studies were done in 7 healthy subjects, 10 patients undergoing bronchoscopy for a lung mass or persistent pulmonary infiltrate but without active infection, and 8 patients with bacterial pneumonia. Endobronchial pH was measured with a flexible pH electrode that had an outer diameter of 1.6 mm.

The mean endobronchial pH in controls was 6.58. The patients with chronic lung problems had a mean of 6.64. Those with pneumonia had

---

(9–6) Am. Rev. Respir. Dis. 127:39–41, January 1983.

an overall mean airway pH of 6.62, not significantly different from that of the other groups. The presence of bronchial inflammation, however, significantly altered the pH between pneumonic and normal airways (6.48 vs. 6.69). All subjects had arterial blood gas values within the normal clinical range. Studies in dogs showed a slight increase in endobronchial pH after aerosolization or instillation of lidocaine, which was used in some of the clinical studies.

Pneumonic airways are slightly more acidic than noninvolved airways, and this may contribute to a lack of response or relapse of GNBP after aminoglycoside therapy. Underdosing with aminoglycosides should be avoided, or antimicrobial agents that are less influenced by an acid milieu should be used. The influence of an acidic lung environment on antimicrobial activity and on the response to treatment is uncertain.

▶ [Without question gram-negative bacillary pneumonia responds poorly to therapy, no matter what antimicrobials are used. As such infections often arise in debilitated hospitalized patients with poor underlying host defenses, failure cannot be wholly ascribed to antimicrobial ineffectiveness. There is evidence to suggest, however, that compared to other gram-negative bacilli, pneumonia due to *Pseudomonas aeruginosa* is more resistant to therapy. Case-fatality rates are reported to be as high as 80%. The usual pattern of in vitro sensitivities of *Pseudomonas aeruginosa* dictates that, more often than not, the only effective antimicrobials are the aminoglycosides. Here the investigation summarized above raises an important point: endobronchial pH is acidotic, in the range of 6.6, and the activity of all aminoglycosides is severely compromised in an acid environment. In 1973 Young and Hewitt demonstrated that minimal inhibitory concentrations of aminoglycosides rose as much as 32-fold against certain organisms as the pH fell from 7.4 (the pH at which tube-dilution sensitivity testing is usually performed) to 6.4 (the pH of the endobronchial environment.[4] Thus failure of aminoglycosides in the therapy of gram-negative pneumonia, especially *Pseudomonas aeruginosa* pneumonia, may be related to the impotence of these antibiotics in the low pH environment of bronchial tissues.

The authors offer no solution to this dilemma. Certainly, in approaching the therapy of patients with gram-negative pneumonia, every effort should be made to provide maximal aminoglycoside dosing and, if possible, to use at least one additional antimicrobial with good in vitro activity. Beneficial effects of aerosolized gentamicin and carbenicillin in high concentrations in patients with cystic fibrosis and *Pseudomonas* pulmonary infection have recently been documented (1983 YEAR BOOK, p. 62). Prospective trials of aerosolized aminoglycosides are indicated. "Alkalinization" of the endobronchial environment was discussed by the authors, but having tried unsuccessfully for years to "acidify" the urine in patients with chronic urinary tract infections on Mandelamine therapy, I am less than optimistic that the pH of bronchial secretions can be altered.] ◀

9–7 **The Use of Rifampin in Treatment of Nontuberculous Infections: An Overview** is presented by Merle A. Sande (San Francisco). The use of rifampin has increased recently, and the drug is now prescribed to treat infections due to a wide range of organisms, including *Chlamydia, Legionella,* and even fungi. Many new applications, however, have evolved without clinical trials. Rifampin acts uniquely by binding to and inactivating bacterial DNA-dependent RNA polymerase. Usually, bactericidal effect at very low concentrations results. Resistance can emerge rapidly by slight modifications in the target enzyme, especially when many organisms are present, as in endocarditis. Rifampin is highly lipid soluble, thus it is able to penetrate

(9–7) Rev. Infect. Dis. 5(Suppl. 3):S399–S401, July–Aug. 1983.

various hidden recesses, including the CNS and abscess cavities. It appears capable of killing bacteria within phagocytic cells. Rifampin induces hepatic microsomal enzymes, and accelerates its own metabolism and excretion.

Both a fear of generating resistance of *mycobacterium tuberculosis* and complex interactions with other antimicrobial agents have retarded the development of rifampin for use in other conditions. Rifampin has been used to treat a variety of staphylococcal infections because of its exceptional activity against methicillin-resistant *Staphylococcus aureus* and *Staphylococcus epidermidis* and its ability to penetrate sites of infection. It can also eliminate staphylococci from nasal carriers. The drug could prove useful in treating both endocarditis and osteomyelitis due to *S. aureus*. Nasal carriage of meningococci is eliminated by rifampin, and it seems useful in aborting outbreaks of meningococcal disease. The drug also can eliminate nasopharyngeal carriage of *Hemophilus influenzae* type b. Rifampin has been administered to patients with chronic granulomatous disease. It is under study for use in treating disease caused by intracellular parasites (e.g., leprosy, chancroid, and chlamydial infections). Whether rifampin will prove of benefit when combined with trimethoprim to treat difficult chronic urinary tract infections remains to be seen.

▶ [Most of us were introduced to rifampin years ago as a welcome addition to isoniazid in the therapy of tuberculosis. Side effects were extremely rare: we had only to advise our contact lens–wearing patients that orange-red tears might develop, irreversibly staining their lenses. Fifteen years later it is as if the drug has just been introduced. Numerous studies are in progress evaluating rifampin's effectiveness in a wide variety of clinical situations. However, despite frequent reports that "after days of therapeutic stalemate with such and such a regimen, the addition of rifampin resulted in dramatic improvement and cure," great caution should be used before employing rifampin in any unproved clinical situation. First, in vitro, low-dose rifampin frequently antagonizes the bactericidal activity of a wide variety of antimicrobials, particularly the cell wall–active antibiotics. Second, in vitro studies correlate poorly with in vivo results whether rifampin is tested alone or in combination with other antibiotics. Third, failures are often due to the emergence of rifampin resistance. Resistance can develop despite concomitant therapy with other effective antibiotics. Finally, allergic and toxic reactions do occur. Specifically, hepatotoxicity with jaundice may occur in patients with preexisting liver disease and an immunoallergic effect (influenza-like syndrome, hemolytic anemia, renal failure) occurs in occasional patients who have received prolonged and/or intermittent therapy.

Rifampin will clearly have an important place in the management of certain nontuberculous infections. That place is currently being defined through carefully designed prospective studies (see Chapter 3—Staphylococcal Infections). Until the answers are in, it must be remembered that rifampin has the potential to aggravate as well as augment standard therapy of infectious processes.] ◀

Chapter 9 References

1. Bang N.U., Tessler S.S., Heidenreich R.O., et al.: Effects of moxalactam on blood coagulation and platelet function. *Rev. Infect. Dis.* 4(Suppl.):S546–S554, 1982.
2. Goldstein E.J.C., Cherubin C.E., Corrado M.L., et al.: Comparative susceptibility of *Yersinia enterocolitica, Eikenella corrodens,* and penicillin-resistant and penicillin-susceptible *Streptococcus pneumoniae* to β-lactam and alternative antimicrobial agents. *Rev. Infect. Dis.* 4(Suppl.):S406–S410, 1982.

3. Sanders C.C., and Sanders W.E.: Emergence of resistance during therapy with the newer β-lactam antibiotics: role of inducible β-lactamases and implications for the future. *Rev. Infect. Dis.* 5:639–648, 1983.
4. Young L.S., Hewitt W.L.: Activity of five aminoglycoside antibiotics in vitro against gram-negative bacilli and *Staphylococcus aureus*. *Antimicrob. Agents Chemother.* 4:617–625, 1973.

10. Miscellaneous

▶ ↓ In 1975 a cluster of children in Lyme, Connecticut, developed a peculiar and troubling syndrome characterized by unique skin lesions, often accompanied by headache, stiff neck, myalgia, and arthralgia. Weeks or months later, some of the children had neurologic symptoms and myocarditis, and still later, some had frank arthritis.

Steere and the group at Yale began work on this puzzle and were soon joined by colleagues at the Centers for Disease Control in Atlanta and the National Institute of Allergy and Infectious Disease. That they have done a splendid job in sleuthing out its infectious origin, the agent that transmits it, its treatment, and now, at last, its specific microbial etiology, is elegantly documented in the following article. ◀

10–1 **Spirochetal Etiology of Lyme Disease.** Lyme disease, first described in 1975, usually begins with an erythema chronicum migrans (ECM) skin lesion, which may be accompanied by headache, stiff neck, fever, myalgia, arthralgia, malaise, fatigue, or lymphadenopathy. Later on, patients may develop meningoencephalitis, cranial or peripheral neuropathies, myocarditis, or migratory musculoskeletal pain. Frank arthritis also may develop. Early findings suggested that the disease may be transmitted by an arthropod and that the causative agent was a nonpyogenic, penicillin-sensitive bacterium such as a spirochete. In 1982 a previously unrecognized spirochete was isolated from *Ixodes dammini* ticks collected on Shelter Island, New York, an area known to be endemic for Lyme disease. Allen C. Steere, Robert L. Grodzicki, Arnold N. Kornblatt, Joseph E. Craft, Alan G. Barbour, Willy Burgdorfer, George P. Schmid, Elizabeth Johnson, and Stephen E. Malawista report the isolation of this same spirochete from the blood, skin, and cerebrospinal fluid (CSF) of patients with Lyme disease and describe the characteristic IgM and IgG antibody response to the organism.

Three of 142 culture specimens from 56 patients yielded spirochetes. These 3 isolates were recovered from different patients and from different parts of the body: 1 from blood, 1 from a skin biopsy specimen of ECM, and 1 from CSF. Examination by immunofluorescence with the use of monoclonal antibody to the original isolate showed that the 3 isolates from patients, the 3 isolates from *I. dammini* ticks in Connecticut, and the original isolate from *I. dammini* on Shelter Island were identical in appearance, with a titer of 1:1,024 in each instance. Specific IgM antibody titers in patients usually peaked between 3 and 6 weeks after the onset of disease, whereas specific IgG antibody titers increased slowly and were generally highest months later when arthritis had developed. Of 40 patients who had ECM alone, 90% had an elevated IgM titer (greater than or equal to 1:128) between the ECM phase of the disease and the convalescent

---

(10–1) N. Engl. J. Med. 308:733–740, Mar. 31, 1983.

phase. Ninety-four percent of 95 patients with involvement of the nervous system, heart, or joints and all 60 patients with arthritis had IgG titers of 1:128 or greater. In contrast, none of 80 control subjects had elevated IgG titers, and only 3 of 20 control patients with infectious mononucleosis had elevated IgM titers.

It is concluded that the *I. dammini* spirochete is the etiologic agent in Lyme disease and that in such cases the number of organisms in affected tissues is small.

▶ [Congratulations—this looks very solid.

It seems confirmed by similar findings in Long Island and Westchester County (see the next article). Read that abstract now, and then I will comment on both.] ◀

10–2 **Spirochetes Isolated From the Blood of 2 Patients With Lyme Disease.** Lyme disease, a chronic inflammatory syndrome, is characterized by an expanding skin lesion, erythema chronicum migrans, at times accompanied or followed days to weeks later by monoarticular or oligoarticular arthritis, neurologic manifestations, or cardiac abnormalities. Since 1977, numerous cases of Lyme disease occurring in Long Island and Westchester County, New York, have been reported. The tick *Ixodes dammini* has been epidemiologically implicated as the vector. Jorge L. Benach, Edward M. Bosler, John P. Hanrahan, James L. Coleman, Gail S. Habicht, Thomas F. Bast, Donald J. Cameron, John L. Ziegler, Alan G. Barbour, Willy Burgdorfer, Robert Edelman, and Richard A. Kaslow report the isolation and subsequent identification of *I. dammini* spirochetes from the blood of 2 of 36 patients in Long Island and Westchester County with signs and symptoms suggestive of Lyme disease.

Man, 21, a summer resident of Fire Island, New York, incurred a tick bite on his lower back on June 20, 1982. During the next 2 days a circular rash, 7.6 cm in diameter, developed near the site of the bite. Four days later the patient felt feverish, with muscle aches and pains; serum and citrated whole blood specimens were obtained at this time. Because of pain in the cervical spine and enlargement of the rash, the patient was started on oral penicillin VK (250 mg 4 times a day for 10 days) on June 26. After 7 days of antibiotic therapy, the rash and symptoms disappeared. A convalescent-phase serum specimen was obtained on July 27, at which time the patient reported being well.

Subcultures of inoculated blood from both patients grew numerous spirochetes. Long forms, which were poorly motile, predominated. The identity of the isolate, both after initial detection and after further cultivation, was determined by identical dilution end points of the direct (titer, 1:128) and indirect (titer, 1:512) immunofluorescence procedures in paired tests using the human isolate and the *I. dammini*–derived spirochete as antigens. Monoclonal antibody also was found to be reactive to the human isolate (Fig 10–1). The spirochetes were not detectable by direct immunofluorescence of frozen sections of the skin lesion.

The findings support the likelihood that the spirochete derived from *I. dammini* is the etiologic agent for one or more of the clinical manifestations of Lyme disease.

(10–2) N. Engl. J. Med. 308:740–742, Mar. 31, 1983.

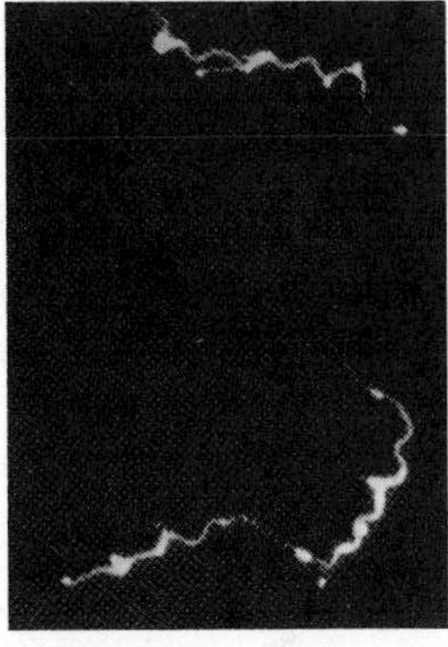

Fig 10–1.—Direct immunofluorescent stain FITC-labeled murine monoclonal antibody raised against strain B31 of the *Ixodes dammini* (spirochete of a Tick-derived spirochete (×850). (Courtesy of Benach, J. L., et al.: N. Engl. J. Med. 308:740–742, Mar. 31, 1983. Reprinted by permission of The New England Journal of Medicine.)

▶ [One of the remaining puzzles is the low frequency of recovery of the spirochete—successful in only 3 of 56 patients studied in New Haven, and in only 2 of 36 in New York. The authors discuss this in some detail. Clearly, the development of appropriate media and isolation procedures was initially troublesome. But it was easy to culture the microorganism from ticks—much tougher from humans. Both sets of authors thus suggest that spirochetemia may be transient or of low density in human disease. They also suggest another intriguing possibility that I'm sure they are hard after. Obviously the late manifestations of Lyme disease may mimic any of several immune-mediated disorders including juvenile or adult rheumatoid arthritis, Reiter's syndrome, rheumatic fever, the Guillain-Barré syndrome, or multiple sclerosis. There is also some evidence to suggest that there may be some HLA-related pathogenetic susceptibility among patients. At present it is unknown whether the *I. dammini* spirochete is present when the arthritis becomes manifest.

This opens up some exciting possibilities. Is the inciting agent (the spirochete) necessary for that continuing disease activity or is this a late autoimmune manifestation? This question remains of primary interest and importance in many immune-mediated diseases. Maybe this is the disease that can help solve the riddle.

As a final gift to clinicians, late in 1983 the Yale group published more definitive data on the results of treatment of the early manifestations of Lyme disease.[1] Here are their findings: (1) Erythema chronicum migrans and its associated symptoms resolved almost twice as fast in patients treated with tetracycline or penicillin than in those given erythromycin (5.5 vs. 9.2 days). (2) *None* of 39 patients given tetracycline (in 1980–1981) developed late major complications (meningoencephalitis, myocarditis, or arthritis). These complications occurred in 3 of 40 penicillin-treated patients and in 4 of 29 given erythromycin. This just missed statistical significance ($P = .07$). (3) In 1982 *all* 49 patients were given tetracycline, and, to date, none have developed late complications. (4) The authors' current choices are (a) tetracycline, (b) penicillin, (c) erythromycin.

Good work!] ◀

10–3 **Transfusion Malaria in the United States, 1972–1981.** Transfusion malaria is an uncommon condition that can cause serious illness and death. Isabel C. Guerrero, Bruce C. Weniger, and Myron G. Schultz (Centers for Disease Control) reviewed findings in 26 patients with transfusion-induced malaria reported in the United States between 1972 and 1981. Malaria caused by *Plasmodium malariae* in 9, *Plasmodium falciparum* in 8, *Plasmodium vivax* in another 8, and *Plasmodium ovale* in 1. The median patient age was 55 years. Most patients had intermittent fever and chills. Of the 4 who died of ma-

(10–3) Ann. Intern. Med. 99:221–226, August 1983.

Characteristics of Implicated Donors* in Cases of Transfusion Malaria, by Species, United States, 1972–1981

Infecting *Plasmodium* Species	Patient	Year	Implicated Donor Age/Sex	Implicated Donor Native Country	Length of Residence in United States	Most Recent Trip to a Malarious Country	Presumed Country of Malaria Acquisition	Malaria History or Illness	Malaria Smear Result	IFA Titers‡ of Implicated Donor *P. falciparum*	*P. malariae*	*P. vivax*	*P. ovale*
P. falciparum	3	1972	. . . M	United States	Life	. . .	Vietnam	. . .	–	4096	. . .	. . .	. . .
	9	1976	28/M	United States	Life	5 yrs	Vietnam	Yes		4096	. . .	. . .	. . .
	10	1976	26/M	Liberia	5 yrs	4 mos	Liberia	Yes	–	4096	256	64	. . .
	12	1977	. . . M	United States	Life	1 mo	Togo	No	+				
	15	1978	. . . M	Ghana	6 yrs	9 mos	Ghana	Yes		Negative	Negative	Negative	. . .
	23	1980	38/F	El Salvador	5 mos	5 mos	El Salvador	Yes	–	4096	1024	1024	. . .
	25	1981	26/M	Upper Volta	2 yrs	2 yrs	Upper Volta	Yes	–	≥ 4096	256	64	. . .
P. malariae	5	1974	28/M	Nigeria	8 yrs	8 yrs	Nigeria	No	–	High	High	Low	. . .
	6	1974	38/M	Cyprus	4 yrs	4 yrs	Cyprus	No	–	. . .	1024	. . .	. . .
	7	1974	53/F	Greece	22 yrs	22 yrs	Greece	Yes	–	. . .	4096	. . .	. . .
	8	1975	33/M	United States	27 yrs	27 yrs	Mexico	No	–	. . .	4096	. . .	. . .
	16	1978	. . . M	Mexico	10 yrs	1 yr	Mexico	No	. . .	. . .	4096	. . .	. . .
	24	1980	. . . M	Nigeria		7 yrs	Nigeria	Yes	+	256	1024	< 16	. . .
P. vivax	1	1972	. . . M	United States	Life	3 yrs	Vietnam	Yes	. . .	. . .	. . .	. . .	. . .
	14	1978	25/M	Nigeria	2 yrs	7 mos	Africa	. . .	–	1024	1024	64	
	21§	1980							+				
	26	1981	40/M	India	3 yrs	3 yrs	India	Yes	. . .	16	16	256	. . .
P. ovale	17	1979	33/M	Nigeria	7 yrs	7 yrs	Nigeria	Yes	. . .	64	64	16	64

*Two donors to patient 4 and 4 donors to patient 11 had positive malaria antibody titers, but are not included here because none could be implicated specifically as the infective donor.

‡Reciprocal titer by indirect fluorescent antibody test (IFA).

§Additional data unavailable.

(Courtesy of Guerrero, I. C., et al.: Ann. Intern. Med. 99:221–226, August 1983.)

laria, 2 had *P. falciparum* and 2 had *P. malariae* infection. Three other patients died of various causes shortly after apparently being cured of malaria. The estimated rate of transfusion malaria during the review period was 0.25 cases per million donor units collected. A specific donor was implicated as the source of infection in 18 instances (table). At least 9 of these donors should have been rejected because of recent residence in or travel to a malarious area. Twelve of 17 evaluable patients received blood from a donor born in a malarious country.

Microscopic examination of blood smears to detect malaria is too tedious and insensitive for use as a screening measure in asymptomatic blood donors. Serologic screening of donor blood is a sensitive method, but probably would not be cost-effective unless significant numbers of potential donors of rare blood types were excluded from donation by the standards. The country of birth should be part of the written information required of blood donors. Potential donors born in malarious countries should be questioned about their most recent visit home. Persons who have had an unexplained febrile illness within a year of being in a malarious country should not donate blood. Also, those visiting a malarious country in the preceding 6 months who did not take antimalarial drugs should be excluded as blood donors.

▶ [This article was chosen primarily to bring malaria to your attention once again. Sadly, the global effort by WHO to contain malaria was unsuccessful, and malaria is resurgent in many countries. My colleagues are full of anecdotes that confirm that many Americans travel to malarious areas without taking appropriate prophylactic medication. There are several reasons for this. Travelers often are not advised to see their physicians before they leave. Indeed, some travel brochures may even suggest that malaria is not a hazard, even though it clearly is. And, although some physicians neglect malaria prophylaxis, it must be acknowledged that precise information may not be readily available. I recommend the telephone. Local and state health departments have access to the latest information, and if this fails, I suggest you call the Centers for Disease Control in Atlanta at (404) 329-3336. Dr. Schultz, one of the authors of this article, has a special interest in the health of travelers and has all the answers.] ◀

10–4 ***Mycobacterium fortuitum* Infection: Evidence of Bactericidal Defect Due to Hyperactive Antigen-Specific Suppressor Cells.** *Mycobacterium fortuitum,* a common saprophyte found in water and soil, is a Runyon group IV, rapidly growing atypical (nontuberculous) *Mycobacterium.* Although uncommon in man, *M. fortuitum* infection is a common cause of mycobacterial infection in patients with malignancy, which suggests that an underlying abnormality in host defense could be an important predisposing factor. J. Douglas Gardner, Marilyn Ousley, William Godfrey, Norma J. Lindsey, and Nabih I. Abdou describe a case of *M. fortuitum* infection in a patient with evidence of a bactericidal defect due to hyperactive antigen-specific suppressor cells.

Woman, 23, was admitted for evaluation of chronic granulomatous lymphadenitis, chronic anterior uveitis, monoarticular arthritis, and a skin rash over the legs, back, and abdomen. Firm, enlarged lymph nodes were present in the anterior and posterior cervical area and supraclavicular fossa. Labo-

(10–4) Am. J. Med. 73:756–764, November 1982.

BACTERICIDAL CAPACITY: EFFECTS OF CHOLINERGIC AGONIST, INDOMETHACIN, OR BOTH

Phagocytic cells		No. of Colonies (mean* ± SD)	
Source	Manipulation	M. fortuitum	E. coli
Patient	None	107 ± 17	30 ± 7
Patient	In vitro carbachol 10^{-5} M	105 ± 30	35 ± 2
Patient	In vitro indomethacin 1 μg	101 ± 9	36 ± 5
Patient	In vitro carbachol + indomethacin	22 ± 20†	37 ± 9
Patient	In vivo bethanechol + indomethacin	4, 5, 6‡	ND
Normal subject§	None	31 ± 6†	28 ± 2
Normal subject	In vitro carbachol 10^{-5} M	22 ± 3†	26 ± 5
Normal subject	In vitro indomethacin 1 μg	25 ± 11†	26 ± 7
Normal subject	In vitro carbachol + indomethacin	22 ± 7†	28 ± 3

*Mean of 3 experiments.
†$P<.01$ when compared with number of *M. fortuitum* colonies incubated with patient's phagocytic cells in absence of drugs or in presence of either carbachol or indomethacin alone.
‡Tested 10 weeks, 3 months, and 6 months after initiation of bethanechol chloride, 30 mg per day, and indomethacin, 75 mg per day, respectively.
§Same normal subject was tested in all the experiments.
(Courtesy of Gardner, J. D., et al.: Am. J. Med.: 73:756–764, November 1982.)

ratory studies showed a white blood cell count of 13,600/μl, an erythrocyte sedimentation rate of 30 mm/hour, and negative results for antinuclear antibody and rheumatoid factor negative. Synovial fluid from the left knee was yellow and cloudy with a poor mucin clot, but did not contain crystals or organisms. Cultures of the synovial fluid did not show any growth. Microscopic examination of a lymph node removed from the neck revealed necrotizing granulomas. Culture of the lymph node yielded *M. fortuitum.* Sensitivity studies disclosed resistance to antituberculous drugs and moderate sensitivity to minocycline and sulfamethoxasole-trimethoprim. The administration of bethanechol chloride (30 mg/day) and indomethacin (75 mg/day) was followed by a marked reduction in the size of the patient's lymph nodes, improvement of the inflammatory changes in the eyes, and resolution of the chronic left knee effusion and the skin rash.

This patient was found to have normal numbers of total T cells, T inducers, T suppressors, B cells, and monocytes. Compared with a control subject, the patient's phagocytic cells had higher numbers of *M. fortuitum* colonies ($P<.01$), indicating a poor bactericidal capacity of her phagocytic cells. This bactericidal abnormality was not corrected by the addition of either carbachol or indomethacin to the patient's phagocytic cells (table). However, the simultaneous addition in vitro of carbachol and indomethacin or in vivo treatment with bethanechol and indomethacin corrected the abnormality. Bactericidal capacity against *Escherichia coli* did not differ significantly from that in the control subject. *M. fortuitum,* but not concanavalin A, activation of blood mononuclear cells worsened the bactericidal capacity of the patient's autologous cells. This bactericidal defect was not noted during in vitro drug treatment of mononuclear cells or in vivo treatment of the patient.

Systemic atypical (nontuberculous) mycobacterial infection may activate specific suppressor cells, thereby compromising the host's phagocyctic cell function. Modulation of these suppressor cells by use of a cholinergic agonist and prostaglandin synthetase inhibitor in combination appears to be able to reverse this abnormality and may be of benefit to the patient.

▶ [This study is one of a growing number of publications dealing with prostaglandins and the immune response. Less than ten years ago prostaglandins were first shown to be important mediators of the inflammatory response, finally identifying the probable mode of action of aspirin and other nonsteroidal antiinflammatory drugs. It is now known that prostaglandins also modulate immunologic responses and, as noted in this article, may become mediators of *abnormal* immunologic responses.

The authors noted in their evaluation of this patient that suppressor cell activity extended to both mononuclear phagocytes and polymorphonuclear leukocytes. I cannot help but wonder if, in time, that seemingly endless line of patients with recurrent furunculosis may throw away their hexachloraphene baths and Neosporin ointments and find relief through a combination of prostaglandin inhibitors!] ◀

▶ ↓ Physicians who have reached that stage in life where they find themselves struggling with the "new math" as they attempt to "help" their youngsters with homework may also find themselves trying to assimilate what I call the "new microbiology" in clinical practice. Bacterial pathogens keep turning up which were not mentioned in my medical school bacteriology course. *Pasteurella multocida* is one of these. This small pleomorphic gram-negative bacillus is a common inhabitant of the oral cavities of cats and dogs. Our veterinarian colleagues have long known it as a cause of sepsis in many wild and domestic animals. The following is an account of how man's best friend, lying at *he patient's feet (and licking a wound on his toe), inoculated him with this pathogen, causing life-threatening infection. ◀

10–5 ***Pasteurella multocida* Infection of a Prosthetic Vascular Graft.** *Pasteurella multocida* is a gram-negative pleomorphic coccobacillus found in a wide variety of infections. It is a frequent cause of disease in pets and is being reported increasingly as a cause of human infections. Steve B. Kalish and Michael L. Sands (Northwestern Univ.) report data on what is thought to be the first case of vascular graft infection by *P. multocida.*

Man, 61, was admitted with fever, chills, and right groin pain 11 years after aortobifemoral bypass graft surgery for atherosclerotic peripheral vascular disease. A false aneurysm of the left femoral graft had caused total occlusion of the right limb of the graft 2 months before, and repair had been done with an interposition polytetrafluoroethylene (PTFE) graft. The occluded limb was corrected by a crossover femoral-femoral PTFE bypass graft, but a thombus developed and another bypass was made from the right limb of the femoral-femoral crossover graft to the native popliteal artery by using autogenous saphenous vein. The distal part of the right second toe had been removed for ischemic gangrene a week before the current symptoms developed. Several pet dogs frequently licked the patient's feet. Swelling was present in the right groin. White blood cell count was 13,000/cu mm. Incision and drainage were carried out. A sinogram showed communication between the skin lesion and the aortobifemoral graft. The right limb of the graft, which contained purulent material, was removed. Cultures of the graft and of pus from the groin yielded *P. multocida.* Blood cultures were negative. The patient did well on treatment with intravenous ampicillin sodium for 19 days, followed by oral ampicillin for several months.

Infection elsewhere in the body raises the risk of graft infection. Patients with foot lesions are at particular risk for infection when there is an anastomosis in the groin. Penicillin is the preferred agent for treating *P. multocida* infections. A history of animal contact should increase suspicion of infection by this organism.

▶ [This was a highly unusual infection, but the case report dramatically calls attention to the source of *P. multocida:* the mouths of dogs and cats. This organism is

---

(10–5) JAMA 249:514–515, Jan. 28, 1983.

one of the most common causes of local and systemic infection following dog and cat bites and scratches.

One of my colleagues recently encountered this organism on infectious disease consultation rounds. The patient was a 75-year-old woman who had chronic lymphedema in her left arm subsequent to a past mastectomy. She had suddenly developed shaking chills, fever, and confusion. The left arm was involved, with hot erythema from shoulder to wrist. A 2-cm laceration scar was evident on the left forearm where, it was thought, she had been scratched by her cat at some time during the previous week. The house officer was concerned and offered a lengthy differential diagnosis. Now, contemporary house officers are very sharp, and it takes some doing to impress them. My colleague seized the opportunity. After hearing the case presentation, he affected a bland expression and murmured, "classic case," and with an arched eyebrow, "Don't you recognize it?" The resident's jaw dropped. My colleague continued, "This should be *Pasteurella multocida* sepsis." The resident's quiet confusion over the name was evident. A quick walk to the clinical microbiology laboratory confirmed that a small pleomorphic gram-negative bacillus had just been recovered from a blood culture. A helpful discussion, with literature references, followed. Predictably this case became the one most discussed over lunch that week by the house staff. It is not often that one can recognize a "classical" clinical presentation of an infection by a pathogen unfamiliar to today's well-trained house officers. You have to seize dramatic teaching opportunities when they come along!

Oh yes, the patient recovered. The organism is very sensitive to penicillin and many other antimicrobials. Penicillin-allergic patients can be treated with your least expensive cephalosporin.] ◀

▶ ↓ The traditional gumshoe sleuthing of epidemiologists has provided insight into how many communicable diseases are spread. Every technique has its limitations, however, and epidemiologic investigation has been powerfully aided by the increasing sophistication of the laboratory. The isolation of pathogens from clinical specimens and environmental sources and the characterization of pathogens by antibiotic sensitivity patterns, serotyping, and the like have provided important data supporting the field investigations. The recent marriage of molecular biology and epidemiology promises to provide an increased level of precision to epidemiologic investigations. An example follows. ◀

10–6 **Evaluation of Isolated Cases of Salmonellosis by Plasmid Profile Analysis: Introduction and Transmission of Bacterial Clone by Precooked Roast Beef.** More than 90% of *Salmonella* infections do not occur in recognized outbreaks. Several outbreaks in late 1981 were traced to precooked roast beef and, because these products are widely distributed, additional reports of salmonellosis not recognized as part of the same outbreaks were probably also caused by the product. Lee W. Riley, George T. DiFerdinando, Jr., Thomas M. DeMelfi, and Mitchell L. Cohen examined the plasmid profiles of *Salmonella* isolates from incriminated food and from patients affected in outbreaks occurring in New Jersey and Pennsylvania during the summer of 1981. Plasmid DNA fragments cleaved by a restriction endonuclease were analyzed by electrophoresis.

The 2 outbreaks under study, caused by the same *Salmonella* serotypes, were traced to a single brand of precooked roast beef. *Salmonella newport* isolates from the meat and from patients affected in both outbreaks were identified by a unique profile present in 45% of reported strains from isolated cases in the area in the same period (Fig 10–2). Review of food exposure histories in isolated cases indicated an association between the plasmid profile and the consumption

---

(10–6) J. Infect. Dis. 148:12–17, July 1983.

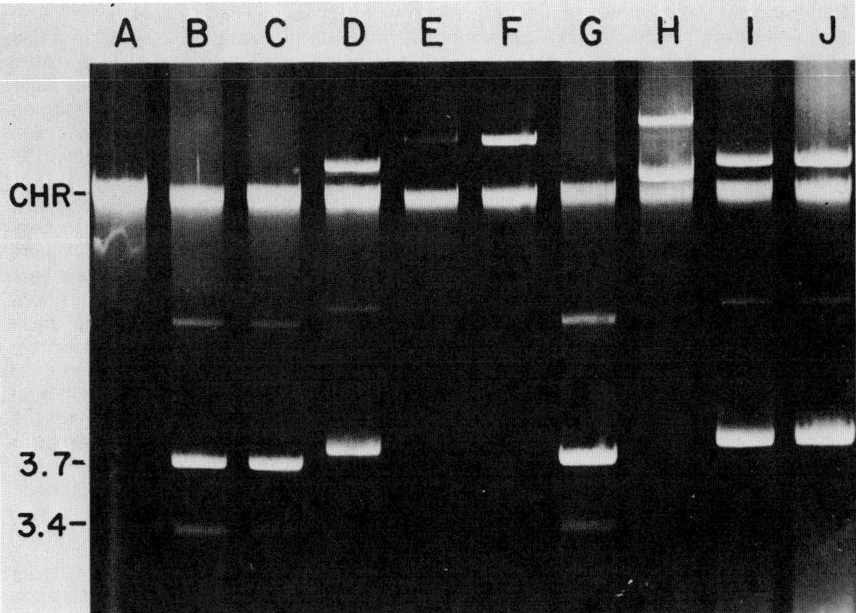

Fig 10–2.—Agarose gel electrophoresis of *Salmonella newport* from isolated cases in 2 areas in the summer of 1981. Lanes B, C, and G represent the epidemic strains with 2 plasmids of 3.7 and 3.4 megadaltons, respectively. (The faint band seen between the chromosomal band [CHR] and the 3.7-megadalton plasmid band represents an open circle of the 3.7-megadalton plasmid.) Other lanes represent a sample of all *S. newport* strains isolated from patients in the 2 areas in the summer of 1981. (Courtesy of Riley, L. W., et al.: J. Infect. Dis. 148:12–17, July 1983.)

of precooked roast beef. Analysis of *S. newport* strains from other areas and other times indicated that the strain in question was introduced into the area within a few months of the outbreaks.

Plasmid profile analysis was useful in elucidating the epidemiology of isolated cases of salmonellosis caused by a sensitive common serotype. Precise determinations of clones of *Salmonella* may be an important part of future studies of salmonellosis epidemics in man.

▶ [First, perhaps we ought to provide a bit of background information to bring everyone up to speed. You will recall that plasmids are bits of extrachromosomal DNA and that bacteria may contain more than one plasmid. Plasmid DNA, like chromosomal DNA, is passed on to subsequent generations of bacteria as they multiply. Thus, if a bacterial strain responsible for an epidemic contains a plasmid collection which is distinctive, one could use this plasmid "fingerprint" as a marker to follow the epidemic strain around. These molecular methods are particularly useful when the other conventional methods (antibiotic sensitivity, phage typing, serotyping, etc.) are not helpful in distinguishing the epidemic strain from the run-of-the-mill strains in the background.

The plasmid fingerprint is determined by lysing the bacteria, collecting the plasmid DNA, and noting its movement through agarose gel under an electrophoretic current. The plasmids move varying distances, depending on their size. This procedure will determine how many plasmids are snuggling within the bacterium and how large they are. The figure gives you an idea of what the several lanes of an agarose gel electrophoresis look like. It takes a while to get used to looking at these things and they are easier to interpret when you have them in your hand than from a photograph.

Now, because different plasmids can be the same size, one more step is required, the use of restriction endonucleases to cut up the plasmids into small pieces. Restriction endonucleases are enzymes that attach to the plasmid DNA at specific recognition sites, producing plasmid fragments of various numbers and sizes which are displayed on another agarose gel. Because the attachment sites of the enzyme to the plasmid DNA are specific, if plasmids of the same size from two bacteria yield identical patterns after restriction endonuclease digestion, the two plasmids are assumed to be identical. Voilà—now you have the "fingerprint"! That sounds like a fair amount of work, but the results are elegant and this "molecular epidemiology" is a powerful tool which is seeing increasing use.

To the present case: During late 1981 several outbreaks of *Salmonella newport* infections occurred in the Pennsylvania–New Jersey area. They were traced to contaminated precooked roast beef which had been imported from abroad. The problem was identified by public health authorities, the contaminated products were recalled, and cases fell off but did not stop completely. Some of the new cases had no connection with the roast beef product. The authors wished to determine whether these cases were the consequence of person-to-person transmission of the epidemic strain as it meandered through the populace after the outbreak.

The plasmid analysis revealed that *S. newport* strains isolated from the roast beef and from patients during the outbreak had a distinctive plasmid profile. Many of the new cases shared this plasmid fingerprint, whereas *S. newport* isolates obtained prior to the outbreak did not. This is the best demonstration to date that outbreaks frequently originate from nonhuman reservoirs of salmonella (the beef in this instance), whereas later transmission of the same pathogen is via human-to-human contacts.

There has been a debate regarding the relative importance of animal and human sources of salmonellosis. This study diplomatically supports both views.] ◀

10–7 **Epidemic Listeriosis: Evidence for Transmission by Food.** *Listeria monocytogenes* is a motile, gram-positive coccobacillus which, in adults, is an uncommon cause of bacterial meningitis and a rare cause of sepsis, endocarditis, peritonitis, or focal abscess. In neonates, however, it is the third most common cause of bacterial meningitis. The mode by which *L. monocytogenes* is acquired from the environment remains unclear. To investigate the risk factors for the acquisition of *L. monocytogenes* infection, Walter F. Schlech III, Pierre M. Lavigne, Robert A. Bortolussi, Alexander C. Allen, E. Vanora Haldane, A. John Wort, Allen W. Hightower, Scott E. Johnson, Stanley H. King, Eric S. Nicholls, and Claire V. Broome analyzed an outbreak of infection due to *L. monocytogenes* (serotype 4b) infection involving 7 adults and 34 perinatal cases in the maritime provinces of Canada between March 1 and September 1, 1981.

Although the peak epidemic period occurred during the summer months of 1981, an increase in the incidence of listeriosis was also noted in the summer of 1980. Perinatal cases were characterized by acute febrile illness in a pregnant woman, which was followed by spontaneous abortion in 5 cases, stillbirth in 4, live birth of a seriously ill premature or term infant in 23, or live birth of a well infant in 2. Despite aggressive supportive care and appropriate antibiotic therapy, 27% of the infants born alive died. In only 1 case did the onset of illness occur more than 24 hours after delivery. In the 7 adult cases, 6 patients had bacterial meningitis and 1 had aspiration pneumonia and sepsis. The mortality rate among the 6 adult patients with meningitis was 33%. Analysis of a case-control survey revealed that cases were more likely than controls to have consumed coleslaw (P =

(10–7) N. Engl. J. Med. 308:203–206, Jan. 27, 1983.

.02) or radishes (P = .03) in the 3 months preceding the onset of illness. Multivariate analysis showed that ingestion of radishes was associated with coleslaw consumption, rather than with illness. Repeat interview with cases and controls showed that all patients, but only 40% of controls, recalled having eaten coleslaw. Cultures of coleslaw obtained from the refrigerator of 1 patient yielded *L. monocytogenes,* serotype 4b, which was the epidemic strain and the strain isolated from the blood of this patient. Attempts to identify the epidemiologic vector led to a farmer who both raised cabbage and kept a flock of sheep. Two sheep had died of listeriosis, 1 in 1979 and 1 in March 1981. A shipment of 5,000 pounds of cabbage during the period before the outbreak was traced through a wholesaler to the implicated coleslaw processing plant. Fifty-three of 55 clinical isolates of *L. monocytogenes* available from the outbreak were of serotype 4b, compared with 3 of 8 isolates from other provinces in Canada (P<.001).

The findings suggest that the source of infection leading to this large outbreak of listeriosis was the ingestion of raw vegetable products, specifically coleslaw, during the period preceding the onset of illness. It is recommended that vegetable growers be careful in the use of raw manure to fertilize crops that are subject to prolonged cold storage and that are usually consumed uncooked.

▶ [This is a nice sleuthing job, and the results look very persuasive to me. It would certainly appear that humans may be able to acquire this very serious infection via the oral route.

L. monocytogenes is a common cause of meningoencephalitis and abortion in ruminants, but fortunately rare in man. That it can wreak dreadful havoc on infants when acquired by pregnant women is dramatically illustrated by the outbreak reported here. Studies have shown that about 5% of the general population harbor this microbe in their stools. What conditions permit it to become invasive are not known, but clearly pregnancy is a risk factor of significance.

That consumption of raw vegetables might be linked to listeriosis in hospitalized immunosuppressed patients was suggested by Ho three years ago.[2] In the present outbreak it certainly appeared that the use of untreated sheep manure to fertilize the cabbage patch did the damage.] ◀

10–8 **Economic Impact of a Botulism Outbreak: Importance of the Legal Component in Food-Borne Disease.** Reports on the economic cost of food-borne disease outbreaks have focused on epidemic investigation and control, direct medical costs, and indirect costs to victims, but have not been concerned with settlements and other legal expenses resulting from such outbreaks. Jonathan M. Mann (New Mexico Health and Environment Department, Santa Fe, New Mexico), George D. Lathrop (Brooks AFB, Texas), and John A. Bannerman (Albuquerque) review the legal expenses arising from a food-borne botulism outbreak involving 34 persons who ate at a restaurant in Clovis, New Mexico, during the period April 9 through April 13, 1978.

Type A botulism was verified by laboratory analysis of clinical specimens. All patients required hospitalization and 2 (6%) died. A total of 1,272 hospital days were required, and the median hospital

(10–8) JAMA 249:1299–1301, Mar. 11, 1983.

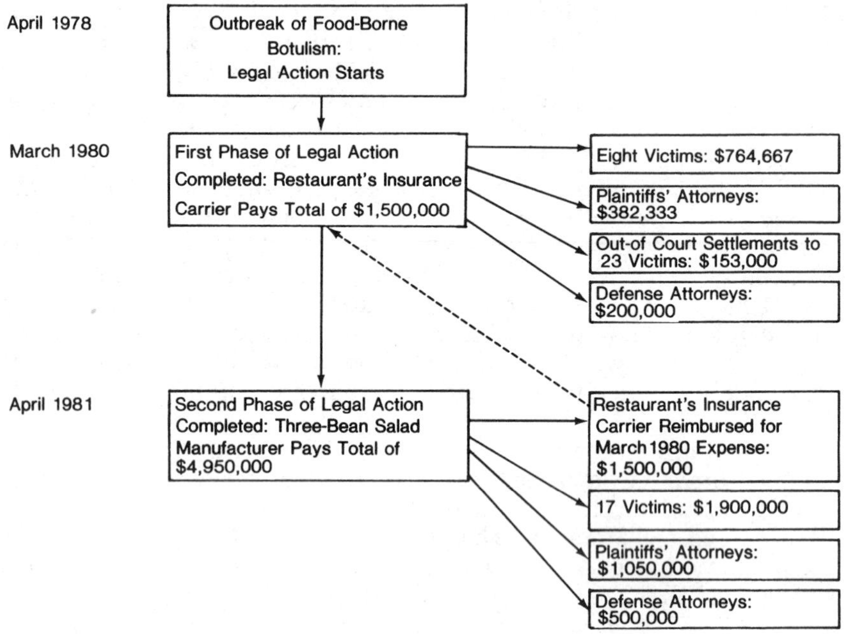

Fig 10–2.—Summary of legal actions and expenses (April 1978 through October 1981) in botulism outbreak in New Mexico. (Courtesy of Mann, M., et al.: JAMA 249:1299–1301, Mar. 11, 1983; copyright 1983, American Medical Association.)

stay was 89.5 days for the 11 severe cases and 7.5 days for the 23 moderate cases. Major legal activity occurred in two phases. The first phase began shortly after the outbreak when 8 victims brought suit against the restaurant, and the restaurant named as additional defendants the wholesaler and manufacturer of the three-bean salad and the suppliers of three ingredients in a second implicated food (potato salad). The second phase began after resolution of the first, with the original 8 plaintiffs, along with 9 other victims, joining the restaurant's insurance carrier in a lawsuit against the manufacturer of the three-bean salad. The total cost of this botulism outbreak was $5,861,800. Legal-phase settlements and charges totaled $4,950,000, of which approximately $2.82 million (57%) was eventually received by victims and $2.13 million (43%) was paid for plaintiffs' and defense attorneys' fees and other costs (Fig 10–2).

The legal implications of food-borne disease outbreaks must be recognized for several reasons. First, the interval between the outbreak and the completion of legal activity, which was 3 years in this instance, necessitates prompt and meticulous written documentation of investigation and control work. Second, legal expenses may contribute significantly to the total societal impact of food-borne disease outbreaks. Lastly, awareness of the legal expense underscores the argument for public and private expenditures for food-borne disease prevention in this country.

▶ [Many of you loyal YEAR BOOK readers will recall that both botulism and the economic aspects of medicine are interests of mine. It was inevitable, then, that this article would appear in this section. Previous studies of the economic impact of outbreaks of food-borne disease have been limited to an assessment of costs incurred during and shortly after the outbreak: medical care expenses, time lost from work, the costs of the investigation, and the like. Dr. Mann and his colleagues have followed the fiscal trail much further than has been done before. I confess to emitting a quiet "wow!" when I saw the final price tag of almost 6 million dollars. I was also surprised that medical care costs represented only 12% of the total; 84% of the cash changed hands in the legal arena.

We showed this article to an attorney who represents insurance companies in medical litigation. Her response to it proves once again that one's prejudices are determined by one's prior experience. She did not think the events were extraordinary and emphasized (as did the authors) that the particular circumstances in each case play a large role in the legal and financial outcome.

I think we can all agree that the economic ripple effects of a food-borne disease outbreak can be considerable and that, beyond the adverse effect on human health, they argue for continuing efforts to prevent food-borne infections by both the purveyors of food and the public authorities responsible for food safety.] ◀

Chapter 10 References

1. Steere A.C., et al.: Treatment of the early manifestations of Lyme disease. *Ann. Intern. Med.* 99:22–26, 1983.
2. Ho J.L., et al.: A multihospital outbreak of type 4b *Listeria monocytogenes* infection. *In* Program and abstracts of the 21st Interscience Conference on Antimicrobial Agents and Chemotherapy. American Society for Microbiology, Washington, D.C., 1981.

PART TWO

THE CHEST

ROGER M. DES PREZ, M.D.

Acknowledgment

The editor would like again to acknowledge with gratitude the participation of Dr. Robert Goodwin, Emeritus Professor of Medicine at Vanderbilt University Medical School and former Chief of the Pulmonary Division at the Nashville VA Hospital, in the preparation of this section.

11. Asthma

11–1 **Inhalation Challenge With Ragweed Pollen in Ragweed-Sensitive Asthmatics.** Although plant pollens are generally accepted as a cause of seasonal asthma, particles of this size are effectively filtered out by the nose and do not substantially pass the larynx on mouth-breathing, suggesting that either smaller particles are operative or pollen in the upper airway activates bronchoconstrictor reflexes. Gary L. Rosenberg, Richard R. Rosenthal, and Philip S. Norman (Johns Hopkins Univ.) examined the ability of inhaled ragweed pollen to induce bronchoconstriction in ragweed-sensitive asthmatics. The authors used a turboinhaler to administer pollen quantitatively to 12 adults with ragweed season asthmatic attacks and positive skin test, histamine release, radioallergosorbent test (RAST), and bronchial challenge responses to ragweed extract. Both oral challenge with whole pollen grains and ground pollen and intranasal challenge were administered.

None of the patients had any bronchial response to oral inhalation of whole pollen grains, whereas nasal challenge produced brisk hay-fever responses without bronchospasm. Oral inhalation of ground pollen fragments 1–8 μm in size led to a 35% fall in airways conductance in 6 of 7 patients, with doses ranging from 59 to 20,000 pollen grain equivalents. Atropine pretreatment did not modify the response to pollen fragments.

These findings and the knowledge that no more than a few pollen grains penetrate past the larynx raise questions about the role of whole ragweed pollen in fall asthma in allergic patients. Further, ragweed-allergic asthmatics seem not to have their symptoms at the time of maximal pollen loads in the air. Small-particle allergens other than ragweed pollen should be taken into account in most cases of fall seasonal asthma. There is abundant sporulation of a number of species of fungi in the fall, producing basidiospores and ascospores of sizes that can readily be inhaled into the lungs.

▶ [In last year's YEAR BOOK an article was abstracted which contended that allergy shots were not helpful in children with ragweed sensitivity and asthma.[1, 2] The article abstracted above, from one of the most respected groups working in allergy, states that *aerosol inhalation of ragweed pollen does not cause bronchospasm* in patients with known ragweed sensitivity and both seasonal rhinitis and seasonal asthma. The authors believe that the pollen particles are too large to reach the lower airways, and they demonstrated that inhalation of smaller pollen fragments *did* produce measurable bronchospasm.

These articles strongly suggest that allergy shots usually don't help seasonal (ragweed) asthma. The issue is complicated, however, by some recent observations that *patients with pollen allergy develop increases in nonallergic bronchial responsive-*

(11–1) J. Allergy Clin. Immunol. 71:302–310, March 1983.

ness during the pollen season. This was systematically investigated by Boulet et al., who demonstrated marked increase in sensitivity to inhaled methacholine during the pollen season in patients with established ragweed sensitivity and some combination of asthma and rhinitis.[3] This article emphasized the difference between patients who have a prompt but transient bronchospastic response to inhaled antigen and those who have both an immediate response and a late (6–12 hours after challenge) response. Only those with the dual response demonstrated increased nonspecific bronchial responsiveness to nonallergic challenges such as Mecholyl or cold air. The implication is that in some asthmatics the early response to specific antigen, if repeated, may eventually result in a state of increased nonspecific bronchial reactivity. This article, and another article discussing the same hypothesis,[4] states that patients with only the early bronchial response have trivial asthma which is easily relieved by inhaled bronchodilators, whereas those with the dual response, both immediate and again at 6–8 hours after inhalation of antigen, have more severe asthma; the articles also state that the late response is less influenced by catecholamines and is prevented by cromolyn and steroids only if these are given before the challenge inhalation. This sort of thinking brings into question the traditional separation of extrinsic asthma due to a specific respiratory allergen from intrinsic asthma which has long been regarded as based on other than specific (IgE) antibody. The articles quoted imply that when an IgE-based immune response in the lungs reaches sufficient intensity an immunologically nonspecific state of bronchial hyperreactivity to a variety of stimuli is induced and that this is often associated not only with bronchial smooth muscle hyperreactivity but also with edema and inflammation. This, when severe, is what perennial asthma is.

Whether or not this sequence, from mild immunologically specific extrinsic asthma to severe perennial asthma, can be interrupted by specific allergy shots is not known, but all balanced appraisals seem to indicate that the overall role of allergy treatment in asthma is probably limited.[5, 6]] ◄

11–2 **Position and Diaphoresis in Acute Asthma.** Barry E. Brenner, Edward Abraham, and Robert R. Simon examined the position in bed chosen by asthmatics admitted to an emergency center. This variable was investigated to learn whether it can be used rapidly to identify patients with severe bronchospasm. Consecutive patients seen with acute asthma in 1 year were studied. Only those with onset of acute asthma before age 35 years and those without bronchitis, emphysema, or other lung disease were included. The head of the bed was elevated 20 degrees. Patients were initially told to lie back on the bed. The 27 females and 22 males studied had a mean age of 31 years.

Twenty of the patients were upright when they arrived at the emergency center; the other 29 were able to be recumbent. The upright patients had higher pulse and respiratory rates than those who were able to lie down. They had a more acidotic pH because of an elevated P_{CO_2} and were significantly more hypoxemic than recumbent patients (table). Pulsus paradoxus was much more marked in the upright group. Sternocleidomastoid muscle retraction was universal in upright patients. Peak expiratory flow rates were about twice as great in the recumbent patients. All 9 patients who were sweating profusely were in the upright group, and peak expiratory flow rates were the lowest in these patients. The mean Fischl index scores at presentation were 1.4 for recumbent patients, 4.9 for the upright group, and 5.6 for those with profuse diaphoresis.

Retention of an upright posture by an acutely asthmatic patient

(11–2) Am. J. Med. 74:1005–1009, June 1983.

Presenting Clinical and Laboratory Values in Patients With Acute Asthma*

Factor	Value Recumbent	Value Upright	p Value
Patients (n)	29	20	
Pulse rate (beats per minute)	108.1 ± 2.6	122.5 ± 2.8	<0.01
Respiratory rate	28.2 ± 0.5	33.4 ± 1.1	<0.001
Pulsus paradoxus (mm Hg)	10.5 ± 0.6	25.1 ± 6.1	<0.01
Peak expiratory flow rate (liters per minute)	225.3 ± 7.5	113.2 ± 13.5	<0.001
Arterial pH	7.47 ± 0.01	7.41 ± 0.02	<0.001
Partial pressure of arterial oxygen (mm Hg)	75.9 ± 1.2	66.4 ± 1.1	<0.001
Partial pressure of arterial carbon dioxide (mm Hg)	30.8 ± 0.5	39.7 ± 1.6	<0.001

*All values expressed as mean ± SEM.
(Courtesy of Brenner, B. E., et al.: Am. J. Med. 74:1005–1009, June 1983.)

suggests relatively severe airway obstruction, as does profuse sweating. The upright position may assist these patients in breathing through a more effective action of the accessory respiratory muscles. The sweating may be due to the increased work of breathing required of patients with severe bronchospasm, sympathetic stimulation from airway obstruction, or hypercapnia.

▶ [This is another clinical point to help to determine which asthmatic patients will require admission or prolonged therapy in the emergency room. The Fischl Index, mentioned in the abstract and discussed in the 1983 Year Book,[7, 8] was an attempt to develop a multifactorial index concerning prognosis in acute asthma. One point was assigned for each of the following: pulse over 120; respiratory rate over 30; pulsus paradoxus over 18 mm Hg; peak expiratory flow rate (PEFR) under 120 L per min; moderate or severe dyspnea; moderate or severe use of accessory muscles; and moderate or severe wheezing. Almost all patients with a score of 4 or more required hospitalization or relapsed after initial treatment. The mean score of those who quickly did well was 1.6. In the same Year Book another article from the Brigham and Women's Hospital was discussed, which indicated that all patients who developed an FEV_1 greater than 40% of predicted after 1 hour of intensive therapy did not need hospitalization.[9, 10] In the 1982 Year Book an article by Brandstetter et al. was discussed that indicated that 35% of those whose initial PEFR was under 100 L required admission as opposed to only 10% of those with a greater PEFR value.[11, 12] McFadden et al. indicated that retraction of the sternocleidomastoid muscles indicated an FEV_1 of less than 1 L.[13, 14] Rebuck and Read stated that significant pulsus paradoxus always indicated an FEV_1 of less than 1.25 L and usually less than 0.9 L.[15, 16]

Nowak et al. have published a very useful article indicating the limitations of blood gas testing in deciding which asthmatic to admit.[17] They defined three groups by outcome: group 1, which had to be hospitalized; group 2, which had substantial residual distress after treatment; and group 3, which did well. The mean initial FEV_1 and PEFR values in these three groups were 0.68 and 134, 0.86, and 128, and 1.12 and 176, respectively, again indicating the powerful prognostic discrimination of flow studies. There was *almost no difference in the initial blood gas values in these three groups;* all showed moderate hypoxemia and low to normal Pa_{CO_2} values. Only 16% of the group 1 (worst) patients had pretreatment hypercarbia or severe hypoxemia or both, and "virtually all of these patients could be detected by specific pulmonary function testing guidelines" (FEV_1 less than 1.0 L or and PEFR less than 200 L/min). There were many patients with this severe impairment of flow who did not have elevation of the Pa_{CO_2}. A number of patients demonstrated falling Pa_{O_2} values as their flow study values improved, presumably owing to V/Q changes as a consequence of catecholamine therapy. Patients with a posttreatment PEFR above 300 L or FEV_1 above 2.1 L could be confidently discharged without further blood gas testing, and once the FEV_1 was above 1.0 L or the PEFR above 200 L/min there was also no need for repeated arterial blood gas analysis in the emergency room. To quote: "In summary, arterial blood gas analysis correlates poorly with pulmonary function testing and is thus of little predictive value in determining patients' outcome. Hypercarbia and/or severe hypoxia is seen only in patients exhibiting specific pulmonary function testing abnormalities. These include an FEV_1 below 1.0 L (25% of predicted value) or a PEFR below 200 L/min (30% of predicted value)."] ◄

11–3 **Glucocorticoids in Acute Asthma: A Critical Controlled Trial.** Although steroids are accepted as being useful in the treatment of acute asthma refractory to standard bronchodilator therapy, the time of onset of action and the relative efficacy of steroids have not been objectively verified. Christopher H. Fanta, Thomas H. Rossing, and E. R. McFadden, Jr. (Harvard Med. School) administered infusions of hydrocortisone and placebo in a double-blind manner to acutely ill, hospitalized, asthmatic patients who were refractory to 8 hours of intensive conventional treatment. For 24 hours the patients received identical bronchodilator therapy concurrently with the test infusion. The 20 patients were aged 18–45 years. Initial treatment was with intravenous aminophylline, injected terbutaline, isoproterenol inhalation, aerosolized isoetharine, and supplemental oxygen. Eleven patients received hydrocortisone in a bolus of 2 mg/kg, followed by 0.5

Fig. 11–1.—Effects of therapy with glucocorticoids or placebo on pulmonary mechanics. The data points are mean values and the brackets represent 1 standard error. Results are expressed as percentage change in 1-second forced expiratory volume (% Δ FEV_1). Zero time is the point at which subjects received the test infusions. (Courtesy of Fanta, C. H., et al.: Am. J. Med. 74:845–851, May 1983.

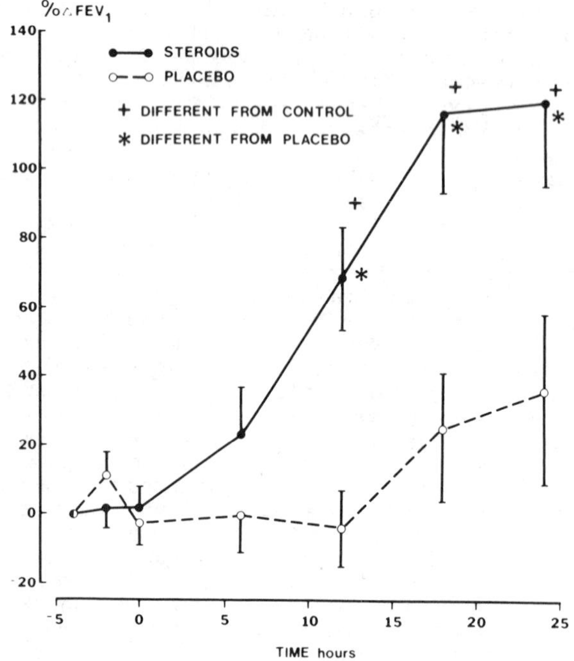

(11–3) Am. J. Med. 74:845–851, May 1983.

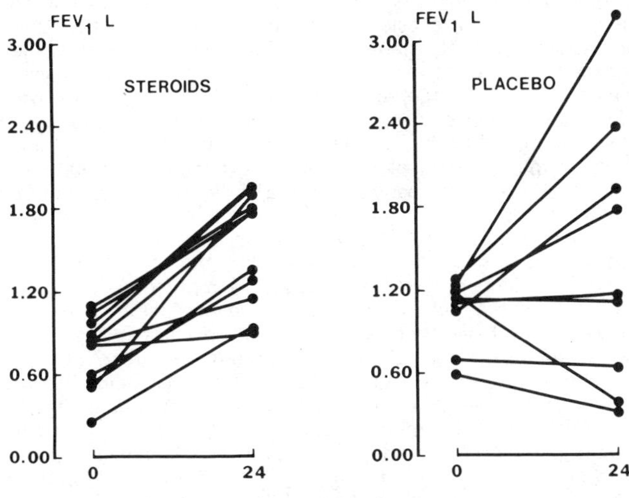

Fig. 11–2.—Individual responses to corticosteroid or placebo therapy. *FEV_1*, 1-second forced expiratory volume. (Courtesy of Fanta, C. H. et al.: Am. J. Med. 74:845–851, May 1983.)

mg/kg/hour for 24 hours, and 9 received saline. Other treatment was identical in the two groups.

All patients had severe, persistent airway obstruction at the outset of the study. The mean FEV_1 was 28% of normal. Hypoxemia and respiratory alkalosis were present. Airway obstruction was significantly relieved by glucocorticoid therapy after an initial lag of 6 hours or more (Fig 11–1). After 24 hours the mean FEV_1 had increased by 118% over baseline in the steroid-treated group and by 36% in the group receiving placebo. Individual responses are compared in Figure 11–2. Adrenal-pituitary function was unchanged during the study in the patients receiving placebo, but pituitary function was significantly suppressed by steroid therapy. Minor medication side effects were frequent in both patient groups.

This study objectively documents the more rapid resolution of severe exacerbations of refractory asthma with glucocorticoid therapy. No dose-response effect was apparent, and the optimal dose regimen remains to be determined. There is a delay of several hours before benefit is apparent, necessitating an effort to identify persons who will require this treatment early in the course. Prompt steroid therapy may minimize morbidity in patients who continue to have an FEV_1 below 40% of normal after intensive conventional therapy.

▶ [Although there are still articles published which contend that steroids are not useful in acute asthma,[18] almost everyone now believes that they are indicated in all acute asthmatic attacks except those that respond completely and promptly (within two or three hours) to bronchodilator agents. The article abstracted above is probably the best study on steroids in emergency room asthma treatment published to date. The effects of steroids are delayed, usually by several hours, and the benefits continue to accrue at least for 3 or 4 days and perhaps for as long as a week.[19, 20] The mechanisms are not known in detail, but the delay of onset probably indicates that synthesis of new protein is involved. It seems almost certain that patients who respond to steroids will be "dual responders" with both immediate and delayed bronchospastic responses (see discussion following abstract 11–1) and that some of the beneficial effects are due to steroid-antiinflammatory action, whatever that is.

The best dose of steroids to use has always been an issue. The dose used in the study abstracted above was large, amounting to well over a gram of hydrocortisone in 24 hours in a moderate sized person. Haskell and associates have published a nice study in patients admitted to the hospital with "status asthmaticus," comparing 15, 40, and 125 mg of methylprednisolone given intravenously over 30 minutes every 6 hours.[21] The highest dose was clearly superior after 24 and 36 hours of treatment. By 60 hours the two higher doses looked alike, but the low dose was clearly inferior. Taking into account relative potency and duration of action, the highest dose was said to be equivalent to 500 mg of cortisone or 25 mg of dexamethasone every 6 hours. No untoward effects of the higher dosage were noted.

It is well established that patients who subjectively are improved by acute asthma treatment probably will have considerable residual disease for several more days, with persisting changes in the small (under 2 mm) airways, which are not reflected in flow studies such as the FEV_1 or PEFR but do result in persisting hypoxemia and a tendency to relapse.[13, 14] Fiel et al. studied the effect of continued steroid treatment after successful outpatient therapy of acute asthma attacks.[22] Therapy in the emergency room was standard with theophylline and catecholamines. Upon discharge from the emergency room, all patients were put on a regimen of oral theophylline, and they were "randomly assigned in double-blind manner to either a placebo treatment (42 patient episodes) or a corticosteroid treatment group (34 patient episodes). The latter were given an intravenous bolus of methylprednisolone followed by an 8-day tapering course of oral methylprednisolone, starting at 32 mg twice a day." They were followed up in 7 to 10 days after emergency room treatment. Relapse could not be predicted from emergency room flow studies. "Those patients who received corticosteroids had a decrease in the need for repeated emergency care (5.9 percent versus 21 percent for placebo) and fewer respiratory symptoms (15.6 percent versus 36.4 percent for placebo)." The implication is that virtually all moderately severe asthmatic attacks treated in the emergency room would benefit from a short course of steroids given in this fashion.] ◀

11–4 **Theophylline-Induced Seizures: Clinical and Pathophysiologic Aspects** are discussed by Tsutomu Nakada, Ingrid L. Kwee, Alfred M. Lerner, and Michael P. Remler. Seizures are a potentially fatal complication of theophylline therapy, but their clinical diagnosis and management are not well appreciated.

Man, 75, with long-standing chronic obstructive lung disease and no history of neurologic disease, had a serum theophylline concentration at admission of 11 μg/ml. The drug was given intravenously at a rate of 20 mg/hour, but 350 mg was accidentally given in 6 hours 6 days after admission, and right focal seizures ensued. The serum theophylline level was 17 μg/ml, with a serum albumin level of 2.2 gm/dl. A metabolic work-up for seizures was negative. Intravenous phenytoin was given, but the patient remained comatose, with occasional right facial twitching and pinpoint pupils. A nuclide scan and computed tomographic study were negative, but an EEG showed periodic left hemispheric epileptiform discharges. Theophylline was discontinued and then reinstituted at a rate of 20 mg/hr. Seizures stopped 2 days later, and consciousness returned within a week. The serum theophylline was 8.8 μg/ml. The patient died a month later of his lung disease. No brain or meningeal abnormalities were found at autopsy.

Theophylline-induced seizures are nearly always focal, with or without secondary generalization. Patients subsequently become stuporous or comatose. If the motor phenomenon persists, it takes the form of par-

(11–4) West. J. Med. 138:371–374, March 1983.

tial continual epilepsy. The seizures tend to be the only manifestation of theophylline toxicity. There are few neurologic sequelae if the encephalopathy is controlled early. Immediate adjustment of the drug dose is the only effective means of controlling the condition. An extensive work-up for a structural brain lesion may be unrewarding.

The mechanism by which theophylline produces seizures is not well understood. Patients with chronic obstructive lung disease have elevated CNS endorphin levels, and this may predispose to seizures. The cyclic guanosine monophosphate excess induced by the hyperactive endorphin state may be further enhanced by theophylline.

▶ [Theophylline seizures, according to the above article, usually start out as focal, may generalize from that, cause a type of electroencephalographic abnormality typical of focal brain lesions, are not affected by dilantin, and when prolonged are often fatal. Zwillich et al. reported 8 patients with theophylline seizures, 4 of whom died.[23, 24] These patients had cor pulmonale, heart failure, and liver dysfunction in some combination which were thought to contribute to the abnormal theophylline metabolism.

In last year's YEAR BOOK a fatal case attributed to cimetidine-theophylline interaction was mentioned.[25, 26] Another fatal case was reported this year.[27] The patient, an 80-year-old man with chronic obstructive pulmonary disease (COPD), was doing well on aminophylline (long-acting), 100 mg 3 times a day, and cimetidine, 300 mg taken at bed time. To simplify his regimen, his aminophylline was changed to 200 mg twice daily. He developed headache, nausea, and vomiting, which were attributed to his peptic ulcer disease, and cimetidine was increased to 300 mg four times daily. (The frequency with which theophylline toxicity mimics peptic ulcer disease is emphasized by all of these reports.) Three days later he was worse; he became confused and had a seizure. He died 24 hours after admission with refractory atrial fibrillation and coma. His serum theophylline concentration was 80 mg/L.

Lalonde et al. have demonstrated that cimetidine decreases the apparent total body clearance of theophylline an average of 29% and increases the half-life from an average of 7.3 to 10.1 hours.[28] Cimetidine is now known to prolong the half-life of a number of drugs that are metabolized by the hepatic mitochondrial mixed-oxidase drug detoxifying system. "Most factors that alter theophylline plasma clearance affect hepatic function, either directly, by action on the biotransformation enzyme system, or indirectly, by changes in hepatic blood flow. Factors changing plasma clearance of theophylline include age, chronic cirrhosis and other hepatic pathologic conditions, congestive heart failure, COPD, macrolide antibiotic administration, upper respiratory tract infections, obesity, ingestion of charcoal-cooked meats, and administration of cimetidine."[27] The erythromycin problem was discussed by Reisz et al. this past year.[29] The degree of inhibition of theophylline catabolism by erythromycin was about the same as with cimetidine. The authors pointed out that a lot of COPD patients who receive theophylline are being given erythromycin now for upper respiratory tract infections, and they recommend a 25% reduction in theophylline dosage if the serum level is known to be in the higher (15–20 mg/L) range.

If what is known about alcohol and the P_{450} system is relevant to theophylline, one would expect that acute intoxication would prolong theophylline half-life and that chronic alcohol ingestion would shorten it. Cigarette smoking is supposed to shorten it, as do isoproterenol[30] and dilantin.[31]

Sahney et al. have reported their experience with hemoperfusion to counteract theophylline neurotoxicity.[32] The use of commercially available charcoal or resin columns resulted in a theophylline clearance at least three times greater than could be achieved by hemodialysis. They recommended its use in any case of theophylline-induced seizures and thought it should be done when serum concentrations were very high, even in the absence of seizures. Therapeutic hemodialysis for renal failure will double usual body theophylline elimination. Kradjan et al. recommend beginning dialysis at the time of a trough theophylline level and giving 150% of the usual dose prior to initiating dialysis.[33]

Brown et al. say that theophylline loading and blood levels in the therapeutic range can be rapidly produced by giving 6 mg/kg of aminophylline (4.8 mg/kg of theophylline) as an oral loading dose and then 6 mg/kg of a sustained-release theophylline preparation 2 hours later and then twice daily.[34] They proposed that this would be a valuable alternative to intravenous therapy.

How essential theophylline is remains a matter of controversy. It has frequently been reported that the effects of catecholamines and theophylline are additive and that one should strive for theophylline concentrations on the high side (15–20 mg/L) to get maximum benefit from the drug. Klein et al. have published a well-done study that indicates that there is significant improvement in bronchodilation when one moves from a level of 6 mg/L to 12 mg/L, but no further improvement when one goes to 19 mg/L.[35] Also, and perhaps more importantly, they could not demonstrate any appreciable improvement in bronchodilation with any dose of theophylline when full-dose catecholamine bronchodilator was used. They thought that there was no benefit to maximizing serum theophylline levels in stable asthmatics receiving catecholamine bronchodilators. A similar less than enthusiastic attitude towards theophylline was taken by Shim and Williams.[36, 37]

How theophylline works is unknown. It has been pointed out in several places that theophylline is a poor phosphodiesterase inhibitor and that better phosphodiesterase inhibitors are not bronchodilators. It has been proposed that theophylline acts on adenosine receptors, as adenosine is apparently a potent bronchoconstrictor.[38] However, the European literature is enthusiastic about a new theophylline, enprofylline, which is a good bronchodilator but lacks any antagonistic effect on adenosine receptors In in vitro experiments.[39, 40] The lack of adenosine antagonism is thought to render it free from tremor-producing effects and free from CNS-stimulating effects, including fits, making it a very attractive drug. However, this apparently shoots down the theory that the bronchodilation of xanthine derivatives is due to adenosine antagonism.] ◀

Chapter 11 References

1. 1983 YEAR BOOK OF MEDICINE, p. 108.
2. Hill D. J., Hosking C. S., Shelton M. J., et al.: Failure of hyposensitisation in treatment of children with grass-pollen asthma. *Br. Med. J.* 284:306, 1982.
3. Boulet L. P., Cartier A., Thomson N. C., et al.: Asthma and increases in nonallergic bronchial responsiveness from seasonal pollen exposure. *J. Allergy Clin. Immunol.* 71:399, 1983.
4. Cockcroft D. W.: Mechanism of perennial allergic asthma. *Lancet* 2:253, 1983.
5. 1983 YEAR BOOK OF MEDICINE, p. 110.
6. Davies R. J., Immunotherapy in respiratory allergy. *Thorax* 38:401, 1983.
7. 1983 YEAR BOOK OF MEDICINE, p. 106.
8. Fischl M. A., Ptichnik A., Gardner L. B.: An index predicting relapse and need for hospitalization in patients with acute bronchial asthma. *N. Engl. J. Med.* 305:783, 1981)
9. 1983 YEAR BOOK OF MEDICINE, p. 105.
10. Fanta C. H., Rossing T. H., McFadden E. R., Jr.: Emergency room treatment of asthma: relationships among therapeutic combinations, severity of obstruction, and time course of response. *Am. J. Med.* 72:416, 1982.
11. 1982 YEAR BOOK OF MEDICINE, p. 120.
12. Brandstetter R. D., Gotz V. P., Mar D. D.: Identifying the acutely ill patients with asthma. *South. Med. J.* 74:713, 1981.
13. 1973 YEAR BOOK OF MEDICINE, p. 181.
14. McFadden E. R., Kiser R., deGroot W. J.: Acute bronchial asthma: relations between clinical and physiologic manifestations. *N. Engl. J. Med.* 288:221, 1973.
15. 1972 YEAR BOOK OF MEDICINE, p. 164.
16. Rebuck A. S., Read J.: Assessment and management of severe asthma. *Am. J. Med.* 51:788, 1971.

17. Nowak R. M., Tomianovich M. C., Sarkar D. D., et al.: Arterial blood gases and pulmonary function testing in acute bronchial asthma: predicting patient outcomes. *JAMA* 249:2043, 1983.
18. Kuksza, A. R.: Acute asthma treated without steroids. *Br. J. Dis. Chest* 76:15, 1982.
19. 1976 YEAR BOOK OF MEDICINE, p. 167.
20. Shenfield G. M., Hodson M. E., Clarke S. W. et al.: Interaction of corticosteroids and catecholamines in treatment of asthma. *Thorax* 30:430, 1975.
21. Haskell R. J., Wong B. M., Hansen J. E.: A double-blind, randomized clinical trial of methylprednisolone in status asthmaticus. *Arch. Intern. Med.* 143:1324, 1983.
22. Fiel S. B., Swartz M. A., Glanz K., et al.: Efficacy of short-term corticosteroid therapy in outpatient treatment of acute bronchial asthma. *Am. J. Med.* 75:259, 1983.
23. Zwillich C. W., Sutton, F. D. Jr., Neff T. A., et al.: Theophylline-induced seizures in adults: correlation with serum concentrations. *Ann. Intern. Med.* 83:784, 1975.
24. 1976 YEAR BOOK OF MEDICINE, p. 167.
25. 1983 YEAR BOOK OF MEDICINE, p. 107.
26. Bauman J. H., Kimbelblatt B. J., Caraccio T. R., et al.: Cimetidine-theophylline interaction: report of four patients. *Ann. Allergy* 48:100, 1982.
27. Anderson J. R., Poklis A., Slavin R. G.: A fatal case of theophylline intoxication. *Arch. Intern. Med.* 143:559, 1983.
28. Lalonde, L., Koob R. A., McLean W. M. et al.: The effects of cimetidine on theophylline pharmacokinetics at steady state. *Chest* 83:221, 1983.
29. Reisz G., Pingleton S. K., Melethil S., et al.: The effect of erythromycin on theophylline pharmacokinetics in chronic bronchitis. *Am. Rev. Respir. Dis.* 127:581, 1983.
30. Hemstreet M. P., Miles M. V., Rutland R. L.: Effect of intravenous isoproterenol on theophylline kinetics. *J. Allergy Clin. Immunol.* 69:360, 1982.
31. Marquis J. F., Carruthers S. G., Spence J. D., et al.: Phenytoin-theophylline interaction. *N. Engl. J. Med.* 307:1189, 1983.
32. Sahney S., Abarzua J., Sessums L.: Hemoperfusion in theophylline neurotoxicity. *Pediatrics* 71:615, 1983.
33. Kradjan W. A., Martin T. R., Delaney C. J., et al.: Effect of hemodialysis on the pharmacokinetics of theophylline in chronic renal failure. *Nephron* 32:40, 1982.
34. Brown D. L., Maddux M. S., Organek H. W., et al.: Rapid and sustained oral theophylline loading: an alternative to intravenous aminophylline therapy. *Arch. Intern. Med.* 143:794, 1983.
35. Klein J. J., Lefkowitz M. S., Spector S. L., et al.: Relationship between serum theophylline levels and pulmonary function before and after inhaled beta-agonist in "stable" asthmatics. *Am. Rev. Respir. Dis.* 127:413, 1983.
36. 1983 YEAR BOOK OF MEDICINE, p. 106.
37. Shim C., Williams M. H. Jr.: Comparison of oral aminophylline and aerosol metaproterenol in asthma. *Am. J. Med.* 71:452, 1981.
38. Cushley M. J., Tattersfield A. E., Holgate S. T.: Inhaled adenosine and guanosine on airway resistance in normal and asthmatic subjects. *Br. J. Clin. Pharmacol.* 15:161, 1983.
39. Pauwels R.: Enprofylline, a new bronchodilating xanthine derivative. *Eur. J. Respir. Dis.* 64:331, 1983.
40. Lunell E., Svedmar N., Andersson K. E., et al.: A novel bronchodilator xanthine apparently without adenosine receptor antagonism. *Eur. J. Respir. Dis.* 64:333, 1983.

12. Chronic Obstructive Pulmonary Disease and Respiratory Failure

▶ ↓ The border between chronic perennial asthma and chronic obstructive pulmonary disease (COPD) due to chronic bronchitis is often quite vague. The article abstracted below contends that patients with chronic bronchitis who suffer from periodic exacerbations have a baseline state of bronchial hyperreactivity and that their clinical course may be improved by maintenance bronchodilator therapy even when they are not isoproterenol responsive between exacerbations. ◀

12–1 **Bronchial Hyperreactivity in Chronic Obstructive Bronchitis.** Many patients with chronic bronchitis will have persistant bronchospasm responsive to bronchodilator therapy and are appropriately described as having asthmatic bronchitis. Other patients, although they demonstrate no response to bronchodilator agents during relatively asymptomatic periods, have episodic acute episodes of cough, wheezing, and dyspnea with demonstrable bronchospasm only during such episodes. Such patients are often not treated with maintenance bronchodilator drugs. Joe W. Ramsdell, Frederick J. Nachtwey, and Kenneth M. Moser (Univ. of California, San Diego) postulated that bronchial hyperreactivity may be present all of the time in such patients and that acute exacerbations may be due to a variety of bronchial irritants including infection in persons with such baseline bronchial hyperreactivity. They therefore determined response to inhaled methacholine in 22 patients with chronic bronchitis who did not demonstrate improvement in FEV_1 after inhaled isoproterenol. The patients were carefully selected to exclude persons with typical asthma or asthmatic bronchitis, but all had significant baseline airway obstruction that did not improve after isoproterenol.

All subjects demonstrated significantly increased sensitivity to inhaled methacholine. Changes in FEV_1 and FVC induced by methacholine were immediately reversible after administration of isoproterenol. Twelve of the 22 patients reported that the symptoms associated with methacholine response were typical of their acute spontaneous exacerbations, and all reported symptomatic improvement after inhalation of isoproterenol. The findings suggest that this group of patients can benefit from maintenance bronchodilator therapy even when response to bronchodilators cannot be demonstrated in relatively asymptomatic periods. It seems reasonable to assume that periodic exacerbations in such patients, which resemble symptomatically the response to inhaled Mecholyl, can be prevented or substantially mitigated by maintenance bronchodilator therapy.

▶ [It seems at least possible, and certainly testable, that the state of chronic bronchial hyperreactivity demonstrated above constitutes one aspect of steroid respon-

---

(12–1) Am. Rev. Respir. Dis. 126:829–832, November 1982.

siveness in chronic obstructive pulmonary disease (COPD). Lam et al. have published a good article which reviews previous studies on this subject and states that 56% of their (small) COPD series were significant steroid responders.[1] This is higher than previous estimates which have ranged from 13% to 20%.[2–5] Also, Lam and associates stated that none of the previously reported clues to steroid responsiveness (variability of symptoms, skin test positivity to usual allergy tests, bronchodilator response to isoproterenol, blood or sputum eosinophilia, or both, serum and sputum IgE levels) had any predictive value in their patients.

In the following abstract another agent that might be helpful in counteracting chronic bronchial hyperreactivity is discussed.] ◀

12–2 **Inhibition of Airway Reactivity by Nifedipine in Patients With Coronary Artery Disease.** Calcium antagonists, which block smooth muscle contraction, might minimize bronchospasm induced by a variety of agents. Jorge M. Gonzalez, Rodolfo C. Morice, Kim Bloom, S. Akers, Albert E. Raizner, and Paul M. Stevens (Houston) used methacholine to quantify bronchial reactivity before and after nifedipine administration in 9 men, aged 45–61 years, with symptomatic coronary artery disease, who were in otherwise stable condition and had no history of airway hyperreactivity. All had failed to respond to conventional antiangina therapy, including coronary bypass. Four patients were taking β-blockers. Bronchoprovocation studies were done with concentrations of methacholine or 2.5–10 mg/ml, 6–12 hours before and 3 days after the start of oral nifedipine therapy in a dosage of 10 mg every 8 hours.

Baseline ventilatory function was normal in 6 patients. Methacholine initially produced a progressive rise in airway resistance and a decrease in specific airway conductance. These changes were significantly less marked at all methacholine doses after 3 days of nifedipine. The FEV_1 and FEF_{25-75} responses to methacholine were also attenuated by nifedipine. All patients had blunted responses to methacholine after nifedipine. No significant differences were seen in the patients receiving β-blockers and the others, either before or after nifedipine therapy.

Nifedipine in relatively low dosage inhibits methacholine-induced bronchospasm in patients with coronary artery disease. If calcium antagonists prove to be useful alternatives to β-blockers in some cardiac diseases, they may be the agents of choice for use in patients with coexistent airway obstruction. Calcium channel antagonists may benefit both cardiovascular and airway disorders in patients with both conditions.

▶ [In the 1982 Year Book a nice article was discussed which said that all chronic obstructive pulmonary disease (COPD) patients got measurably worse on propranolol, that only some did so on metoprolol, and that none did on metoprolol plus terbutaline.[6, 7] This seemed a useful thing to know in view of the large number of angina or hypertension patients who also have COPD. A lot of interesting documentation of the harmful effects of propranolol in "hidden asthmatics" and COPD patients was included in the discussion.[8] The above abstract puts forth a possibly even better solution, at least in the angina-COPD patient, which is sufficient reason for its inclusion here. However, it is of even more interest that the effectiveness of nifedipine was demonstrated by inhibition of response to methacholine inhalation. If one can extrapolate from methacholine responsiveness to "bronchial hyperreactivity," as discussed

(12–2) Am. Rev. Respir. Dis. 127:155–157, February 1983.

above, then the potential role for calcium channel blockers in COPD might be much broader than just in the COPD-angina subset.

There have been a lot of articles on calcium blockers in asthma this past year with such differing results that they really cannot be summarized briefly. However, there have been good reviews by Barnes[9] and by Triggle[10] which discuss receptor-operated calcium channels, potential dependent channels, calmodulin, how cyclic adenosine monophosphate works, and many other things. Triggle stated that "bronchial hyperreactivity" might be a fundamental perturbation at the level of calcium metabolism analogous to what is thought to be the case with respect to vascular smooth muscle in essential hypertension. The fact that almost every step in bronchospasm and bronchial inflammation (mediator release from a variety of cells, smooth muscle contraction, and bronchial secretion) can be viewed as calcium dependent in some sense makes the whole sequence enormously complicated. Nevertheless, the idea that bronchial hyperreactivity may be some sort of even more fundamental defect, detectable by response to methacholine and possibly reversible to some extent by slow channel blockers, is exciting.] ◀

12–3 **Respiratory Muscle Contribution to Lactic Acidosis in Low Cardiac Output.** Respiratory muscle blood flow may decline because of low perfusion during low cardiac output, and the oxygen supply to the muscles may not meet energy demands. The prognosis of low cardiac output correlates with the arterial lactic acid concentration. M. Aubier, N. Viires, G. Syllie, R. Mozes, and Ch. Roussos (McGill Univ.) examined the role of the respiratory muscles in the course of low cardic output and lactic acidosis in 6 dogs that were paralyzed and artificially ventilated and 6 that breathed spontaneously when shock was induced by cardiac tamponade to reduce cardiac output to 25%–35% of baseline. Arterial pressure averaged 55 mm Hg. The mixed venous P_{O_2} was maintained at about 25 mm Hg.

All the spontaneously breathing dogs died of ventilatory failure, after a mean of 2 hours, whereas the ventilated dogs were alive 3 hours after the onset of cardiogenic shock. Arterial pH was significantly lower in the spontaneously breathing dogs at all intervals because of a greater increase in arterial blood lactate concentrations in this group. The mean 2-hour lactate values were 9.5 mmole/L in spontaneously breathing dogs and 4.7 mmole/L in ventilated dogs. Muscle glycogen concentrations fell significantly only in the spontaneously breathing dogs. Muscle lactate concentrations increased significantly in these dogs and much less markedly in those that were artificially ventilated.

Artificial ventilation during cardiogenic shock in the dog reduces the severity of lactic acidosis and prolongs survival. The respiratory muscles are fairly resistant to anaerobic metabolism; however, glycogen stores are the chief source of energy when these muscles work anaerobically, and breakdown of glycogen by anaerobic metabolism produces lactate, as in other skeletal muscles. Excess lactate production is probably an important factor in the death of spontaneously breathing dogs in cardiogenic shock. It may be that resting the respiratory muscles by artificial ventilation will reduce lactate production and promote survival in the clinical setting as well.

▶ [The concept that respiratory failure is actually often diaphragmatic failure caused by energy requirements in excess of energy supplies (oxygen) has been discussed in

(12–3) Am. Rev. Respir. Dis. 126:648–652, October 1982.

each of the last two YEAR BOOKS. An article abstracted in the 1982 YEAR BOOK showed that dogs in low cardiac output shock (produced by saline pericardial tamponade) developed combined respiratory and metabolic acidosis and that this was prevented to some degree by mechanical ventilation.[11, 12] The article abstracted above is a more extensive analysis of the same experimental model. It contains much more information than could be presented in the abstract. Some points it makes will be discussed a little more here.

(1) When the demand for work is increased, the diaphragm cannot increase oxygen extraction from blood. Its relative resistance to development of anaerobic metabolism as compared to nonrespiratory muscles (as mentioned in the abstract) is rather due to its ability to increase its blood flow to meet rising oxygen requirements, sometimes to the disadvantage of nonrespiratory muscles and other tissues. This preferential increase in blood flow to the diaphragm as respiratory work increases obviously requires a normal oxygen delivery system (heart, blood, and lungs).

(2) When a disproportionate amount of the blood flow is diverted to the diaphragm and away from other muscles and tissues, these will tend to shift to anaerobic metabolism and produce lactic acid. Data in the abstracted article supported this. The measured quadriceps lactate level in spontaneously breathing dogs during cardiogenic shock was much greater (5.27 ± 0.89 mmole/kg of tissue) than in artificially ventilated dogs (3.94 ± 0.71 mmole/kg of tissue). In other words, artificial ventilation in cardiogenic shock decreases lactate production both by putting the diaphragm at rest and by avoiding diaphragmatic monopolization of the limited cardiac output.

(3) It should be emphasized that the beneficial effects of artificial ventilation were *not* due to increased oxygen delivery in these experiments; the whole body oxygen uptake was the same in ventilated and spontaneously breathing animals until the very end when the nonventilated animals died.

(4) Figure 3 in the article (not illustrated in the above abstract) demonstrated that the fall in cardiac output was initially associated with a marked increase in minute ventilation in the spontaneously breathing dogs, rising from a baseline of 5L per minute to three times that after one hour. Minute ventilation then progressively fell and by 2½ hours had fallen below the baseline. The conditions of these experiments (normal lungs, falling cardiac output) place the diaphragm in a no-win situation. Hyperventilation in response to metabolic acidosis further compromises the diaphragmatic energy supply-demand problem, generates more lactic acid as a result of diaphragmatic anaerobic metabolism, and exacerbates the defect in oxygen delivery to nonrespiratory muscles by diverting blood to the diaphragm. As the diaphragm itself becomes unable to sustain this work, the situation is compounded by hypoventilation and respiratory acidosis superimposed on the metabolic acidosis. It is generally agreed that heart failure with pulmonary edema can cause CO_2 retention as a result of alveolar flooding and interference with gas exchange. This might be called *respiratory failure due to backward heart failure.* The sequence of events leading to CO_2 retention in the abstracted article might be thought of as *respiratory failure due to foreward cardiac failure.*

(5) The article also pointed out that the liver clears blood lactate and that any liver problems due to decreasing liver perfusion and hypoxia would favor further accumulation of lactic acid in the blood.

Retention of CO_2 in COPD is only uncommonly an indication for ventilator therapy. In most instances of COPD, the cardiac output is normal or elevated, and any energy supply-demand problems that the diaphragm develops in those circumstances are usually due to mechanical inefficiency (flattened diaphragm) or to excess mechanical load (obstruction to the airways, stiff chest cage, etc.), problems not easily resolved by mechanical ventilation. (Mechanical diaphragm problems can be made worse by arterial hypoxemia.) The clinical implication of the abstracted article is that CO_2 retention with low cardiac output may *require* ventilator therapy.

An article abstracted last year showed that the oxygen cost of breathing went up as the FEV_1 fell and that mechanical ventilation did in fact result in decreased oxygen uptake, thus supporting the idea that mechanical ventilation would spare substantial amounts of oxygen for use in other body tissues in situations of compromised oxygen delivery such as low output cardiac failure.[13, 14] Another article that was mentioned supported the concept that one of the benefits of oxygen therapy might be delay or prevention of development of diaphragmatic failure.[15, 16]] ◀

12–4 **Force Reserve of the Diaphragm in Patients With Chronic Obstructive Pulmonary Disease.** The fatigue threshold of the human diaphragm in normal subjects (Fig 12–1) corresponds to a transdiaphragmatic pressure (Pdi)-inspiratory time integral (TTdi) of about 15% of maximal Pdi. When the diaphragm contracts at a TTdi higher than threshold, changes on the electromyogram that herald the onset of muscle failure are immediately noted. F. Bellemare and A. Grassino (Montreal) measured the TTdi of resting ventilation in 20 patients with chronic obstructive pulmonary disease (COPD). Five patients were asked to change the ratio of inspiratory time to total cycle duration (TI-TT) so as to approach or exceed the critical TTdi of 0.15.

The results are given in the table. The TTdi of resting ventilation ranged from 1% to 12% of maximal Pdi, the mean being 5%. The TTdi was significantly related to total airway resistance. The 5 patients who modified their TI-TT ratios so as to increase their TTdi from 8% to 17% (Fig 12–2) showed a progressive decline in the high-frequency–low-frequency power ratio of the diaphragmatic electromyogram, indicating fatigue. Decline in the high-frequency–low-frequency ratio was followed by a progressive fall in mean Pdi, due chiefly to a decrease in gastric pressure swings.

These findings suggest that the force reserve of the diaphragm in patients with COPD is decreased because of a lowered maximal Pdi.

Fig 12–1.—Iso-TTdi diagram: relationship between duty cycle (TI/TT) and mean transdiaphragmatic pressure ($\bar{P}di/Pdi_{max}$) for different TTdi isopleths: 0.02, 0.15, 0.20, and 0.35. The TTdi is equal to transdiaphragmatic pressure time integral per breath normalized to maximal Pdi (Pdi_{max}). Each TTdi isopleth describes an iso-endurance time relationship (T_{lim}). *Dotted band* describes critical zone in which breathing pattern sustained with any combination of $\bar{P}di/Pdi_{max}$ and TI/TT leads to diaphragmatic failure in about 1 hour. A TTdi lower than 0.15 ($TTdi_{crit}$) can be sustained indefinitely. Difference between TTdi during resting (★) breathing and $TTdi_{crit}$ determines force reserve of diaphragm.

(Courtesy of Bellemare, F., and Grassino, A.: J. Applied Physiol. 55:8–15, July 1983.)

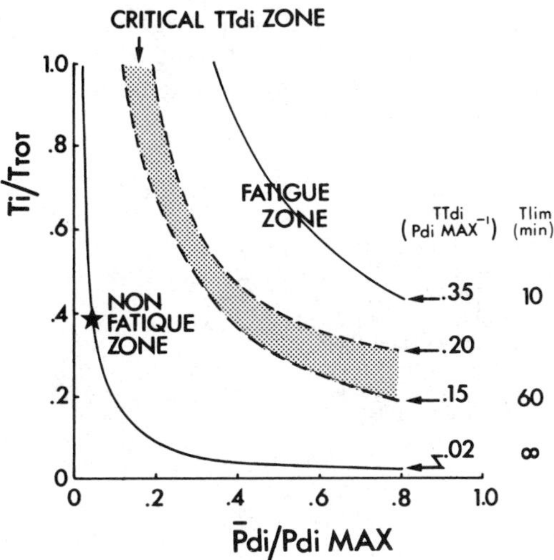

(12–4) J. Applied Physiol. 55:8–15, July 1983.

BREATHING CYCLE PARAMETERS IN PATIENTS WITH COPD WHILE BREATHING ROOM AIR

Patient No.	$\dot{V}_E$, l/min	V_T, liter	f, breaths/min	T_I, s	T_I/T_T, %	V_T/T_I, l/s	$\bar{P}di$, cmH_2O	Peak Pdi, cmH_2O	Pdi_{max}, cmH_2O	Pm_{max}, cmH_2O
1	9.6	0.620	15.4	1.50	0.38	0.415	11.0	15.0	127	94
2	8.1	0.550	14.8	1.53	0.38	0.360	9.5	13.4	67	40
3	14.9	0.760	19.5	0.99	0.33	0.770	9.3	15.8	98	45
4	14.3	0.670	21.4	1.04	0.38	0.640	7.7	14.0	170	92
5	11.6	0.710	16.3	1.27	0.34	0.560	4.6	6.5	77	
6	19.5	0.890	21.8	0.95	0.35	0.940	14.1	17.5	71	19
7	7.5	0.490	15.5	1.62	0.46	0.300	15.4	20.0	157	102
8	7.8	0.500	15.4	1.10	0.30	0.460	6.9	11.5	125	66
9	14.1	0.700	20.1	1.08	0.37	0.640	19.5	22.0	62	75
10	15.3	0.670	22.9	1.05	0.35	0.640	9.5	15.0	121	70
11	13.5	0.620	21.9	1.10	0.40	0.560	5.5	10.0	54	
12	8.8	0.900	9.8	1.85	0.28	0.490	10.2	14.6	68	76
13	13.1	0.410	31.9	0.66	0.35	0.620	16.3	20.0	44	
14	12.0	1.020	11.8	2.15	0.42	0.470	3.5	6.3	120	95
15	14.5	1.010	14.4	1.82	0.44	0.555	8.8	14.0	47	
16	9.2	0.580	15.7	1.47	0.38	0.400	8.0	11.0	62	67
17	11.0	0.500	22.0	1.10	0.41	0.450	12.1	16.0	75	
18	14.3	0.590	25.0	0.70	0.29	0.820	20.0	25.0	69	28
19	13.6	0.530	24.6	0.86	0.37	0.610	22.0	27.5	90	65
20	8.5	0.850	8.8	1.58	0.20	0.630	14.9	19.0	77	48

V_E = minute ventilation; V_T = tidal volume; f = breathing frequency; T_I = inspiratory time; T_I/T_T = ratio inspiratory time to total cycle duration; V_T/T_I = mean inspiratory flow; $\bar{P}di$ = mean transdiaphragmatic pressure; Peak Pdi = peak Pdi inspiration; Pdi_{max} = maximal Pdi at FRC; Pm_{max} = maximal mouth pressure at FRC during an occluded inspiratory effort.

(Courtesy of Bellemare, F., and Grassino, A.: J. Applied Physiol. 55:8–15, July 1983.)

The residual force reserve of the diaphragm can be exhausted by minor modifications in the pattern of breathing. The reduced maximal Pdi may be due at least in part to an increase in functional residual capacity. Increased airway resistance in these patients will tend to decrease the force reserve of the diaphragm by increasing the Pdi generated at each inspiration. Recruitment of other inspiratory muscles can provide a period of recovery for the diaphragm and may delay the onset of diaphragmatic fatigue.

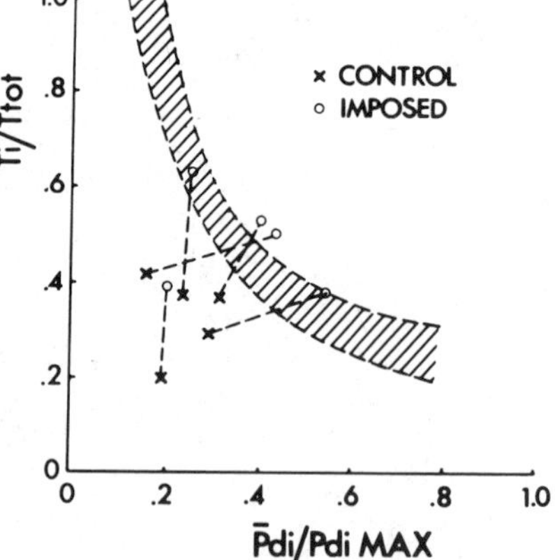

Fig 12–2.—Relationship between T_I/T_T and the $\bar{P}di/Pdi_{max}$ in 5 patients with COPD during spontaneous control breathing *(x)* and during imposed pattern of breathing *(o)*. In 4 patients imposed pattern of breathing brought their diaphragm within or above fatigue threshold.

(Courtesy of Bellemare, F., and Grassino, J.: J. Applied Physiol. 55:8–15, July 1983.)

▶ [This article was selected because of Figure 12–1 which is worth looking at a lot. The authors' analysis uses terms and concepts from classical muscle physiology. "Skeletal muscles, including the diaphragm, will develop fatigue if they contract beyond a given tension-time threshold. During continuous contractions the tension threshold of fatigue for the biceps and the diaphragm is about 0.15 of the maximal tension those muscles can develop. If the contractions are intermittent, the tension threshold is an inverse function of the ratio of contraction time to total cycle time (duty cycle) and the mean tension developed."

As illustrated in Figure 12–1, the tension-time index of the diaphragm (TTdi) is a function of two factors: (1) the integral of the transdiaphragmatic pressure over the time of contraction during one breath (Pdi) expressed as a fraction of the maximal pressure that the diaphragm can generate for an instant (Pdi_{max}) (the ratio Pdi-Pdi_{max} is on the horizontal axis); (2) the duty cycle—inspiratory time divided by the total time from the beginning of one breath to the beginning of the next (this ratio [TI-TT] is on the vertical axis). Obstruction to airflow or mass loading such as in obesity would increase Pdi. Mechanical disadvantages, such as those caused by flattened diaphragms in emphysema, would decrease Pdi_{max}. Any of these would result in an increase in the ratio, Pdi-Pdi_{max}, moving the TTdi to the right towards the fatigue zone. Obstruction to inspiration could also increase TI; tachypnea would decrease TT; either of these would increase the ratio TI-TT, moving the TTdi upwards, again towards the fatigue zone.

The authors trained 5 of their COPD patients to breathe in a manner different from their spontaneous pattern but in such a way that they preserved their minute volume. This generally was done by increasing the tidal volume and time of inspiration. As illustrated in Figure 12–2, this change from their spontaneous pattern resulted in movement of the TTdi towards or into the fatigue zone. In other words, the pattern of breathing that is spontaneously selected by patients is optimal for their own situation.

The information in the table is valuable. Note the peak diaphragm pressures in these patients (second to last column). These were generated by breathing out against a fixed resistance from FRC (lung volume at the end of normal exhalation). The pressures generated on inspiration at FRC were only about two thirds of those generated on expiration, which we did not know. The authors estimated that 200 cm H_2O would be a reasonable normal value. These patients had a lot of wasted ventilation (column 1), and the data on duty cycle (TI-TT; column 5) are interesting. In normals this is well under 0.2 (see Fig 12–1). In last year's YEAR BOOK, an article by Cohen et al. was mentioned which stated that one of the physical signs of impending diaphragmatic failure was breath-by-breath alternating between abdominal and rib cage breathing, which the authors termed *respiratory alternans*.[17] The meaning of this becomes clear. Such patients are cutting their duty cycle (TI-TT) in half by making TT comprise two breaths instead of one.

Aubier et al. reported an elegant series of observations which indicated that improved ventilation caused by aminophylline in therapeutic plasma concentrations was entirely due to improved diaphragmatic contractility.[18] In terms of Figure 12–1 again, this would be an increase in Pdi_{max} and a consequent decrease in the ratio (Pdi-Pdi_{max}). Increased central drive did not occur until plasma aminophylline concentrations rose to the toxic range. The same authors have demonstrated that the enhance ment of diaphragmatic contractility produced by aminophylline is abolished by verapamil and is therefore presumably dependent on calcium flux.[19] It seems quite possible that these pharmacologic interactions may be important in some cases of respiratory failure.

Oliven et al. reported that COPD patients who develop hypercapnia in response to flow-resistant loads (external obstruction to inspiration) shorten their inspiratory time (TI).[20] They apparently choose to avoid diaphragmatic fatigue by decreasing the TI-TT ratio even at the cost of CO_2 retention.

Diaphragmatic weakness may be an important clinical feature of polymyositis[21] and systemic lupus.[22] Roussos and Macklem have written another excellent review of the respiratory muscles.[23]] ◀

12-5 **Mixed Venous Oxygen Saturation: Its Role in Assessment of the Critically Ill Patient** is discussed by Gabor Kandel and Arnold

(12–5) Arch. Intern. Med. 143:1400–1402, July 1983.

Aberman (Toronto). Mixed venous blood ideally is derived from a pool of venous blood that has traversed capillary beds capable of extracting oxygen from blood and excludes any blood that has not traversed such capillary beds. A decreasing mixed venous oxygen saturation ($S\bar{v}O_2$) is a common compensatory mechanism regardless of which component of oxygen delivery is threatened. Once the $S\bar{v}O_2$ falls below a critical value, lactic acidosis occurs, and the value reflects the degree to which compensatory mechanisms are being used to match oxygen consumption with oxygen demand. A fall in $S\bar{v}O_2$ in a critically ill patient indicates that at least one component of the oxygen delivery system has been compromised. If the value is below 40%, the limits of compensation are being reached. The $S\bar{v}O_2$ has been related to the prognosis in respiratory failure, myocardial infarction, and septic shock. Occasionally the $S\bar{v}O_2$ is elevated in patients who by other criteria have compromised tissue oxygenation; sepsis is an example. The effect may be due to abnormalities in the distribution of blood flow or to contamination of mixed venous blood by arterial blood due to peripheral shunting.

The $S\bar{v}O_2$ measurement is preferable to that of mixed venous oxygen pressure ($P\bar{v}O_2$) because it is determined only by components of the oxygen transport system, whereas the $P\bar{v}O_2$ can change solely because of a shift in the oxygen-hemoglobin dissociation curve. The SvO_2 should be measured directly rather than being calculated from the $P\bar{v}O_2$. The cardiac output is not an accurate indicator of whether the body's oxygen needs are being met. The $S\bar{v}O_2$ may be helpful in interpreting the measured cardiac output. It also is valuable in states such as tricuspid insufficiency where thermodilution measurements of cardiac output are inaccurate. A complete assessment of tissue oxygenation includes the cardiac output, hemoglobin concentration, arterial oxygen saturation, and $S\bar{v}O_2$.

▶ [This is a good and clinically helpful review article with a lot of good information. It says that mixed venous P_{O_2} ($P\bar{v}O_2$) is not a very good measurement, since the values typically found in health and disease occur on the steep part of the oxyhemoglobin dissociation curve and therefore minor errors in $P\bar{v}O_2$ measurement are magnified when converted to mixed venous oxygen saturation ($S\bar{v}O_2$). Furthermore, the position of the oxyhemoglobin dissociation curve, which determines the relationship of oxygen tension to oxyhemoglobin saturation, is variable depending on some factors that can be determined (temperature, pH) and some that usually are not (concentration of erythrocyte 2, 3-diphosphoglycerate and abnormal hemoglobin).

Oxygen transport to tissues is determined by cardiac output, hemoglobin concentration, and the arterial oxygen saturation. With normal cardiac output (5L/minute), normal hemoglobin concentration, and normal arterial oxyhemoglobin saturation (97%), the $S\bar{v}O_2$ is approximately 75%. With falling delivery of oxygen, the body can compensate by one or both of two mechanisms: increasing cardiac output and increasing tissue oxygen extraction. A normal heart can increase the cardiac output threefold (15L/minute), and increased tissue extraction of oxygen can result in an $S\bar{v}O_2$ as low as 31% (other variables being equal) before tissue hypoxia supervenes, which is a tripling of the arterial-venous oxygen saturation difference—from a normal value of 22% (difference between 97% and 75%) to 66% (difference between 97% and 31%). These two mechanisms provide ninefold protection so that if anemia is the only abnormality the hemoglobin level can fall to 3 gm/dl before lactic acidosis develops on that account; and if arterial hypoxemia is the only abnormality the Pa_{O_2} can fall to 26 mm Hg before lactic acidosis develops. A fall in cardiac output is less well tolerated than either anemia or arterial hypoxemia, since increased cardiac output is one of the two compensatory mechanisms to adjust to falling oxygen delivery. Perfusion failure is accordingly a much more common clinical cause of lactic acidosis than is anemia or hypoxia.

Focus on the $S\bar{v}O_2$ makes it necessary to think about all components of the oxygen delivery system and their interrelationships and to appreciate when other things might be going on. As mentioned in the abstract, occasionally the $S\bar{v}O_2$ will be inappropriately high (60% or more) in the presence of lactic acidosis. The authors say that this represents redistribution of blood flow to tissues characterized by low oxygen extraction, such as the skin, and away from organs characterized by high oxygen extraction, such as the viscera (especially the kidneys), usually as a result of shock complicating sepsis. Danek and associates[24, 25] say that this is exactly what is going on in adult respiratory distress syndrome, and they speculate that diffuse lung injury disorganizes distribution of blood flow to the periphery, possibly owing to failure of the injured lung to modify vasoactive agents (bradykinin, angiotensin I, and perhaps others) as it does in health.[26, 27] A high $S\bar{v}O_2$ in the presence of hypotension has a poor prognostic import. Oxygen extraction can be increased by fever or other causes of hypermetabolism favoring the development of lactic acidosis, a consideration that might be missed if $S\bar{v}O_2$ were not measured.

On a loosely related subject, Covelli et al. have published data to indicate that the ratio of arterial oxygen tension to fraction of inspired oxygen (Pa_{O_2}-Fi_{O_2}) is a fairly accurate predictor of pulmonary arteriovenous shunt fraction, whereas the alveolar-arterial gradient is not.[28] A ratio of 200 corresponded fairly well to a shunt fraction of 20%, and 100 to about 40%. Another article in the same issue of *Critical Care Medicine* attempted to quantify the important and often neglected influence of mixed venous oxygen tension on arterial oxygen saturation or tension; the statistical analysis showed that pulmonary venous admixture (pulmonary shunting) accounted for only 48% of the observed arterial hypoxemia in acute respiratory failure patients and that the mixed venous oxygen tension accounted for almost as much, another 32%.[29]] ◀

12–6 **α_1-Antitrypsin Deficiency: Clinical and Physiologic Features of Pulmonary Emphysema in Subjects Homozygous for Pi Type Z. A Survey by the British Thoracic Association** is reported by M. J. Tobin, P. J. L. Cook, and D. C. S. Hutchison (London). Hereditary deficiency of α_1-antitrypsin (AT), the main serum inhibitor of proteolytic enzymes, is associated with pulmonary emphysema of early onset. A multicenter survey begun in 1976 included 166 subjects homozygous for the Z phenotype, 126 index cases identified at chest clinics, and 40 nonindex cases identified through family studies. Persons homozygous for type Z have 10%–20% of normal serum AT activity.

The index cases and many nonindex cases had marked radiologic and physiologic abnormalities. Nineteen of 23 deaths were reportedly directly due to emphysema. Twenty deaths occurred among index smokers. A history of cigarette smoking significantly influenced the prognosis, but sex and occupational exposure to dust or fumes did not. Wide variation in lung function was evident, even among those who had never smoked. Chronic bronchitis was present in 53% of all subjects. Asthma was described in 14 (11%) of 129 subjects.

Smoking significantly worsens the prognosis for persons homozygous for type Z. Treatment for this form of emphysema is limited at present. It is reasonable to advise affected persons to avoid smoking and work involving any type of atmospheric pollution. Emphysematous patients may obtain benefit from a bronchodilator. Danazol has increased the serum AT activity but does not completely correct the

---

(12–6) Br. J. Dis. Chest 77:14–27, January 1983.

EMPHYSEMA IN PATIENTS POSITIVE FOR PI TYPE Z.

	Smokers		Nonsmokers	
	COPD	No COPD	COPD	No COPD
Males (n = 141)	88	12	71	29
Females (n = 105)	72	28	46	54

Data are percentages of patients with emphysema.
Adapted from Larson, C.: Acta Med. Scand. 204:345, 1978.

defect. Lung transplantation is the only radical treatment available for severe emphysema. Liver transplantation could correct the primary metabolic disorder. Neither of these procedures, however, is likely to be commonly used in the forseeable future.

▶ [The article abstracted above was selected because of the size of the population (166 patients) collected from chest clinics all over England. PiZZ homozygotes constitute about 0.03% of the newborn population in the United Kingdom. Twenty-three of the 166 adult patients died during the study at a mean age of 53; almost all deaths were due to emphysema. Nonsmokers were older (mean age, 56) than smokers (mean age, 48), suggesting that smokers sought help earlier. There were more men than women (1.9:1), but this was owing to the fact that more males smoked. The sex incidence was equal when smoking was factored out. Also there was no sex predominance in the group discovered by family screening (nonindex cases) rather than by attendance at a chest clinic (index cases). The mean age of onset of dyspnea was 41 years overall, and onset occurred 7 years sooner in smokers than in nonsmokers. Eleven percent were thought to have asthma. Chronic bronchitis, defined by sputum production, was present in 59% of the smokers but also in 29% of the nonsmokers. Radiologic emphysema was present in 90% of the index cases and 73% of the nonindex cases, and was more frequent in smokers (90%) than nonsmokers (65%). The lower lung zones were involved in 98% of patients with emphysema, all lung zones in 23%, and both lower and upper zones in 13%, sparing the midlung. This predominance of lower lobe emphysema is attributed to increased perfusion in the bases with increased delivery of leukocytes, the elastase of which is thought to cause the emphysema in the absence of α_1-antitrypsin (AT). Liver disease was present in only 9 patients, and peptic ulcer, which has been reported in increased incidence in other studies, in 8.

Homozygotes (PiZZ) have 10%–20% of normal serum AT activity, and heterozygotes of the PiMZ or PiMS type have 60%–80%, but the uncommon PiSZ type (0.2% of the newborn population) have only 30%–40% of normal serum AT activity. It has been stated in the past that PiSZ patients are also at greater risk for emphysema. If this is so, it could not be demonstrated in a companion article based on the same chest clinic population.[30] These patients seemed no different from the general population in terms of the incidence and type of emphysema they developed.

The other important clinical manifestation of AT deficiency is liver disease. Between 15% and 20% of newborn PiZZ patients develop conjugated hyperbilirubinemia, and 15%–20% of these (or 4%–5% of the total) develop cirrhosis during childhood. A much more important consideration for internists is the risk of liver disease (chronic active hepatitis, cryptogenic cirrhosis, and hepatoma) in adults, which, in contrast to emphysema, is *not* confined to homozygotes. A large Scandinavian study[31] similar to the one abstracted above cataloged the incidence of emphysema in 246 PiZZ patients according to sex and smoking history (table). Thirty-four of these patients initially were ill with recurrent pneumonia before the diagnosis of chronic obstructive pulmonary disease (COPD) was made. Twenty-eight had bronchiectasis in addition to COPD. Smokers became dyspneic 13–15 years earlier than nonsmokers. However, this series, in contrast to the series in the abstracted article, demonstrated a lot of liver disease. Twenty-nine patients (12%) had cirrhosis, mostly developing after the age of 50 (27 of 29), and 8 of the 29 (3.2% of the 246) had hepatoma. The authors stated that 19% of all PiZZ patients who live past age 50 will develop cirrhosis. The cause of death in 54 was respiratory insufficiency and in 12 was cirrhosis (9, liver failure; 3, bleeding esophageal varices). None of the patients with cirrhosis had had childhood liver disease.

Triger et al. described 13 adult patients with AT deficiency and cirrhosis.[32] One had a hepatoma, and 2 died from intraperitoneal hemorrhage from a large cirrhotic nodule. (The tendency of cirrhosis in AT deficiency to be macronodular has been commented on elsewhere.) Eleven of the patients were homozygotes and 2 were heterozygotes. Eriksson and Hagerstrand[33] collected data on 9 cases of cirrhosis. All of the patients were over 50 (mean age, 62), and none had had previous episodes of jaundice or liver disease. The course was rapidly progressive, terminating either in coma or esophageal bleeding, and only one patient survived more than 2 years after diagnosis. Six had hepatoma, and in 2 the tumor was multifocal. Emphysema was common but not usually advanced in these patients, and in some it had not been clinically recognized. Serum autoantibodies (antinuclear factor, anti-smooth-muscle antibody, or antimitochondrial antibody) were not present. At autopsy, nodular regeneration was prominent, as mentioned above, and cholestasis was minimal, another point mentioned by several authors. These 9 patients constituted about 5% of all PiZZ patients registered at Malmö, Sweden, where the authors work.

Hodges et al. have published an article that also indicates that *heterozygous* AT deficiency may be a relatively common association with chronic liver disease in adults.[34] They recorded the occurrence of the PiMZ phenotype in 9.2% of cirrhotics (compared to a 2.5% incidence of this phenotype in the general population), in 20.5% of patients with chronic active hepatitis, and in 21% of patients with cryptogenic cirrhosis. All of the chronic active hepatitis patients and all of the patients with cryptogenic cirrhosis were negative for hepatitis B surface antigen. The hepatocyte inclusions (diastase resistant and positive for para-aminosalicylic acid, confirmed by immunologic staining) on which the diagnosis was based were said to be much smaller and less conspicuous in the heterozygotes than in homozygotes. (The authors quoted other studies that indicated that cirrhosis develops in 10%–20% of PiZZ homozygotes.) It is usually assumed that the presence of the AT-like material in the hepatocytes has something to do with the development of cirrhosis; but that is not entirely clear, as cirrhosis also develops in the rare Pi Null population, which has a very low concentration of serum AT activity but no inclusions in the hepatocytes.

Some recent literature indicates that AT deficiency may also be associated with Weber-Christian disease (febrile nonsuppurative recurrent panniculitis). The reasoning is that AT is required to limit inflammation and that in its absence or deficiency these inflammatory subcutaneous areas can develop as an overshoot in a number of inflammatory conditions.[35–37]] ◀

12–7 **Diffuse Panbronchiolitis: Disease of the Transitional Zone of the Lung.** Diffuse panbronchiolitis (DPB) is characterized by chronic inflammation mainly in the region of the respiratory bronchiole, just distal to the terminal bronchiole. Hiomi Homma, Akira Yamanaka, Shinichi Tanimoto, Masashi Tamura, Yoichi Chijimatsu, Shiro Kira, and Takahide Izumi reviewed the findings in 49 definite and 33 highly probable cases of DPB. Pathologic features, including thickening of the respiratory bronchiolar wall, infiltration of lymphocytes, plasma cells, and histiocytes, and extension of inflammation toward the peribronchiolar area, were confirmed by autopsy in 42 cases, open lung biopsy in 10, and transbronchial biopsy in 30.

More than three fourths of patients had a history of or had chronic paranasal sinusitis. The most prominent clinical features were exertional dyspnea, chronic cough, and sputum production. *Pseudomonas aeruginosa* was isolated from the sputum in nearly two thirds of the patients. Roentgenograms typically showed disseminated small nodular

(12–7) Chest 83:63–69, January 1983.

CLINICAL STAGING AND RESPIRATORY FUNCTIONS IN 82 PATIENTS WITH DPB

	Staging		
	I	II	III
%VC	64.3±14.4 (8)	67.2±20.2 (53)	61.7±16.2 (12)
FEV_1	62.4±13.3 (8)	57.3±11.3 (53)	52.5±13.7 (12)
RV/TLC	39.8±13.5 (4)	46.0±11.5 (38)	49.3±12.2 (9)
DLCO	15.3 (1)	18.1±7.7 (23)	14.5±8.6 (3)
PaO_2	65.1±15.8 (3)	62.5±11.1 (45)	52.9±11.8 (12)
$PaCO_2$	43.1±6.2 (3)	40.3±7.3 (45)	47.0±5.7 (12)
$\dot{V}_{50}$	1.11±0.54 (3)	0.92±0.85 (23)	0.49±0.35 (3)
$\dot{V}_{25}$	0.35±0.13 (3)	0.40±0.34 (23)	0.22±0.16 (3)
C_{st}	—	0.159±0.093 (6)	0.191±0.116 (3)
RRES	5.9±2.3 (2)	6.0±2.1 (17)	4.4 (1)
RAW	3.7 (1)	6.3±2.1 (4)	5.3±2.8 (2)

(Courtesy of Homma, H., et al.: Chest 83:63–69, January 1983.)

shadows in both lung fields. The 5-year survival rates of patients with and without lung infection by *P. aeruginosa* were 70% and 80%, respectively. The respective 10-year survival rates were 30% and 71%.

Marked obstructive and slight restrictive impairments are observed in patients with DPB (table). Differentiation from chronic obstructive lung disease is important. The prognosis formerly was poor, but today milder forms are being diagnosed. Further studies are needed to determine the cause of DPB, but it appears to be a definite entity, even in adults.

▶ [Judging from the number of articles that have appeared, bronchiolitis obliterans is being recognized more and more.[38, 39] It is supposed to have a typical clinical picture of rapidly progressing shortness of breath and typical pulmonary function tests. We have never diagnosed a case and find a little unsettling the fact that there is some sort of epidemic in Japan, as reported in the abstract above.

Epler and Colby have published a good general article listing the causes as fume inhalation, postinfectious (presumably the etiology of the Japanese series), connective tissue disease (most notably rheumatoid arthritis), "localized," and "idiopathic."[40] Seggev et al. report detailed physiologic studies in three patients[41]; they demonstrated increased total lung capacity, increased residual volume, decreased force vital capacity, decreased forced expiratory volume in 1 second, increased airways resistance, a slightly depressed diffusion capacity which was "normal when adjusted for alveolar volume," and significant hypoxemia. Obstruction at low lung volumes and some representative flow-volume curves with greatly flattened terminal portions have been demonstrated. All reports indicate that the chest roentgenogram may simply show hyperinflation or may have nodular or alveolar infiltrates scattered throughout.

The association of bronchiolitis obliterans and rheumatoid arthritis was also discussed at some length in the 1983 YEAR BOOK.[42, 43] At least three more articles reporting this association[44–46] and one discussing its occurrence in lupus[47] have been published during the past year.

The clinical, x-ray, and physiologic picture discussed above should be recognizable. Some patients have responded very rapidly to steroids, some not at all, and some have been treated with azathioprine after failing to improve with steroids. Attempts at diagnosis by transbronchial biopsy have not been productive in the few cases in which they have been made.] ◀

12–8 **Spirometric Diagnosis of Upper Airway Obstruction.** Flow-volume loops are useful in diagnosing upper airway obstruction

(12–8) Arch. Intern. Med. 143:1331–1334, July 1983.

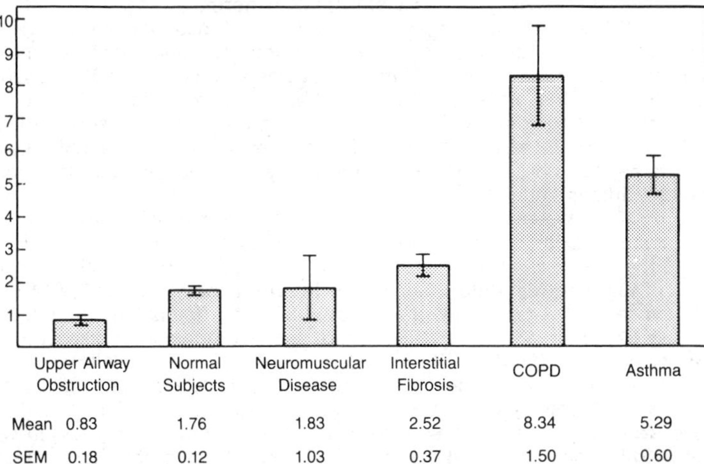

	Upper Airway Obstruction	Normal Subjects	Neuromuscular Disease	Interstitial Fibrosis	COPD	Asthma
Mean	0.83	1.76	1.83	2.52	8.34	5.29
SEM	0.18	0.12	1.03	0.37	1.50	0.60

Fig 12–3.—Ratio of forced inspiratory flow between 25% and 75% of vital capacity to forced expiratory flow between 25% and 75% of vital capacity in patients with upper airway obstruction compared with normal subjects, patients with neuromuscular disease, interstitial fibrosis, chronic obstructive pulmonary disease *(COPD),* and asthma. (Courtesy of Owens, G. R., and Murphy, D. M. F.: Arch. Intern. Med. 143:1331–1334, July 1983; copyright 1983, American Medical Association.)

(UAO) but are not always available or routinely used. Gregory R. Owens and David M. F. Murphy (Univ. of Pennsylvania) reviewed the routine spirometric findings in 15 patients seen in 1977–1979 for possible UAO because of dyspnea associated with known upper airway disease or unexplained dyspnea. Their mean age was 49 years. The most common diagnoses were cancer of upper airway structures and vocal cord paralysis. Obstruction was extrathoracic in all but 1 of the patients. Luminal narrowing was estimated at bronchoscopy to be 33%–80% in all patients.

The FEV_1 was mildly reduced in patients with UAO, and the maximal voluntary ventilation (MVV) was moderately decreased. Seven of the 10 patients studied had flow-volume loop abnormalities consistent with UAO. The only spirometric abnormalities noted in patients with UAO were also present in the comparison groups. Two thirds of patients with UAO and 1 of 20 patients with neuromuscular disease had a ratio of MVV to FEV_1 of less than 25. The ratio of forced inspiratory to expiratory flow distinguished patients with UAO from the other groups of patients except those with neuromuscular disease (Fig 12–3). At least 1 of these ratios was abnormal in all the patients with UAO and in 5% of the patients in comparison groups. Three of the 5 control patients with an abnormal ratio had neuromuscular disease.

Routine spirometry is of use in diagnosing extrathoracic UAO. Flow-volume loops provide visual evidence of obstruction but may not be necessary to make the diagnosis in a majority of cases. Estimation of the MVV-FEV_1 and FIF_{25-75}-FEF_{25-75} ratios from the spirometric data is a sensitive and highly specific means of diagnosing UAO.

▶ [In the 1974 YEAR BOOK the usefulness of the ratio of maximum midinspiratory flow (MMIF) to maximum midexpiratory flow (MMEF) in the diagnosis of upper airways obstruction was discussed.[48] It was stated that in normals the ratio is 1.5, and in patients with COPD it is much larger; whereas in 8 of 9 patients with upper airways obstruction it was less than 1. A much more complicated and extensive analysis of upper airways obstruction by flow-volume loops was abstracted and discussed in the 1977 YEAR BOOK.[49, 50] Nevertheless this subject was selected again this year, in part because these patients continue to turn up after long periods of mistaken diagnosis, usually of COPD, and in part because the data analyzed in the abstracted article were not flow-volume loops but rather simple spirometry of a sort that can be obtained in most doctors' offices.

Maximum voluntary ventilation (MVV) was lower in patients with UAO and in COPD than in patients with the other causes of shortness of breath investigated. However, as stated in the abstract, a low ratio of MVV to FEV_1 appeared to be characteristic of UAO. In all of the other conditions, as well as in *normal* persons, the MVV-FEV_1 ratio was pretty close to 40, and in UAO it was about 20. Only one patient with neuromuscular disease had such a low MVV-FEV_1 ratio, and neuromuscular disease has such characteristic findings (fall in FVC and FEV_1 in recumbency, radically decreased inspiratory force, etc.) that the diagnosis—once considered—should not be difficult although it often seems to be.[51] The second point, illustrated in Figure 12–3, is that the ratio of forced inspiratory flow to forced expiratory flow is very low in UAO (of the usual extrathoracic sort) and very high in COPD, the two conditions most likely to be confused. The causes of UAO are multiple. The association with rheumatoid arthritis[52] and with prior tracheostomy[53] merits emphasis.] ◀

12–9 **Increased Respiratory Chemosensitivity Induced by Oral Almitrine in Healthy Man.** Almitrine is a piperazine derivative that stimulates respiration in animals by an effect on the peripheral chemoreceptors and has no central activity. It increases neural discharge from the carotid body chemoreceptors in anesthetized dogs. The chief function of the peripheral chemoreceptors is to increase ventilation in hypoxia. N. N. Stanley, J. M. Galloway, K. C. Flint, and D. B. Campbell (England) examined the respiratory effects of almitrine in 12 healthy men aged 24–42 years. A double-blind crossover design was used with 50-mg and 100-mg doses of almitrine, representing approximate weight-related doses of 0.7 and 1.4 mg/kg, respectively. The drug and placebo were given orally with an empty stomach 1–3 weeks apart.

Almitrine caused no significant changes in ventilation, mixed venous CO_2 tension, metabolic rate, heart rate, or blood pressure in resting subjects breathing room air. With progressive hypercapnia induced by rebreathing 6% CO_2 in oxygen, the ventilatory response increased by 5% after 50 mg of almitrine and by 27% after the 100-mg dose. The response to progressive hypoxia was increased 78% after the lower dose of almitrine and 120% after the higher dose. Both responses to 100 mg of almitrine were significantly greater than those to the lower dose of the drug. Responses to hypoxia could not be related to the plasma almitrine level. The degree of respiratory stimulation by almitrine was, however, influenced by the subject's constitutional sensitivity to hypoxia.

Almitrine causes a large, dose-related increase in the ventilatory response to hypoxia in normal men, and a smaller increase in the response to hypercapnia. No stimulation of ventilation is evident in subjects breathing room air. No ill effects have been observed. The findings are consistent with an agonist action of almitrine on the pe-

(12–9) Br. J. Dis. Chest 77:136–146, April 1983.

ripheral chemoreceptors. The drug may have clinical value in the treatment of patients with respiratory failure due to hypoventilation. In patients with chronic airways obstruction, almitrine also may act by improving impaired ventilation-perfusion relationships.

▶ [It seems likely that this agent, which acts in a unique way (stimulation of peripheral chemoreceptors) will become important. It has been around for almost 10 years but until a year or two ago was mostly studied in Europe. The abstracted article together with a companion study using intravenous infusions[54] demonstrated marked enhancement of the ventilatory response to experimental hypoxia and a much smaller response to experimental hypercapnia in normal people. As mentioned, its major action is thought to be enhancement of the peripheral chemoreceptors (aortic and carotid bodies) which respond to hypoxia and to a much smaller degree to hypercapnia. Almitrine has no effect on normal persons breathing room air. It is very active when infused locally around the carotid body and totally inactive when instilled directly in the cerebral ventricles. Its major effect is on tidal volume rather than respiratory frequency. The now extensive experience in Europe suggests that almitrine has almost no side effects.

Powles et al. studied a number of patients with stable hypoxic chronic obstructive pulmonary disease (COPD) with intravenous infusions of the drug (0.5 mg/kg/hour).[55] The mean minute ventilation increased from 8.2 to 11.6 L, the oxygen saturation from 83% to 90%, the Pa_{O_2} from 48 to 55 mm Hg, and the mean Pa_{CO_2} fell from 54 to 47 mm Hg. However, the venous admixture decreased from 38% to 22%, an effect not easily understood if the drug's action is only on peripheral chemoreceptors. Further, there was a subgroup of 4 patients in this study who *did not increase ventilation but nevertheless improved their blood gases.* The authors mentioned a number of studies that had also demonstrated improvement in ventilation-perfusion V/Q mismatch, a property that is apparently well established but not well understood. A study by Melot et al. showed almost identical effects including improved V/Q matching when almitrine (100 mg) was given by mouth to 6 patients with hypoxic hypercapnic COPD.[56] Melot et al. thought that it might not be a good drug in patients with advanced pulmonary hypertension and cor pulmonale.

An article by Dull et al. focused directly on the hemodynamic effects of almitrine given intravenously (1 mg/kg) in 7 COPD patients (mean FEV_1, 0.67).[57] All had baseline pulmonary hypertension (mean PAP, 30 mm Hg) and baseline elevated pulmonary vascular resistance. During almitrine infusion the mean PAP rose to 45 mm Hg, and stroke work was also increased. Interestingly, the authors stated that oxygen delivery and consumption did not change in spite of the beneficial effects on ventilation and arterial blood gases, and the cardiac output fell slightly. So it is clear that although the major action appears to be enhancement of hypoxic stimulation of the peripheral chemoreceptors, it does a lot of other things and a lot more studies will doubtless appear soon. However, the authors stated that they have used the drug extensively over the past few years in acute-on-chronic respiratory failure with no untoward results.

Naeije et al. report a patient with central hypoventilation whom they felt was benefited, but the patient signed out.[58] Krieger et al. in a letter to Lancet say that almitrine did not help several patients with the sleep apnea hypersomnolence syndrome whom they treated, as it would be expected to do.[59]] ◀

12–10 **Comparative Studies of IPPV and HFPPV With PEEP in Critical Care Patients: I. A Clinical Evaluation.** L. Magnus Wattwil, Ulf H. Sjöstrand, and Ulf R. Borg compared the effects of a conventional ventilator and a low-compression ventilator in 12 adult patients with respiratory failure who were seen at Regional Hospital of Örebro, Örebro, Sweden. All were critically ill (Table 1), and most were studied after achieving some degree of stability. The 8 men and 4 women had a mean age of 66 years. All required an inspired oxygen

---

(12–10) Crit. Care Med. 11:30–37, January 1983.

TABLE 1.—DIAGNOSES OF PATIENTS

Patients	Diagnoses
1	Bilateral pneumonia
2	Pancreatitis
3	Chronic bronchitis
	Cardiac decompensation
	Carcinoma of the rectum (postoperative ventilation)
4	Sarcoidosis
	Pancreatic cyst (postoperative ventilation)
5	Acute nephritis
	Cardiac decompensation
6	Rheumatoid arthritis
	Diverticulitis of sigmoid colon with perforation and peritonitis
7	Coronary arteriosclerosis
	Abdominal aortic aneurysm (postoperative ventilation)
8	Chemical pneumonitis secondary to phosgene inhalation
9	Ruptured abdominal aortic aneurysm (postoperative ventilation)
10	Bilateral pneumonia
11	Cardiac decompensation
	Pneumonia right side
12	Drug intoxication with pulmonary edema

(Courtesy of Wattwil, L. M., et al.: Crit. Care Med. 11:30–37, January 1983.)

fraction of 0.4 or above despite adequate positive end-expiratory pressure (PEEP) to achieve an acceptable arterial oxygen tension. Volume-controlled ventilation was carried out at frequencies of 20 breaths per minute with a conventional ventilator and at 20 and 60 breaths per minute with a low-compression system. Inspiration constituted 25% and 22% of the ventilatory cycle, respectively.

Five patients died, none directly because of hypoventilation or hypoxia. Respiratory variables with the conventional and low-compression systems are compared in Table 2. Intratracheal and intrapleural pressures are shown in Figure 12–4. Low-compression ventilation at a rate of 60 breaths per minute provided smaller tidal volumes and lower mean intratracheal pressures than the other modes. Cardiac index and oxygen transport were unaffected by changes in the ventilatory pattern. Respiration-synchronous variations in central venous and pulmonary artery pressures and pulmonary capillary wedge pressure during ventilation at 20 breaths per minute were abolished during high-frequency positive pressure ventilation (HFPPV). Long-term HFPPV was uneventful in the most severely ill patients.

Ventilation by the HFPPV technique is well accepted by critically ill patients in respiratory failure and is as efficient as conventional ventilation in terms of cardiac performance and oxygen transport. Barotrauma may be less frequent with HFPPV. Simple, versatile low-compression ventilators that use ventilatory frequencies less than 2 Hz may improve patient acceptance of mechanical ventilation, reduce the need for sedation, and facilitate weaning.

▶ [The article abstracted above gave some details about a "low-compression, low-compliance" ventilator which the authors have developed for use in high frequency

TABLE 2.—MEASURED AND CALCULATED RESPIRATORY VARIABLES UNDER STEADY STATE CONDITIONS DURING VENTILATION*

Patient	SV-20							H-20							H-60						
	F_{IO_2}	Pa_{O_2} (torr)	Pa_{CO_2} (torr)	ITP (cm H_2O) Max	ITP (cm H_2O) Mean	Ppl (cm H_2O) Max	Ppl (cm H_2O) Mean	F_{IO_2}	Pa_{O_2} (torr)	Pa_{CO_2} (torr)	ITP (cm H_2O) Max	ITP (cm H_2O) Mean	Ppl (cm H_2O) Max	Ppl (cm H_2O) Mean	F_{IO_2}	Pa_{O_2} (torr)	Pa_{CO_2} (torr)	ITP (cm H_2O) Max	ITP (cm H_2O) Mean	Ppl (cm H_2O) Max	Ppl (cm H_2O) Mean
1	0.57	60	37	25.4	17.5	7.2	5.9	0.57	61	41	26.0	15.6	6.5	4.9	0.57	73	37	21.8	15.3	8.4	5.7
2	0.39	86	42	28.5	15.3			0.43	81	42	28.5	15.3			0.43	88	41	22.0	11.1		
3	0.49	80	51	18.1	10.8	4.7	3.3	0.52	74	53	16.8	9.8	3.7	3.1	0.52	89	52	19.4	10.3	5.7	3.6
4	0.37	105	41	16.5	10.5			0.42	84	41	18.1	10.3			0.42	84	40	11.0	8.3		
5	0.49	58	41	26.2	14.6			0.49	61	38	23.8	14.6			0.49	59	38	23.0	14.0		
6	0.36	73	39	20.6	11.1			0.42	64	40	17.0	10.2			0.42	64	38	17.7	11.2		
7	0.34	137	39	19.7	14.8			0.33	131	35	21.4	13.3			0.33	140	36	15.3	10.3		
8	0.49	111	39	27.9	19.4			0.51	93	39	42.2	26.5			0.51	81	40	31.3	20.7		
9	0.29	67	41	19.7	14.8	5.1	4.3	0.30	67	40	19.4	12.0	5.1	3.3	0.30	70	41	17.0	10.7	3.7	2.4
10	0.73	88	42	48.3	25.2			0.71	89	40	51.7	25.3			0.71	74	40	32.3	19.7		
11	0.29	74	41	19.7	12.9	9.9	7.3	0.29	77	44	18.7	11.7	6.0	3.7	0.29	68	41	22.4	11.7	3.6	2.0
12	0.48	60	32	23.5	20.6			0.50	74	34	29.2	20.7			0.50	60	35	24.2	18.7		
Mean ± SD				24.5±8.5	15.4±4.5	6.7	5.2				25.4±6.0	14.9±6.0	5.3	3.8				21.5±6.1	13.5±4.1	5.4	3.4

Note. Volume = controlled ventilation was carried out at a frequency of 20 breaths per minute with a conventional ventilator (SV-20) and at 20 and 60 breaths per minute with a low-compression system (H-20 and H-60).

*F_{IO_2} was set in order to obtain an acceptable Pa_{O_2} with respect to patient's clinical condition.

(Courtesy of Wattwil, L. M., et al.: Crit. Care Med. 11:30–37, January 1983.)

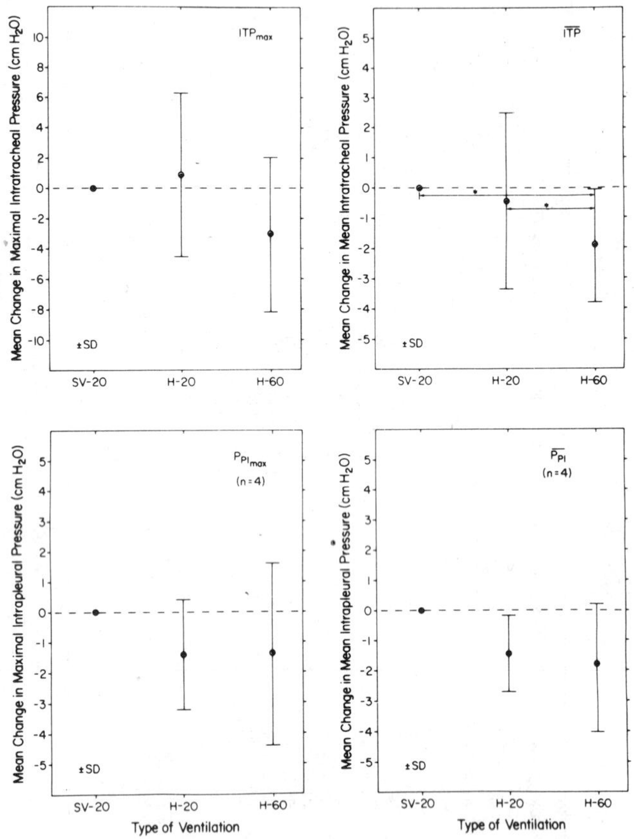

Fig 12–4.—Changes (mean ± SD in cm H_2O) in maximum and mean intratracheal (12 patients) and maximum and mean intrapleural (4 patients) pressures during ventilation with H-20 and H-60 in relation to conditions during ventilation with SV-900 (SV-20, Table 2); ITP_{mean} was significantly lower during ventilation with H-60 (*$P \leq .01$) compared to SV-20 and H-20. (Courtesy of Wattwil, L. M., et al.: Crit. Care Med. 11:30–37, January 1983.)

positive pressure ventilation (HFPPV). Its essence is that the volume of gas in the machine is very low compared to conventional ventilators and the tubing is stiff. Therefore, sudden application of force to the gas does not result in a lot of compression, and small volumes can be delivered at flow rates that reach their (quite high) maximum almost immediately. In a companion article, the superiority of this system as compared to conventional ventilation was documented in terms of nitrogen washout and carbon dioxide elimination.

The term *high frequency ventilation* actually is now applied to three quite different treatment modalities, although the essence of each seems to be mechanical disturbance of lung gas so as to enhance diffusion. The modalities are HFPPV as discussed in the abstracted article, high frequency jet ventilation (HFJV), and high frequency oscillation (HFO). All share the characteristics of ventilation at greater than normal frequencies and at tidal volumes less than anatomic dead space, and all produce lower peak airways pressures than conventional ventilators, which is thought to minimize the cardiodepressive effects of mechanical ventilation. HFPPV, which is the oldest, utilizes respiratory frequencies between 60 and 120 per minute and tidal volumes about equal to dead space or a little less. It is at present administered in a closed system (cuffed endotracheal tube) in a manner quite similar to conventional controlled ventilation.

The authors of the abstracted article believe that ordinary ventilators are not suitable for delivery of HFPPV because of their large gas content and consequent compressibility which hampers the instantaneous development of high velocity (square wave) ventilatory pattern. The "low-compression" systems, which they advocate, appear to be very simple mechanically and probably less expensive than conventional ventilators but are not widely available yet. On the other hand, some Israeli authors have published several articles which indicate that they, at least, *could use the usual Bennett machines (MA-1B and MA-2) in a HFPPV mode* and that this was very helpful to several sorts of patients. Their most recent article described treatment of 50 patients in this way.[60] They turned both the rate and flow dials all the way up, put the tidal volume control to between 0 and 200, shut off the VT control button, set the inspiratory-expiratory ratio to under 0.3 (something that we are not sure could be done on our MA-2 machines), and used special low-compliance tubing. They aimed at a tidal volume between 1 and 3 ml per kg of body weight. The frequency they achieved was 66 to 70. Their data indicated lower intratracheal peak pressures, lower shunt fraction, higher cardiac output, and lower pulmonary artery and pulmonary wedge pressures on HFPPV than on conventional ventilation; and gas exchange was improved. This is not mentioned to encourage the reader to run back to the intensive care unit and try it, but these people seemed to know what they were doing; and if this can be done on machines already in place, one can be certain that the next generation of ventilators will incorporate modifications making it easy to do. It should be emhasized again that the group with the longest experience with HFPPV contend that usual ventilators are *not* suitable,[61] which was one of the messages of the abstracted article.

High frequency jet ventilation (HFJV) is another modality with which there is a lot of experience, most notably from the Pittsburgh Intensive Care group.[62, 63] This is based on delivery of a short blast of gas at high pressure through a narrow tube (about like a no. 15 needle) directly into the trachea. This entrains ambient air by the Venturi effect. It actually has been done and can be done simply by placing a large-bore needle through the neck into the trachea. Now there are endotracheal catheters specially adapted to delivery of a similar jet, but the principle is the same and the mechanics of the ventilator pumps are simple. This is used widely in Europe for ventilation during bronchoscopy and during laryngeal operations. It has proved to be *very successful* in ventilation of patients with disrupted airways or with bronchopleural fistulas who could not be adequately ventilated by conventional techniques.[64, 65] The frequencies generally used for HFJV are somewhat higher than for HFPPV, ranging from 100 to 200 per minute.

High frequency oscillation (HFO) is the most unusual of all. It utilizes extremely high frequencies, 10–50 Hz (600–3,000 per minute) developed by an oscillating diaphragm or, more recently, by a special pump. The system essentially involves vibrating the same gas backward and forward. Oxygen and nitrogen are added by side tubes between the oscillator and the patient, and carbon dioxide is removed in some way which I could not quite understand. Originally, carbon dioxide was removed by putting a carbon dioxide absorber in stream, but that raised technical problems and some other system has been devised. This seems much the most complicated and farthest from practical widespread application, but it is also the most interesting physiologically.[66] However, it is being used clinically in some places. One report says that there is a machine which will deliver *both* HFPPV and HFO together and says that the authors had one patient in whom this combined therapy appeared to be necessary.[67]

The principle of all these modalities (HFPPV, HFJV, and HFO) seems to be increasing diffusion by shaking up the gas in the lung, and they all work well in terms of gas exchange. As mentioned, their use in major airways disruption and in cases of bronchopleural fistula requiring ventilatory support appears to have been life-saving. Their use in thoracic surgery is also apparently very promising. (It is claimed that HFJV makes it possible to operate on a single lung.) Jet ventilation has been widely used in bronchoscopy and laryngeal surgery in Europe. It is suggested that these modalities will have a major application in delicate neurosurgical procedures, since the usual sort of ventilation causes the brain to expand and contract. What role they will eventually play in acute and chronic respiratory failure of the usual sort is not yet established, but the movement of the literature makes it likely that more and more indications will develop.[63, 68, 69] As mentioned, the fact that the usual ventilators to which all of us have access have been used successfully in a HFPPV mode for a variety of clinical conditions seems very imporant as the manufacturers will almost certainly add "low-compression, low-compliance" capabilities to the next generation of ventilators, providing the mechanical situation advocated in the abstracted article. So it seems that high frequency ventilation will soon be upon all of us.

There are a number of good recent reviews.[61, 63, 70–73]] ◀

Chapter 12 References

1. Lam W. K., So S. Y., Yu D. Y. C.: Response to oral corticosteroids in chronic airflow obstruction. *Br. J. Dis. Chest* 77:189, 1983.
2. 1983 YEAR BOOK OF MEDICINE, p. 123.
3. Mendella L. A., Manfreda J., Warren C. P. W., et al.: Steroid response in chronic obstructive pulmonary disease. *Ann. Intern. Med.* 96:17, 1982.
4. 1980 YEAR BOOK OF MEDICINE, p. 108.
5. 1981 YEAR BOOK OF MEDICINE, p. 122
6. 1982 YEAR BOOK OF MEDICINE, p. 139.
7. Wunderlich J., Macha H. H., Wudicke H., et al.: β-Adrenoceptor blockers and terbutaline in patients with chronic obstructive lung disease: effects and interaction after oral administration. *Chest* 78:714, 1980.
8. 1982 YEAR BOOK OF MEDICINE, p. 140.
9. Calcium-channel blockers and asthma, editorial. *Thorax* 38:481, 1983.
10. Triggle D. J.: Calcium, the control of smooth muscle function and bronchial hyperreactivity. *Allergy* 38:1, 1983.
11. 1982 YEAR BOOK OF MEDICINE, p. 124.
12. Aubier M., Trippenbach T., Roussos, C.: Respiratory muscle fatigue during cardiogenic shock. *J. Appl. Physiol.* 51:499, 1981.
13. 1983 YEAR BOOK OF MEDICINE, p. 115.
14. Field S., Kelly S. M., Macklem, D. J.: The oxygen cost of breathing in patients with cardiorespiratory disease. *Am. Rev. Respir. Dis.* 126:9, 1982.
15. 1983 YEAR BOOK OF MEDICINE, p. 116.
16. Jardim J., Farkas G., Prefaut C., et al.: The failing respiratory muscles under normoxic and hypoxic conditions. *Am. Rev. Respir. Dis.* 124:274, 1981.
17. 1983 YEAR BOOK OF MEDICINE, p. 118.
18. Aubier M., Murciano D., Viires N., et al.: Increased ventilation caused by improved diaphragmatic efficiency during aminophylline infusion. *Am. Rev. Respir. Dis.* 127:146, 1983.
19. Aubier M., Murciano D., Viires H., et al.: Diaphragmatic contractility enhanced by aminophylline: role of extracellular calcium. *J. Appl. Physiol.* 54:460, 1983.
20. Oliven A., Kelsen S. G., Deal E. C., et al.: Mechanisms underlying CO_2 retention during flow-resistive loading in patients with chronic obstructive pulmonary disease. *J. Clin. Invest.* 71:1442, 1983.
21. Braun N. M. T., Arora N. S., Rochester D. F.: Respiratory muscle and pulmonary function in polymyositis and other proximal myopathies. *Thorax* 38:616, 1983.
22. Martens J., Demedts M., Vanmeenen M. T., et al.: Respiratory muscle dysfunction in systemic lupus erythematosis. *Chest* 84:170, 1983.
23. Roussos C., Macklem P. T.: The respiratory muscles. *N. Engl. J. Med.* 307:786, 1982.

24. Danek S. J., Lynch J. P., Weg J. G., et al.: Dependence of oxygen uptake on oxygen delivery in adult respiratory distress syndrome. *Am. Rev. Respir. Dis.* 122:387, 1980.
25. 1981 YEAR BOOK OF MEDICINE, p. 130.
26. O'Brodovich H. M., Salcup A., Pang L. M., et al.: Hemodynamic and vasoactive mediator response to experimental respiratory failure. *J. Appl. Physiol.* 52:1230, 1982.
27. 1983 YEAR BOOK OF MEDICINE, p. 85.
28. Covelli H. D., Nessan V. J., Tuttle W. K.: Oxygen derived variables in acute respiratory failure. *Crit. Care Med.* 11:646, 1983.
29. Giovannini I, Boldrini G., Sganga G., et al.: Quantification of the determinants of arterial hypoxemia in critically ill patients. *Crit. Care Med.* 11:644, 1983.
30. Hutchinson D. C. S., Tobin M. J., Cook P. J. L.: α_1-Antitrypsin deficiency: clinical and physiological features in heterozygotes of Pi type SZ. *Br. J. Dis. Chest* 77:28, 1983.
31. Larsson C.: Natural history and life-expectancy in severe α_1-antitrypsin deficiency. Acta Med. Scand. 204:345, 1978.
32. Triger D. R., Millward-Sadler G. H., Czaykowski A. A., et al.: α-Antitrypsin deficiency and liver disease in adults. *Q. J. Med.* 45:351, 1976.
33. Ericksson S., Hagerstrand I.: Cirrhosis and malignant hepatoma in α_1-antitrypsin deficiency. *Acta Med. Scand.* 195:451, 1974.
34. Hodges J. R., Millward-Sadler G. H., Barbatis C., et al.: Heterozygous MZ α_1-antitrypsin deficiency in adults with chronic active hepatitis and cryptogenic cirrhosis. *N. Engl. J. Med.* 304:557, 1981.
35. Breit S. N., Clark P., Robinson J. P., et al.: Familial occurrence of α_1-antitrypsin deficiency and Weber-Christian disease. *Arch. Dermatol.* 119:198, 1983.
36. Clark P., Breit S. N., Dawkins R. L., et al.: Genetic study of a family with two members with Weber-Christian disease (panniculitis) and α_1-antitrypsin deficiency. *Am. J. Med. Genet.* 13:56, 1982.
37. Pottage J. C., Trenholm G. M., Aronson I. K., et al.: Panniculitis associated with histoplasmosis and α_1-antitrypsin deficiency. *Am. J. Med.* 75:150, 1983.
38. 1983 YEAR BOOK OF MEDICINE, pp. 157–158.
39. Hawley P. C., Whitcomb M. E.: Bronchiolitis fibrosa obliterans in adults. *Arch. Intern. Med.* 141:1324, 1981.
40. Epler G. R., Colby T. V.: The spectrum of bronchiolitis obliterans. *Chest* 83:161, 1983.
41. Seggev J. X., Mason U. G. III, Worthen S., et al.: Bronchiolitis obliterans: report of three cases with detailed physiologic studies. *Chest* 83:169, 1983.
42. 1983 YEAR BOOK OF MEDICINE, pp. 125–127.
43. Begin R., Masse S., Cantin A., et al.: Airway disease in a subset of nonsmoking rheumatoid patients: characterization of the disease and evidence for an autoimmune pathogenisis. *Am. J. Med.* 72:743, 1982.
44. Penny W. J., Knight R. K., Rees, A. M., et al.: Obliterative bronchiolitis in rheumatoid arthritis. *Ann. Rheum. Dis.* 41:469, 1982.
45. McCann B. G., Hart G. J., Stokes T. C., et al.: Obliterative bronchiolitis and upper-zone pulmonary consolidation in rheumatoid arthritis. *Thorax* 38:73, 1983.
46. Forman M. B., Zwi S., Gear A. J., et al.: Severe airway obstruction associated with rheumatoid arthritis and Sjogren's syndrome. *S. Afr. Med. J.* 61:674, 1982.
47. Kinney W. W., Angelillo V. A.: Bronchiolitis in systemic lupus erythematosus. *Chest* 82:646, 1982.

48. 1974 Year Book of Medicine, pp. 115–116.
49. 1977 Year Book of Medicine, pp. 107–109.
50. Kryger M., Bode F., Antic R., et al.: Diagnosis of obstruction of upper and central airways. *Am. J. Med.* 61:85, 1976.
51. 1977 Year Book of Medicine, pp. 107–111.
52. 1978 Year Book of Medicine, p. 126.
53. 1982 Year Book of Medicine, p. 143.
54. Stanley N. N., Galloway J. M., Gordon B., et al.: Increased respiratory chemosensitivity induced by infusing almitrine intravenously in healthy man. *Thorax* 38:200, 1983.
55. Powles A. C., Tuxen D. V., Mahood C. B., et al.: The effect of intravenously administered almitrine, a peripheral chemoreceptor agonist, on patients with chronic air-flow obstruction. *Am. Rev. Respir. Dis.* 127:284, 1983.
56. Melot C., Naeije R., Rothschild T., et al.: Improvement in ventilation-perfusion matching by almitrine in COPD. *Chest* 83:528, 1983.
57. Dull W. L., Polu J. M., Sadoul P.: The pulmonary haemodynamic effects of almitrine infusion in men with chronic hypercapnia. *Clin. Sci.* 64:25, 1983.
58. Naeije N., Melot C., Naeije R., et al.: Ondine's curse: report of a patient treated with almitrine, a new respiratory stimulant. *Eur. J. Respir. Dis.* 63:342, 1982.
59. Krieger J., Mangia P., Kurtz D.: Almitrine and sleep apnea. *Lancet* 2:210, 1982.
60. Abu-Dbal J., Flatau E., Lev A., et al.: The use of conventional ventilators for high frequency positive pressure ventilation. *Crit. Care Med.* 83:356, 1983.
61. Sjöstrand U. H., Smith R. B.: Development and clinical application of low-compression ventilation. *Opuscula Medica* 62(Suppl. 62):32, 1983.
62. Schuster D. P., Snyder J. V., Klain M.: Comparison of venous admixture during high frequency ventilation and conventional ventilation in oleic acid-induced pulmonary edema in dogs. *Anesth. Analg.* 61:735, 1982.
63. Schuster D. P., Klain M., Snyder J. V.: Comparison of high frequency jet ventilation to conventional ventilation during severe acute respiratory failure in humans. *Crit. Care Med.* 10:625, 1982.
64. Derderian S. S., Rajagopat K. R., Abbrecht P. H., et al.: High frequency positive pressure jet ventilation in bilateral bronchopleural fistulas. *Crit. Care Med.* 10:119, 1982.
65. 1983 Year Book of Medicine, pp. 147–148.
66. Rossing T. H., Slutsky A. S., Ingram R. H. Jr., et al.: CO_2 elimination by high frequency oscillations in dogs: effects of histamine infusion. *J. Appl. Physiol.* 53:1256, 1982.
67. El-Baz N., Faber L. P., Doolas A.: Combined high-frequency ventilation for management of terminal respiratory failure: a new technique. *Anesth. Analg.* 62:39, 1983.
68. Flatau E., Shumani Z., Antinelli D., et al.: Treatment of cardiogenic shock with nitgroglycerine infusion and high frequency positive pressure ventilation. *Isr. J. Med. Sci.* 18:878, 1982.
69. Flatau E., Barzilay F., Kaufmann N., et al.: Adult respiratory distress syndrome treated with high frequency ventilation. *Isr. J. Med. Sci.* 17:453, 1981.
70. Gallagher T. J.: High-frequency ventilation. *Ariz. Med.* 40:319, 1983.
71. Gillespie D. J.: High-frequency ventilation, a new concept in mechanical ventilation. *Mayo Clin. Proc.* 58:187, 1983.

72. Quan S. F., Otto C. W., Calkins J. C., et al.: High-frequency ventilation: a new method of ventilation. *Heart Lung* 12:152, 1983.
73. Smith, R. B.: Ventilation at high respiratory frequencies: high frequency positive pressure ventilation, high frequency jet ventilation, and high frequency oscillation. *Anaethesia* 37:1011, 1982.

13. Sleep Apnea Hypersomnolence Syndrome

▶ ↓ In last year's YEAR BOOK a lot of new material on the sleep apnea hypersomnolence syndrome (SAHS) was reviewed.[1] The concept that all SAHS cases have some decreased respiratory center activity was discussed. Peripheral (obstructive) apneic events are due in part to decreased neural drive to the muscles of the upper airways (nasopharynx, oropharynx, and hypopharynx) and the tongue; the normal function of these muscles is to keep the upper airways from collapsing as a result of falling pressure with inspiration. The fact that hypoxia per se causes a *decrease* in the responsiveness of the respiratory center was emphasized in several studies. The importance of this is that episodes of hypoxia themselves can cause further respiratory center depression, producing a vicious cycle of decreasing responsiveness and more frequent hypoxic episodes. It was demonstrated that prevention of episodes of serious hypoxia by tracheostomy or by administration of oxygen at night often reintegrated sleep patterns by improving the CNS response to hypercapnia. This beneficial effect is progressive over a period of weeks or even longer. The fear that administration of oxygen in these patients might cause them to cease breathing was shown to be generally without foundation. Hypoxia itself is a very weak arousal stimulus, both patients and normal individuals being able to tolerate serious hypoxia without arousal as long as the carbon dioxide tension does not rise. Arousal is principally due to hypercapnia and acidosis. Measures such as the use of drugs can be construed as acting to improve CNS response to hypercapnia, which results in less hypoxia and improved respiratory center function.

Other points that were mentioned include the occurrence of SAHS in myxedema and its correction with thyroid replacement, the effect of protriptyline, the effect of progesterone, production of systemic hypertension by the SAHS, and production of noncardiogenic pulmonary edema in SAHS. The article abstracted below demonstrates the effect of weight loss in morbidly obese SAHS patients. ◀

13–1 **Effect of Weight Loss on Sleep-Disordered Breathing and Oxygen Desaturation in Morbidly Obese Men.** Sleep-disordered breathing and oxygen desaturation have been observed in a significant proportion of morbidly obese men, but the relation of obesity to the sleep apnea syndrome is unclear. Eloise M. Harman, James W. Wynne, and A. Jay Block (Univ. of Florida) performed repeated sleep studies on 4 morbidly obese men with sleep apnea who underwent massive weight reduction after jejunoileal bypass. They were evaluated about 2 years after operation, when they had had an average weight loss of 108 kg. Average age was 36 years, and mean initial body weight was 231 kg.

The 2 heaviest subjects were symptomatic, with daytime somnolence and peripheral edema before surgery. All were asymptomatic at follow-up, and repeat arterial blood gas and pulmonary function tests gave normal results (Table 1). The number of hourly episodes of sleep-disordered breathing decreased in all patients. In 3 of 4 there was a decrease in the severity of desaturation during episodes of dis-

(13–1) Chest 82:291–294, September 1982.

TABLE 1.—Disordered Breathing and Desaturation Before and After Weight Loss

Patient	Weight (Kg)	Sleep Period Time (Hours)	Total No. Episodes per hour	Desaturations* per hour	Hypopneas per hour	Apneas per hour	Low Sat (%)
1 Initial	228	2.0	81	2	—	79	<50
Repeat	128	3.27	2.75	1.22	1.22	.31	89
2 Initial	264	NA	196	—	—	196	<50
Repeat	109	3.67	.27	0	0.27	0	90
4 Initial	182	1.75	29	6	0	23	77
Repeat	129	5.08	5.71	4.33	1.18	0.20	75
5 Initial	180	2.5	15	0	0	15	85
Repeat	125	5.08	3.94	1.38	1.58	0.98	82
Mean initial	231		78	2		78	65.5
Repeat	123		1.4	1.74		.37	84
p (based on means)	.063		.063	.375	—	.063	0.125

*Desaturations means oxygen desaturation without abnormal breathing.
(Courtesy of Harman, E. M., et al.: Chest 82:291–294, September 1982.)

ordered breathing, and this was most marked in the previously symptomatic subjects. A trend toward deeper sleep with fewer awakenings was evident at follow-up (Table 2). Overall sleep quality was improved after weight reduction.

Massive weight loss by morbidly obese men with sleep apnea re-

TABLE 2.—SLEEP CHARACTERISTICS

	Sleep Period Time (min)	% of Time in Each Stage 0	1	2	3	4	REM
Baseline	125	25	13	29	14	13	8
After weight loss	247	8	6	45	7	24	10
Age-matched normals	428	2	5	55	7	8	20

(Courtesy of Harman, E. M., et al.: Chest 82:291–294, September 1982.)

sults in a significant reduction in sleep-disordered breathing events. The findings may be explained by removal of upper airway obstruction by fat tissue, by improvement in oxygenation, or by lessening of the mass load on the chest wall and abdomen, with resultant improvement in respiratory muscle function. It seems appropriate to attempt weight reduction in adequately motivated patients with obesity-related sleep apnea before tracheostomy is recommended, if a delay is feasible. The degree of weight reduction necessary to obtain improvement requires further study.

▶ [Only 6 of the 14 patients undergoing jejunoileal bypass had SAHS. In the discussion the authors stated that this was probably a result of decreased respiratory center responsiveness to hypercapnia in those six and not in the others. The ventilatory response to hypercapnia differs in degree among individuals. For instance, it has been proposed that crib deaths and other sudden deaths occur in kindreds with decreased CO_2 responsiveness.[2, 3] A study by Sampson and Grassino supports this concept.[4] They studied two groups of matched obese subjects thought to be similar in all respects except that one had a history of prior alveolar hypoventilation. They demonstrated that the diaphragmatic response to CO_2 rebreathing was blunted in those with a history of alveolar hypoventilation but was *greater* than normal in those obese individuals without such a history. They reasoned that the increased neuromuscular respiratory drive in the obese persons who had avoided hypoventilation problems was essentially a compensation for the handicap of the thoracic mass-loading effect of obesity. An essentially similar study was published by Lopata and Onal.[5] Both of these studies indicate that the mass-loading consequences of obesity, whether naturally occurring or experimentally simulated, normally produce an *increase* in the CO_2 response curve as a compensatory mechanism and that persons who are unable to respond in the normal fashion are at risk to develop SAHS. (In addition to these mechanical disadvantages, obesity also favors hypoxia as a result of ventilation-perfusion abnormalities of the shunt sort due to loss of functional residual capacity and premature closure of the basilar airways; and also obese individuals with fat necks are more prone to collapse of the upper airways.) As mentioned, what emerges from all of the above is the concept that decreased CO_2 responsiveness is the essential factor leading to development of SAHS, on which basic defect the handicaps due to obesity or (functional or anatomic) upper airways obstruction are superimposed. When this results in episodes of serious hypoxemia, the respiratory center is further compromised, the architecture of sleep disintegrates further, and the full-blown SAHS develops.

Focusing on the upper airways defect, Suratt et al. have demonstrated that obese SAHS patients have increased resistance to airflow in the upper airways while awake.[6] Haponik et al. have demonstrated that narrowed upper airways can be demonstrated by computed tomographic scan in these patients.[7] They were able to demonstrate which anatomic area was most compromised (nasopharynx, oropharynx, or hypopharynx), an observation of importance when operations such as uvulopalatopharyngoplasty are contemplated. The same group indicated that flow-volume curves obtained during waking can be used to diagnose and follow SAHS patients with obstructive components to their apneic events.[8] They found that 40% of their SAHS patients demonstrated decreased inspiratory flow rates and a flow-volume loop configuration consistent with variable extrathoracic obstruction (flattening of the inspiratory part of the loop and decrease in the rate of inspiratory flow). Patients demonstrating that pattern had more severe desaturation during apneic events and were more liable to require surgery. The peak expiratory flow was no different in the surgical and nonsurgical patients, but the peak inspiratory flow was lower (4.08 L/second) and the ratio of forced expiratory flow to forced inspiratory flow at 50% of vital capacity (FEF_{50}/FIF_{50}) was higher (1.41) than in the nonsurgical patients (5.55 L/second and 0.82 respectively). The "sawtooth sign," a fluttering of the flow-volume loop just after peak flow in expiration, was present in 50% of their patients, more often in those requiring surgery (60%) than in those who did not (45%). The indications for surgery which they utilized were anatomical obstruction, severe arrhythmias, severe cor pulmonale, and incapacitating somnolence refractory to medical therapy, which were present in some combination in 25 of their 72 patients.

With regard to medical therapy, Smith et al.[9] have demonstrated decrease in the proportion of REM sleep and decrease in the amount of apnea in sleep-disordered-breathing events under the influence of protriptyline. Both nocturnal oxygenation and daytime hypersomnolence were improved. The authors felt that the drug was not a respiratory stimulant. Detailed dosage was not given. White et al. published an impressive article indicating that 250 mg of diamox given four times daily produced better sleep and less daytime somnolence in 5 of 6 patients.[10] The total number of sleep-disordered-breathing events was decreased by 69%. The group's mean pH decreased from 7.42 to 7.34, and their response to hypercapnia was significantly increased, which latter effect the author's attributed to the metabolic acidosis. These observations raise the question as to whether or not diuretic-induced metabolic alkalosis might in some instances have the opposite effect, contributing to decreased CO_2 responsiveness, a consideration of potential importance in view of the frequency with which alkalosis-producing diuretics are given to these patients. Rapoport et al. report good results with a complicated mask device, resulting in increased pressure in the upper airways, presumably acting against the tendency for upper airways collapse on inspiration.[11] Progesterone therapy was discussed in last year's YEAR BOOK,[12, 13] as was, most importantly, the beneficial effects of nocturnal oxygen.[14, 15] So there now is an impressive list of drugs (progesterone, amitriptyline, and diamox) and maneuvers (nocturnal oxygen, weight loss, and increase in pharyngeal airways pressure) which can be assessed before resorting to surgery. On the other side of the coin, the Florida group warn against the untoward effects of sleep-inducing medicines and alcohol in these patients, suggesting that sometimes these may be fatal.[16, 17]

Davies and Iber report a case of SAHS due to micrognathia complicating rheumatoid arthritis.[18] Millman and associates reported another case of SAHS in hypothyroidism.[19] The importance of this case is that central respiratory center defects were demonstrated while the patient was hypothyroid.] ◀

13–2 **Nocturnal Oxygen Desaturation in Patients With Sickle Cell Anemia.** Mild oxygen desaturation, with and without apnea, occurs regularly during normal sleep and may lead to vaso-occlusive episodes in patients with sickle cell disease. Milton B. Scharf, Jeffrey S. Lobel, Elsy Caldwell, Bruce F. Cameron, Milton Kramer, Jane De Marchis, and Charles Paine (Cincinnati) encountered 2 patients with sickle cell disease who had periods of notable oxygen desaturation during sleep without concurrent apnea. A temporal relation was found between desaturation and painful sickle cell disease crisis. The patients had notably reduced arterial oxygen saturation (Sa_{O_2}) de-

(13–2) JAMA 249:1753–1755, Apr. 1, 1983.

spite normal respiratory rates during sleep. One patient had reductions to as low as 55%, whereas the other had Sa_{O_2} values below 50%, the sensitivity of the oximetry instrument. Oxygen saturation returned to baseline values during intermittent wakefulness. In neither patient were reductions in Sa_{O_2} related to episodes of apnea or hypopnea.

It appears that abnormal gas exchange patterns during sleep may contribute to the morbidity of sickle cell disease. Both patients in this study had been hospitalized for recurrent vaso-occlusive crisis. Each had a history of what appeared to be ischemic pain on awakening, consistent with a vaso-occlusive process. A recent report on the use of oxygen to reverse nocturnal oxygen desaturation and associated clinical signs in adults with chronic obstructive airway disease suggests the possible use of a similar intervention in selected patients with sickle cell disease to prevent vaso-occlusive crisis. Further studies are needed to clarify the relation between oxygen saturation and sleep stages in patients with sickle cell disease.

▶ [A large postmortem study from Johns Hopkins abstracted in last year's YEAR BOOK emphasized the number of pathologic pulmonary findings (alveolar wall necrosis, diffuse pulmonary edema, focal parenchymal scars, and emboli from necrotic marrow) found much more frequently during autopsies of 72 patients with sickle cell disease than during those of 72 matched controls.[20, 21] It was noteworthy that 20% of these 72 patients died in the setting of a recent painful crisis (infarct crisis) with no ready explanation for death. The interactions between pneumonia and sickle cell disease were discussed in an article abstracted in the 1975 YEAR BOOK.[22, 23] The subject of sickle cell disease was selected again this year, first because of the interesting association between nocturnal desaturation and symptoms of sickle cell disease crisis reported in the abstracted article, and second because of criticism recently received from our hematologist for not using partial exchange transfusion in a fatal case of sickle cell disease. Since the lung is a pivotal organ in sickle cell disease, both as a target organ where damage can occur and often as the cause of the hypoxia which leads to red blood cell changes, it seemed worthwhile to discuss the subject again.

Crises in the sickle states are of several kinds. Painful crises occur with tissue infarction, involving most frequently the bones, chest, and abdomen. Aplastic crises occur when intercurrent viral infections depress erythropoiesis to the point that the marrow can no longer keep up with the excessive demand due to shortened red blood cell survival. Megaloblastic crises are attributed to folate deficiency associated with increased erythropoiesis, and folate therapy is indicated in all patients with sickling disorders producing chronic hemolysis. Hemolytic crisis associated with a falling hematocrit and rising bilirubin and reticulocyte count are thought to be rare. And finally, hypersequestration crisis in which there is a sudden pooling of blood with fall in the hematocrit in the absence of hemolysis is common in the spleen in children and probably occurs in other vascular beds in adults.[24] The patient mentioned above had a 12% fall in hematocrit without reticulocytosis, hyperbilirubinemia, or evidence of blood loss in the 24 hours before death.

Careful old in vitro studies have outlined the Pa_{O_2} values at which important red blood cell changes take place. In SS disease, hemoglobin tactoid formation and increase in the percentage of sickle cells begin at a Pa_{O_2} of about 60 mm Hg. In SC disease tactoid formation is observed at a Pa_{O_2} of 40 mm Hg and increase in the percentage of sickle cells at about 30 mm Hg. In patients with AS hemoglobin tactoid formation begins at a Pa_{O_2} of 30. However, sickling does not occur until the Pa_{O_2} falls to 10–15 mm Hg. Increased erythrocyte mechanical fragility, interestingly, begins at a somewhat higher Pa_{O_2}, 50 mm Hg for both SS and SC hemoglobin, indicating that this is probably a more sensitive index of tactoid formation. Sickle cell–thalassemia disease often resembles SC disease in its oxygen relationships.[25]

The recommendation for partial exchange transfusion and the method by which this can be done (essentially, removal of one unit from the patient, infusion of 500 ml of saline, removal of another unit, and then replacement with 5 units of packed red blood cells) comes from an article by Charache.[26] He states, "Since hypoxemia produced by the lung lesion can lead to further sickling (in pneumonia), it is important to monitor the arterial Pa_{O_2}. If it is less than 75 mm Hg and does not rise into the normal range with oxygen therapy, partial exchange transfusion should be done promptly. Patients with advancing disease should have the Pa_{O_2} monitored very closely, and vigorous measures (intubation, positive end-expiratory pressure, etc.) should be instituted if the situation deteriorates." He does not mention the importance, if any, of mixed venous oxygen tensions, although on the face of it these should be important. It seems that there is a lot of work waiting to be done in the pulmonary physiologic aspects of sickle cell disease. It should be noted that sometimes crises can be worse in SC disease than in SS disease, since SC patients are usually not as anemic and therefore more cells are present to sickle when the Pa_{O_2} is low enough to begin the process.

Collins and Orringer reported 3 relatively young sicklers, all of whom died with pulmonary hypertension and cor pulmonale, and found 3 more in the literature.[27] The patients were both SS and SC. The authors used the term "acute chest syndrome" to indicate episodes of pulmonary distress, which might be due to infection, infarction, or hypersequestration in any combination, and said that these were associated with transient pulmonary hypertension. They also referred to statements that 10 of 12 patients with sickle cell disease over age 15 had pulmonary thromboemboli and arterial intimal proliferation at postmortem examination, and the authors cited statements that sickled erythrocytes accelerate clotting in vitro. They thought that these patients would also benefit from nocturnal oxygen therapy.] ◀

Chapter 13 References

1. 1983 Year Book of Medicine, pp. 118–123.
2. Strohl K. P., Saunders N. A., Feldman N. T., et al.: Obstructive sleep apnea in family members. *N. Engl. J. Med.* 299:969, 1978.
3. 1982 Year Book of Medicine, p. 129.
4. Sampson M. G., Grassino A.: Neuromechanical properties in obese patients during carbon dioxide rebreathing. *Am. J. Med.* 75:81, 1983.
5. Lopata M., Onal E.: Mass loading, sleep apnea, and the pathogenesis of obesity hypoventilation. *Am. Rev. Respir. Dis.* 126:640, 1982.
6. Suratt P. M., Wilhoit S. C., Atkinson, R. L.: Elevated pulse flow resistance in awake obese subjects with obstructive sleep apnea. *Am. Rev. Respir. Dis.* 127:162, 1983.
7. Haponik E. F., Smith P. L., Buhlman M. E., et al.: Computerized tomography in obstructive sleep apnea. Correlation of airway size with physiology during sleep and wakefulness. *Am. Rev. Respir. Dis.* 127:221, 1983.
8. Haponik E. F., Smith P. L., Kaplan J., et al.: Flow-volume curves and sleep-disordered breathing: therapeutic implications. *Thorax* 38:609, 1983.
9. Smith P. L., Haponik E. F., Allen R. P., et al.: The effects of protriptyline in sleep-disordered breathing. *Am. Rev. Respir. Dis.* 127:8, 1983.
10. White D. P., Zwillich C. W., Pickett C. K., et al.: Central sleep apnea: improvement with acetazolamide therapy. *Arch. Inter. Med.* 142:1816, 1982.
11. Rapoport D. M., Sorkin B., Garay S. M., et al.: Reversal of the "Pickwickian Syndrome" by long-term use of nocturnal nasal airways pressure. *N. Engl. J. Med.* 307:931, 1982.
12. 1983 Year Book of Medicine, p. 121–123.
13. Strohl K. P., Hensley M. J., Saunders N. A., et al.: Progesterone administration and progressive sleep apneas. *JAMA* 245:1230, 1981.
14. Martin R. J., Sanders M. H., Gray B. A., et al.: Acute and long-term ventilatory effects of hyperoxia in the adult sleep apnea syndrome. *Am. Rev. Respir. Dis.* 125:175, 1982.

15. 1983 YEAR BOOK OF MEDICINE, pp. 120–121.
16. Dolly F. R., Block A. J.: Effect of flurazepam on sleep-disordered breathing and nocturnal oxygen desaturation in asymptomatic subjects. *Am. J. Med.* 73:239, 1982.
17. Dolly E. R., Block A. J.: Increased ventricular ectopy and sleep apnea following ethanol ingestion in COPD patients. *Chest* 83:469, 1983.
18. Davies S. F., Iber S. F.: Obstructive sleep apnea associated with adult-acquired micrognathia from rheumatoid arthritis. *Am. Rev. Respir. Dis.* 127:245, 1983.
19. Millman R. P., Bevilacqua J., Peterson D. D., et al.: Central sleep apnea in hypothyroidism. *Am. Rev. Respir. Dis.* 127:504, 1983.
20. Haupt H. M., Moore G. W., Bauer T. W., et al.: The lung in sickle cell disease. *Chest* 81:332, 1982.
21. 1983 YEAR BOOK OF MEDICINE, pp. 211–222.
22. Brombert P. A.: Pulmonary aspects of sickle cell disease. *Arch. Intern. Med.* 133:6652, 1974.
23. 1975 YEAR BOOK OF MEDICINE, p. 222.
24. Beutler E.: The sickle cell diseases and related disorders, Williams W. J., Beutler, E., Enslev A. J., Lichtman M. A. (eds.): *Hematology,* ed. 3. New York, McGraw-Hill, 1983.
25. Griggs R. C., Harris J. W.: The biophysics of the variants of sickle-cell disease. *Arch. Intern. Med.* 97:315, 1956.
26. Charache S.: Treatment of sickle cell anemia. *Ann. Rev. Med.* 32:195, 1981.
27. Collins F. S., Orringer E. P.: Pulmonary hypertension and cor pulmonale in the sickle hemoglobinopathies. *Am. J. Med.* 73:814, 1982.

14. Adult Respiratory Distress Syndrome

14-1 **Adult Respiratory Distress Syndrome: Risk With Common Predispositions.** Alpha A. Fowler, Richard F. Hamman, James T. Good, Kim N. Benson, Michael Baird, Donald J. Eberle, Thomas L. Petty, and Thomas M. Hyers (Univ. of Colorado) prospectively identified 993 patients who had one or more of eight conditions thought to predispose to respiratory failure, 57 of whom had more than one predisposing factor, and followed them to ascertain incidence rates for adult respiratory distress syndrome (ARDS). The predisposing states included cardiopulmonary bypass, burn, bacteremia, hypertransfusion, fracture, disseminated intravascular coagulation, pneumonia requiring intensive care, and pulmonary aspiration. Patients with interstitial lung disease or pulmonary carcinomatosis were excluded, as were those with a FEV_1 of less than 1.5 L.

Sixty-eight patients developed ARDS, and 20 others developed the syndrome from causes other than the identified predispositions. The risk was higher for women than for men among patients with burns and with multiple risk factors. Incidence and case-fatality rates are given in the table. There was a strong relation between incidence rates and number of predisposing factors (Fig 14–1). The overall case-

INCIDENCE AND CASE-FATALITY RATES BY PREDISPOSED GROUP

Risks for Predisposition	Patients at Risk	Patients with the Syndrome	Incidence Rate* (per 100)	Patients Who Died	Case-Fatality Rate (per 100)
			n		
Cardiopulmonary bypass	237	4	1.7	2	50.0
Burn	87	2	2.3	1	50.0
Bacteremia	239	9	3.8	7	77.8
Hypertransfusion	197	9	4.6	4	44.4
Fracture	38	2	5.3	0	...
Pneumonia in intensive care	84	10	11.9	6	60.0
Disseminated intravascular coagulation	9	2	22.2	1	50.0
Pulmonary aspiration	45	16	35.6	15†	93.8
All single-risk patients	936	54	5.8	36	66.7
Multiple-risk patients	57	14	24.6	10	71.4
Total of patients with known risks	993	68	6.8	46	67.6
Other patients with syndrome‡	...	20	...	11	55.0

*Incidence rates for the eight predisposed groups were significantly different overall (χ^2, 110.9; $P < .000001$).
†Includes 2 deaths in 6 mos after extubation.
‡Patients at risk were not prospectively identified.
(Courtesy of Fowler, A. A., et al.: Ann. Intern. Med. 98:593–597, May 1983.)

(14–1) Ann. Intern. Med. 98:593–597, May 1983.

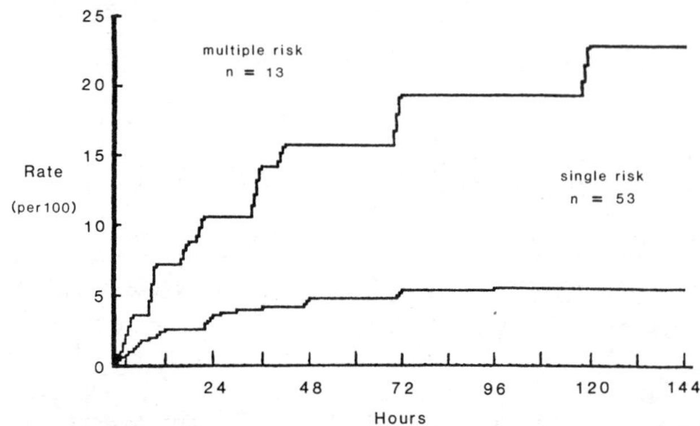

Fig 14–1.—Cumulative incidence rates (per 100) from onset of predisposition to development of syndrome, by number of risks. Two patients with syndrome had missing onset time. (Courtesy of Fowler, A. A., et al.: Ann. Intern. Med. 98:593–597, May 1983.)

fatality rate after onset of the syndrome was 65%. Differences in case-fatality rates among the various predisposed groups were not significant. Case-fatality rates in patients with identified risk factors did not differ significantly from those in patients with causes other than identified predisposing factors.

Rates of ARDS are highest after direct pulmonary injury, such as results from aspiration of gastric contents. The risk is markedly increased in the presence of multiple predisposing factors. Mortality is high in all subgroups. Relatively simple clinical designations can be used in combination to identify patients at high risk of ARDS.

▶ [The interval between the predisposing insult and the development of ARDS was analyzed. Although this ranged from 1 hour to 303 hours, 90% of ARDS episodes had developed by 72 hours. The median interval in the entire patient population was 22 hours but was shorter after aspiration (5.5 hours) and after burns (6 hours). Of those who required intubation, 90% had this accomplished within 72 hours, and 90% of fatal cases died by 14 days. It should be emphasized that the authors' definition of ARDS was quite rigorous, requiring all of the following criteria: "acute respiratory failure requiring mechanical ventilation; sudden onset of bilateral pulmonary infiltrates on roentgenogram; pulmonary capillary wedge pressure of 12 mm Hg or less; total static pulmonary compliance of 50 ml/cm or less; arterial to alveolar partial pressure of oxygen ratio of 0.2 or less." Disseminated intravascular coagulation (DIC) was defined as a platelet count of less than 50,000/cu mm with spontaneous bleeding from 2 or more sites; hypertransfusion was defined as 10 or more units of blood in 24 hours. Studies reporting better results are probably based on less advanced disease. The only other similar epidemiologic study by Pepe et al.[1] was briefly commented on in last year's YEAR BOOK.[2]

Bell and associates[3] from San Antonio have published another good ARDS study analyzing outcome in terms of cause and complications. The overall message was that multiple organ failure (coagulation system, gastrointestinal system with bleeding, CNS abnormalities, pancreatitis, renal failure, or liver failure) was more common in infected patients and that both infection and multiple organ involvement were important determinants of mortality, which was 73.8% overall. Eight of 9 patients with DIC at the outset died, which made DIC the worst prognostic feature at time of diagnosis. Sixty-four of 69 infected patients had some extrapulmonary organ failure compared to only 7 of 15 without infection. From these numbers it is clear that the majority were infected. All patients with bacteremia from a clinically known site of infection lived, whereas all those with bacteremia from an inapparent site died. In 9 such patients who came to autopsy, the site of infection was peritoneal in 7, pericardial in 1, and pleural in 1. This is an important clinical observation since it suggests where to look and implies that drainage might have made a big difference. They discussed an important group of patients which they, and others, have defined as "nonbacteremic clinical sepsis" defined by sudden hypoxemia, hyperbilirubinemia, renal failure, and transient hypotension without a positive blood culture or clinically apparent site of infection. Seventy-one percent of such patients died; in those in whom postmortem examination was done, the site of infection turned out to be the lung in 8, pleura in 1, and meninges in 1. The difficulty of diagnosing pneumonia in ARDS and its untoward effect on outcome was the subject of an article briefly noted in last year's YEAR BOOK.[4, 5]

Two more good articles emphasizing the vascular abnormalities in ARDS have appeared this year. Pinet and associates examined 17 cases of ARDS from ultimately fatal trauma by injecting the pulmonary vasculature with contrast material and by histologic analysis.[6] Microthrombi leading to pulmonary vascular ischemia and to alveolar rupture with hemorrhagic alveolitis were present in all. Bronchopulmonary infection developed in 16 of the 17 patients. All lungs showed some degree of what the authors termed fibroleukocytic alveolitis and attributed to infection. The authors mentioned the theory of Colonel Hardaway that hypotension, when severe, becomes complicated by intravascular coagulation. Actually Hardaway maintained that shock became irreversible when it was followed by disseminated intravascular coagulation, and he wrote a good book about it.[7] In another study of basically the same thing, Snow and associates did an extensive histologic analysis of the lungs of patients dying of ARDS.[8] They noted numerous arterial filling defects, marked reduction of the normal fine peripheral vasculature seen both in areas with thrombi and in areas free of thrombi, extensive fibrin microthrombi, and conversion of nonmuscular vessels to muscular vessels with loss of overall luminal area. The disruption of the pulmonary vascular bed was extensive, and recovery tended to be associated with markedly reduced diffusing capacity and elevated pulmonary vascular resistance. Other references to pulmonary vascular loss in ARDS were discussed in last year's YEAR BOOK.[9]

A new anatomic consequence of treated ARDS, bronchiolectasis, was reported by Slavin et al.[10] Most interestingly, they attributed this to high levels of positive end-expiratory pressure (PEEP). Although many recommend not using more than 15 or 20 mm Hg of PEEP, others continue to recommend "super-PEEP" up to 50 mm Hg when suitable oxygenation cannot be otherwise obtained.[11] The article by Slavin and associates described dilatation of terminal and respiratory bronchioles in autopsy material and correlated its severity with levels of PEEP used, the highest in their group being 45 mm Hg. Also they indicated that *this process caused increased physiologic deadspace.* Patients with a "bronchiolectasis score" of 0 had had deadspace–tidal volume (VD/Vt) values of about 0.3 recorded during life; those with a score of 2 (arbitrary anatomic scoring) had VD/Vt values up to 0.7 and those with scores of 8 had VD/Vt values of greater than 0.8. We have been greatly puzzled by patients who late in the course of ARDS developed very large VD/Vt values with a huge amount of wasted ventilation, and we had never understood what was going on. Bronchiolectasis should be added to obliteration of the vascular bed and interstitial fibrosis as chronic anatomic complications of severe ARDS.

Most instances of ARDS are clearly more severe and widespread insults than just noncardiogenic pulmonary edema as discussed above. However, some problems subsumed under this overall title, such as pulmonary edema due to low oncotic pressure, do not seem to be this sort of total lung injury, and we have always considered neurogenic pulmonary edema to be this sort of less severe problem. Lagerkranser et al. have published a good recent review of the problem.[12] The authors accepted it as established that increased intracranial pressure causes a massive sympathetic discharge with sudden increase in left ventricular preload and afterload, massive shift of blood to the central circulation, and left ventricular failure. They quoted an incidence of 71% in subarachnoid hemorrhage patients, but only a third of these were clinically important. They thought that therapy with α-adrenergic blockers was theoretically attractive but chancy because of the possible hypotensive effect. Also, and this seemed clinically important, they warned against the use of more than 5 or 6 mm Hg of PEEP because of its possible untoward effects on cerebral perfusion when the intracranial pressure is increased. They thought that diuretics also should be used with caution, as the problem is not fluid overload but fluid redistribution. Some patients with neurogenic pulmonary edema will develop some capillary damage which has been sort of loosely attributed to overperfusion. As mentioned, whether or not they go on to the graver complications of ARDS, such as loss of pulmonary vasculature, interstitial fibrosis, and the like is not known but seems unlikely. Lagerkranser et al. say that β-adrenergic blockade is bad for this problem. In contrast Colgan et al. say it is helpful.[13] This was an experimental study in dogs. Outpouring of catecholamines continued as long as the intracranial pressure was elevated, and considerable pulmonary arteriovenous shunting was present. Both arteriovenous shunting and pulmonary hypertension appeared to be ameliorated by β blockade. It was an interesting but complicated study. Probably the vast majority of patients with neurogenic pulmonary edema do well if diagnosed and treated with low levels of PEEP and supplemental oxygen.

Walters and associates published a very good article on salicylate-induced pulmonary edema.[14] They had 111 patients with salicylate intoxication, 6 of whom developed pulmonary edema. All were older people who smoked. The authors said that pulmonary edema is a rare complication of salicylate intoxication in children and that smoking is an added risk factor. A very interesting point was their contention that acidosis enhanced the pulmonary edema. They pointed out that it is only the nonionized form of aspirin which penetrates biologic membranes and that a shift of pH from 7.4 to 7.2 doubles the nonionized salicylate level. Also they state that brain salicylate levels are increased by acidosis. The average pH in their patients with pulmonary edema was 7.37, whereas those without pulmonary edema had an average pH of 7.41 (all had comparable levels of salicylate). Those with pulmonary edema also had prominent neurologic changes (lethargy, confusion, and disorientation) which the authors felt were due to direct action of salicylate on the brain. Pulmonary edema was more frequent in chronic ingesters of aspirin than in those who took a large dose acutely, and chronic ingesters also had a lower pH. The authors mentioned the clinical fact that salicylate intoxication is also associated with proteinuria, and they think that it is caused by the same membrane-toxic effect.

Mountain et al. report a case of noncardiac pulmonary edema due to paraldehyde, 23 ml, administered in 5 intramuscular injections over 9 hours.[15] They say that the analogous hypnotic ethchlorvynol can do the same thing. Paraldehyde is cleared by the lungs in substantial degree, and the authors feel that this might result in a direct toxic effect on the alveolar membrane. They reviewed several other cases, some of which occurred at quite modest dosage, and felt that the toxic-therapeutic ratio of this drug was pretty narrow. Bernstein et al. report a case of ARDS following *intrathecal injection of methotrexate.*[16] Perez et al. believe that *pulmonary edema complicating pancreatitis* is due to complement activation.[17]] ◀

Chapter 14 References

1. Pepe P. E., Potkin R. J., Reus D. H., et al.: Clinical predictors of the adult respiratory distress syndrome. *Am. J. Surg.* 144:124, 1982.
2. 1983 Year Book of Medicine, p. 135.
3. Bell R. C., Carlson J. J., Johanson W. G. Jr.: Multiple organ system failure and infection in adult respiratory distress syndrome. *Ann. Intern. Med.* 99:293, 1983.
4. Andrews C. P., Coalson J. J., Smith J. D., et al.: Diagnosis of nosocomial bacterial pneumonia in acute, diffuse lung injury. *Chest* 80:254, 1981.
5. 1983 Year Book of Medicine, p. 136.
6. Pinet F., Tabit A., Clermont A., et al.: Post-traumatic-shock lung: postmortem microangiographic and pathologic correlation. *A.J.R.* 139:449, 1982.
7. Hardaway, R. M., *Syndromes of Disseminated Intravascular Coagulation With Special Reference to Shock and Hemorrhage.* Springfield, Ill., Charles C Thomas Publisher, 1966.
8. Snow R. L., Davies P., Pontoppidan H., et al.: Pulmonary vascular remod-

eling in adult respiratory distress syndrome. *Am. Rev. Respir. Dis.* 126:887, 1982.

9. 1983 YEAR BOOK OF MEDICINE, p. 135.
10. Slavin G., Nunn J. F., Crow J., et al.: Bronchiolectasis—a complication of artificial ventilation. *Br. Med. J.* 285:931, 1982.
11. van Rooyen W., Bruining H. A.: Respiratory distress syndrome and its treatment with high positive end-expiratory pressure ventilation. *Int. Surg.* 67:245, 1982.
12. Lagerkranser M., Petersson K., Slyven C., Neurogenic pulmonary oedema. A review of the pathophysiology with clinical and therapeutic implications. *Acta Med. Scand.* 212:267, 1982.
13. Colgan F. J., Sawa J., Teneytck L. G., et al.: Protective effect of β blockade on pulmonary function when intracranial pressure is elevated. *Crit. Care Med.* 11:368, 1983.
14. Walters J. S., Woodring J. H., Stelling C. B., et al.: Salicylate-induced pulmonary edema. *Radiology* 146:289, 1983.
15. Mountain R., Ferguson S., Fowles A., et al.: Non-cardiac pulmonary edema following administration of parenteral paraldehyde. *Chest* 82:371, 1982.
16. Bernstein M. L., Sobel D. B., Wimmer R. S.: Non-cardiogenic pulmonary edema following injection of methotrexate into the cerebrospinal fluid. *Cancer* 50:866, 1982.
17. Perez H. P., Horn J. K., Ong R., et al.: Complement (C5)-derived chemotactic activity in serum from patients with pancreatitis. *J. Lab. Clin. Med.* 101:123, 1983.

15. Interstitial Lung Disease

15–1 **Role of Alveolar Macrophages in Asbestosis: Modulation of Neutrophil Migration to the Lung After Acute Asbestos Exposure.** Asbestosis is a chronic interstitial lung disorder of the alveolar structures characterized by accumulation of inflammatory and immune effector cells. Most noninfectious, nonmalignant alveolar diseases are mediated by inflammatory and immune effector processes. Carl I. Schoenberger, Gary W. Hunninghake, Oichi Kawanami, Victor J. Ferrans, and Ronald G. Crystal (Natl. Inst. of Health) undertook to characterize the alveolitis of acute asbestosis in an experimental guinea pig model, in which short chrysotile asbestos was injected intratracheally. The alveolitis was assessed by bronchoalveolar lavage and by lung sectioning for microscopic examination. In controls, only saline was instilled.

Instillation of asbestos led to a widespread, acute alveolitis with large numbers of neutrophils and eosinophils and an increased number of alveolar macrophages. Septal thickening was apparent after 6 weeks, when polymorphonuclear leukocyte infiltration of the lungs persisted. Polymorphonuclear cells comprised 21% of all leukocytes in bronchoalveolar lavage specimens at 3 days and 28% at 6 weeks. Guinea pig alveolar macrophages released appreciable amounts of neutrophil chemotactic factor when exposed in vitro to short or intermediate chrysotile fibers or amosite or crocidolite fibers. Release was augmented by prior exposure of the asbestos fibers to normal serum. The chemotactic factor was lipid soluble and resembled that released spontaneously by alveolar macrophages from animals exposed in vivo to short chrysotile fibers.

The findings suggest that alveolar macrophages may have an important role in the early stages of asbestosis, modulating the migration of neutrophils to the lungs. At least some of the alterations in alveolar structures associated with asbestosis may be related to the ability of asbestos fibers to stimulate alveolar macrophages to attract neutrophils to the lower respiratory tract. Neutrophils are known to be cytotoxic to lung parenchymal cells.

▶ [It has become popular to divide the fibrogenic diseases into "lymphocyte predominant" and "polymorphonuclear leukocyte predominant," following the hypotheses of Dr. Ronald Crystal's group at the NIH. In last year's YEAR BOOK, a study on bronchoalveolar lavage (BAL) cells in berylliosis by Dauber et al. was abstracted which argued that this condition was a hypersensitivity pneumonitis and best grouped in the lymphocyte predominant category with sarcoidosis and allergic alveolitis due to inhalation of organic dusts.[1,2] It was demonstrated that BAL lymphocytes (actually in a macrophage-lymphocyte mixture) were activated (proliferation and thymidine uptake) by soluble beryllium salts. This was thought to conform to the sequence in the

---

(15–1) Thorax 37:803–809 November 1983.

granulomatous lung diseases in which immunologically specific or nonspecific stimulation of T cells attracted to the lung from the circulation results in elaboration of materials (lymphokines) that are chemotactic for macrophages and for other lymphocytes. This causes cellular alveolitis early, granuloma formation later, and eventually bland fibrosis. Also another T-cell-derived material stimulates alveolar B cells to produce a broad and essentially nonspecific hypergammaglobulinemia (although specificity for certain ubiquitous antigens such as the Epstein-Barr virus can be found with regularity in sarcoidosis). Rankin et al. have correlated the level of *serum* IgG with the number of IgG-producing cells in the BAL but *not* in nonpulmonary lymphatic tissue.[3] This appears to support the notion that the serum hypergammaglobulinemia in sarcoid spills over from the lung to the systemic circulation. A similar pulmonary-extrapulmonary disparity is also said to be true with respect to helper T lymphocytes, which are way up in BAL fluid but abnormally low in circulating blood, leading to pulmonary hyperreactivity of cellular immune mechanisms but systemic hyporeactivity of the same mechanisms as illustrated by cutaneous anergy.

The article by the NIH group, abstracted above, indicates that asbestosis is an example of the other general category of interstitial disease, leukocyte predominant, resembling in this respect idiopathic interstitial fibrosis. To quote another good general article on the same subject, "The effect of asbestos fibers on pulmonary cells is as follows: (1) pulmonary alveolar macrophages are activated to produce lysosomal enzymes, produce neutrophil chemotactic factor, augment fibroblast replication, cause the increased uptake of ^{67}Ga, cause the induction of lymphocyte proliferation, cause increased IgG and C3 receptors; (2) neutrophils become increased in numbers in alveolitis and cause the release of lysosomal enzymes, toxic oxygen metabolites, and collagenase; (3) fibroblasts stimulate collagen synthesis; (4) for lymphocytes, peripheral blood studies suggest impaired mitogenic response and T-cell counts." These authors suggest that when asbestosis is associated with a positive gallium scan, indicating cellular alveolitis, perhaps steroids might be of use. They do not recommend it but say that it is a reasonable subject for study.[4]

Although silica, beryllium, and asbestos are the classic fibrogenic dusts, it is reasonable to ask whether or not *any* inorganic dust which persists for any period of time in the lung is truly free of fibrogenic potential. Lapenas et al. report on the use of analytic scanning electron microscopy to detect talc, mica, graphite, and mixed inorganic dusts in cases of advanced pulmonary fibrosis.[5] Davison et al. report that hard metal, which is an "alloy of tungsten, cobalt, and occasionally other metals such as titanium and tantalum" can cause asthma, interstitial fibrosis with an active alveolitis containing multinucleated giant cells, or both, the suspect agent being cobalt.[6]] ◀

15–2 **Wegener's Granulomatosis: Prospective Clinical and Therapeutic Experience With 85 Patients for 21 Years** is reported by Anthony S. Fauci, Barton F. Haynes, Paul Katz, and Sheldon M. Wolff (Natl. Inst. of Health). Eighty-five patients with Wegener's granulomatosis were studied during a 21-year period in conjunction with long-term low-dose cyclophosphamide and alternate-day corticosteroid therapy. All patients had either upper airway or lung involvement, and most had both. Lung biopsies showed granulomas and vasculitis. Renal disease was documented in 85% of patients. Only about one fifth of patients had nervous system involvement. Ten patients had cardiac involvement. There are no diagnostic laboratory findings in Wegener's granulomatosis, but all patients had an elevated sedimentation rate before treatment. Elevations of IgE concentration were rare.

Treatment was initiated with 2 mg of cyclophosphamide per kg daily and prednisone in a daily dose of 1 mg/kg, followed by alternate-day treatment with 60 mg and then gradually reduced doses until

---

(15–2) Ann. Intern. Med. 98:76–85, January 1983.

cyclophosphamide only was given. The dosage was adjusted to maintain the leukocyte count at greater than 3,000/cu mm. Complete remission was achieved in 93% of patients. Remission was induced less often in the small group of patients given azathioprine than in those given cyclophosphamide. Mean duration of remission in surviving patients was 4 years. Twenty-three patients are presently off all treatment after a mean of nearly 3 years. Seven patients had 9 episodes of herpes zoster while they were in remission. Gonadal dysfunction remains a serious problem. Hemorrhagic cystitis was a frequent side effect of cyclophosphamide therapy.

Long-term remissions can be induced and maintained in a high proportion of patients with Wegener's granulomatosis by combined daily cyclophosphamide and alternate-day prednisone therapy. Serious side effects continue to occur, but promising results have been obtained in patients with this previously fatal illness.

▶ [Some points of interest not covered in the abstract: (1) Most patients initially presented with severe and persistent rhinorrhea, sometimes with pain. Otitis media due to eustachian tube blockage was present in 25%. Biopsy of upper airway lesions was not a very good way to make the diagnosis. Half showed either vasculitis or granuloma but rarely both, and in the other half biopsy revealed only chronic, nonspecific inflammation. Biopsy of oral ulcers showed only nonspecific changes. Twenty-eight percent developed some degree of saddle-nose deformity. All of the patients with serious sinus or nasal disease developed secondary infection, usually with *Staphylococcus aureus.* The authors emphasized that nasal problems due to infection should be distinguished from relapse, with the latter's implication for retreatment or dosage adjustment. They feel that Wegener's is distinctly different from midline granuloma. Wegener's can cause sinus wall perforation and destruction of the bridge of the nose but is *not,* in their experience, the cause of hard palate perforation or erosion through the skin of the nose such as can be seen in lethal midline granuloma or in midline malignant reticulosis.

(2) Half of the 80 patients with pulmonary infiltrates had no symptoms of lung disease. The usual x-ray pattern was single or multiple pulmonary nodules with a tendency to cavitation. Pleural effusions were seen in 20%, and 15% had endobronchial involvement although bronchoscopic biopsy of the latter usually revealed nonspecific findings. The endobronchial lesions could cause atelectasis.

(3) Signs and symptoms of renal involvement were usually late manifestations, often developing after diagnosis had been established, but renal disease is probably the most serious long-term consequence of Wegener's. Only 11% of patients presented initially with functional renal impairment. In those who had glomerulonephritis and azotemia before starting immunosuppressive therapy, the risk of progressing to renal failure was 30%. Renal biopsy was *not* specific for Wegener's, granulomata and true arteritis being found extremely rarely. The histologic picture ranged from mild focal segmental glomerulonephritis, often without any urinary abnormalities, to diffuse necrotizing glomerulonephritis with crescent formation. The authors emphasized that renal disease could progress from mild to severe, sometimes within a matter of days, and implied that one of the reasons for diagnostic urgency is prompt treatment in order that renal involvement might be avoided or mitigated.

(4) Various sorts of rather nonspecific eye involvement were seen in 58%. Proptosis from a retro-orbital mass occurred in 15 patients and was slow to respond to therapy. Mononeuritis multiplex, a clinical hallmark of all sorts of vasculitis, was present in 9 patients.

(5) The authors' treatment protocol was *extremely meticulous.* White blood cell counts were obtained every other day at the start of therapy in order to adjust the cyclophosphamide dosage so as to avoid counts lower than 3,000. When counts fell below this, which the authors felt could be avoided with this sort of observation, then serious and prolonged leukopenic periods inevitably followed, often with sepsis. The article should be consulted for details of therapy and how it is tapered. Hemorrhagic

cystitis was a frequent, but not usually serious, problem. They felt that they had clear evidence that azathioprine was not as good as cyclophosphamide.

It is unusual that so much of the experience with treatment of this uncommon but important disease should have been accumulated by one group, but that seems to have been the case and we are fortunate that the group has persevered. Everyone who undertakes management of Wegener's granulomatosis should read this article in the original and know it well.

A distinctly less favorable picture was presented in a small series by Brandwein et al. from McGill.[7] Four of their 13 patients were very sick on presentation and died before therapy could really be instituted. Two of these had a fulminant pulmonary-renal syndrome with massive hemoptysis and acute renal failure resembling Goodpasture's syndrome but with no antiglomerular basement membrane antibody. Nine patients lived long enough to have proper therapy, but only 5 of these survived a year. Of the 4 who died, 1 had a hemorrhaging duodenal ulcer, 1 had mesenteric and portal vein thrombosis, 1 died of peritonitis and sepsis occurring during treatment of chronic renal failure, and 1 died of respiratory failure thought to be due to cyclophosphamide. Of the 5 who survived a year, 4 had chronic renal failure. Only one could be thought of as well. The authors felt that renal failure and hypertension were the major causes of morbidity and that these were often late manifestations, occurring after apparent control of the vasculitis and granulomatosis.

A good study from the Mayo Clinic emphasized involvement of the subglottis and upper portion of the trachea.[8] Seventeen of the 108 patients with Wegener's had subglottic or tracheal stenosis or both. Fourteen of these had tracheal symptoms and signs, usually hoarseness with increasing stridor occurring at the same time as or a little after the presenting nasal manifestations. Direct laryngoscopy showed a reddish, friable narrowing just below the cords, tracheal tomograms delineated the narrowed area, and biopsy in 3 showed changes consistent with Wegener's. Tracheotomy was necessary in 9. All survived, but 5 continued to use tracheotomy tubes. (Some people think that the floppy trachea syndrome is burnt out Wegener's).

Gephart et al. report a careful immunohistologic study of a case of Wegener's confined to the lungs.[9] The vasculitic lesions contained T cells and monocytes, but there was no evidence of antibody, immune complexes, or complement. The authors suggest that the pulmonary vasculitis is based on cellular rather than humoral reactions. This seems clearly not the case in the glomerulonephritis. Perhaps the clinical suggestion that the pulmonary process is easier to treat than the renal reflects a difference in pathogenesis, the renal process being due to circulating immune complexes rather than round cell infiltration.

Jaspan et al. report a case of Wegener's with spontaneous pneumothorax progressing to pyopneumothorax with bronchopleural fistula.[10] They note that pneumothorax has been reported in 3%–5% of other series.

The experience of the NIH group with treatment of lymphomatoid granulomatosis, which is often confused with Wegener's, but is not, according to them, as easy to treat was discussed in the 1983 Year Book,[11, 12] and the difficult interrelationships of the various diseases characterized by lymphoid infiltration of the lung were commented on and briefly referenced. Two interesting articles on this subject will be briefly mentioned here. Taveira Da Silva et al. report a case of lymphomatoid granulomatosis presenting as ARDS.[13] Kohler et al. report a case of lymphoid interstitial pneumonitis associated with common variable hypogammaglobulinemia which presented with interstitial lung disease causing hypoxia and responded, in terms of oxygenation, etc., to treatment with prednisone.[14]] ◀

15–3 **Bronchocentric Granulomatosis: A Review and Thoughts on Pathogenesis** are presented by Martin D. Clee, David Lamb, and Roland A. Clark (Scotland). Bronchocentric granulomatosis is characterized by a necrotizing granulomatous reaction centered around both large and small airways. It is most severe peripherally, where irregular necrotic lesions are found within collapsed, consolidated lung tissue. The ulcerated bronchial walls may exhibit an eosino-

---

(15–3) Br. J. Dis. Chest 77:227–234, July 1983.

philic necrotic lining with palisaded histiocytes and giant cells. Occasional true epithelioid granulomas are seen. Peribronchial inflammatory infiltrates may include eosinophils as a prominent feature. Proximal bronchi may be plugged by inspissated material, and may exhibit chondritis and cartilage destruction. Arteritis is not a major feature. The bronchocentric pathology contrasts with the angiocentric nature of other pulmonary granulomatides.

A majority of cases have been reported from the United States. Some patients have associated asthma, and they may have strongly positive skin test responses to *Aspergillus*. Increased serum levels of IgE and specific IgE antibody to *A. fumigatus* have been described. Tissue eosinophilia is characteristic of asthmatic patients, while in nonasthmatics polymorphonuclear leukocytes predominate. A wide range of radiologic findings has been reported. The lesions often are unilateral, with a predilection for the upper lobes. A majority of patients have been diagnosed at thoracotomy. Removal of the involved lobe often is curative, although some patients require steroids postoperatively. Regular follow-up is necessary; death from progressive disease has been described.

Bronchocentric granulomatosis may represent one of a limited number of ways in which the bronchi can respond to insult, and a variety of stimuli may produce it. The essential condition is a sustained inflammatory process within the lumen, often in association with proximal bronchial obstruction and distention of distal airways by retained secretions and cellular debris. In asthmatics, bronchocentric granulomatosis may represent one end of a spectrum of allergic bronchopulmonary aspergillosis.

▶ [The term *bronchocentric granulomatosis* (BG) was introduced by Dr. A. A. Liebow in a landmark lecture in 1973.[15] At that time he discussed it as closely associated with what he termed the angiocentric granulomatoses, which included Wegener's, lymphomatoid granulomatosis, and necrotizing sarcoid granulomatosis. Two years later Katzenstein and associates, including Liebow, separated bronchogenic granulomatosis from those other processes and presented the concept that it was one of a group of closely related illnesses based on allergic reactions to fungi (or other material) chronically present in the bronchi. These often overlapping illnesses include allergic bronchopulmonary aspergillosis (ABA), mucoid impaction of the bronchus, and at least some instances of hypersensitivity pneumonitis.[16]

As pointed out by Dr. Liebow, not all cases of BG are due to saphrophytic contamination of the bronchi with *Aspergillus*. In those cases that are due to *Aspergillus* (approximately half of the total), there is almost always a history of asthma, peripheral and sputum eosinophilia, and immunologic features (positive skin test to *Aspergillus* antigen, *Aspergillus* precipitins) characteristic of ABA. In point of fact it is very difficult to differentiate those cases of BC associated with asthma and eosinophilia from ABA, except that in BC the radiologic shadows are more chronic and histologic study shows bronchial wall destruction and granulomatous and often eosinophilic infiltration with tissue destruction extending beyond the bronchus into the surrounding parenchyma. Also, as pointed out by Katzenstein et al., 70%–80% of patients with mucoid impaction of the bronchus have asthma or chronic bronchitis, and many will have eosinophilia, *Aspergillus* in the mucoid bronchial cast, and the immunologic features of ABA.[16] Since patients with ABA characteristically cough up mucus plugs, the overlap between ABA and at least many cases of mucoid impaction is obviously great. The difference is that most cases of mucoid impaction (in which there is no permanent destruction of the bronchial wall and no peribronchiolar inflammation), as well as most cases of BC (which is more or less defined by these destructive features), are diagnosed because they are resected on suspicion of a neoplastic mass lesion. In the series of 23 BC patients discussed by Katzenstein et al., the 10 patients who were asthmatic had a clinical picture of fever, cough, chest pain, anorexia, and malaise in some combination superimposed on chronic asthma. The 13 patients who were not asthmatic tended to be older (onset age 50 or so), had no evidence of atopy, had vague symptoms present about 3 months before surgery, and had a variety of organisms recovered from the surgical specimen. The prominent eosinophilia characteristic of the asthmatic cases was not present, but otherwise the histology was pretty much the same.

The abstracted article emphasized that BC, unlike the angiocentric granulomatoses, does not have extrapulmonary manifestations and usually follows a relatively benign course. As mentioned, BC is usually diagnosed after resection, and it seems unlikely that fiberoptic bronchoscopy will significantly contribute to the diagnosis of either BC or mucoid impaction except in a negative sense. A CPC in the *New England Journal of Medicine* records one instance in which fiberoptic bronchoscopy was done: the involved segment was narrowed and extruded a little pus and blood, findings which are pretty nonspecific.[17] In terms of prognosis, the abstracted article states, "Should the histological features in resected lung tissue suggest bronchocentric granulomatosis, long-term follow-up of asthmatic patients is required with early use of steroids on clinical or radiological suspicion of recurrence. Such long-term stringency is probably unnecessary in the non-asthmatic patient."

Robinson et al. state that the shadows are upper lobe in 60%, unilateral in 73%, and solitary in most patients.[18] Nine of their 15 patients had mass lesions, 7 solitary, 1 with 2 and 1 with 3 separate masses, and 4 had pneumonic shadowing with the features of an alveolar filling process. The remaining 2 patients, however, had disseminated nodular densities due to involvement of much smaller bronchi. The clinical features in these 15 patients included asthma in 3, chest pain in 6, cough in 10, fever in 9, leukocytosis in 5, and eosinophilia in 2.] ◄

► ↓ Two notable advances in the area of nonspecific interstitial lung diseases are the analysis of material obtained by bronchoalveolar lavage (BAL) and the use of gallium scanning to estimate disease "activity" and by inference the expectations of therapy. As discussed above, the BAL cell studies of the NIH group led to the concept that these diseases could be divided into two broad categories, lymphocyte predominant (sarcoidosis and hypersensitivity pneumonitis) and polymorphonuclear leukocyte predominant (mostly nonspecific interstitial fibrosis or—the English term for this disease—cryptogenic fibrosing alveolitis). The pathogenic concepts built on study of these cells and the fluid contents of alveolar wash specimens were outlined in some detail in the 1982 YEAR BOOK.[19] The same group made the observation that active cellular infiltration of the lung was associated with uptake of gallium, whereas more fibrotic processes were not. These observations inevitably led to the notion that both BAL studies and gallium scanning would have clinical value as indices both for diagnosis and monitoring the results of therapy. The following abstract speaks to this point with respect to sarcoidosis. ◄

15–4 **Serial Changes in Markers of Disease Activity With Corticosteroid Treatment in Sarcoidosis.** A variety of independent markers of disease activity have been recommended in the management of patients with sarcoidosis, but relative merit of such markers remains unclear. E. Clinton Lawrence, Robert B. Teague, Marc S. Gottlieb, Satish G. Jhingran (Baylor Coll. of Medicine, Houston) and Jack Lieberman (VA Med. Ctr., Sepulveda, Calif.) followed 12 patients having sarcoidosis, diagnosed by lung biopsy. Patients were treated with 40 mg of prednisone daily for 6 weeks. Initially, all had abnormal ^{67}Ga uptake in the lung parenchyma, abnormal bronchoalveolar lavage fluid, elevated serum angiotensin-converting enzyme level, or a combination of these findings. All patients had radiographic stage-II or stage-III disease.

(15–4) Am. J. Med. 74:747–756, May 1983.

All patients but 1 improved symptomatically and radiographically after 6 weeks of steroid therapy. The forced vital capacity increased in patients who responded. Uptake of ^{67}Ga in the lung parenchyma decreased in all patients (Fig 15–1). Converting enzyme levels decreased substantially. Serum gamma globulin levels also decreased. The mean erythrocyte sedimentation rate decreased from 27 to 15 mm/hour. Changes in cell counts in bronchoalveolar lavage fluid analysis were variable. Five patients given decreasing doses of prednisone therapy on alternate days for several months had their course best reflected by changes in ^{67}Ga uptake. Converting enzyme levels were the next best measure (table).

Sarcoidosis should be treated only in patients with symptomatic pulmonary disease or critical extrapulmonary involvement, rather than in all patients with abnormalities of a single measure of disease activity. The response to treatment can be objectively assessed from ^{67}Ga lung uptake or the serum angiotensin-converting enzyme level. The latter may be preferable if initially abnormal, since it is less ex-

Fig 15–1.—Effects of 6 weeks of daily prednisone treatment on ^{67}Ga lung scanning scores, serum angiotensin-converting enzyme *(SACE)* levels, serum γ globulin levels, and erythrocyte sedimentation rate *(ESR)*. Solid circles represent results for each patient before and after treatment with 40 mg/day of prednisone. Mean values for each test are indicated by open circles. *P* values represent results of paired *t*-test analysis. (Courtesy of Lawrence, E. C., et al.: Am. J. Med. 74:747–756, May 1983.)

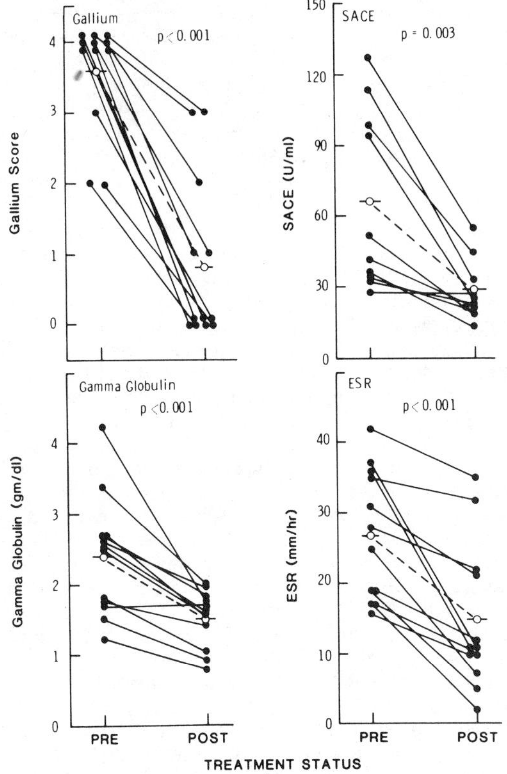

SUMMARY OF CORRELATION OF VARIOUS MARKERS OF DISEASE ACTIVITY WITH CLINICAL COURSE

		Parameters of Disease Activity					
Patient*	Clinical Response	^{67}Gallium Lung Scan	Serum Angiotensin-Converting Enzyme	Bronchoalveolar Lavage Fluid (% Lymphocytes)	Bronchoalveolar Lavage Fluid-IgG-Secreting Cells	Gamma Globulin	Erythrocyte Sedimentation Rate
1	Yes	+	0	0	0	+	0
2	Yes	+	+	0	0	0	0
4	Yes	+	+	0	+	0	+
6	Yes	+	+	+	0	+	0
3	No	+	+	+	+	?	0

*Patients treated for 12 months with decreasing doses of prednisone.

+, Positive correlation with clinical course; *?,* equivocal correlation with clinical course; *0,* lack of correlation with clinical course.

(Courtesy of Lawrence, E.C., et al.: Am. J. Med. 74:747–756, May 1983.)

pensive than lung scanning. Further study is needed to determine the benefits of bronchoalveolar lavage in terms of its cost and the risk to individual patients.

▶ [This useful article requires more analysis than could be provided in the abstract. First, the vital capacity was again found to be a very useful test to follow response to steroids in sarcoidosis, and total lung capacity studies did not add to this. Diffusion capacity was really less useful than vital capacity, as was serial arterial oxygen tension measurement. The studies on BAL content, both cell type and number of immunoglobulin-producing cells, were *too variable to be clinically useful,* a very important point. Serum angiotensin-converting enzyme (SACE) was a useful marker of response to therapy when it was elevated at the outset, but this was the case in only 7 of 10 patients in whom serial measurements were made and who were judged on other grounds to have been steroid responders. Gallium scan seemed to be the best indicator of clinical activity and also the best index of response to steroids. In one interesting case the patient had only skin disease clinically, but he wanted to be treated and accordingly was studied. He was found to have a positive gallium scan which decreased in intensity with treatment.

The authors of the abstracted article quote others who contend that steroid therapy probably does not alter the long-term outcome in sarcoidosis (see also Harkleroad et al.[20]), and recommend treatment only in "those patients with symptomatic pulmonary disease or other critical extrapulmonary involvement, rather than abnormalities in any single (laboratory) parameter of disease activity." However, the message of the article is that vital capacity, SACE levels, and gallium scanning are all useful parameters to follow when steroid therapy is to be used. The authors thought that gallium scanning could be eliminated when cost was a major factor. However, steroid therapy in sarcoidosis is a risky, uncertain, and of itself costly undertaking, and any guidance seems worth the cost, especially with respect to when to quit and when or whether to start again. A lot more material that provided interesting information on treatment in sarcoidosis was briefly mentioned in the 1983 YEAR BOOK.[21] The pregallium pre-BAL sarcoid-steroid article that we keep returning to is one by Johns et al. from Johns Hopkins, which was discussed in the 1975 YEAR BOOK.[22, 23] Since it relates to SACE and sarcoid, one interesting article on a fine clinical point with surprising results will be mentioned here. Workers at the Mayo Clinic tried to determine whether the combination of hypercalcemia and elevated SACE activity was specific for sarcoidosis.[24] They found it was not, elevated SACE levels being found in some cases of hyperparathyroidism and tumor-induced hypercalcemia as well.

A study concerning the usefulness of these laboratory markers in interstitial fibrosis but focusing on prediction of response to therapy was reported by Gelb et al.[25] In the summary they state that "positive gallium lung scans, BAL, circulating immune complexes, and to a lesser extent lung immune complexes are associated with the cellular phase of interstitial pneumonia, but do not reliably identify a corticosteroid-responsive group." Their data showed improvement in only 2 of 16 patients with predominantly cellular processes, one of whom had a *negative* gallium scan, and in none of 4 with predominantly fibrotic processes. (The article has a lot of excellent, hard-to-come-by data, particularly with regard to circulating and tissue-fixed immune complexes).

In view of the lack of predictive value of these various tests, Gelb et al. feel that open-lung biopsy is necessary to decide on whether or not to treat. In support of the opposite view, Tukiainen et al. in a restrospective analysis report that the "main factor influencing the long-term prognosis was the short-term response to steroid treatment."[26] They reported 21 steroid responders, 13 with a cellular and 8 with a fibrotic histology, and 43 nonresponders, 9 with cellular and 34 with fibrotic histology. They stated that the main purpose of lung biopsy was diagnosis rather than making a determination as to whether or not to treat. Other factors which they found had some predictive value regarding response to therapy were younger age, less radiographic abnormality, a higher diffusing capacity, and a shorter duration of symptoms before presentation, but none of these in any combination was sufficiently discriminatory to warrant a decision not to treat. A similar view concerning the lack of definitive usefulness of lung biopsy was expressed by the Brompton group in a series of excellent articles about interstitial fibrosis.[27]

An editorial concerning bronchoalveolar lavage by Fulmer will be mentioned here.[28] He states that it is useful in the diagnosis of lung hemorrhage (hemosiderin-laden macrophages), some infections, alveolar proteinosis (sometimes), and, with ultrastructural studies, histiocytosis X; but that the considerable overlap in lymphocyte-predominant and leukocyte-predominant patterns makes it not yet useful for diagnosis or prognosis in the nonspecific interstitial diseases, including sarcoidosis.] ◀

15–5 **Association of Progressive Multifocal Leukoencephalopathy and Sarcoidosis.** Despite abnormalities of cell-mediated immunity, the only well-documented infectious complication of sarcoidosis is aspergilloma. Mark A. Rosenbloom and Dean F. Uphoff (Hartford Hosp., Conn.) describe a patient with both well-documented progressive multifocal leukoencephalopathy (PML), a viral infection, and sarcoidosis.

Woman, 59, previously healthy, had visual and memory difficulties for 5 months, starting a month before an automobile accident. A right homonymous hemianopia was present, and computed tomography (CT) 2 months after the accident showed an extremely small hypodense area in the left parieto-occipital lobe. A brain scan yielded normal findings. The patient could not subtract serial 7s and had difficulty in recalling numbers. A chest x-ray film showed extensive, bilateral reticulonodular infiltrates. The CT lesion in the cerebrum had become larger. The sedimentation rate was 59 mm/hour. Open-lung biopsy showed changes consistent with sarcoidosis. Prednisone was given, but progressive confusion developed, a new, nonenhancing CT lesion was seen on the opposite side, and brain biopsy showed myelin destruction. The patient became comatose and died.

Autopsy showed small, nodular, fibrotic foci in the lungs that appeared to be residua of sarcoid granulomas. Nodules were also found in the spleen. Extensive demyelination of the cerebral white matter was observed, with typical microscopic features of PML. Numerous intranuclear inclusions were seen in oligodendroglia, and electron microscopic examination showed intranuclear virions typical of papovavirus.

This patient had many typical features of PML, a disease most often associated with chronic lymphocytic leukemia, Hodgkin's disease, and non-Hodgkin's lymphoma. An association with sarcoidosis has previously been suggested. Such an association does appear to exist, and corticosteroid therapy would seem to be unnecessary. Progressive

(15–5) Chest 83:572–575, March 1983.

multifocal leukoencephalopathy should be considered in any patient thought to have CNS sarcoidosis, especially if the cerebrospinal fluid is normal. An aggressive approach is warranted in evaluating patients with sarcoidosis who have atypical neurologic deficits.

▶ [This is an unusual association. The handful of other such cases are referenced in the article. It seems important to know this, since a superficially similar picture can be caused by sarcoidosis itself, for which the treatment—steroids and possibly radiotherapy, as discussed below—would be very different.

It is estimated that about 5% of sarcoid patients will have neurologic involvement.[29] Evidence for sarcoidosis in other organs will be present in the majority but not in all. The most typical clinical syndromes are due to involvement at the base of the brain and include diabetes insipidus, single or multiple cranial nerve palsies (VII, II, IX and X together, and VIII, in that order), mass lesions resembling tumor in the brain or spinal cord, chronic meningitis, and seizures. One recent and probably very important paper from the Bronx Municipal Hospital reported a patient with meningitis (mononuclear pleocytosis, high levels of protein in cerebrospinal fluid [CSF] and seizures who did not improve with steroids.[30] Reasoning from the fact that other sarcoid tissue shrinks with radiotherapy, the authors treated that patient with 1,000 rads to the head in 200-rad doses over a week with good response. They quote opinions in the literature indicating that seizures in sarcoidosis tend to be refractory to steroid therapy and indicate a very poor prognosis.[31]

Although in most instances neurologic sarcoidosis will have some sort of focal symptomatology, patients have been reported with simple dementia not unlike the case of PML discussed in the abstracted article.[32, 33] An important difference between patients with dementia caused by PML complicating sarcoidosis and patients in which the dementia is due to sarcoidosis itself is that in the latter the CSF almost always shows the findings of chronic meningitis (mononuclear pleocytosis, elevated CSF protein, and often, although not always, hypoglycorrhachia). Also the computed tomographic (CT) scan may be different. The CT scan in the PML case reported showed "a small hypodense area." In sarcoidosis it may show contrast-enhancing lesions looking just like metastatic carcinoma. One sort of exciting case report had the title of "Nodular Cerebral Sarcoidosis Simulating Metastatic Carcinoma."[34] The picture looked just the same as that discussed below in the abstract on tuberculomas (18–4). The patient had seizures. Diagnosis was made by blind bronchial biopsy. The CT lesions and the seizures went away after 4 months of prednisolone therapy. Thus sarcoidosis, tuberculosis, and fungus disease, particularly histoplasmosis, may all cause enhancing nodular lesions on CT scan with or without chronic basilar meningitis.

Reasoning from experience with tuberculosis and histoplasmosis, one would expect a chronic sarcoid meningitis to light up on gallium scan. Also the CT scan should show hydrocephalus when this develops. There are two articles which are not accessable to us on these radiologic subjects.[35, 36]

Finally, some cases of neurosarcoid will be associated with granulomatous lesions of bone, which in the skull may resemble the punched-out lesions of multiple myeloma.[37, 38]] ◀

15–6 **Lung Disease Caused by Amiodarone, a New Antiarrhythmia Agent.** Amiodarone is effective in controlling recurrent, potentially life-threatening ventricular tachyarrhythmias. Serious pulmonary reactions are among the adverse side effects of the drug. Warren B. Gefter, David M. Epstein, Giuseppe G. Pietra, and Wallace T. Miller (Univ. of Pennsylvania) recently saw 4 patients who had abnormalities visible on chest roentgenograms and clinical findings consistent with amiodarone-induced lung disorder. They were among 90 patients treated for refractory ventricular tachyarrhythmias. None had underlying lung disease or other systemic illness. An initial loading

---

(15–6) Radiology 147:339–344, May 1983.

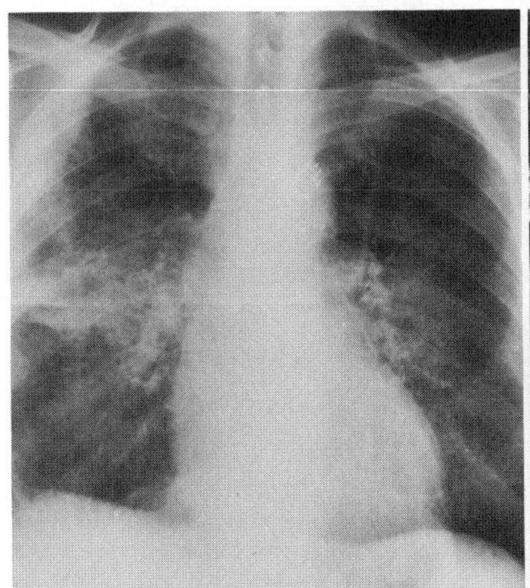

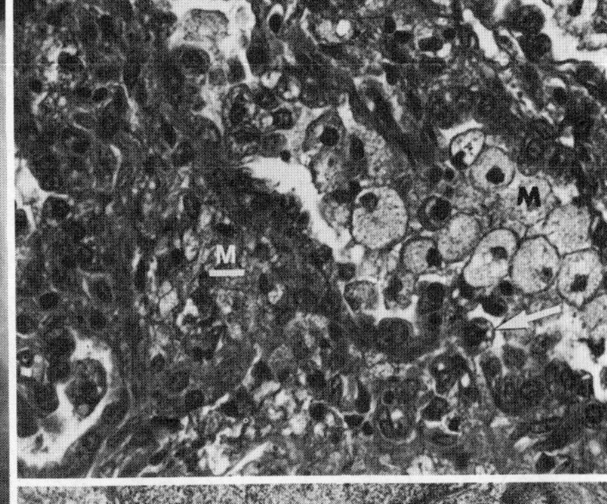

Fig 15–2 (left).—Peripheral consolidation of right upper lobe and superior segments of lower lobes developed after 7 months of amiodarone therapy. There is background of diffuse interstitial disease.

Fig 15–3 (top right).—Open lung biopsy. Foamy macrophages *(black M)* in alveolus lined by hyperplastic and finely vacuolated type II pneumocytes *(arrow)*. Alveolar walls are widened with accumulation of macrophages *(white M)* and rare lymphocytes. Hematoxylin-eosin; original magnification ×300.

Fig 15–4 (bottom right).—Open lung biopsy. Large osmiophilic lamellar bodies *(LB)* in cytoplasm of interstitial cell. Lead citrate-uranyl acetate; original magnification ×20,000. (Courtesy of Gefter, W. B., et al.: Radiology 147:339–344, May 1983.)

dose of 1,400 mg of amiodarone for about 2 weeks was followed by treatment with 600–800 mg daily. The clinical features are summarized in the table. Three patients recovered, but 1 died a few days after biopsy. The findings in that patient are shown in Figures 15–2, 15–3, and 15–4.

Eight cases of pulmonary reaction to amiodarone have been reported. The estimated incidence of pulmonary toxicity is about 1.4%. Patients with toxicity have received somewhat higher maintenance dosages than those without. The most common clinical manifestation of amiodarone-induced lung disease is exertional dyspnea. There may also be muscle weakness and anorexia with weight loss. Fever is not prominent. Several patients have had pleuritic chest pain. Abnormalities are seen in chest roentgenograms a mean of 6 months after the start of treatment. The most common are multiple peripheral areas of alveolar consolidation, predominantly in an upper lobe, which are often superimposed on diffuse interstitial disease. A diffuse, predominantly interstitial pattern may also be seen, and pleural abnormalities may occur. Lung function tests may show a restrictive pattern with severely impaired gas transfer and hypoxemia.

The roentgenographic abnormalities are completely reversible on

CLINICAL AND ROENTGENOGRAPHIC FEATURES OF AMIODARONE TOXICITY

Case	Age/Sex	Maintenance Dose (mg/day)*	Duration to Onset of Pulmonary Symptoms (mos)	Symptoms	Chest Radiographic Findings	Response to Drug Withdrawal, Steroids
I	73/M	600	10	Anorexia, muscle weakness, dyspnea on exertion	Peripheral consolidation right apex, anterior segment left upper lobe	Symptoms resolved over three weeks; infiltrates cleared over three months
II	55/M	800	7	Anorexia, weight loss, muscle weakness, dyspnea on exertion	Peripheral consolidation right upper lobe, superior segment both lower lobes, diffuse interstitial infiltrate	Died four days postbiopsy
III	44/M	800	9	Nonproductive cough, mild dyspnea on exertion, bilateral pleuritic pain	Bilateral peripheral consolidation with adjacent pleural thickening	Symptoms improved over two weeks; chest radiograph cleared at three months
IV	67/M	600	6.5	Anorexia, weight loss, muscle weakness, mild dyspnea on exertion	Coarse reticular interstitial infiltrate lower lung zones with confluence in right lower lobe	Symptoms improved over one month; chest radiograph resolved over three months

*Note that this column is expressed in terms of maintenance dose rather than total dose.
(Courtesy of Gefter, W. B., et al.: Radiology 147:339–344, May 1983.)

withdrawal of the drug and institution of corticosteroids. Resolution is generally slow, presumably reflecting the long biologic half-life of amiodarone. The symptoms resolve more rapidly than the roentgenographic findings.

▶ [There have been a lot of articles on amiodarone pulmonary toxicity this year. One good one by Marchlinsky et al. reported an incidence of 6% (4 of 70 patients).[39] The dose ranged from 400 or 600 mg on alternate days to as much as 800 mg daily, and the duration of therapy was 6 to 11 months. None of the patients had toxicity at a dose of 400 mg daily or less, and the authors noted that 7 of 8 cases reported prior to their writing were receiving doses of 600 mg. All 4 of their cases had some nonpulmonary toxicity as well (neurologic changes in 3, hepatic enzyme elevations in 3, and hypothyroidism in 1). Laboratory evaluation revealed hypoxemia, hypocapnia, leukocytosis, *no* eosinophilia, and negative results in antinuclear antibody studies. The course was resolution with steroids in 2–3 months. The histology was alveolar thickening, intraalveolar foamy macrophages, and hyperplasia of type II cells. There was no evidence of immunoglobulin, complement, or fibrinogen deposits in the tissues. The authors questioned the need for steroids. They thought that it probably was a metabolic rather than an allergic process and that patients would get well simply with withdrawal of drug. Antolin et al. record a patient who did get well simply with drug withdrawal.[40] The dosage in this case was only 200 mg per day, however. Other things that amiodarone can cause are photodermatitis, a blue-gray skin discoloration, hypothyroidism, hyperthryoidism, corneal deposits, neurotoxicity (neuropathy, proximal myopathy, and extrapyramidal symptoms), elevation of liver function tests, bradyarrhythmias, and cardiac muscle depression. Sounds like a winner.

Some other drug toxicities: Krowka et al. report a patient receiving azathioprine who was admitted for spiking fever, leukocytosis of 15,500 without eosinophilia, and negative collagen vascular serologies.[41] A gallium scan was done to look for an abdominal abscess, but the authors were surprised to find that the lung lit up "spectacularly" at 6–48 hours. The diffusion capacity was 45%, and pulmonary function studies showed restriction. The medicine was stopped and prednisone administered, and 2 months later the gallium scan and diffusion studies were normal. The accidental detection of the cause of a fever of unknown origin by gallium scanning has been recorded with *Pneumocystis* infections without x-ray abnormalities, but this is the first instance that we know of pulmonary drug reaction discovered in that way. Nader and Schellaci record pulmonary infiltration with eosinophilia and fever due to naproxen, which was proved by rechallenge.[42] Sigvaldason and Sorenson record a similar case due to sulfasalazine.[43]] ◀

Chapter 15 References

1. 1983 YEAR BOOK OF MEDICINE, pp. 151.
2. Dauber J. H., Rossman M. D., Daniele R. P.: Bronchoalveolar lavage in a patient with chronic berylliosis: evidence for hypersensitivity pneumonitis. *Ann. Intern. Med.* 97:213, 1982.
3. Rankin J. D., Naegel G. P., Schraeder C. E., et al.: Air-space immunoglobulin production and levels in bronchoalveolar lavage fluid of normal subjects and patients with sarcoidosis. *Am. Rev. Respir. Dis.* 127:442, 1983.
4. Rebuck A. S., Braude A. C.: Bronchoalveolar lavage in asbestosis. *Arch. Intern. Med.* 143:950, 1983.
5. Lapenas D. J., Davis G. S., Gale P. N., et al.: Mineral dusts as etiologic agents in pulmonary fibrosis: the diagnostic role of analytical scanning electron microscopy. *Am. J. Clin. Pathol.* 78:701, 1982.
6. Davison A. G., Haslam P. L., Corrin B., et al.: Interstitial lung disease and asthma in hard-metal workers: bronchoalveolar lavage, ultrastructural, and analytical findings and results of bronchial provocation tests. *Thorax* 38:119, 1983.

7. Brandwein S., Esdaile J., Danoff D., et al.: Wegener's granulomatosis: clinical features and outcome in 13 patients. *Arch. Intern. Med.* 143:476, 1983.
8. McDonald T. J., Neel H. B. III, DeRemee R. A.: Wegener's granulomatosis of the subglottis and the upper portion of the trachea. *Ann. Otol. Rhinol. Laryngol.* 91:588, 1982.
9. Gephardt C. H., Armad M., Tubbs R. R.: Pulmonary vasculitis (Wegener's granulomatosis): immunohistochemical study of T and B cell markers. *Am. J. Med.* 74:700, 1983.
10. Jaspan T., Davidson A. M., Walker W. C.: Spontaneous pneumothorax in Wegener's granulomatosis. *Thorax* 37:774, 1982.
11. 1983 Year Book of Medicine, pp. 155–157.
12. Fauci A. S., Haynes B. F., Costa J., et al.: Lymphomatoid granulomatosis: Prospective clinical and therapeutic experience over 10 years. *N. Engl. J. Med.* 306:68, 1982.
13. Taveira Da Silva A. M., Weiner J., Dean P., et al.: Lymphomatoid granulomatosis beginning as the adult respiratory distress syndrome and rapidly progressing to lymphoma. *South. Med. J.* 76:805, 1983.
14. Kohler P. F., Cook R. D., Brown W. R., et al.: Common variable hypogammaglobulinemia with T-cell nodular lymphoid interstitial pneumonitis and B-cell nodular lymphoid hyperplasia: different lymphocyte populations with a similar response to prednisone therapy. *J. Allergy Clin. Immunol.* 70:299, 1982.
15. Liebow A. A.: The J. Burns Amberson Lecture: pulmonary angiitis and granulomatosis. *Am. Rev. Respir. Dis.* 108:1, 1973.
16. Katzenstein A., Liebow A. A., Friedman P. J.: Bronchocentric granulomatosis, mucoid impaction, and hypersensitivity reactions to fungi. *Am. Rev. Respir. Dis.* 111:497, 1975.
17. Case Records of the Massachusetts General Hospital, Case 24–1982. *N. Engl. J. Med.* 306:1471, 1982.
18. Robinson R., Wehunt W. D., Tsou E., et. al.: Bronchocentric granulomatosis: roentgenographic manifestations. *Am. Rev. Respir. Dis.* 125:751, 1982.
19. 1982 Year Book of Medicine, pp. 105–110.
20. Harkleroad L. E., Young R. L., Savage P. J., et al.: Pulmonary sarcoidosis: long-term follow-up of the effects of steroid therapy. *Chest* 82:84, 1982.
21. 1983 Year Book of Medicine, pp. 158.
22. Johns C. J., Zarchary J. B., Ball W. C. Jr.: Ten-year study of corticosteroid treatment of pulmonary sarcoidosis. *Johns Hopkins Medical Journal* 134:271, 1974.
23. 1983 Year Book of Medicine, pp. 158–159.
24. Lufkin E. G., DeRemee R. A., Rohrback M. S.: The predictive value of serum angiotensin-converting enzyme activity in the differential diagnosis of hypercalcemia. *Mayo Clin. Proc.* 58:447, 1983.
25. Gelb A. F., Dreisen R. B., Epstein J. D., et al.: Immune complexes, gallium lung scans, and bronchoalveolar lavage in idiopathic interstitial pneumonitis-fibrosis: a structure-function clinical study. *Chest* 84:148, 1983.
26. Tukiainen P., Taskinen E., Holsti P., et al. Prognosis of cryptogenic fibrosing alveolitis. *Thorax* 38:349, 1983.
27. 1981 Year Book of Medicine, pp. 174–178.
28. Fulmer J. D.: Bronchoalveolar lavage. *Am. Rev. Respir. Dis.* 126:961, 1982.
29. Delaney P.: Neurological manifestations in sarcoidosis. *Ann. Intern. Med.* 87:336, 1977.

30. Grizzanti J. N., Knapp A. B., Schecter A. J., et al.: Treatment of sarcoid meningitis with radiotherapy. *Am. J. Med.* 73:605, 1982.
31. Delaney P.: Seizures in sarcoidosis: a poor prognosis. *Ann. Neurol.* 7:494, 1980.
32. Thompson C., Checkley S.: Short term memory deficit in a patient with cerebral sarcoidosis. *Br. J. Psychiatry* 139:160, 1981.
33. Cordingley G., Navarro C., Brust J. C., et al.: sarcoidosis presenting as senile dementia. *Neurology* 31:1148, 1981.
34. Karnik A. S.: Nodular cerebral sarcoidosis simulating metastatic carcinoma. *Arch. Intern. Med.* 142:385, 1982.
35. Makhija M. C., Anayiotos C. P.: Gallium scan in intracerebral sarcoidosis. *Clin. Nucl. Med.* 6:324, 1981.
36. Morehouse H., Danziger A.: CT findings in intracranial neurosarcoid. *Comput. Radiol.* 4:267, 1980.
37. Case Records of the Massachusetts General Hospital. *N. Engl. J. Med.* 307:1257, 1983.
38. Rohatgi P. K., Archutowska-Kempa M.: Combined calvarial and CNS sarcoidosis: report of two cases. *Arch. Neurol.* 38:261, 1981.
39. Marchlinsky F. F., Gansler T. S., Waxman H. L., et al.: Amiodarone pulmonary toxicity. *Ann. Intern. Med.* 97:839, 1982.
40. Antolin J., Cabrera P., Amerigo M. J., et al.: Amiodarone and the lung. *Ann. Intern. Med.* 99:278, 1983.
41. Krowka M. J., Brever R. I., Kehoe T. J.: Azathiaprine-associated pulmonary dysfunction. *Chest* 83:696, 1983.
42. Nader D. A., Schellaci R. F.: Pulmonary infiltrates with eosinophilia due to naproxen. *Chest* 83:208, 1983.
43. Sigvaldason A., Sorenson S.: Interstitial pneumonia due to sulfasalazine. *Eur. J. Respir. Dis.* 64:229, 1983.

16. Pulmonary Vascular Disease Including Pulmonary Embolism

16–1 **Acute Hemodynamic Effects of Nitroglycerin in Pulmonary Hypertension.** Pulmonary vasodilator therapy has not been widely used in disease states associated with elevated pulmonary vascular resistance. Ronald G. Pearl, Myer H. Rosenthal, John S. Schroeder and J. P. A. Ashton (Stanford Univ.) report data concerning 9 patients in whom acute intravenous nitroglycerin administration improved pulmonary hemodynamics. All patients had severe symptomatic pulmonary hypertension, and 4 were bedridden. All patients had normal left ventricular filling pressures. Trials of agents other than nitroglycerin had been uniformly unsuccessful. After placement of a right main pulmonary artery catheter, nitroglycerin was infused in increasing doses until headache, systemic hypotension or arrhythmia developed.

Nitroglycerin infusion increased the cardiac index and reduced pulmonary vascular resistance in all patients but 1 (Table 1). The rise in cardiac index was due to an increase in stroke volume. Mean pulmonary artery pressure declined in 6 patients. Systemic arterial pressure and systemic resistance declined in all cases. The highest infusion rate of nitroglycerin increased the cardiac index by 40%, reduced pulmonary vascular resistance by 40%, and reduced the mean pulmonary artery pressure by 15%. Topical nitroglycerin therapy had hemodynamic effects similar to those of infused nitroglycerin (Table 2). All but 1 of 6 patients discharged taking long-acting nitrate preparations responded to some degree.

The efficacy of nitroglycerin in these patients with pulmonary hypertension and the relative lack of efficacy of other vasodilators can be explained in terms of preferential right-sided vs. left-sided afterload reduction. Nitroglycerin produces systemic venodilation at doses that produce only minimal systemic arterial dilatation. Topical nitroglycerin therapy has produced hemodynamic benefit similar to that obtained from infusions. Further study is needed of both the acute and chronic effects of nitroglycerin in a larger number of patients.

▶ [Drug treatment of pulmonary hypertension was discussed in last year's YEAR BOOK.[1] The problem is that since pulmonary hypertension with increased pulmonary vascular resistance is essentially a low-cardiac-output state with very little ability to adjust to a fall in systemic pressure, it makes a big difference whether or not the agent being given causes systemic vasodilation. Results are bad when this occurs. All of the drugs mentioned last year had produced some good results but also some very bad results with some deaths. Therefore the above article seems very promising. The authors state that nitroglycerin reduces pulmonary vascular resistance at a dose

(16–1) Ann. Intern. Med. 99:9–13, July 1983.

TABLE 1.—HEMODYNAMIC EFFECTS OF NITROGLYCERIN ADMINISTRATION*

Patient	Dose	Cardiac Index	A-V $O_2\Delta$	Heart Rate	Stroke Volume	PVR	SVR	MPAP	MAP	CVP	PAWP
	µg/min	*L/min/m²*	*mL/dL*	*beats/min*	*mL/beat*	*dynes · s/cm⁵*		*mm Hg*			
1	0	1.84	9.4	99	32	1050	1550	54	75	13	12
	30	3.45	7.4	102	59	547	786	53	70	11	12
2	0	2.49	7.6	97	52	640	1168	55	83	10	15
	24	3.98	6.7	94	85	340	670	49	77	10	15
3	0	1.69	8.8	97	27	1686	2330	63	82	6	8
	100	2.76	7.1	93	46	678	1280	44	66	−2	8
4	0	2.80	3.4	73	63	998	1225	67	75	5	10
	90	3.96	4.3	72	90	509	930	48	74	−1	7
5	0	1.58	11.1	108	25	2000	3134	77	122	17	10
	120	1.90	9.2	108	30	1468	1933	70	93	14	10
6	0	3.12	5.3	90	60	496	1067	38	80	8	4
	300	3.76	5.1	90	72	252	763	25	64	2	4
7	0	1.36	9.0	120	20	1600	3404	55	117	17	8
	120	1.90	7.7	121	27	1049	2073	54	97	12	11
8	0	1.86	6.4	84	40	706	1741	36	77	3	6
	120	1.96	5.4	85	42	646	1448	35	68	3	6
9	0	2.07	5.5	77	45	812	1484	41	71	7	6
	120	2.59	4.6	79	55	500	963	34	58	6	7
Mean	0	2.09 ± 0.20	7.4 ± 0.8	94 ± 5	40 ± 5	1110 ± 176	1900 ± 288	54 ± 5	87 ± 6	10 ± 2	9 ± 1
± SEM	Doses	2.92 ± 0.30†	6.4 ± 0.5‡	94 ± 5	56 ± 8†	665 ± 126†	1205 ± 172†	46 ± 4†	74 ± 4†	6 ± 2†	9 ± 1

A-V $O_2\Delta$, arteriovenous oxygen difference; *PVR*, pulmonary vascular resistance; *SVR*, systemic vascular resistance; *MPAP*, mean pulmonary artery pressure; *MAP*, systemic mean arterial pressure; *CVP*, central venous pressure; *PAWP*, pulmonary artery wedge pressure.

†$P < .01$ compared with control value (no nitroglycerin).

‡$P < .05$ compared with control value (no nitroglycerin).

(Courtesy of Pearl, R.G., et al.: Ann. Intern. Med. 99:9–13, July 1983.)

TABLE 2.—HEMODYNAMIC EFFECTS OF TOPICAL NITROGLYCERIN PREPARATIONS*

Patient	Dose†	Cardiac Index	Heart Rate	Stroke Volume	PVR	SVR	MPAP	MAP	CVP	PAWP
		L/min·m²	*beats/min*	*mL/beat*	*dynes · s/cm⁵*			*mmHg*		
2	0	2.29	95	48	690	1270	55	85	12	15
	1 h after 2 in	3.23	93	70	440	800	54	78	12	8
3	0	2.08	95	34	1150	1625	54	70	5	8
	0.5 in every 4 h	3.90	94	64	400	944	35	68	−3	5
5	0	1.58	103	26	1990	3134	77	122	17	10
	0.75 in every 6 h	1.82	98	34	1281	2719	56	117	12	7
9	0	1.97	80	41	900	1532	41	70	7	4
	20 mg every 24 h	2.91	82	55	583	1219	38	73	4	5

**PVR*, pulmonary vascular resistance; *SVR*, systemic vascular resistance; *MPAP*, mean pulmonary artery pressure; *MAP*, systemic mean arterial pressure; *CVP*, central venous pressure; *PAWP*, pulmonary artery wedge pressure.

†Dose in inches of 2% nitroglycerin ointment (Nitrol Ointment; Kremers-Urban, Milwaukee, Wis.); or in delivered milligrams of Transderm-Nitro (CIBA, Summit, N.J.).

(Courtesy of Pearl, R.G., et al.: Ann. Intern. Med. 99:9–13, July 1983.)

much lower than that which affects systemic resistance vessels and that that may be the reason that it works well. (Nitroglycerin does affect the systemic capacitance vessels at low dose). As indicated in Table 1, dosage in the intravenous part of the study was incremental; they kept going until the desired effect was obtained. Only one patient had a hypotensive episode (nonfatal) at a dosage of 8 μg/kg/minute, and thereafter the authors limited dosage to half that. All but 1 of their patients had measurable benefit in terms of pulmonary pressures and resistance.

The results with chronic outpatient therapy, undertaken because of the success of the intravenous therapy, were also very impressive. Three patients who had been bedridden returned to full activity, and although 2 eventually died (at 9 months and 2 years), one was still employed 4 years after therapy was initiated. Even one such result in a disease that is almost always relentlessly downhill is worth attention. Another nice thing is that most doctors know how to use long-acting nitrates and feel relatively comfortable with them.

A somewhat similar study indicating a possible good effect of nitroglycerin (isosorbide) was published by Hermiller et al.[2] This was an acute study of several oral agents, and hemodynamic monitoring was carried out. Of the agents tested (phentolamine, diazoxide, hydralazine, isoproterenol, isosorbide, isosorbide with isoproterenol, tolazoline, and prostaglandin-active agents), only isosorbide reduced both the pulmonary vascular pressures and resistance. The prostaglandin inhibitors (aspirin and dipyridamole) did not help, and indomethacin administration was associated with hemodynamic deterioration. The best results were seen when isosorbide and isoproterenol were given together. How sick these people were, and how dangerous it is to study them with vasoactive agents is very clear from the fact that 3 of the 10 patients died during the study, one after diazoxide, one after phentolamine, and one during a venous cut-down. The authors emphasize the central problem that many of the drugs given for primary pulmonary hypertension produce systemic hypotension and that this "in the face of elevated right heart pressures, reduces coronary perfusion pressure and flow to the hypertrophied right heart below a critical or marginal level," resulting in right heart and possibly sinoatrial dysfunction.

All of the collagen vascular diseases can cause pulmonary hypertension, but scleroderma (progressive systemic sclerosis [PSS]) is the worst in this respect. Ungerer et al. state that significant pulmonary hypertension occurs in one third of PSS patients and in one half of those with the CREST syndrome.[3] Looking for noninvasive ways to assess the pulmonary vasculature in scleroderma patients, they found that a combination of a chest x-ray showing definite dilatation of the descending right pulmonary artery, a diffusion capacity of 50% or less of predicted, and EKG abnormalities suggesting right heart strain (complete or incomplete right bundle branch block, right ventricular hypertrophy, or right atrial hypertrophy) identified 75% of those with definite pulmonary hypertension (proved at catheterization) and that absence of all of these features identified 97% of those with a normal pulmonary vascular bed. There were a lot of other good clinical points in this article. Ettinger et al. made the interesting observation that diffusing capacity adjusted for alveolar volume goes up in normal persons when they lie down but does not do so in scleroderma patients.[4] The authors regarded this as an early indicator of a nondistensible pulmonary vascular bed. (Whether or not any therapeutic intervention will be indicated if early pulmonary vascular involvement in the collagen vascular diseases can be diagnosed is a matter for future study.) Perez and Kramer report pulmonary hypertension, probably unrelated to interstitial fibrosis, in 4 of 43 patients with systemic lupus erythematosus.[5] Pulmonary vascular disease in patients with scleroderma and other collagen vascular diseases and arteritides was also discussed in the 1979 YEAR BOOK.[6]

The still poorly understood association between pulmonary hypertension and cirrhosis and the relevant literature was discussed again by McDonnell and associates.[7] Among 2,459 patients with clinical evidence of cirrhosis they found pulmonary hypertension in 15 (0.61%), and among 1,241 patients with cirrhosis examined at autopsy they found pulmonary hypertension in 0.73%, compared to 0.13% in all patients examined at autopsy, a significant difference. Importantly, none of the cases with these two diseases had any evidence at all of pulmonary thromboembolic disease when this was specifically looked for at postmortem examination, fairly strong evidence for the vasospastic and against the thromboembolic theory of this association. The two diseases occurred together most frequently in young women. Pare et al. report a patient with cirrhosis who also had pulmonary hypertension in whom microangiopathic hemolytic anemia occurred at the end of the illness.[8] They attributed it to red blood cell damage in the fibrin-containing plexiform pulmonary arteriopathic lesions. Pulmonary hypertension in liver disease was also discussed in the 1981 YEAR BOOK.[9]

A problem that seems as if it will never go away is how can one be sure that pulmonary hypertension is not actually due to thromboembolic disease. As discussed in previous YEAR BOOKS,[10, 11] it is probably not very difficult to tell when pulmonary hypertension develops due to fairly large emboli, but those due to microemboli are practically impossible to sort out, and it has been proposed that these microemboli can come from the right atrium. This is discussed in a good article by James.[12]

Two good reviews will be mentioned here for reference.[13, 14]] ◀

16–2 **Thromboxane Mediation of Cardiopulmonary Effects of Embolism.** The cardiopulmonary dysfunction resulting from pulmonary embolism is thought to be due in part to platelet interactions with clot and the resultant platelet release reaction. Takayoshi Utsunomiya, Michael M. Krausz, Lawrence Levine, David Shepro, and Herbert B. Hechtman examined the cardiopulmonary dysfunction that followed embolism in dogs as moderated by prostacyclin (PGI_2) and thromboxane A_2 (TxA_2). Embolism was induced with 0.5 gm of autologous clot per kg. Groups of dogs were pretreated with the Tx synthetase inhibitor imidazole or with the cyclooxygenase inhibitor indomethacin or were treated with PGI_2 after embolization.

The rise in pulmonary vascular resistance that followed embolization was significantly inhibited by both imidazole and indomethacin pretreatment (Fig 16–1). Physiologic shunting rose only transiently in pretreated dogs, and PGI_2 administration rapidly restored it to baseline (Fig 16–2). Pretreatment with both imidazole and indomethacin prevented an increase in dead space, and PGI_2 rapidly restored it to baseline (Fig 16–3). Imidazole infusion blocked production of TxA_2, but concentrations of 6-keto-prostaglandin $F_{1\alpha}$ ($PGF_{1\alpha}$) were

Fig 16–1.—Increase in pulmonary vascular resistance *(PVR)* 1 hour after embolization was significantly less in imidazole- and indomethacin-pretreated dogs ($P < .005$). Prostacyclin (PGI_2) lowered PVR, but not significantly. (Courtesy of Utsunomiya, T., et al.: J. Clin. Invest. 70:361–368, August 1982; copyright 1982 by the American Society for Clinical Investigation.)

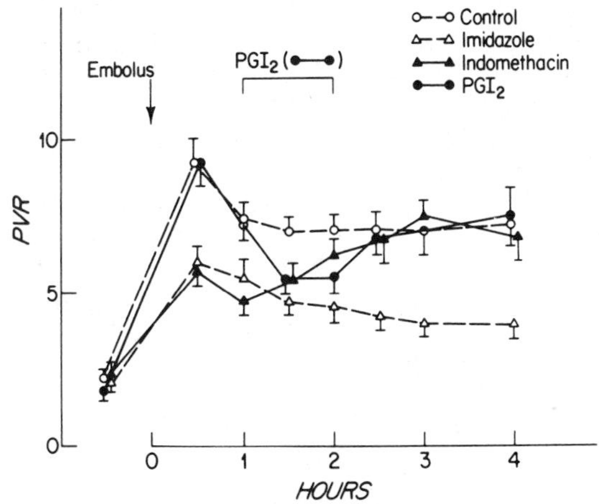

(16–2) J. Clin. Invest. 70:361–368, August 1982.

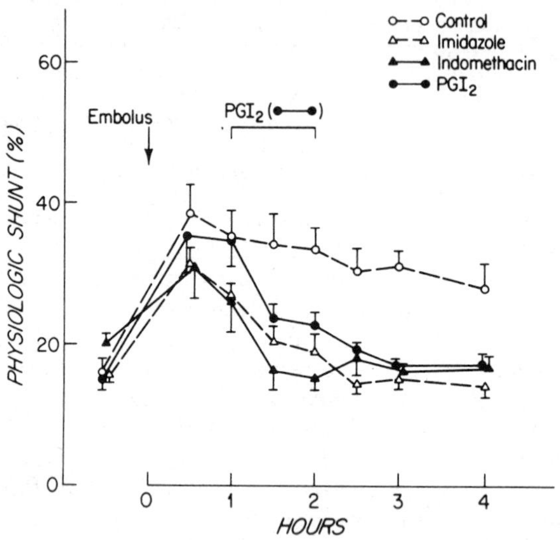

Fig 16–2.—Relative to untreated controls, rise in physiologic shunt after imidazole or indomethacin was transient. Prostacyclin (PGI_2) rapidly restored physiologic shunt to baseline. (Courtesy of Utsunomiya, T., et al.: J. Clin. Invest. 70:361–368, August 1982; copyright 1982 by the American Society for Clinical Investigation.)

similar to those in control dogs. Baseline 6-keto-$PGF_{1\alpha}$ values were much lower in indomethacin-pretreated dogs and did not change after embolization. Prostacyclin infusion led to a rise in 6-keto-$PGF_{1\alpha}$ concentrations.

Many of the cardiopulmonary effects of embolism seem to be re-

Fig 16–3.—Imidazole and indomethacin prevented rise in physiologic dead space, whereas prostacyclin (PGI_2) rapidly restored this variable to baseline. Transient increase in physiologic dead space followed cessation of PGI_2. (Courtesy of Utsunomiya, T., et al.: J. Clin. Invest. 70:361–368, August 1982, copyright 1982 by the American Society for Clinical Investigation.)

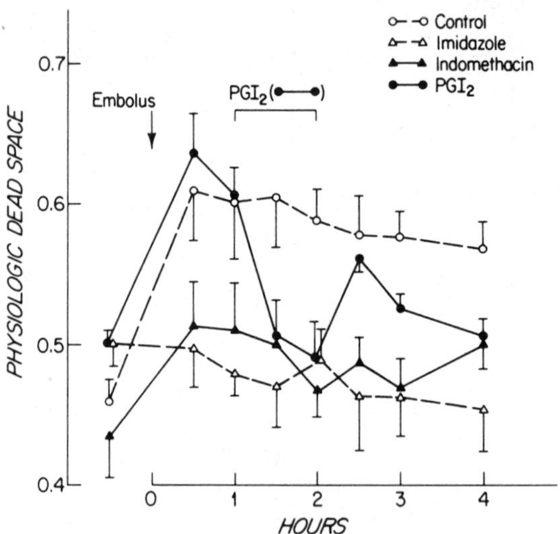

PRESENCE OF EMBOLI IN PATIENTS WITH LOW-PROBABILITY SCAN PATTERNS

Scan	Positive pulmonary arteriogram	Positive leg venogram
Large defect, ventilation mismatch	86	51
Large defect, matched ventilation defect	23	31
Small multiple perfusion defects	27	19

Data are percentages of patients with emboli.
Adapted from Hull, R. D., et al.: Ann. Intern. Med. 98:8891, 1983.

lated to platelet secretions, but the findings in this study must be cautiously applied to the clinical setting. Cardiopulmonary function is also altered in other states in which platelets are entrapped in the lungs, such as sepsis and microembolism. That lung parenchyma can be stimulated by antigen-antibody reaction to release Tx indicates that pulmonary metabolic events may influence cardiopulmonary function.

▶ [It is superficially reasonable to attribute the physiologic abnormalities caused by pulmonary embolization to the embolized areas of the lung, but further thought raises problems. Cessation of blood flow to an area of lung could certainly contribute to increased dead space, since that area would be ventilated but not perfused. However, attribution of pulmonary hypertension solely to interruption of blood flow has always been a little more difficult to maintain since the surgeons have taught us that the pulmonary blood flow to an entire lung can be interrupted without causing pulmonary hypertension in otherwise normal persons. It has also always been a stumbling block to attribute hypoxemia to functional changes in those areas of the lung that have been embolized, since they have thereby been excluded from participation in gas exchange. Therefore it is necessary to seek the cause of hypoxemia in those areas that have *not* been embolized, In last year's YEAR BOOK, a study from the University of Michigan was briefly discussed which indicated that hypoxia following pulmonary embolization was largely due to perfusion of poorly ventilated areas (areas with low ventilation-perfusion [V/Q] values).[15] This past year the same group studied two patients in detail using the technique of multiple inert gas elimination to determine the distribution of V/Q ratios and concluded that in these patients hypoxemia was largely due to arteriovenous shunting.[16] They thought that the shunting was probably due to pulmonary edema or atelectasis or some combination of the two occurring *in the nonembolized areas of the lung.*

The article abstracted above suggests that the substance generated as a consequence of embolization which alters the nonembolized part of the lung is platelet thromboxane. The data also indicate that not only hypoxemia but also changes in physiologic dead space and pulmonary vascular resistance are caused at least in part by these humoral effects on nonembolized parts of the lung and are reversible to some degree by maneuvers that prevent the generation of thromboxane or by administration of its opposing prostaglandin, prostacycline. Another excellent study makes the same point in a very different experimental system.[17] The experimental model used was perfusion of rabbit lungs by material containing human platelets. Pulmonary hypertension resulted when platelet activating factor (acetyl glyceryl ether phosphorylcholine), a substance derived from macrophages and neutrophils which causes platelet activation (aggregation and release of platelet factors) and neutrophil degranulation, was included in the perfusate. A number of pharmacologic maneuvers were carried out to establish that the important result of platelet activation with respect to causing pulmonary hypertension was generation of thromboxane and that neutrophils were not involved. Pulmonary edema also occurred in some animals, but the character of the edema fluid indicated that it was due to increased microvascular pressure rather than increased microvascular permeability. An experimental study that contends that serotonin rather than thromboxane is the important humoral principle released from platelets was also published this last year by a surgical group.[18] This was a less convincing study in our opinion, but in any event it seems clear that release of something (thromboxane, serotonin, or both) from blood platelets is responsible for the pulmonary hypertension and hypoxemia which result from pulmonary embolism and that the effects of this agent or agents are on the nonembolized parts of the lung. Since blood platelets are also activated by immune complexes, thrombin, epinephrine, and some microbial products, most notably endotoxin, this mechanism probably has importance beyond the pathophysiology of pulmonary embolism. It has been shown by Brigham, Snapper, and the Vanderbilt group that the immediate pulmonary hypertension and bronchospasm that follow endotoxin injections in sheep are preventable by pharmacologic maneuvers which prevent thromboxane generation, whereas the late (4–6 hours) development of increased microvascular permeability is not.[19] The late endothelial permeability effect is probably attributable to materials released from polymorphonuclear leukocytes. Whether or not these physiologic insights will have therapeutic implications with respect to pulmonary embolism is not clear, but it is certainly possible.

Diagnosis of pulmonary embolism continues to be an evolving field. An autopsy study by Goldhaber et al. states that only 30% of their cases of *major* pulmonary embolism were diagnosed during life.[20] None of 21 patients with major pulmonary embolism plus pneumonia, only 2 of 18 with major pulmonary embolism and congestive heart failure, and only 2 of 21 patients over age 70 had the correct diagnosis established. Correct diagnosis was most frequently established in postoperative patients (7 of 11) and in those with clinical evidence of venous thrombosis (11 of 20). Lung scan and pulmonary arteriogram done in the 10 days before death resulted in correct diagnosis in 9 of 11 and in 4 of 5 respectively. Both patients with misleading results (1 studied only by scan and 1 by scan plus pulmonary arteriogram) had multiple segmental emboli at autopsy.

Most studies concerning the use of lung scanning and pulmonary arteriography in the diagnosis of pulmonary embolism advise that high-probability scans (segmental or greater defect on perfusion but no matching defect on ventilation) have a greater than 90% chance of being pulmonary emboli, that low-probability scans (multiple subsegmental defects with matching ventilation defects) have a greater than 90% chance of *not* representing emboli, and that normal scans exclude the presence of emboli. They state that in these three scan categories further diagnostic tests are not required for therapeutic decisions, but in all others they are.[21–24] The role of leg vein studies by invasive and noninvasive techniques is also not entirely agreed upon.[25, 26] Recognizing some continuing uncertainty, Hull and associates did a multihospital study in which all patients suspected of having a pulmonary embolism and having an abnormal ventilation lung scan were studied by ascending contrast venograms *and* impedance plethysmography of the legs and by pulmonary arteriography.[27] The study has far too many data to attempt to summarize here, but a few things will be mentioned. There were a number of patients with positive scans and arteriograms and negative leg vein studies, some other patients with positive scans and leg vein studies and negative pulmonary arteriograms, and a sizable number with low-probability scan patterns who did in point of fact have emboli, leg vein thrombi, or both (table). The authors recommended that a patient with a high-probability scan (ventilation mismatch) treated, that a normal scan be regarded as excluding pulmonary embolism, and that other patients be further studied. They thought it wise to begin with study of the leg veins, since a positive study made it very likely that a pulmonary embolism was present; and even if it were not, the treatment would be the same, given the bad prognosis of thigh-vein thrombosis. They also said that impedance plethysmography was positive in 86% of those who were also positive on contrast ascending venography, that the false negatives were in patients with very small clots, and that it was negative in 97% of those with negative venograms. With a negative venographic study in a patient thought likely to have pulmonary embolism they would do pulmonary arteriograms, a more invasive and expensive procedure and one which carries a little more risk. In their opinion any scan pattern other than cold normal should be investigated further in situations in which pulmonary embolism seems likely.

Data concerning how often patients with exacerbations of chronic obstructive pulmonary disease (COPD) have pulmonary embolism as a part of their problem are conflicting.[28] Winter and associates demonstrated deep venous thrombosis in 13 of 29 such patients, and 1 patient died of a pulmonary embolism.[29] They thought that the association was sufficiently great to warrant prophylactic anticoagulation.

Sasahara has published another of his excellent reviews which emphasizes the usefulness of impedance plethysmography.[30] He states that 95% of patients with angiographically confirmed pulmonary embolism have positive impedance plethysmography, that 90% of patients with abnormal plethysmography have pulmonary embolism on pulmonary arteriogram, and that a normal plethysmographic study excludes pulmonary embolism in 90% of patients. It has become his practice to follow patients after discharge on anticoagulation with monthly scans and plethysmograms. He feels that anticoagulation can be discontinued when these are normal. Some patients might be spared several months of anticoagulation thereby, since most people generally keep it up for at least three, and more often six, months after discharge. His recommendations concerning thrombolytic therapy are more conservative than in the past: he states that it is certainly indicated in massive pulmonary emboli with a clinical picture of acute cor pulmonale. Where the thrombolytic story will end up is certainly not any clearer now than it was three years ago.[31] The repeated use of streptokinase may carry more allergic risk than its one-time use.[32]] ◀

16–3 **Familial Antithrombin III Deficiency: Its Natural History, Genetics, Diagnosis, and Treatment.** One of the components of plasma that inhibits thrombin is the same as the plasma cofactor that is necessary for the antithrombin effect of heparin; the substance, an alpha 2-globulin glycoprotein, is now called antithrombin III (AT III). This inhibits not only thrombin but also factors XIIa, XIa, Xa, and IXa as well as platelet aggregation. Familial AT III deficiency is a serious, sometimes lethal, disorder inherited in an autosomal dominant pattern. T. M. Cosgriff, D. T. Bishop, E. J. Hershgold, M. H. Skolnick, B. A. Martin, B. J. Baty, and K. S. Carlson (University of Utah) report data on 5 clinical cases of AT III deficiency occurring in a single family together with an analysis of the pedigree. Patient 1 died with diffuse thrombosis of the abdominal veins (portal, gastric, pancreatic, and mesenteric); patient 2 had 2 episodes of thrombophlebitis widely separated but was otherwise well; patient 3 had episodes of small bowel infarction due to mesenteric vein thrombosis, left arm thrombophlebitis, and central retinal vein thrombosis at different times; patient 4 developed pulmonary embolism which progressed under treatment to fatal venous thrombosis of lungs, heart, and kidneys. Patient 5 developed early onset (age 21) recurrent thrombophlebitis with stasis ulcers requiring continuous oral anticoagulation.

A variety of assays for AT III are available. Functional assays are thought by some to be superior to immunologic assays because one variety of the disorder demonstrates functional deficiency of the protein but not quantitative deficiency. (A third subcategory of AT III deficiency demonstrates normal immunoreactivity and antithrombin activity but is deficient in terms of its heparin-cofactor activity). The AT III level in family members of AT III–deficient pedigrees averages 50% of normal but is highly variable. The most frequent clinical manifestation of the deficiency is lower extremity thrombophlebitis, often

---

(16–3) Medicine 62:209–220, July 1983

bilateral and recurrent, leading to venous insufficiency, sometimes complicated by crural ulcers. Pulmonary embolism is also common. Other consequences include upper extremity thrombophlebitis, mesenteric venous thrombosis (surprisingly frequently), the Budd-Chiari syndrome, priapism, retinal central vein thrombosis, and disseminated intravascular coagulation. The age of greatest risk is the third decade. Pregnancy, immobility, and surgery all constitute additive risks. In addition, AT III deficiency may be seen in coronary artery, cerebral artery, and peripheral artery disease and in thromboembolism, renal diseases, cancer, severe liver disease, and disseminated intravascular coagulation.

Familial AT III deficiency may be implicated in as many as 2% of thromboembolic episodes. Recognition begins with a history and especially a family history of a clustering of thromboembolic events and is confirmed by specific assay. Diagnosis is important since in some (although not in all) cases, heparin, which requires AT III for its action, is partially or seriously ineffective and oral anticoagulation is required. Once diagnosed, patients should probably be treated for life. Replacement therapy with AT III concentrate is practicable and will be available in the future.

▶ [An editorial by Rothschild adds some other information.[33] He states that AT III is decreased in certain forms of vasculitis and mentioned particularly Behçet's disease. He notes that oral anticoagulants usually increase AT III levels; and if they don't, a thrombotic tendency may persist even with a therapeutic prolongation of the prothrombin time. In other words, it is implied that increases in AT III levels produced by oral anticoagulants may be an important part of their action and that this action of AT III is independent of its heparin cofactor activity. AT III levels are down after operations with major tissue damage such as total hip replacement, which, it is implied, is one of the reasons why anticoagulation may be difficult and at times unsuccessful in such patients. The fact that heparin per se causes decreases in AT III levels was again emphasized. The importance of knowing the AT III level when low-dose heparin is to be used is also implied. Dr. Rothschild feels that AT III determination should be a part of the initial evaluation of every patient in whom anticoagulation therapy is contemplated and should be followed in assessing the response to therapy. In contrast to the authors of the abstracted article, he feels that the (commercially available) immunodiffusion test is so easy and inexpensive that it is the one to be used; he also believes that it only rarely disagrees with functional assays except in very young children.] ◀

16–4 **Pulmonary Endarterectomy for Chronic Thromboembolic Obstruction: Recent Surgical Experience.** A few patients with pulmonary embolism develop chronic symptoms and are candidates for pulmonary artery endarterectomy. Joe R. Utley, Roger G. Spragg, William B. Long III, and Kenneth M. Moser (Univ. of California, San Diego) report data on 10 patients who had pulmonary thromboendarterectomy for chronic pulmonary embolism in 1977–1981. Age range was 20–67 years. All patients reported exercise intolerance and dyspnea. Five were in New York Heart Association functional class III, and 5 were in class IV. All had evidence of severe central vascular obstruction on angiography; the lobar arteries or more central vessels were involved. All had pulmonary hypertension and elevated pulmonary vascular resistance. Five patients had complete obstruction of

(16–4) Surgery 92:1096–1102, December 1982.

the right or left pulmonary artery. Five had more peripheral obstruction in both lungs. Surgery was performed under hypothermic bypass with cold blood cardioplegia.

All patients had edema in the area of thrombectomy after operation. One patient developed respiratory distress syndrome and infection and died. No neurologic deficits developed. All surviving patients had improvement in pulmonary hypertension and in pulmonary vascular resistance. Seven patients improved by two functional classes, 1 by one class, and 1 by three classes. Two patients had episodes of pulmonary infection late in the postoperative period.

Thrombectomy of the pulmonary vessels appears to be an effective approach to chronic embolic obstruction. Long-term anticoagulation is maintained after operation in all patients. The degree of rehabilitation varies, but most patients have returned to their previous level of employment.

▶ [An article briefly mentioned in the 1972 YEAR BOOK quotes a surgical mortality in collected cases of 35%–40%,[34, 35] much more than the 10% in the abstracted article. Sabiston et al. record personal experience with six patients, all of whom lived, five with good to excellent results.[36]

Bomalaski and associates have written a useful review on surgical vena cava interruption which summarizes a lot of data.[37] They record an operative mortality of 15.5% and recurrent pulmonary embolization in 6.4% of 1,358 cases treated with inferior vena cava ligation, and 7.3% mortality and 5.2% recurrence in 1,108 cases treated with plication. In 2,966 cases treated with the Mobin-Uddin umbrella there was an operative mortality of 0.6% recurrent pulmonary embolism in 3.4%, new or worsened sequelae in 9% (complications of the umbrella itself), and inferior vena cava patency in only 40%. In 141 cases treated with the Greenfield filter there was an operative mortality of 3.5%, recurrent embolization in 2%, new or worsened sequelae in 15%, and patency of the cava in 96%. The Greenfield filter got a worse report in this review than it ordinarily gets.[38] Experience with it is limited, of course, but its record with respect to caval patency and prevention of reembolization has been good in most studies.

Septic embolization has been usually taken as one indication for caval ligation. An article by Peyton et al. gives some experimental data in dogs which indicate that the Greenfield filter can be sterilized by antibiotics and that its insertion, together with prolonged antibiotic therapy, might be a conservative alternative to vena cava ligation.[39]] ◀

Chapter 16 References

1. 1983 YEAR BOOK OF MEDICINE, pp. 97–98.
2. Hermiller J.B., Bambach D., Thompson M.J., et al.: Vasodilators and prostaglandin inhibitors in primary pulmonary hypetension. *Ann. Intern. Med.* 97:480, 1982.
3. Ungerer R.G., Tshkin D.P., Furst D., et al.: Prevalence and clinical correlates of pulmonary arterial hypertension in progressive systemic sclerosis. *Am. J. Med.* 75:65, 1983.
4. Ettinger W.H., Wise R.A., Stevans M.B., et al.: Absence of positional change in pulmonary diffusing capacity in systemic sclerosis. *Am. J. Med.* 75:305, 1983.
5. Perez D., Kramer N.: Pulmonary hypertension in systemic lupus erythematosus: report of four cases and review of the literature. *Semin. Arthritis Rheum.* 11:177, 1981.
6. 1979 YEAR BOOK OF MEDICINE, pp. 153–154.
7. McDonnell P.J., Toye P.A., Hutchins G.M.: Primary pulmonary hypertension and cirrhosis: are they related? *Am. Rev. Respir. Dis.* 127:437, 1983.

8. Pare P.D., Chan-Yan C., Wass H., et al.: Portal and pulmonary hypertension with microangiopathic hemolytic anemia. *Am. J. Med.* 74:1093, 1983.
9. 1981 YEAR BOOK OF MEDICINE, pp. 161–165
10. 1983 YEAR BOOK OF MEDICINE, pp. 98–99.
11. 1982 YEAR BOOK OF MEDICINE, p. 149.
12. James T.: Thrombi in antrum atrii dextri of human heart as clinically important source for chronic microembolization to lungs. *Br. Heart J.* 49:122, 1983.
13. Haworth S.G.: Primary pulmonary hypertension. *Br. Heart J.* 49:517, 1983.
14. Fulmer J.D., Kaltreider H.B.: The pulmonary vasculitides. *Chest* 82:615, 1982.
15. 1983 YEAR BOOK OF MEDICINE, p. 95.
16. D'Alonzo G.E., Bower J.S., DeHart P., et al.: The mechanisms of abnormal gas exchange in acute massive pulmonary embolism. *Am. Rev. Respir. Dis.* 128:170, 1983.
17. Heffner J.E., Shoemaker S.A., Canham E.M., et al.: Acetyl glyceryl ether phosphorylcholine-stimulated human platelets cause pulmonary hypertension and edema in isolated rabbit lungs: role of thromboxane A1. *J. Clin. Invest.* 71:351, 1983.
18. Huval W.V., Mathieson M.A., Stemp L.I., et al.: Therapeutic benefits of 5-hydroxytryptamine inhibition following pulmonary embolism. *Ann. Surg.* 197:220, 1983.
19. Snapper J.R., Ogletree M.L., Hutchison, A.A., et al.: Meclofenamate prevents increased resistance of the lung (RL) following endotoxemia in unanesthetized sheep. *Am. Rev. Respir. Dis.* 123(Suppl.):200, 1981.
20. Goldhaber S.Z., Hennekens C.H., Evans D.A., et al.: Factors associated with correct antemortem diagnosis of major pulmonary embolism. *Am. J. Med.* 73:822, 1982.
21. Biello D.R., Mattai A.G., McKnight R.C., et al.: Ventilation-perfusion studies in suspected pulmonary embolism. *A.J.R.* 133:1033, 1979.
22. McNeil B.J.: Ventilation-perfusion studies and the diagnosis of pulmonary embolism: concise communication. *J. Nucl. Med.* 21:319, 1980.
23. 1983 YEAR BOOK OF MEDICINE, pp. 94–95.
24. 1981 YEAR BOOK OF MEDICINE, p. 155.
25. 1983 YEAR BOOK OF MEDICINE, p. 95.
26. 1982 YEAR BOOK OF MEDICINE, p. 147.
27. Hull R.D., Hirsh J., Carter C.J., et al.: Pulmonary angiography, ventilation lung scanning, and venography for clinically suspected pulmonary embolism with abnormal perfusion lung scan. *Ann. Intern. Med.* 98:891, 1983.
28. 1982 YEAR BOOK OF MEDICINE, pp. 150–151.
29. Winter J.H., Buckler P.W., Bautista A.P., et al.: Frequency of venous thrombosis in patients with an exacerbation of chronic obstructive lung disease. *Thorax* 38:605, 1983.
30. Sasahara A.A., Sarma G.V.R.K., Barsamian E.M., et al.: Pulmonary thromboembolism. *JAMA* 249:2945, 1983.
31. 1981 YEAR BOOK OF MEDICINE, pp. 158–159.
32. Pick R.A., Joswig B.C., Cheung A.K., et al.: Acute renal failure following repeated streptokinase therapy for pulmonary embolism. *West. J. Med.* 138:878, 1983.
33. Rothschild B.M.: The role of antithrombin III in clinical management of pulmonary embolization. *Am. J. Med.* 74:529, 1983.

34. Shuck J.W., Walder J.S., Kam T.H., et al.: Chronic persistent pulmonary embolism: report of three cases. *Am. J. Med.* 69:790, 1983.
35. 1982 YEAR BOOK OF MEDICINE, p. 152.
36. Sabiston D.C., Wolfe W.G., Oldham H.N. Jr., et al.: Surgical management of chronic pulmonary embolism. *Ann. Surg.* 185:699, 1977.
37. Bomalaski J.S., Martin G.J., Hughes R.L., et al.: Inferior vena cava interruption in the management of pulmonary embolism. *Chest* 82:767, 1982.
38. 1983 YEAR BOOK OF MEDICINE, pp. 93–94.
39. Peyton J.W.B., Hylemon M.B., Greenfield L.J., et al. Comparison of Greenfield filter and vena caval ligation for experimental septic thromboembolism. *Surgery* 93:533, 1983.

17. Lung Cancer

▶ ↓The only thing certain about the treatment of non-small-cell lung cancer (NSCLC) is that total resection is beneficial. The other many issues, such as whether or not mediastinal metastases contraindicate surgery, what constitutes proper mediastinal preoperative staging, the role of radiotherapy and/or chemotherapy as adjunctive therapy to surgery, and whether or not either chemotherapy or radiotherapy actually helps in nonresectable cases are open questions.

The surgical staging system for NSCLC now used by almost everyone is presented in the table, as it is really necessary to use it to speak meaningfully about different treatment options. The system was arrived at by retrospective analysis of 5-year survivorship after surgery, stage I being 50%–70%, stage II 20%–35%, and stage III 2%–19%.

For a long time American surgical practice held that *any* mediastinal nodal metastases (stage III by virtue of N2) indicated inoperability. This has obvious implications for how vigorously the mediastinum should be investigated before operation. As discussed at some length in last year's YEAR BOOK there has been a recent swing away from this attitude, and operations for this subset (N2) of stage III cancers are being done, although major surgical groups continue to differ quite a lot concerning details.[1] Kirsh, from Michigan, advises resection with attempt for cure when the histology is squamous cell and the mediastinal metastasis is ipsilateral and below midtracheal level; and he uses postoperative irradiation. He does not resect such cases when the histology is adenocarcinoma. He recommends mediastinoscopy only when the chest x-ray is suggestive of mediastinal involvement or when the histology is known to be adenocarcinoma. Pearson, from Canada, seems to advise resection for cure with postoperative irradiation in patients with negative mediastinoscopy who are found to have mediastinal node involvement at thoracotomy. His experience with those who were mediastinoscopy positive was much less good, although he treated them with preoperative rather than postoperative irradiation, possibly a significant difference itself. Pearson also felt that the prognosis of adenocarcinoma with mediastinal nodes was poor. Martini, from Memorial, in contrast, reported very good results in patients with mediastinal metastases resected and treated with postoperative irradiation, and he specifically stated that patients with adenocarcinomas did as well as those with squamous cell cancers. The explanation for the difference between Martini's results and those of practically everyone else almost certainly has to do with some major differences in patient population and treatment policies. First, at Memorial they use implantation of radon seeds in many patients found to be too advanced for resection at operation. Those whom they chose to resect rather than implant obviously represent a population selected for resection at the time of thoracotomy. Also, Memorial is one of the institutions deeply involved in lung cancer screening (periodic cytologic and x-ray examinations), and it seems almost certain that at least some of their patients derive from this screening effort and, accordingly, are earlier in the course of their disease than patients who come to the attention of doctors in other ways. Abbey-Smith, who is representative of the quite homogenous attitudes and practices on the part of British thoracic surgeons, feels that operability, including nodal resection when needed, can only really be determined at thoracotomy and follows a policy of "operate at all costs." He decries the use of mediastinoscopy, since patients who might otherwise be helped are often denied the attempt on the basis of this examination, and he does not use postoperative irradiation.

The highly uniform British experience with over 8,000 cases operated on over a period of 30 years by six enormously experienced surgeons who use mediastinoscopy very sparingly, who follow the policy of "operate at all costs", and who do not use postoperative irradiation was reported in an article by Belcher.[2] They reported an operative mortality of 5.7% for lobectomy, which did not change over the years,

TNM CLASSIFICATION OF LUNG CANCER

Primary Tumor (T)
- T1 A tumor that is 3.0 cm or less in greatest diameter, surrounded by lung or visceral pleura, more than 2 cm from carina
- T2 A tumor more than 3.0 cm in greatest diameter, more than 2 cm from carina, or tumor of any size that either invades the visceral pleura or has associated atelectasis or obstructive pneumonitis extending to the hilar region. Any associated atelectasis or obstructive pneumonitis must involve less than an entire lung; no pleural effusion.
- T3 A tumor of any size with direct extension into parietal pleura, chest wall, the diaphragm, or the mediastinum and its contents; or a tumor within 2 cm of the carina or a tumor with atelectasis or obstructive pneumonitis of an entire lung or plural effusion.

Nodal Involvement (N)
- N0 No lymph node metastasis
- N1 Metastasis to hilar or peribronchial lymph nodes
- N2 Metastasis to mediastinal lymph nodes.

Distant Metastases (M)
- M0 No (known) distant metastasis
- M1 Distant metastasis present

Staging of lung cancer

Stage I—T1, N0, M0, T2, N0, M0; T1, N1, M0
Stage II—T2, N1, M0
Stage III—T3, N0, M0; T1–3, N2, M0; T1–3, N1–2, M1

and a mortality of 11.7% for pneumonectomy during the early period which fell to 7.0% during the later period, a change attributed to better respiratory care techniques. There was no change in survival over the 30-year period, which ranged from 25.5% to 26.8% at 5 years and 13.6% to 17.8% at 10 years. It is noteworthy that their resection rate was quite high (ranging from 83% to 97.5% in the six different hospitals) so that their neglect of intensive preoperative mediastinal evaluation did not result in a large number of thoracotomies without resection. (An important difference in British and American practice may figure in these very good results, however. British patients have to pass through a general practitioner and often through a thoracic medical specialist before getting to the surgeon, decreasing the proportion of obviously unfavorable cases.)

The article abstracted below is based on two new concepts. The first is that inclusion of T1 N1 M0 lesions in stage I is inappropriate since the presence of hilar nodes indicates just as poor a surgical prognosis as does the presence of mediastinal (N2) nodes. (T1 N1 M0 lesions were initially included in stage I, in part because it was thought that hilar metastases, as opposed to mediastinal metastases, would be included in a pneumonectomy). Accordingly, the authors have coined the term *"modified" stage II* to include T1 N1 M0 lesions with T2 N1, M0 lesions. The second new concept is that postoperative adjunctive therapy (radiotherapy, chemotherapy, or both) would be as beneficial when hilar nodes are present as it is now widely assumed to be when mediastinal nodes are present and resected in stage III (N2) lesions. ◀

17–1 **Treatment of Modified Stage II (T1 N1 M0, T2 N1 M0) Non-Small-Cell Bronchogenic Carcinoma: A Combined Modality Approach.** Stage II non-small cell bronchogenic carcinoma accounts for about 10% of all patients with non-small-cell lung cancer in the United States. Resection alone has yielded an expected 5-year survival of 15%–30%. Steven B. Newman, Tom R. DeMeester, Harvey M. Golomb, Philip C. Hoffman, Alex G. Little, and Vathsala Raghavan (Univ. of Chicago) reviewed data on 20 consecutive, previ ously untreated patients seen in 1974–1981 with modified stage II

(17–1) J. Thorac. Cardiovasc. Surg. 85:180–185, August 1983.

SURVIVAL BY TREATMENT MODALITY

	No. of patients	*No. of patients alive*	*Median survival (mo)*
Surgical resection alone (SR)	8	1	12.0
SR + radiation therapy (RT)	4	2	37.0 (+)
SR + RT + chemotherapy	8	6	72.0 (+)
Total	20	9	20.3

(Courtesy of Newman, S. B., et al.: J. Thorac. Cardiovasc. Surg. 86:180–185, August 1983.)

non-small-cell bronchogenic carcinoma. Fifteen patients had T2 N1 M0 lesions; 5 had T1 N1 M0 disease. The 14 men and 6 women had a median age of 63 years.

The first 8 patients had surgical resection only, but later patients were offered resection, postoperative radiation therapy consisting of 3,000 rads in 15 fractions, and 12 monthly cycles of combination chemotherapy consisting of cyclophosphamide, doxorubicin, methotrexate, and procarbazine (CAMP). Chemotherapy was begun 2 weeks after radiation therapy was completed. Pneumonectomy was done in 11 cases and lobectomy in 9. Fifteen patients had adenocarcinoma, 4 had squamous cell cancer, and 1 had a large cell undifferentiated carcinoma.

There were no perioperative deaths. Eight patients received an average of 10 cycles of CAMP therapy at 80% of calculated full dosage. None required hospital care for complications of treatment. All patients had what was considered a curative resection. Survival is related to treatment in the table. Actuarial survival was better in patients given adjunctive radiation therapy with or without chemotherapy than in those having resection alone. Disease-free intervals were comparable in the various treatment groups. All but 1 of the 12 relapses occurred within 14 months of operation. Eleven patients have died with progressive non-small-cell bronchogenic carcinoma.

Combined treatment appears to be indicated for patients with "modified" stage II non-small-cell bronchogenic carcinoma. Those with early progression of previously localized disease are most likely to benefit from adjuvant therapy. A study is underway to evaluate prophylactic whole brain irradiation because of the high incidence of CNS relapse in these patients.

▶ [There are a lot of reasons for hoping that postoperative irradiation will sterilize micrometastases in the hilar and mediastinal nodes, as appears to have been the case here.[3,4] The contention in the abstracted article that adjunctive chemotherapy is additive to adjunctive radiotherapy has not been demonstrated elsewhere as far as we know. No patient treated with adjunctive therapy had a recurrence at the initial tumor site (but only one treated with surgery alone did so). Of 11 patients in whom therapy failed as a result of metastatic disease, 5 had isolated CNS metastases. Many authors have suggested that prophylactic cranial irradiation might be more appropriate for adenocarcinoma, which cell type comprised the majority of the reported cases, than for small cell carcinoma in which prophylactic cranial irradiation is widely used (see below), since cranial metastases are almost as frequent in adenocarcinoma as in oat cell and, in contrast to small cell, are often isolated, single-organ metastases.[5] Obviously this very small series of cases cannot serve as the basis for any major conclusions. However, it will take a much larger study to prove that the most appropriate therapy for "modified" stage II lung cancer is *not* adjunctive treatment with radiotherapy or both radiotherapy and chemotherapy plus prophylactic cranial irradiation in the case of adenocarcinoma.] ◀

17–2 **Bronchogenic Carcinoma With Chest Wall Invasion: Factors Affecting Survival Following en Bloc Resection.** Invasion of the chest wall by bronchogenic carcinoma is not rare, but the prognosis of such cases has been controversial. Jeffrey M. Piehler, Peter C. Pairolero, Louis H. Weiland, Kenneth P. Offord, W. Spencer Payne, and Philip E. Bernatz report data on 93 patients who had an en bloc chest wall and pulmonary resection for bronchogenic carcinoma. In 66 of the patients, all tumor was thought to have been removed. Chest wall reconstruction was by autologous tissue or Marlex mesh. The diameter of the neoplasms ranged from 2 to 10 cm. Lobectomy was performed in 72%, pneumonectomy in 24%, and resection in the remainder. Overall operative mortality was 15.2%, 19.6% for patients over 60 years of age and 5.0% for those under 60. Actuarial 5-year survival for those patients without hilar or mediastinal node involvement who had a complete resection was 53.7%, and for those patients with either hilar or mediastinal node involvement it was 7.4%. Only age and the presence or absence of hilar or mediastinal nodes had a significant impact on survival. Postoperative irradiation was used in some patients, but no effect was apparent regardless of the TNM classification. Patients with T3 N0 M0 bronchogenic carcinoma invading the chest wall represent a very favorable subset of patients with stage III disease that has a favorable prognosis, but only in the absence of hilar or mediastinal lymph node involvement.

▶ [Pearson and his associates from Toronto have reported the same general experience in an article by Patterson et al. in the same journal issue.[6] They note that chest wall involvement occurs in 2%–8% of patients undergoing thoracotomy for lung cancer. Their operative mortality in 35 patients was 8.5%, and the overall (actuarial) 5-year survival was 38%. However, none of 5 patients with N2 disease survived, and only one (who had developed metastatic disease at the time of the report) in 6 patients with N1 disease survived. The actuarial 5-year survival in 13 patients who received postoperative irradiation was 56% and 30% in those who did not. Seven of 9 patients who received postoperative irradiation and had no nodal involvement (T3 N0 M0) were alive and free of disease. Local extension did not develop in any irradiated patient.

English surgeons have long contended that not only chest wall but also mediastinal involvement should be resected when this is technically possible, following the policy of "operate at all costs."[7] And, as mentioned, they do not usually use postoperative irradiation. Patients with chest wall involvement represent another subset of Stage III cancers (T3 N0 M0) in which prognosis is not all that bad. These results, together with the acceptable results of some stage III disease by virtue of being N2 lesions (T1–2 N2 M0) as discussed last year,[1] clearly show that it is really not helpful to group these two subcategories with other stage III lesions such as those with extrathoracic metastases (M1) or other far advanced tumors. As indicated in the article by Newman (17–1), stage I, as presently defined, also lacks homogeneity, grouping tumors with no node involvement and small primaries—for which the results with surgery without adjunctive radiotherapy are ex-

---

(17–2) Ann. Thorac. Surg. 34:684–691, December 1982.

cellent (T1 N0 M0)—together with tumors with hilar node involvement, for which the prognosis is much less good and for which, if the data in Newman's article are born out, the therapy may be different (adjunctive therapy indicated). Further, even the stage III subcategory of T1 N2 M0 is itself too broad, as it includes tumors with a quite acceptable 5-year survivorship, such as squamous cell tumors with ipsilateral low mediastinal nodal involvement, and tumors with quite poor prognosis, such as extensive mediastinal node involvement (at more than one level) or involvement of the nodes in the aortopulmonary window or in the posterior subcarinal area. Description of tumors by the TNM system has proved very effective in describing surgical results, designing treatment, and estimating prognosis. The grouping of these various lesions into the three stages has perhaps outlived its usefulness.

The editors are aware that the character of their selections indicate an increasingly activist bias in the treatment of NSCLC. This has been a slow process, and there are good reasons for adopting the opposite stance, a sort of biologic determinism which assumes that patients with good tumors live a long time and patients with bad tumors don't, regardless of what is done for them. This was the implicit message of a large retrospective review of more than 6,000 lung cancer cases recorded in the Armed Forces Registry.[8] In that study all of the survival curves had two components: an early rapidly decreasing slope and a later flat slope. The authors entertained the notion, as have others, that prolonged survival after surgery might be more a result of the fact that surgical patients come from the long-lived group rather than that surgery prolongs lives. This also is the implicit lesson of the distinguished Philadelphia Pulmonary Neoplasm Research Project.[9] However, lung cancer is now epidemic, detailed knowledge about it is increasing, and some therapeutic results based on staging and intensive treatment are surprisingly good. It is impossible to be dogmatic about either rigorous therapeutic nihilism or its opposite, and there remains a great deal to be learned.

Some other good articles about NSCLC: The *role of computed tomographic (CT) scanning in preoperative staging,* discussed a little negatively in last year's YEAR BOOK,[1] depends in part on how aggressive one's therapeutic attitudes are. Goldstraw et al. state that when the mediastinum is negative on CT scan it almost always is also negative at surgery.[10] They found that CT scan was superior to mediastinoscopy with lower lobe tumors, the nodal deposits from which are often inaccessable at mediastinoscopy (posterior, subcarinal, etc.). As pointed out in the article, mediastinoscopy as a staging procedure in all cases, which many at first believed might be its role, has really not ever caught on. It is not without risk, provides only a limited evaluation of the mediastinum, requires frozen section and prolongation of the operation when done tandem to thoracotomy, and, if done some days before surgery, leaves an inflamed and altered mediastinum which may be difficult to evaluate at thoracotomy. Its greatest use may be when there is an abnormal mediastinal contour on chest x-ray (or CT scan) in patients in whom radical surgery would not be contemplated for some reason (small cell histology or perhaps adenocarcinoma or old age, in which tolerance of pneumonectomy is definitely decreased). Baron et al. stated that the CT scan was almost always right in predicting operability or inoperability but that the findings in 35% were inconclusive, showing tumor abutting but not definitely invading the mediastinum or nodes less than 2 cm in diameter, which can be either benign or malignant.[11] An article from Italy states that CT scans of the chest, brain, and upper abdomen are all needed for staging.[12] Twenty-one of 85 patients were said to have intraabdominal disease contraindicating operation (adrenals, liver, subdiaphragmatic nodes, spleen). It seems likely to the editors that extensive CT scanning will inevitably become a part of preoperative staging in all but the least advanced cases and that the results will get progressively more reliable. The results of *aspiration needle biopsy* in 146 cases were discussed by Gibney et al.[13] Accuracy of diagnosis was 73% in malignant disease and 17.5% in benign disease; there were no false positives in their series; pneumothorax occurred in 30%, and a tube was required in 14%. Michel et al. reported a series of 239 patients.[14] There were 12 false negative aspirations in 152 cancers (about 8%) and one false positive (for malignancy) aspiration in benign disease. The authors were good at telling metastatic disease, particularly when a slide from the primary tumor was available for comparison and particularly with colon cancers, even without comparative slides. Needle biopsy seems to us to be seldom indicated in patients in whom cancer is suspected and exploratory surgery is therefore planned; this is because (1) the decision to operate is not changed by a positive result, (2) it is uncommon to get a reliable benign diagnosis, and (3) false negatives for malignancy occur sufficiently frequently that operation cannot be avoided on that basis. Needle biopsy would seem to be useful in studying patients who would not be operated on and sometimes in determining whether a lesion is metastatic from a previous carcinoma. Ellis et al. have reported on the usefulness of *lung perfusion scanning in determination of resectability.*[15] They state that when the perfusion of a lung containing a central tumor is less than 25% of the total, resectability is unlikely, that ventilation studies do not add helpful information, and that the presence of airways obstruction does not invalidate the data.

Last year the difficulty in assessing the results of *chemotherapy in NSCLC* because of the lack of a controlled study was noted.[16] A small but good randomized study appeared this past year from France.[17] The medicines were methotrexate, adriamycin, cyclophosphamide, and lomustine. Median survival was 30 weeks in the treated group and 8 weeks in the nontreated group. These are not great results, but some (relatively well) patients with disseminated SCLC will get some good from chemotherapy, and a couple of cycles to determine response is certainly reasonable in those who wish to pay a reasonably high price in expense, discomfort, and toxicity for what is usually quite limited benefit. Some may be lucky and have quite prolonged survival. Several in the treated group had survived one year, and 1 patient had survived almost 2 years at the time of the report. The decision has to be highly individualized, and it remains consonant with good practice to avoid the use of chemotherapy in patients who have been informed of the benefits and risks and choose not to take it and in those in whom, for reasons of age or general debility, the results may be expected to be minimal.] ◀

17–3 **Surgical Resection in Management of Small Cell Carcinoma of the Lung** is being increasingly used. Thomas W. Shields, George A. Higgins, Jr., Mary J. Matthews, and Robert J. Keehn reviewed the experience of the VA Surgical Oncology Group, which included 148 patients with small cell carcinoma of the lung who underwent potentially "curative" resection in the past 25 years. They represented 4.7% of all patients undergoing resection in this period. The first 101 patients were randomized to chemotherapy or no chemotherapy at the time of operation and the other 47 from 10 to 13 days after operation, excluding early postoperative mortality. Sixteen of the earlier patients died within 30 days of operation.

When the data were analyzed by the life table method, the 5-year survival was 23% for the 132 patients who lived and were evaluated. Survival is related to the TNM classification in Figure 17–1. Only the difference between T1 N0 M0 and the other categories was significant; the 5-year survival for this group was 59.5%. No benefit from adjuvant postoperative chemotherapy was apparent when a one- or two-course regimen of nitrogen mustard or cyclophosphamide was used. Prolonged intermittent therapy with cyclophosphamide, alone or alternating with methotrexate, may have given some benefit. A recent trial of prolonged intermittent courses of CCNU (nitrosourea) and hydroxyurea resulted in 5-year survival rates of 80.0% for treated patients and 38.1% for controls.

Selected patients with undifferentiated small cell carcinoma of the lung benefit from resection of local disease. Patients with a T1 lesion and no nodal metastases have the best prospect of satisfactory long-

(17–3) J. Thorac. Cardiovasc. Surg. 84:481–488, October 1982.

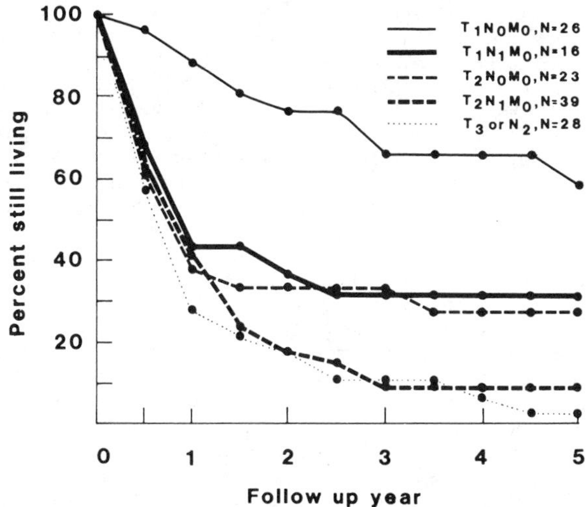

Fig 17–1.—Survival, computed by life table method, from postoperative day 30 (early trials) or from randomization (recent trials) by TNM classification for patients with undifferentiated small-cell carcinoma who had undergone "curative resection" in VA Surgical Oncology Group lung trials. (Courtesy of Shields, T. W., et al.: J. thorac. Cardiovasc. Surg. 84:481–488, October 1982.)

term survival. Resection is definitely indicated for patients with T1 N0 M0 lesions and is probably indicated for those with T1 N1 M0 or T2 N0 M0 lesions. Primary resection is contraindicated for patients in any other TNM category. After operation, it seems reasonable to try a regimen of three or four effective chemotherapeutic agents in repeated courses over 6 months or longer. Prophylactic cranial irradiation should also be considered.

▶ [For many years the poor overall results with surgery in small cell lung cancer (SCLC) together with the growing enthusiasm for chemotherapy resulted in the widely held opinion that preoperative demonstration of this cell type constituted a contraindication to operation regardless of the stage of the tumor. This was so much the belief that quite recently it was taught that one reason that a preoperative histologic diagnosis was required was that if small cell lung cancer were discovered an unrewarding operation could be avoided. Only a minority (less than 10%) of SCLC patients present with low stage lung cancers (stage I or II), but in these there is now good evidence that surgery is beneficial. In 1975, Higgins and associates reported the extensive VA experience with solitary pulmonary nodules.[18] These included 11 SCLC cases that demonstrated a *36% 5-year survival.* Similar findings have been reported by Shore and Paneth.[19, 20] Forty of approximately 400 patients with SCLC seen at the Brompton Hospital over a 15 year period were resected for cure, including some with hilar and mediastinal nodes. Ten (25%) survived 5 years. No adjunctive therapy (radiotherapy or chemotherapy) was used in this experience, although the authors now say that they would use chemotherapy.

The article abstracted above contains additional convincing evidence that low stage SCLC tumors should be resected. Note that the results with even the less favorable T1 N1 M0 and T2 N0 M0 cases were much more favorable than even the best results that can be expected from chemotherapy in limited SCLC. Everyone would now advise that if resection is carried out it should be followed by chemotherapy, and it is certainly possible that in patients with hilar nodes postoperative irradiation may work out to be beneficial as well; that is really an unanswered question and one that, given the relative rarity of low stage SCLC, probably will remain so. It should be mentioned that this attitude about low stage SCLC is not agreed upon by everyone.

Some believe that good surgical results are all in the polygonal histologic subtype.[21] Others say that these successfully operated cases are really all atypical carcinoids.[22] However, present evidence indicates that low stage SCLC should be resected.

A combination of chemotherapy and surgery for more advanced disease is being investigated by a number of centers now. The most successful and as yet unconfirmed results have been published from Syracuse.[23] They report data on 2 patients with T1 N0 M0, 4 with T2 N0 M0, and 4 with T2 N1 M0 tumors treated with surgery and intensive, multiple-drug chemotherapy. One patient died of a surgical complication, 1 died more than 4 years after therapy with an unrelated malignancy, and one relapsed in the CNS. The other 7 remain well, 3 surviving more than 5 years at the time of this most recent report. Other centers are now investigating preoperative chemotherapy in order to attempt to convert inoperable tumors to operable ones, but results of this approach are preliminary and so far not too promising.

The results of surgery reported above have to be put in the context of what can be expected from chemotherapy, the current status of which has recently been reviewed by the International Association for the Study of Lung Cancer (IASLC).[24] They concluded that multiple-drug therapy is preferable to single-agent chemotherapy, three drugs are better than two, and maximal results *require* drug dosage sufficient to produce a certain degree of serious toxicity with a predictable fall in hematologic parameters in all patients, infection in some, and a few deaths. Complete response, defined as disappearance of all measurable disease, should be observed in 50% of "limited disease" patients (disease confined to one hemithorax and the supraclavicular nodes on that and the opposite side) and in 25% of "disseminated disease" patients (more than limited). Partial response should be observed in 20% of limited disease and 50% of disseminated disease patients. Either complete response or partial response should be observed in 80% of limited and 75% of disseminated disease patients. The overall median survival should be 14 months in limited and 7 months in disseminated disease, and the 3 year survival, all in limited disease patients, should be 15%–20%. The *role of radiation therapy as adjunctive to chemotherapy* in SCLC was also recently reviewed by the IASLC.[25] They conclude that "no advantage [of addition of radiation therapy to chemotherapy] in short-term [median] survival has been shown in randomized studies, but current data suggest a possible advantage in long-term control of loco-regional disease." It is our opinion that some advantage in long-term survivorship in limited-stage SCLC will be demonstrated with combined therapy but that is based on very partial data. Adjunctive radiation has, of course, no role in the treatment of disseminated disease.] ◀

17–4 **Role of Prophylactic Cranial Irradiation in Prevention of Central Nervous System Metastases in Small Cell Lung Cancer: Potential Benefit Restricted to Patients With Complete Response.** Steven T. Rosen, Robert W. Makuch, Allen S. Lichter, Daniel C. Ihde, Mary J. Matthews, John D. Minna, Eli Glatstein, and Paul A. Bunn, Jr. (Natl. Cancer Inst.) reviewed the records of 332 patients treated by National Cancer Institute protocols for small-cell lung cancer (SCLC) between 1969 and 1980 to evaluate prophylactic cranial irradiation. Group I (76 patients) received prophylactic cranial irradiation from day 1 of induction therapy; in group II (80) patients who responded received prophylactic irradiation at week 12 or 24 and nonresponders received no irradiation; group III (176) received no cranial irradiation and was used as a control population. Autopsy data were available for 111 patients. All patients received combination chemotherapy. Some received thoracic irradiation, and some, thymosin immunotherapy. Cranial irradiation was with doses of 2,000 or 2,400 rads.

Pretreatment risk factors for CNS metastasis are analyzed in Table

(17–4) Am. J. Med. 74:615–624, April 1983.

TABLE 1.—PRETREATMENT RISK FACTORS IN 332 PATIENTS

Factor	Number of Patients	Relative Failure Rate, O/E*	Univariate Significance†	Multivariate Significance‡
Age				
<60 years	114	1.08	p = 0.24	p = 0.16
≥60 years	218	0.85		
Sex				
Male	272	1.09	p = 0.06	p = 0.40
Female	60	0.67		
Race				
White	274	0.95	p = 0.21	p = 0.41
Non-white	58	1.28		
Stage				
Limited	136	0.51	p <0.001	p <0.001
Extensive	196	1.49		
Bone marrow				
Negative results	255	0.80	p <0.001	p <0.001
Positive results	77	1.93		
Bone				
Negative results	218	0.80	p <0.001	p = 0.009
Positive results	114	1.47		
Liver				
Negative results	233	0.50	p <0.001	p <0.001
Positive results	99	1.67		
Response				
Complete	123	0.68	p <0.001	p <0.001
Less than complete	209	2.06		

*Ratio of observed no. of CNS relapses and extent of exposure to risk of CNS relapse.
†Mantel test.
‡Significance level after adjustment for type of CNS treatment.
(Courtesy of Rosen, S. T., et al.: Am. J. Med. 74:615–624, April 1983.)

TABLE 2.—AUTOPSY RESULTS BY GROUP

	Percent Positive Results			
	Group I (n = 17)	Group II (n = 17)	Group III (n = 77)	Significance Level
Intracerebral	41	53	61	0.31
Spinal cord	18	12	14	0.89
Leptomeningeal	18	29	29	0.64
Total positive results	47	59	61	0.57

(Courtesy of Rosen, S. T., et al.: Am. J. Med. 74:615–624, April 1983.)

1. Significant factors included stage of disease; involvement of liver, marrow, and bone; and degree of response to systemic therapy. Cranial irradiation was associated with a significant reduction in intracerebral metastases but no change in leptomeningeal, spinal, or epidural metastases. The course of patients with a complete response to systemic therapy is shown in Figure 17–2, and that of patients who failed to respond completely is shown in Figure 17–3. Overall survival was significantly improved in patients given cranial irradiation, who had an actuarial 2-year survival of 18%–20% compared with 5% for controls. Evidence of CNS tumor was present in 59% of patients

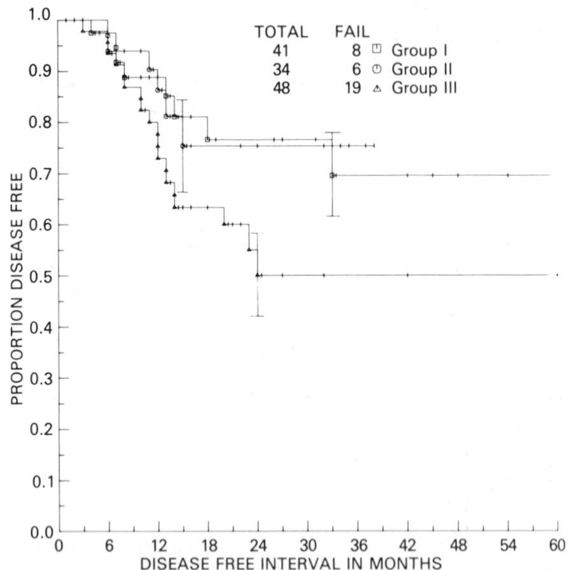

Fig 17–2.—Life table analysis of probability of remaining free from CNS metastases as function of time from onset of therapy for patients who achieved complete response to systemic therapy. Bars representing ±1 SE for each group are shown at "plateau" region of curves and are 0.10, 0.12, and 0.06 for groups I, II, and III, respectively. (Courtesy of Rosen, S. T., et al.: Am. J. Med. 74:615–624, April 1983.)

Fig 17–3.—Life table analysis of probability of remaining free from CNS metastases as function of time from onset of therapy for patients who did not achieve complete response to systemic therapy. Bars representing ±1 SE for each group are shown at "plateau" region of curves. (Courtesy of Rosen, S. T., et al.: Am. J. Med. 74:615–624, April 1983.)

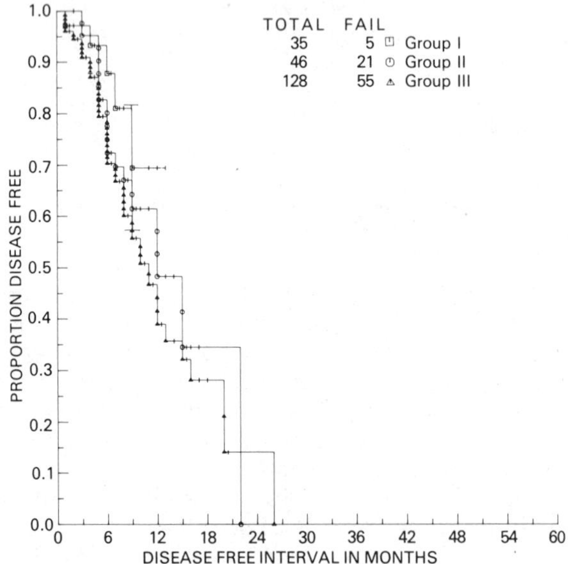

at autopsy. It was less frequent in patients in groups I and II than in patients in group III (Table 2).

It may be prudent to give prophylactic cranial irradiation to patients with SCLC who respond completely to systemic therapy, pending results of randomized trials. Elective irradiation is not recommended for those who do not respond completely to systemic therapy. Therapeutic brain irradiation effectively controls intracerebral relapse in most patients with SCLC.

▶ [Ten percent of all patients with SCLC will have a CNS metastasis when initially diagnosed, and 20%–50% will develop such during the course of their disease.[26–28] Between 60% and 80% of SCLC patients surviving more than two years will have developed brain metastases.[27, 29] Since most drugs used to treat SCLC are excluded from the CNS, the treatment strategy of prophylactic cranial irradiation (PCI) became popular quite early in the SCLC chemotherapy era. Usually 2,500–3,000 rads are administered, and complications are for the most part minimal and transient.[30]

Although the rationale for the use of PCI seems sound, its proper role is still not agreed upon. Seven randomized trials of the effect of PCI in SCLC have recently been summarized, again by members of the International Association for the Study of Lung Cancer.[31] These studies all demonstrate significant reduction in the frequency of CNS metastasis by PCI but no prolongation of life, since development of CNS metastases is almost always associated with simultaneous development of metastatic disease elsewhere in the body. Furthermore, treatment of CNS metastases when they become clinically apparent is really very successful, especially when begun promptly after the appearance of symptoms. Patients in whom the only symptom of intracranial metastasis is headache are very likely to be totally relieved and to remain free of neurologic symptoms for the rest of their lives after symptomatic cranial irradiation (SCI); similar good results are seen in 65%–90% of *all* patients with CNS metastases regardless of the severity of their symptoms.[27, 32] The effectiveness of SCI together with the apparent lack of prolongation of life by PCI (as judged by median survival) has led to the argument that cranial irradiation should be deferred until symptoms develop (SCI).

The article abstracted above takes a different tack. It focuses on the very important group of patients with limited disease and complete response to chemotherapy in whom, as has been mentioned above, prolonged (3-year) survival should be observed in 15%–20%. In contrast to SCLC patients taken as a whole, 17% of CNS relapses in this most favorable group are single-organ metastases. The use of PCI in *limited-disease complete-response* patients reduced the incidence of CNS metastasis from 52% to 25% and was associated with a 2-year survival rate of 38% compared to 16% in a comparable group not given PCI. It is their opinion that PCI should be reserved for this group of patients who have some hope of prolonged survival and administered only after demonstration of complete response, usually 2 to 4, but less than 6, months after beginning treatment.] ◀

Chapter 17 References

1. 1983 YEAR BOOK OF MEDICINE, pp. 169–172.
2. Belcher J.R.: Thirty years of surgery for carcinoma of the bronchus. *Thorax* 38:428, 1983.
3. 1982 YEAR BOOK OF MEDICINE, pp. 163–166.
4. Hande K.R., Des Prez R.M.: Chemotherapy and radiation therapy for non-small cell lung carcinoma. *Clin. Chest Med.* 3:399, 1982.
5. 1982 YEAR BOOK OF MEDICINE, pp. 171–172.
6. Patterson G.A., Ilves R., Ginsberg R.J., et al.: The value of adjuvant radiotherapy in pulmonary and chest wall resection for bronchogenic carcinoma. *Ann. Thorac. Surg.* 34:692, 1982.
7. Abbey-Smith, R.: The importance of mediastinal lymph node invasion by pulmonary carcinoma in selection of patients for resection. *Ann. Thorac. Surg.* 25:5, 1978.

8. Rossing T.H., Rossing R.G.: Survival in lung cancer: analysis of the effects of age, sex, resectability, and histopathologic type. *Am. Rev. Respir. Dis.* 126:771, 1982.
9. Weiss W., Boucot K.R., Seidman H.: The Philadelphia pulmonary neoplasm research project. *Clin. Chest Med.* 3:243, 1982.
10. Goldstraw P., Kurzen M., Edwards D.: Preoperative staging of lung cancer: accuracy of computed tomography versus mediastinoscopy. *Thorax* 38:10, 1983.
11. Baron R.L., Levitt R.G., Sagel S.S., et al.: Computed tomography in the preoperative evaluation of bronchogenic carcinoma. *Radiology* 145:727, 1982.
12. Modini C., Passariello R., Iasconi C., et al.: TNM staging in lung cancer: Role of computed tomography. *J. Thorac. Cardiovasc. Surg.* 84:569, 1982.
13. Gibney R.T.N., Man G.C.W., King E.G.: Aspiration biopsy in the diagnosis of pulmonary disease. *Chest* 80:300, 1981.
14. Michel R.P., Lushpihan A., Ahmed M.N.: Pathologic findings of transthoracic needle aspiration in the diagnosis of localized pulmonary lesions. *Cancer* 51:1663, 1983.
15. Ellis D.A., Hawkins T., Gibson G.J., et al.: Role of lung scanning in assessing the resectability of bronchial carcinoma. *Thorax* 38:261, 1983.
16. 1983 YEAR BOOK OF MEDICINE, pp. 167–168.
17. Cormier Y., Bergeron D., La Forge J., et al.: Benefits of polychemotherapy in advanced non small cell bronchogenic carcinoma. *Cancer* 50:845, 1982.
18. Higgins G.A., Shields T.W., Keehn R.J.: The solitary pulmonary nodule: ten year follow-up of Veterans Administration Armed Forces Cooperative Study. *Arch. Surg.* 110:570, 1975.
19. Shore D.F., Paneth, M.: Survival after resection of small cell carcinoma of the bronchus. *Thorax* 35:819, 1980.
20. 1982 YEAR BOOK OF MEDICINE, p. 173.
21. Mayer J.E. Jr., Ewing S.L., Ophoven J.J., et al.: Influence of histologic type on survival after curative resection for undifferentiated lung cancer. *J. Thorac. Cardiovasc. Surg.* 84:641, 1982.
22. Kron I.L., Harman P.K., Mills S.E., et al.: A reappraisal of limited-stage undifferentiated carcinoma of the lung: does Stage I small cell undifferentiated carcinoma exist? *J. Thorac. Cardiovasc. Surg.* 84:734, 1982.
23. Meyer J.A., Comis R.L., Ginsberg S.J., et al.: The prospect of disease control by surgery combined with chemotherapy in stage I and stage II small cell carcinoma of the lung. *Ann. Thorac. Surg.* 36:37, 1983.
24. Aisner J., Alberto P., Bitran J., et al.: Role of chemotherapy in small cell lung cancer: a consensus report of the International Association for the Study of Lung Cancer workshop. *Cancer Treat. Rep.* 67:37, 1983.
25. Bleehen N.M., Bunn P.A., Cox J.C., et al.: Role of radiation therapy in small cell anaplastic carcinoma of the lung. *Cancer Treat. Rep.* 67:11, 1983.
26. Bunn P.A. Jr., Cohen M.H., Ihde D.C., et al.: Advances in small cell bronchogenic carcinoma. *Cancer Treat. Rep.* 61:333, 1977.
27. Nugent J.L., Bunn P.A. Jr., Matthews M.J., et al.: CNS metastases in small cell bronchogenic carcinoma: increasing frequency and changing pattern with lengthening survival. *Cancer* 44:1885, 1979.
28. Komaki R., Cox J.D., Whitson W.: Risk of brain metastasis from small cell carcinoma of the lung related to length of survival and prophylactic irradiation. *Cancer Treat. Rep.* 65:811, 1981.
29. Baglan R.J., Marks J.E.: Comparison of symptomatic and prophylactic irradiation of brain metastases from oat cell carcinoma of the lung. *Cancer* 47:41, 1981.

30. Abeloff M.D., Klastersky J., Drings P.D., et al.: Complications of treatment of small cell carcinoma of the lung. *Cancer Treat. Rep.* 67:21, 1983.
31. Bleehen N.M., Bunn P.A., Cox J.D., et al.: Role of radiation therapy in small cell anaplastic carcinoma of the lung. *Cancer Treat. Rep.* 67:11, 1983.
32. Baglan R.J., Marks J.E.: Comparison of symptomatic and prophylactic irradiation of brain metastases from oat cell carcinoma of the lung. *Cancer* 47:41, 1981.

18. Mycobacterial Disease

18–1 **Tuberculosis Among Indochinese Refugees in the United States.** The admission of Indochinese refugees to the United States increased markedly in mid-1979, and a high prevalence of tuberculosis of 1%–2% was found among entrants. Kenneth E. Powell, E. Donald Brown, and Laurence S. Farer (Centers for Disease Control, Atlanta) surveyed state tuberculosis control programs to determine the occurrence of tuberculosis in 263,000 Indochinese refugees who entered the country in 1979 and 1980. About 1.5% either had tuberculosis at entry or developed it by the end of 1980, and in another 18% prophylaxis was begun. The refugees accounted for more than 5% of nationally counted cases in this 2-year period. Age- and sex-specific incidence rates were 30 to 200 times higher than those for other persons in the United States. Bacteriologic confirmation of the diagnosis was reported for only 26% of refugees, compared with 79% of other patients in the United States. Age-specific rates of bacteriologically proved tuberculosis were 14 to 70 times higher than rates for the country as a whole.

Indochinese refugees have substantially increased rates of tuberculosis even when only bacteriologically documented cases are considered. About one third of Indochinese patients have organisms resistant to at least one antituberculosis drug. The low rate of bacteriologic confirmation suggests overdiagnosis by physicians in the United States. Some of the refugees being treated for tuberculosis may require only prophylaxis, and some may require no treatment. Some may have other diseases.

▶ [In those areas where they were concentrated, the Indochinese accounted for a very large part of the new cases added to tuberculosis registers, more than 25% in Colorado, Kansas, Minnesota, Utah, and Washington, and more than 50% in Orange County, Calif., St. Paul, and Wichita, Kan. Most of the refugees were young, and most of the cases were therefore in younger individuals. But the age-specific rates of prevalence (disease present on immigration) and incidence (development of active disease after immigration) make it clear that older persons are at greatest risk. Of those older than 65 years of age, 6.8% had active tuberculosis on arrival, and a further 1.6% developed it later. Data from the Centers for Disease Control for the year 1979 indicate that among Indochinese persons the risk is greatest in the older male; the prevalence per 100,000 in the age group 56 years and older was 3,478 in women but an astounding *14,180 (14%)* in men.[1]

The problem is compounded by the high rate of drug resistance in Oriental immigrants with active tuberculosis, whether from Indochina or elsewhere. Carpenter et al. report the following resistances in Korean immigrants with previously untreated active tuberculosis: isoniazid (INH), 33%; ethambutol (EMB), 13%; rifampin (RMP), 5%; streptomycin (STM) 22%.[2] They suggest a regimen of INH, RMP, pyrazinamide, and capreomycin for these patients. Whether or not this would be best for all Asians, for whom a regimen of INH-RMP-EMB has usually been suggested, is not certain.

(18–1) JAMA 249:1455–1460, Mar. 18, 1983.

High rates of drug resistance in Orientals,[3] in Haitians,[4] and other groups[5] have obvious implications for both therapy and chemoprophylaxis.

It is generally agreed that worldwide the group at greatest risk for tuberculosis is the nonwhite elderly male. The abstract that follows indicates that it is a special problem in all older individuals.] ◀

18–2 **Does the Risk of Tuberculosis Increase in Old Age?** William W. Stead and J. P. Lofgren (Arkansas Dept. of Health, Little Rock) examined age-specific case rates for tuberculosis in Arkansas, the state with the second-highest proportion of elderly persons in the United States, over the two decades since 1961. There has been a decline in the overall case rate in each decade and in the rate for each age group through age 69 years, but the apparent incidence has increased for those older than 69. A modest increase in 1976 was followed by a much more pronounced increase in 1980–1981. Most tuberculosis in the elderly is a result of recrudescence of long-dormant infection. Age-specific case rates are shown in Figure 18–1, and rates

Fig 18–1.—Age-specific case rates of tuberculosis per 100,000 population in Arkansas for the 3 census years of the last 2 decades. Each point represents an average of the data for 2 consecutive years. Although the 1976 figures required the use of interpolated census data, the last 2 points of the curve for 1976 are included to show that the increased incidence of the disease in the elderly had already started by then. (Courtesy of Stead, W.W., and Lofgren, J.P.: J. Infect. Dis. 147:951–955, May 1983.)

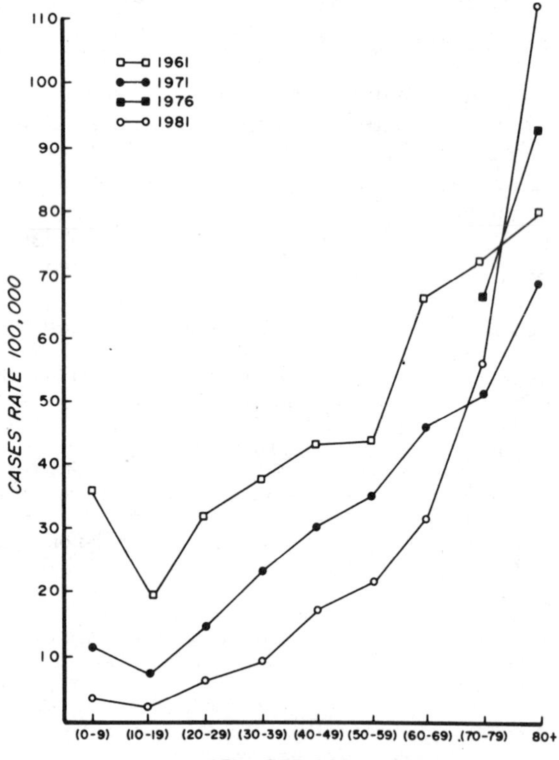

(18–2) J. Infect. Dis. 147:951–955, May 1983.

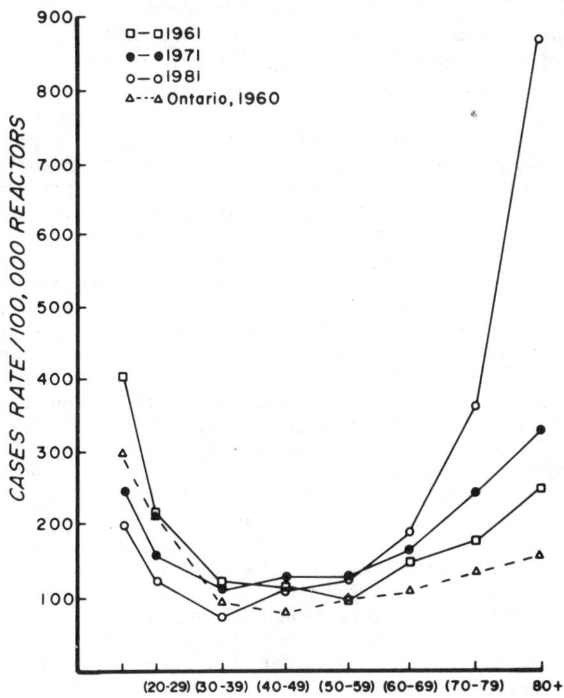

Fig 18–2.—Age-specific case rate of tuberculosis in Arkansas per 100,000 tuberculin-positive persons for 1961, 1971, and 1981. The curve for 1960 obtained from the Ontario survey of Grzybowski and Allen (*Am. Rev. Respir. Dis.* 90:707–720, 1964) is shown for comparison. The closeness of fit is remarkable through the age of 69 years, after which the curve for 1981 deviates upward in a significant manner. (Courtesy of Stead, W.W., and Lofgren, J.P.: J. Infect. Dis. 147:951–955, May 1983.)

in tuberculin-positive persons in Figure 18–2. A large majority of elderly persons can develop a reaction that usually exceeds 15 mm of induration with 5 units of purified protein derivative (PPD) when newly infected. The increased prevalence of tuberculosis in the elderly is not attributable to overdiagnosis of the disease. Men have predominated among elderly patients with tuberculosis, but the important factor appears to be the presence of a positive skin test, not sex.

Tuberculosis should receive more consideration in the differential diagnosis of pulmonary symptoms or fever of obscure origin in elderly patients. The tuberculin status should be determined by the dual test method in all persons admitted to or employed by nursing homes and similar facilities. Tuberculin-positive subjects should have a chest roentgenogram. Even if this is negative, the sputum should be studied if a cough develops and persists. Infection is not highly contagious, and reasonably early detection of infectious cases will largely prevent spread to others. A negative result of dual testing indicates a person who is susceptible to infection if exposed, regardless of whether infection occurred previously. Tuberculin-negative persons can develop very serious disease if not given preventive treatment with isoniazid. In addition, the infection may spread to personnel and to frequent visitors, and thence into the community.

▶ [These data have been criticized by some because the numbers are small, but they do accurately represent what is the case in Arkansas, which has an excellent statewide tuberculosis program. Note that in Figure 18–1 the case rate in the oldest group is over 100 per 100,000 population, and in Figure 18–2, which presents case rates in *tuberculin-positive* persons, it is almost 900 per 100,000. This is much much higher than the case rate for tuberculin-positive adolescents and young adults, long regarded as most at risk for progression of infection to active disease.

There are several important points to make about tuberculosis in the elderly. First, the majority of elderly persons are quite susceptible to infection from the environment. In the last Centers for Disease Control statistical publication concerning tuberculosis in the United States, tuberculin reactivity in the 65 and older group countrywide was just at 10%, and the urban rate, determined in 13 cities of 250,000 or greater, was less than 30%. A survey of tuberculin reactivity of entering patients in several Arkansas nursing homes was reported in Dr. Stead's now classic article on nursing home tuberculosis.[6, 7] Six percent were positive when tested the first time, and another 6% had become positive when retested a week later, providing firm data on tuberculin reactivity and also on the magnitude of the "booster effect" of a tuberculin test in that population at that time. A negative tuberculin test in an older individual may represent (1) a waned state of hypersensitivity which will be recalled one week after tuberculin test; (2) no prior infection at all; or (3), and this is the least well known point, *the complete disappearance of an ancient infection with complete loss of tuberculin reactivity* and probably specific cellular immunity as well. This last point has been recently emphasized in an excellent review by Dr. S. Grzybowski, who ranks with Dr. Stead as one of the handful of real tuberculosis scholars still writing.[8] Dr. Grzybowski had the opportunity of participating in a large-scale Canadian tuberculin survey in 1957–1959.[9] He was able to find some precise survey data from earlier years which made it possible to compare reactivity in single age cohorts as they aged. One group of women (nurses), who had demonstrated 51% positivity when surveyed in 1933 at an average age of 20, demonstrated only 27% positivity when tested again 26 years later. Also a 15–20-year-old cohort from two rural Ontario townships with a tuberculin positivity rate of 52% in 1923 demonstrated only 40% positivity when retested 36 years later. If all reactions had been permanent, it could be calculated that the positivity rate should have increased to over 90% rather than decreased, given what was known about the risk of infection. The most compelling data, however, came from a program, which is described in the same article, of retesting persons with known reactions in different age groups one year later; the results are shown here in Tables 1 and 2.

The first table gives an index of the infectiousness of that environment. The excess of "conversions" in the older group was attributed by Dr. Grzybowski to the "booster effect" in older persons. The second table is the most interesting one, however. It says that in any adult age group roughly between 5% and 10% of tuberculin reactors

TABLE 1.—Annual Tuberculin CONVERSION Rates According to Age Groups, Victoria County 1959–1962

Age groups	Negative reactors retested after one year	Number of conversions	Conversion rate
0-19	8,381	22	0.3%
20-39	2,459	38	1.5%
40-59	1,988	78	4.1%
60 and older	640	61	9.5%
Total	13,368	199	1.5%

(Courtesy of Grzybowki, S., and Allen, E.A.: Am. Rev. Respir. Dis. 90:707–720, November 1964.)

TABLE 2.—ANNUAL TUBERCULIN REVERSION RATES ACCORDING TO AGE GROUPS, VICTORIA COUNTY 1959–1962

Age groups	Positive reactors retested after one year	Number of reversions	Reversion rate
0-19	99	22	22.2%
20-39	200	16	8.0%
40-59	525	25	4.8%
60 and older	377	34	9.0%
Total	1,201	97	8.1%

(Courtesy of Grzybowski, S., and Allen, E.A.: Am. Rev. Respir. Dis. 90:707–720, November 1964.)

will be tuberculin-negative when retested a year later. It has long been known that the maintenance of histoplasmin reactivity requires continual reinfection, as there is a great tendency for the relatively effete (as compared to tuberculosis) histoplasmosis yeast form to die off and it is known in a variety of ways that such individuals respond to new infection just as if they had never been infected at all. It seems certain that the same thing is true about tuberculosis, the only difference being that there is a much greater tendency for the intrinsically long-lived tubercle bacillus to remain viable. But ancient tuberculosis infections do die off, and when they do the host almost certainly loses cellular immunity as well as hypersensitivity.

Older persons accordingly have several sorts of special tuberculosis risks. Those who have old infections with persisting viable bacilli in the lung apex can relapse as aging immune mechanisms become inadequate for the containment of infection. If the focus of infection is in an extrapulmonary site, they are liable to the development of the clinically very subtle late hematogenous tuberculosis.[10, 11] Also, ancient infections can die off entirely, rendering the individual as susceptible as if he had never been infected. And in the present epidemiologic circumstances, many older individuals have never been infected at all. When infection does occur in advanced years it looks clinically different from that in younger individuals. All of the active cases discovered in Stead's nursing home epidemic were nondescript lower lobe chronic pneumonitis, resembling lower lobe tuberculosis in childhood except for less of a tendency to mediastinal lymphadenitis.[6] Another important piece of data from that study is that when infection occurs in this age group the likelihood of disease resulting (high degree of infection penetrance) is very great, equal to that in adolescents and perhaps greater.

So infection in elderly persons who have either never been infected or who have lost the protection of a remote and extinguished infection is very apt to produce disease, and the disease does not resemble what we have come to think of as tuberculosis in the adult. Moreover, diagnosis is often difficult because these lower lobe lesions are not associated with the huge bacillary populations characteristic of apical cavitary disease.] ◀

18–3 **Efficacy of Various Durations of Isoniazid Preventive Therapy for Tuberculosis: Five Years of Follow-up in the IUAT Trial** are reported by the International Union Against Tuberculosis Committee on Prophylaxis. Because 1 year of daily pill-taking is difficult for both patients and those supervising treatment, shorter terms of isoniazid prophylaxis have been evaluated in persons with fibrotic lesions who were followed up over 5 years. A total of 27,830 subjects with well-delineated lesions of probable tuberculous origin that had been stable over the previous year were assigned to receive isoniazid

(18–3) Bull. WHO 60:555–564, 1982.

TABLE 1.—RISK OF HEPATITIS BY QUARTER (PER 1,000 PERSONS)

Weeks	Risk by quarter: Placebo (P)	Isoniazid (I)	Excess (I-P)	Cumulative risk: Placebo (P)	Isoniazid (I)	Excess (I-P)	Risk reduction (cases prevented per 1000 persons)
1–12	0.7	3.2	2.5	0.7	3.2	2.5	2.7
13–24	0.5	1.6	1.1	1.2	4.8	3.6	1.6
25–36	0.0	0.8	0.8	1.2	5.6	4.4	0.8
37–52	0.0	0.8	0.8	1.2	6.4	5.2	standard

(Courtesy of International Union Against Tuberculosis Committee on Prophylaxis: Bull. WHO 60:555–564, 1982.)

TABLE 2.—EFFICACY OF VARIOUS DURATIONS OF ISONIAZID THERAPY OR PLACEBO FOR ALL ASSIGNED PARTICIPANTS

Regimen	No. of participants entering regimen	Cumulative no. of cases	5-Year incidence[a]	Percentage reduction	Relative risk
Placebo	6990	97[b]	14.3	0	4.0
12-I	6956	76	11.3	21	3.1
24-I	6965	34[b]	5.0	65	1.4
52-I	6919	24[c]	3.6	75	1.0

*Culture-positive tuberculosis per 1,000 persons at risk.
†Includes 1 case during the first 6 months of pill-taking.
‡Includes 2 cases during the first 6 months of pill-taking.
(Courtesy of International Union Against Tuberculosis Committee on Prophylaxis: Bull. WHO 60:555–564, 1982.)

TABLE 3.—BENEFIT-TO-RISK RATIO BY REGIMEN AND YEAR

Year of follow-up	Regimen	Cumulative no. of tuberculosis cases prevented[a]	Cumulative no. of hepatitis cases incurred[b]	Benefit-to-risk ratio
First	12-I	2.6	2.5	1.0
	24-I	3.9	3.6	1.1
	52-I	3.6	5.2	0.7
Second	12-I	2.9	2.5	1.2
	24-I	5.5	3.6	1.5
	52-I	5.3	5.2	1.0
Third	12-I	3.6	2.5	1.4
	24-I	7.6	3.6	2.1
	52-I	8.0	5.2	1.5
Fourth	12-I	3.9	2.5	1.6
	24-I	8.8	3.6	2.4
	52-I	9.3	5.2	1.8
Fifth	12-I	3.0	2.5	1.2
	24-I	9.3	3.6	2.6
	52-I	10.7	5.2	2.1

[a]Reduction in cases over placebo regimen per 1,000 persons.
[b]Excess of cases over placebo regimen per 1,000 persons.
(Courtesy of International Union Against Tuberculosis Committee on Prophylaxis: Bull. WHO 60:555–564, 1982.)

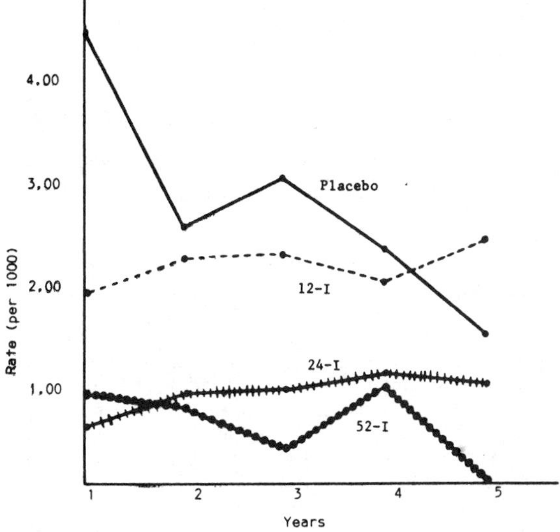

Fig 18–3.—Annual incidence of culture-positive tuberculosis: all participants, by regimen. (Courtesy of International Union Against Tuberculosis Committee on Prophylaxis: Bull. WHO 60:555–564, 1982.)

or placebo for 12, 24, or 52 weeks. The daily dose of isoniazid was 300 mg. The median age of the subjects at entry to the trial was 50 years, and 38% of the participants were aged 55–65 years.

There were few side effects. Hepatitis occurred in 0.5% of subjects given isoniazid and in 0.1% of those given placebo. Two patients given isoniazid for 12 weeks and 1 treated for 52 weeks died of hepatitis. The risk of hepatitis is shown in Table 1. The efficacy of the various isoniazid regimens is shown in Table 2. The risk of tuberculosis was reduced by 21% on the 12-week regimen, 65% by 24 weeks of prophylaxis, and 75% by the 1-year regimen, compared with placebo. The risk of tuberculosis declined during the follow-up period (Fig 18–3). Benefit-to-risk ratios are given in Table 3. Among placebo recipients, tuberculosis was less frequent in those with small lesions than in those with large ones.

The prevention of tuberculosis in relation to cases of hepatitis was most efficient with 24 weeks of isoniazid prophylaxis in this study. It is estimated that, where prophylaxis is currently given for 1 year, adoption of a 24-week regimen would increase tuberculosis by 40% and reduce cases of hepatitis by one third. It remains unclear how long beyond 5 years isoniazid will continue to provide protection. A 52-week regimen is most effective in preventing tuberculosis in highly compliant populations and populations with large fibrotic lesions.

▶ [There is general agreement that "chemoprophylaxis" is indicated in at least two groups: *(1)* contacts of known active cases and *(2)* persons thought to have inactive pulmonary tuberculosis either because of apical infiltrates compatible with tuberculosis and a positive tuberculin test or because of known, usually remote, pulmonary tuberculosis never treated with an acceptable course of chemotherapy. The article abstracted above is the last and in many ways the best of the studies used as justification for treatment of patients in the second group. In the Table the results of this study are listed along with the two other usually quoted studies of this problem.[12, 13]

	Relapse Rate per 100,000 Population	
Author	*Untreated*	*Treated*
Grzybowski et al.[12]	2,450 over 5 years	350 over 5 years
Falk and Fuchs[13]	1,940 over 7 years	560 over 7 years
IUAT (abstracted study)	1,430 over 5 years 450 in year 1 150 in year 5	360 over 5 years

In all of these studies the incidence is over a stated number of years, not annual incidence. The fact that this "prophylactic" treatment is only partially successful is clear. The IUAT study is the only one which describes the incidence of relapse by year of observation. Note that there was a progressive decrement in relapse rate with time and that by year 5 this had dropped substantially below the incidence of isoniazid (INH)-induced hepatitis observed in the study (520 per 100,000). In other words, a person with a lung lesion that has been stable under observation for a period of 5 years is really less at risk of relapse than of acquiring hepatitis from a year's treatment with INH. This is another piece of evidence that chemoprophylaxis in this situation is really treatment of low-grade active disease. It actually is probable that chemoprophylaxis is only effective when it is actually treatment of active disease, both in this situation and in treatment of a contact or tuberculin reactor.

If that is true, it becomes reasonable to ask whether or not INH alone is enough for what is really treatment of low-grade but active pulmonary tuberculosis. The only study which has raised that question is Grzybowki's.[12] He treated one group of his patients with INH alone and one with INH plus PAS. No relapses were observed with double-drug therapy, but 3 relapses were seen in the patients treated with INH alone, and in 2 of these INH resistance had developed. This constituted a relapse rate of 1,909 per 100,000. Dr. William Stead tells us that he is approaching these pulmonary lesions of unknown activity by obtaining several cultures and then putting the patients on INH, rifampin, streptomycin, and pyrazinamide for three months. If at the end of that time the cultures are negative and the chest x-ray has not changed, he stops, knowing that he has given sufficient therapy for that sort of active pulmonary tuberculosis which is both smear- and culture-negative.] ◀

18–4 **Intracranial Tuberculoma: Conservative Management.** Edward Harder, M. Zuheir Al-Kawi, and Peter Carney (Riyadh) reviewed 20 cases of intracranial tuberculoma seen between 1978 and 1980 in Saudi Arabia. Ten patients had craniotomy, followed by antituberculosis therapy, and 10 were managed medically. Corticosteroids and anticonvulsant therapy were used where necessary in both treatment groups. Most patients had symptoms for 6 months or less. Headache was the chief symptom of 12 patients. Five patients reported seizures only. A history consistent with tuberculosis was seldom obtained. Eleven patients had papilledema, 3 had hemiparesis, and 2 were ataxic. Three patients had normal neurologic findings. The computed tomographic appearances of the tuberculomas were variable. Lesions were supratentorial in 16 patients. A pretreatment bacteriologic diagnosis was made in only 2 patients.

The medically treated patients received isoniazid, ethambutol, and rifampin. Hepatitis developed within the first few weeks in 3 of 4 patients given 600–900 mg of isoniazid daily. Subsequent treatment

(18–4) Am. J. Med. 74:570–576, April 1983.

with 300 mg daily was tolerated without difficulty. Pyridoxine was given to all patients. Dexamethasone was given to all patients who were operated on and to half of those who were managed medically. Treatment lasted 3–24 months. Six medically treated patients and 1 patient who was operated on returned to normal. Six other surgical patients showed some improvement. Three medically treated patients improved and 1 remained the same.

Normal chest roentgenograms and lack of clinical evidence of extrapulmonary tuberculosis do not rule out intracranial tuberculoma. Tuberculomas appear to grow without causing the destruction that usually accompanies a malignant tumor and to resolve with minimal residual deficit. Corticosteroids rapidly counter symptoms of increased intracranial pressure in these cases, permitting conservative management. Treatment with isoniazid, ethambutol, and rifampin over 1 year is adequate. Computed tomography is useful in monitoring these patients.

▶ [CNS tuberculoma is an unusual clinical problem in the Western world, and not many people have an opportunity to gain experience with it. This large series from Saudi Arabia, where it is not rare, is accordingly welcome. The article shows that medical therapy is superior to surgical therapy when the diagnosis is known or strongly suspected. The degree of neurologic deficit at the outset of treatment was just as great in those treated medically as in the surgical group, each of which had equal numbers (4) of cases defined as "grade 3" disability (decreased level of consciousness, signs of increased intracranial pressure, and daily seizures or status epilepticus). Six of 10 medically treated patients but only 1 of 10 surgically treated patients became completely normal neurologically. The authors state that symptoms often were less than would be expected with computed tomographic (CT) scan lesions of equal size due to other pathologic processes (tumors or abscesses). The defects on CT scan were both single and multiple. They began to decrease in size by 2 months of drug treatment and were gone entirely by 12 months. Steroids were thought to be very effective in reducing edema and intracranial pressure. The authors advise trying medical therapy before resorting to surgery in cases in which the diagnosis is known and advise using biopsy followed by medical treatment rather than resection when craniotomy is required for diagnosis.

The CT scan has enlarged concepts of the pathogenesis of tuberculomas and their relationship to meningitis. One article reported that enhanced CT scan in a case of miliary disease with *no* clinical meningitis demonstrated multiple small cerebral lesions that were compatible with tuberculomas and that disappeared with treatment.[14] Another report concerned a case of meningitis with no clinical evidence of a cerebral mass. The CT scan showed multiple lesions compatible with tuberculomas and early hydrocephalus on the fifth week of illness, all of which abnormalities disappeared after 8 months of treatment.[15] It seems likely that any blood stream spread of tuberculosis may be associated with cerebral parenchymal foci which on CT scan can cast a shadow; these may involute entirely, may progress to cause symptoms of a space-occupying lesion, or may rupture into the subarachnoid space, producing meningitis.

The CT scan is also enlarging concepts concerning histoplasmosis in ways that are analogous and therefore possibly worth mentioning here. One patient seen by us this year had been taking steroids for one year on the basis of a clinical diagnosis of cerebral metastatic disease. Since the patient was a smoker, it was reasonably concluded that he either had lung cancer as a primary source or at least deserved to have it. A year later he developed a mouth ulcer, which led to the diagnosis of disseminated histoplasmosis. A craniotomy was then done, and the cerebral lesions were found to be histoplasmosis as well. There are a handful of reports, mostly in the neurosurgical literature, of mass lesions turning out to be histoplasmosis,[16] and one case like ours was reported in an osteopathic journal.[17]

Some other mycobacterial topics will be mentioned here. A lot of information about *short-course chemotherapy* was discussed in last year's YEAR BOOK.[18] This year a large British Thoracic Association study was published indicating that ethambutol (EMB) is as good as streptomycin (STM) in 4-drug chemotherapy.[19] The authors compared two groups treated with 4 drugs (one group treated with isoniazid [INH], rifampin [RMP], STM, and pyrazinamide [PZA]; and the other with INH, RMP, EMB, and PZA) for 2 months and then with INH-RMP for 4 more months. The EMB dosage was 25 mg/kg, a level at which the incidence of optic neuritis is usually stated to be 2%.[20] They also included a group treated with EMB-INH-RMP for 2 months and then INH-RMP for 7 months, the now standard treatment regimen in England. This made it possible to show that sputum conversion was definitely more prompt in PZA-containing regimens and that the incidence of hepatitis was no greater in regimens containing PZA than in those that did not. The authors noted that the occurrence of positive smears with negative cultures in the later months of treatment had some predictive value for late relapse, which was observed in 2 (14%) of 14 patients with this finding but in only 4 (1.0%) of 379 patients without it. Another good and fairly large short-course article was published from India.[21] One point of possible importance to emerge was that when the continuation phase was twice weekly (INH-RMP-STM-PZA daily for 2 months and then INH-RMP twice weekly for the remainder of the treatment), relapse was greater (5.4%) with a total of 5 months than with a total of 7 months of therapy (0%). As their purpose is economy in that area, the authors also compared a 9-month regimen without RMP (INH-STM-PZA daily for 2 months and then twice weekly for 7 more months). The results were surprisingly good. The contribution of RMP to early sputum conversion was clear, being observed in 92% at 2 months in regimens containing RMP and in only 72% at 2 months in regimens without RMP. Hepatitis occurred in 4% of patients treated with RMP-containing regimens and in only 1% of those treated without RMP. The authors made the interesting observation that arthralgias, which they observed in a large percentage (43%) of patients who received PZA without RMP, were substantially less frequent in patients receiving both PZA and RMP, and they stated that RMP enhances uric acid excretion, opposing the hyperurecemic effect of PZA. On the basis of the above information, one can conclude (1) that EMB can probably substitute for STM in the intensive 4-drug bactericidal phase of short-course chemotherapy, making it an entirely oral regimen; (2) that 5 months is too short when the continuation phase is intermittent (twice weekly); and (3) that there is increased hepatotoxicity due to RMP but not due to PZA.

Dr. Dixie Snider, in commenting on the British Thoracic Association studies, sounded a note of caution conçerning the applicability of British findings to the United States.[22] He noted that only 3% of British patients defaulted and that the median hospital stay was 55 days—as contrasted to 17% defaulters and a median stay of 12 days in this country. We strongly agree, and we believe that the major use of "ultra-short-course" chemotherapy (6 months), in our practice at least, is in the patient who cannot be trusted to take medicines without supervision. It is a major tragedy when drug resistance to both major agents (RMP and INH) develops because of irregular drug taking, a risk that is greater when the continuation phase is intermittent. It is always worth repeating that with reliable drug takers and drug-sensitive infections one cannot improve on the results of INH plus EMB for 18–24 months, "reinforced" with STM for the first 2 months in extensive disease.

Bartelink et al. report a case of *fatal hepatitis* in a patient put on INH and RMP while receiving phenobarbital and dilantin, which occurred 9 days after antituberculous chemotherapy was begun.[23] The patient also had an operation (halothane anesthesia) 2 days into treatment. They referred to another (nonfatal) case in the literature in which the patient developed severe hepatitis and coma 6 days after beginning INH and RMP while receiving maintenance anticonvulsants. The authors also quote earlier literature concerning these fulminant INH-RMP hepatic reactions in surgical patients. It seems probable to us, although not established, that both chronic therapy with other inducers of the hepatic P_{450} mixed-oxidase system such as dilantin and phenobarbital (RMP itself is a potent inducer, to which property some people have attributed the increased risk of early hepatitis in INH-RMP regimens) and surgery may constitute added hepatotoxic risks when INH and RMP are given. As mentioned, the hepatitis in such cases has been early in onset (within a week or two) and often fulminant, associated with coma. Powell-Jackson et al. believe that RMP makes the management of *steroid-dependent asthma* much more difficult, decreasing steroid half-life by 43% and doubling the dose of prednisolone required to prevent symptomatic deterioration.[24]

Three important articles concerning *nontuberculous mycobacterial disease* will be mentioned. Banks et al. report a series of 35 patients with *Mycobacterium kansasii* pulmonary disease in Britain.[25] Most of the patients were older (mean age, 52), male (31 of 35), and had underlying pulmonary disease (66%). All organisms were sensitive to RMP (but were 8 times as resistant to INH as standard *Mycobacterium tuberculosis* strains) and all got well with RMP-EMB. *M. kansasii* is the most drug susceptible of the nontuberculous mycobacteria. Smith and Citron report that *Mycobacterium zenopi* is also more drug susceptible than other "atypicals," with the exception of *M. kansasii.*[26] They studied isolates from 27 patients, 68% of which were susceptible to RMP, 73% to EMB, 59% to INH, and 77% to STM. Of the 15 patients with active disease due to the infection (the other isolates were regarded as not significant), 9 had a prolonged chronic course and 6 were acute. All those treated with at least 2 drugs to which the organism was sensitive got better. Two patients with resistant organisms remained positive throughout chemotherapy. The thermophilic character of the organism, the microepidemics attributed to contamination of hospital hot-water systems,[27] and the possibility that cases of person-to-person spread have been observed with this organism (in contrast to all other "atypicals") were mentioned. Clegg et al. have reported the problem of infections with the *Mycobacterium fortuitum* complex (*M. fortuitum* and *M. chelonei*) complicating augmentation mammaplasty, which was mentioned briefly in the 1982 Year Book.[28, 29] They had 17 cases. The incubation period (following operation) averaged 28 days but extended up to 2 years. Symptoms were only local. The discharge was odorless and contained polymorphonuclear leukocytes and sometimes gram-variable organisms called "diphtheroids" on the basis of morphology; the acid-fast stain was positive in 5 of 7 cases in which it was done, and the infection persisted in spite of reoperation and reimplantation of new prostheses. The organisms were not susceptible to the usual first- and second-line antimycobacterial drugs, and therapy with aminoglycosides, tetracyclines, and sulfa drugs was recommended although its efficacy was not demonstrated.

Lichtenstein and MacGregor have reviewed the problem of *mycobacterial infection in renal transplantation patients.*[30] They found 47 cases in the literature, including 5 of their own. Sixty-six percent were due to *M. tuberculosis,* the others being distributed among several different mycobacterial species. Forty-three percent of the *M. tuberculosis* cases were disseminated. The mean interval between transplantation and emergence of disease was 17 months. The authors calculated an overall incidence of about 500 per 100,000 and recommended chemoprophylaxis when either donor or recipient was tuberculin positive. Others, including ourselves, would not so recommend, given the fact that the incidence of hepatotoxicity due to INH is about that figure in normal persons. Haanaes and Bergmann take issue with the notion that *tuberculin-positive individuals on steroids necessarily require chemoprophylaxis* and review such data as are available.[31] Kitrou et al. have observed *hypercalcemia in 24 of 50 consecutive tuberculosis patients on therapy.*[32] They state that it peaks 3 weeks after initiation of drug treatment. This subject, together with the interesting literature concerning hypercalcemia in infectious granulomatous disease, was discussed in the 1981 YEAR BOOK.[33]] ◄

Chapter 18 References

1. *1979—Tuberculosis in the United States.* Atlanta, Centers for Disease Control, 1979, p. 40.
2. Carpenter J.L., Covelli H.D., Avant M.E., et al.: Drug resistant *Mycobacterium tuberculosis* in Korean isolates. *Ann. Rev. Respir. Dis.* 128:1092, 1982.
3. Byrd R.B., Fisk D.E., Roethe R.A., et al.: Tuberculosis in Oriental immigrants: a study in military dependents. *Chest* 76:136, 1979.
4. Pitchenik A.E., Russell B.W., Cleary T., et al.: The prevalence of tuberculosis and drug resistance among Haitians. *N. Engl. J. Med.* 307:162, 1982.

5. Glassroth J., Robins A.G., Snider D.E. Jr.: Tuberculosis in the 1980s. *N. Engl. J. Med.* 301:1441, 1980.
6. Stead W.W.: Tuberculosis among elderly persons: an outbreak in a nursing home. *Ann. Intern. Med.* 94:606, 1981.
7. 1982 YEAR BOOK OF MEDICINE, pp. 189–192.
8. Grzybowski S.: The value and limitations of the tuberculin test. *S. Afr. Med. J.* 62:19, 1982.
9. Grzybowski S., Allen E.A.: The challenge of tuberculosis in decline: a study based on the epidemiology of tuberculosis in Ontario, Canada. *Am. Rev. Respir. Dis.* 90:709, 1964.
10. Slavin R.E., Walsh T.J., Pollack A.D.: Late generalized tuberculosis: clinical pathologic analysis and comparison of 100 cases in preantibiotic and antibiotic eras. *Medicine* 59:352, 1980.
11. 1981 YEAR BOOK OF MEDICINE, pp. 187–190.
12. Grzybowski S., Ashley M.J., McKinnon N.E., et al.: A trial of chemoprophylaxis in inactive tuberculosis. *Can. Med. Assoc. J.* 101:81, 1969.
13. Falk A., Fuchs G.F.: Prophylaxis with isoniazid in inactive tuberculosis: a Veterans Administration Cooperative Study XII. *Chest* 76:44, 1978.
14. Witham R.R., Johnson R.H., Roberts D.L.: Diagnosis of miliary tuberculosis by cerebral computerized tomography. *Arch. Intern. Med.* 139:479, 1979.
15. Stevens D.L., Everett E.D.: Sequential computerized axial tomography in tuberculous meningitis. *JAMA* 239:642, 1978.
16. Vakill S., Eble J.H., Richomond B.D., et al.: Cerebral histoplasmoma: case report. *J. Neurosurg.* 59:332, 1983.
17. Dubes R.D., Schnitzer M.: Histoplasmosis appearing as multiple mass lesions of the brain: report of a case. *J. Am. Osteopath. Assoc.* 81:554, 1982.
18. 1983 YEAR BOOK OF MEDICINE, pp. 183–185.
19. British Thoracic Association: A controlled trial of six months chemotherapy in pulmonary tuberculosis. *Am. Rev. Respir. Dis.* 126:460, 1982.
20. Citron K.M.: Ethambutol: a review with special reference to ocular toxicity. *Tubercle* 51:32, 1969.
21. Tuberculosis Research Center: Study of chemotherapy regimens of 5 and 7 months duration and the role of corticosteroids in the treatment of sputum-positive patients with pulmonary tuberculosis in south India. *Tubercle* 64:73, 1983.
22. Snider D.E. Jr.: A controlled trial of six months chemotherapy in pulmonary tuberculosis. *Am. Rev. Respir. Dis.* 127:254, 1983.
23. Bartelink A.K.M., Lenders, J.W.M., van Herwaarden C.L.A., et al.: Fatal hepatitis after treatment with isoniazid and rifampicin in a patient on anticonvulsant therapy. *Tubercle* 64:125, 1983.
24. Powell-Jackson R.R., Gray B.J., Heaton R.M., et al.: Adverse effect of rifampicin administration on steroid-dependent asthma. *Am. Rev. Respir. Dis.* 128:307, 1983.
25. Banks J., Hunter A.M., Campbell I.A., et al.: Pulmonary infection with *Mycobacterium kansasii* in Wales, 1970–9: review of treatment and response. *Thorax* 38:271, 1983.
26. Smith M.J., Citron K.M.: Clinical review of pulmonary disease caused by *Mycobacterium xenopi. Thorax* 38:373, 1983.
27. Costrini A.M., Mahler D.A., Gross W.M., et al.: Clinical and roentgenographic features of nosocomial pulmonary disease due to *Mycobacterium xenopi. Am. Rev. Respir. Dis.* 123:104, 1981.
28. Clegg H.W., Foster M.T., Sanders W.E. Jr., et al.: Infection due to organisms of the *Mycobacterium fortuitum* complex after augmentation mam-

maplasty: clinical and epidemiologic features. *J. Infect. Dis.* 147:427, 1983.
29. 1982 YEAR BOOK OF MEDICINE, p. 197.
30. Lichtenstein I.H., MacGregor R.R.: Mycobacterial infections in renal transplant recipients: report of five cases and review of literature. *Rev. Infect. Dis.* 5:216, 1983.
31. Haanaes O.C., Bergmann A.: Tuberculosis emerging in patients treated with corticosteroids. *Eur. J. Respir. Dis.* 64:294, 1983.
32. Kitrou M.P., Phytou-Palikari, A., Tzannes S.E., et al.: Serum calcium during chemotherapy for active pulmonary tuberculosis. *Eur. J. Respir. Dis.* 64:347, 1983.
33. 1981 YEAR BOOK OF MEDICINE, pp. 196–198.

19. Other Infections

19–1 **Treatment of Systemic Mycoses With Ketoconazole: Emphasis on Toxicity and Clinical Response in 52 Patients.** The National Institute of Allergy and Infectious Diseases Collaborative Antifungal Study, a phase-II evaluation, is reported by William E. Dismukes, Alan M. Stamm, John R. Graybill, Philip C. Craven, David A. Stevens, Robert L. Stiller, George A. Sarosi, Gerald Medoff, Clark R. Gregg, Harry A. Gallis, Branch T. Fields, Jr., Robert L. Marier, Thomas A. Kerkering, Lisa G. Kaplowitz, Gretchen Cloud, Cyndi Bowles, and Smith Shadomy. Ketoconazole, an oral imidazole anti-

TABLE 1.—Sites of Involvement

	Lung	Bone and Joint	Skin and Soft Tissue	Disseminated	Total
			n(%)		
Blastomycosis	8	2	3	3	16 (31)
Coccidioidomycosis	4	2	5	2	13 (25)
Cryptococcosis	3	1	3	...	7 (13)
Histoplasmosis	5	...	2	1	8 (16)
Sporotrichosis	...	4	3	...	7 (13)
Blastomycosis and coccidioidomycosis	...	...	...	1	1 (2)
Total	20(38.5)	9(17)	16(31)	7(13.5)	52(100)

(Courtesy of Dismukes, W.E., et al.: Ann. Intern. Med. 98:13–20, January 1983.)

TABLE 2.—Adverse Effects of Ketoconazole in 52 Patients

Adverse Effect	Patients
	n(%)
No adverse effect	35(67)
Nausea, vomiting, or anorexia	11(21)
Skin rash	2 (4)
Photophobia	1 (2)
Paresthesias	1 (2)
Abdominal discomfort	1 (2)
Gingival bleeding	1 (2)
Gynecomastia	1 (2)
Hepatic dysfunction	1 (2)
Thrombocytopenia	1 (2)
Adverse effects leading to termination of therapy	3 (6)

(Courtesy of Dismukes, W.E., et al.: Ann. Intern. Med. 98:13–20, January 1983.)

(19–1) Ann. Intern. Med. 98:13–20, January 1983.

TABLE 3.—OUTCOME AFTER TREATMENT FOR SPECIFIC MYCOSIS

Outcome	Patients with						All Patients
	Blastomycosis	Coccidioidomycosis	Cryptococcosis	Histoplasmosis	Sporotrichosis	Blastomycosis and Coccidioidomycosis	
	n						*n*(%)
Cured	7	...	3	5	1	...	16 (31)
Improved	...	7*	2	1	1†	...	11 (21)
Failed	4	4	2	1	3	...	14 (27)
Relapsed	5	2	...	1	2	1‡	11 (21)
Total	16	13	7	8	7	1	52(100)

*Two patients remain on ketoconazole therapy.
†Patient remains on ketoconazole therapy.
‡Although blastomycosis in this patient was cured, the patient had a relapse of coccidioidomycosis; thus, the patient is considered as having had a relapse.
(Courtesy of Dismukes, W.E., et al.: Ann. Intern. Med. 98:13–20, January 1983.)

fungal agent, is potentially preferable to amphotericin B because of less toxicity, ease of long-term administration to outpatients, and a broad spectrum of antifungal activity. It was evaluated in 52 patients with systemic mycoses, most commonly blastomycosis and nonmeningeal coccidioidomycosis. Sites of involvement are given in Table 1. The mean patient age was 44 years. Pregnant women and patients with moderate or severe liver disease were excluded from the study. Treatment began with 200 mg of ketoconazole daily in most instances. The maximum daily dose was 600 mg. Seven patients were treated for longer than a year, and 3 remain on ketoconazole therapy.

Toxicity from ketoconazole was minimal (Table 2). Treatment was stopped in 3 cases because of possible adverse reactions. The serum triglycerides were significantly elevated after treatment for 3 months or longer. The results are given in Table 3. Cure or improvement was obtained in 52% of cases. Primary failure occurred in 27% of cases, and 21% of patients relapsed after ketoconazole therapy was discontinued. The outcome did not correlate significantly with the susceptibility of the pretreatment fungal isolate to ketoconazole. Prolonged treatment appeared to be beneficial.

Ketoconazole seems to be a well-tolerated antifungal agent with minimal toxicity. It holds promise as an alternative to amphotericin B in the treatment of histoplasmosis and nonmeningeal cryptococcosis, but its role in patients with blastomycosis and nonmeningeal coccidioidomycosis requires further study. Ketoconazole acts as a fungistatic, not a fungicidal, agent. The outcome of treatment has not been predictable from the results of in vitro susceptibility testing.

▶ [Ketoconazole is not as strong a drug as amphotericin for the treatment of systemic mycoses, but it has the advantage of being suitable for long-term administration by mouth. In spite of the published data, the editors have some reservation about its use in histoplasmosis. Chronic pulmonary histoplasmosis is such a complicated process that it is really difficult to be certain that amphotericin itself substantially modifies its course and prognosis.[1] Disseminated histoplasmosis is a disease spectrum ranging from an extremely long-term chronic process measured in years to an acute overwhelming illness fatal in weeks. In the latter we would be very hesitant to depend on less than maximal therapy. Although ketoconazole has been only moderately successful in coccidioidomycosis overall, and CNS levels are very low at usual (400 ng/day) doses, one recent study has claimed good results in treating 5 patients who had coccidioidal meningitis with prolonged high-dose (1,200 mg/day) ketoconazole.[2] If this is so, it will be a major advance over intrathecal amphotericin therapy.

Ketoconazole is the agent of choice in mucocutaneous candidiasis in patients with immunodeficiency syndromes. It is better than amphotericin in this situation because it can be given by mouth indefinitely.[3] It has been reported to produce effective maintenance prophylaxis against fungal infections in immunocompromised hosts.[4] Good results have been reported treating candidal esophagitis with low doses (200 mg) for a period of only two or three weeks.[5, 6] Ketoconazole is very good for dermatomycoses.[7]

The trivial complications are outlined in Table 2 above. The most significant one is hepatitis. Its incidence has been estimated at 1 per 10,000, but that is a soft figure and probably underestimates the problem. Fatalities have been observed, and monitoring the liver function tests is recommended. The most interesting complication is endocrinological. Gynecomastia, which occurs in a fairly large proportion, and decreased libido have been attributed to interference with testosterone synthesis. This side effect has been used therapeutically in disseminated prostatic cancer; one patient treated with high-dose (400 mg every 8 hours) ketoconazole demonstrated a fall in testosterone levels from 562 ng/dl to 53 ng/dl (castrate range) in 48 hours associated with prompt relief of bone pain.[8] Cortisol levels are also lowered by a now well-worked-out mechanism.[9, 10]

The drug inhibits mitochondrial P_{450}-dependent enzymes.[9] Accordingly a number of clinically important drug-drug interactions will probably emerge. One significant one is increase in the level of cyclosporin caused by ketoconazole. This has resulted in nephrotoxicity in some renal transplant patients.[11] An antabuse-like reaction has also been reported.[5]] ◀

19–2 **Diagnostic Laboratory Tests for Histoplasmosis: Analysis of Experience in a Large Urban Outbreak.** Histoplasmosis frequently is difficult to diagnose. Joseph Wheat, Morris L. V. French, Richard B. Kohler, Sarah E. Zimmerman, Warren R. Smith, James A. Norton, Harold E. Eitzen, Coy D. Smith and Thomas G. Slama (Indianapolis) evaluated standard diagnostic tests in the course of a large outbreak of histoplasmosis occurring in Indianapolis in 1978 and 1979. Of 495 patients reported, the cases of 276 whose serologic tests were done at a single laboratory were analyzed. Control subjects included young adults and older adults without pulmonary disease and patients with pulmonary disease.

Peak yeast-phase complement fixation (CF) titers are given in Table 1, and mycelial-phase titers in Table 2. Nearly 95% of all patients had CF titers of 1:8 or greater to at least 1 of the antigens, and 71% had titers of 1:32 or higher. Immunodiffusion testing was more often positive in patients with disseminated disease (Table 3). Weak serologic responses occurred more often in immunosuppressed patients (Table 4). Fungal cultures were positive in nearly two thirds of patients with cavitary disease and in three fourths of those with disseminated disease (Table 5). The histologic findings are given in Table 6. Extrapulmonary granulomas were present in more than half the patients with disseminated histoplasmosis, but in only about 10% of the other patients.

Isolation of *Histoplasma capsulatum* is the strongest evidence for histoplasmosis, but cultures often are negative, and usually require 2–4 weeks for identification even when positive. Complement fixation testing has been more sensitive than immunodiffusion testing in cases of subclinical infection. Serologic titers are higher in patients with cavitary disease, and tend to be higher in blacks and in immunocompetent patients. Fourfold increases or falls in titers have not been of prognostic significance. Further study is needed to determine whether persistently high titers are related to the development of late complications of the disease.

▶ [The article abstracted above and the one that appears below are two of the several more detailed reports that have followed the initial description of the large "epidemic" of acute pulmonary histoplasmosis in Indianapolis.[12] It is important to be reminded that clinically significant histoplasmosis undoubtedly occurs far more often than is recognized, both as sporadic cases and in small epidemics. Since symptoms are nonspecific, diagnosis depends first of all on constant awareness of the possibility of histoplasmosis in any febrile illness in endemic areas. If histoplasmosis is a reasonable consideration and particularly if a possible history of exposure is elicited, a chest x-ray showing scattered small infiltrates and/or mediastinal lymphadenopathy and a significantly positive histoplasmin complement fixation test are the most help-

---

(19–2) Ann. Intern. Med. 97:680–685, November 1982.

TABLE 1.—HIGHEST YEAST-PHASE COMPLEMENT FIXATION TITERS IN PATIENTS WITH DIFFERENT CLINICAL FORMS OF HISTOPLASMOSIS

Yeast-Phase Complement Fixation Titer	Noncavitary pulmonary (n = 176)	Pericardial (n = 23)	Rheumatologic (n = 12)	Histoplasmosis Asymptomatic (n = 29)	Cavitary (n = 15)	Disseminated (n = 21)	Total (n = 276)
				n patients (%)			
≤8	25 (14.2)	3	2	4	9	9	52 (18.8)
8	16 (9.1)	1	1	6	0	1	25 (9.1)
16	20 (11.4)	5	2	4	2	2	35 (12.7)
32	34 (19.3)	3	0	10	1	2	50 (18.1)
64	39 (22.2)	7	1	4	2	3	56 (20.3)
128	27 (15.3)	2	5	1	1	3	39 (14.1)
256	14 (8.0)	2	1	0	0	0	17 (6.2)
512	1 (0.6)	0	0	0	0	1	2 (0.7)
1024	0	0	0	0	0	0	0

*For purposes of statistical analysis, noncavitary pulmonary, pericardial, and rheumatologic groups were combined as self-limiting symptomatic histoplasmosis. Yeast-phase titers were lower in the cavitary, disseminated, and asymptomatic groups (P = .0008).

(Courtesy of Wheat, J., et al.: Ann. Intern. Med. 97:680–685, November 1982.)

TABLE 2.—HIGHEST MYCELIAL-PHASE COMPLEMENT FIXATION TITERS IN PATIENTS WITH DIFFERENT CLINICAL FORMS OF HISTOPLASMOSIS

Mycelial-Phase Complement Fixation Titer	Histoplasmosis						
	Noncavitary Pulmonary (n = 176)	Pericardial (n = 23)	Rheumatologic (n = 12)	Asymptomatic (n = 29)	Cavitary (n = 15)	Disseminated (n = 21)	Total (n = 276)
				n patients (%)			
≤8	38 (21.6)†	5	3	11	1	4	62 (22.2)
8	19 (10.8)	5	1	9	2	5	41 (14.9)
16	33 (18.8)	2	3	4	3	1	46 (16.7)
32	23 (13.1)	4	2	1	1	4	35 (12.7)
64	28 (15.9)	3	2	2	3	1	39 (14.1)
128	18 (10.2)	1	1	1	4	3	28 (10.1)
256	11 (6.3)	3	0	1	1	2	18 (6.5)
512	5 (2.8)	0	0	0	0	0	5 (1.8)
1024	1 (0.6)	0	0	0	0	1	2 (0.7)

*For purposes of statistical analysis, noncavitary pulmonary, pericardial, and rheumatologic groups were combined as self-limiting symptomatic histoplasmosis. Patients with cavitary histoplasmosis tended to have higher titers, and asymptomatic patients and those with disseminated infection tended to have lower titers than those in the self-limiting symptomatic histoplasmosis group (P = .008).

(Courtesy of Wheat, J., et al.: Ann. Intern. Med. 97:680–685, November 1982.)

TABLE 3.—IMMUNODIFFUSION RESULTS IN PATIENTS WITH DIFFERENT CLINICAL FORMS OF HISTOPLASMOSIS

Histoplasmosis Syndrome	Total Patients	Patients with M Band	M and H Bands	Neither M nor H Bands
			n	
Noncavitary pulmonary	176	131	19	26
Pericardial	23	15	3	5
Rheumatologic	12	7	3	2
Asymptomatic	29	16	1	12
Cavitary	15	15	0	0
Disseminated	21	12	5	4

*Patients with asymptomatic histoplasmosis had a lower positivity rate, and those with disseminated infection had a higher frequency of H-precipitin bands ($P = .0023$).

(Courtesy of Wheat, J., et al.: Ann. Intern. Med. 97:680–685, November 1982.)

ful findings leading to the clinical diagnosis. The experience with diagnostic laboratory tests in Indianapolis is reported in the article abstracted above and is summarized in the tables. The complement fixation test has generally proved to be the most useful diagnostic laboratory test. However, if one combines the first four columns of Tables 1 and 2, it is apparent that there is a small (perhaps 5%–10%) group of false negative tests to both antigens, and the remainder vary widely in titer with either antigen. Since titers of 1:8 and 1:16 (and rarely 1:32) can sometimes represent old rather than recent infections, this range must be considered as only suggestive diagnostically. The range of 1:32 and higher (71% in this series) is generally regarded as highly suggestive. It should be noted that less than an average of 2 tests per patient were obtained in this study. A larger number of samples during the first 8–10 weeks after onset would have undoubtedly revealed a somewhat higher percentage of titers of 1:32 or above. Aside from the diagnostic value of a significantly high titer, a four-fold increase in titer at any level is regarded as highly suggestive. For this purpose it is necessary to obtain a baseline specimen within 2–3 weeks of onset of illness and a subsequent specimen 6–10 weeks after onset.

Table 6 merits some comment. The number of cases of disseminated histoplasmosis reported from Indianapolis in nonimmunosuppressed individuals is unexpectedly high. In our opinion, the low incidence of organisms (2/16 and 0/11) in liver and bone marrow biopsies in cases diagnosed as disseminated histoplasmosis is more in keeping with extrapulmonary organized granulomas found in many persons living in endemic areas than with the histologic picture of histiocytes containing large numbers of organisms, which is characteristic of progressive disseminated disease. One series of consecutive autopsies in Cincinnati demonstrated splenic and hepatic calcifications often containing *H. capsulatum* organisms in 43 of 92 patients dying from unrelated causes.[13] Such foci are undoubtedly established in the preallergic phase of both symptomatic and asymptomatic infections and are only incidental findings.

Some other articles on the diagnosis of fungal disease which have appeared this year merit comment. Warlick and his associates have shown that cytologic preparations are more sensitive than potassium hydroxide preparations in demonstration of spherules of *Coccidiodes immitis* in sputum[14]; they recommend the use of both tests for rapid diagnosis of pulmonary coccidioidomycosis. Cytologic techniques were recently recommended as the best method for diagnosis of pulmonary blastomycosis.[15] Penn and associates have provided a good up-to-date review of the use of serologic tests in invasive fungal infections, including aspergillosis, blastomycosis, candidiasis, coccidioidomycosis, cryptococcosis, and histoplasmosis.[16]] ◀

TABLE 4.—FACTORS INFLUENCING COMPLEMENT FIXATION TITERS AND FUNGAL IMMUNODIFFUSION TEST RESULTS

Factor	Total Patients	Patients with Complement Fixation Titer ≥ 1:64*		Patients with Fungal† Immunodiffusion	
		Yeast	Mycelial	M Band	M and H Band
			n (%)		
Residence					
Inner city	125	53(42.4)	49(39.2)	95(76.0)	12(9.6)
Outer city	140	56(40.0)	49(27.9)‡	93(66.4)	19(13.6)
Age					
≤ 35 years	213	99(46.4) ‖	69(32.4)	156(73.2)	22(10.3)
≥ 36 years	62	14(22.5)	22(35.5)	39(62.9)	9(14.5)
Race					
Black	173	86(49.7)	74(42.8)	130(75.2)	22(12.7)
White	98	25(25.5)	17(17.3) ‖	61(62.2)	9(9.2)‡
Immunosuppression					
Yes	18	3	2	10	2
No	258	111(43.0)§	90(34.9)‡	186(72.0)	29(11.2)
Duration of illness					
< 8 weeks	111	55(49.5)	33(26.4)	76(68.5)	13(11.7)
≥ 8 weeks	68	30(44.1)	31(45.5)§	49(72.1)	10(14.7)
Culture					
Positive	24	8	11	15	5
Negative	86	39(45.3)	29(33.7)	57(66.3)	11(12.8)

*Analysis of complement fixation response compares the frequency of titers of 1:64 or greater to the yeast or mycelial antigens in groups created by the factors listed in the left-hand column using the Fisher's exact test for 2 × 2 tables.

†For analysis of the response in the immunodiffusion assay, P values were calculated using contingency χ^2 statistic for 2 × 3 tables for these serologic groups: M band only, M and H band, neither M nor H band.

‡$P < .05$.

§$P < .025$.

¶$P < .0001$.

(Courtesy of Wheat, J., et al.: Ann. Intern. Med. 97:680–685, November 1982.)

TABLE 5.—FUNGAL CULTURES IN PATIENTS WITH ACUTE HISTOPLASMOSIS

Culture Source	Patients with Clinical Syndrome of Histoplasmosis		
	Noncavitary Pulmonary, Pericarditis, Rheumatologic, Asymptomatic	Cavitary	Disseminated
	n positive/n tested		
Sputum	7/72	9/16	5/7
Bronchial washing	0/35	3/5	0/1
Pleural fluid	0/9	0/2	1/4
Lung	3/14	2/3	1/4
Lymph nodes	1/9	ND	1/2
Pericardial fluid	0/7	ND	ND
Pericardium	0/4	ND	ND
Bone marrow	0/16	1/4	9/14
Liver	0/2	ND	1/3
Cerebrospinal fluid	0/13	0/1	1/11
Urine	0/5	0/1	0/2
Blood	0/15	0/1	4/10
Any site	11/128	11/17	15/20

**ND*, not done.
(Courtesy of Wheat, J., et al.: Ann. Intern. Med. 97:680–685, November 1982.)

19–3 **Pericarditis as a Manifestation of Histoplasmosis During Two Large Urban Outbreaks.** Only 55 cases of pericarditis that complicated the course of histoplasmosis have been reported. Lawrence J. Wheat, Leon Stein, Betty C. Corya, Justin L. Wass, James A. Norton, Kathy Grider, Thomas G. Slama, Morris L. French, and Richard B. Kohler reviewed data on 712 cases of histoplasmosis in two large outbreaks in Indianapolis, including 45 (6.3%) patients who presented with pericarditis. Pericarditis occurred more often in immunocompetent than in immunosuppressed patients.

Findings in the 38 evaluated patients are listed in Table 1. Respiratory illness preceded the pericarditis in most cases. Characteristics of the pericardial fluid are given in Table 2. Peak complement fixation titers were present initially in 18 of 23 patients (Table 3), and 5 patients had a fourfold or greater rise.

Pericarditis usually was a late feature of histoplasmosis in these patients. The clinical features of pericarditis usually resolved within 2 weeks of admission. Nine patients developed pericardial tamponade and required intensive care. More than 40% of all patients with pericarditis had some evidence of hemodynamic compromise, either hypotension or pulsus paradoxus. Most patients responded to bed rest and antiinflammatory drugs. Corticosteroids were given to some patients for less than a month and did not appear to cause progression of pericarditis or dissemination of disease. None of the 16 patients

(19–3) Medicine (Baltimore) 62:110–119, March 1983.

TABLE 6.—HISTOPATHOLOGIC EXAMINATION OF TISSUES IN PATIENTS WITH HISTOPLASMOSIS

Tissue	Noncavitary Pulmonary, Pericarditis, Rheumatologic, or Asymptomatic Histoplasmosis		Cavitary Histoplasmosis		Disseminated Histoplasmosis	
	Granulomas	*H. capsulatum*	Granulomas	*H. capsulatum*	Granulomas	*H. capsulatum*
			n positive/n tested			
Lung	20/34	13/34	1/2	0/2	1/1	1/1
Intrathoracic lymph node	17/19	9/19			2/2	0/2
Bone marrow	0/24	0/24	0/3	0/3	7/16	2/16
Liver	4/9	0/9			7/12	0/11
Other	4/24	2/24			1/1	1/1

(Courtesy of Wheat, J., et al.: Ann. Intern. Med. 97:680–685, November 1982.)

TABLE 1.—CLINICAL AND LABORATORY FINDINGS

Clinical findings	Positive/ total	%
Preceding pulmonary illness	24/38	63.2
Pericardial pain	36/38	94.7
Fever	30/38	78.9
Pericardial friction rub	29/38	76.3
Pulsus paradoxus ≥10 mm Hg	12/38	38.6
Jugular venous distension	10/38	26.3
Systolic blood pressure <100 mm Hg	13/38	34.2
Elevation sedimentation rate	28/30	93.3
Elevation alkaline phosphatase	15/30	50.0
Elevation SGOT	11/31	35.4
Elevation CPK	6/19	31.5
Anemia, ≤12 g	22/38	57.9
Electrocardiogram:		
ST segment elevation	25/38	65.8
ST segment depression	3/38	7.9
T wave depression	26/38	68.4
T wave flattening	2/38	5.2
PR segment depression	16/38	42.1
QRS alternans	2/38	5.2
Normal	1/38	2.6
Echocardiogram:		
Pericardial effusion	32/38	84.2
Pericardial thickening	7/38	18.4
"Swinging heart"	2/38	5.2
Normal	5/38	13.1

(Courtesy of Wheat, L.J., et al.: Medicine (Baltimore) 62:110–119, March 1983.)

reevaluated a year or more after the initial episode had recurrent or constrictive pericarditis.

Pericarditis may occur as a late complication of histoplasmosis in outbreaks of the disease. Risk factors for the complication include young age, immunocompetence, and male sex in those aged 20–39 years. The course usually is benign, but tamponade and constrictive pericarditis may develop. A noninfectious inflammatory basis for pericarditis in this setting seems likely. Histoplasmosis should be considered in patients presenting with pericarditis in endemic areas, especially when it is associated with intrathoracic adenopathy. Follow-up is necessary to detect late constriction.

▶ [This is, in our opinion, the most interesting study to come out of the Indianapolis experience with acute pulmonary histoplasmosis. It almost doubles the number of cases of histoplasma pericarditis reported in the medical literature. It is quite clear that the majority of the 45 cases, largely diagnosed by physicians in the community, would not have been recognized without the knowledge that there was an "epidemic" of acute histoplasmosis in their midst. Since the process tends to resolution without therapy, it is certain that many such cases occur and are not recognized in other endemic areas.

It is likely that the pathogenesis is spread to the pericardium from a contiguous infected lymph node, as is thought to be usually the case with tuberculous pericarditis. In most cases it appears that only an acute fibrinous pericarditis is induced, but in some it is likely that the lymph node breaks down and empties antigenic material and viable organisms into the pericardium resulting in a granulomatous pericarditis. The pericardial infection per se is not progressive, and the inflammatory reaction, whether fibrinous or granulomatous, is self-limited. A characteristic feature emphasized in this study was the latent period, averaging six weeks, between the onset of

TABLE 2.—PERICARDIAL FLUID ANALYSIS IN HISTOPLASMAL PERICARDITIS

No.	RBC/mm^3	WBC/mm^3	%PMN	Protein, g/dl	LDH, units
1	775,000	30,200	91	6.5	500
2	3,750	5,250	40	—	—
3	4,080	552	36	—	1235
4	90,000	6,900	27	5.6	500
5	6,050	2,020	24	6.0	772
6	3,400	1,080	89*	6.4	—

*Forty percent were bond forms.

(Courtesy of Wheat, L.J., et al.: Medicine (Baltimore) 62:110–119, March 1983.)

TABLE 3.—SEROLOGIC EVIDENCE FOR HISTOPLASMOSIS

Complement fixation titers

Titer	Highest mycelial	Highest yeast	Highest yeast or mycelial*
<1:8	8	7	1
1:8	8	2	1
1:16	2	10	7
1:32	10	7	9
1:64	4	6	10
1:128	4	3	6
≥1:256	2	3	4
Total	38	38	38

Immunodiffusion test

	No.	%
M band	25	69.4
M + H band	4	11.1
Neither	7	19.51
Total	36	100

*Patient distribution using highest titer to either the yeast or mycelial antigen. For example, 8 patients had titers of <1:8 to the yeast antigen, 7 had titers of <1:8 to the mycelial antigen, but only 1 had titers of <1:8 to both antigens, and that patient had an M band by immunodiffusion.

(Courtesy of Wheat, L.J., et al.: Medicine (Baltimore) 62:110–119, March 1983.)

the acute pulmonary illness and symptoms of pericarditis. Once considered, diagnosis can be reasonably firmly established by the demonstration of a significant complement fixation titer or a fourfold increase in titer. Mediastinal adenopathy is usually visible on x-ray, which is a helpful diagnostic point.

Previous case reports had tended to emphasize the severity of histoplasma pericarditis. The great value of this article is the demonstration that it is actually usually benign. A few years ago the editors evaluated all reported cases and found that 14% went on to constriction. There was only one case (of 45) that progressed to constriction in the abstracted report, making it clear that the severity of the process, as previously construed, was actually a result of looking at only the most severe cases. The real figure is probably even lower than the 2% in this series, since the mildest cases are apt to escape detection entirely.

No controlled analysis of treatment approaches was possible in the reported experience. The authors recommend the use of nonsteroidal antiinflammatory agents (aspirin or indomethacin) in most cases and use corticosteroids only in those patients demonstrating tamponade. We would add that resection of a small part of the pericardium and drainage of the fluid through a subxiphoid incision is a very benign procedure providing a very high level of diagnostic certainty and usually solving problems of tamponade and constriction (we believe) as well. We prefer this to administration of corticosteroids in situations in which etiologic diagnosis is less than certain.] ◀

19–4 **Pulmonary Aspergilloma: Analysis of Prognosis in Relation to Hemoptysis and Survey of Treatment.** Jonathan Jewkes, Philip H. Kay, Mathias Paneth, and Kenneth M. Citron reviewed the records of 85 patients seen at Brompton Hospital, London, in 1956–1980 with pulmonary aspergilloma. The 53 men and 32 women had a mean age at diagnosis of 45 years. The most common preceding lung lesion, present in 24 patients, was an open healed tuberculous cavity (Table 1). Skin testing with *Aspergillus fumigatus* extract gave an immediate positive response in 39 (70%) of 56 patients tested. Ten patients had allergic bronchopulmonary asperigillosis. Most aspergillomas were in the upper lobes. Nineteen (22%) patients had more than 1 lesion.

Spontaneous resolution of the aspergilloma was observed in 2 patients. Among the 72 patients followed up for 5 years or longer, mortality was 31% at 5 years and 56% at 10 years. Causes of death are listed in Table 2. Three (7%) of 41 patients died after pulmonary resection. Sixty-six (78%) patients had hemoptysis at some time. Steroids were given to 10 patients, and specific antifungal agents to 33. Ten patients had antifungal drugs instilled directly into the cavity.

TABLE 1.—PREEXISTING PULMONARY DISEASE IN 85 PATIENTS WITH ASPERGILLOMA

Disease		*No of patients*
Healed pulmonary tuberculosis		24
Mycobacterium kansasii infection		3
Sarcoidosis		10
Allergic bronchopulmonary aspergillosis		10
Bronchiectasis		6
Pneumonia and lung abscess		8
Idiopathic upper lobe fibrosis and/or cavitation		13
Associated with rheumatoid arthritis	2	
ankylosing spondylitis	2*	
Marfan's syndrome	2†	
No other disease present	7	
Miscellaneous		6
Pulmonary infarction	2	
Polyarteritis	1	
Fibrosing mediastinitis	1	
Eosinophilic granuloma	1	
Bullous emphysema	1	
No known pre-existing pulmonary disease		5
Total		85

*One former patient with a lung abscess also had ankylosing spondylitis.

†Two further patients who had tuberculosis also had Marfan's syndrome.

(Courtesy of Jewkes, J., et al.: Thorax 38:572–578, August 1983.)

(19–4) Thorax 38:572–578, August 1983.

TABLE 2.—CAUSES OF DEATH AMONG 85 PATIENTS WITH ASPERGILLOMA

Cause of death		*No of patients*
Respiratory disease other than aspergilloma		17
Acute pneumonia	6	
Chronic suppurative pneumonia*	5	
Chronic respiratory insufficiency	6	
After surgery for aspergilloma		7
Pulmonary resection	3	
Cavernostomy	4	
Bleeding from aspergilloma		3
Non-respiratory causes		9
Not known		5
Total deaths		41

(Courtesy of Jewkes, J., et al.: Thorax 38:572–578, August 1983.)

Results of treatment and relation to the severity of hemoptysis are shown in Table 3. Patients who had pulmonary resection lived longer than those who were managed medically (Fig 19–1). It appears that resection would have been feasible in 12 of the 17 medically treated patients.

The better survival rate of patients in this series who had an operation may reflect the selection of patients with better lung function and more localized pulmonary disease for operation. Resection of aspergilloma should be restricted to patients having severe hemoptysis and adequate pulmonary function. Cavernostomy is hazardous in patients unsuited for resection. If bronchial artery embolization fails in patients with major hemoptysis who are unfit for resection, cavernostomy may need to be attempted despite the high operative risk.

▶ [Attitudes concerning treatment of aspergillomas have become increasingly conservative.[17] A recent review by Glimp and Bayer collected 208 cases, 110 of which were resected.[18] The operative mortality was 8.2%, and 24.5% of patients had major complications. The high complication rate is due to the fact that almost all patients have serious underlying lung disease, and in addition there is almost always marked pleural thickening over an aspergilloma. The opinion expressed in the review by Glimp and Bayer was that resection should be reserved for those with major hemoptysis. They quoted Faulkner's paper,[17] which recounted data on 31 patients followed without operation. Twenty-four had hemoptysis, 13 severe in degree; 3 had recurrent hemoptysis; and only 1 died. Glimp and Bayer also discussed in some detail an article outlining the special and surgically quite difficult problem of aspergilloma in advanced sarcoidosis.[19]

The article abstracted above, which was not included in the review by Glimp and Bayer, is the largest series of cases from a single hospital that we know of. It is widely assumed, perhaps incorrectly, that the only way aspergillomas can cause trouble is from hemoptysis, and the data are analyzed from that point of view. Twenty-four of the patients had "frank hemoptysis," defined as expectoration of less than 150 cc of pure blood (in other words, more than blood streaking). Half of these 24 went on to "major hemoptysis" (greater than 150 cc) in 6 months to 2 years. Of 8 patients with "major hemoptysis" who were not treated by surgery, 3 (37%) died from subsequent hemoptysis, 3 died of unrelated disease, and 2 lived for at least 10 years. The other causes of death would not be expected to be modified favorably by surgery, and at least one very important one, respiratory insufficiency, would probably be made worse thereby. The forbidding surgical mortality they noted with cavernostomy is useful information, as is the generally poor result of intracavitary instillation of fun-

TABLE 3.—RESULTS OF TREATMENT ACCORDING TO SEVERITY OF HEMOPTYSIS

		Medical treatment (n = 36)			*Surgical resection (n = 40*)*			
		Died within 5 y	*Alive at 5 y*	*Alive at follow-up >5 y*	*Died after operation*	*Died within 5 y*	*Alive at 5 y*	*Alive at follow-up >5 y*
Group 1 n = 12	No haemoptysis	3	3	2	0	1	2	1
Group 2 n = 24	Blood staining	3	8	0	1	1	7	4
Group 3 n = 20	Frank blood	5	4	0	0	0	8	3
Group 4 n = 20	Major haemoptysis	5	3	0	2	1	8	1

*Nine patients treated by cavernostomy not included.
(Courtesy of Jewkes, J., et al.: Thorax 38:572–578, August 1983.)

gistatic materials. Their recommendation for resection in persons with major hemoptysis who are reasonable surgical candidates with acceptable pulmonary function seems to be supported by their data and generally in accord with most other peoples' opinion.

Another recent English study, which was presented in an article by Rafferty et al., will be mentioned here, as it is really out of step in important ways with what is usually written.[20] To quote the authors' abstract, "The problems associated with pulmonary aspergilloma were assessed retrospectively in 23 patients presenting from 1953 to 1982. Hemoptysis occurred in over half the patients and in two it was fatal. Invasive aspergillosis occurred in five patients, a higher proportion than in earlier reports, and two of these died. Amphotericin B in combination with either flucytosine or natamycin and, more recently, ketoconazole have proved useful in the treatment of this condition." Note that only 3 had major hemoptysis and 2 of these died, a

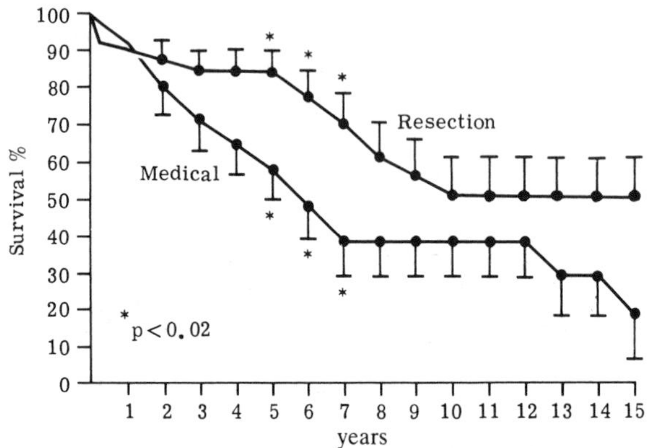

Fig 19–1.—Actuarial survival curves for 40 patients treated by pulmonary resection and 36 treated medically. Points show probability of survival, and bars show standard error. (Courtesy of Jewkes, J., et al.: Thorax 38:572–578, August 1983.)

fatality rate of 66%. What makes this report different from the vast majority is the contention that invasive aspergillosis occurred in 5 of 23 patients and that some were benefited by antifungal therapy. The notion that aspergilloma carries the risk of invasive aspergillosis is not widely accepted. However, data on one patient with this sequence were reported by Rosenberg et al. this year.[21] The patient was a fairly healthy man with an aspergilloma in an old tuberculosis cavity. The cavity ruptured at operation, contaminating the pleural space. The patient died on day 28. At postmortem he had *A. fumigatus* in the pleural space, invasive aspergillus pneumonia throughout the opposite lung, and myocardial and brain aspergilla abscesses. It will be important to watch for other patients with this sequence, since if it really is observed with any frequency, then treatment policies may have to be changed.

The article by Rafferty et al. had another concept that was new to us at least. They said that 8 patients had serious chronic bronchitis with only *Aspergillus* organisms in the sputum and that these improved with antifungal therapy. How this syndrome of "aspergillus bronchitis" relates to allergic bronchopulmonary aspergillosis (which does not benefit from antifungal therapy) and whether or not it actually exists is really not known. Buchanan and Lamb have reported 5 pretty convincing cases of invasion of a pulmonary infarct by *Aspergillus* causing an aspergilloma,[22] another thought that is sort of new but perfectly reasonable.

The traditional separation of pulmonary aspergillosis into aspergilloma, allergic bronchopulmonary aspergillosis, and invasive aspergillosis is breaking down at the edges. Invasive aspergillosis can complicate an aspergilloma, even in normal hosts as mentioned above. Also there is the syndrome of "semi-invasive aspergillosis,"[23, 24] or in the terminology of Glimp and Bayer, "chronic necrotizing aspergillosis,"[18] in which an area of aspergillus pneumonia in a normal host breaks down leaving an aspergilloma. The coexistance of allergic bronchopulmonary aspergillosis and aspergilloma has been recognized for some time as discussed by Ein et al. and referenced in the 1979 YEAR BOOK.[25] And, as discussed above (abstract 15–3), some instances of bronchocentric granulomatosis are thought to be caused by allergic bronchopulmonary aspergillosis. Finally, inhalation of *Aspergillus* is one cause of a hypersensitivity pneumonitis picture.] ◀

19–5 **Pneumonia Due to the Pittsburgh Pneumonia Agent: New Clinical Perspective With a Review of the Literature.** Robert R. Muder, Victor L. Yu, and Jeffrey J. Zuravleff (Pittsburgh) encountered 26 cases of pneumonia due to Pittsburgh pneumonia agent

(19–5) Medicine (Baltimore) 62:120–128, March 1983.

(PPA) in a 20-month period. Seventeen cases were documented by culture, direct fluorescent antibody testing, or both, and 9 cases were diagnosed because of seroconversion. In 7 cases *Legionella pneumophila* also was demonstrated. All the patients were men, with a mean age of 62 years. A large majority were smokers, but only half were immunosuppressed. All patients had at least one serious chronic illness. The clinical characteristics are given in Table 1. Infection was nosocomial in 77% of cases.

The most common features were fever, cough, and sputum production (Table 2). A majority of patients had an abnormal mental status. The laboratory findings were not distinctive, and chest radiography generally was not specific. Half the patients died in hospital. Mortal-

TABLE 1.—CLINICAL CHARACTERISTICS OF 26 PITTSBURGH PNEUMONIA PATIENTS

Hospital acquisition of PPA	88%	
Smoking history	85%	
Immunosuppression*	50%	
Simultaneous infection with *L. pneumophila*	27%	
Underlying chronic illness	100%	
Chronic pulmonary disease		54%
Malignancy (all types)†		46%
Alcoholism		31%
Heart disease		14%
Chronic renal disease		12%
Systemic vasculitis		12%
Cirrhosis		8%
Diabetes		8%

*Corticosteroid therapy; cytotoxic chemotherapy or hematologic/lymphatic malignancy, or both.

†Lung carcinoma, 15%; other solid tumors, 23%; leukemia/lymphoma, 8%.

(Courtesy of Muder, R. R., et al.: Medicine (Baltimore) 62:120–128, March 1983.)

TABLE 2.—CLINICAL FEATURES OF PITTSBURGH PNEUMONIA AGENT PNEUMONIA

	Number*	%
Fever	20/23	87
Cough	19/23	83
Sputum production	18/22	82
Abnormal mental status	15/25	60
Abdominal pain	8/22	36
Diarrhea	6/23	26
Pleuritic pain	5/23	22
Abnormal liver function	12/17	71
Leukocyte count >10,000/mm^3	18/26	69
Serum Na <130 m Eq/l	9/24	38
Simultaneous infection with *L. pneumophila*	7/26	27

*Number of cases with finding per number of cases for whom data were recorded.

(Courtesy of Muder, R. R., et al.: Medicine (Baltimore) 62:120–128, March 1983.)

TABLE 3.—COMPARISON OF PITTSBURGH PNEUMONIA (PPA) PATIENTS WITH LEGIONNAIRES' DISEASE (LD) PATIENTS*

	PPA patients		LD patients		Significance Fisher's exact test
	Number†	%	Number	%	
Age >60 years	8/19	42	24/43	56	NS‡
Smoking history	17/19	89	36/40	90	NS
Nosocomial infection	16/19	84	27/41	66	NS
Immunosuppressed§	10/19	53	8/42	19	$p < 0.02$
Malignancy (all types)	9/19	47	11/43	26	NS
Prior surgery	8/19	42	6/42	14	$p < .025$
Prior hospital stay >14 days (nosocomial cases only)	12/16	75	7/27	26	$p < .005$

*Patients with dual infection are excluded.
†Number positive per number in whom observation was made.
‡*NS*, not significant ($P < .05$).
§Steroid therapy, cytotoxic chemotherapy, hematologic/lymphatic malignancy.
(Courtesy of Muder, R. R., et al.: Medicine (Baltimore) 62:120–128, March 1983.)

ity was higher in patients with coexisting *L. pneumophila* infection, but this difference was not statistically significant. A majority of patients received erythromycin for at least 24 hours, and most of the others received a penicillin or cephalosporin, and sometimes an aminoglycoside as well. The findings are compared with those in patients with Legionnaires' disease in Table 3.

PPA infection is not distinct from Legionnaires' disease or other bacterial pneumonias on the basis of the presenting clinical features. PPA infection is not limited primarily to patients who are greatly immunosuppressed by drug therapy. The reservoir for the organism probably is within the hospital. Patients with PPA infection tend to have more severe underlying disease than those with *L. pneumophila* infection. Erythromycin appears to benefit patients with PPA pneumonia more than does conventional treatment for undiagnosed pneumonia, making the diagnosis of PPA particularly important.

▶ [Experience with direct fluorescent antibody (DFA) in the diagnosis of pneumonia due to Pittsburgh Pneumonia Agent (PPA) was one important feature of this report. The antibody came from the Centers for Disease Control. DFA was positive on 16 specimens from 14 patients and was accepted as diagnostic; 10 DFA exams were on sputum, 2 on pleural fluid, and 3 from lung tissue (does not add up). Specimens were cultured (6 positives) with the use of a commercially available special buffered charcoal yeast extract agar containing inhibitory antibiotics and dyes allowing species identification. Seroconversion, a fourfold rise to 1:160, was the basis for diagnosis in 14. It was observed from 9 to 60 days after the outset of the illness. Two patients, both very ill with underlying disease, were seronegative although culture positive. The authors emphasized that neither Legionnaires' disease nor Pittsburgh Agent pneumonia could be reliably diagnosed on the basis of symptoms or laboratory findings including x-ray. The fact that only half of these patients were immunosuppressed (although all had significant underlying illness) was felt to set this experience apart from previously recorded series, almost all of which concerned immunocompromised patients, mainly renal transplant recipients. The organism is water associated, as is *Legionella,* and contamination of the hospital hot water system with both organisms was thought to be the likely reason for the 7 instances of double infection (*Legionella* plus PPA).[26, 27] The authors said that the reason to make the diagnosis was that 60% of patients who were treated with erythromycin lived (compared with only 36% of those who were not) and that erythromycin was not part of the antibiotic cocktail ordinarily administered to patients with hospital acquired pneumonia, although perhaps it should be. Rifampin and trimethoprim sulfamethoxazole are also thought to be effective, possibly because they get into cells in high concentration, and both PPA and *Legionella* are intracellular parasites.

Although DFA has been to date the mainstay of diagnosis for both PPA and Legionnaires' disease, recent advances in culture technique, as mentioned in the discussion of the abstracted article, may bring it about that culture comes in first. The same group from Pittsburgh indicate that culture was positive in 80% of serologically determined cases of Legionnaires' disease, whereas DFA was positive in only 47%.[28] There were some DFA-negative, culture-positive cases, and in general DFA tended to be positive with heavier bacterial content of the sputum and with more extensive roentgenographic involvement.[29] The best sample for culture, in their experience, was a transtracheal aspirate, but sputum was good also. They thought that all three methods, DFA, culture, and serologic analysis, were required for accurate diagnosis. Sathapataravongs et al. report that antigenuria can be diagnosed by simple latex agglutination techniques.[30] Kahorst et al. say that a pellet from bronchoalveolar lavage is a very good sample both for DFA and for culture.[31]

Although, as mentioned, all authors say you cannot diagnose either of these pneumonias on clinical grounds, the article by Kroboth et al. provides a very nice roentgenographic summary of Legionnaires' disease.[29] They say that the process begins as a peripheral patchy infiltrate (in 76%) and progresses to consolidative pneumonia (70%); there is initial or eventual involvement of noncontiguous lobes in 50%; the process is bilateral in 50%; pleural effusions (small) are present in 32%; and in 12% bilateral diffuse disease develops.] ◀

19–6 **Herpes Simplex Virus Pneumonia: Clinical, Virologic, and Pathologic Features in 20 Patients.** Paul G. Ramsey, Kenneth H. Fife, Robert C. Hackman, Joel D. Meyers, and Lawrence Corey (Seattle) reviewed the autopsy findings in 20 patients who had pneumonia in 1974 to mid-1980 and in whom herpesvirus was isolated from lung specimens. The 14 male and 6 female patients were aged 9 months to 49 years. Sixteen had received bone marrow transplants, 12 for hematologic malignancy and 4 for aplastic anemia. Eighteen patients received immunosuppressive or cytotoxic drugs for a week or longer before the onset of pneumonia. All the marrow transplant recipients developed pneumonia within 2 months after transplantation.

The most common initial features were dyspnea and cough. Thirteen patients had concomitant pulmonary infections with other agents in addition to herpesvirus. Mucocutaneous herpesvirus infection was present in 18 patients, in 16 before the onset of pneumonia. Twelve patients showed focal or multifocal infiltrates on chest roentgenography, and 8 had a diffuse interstitial infiltrate. Five patients had a fourfold or greater fall in neutralizing antibody to herpesvirus during the course of infection. All patients had a pulmonary inflammatory infiltration, parenchymal necrosis, and hemorrhage at autopsy. Fifteen had cellular changes characteristic of herpetic infection, including intranuclear inclusions. Herpesvirus antigen was detected by direct immunofluorescence in half of the 14 lung specimens examined. Necrotizing herpetic tracheitis was observed in 10 of 17 patients. Five patients had evidence of disseminated herpesvirus infection at sites other than the lungs and gastrointestinal tract.

Localized herpesvirus pneumonia may result from direct spread of

(19–6) Ann. Intern. Med. 97:813–820, December 1982.

virus from the upper to the lower respiratory tract, whereas diffuse pneumonia appears to result from dissemination from genital or oral lesions, probably by the hematogenous route. Restriction enzyme patterns have shown the mucosal and lung isolates to be identical. Rapid diagnosis of herpesvirus pneumonia may permit effective treatment.

▶ [This is an impressive collection of cases. *None* of the patients had diagnosis before death, and *all* died of respiratory insufficiency. The argument for spread from above in patients with oral herpetic lesions and focal (single focus or multifocal) pneumonia is compelling. It is clear that herpesvirus pneumonia should be considered when fever, cough, and dyspnea develop in immunocompromised patients with oral or genital herpetic lesions. The coexistence of tracheitis or esophagitis strengthens the case. The authors agreed with the notion that intubation may weaken local tracheal mucosal defense mechanisms, favoring spread from an oral lesion to the trachea and thence to the lungs. In a separate sort of experience in the same laboratory, herpesvirus was isolated from 9 (5%) of 183 lung specimens in a transplant population. This is to be compared with isolation of cytomegalovirus in 46%. So it is a very uncommon pneumonia. Open lung biopsy in the population described in the abstracted article did not result in diagnosis (6 patients). These were very compromised people. Thirteen had other serious pulmonary infections (*Aspergillus, Candida,* cytomegalovirus, and a variety of bacterial species), and therefore the suggestion that early diagnosis might permit effective treatment (acyclovir) remains to be established. However the authors felt that those with just herpesvirus infection were just as sick as those with multiple infection.

Two studies this year indicate that prophylaxis with acyclovir works. Saral et al. did a double-blind study in leukemia patients under treatment.[32] The patients were selected on the basis of pretreatment antibody titers of 1:16 or greater. Patients in the treated arm received *32 days* of intravenous acyclovir. *All* placebo-treated patients developed typical oral herpes simplex virus lesions, and 11 of 15 were culture positive. None of the 14 who were treated with acyclovir developed oral lesions, although 6 did so after treatment was stopped. The authors recommended acyclovir prophylaxis in leukemic patients with pretreatment herpesvirus antibody titers of 1:16 or greater during periods of intensive chemotherapy. Essentially similar results were reported by Hann et al.[33] These authors said that leukopenia was less marked in those receiving acyclovir, and they believed that this might be due to prevention of systemic viremia. It should be emphasized that both of these studies had prevention of oral lesions in antibody-positive patients (prevention of relapse) as the end point studied and that they did not speak to the pneumonia question. The risk of an oral (or genital) lesion with respect to development of pneumonia and how much this is increased, if any, by tracheal intubation are important questions to which the answers are unknown. It is hoped that subsequent trials will address these questions, as the use of intravenous acyclovir is an enormous effort and expense. Trials are now underway with oral acyclovir. If these are equally successful, it will certainly come to be widely used (acycloketoconomycin?).

A report of 6 cases and an extensive review of the literature was published by Graham and Snell.[34] Oropharyngeal herpes was present in 5. An interesting feature was a gray adherent "pseudomembrane" between the larynx and the carina in 2 patients, which was seen clinically in 1 and described at autopsy in the other. Three of the 6 patients with well-proved disease survived without any specific antiherpes treatment. Pericardial effusion was present in 1 of the patients with no underlying illness and complete recovery.

Chapter 19 References

1. Goodwin R.A. Jr., Owens F.T., Snell J.D., et al.: Chronic pulmonary histoplasmosis. *Medicine* 55:1, 1976.
2. Craven P.C., Graybill J.R., Jorgensen J.H., et al.: High-dose ketoconazole for treatment of fungal infections of the central nervous system. *Ann. Intern. Med.* 98:160, 1983.
3. Petersen E.A., Alling D.W., Kirkpatrick C.H.: Treatment of chronic mu-

cocutaneous candidiasis with ketoconazole. *Ann. Intern. Med.* 93:791, 1980.

4. Hann I.M., Corringham R., Kearney M.: Ketoconazole versus nystatin plus amphotericin B for fungal prophylaxis in severely immunocompromised patients. *Lancet* 2:826, 1982.
5. Fazio R.A., Wickremesinghe P.C., Arsura E.L.: Ketoconazole treatment of *Candida esophagitis:* a prospective study of 12 cases. *Am. J. Gastroenterol.* 78:261, 1983.
6. Hughes W.T., Bartley D.L., Patterson G.G., et al.: Ketoconazole and candidiasis: a controlled study. *J. Infect. Dis.* 147:1060, 1983.
7. Jolly H.W. Jr., Daily A.D., Rex, I.H.: A multicenter double-blind evaluation of ketoconazole in the treatment of dermatomycoses. *Cutis* 31:208, 1983.
8. Trachtenberg J., Halpern N., Pont, A.: Ketoconazole: a novel and rapid treatment for advanced prostatic cancer. *J. Urol.* 130:152, 1983.
9. Loose D.S., Kan P.B., Hirst M.A., et al.: Ketoconazole blocks adrenal steroidogenesis by inhibiting cytochronic P_{450} dependent enzymes. *J. Clin. Invest.* 71:1495, 1983.
10. Englehardt D., Mann K., Hormann R., et al.: Ketoconazole inhibits cortisol secretion of an adrenal adenoma in vivo and in vitro. *Klin. Wochenschr.* 61:373, 1983.
11. Cunningham C., Burke M.D., Whiting P.H., et al.: Ketoconazole, cyclosporin, and the kidney. *Lancet* 2:1464, 1982.
12. 1982 YEAR BOOK OF MEDICINE, p. 203.
13. Okudaika M., Straub M., Schwarz J.: The etiology of discrete splenic and hepatic calcifications in an endemic area of histoplasmosis. *Am. J. Pathol.* 39:599, 1961.
14. Warlick M.A., Quan S.F., Sobonya R.E.: Rapid diagnosis of pulmonary coccidioidomycosis. *Arch. Intern. Med.* 143:723, 1983.
15. 1982 YEAR BOOK OF MEDICINE, p. 201.
16. Penn R.L., Lambert R.S., George R.B.: Invasive fungal infections: the use of serologic tests in diagnosis and management. *Arch. Intern. Med.* 143:1215, 1983.
17. Faulkner W.L., Vernon R., Brown P.P., et al.: Hemoptysis and pulmonary aspergillomas: operative and nonoperative treatment. *Ann. Thorac. Surg.* 25:389, 1978.
18. Glimp R.A., Bayer A.S.: Pulmonary aspergilloma: diagnostic and therapeutic considerations. *Arch. Intern. Med.* 143:303, 1983.
19. Israel H.L., Lenchner G.S., Atkinson G.W.: Sarcoidosis and aspergilloma: role of surgery. *Chest* 82:430, 1982.
20. Rafferty P., Biggs, B., Crompton G.K., et al.: What happens to patients with pulmonary aspergilloma? Analysis of 23 cases. *Thorax* 38:579, 1983.
21. Rosenberg R.S., Creviston S.A., Schonfeld A.J.: Invasive aspergillosis complicating resection of a pulmonary aspergilloma in a nonimmunocompromised host. *Am. Rev. Respir. Dis.* 126:1113, 1982.
22. Buchanan D.R., Lamb D.: Saphrophytic invasion of infarcted pulmonary tissue by *Aspergillus* species. *Thorax* 37:693, 1982.
23. Gefter W.B., Weingrad T.R., Epstein D.M., et al.: "Semi-invasive" pulmonary aspergillosis: A new look at the spectrum of *Aspergillus* infections of the lung. *Radiology* 140:313, 1981.
24. 1982 YEAR BOOK OF MEDICINE, pp. 207–209.
25. 1979 YEAR BOOK OF MEDICINE, p. 134.
26. Muder R.R., Yu V.L., Vickers R.M.: Simultaneous infection with *Legionella pneumophila* and Pittsburgh Pneumonia Agent. *Am. J. Med.* 74:609, 1983.

27. Helms C.M., Massanari R.M., Zietler R., et al.: Legionnaires' disease associated with a hospital water system: a cluster of 24 nosocomial cases. *Ann. Intern. Med.* 99:172, 1983.
28. Zuravleff J.J., Yu V.L., Shannard J.W., et al.: Diagnosis of Legionnaires' disease. *JAMA* 250:1981, 1983.
29. Kroboth F.J., Yu V.L., Reddy S.C., et al.: Clinicoradiographic correlation with the extent of Legionnaires' disease. *A.J.R.* 141:263, 1983.
30. Sathapatayavongs B., Kohler R.B., Wheat L.J., et al.: Rapid diagnosis of Legionnaires' disease by latex agglutination. *Am. Rev. Respir. Dis.* 127:559, 1983.
31. Kahorst W.R., Schonfeld S.A., Macklin J.E., et al.: Rapid diagnosis of Legionnaires' disease by bronchoalveolar lavage. *Chest* 84:186, 1983.
32. Saral R., Ambinder R.F., Burns W.H., et al.: Acyclovir prophylaxis against herpes simplex virus infection in patients with leukemia. *Ann. Intern. Med.* 99:773, 1983.
33. Hann I.M., Prentice H.G., Blacklock H.A., et al.: Acyclovir prophylaxis against herpes virus infections in severely immunocompromised patients: randomized double blind trial. *Br. Med. J.* 287:384, 1983.
34. Graham B.S., Snell J.D. Jr.: Herpes simplex virus infection of the adult lower respiratory tract. *Medicine* 62:384, 1983.

20. Miscellaneous

20–1 **Comparison of Medical Versus Surgical Treatment of Major Hemoptysis.** Aggressive surgery generally is recommended for severe hemoptysis, but interest in medical management has recently increased. Isidore D. Bobrowitz, Srinivasarao Ramakrishna, and Young-Soo Shim (Albert Einstein Coll. of Medicine) reviewed the cases of 113 patients with hemoptysis of at least 1 dl of blood a day at least once in hospital. Thirty-one were operated on, and 82 were managed medically. Eighty patients, including 21 in the operated group, had active tuberculosis. Only 12 patients had neither tuberculosis nor bronchiectasis.

Nineteen lobectomies and 7 pneumonectomies were carried out, as well as 2 bilobectomies, 2 bronchial ligations, and 1 segmentectomy. Seven patients had complications following surgery. Three patients developed bronchopleural fistulas. There were 4 deaths in this group. Eighteen medically treated patients died. Eight of them died of a sudden first hemoptysis. Nine of the 10 patients with terminal hemoptysis after previous bleeding had absolute contraindications to surgery. The maximum daily hemoptysis in medically managed patients is given in Table 1, and the duration of hemoptysis in Table 2. Hemoptysis was controlled medically in 64 patients, most of whom had a steady decline in bleeding and did not bleed further after 4 days. Half the patients were followed up; only 1 of them had recurrent hemoptysis.

A majority of patients with serious hemoptysis can be successfully managed conservatively, and massive hemoptysis and aspiration are not in themselves indications for operation. Surgery can be life-saving where hemoptysis is not controlled by adequate medical care or when aspiration is severe and progressive. Surgery should be restricted to patients with a localized, identified site of bleeding and with adequate pulmonary function. Patients with bilateral disease and hemoptysis from a lesion on one side can also be operated on.

▶ [This is a more conservative approach to the management of hemoptysis than has been the usual recent recommendation. The authors eliminated from consideration patients who died too quickly to be operated on and those who had absolute contraindications to surgery. They had an operative mortality of 13% (4 of 31 patients) and in the nonoperated group a mortality of 1.5% (1 of 64 patients). It's hard to really tell without being there, but they claim to have managed 63 of 64 patients who could have been operated successfully without surgery. Another conservative article about the treatment of hemoptysis last year, also from the Bronx Municipal Hospital, recommended the use of pitressin.[1, 2]] ◀

(20–1) Arch. Intern. Med. 143:1343–1346, July 1983.

TABLE 1.—MAXIMUM DAILY HEMOPTYSIS

	Surgical Group		Medical Group					
Total Amount, dL	Total Patients	%	Tuberculosis Treated for First Time	Tuberculosis Treated Previously	Bronchiectasis	Miscellaneous	Patients	%
1-2	5	16.1	9 (1)*	5 (2)	4 (2)	2 (2)	20 (7)	31.2
2-3	7	22.6	5 (1)	5 (2)	4	2 (2)	16 (5)	25.0
3-4	5	16.1	...	4 (2)	2 (1)	1 (1)	7 (4)	10.9
4-5	1	3.2	1	1	2	...	4	6.2
5-6	3	9.7	...	1	1	...	2	3.1
6-7	2	6.4	2	3 (1)	...	...	5 (1)	7.8
7-8	4	12.9	3 (1)	...	1 (1)	1 (1)	5 (3)	7.8
8-9	...	...	...	1	1 (1)	...	2 (1)	3.1
9-10	2	6.4	...	...	...	...	...	...
10-11	1	3.2	1	...	...	...	1	1.5
13-14	...	...	...	1	...	...	1	1.5
14-15	...	...	1 (1)	...	...	...	1 (1)	1.5
30	1	3.2	...	...	...	...	...	...
Total	**31**		**22 (4)**	**21 (7)**	**15 (5)**	**6 (6)**	**64 (22)**	

*Numbers in parentheses represent patients ineligible for surgery.
(Courtesy of Bobrowitz, I.D., et al.: Arch. Intern. Med. 143:1343–1346, July 1983; copyright 1983, American Medical Association.)

20–2 **Inflammatory Pseudotumors of the Lung** are poorly understood. Romeo S. Berardi, Steve S. Lee, Hammond P. Chen, and Guy J. Stines (VA Med. Center, Des Moines) reviewed 181 cases of inflammatory pseudotumor of the lung. Average patient age was 29.5 years. Sex distribution was equal. Nearly a third of evaluable patients had a history of previous lung disease. Symptoms were present initially

(20–2) Surg. Gynecol. Obstet. 156:89–96, January 1983.

TABLE 2.—DURATION OF HEMOPTYSIS FOR 64 MEDICAL PATIENTS*

Days	Tuberculosis Treated for First Time	Tuberculosis Treated Previously	Bronchiectasis	Miscellaneous	Total Patients	%
1	8	7	4	1	20	31.2
2	5	3	1	2	11	17.1
3	5	5	4	3	17	26.5
4	1	4	3	. . .	8	12.5
5	2	1	. . .	. . .	3	4.6
6	. . .	1	1	. . .	2	3.1
Total	**22**	**21**	**15**	**6**	**64**	

*There were 2 patients with bronchiectasis with hemoptysis for 7 and 11 days, respectively, and 1 patient with tuberculosis treated for the first time who had bleeding for 12 days.

(Courtesy of Bobrowitz, I.D., et al.: Arch. Intern. Med. 143:1343–1346, July 1983; copyright 1983, American Medical Association.)

in about one fourth of patients; cough was the most common. Fifteen patients had hemoptysis. Few patients had pathogens isolated from the sputum. The most common roentgenographic finding was a well-defined, circumscribed nodule, mass, or coin lesion, seen in 77 patients. Bronchoscopy yielded abnormal findings in 9 of 32 patients. Lung cancer was explicitly suspected in 25 patients before operation.

Lobectomy was the most common procedure. Twenty-three patients had pneumonectomy, and 9 had segmetal resections. Enucleation of the lesion was possible in 8 patients. The predominant cells were usually plasma cells or spindle-shaped cells. Mitoses were seen in eight sections. Two of 38 patients followed up for an average of 3½ years had recurrences. Two patients died perioperatively.

The true incidence of inflammatory pseudotumor of the lung is difficult to establish. Its cause and pathogenesis are obscure. Bacteriologic evaluation of sputum is helpful in ruling out an active inflammatory process, especially tuberculosis, and cytologic evaluation can help to rule out malignancy. Inflammatory pseudotumor is benign; no malignant degeneration has been described. The lesions are generally static, but spontaneous resolution has been observed. The lesions may respond to radiotherapy. The prognosis of patients with inflammatory pseudotumor of the lung is usually excellent.

20–3 **Unexplained Diaphragmatic Paralysis: Harbinger of Malignant Disease?** Occasionally the cause of diaphragmatic paralysis is unexplained, raising the possibility of malignancy or disabling neuromuscular disease. Jeffrey M. Piehler, Peter C. Pairolero, Douglas R. Gracey, and Philip E. Bernatz (Mayo Clinic, Rochester, Minn.) reviewed the records of 247 patients seen between 1960 and 1980 with diaphragmatic paralysis producing an elevated hemidiaphragm that failed to contract during fluoroscopy. The cause was suggested by initial evaluation in 105 patients, about a third of whom had a history compatible with lung cancer. Symptoms such as dyspnea, cough, and chest wall pain were present in 45% of the other 142 patients. Intrathoracic malignancy with phrenic nerve involvement was subse-

CAUSES OF DIAPHRAGMATIC PARALYSIS*

- Postsurgical
  - Inadvertent after cervical or thoracic procedures
  - Intentional phrenic transection
- Neoplastic
  - Direct phrenic invasion
  - Metastatic involvement
- Neuromuscular
  - Sequelae of myelitis, encephalitis, poliomyelitis, or diphtheria
  - Degenerative neurologic diseases
- Posttraumatic
- Mechanical: Compression from aortic aneurysm or substernal thyroid
- Infectious: Sequelae of bacterial, viral, syphilitic, or tuberculous infection
- Miscellaneous
  - Reaction to tetanus antitoxin
  - Congenital anomalies
- Idiopathic

*Modified from Riley, E.A.: Idiopathic diaphragmatic paralysis: a report of eight cases. Am. J. Med. 32:404, 1962.

(Courtesy of Piehler, J.M., et al.: J. Thorac. Cardiovasc. Surg. 84:861–864, December 1982.)

(20–3) J. Thorac. Cardiovasc. Surg. 84:861–864, December 1982.

quently diagnosed in 5 (3.5%) patients and progressive neurogenic atrophy in 1 patient. A normal diaphragmatic position returned in only 12 instances. Prognosis was best for patients with chest wall pain and cough. Dyspnea improved in ony one third of patients with this symptom.

Causes of diaphragmatic paralysis are listed in the table. If the history, physical findings, and chest roentgenogram fail to suggest the cause, further investigation is unlikely to be helpful, except in patients with ipsilateral vocal cord paralysis. Intrathoracic malignancy was diagnosed in 2 of 4 patients with this finding. The prognosis for most patients with unexplained diaphragmatic paralysis is excellent. Phrenic nerve paralysis from bronchogenic carcinoma in the presence of a normal chest x-ray film tends to be caused by mediastinal node disease, which may preclude curative resection. It is difficult to justify extensive ongoing evaluation of patients with unexplained diaphragmatic paralysis. Computed tomographic scanning of the neck and mediastinum is appropriate as part of the initial evaluation and follow-up. Exploratory thoracotomy is not indicated unless specific intrathoracic abnormalities other than diaphragmatic elevation are found.

20–4 **Serial Pulmonary Function in Patients With Acute Heart Failure.** It has been suggested that serial determinations of vital capacity be used as an empirical measure of fluid accumulation in the lungs of patients with left ventricular failure. Richard W. Light and Ronald B. George examined the effects of congestive heart failure on pulmonary function in 28 patients with heart failure and no history of chronic obstructive lung disease who were admitted to Louisiana State University Medical Center, Shreveport, between December 1974 and July 1977. Lung function tests were repeated during treatment of heart failure. Spirometry was carried out, and lung volumes and diffusing capacity were measured. Mean patient age was 62 years. About one half were smokers. All patients but 1 had hypertensive or arteriosclerotic cardiovascular disease. Most had severe heart failure. Average follow-up was 310 days.

Both obstructive and restrictive ventilatory dysfunctions were present on initial evaluation. Pulmonary function tended to improve with treatment. Mean FEV_1 was 29% above baseline after 4 weeks. The FEV_1-FVC ratio tended to improve over time in nonsmoking patients. Obstructive ventilatory dysfunction did not improve after bronchodilator nebulization in most patients, whether or not they smoked. At least part of the increase in FVC observed with treatment appeared to be due to less air trapping.

Patients with acute heart failure have markedly abnormal pulmonary function. The present patients were treated for 2–4 days before initial lung function testing. Lung function tended to improve rapidly when the heart failure was treated, but the time course of improvement varied widely. A substantial number of nonsmoking patients had residual evidence of obstructive ventilatory dysfunction for rea-

(20–4) Arch. Intern. Med. 143:429–433, March 1983.

sons that were not clear, but this may not have substantial clinical importance.

▶ [These are excellent clinical data concerning the restrictive and obstructive changes in pulmonary function due to congestive heart failure. For a number of years there has been an argument as to whether or not congestive heart failure causes airways obstruction, and if it does, whether or not there is an element of bronchospasm associated with it, the alternative being simple mechanical obstruction due to edema in the peribronchiolar tissues. Many excellent doctors don't believe in cardiac asthma in the sense of reversible bronchospasm, and many good laboratory studies in animals argue against it as well. The issue has been discussed at some length in past YEAR BOOKS.[3, 4] The editors incline to the old view that "cardiac asthma," implying functional bronchospasm reversible by bronchodilator agents, does exist some of the time in some patients but recognize that this is still an unproved notion. The data in the abstracted article certainly support increased airways resistance in congestive heart failure, although this did not appear to be reversible by bronchodilators.] ◀

Chapter 20 References

1. Magee G., Williams M.H. Jr.: Treatment of massive hemoptysis with intravenous pitressin. *Lung* 160:165, 1982.
2. 1983 YEAR BOOK OF MEDICINE, pp. 213–214.
3. 1976 YEAR BOOK OF MEDICINE, pp. 135–173.
4. 1978 YEAR BOOK OF MEDICINE, pp. 132–135.

PART THREE

THE BLOOD AND BLOOD-FORMING ORGANS

MARTIN J. CLINE, M.D.

21. Erythrocytes, Aplasia, and Bone Marrow Transplantation

21–1 **Human Parvovirus-Like Virus Inhibits Hematopoietic Colony Formation in Vitro.** Cossart et al. identified a serum parvovirus-like virus (SPLV) in human serum, and subsequently evidence of active infection with the virus was found in children with transient aplastic crisis of sickle cell disease. Philip P. Mortimer, R. Keith Humphries, Jeffrey G. Moore, Robert H. Purcell, and Neal S. Young (Natl. Inst. of Health, Bethesda, Md.) examined the effects of virus-containing material on hematopoiesis using in vitro colony-forming assays. Seven sera found to contain SPLV by countercurrent immunoelectrophoresis and electron microscopy were evaluated. Five were from blood donors, and 2 were from patients with brief febrile illnesses.

Sera containing SPLV were found to inhibit erythropoiesis in culture. Six of the 7 sera caused more than 50% mean inhibition of colony formation from later erythroid progenitors. Three sera led to similar inhibition of colony formation from the more primitive progenitor. None of the sera inhibited the formation of myeloid colonies to the same degree. The degree of inhibition of colony formation was not closely related to the antigenic titer of SPLV. Acute-phase sera from the patients with febrile illness inhibited the formation of colonies derived from the later erythroid progenitor, but convalescent sera did not. Serum from a child with hereditary spherocytosis and transient aplastic crisis had a strong inhibitory effect on erythropoiesis, correlating with the presence of virus.

These findings provide evidence for a suppressive effect of a human virus on hematopoiesis in vitro. SPLV-associated aplastic crises of hemolytic anemias may result directly from viral cytotoxicity for erythroid progenitors in the bone marrow. The effect may occur in all infected persons, but it probably is apparent only when coexisting hemolysis causes rapid destruction of circulating red blood cells and increases the requirement for erythrocyte production by the marrow. Abrupt recovery from aplastic crises would seem to be due to inactivation of virus. Transient erythroblastopenia and aplastic anemia of childhood, both of which often follow viral infection, may also be due to a viral effect on hematopoietic cells.

▶ [Viruses have been shown to be one cause of bone marrow aplasia in certain diseases of cats and horses and have recently been implicated in some types of bone marrow failure in man. In 1975 Cossart and his colleagues found a serum parvovirus-like virus (SPLV) in human serum. Antibodies to this virus were present in the sera of 30%–45% of healthy adults. Subsequently, Pattison and his colleagues found five children with transient aplastic crisis of sickle cell disease and evidence of active

(21–1) Nature 302:426–429, Mar. 31, 1983.

infection with SPLV. The association of this virus with aplastic crisis was later confirmed in a large series of children with sickle cell disease in Jamaica.

Infection with SPLV is common, occurring most frequently in children, and may be associated with headache, fever, malaise, and rash. Temporary cessation of erythropoiesis is probably common in parvovirus infection, although the aplastic crisis is not seen in normal individuals because of the long red blood cell life span and the self-limiting nature of the suppression of red blood cell production. One would only anticipate seeing aplastic crisis in conditions with markedly shortened red blood cell survival, as in hereditary pyruvate kinase deficiency described in the next article.] ◀

21–2 **Aplastic Crisis Due to Parvovirus Infection in Pyruvate Kinase Deficiency.** Infection with serum parvovirus-like virus (SPLV) is a cause of aplastic crisis in sickle cell anemia, and possibly in crises occurring in hereditary spherocytosis. J. R. Duncan, C. G. Potter, M. D. Cappellini, J. B. Kurtz, M. J. Anderson, and D. J. Weatherall report an aplastic crisis in pyruvate kinase (PK) deficiency associated with proved infection by SPLV in a boy with congenital hemolytic anemia.

Boy, 13, diagnosed at age 3 years as having congenital nonspherocytic hemolytic anemia due to PK deficiency, and maintained on folic acid supplements, presented with upper abdominal pain, vomiting, and severe headache.

Fig 21–1.–Parvovirus-like particles from plasma on day 3 of aplastic crisis, clumped by serum taken on day 15. Bar = 100 nm. (Courtesy of Duncan, J. R., et al.: Lancet 2:14–16, July 2, 1983.)

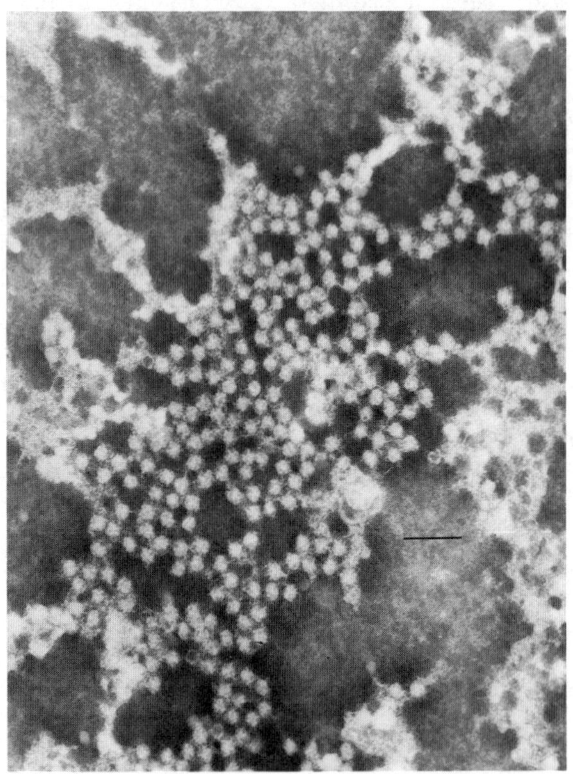

(21–2) Lancet 2:14–16, July 2, 1983.

Splenomegaly of 2 cm was noted. Pancytopenia and reticulocytopenia were documented 3 days after the onset of symptoms. White blood cell and platelet counts improved rapidly, but the hemoglobin fell to 5.8 gm/dl before recovery. Transfusions were not necessary. Striking reticulocytosis was observed on day 11. A brief, acute exacerbation of symptoms occurred on day 15, 3 days after discharge. High-grade fever coincided with a fall in reticulocytes at this time.

Blood taken 3 days after the onset of symptoms contained parvovirus-like particles. Serum taken on day 8 contained an antibody which, on immune electron microscopy, clumped both the parvovirus-like particles in the patient's blood (Fig 21–1) and prototype B19 parvovirus. Serum IgM antibody persisted until 7 weeks after the crisis, at which time only IgG antibody remained. The patient's sister had IgM antibody to parvovirus; she was also known to have homozygous PK deficiency. Virus-containing plasma from the patient inhibited the formation of burst-forming units erythroid from nonimmune subjects, and this effect was neutralized by convalescent-phase serum. Colony forming units granulocyte-macrophage also were inhibited, but neutralization did not reverse the effect.

A selective effect of SPLV at the stage of erythroid progenitors seems likely in this case. Patients with congenital hemolytic anemia should be screened for evidence of immunity in order to identify those at risk. When propagation of human parvovirus in tissue culture is achieved, it should be possible to develop a vaccine to prevent aplastic crisis in hemolytic anemia.

▶ [An understanding of the mechanisms underlying aplastic crisis in hemolytic diseases offers the opportunity for prevention. Once tissue culture techniques for propagation of human parvoviruses are developed, it should be possible to develop a vaccine that might be used to prevent aplastic crisis in hemolytic anemias. In the meantime, patients with chronic hemolytic anemia should be screened for evidence of antibodies to SPLV in order to determine who is at risk. In such patients the low reticulocyte count often warrants admission to a hospital. Transfusion should be used if the hemoglobin count falls substantially below the steady-state value for the patient. Other family members at risk of aplasia should be observed closely.] ◀

21–3 **Antithymocyte Globulin Treatment in Patients With Aplastic Anemia: Prospective Randomized Trial.** Currently, there is no proved effective treatment for patients with aplastic anemia who are not candidates for bone marrow transplantation. Interest in a potential role of immune suppression of hematopoiesis in the pathogenesis of aplastic anemia has increased recently, and several studies have found evidence of lymphocyte- or antibody-mediated suppression as a cause of some cases of aplastic anemia. Richard Champlin, Winston Ho and Robert Peter Gale (Univ. of California, Los Angeles) undertook a prospective trial of antithymocyte globulin in patients with moderate or severe aplastic anemia who had no evidence of spontaneous hematologic recovery and who were not candidates for bone marrow transplantation. After stratification for the duration and severity of aplasia, the patients were randomized to receive immediate treatment with equine antihuman thymocyte globulin or were followed as controls. A dose of 20 mg/kg daily was given by infusions on 8 consecutive days. Following premedication with acetaminophen and diphenhydramine, each dose was infused in normal saline over 4–6 hours.

(21–3) N. Engl. J. Med. 308:113–118, Jan. 20, 1983.

Eleven of 21 patients randomized to immediate treatment with antithymocyte globulin showed hematologic improvement within 3 months of entry into the study. Two others improved later. Actuarial survival of this group was 62% at 2 years. No control patient improved within 3 months of randomization, and 7 of the 21 patients died of bleeding or infection in this period. Six of 12 who subsequently were treated improved within 3 months, and 2 others survived but did not improve. The actuarial survival of controls was 41% at 2 years. Only 4 of 24 patients not meeting criteria for response have survived. All but 1 of 17 responders have sustained hematologic improvement for 5–27 months after treatment. Most have improved levels of granulocytes, erythrocytes, and platelets and require no transfusions. Substantial toxicity resulted from antithymocyte globulin therapy, but there were no treatment-related deaths. The only clinical variable correlated with the outcome was the interval from diagnosis to treatment, and this association was not significant.

Antithymocyte globulin improves hematopoiesis in some patients with aplastic anemia. The treatment should be considered for patients who lack an HLA-identical bone marrow donor. It also may be an appropriate alternative to bone marrow transplantation in selected groups of patients such as those with moderate aplastic anemia or those older than age 40 who have an increased risk of complications after transplantation.

▶ [Aplastic anemia is a life-threatening hematologic disorder characterized by pancytopenia in the peripheral blood and reduced numbers of hematopoietic cells in the bone marrow. In the United States at the present time the cause of most cases of aplastic anemia is unknown. Several potential pathogenetic mechanisms have been suggested, including viral suppression of hematopoiesis, chemical or drug injury of stem cells, and defects in the bone marrow microenvironment. It has also been suggested that abnormalities of hematopoietic regulatory cells may cause failure of hematopoiesis. The nature of these regulatory cells has not been defined with certainty, but several investigators have suggested that they are a subset of lymphocytes.

The idea of using immunosuppression to treat bone marrow failure arose from the concept that some cases of aplasia develop as a consequence of suppression of hematopoiesis by lymphocyte-mediated or antibody-mediated mechanisms. Initial clinical trials in Europe suggested that antithymocyte globulin might be of benefit to patients with aplasia; however, these studies were not well controlled. This study from UCLA suggests that the European investigators were indeed correct and that antithymocyte globulin may be of value in the treatment of this frustrating disorder.] ◀

21–4 **Graft-Versus-Host Disease and Survival in Patients With Aplastic Anemia Treated by Marrow Grafts From HLA-Identical Siblings: Beneficial Effect of a Protective Environment.** Graft-versus-host disease (GVHD) and associated infections are the chief causes of treatment failure in patients with aplastic anemia who have successful marrow engraftment. Rainer Storb, Ross L. Prentice, C. Dean Buckner, R. A. Clift, Fred Appelbaum, Joachim Deeg, Kristine Doney, John A. Hansen, Mark Mason, Jean E. Sanders, Jack Singer, Keith M. Sullivan, Robert P. Witherspoon, and E. Donnall Thomas (Univ. of Washington) attempted to identify factors associ-

---

(21–4) N. Engl. J. Med. 308:302–307, Feb. 10, 1983.

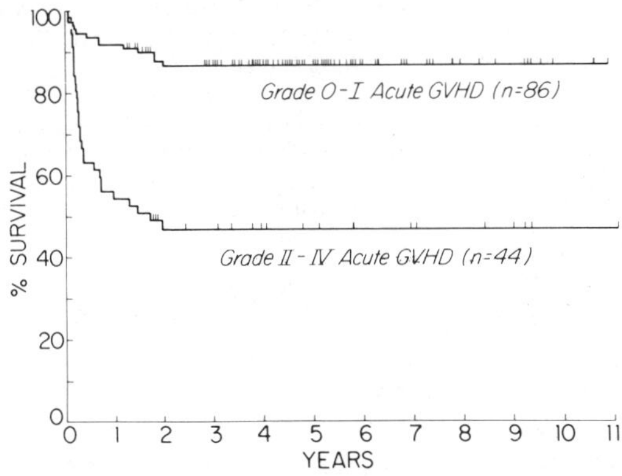

Fig 21–2.—Survival of 86 patients (9 deaths) without or with grade-I acute graft-versus-host disease *(GVHD)* compared with survival of 44 patients (24 deaths) with more acute GVHD. Grade I, mild, transient skin rash; grade II, severe skin rash or mild rash with evidence of liver or gastrointestinal involvement; grade III, severe involvement of skin, liver, or gastrointestinal tract; grade IV, life-threatening involvement. (Courtesy of Storb, R., et al.: N. Engl. J. Med. 308:302–307, Feb. 10, 1983. Reprinted by permission of The New England Journal of Medicine.

ated with GVHD and survival in a series of 130 consecutive patients with aplastic anemia whose marrow grafts were accepted and who lived for at least 2 weeks after transplantation. Thirty-nine patients were managed in laminar airflow rooms and given "sterile" food and oral nonabsorbable antibiotics, and skin cleansing was carried out.

All but 4 of the 33 patients who died had moderately severe or severe acute or chronic GVHD. The most common proximate causes of death were gram-negative infection, interstitial pneumonitis, and undiagnosed infection. Survival is related to the degree of GVHD in Figure 21-2. Survival was significantly associated with refractoriness to random-donor platelet infusions, laminar airflow isolation, patient age, and acute GVHD. The protective environment was related to significantly reduced mortality, corresponding in part to a reduction in the incidence, and delayed onset of acute GVHD. Refractoriness to platelet infusions particularly influenced survival negatively in patients with acute GVHD. Mortality increased with advancing age.

Moderate to severe acute GVHD compromised survival significantly in patients in this study with sustained bone marrow grafts for aplastic anemia. Mortality was reduced by laminar airflow isolation. Patients in a protective environment can be expected to have fewer infections even in the absence of GVHD, and GVHD was less frequent in these patients. The effect of refractoriness to random-donor platelet infusions on survival may be related to differences in immune responsiveness among patients.

▶ [The survival rate among young patients with aplastic anemia treated by high-dose cyclophosphamide and allogeneic bone marrow transplantation is about 70% for those who have been transfused and more than 80% for those who have not received previous transfusions. In the current study of 130 patients with aplastic anemia, 97 were still alive between 1.4 and 11 years after bone marrow transplantation. Of the 33 who died, 29 had either acute or chronic GVHD. One of the principal observations in this study is that a protective environment significantly reduces mortality, probably as a result of the reduction in and delayed onset of acute GVHD, as well as a reduction in the incidence of infection. Mortality among germfree mice given allogeneic incompatible bone marrow is significantly reduced, as compared with mortality among conventionally treated mice given similar transplants. Reduction in the incidence of GVHD has recently been claimed by several groups of investigators utilizing donor marrow treated with antibody cytotoxic for T lymphocytes. All the consequences of immunodepletion induced by such maneuvers are not yet known. A high incidence of lymphoma has been reported by one group.] ◀

21–5 **Transplantation for Severe Combined Immunodeficiency With HLA-A, B, D, DR Incompatible Parental Marrow Cells Fractionated by Soybean Agglutinin and Sheep Red Blood Cells.** It is possible to remove T lymphocytes from human bone marrow aspirates by the selective removal of cells agglutinable by soybean agglutinin and the subsequent removal of residual T lymphocytes by differential sedimentation of cells forming rosettes with sheep red blood cells. Yair Reisner, Neena Kapoor, Dahlia Kirkpatrick, Marilyn S. Pollack, Susanna Cunningham-Rundles, Bo Dupont, Marquis Z. Hodes, Robert A. Good, and Richard J. O'Reilly (Meml. Sloan-Kettering Cancer Center, New York) used this technique to prepare bone marrow transplants from HLA-haploidentical, mixed lymphocyte culture-incompatible parental donors for 3 children with severe combined immunodeficiency (SCID). Two of these patients have had sustained engraftment and immunologic reconstitution without graft-versus-host disease (GVHD). The third patient had early transient engraftment only. Mitogen-responsive lymphocytes of paternal origin developed in this case. This patient subsequently was engrafted and reconstituted by a transplant of HLA haplotype-mismatched maternal bone marrow after immunosuppression. Three further patients with SCID were engrafted more recently, and immune function was restored in 2 of them. None of the patients have had GVHD.

Depletion of T lymphocytes by differential agglutination with soybean agglutinin and subsequent E-rosette depletion can abrogate the potential of histoincompatible bone marrow grafts to induce lethal GVHD without restricting the possibility of immunologic reconstitution in bone marrow recipients. In some patients, engraftment and the development of parental lymphoid cells were associated with normalization of T cell numbers, full reconstitution of in vitro transformation responses to mitogens and antigens, development of the ability to generate lymphokines in vitro, and in vivo delayed-type hypersensitivity responses to dinitrochlorobenzene.

Further experience is needed to determine the general applicability of this approach to patients with SCID or other lethal congenital or acquired blood disorders.

▶ [Acute GVHD is presumed to be triggered by differences between recipients and donors in polymorphic non-HLA determinants. The syndrome is manifested by lesions throughout the skin, gastrointestinal tract, liver, and lymph nodes. Fatal complications may arise as a consequence of deranged organ function per se, but more often result from infectious complications. Opportunistic infections in GVHD presumably arise from injury to the integrity of the body surfaces and from impaired granulocyte

---

(21–5) Blood 61:341–348, February 1983.

and immunologic defense functions. Acute GVHD may also predispose to chronic GVHD, which is also often associated with infectious complications. Acute and chronic GVHD are thought to arise from immunologically reactive T-lymphoid cell in the donor bone marrow. The traditional approach to treating established GVHD is to use glucocorticoids, sometimes in combination with immunosuppressive agents such as antithymocyte globulin or cyclosporin A. Over the past decade a number of investigators have attempted to reduce the immunologically reactive cells in the donor's bone marrow by a variety of techniques, including separation of cell based on size, density, reaction with monoclonal antibodies, etc. In this report the investigators describe depleting T cells from the bone marrow by the use of soybean agglutinin and rosetting with sheep red blood cells. Their level of success appears to be pretty impressive. If these results can be confirmed and more widely applied, then there has indeed been a breakthrough in the number of patients that can be considered for bone marrow transplantation.] ◀

21–6 **Mismatched Family Donor for Bone Marrow Transplantation as Treatment for Acute Leukemia.** Although matched marrow grafting is, along with irradiation and cyclophosphamide, a successful treatment of acute myeloid leukemia, patients are not likely to have a histocompatible sibling; also, even matched grafts usually do not succeed in recipients who are more than 45 years of age. R. L. Powles, G. R. Morgenstern, H. E. M. Kay, T. J. McElwain, H. M. Clink, P. J. Dady, A. Barrett, B. Jameson, M. H. Depledge, J. G. Watson, J. Sloane, M. Leigh, H. Lumley, D. Hedley, S. D. Lawler, J. Filshie, and B. Robinson (Sutton, England) used allogeneic bone marrow grafts from a relative mismatched at the major histocompatibility complex in 35 patients with acute myeloid or, in 2 instances, lymphoblastic leukemia. The patients were aged 3–45 years. Fourteen were in first remission at the time of grafting, 15 were in a later remission, and 6 were in relapse. All patients but 1 shared 1 HLA haplotype with the donor, and 19 of these shared 1 or more antigens of the nonidentical haplotype with the donor. Thirty-one patients were conditioned with cyclophosphamide and total-body radiation. Four received melphalan in place of irradiation. Cyclosporin A was given intramuscularly or orally in daily doses of 12.5–37.5 mg/kg for 5 days, starting 24 hours before marrow infusion. Oral treatment with 12.5 mg/kg daily ensued for 6 months. Fifteen patients received methotrexate as well.

Eleven patients were alive for 6 months or longer after marrow transplantation, 5 of them after more than 2 years. Eight of the 15 patients younger than age 20 at the time of transplantation were well from 6 months to 3 years later. Acute graft-vs.-host disease caused 1 death and contributed importantly to 2 others. Graft failure caused 2 deaths. Four patients died of recurrent leukemia. Twelve patients had fatal pulmonary edema, often associated with seizures, intravascular hemolysis, and renal failure. Infection was not apparent in most of these patients. However, 3 patients died of lung disease in which infection was a factor. At least 1 patient appeared to have autologous reconstitution of the marrow.

Complete major histocompatability complex identity appears unnecessary for successful bone marrow transplantation in leukemic patients, and attempts at continued mismatched marrow transplanta-

(21–6) Lancet 1:612–615, Mar. 19, 1983.

tion seem warranted. Young patients with acute myelogenous leukemia in first remission may be the most likely to benefit. Complications may be reduced by optimizing radiation schedules and the dose of cyclosporin A and by the use of supportive measures such as large albumin infusions.

▶ [This is another report on the use of mismatched bone marrow in transplantation. These investigators did not treat the mismatched marrow before transplantation, but rather attempted to modify graft-vs.-host disease in the recipient by treatment with cyclosporin A. In this study, 11 of 35 patients are alive 6 months after grafting, and 5 of them are alive at more than 2 years. It should be noted that 6 months is too early to evaluate the success or failure of the transplantation process. Nevertheless, the results appear promising. The problem is obviously important, since most patients who are candidates for bone marrow transplantation either for leukemia or for bone marrow failure do not have a suitably matched sibling to serve as a potential donor.] ◀

21–7 **5-Azacytidine Selectively Increases γ-Globin Synthesis in a Patient With β^+-Thalassemia.** β-Thalassemia is characterized by decreased or absent production of the β subunit of adult hemoglobin, resulting in a relative excess of α-globin molecules, which precipitate in erythroid cells and form inclusions that impair erythroid cell replication, membrane function, and red blood cell survival, resulting in ineffective erythropoiesis, hemolysis, and severe anemia. Timothy J. Ley, Joseph DeSimone, Nicholas P. Anagnou, George H. Keller, R. Keith Humphries, Patricia H. Turner, Neal S. Young, Paul Heller, and Arthur W. Nienhuis examined the effect of 5-azacytidine, a cytidine analogue that can activate repressed gene in tissue-cultured cells, on hemoglobin F synthesis in baboons, in which the globin genes are structurally and functionally similar to those of human beings. The drug was also given to a patient with severe homozygous β-thalassemia and markedly imbalanced globin chain production.

Adminstration of 5-azacytidine increased hemoglobin F production in anemic baboons. In the patient, who had daily phlebotomies for 5 days before a week of treatment by infusion of 5-azacytidine in a dosage of 140 mg daily. γ-Globin synthesis increased about sevenfold, temporarily returning to normal. Erythropoiesis became more effective, with a rise in hemoglobin concentration from 8.0 to 10.8 gm/dl. Hypomethylation of bone marrow DNA near both the γ-globin and ε-globin genes was demonstrated. At the time of peak effect, about 7,000 γ-globin messenger RNA molecules per erythroid marrow cell were present, compared with 10 to 15 ε-globin messenger RNA molecules per cell.

A selective increase in γ-globin synthesis is obtained with 5-azacytidine, and this may provide a new approach to the treatment of severe β-thalassemia, although further studies are needed to evaluate the risks and long-term toxicity of this treatment. The effect of treatment appeared to be relatively specific in this patient, and it was well tolerated.

▶ [Genes that are transcriptionally inactive usually have high levels of methylation of DNA bases in the area of the gene. Conversely, genes in which messenger RNA is being actively transcribed tend to be relatively undermethylated. 5-Azacytidine is an analogue of cytidine that is incorporated into newly synthesized DNA. Incorporation

---

(21–7) N. Engl. J. Med. 307:1469–1475, Dec. 9, 1982.

leads to a decrease in DNA methyltransferase activity which reduces the methylation of newly synthesized DNA. In some animal model systems 5-azacytidine exposure can reactivate genes that have been repressed.

It has been realized for a long period of time that a fetal pattern of hemoglobin production would benefit patients with severe sickle cell disease and severe β-thalassemia. Ley and his colleagues now report that 5-azacytidine can selectively increase γ-globin synthesis in β-thalassemia. The observations are intriguing, although they have been the subject of some criticism. As noted in a *Lancet* editorial (*Lancet* 1:36, 1983), "there could be no obvious lasting benefit to the patient from this experiment and the use in these circumstances of a potent cytotoxic drug with a known propensity for activating latent viruses seems dubious." 5-Azacytidine is highly carcinogenic in some animal model systems.] ◀

1–8 **A Genetic Defect in the Binding of Protein 4.1 to Spectrin in a Kindred With Hereditary Spherocytosis.** Hereditary spherocytosis is considered a disorder of the red blood cell membrane whose structural stability depends on a filamentous meshwork of proteins lining the inner membrane surface. The membrane skeleton consists chiefly of four proteins: spectrim, actin, protein 4.1, and ankyrin. Lawrence C. Wolfe, Kathryn M. John, John C. Falcone, Ann M. Byrne, and Samuel E. Lux (Harvard Med. School) examined spectrin interactions in 16 members of 6 kindreds with autosomal dominant hereditary spherocytosis.

A defect was found in the interaction of spectrin, actin, and protein 4.1 in all 4 members of these kindreds, and the defect was caused by the presence of abnormal spectrin molecules incapable of binding protein 4.1. The binding of normal protein 4.1 by the defective spectrin was reduced by 39% in these cases. The defective spectrin was separated into two populations by affinity chromatography on immobilized normal protein 4.1; one population lacked the ability to bind protein 4.1. The nonfunctional spectrin presumably was a product of the autosomal dominant gene reponsible for hereditary spherocytosis in this kindred. All the patients are presently well, 1 after splenectomy done during an aplastic crisis.

A qualitative defect in the interactions of spectrin, the major protein of the red blood cell skeleton, was found in 1 of 6 kindreds with hereditary spherocytosis in this study. The fact that the proportion of nonfunctional spectrin did not increase with red blood cell age or decrease after splenectomy in these patients strongly suggests that it was not simply a secondary manifestation of the disease.

Hereditary spherocytosis is clearly a biochemically heterogeneous disorder. The lesion responsible for the condition in the kindreds with normal spectrin function is unknown, but these patients probably also have defective membrane skeletons. The possibility that they lack the ability to form a normal spectrin-actin-protein-4.1 complex because of a dysfunction of protein 4.1 or actin is under study.

▶ [Hereditary spherocytosis is thought to result from a disorder or disorders of the red blood cell membrane. Despite several decades of investigation, the precise molecular defect in hereditary spherocytosis has not been defined. The present study helps to elucidate this murky situation. This and other recent investigations clearly show that hereditary spherocytosis is biochemically heterogeneous.] ◀

(21–8) N. Engl. J. Med. 307:1367–1374, Nov. 25, 1982.

21-9 **Ocular Toxicity of High-Dose Intravenous Desferrioxamine.** Sally C. Davies, R. E. Marcus, J. L. Hungerford, M. H. Miller, G. B. Arden, and E. R. Huehns gave large doses of desferrioxamine by continuous infusion to counter the effects of transfusion-induced iron overload in 4 patients with β-thalessemia major. All 4 had serious cardiac involvement. Ocular complications developed in 2 of the 4. One case is described below.

Woman, 19, had received regular transfusions since age 6 months and had an average hemoglobin value of 9.5 gm/dl. Splenectomy was done at age 7 years, and intramuscular desferrioxamine was started at age 15 years. Compliance was intramuscular, and later with subcutaneous infusion, therapy had been poor. Angina had developed at age 11 years, hypoparathyroidism at age 14, and diabetes mellitus at age 19, when the serum ferritin level was 6,000 μg/L. Intravenous desferrioxamine was given over 50 days with a 4-day break in doses as high a 235 mg/kg/24 hours. She excreted a total of 7 gm iron in the urine and feces, and the serum ferritin level fell to 4,500 μg/L.

Blurred vision was reported in the fifth week of treatment, and posterior lens opacities were noted in both eyes. Subsequently the patient was unable to see in dim light, and peripheral vision was impaired bilaterally. Retinal pigmentary changes were noted, with thinning of the retinal vessels. Peripheral visual field loss was documented; bilateral annular scotomas were present. Dark adaptation was defective, and findings on the electro-oculogram were grossly subnormal, as were those on the electroretinogram. The pattern visually evoked response was normal in both eyes. The symptoms resolved within 3 weeks after high-dose desferrioxamine was discontinued. Some field loss remained at 3 months. Dark adaptation improved, as did findings on the electroretinogram, but findings on the electro-oculogram remained grossly subnormal. The lens opacities were less evident, but the retinal pigmentation was unchanged.

The second patient had a central scotoma in each eye and severely impaired color vision. Rapid improvement in vision followed withdrawal of high-dose desferrioxamine.

Lens opacities have previously been described, but rapid visual failure has not been reported as a toxic effect of desferrioxamine. The mechanism of this form of retinal toxicity is unclear. High-dose desferrioxamine therapy is warranted in selected cases, but the dose should be increased gradually to a maximum of 125 mg/kg/24 hours. If ophthalmic complications occur, the treatment should be stopped and later reinstituted in a lower dose.

▶ [The admonitions about the maximal dose and rate of dosage increase of desferrioxamine clearly should be noted.] ◀

(21–9) Lancet 2:184, July 23, 1983.

22. Leukocytes and Immunodeficiency

22–1 **National Case-Control Study of Kaposi's Sarcoma and *Pneumocystis carinii* Pneumonia in Homosexual Men.**—*Part 1.—Epidemiologic results.*—Harold W. Jaffe, Keewhan Choi, Pauline A. Thomas, Harry W. Haverkos, David M. Auerbach, Mary E. Guinan, Martha F. Rogers, Thomas J. Spira, William W. Darrow, Mark A. Kramer, Stephen M. Friedman, James M. Monroe, Alvin E. Friedman-Kien, Linda J. Laubenstein, Michael Marmor, Bijan Safai, Selma K. Dritz, Salvatore J. Crispi, Shirley L. Fannin, John P. Orkwis, Alexander Kelter, Wilmon R. Rushing, Stephen B. Thacker, and James W. Curran report results of a case-control study that was carried out in 4 metropolitan centers (Atlanta, New York, San Francisco, and Los Angeles) to identify risk factors for the development of Kaposi's sarcoma and *P. carinii* pneumonia in homosexual men.

Thirty-nine patients with Kaposi's sarcoma, 8 with *P. carinii* pneumonia, and 3 with both were matched for age and race with 120 homosexual male control subjects who had never had either disease and had not received immunosuppressive therapy in the past year. Controls were obtained from venereal disease clinics and private practices and also from among friends of the patients.

Cases were nearly twice as likely as controls to have a history of syphilis, and they also were more likely to have had hepatitis other than hepatitis B. Illicit substances were commonly used by both groups, but cases more often had used "street" drugs. Cases had had more than twice as many sexual partners as controls in the year before the onset of illness. This factor correlated with both a history of syphilis and the use of "street" drugs. The variables most closely associated with Kaposi's sarcoma or pneumocystic pneumonia were the number of male sex partners and meeting of partners in bathhouses. Possible exposure to feces was more prevalent in the cases than in controls. Nitrite use was comparable in the two groups.

The occurrence of Kaposi's sarcoma and pneumocystic pneumonia in homosexual men appears to be associated with the number of sex partners and other aspects of their life-style. The significance of various risk factors may not be fully clear until more is known of the cause of the underlying acquired immunodeficiency.

Part 2.—Laboratory results.—Rogers, David M. Morens, John A. Stewart, Rose M. Kaminski, Spira, Paul M. Feorino, Sandra A. Larson, Donald P. Francis, Marianna Wilson, Leo Kaufman, and the Task Force on Acquired Immune Deficiency Syndrome (Centers for Disease Control, Atlanta) obtained biologic specimens from patients

(22–1) Ann. Intern. Med. 99:145–158, August 1983.

with Kaposi's sarcoma and *P. carinii* pneumonia and from matched control subjects in the course of this case-control study of homosexual men. Patients were aged 15 to 60 years. None had known risk factors for immunodeficiency or had received treatment with immunosuppressive drugs. Thirty-nine patients had Kaposi's sarcoma only, 8 had *P. carinii* pneumonia only, and 5 had both. Mean duration of symptoms was slightly more than 1 year. An attempt was made to find four control subjects for each patient, matched for age, sex, homosexuality, race, and area of residence.

Cases had lower total lymphocyte and T-lymphocyte counts, particularly T-helper cells, than controls. The ratio of T-helper to suppressor cells was reversed in the patient group. Lymphocyte responsiveness to antigens was less evident in the case group. Levels of IgG and IgA were higher in cases than in controls. Cases had higher titers of IgG antibody to Epstein-Burr virus, as well as higher titers of antibody to cytomegalovirus. Antibodies to hepatitis A virus and *Treponema pallidum* were more prevalent in the case group, but antibody to varicella-zoster virus was less prevalent in cases. Cytomegalovirus was isolated more often from urine and throat swab specimen in the case group.

Depressed cellular immune function appears to underlie the outbreak of opportunistic infections and Kaposi's sarcoma in homosexual men in American cities. Epstein-Barr virus, cytomegalovirus, and *T. pallidum* can depress cellular immune function. Sexual contact and the infection transmitted by sexual exposures may be confounding variables that are highly correlated with another, as yet unidentified, cause of immunosuppression. In future studies an attempt should be made to identify an infectious agent that can circulate in the blood or within peripheral blood leukocytes and that may also be present in rectal secretions, semen, or other secretions in homosexual men.

▶ [This and the accompanying article provide good summaries of the epidemiology and serologic abnormalities in the acquired immunodeficiency syndrome (AIDS). In the articles that follow, epidemiology, immunologic abnormalities, and potential pathogenetic agents are considered in more detail.] ◀

22-2 **T-Lymphocyte Subpopulation in Homosexual Men.** An outbreak of Kaposi's sarcoma, *Pneumocystis carinii* pneumonia, and other opportunistic infections has recently occurred in male homosexuals and drug addicts in the United States. If these are the result of acquired immunodeficiency, many persons may be at risk of serious illness. Hardy Kornfeld, Robert A. Vande Stouwe, Michael Lange, M. Mohan Reddy, and Michael H. Grieco (St. Luke's-Roosevelt Hosp. Center, New York) examined T-lymphocyte subpopulations in 81 healthy male homosexuals in New York City and in 20 heterosexual men. The respective mean ages were 35 and 31 years. None of the homosexuals had a history of serious systemic illness or immunosuppressive therapy. Thirty-one of the homosexuals had a history of symptoms or signs, most often amebiasis and lymphadenopathy.

Homosexuals had lower absolute and relative counts of OKT4-positive lymphocytes (helper cells) and lower ratios of OKT4 to OKT8

(22–2) N. Engl. J. Med. 307:729–731, Sept. 16, 1982.

(suppressor) cells than heterosexuals. Only 17.3% of homosexuals had normal ratios, and 12 of these 14 subjects were asymptomatic. Tests for cytomegalovirus antibody were positive in all but 2 homosexuals, and more than three fourths had a titer above 1:16. One fourth of the heterosexuals had antibody tests; none had a titer above 1:16. Sexual promiscuity was associated with reduced OKT4-OKT8 ratios. The ratio was not related to long-term use of amyl or butyl nitrite.

Abnormality in the distribution of T-cell subsets was found in over 80% of healthy male homosexuals in this study, suggesting the existence of a greater public health problem than has generally been appreciated. A reduced OKT4-OKT8 ratio may be found in a large number of homosexual men in the community. The cause of the reduced ratios in these subjects is unclear, but reductions have been described in a variety of diseases, including cytomegalovirus-induced mononucleosis, Epstein-Barr virus infection, influenza, acute and chronic hepatitis B infection, and primary biliary cirrhosis.

▶ [The initial four patients with AIDS were described by Gottlieb et al. in 1981 (*N. Engl. J. Med.* 305:1425–1431,1981). The original four patients had altered distribution of T-cell subsets, determined by immunofluorescent staining with monoclonal antibodies. The ratio of helper-suppressor lymphocytes was reduced. The study by Kornfeld et al. that is abstracted above was reported late in 1982 and was one of the first to examine lymphocyte subpopulations in a large group of homosexual men. The observations reported in the study have since been widely confirmed.

Four principal immunologic features have been described in the AIDS syndrome. First, the helper-suppresor cell ratio of T-lymphocytes is reversed. Second, natural killer cell activity is reduced. Third, autoimmune phenomena are sometimes seen; for example, the features of systemic lupus erythematosus. The fourth feature is an extraordinary immunodeficiency that equals and usually surpasses in magnitude that associated with treatment with immunosuppressive drugs. This profound disturbance in cell-mediated immunity contrasts with a relatively normal humoral immunity. The cellular immunodeficiency is reflected in lymphopenia, defective skin sensitivity to various antigens, and defective in vitro lymphocyte transformation.] ◀

22–3 **Acquired Immune Deficiency in Haitians: Opportunistic Infections in Previously Healthy Haitian Immigrants.** Over 700 cases of acquired immunodeficiency syndrome (AIDS) have been reported to the Centers for Disease Control (CDC) since June 1981, including 34 cases among Haitian immigrants. Jeffrey Vieira, Elliot Frank, Thomas J. Spira and Sheldon H. Landesman reviewed findings in 10 Haitians with AIDS and opportunistic infections, seen in 1981–1982. The patients were previously healthy men with no history of homosexuality or drug abuse. Mean age at diagnosis was 29 years, and mean time of residence in the United States before the illness was 2.7 years.

Six of the 10 patients died, and 2 survivors were ill at follow-up. Most patients presented with fever and weight loss; several had mild gastrointestinal symptoms. Three patients had localized adenopathy due to *Myobacterium tuberculosis,* and 1 had *Cryptococcus neoformans* infection. Four patients had intracerebral lesions due to *Toxoplasma gondii.* All 6 patients with *M. tuberculosis* infection developed opportunistic infection within months after the start of isoniazid and rifam-

(22–3) N. Engl. J. Med. 308:125–129, Jan. 30, 1983.

pin therapy. All 10 patients were anergic to skin-test antigens. A marked reduction in helper-inducer lymphocytes was found; the ratio of helper to suppressor cells was decreased more than 10-fold compared with normal heterosexual men. Mitogen stimulation was impaired in all 3 patients tested. Serologic evidence of previous infection by cytomegalovirus, herpes simplex virus, *Toxoplasma gondii* or hepatitis A virus was present in several patients.

Acquired immunodeficiency syndrome was manifested by a variety of opportunistic infections in these heterosexual Haitian men. The infections present were those against which cell-mediated immunity ordinarily has the major role in host defense. The pathogenesis of AIDS is unclear. The usual epidemiologic features were generally absent in these Haitian patients, but cytomegalovirus infection is a possible factor. It is possible, though unlikely, that the pathogenesis differs in homosexual men and Haitians. Aggressive patient evaluation is necessary if the diagnosis is not readily apparent or empiric therapy fails to induce a prompt response.

▶ [The manifestations of acquired immunodeficiency syndrome (AIDS) first surfaced about 1979, with the major foci in New York and in California. Of the first 300 patients described, over 290 came from the United States. Recent cases have appeared, however, throughout many parts of the world, including the Caribbean basin, the Far East, and parts of Africa. The reason for the apparently high incidence of AIDS among Haitians is unknown. Apparently none of the patients reported in this study were homosexual or used illicit drugs. The authors note that an interesting common epidemiologic feature linking the groups susceptible to AIDS, including Haitians, homosexuals, intravenous drug abusers, and hemophiliacs, is a high incidence of hepatitis B viral markers.] ◀

22–4 **Immunodeficiency in Female Sexual Partners of Men With the Acquired Immunodeficiency Syndrome.** The current outbreak of acquired immunodeficiency syndrome (AIDS) among previously healthy adults may be due to a transmissible agent and may be preceded by immunologic abnormalities. Carol Harris, Catherine Butkus Small, Robert S. Klein, Gerald H. Friedland, Bernice Moll, Eugene E. Emeson, Ilyâ Spigland, and Neal H. Steigbigel assessed 7 female sexual partners of men with AIDS. All the patients were previously healthy men under age 60 years who were drug abusers and who had evidence of cellular immunodeficiency and of severe opportunistic infection or Kaposi's sarcoma or both. One of the women was found to have the complete syndrome, and a second had features consistent with the prodrome of AIDS, including generalized lymphadenopathy, lymphopenia, and a decreased ratio of helper to suppresor T cells. Four other subjects had generalized lymphadenopathy or lymphopenia, with or without a decreased ratio of helper to suppressor T cells. Only 1 woman was free of all abnormalities. One subject had manifestations of cutaneous anergy. Two women had markedly increased IgG levels, and 1 of them also had a marked increase in IgA.

Subjects who are sexual partners of heterosexual men with AIDS appear to be at risk of acquiring the syndrome. The findings in this study suggest that AIDS may be sexually transmitted between het-

(22–4) N. Engl. J. Med. 308:1181–1184, May 19, 1983.

erosexual men and women. Further observations are necessary to determine whether opportunistic infections or Kaposi's sarcoma will eventually develop in the women who were assessed. The recent finding of a cluster of men in California with Kaposi's sarcoma and *Pneumocystis carinii* pneumonia supports the view that an agent transmissible to sexual contacts may be responsible for abnormalities in cellular immunity in AIDS, but all these patients were homosexuals and had had many sexual partners. The present female subjects denied having had sexual contact with anyone other than their male partners for a mean of about 8 years.

▶ [This study suggests that AIDS may be sexually transmitted between heterosexual men and women.] ◀

22–5 **T-Lymphocyte Subpopulations in Patients With Classic Hemophilia Treated With Cryoprecipitate and Lyophilized Concentrates.** The clustering of acquired immunodeficiency syndrome (AIDS) in patients with common sexual contacts and the occurrence of *Pneumocystis carinii* pneumonia in hemophilic users of factor VIII concentrates have suggested that AIDS may be transmitted to hemophiliacs through factor VIII infusion. Jay E. Menitove, Richard H. Aster, James T. Casper, Stephen J. Lauer, Jerome L. Gottschall, James E. Williams, Joan C. Gill, Dana V. Wheeler, Vicki Piaskowski, Phyllis Kirchner, and Robert R. Montgomery (Milwaukee) examined this possibility by immunologic analysis of healthy hemophiliacs treated with cryoprecipitate from volunteer blood donors or commercial lyophilized factor VIII concentrates. None of the 22 patients studied was known to be homosexual. Sixteen age-matched normal subjects were also studied.

An abnormal ratio of helper (T4) to suppressor (T8) lymphocytes was found in 36% of patients, and this was the most powerful discriminator between patients given cryoprecipitate and those given commercial concentrate. The T4-T8 ratios in cryoprecipitate users differed significantly from those in patients given factor VIII concentrate. The amount of exposure to factor VIII did not correlate with the T4-T8 ratio in the concentrate group. Natural killer cells were slightly but not significantly reduced in hemophiliacs compared with control subjects. Patients with abnormal T4-T8 ratios had higher serum IgG concentrations than those with normal ratios. Only 2 patients had absolute lymphocyte counts of less than 1,500/cu mm. Only 1 had hepatitis B surface antigen; he used only cryoprecipitate and had a normal T4-T8 ratio.

These findings are consistent with the possibility that commercial lyophilized factor VIII concentrate can induce an AIDS-like condition. The clinical sequelae, if any, are unclear, but patients using factor VIII concentrate should be closely monitored for signs of AIDS and changes in immunologic status.

22–6 **Immunologic Evaluation of Hemophiliac Patients and Their Wives: Relationships to the Acquired Immunodeficiency Syndrome.** The acquired immunodeficiency syndrome, possibly due to a

(22–5) N. Engl. J. Med. 308:83–86, Jan. 13, 1983.
(22–6) Ann. Intern. Med. 99:159–164, August 1983.

sexually transmittable infectious agent, also has been observed in heterosexual drug abusers and their consorts, in Haitian refugees, and in at least 8 hemophiliacs given factor concentrate therapy. Richard D. deShazo, W. Abe Andes, Judy Nordberg, Julie Newton, Carolyn Daul, and Brian Bozelka (Tulane Univ.) undertook an immunologic study of 24 patients with classic hemophilia and 5 with factor IX deficiency. Twenty of the patients with classic hemophilia had severe and 4 had mild factor VIII deficiency. Three patients had mild and 2 had severe factor IX deficiency. Age range was 10–66 years. No patient had recently been ill. None were homosexuals or drug abusers. There was wide variation in the amount of lyophilized factor concentrate used by the patients. Studies also were done in 5 apparently healthy wives of classic hemophiliacs and 17 healthy male volunteers, matched for age with the hemophiliacs.

Both groups of patients had decreased percentages and numbers of helper-inducer lymphocytes and increased percentages of suppressor-cytotoxic T cells, with depressed helper-suppressor ratios. The abnormalities were most marked in 7 classic hemophiliacs with lymphadenopathy who also had an increase in Ia+ cells and suppressed lymphocyte responses to mitogens. The helper-suppressor T-cell ratio was not related to lymphocyte responsiveness or to the amount of factor VIII concentrate used in a year. The wives who were studied had decreased percentages of helper T cells but had normal lymphocyte mitogenic responses. Serum levels of IgG were elevated in classic hemophiliacs but not in their wives or in factor IX–deficient patients.

The changes in mononuclear cell populations described in acquired immunodeficiency syndrome have been observed in treated hemophilic patients without the apparent risk factors identified in homosexual men. The findings support the hypothesis that chronic infection with a blood product-transmissible agent is the most likely cause of the abnormalities observed. Further studies of hemophiliacs should help elucidate the cause of the syndrome in persons with nontraditional life-styles.

▶ [This and the previous study indicate that T-lymphocyte subpopulation abnormalities exist in asymptomatic hemophilic patients. Lymphocyte mitogenic responses are also depressed. These abnormalities apparently correlate with administration of factor VIII or factor IX concentrates. The abnormalities tend to be most severe in otherwise asymptomatic hemophilic patients who develop lymphadenopathy. Because consorts of patients with acquired immunodeficiency syndrome (AIDS) have apparently acquired the disease through contact, the writers of this report investigated the wives of five hemophilic patients receiving factor VIII replacement therapy. They observed that the lymphocyte-proliferative responses of the wives were normal and that their lymphocyte population ratios, although lower, were not significantly different from control values.

The etiology of AIDS is, of course, still uncertain, although a strong case can be made for the syndrome being linked to an infectious agent of some sort. Cytomegalovirus, Epstein-Barr virus, enteroviruses, and, as we shall see, human T-cell leukemia virus have been put forward as possible candidates. An intriguing question is whether this is a "new" disease syndrome. Other "new" infectious diseases have been brought to light as a consequence of changed technical or social practices. For example, the Marburg virus infected some laboratory workers preparing polio vaccine from vervet monkey kidney cell lines in the late 1960s. This disease may have been rife in the African jungles for centuries but would not have come to medical attention except for the introduction of a particular technical procedure. Recognition of the viral hepatitis B syndrome followed the widespread introduction of blood transfusion practices in the 1920s. It was some three decades before its clinical course was well defined. Had it not been for the use of blood and blood products, hepatitis B might have first appeared to be a sexually transmitted disease.] ◀

22–7 **Acquired Immunodeficiency Syndrome in a Colony of Macaque Monkeys.** The acquired immunodeficiency syndrome (AIDS) in man represents a breakdown of normal immune function that can provide a model for examining the role of the immune system in protecting individuals against infections and tumors. Norman L. Letvin, Kathryn A. Eaton, Wayne R. Aldrich, Prabhat K. Sehgal, Beverly J. Blake, Stuart F. Schlossman, Norval W. King, and Ronald D. Hunt describe a naturally occurring immunodeficiency syndrome in macaque monkeys, primarily *Macaca cyclopis*. Affected animals died of lymphoma, which is rare in macaques, or of such opportunistic infections as *Pneumocystis carinii* and noma (necrotizing gingivitis). The animals had anemia, neutropenia, and a circulating bizarre immature monocyte with vacuolated cytoplasm. Results of liver function studies suggested hepatitis. The sites where the animals were housed appeared related to the risk of development of the syndrome. Lymphocyte proliferative responses were markedly reduced in affected animals. The ratio of helper to suppressor T cells in *M. cyclopis* was lower than in either *Macaca mulatta* in the same colony or in normal human beings.

There is epidemiologic evidence for a common source agent in this syndrome that may provide a useful model for studying human AIDS. The finding of bizarre immature monocyte forms in the marrow and in the peripheral blood, however, is unique to the monkeys. These cells may be transformed by an unidentified viral agent that may be etiologically important in the disease process, or they may reflect reactive changes by the monocytes to an infectious process. The hepatitis in macaques also differs from human AIDS. Disease transmission similar to that in human AIDS is a possibility in macaques, which exhibit bisexual activity in captivity. Further studies of the disease in monkeys may yield insights into the mechanisms by which immune surveillance can break down.

▶ [Opportunistic infections in the affected monkeys included *Pneumocystis carinii*. In human AIDS a striking feature has been the range of infectious agents that have been implicated. These include protozoa (*P. carinii* and *Entamoeba histolytica*), yeast (*Candida albicans* and *Candida neoformans*), bacteria (*Mycobacterium tuberculosis* and *Mycobacterium avium-intracellulare*), and viruses (for example, *Herpesvirus hominis* and cytomegalovirus).] ◀

22–8 **Isolation of Human T-Cell Leukemia Virus in Acquired Immune Deficiency Syndrome (AIDS).** The human T-cell leukemia-lymphoma virus (HTLV) was first isolated from mature T cells associated with certain T-cell malignancies in adults. Several isolates of a human type C retrovirus belonging to the HTLV group were obtained from adults with T-cell leukemia or lymphoma. Robert C. Gallo, Prem S. Sarin, E. P. Gelmann, Marjorie Robert-Guroff, Ersell

(22–7) Proc. Natl. Acad. Sci. USA 80:2718–2722, May 1983.
(22–8) Science 220:865–867, Apr. 19, 1983.

Richardson, V. S. Kalyanaraman, Dean Mann, Gurdip D. Sidhu, Rosalyn E. Stahl, Susan Zolla-Pazner, Jacque Leibowitch, and Mikulas Popovic sought HTLV in patients with the epidemic T-cell disorder known as acquired immunodeficiency syndrome (AIDS), because of the T-cell tropism of HTLV and its prevalence in the Caribbean basin.

Peripheral blood lymphocytes from a patient in the United States and 2 patients in France, when cultured with T-cell growth factor, expressed HTLV antigens. The virus isolated from the American patient was related to HTLV subgroup I. The virus was transmitted to normal human T cells from umbilical cord blood of a newborn infant. The HTLV antigens were identified by indirect immunofluorescence with a highly specific monoclonal antibody and also by a competitive radioimmunoprecipitation assay in both the umbilical cord blood T-cell line and the donor cell line.

Whether or not HTLV subgroup I or other retroviruses with T-cell tropism cause AIDS, patients from whom the virus is isolated may be able to transmit it to others. The high rate of AIDS in homosexuals who have not received blood or used intravenous drugs suggests that the agent is transmitted during sexual contact by sperm or saliva; it may be possible to detect HTLV antigen in these secretions and to transmit the virus to cord blood by coculturing. Also, HTLV can infect marmoset and other primate T cells, suggesting that an animal model of AIDS might be developed.

▶ [In the next chapter we shall review several articles about the human T-cell leukemia virus and its association with certain types of leukemia and lymphoma. Here we are concerned with a possible role for this virus in the pathogenesis of AIDS. Five reports in a single issue of *Science* (vol. 221, Sept. 9, 1983) suggested a possible link between AIDS and human T-cell leukemia virus. Several observations suggest a link between HTLV and AIDS: First is the prevalence of HTLV in the Caribbean basin and in Africa, where AIDS has frequently been reported. Second is the observation that HTLV primarily infects T lymphocytes—a cell that is defective in AIDS. A third point of similarity is transmission by intimate contact and through blood products. Finally, there are the numerous examples of viruses causing both leukemia and immunosuppression.

Arguing against a causal relationship between HTLV and AIDS is the relatively short time required for the immunodeficiency disease to develop. The T-cell leukemia caused by HTLV may require years to develop. Furthermore, there is no evidence for an increase in AIDS in the southern area of Japan, where HTLV infection rates are very high.] ◀

22–9 **Disorders of B Cells and Helper T Cells in the Pathogenesis of the Immunoglobulin Deficiency of Patients With Ataxia Telangiectasia.** Recurrent infections are a major feature of ataxia telangiectasia (AT), an autosomal recessive multisystem disorder that includes a high incidence of neoplasia and a variable immunodeficiency state. Both the cellular and humoral immune systems are affected. T. A. Waldmann, S. Broder, C. K. Goldman, K. Frost, S. J. Korsmeyer, and M. A. Medici investigated the pathogenesis of immunoglobulin deficiency in 10 patients with AT, using an invitro immunoglobulin biosynthetic system. Fourteen patients had an in-

(22–9) J. Clin. Invest. 71:282–295, February 1983.

creased incidence of sinopulmonary infections. Ten patients had no serum IgA detected by radial diffusion in agar, and 3 others had reduced concentrations.

On culturing peripheral blood mononuclear cells with pokeweed mitogen, immunoglobulin synthesis was below normal for IgM in 5 of 17 patients, for IgG in 8, and for IgA in 14. Mononuclear cells from 9 of the 10 patients with no detectable serum IgA failed to synthesize IgA in vitro. No patient had excessive suppressor-cell activity. All had measurable, though reduced helper T-cell activity for immunoglobulin synthesis by cocultured normal pokeweed mitogen-stimulated B cells. Addition of normal irradiated T cells to patient mononuclear cells led to augmented IgM synthesis in 15 of 17 cases, and increased IgG synthesis in 9 of 17 cases. Synthesis of IgA was increased in all 8 patients tested who had undetectable serum IgA. No IgA synthesis was seen in 9 of 10 of these cases on coculture with normal T cells, and these cells failed to produce IgA when stimulated with the relatively helper T-cell-independent polyclonal activators, *Nocardia opaca* water-soluble mitogen and Epstein-Barr virus.

A helper T-cell defect seems to contribute to decreased immunoglobulin synthesis in AT but is not the sole cause. A B-cell defect also may contribute. The existence of a broad defect in lymphocyte maturation and observations of persistent α-feto-protein production by AT patients indicate a generalized defect in tissue differentiation in this disorder. Failure of an enzyme system could account for both increased x-ray sensitivity and the failure of normal maturation of certain tissues critical for immunoglobulin production.

▶ [Ataxia telangiectasia is an autosomal recessive disorder affecting multiple organ systems. It is characterized by cerebellar ataxia, oculocutaneous telangiectasia, a high incidence of neoplasms, recurrent sinopulmonary infection, and a variable immunodeficiency state. The disorder is associated with increased sensitivity to ionizing irradiation that may result from a defect in the ability to repair DNA. Other characteristics of the disorder include an embryonic-appearing thymus and persistent production of fetal hepatic protein. On the basis of these observations it has been postulated that the disorder may result from a defect in tissue differentiation. The studies reported in this article indicate a broad defect in lymphocyte maturation in patients with this disorder.] ◀

22–10 **X-linked Lymphoproliferative Syndrome: Natural History of the Immunodeficiency.** The X-linked lymphoproliferative syndrome is characterized by immunodeficiency to Epstein-Barr virus (EBV), which is manifested by severe or fatal infectious mononucleosis and acquired immunodeficiency. John L. Sullivan, Kevin S. Byron, Frank E. Brewster, Sharon M. Baker, and Hans D. Ochs examined immune responsiveness in 6 male subjects from a kindred with the X-linked lymphoproliferative syndrome. Two subjects were studied before and during acute fatal EBV infection, and 4 years after they had survived EBV infection.

Both deaths were due to liver failure; 1 patient had extensive liver necrosis, and the other developed massive hepatic infiltration by EBV-infected immunoblasts after aggressive immunosuppressive

(22–10) J. Clin. Invest. 71:1765–1778, June 1983.

therapy. Both patients developed vigorous cytotoxic cellular responses against both infected and uninfected target cells during acute EBV infection. Anomalous killer and natural killer T-cell activity against a variety of lymphoid cell lines, autologous fibroblasts, and autologous hepatocytes was demonstrated. The effector cells responsible for anomalous killing belonged to the OKT8 T-cell subset. The 4 surviving subjects exhibited global cellular immune defects with deficient lymphocyte responses to mitogens and antigens, humoral immune deficiencies, abnormalities of regulatory T-cell subsets, and deficient natural killer cell activity.

It appears that an aberrant immune response is triggered by acute EBV infection in subjects with the X-linked lymphoproliferative syndrome, resulting in unregulated anomalous killer and natural killer cell activity directed against EBV-infected and uninfected cells. Secondary immune deficits in surviving subjects may predispose them to bacterial infections and perhaps to lymphoreticular malignancies. Studies of regulatory mechanisms for anomalous killer and natural killer cells activated during infectious mononucleosis in normal persons may increase understanding of acquired immunodeficiency in man.

▶ [In 1974 and 1975 three families were described in which an X-linked immunodeficiency to EBV resulted in fatal infectious mononucleosis in affected males (Purtillo et al., *Lancet* 1:935, 1975). Subsequent studies of these families have demonstrated that fatal infectious mononucleosis, acquired immunodeficiency, and lymphoproliferative disorders occur with high frequency in males. Approximately 70% of affected males die with a fatal infectious mononucleosis syndrome, with severe hepatitis and liver failure accounting for most deaths. The majority of those who survive their initial infection with EBV develop an immunodeficiency disorder characterized by hypogammaglobulinemia and recurrent infections.

In the study abstracted above, two affected males had normal cellular and humoral immunity before EBV infection. The demonstration of major defects in the immune system of individuals surviving infection is good evidence for an aberrant immune response specifically triggered by EBV.] ◀

23. Leukemia and Lymphoma

23–1 **Survey of Human Leukemias for Sequences of a Human Retrovirus.** Human T-cell leukemia-lymphoma virus (HTLV) is a human retrovirus closely linked with a subtype of adult T-cell malignancy. It can be transmitted to cord blood T lymphocytes in vitro, and the infected cells exhibit features of transformed neoplastic T cells. Flossie Wong-Staal, Beatrice Hahn, Vittorio Manzari, Sandra Colombini, Genoveffa Franchini, Edward P. Gelmann, and Robert C. Gallo (Natl. Cancer Inst., Bethesda, Md.) recently cloned DNA sequences derived from 1 kilobase (kb) of the 5′ and 3′ termini of the HTLV genome, as well as a 4–5-kb defective HTLV provirus flanked by cellular sequences. These probes have been used in a limited survey of fresh or cultured cells from patients with various lymphoid and myeloid malignancies to seek HTLV-related DNA sequences.

DNA from 5 Japanese patients with adult T cell leukemia contained 1 or 2 copies of HTLV provirus. One of the patients had no circulating antibody against HTLV antigen. A patient with T-cell acute lymphocytic leukemia had antibody reactive with HTLV antigen although his leukemic cells were immature T cells, which are usually not the target for HTLV infection. On hybridization the leukemic cells lacked HTLV DNA sequences. Positive samples also were obtained from leukemic cells of an Israeli patient with peripheral diffuse lymphoma, and a skin biopsy from a Brazilian patient with mycosis fungoides. Samples from patients with Sézary syndrome and cutaneous T-cell lymphoma, and 20 acute and chronic lymphocytic leukemia samples were negative.

It is concluded that all HTLV-positive fresh leukemic cells and cultured cell lines are clonal populations of infected cells. The tumor cells appear to be clonal expansions of single infected cells. Although the prototype HTLV is specifically associated with mature T-cell malignancies, cloned HTLV sequences may prove useful in detecting cross-reactive putative human retroviruses involved in other malignancies.

▶ [The human T-cell leukemia virus (HTLV) initially described in 1980 was isolated from an American patient with mycosis fungoides—a form of T-cell lymphoma with extensive skin involvement. Subsequently, the same virus was found in patients with lymphoid malignancies of a variety of types, both in the United States and in other geographical areas including southern Japan, the Caribbean, and the Middle East. Most of the viruses are of a single type (type I), although a second type has recently been described in a patient with hairy-cell leukemia. HTLV is distinct from other previously identified animal retroviruses. It appears to be acquired by postnatal, or at least postzygotic, infection. The virus has been cloned, but the genetic sequences responsible for malignant transformation have not yet been identified with certainty.

(23–1) Nature 302:626–628, Apr. 14, 1983.

It has been suggested, however, that these oncogenic sequences lie near the 3′ (right-hand) end of the virus. A recent observation of interest is that cell lines producing HTLV showed altered HLA expression. This phenomenon may be the result of homology between HTLV virus envelope proteins and class I HLA genes.

In the articles that follow we shall review some of the clinical features of the HTLV disease syndromes.] ◀

23–2 **Antibodies to Human T-Cell Leukemia Virus Membrane Antigens in Hemophiliacs.** Hemophiliacs are one of the groups at risk for acquired immunodeficiency syndrome (AIDS). Most researchers suspect that AIDS may be due at least in part to an infectious agent, and human T-cell leukemia virus (HTLV) is one candidate for such

Fig 23–1.—Reactivity of serum samples from asymptomatic hemophiliacs positive for antibody to human T-cell leukemia virus membrane antigens (HTLV-MA), as determined by sodium dodecyl sulfate–polyacrylamide gel electrophoresis. Samples were tested by radioimmunoprecipitation of Hut 102 cells (lanes a–i) and T8402 cells (lanes j–o) exposed to ^{35}S-cysteine. Lysate supernatant was cleared once with 50 μl of Protein-A Sepharose CL-4B (Protein-A beads) before portions were reacted with the following serum samples preabsorbed with Protein-A beads: *a*, representative serum negative for antibodies to HTLV-MA from healthy resident of Kyushu, Japan (HTLV-endemic region) (10 μl); *b*, reference goat antiserum to purified p24 of HTLV (3 μl); *c and j*, representative serum positive for antibodies to HTLV-MA from healthy resident of Kyushu (3 μl); *d and k*, representative serum sample positive for antibodies to HTLV-MA from Japanese patient with adult T-cell leukemia (5 μl); *e and l*, representative serum positive for antibodies to HTLV-MA from patient with acquired immunodeficiency syndrome (10 μl); *f and m*, representative sample positive for antibodies to HTLV-MA from asymptomatic hemophiliac (10 μl); *g and n*, representative sample positive for antibodies to HTLV-MA from asymptomatic hemophiliac (10 μl); *h and o*, representative serum sample negative for antibodies to HTLV-MA from asymptomatic hemophiliac (10 μl); *i*, representative serum sample negative for antibodies to HTLV-MA from asymptomatic hemophiliac (10 μl). Molecular weight markers were ^{14}C-phosphorylase b (92,500), bovine serum albumin (68,000), ovalbumin (46,000), carbonic anhydrase (30,000), and cytochrome *c* (12,000); arrow indicates 61,000-dalton glycoprotein. (Courtesy of Essex, M., et al.: Science 221:1061–1064, Sept. 9, 1983; copyright 1983 by the American Association for the Advancement of Science.)

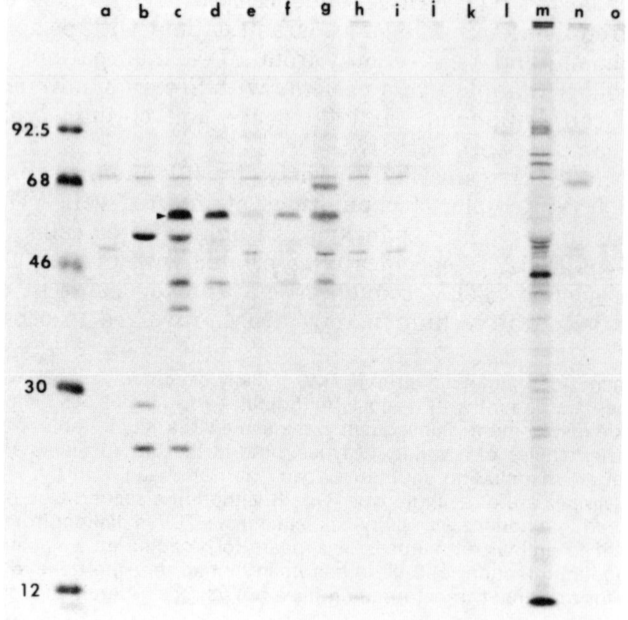

(23–2) Science 221:1061–1064, Sept. 9, 1983.

an agent. M. Essex, M. F. McLane, T. H. Lee, N. Tachibana, J. I. Mullins (Harvard Univ.), J. Kreiss (Los Angeles), C. K. Kasper (Univ. of Southern California), M.-C. Poon, A. Landay (Univ. of Alabama), S. F. Stein (Emory Univ.), D. P. Francis, C. Cabradilla, D. N. Lawrence, and B. L. Evatt (Centers for Disease Control) examined serum samples from 172 hemophiliacs who were asymptomatic, 2 with AIDS, and 1 with severe lymphadenopathy for the presence of antibodies to cell membrane antigens associated with HTLV (HTLV-MA). A previous study showed antibody to HTLV-MA in 36% of a group of patients with AIDS. Antibodies to HTLV-MA were detected in 5%–19% of hemophiliacs from 4 geographic locations. Representative findings are shown in Figure 23–1. Antibodies were found in 1% or fewer of laboratory workers, normal blood donors, donors receiving hemodialysis, and donors with chronic active hepatitis.

These findings are consistent with earlier observations that patients with AIDS have increased rates of exposure to HTLV compared with control subjects. The data do not, however, necessarily support the hypothesis that HTLV is etiologically associated with AIDS. Hemophiliacs may have immune system abnormalities before exposure to HTLV that enhance the risk of infection when HTLV-carrier blood or blood products are infused. Because hemophiliacs have frequent contact with major medical centers, they may be a good population in which to determine prospectively whether persons exposed to HTLV are at increased risk for disease.

▶ [This is one of the articles that attempts to link HTLV with exposure to blood products and perhaps to AIDS.] ◀

23–3 **Human T-Cell Leukemia-Lymphoma Virus, Lymphoma, Lytic Bone Lesions, and Hypercalcemia.** The human T-cell leukemia-lymphoma (HTLV) virus is the first type C retrovirus to be consistently associated with human malignancy. Douglas W. Blayney, Elaine S. Jaffe, Richard I. Fisher, Geraldine P. Schechter, Jeffrey Cossman, Marjorie Robert-Guroff, V. S. Kalyanaraman, William A. Blattner, and Robert C. Gallo describe three patients with a subset of mature T-cell lymphomas associated with HTLV. All had advanced peripheral T-cell lymphoma and hypercalcemia and were identified as positive for antibody to HTLV when stored serums were retrospectively analyzed. The virus was isolated from malignant cells in two cases when previously frozen tumor cells were placed in tissue culture.

One patient had hypercalcemia of 6 months' duration, and 2 patients had circulating malignant lymphocytes. The malignant cells in all cases had surface markers characteristic of T lymphocytes. All patients had natural serum antibodies to disrupted HTLV and to one or both of the viral structural proteins p19 and p24. All patients had node biopsy findings of diffuse, aggressive non-Hodgkin's lymphoma. One tumor was classified as the "histiocytic" type, and 2 tumors were classed as the diffuse, mixed-cell type.

These cases indicate that patients with adult peripheral T-cell lym-

---

(23–3) Ann. Intern. Med. 98:144–151, February 1983.

phomas, especially those with lytic bone lesions and hypercalcemia, may have antibodies to HTLV, a type C RNA human tumor virus. Two of the authors' patients were from areas where HTLV has not previously been recognized. There is strong evidence that HTLV can cause malignant lymphoma. Longitudinal studies are needed to clarify the role of HTLV in malignant lymphoma, the lymphoma attack rate in antibody-positive persons, and the mode of HTLV transmission.

▶ [As noted earlier, HTLV has been implicated not only in a variety of T-cell malignancies but also in the AIDS syndrome. Antibodies to cell membrane antigens associated with human T-cell leukemia virus have been detected in patients with AIDS (see Essex et al., *Science* 220:859, 1983).] ◀

23–4 **Clinical Course of Retrovirus-Associated Adult T-Cell Lymphoma in the United States.** A human type C retrovirus has been isolated from patients with T-cell lymphomas and an "adult T-cell leukemia," characterized by frequent skin lesions, high white blood cell count, and a rapidly fatal terminal course, has been described. Paul A. Bunn, Jr., Geraldine P. Schechter, Elaine Jaffe, Douglas Blayney, Robert C. Young, Mary J. Matthews, William Blattner, Samuel Broder, Marjorie Robert-Guroff, and Robert C. Gallo report data on 11 patients with serum antibody to human T-cell lymphoma virus who had an aggressive form of T-cell non-Hodgkin's lymphoma in association with a paraneoplastic syndrome. Most patients were young. Median age was 33 years. All but 2 were black. Seven of the 11 were men. Seven patients had been born in the southeastern part of the United States, 2 in Jamaica, 1 in Israel, and 1 in Ecuador.

Median duration of symptoms at the time of diagnosis was 2 months. Six patients had cutaneous nodules, plaques, papules, or erythroderma. Skin biopsy specimens were diagnostic of lymphoma in all patients but 1. A polymorphic lymphoid infiltrate of the dermis and Pautrier microabscesses were present in some cases. Five patients had symptoms and signs of hypercalcemia, and most of the patients who presented with skin lesions developed hypercalcemia within several weeks or months. All patients had elevated alkaline phosphatase levels, and bone scans suggested metabolic bone disease with increased bone turnover. Renal and hepatic dysfunction and increased cellular turnover were prominent features. Circulating malignant cells were readily recognized in 9 patients. All patients had stage IV disease before treatment. Node biopsy specimens showed diffuse malignant lymphoma. Five patients had diffuse interstitial pulmonary infiltrates at the onset, and 3 had lymphomatous leptomeningitis. Opportunistic infections such as *Pneumocystis carinii* pneumonia were frequent. Intensive combination chemotherapy led to prompt remissions, but these generally were of short duration. Seven patients have died; 4 remain alive after 2–42 months.

Retrovirus-associated T-cell lymphoma should be suspected in patients who have an acute onset of generalized skin lesions or hypercalcemia with metabolic bone abnormalities. Intensive combination

---

(23–4) N. Engl. J. Med. 309:257–264, Aug. 4, 1983.

chemotherapy is indicated, with prophylactic treatment of the CNS when a complete response is obtained.

▶ [This is the best overall clinical description of this syndrome that I have found thus far. Hypercalcemia as a manifestation should be underlined; the lytic bone lesions are often extremely extensive.] ◀

23–5 **A Randomized Study of Radiotherapy Versus Radiotherapy Plus Chemotherapy in Stage I–II Non-Hodgkin's Lymphoma.** In most studies of non-Hodgkin's lymphoma, the relapse rate remains disappointingly high. Nis I. Nissen, Jens Ersbøll, Hanne Sand Hansen, Sven Walbom-Jørgensen, Jens Pedersen-Bjergaard, Mogens Mørk Hansen, and Jørgen Rygård (Copenhagen) reported a randomized prospective trial conducted in 1974–1978 in 73 patients with non-Hodgkin's lymphoma in clinical stages I and II who received extended-field radiotherapy alone or with adjuvant chemotherapy with vincristine, streptonigrin, cyclophosphamide, and prednisone. All subclasses of lymphoma were included in the study. A total central tumor dose of 3,700–4,300 rads of 6-MeV irradiation was delivered over a period of 4–5 weeks, with further doses in cases of persistent tumor. Chemotherapy was begun at the same time as radiotherapy, and was given for 3 years after a 6-week induction regimen. The median follow-up was 5 years.

Adjunctive chemotherapy was given to 40 of the 73 study patients. Prognostic variables were fairly evenly distributed in the two treatment groups. All patients except possibly 2 in the radiotherapy group had complete remissions. The relapse rate was 54% with radiotherapy and 10% with combined treatment. Recurrences of both stage I and stage II disease were significantly less with combined treatment. The difference persisted after adjustment for age and sex. Most relapses in the radiotherapy group occurred in the first year of follow-up (Fig 23–2). All but 5 of 18 radiotherapy patients who relapsed died of progressive disease, despite altered treatment. Complications were more frequent in the combined-treatment group. Hematologic toxicity

Fig 23–2.—Relapse-free survival in patients with stage I–II non-Hodgkin's lymphoma treated with radiotherapy (RT) or RT and chemotherapy (RT + CT). (Courtesy of Nissen, N.I., et al.: Cancer 52:1–7, July 1, 1983.)

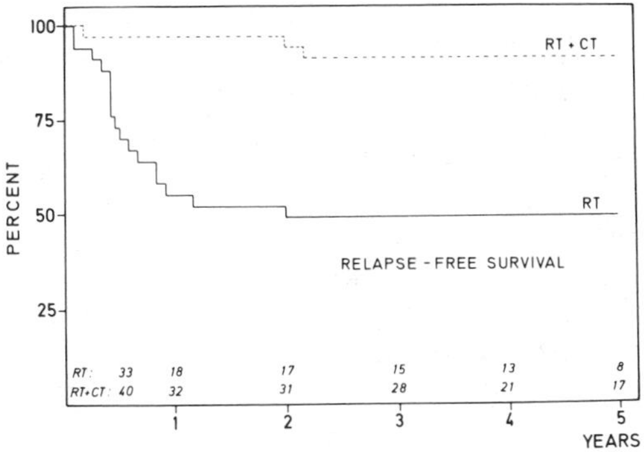

(23–5) Cancer 52:1–7, July 1, 1983.

and infections continued to occur during prolonged "maintenance" chemotherapy. No secondary malignant neoplasms developed. Three combined-treatment patients died of progressive disease.

It is suggested that adjuvant chemotherapy be used with radiotherapy in patients with stage I–II non-Hodgkin's lymphoma of unfavorable histologic characteristics. Salvage chemotherapy remains a possibility in patients who relapse, especially those with nodular lymphoma. Further work is needed to determine whether chemotherapy alone is as effective as combined treatment in patients with unfavorable histologic findings.

▶ [The results appear to be impressive and should be noted. Clearly they should be tested in a larger series of patients before this aggressive program becomes the standard approach to stage I and II poor-prognostic categories of non-Hodgkin's lymphoma.] ◀

23–6 **Comparison of Adriamycin-Containing Chemotherapy (MOP-BAP) With MOPP-Bleomycin in Management of Advanced Hodgkin's Disease: A Southwest Oncology Group Study.** Preliminary study indicated that Adriamycin can safely be added to the nitrogen mustard, vincristine, procarbazine, prednisone plus bleomycin (MOPP-Bleo) chemotherapeutic regimen for Hodgkin's disease. Stephen E. Jones, Arthur Haut, James K. Weick, Henry E. Wilson, Petre Grozea, Carol J. Fabian, Eugene McKelvey, Gerald E. Byrne, Jr., Robert Hartsock, Dennis O. Dixon, and Charles A. Coltman, Jr., randomly assigned 315 patients with advanced Hodgkin's disease who had not received chemotherapy to treatment with MOPP-Bleo or the same agents plus Adriamycin (MOP-BAP). All patients completed remission induction therapy, the median time in the study being 47 months.

The complete remission rate was 77% for 166 evaluable patients treated with MOP-BAP and 67% for 125 given MOPP-Bleo. The former regimen was more successful in patients with better pretreatment prognostic features, e.g., a hemoglobin value of 12 gm/dl or higher, a performance status of 70%–100%, lack of marrow involvement, age of more than 40 years, lack of symptoms, and lack of previous treatment. The duration of complete responses was similar with the two treatments, as was overall survival; but survival was better for patients with favorable pretreatment prognostic factors who were treated with MOP-BAP. Less vomiting and thrombocytopenia occurred with MOP-BAP therapy than with the MOPP-Bleo regimen. Six patients in each treatment group may have had bleomycin-induced pulmonary reactions. Only 1 patient had possible Adriamycin-induced cardiac toxicity.

Patients with prognostically more favorable advanced Hodgkin's disease obtain complete remission more often with MOP-BAP chemotherapy than with MOPP-Bleo; in addition, their survival is improved and they experience less acute toxicity. Further studies are needed to compare chemotherapy alone with combined treatment in patients with advanced Hodgkin's disease.

(23–6) Cancer 51:1339–1347, Apr. 15, 1983.

▶ [It looks as if MOP-BAP is marginally better than MOP-bleo. I still wonder whether it wouldn't be better to hold the Adriamycin in reverse for those who fail therapy (about 20%–30%). As shown by the next abstract, salvage therapy is frequently successful.] ◀

23–7 **Treatment of MOPP-Refractory Hodgkin's Disease With Vinblastine, Doxorubicin, Bleomycin, CCNU, and Dacarbazine.** As many as 50% of the patients with advanced Hodgkin's disease are candidates for some form of salvage therapy. Lawrence H. Einhorn, Stephen D. Williams, Eugene E. Stevens, William H. Bond, and Linda Chenoweth (Indiana Univ.) administered chemotherapy consisting of vinblastine, Adriamycin, bleomycin, 1,(2-chloroethyl) 3 cyclohexyl-1-nitrosurea, and dacarbazine (VABCD) to 18 patients with advanced Hodgkin's disease that was refractory to chemotherapy with combined nitrogen mustard, vincristine, prednisone, and procarbazine (MOPP). Seven patients had progressive disease during MOPP induction, and 11 relapsed within 6 months of completing treatment. Fifteen patients had stage IV disease. The median age was 26 years. Eleven patients had systemic symptoms. Previously, 11 had received radiotherapy in addition to MOPP chemotherapy.

Significant myelosuppression occurred with VABCD therapy, but there was no drug-related mortality. Bleomycin-induced pulmonary fibrosis developed in 6 patients but always was reversible. Eight patients experienced complete remission, and 5 currently are in remission after 5–36 months. Another patient had a complete remission for 30 months, relapsed with local adenopathy, and presently is free of disease at 46 months after receiving involved-field radiotherapy. The overall response rate was 88%. The median duration of partial remissions was 6 months. Complete remission was achieved in 6 of 15 patients with visceral disease. Thus, long-term disease-free survival and potential cure can be attained with VABCD chemotherapy in patients with advanced Hodgkin's disease resistant to MOPP therapy.

▶ [This aggressive chemotherapeutic combination appears to be effective in treatment of MOPP-resistant Hodgkin's disease. As the authors point out, this is a frequent problem, with approximately 40%–50% of advanced Hodgkin's disease patients ultimately requiring some form of salvage therapy. The combination of ABVD was initially put forth as the standard salvage regimen for MOPP-resistant Hodgkin's disease. The initial high success rate reported from Milan was not, however, subsequently confirmed in other treatment centers. Of a total of 74 patients with resistant disease, only 9% achieved a complete remission with ABVD in a multi-institutional study. Clearly VABCD appears to be a more promising regimen.] ◀

23–8 **Distinctive Chromosomal Abnormalities in Histologic Subtypes of Non-Hodgkin's Lymphoma.** Nonrandom chromosomal abnormalities have been described in lymphomatous lymph nodes, but adequate cytogenetic analysis has been possible in fewer than 70% of lymphoma patients. Jorge J. Yunis, Martin M. Oken, Manuel E. Kaplan, Kathy M. Ensrud, Robert R. Howe, and Athanasios Theologides (Univ. of Minnesota) have used the methotrexate synchronization technique in conjunction with immunologic cell markers to assess cytogenetic abnormalities in lymph nodes from 44 patients with non-

---

(23–7) Cancer 51:1348–1352, Apr. 15, 1983.
(23–8) N. Engl. J. Med. 307:1231–1236, Nov. 11, 1982.

Hodgkin's lymphoma. All but 2 patients had successful chromosomal analyses of node biopsy specimens. Twenty-seven patients were assessed before treatment. All but 2 patients were adults. A large majority of the lymphomas were of B-cell origin.

All 42 evaluable patients had clonal abnormalities in their chromosomes. Most of the structural defects could be fully delineated from finely banded and elongated mitoses (Fig 23–3). A translocation between chromosomes 18 and 14 was identified in 16 of 19 patients with follicular lymphomas. A translocation between chromosomes 8 and 14 was found in 5 of 6 patients with small noncleaved-cell (non-Burkitt's) or large-cell immunoblastic lymphomas. Trisomy 12 was identified in 4 of 11 patients with small-cell lymphocytic lymphoma.

Characteristic chromosomal defects apparently occur in certain subtypes of lymphoma. High-resolution chromosomal analysis may become an important means of enhancing understanding of lymphoid cancers. All evaluable patients in this present study had chromosomal abnormalities in lymph node specimens. The abnormalities

Fig 23–3.—A G-banded mitosis from a patient with small noncleaved-cell (non-Burkitt's) lymphoma, showing the average degree of chromosome elongation, banding quality, and complexity of chromosomal defects found with the methotrexate technique of cell synchronization. (Courtesy of Yunis J.J., et al.: N. Engl. J. Med. 307:1231–1236, Nov. 11, 1982; reprinted by permission of The New England Journal of Medicine.)

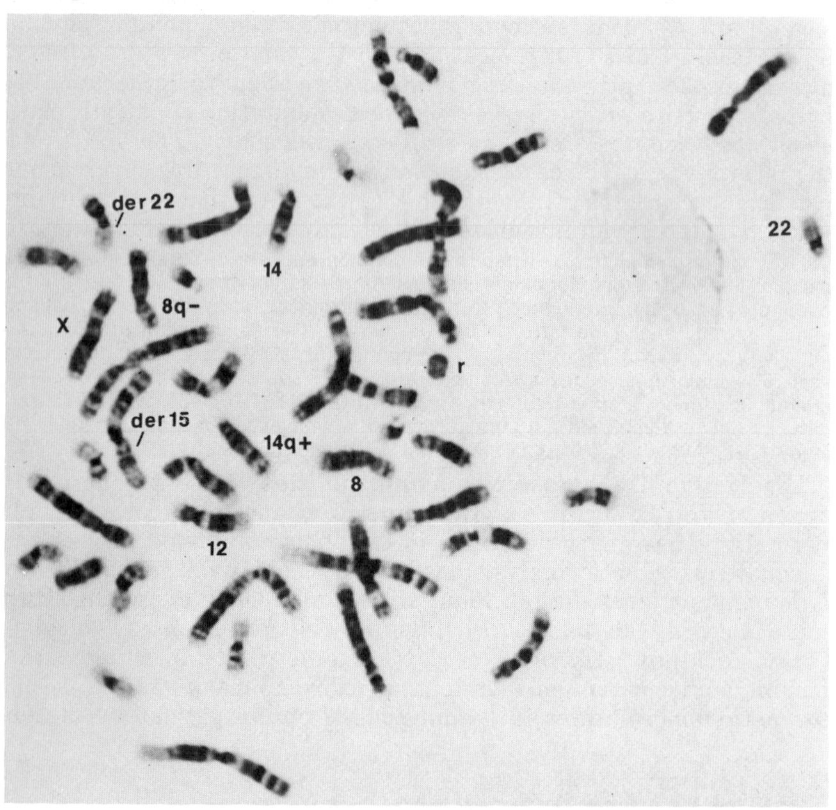

were not present in cultured lymphocytes, suggesting that they were not constitutional. In all 25 patients with a 14q+ marker chromosome, the break point was at band q32, and the donor chromosome was recognized in all instances. The constancy of the chromosome 14, band q32 break point in both Burkitt's and non-Burkitt's lymphomas suggests that an abnormality at this site may confer a proliferative advantage.

▶ [The suggestion that chromosome 14 translocations in both Burkitt's and non-Burkitt's lymphoma may confer a proliferative advantage on cell with the translocation is supported by other evidence that indicates that one of the cellular oncogenes (c-*myc*) is activated by the translocation. C-*myc* is one of a pair of oncogenes which, when introduced into normal fibroblasts, will induce a malignant transformation in vitro. The subject of oncogenes is discussed in more detail in Chapter 24, "Oncology."] ◀

23–9 **Diffuse Aggressive Lymphomas: Increased Survival After Alternating Flexible Sequences of ProMACE and MOPP Chemotherapy.** Richard I. Fisher, Vincent T. DeVita, Jr., Susan M. Hubbard, Dan L. Longo, Robert Wesley, Bruce A. Chabner, and Robert C. Young (Natl. Inst. of Health) developed a new treatment program for previously untreated patients with advanced diffuse aggressive lymphoma. Varying numbers of cycles of 2 combination chemotherapy programs, ProMACE (prednisone, methotrexate, doxorubicin, cyclophosphamide and epipodophyllotoxin VP-16) and MOPP (mechlorethamine, vincristine, procarbazine and prednisone) were followed by late intensification with the ProMACE regimen. The duration of each phase was determined by the rate of tumor response. Eighty-one consecutive patients with diffuse aggressive non-Hodgkin's lymphoma were entered into the study in 1977–1981. Seventy-nine patients having a median age of 44 years were evaluable. Fifty-six had diffuse histiocytic; 14, diffuse mixed; 7, diffuse undifferentiated; and 2, diffuse poorly differentiated lymphocytic lymphoma. Five patients had relapsed after involved-field radiotherapy.

The median time in the study now exceeds 31 months. Of 74 pa-

Fig 23–4.—Disease-free interval for the 55 patients who achieved complete remission. A single vertical line may represent 1 or more patients free of disease at the given interval. (Courtesy of Fisher, R.I., et al.: Ann. Intern. Med. 98:304–309, March 1983.)

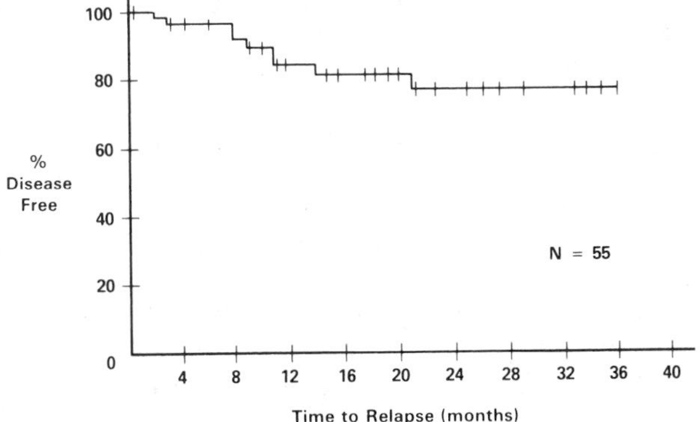

(23–9) Ann. Intern. Med. 98:304–309, March 1983.

tients who have completed all treatment, 55 (74%) achieved complete remission, and 16 others had partial responses. Disease-free intervals for the complete responders are shown in Figure 23–4. Patients with all histologic types of lymphoma achieved complete remission. Remissions occurred at various times during treatment. The actuarially predicted median survival will exceed 4 years, with 65% of all patients alive at that time. The dose-limiting toxicity was myelosuppression. Eight patients died of sepsis while leukopenic. Platelet toxicity was less than leukocyte toxicity.

Three fourths of patients in this study had complete remissions compared with 46% of patients in a previous study. The survival at 4 years is predicted as 65% compared with a previous rate of 38%. ProMACE-MOPP chemotherapy represents a substantial improvement in the management of patients with diffuse aggressive lymphomas.

▶ [A complete remission rate of 74% in patients with poor prognostic diffuse lymphomas is pretty impressive; however, so is a mortality of 10% (8 of 79 patients) from sepsis associated with leukopenia. This must be at or beyond the limit of acceptable toxicity. The authors of this article make several points. The first is that other aggressive multidrug regimens achieve remission in fewer than 50% of all patients, and thus median survival is less than 1 year. Only 35%–40% of patients achieve long-term survival. The second is that essentially all relapses occur within the first two years of completion of therapy and that relapse-free survival beyond two years is considered tantamount to cure. It will be interesting to see if these results are confirmed in multicenter trials. Previous reports from this same group suggested that they had pretty much gotten ovarian carcinoma under control; subsequent experience did not bear out this contention.] ◀

23–10 **Childhood Non-Hodgkin's Lymphoma: Results of a Randomized Therapeutic Trial Comparing a 4-Drug Regimen (COMP) With a 10-Drug Regimen (LSA_2-L_2)** in children with untreated biopsy-proved non-Hodgkin's lymphoma are reported by James R. Anderson, John F. Wilson, R. Derek T. Jenkin, Anna T. Meadows, John Kersey, Robert R. Chilcote, Peter Coccia, Philip Exelby, Joseph Kushner, Stuart Siegel, and Denman Hammond (Childrens Cancer Study Group, Los Angeles). A total of 234 patients under age 18 with any pathologic type of non-Hodgkin's lymphoma was assigned to treatment with either the 4-drug COMP (cyclophosphamide, vincristine, methotrexate, prednisone) regimen or a 10-drug regimen, the modified LSA_2-L_2 program. The latter regimen included cyclophosphamide, vincristine, methotrexate, daunomycin, prednisone, cytarabine, thioguanine, asparaginase, carmustine, and hydroxyurea. Radiotherapy was the same for both chemotherapeutic groups. About one third of patients had localized disease. The lymphoblastic and undifferentiated pleomorphic types were most prevalent.

Overall survival is shown in Figure 23–5. Failure-free survival for all patients was estimated as 64% at 1 year and 60% at 2 years. Failure-free survival was clearly related to the extent of disease at diagnosis (Fig 23–6). The 2 regimens were comparably effective in patients with localized disease and also in those with nonlocalized disease. In the latter group, however, patients with lymphoblastic

(23–10) N. Engl. J. Med. 308:559–565, Mar. 10, 1983.

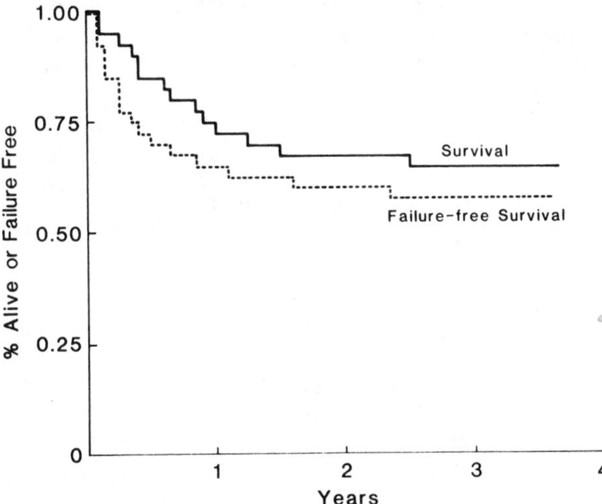

Fig 23–5.—Failure-free and overall survival in 234 patients with childhood non-Hodgkin's lymphoma. (Courtesy of Anderson, J.R., et al.: N. Engl. J. Med. 308:559–565, Mar. 10, 1983; reprinted by permission of The New England Journal of Medicine.)

lymphoma did better with the modified LSA_2-L_2 regimen, and those with nonlymphoblastic lymphoma did better with COMP therapy. Intrathecal methotrexate satisfactorily prevented isolated CNS relapse. Only 1 of 54 patients with localized disease relapsed after completing treatment. Seven of 61 patients with disseminated disease relapsed; 6 had received COMP therapy. Nine patients died from treatment-related sepsis. Nonfatal toxicity was mainly hematologic.

Long-term control now can be achieved in a majority of children

Fig 23–6.—Failure-free survival according to extent of disease at diagnosis and treatment regimen. Figures in parentheses indicate numbers of patients. (Courtesy of Anderson, J.R., et al.: N. Engl. J. Med. 308:559–565, Mar. 10, 1983; reprinted by permission of The New England Journal of Medicine.)

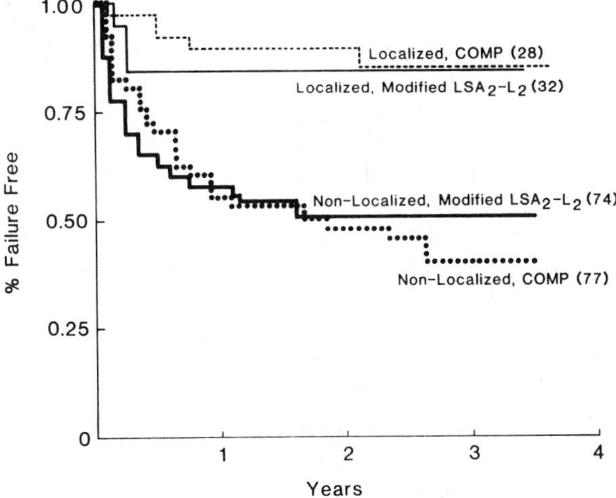

with non-Hodgkin's lymphoma. Both COMP therapy and the modified LSA_2-L_2 regimen were effective in patients in the present study with localized disease. Among those with nonlocalized disease, patients with lymphoblastic lymphoma had best results with the modified LSA_2-L_2 regimen, and the others with COMP therapy.

▶ [The use of aggressive combination chemotherapy in conjunction with radiation therapy has changed the outlook for children with non-Hodgkin's lymphoma. Wollner and colleagues treated 39 children with a 10-drug leukemia program and reported a long-term disease-free survival of 73% (*Cancer* 44:1990, 1979). Weinstein and colleagues obtained an 82% 2-year survival rate with a combination of doxorubicin, vincristine, prednisone, asparaginase, and 6-mercaptopurine (*Clin. Haematol.* 8:669, 1979). This report is a useful summary of a large experience and can be used as a statement of the current standards of treatment of childhood non-Hodgkin's lymphoma.] ◀

23–11 **Current Status of the Biology and Treatment of Acute Nonlymphocytic Leukemia in Children: Report From the ANLL Strategy Group of the Children's Cancer Study Group** is presented by Beatrice C. Lampkin, William Woods, Ronald Strauss, Stephen Feig, Gussie Higgins, Irwin Bernstein, Giulio D'Angio, Ronald Chard, Archie Bleyer and Denman Hammond (Children's Cancer Study Group, Los Angeles). Acute nonlymphocytic leukemia (ANLL) is a clonal disease. There is evidence that, in some cases, the primary defect may be one of differentiation. Little is known of surface receptors on the leukemic cells in ANLL. Bactericidal defects occur, but neutrophils from some patients with ANLL exhibit normal microbicidal functions. The morphologic subtype of leukemia depends on the type of leukemic "stem cell" that clonally expands. More than half of patients with ANLL have chromosome abnormalities, and those abnormalities have been associated with a poor prognosis in children. A white blood cell count of 20,000 or above also seems to indicate a poor prognosis.

The most effective single drugs for inducing remission in both children and adults with ANLL are daunorubicin, doxorubicin, cytosine arabinoside, and 5-azacytidine. Currently drug combinations are used to induce remission; most studies have utilized cytosine arabinoside plus an anthracycline, with or without other drugs. More than 70% of children have achieved remission. Currently it is necessary to produce marked marrow aplasia to achieve remission. The value of CNS prophylaxis has been confirmed by individual workers but is not definitively established. Intensification of therapy during remission appears to reduce the number of residual leukemic cells. Most workers have used various drug combinations to maintain remissions. The current median remission time is less than 2 years. Marrow transplantation in initial remission is under study; the preliminary results are encouraging. Many children who relapse can be induced into a second remission, and a few have been long-term survivors.

▶ [This is a useful exposition of the current state of the art. The 156 references provide a useful bibliography for those interested in more details concerning biology and treatment programs. The last statement—about the encouraging results of bone marrow transplantation—should be amplified. Of 13 children who received transplants in

(23–11) Blood 61:215–228, February 1983.

Seattle, 10 were in remission 20–53 months later. At the City of Hope, 14 of 16 children and adults with AMML were still in remission 2–48 months after bone marrow transplantation.] ◀

23–12 **Intensification Therapy for Acute Nonlymphoblastic Leukemia in Adults.** Despite improvements in remission induction, the median remission duration in acute nonlymphoblastic leukemia (ANL) in adults remains quite short. Harold Glucksberg, Martin A. Cheever, Vernon T. Farewell, Alexander Fefer, and E. Donnall Thomas examined the efficacy of intensification therapy with high-dose combination chemotherapy in 23 adults with ANL who remained in complete remission for at least 6 months. All had received a high-dose remission-induction regimen of daunorubicin, cytosine arabinoside, 6-thioguanine, prednisone, and vincristine, followed by a consolidation course of the same drugs at lower doses and then monthly maintenance courses of low-dose chemotherapy. Intensification therapy consisted of high-drug doses in place of the 6th and 12th monthly courses of post-remission-induction therapy. Sixteen other patients received only monthly therapy.

The median remission duration for the 23 patients given intensification therapy was 157 weeks, and 9 patients remain in continuous first remission after periods as long as 285 weeks. The median remission duration for the 16 control patients was 73 weeks (Fig 23–7). Estimates of median remission duration made by including patients who either relapsed or received marrow transplants before intensification were 100 and 37 weeks, respectively, for study and control patients. The respective estimates of survival from the time of remission were 172 and 70 weeks. Considerable toxicity resulted from intensification therapy. All patients had profound marrow suppression. Neurologic toxicity from vincristine was minimal. One patient had daunomycin-related heart failure.

These preliminary findings strongly suggest that high-dose combination chemotherapy, used for intensification, can prolong remission duration and survival in adults with ANL. Further follow-up is necessary, however, before intensification can be recommended as standard therapy. A study has been started in adults younger than age

Fig 23–7.—Remission duration of all patients younger than age 50. (Courtesy of Glucksberg, H., et al.: Cancer 52:198–205, July 15, 1983.)

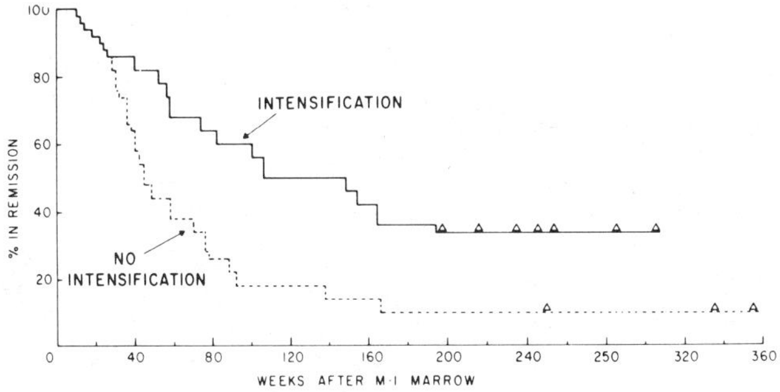

(23–12) Cancer 52:198–205, July 15, 1983.

50 with ANL to compare intensification therapy with chemoradiotherapy and bone marrow transplantation.

▶ [This is a useful report. The results achieved with intensification therapy are consistent with our own experience.] ◀

23–13 **Induction of Differentiation in a Case of Common Acute Lymphoblastic Leukemia.** There is evidence that many cases of "common" non-T, non-B acute lymphoblastic leukemia (ALL) are neoplasms of early B cells. Jeffrey Cossman, Leonard M. Neckers, Andrew Arnold, and Stanley J. Korsmeyer (Natl. Inst. of Health) attempted to manipulate the leukemic cells in such a case to differentiate in vitro into an immunoglobulin-synthesizing B cell. The phorbol diester 12-0 tetradecanoylphorbol 13-acetate (TPA), an effective inducer of differentiation in T-cell ALL and in the B cells of chronic lymphocytic leukemia, was utilized.

Cells were obtained from the peripheral blood of a man, aged 23, with a white blood cell count of 45,000/μl, lymphoblastic infiltration of the bone marrow, and typical ALL morphology without a Philadelphia chromosome. The lymphoblasts expressed the phenotype of common ALL but were without surface or cytoplasmic immunoglobulin. They were unreactive with monoclonal antibodies to T cells, and they exhibited no B-cell-associated antigens. Under the influence of TPA, the cells began expressing intracytoplasmic and surface μ and κ chains, a B-cell antigen recognized by BA2, and OKM1 reactivity. The proportion of cells containing terminal deoxynucleotidyl transferase (TdT) declined markedly. Cells cultured without TPA showed increases in BA2 reactivity and OKM1 reactivity. Retention of CALLA (J5) throughout the period of TPA exposure was observed.

Lymphoblasts of common ALL were, on exposure to TPA, induced to develop from the primitive cell stage to the phenotypic pre-B-cell and early B-cell stages. The findings support the view that the cells of common non-T, non-B ALL are primitive B cells. Leukemic cells capable of such induced differentiation provide a model of early B-cell differentiation and a means of examining the genetic events that prevent the maturation of leukemic cells in vivo.

▶ [The present study indicates that lymphoblasts of the common ALL variety were induced to differentiate along the B-cell pathway of development under the influence of TPA. The same phenomenon has been observed in other laboratories and was first defined by experimental model systems in which an acute myeloid leukemia cell line was induced to differentiate either with dimethylsulfoxide or with TPA. Freshly isolated blast cells from patients with acute nonlymphocytic leukemia often undergo some degree of differentiation on exposure to TPA. Such model systems indicate that many types of leukemia cells are still capable of some degree of normal differentiation despite intrinsic abnormalities resulting from chromosomal rearrangements and oncogene amplification or activation. Clearly many investigators would like to be able to apply agents that induce cell differentiation to the treatment of malignant disease in vivo. As the next article shows, this is already being attempted in some hematologic neoplasms.] ◀

23–14 **Treatment of Cutaneous T Cell Lymphoma (Mycosis Fungoides) With 13-*cis*-Retinoic Acid.** Previous work has indicated possible benefit from retinoids in treating mycosis fungoides. John F.

(23–13) N. Engl. J. Med. 307:1251–1254, Nov. 11, 1982.
(23–14) Lancet 1:1345–1347, June 18, 1983.

Kessler, Frank L. Meyskens, Jr., Norman Levine, Peter J. Lynch, and Stephen E. Jones (Univ. of Arizona, Tucson) evaluated the use of 13-*cis*-retinoic acid, which has potent effects on various malignant and nonmalignant skin conditions, in 4 patients with generalized plaques and erythroderma due to mycosis fungoides. Nearly complete clearing of extensive tumors and plaques occurred in 1 patient, who remains in partial remission after 15 months. Two others had improvement in pruritus and a 50% reduction in plaques after 4 and 6 weeks, respectively. A fourth patient had improvement in pruritus and clearing of plaques, but dryness and scaling necessitated a reduction in dosage and eventual withdrawal of the drug.

There is ample evidence that retinoids could influence tumor activity by their effects on immunity. They influence the immune function of epidermal mononuclear cells, and the lesions of cutaneous T-cell lymphoma are characterized by epidermal infiltration with atypical mononuclear cells. Dennert found that retinoic acid enhances antigen-specific cytotoxic T-cell activity. Further clinical study of retinoids in the treatment of cutaneous T-cell lymphoma is warranted.

▶ [This is an extremely impressive report. The studies were based upon recent descriptions of treatment of mycosis fungoides with retinoic acid (*Arch. Dermatol. Res.* 273:37, 1982; *Acta Dermatologica* 62:162, 1982). Whether or not the activity of retinoic acid is based on alterations of immune function is a moot point—the results appear to be impressive.] ◀

24. Oncology

24–1 **Evaluation of Tamoxifen Doses With and Without Fluoxymesterone in Advanced Breast Cancer.** Tamoxifen has been widely used as a single nonsteroidal antiestrogenic agent in the treatment of breast cancer. Douglass C. Tormey, Marc E. Lippman, Brenda K. Edwards, and Jane G. Cassidy (Natl. Inst. of Health) evaluated the combination of tamoxifen and fluoxymesterone because of the presence of androgen-receptor activity in some tumors. Women with biopsy-proved breast cancer and progressive metastatic disease were included in the trial. Fifty-two patients received tamoxifen in doses of 2–100mg/sq m of body surface area, given orally twice a day. Fifty-six patients received both tamoxifen and fluoxymesterone, the latter in a dose of 7 mg/sq m orally twice a day. Chemotherapy had been used previously in 85% of cases; hormonal therapy, in 60%. The 2 treatment groups were clinically comparable.

Combined treatment caused significantly more masculinization than tamoxifen alone. Major hematologic toxicities were comparable with the two regimens. The overall remission rate was 38% with combined treatment and 15% with tamoxifen only (table). Complete remissions occurred only with combined treatment. The rate of remission and improvement was 50% with combined treatment and 25% with tamoxifen alone. Median survival was 380 days in the combined treatment group and 330 days in the tamoxifen group. Patients given tamoxifen alone tended to do better with increasing doses; no such effect was apparent with combined treatment.

Combined treatment with tamoxifen and fluoxymesterone appeared to be superior to tamoxifen alone in this study of patients with advanced breast cancer. Side effects did not differ except for more an-

RESPONSE RATES TO TAMOXIFEN AND TO TAMOXIFEN AND FLUOXYMESTERONE*

Regimen	Patients	CR	PR	IMP	NC	PD
	n	←		%		→
Tamoxifen	52	0	15	10	25	50
Tamoxifen and fluoxymesterone	56	5	32	12	25	25

*Abbreviations used: CR, complete remission; PR, partial remission; IMP, improvement; NC, no change; PD, progressive disease. Overall trend, P = .0025; CR + PR, P = .016; CR + PR + IMP, P = .013.

(Courtesy of Tormey, D.C., et al.: Ann. Intern. Med. 98:139–144, February 1983.)

(24–1) Ann. Intern. Med. 98:139–144, February 1983.

drogenic effects from combined treatment. No significant dose-response relationships were observed.

▶ [The trial described in this report was designed as a phase I evaluation of Tamoxifen dosage and a limited phase III comparison of tamoxifen alone and in combination with fluoxymesterone. Among the pretreatment characteristics evaluated, the tamoxifen and fluoxymesterone combination tended to produce higher remission rates in all categories. Of particular interest was the higher remission rate irrespective of previous hormone effect or estrogen receptor status.] ◀

24–2 **5-Fluorouracil + Oncovin + Adriamycin + Mitomycin C (FOAM): An Effective Program for Breast Cancer, Even for Disease Refractory to Previous Chemotherapy: Northern California Oncology Group (NCOG) Study** is discussed by M. A. Friedman, F. S. Marcus, M. J. Cassidy, K. J. Resser, M. Kohler, C. G. Hendrickson, R. Reynolds, D. Johnson, T. Kilbridge, K. Yu, and M. Cruicitt. In this study a total of 118 patients with disseminated breast cancer were evaluated in conjunction with FOAM combination chemotherapy. All had biopsy-proved adenocarcinoma of the breast and were expected to live for 2 months or longer. The upper age limit was 75 years.

Treatment courses, repeated at 8-week intervals, consisted of 5-fluorouracil in 4 doses of 400 mg/sq m; Oncovin, 2 doses of 1 mg/sq m to a maximum of 2 mg per dose; Adriamycin, 2 doses of 40 mg/sq m; and mitomycin C in a single dose of 10 mg/sq m. The total cumulative dose of Adriamycin was limited to 450 mg/sq m in patients given mediastinal irradiation previously. All drugs were given intravenously. Doses were adjusted according to blood cell counts and serum bilirubin level.

For 38 patients, FOAM was the first chemotherapy treatment. Seven of 36 evaluable patients had complete and 13 had partial responses. Median time to failure was 10.6 months. Eighteen patients are still alive. Median survival for responders was 22.7 months and for nonresponders, 12 months. Of the 82 patients in whom previous chemotherapy had failed, 7 had complete and 22 had partial responses to FOAM therapy. Median time to failure was 5.6 months, and median survival was 9.4 months. Twenty-six patients in this group remain alive. Survival curves did not differ significantly in the responders and the other patients. Hematologic toxicity was generally mild and acceptable. Two patients had significant leukopenia-associated infection, 4 had CNS toxicity, and 2 had cardiac toxicity. No renal toxicity was noted.

It appears that FOAM therapy is an effective approach to patients with breast cancer resistant to treatment with cyclophosphamide, methotrexate, and 5-fluorouracil.

▶ [In a number of previous studies of patients with breast cancer refractory to Cytoxan plus methotrexate plus 5-fluorouracil (CMF), single agents or combination of drugs have usually resulted in response rates of 20%–40%, and responses have lasted from 4 to 6 months. FOAM seems a little better than most of these programs; however, it is apparent that all second-line therapies in advanced cancer are less than satisfactory.] ◀

24–3 **Prospective Randomized Evaluation of Adjuvant Chemotherapy in Adults With Soft Tissue Sarcomas of the Extremities.** Most

(24–2) Cancer 52:193–197, July 15, 1983.
(24–3) Ibid., pp. 424–434, Aug. 1, 1983.

patients with soft tissue sarcoma have residual microscopic foci of tumor after definitive treatment of local disease. Steven A. Rosenberg, Joel Tepper, Eli Glatstein, Jose Costa, Robert Young, Alan Baker, Murray F. Brennan, Ernest V. Demoss, Claudia Seipp, William F. Sindelar, Paul Sugarbaker, and Robert Wesley (Natl. Inst. of Health) undertook a prospective study of chemotherapy with doxorubicin, cyclophosphamide, and high-dose methotrexate in 65 patients seen in 1977–1981 with high-grade soft tissue sarcoma of the extremities. All had lesions distal to the shoulder or hip joint, and all underwent either amputation alone or wide local excision and radiotherapy. Chemotherapy was given to 37 patients. Doses of methotrexate as high as 250 mg/kg of body weight were given with leucovorin rescue. The median follow-up period was nearly 2 years.

Actuarial analysis indicated better continuous disease-free survival and overall survival in the chemotherapy group. Continuous disease-free survival rates at 3 years were 92% in the chemotherapy group and 60% in the control group, and the overall survival rate were 95% and 74%, respectively. Chemotherapy was associated with improved disease-free survival both in the 42% of patients who had amputation (Fig 24–1) and in the patients who had limb-sparing surgery plus

Fig 24–1.—Actuarial analysis of results in patients who underwent amputation and were then randomly assigned either to receive or not to receive chemotherapy. Significant benefit was conferred on patients who received chemotherapy (P = .006). (Courtesy of Rosenberg, S.A., et al.: Cancer 52:424–434, Aug. 1, 1983.)

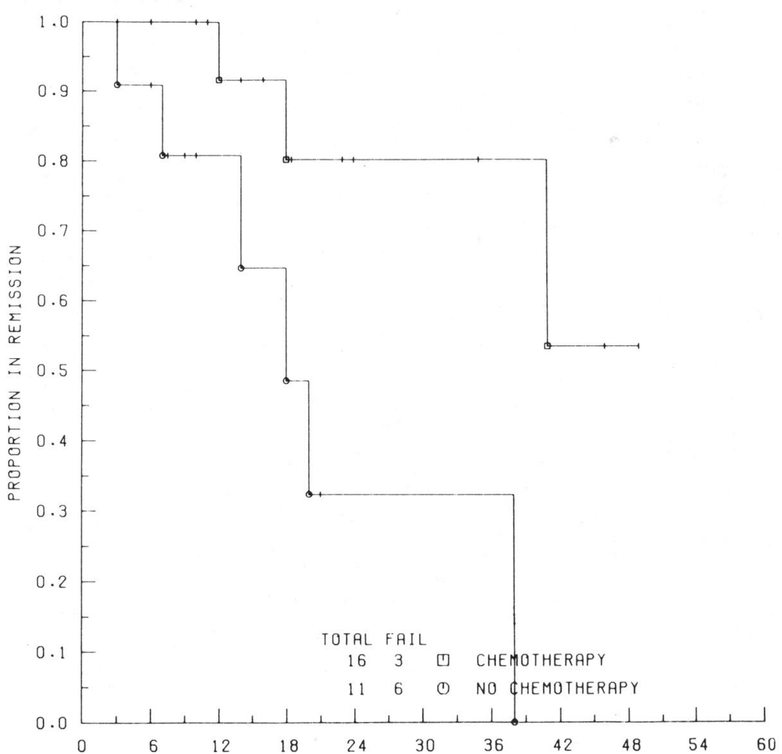

radiotherapy. Two local failures occurred in patients not given chemotherapy but none in the chemotherapy group. A review of 26 patients who participated in a pilot trial and were followed-up for at least 4 years confirmed improved disease-free survival and overall survival in association with chemotherapy.

Adjuvant chemotherapy appears to be a useful part of the management of adults with soft tissue sarcoma of the extremity. Cardiomyopathy and permanent infertility are important side effects, and future efforts should be devoted to developing regimens with minimal toxicity. A prospective trial of adjuvant chemotherapy in patients with head, neck, and trunk sarcomas is underway.

▶ [Soft tissue sarcomas arise in mesodermally derived connective tissues. In about 95% of cases these sarcomas initially appear as localized soft tissue masses without evident clinical metastases. They are characterized by a tendency to aggressively invade local tissues and by early micrometastatic spread, usually to the lungs. In most reported series, local recurrence rates following surgery with or without local irradiation vary from 20% to 50%. In these series, the overall 5-year survival rate is in the range of 35%–45%. The present study presents reasonably convincing evidence that this is one of the few malignancies in which adjuvant chemotherapy appears to offer an obvious advantage. The authors and many others feel that adjuvant chemotherapy should be the standard of management of adult patients with soft tissue sarcomas of the extremity.] ◀

24–4 **Cisplatin, Vindesine, and Bleomycin (CVB) Combination Chemotherapy of Advanced Non-Small-Cell Lung Cancer.** Conventional chemotherapy for advanced non-small-cell lung cancer (NSCLC) continues to be unsatisfactory. Loretta M. Itri, Richard J. Gralla, David P. Kelsen, Robert A. Chapman, Ephraim S. Casper, David W. Braun, Jr., Jane E. Howard, Robert Golbey, and Robert T. Heelan (Meml. Sloan-Kettering Cancer Center) evaluated a CVB regimen in 54 patients with measurable advanced squamous or large-cell carcinoma or adenocarcinoma of the lung, none of whom had previously received chemotherapy. All were less than age 70 and had stage III disease. Forty-four of the 52 evaluable patients had distant metastases. Cisplatin was given in a dose of 120 mg/sq m with mannitol-induced diuresis on days 1 and 29 and then every 6 weeks. Vindesine was given intravenously in a dose of 3 mg/sq m each week for 5 weeks and then every 2 weeks. Bleomycin was given only in the first 2 cycles in an intravenous injection of 10 mg/sq m starting on day 3, followed by a 4-day infusion of 10 mg/sq m daily for a total dose of 50 mg/sq m per cycle. Treatment was continued until progressive disease or unacceptable toxicity appeared.

The patients received a median of 3 treatment cycles and were followed-up for 3–18 months. A complete or partial remission occurred in 38% of patients. Responses were seen at all sites of disease. Median response duration was 8 months; 8 patients were in remission after as long as 19 months. Moderate hemorrhagic toxicity occurred. Nearly one third of patients had nephrotoxicity, and 3 deaths were due to renal failure. All patients had some peripheral neuropathy, but none had clinical pulmonary toxicity. Half the patients had severe nausea and vomiting.

(24–4) Cancer 51:1050–1055, Mar. 15, 1983.

A combination of vindesine and high-dose cisplatin appears to be useful in the treatment of NSCLC. Addition of bleomycin has caused increased hematologic and renal toxicity without improving response rate, median response duration, or survival of responding patients. The simultaneous or sequential use of other drugs may be useful in this setting.

▶ [In previously treated patients with non-small-cell carcinoma of the lung, vindesine (a new vinca alkaloid) has produced objective responses of about 23%–29%; cisplatin has produced objective responses in about 20% of the patients. Recently, vindesine and cisplatin were combined in a group of 83 previously untreated patients, and a 43% objective response rate was observed. It appears that we are making slow but steady progress in the treatment of this type of lung cancer.] ◀

24–5 **Randomized Comparison of Melphalan Versus Melphalan Plus Hexamethylmelamine Versus Adriamycin Plus Cyclophosphamide in Ovarian Carcinoma.** G. A. Omura, C. P. Morrow, J. A. Blessing, A. Miller, H. J. Buchsbaum, H. D. Homesley, and L. Leone undertook a prospective study of combination chemotherapy vs. melphalan alone in women with suboptimal (residual tumor at least 3 cm in size) stage III, stage IV, or recurrent ovarian adenocarcinoma. Sixty-four patients received melphalan alone, 97 received hexamethylmelamine in addition to melphalan, and 72 received Adriamycin and cyclophosphamide. Responding patients given either melphalan regimen continued to receive the drug until relapse or for 18 months. Those given Adriamycin and cyclophosphamide discontinued Adriamycin after 9 courses; the dose of cyclophosphamide was increased and treatment was continued until relapse or for 18 months.

Complete clinical responses occurred in 20% and partial responses in 17% of patients given melphalan alone. The respective figures for patients given melphalan plus hexamethylmelamine were 28% and 24%, and for those given Adriamycin and cyclophosphamide, 32% and 17%. When another 136 patients were included in whom measurable disease was not present, Adriamycin-cyclophosphamide therapy did not improve the median survival over that achieved by the other regimens. More hematologic and gastrointestinal tract toxicity occurred with combination therapy than with melphalan alone. More severe platelet toxicity occurred with melphalan-hexamethylmelamine therapy, and more severe vomiting with Adriamycin-cyclophosphamide therapy.

Some progress has been made in improving the complete response rate in patients with advanced ovarian cancer, but entirely satisfactory combination chemotherapy is yet to be devised. Better results may be obtained using cisplatin in these patients.

▶ [The most active drugs in ovarian adenocarcinoma include the ones used in this study, as well as cisplatin. In combination chemotherapy which included 5-fluorouracil, actinomycin, and methotrexate, the results have been no better than those achieved with melphalan alone. Toxicity has generally been greater with the combination chemotherapy regimens. Recently Parker, Griffiths, and Yankee reported that adriamycin and cytoxan achieved an 83% response rate in previously untreated patients (*Cancer* 46:669, 1980). Similarly, hexamethylmelamine plus methotrexate plus 5-fluorouracil plus cytoxan has been reported to result in response rates of 80%–85%

(24–5) Cancer 51:783–789, Mar. 1, 1983.

(Young et al.: *N. Engl. J. Med.* 299:1261, 1978). Unfortunately these high response rates have not generally been sustained when examined in multi-institution studies or in clinical practice. The Gynecologic Oncology Study Group compared the combination of melphalan plus 5-fluorouracil plus or minus actinomycin plus cytoxan with melphalan alone; there appeared to be no advantage for the combination chemotherapy. In contrast to these rather negative results with combination chemotherapy, recent reports of combinations that include cisplatin are more encouraging (see, for example, *Cancer Treat. Rep.* 63:307, 1979 and 63:311, 1979).] ◀

24–6 **Randomized Trial of Adjuvant Chemotherapy and Immunotherapy in Cutaneous Melanoma.** Conflicting reports have appeared on the efficacy of both adjuvant chemotherapy and immunotherapy against melanoma. U. Veronesi, J. Adamus, C. Aubert, E. Bajetta, G. Beretta, G. Bonadonna, R. Bufalino, N. Cascinelli, G. Cocconi, J. Durand, J. De Marsillac, R. L. Ikonopisov, B. Kiss, F. Lejeune, R. MacKie, G. Madej, H. Mulder, Z. Mechl, G. W. Milton, A. Morabito, H. Peter, J. Priario, E. Paul, P. Rumke, R. Sertoli, and R. Tomin report the results of a prospective clinical trial conducted by the WHO International Melanoma Group to evaluate the effects of adjuvant therapy with dacarbazine, bacille Calmette-Guérin (BCG), and both after conventional surgery for melanoma. A total of 761 patients at high risk of recurrence were randomized. Histologic stage II disease was present in 663 patients; the other 98 had pathologic stage I disease with Clark-level 3–5 melanoma of the trunk and uninvolved regional nodes. The primary tumor was excised with 3–5-cm borders, and "radical" node dissection was carried out. Chemotherapy was begun 10–20 days later in an initial dosage of 200 mg/sq m daily for 5 days, with cycles repeated at 4-week intervals for 24 cycles. Adjuvant immunostimulation with BCG was given weekly until a 2+ skin reaction occurred and then was given monthly.

Dacarbazine therapy had to be discontinued or reduced because of nausea and vomiting in nearly one fifth of cases. Survival was not influenced by any adjuvant treatment, although patients with two or three involved nodes survived better with both adjuvant treatments than with surgery alone. Immunostimulation alone did not appear to influence survival significantly.

Neither overall survival nor the disease-free interval was significantly modified by adjuvant treatment for melanoma in this series of pathologic stage I and stage II cases. Any benefit from adjuvant chemotherapy or immunostimulation was of limited clinical importance.

▶ [A refreshingly honest article in a field in which hype has been the standard of the day. It is interesting in retrospect to observe that it has taken more than a decade to decide that immunotherapy as currently conceived is of no value in the treatment of malignant melanoma.] ◀

24–7 **Chemotherapy in Advanced Kaposi's Sarcoma: Implications For Current Cases in Homosexual Men** are discussed by Paul Volberding, Marcus A. Conant, Raphael B. Stricker, and Brian J. Lewis (Univ. of California, San Francisco). Until recently, Kaposi's sarcoma has occurred chiefly in elderly men of Italian or Jewish origin, but it now appears more frequently in young male homosexuals in major

(24–6) N. Engl. J. Med. 307:913–916, Oct. 7, 1982.
(24–7) Am. J. Med. 74:652–656, April 1983.

CLASSIFICATION OF KAPOSI'S SARCOMA*

Type	Histologic Characteristics	Clinical Features	Prognosis
Nodular	Mixed (92%) Monocellular (8%)	Violaceous cutaneous and subcutaneous nodules, often in lower extremities	Prolonged course; responsive to local therapy
Florid (infiltrative, locally aggressive)	Mixed (23%) Monocellular (63%) Anaplastic (14%)	One or more large, ulcerated or exophytic cutaneous lesions; often invade subcutaneous tissues and bone	36% three-year mortality in Africa
Generalized (lymphadenopathic)	Mixed (100%)	Disease involves lymph nodes, viscera	Rapidly fatal; less responsive to therapy

*Data from Templeton, A.C. and Bhana, D.: J. Natl. Cancer Inst. 55:1301–1304, 1975. (Courtesy of Volberding, P., et al.: Am. J. Med. 74:652–656, April 1983.)

urban areas, in association with illnesses of defective immunity as part of the acquired immunodeficiency syndrome (AIDS). Affected patients often present with widespread cutaneous lesions and visceral involvement. Most current cases appear to represent the generalized form of Kaposi's sarcoma (table), which is the most aggressive variant. Viscera and lymph nodes are involved, and a mixed histologic pattern is found.

Treatment for generalized Kaposi's sarcoma, as found in patients with AIDS, is systemic rather than local in nature. Affected homosexuals appear to be unique etiologically and immunologically. Systemic therapy will involve both an attempt to control the tumor with cytotoxic drugs and an alteration of host resistance with biologic response modifiers. Current reports of chemotherapy for Kaposi's sarcoma are, at best, in the phase II stage. Solid data have been obtained mainly for vinblastine, dacarbazine, and actinomycin D. Chemotherapy trials will have to be appropriately aggressive but as sparing of the immune system as possible. There is reason to hope that continued research will lead to the development of effective treatment with acceptable toxicity.

▶ [Several chemotherapeutic agents have been tried in small groups of patients with Kaposi's sarcoma. The following agents have produced responses: vinblastine (89%), actinomycin-D (89%), bleomycin (60%), dacarbazine (56%), and carmustine (38%). Actinomycin and vincristine have produced responses in nearly 100% of patients, and vinblastine and bleomycin have been equally effective. Although on the surface these results appear to be promising, it must be realized that the responses are usually of a transient nature and that the disease soon recurs with full virulence. The authors are undoubtedly right in concluding that multiagent aggressive chemotherapy programs will have to be examined. I have seen one patient who received lethal doses of total-body irradiation and cyclophosphamide followed by bone marrow transplantation from an identical twin. Even this ultra-aggressive cytotoxic therapy had a transient effect on the sarcoma. As shown in the next article, interferon is the latest "magic" drug for Kaposi's sarcoma.] ◀

24–8 **Preliminary Observations on the Effect of Recombinant Leukocyte A Interferon in Homosexual Men With Kaposi's Sarcoma.** Kaposi's sarcoma has been associated with the syndrome of cellular immunodeficiency and susceptibility to opportunistic infec-

(24–8) N. Engl. J. Med. 308:1071–1076, May 5, 1983.

tion in young homosexual men. Persistent cytomegalovirus infection is considered a possible cause of both the immunodeficiency and the sarcoma in these patients. Susan E. Krown, Francisco X. Real, Susanna Cunningham-Rundles, Patricia L. Myskowski, Benjamin Koziner, Seymour Fein, Abraham Mittelman, Herbert F. Oettgen, and Bijan Safai examined the effects of recombinant leukocyte A interferon (IFLrA), a purified human interferon, on immune function and tumor growth in 13 patients in a phase I trial. All patients had measurable biopsy-proved Kaposi's sarcoma. Intramuscular injections of IFLrA were given for 28 days in a daily dose of 36×10^6 units or, in 4 cases, 54×10^6 units. When tumor regressed or was stable, treatment was continued 3 days a week. All patients were homosexual or bisexual men aged 32–50 years. Two patients had previously been treated unsuccessfully for Kaposi's sarcoma.

Five of the 12 evaluable patients had major objective responses, of which 3 were complete. Three patients had minor responses, and 4 had progressive disease. Side effects were similar to those observed previously with both partially purified and recombinant-DNA-produced interferons. Major episodes of infection were infrequent during interferon therapy. Augmentation of natural killer-cell activity was noted during treatment in several patients. Lymphocyte responses to PHA increased to normal in several patients.

It would appear that IFLrA can induce tumor regression in patients with AIDS and Kaposi's sarcoma. Treatment was well-tolerated by the present patients. There is preliminary evidence to suggest that interferon therapy can restore at least some aspects of cell-mediated immune function in these patients. It may be worth considering the addition of IFLrA to cytoreductive or other immunomodulatory agents in the treatment of Kaposi's sarcoma.

24–9 **Critical Appraisal of the "Human Tumor Stem-Cell Assay"** is presented by Peter Selby, Ronald N. Buick, and Ian Tannock (Toronto). The human tumor stem-cell assay has been proposed as an in vitro method by which anticancer agents can be selected for activity against a given patient's tumor cells. Although the ability to generate colonies from human tumor cells is a major advance in human tumor biology, use of the assay in routine selection of anticancer drug therapy would seem to be premature. Much evidence supports the validity of the stem-cell model for human cancer. There is preliminary evidence that the growth of tumor-cell colonies from bone marrow or body fluids may be useful in diagnosis or staging, but current clonogenic assays have been used mainly in attempts to predict the clinical response of tumors to drug therapy.

Problems in the use of clonogenic assays include a low plating efficiency, a small proportion of tumors suitable for testing, and difficulties in preparing single-cell suspensions. Criteria for defining a colony are arbitrary, and the in vitro criteria for drug sensitivity are uncertain. The in vitro treatment of cell suspensions with drugs presents substantial problems because the in vitro cell environment dif-

---

(24–9) N. Engl. J. Med. 308:129–134, Jan. 20, 1983.

fers from that in vivo and may alter the chemosensitivity of the cells. The optimal concentration and exposure time for the drugs are unknown. The various technical and conceptual limitations to individual chemosensitivity tests also apply to drug screening.

Clonogenic assays appear to have potential value for study of the biology of human cancers and the chemosensitivity of human tumors, but assay systems for each type of tumor to be studied must be improved before the large-scale clinical use of this approach is warranted. Many technical problems remain to be solved before any clonogenic assay can be considered to be optimal for the growth of colonies or for use as a chemosensitivity test. Validation of these assays as a means of selecting treatment will require randomized, controlled clinical trials.

▶ [This is a level-headed evaluation of a technique that has been in vogue for the past 5 years. At the moment, the applications of the stem-cell assay to clinical oncology appear to be limited. Much more experimental work has to be done. The proliferation of commercial laboratories providing stem-cell assays on a fee-for-service basis to practicing oncologists would seem to be unwarranted at the present time.] ◀

24–10 **Antibodies to Human Leukocyte Interferons in Cancer Patients.** Vallbracht et al. have described the development of antibody to human fibroblast interferon in a treated patient. Patrick W. Trown, Michael J. Kramer, Robert A. Dennin, Jr., Edward V. Connell, Alicia V. Palleroni, Jorge Quesada, and Jordan U. Gutterman detected neutralizing IgG antibodies to human leukocyte interferon in the course of a study of partly purified interferon in 3 cancer patients. Two had serum antibody before treatment, and 1 developed antibody during treatment. Titers of antibody to six recombinant human leukocyte interferon subtypes and one recombinant hybrid human leukocyte interferon differed in the 3 patients.

Both endogenous and exogenous human leukocyte interferons are immunogenic in some patients. The presence of interferon antibodies in these 3 patients was not associated with clinical abnormalities such as immune complex disease or increased susceptibility to viral infection. In 2 patients, however, the antibodies presumably resulted in the absence of detectable serum interferon after treatment and may have thereby prevented biologic activity of the administered product. The antibodies most likely resulted from previous viral infection that induced endogenous interferon, but it is unclear why interferon antibody was produced in these patients. Besides malignancy, 1 of the patients had insulin-dependent diabetes, and the other had chronic rheumatic heart disease.

▶ [The phenomenon described here is not restricted to leukocyte (α) interferons. Patients receiving recombinant interferon-β also frequently develop high titers of antibody to interferon.] ◀

24–11 **Immunotoxins: A New Approach to Cancer Therapy** is discussed by Ellen S. Vitetta, Keith A. Krolick, Muneo Miyama-Inaba, William Cushley, and Jonathan W. Uhr (Univ. of Texas, Dallas). Ehr-

(24–10) Lancet 1:81–84, Jan. 15, 1983.
(24–11) Science 219:644–650, Feb. 11, 1983.

lich, about 75 years ago, discussed the possible use of antibodies as carriers of pharmacologic agents. An immunotoxin is a cell-binding antibody or antigen covalently bound to a plant or bacterial toxin. Immunotoxins of improved effectiveness may depend on increasing both endocytosis of the conjugate and the ability of the A chain to traverse the membrane of the endocytic vesicle before inactivation by enzymes. Immunotoxin efficacy has been tested in the murine BCL_1 model. In vivo studies have suggested that, in the clinical setting, the tumor burden is a major consideration, at least until the therapeutic index of immunotoxins can be substantially increased. Specific immunologic unresponsiveness can be induced with soluble antigen-containing immunotoxins. This could be useful both in cancer patients and in patients with autoimmune disease. Immunotoxins directed against T suppressor cells might be effective in stimulating immune responsiveness in patients with tumor immunity due to a hyperreactive T suppressor system and in those with some persistent viral infections such as herpes simplex infection.

Further studies on the pharmacokinetics of immunotoxins are needed. The possible representation of target antigens on normal tissues is a potentially major problem in predicting the efficacy of immunotoxins in any type of in vivo therapy. It is not clear whether immunotoxins can gain access to cancer cells forming solid tumors, especially those with a dense connective tissue component. Tumor cell heterogeneity, including the emergence of mutants lacking particular surface antigens or resistant to the toxic effects of ricin A chain, is another potential problem in immunotoxin therapy. A further obstacle to the treatment of cancer or the induction of tolerance in autoimmune disease is the presence of tumor-associated antigens or autoantibody, respectively, in the circulation. These may have to be partly removed by plasmapheresis or the injection of unconjugated antibody, or antigen in the case of autoimmune disease, before the appropriate immunotoxin is administered.

▶ [The "toxic" moiety of an immunotoxin may be either a whole molecule or a peptide portion of a molecule which carries the toxic activity. The best-studied toxin in mammalian cell systems is the diphtheria toxin. However, because most individuals have been immunized against diphtheria, the presence of antitoxin militates against the use of diphtheria in clinically applicable immunotoxin preparations. For that reason, most investigators have concentrated on ricin, a plant toxin. Like most toxic proteins produced by bacteria and plants, ricin has a toxic polypeptide (the A chain) attached to a polypeptide chain (B chain) which binds to the cell. The ricin B chain is a lectin that binds to galactose-containing glycoproteins or glycolipids on the cell surface. The mechanism of entry of the A chain is not completely elucidated. It is known, however, that the ricin A chain is one of the most potent toxins recognized in nature. It inhibits protein synthesis by enzymatically inactivating a portion of one of the ribosomal subunits. The A chain is nontoxic until it enters the cytoplasm of the cell. Therefore, conjugates of antibody and A chain should be relatively nontoxic to cells lacking the specific cell surface receptor molecules. A number of observations have been made with the ricin-antibody system. For those interested in the details, the article abstracted above includes a summary of the preparation of immunotoxins, strategies for testing the efficacy of immunotoxins, and the use of such immunotoxins in animal tumor model systems. The authors also consider the problems with these techniques and their future potentials.] ◀

24–12 **Monoclonal Antibody and an Antibody-Toxin Conjugate to a Cell Surface Proteoglycan of Melanoma Cells Suppress In Vivo Tumor Growth.** Several monoclonal antibody-toxin conjugates directed against human and animal tumor cell surface antigens have been found to have specific toxicity toward target cells in vitro. T. F. Bumol, Q. C. Wang, R. A. Reisfeld, and N. O. Kaplan examined a monoclonal antibody directed against a cell surface chondroitin sulfate proteoglycan of human melanoma cells, 9.2.27, and its diphtheria toxin A chain (DTA) conjugate for their effects on in vitro protein synthesis and the in vivo growth of human melanoma cells. The 9.2.27 IgG and its DTA conjugate exhibited similar serologic activities against melanoma target cells, but only the conjugate consistently induced inhibition of protein synthesis and toxicity in vitro in M21 melanoma cells. Both elements significantly suppressed M21 tumor growth in vivo in a model of rapidly growing tumor in athymic *nu/nu* mice.

The target antigen for this monoclonal antibody and its DTA-conjugate is a core glycoprotein of the chondroitin sulfate proteoglycans, representing the extracellular/pericellular matrix components that have been shown to be membrane associated. These components have been implicated in many cellular processes including cell motility, differentiation, and growth control. A monoclonal antibody and its DTA conjugate can inhibit the growth of an established, rapidly growing melanoma in an immunotherapy model in athymic mice. Complete regression of established tumor has not been achieved, but significant inhibition of tumor growth is obtained with both the antibody and its DTA conjugate. More work is needed on the use of toxin conjugates as immunotherapeutic agents, especially in the intact animal.

▶ [This is an example of one of the model systems in which immunotoxins are used to treat tumors. Because of the potential toxicity of the toxin moiety to normal cells, efforts have been directed at ensuring that the toxins are delivered only to cancer cells. Monoclonal antibodies seem to be the best candidates for this task. The toxin, either diphtheria toxin A chain (as in this study) or the ricin A chain (as in the previous article), is covalently linked to a specifically directed monoclonal antibody. Efficient killing of the target cell seems to depend on the target antigen chosen, and this represents the inherent limitation in this system. Most antigens that were initially considered as tumor specific have turned out to be tumor-related antigens that are also associated with differentiation of normal tissues. Only the idiotypic determinants of the surface immunoglobulin B-cell lymphomas have thus far been shown to be truly tumor specific. It is only in this system that monoclonal antibodies have had a useful therapeutic effect.

A potential obstacle to successful immunotherapy is antigenic modulation of tumor cells whereby those cells with a relative lack of the antigen survive the immunologic attack and proliferate to yield progeny that are deficient in the target surface antigen. Other obstacles include circulating antigen which can bind the immunotoxin before it reaches its target.] ◀

24–13 **Patient With 13 Chromosome Deletion: Evidence That the Retinoblastoma Gene Is a Recessive Cancer Gene** is presented by William F. Benedict, A. Linn Murphree, Ashutosh Banerjee, Celsa A.

(24–12) Proc. Natl. Acad. Sci. USA 80:529–533, January 1983.
(24–13) Science 219:973–975, Feb. 25, 1983.

Spina, Maryellen C. Sparkes, and Robert S. Sparkes (Los Angeles). A small proportion of patients with hereditary retinoblastoma have a constitutional deletion of the chromosomal region 13q14. The enzyme esterase D (ESD), present in most tissues but of unknown function, has been assigned to the same region by deletion mapping. The chromosomal deletion has been identified in all retinoblastoma patients with ESD activity that is only 50% of normal; however, a child aged 3 years was encountered with bilateral retinoblastoma and 50% ESD activity in all normal cells examined but no deletion of 13q14 at the 550-band level. She had the smallest constitutional chromosomal deletion within 13q14 yet reported in association with susceptibility to retinoblastoma. Two stem lines were identified in tumor tissue from this patient; each had a missing 13 chromosome. No ESD activity was detected in the tumor, indicating that the normal nondeleted 13 chromosome was lost in both stem lines.

This is the first individual in whom total loss of genetic material has been shown at a chromosomal locus known to contain a cancer gene for a specific human malignancy. The findings imply that recessive genes may have an important role in the development of certain human tumors, including retinoblastoma. The patient's tumor cells, which contain only the deleted 13 chromosome, may provide valuable target cells for probes being developed to identify key genetic differences within 13q14 between normal 13 chromosomes and those containing small deletions or mutations responsible for susceptibility to retinoblastoma.

▶ [The authors present evidence that there is only one retinoblastoma gene and that this gene represents a prototype of the class of human cancer genes characterized by loss of genetic information at the constitutional or tumor level. This class of cancer genes includes those related to Wilms' tumor, neuroblastoma, small-cell carcinoma of the lung, and renal cell carcinoma. The authors contrast these findings with the second class of potential human "cancer genes" which may function by gene activation rather than by gene inactivation or loss. Such a "cancer gene" is described in the next article.] ◀

24–14 **Point Mutation Is Responsible for the Acquisition of Transforming Properties by the T24 Human Bladder Carcinoma Oncogene.** E. Premkumar Reddy, Roberta K. Reynolds, Eugenio Santos, and Mariano Barbacid (Natl. Inst. of Health) point out that more than 10 different human oncogenes have been identified to date. One of them, present in the T24 and EJ bladder carcinoma cell lines, has been isolated by molecular cloning methods. It is a small oncogene that has not undergone major genetic rearrangements. Comparative analysis of this oncogene with retroviral transforming *(onc)* genes has shown that an internal fragment of the T24 oncogene is closely related to the *onc* genes of the Harvey and BALB murine sarcoma viruses. A single point mutation of guanosine into thymidine now has been found to lead to activation of the oncogene in T24 human bladder carcinoma cells. The substitution results in incorporation of valine rather than glycine as the twelfth amino acid residue of the T24 oncogene-encoded p21 protein.

(24–14) Nature 300:149–152, Nov. 11, 1982.

A single amino acid substitution appears to suffice in conferring transforming properties on the gene product of the T24 human bladder carcinoma oncogene. It is possible that activation of the T24 oncogenes represents a late, irreversible step in oncogenesis, but the possibility that the oncogene has a role in the onset of certain human cancers cannot be ruled out. The development of biochemical and immunologic reagents that can specifically detect the presence of the T24 bladder carcinoma oncogene or its gene product in both naturally occurring and experimentally induced neoplasms should help define the role of this dominant transforming gene in carcinogenesis.

▶ [Oncogenes are now getting wide display in the biologic literature. They are a small family of genes normally present in the cells of all vertebrates thus far examined, and they are also found in some invertebrates. They code for proteins with a variety of functions, including enzymatic activity (phosphorylation of tyrosine residues), DNA-binding activity, and growth factor activity. These normal cellular genes, when incorporated into certain retroviruses, are capable of inducing malignant transformation. It has also been suggested that under some circumstances the cellular oncogenes may become activated or undergo mutation. Under these circumstances they can also induce malignancy. A frequently used test system to detect such "cancer genes" is the introduction (transfection) of gene sequences into mouse fibroblasts designated NIH3T3 cells. When some of the activated or mutated oncogenes are introduced into such cells, they induce transformations typical of neoplasia. These transformations include unrestrained cellular proliferation in which cells pile up on one another. The present study, which has been confirmed in several laboratories, indicates that a single point mutation may be responsible for converting one of the normal oncogenes into a "cancer gene" with the property of inducing neoplastic transformation in the 3T3 assay system.] ◀

4–15 **Detection of Human Papillomavirus Type 5 DNA in Skin Cancers of an Immunosuppressed Renal Allograft Recipient.** Copies of the human papillomavirus type 5 (HPV-5) genome have been found in primary and metastatic squamous cell cancers of the skin in epidermodysplasia verruciformis. Marvin A. Lutzner, Gérard Orth, Vi-

Fig 24–2.—Early invasive squamous cell carcinoma of cheek. Invading lesion is surrounded by dermal infiltrate. (Hematoxylin-eosin; ×100). (Courtesy of Lutzner, M.A., et al.: Lancet 2:422–424, Aug. 20, 1983.)

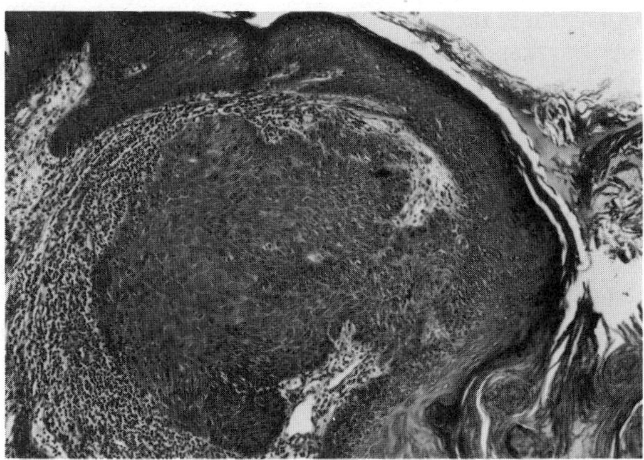

(24–15) Lancet 2:422–424, Aug. 20. 1983.

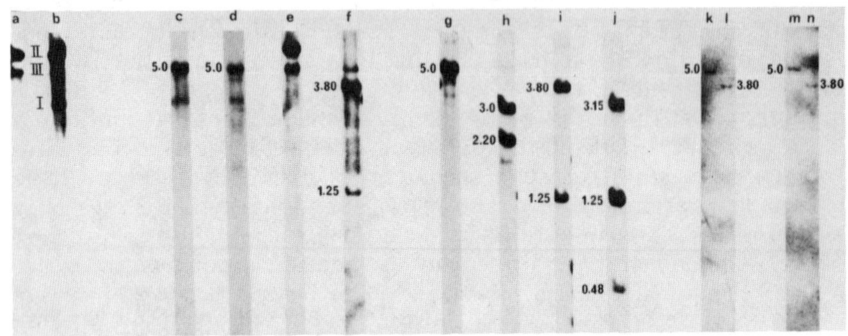

Fig 24–3.—Detection of HPV-5 DNA in benign lesions and skin cancers of renal allograft recipient, with use of Southern blot technique. Lane a contains uncleaved DNA extracted from patient's benign lesions; lanes c–f contain this DNA cleaved with SacI, BamHI, EcoRI, and PstI restriction endonucleases, respectively. Lane b contains uncleaved DNA extracted from benign lesions of patient with HPV-5 infection and epidermodysplasia verruciformis; lanes g–j contain this DNA cleaved with same 4 endonucleases. Lanes k and l contain DNA from renal allogaft recipient's in situ cancer, cleaved with BamHI and PstI, respectively; lanes m and n contain DNA from patient's early invasive carcinoma, cleaved with same 2 endonucleases. Arabic numerals indicate molecular weights of fragments, expressed in megadaltons; roman numerals indicate DNA forms I (circular, supercoiled molecules), II (circular, relaxed molecules), and III (linear molecules). Smallest HPV-5 PstI fragment (lane j) ran off gel. (Courtesy of Lutzner, M.A., et al.: Lancet 2:422–424, Aug. 20, 1983.)

viane Dutronquay, Marie-Francoise Ducasse, Henri Kreis, and Jean Crosnier (Paris) report the case of a renal allograft recipient with a syndrome resembling epidermodysplasia verruciformis who was found to have HPV-5 in his benign warty lesions and HPV-5 DNA in 2 skin cancers. The patient, a man aged 35, had received a cadaver kidney because of renal failure due to glomerulonephritis and had been receiving immunosuppressive agents for 13 years. There were several macular, scaly lesions that looked like the benign lesions of epidermodysplasia verruciformis, which resemble pityriasis versicolor. There were also 2 cancers on the cheek (Fig 24–2), which were excised. The detection of HPV-5 DNA in the benign lesions and the skin cancers is illustrated in Figure 24–3. The intensity of the bands in the cancers corresponded to 1 or 2 copies of viral DNA per diploid-cell DNA content, as deduced from reconstruction studies.

The findings in this patient suggest a role for HPV-5 in the pathogenesis of skin cancers in renal transplant recipients. Skin cancers in these patients and in those with epidermodysplasia verruciformis arise almost exclusively in sun-exposed skin, and the frequency of skin cancer in renal allograft recipients is proportional to both the duration of immunosuppression and the duration of sunlight exposure, indicating that ultraviolet light may serve as a cofactor for oncogenesis. Papillomavirus is found in ocular tumors of sun-exposed cattle and also in solar keratoses in man. Another cofactor role of solar exposure may be further immunosuppression by ultraviolet light.

▶ [Very interesting indeed. Further observations in this area will obviously be followed with interest.] ◀

25. Platelets and Bleeding Disorders

25–1 **Congenital Protein C Deficiency and Venous Thromboembolism: A Study of Three Dutch Families.** Protein C is the zymogen of a serine protease involved in blood coagulation, and it has been proposed that its deficiency will be associated with an increased risk of thrombosis because of impaired inactivation of activated factors V and VIIIC and reduced fibrinolytic capacity. André W. Broekmans, Jan J. Veltkamp, and Rogier M. Bertina (Leiden Univ., The Netherlands) used an immunologic assay for protein C to identify 18 patients (11 male and 7 female) in 3 unrelated Dutch families who had isolated protein C deficiency. Deficiency was diagnosed by a protein C antigen concentration below 0.65 unit per ml in patients who were not receiving oral anticoagulants and by a concentration below about 0.25 unit per ml in patients who were.

Mean protein C antigen level was 0.48 unit per ml in 12 patients not receiving oral anticoagulants and 0.17 unit per ml in 6 patients who were receiving such therapy and who had stable anticoagulation. (Normal value is 0.98 unit per ml in healthy patients.) All but 4 of the 18 patients had a history of venous thromboembolism, usually superficial thrombophlebitis. Deep venous thrombosis and pulmonary embolism also had occurred. Most manifestations of thromboembolism had appeared at a relatively young age, without apparent cause. No patient had evidence of symptomatic arterial thrombotic disease. Pedigree analysis suggested an autosomal dominant trait with variable expressivity.

Congenital protein C deficiency should be considered in patients with a family history of venous thromboembolism, especially superficial thrombophlebitis. Patients receiving oral anticoagulant therapy should be stabilized before an attempt is made to diagnose isolated protein C deficiency. The deficiency appears to be inherited as an autosomal dominant trait with variable expressivity at the laboratory level and incomplete penetrance at the clinical level.

▶ [Protein C is synthesized in the liver in the presence of adequate amounts of vitamin K. It is activated by thrombin, and this activation reaction is accelerated by a protein present on endothelial cell surfaces. Activated protein C has potent anticoagulant properties. In vitro, activated protein C has inhibitory activity against activated factors V and VIIIC, and it stimulates fibrinolysis. The observations reported in this article confirm a previously described association between isolated protein C deficiency and thrombotic disease (Griffin et al.: *J. Clin. Invest.* 68:1370, 1980). This relationship is similar to that seen in congenital antithrombin III deficiency. About half of the patients with protein C deficiency have thrombotic episodes before the age of 33 years.] ◀

25–2 **Deamino-8-D-Arginine Vasopressin Shortens the Bleeding Time in Uremia.** Cryoprecipitate has shortened the prolonged bleed-

(25–1) N. Engl. J. Med. 309:340–344, Aug. 11, 1983.
(25–2) Ibid., 308:8–12, Jan. 6, 1983.

ing time in uremic patients, allowing surgery without excessive blood loss. If it acts by increasing factor VIII (FVIII):Willebrand factor (VWF), 1-deamino-8-D-arginine vasopressin (DDAVP) may by an alternative, since it causes the release of autologous FVIII:VWF from storage sites into plasma. Pier Mannuccio Manucci, Giuseppe Remuzzi, Fiorenza Pusineri, Rossana Lombardi, Carla Valsecchi, Giuliano Mecca, and Theodore S. Zimmerman undertook a double-blind study of DDAVP and placebo in 12 patients with chronic renal failure and a history of bleeding associated with a bleeding time of 10 minutes or longer. Median age was 34 years. Coagulation screening tests gave normal results, and platelet counts were normal. All the patients were undergoing regular hemodialysis. Nine other patients received DDAVP before surgery, usually renal biopsy. Patients in the double-blind trial received DDAVP (0.3 μg/kg) or placebo by infusion over 30 minutes. Surgical patients were treated just before the procedure.

Bleeding times were shorter 1 hour after the start of DDAVP infusion in all patients and after placebo in only 1 patient. Seven patients still had shortened bleeding times at 8 hours. Infusion of DDAVP led to about twofold increases in both FVIII-related antigen and ristocetin cofactor and a greater increase in factor VIII coagulant activity. Larger FVIII:VWF multimers appeared in the plasma after DDAVP infusion. No serious side effects occurred. All the surgical patients had shorter bleeding times 1 hour after DDAVP administration, and no undue blood loss occurred during or after the procedures.

It appears that DDAVP is a promising agent for prevention of bleeding after renal biopsy in uremic patients with a prolonged bleeding time. It might also be considered for the treatment of spontaneous hemorrhage in these patients.

▶ [Prolongation of the skin bleeding time and normal laboratory coagulation tests are characteristic of the hemostatic derangement in uremia. These were interpreted as indicating a defect in plug formation in injured blood vessels. It has been suggested that the bleeding time is the most useful platelet function test to discriminate bleeders from nonbleeders in uremia. A variety of approaches have been used to treat this hemorrhagic disorder. Hemodialysis reduces the frequency and severity of spontaneous or postoperative bleeding but cannot be relied upon to do so. Janson et al. (*N. Engl. J. Med.* 303:1318, 1980) described the correction of uremic bleeding in patients given plasma cryoprecipitate. The mechanism of action of cryoprecipitate in this setting is not well defined but may involve increases in factor VIII:von Willebrand factor. Based on this assumption, the authors of the article abstracted above undertook this clever study with DDAVP.] ◀

25–3 **Effects of Acetylsalicylic Acid Ingestion on Maternal and Neonatal Hemostasis.** Acetylsalicylic acid crosses the placenta after maternal ingestion, and has been associated with hemostatic abnormalities in both full-term and premature infants. Marie J. Stuart, Steven J. Gross, Haim Elrad, and Janet E. Graeber (Upstate Med. Center, Syracuse, N.Y.) examined the effects of aspirin on maternal and neonatal hemostasis in a prospective case-control study of mothers taking aspirin within 10 days of delivery. Thirty-four control mother-infant pairs were compared with 10 pairs in which 5–10 gm

---

(25–3) N. Engl. J. Med. 307:909–912, Oct. 7, 1982.

of aspirin was ingested by the mother within 5 days before delivery, 7 in which the mother took 5–15 gm 6–10 days before delivery, and 7 in which ingestion was documented during the immediate postpartum period only.

Only 1 control pair had hemostatic abnormalities. Six of 10 mothers who took aspirin within 5 days before delivery and 9 of their 10 infants had bleeding tendencies. No clinical bleeding occurred when aspirin was ingested 6–10 days before delivery. Four of 7 mothers who ingested aspirin in the postpartum period only had impaired hemostasis. Maternal bleeding was confirmed to excessive intrapartum or postpartum blood loss. Infants exhibited petechiae over the presenting part, hematuria, a cephalhematoma, subconjunctival hemorrhage, and bleeding from a circumcision site. Four infants whose mothers used aspirin within 5 days before delivery had profuse petechiae over the presenting part.

Aspirin should be avoided during pregnancy. If the mother has ingested aspirin within 5 days before delivery, the neonate should be assessed for bleeding. Serious internal bleeding did not occur in the full-term infants in this study, but the risk of life-threatening hemorrhage may be increased in small premature infants.

5–4 **Danazol Increases Factor VII and Factor IX in Classic Hemophilia and Christmas Disease.** Factor concentrates used to treat patients with hemophilia can cause several abnormalities such as chronic liver disease and unexplained hypertension. Abnormal T-cell function has recently been documented, possibly predisposing patients to opportunistic infection. Harvey R. Gralnick and Margaret E. Rick (Natl. Inst. of Health) evaluated the androgen derivative danazol in 4 patients with classic hemophilia and 1 with Christmas disease. All patients were older than 18 years of age and had lifelong histories of hemorrhage. None had other marked medical problems. The patients had been on a program of infusion on demand, which was continued during the 2-week period of danazol therapy. The drug was given orally in a dose of 600 mg daily.

The response of factor VIII levels to danazol therapy is shown in Figure 25–1. Deficient coagulation factor levels increased markedly in all instances, and the increase persisted throughout treatment. The activated partial thromboplastin time declined as the deficient coagulation factor level increased. Two patients with classic hemophilia who had averaged 1 and 2½ infusions per week, respectively, gave themselves infusions on the first day of danazol therapy. The remaining 2 required an average of 1 transfusion every 2 weeks. Two patients required infusion within 6 days of stopping danazol therapy; in each instance the factor level had returned to near baseline.

Danazol may reduce the bleeding tendency and the need for transfusions of plasma products in patients with classic hemophilia and Christmas disease. The present results are similar to those obtained with danazol in hereditary angioedema and α_1-antitrypsin deficiency.

(25–4) N. Engl. J. Med. 308:1393–1395, June 9, 1983.

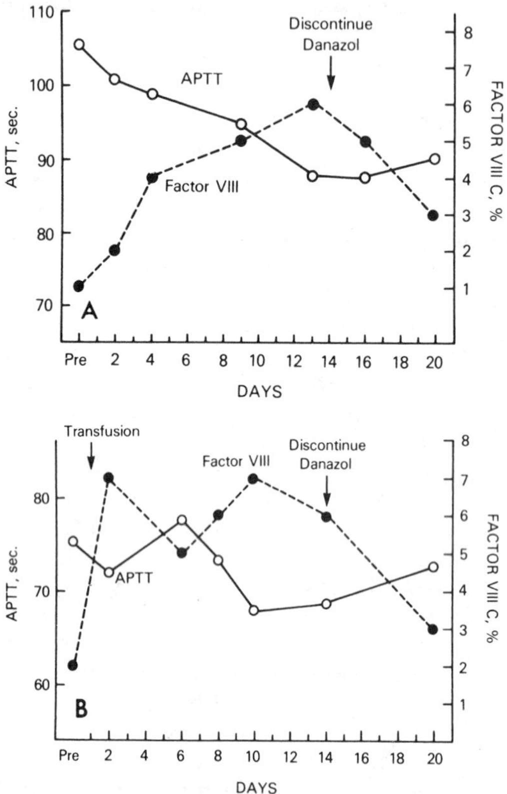

Fig 25–1.—Response of factor VIII to danazol in classic hemophilia. **A,** patient with classic hemophilia had a baseline factor VIII level of 1% that rose to a peak of 6% on day 13. Apparent half-life after discontinuation of the drug was 5 days. By day 4 of therapy, the factor VIII level increased to 4%. **B,** patient with classic hemophilia after infusion on day 1 had a factor VIII level of 7%. After 4 days, his factor VIII level was 5%, despite the fact that he had received no further transfusions. The factor VIII level peaked at day 10. Apparent half-life after discontinuation of the drug was approximately 4 days. *APTT,* activated partial thromboplastin time. (Courtesy of Gralnick, H.R. and Rich, M.E.: N. Engl. J. Med.: 308:1393–1395, June 9, 1983; reprinted by permission of The New England Journal of Medicine.)

Higher doses of danazol or longer periods of treatment might result in higher levels of deficient coagulation factor or factors.

▶ [These studies with Danazol indicate that with a dosage of 600 mg daily there was a selective rise in a deficient coagulation factor protein in four patients with classic hemophilia and in one with Christmas disease. The percentage increases over the baseline levels were 100%–500%.] ◀

25–5 **Danazol for Treatment of Idiopathic Thrombocytopenic Purpura.** Idiopathic thrombocytopenic purpura (ITP) is not adequately controlled despite both splenectomy and glucocorticoid therapy in about 25% of the affected patients. Conventional androgen therapy is limited by the fact that it causes masculinization in women. Yeon S. Ahn, William J. Harrington, Sheryl R. Simon, Ravindra Mylva-

(25–5) N. Engl. J. Med. 308:1396–1399, June 9, 1983.

ganam, Lorraine M. Pall, and Antero G. So (Miami) evaluated the effect of danazol, an impeded androgen having a reduced capacity for masculinization, in 22 patients (12 women) with ITP. Fifteen patients had undergone splenectomy. All had thrombocytopenia that was inadequately controlled by tolerable doses of glucocorticoids. Danazol was given orally in a dose of 200 mg 2–4 times daily for 2 months or longer.

There were 11 excellent, 2 good, 2 fair, 3 transient, and 4 poor responses. In those with excellent responses, the platelet count rose to 100,000/cu mm or higher and remained there for 2 months or longer with continued therapy. Improvement was maintained for as long as 13 months. Both sexes were benefited by danazol therapy. Responses could not be related to duration of disease or to failure of splenectomy or various medical measures. Six patients remained in remission taking danazol only. Most patients tolerated the treatment well. Weight gain was the most common side effect. Two women had menstrual spotting during danazol therapy, 2 reported oiliness of the skin, and 1 experienced a generalized skin eruption.

Danazol benefited most patients with ITP in this series, regardless of previous treatment. The drug appears to be superior to glucocorticoids in the long-term management of ITP, but exact indications for its use remain to be determined. Danazol should not be used in pregnant women. The optimal dosage and duration of danazol therapy require further study.

▶ [Danazol appears to be the "Drug of the Year" in hematology. The results in ITP appear to be impressive. The mechanism of action of danazol in this disease is entirely unknown, although the authors go into a lengthy discussion of the relationship between sex hormone status and autoimmune phenomena.] ◀

5–6 **Diagnosis of Bernard-Soulier Syndrome and Glanzmann's Thrombasthenia with Monoclonal Assay on Whole Blood.** Certain hereditary platelet disorders are characterized by a deficiency of specific platelet membrane glycoproteins (GPs) in the Bernard-Soulier syndrome, the platelets lack the platelet membrane GPIb, whereas in Glanzmann's thrombasthenia there is a deficiency of GPIIb and GPIIIa. Robert R. Montgomery, Thomas J. Kunicki, Cynthia Taves, Domonique Pidard, and Michael Corcoran (Med. College of Wisconsin, Milwaukee) developed murine monoclonal antibodies GPIb and the GPIIb/GPIIIa complex and developed a rapid whole-blood assay for identifying GP deficiencies. The assay was used to study whole blood from 6 patients with Glanzmann's thrombasthenia and 3 with Bernard-Soulier syndrome. Patients with both type I and type II Glanzmann's thrombasthenia were readily detected within 2 hours of sampling, using 200 μl of whole blood.

Studies of heterozygotes or carriers of Glanzmann's thrombasthenia and Bernard-Soulier syndrome may provide a means of carrier detection without the need for more elaborate GP analysis.

▶ [Diagnosis of Bernard-Soulier syndrome is suggested by giant platelets and an absence of ristocetin-induced platelet aggregation. The diagnosis is confirmed by detailed analysis of platelet membrane glycoproteins. These latter studies are difficult

(25–6) J. Clin. Invest. 71:385–389, February 1983.

to perform, since Bernard-Soulier platelets are difficult to separate from whole blood. The technique described in this paper represents a clear advance in methodology.

In Glanzmann's thrombasthenia, platelet aggregation is reduced or absent, clot retraction is decreased, and the bleeding time is prolonged. In this disorder, platelet GPIIb and GPIIIa are reduced. Analysis of these platelet membrane glycoproteins is not routine; therefore, the use of monoclonal antibodies appears to be a step forward.] ◀

PART FOUR

THE HEART AND BLOOD VESSELS

EUGENE BRAUNWALD, M.D.

26. Ischemic Heart Disease

Coronary Risk Factors

26–1 **Coronary Atherosclerosis and Myocardial Infarction in Young Women—Role of Oral Contraceptives.** Coronary heart disease in young women is not as infrequent as previously thought. Oral contraceptives appear to significantly increase the risk of cardiovascular morbidity and mortality. H.-J. Engel, E. Engel, and P. R. Lichtlen reviewed the findings in 76 women aged 50 years and younger who had a history of acute myocardial infarction. Twenty-seven patients had infarction during oral contraceptive medication without significant angiographic abnormalities. Fifteen others had infarction during oral contraceptive medication and typical diffuse coronary atherosclerosis with 50% or greater stenoses. Twenty-seven patients had advanced diffuse coronary disease and a history of infarction not associated with oral contraceptive medication. Seven patients had had infarction without substantial coronary disease or history of oral contraceptive use.

All but 7 of 34 patients without significant coronary atherosclerosis had used oral contraceptives at the time of myocardial infarction, and except for cigarette smoking, the incidence of atherogenic risk factors was low in this group. The women with typical coronary atherosclerosis had an unusually high incidence of atherogenic risk factors. Oral contraceptives were used by 15 of these 42 patients. Coronary disease was not present in about two thirds of patients who had sustained myocardial infarction during oral contraceptive use.

Myocardial infarction in relatively young women who use oral contraceptives may be a distinct entity unrelated to coronary atherosclerosis. Oral contraceptives appear to increase the risk of myocardial infarction, but they are not a typical atherogenic risk factor. Coronary atherosclerosis is rare in premenopausal women, and is associated with a high number of atherogenic risk factors.

▶ [Previous studies have suggested that the risk of myocardial infarction (MI) in women taking oral contraceptive medications occurred predominantly in those with one or more of the common risk factors, i.e., a history of cigarette smoking, hypertension, hypercholesterolemia, and diabetes mellitus. The present important study raises questions about this notion, since almost half of the young women with MI did *not* have serious coronary atherosclerosis on angiographic examination but most of these had been using oral contraceptives. Conversely, a second large subgroup of young women with MI *without* a history of oral contraceptive medication had advanced diffuse coronary atherosclerosis. These findings suggest that oral contraceptives may not be a risk factor for coronary atherosclerosis but may instead be responsible for causing coronary thrombosis and thereby MI. In an editorial accompanying the above article, M. F. Oliver[1] raises the important question of whether the discrete

(26–1) Eur. Heart J. 4:1–6, January 1983.

isolated occlusive vascular lesions in patients using oral contraceptives might have been a local inflammatory or autoimmune reaction or could be related to a transient systemic increase in intravascular coagulation.

Wei and Bulkley[2] compared 19 women, aged 18–35 years, with documented MI with twenty young men with a history of MI. Atherosclerosis was more advanced and accounted for most MIs in young men but was less evident and accounted for only a minority of MI's in young adult women, who appeared to have a greater preponderance of nonatherosclerotic related infarcts. In a study of MI in young adults, Uhl and Farrell[3] also found that young women with MI had a lower incidence of risk factors for atherosclerosis than did men of similar age.] ◀

26–2 **Platelet Function, Thromboxane Formation, and Blood Pressure Control During Supplementation of the Western Diet With Cod Liver Oil.** There is considerable evidence for a protective effect of dietary eicosapentaenoic acid against cardiovascular disease. This substance interferes with the balance between proaggregatory and vasoconstrictor thromboxane A_2 and anti-aggregatory and vasodilator prostacyclin. This could lead to less reactive platelets and lowered pressure reactivity of the vascular system. Reinhard Lorenz, Ullrich Spengler, Sven Fischer, Jochen Duhm, and Peter C. Weber used a small cod liver oil supplement to add long-chain ω-3 polyunsaturated fatty acids to an otherwise unchanged Western diet in 8 healthy men aged 22–42 years. Cod liver oil (20 ml) was given twice daily for 25 days. The oil contained about 11% eicosapentaenoic acid and 16% doxosahexaenoic acid.

A significant increase in ω-3 polyunsaturated fatty acids occurred with cod liver oil ingestion, whereas most ω-6 polyunsaturated fatty acids decreased in plasma, red blood cell membranes, and platelet microsomal phospholipids. The changes were reversed within 4 weeks after cessation of supplementation. The plasma cholesterol, triglycerides, and lipoprotein fractions did not change despite an increase in total fat intake of about 300 kcal daily. Bleeding time increased, platelet count fell, and plasma thromboxane B_2 declined during supplementation. Platelet aggregation with adenosine diphosphate and collagen also decreased. Baseline blood pressure and blood pressure response to norepinephrine and angiotensin II decreased during supplementation. There were no significant changes in plasma catecholamines, renin, urinary aldosterone, kallikrein, prostaglandins E_2 and $F_2\alpha$, or red blood cell cation fluxes.

Cod liver oil supplementation of a Western diet to provide ω-3 polyunsaturated fatty acids leads to changes paralleling those seen in Eskimos, who have low morbidity from atherothrombotic disease. Moderate supplementation causes marked changes in membrane phospholipids, a shift toward less reactive platelets, and blunted circulatory responses to pressure-regulating hormones.

▶ [It has long been known that Greenland Eskimos, and to a lesser extent some Japanese, enjoy a particularly low incidence of coronary disease, a favorable pattern of serum lipids, and a mild hemostatic defect characterized by a bleeding tendency and reduced platelet aggregability. It has been suggested that these changes are related to their unique diet of sea food rich in ω-3 polyunsaturated fatty acids. The low dose of cod liver oil given in this study (40 ml/day) produced beneficial biochem-

---

(26–2) Circulation 67:504–511, March 1983.

ical effects, but did not produce weight gain. Other investigations support some of the interesting and potentially important findings of this study. Thus, Brox et al.[4] treated patients with familial hypercholesterolemia (type II-A) with cod liver oil for six weeks. Collagen-induced platelet aggregation and thrombin-stimulated thromboxane B_2 generation in platelets in vitro were both reduced; primary bleeding time was not significantly prolonged. There was a statistically significant increase in eicosapentaenoic acid/arachidonic acid ratios in platelet phospholipids. These observations are of great interest, since patients with type II-A hypercholesterolemia have platelets with increased sensitivity to various aggregating agents. I think that given the information available, it would now be of great interest to carry out primary or secondary prevention studies or both to determine the effects of cod liver oil on the development of atherosclerosis.] ◀

6–3 **Effect of Long-Term Moderate Physical Exercise on Plasma Lipoproteins: National Exercise and Heart Disease Project.** John C. LaRosa, Patricia Cleary, Richard A. Muesing, Patrick Gorman (George Washington Univ., Washington, D.C.), Herman K. Hellerstein (Case-Western Reserve Univ.), and John Naughton (State Univ. of New York, Buffalo) report that 223 men, aged 30–64, who had had a myocardial infarction 2 months to 3 years before entering the study were randomly assigned to moderate exercise or control groups. Levels of total plasma cholesterol, high- and low-density lipoprotein (HDL and LDL) cholesterol, and triglycerides were measured.

At baseline, body weight and skin-fold thickness were directly correlated with triglyceride levels and inversely correlated with HDL cholesterol levels. Alcohol consumption correlated directly with HDL cholesterol levels. Smoking, work capacity, and elapsed time from myocardial infarction to study entry were not substantially correlated with lipid and lipoprotein levels.

After 1 year, even though body weight was not different, a statistically significant difference in skin-fold thickness was evident, implying an increase in lean body mass in the exercise group. The exercise group showed a significant increase in work capacity (fitness), whereas the control group showed a significant decrease. No clinically important change in lipid levels was noted in either group after 1 year. A trend toward slightly lower total and LDL cholesterol levels in the exercise group was apparent. Triglyceride levels were slightly lower in the exercise group and increased in the control group; the values between groups differed significantly. Failure to comply with the exercise or control regimen could have obscured the relationship between lipoprotein changes and other variables.

Changes in body weight were weakly correlated with changes in cholesterol levels, but not with triglyceride levels. Diuretic use was negatively correlated with HDL cholesterol change at 1-year follow-up. When multiple regression analysis of the combined groups was used, changes in several independent variables, including work capacity, were not predictive of changes in lipid levels. When plasma lipoprotein levels at 1 year were examined in subjects classified by 3 levels of work capacity, there was a modest but significant increase in HDL cholesterol level with increasing work capacity, as well as a trend toward increasing LDL cholesterol level.

(26–3) Arch. Intern. Med. 142:2269–2274, December 1982.

Changes in levels of fitness or regular exercise or both did not substantially influence HDL cholesterol or other lipid levels. It is possible that exercising subjects ingested foods higher in animal fat and that the higher levels of HDL and LDL cholesterol were related to dietary changes. The data do not disprove the notion that physical activity can alter lipoprotein levels, but they do indicate that the levels of fitness that can be sustained in many patients after infarction are unlikely to alter substantially plasma lipoprotein levels.

▶ [The results of this investigation of the effect of physical exercise are important, since previous studies have shown that physically active healthy persons have lower levels of total triglycerides and total lipoproteins and higher levels of HDL cholesterol (HDL-C) than their sedentary peers. Surprisingly, a full year of moderate exercise appears to have no effect on these biochemical parameters. In accord with these findings are the observations of Ready and Quinney[5] who demonstrated that 9 weeks of high-intensity endurance training in young normal subjects also did not alter lipid or lipoprotein metabolism. In contrast, Lobstein et al.[6] found that exercise training did lower LDL cholesterol (LDL-C) and raise HDL-C in normal middle-aged men, whereas Gordon et al.[7] found that physical activity correlated directly with HDL-C in men with primary type II hyperlipoproteinemia. Similarly, Penny et al.[8] found such a relationship between HDL-C and physical activity in normal male marathon runners and joggers. It is possible that the prolonged and intense physical activity in the latter study was much greater than that used by LaRosa et al. in the study abstracted above.

The important clinical question raised by these studies, of course, is whether exercise alters the rate of myocardial infarction in men. The Ontario Exercise-Heart Collaborative Study found that the 4-year recurrence rate among 379 patients on a program of high-intensity exercise did not differ significantly from that among 354 control patients on a program of light exercise.[9] Naughton[10] has summarized the effects of five clinical exercise trials designed to study the effects of regular physical activity on the outcome of patients with a history of myocardial infarction. There was only the suggestion of a favorable effect on mortality and little evidence to suggest that physical activity affects the rate of cardiac or noncardiac morbid events. Naughton indicated that there is no evidence that physical activity affects cardiovascular morbidity, and no information is available to support its routine use.

It is not easy to put all of this together, but, as I now see it, individuals who have been physically active all of their lives or who have undergone a prolonged (1 year) program of intense physical training, tend to have lower lipid risk factors (higher HDL-C and lower LDL-C) than do sedentary persons. On the other hand, a short program of intense exercise or a longer (one year) program of moderate physical activity may be insufficient to alter the lipid profile. Thus, although a life-long behavior pattern of exercise may well lower the risk of atherosclerosis, once an infarction occurs it may be difficult to make up for past sins, i.e., postinfarction exercise activity does not appear to have a major effect on serum lipids or recurrence of myocardial infarction. Although the incidence of myocardial infarction does not appear to be altered by postinfarction activity, there is some evidence that previous physical activity does improve survival of patients who have suffered a myocardial infarction.[11]

26–4 **Obesity as Independent Risk Factor for Cardiovascular Disease: 26-Year Follow-Up of Participants in the Framingham Heart Study.** The relationship between obesity and the incidence of cardiovascular disease (CVD) remains unclear. Helen B. Hubert, Manning Feinleib, Patricia M. McNamara, and William P. Castelli reexamined this relationship in the 5,209 members of the original Framingham cohort. The 2,252 men and 2,818 women, aged 28–62 years, were free of apparent CVD at initial examination in 1949 or 1950. The population was characterized by Metropolitan Relative

(26–4) Circulation 67:968–977, May 1983.

Weight (MRW), or percent desirable weight (ratio of actual to desirable weight × 100). Clinical CVD developed in 870 men and 688 women during the 26-year follow-up. Coronary heart disease accounted for 75% of events in men and 66% of those in women.

The cohort appeared to be about 20% above desirable weight at entry into the study, and women became progressively heavier with advancing age. The risk of CVD increased with increasing MRW in both men and women. The association was most marked in those under age 50 years. Similar relationships were evident between MRW and coronary disease, and there was a particularly strong gradient of risk of sudden death with increasing MRW in both sexes and all age groups. Multivariate logistic regression analyses showed MRW to be a significant predictor of total CVD in both men and women after adjusting for risk factors. The degree of obesity was one of the best predictors of total CVD in women.

The degree of obesity was an important long-term predictor of the incidence of CVD in the Framingham cohort. Obesity did not act solely through its association with other risk factors in influencing the risks of coronary disease and congestive heart failure. Obesity appears to have predisposed this population to the premature development of CVD. Leanness and avoidance of weight gain before middle age would appear to be advisable for preventing CVD in Americans. Intervention in established risk factors for CVD should be accompanied by weight loss in overweight persons.

▶ [It has been known for many years that the incidence of coronary heart disease and stroke is greater in the obese, but it has been debatable whether obesity by itself makes an additional contribution to risk once the level of coexisting risk factors such as hypertension, elevated blood lipids, and blood glucose are taken into account. In the past, it has been believed that the increased cardiovascular risk seen in heavier persons is due primarily to the influence of the associated risk factor profile and not to the obesity per se. For example, it is clear from many studies (e.g., Knuiman et al.[12]) that the body mass index is related directly to the concentration of total cholesterol and inversely to the concentration of high-density lipoprotein cholesterol. This study is important in that it shows that obesity does not exert its influence on risk solely through its association with coexisting risk factors.] ◀

26–5 **Relationship of Education to Major Risk Factors and Death From Coronary Heart Disease, Cardiovascular Diseases, and All Causes: Findings of Three Chicago Epidemiologic Studies.** Several studies have reported an association between education and the risk of coronary heart disease (CHD), but it is not clear whether education is related to CHD beyond its influence on the well-established major coronary risk factors. Kiang Liu, Lucila B. Cedres, Jeremiah Stamler, Alan Dyer, Rose Stamler, Serafin Nanas, David M. Berkson, Oglesby Paul, Mark Lepper, Howard A. Lindberg, John Marquardt, Elizabeth Stevens, James A. Schoenberger, Richard B. Shekelle, Patricia Collette, Sue Shekelle, and Dan Garside examined the relation of education to risk factors at baseline and to long-term mortality from CHD, cardiovascular diseases, and all causes in 3 cohorts of middle-aged employed white men in Chicago. There were 8,047 subjects from the Chicago Heart Association (CHA) Detection

---

(26–5) Circulation 66:1308–1314, December 1982.

Project in Industry; 1,250 from the Peoples Gas Company Study; and 1,730 from the Western Electric Study.

In all 3 cohorts, an inverse relation was evident at baseline between education and blood pressure. For 2 cohorts, the relationship was significant and was independent of age and relative weight. A significant inverse association between education and cigarette use was noted at entry in all cohorts. No clear pattern was noted for serum cholesterol level. The CHA cohort exhibited an inverse association between education and relative weight and was the only cohort with a significant inverse relation between education and the prevalence of ECG abnormalities at entry. Five-year follow-up data in the CHA cohort showed that education was inversely related to the age-adjusted mortality from CHD, cardiovascular diseases, and all causes. A lesser but still significant relationship for cardiovascular disease mortality persisted in this cohort after adjustment for entry age, diastolic blood pressure, cigarette smoking, serum cholesterol level, relative weight, and ECG abnormalities. In the other 2 cohorts together, with follow-up for 20–21 years, education was inversely related to all 3 mortality end points in univariate analyses.

Education appears to be inversely correlated with cardiovascular risk factors related to life-style and to the long-term risk of death from CHD, cardiovascular disease, and all causes. The relation between education and mortality is not fully explained by established major biomedical risk factors. Further work is needed to assess the mechanisms of these relationships.

▶ [As the pandemic of coronary disease increased during the first half of the 20th century, it was related to a change in life-style—affluence, decreased physical activity, "improved" nutrition, increased stress, etc. Much of this was related to an improvement of social conditions, which is, of course, associated with better education. During the last 30–35 years, the incidence of coronary artery disease and indeed of all atherosclerotic diseases has diminished strikingly in the United States, despite continued improvement of social conditions. Now we see that the better educated—and therefore the more affluent—members of our society appear to have a lowered risk of coronary artery disease! The general reduction in coronary atherosclerosis during the past 35 years may well be due to the healthier lifestyle resulting from widespread public education programs. Since education correlates inversely with body weight and since obesity is a risk factor for coronary disease (see abstract 26–4), the lower risk of the educated might be related, in part, to their lower body weight.] ◀

26–6 **The Tromsø Heart Study: Does Coffee Raise Serum Cholesterol?** Although several studies have reported a relation between coronary heart disease and coffee intake, the apparent risk has generally been ascribed to other factors operating concurrently. Dag S. Thelle, Egil Arnesen, and Olav H. Førde (Univ. of Tromsø, Norway) undertook a survey of coronary risk factors in 7,213 women and 7,368 men, aged 20–54 years, in northern Norway. Coffee consumption correlated positively with concentrations of both total cholesterol and triglycerides in both men and women and correlated inversely with concentrations of high-density lipoprotein (HDL) cholesterol in women. The relation between HDL cholesterol concentrations and coffee con-

(26–6) N. Engl. J. Med. 308:1454–1457, June 16, 1983.

sumption in men was inconsistent. The relations remained evident after adjustment for age, body mass index, physical activity, smoking, and alcohol consumption. The mean total cholesterol concentrations were 5.6 mmole/L in men drinking less than 1 cup of coffee a day and 6.2 mmole/L in those taking more than 9 cups. The respective figures for women were 5.3 and 5.9 mmole/L.

Coffee consumption appears to be a major factor contributing to variations in concentrations of total cholesterol in this population. A relation between coffee consumption and coronary heart disease has not yet been established, but these findings suggest that such an association exists in the Norwegian population. Coffee contains many substances other than caffeine that could influence plasma lipid concentrations, and additives such as cream and sugar may be of importance.

▶ [Although previous studies have reported a relation between coronary heart disease and coffee intake, the apparent risks of coffee consumption (like obesity) have previously been ascribed to concomitantly acting factors rather than to coffee per se. The key finding in this investigation is that after adjustment for all known variables, total cholesterol was related to coffee consumption. Acute caffeine ingestion does not have any significant effect on water loss, changes in plasma volume and rectal temperature during endurance performance, or pathologic electrocardiographic changes in normal subjects. Caffeine has been shown to increase plasma free fatty acid levels, resulting in a diminished dependence on muscle glycogen during exercise, and this glycogen-sparing effect is thought to account for the well-known increase in physical endurance following coffee ingestion.[13] In an interesting study of the electrophysiologic effects of caffeine, Dobmeyer et al. found that the administration of a quantity of caffeine equivalent to that in two cups of coffee reduced the effective refractory period of the atria and right ventricle, and sometimes enhanced the development of atrial flutter or fibrillation and of unsustained ventricular tachycardia in response to programmed atrial or ventricular stimulation.[14]] ◀

26–7 **Familial Aggregation of Coronary Heart Disease and Its Relation to Known Genetic Risk Factors.** Coronary heart disease and myocardial infarction tend to run in families, but it is not clear whether the familial aggregation of coronary heart disease can be fully explained by the presence of currently recognized major genetic risk factors such as hypertension, diabetes, and hyperlipidemia. Leo P. ten Kate, Helge Boman, Stephen P. Daiger, and Arno G. Motulsky (Univ. of Washington) have obtained evidence for familial aggregation independent of these risk factors. A case-control study was carried out in 145 white male survivors of myocardial infarction, 145 age-matched white male blood donors, and the first-degree relatives of both groups.

Risk factors other than high blood pressure were significantly more frequent in patients than in control subjects. The incidence of myocardial infarction was 16% in first-degree relatives of patients and 8.9% in relatives of control subjects. The rates of coronary heart disease were 20.5% and 14.7%, respectively. When the data were stratified according to confounding risk variables and a pooled relative risk estimate was calculated by the Mantel-Haenzel method, a greater than 2-fold relative risk for myocardial infarction was found

---

(26–7) Am. J. Cardiol. 50:945–953, November 1982.

for relatives of patients. Their relative risk for coronary heart disease was 1.7. Classic risk factors also did not predict the familial occurrence of myocardial infarction or coronary heart disease when Cox's life-table regression analysis was employed.

These findings indicate that the familial aggregation of coronary heart disease is not fully explained by familial clustering of recognized coronary risk factors. Aggregation could be due to undefined genetic factors, environmental factors common to family members, or an interaction of genetic factors with environmental agents. Future studies of familial clustering of coronary heart disease should take lipoprotein characteristics into account.

▶ [Until I read this paper, I had always thought that the familial association of coronary heart disease was related simply to the familial aggregation of coronary risk factors, i.e., cigarette smoking, hypercholesterolemia, hypertension, and diabetes mellitus. Clearly, something else is operating which has not yet been identified. It could be related to education (see abstract 26–5). Thus, it does appear that there are important, thus far unidentified familial risk factors for coronary heart disease. It must be recalled that familial aggregation is not necessarily genetic because many environmental factors are common to family members.

There have been a number of other interesting studies relating to the risk of developing coronary artery disease. Thus, Brook et al.[15] have found that not only the level of high-density lipoprotein cholesterol (HDL-C) but those of the HDL-2C and HDL-3C subclasses are depressed in patients with coronary disease. In turn, obesity and daily consumption of tobacco are inversely associated with the serum HDL-C, whereas the consumption of beer is directly associated.[16] Another important risk factor is psychosocial stress, as recently reviewed by Boman.[17] The type A personality, which is associated with a high incidence of coronary disease, is characterized by enhanced secretion of catecholamines and cortisol during mental work.[18] The Framingham investigators have reported that the incidence of cardiovascular disease is inversely related to the amount of alcohol regularly consumed.[19] Although it has long been known that there is a relationship between hematocrit values and morbidity and mortality due to coronary artery disease, this relationship disappears after adjustment of other risk factors.[20] Also, there is no evidence that vasectomy predisposes to cardiovascular disease.[21] Although the effects of cigarette smoking on the risk of myocardial infarction are well known, an interesting new finding is that men who smoke the newer cigarettes with reduced concentrations of nicotine and carbon monoxide do *not* have a lower risk of myocardial infarction than those who smoke cigarettes containing larger amounts of these substances.[22]] ◀

26–8 **Coronary Artery Disease Following Mediastinal Radiation Therapy.** Lon S. Annest, Richard P. Anderson, Wei-i Li, and Mark D. Hafermann (Mason Clinic, Seattle) observed 4 men (average age, 41) with coronary artery disease who had received curative radiotherapy for mediastinal malignancy 12–18 years previously, the mean interval being 15 years. Three of the patients were among 558 undergoing coronary bypass surgery between 1978 and 1982. Estimated radiation exposure of the heart ranged from 1,500 to 3,300 rad. None of the patients was at high risk for coronary disease by Framingham criteria.

All 4 patients had angina, and 2 reported previous myocardial infarction. Angiograms showed obstruction of the proximal right coronary artery in each case. Three patients also had obstruction of the proximal left anterior descending artery, and 1 had proximal circum-

(26–8) J. Thorac. Cardiovasc. Surg. 85:257–263, Feburary 1983.

flex involvement. The radiation dose to the anterior myocardium averaged 1.8 times higher than that to the posterior myocardium in the 3 evaluable patients. A patient with lung cancer had obliterative pericarditis and tumor invasion of the heart. One other patient had dense pericardial adhesions, but no additional technical difficulties were encountered. The 3 patients who had bypass surgery remained asymptomatic for at least 10–43 months. The patient with cancer received radiotherapy but died of progressive disease after 2 years. Among 163 patients given mediastinal irradiation for lymphoma or thymoma between 1959 and 1980, survival was 10 years or longer in 29, and in 5 of these, severe coronary artery disease developed.

Many long-term survivors of mantle irradiation for lymphoma may be at an increased risk for the development of coronary artery disease. Standard surgical treatment may be beneficial to affected patients because of their relatively young age, and because the typically proximal distribution of lesions enhances the likelihood of complete revascularization. Normal wound healing and satisfactory early symptomatic results can be expected. Coronary bypass surgery should not be withheld because of a past history of mediastinal radiotherapy.

▶ [In the past, the heart has been thought to be relatively resistant to radiation, but now there is an increasing number of well-documented instances of pericarditis with effusion, tamponade, and chronic constriction as well as of coronary artery thrombosis and myocardial infarction following irradiation. Gottdiener et al.[23] found that echocardiographic and radionuclide cineangiographic evidence of left ventricular dysfunction was common in asymptomatic persons 5–15 years after therapeutic anterior radiation of the mediastinum. Similarly, Burns et al.[24] studied asymptomatic adults 7–20 years after mediastinal irradiation for Hodgkin's disease; the majority had abnormal function of the left or right ventricle, or both, at rest or during exercise. These techniques are more sensitive than are the clinical means of assessing ventricular performance, and they indicate the high incidence of cardiomyopathy secondary to previous radiotherapy. Miller et al.[25] reported yet another complication: ergonovine-induced severe coronary spasm following radiotherapy for Hodgkin's disease.] ◀

ACUTE MYOCARDIAL INFARCTION

26–9 **Intravenous Short-Term Infusion of Streptokinase in Acute Myocardial Infarction.** Early restoration of coronary blood flow may be the best means of limiting myocardial necrosis in evolving myocardial infarction. Rolf Schröder, Giancarlo Biamino, Enz-Rüdiger v. Leitner, Thomas Linderer, Thomas Brüggemann, Jörg Heitz, Hans-Friedrich Vöhringer, and Karl Wegscheider (Free Univ. of Berlin, West Germany) evaluated the use of short-term, high-dose intravenous streptokinase therapy in a series of 93 patients with acute myocardial infarction. Twenty-six patients had angiography before and up to 3 hours after the start of streptokinase infusion and, usually, after 24 hours and 3 weeks. Fifty-two others had angiography only in the fourth week after infarction. Some of these patients, like all those in the first group, received 500,000 IU of streptokinase in 30 minutes, whereas others received 1.5 million IU in 1 hour. Fifteen patients not having angiography received either dose of streptoki-

---

(26–9) Circulation 67:536–548, March 1983.

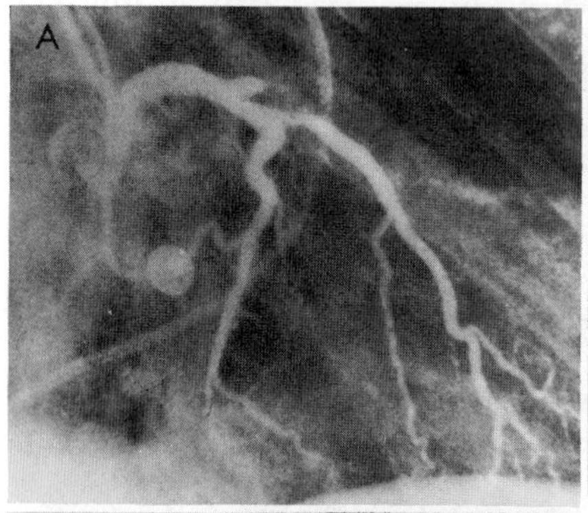

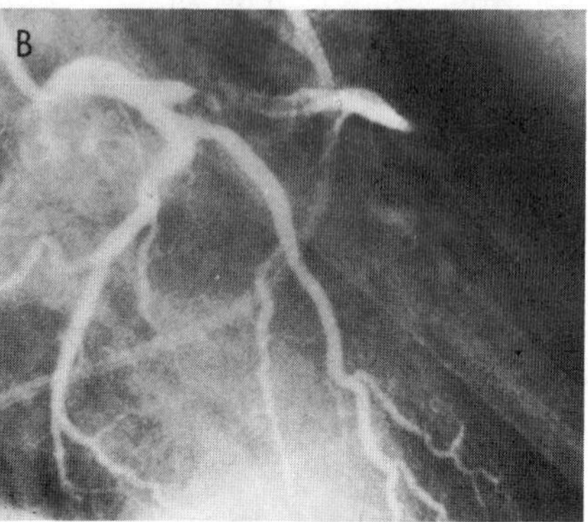

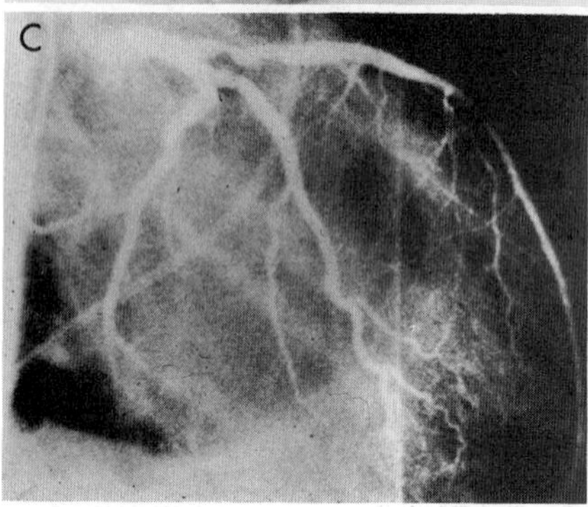

Fig 26–1.—A, complete occlusion of the left anterior descending coronary artery. **B,** 20–40 minutes after beginning intravenous streptokinase infusion, contrast material flows around a large thrombus; peripheral filling (not seen) is delayed. **C,** complete visualization of the vessel periphery 80–100 minutes after initiation of streptokinase infusion. (Courtesy of Schröder, R., et al.: Circulation 67:536–548, March 1983; by permission of the American Heart Association, Inc.)

nase. Heparin, acetylsalicylic acid, and methylprednisolone were given before streptokinase, and heparin was infused for up to 96 hours afterwards. Phenprocoumon was given subsequently.

Occluded coronary arteries were opened within an hour after streptokinase infusion was begun in 11 of 21 of the patients monitored (Fig 26–1). In 84% of all patients having angiography, the infarct-related vessel was patent in the fourth week after infarction. Three fourths of patent arteries had residual luminal stenosis of less than 70%. Serial serum creatine kinase myocardial-specific isoenzyme (CK-MB) estimates indicated that recanalization usually was achieved within 1 to 2 hours. Localized disorders of contraction resolved in patients exhibiting recanalization. Seven patients died in hospital, and 6 had nonfatal reinfarctions. No serious bleeding complications occurred. There were no pyretic or allergic reactions to streptokinase. Most of the patients who did not have further surgery were quite free of symptoms at follow-up, although some had severe residual stenosis of major coronary vessels.

Coronary blood flow can be rapidly restored by high doses of intravenous streptokinase in patients with evolving myocardial infarction. The earlier application of this treatment may compensate for the shorter time to lysis with intracoronary administration. The optimal dose of streptokinase remains unknown.

▶ [The use of intracoronary streptokinase in the lysis of coronary thrombi in patients with acute myocardial infarction (MI) was described in the 1981 YEAR BOOK OF MEDICINE (p. 318). Since then, interest in this subject has grown enormously. Insofar as the intracoronary administration of streptokinase is concerned, Schwarz et al.[26, 27] demonstrated that if reperfusion is carried out within 4 hours of the onset of infarction, myocardial function, as reflected in both the global and the regional ejection fraction, improved; myocardial function did not improve if reperfusion was successful but the time lag exceeded four hours. Ganz et al.[28] reported that intracoronary administration of streptokinase resulted in successful reperfusion in 80% of 81 patients; reocclusion occurred in 4 patients. Elective bypass operation was carried out following thrombolysis in 18 patients because of multiple vessel involvement. Smalling et al.[29] treated 136 patients with acute MI with intracoronary streptokinasae. Ejection fraction increased when reperfusion was successful but failed to increase in patients not achieving successful reperfusion. There was a suggestion of a lower mortality and of sustained improvement in left ventricular function among successfully reperfused patients. MI size, as estimated by analysis of serial creatine kinase activity, was also significantly reduced.

Bergmann et al.[30] produced coronary thrombi experimentally in dogs and demonstrated that positron-emission tomography of the uptake of ^{11}C-palmitate could show the beneficial effects of streptokinase-induced thrombolysis and is a potentially useful technique for assessing the efficacy of thrombolytic therapy.

One of the complications of coronary thrombolysis is the development of reperfusion arrhythmias; at the time of coronary revascularization, transient arrhythmias, usually idioventricular rhythm and sinus bradycardia, occur commonly. These arrhythmias are useful noninvasive markers of successful reperfusion.[31]

The importance of the article abstracted above is that it suggests that intravenous streptokinase may be useful in coronary thrombolysis as well. Since maximal benefit from thrombolysis will be obtained by the earliest possible restoration of coronary blood flow, intravenous streptokinase may be associated with a shorter delay than intracoronary streptokinase because the former can be instituted without preceding coronary angiography. Also, intravenous streptokinase can be administered in any community hospital and, indeed, can be begun in the ambulance or even in the patient's home in order to shorten the duration of coronary occlusion and thereby enhance the quantity of myocardium that is salvaged.] ◀

26–10 **Clot-Selective Coronary Thrombolysis With Tissue-Type Plasminogen Activator.** Intracoronary administration of fibrinolytic activators such as streptokinase induces proteolysis in the circulating blood and can produce a lytic state, resulting in systemic bleeding. Steven R. Bergmann, Keith A. A. Fox, Michel M. Ter-Pogossian, Burton E. Sobel (Washington Univ.), and Désiré Collen (Univ. of Leuven, Belgium) used a clot-selective tissue-type plasminogen activator (tPA) purified from cultures of a melanoma cell line in an attempt to lyse coronary thrombi in dogs without inducing a systemic lytic state. Myocardial perfusion and metabolism were assessed by positron-emission tomography before and after administration of tPA to dogs with occlusive coronary thrombi induced by a copper coil in the left anterior descending coronary artery. Intracoronary or intravenous streptokinase or tPA was administered 1–2 hours after thombus induction.

Coronary thrombolysis was achieved within 10 minutes of intravenous tPA administration. Streptokinase also was effective, but its intravenous administration took much longer than did intracoronary streptokinase to lyse thrombi. Thrombolysis by tPA was accompanied by restoration of myocardial perfusion and metabolism. Myocardial salvage was greater than in dogs given streptokinase. Neither agent

---

(26–10) Science 220:1181–1183, June 10, 1983.

led to significant depletion of fibrinogen. No systemic lytic state was identified in tPA-treated animals, but streptokinase induced a mild systemic lytic state, as reflected by elevated levels of fibrin degradation products.

Intravenous administration of tPA produces prompt coronary thrombolysis in dogs, with resultant salvage of myocardial metabolism and perfusion and no induction of a systemic lytic state. Intravenous administration is as effective as the intracoronary route. It may be possible to produce tPA by recombinant DNA technology. The agent then would offer promise for promptly and safely lysing coronary thrombi and restoring the metabolism of jeopardized myocardium in patients.

▶ [One of the hazards of intravenous or intracoronary streptokinase or urokinase is that these substances can induce a systemic lytic state that may lead to serious bleeding. Physiologically, fibrinolysis occurs when tissue plasminogen activator is bound to fibrin. This complex then binds circulating plasminogen which produces plasmin at the fibrin surface. The presence of fibrin increases the local plasminogen concentration by creating an additional interaction between tissue-type plasminogen activator (tPA) and circulating plasminogen. Streptokinase and urokinase have no specific affinity for fibrin and therefore activate circulating and fibrin-bound plasminogen equally. The use of recombinant techniques to produce tPA would be a great boon for the management of acute myocardial infarction. Pennica et al.[32] have recently synthesized and cloned the human tPA gene. It is to be hoped that a translation product of this gene will induce thrombolysis when administered intravenously. It is likely that by the time these comments are published this will have been achieved clinically.

The potential hazard of streptokinase therapy is reflected in the evidence of systemic fibrinolytic activity that appears even in patients receiving low-dose intracoronary streptokinase which alters coagulation variables for as long as 48 hours.[33] On the other hand, there is electrocardiographic evidence, from regression of Q waves and increase in R waves in patients undergoing thrombolysis, that damaged myocardium may be salvaged by perfusion induced by intracoronary streptokinase.[34]

There is considerable argument about how to treat the patient who has undergone successful thrombolytic reperfusion. Some investigators advise early surgical treatment because of the presence of other critical coronary lesions and concern about reinfarction.[35–38] Others feel that coronary artery bypass grafting is necessary in only a minority of patients.] ◀

26–11 **Left Ventricular Function and Rapid Release of Creatine Kinase MB in Acute Myocardial Infarction: Evidence for Spontaneous Reperfusion.** Angiographic studies have suggested that early coronary recanalization may occur spontaneously in a substantial number of patients with acute myocardial infarction, and spontaneous improvement in left ventricular (LV) systolic function does not seem to be uncommon during infarction. Lawrence Ong, Peter Reiser, James Coromilas, Lawrence Scherr, and John Morrison examined the relation between rapid release of creatine kinase MB isoenzyme (CK-MB), used as a marker for spontaneous reperfusion, and improvement in left ventricular function in 52 patients with early transmural myocardial infarction. All were admitted before the serum CK-MB was above 5 mIU/ml. The 43 men and 9 women had a mean age of 57 years. Ventricular function was assessed by equilibrium-gated radionuclide ventriculography.

(26–11) N. Engl. J. Med. 309:1–6, July 7, 1983.

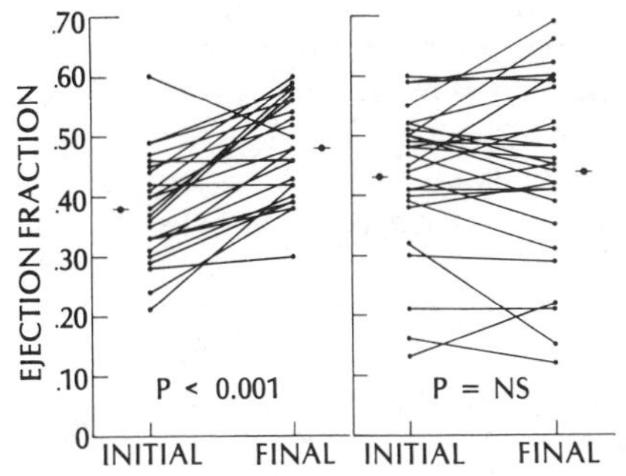

Fig 26–2.—Initial and final left ventricular ejection fraction in patients with rapid *(left panel)* and slow *(right panel)* release of creatine kinase MB. NS = not significant. (Courtesy of Ong, L., et al.: N. Engl. J. Med. 309:1–6, July 7, 1983; reprinted by permission of The New England Journal of Medicine.)

The degree of spontaneous improvement in LV ejection fraction was inversely related to the time to peak CK-MB. Neither parameter was related to the degree of initial LV damage. Ventricular function in patients with rapid (12 hours or less to peak) and slow release of CK-MB is shown in Figure 26–2. Significant increases in the LV ejection fraction was evident in the rapid release group. Mean initial global and regional ejection fractions did not differ significantly in the 2 groups.

These findings, in a small select population of survivors of acute infarction, emphasize the heterogeneous nature of evolving acute infarction in man. Spontaneous reperfusion that results in altered CK-MB release and improvement in ventricular function does not appear to be uncommon after acute myocardial infarction. Patients likely to have spontaneous reperfusion may be those who respond to intracoronary thrombolysis.

▶ [A number of years ago DeWood et al.[39] demonstrated that total occlusion of the infarct-related vessel is frequent during the early hours of transmural myocardial infarction (MI) and decreases in frequency during the initial 12–24 hours, suggesting spontaneous recanalization. This interesting study by Ong et al. not only provides support for this notion but, even more importantly, indicates that such spontaneous reperfusion is quite common. De Feyter et al.[40] also found evidence for spontaneous recanalization in patients with acute MI and observed that in these patients, left ventricular function was significantly better than in those with persistent occlusion. If spontaneous reperfusion is as common as these studies suggest, then it is logical to utilize thrombolytic therapy in patients with acute MI in order to give a little "nudge" to the normal fibrinolytic system and thereby limit myocardial damage.] ◀

26–12 **Indomethacin-Induced Scar Thinning After Experimental Myocardial Infarction.** The nonsteroidal, antiinflammatory agent ibuprofen can induce scar thinning when given after experimental myocardial infarction. Haim Hammerman, Robert A. Kloner, Frederick J. Schoen, Edward J. Brown, Jr., Sharon Hale, and Eugene Braunwald (Harvard Med. School) examined the effects of indomethacin, a potent prostaglandin synthesis inhibitor, on scar formation after the production of myocardial necrosis in dogs by occlusion of the left anterior descending coronary artery. Experimental animals received indomethacin, 10 mg/kg, intravenously 15 minutes and 3 hours after occlusion; controls received saline only. The animals were killed 6 weeks later.

(26–12) Circulation 67:1290–1295, June 1983.

The mean scar thickness was 7.2 mm in controls and 3.6 mm in indomethacin-treated animals. The ratio of scar thickness to uninfarcted wall thickness was significantly less in indomethacin-treated dogs. Infarct size was similar in the two groups. The hydroxyproline content of scar tissue was not significantly altered by indomethacin therapy. The microscopic findings were qualitatively similar in the treated and control dogs.

Severe thinning of myocardial scars was observed 6 weeks after coronary ligation in indomethacin-treated dogs in this study. Indomethacin, in addition to its antiinflammatory action, may inhibit collagen synthesis in some situations, but it is not likely that this is responsible for the scar thinning noted in the present study. The healing of myocardial infarctions might be altered by administering antiinflammatory agents early in the course of infarction. The functional significance of induced scar thinning remains to be determined, but it may well cause infarct expansion. Scar thinning might predispose to late aneurysm formation and deterioration of left ventricular function.

▶ [In a corollary study, Hammerman et al.[41] examined the effects of multiple, large doses of methylprednisolone and a single dose of methylprednisolone following acute coronary occlusion on infarct size, scar formation and ventricular function. The former resulted in depressed left ventricular function and infarct thinning, just as is the case with indomethacin. A single dose of methylprednisolone exhibited some reduction of infarct size. Fortunately, aspirin does not affect scar formation. Taking all of these studies together, it seems unwise to use large doses of ibuprofen, indomethacin, or methylprednisolone in the early postinfarct state—particularly for the treatment of acute pericarditis. It is probably more appropriate to use aspirin whenever possible.] ◀

26–13 **Implications of Increased Myocardial Isoenzyme Level in the Presence of Normal Serum Creatine Kinase Activity.** It is not clear whether patients with normal total creatine kinase (CK) activity but elevated myocardial-specific isoenzyme (CK-MB) activity have subtle myocardial injury. Gary V. Heller, Alvin S. Blaustein, and Jeanne Y. Wei (Harvard Med. School), with the technical assistance of Daniel Geer, attempted to correlate peak serum CK and CK-MB levels with other clinical criteria for acute infarction in 335 consecutive patients suspected of having infarction and 71 control subjects. The other criteria included typical chest pain, increased myocardial lactic dehydrogenase concentration, acute ECG changes, and an elevated CK-MB value on 2 or more occasions or a typical CK curve.

The presence of criteria for myocardial injury is related to the CK and CK-MB findings in the table. No control subjects had increased CK or CK-MB values or any of the criteria for myocardial infarction. None of the patients with normal CK and CK-MB values had more than 2 criteria consistent with myocardial injury, whereas more than 90% of those with elevated CK and CK-MB levels had 2 or more criteria for injury, and more than 80% had 3 or more criteria. Two or more criteria were met by two thirds of patients with elevated CK-MB and normal CK values; about three fourths of these patients had

(26–13) Am. J. Cardiol. 51:24–27, Jan. 1, 1983.

DIAGNOSTIC CRITERIA*

Criteria Number	Study Patients† Group 1: CK–MB–†	Group 2: CK+MB+	Group 3: CK–MB+	Control Patients† Group A: CK–MB–
0	43	1	6	100
1	46	6	29	0
2	11	12	33	0
3	0	27	24	0
4	0	54	3	0

*Criteria are typical chest pain, new ECG changes, ratio of cardiac isoenzymes of lactic dehydrogenase to liver isoenzymes ≥1, and typical creatine kinase (CK) curve or increased level of myocardial-specific isoenzyme of creatine kinase (CK-MB) more than once. Maximum of 4 criteria per patient. Abbreviations: CK – MB –, normal CK and CK-MB values; CK – MB +, normal CK and elevated CK-MB; CK + MB +, elevated CK and CK-MB.

†Values indicate percentage of total in each group with designated number of criteria.

(Courtesy of Heller, G.V., et al.: Am. J. Cardiol. 51:24–27, Jan. 1, 1983.)

subendocardial ECG changes. Elevated CK-MB and normal CK values were found in 20% of patients aged 70 years and older and in 10% of younger patients.

It appears that an elevated CK-MB level with normal total CK activity indicates definite myocardial injury. These findings should be considered part of the spectrum of nontransmural myocardial infarction. Elderly patients with atypical ischemic symptoms are affected relatively often. Each patient's basal CK level should serve as his or her reference, since most patients in this study with elevated CK-MB and normal CK values had elevations to at least twice baseline although the maximal CK value remained normal.

▶ [Creatine kinase myocardial-specific isoenzyme is a mainstay of the diagnosis of acute myocardial infarction. The results of this interesting study show that an elevated CK-MB level in the face of a normal total CK is consistent with a small infarction. Clearly, the isoenzyme, i.e., CK-MB, is a more sensitive index of myocardial necrosis than is CK. In a cost-effectiveness study of routine use of serum enzyme analysis in the diagnosis of myocardial infarction, Fisher et al.[42] concluded that serial CK-MB determinations are sufficient and that routine serial determinations of serum glutamic oxaloacetic transaminase and lactic dehydrogenase values are not justified.] ◀

26–14 **Value of Electrocardiogram in Diagnosing Right Ventricular Involvement in Patients With an Acute Inferior Wall Myocardial Infarction.** Until recently, right ventricular infarction was diagnosed only at autopsy. Simon H. Braat, Pedro Brugada, Christoffel de Zwaan, Joseph M. Coenegracht, and Hein J. J. Wellens (Univ. of Limburg, The Netherlands) evaluated various ECG criteria for diagnosing right ventricular infarction in patients with inferior wall infarction when ^{99m}Tc-pyrophosphate scintigraphy indicated right ventricular involvement. Sixty-seven consecutive patients with acute inferior wall infarction were studied. A 12-lead ECG and 4 additional right precordial leads (Fig 26–3) were recorded at admission and then every 8 hours for 3 days.

All patients had abnormal uptake of ^{99m}Tc in the inferior wall, and

(26–14) Br. Heart J. 49:368–372, April 1983.

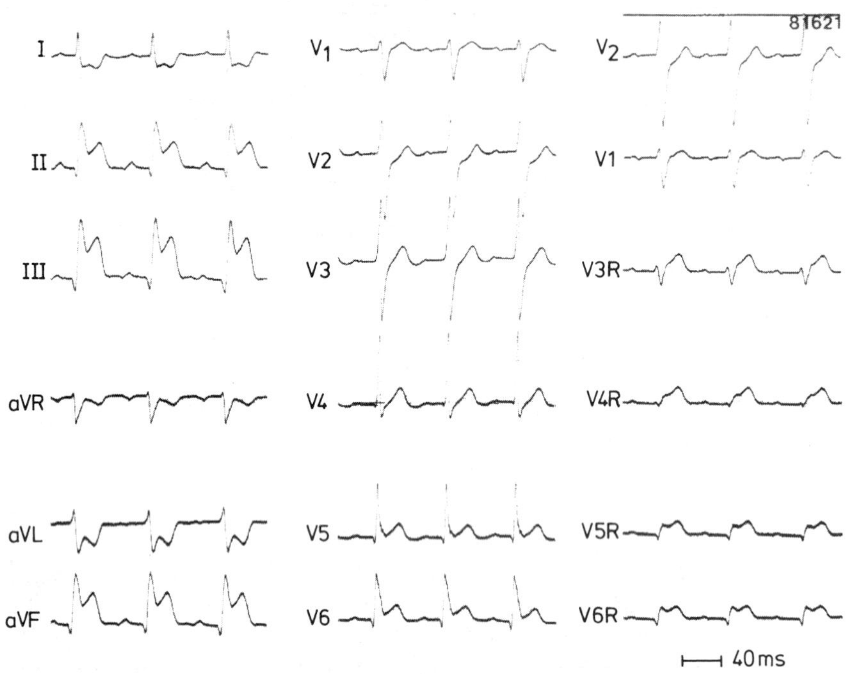

Fig 26–3.—This simultaneous recording of electrocardiogram leads shows acute inferoposterior wall myocardial infarction. Right precordial leads show ST-segment elevation in leads V_3R, V_4R, V_5R, and V_6R in the absence of a QS pattern in lead V_3R or V_4R or ST-segment elevation in lead V_1. (Courtesy of Braat, S.H., et al.: Br. Heart J. 49:368–372, April 1983.)

43% also had right ventricular involvement. All but 1 of the 21 patients with ST-segment elevation of 1 mm or more in lead V_3R had right ventricular involvement, as did 27 of the 29 patients with ST elevation in lead V_4R. This elevation very seldom persisted longer than 72 hours, and in some cases it lasted less than 10 hours after the onset of chest pain. Three of 29 patients with ST elevation in lead V_5R had no pathologic uptake in the right ventricle. The same was true of 3 of 27 patients with significant ST elevation in lead V_6R. Several patients had false-positive QS patterns in leads V_3R and V_4R or false-positive ST elevation in lead V_1. The degree of enzyme elevation was not helpful in identifying patients with right ventricular involvement. One patient with right ventricular involvement died in hospital with cardiac tamponade.

The most consistent finding in patients in this study with right ventricular infarction was ST-segment elevation of 1 mm or more in the right precordial leads. Right ventricular infarction occurs almost exclusively in patients with inferior wall infarction in combination with posteroseptal involvement. A recording of lead V_4R is the best means of diagnosing right ventricular involvement in patients admitted with acute myocardial infarction.

▶ [Infarction of the right ventricle has been reported to occur in 5%–18% of all patients with myocardial infarction; it occurs exclusively as a complication of posterior-inferior infarction and is usually associated with complete occlusion of the right coronary artery. However, right ventricular infarction occurs in only a minority of cases of obstruction of the right coronary artery. It has been proposed that the low oxygen requirements of the right ventricle, the greater blood flow to the right ventricle during systole, and the more extensive collateralization of the right ventricle are responsible for the frequency in which the right ventricle is spared when total occlusion of the right coronary artery occurs. Haupt et al.[43] showed at autopsy that collateral flow to the right ventricle from the left coronary artery, particularly through the moderator band artery, protects against massive right ventricular infarction in the presence of acute proximal right coronary artery occlusion. Thus, with severe obstructive disease of the proximal left coronary artery, i.e., proximal to the origin of the moderator band artery, complete right coronary artery occlusion is likely to produce a massive right ventricular infarction.

The recognition of right ventricular infarction has important therapeutic implications, since it may cause hypotension as a result of a low cardiac output with a normal or near normal left ventricular filling pressure; this condition is often responsive to massive administration of fluid. The findings in the article by Braat et al. abstracted above, were in large part confirmed by Klein et al.[44] who also found ST-segment elevation in right precordial leads to be an accurate indicator of right ventricular infarction. In 110 patients with acute inferior myocardial infarction, the sensitivity was 82.7%; the specificity, 76.9%; and the negative predictive value, 87.7%. Therefore, I agree that because of its simplicity and relative accuracy, the recording of right precordial leads (V_3R and V_4R) should be an intrinsic part of the early evaluation of all patients with acute inferior wall infarction.

Insofar as pure right ventricular infarction is concerned, an experimental study in the dog by Chou et al.[45] indicated that this causes transient ST-segment elevations in right precordial leads, right bundle branch block, and abnormal Q waves or small R waves in right precordial leads. It is possible that these findings, although not yet extended to man, may help to identify the rare cases of isolated or predominant right ventricular infarction.] ◀

26–15 **Precordial ST-Segment Depression in Patients With Inferior Myocardial Infarction: Clinical Implications.** Precordial ST-segment depression associated with inferior myocardial infarction may indicate anteroseptal or posterior left ventricular ischemia or infarction, or may be "reciprocal" to ST changes in the inferior leads. J. S. Gelman and A. Saltups (Melbourne) undertook a prospective study of precordial ST-segment depression in 110 consecutive patients with acute transmural inferior infarction or no previous infarction. Thirty-five patients had inferior or inferolateral infarction with no precordial ST depression. Fifty-nine patients had ST depression of 1 mm or more, which in 23 lasted for 48 hours or longer after hospital admission. Sixteen patients had definite inferoposterior or inferoposterolateral infarction. The mean follow-up was 17 months.

Patients with ST depression were older than those without, had higher peak creatine kinase levels, and more often required treatment for atrial fibrillation and atrioventricular (AV) block. These differences were largely restricted to patients with lasting ST depression, and this group included more patients with ventricular fibrillation and left ventricular failure. Group differences in hospital mortality were not significant. Left ventricular failure was most frequent in the group with lasting ST depression or follow-up, as was recurrent infarction. Three (5%) patients in this group died. There were no late deaths in patients without ST depression or in those with inferoposterior or inferoposterolateral infarction.

(26–15) Br. Heart J. 48:560–565, June 1982.

Precordial ST depression is a reliable indicator of a relatively unfavorable hospital and postdischarge course in patients with inferior myocardial infarction. Even transient ST depression is associated with higher enzyme levels and more frequent AV block; it should not be dismissed as merely a "reciprocal" event.

▶ [In patients with inferior myocardial infarction (MI), precordial ST-segment depressions may indicate (1) ischemia or infarction of the anterior septal wall due to associated disease of the left anterior descending coronary artery; (2) reciprocal electrical changes; or (3) a large inferior infarct. Gibson et al.[46] reported that patients with inferior MI and precordial ST-segment depressions had more prolonged chest pain, greater ST-segment elevations in inferior leads, higher plasma creatine kinase levels, a higher prevalence of true posterior infarction by ECG criteria, a lower left ventricular ejection fraction, more extensive infarct related asynergy, greater thallium-201 perfusion abnormalities, more complications during hospitalization and more cardiac events at three months. However, they did *not* have a higher incidence of left anterior descending coronary artery disease, thallium-201 defects or wall motion abnormalities involving anterior or septal segments. All of these findings, together with those of the article abstracted above, suggest that patients with acute inferior MI who have associated precordial ST-segment depression have greater global and regional left ventricular dysfunction owing to more extensive inferior wall infarction rather than to concomitant anterior septal ischemic injury. In any event, regardless of the mechanism of the ST-segment depression, these patients are at a higher risk for subsequent morbid events than patients with inferior wall infarctions who do not exhibit this ECG change. Therefore, one can make a good case for an aggressive approach to these high-risk patients, i.e., early coronary arteriography, and—if the anatomy dictates—coronary bypass surgery.] ◀

26–16 **Double-Blind Trial of Metoprolol in Acute Myocardial Infarction: Effects on Ventricular Tachyarrhythmias.** Recent studies indicate that β-blocking agents may reduce mortality in patients having acute myocardial infarction. L. Rydén, R. Ariniego, K. Arnman, J. Herlitz, Å. Hjalmarson, S. Holmberg, C. Reyes, P. Smedgård, K. Svedberg, A. Vedin, F. Waagstein, A. Waldenström, C. Wilhelmsson, H. Wedel, and M. Yamamoto evaluated the β_1-selective adrenoceptor antagonist metoprolol in a double-blind, placebo-controlled trial in 1,395 patients with symptoms suggestive of acute infarction. A total of 698 patients received metoprolol in a dosage of 15 mg intravenously, followed by 50 mg orally every 6 hours for 2 days, and then 100 mg twice daily for 3 months. Continuous ECG monitoring was carried out in 145 patients with definite or suspected infarction, 73 of whom received metoprolol.

Definite acute infarction occurred in 809 patients, and probable infarction in 162 others. Metoprolol did not influence the occurrence of premature ventricular contractions (PVCs) or short bursts of ventricular tachycardia, however, ventricular fibrillation occurred in 17 placebo patients and 6 metoprolol-treated patients. Significantly fewer metoprolol patients required lidocaine for ventricular fibrillation or sustained ventricular tachycardia while in hospital. Metoprolol did not alter the occurrence of PVCs or brief ventricular tachycardia during the first 24 hours of treatment in patients having continuous ECG monitoring.

Metoprolol appeared to protect against ventricular fibrillation in

(26–16) N. Engl. J. Med. 308:614–618, Mar. 17, 1983.

hospitalized patients with myocardial infarction. The mechanism of the antifibrillatory action of metoprolol is not clear, but it may counteract a rise in cyclic adenosine monophosphate that provides an electrophysiologic substrate for ventricular fibrillation. Prevention of fibrillation may be a major factor in the reduced mortality related to β-blocking agents in patients with myocardial infarction. β-Blocking agents provide a means of preventing arrhythmias in coronary care units.

▶ [It is now well established that mortality during the year after acute myocardial infarction is relatively high and that many of the deaths are sudden and are probably caused by ventricular fibrillation. Similarly, there is agreement that β-adrenergic blockade begun about three weeks after acute myocardial infarction reduces the mortality during the subsequent year.[47] The results of the Norwegian Multicenter Study Group using timolol in patients who had sustained a myocardial infarction were reported in the 1982 YEAR BOOK OF MEDICINE (p. 329) and the results of the randomized trial using propranolol, the so-called BHAT trial, were reported in the 1983 YEAR BOOK OF MEDICINE (p. 339); both showed favorable effects of β-blockade on survival. Although the mechanism of this protective effect is not yet understood, it may be related to a reduction of ischemia and resultant infarction or arrhythmia or both.[47] The Swedish trial summarized by Ryden et al. in the article abstracted above has also shown a reduced mortality with metoprolol treatment begun immediately upon arrival in the coronary care unit and continued for 90 days. One of the beneficial effects of β-blockade was a marked reduction in the incidence of ventricular fibrillation and in the need for intravenous lidocaine. However, metoprolol did not influence the occurrence of premature ventricular contractions or short bursts of ventricular tachycardia.

Although the prevention of ventricular fibrillation in the coronary care unit does not necessarily improve survival, it does imply a potent stabilizing effect on the heart's electrical activity which probably persists to the period after the patient leaves the coronary care unit and thereby explains the reduction in the late incidence of sudden death.

There has been a suspicion that long-term β-blockade is less effective in patients more than 65 years of age. An earlier study with alprenolol had shown that treatment with this β-blocker actually increased the mortality in this age group. Therefore, it is of interest that Gundersen and the Norwegian Multicenter Group compared the effects of timolol in patients under age 65 with those over 65. They noted that the incidence of side effects, the number of withdrawals, and the reasons for withdrawal were similar in older and younger patients.[48] They therefore concluded that age should not be decisive in determining whether or not to treat postinfarction patients with a β-blocker.] ◀

26–17 **First Ultra-Short-Acting β-Adrenergic Blocking Agent: Its Effect on Size and Segmental Wall Dynamics of Reperfused Myocardial Infarcts in Dogs.** β-Blockers may be useful in treating patients with myocardial ischemia, but heart failure and bronchospasm may restrict their use in some patients with infarction or those having coronary bypass surgery. Rüdiger Lange, Robert A. Kloner, and Eugene Braunwald (Harvard Med. School) evaluated a new cardioselective ultra-short-acting β-blocker, ASL-8052, which permits the abolition of β-blockade within 16 minutes of termination of an infusion. The drug was evaluated in dogs subjected to occlusion of the left anterior descending coronary artery for 3 hours, followed by 3 hours of reperfusion. Study animals received ASL-8052 by infusion starting 15 minutes after occlusion, in a dose adjusted to reduce the heart rate

(26–17) Am. J. Cardiol. 51:1759–1767, June 1983.

by about 20%. The extent of myocardial necrosis was determined by tetrazolium staining and autoradiography. Regional myocardial blood flow was estimated using labeled microspheres.

Treated dogs received ASL-8052 in doses of 100–150 μg/kg/minute. The amount of myocardial tissue necrosis was significantly lower in treated than control dogs after 3 hours of reperfusion, as related to the in vivo area at risk (48% vs. 73%). Segment shortening decreased in control dogs after 2 hours of reperfusion, but no such functional deterioration was seen in treated animals. The rate of increase of left ventricular pressure (LV dP/dt) declined by 22% during infusion of ASL-8052. The heart rate decreased 22% in treated dogs and did not change on reperfusion, whereas in control dogs it increased 26% on reperfusion. Regional myocardial blood flow was similar in the treated and control groups throughout the study.

It appears that ASL-8052 may be useful in the early treatment of patients with acute myocardial infarction who are to undergo either thrombolysis or surgical revascularization. Its brief duration of action would permit its use to reduce myocardial oxygen consumption maximally with less risk of seriously depressing cardiac function. Hypertension and tachycardia that occur postoperatively with increased sympathetic tone could be treated safely with ASL-8052.

▶ [β-Blockers are useful for reducing ischemia, increasing atrioventricular block, reducing the sinus rate and diminishing ventricular arrhythmias in many forms of heart disease, particularly those associated with myocardial ischemia. However, these drugs are not devoid of adverse effects. Thus, they may produce bronchoconstriction in patients with a history of asthma or chronic obstructive pulmonary disease, intensification of left ventricular failure in patients with borderline compensation, hypotension in patients with borderline arterial pressure, and various forms of bradyarrhythmias and atrioventricular block in patients predisposed to these conditions. The experimental drug utilized in this study is of considerable interest, since it is very rapidly metabolized. Indeed, 16 minutes after discontinuation of its infusion, the heart rate response to isoproterenol and evidence of β-blockade had essentially disappeared. Therefore, it is possible to use this agent to test acutely the potential risks of β-blockade. If the patient responds well to the ultra-short-acting drug, then it is possible either to continue its infusion or to switch to one of the standard longer acting β-blockers.

As outlined in abstracts 26-9 and 26-10, there is now considerable interest in the salvage of ischemic myocardium by thrombolysis. In the present experimental study, reperfusion was carried out after 3 hours of coronary occlusion and administration of the ultra-short-acting β-blocker was found to increase the amount of myocardium salvaged. This finding suggests that combination therapy—intravenous (or intracoronary) streptokinase (or tissue plasminogen activator) accompanied by an agent that prolongs the survival of ischemic cells, such as a β-blocker (an ultra-short-acting β-blocker to be on the safe side in a patient who might sustain adverse effects with acute myocardial infarction), might be very efficacious.] ◀

26–18 **Risk Stratification and Survival After Myocardial Infarction.** The Multicenter Postinfarction Research Group examined the role of physiologic parameters of cardiac function in predicting mortality after myocardial infarction in a series of 866 patients under age 70 who survived the coronary care unit phase of acute myocardial infarction at 9 participating centers. Most patients had 24-hour Holter monitoring and determination of the resting nuclide ventricular ejection frac-

(26–18) N. Engl. J. Med. 309:331–336, Aug. 11, 1983.

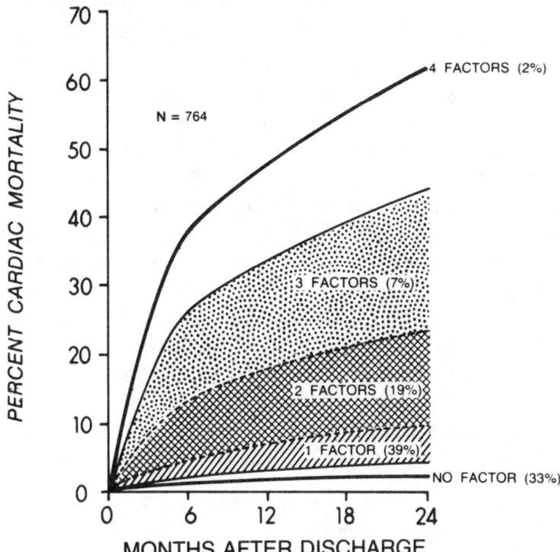

Fig 26–4.—Mortality curves after discharge and zones of risk according to the number of risk factors. Variation of risk within each zone reflects the spectrum of relative risk for individual factors as well as the range of multiplicative risks for combinations of factors. Numbers in parenthesis denote percentage of population with specified factors. (Courtesy of the Multicenter Postinfarction Research Group: N. Engl. J. Med. 309:331–336, Aug. 11, 1983; reprinted by permission of The New England Journal of Medicine.)

tion before discharge. A total of 452 clinical variables were assessed for each patient. Treatment at the time of discharge included antiarrhythmic drugs, β-blockers, cardiac glycosides, and diuretics. Thirteen percent of patients had coronary bypass surgery in the first year after discharge.

Univariate analyses indicated a progressive increase in cardiac mortality over 1 year after infarction as the ejection fraction fell below 0.40 and as the number of ventricular ectopic depolarizations exceeded 1 per hour. The only risk factors that were independent predictors of mortality were an ejection fraction below 0.40, ventricular ectopy of 10 or more depolarizations per hour, an advanced New York Heart Association (NYHA) functional class before infarction, and rales in the upper two thirds of the lung fields during the stay in the coronary care unit. Zones of risk associated with these risk factors are shown in Figure 26-4. Patients with no risk factors (33% of the study population) had a 2-year mortality below 3%, whereas patients with all 4 risk factors (2% of the study population) had a 2-year mortality of 60%.

Both nuclide ejection fraction and ventricular ectopic depolarization have been confirmed as risk stratifiers in patients having myocardial infarction. Pulmonary rales are also an independent risk factor. No strong association between anterior infarction and death was found in this study. NYHA functional class probably includes functional information that is related to an unfavorable outcome in patients with anterior infarction.

▶ [It is critical to evaluate the risk of death in patients following acute myocardial infarction in order to determine which patients require invasive studies, i.e., catheterization and arteriography, and depending on the anatomic findings, which patients should undergo coronary artery bypass grafting. Besides the variables discussed in the article summarized above, an additional test, which was not utilized by this research group but which may be very helpful in predicting mortality in patients with acute myocardial infarction, is an early postinfarction thallium-201 scintigram. Becker et al.[49] found that a thallium defect involving 40% or more of the left ventricular circumference identified a subgroup of patients with a high (64%) 6-month mortality. The thallium scan was more sensitive in detecting nonsurvivors than was a reduced ejection fraction. These investigators also reported that the combination of three variables—the development of Q waves, the ejection fraction, and the size of the thallium defect—was more useful than any single variable for prognosis. Gibson et al.[50] also evaluated the utility of the exercise thallium-201 scintigram prior to hospital discharge in postinfarct patients. They observed that submaximal exercise scintigraphy can distinguish between high and low risk groups. Thallium defects in more than one region of the myocardium, the presence of delayed redistribution, or increased lung thallium uptake are more sensitive predictors of subsequent cardiac events than ST-segment depression, angina, or even the extent of disease as determined angiographically.] ◀

Chronic Coronary Artery Diseases

26–19 **Can Noninvasive Exercise Test Criteria Identify Patients With Left Main or 3-Vessel Coronary Disease After a First Myocardial Infarction?** Randolph E. Patterson, Steven F. Horowitz, Calvin Eng, Jose Meller, Stanley J. Goldsmith, Augusto D. Pichard, Doris A. Halgash, Michael V. Herman, and Richard Gorlin (Mount Sinai Med. Center, New York) investigated whether exercise treadmill testing with clinical, ECG, and thallium-201 myocardial perfusion imaging data can identify patients who have left main or 3-vessel (anatomically high-risk) coronary artery disease (CAD) 3–24 months after their first transmural myocardial infarction (MI). Twelve exercise test criteria for high-risk disease were compared in 40 patients referred for cardiac catheterization; 34 had a history of chest pain, and 17 had angiographically defined high-risk CAD.

A thallium image defect outside the vascular distribution of the MI was the most reliable criterion to distinguish patients with high-risk CAD (P = .00052, Fisher's exact test of discrimination). Thallium imaging was somewhat more sensitive (92% vs. 65%) when patients with negative thallium imaging criteria who failed to achieve 85% of the age-predicted maximal heart rate were excluded. Failure to achieve 85% of predicted heart rate was by itself a useful criterion for detecting high-risk CAD, especially in patients who were not receiving propranolol. Development of positive ST-segment depression at less than 70% of predicted heart rate also discriminated left main or 3-vessel disease from less extensive CAD. Patients who do not meet these criteria have a very low probability of having high-risk CAD and probably do not need coronary angiography for the purpose of excluding these high-risk coronary lesions after a first MI.

Other criteria failed to discriminate significantly between high-risk and less extensive CAD in patients after their first MI. Chest pain or ST-segment depression during exercise testing was particularly un-

(26–19) Am. J. Cardiol. 51:361–372, February 1983.

reliable. None of the criteria for high-risk CAD was influenced by irreversible left ventricular dysfunction. Although neither chest pain during an exercise test nor a history of typical angina pectoris provided a reliable indicator of anatomically high-risk CAD in these patients, the results may not hold true in all patients. Exertional angina may be an indication for coronary angiography and surgery to relieve symptoms. Exercise testing with thallium imaging appears to be a cost-effective approach to screening patients for high-risk CAD after MI.

▶ [The classical exercise ECG may also be of some value in the detection of left main coronary artery disease; Schneider et al.[51] reported that an early positive treadmill test, i.e., during stage 1 or 2 of the Bruce protocol, identifies patients who have an increased likelihood of having left main coronary stenosis even if they are minimally symptomatic. I agree with Schneider et al. that coronary arteriography should be carried out in patients who have mild angina pectoris if they have an early positive treadmill response. If left main coronary artery stenosis has been excluded by arteriography, these patients may be treated medically with little risk, as indicated in the report from the Coronary Artery Surgery Study (see abstract 26-31). However, the absence of a positive early treadmill exercise test does not exclude left main coronary artery disease, since 10% of patients with coronary disease without early positive treadmill tests had left main coronary disease.

In addition to the criteria described in the abstract above (i.e., thallium imaging defects outside the region of the MI, a fall in blood pressure during exercise, failure to achieve 85% of the predicted heart rate, and ST-segment depression at less than 70% of predicted heart rate during exercise), other findings on exercise study may be useful in identifying postinfarction patients at high risk of death. These include a left ventricular ejection fraction on a radionuclide ventriculogram less than 0.40, failure of the left ventricular ejection fraction to increase by 0.05 units, and an increase in left ventricular end-systolic volume index during exercise greater than 5% above levels at rest. These exercise-induced abnormalities of left ventricular function may have even greater prognostic significance than the delineation of coronary arterial anatomy or the assessment of left ventricular function at rest.[52]

Epstein et al.[53] have developed a rational strategy for the evaluation of patients three weeks after myocardial infarction. They suggest that if such patients have recurrent angina and/or a positive exercise ECG they should undergo catheterization. Patients with normal left ventricular function on echocardiography or radionuclide angiography should undergo exercise studies (radionuclide or ECG); those who have inducible ischemia, i.e., either abnormalities in the ejection fraction or ST-segment depression should also undergo catheterization. Patients with normal left ventricular function who do not exhibit ischemia as defined above can undergo medical follow-up.] ◀

26–20 **Percutaneous Transluminal Coronary Angioplasty: Report of Complications From the National Heart, Lung, and Blood Institute PTCA Registry.** G. Dorros, M. J. Cowley, J. Simpson, L. G. Bentivoglio, P. C. Block, M. Bourassa, K. Detre, A. J. Gosselin, A. R. Grüntzig, S. F. Kelsey, K. M. Kent, M. B. Mock, S. M. Mullin, R. K. Myler, E. R. Passamani, S. H. Stertzer, and D. O. Williams analyzed the complications occurring in the first 1,500 patients enrolled in the National Heart, Lung, and Blood Institute (NHLBI) Percutaneous Transluminal Coronary Angioplasty (PTCA) Registry over 3½ years, starting in 1977. The data were contributed by 73 participating centers. A total of 543 in-hospital complications occurred in 21% of the patients (Table 1). Significant complications occurred in about 10% of patients. There were 16 hospital deaths.

(26–20) Circulation 67:723–730, April 1983.

TABLE 1.—COMPLICATIONS WITH PERCUTANEOUS TRANSLUMINAL CORONARY ANGIOPLASTY IN 314 PATIENTS

Complication	Episodes	Complication	Episodes
Prolonged angina	121	Miscellaneous	32
Myocardial infarction	72	Conduction defects	5
Coronary occlusion	70	Central nervous system events	5
Coronary spasm	63	Minor arrhythmias	3
Dissection/intimal tear	43	Coronary branch injury	3
Hypotension	31	Pulmonary embolism	2
Bradycardia	25	Coronary air embolism	2
Ventricular fibrillation	24	Allergic reactions	2
Vascular	22	Pulmonary edema	1
Hospital death	16	Respiratory arrest	1
Excessive blood loss	11	Transient hypotension	1
Ventricular tachycardia	8	Febrile episode	1
Coronary embolism	2	Nausea	1
		Minor bleeding	1
		Impending infarction	1
		Total	543

(Courtesy of Dorros, G., et al.: Circulation 67:723–730, April 1983; by permission of the American Heart Association, Inc.)

TABLE 2.—IN-HOSPITAL DEATHS

Mortality statistics	One-vessel disease	Multivessel disease	Total
1. All deaths	10/1177 (0.85%)	6/320 (1.9%)	16/1497 (1.1%)
2. Patients without previous bypass surgery	9/1135 (0.8%)	2/262 (0.8%)	11/1397 (0.8%)
3. Patients with previous bypass surgery	1/42 (2.4%)	4/58 (6.9%)	5/100 (5.0%)

Relationship of the 16 deaths to PTCA

Causes of death

1. Related (11 patients)
   - Guiding catheter dissection of the left main coronary
   - Failure to administer anticoagulation
   - Probable coronary spasm
   - Myocardial revascularization in an unstable patient
   - Coronary artery dissection
   - Coronary occlusion
   - Prolonged angina
2. Probably not related (5 patients)
   - Disseminated intravascular coagulopathy
   - Perioperative myocardial infarction during elective surgery
   - A difficult elective second CABG

CABG, coronary artery bypass grafting; *PTCA*, percutaneous transluminal coronary angioplasty.

(Courtesy of Dorros, G., et al.: Circulation 67:723–730, April 1983; by permission of the American Heart Association, Inc.)

The rate of myocardial infarction following PTCA was 4.8%. The rate in patients having emergency bypass surgery was 39%. Emergency bypass surgery was done in 6.8% of all patients, most often for coronary dissection or occlusion. The in-hospital deaths are analyzed in Table 2. Eleven of the 16 deaths were related to PTCA. Coronary occlusion was reported in 69 patients after PTCA, and 53 of them had major complications, including the need for emergency surgery. Ventricular fibrillation complicated PTCA in 1.6% of patients. Fatal complications were significantly more frequent in patients having previous bypass surgery. Complications occurred less frequently as investigator experience increased.

These findings support the relative safety of transluminal angioplasty as a means of nonoperative myocardial revascularization in carefully selected patients. However, further follow-up is needed to establish the long-term morbidity and mortality associated with PTCA.

▶ [Percutaneous transluminal coronary angioplasty (PTCA) described by Gruentzig in the late 1970s was considered by many to be little more than a stunt at first, but it is now clear that the procedure is much more than that. It is a legitimate method of treating discrete obstruction in the coronary vascular bed. An excellent up-to-date summary of key references on the subject of PTCA was recently published.[54]

The article by Dorros et al. abstracted above provides a good summary of the complications of the procedure. However, it must be recognized that investigator experience with the technical procedure importantly influences the frequency of complications; as might be anticipated, the incidence of complications diminishes as the investigator experience increases. Meier et al.[55] have shown that eccentric stenoses have a lower rate of primary success than concentric stenoses, and stenoses that are long and eccentric are associated with the highest incidence of complications, whereas stenoses that are short and concentric have the lowest. Ischinger et al.[56] reported that patients who had only mild stenosis (60% or less diameter narrowing) are not ideal candidates for angioplasty, since they carry the same risk of myocardial infarction and emergency operation as do patients with severe stenosis; indeed PTCA may even accelerate the disease process with the frequent development of severe restenosis. Restenosis, which occurs in about 30% of patients within 7 months of angioplasty remains one of the major problems with the procedure. Fortunately, restenosis can be treated by a second angioplasty. Usually PTCA is very efficacious. Thus, Kanemoto et al.[57] found that if the luminal diameter is increased by more 20%, coronary perfusion to the ischemic areas, as determined by exercise thallium myocardial scintigraphy, is improved. Bonow et al.[58] found that PTCA increased the ejection fraction as well as left ventricular diastolic filling during exercise.

Several additional points about PTCA might be noted: It has been reported that angioplasty can be carried out on an outpatient basis without increased risk.[59] PTCA has been carried out successfully in patients who have had partially obstructed saphenous vein bypass grafts.[60] Unfortunately, transmural myocardial ischemia following a complicated PTCA is frequently associated with evidence of myocardial infarction, despite prompt surgical revascularization. It is possible that greater salvage of ischemic myocardium may be possible if the intraaortic balloon pump is used in the interval between PTCA-induced coronary occlusion (the principal complication of this procedure) and surgical revascularization; obviously this interval should be as brief as possible.[61]] ◀

26–21 **In Vivo Coronary Angioscopy.** The coronary arteries now can be visualized using a high-resolution 1.8-mm fiberoptic scope and a translucent perfluorocarbon emulsion blood substitute. J. Richard Spears, H. John Marais, Juan Serur, Oleg Pomerantzeff, Robert P.

(26–21) J. Am. Coll. Cardiol. 1:1311–1314, May 1983.

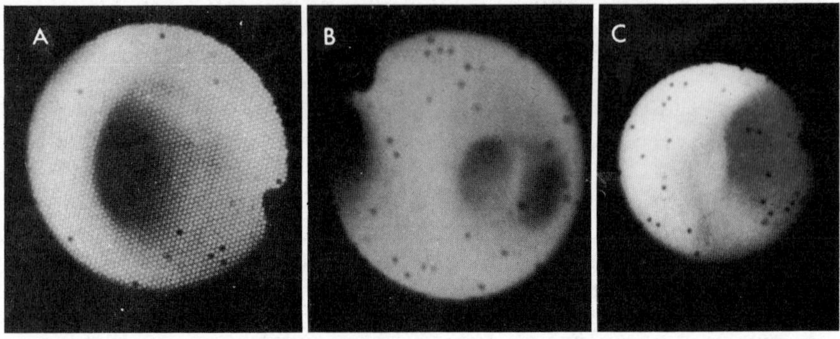

Fig 26–5.—A, left anterior descending coronary artery of postmortem canine heart filled with normal saline solution. **B,** in vivo view of trifurcation of left coronary artery into (from left to right) circumflex, intermediate, and anterior descending branches in the dog during perfusion with oxygenated Krebs-Ringer's lactate solution. **C,** in vivo view of human left anterior descending coronary artery lumen showing encroachment by atherosclerotic plaque. Blood replacement with cardioplegic solution permitted intraluminal visualization. (Courtesy of Spears, J.R., et al.: J. Am. Coll. Cardiol. 1:1311–1314, May 1983.)

Geyer, Robert S. Sipzener, Ronald Weintraub, Robert Thurer, Sven Paulin, Richard Gerstin, and William Grossman (Harvard Med. School) have evaluated this method in postmortem studies, in vivo canine studies, and studies in human patients. An Olympus ultrathin fiberscope was used. The perfluorocarbon-containing blood replacement included electrolytes and hydroxyethyl starch as an oncotic agent. The preparation was sterilized by filtration and equilibrated with 95% oxygen and 5% CO_2. The pH was adjusted to 7.45.

The appearances in postmortem canine studies are shown in Figure 26–5. Comparable findings were obtained in in vivo studies in dogs using oxygenated Ringer's lactate and perfluorocarbon solution. Four human patients were examined during coronary bypass surgery. Plaques were visualized within the lumina of the coronary vessels.

Coronary angioscopy has many possible clinical uses. When done at cardiac catheterization or during heart surgery, the procedure could provide important information on the nature of the underlying disease process. It may be possible to distinguish atheroma from residual thrombus in patients receiving fibrinolytic therapy for acute myocardial infarction. Mechanisms of reclosure could be examined in patients having percutaneous transluminal coronary angioplasty. The patency of vein graft anastomoses could be assessed by angioscopy. Laser-mediated "atheroplasty" under direct vision might be possible. No untoward effects have been observed, but there is likely to be a risk of provoking coronary spasm or producing dissection or perforation. At present, coronary angioscopy should be restricted to experienced angiographers.

▶ [Up to now selective coronary angiography has been the principal diagnostic method for evaluating coronary artery anatomy. Direct visualization of the internal surface of coronary arteries, as carried out by in vivo coronary angioscopy, would permit precise determination of coronary cross-sectional area and identification of different types of vascular disease, i.e., thrombi vs. atheroma. The high resolution, small-diameter (less than 2 mm) fiberoptic scope and the transluscent perfluorocarbon emulsion blood substitutes have allowed the development of this unique and imaginative technique. This opens the door to direct treatment of obstructive lesions by means of laser irradiation, as described in the abstract below.] ◀

26–22 **Effects of Carbon Dioxide, Nd-YAG, and Argon Laser Radiation on Coronary Atheromatous Plaques.** George S. Abela, Sigurd Normann, Donald Cohen, Robert L. Feldman, Edward A. Geiser and C. Richard Conti (Univ. of Florida) examined the effects of laser radiation on atherosclerotic plaques under both wet and dry conditions. Studies were done using fresh autopsy specimens from 15 patients. Plaques were exposed to CO_2 laser radiation as well as to radiation from the neodymium-yttrium, aluminum, and garnet (Nd-YAG) lasers and argon lasers. Split and intact segments were prepared under dry conditions or immersed in saline solution or blood when exposed to laser radiation at varying power and duration settings.

All 3 lasers created controlled injuries in atherosclerotic plaques. The magnitude of injury generally varied with the total energy delivered. Calcified and uncalcified plaques were penetrated at similar exposure levels. A wedge incision was produced in the plaque that was surrounded by zones of thermal and acoustic injury (Fig 26–6). A zone of thermal necrosis and coagulation surrounded the crater and in turn was surrounded by a diffuse region of acoustic or shock injury that gradually faded into uninjured tissue. More energy was needed to produce penetration with the CO_2 laser under saline solution than in the dry condition. Less total energy generally was needed to penetrate a plaque with Nd-YAG laser radiation when tissues were immersed in blood than when saline was used.

Fig 26–6.—Histology of an injury to a fatty atherosclerotic plaque by exposure to 5 J of total energy from a CO_2 laser under dry conditions. **A,** atheroma showing wedge-shaped incision *(arrow);* original magnification, ×52. **B,** same artery (original magnification, × 119) showing laser incision *(1),* and complete penetration of the fatty atheromatous core *(2).* The media also has been partly penetrated *(3).* Note the zone of tissue burn along the laser path and the zone of complete tissue vaporization. Hematoxylin-eosin. (Courtesy of Abela, G.S., et al.: Am. J. Cardiol. 30:1199–1205, December 1982.)

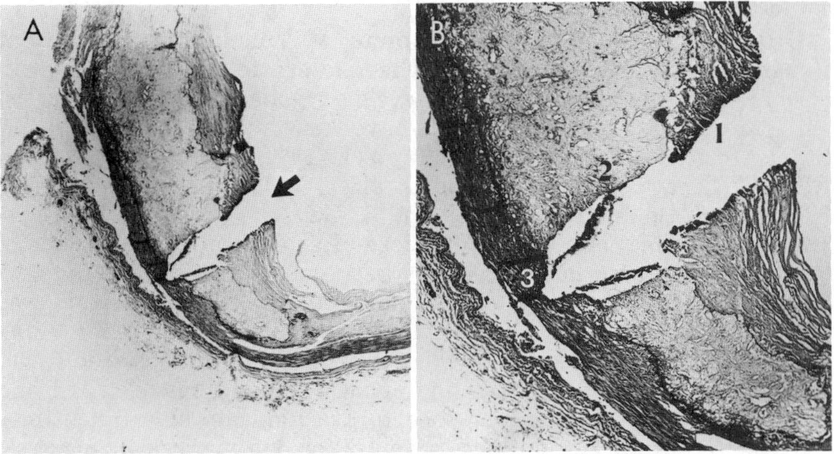

(26–22) Am. J. Cardiol. 30:1199–1205, December 1982.

Laser radiation can be used to damage atherosclerotic plaques. This approach probably can be adapted to intravascular delivery of a laser beam with the use of guidance systems similar to those employed in percutaneous transluminal angioplasty. Further work is warranted on the possible role of laser radiation in improving perfusion through obstructed arteries.

▶ [Cardiology is preparing to enter the 21st century! Up to now only two nonsurgical techniques have been available to recanalize partially or totally occluded arteries: transluminal angioplasty and thrombolytic therapy. Laser irradiation may be a third and possibly ultimately the most effective technique!

Laser light is a monochromatic and coherent light that can be carried by optical fibers. In the past it has been used to destroy hemangiomas, cause hemostasis of bleeding peptic ulcers, and produce photocoagulation in the treatment of retinal neovascularization. In dogs with pulmonary stenosis, the obstruction has been relieved by the use of a laser transmitted through a cardiac catheter. Although this technique may seem "far out," the ability to deliver the laser through a fiber-optic catheter makes it realistic. The hazard of this approach, of course, is that in addition to penetrating the atherosclerotic plaque and/or thrombus, the catheter may injure the wall of the vessel.

At the present time, substantial investigation is going on in many laboratories to determine the applicability of this new therapeutic modality to the relief of atherosclerotic obstructions in the coronary and other vascular beds. Choy et al.[62] described the use of an argon laser through a specialized coronary catheter with a fiberoptic wave guide in a series of animals. A moderate degree of intimal necrosis and some loss of elastic tissue occurred. However, five days later intimal repair had occurred, although focal elastic tissue loss persisted. Lee et al.[63] inserted a flexible catheter equipped with both fiber-optic viewing capabilities and a quartz fiber for laser delivery into the aorta or iliac artery of living dogs and human cadavers with diseased arteries. They vaporized a hyalinized diseased area, demonstrating the feasibility of simultaneous visualization and vaporization of atherosclerotic plaques. They also extracted coronary plaques from fresh human cadaver hearts and subjected them to laser treatment from argon ion and carbon dioxide sources. Fibrous, lipoid, and calcified plaques could all be vaporized! The area and depth of penetration varied directly with the intensity and duration of photoirradiation and inversely with the density of the atherosclerotic tissue.[64] Choy et al.[65] summarized their experience in 60 coronary arteries obtained from cadaver hearts. Successful laser angioplasty was achieved in 14 of 15 arteries, and the authors concluded that damage to the intima and accidental perforation of the arterial wall by the laser catheter are controllable low-incidence risks.] ◀

26–23 **Differential Inhibition by Aspirin of Vascular and Platelet Prostaglandin Synthesis in Atherosclerotic Patients.** Aspirin permanently inactivates platelet cycle-oxygenase, but vascular tissues can rapidly resynthesize cyclo-oxygenase and regain the capacity to form prostaglandins. Babette B. Weksler, Stuart B. Pett, Daniel Alonso, Richard C. Richter, Paul Stelzer, Valavanur Subramanian, Karen Tack-Goldman, and William A. Gay, Jr. (Cornell Univ.) examined the effect of a single low dose of aspirin on the synthesis of prostacyclin in arterial and venous tissue of 70 patients having aortocoronary bypass surgery. A dose of 40, 80, or 325 mg of aspirin was given 12–16 hours before operation.

The serum thromboxane B_2 was reduced 77% from baseline by 40 mg of aspirin, and 99% by the highest dose. All patients except 1 had inhibition of the platelet response to arachidonate. Bleeding times were twice baseline in patients given 80 or 325 mg of aspirin. Pros-

(26–23) N. Engl. J. Med. 308:800–805, Apr. 7, 1983.

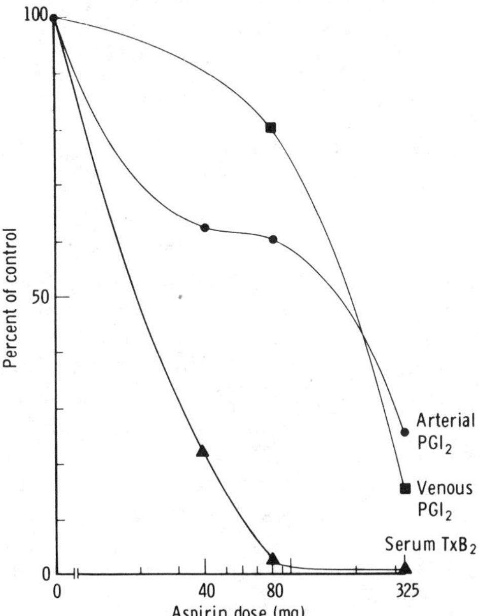

Fig 26–7.—Comparison of the effects of aspirin ingestion on platelet production of thromboxane B_2 *(TxB_2)* and venous and aortic production of prostacyclin *(PGI_2)*. SEM for thromboxane B_2 was ±10% for controls and up to ±30% for aspirin-treated patients; for prostacyclin, it was ±10% for all subjects. (Courtesy of Weksler, B.B., et al.: N. Engl. J. Med. 308:800–805, Apr. 7, 1983; reprinted by permission of The New England Journal of Medicine.)

tacyclin generation by saphenous vein was reduced only after the highest dose of aspirin. Arterial prostacyclin was reduced 35%–40% by the lower doses of aspirin and 75% by the 325-mg dose. The extent of atherosclerosis could not be related to prostacyclin production by aortic tissue. No increase in surgical blood loss was associated with aspirin administration.

A 325-mg dose of aspirin greatly inhibited prostaglandin production by both platelets and aortic and venous tissue for at least 14 hours in this study (Fig 26–7). The recovery of vascular cyclo-oxygenase function after a single dose of aspirin is much slower in vessels than in cultured endothelial cells. Lower doses of aspirin suppress prostaglandin production by platelets much more than that by vascular tissue. The use of multiple drugs in patients with atherosclerosis probably augments the differential effects of low doses of aspirin on prostaglandin synthesis in a beneficial manner. Nitrates enhance prostacyclin production, and both nitrates and β-blockers can reduce the production of thromboxane A_2. Very low doses of aspirin, given before coronary bypass surgery, might best prevent the initiation of platelet thrombi, the release of platelet mediators, and the occurrence of platelet-dependent damage in vascular grafts.

▶ [The principal conclusion from this important study is that very low doses of aspirin (40–80 mg) can inhibit platelet aggregation and the synthesis of thromboxane A_2, a vasoconstrictor and platelet activator, but these doses have much less effect on the inhibition of the synthesis of prostacyclin, a potent vasodilator and platelet inhibitor which is produced by arterial and venous endothelium. Therefore, these low doses of aspirin alter the prostacyclin-thromboxane A_2 equilibrium in favor of prostacyclin. On the other hand, usual doses of aspirin (i.e., 325 mg) prevent synthesis of both prostacyclin and thromboxane A_2 and may not affect the equilibrium between these two substances. Therefore, large doses of aspirin may not prevent clotting, whereas small doses, which inhibit platelet aggregation and thromboxane A_2 synthesis (without inhibiting the synthesis of prostacyclin) would be expected to have potent antithrombotic properties.

In the 1983 YEAR BOOK (p. 343) the effectiveness of aspirin and dipyridamole on the maintenance of patency of aortocoronary vein grafts was reported.] ◀

26–24 **Effect of Aspirin in Large Doses on Attacks of Variant Angina.** Coronary spasm may be important in the production of variant angina and some forms of exertional angina and acute myocardial infarction. Prostaglandin I_2, which is produced by the coronary arteries, reportedly is involved in the modulation of coronary artery tone. Kunihisa Miwa, Hirofumi Kambara, and Chuichi Kawai (Kyoto Univ., Japan) examined the effects of aspirin, which suppresses prostaglandin I_2 synthesis, on attacks of variant angina in 4 patients who experienced more than 5 attacks a week, usually at night. All drugs except for nitroglycerin were withdrawn at least 3 days before the study. Aspirin was given in a dose of 4 gm daily with antacids, and diltiazem was given in a dose of 120–240 mg daily.

Aspirin aggravated attacks of variant angina in all 4 patients, with attacks not only becoming more frequent but also occurring even in the daytime. The results of treadmill testing were negative when testing was done in the afternoon in the control period, but results became positive during aspirin administration in the 3 patients tested. Diltiazem suppressed attacks of variant angina in all 4 patients. Coronary spasm was documented angiographically during attacks in all patients.

Aspirin consistently aggravated attacks of variant angina in patients in this series, and their exercise capacity declined. Apparently, aspirin in large doses can be detrimental in patients with coronary artery spasm. Further studies of the roles of aspirin and prostaglandins in patients with coronary spasm are needed.

▶ [In accord with the findings of the abstract (26–23) of the article by Weksler et al., one would expect that large doses of aspirin which inhibit the production of the vasodilator prostacyclin might upset the balance between coronary constriction and vasodilation and enhance vasoconstriction. This is exactly what occurred in this investigation, which, like the one by Weksler et al., emphasizes that although small doses of aspirin might be beneficial in the prevention of coronary thrombosis, large doses can be detrimental and can induce coronary spasm and aggravate myocardial ischemia.

Mehta et al.[66] have shown that in concentrations that can be achieved clinically, nitroglycerin stimulates prostacyclin released from human saphenous and umbilical vein rings. This may be one of its mechanisms of action.] ◀

26–25 **Protective Effects of Aspirin Against Acute Myocardial Infarction and Death in Men With Unstable Angina: Results of a Veterans Administration Cooperative Study** are reported by H. Daniel Lewis, Jr., James W. Davis, Donald G. Archibald, William E.

(26–24) Am. Heart J. 105:351–356, February 1983.
(26–25) N. Engl. J. Med. 309:396–403, Aug. 18, 1983.

Steinke, Thomas C. Smitherman, James E. Doherty, III, Harold W. Schnaper, Martin M. LeWinter, Esteban Linares, J. Maurice Pouget, Subhash C. Sabaharwal, Elliot Chesler, and Henry DeMots. A double-blind, placebo-controlled trial of aspirin therapy was carried out at 12 centers in 1,266 men with unstable angina, defined as a new onset or sudden worsening of angina without increased activity, occurring at least once a day for longer than 15 minutes, or occurring at rest or on minimal activity. A 324-mg dose of aspirin in buffered solution was given in the form of Alka-Seltzer daily to 625 subjects, and 641 subjects received the buffer alone. The two groups were clinically comparable at the outset.

The rate of death or acute myocardial infarction was 51% lower in the aspirin-treated patients than in placebo patients during the 12-week study period (Fig 26–8). All deaths were cardiac in origin. Six aspirin-treated and 10 placebo patients died suddenly. The reduction in major events in aspirin-treated patients was independent of β-blocker therapy. No significant group differences in epigastric discomfort, decreased hemoglobin levels, or presence of blood in the stool were observed. Mortality at 1 year was 43% lower in the group treated with aspirin.

A significant reduction in deaths or acute infarctions was associated with aspirin administration in this study of patients with unsta-

Fig 26–8.—Sequential analysis for the combined end point death or acute myocardial infarction in patients with unstable angina. This is a sequential plan with a 2-sided overall significance level of 0.01. Each patient receiving aspirin is paired with a patient receiving placebo on the basis of entry date. The abscissa represents the number of pairs in which a preference occurred (within a pair, the patient receiving one treatment died or had an acute myocardial infarction, whereas the other did not). The ordinate represents the direction of preference (plot moves up 1 unit if preference is in favor of placebo). If the sample path had crossed either boundary for no significant difference, we would have had 95% confidence that the reduction in the event rate is not as large as 50%. The significance boundary was crossed on the 75th pair when there were +29 excess preferences (52 preferences in favor of aspirin and 23 in favor of placebo). This insured that the difference between the treatment groups for the end point death or acute myocardial infarction was significant at the 0.01 level even after we allowed for multiple tests during the trial. (Courtesy of Lewis, H.D., Jr., et al.: N. Engl. J. Med. 309:396–403, Aug. 18, 1983; reprinted by permission of The New England Journal of Medicine.)

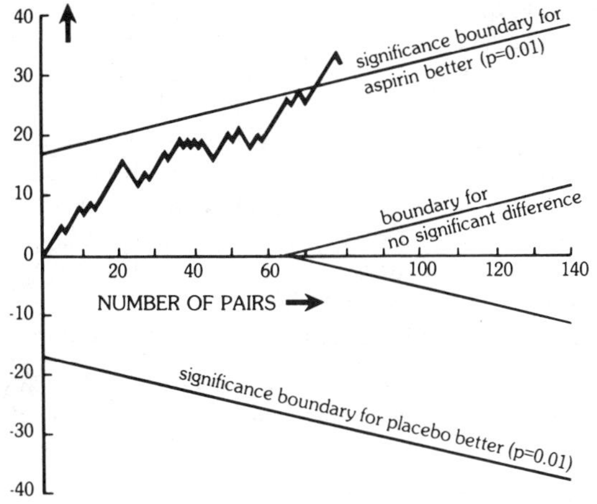

ble angina. The findings should be applicable to most men with unstable angina who are admitted to coronary care units. A reduction in major events to half of baseline was associated with daily treatment with 324 mg of aspirin in buffered solution for 12 weeks. No gastrointestinal side effects occurred. Aspirin is recommended in men, and perhaps in women, with unstable angina if contraindications are not present.

▶ [The results of this study are straightforward and clear-cut. Both death and nonfatal acute myocardial infarction were reduced by half in the aspirin-treated group. Surprisingly, the dose of aspirin was relatively large, i.e., 324 mg/day, a dose that we know from Weksler's study (abstract 26–23) to be sufficient to inhibit not only thromboxane A_2 formation but also prostacyclin synthesis.] ◀

26–26 **Intravenous Nitroglycerin in Treatment of Spontaneous Angina Pectoris: Prospective, Randomized Trial.** It is possible that maintenance of sustained plasma concentrations of a coronary vasodilator by continuous infusion will prevent spontaneous ischemic episodes in patients with unstable angina. Gregory D. Curfman, James A. Heinsimer, Eugene C. Lozner, and Ho-Leung Fung undertook a prospective comparison of intravenous nitroglycerin (TNG) administration with oral isosorbide dinitrate (ISDN) ingestion combined with 2% TNG ointment in patients who had repeated episodes of spontaneous angina. Forty patients with at least 2 episodes of spontaneous myocardial ischemia in a 48-hour control period were included. The TNG was infused at a starting rate of 5 μg/minute, and the rate was increased until the systolic arterial pressure was 20% below baseline or up to 200 μg per minute. Doses of ISDN and TNG ointment were alternated at 3-hour intervals to produce the same pressure reduction. The maximal dosage of ISDN was 60 mg every 6 hours, and that of TNG ointment was 2 inches (23.2 mg of TNG) every 6 hours.

The mean TNG infusion rate in 14 patients was 82 μg/minute. The mean maximal daily doses in the other 18 patients were 187 mg of ISDN and 65 mg of TNG in ointment form. The rate of ischemic episodes decreased 70% in the TNG infusion group and 55% in the control group. One study patient and 3 controls had an increase in ischemic episodes during treatment. Significant hypotension and other side effects were comparably frequent in the two groups. Ischemia was controlled to a similar degree in the first 24 hours in the two groups.

Intravenous TNG infusion appears to be useful in the management of patients with repeated episodes of angina, but much of the therapeutic benefit can be reproduced by conventional nitrate therapy with oral ISDN and topical TNG ointment. Intravenous treatment may be especially helpful in controlling frequent spontaneous ischemia in the initial hours. A substantial number of these patients continue to have ischemia uncontrolled by medical treatment, and coronary artery bypass grafting may have to be considered.

▶ [There has recently been considerable interest in the use of intravenous nitroglycerin for the treatment of angina at rest. Kaplan et al.[67] tested it in patients unresponsive to standard therapy, i.e., the combination of oral or topical nitrates and β-blockers. With intravenous nitroglycerin the number of episodes of angina at rest

(26–26) Circulation 67:276–282, February 1983.

decreased to 10% of control. DePace et al.[68] observed that it caused an 85% reduction in the number of ischemic episodes of patients with rest angina. These authors provided indirect evidence that the mechanism of action may differ among patients; in some patients the nitroglycerin favorably alters the hemodynamic determinants of myocardial oxygen consumption, whereas in others it appears to exert a direct effect on the coronary circulation.] ◀

26–27 **Unstable Angina and Progression of Coronary Atherosclerosis.** Alain Moise, Pierre Théroux, Yves Taeymans, Bénédicte Descoings, Jacques Lespérance, David D. Waters, Guy B. Pelletier, and Martial G. Bourassa (Montreal) attempted to document the progression of coronary artery disease in patients recatheterized during an episode of unstable angina, while factors known to influence the rate of progression were being controlled. The progression of disease was studied in 38 patients who had previously had angiography and later were hospitalized for unstable angina and in 38 matched patients with stable angina who also had had catheterization previously. The two groups were comparable in age and risk factors. The mean interval between angiographic studies was 44 months in the group with unstable angina and 35 months in the comparison group. The mean number of diseased coronary vessels on the first angiogram was 1.5 in both groups. The patients with unstable angina had a mean initial ejection fraction of 65%; those with stable angina, 63%.

PROGRESSION OF CORONARY ARTERY LESIONS IN 2 STUDY GROUPS*

Unmatched Data Display

	Patients with unstable angina	Patients with stable angina
Progression	29	12
No progression	9	26
Total	38	38

Matched Data Display

Progression in patient with stable angina

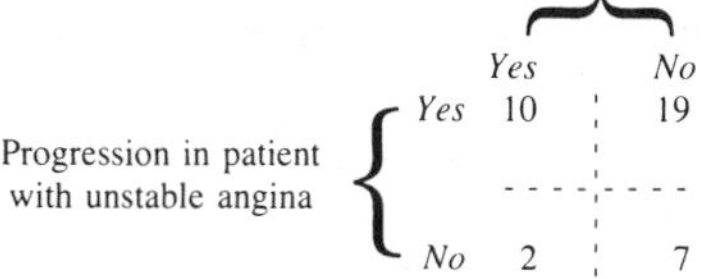

Progression in patient with unstable angina		*Yes*	*No*
	Yes	10	19
	No	2	7

Odds ratio, 9.5
95% confidence interval, 2.28–82.33
$P<0.0005$

*(Courtesy of Moise, A., et al.: N. Engl. J. Med. 309:685–689, Sept. 22, 1983; reprinted by permission of The New England Journal of Medicine.

(26–27) N. Engl. J. Med. 309:685–689, Sept. 22, 1983.

The progression of coronary lesions in the 2 groups is compared in the table. Progression occurred significantly more frequently in patients with unstable angina. Twenty-seven patients with unstable angina and 18 with stable angina had disease in 2 or 3 vessels at the second study. The difference was apparent both in patients given nitroglycerin during the second catheterization and those not so treated. New occlusions occurred in 11 patients with unstable angina and 6 control patients, which was not a significant difference. There were no significant differences in occurrence of new akinesia or change in ejection fraction. Lesions regressed in 3 patients with unstable angina.

Unstable angina is closely associated with progression in the extent and severity of obstructive coronary artery lesions. Unstable angina can be viewed as a hallmark of progressive coronary artery disease, and this should be kept in mind when treatment decisions are made. The narrowings observed appear to represent fixed lesions.

▶ [Although it has been well established that severe atherosclerotic coronary artery disease is present in the vast majority of patients with unstable angina, it had been considered that the *extent* of the coronary artery disease is similar to that in patients with stable angina. The above study generally supports this concept but also indicates that unstable angina is associated with a *more rapid rate of progression* in the severity of coronary atherosclerosis than is stable angina. Therefore, these observations rationalize the more frequent use of surgical treatment for patients with unstable angina.

An interesting recent finding in unstable angina is that thrombolysis with streptokinase may open an occluded vessel, increase the stenotic diameter, or dissolve an intracoronary filling defect in patients with unstable angina, suggesting that intracoronary thrombus formation plays a pathogenic role in some patients with this condition.[69]

Hultgren et al.[70] carried out a prospective, nonrandomized data bank study of the effect of medical vs. surgical treatment of patients with unstable angina. Surgical management appeared preferable to medical therapy insofar as both survival and relief of angina were concerned. The 7-year survival was 65% for the medical group and 85% for the surgical group; at 5 years, 62% of the surgical group had no angina compared with only 37% of the medical group. The incidence of myocardial infarction, however, was similar in both groups.] ◀

26–28 **Variable Threshold Exertional Angina in Patients With Transient Vasospastic Myocardial Ischemia: Repeat Exercise Test Results and Therapeutic Implications.** Stefano de Servi, Giuseppe Specchia, Columba Falcone, Antonello Gavazzi, Antonio Mussini, Luigi Angoli, Ezio Bramucci, Diego Ardissino, Laura Vaccari, Jorge Salferno, and Piero Bobba (Pavia, Italy) report that 35 of 70 patients with vasospastic angina at rest complained of chest pain during exercise or during usual daily activity. In 22, the angina threshold was described as variable during exercise—i.e., the amount of exertion that induced angina was not always the same.

In 12 patients with variable threshold exertional angina, 3 exercise tests performed in the morning on different days yielded different results because chest pain and ischemic ECG changes occurred at different work loads, with a wide range in heart rate–systolic pressure product. Two patients, in whom great cardiac vein flow was measured during exercise before and after administration of nifedipine, toler-

(26–28) Am. J. Cardiol. 51:397–402, February 1983.

ated heavier work loads after receiving the drug and had a more marked increase in flow during exercise.

Variable threshold exertional angina can be demonstrated objectively by repeat exercise tests in patients with vasospastic angina. Variability of the angina threshold may be due to a functional mechanism that causes myocardial ischemia in addition to the increased myocardial metabolic requirements provoked by exercise. Because in such patients fluctuations in coronary arterial tone play an important role in determining the response to exercise, calcium antagonistic drugs, which lower coronary tone and prevent the occurrence of coronary spasm, are effective in increasing exercise capacity, whereas propranolol may be ineffective and even detrimental.

▶ [One classification of angina is into stable, unstable and variant; a second is into fixed threshold and variable threshold. In fixed threshold angina, the amount of activity necessary to induce angina is relatively constant. In these patients the angina is due primarily to fixed coronary atherosclerotic obstruction and the ischemia is provoked by an increase in myocardial oxygen needs which outstrip the available oxygen supply. In contrast, variable threshold angina is associated with a combination of fixed atherosclerotic obstructive lesions and dynamic changes in coronary vascular tone. Thus, in patients with variable threshold angina ischemia is precipitated by a combination of an increase in myocardial oxygen demands occurring on the background of varying coronary vascular tone. When vascular tone is reduced, the patient may have a very high exercise capacity; on the other hand, when vascular tone is increased, the exercise capacity is markedly limited.

Patients with variable threshold angina described in the article abstracted above responded well to the calcium channel blocking agent nifedipine. It may become possible to predict which patients with chronic angina will respond best to calcium channel blockers and which will respond best to β-blockers. Those with fixed threshold angina would be expected to respond best to β-blockade, whereas those with variable threshold angina would be expected to respond best to calcium blockade.

Further evidence for a functional (dynamic or vasoconstrictive) component playing an important role in inducing ischemia in chronic angina is provided by the following abstract.] ◀

26–29 **Silent Myocardial Ischemia During Ambulatory Electrocardiographic Monitoring in Patients With Effort Angina.** Although anginal pain is the chief symptom of acute myocardial ischemia, ischemia can occur without pain or other symptoms in patients with either spontaneous angina or effort angina. Antonio C. Cecchi, Emilio V. Dovellini, Francesco Marchi, Paolo Pucci, Giovanni M. Santoro, and P. Filippo Fazzini (Florence) examined the characteristics of asymptomatic ischemic attacks in 39 patients with effort angina who had 24-hour Holter monitoring. The 35 men and 4 women (average age 55 years) all had a history of induced chest pain and a definitely positive exercise stress test. Sixteen patients had had myocardial infarction. Graded bicycle exercise testing was carried out after Holter monitoring.

All but 7 patients had episodes of ischemic ST depression during Holter monitoring. Eight patients had attacks always accompanied by pain, and 9 had only asymptomatic ischemic episodes (table). In patients with both symptomatic and asymptomatic episodes, the duration of symptomatic episodes was longer, and the mean maximal ST depression was greater. Patients with a delayed response to pain

---

(26–29) J. Am. Coll. Cardiol. 1:934–939, March 1983.

ISCHEMIC EPISODES DURING HOLTER MONITORING OF 39 PATIENTS

Patients (no.)	Episodes (no.) Total	Symptomatic	Asymptomatic
7	0	—	—
8	25	25	—
15	105	29	76
9	40	—	40
Total	170	54	116

(Courtesy of Cecchi, A.C., et al.: J. Am. Coll. Cardiol. 1:934–939, March 1983.)

after the onset of ischemic ST depression during stress testing had a higher ratio of asymptomatic to symptomatic attacks during Holter monitoring, as compared with those who reported pain before or at the appearance of ischemic ECG changes during stress testing. Patients with the longest interval between ST changes and the onset of angina had a greater incidence of previous myocardial infarction.

Most patients with effort angina have asymptomatic episodes of ischemia more often than symptomatic episodes. Angina can no longer be considered a valuable criterion in evaluating patients with ischemic heart disease. Ischemic attacks apparently are not always evoked by factors that increase myocardial oxygen consumption. Other factors such as a primary reduction in blood flow may be operative. Individual factors may explain differences in the predominance of symptomatic or asymptomatic attacks of myocardial ischemia.

▶ [An important finding in the present study was that the heart rate during Holter monitoring at which ST-segment depression (91/minute) and pain (100/minute) occurred were lower than the corresponding values during stress testing (113 and 123/minute). This observation suggests that ischemic episodes during Holter monitoring are associated with a lower myocardial oxygen consumption than during stress testing. Presumably a reduction of coronary blood flow due to coronary vasoconstriction plays a role in their genesis.

Multiple episodes of silent myocardial ischemia in patients with coronary artery disease may cause an ischemic insult that is not of sufficient severity to produce myocardial necrosis, but they may result in prolonged postischemic ventricular dysfunction, i.e., "stunning" of the myocardium.[71] It has been proposed that repeated stunning may lead to myocardial scarring and ischemic cardiomyopathy. Therefore, therapy of myocardial ischemia should be directed not only at eliminating or reducing the number of episodes of symptomatic ischemia (angina), but also of the frequency of episodes of myocardial ischemia characterized by ST-segment depression without angina. Patients who have only silent myocardial ischemia, i.e., a defective anginal warning system, do not differ from those with angina insofar as the severity of coronary obstructive disease, the occurrence of myocardial infarction, as well as the global and regional ejection fraction are concerned.[72] Thus, the extent of abnormalities in both global and regional left ventricular wall motion is similar in patients with and without silent myocardial ischemia.] ◀

26–30 **Long-Term Results of Prospective Randomized Study of Coronary Artery Bypass Surgery in Stable Angina Pectoris.** The European Coronary Surgery Study Group presents the final results (follow-up, 5–8 years) of a prospective study involving 768 men younger

(26–30) Lancet 2:1173–1180, Nov. 27, 1982.

than 65 years of age who had mild to moderate angina, 50% or greater stenosis in at least 2 major coronary arteries, and good left ventricular function; 395 were randomly assigned to coronary bypass surgery and 373, to no treatment. One surgical patient was lost to follow-up. Both groups had high-level medical care. If at any time a patient in the medical group had unacceptable symptoms despite adequate medical therapy, he was eligible for surgery. The original groups were compared regardless of the subsequent outcome of the patients.

Survival was improved significantly by surgery in the total population (the policy of surgery conferred a 53% decrease in 5-year mortality), in patients with 3-vessel disease, and in patients with stenosis of 50% or more in the proximal third of the left anterior descending coronary artery constituting a component of 2- or 3-vessel disease. The improvement was nonsignificant in patients with left main coronary disease. An abnormal ECG at rest, ST-segment depression of 1.5 mm or more during exercise, (Fig 26–9), peripheral arterial disease, and increasing age independently pointed to a better chance of survival with surgery. In the absence of these prognostic variables in patients with 2- or 3-vessel disease, the outlook is so good that early surgery is unlikely to increase the prospect of survival. In terms of anginal attacks, use of β-adrenergic blockers and nitrates, and exercise performance, the surgical group did significantly better than the medical group throughout most of the 5-year follow-up, but the difference between the treatments tended to decrease with time.

The results in patients randomly assigned to the surgical group indicate that coronary bypass grafting is the treatment of choice even when angina pectoris responds adequately to medical management. Surgery is unlikely to improve 5-year survival in patients with good

Fig 26–9.—Survival curves for subset of patients with exertional ST-segment depression of 0–1 mm and for subset with ST-segment depression of 1.5 mm or more. (Courtesy of European Coronary Surgery Study Group: Lancet 2:1173–1180, Nov. 27, 1982.)

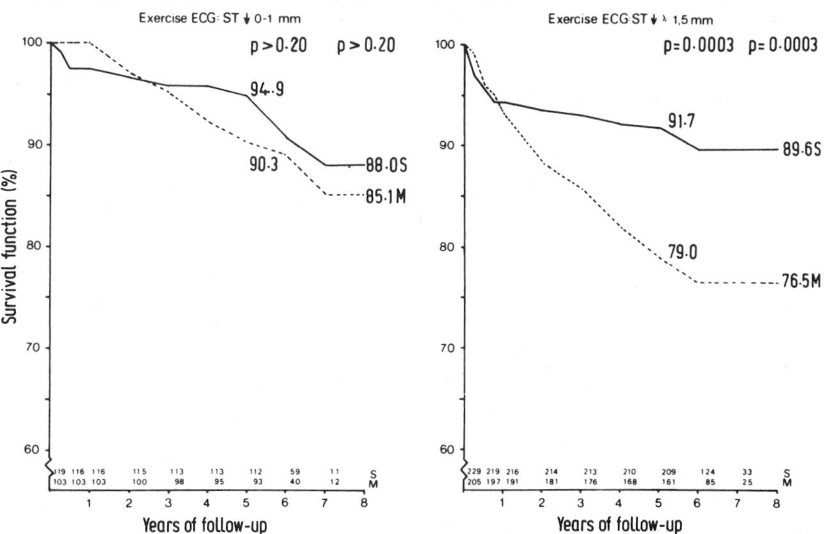

left ventricular function whose ST segment is depressed less than 1.5 mm on exertion, whose resting ECG is normal, and who are free from peripheral arterial disease.

26–31 **Coronary Artery Surgery Study (CASS): Randomized Trial of Coronary Artery Bypass Surgery. Survival Data** are reported by the CASS Principal Investigators and their Associates. The CASS is a multicenter, randomized trial of the effects of coronary bypass graft-

Fig 26–10.—Five-year cumulative survival in groups with single-, double-, and triple-vessel disease, with disease being defined as at least 70% luminal diameter reduction. (Courtesy of CASS Principal Investigators and their Associates: Circulation 68:939–950, November 1983; by permission of the American Heart Association, Inc.)

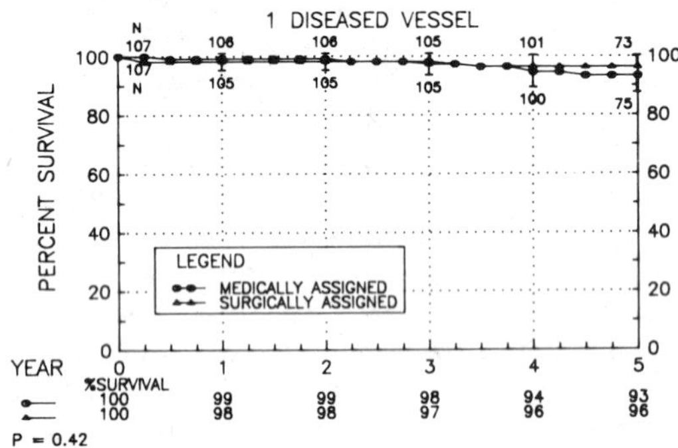

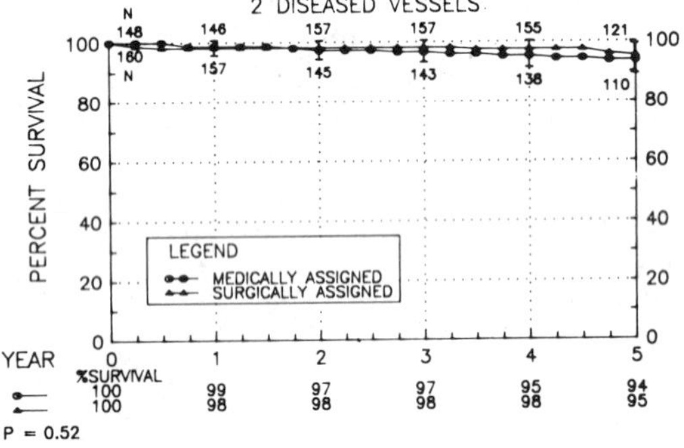

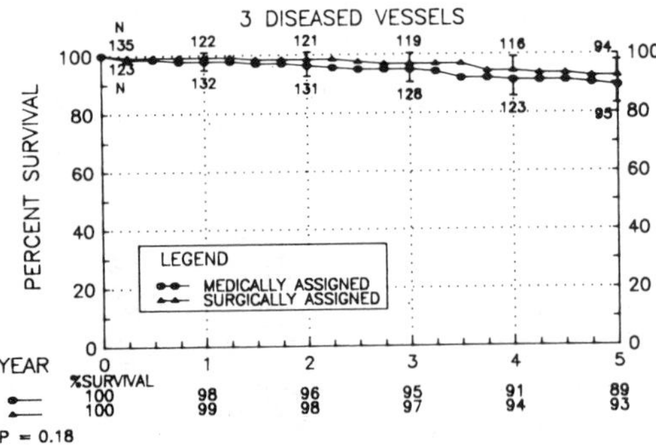

(26–31) Circulation 68:939–950, November 1983.

ing on mortality and other end points in 780 patients with stable ischemic heart disease seen between 1975 and 1979 and followed-up through 1983. The 390 surgically and 390 medically managed patients were comparable in initial baseline clinical and demographic characteristics. More than half the patients had a history of myocardial infarction at entry to the trial. A single major vessel was stenosed by at least 70% in 27% of patients, whereas 40% had two-vessel and 33% had triple-vessel disease.

Operative mortality was 1.4% in the 357 patients actually operated on. Patients received an average of 2.7 grafts. In more than 80% of the 129 patients studied within 2 months of operation, all grafts were patent. Medical management consisted of attempts to modify risk factors and use of nitrates and β-blocking drugs. The 5-year survival rates did not differ significantly in the medical and surgical groups. The estimated annual mortalities were 1.6% for the medical group and 1.1% for the surgical group. The respective rates for patients with single-vessel disease were 1.4% and 0.7%, and for those with triple-vessel disease they were 2.1% and 1.5%. There were no significant group differences in survival according to extent of disease (Fig 26–10), ejection fraction, or both. Mortality in medically treated patients was increased when ventricular function was impaired, but this was not the case in the surgical group.

Comparable survival has been documented in patients in the CASS assigned to coronary bypass grafting and those managed medically. The findings suggest that patients similar to these can safely be treated medically until symptoms worsen to the point at which surgical palliation is necessary. The results are most applicable to patients with mild to moderate angina and to survivors of myocardial infarction without angina but with surgically approachable coronary artery disease.

▶ [The two articles abstracted above deal with the critically important question of whether or not coronary artery bypass grafting (CABG) improves patient survival. Three large multicenter randomized trials have now addressed this question: the VA trial, the European Coronary Surgery Study (ECSS), and the Coronary Artery Surgery Study (CASS). In 1977 the preliminary results of the first of the "big three," i.e., the VA trial, were released.[73] Although operation clearly reduced the incidence and severity of angina in patients other than those with obstructive disease of the left main coronary artery, there was no difference in the survival of patients with chronic stable angina who had been randomized into medically and surgically treated groups. The results of this study aroused considerable controversy, largely because they did not appear to be correct intuitively. It seemed logical that the appropriate way to treat an obstruction is to bypass it. The cardiac surgical community was very critical of the VA trial, in particular of the relatively high surgical mortality of 5.6% (even though it was representative of that observed in most institutions during the period in which the surgery was performed, i.e., 1972–1974).

Despite much subsequent discussion about the interpretation of the VA trial, it has shown no differences—except for patients with lesions of the left main coronary artery—between medical and surgical treatment, with a follow-up now of nine years. There is no statistically significant difference between the results of these two forms of treatment for the group as a whole or for any subgroup, although there are *non-statistically-significant trends* in favor of surgical treatment of two subgroups: patients with three-vessel disease and those with left ventricular dysfunctions.

Between the period of enrollment in the VA trial (1972–1974) and the period of enrollment in CASS (1975–1979), surgical techniques and results improved substantially. Superior methods of myocardial preservation contributed to reductions in operative mortality, which was only 1.4% in CASS compared with 5.6% in the VA trial. (The surgical mortality in ECSS (3.3%) was intermediate.) The performance of multiple grafts leading to more complete revascularization has been responsible for better symptomatic results; even patients with angina and heart failure can now be operated upon in good centers with a mortality of less than 7%. Therefore, when carried out by a skilled team in properly selected patients, coronary artery bypass grafting is a relatively safe operation which is effective in abolishing or reducing angina refractory to medical management in 80%–90% of patients. A companion paper to the one abstracted above confirms the effectiveness of surgical treatment of coronary disease insofar as relief of angina is concerned.[74]

The important conclusion of CASS is that despite the excellence of the surgical results, surgical treatment provided no overall statistical benefit in survival. This important finding applied not only to the total patient group but also to each of the many subgroups analyzed.

It is interesting to consider the steadily improving survival rate of *medically treated* patients with angiographically proved obstructive CAD. Although the patients were not entirely comparable, the annual mortality for patients with three-vessel CAD reported by Reeves et al.[75] was 11.4% in patients studied in the late 1960s; it was 4.8% in the early and mid-1970s in the VA study,[71] 3.5% in the ECSS in the late 1970s, and only 2.1% in CASS.

How do we reconcile the results of CASS with those of other clinical trials? The ECSS showed that surgical treatment resulted in significantly better survival than did medical treatment in patients with three-vessel disease; no significant improvement in prognosis was noted in patients with two-vessel disease, although a nonsignificant trend in favor of surgery in such patients who had involvement of the proximal left anterior descending coronary artery was demonstrated. I cannot account fully for this major difference between the two studies, except to point to the better prognosis of medically treated patients with obstructive coronary artery disease with few or no symptoms in CASS as compared with that of patients with similar anatomic findings in the European trial, who may have been more symptomatic and in whom medical therapy may have been less intensive.

The principal lesson to be learned from CASS, I believe, is that the prognosis for life (and reinfarction) of asymptomatic or mildly symptomatic patients with multivessel coronary artery disease who were treated medically in the late 1970s was much better than we suspected. Therefore, it is difficult for any operation, even a very good one such as coronary artery bypass grafting, to improve on such excellent results. Even if CASS has missed a statistically beneficial effect of surgery on survival or infarction in one or another subgroup, that effect could not have been a very large one. And it may not even be present today when, with widespread use of β-adrenergic and calcium channel blockers, the prognosis of medical therapy is probably even better than it was in the late 1970s.

How should the results of the randomized CASS affect management of patients with obstructive coronary artery disease and stable angina pectoris? The results do not dictate any alteration in the treatment of patients with severe obstruction of the left main coronary artery or of patients with angina that is unacceptable despite intensive medical management or of patients with angina who do not tolerate (or are unwilling or unable to remain on) a strict medical regimen. In the absence of contraindications, such patients should have coronary bypass surgery. CASS also confirms that asymptomatic or mildly symptomatic patients with single vessel disease need not be operated upon. Most important, the results of CASS suggest that operation should not be expected to prolong the survival or prevent myocardial infarction in patients with multivessel disease who are asymptomatic or who have mild angina.] ◀

26–32 **Radionuclide Angiographic Assessment of Global and Segmental Left Ventricular Function at Rest and During Exercise After Coronary Artery Bypass Graft Surgery.** Although coronary bypass surgery relieves angina and improves the quality of life, its

(26–32) Circulation 66:972–979, November 1982.

effects on ventricular function and survival remain controversial. Y. L. Lim, V. Kalff, M. J. Kelly, P. J. Mason, P. J. Currie, R. W. Harper, S. T. Anderson, J. Federman, G. R. Stirling, and A. Pitt (Melbourne) examined the effects of bypass graft surgery on left ventricular (LV) function, assessed by radionuclide angiography at rest and on maximal and graded submaximal exercise, in 20 patients, 18 men and 2 women with a mean age of 54 years. Studies were done before and 3 months after surgery. All patients had New York Heart Association class II–IV angina preoperatively despite adequate medical therapy. Nine had evidence of past myocardial infarction. Fifteen patients had three-vessel disease, and 2 of these had significant left main coronary lesions.

An average of 2.8 grafts were placed per patient. The rate of satisfactory graft function at 3 months was 86%. One patient had acute infarction postoperatively. Only 3 patients had chest pain on postoperative exercise testing, and only 3 had more than 1 mm of ischemic ST-segment depression. Mean work capacity was significantly higher after surgery, as was the mean rate-pressure product at maximal work capacity. The LV ejection fraction fell significantly with sprint maximal exercise before surgery, but increased afterwards (Fig 26–11). A difference also was evident at lower work loads. The LV end-diastolic volume tended to increase less with exercise after bypass surgery. Patients with and those without previous infarction had comparable responses to surgery. Mild impairment of LV functional reserve was observed in a substantial proportion of patients with successful grafts and no evidence of residual ischemia.

Fig 26–11.—First-pass left ventricular (LV) ejection fraction response to sprint maximal exercise (Wmax) in right anterior oblique view before *(left)* and after *(right)* coronary artery bypass graft surgery. (Courtesy of Lim, Y.L., et al.: Circulation 66:972–979, November 1982, by permission of the American Heart Association.)

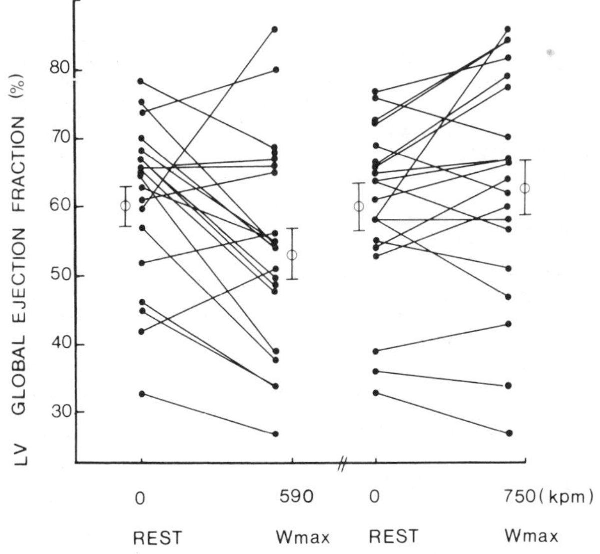

These findings suggest that bypass surgery produces objective functional improvement as well as relief of angina in patients with coronary artery disease. Successful myocardial revascularization substantially improves LV performance during exercise at increased levels of myocardial oxygen requirement in patients with stable angina resistant to conventional medical treatment.

▶ [The key finding in this study is that the ejection fraction at rest was not altered by coronary artery bypass grafting (CABG). However, the *change* in ejection fraction that occurred during exercise was improved decisively. Similarly, Andersen et al.[76] observed that CABG had no effect on the ejection fraction or left ventricular end-diastolic pressure at rest, but did improve myocardial contractility, as reflected in the maximum velocity of myocardial fiber shortening (V_{max}).

One important question surrounding CABG has been whether perioperative myocardial infarction alters the prognosis. Gray et al.[77] reported that the five-year survival rate of patients with and without perioperative infarction was not significantly different, nor was the relief of angina, the degree of dyspnea, or the level of physical activity. An interesting study of patients following CABG was conducted by Pfisterer et al.[78] who reported that serial rest and exercise thallium-201 scintigrams had an 86% accuracy in detecting or excluding graft occlusion. Thus, this noninvasive method can be used to assess graft function and to identify patients with a high likelihood of graft occlusion who may need invasive studies. In patients in whom exercise testing was carried out 5 or 6 years after CABG, a sustained improvement in exercise tolerance was observed.[79, 80] The improvement is usually confined to patients with complete or almost complete revascularization, and as might be anticipated, it is not sustained in patients with incomplete revascularization or in those with occluded grafts.

A number of other interesting articles appeared evaluating the outcomes of CABG. Thus, Loop et al.[81] compared the results of CABG in men and women. Despite the presence of less three-vessel disease and better left ventricular function, women had a higher operative mortality (2% vs. 1%); in addition, after a 2-year interval, women had a lower overall graft patency rate than men, and at 5 and 10 years postoperatively a lower fraction were angina free, although survival for the two sexes was similar. When matched for age, severity of angina, and extent of coronary atherosclerosis, women still had twice the operative mortality rate of men. The CASS study[82] came to a similar conclusion. The operative mortality was 1.9% in men and 4.5% in women. Regardless of gender, body surface area was the strongest predictor of operative risk. Thus, it is the smaller size of women rather than their sex that appears to explain the difference in operative mortality. The CASS study also demonstrated that the risk of CABG is higher in older than in younger patients. A part of this difference was related to the fact that the older patients had a higher incidence of variables independently associated with an increase in perioperative mortality, such as diabetes mellitus, cerebrovascular disease, unstable angina, congestive heart failure, pulmonary rales, cardiomegaly, and left main coronary artery disease, all of which independently increased the operative risk. However, when all of these factors were corrected for, age was still an independent risk factor.[83]

An increasing number of pathologic studies of vein grafts are now appearing. For example, Smith and Geer[84] examined 51 grafts 7 to 116 months after operation and described four pathologic changes: *(1)* fibrous cord lesions that represented early postoperative thrombotic occlusion and organization; *(2)* diffuse intimal thickening, which was present in all grafts that maintained long-term patency; *(3)* frank atherosclerosis, which was found in 79% of grafts studied 39 or more months postoperatively; and *(4)* late vein thrombosis. It will be interesting to determine whether the regimen of early treatment with aspirin and dipyridamole (1983 YEAR BOOK, p. 343) will be helpful in altering this natural course.

Given these pathologic changes, it is apparent that an increasing number of patients who have had CABG will require reoperation 5 or more years after the initial procedure because of late graft closure. Pucci et al.[85] demonstrated that reoperation can be accomplished with a low mortality and morbidity and is potentially beneficial; 69% of their reoperated patients either lost recurrent angina or were improved.

Hertzer et al.[86] reported that combined myocardial revascularization and carotid endarterectomy may be performed in a single sitting and with reasonable safety in patients whose coronary and carotid diseases are considered to be too severe to tolerate staged operations.

The long-term psychosocial effects of CABG are still in dispute. The CASS study showed that surgically treated patients did *not* do better than medically treated patients, insofar as return to work or recreational activity was concerned, yet two articles, one from the United States[87] and the other from Australia,[88] showed a very high incidence of return to normal economic and social functioning within 6 months after CABG.] ◀

26–33 **Mechanism of Relief of Pacing-Induced Angina With Oral Verapamil: Reduced Oxygen Demand.** To evaluate the influence of oral verapamil (80 and 120 mg) on angina threshold, coronary blood flow, myocardial oxygen consumption, and left ventricular function, Jean-Lucien Rouleau, Kanu Chatterjee, Thomas A. Ports, M. Brigid Doyle, Beverley Hiramatsu, and William W. Parmley (Univ. of California, San Francisco) subjected 13 patients with effort angina and fixed obstructive coronary artery disease to atrial pacing at progressively higher heart rates.

After 120 mg of verapamil, the time to onset of angina and the heart rate at the onset of ST-segment depression increased by 18% ($P < .005$) and 10% ($P < .001$), respectively, without any change in the angina threshold (rate-pressure product at the onset of angina). The rate-pressure product, coronary blood flow, and myocardial oxygen consumption were lower at rest and at preangina heart rates but not when the angina threshold was reached.

Thus, the beneficial effect of verapamil was primarily due to decreased myocardial oxygen demand rather than to increased coronary blood flow. The decreased demand resulted from a lower arterial pressure at each pacing rate. In these patients without heart failure, left ventricular pump function did not deteriorate. The beneficial response was less with 80 mg of verapamil. The results suggest that oral verapamil had a potential role in the management of patients with effort angina due to fixed obstructive coronary artery disease. Since regional myocardial blood flow was not determined in this study, a relative increase in blood flow to the ischemic region despite a decrease in global flow cannot be ruled out.

▶ [As discussed in detail in the 1983 Year Book (pp. 340–341) calcium channel blocking agents are extremely useful in the treatment of chronic stable angina, when administered alone or in combination with β-blockers. The present interesting report by Rouleau et al. helps to elucidate the mechanism of the antianginal action of oral verapamil when heart rate is controlled. The threshold of myocardial oxygen consumption, coronary blood flow and the rate-pressure product at the anginal threshold were unchanged by verapamil. This means that verapamil (like β-blockers) acts primarily to reduce myocardial oxygen needs rather than to increase supply. However, the issue of the mechanism of the antianginal action of calcium channel blocking agents is far from settled. Thus, Chew et al.[89] found that *intravenous* verapamil produced moderate dilatation of both systemic and coronary small vessels and mildly dilated large coronary conductance vessels in both normal and disease segments, although significantly less so than did nitroglycerin. These observations suggest that the drug acts in part by augmenting oxygen delivery.

After one year of continuous high-dose therapy (480 mg/day), Weiner and collaborators reported that there is no evidence of tachyphylaxis, nor does verapamil appear to cause an abrupt withdrawal syndrome in patients with chronic stable angina

(26–33) Circulation 67:94–100, January 1983.

pectoris, as is seen occasionally in patients with β-blockers.[90] A helpful article indicating the usefulness of verapamil in the treatment of chronic stable angina was provided by Frishman and Charlap.[91] They point out that among the relative contraindications to its use are sinus node dysfunction and atrioventricular conduction disease.

There has also been considerable concern about the negative inotropic effects of verapamil. However a careful study by Klein et al.[92] showed that although intravenous verapamil does exert a depressant effect on left ventricular function, the transient nature of this depression and the quick recovery indicate that in low doses (up to 0.1 mg/kg, intravenously) it is safe in patients with coronary disease, even in those with ejection fractions less than 35%.

Combination therapy of a β-blocker with verapamil can provide important benefits to many patients with angina pectoris who remain symptomatic on treatment with either drug alone; however, this combination does carry with it the potential for serious adverse reactions. Heart failure may occur when verapamil is administered together with β-blockers to patients having compromised left ventricular function prior to therapy with either agent. Therefore, it is advisable to avoid this combination in patients with left ventricular dysfunction or with intrinisic sinus node or atrioventricular conduction system disease. In that group when both a calcium antagonist and a β-blocker are needed, it may be more useful to employ nifedipine instead of verapamil.] ◀

26–34 **Prognostic Value of Risk Factors and Exercise Testing in Men With Atypical Chest Pain.** Patients with atypical chest pain are a difficult management problem. Kenneth F. Hossack, Robert A. Bruce, Lloyd Fisher, and Verona Hofer (Univ. of Washington) reviewed data on 551 men with atypical chest pain who were enrolled in the Seattle Heart Watch Study. Mean age was 45 years. They were followed up annually for a mean of about 6 years.

Thirty-six subjects had a primary coronary heart disease (CHD) event during follow-up. Only 3 events, all in men older than age 50 years, were fatal. Events tended to occur in older patients, but the association was not statistically significant. The three classical risk factors, i.e., smoking, elevated resting systolic blood pressure, and hypercholesterolemia, all were significantly associated with primary CHD events. A positive family history was not predictive, and obesity and premature atrial or ventricular contraction on the resting ECG were not significant factors. The presence of two or more risk factors was associated with a marked increase in CHD events. The most useful exercise predictors were functional aerobic impairment and ST-segment depression. Ninety-six percent of men who had neither risk factors nor abnormal exercise predictors were free of coronary events at 9 years compared with 76% of men with abnormal exercise findings only, and 86% of those with risk factors only.

Evaluation of both risk factors and exercise responses aids the prognostic assessment of men with atypical chest pain. In the office setting men can readily be classified according to risk. Seventeen percent of the present population were identified as high-risk subjects, and 24% of them had primary CHD events during 9 years of surveillance. Additional evaluative measures might be selectively applied to subjects identified as being at risk.

▶ [Patients with atypical chest pain always pose a difficult management problem. Obviously, coronary angiography is the decisive means of determining whether this symptom is due to angina or not, but this is a complex and expensive procedure for

---

(26–34) Int. J. Cardiol. 3:37–50, April 1983.

a group of patients with a low incidence of coronary artery disease. Similarly, thallium scintigraphy and exercise radioventriculography are alternative methods, but they are of little predictive value in a group with a low prevalence of the disease.

A logical approach to patients with atypical chest pain is simply to follow the low-risk group, i.e., those with no risk factors for coronary disease, and without ST-segment depression or functional aerobic impairment on treadmill exercise. In contrast, a high-risk group, i.e., men with exercise-induced ST-segment depression, or a functional aerobic impairment greater than 30%, deserve extremely careful scrutiny, reduction of risk factors, and if the exercise test is *markedly* abnormal, a thallium-201 scintiscan; if the latter is positive, coronary arteriography is indicated.

One major finding in this study is that the general prognosis of patients with atypical chest pain is excellent. Even though it is symptomatically distressing, 99.3% survived free of cardiac mortality at 9 years.] ◀

6–35 **Esophageal Function in Patients With Angina-Type Chest Pain and Normal Coronary Angiograms.** As many as 10% of patients with angina continue to be symptomatic despite a normal coronary artery status and normal cardiac function. Tom R. DeMeester, Gerald C. O'Sullivan, Gustavo Bermudez, Allen I. Midell, George E. Cimochowski, and Joan O'Drobinak (Univ. of Chicago) evaluated 50 such patients with severe chest pain in an attempt to distinguish clinically between pain of cardiac and pain of esophageal origin. The 34 women and 16 men were aged 33–77 years. Maximal exercise testing was carried out before angiography and cardiac catheterization. The esophageal studies included endoscopy, manometry, and 24-hour pH monitoring of the distal portion of the esophagus.

Squeezing-type chest pain with radiation was shown to be induced by effort in 20 patients. Nine patients had severe T-wave depression on the resting ECG, and in 20 patients the exercise test was stopped because of pain. Twenty-three patients had reflux on esophageal pH monitoring. They did not differ from those without reflux with regard to the incidence or severity of chest pain, esophageal symptoms, or medication use. Twelve patients with reflux and 1 without had chest pain coinciding with an episode of reflux during pH monitoring. All but 1 of 11 patients who had antireflux operations were asymptomatic on follow-up, as were 5 of the other 12 patients with reflux who were managed medically. All patients who had chest pain coinciding with documented reflux did well, 8 of them after antireflux operations.

Gastroesophageal reflux is a frequent cause of angina-type chest pain in patients with normal coronary arteries and normal cardiac function. Patients whose pain coincides with esophageal reflux consistently respond to surgical or medical antireflux treatment. Operation has given the best results, but it does carry some morbidity. Esophageal pH monitoring permits selective management in this setting.

▶ [The preceding two abstracts deal with the very important issue of the clinical diagnosis of ischemic heart disease. Actually about 10% of patients with typical anginal pain have normal coronary arteries on angiography, and no ergonovine-provoked spasm. The syndrome of normal coronary arteries with anginal pain has a favorable prognosis, and the long-term survival of these patients is excellent. However, these patients continue to have many complaints, despite reassurance.

The article by DeMeester et al. abstracted above describes an important approach to identifying a subgroup of these patients with esophageal reflux. The key was the

(26–35) Ann. Surg. 196:488–498, October 1982.

use of 24-hour pH monitoring. A pH electrode was placed 5 cm above the upper border of the lower esophageal sphincter; a reflux episode was defined as a drop in the esophageal pH to less than 4.0. Twenty-four-hour esophageal pH monitoring revealed reflux in almost one half of the patients with anginal chest pain and normal coronary arteries. In many of these patients the reflux, as documented during the pH monitoring episode, was associated with chest pain. Both medical and surgical treatment of reflux resulted in relief of the chest pain in the majority of patients.

To prove that esophageal disease is responsible for the angina-type chest pain, it is necessary to exclude the cardiac basis for symptoms, demonstrate a cause-and-effect relationship between episodes of chest pain and esophageal abnormality, such as reflux, and show that correction of the esophageal abnormality should result in relief from the chest pain. Other causes of angina-like chest pain in patients with normal coronary arteries include cervical ribs, evidence of vascular compression at the thoracic outlet, skeletal deformities, and cervical osteoarthritis.] ◀

26–36 **Beneficial Effect of Labetalol in Hypertensive Patients With Angina Pectoris.** W. F. Lubbe and D. A. White (Univ. of Cape Town, South Africa) evaluated labetalol, an antihypertensive agent with both α- and β-adrenergic antagonistic activities, in 20 hypertensive patients with a long history of effort-induced chest pain responsive to sublingual nitroglycerin use but not relieved by standard antihypertensive therapy. The 17 evaluable patients had moderate to severe hypertension. After an initial placebo period, labetalol was titrated up to a dose of 400 mg three times daily as current antihypertensive medication was withdrawn; thiazide diuretic therapy was continued. Titration was stopped if the blood pressure fell to less than 140/90 mm Hg. Maintenance therapy was continued for 2 months before a second placebo period.

Labetalol did not significantly influence cardiovascular responses to isotonic exercise or cold pressor testing. Angina scores were significantly reduced during labetalol therapy, and several patients had increased angina when labetalol was replaced by the original antihypertensive medication. There were no serious side effects. Two patients with intermittent calf claudication noticed substantial improvement during labetalol administration.

Labetalol improved control of angina in hypertensive patients in this study, which had not been satisfactorily controlled by standard antihypertensive therapy. Further controlled trials are needed to determine how many of such patients will respond to labetalol. The mechanisms of the antiangina effect of the drug are unclear, but an increase in coronary perfusion from a vasodilator may increase the myocardial blood supply. Labetalol has been shown to reduce ischemic damage and infarct size after coronary occlusion in rats. Thallium perfusion scanning could help elucidate the mechanism of the effect of labetalol on angina.

▶ [The treatment of angina pectoris in patients with hypertension may be difficult, since many hypotensive agents can cause a disproportionate reduction in coronary blood flow and exacerbate angina. Labetalol, an interesting new drug that combines both α- and β-adrenergic antagonist activities and is likely to be released soon by the Food and Drug Administration, appears to be ideally suited to the management of patients with hypertension and angina. The α-adrenergic blocking component reduces systemic vascular resistance and thereby blood pressure. Ordinarily, this might

---

(26–36) S. Afr. Med. J. 63:67–71, Jan. 15, 1983.

be accompanied by a reflex tachycardia, but the β-blocking component prevents this. Thus, this drug reduces myocardial oxygen demands in two ways: *(1)* the α-adrenergic antagonistic activity reduces arterial pressure; and *(2)* the β-adrenergic blocking activity reduces heart rate and myocardial contractility. Both actions contribute to the reduction of myocardial oxygen needs and thus help to restore the balance between myocardial oxygen supply and demand.] ◀

Chapter 26 References

1. Oliver M.F.: Oral contraception and coronary heart disease. *Eur. Heart J.* 4:6, 1983.
2. Wei J.Y., Bulkley B.H.: Myocardial infarction before age 36 years in women: predominance of apparent nonatherosclerotic events. *Am. Heart J.* 104:561, 1982.
3. Uhl G.S., Farrell P.W.: Myocardial infarction in young adults: risk factors and natural history. *Am. Heart J.* 105:548, 1983.
4. Brox J.H., et al.: Effects of cod liver oil on platelets and coagulation in familial hypercholesterolemia (type IIa). *Acta Med. Scand.* 213:137, 1983.
5. Ready A.E., Quinney H.A.: The response of serum lipids and lipoproteins to high intensity endurance training. *Can. J. Appl. Sport. Sci.* 7:202, 1982.
6. Lobstein D.D., et al.: Circulating lipoprotein-cholesterol and multivariate adaptation to regular exercise training of middle-aged men. *J. Sports Med. Phys. Fitness* 22:440, 1982.
7. Gordon D.J., et al.: Habitual physical activity and high-density lipoprotein cholesterol in men with primary hypercholesterolemia: the lipid research clinics coronary primary prevention trial. *Circulation* 67:512, 1983.
8. Penny G.D., et al.: Comparison of serum HDL-C and HDL-total cholesterol ratio in middle-aged active and inactive males. *J. Sports Med. Phys. Fitness* 22:432, 1982.
9. Rechnitzer P.A.: Relation of exercise to the recurrence rate of myocardial infarction in men. *Am. J. Cardiol.* 51:64, 1983.
10. Naughton J.: Death rates of cardiac patients: effects of physical activity. *Primary Care* 9:77, 1983.
11. Siltanen P., et al.: The influence of previous physical activity on survival and reinfarction after first myocardial infarction. *Acta Med. Scand.* [Suppl] 688:34, 1982.
12. Knuiman J.T., et al.: Serum total and high density lipoprotein cholesterol concentrations and body mass index in adult men from 13 countries. *Am. J. Epidemiol.* 116:631, 1982.
13. Gordon N.F., et al.: Effects of caffeine ingestion on thermoregulatory and myocardial function during endurance performance. *S. Afr. Med. J.* 62:644, 1982.
14. Dobmeyer D.J., et al.: The arrhythmogenic effects of caffeine in human beings. *N. Engl. J. Med.* 308:814, 1983.
15. Brook J.G., et al.: High-density lipoprotein subfractions in normolipidemic patients with coronary atherosclerosis. *Circulation* 66:923, 1982.
16. Salonen J.T., et al.: Serum HDL cholesterol in a high coronary risk population in Eastern Finland. *Acta Med. Scand.* 213:255, 1983.
17. Boman B.: Psychosocial stress and ischaemic heart disease: a response to Tennant. *Aust. N. Z. J. Psychiatry* 16:265, 1982.
18. Williams R.B., et al.: Type A behavior and elevated physiological and neuroendocrine responses to cognitive tasks. *Science* 218:483, 1982.

19. Gordon T., Kannel W.B.: Drinking habits and cardiovascular disease: the Framingham study. *Am. Heart J.* 105:667, 1983.
20. Carter C., et al.: Hematocrit and the risk of coronary heart disease: the Honolulu heart program. *Am. Heart J.* 105:674, 1983.
21. Goldacre M.J., et al.: Cardiovascular disease and vasectomy. *N. Engl. J. Med.* 308:805, 1983.
22. Kaufman D.W., et al.: Nicotine and carbon monoxide content of cigarette smoke and the risk of myocardial infarction in young men. *N. Engl. J. Med.* 308:409, 1983.
23. Gottdiener J.S., et al.: Late cardiac effects of therapeutic mediastinal irradiation. *N. Engl. J. Med.* 308:569, 1983.
24. Burns R.J., et al.: Detection of radiation cardiomyopathy by gated radionuclide angiography. *Am. J. Med.* 74:297, 1983.
25. Miller D.D., et al.: Symptomatic coronary artery spasm following radiotherapy for Hodgkin's disease. *Chest* 83:284, 1983.
26. Schwarz F., et al.: Intracoronary thrombolysis in acute myocardial infarction: duration of ischemia as a major determinant of late results after recanalization. *Am. J. Cardiol.* 50:933, 1982.
27. Schwarz F., et al.: Intracoronary thrombolysis in acute myocardial infarction: an attempt to quantitate its effect by comparison of enzymatic estimate of myocardial necrosis with left ventricular ejection fraction.
28. Ganz W., et al.: Nonsurgical reperfusion in evolving myocardial infarction. *J. Am. Coll. Cardiol.* 1:1247, 1983.
29. Smalling R.W., et al.: Sustained improvement in left ventricular function and mortality by intracoronary streptokinase administration during evolving myocardial infarction. *Circulation* 68:131, 1983.
30. Bergmann S.R., et al.: Temporal dependence of beneficial effects of coronary thrombolysis characterized by positron tomography. *Am. J. Med.* 73:573, 1982.
31. Goldberg S., et al.: Reperfusion arrhythmia: a marker of restoration of antegrade flow during intracoronary thrombolysis for acute myocardial infarction. *Am. Heart J.* 105:26, 1983.
32. Pennica D., Holmes W.E., Kohr W.J., et al.: Cloning and expression of human tissue-type plasminogen activator cDNA in *E. coli. Nature* 301:213, 1984.
33. Cowley M.J., et al.: Fibrinolytic effects of intracoronary streptokinase administration in patients with acute myocardial infarction and coronary insufficiency. *Circulation* 67:1031, 1983.
34. Blanke H., et al.: Electrocardiographic changes after streptokinase-induced recanalization in patients with acute left anterior descending artery obstruction. *Circulation* 68:406, 1983.
35. Lolley D.M., et al.: Coronary artery surgery and direct coronary artery thrombolysis during acute myocardial infarction. *Am. Surg.* 49:296, 1983.
36. Richardson R.L., et al.: Coronary artery bypass grafts. *Arch. Surg.* 118:970, 1983.
37. Walker W.E., et al.: Streptokinase reperfusion and early surgical revascularization in patients with acute myocardial infarction. *South. Med. J.* 75:1531, 1982.
38. Messmer B.J., et al.: New developments in medical-surgical treatment of acute myocardial infarction. *Ann. Thorac. Surg.* 35:70, 1983.
39. DeWood M.A., et al.: Prevalence of total coronary occlusion during the early hours of transmural myocardial infarction. *N. Engl. J. Med.* 303:897, 1980.
40. De Feyter P.J., et al.: Effects of spontaneous and streptokinase-induced

recanalization on left ventricular function after myocardial infarction. *Circulation* 67:1039, 1983.

41. Hammerman H., et al.: Dose-dependent effects of short-term methylprednisolone on myocardial infarct extent, scar formation, and ventricular function. *Circulation* 68:446, 1983.
42. Fisher M.L., et al.: Routine serum enzyme tests in the diagnosis of acute myocardial infarction. *Arch. Intern. Med.* 143:1541, 1983.
43. Haupt H.M., Hutchins G.M., Moore G.W.: Right ventricular infarction: role of the moderator band artery in determining infarct size. *Circulation* 67:1268, 1983.
44. Klein H.O., Tordjman T., Ninio R., et al.: The early recognition of right ventricular infarction: diagnostic accuracy of the electrocardiographic V_4R lead. *Circulation* 67:558, 1983.
45. Chou T-C., Fowler N.O., Gabel M., et al.: Electrocardiographic and hemodynamic changes in experimental right ventricular infarction. *Circulation* 67:1258, 1983.
46. Gibson R.S., Crampton R.S., Watson D.D., et al.: Precordial ST-segment depression during acute inferior myocardial infarction: clinical, scintigraphic and angiographic correlations. *Circulation* 66:732, 1982.
47. Braunwald E., Muller J.E., Kloner R.A., et al.: Role of β-adrenergic blockade in the therapy of patients with myocardial infarction. *Am. J. Med.* 74:113, 1983.
48. Gundersen T., Abrahamsen A.M., Kjekshus J., et al.: Timolol-related reduction in mortality and reinfarction in patients ages 65–75 years surviving acute myocardial infarction. *Circulation* 66:1179, 1982.
49. Becker L.C., Silverman K.J., Bulkley B.H., et al.: Comparison of early thallium-201 scintigraphy and gated blood pool imaging for predicting mortality in patients with acute myocardial infarction. *Circulation* 67:1272, 1983.
50. Gibson R.S., Watson D.D., Craddock G.B., et al.: Prediction of cardiac events after uncomplicated myocardial infarction: a prospective study comparing predischarge exercise thallium-201 scintigraphy and coronary angiography. *Circulation* 68:321, 1983.
51. Schneider R.M., Seaworth J.F., Dohrmann M.L., et al.: Anatomic and prognostic implications of an early positive treadmill exercise test. *Am. J. Cardiol.* 50:682, 1982.
52. Nicod P., Corbett J.R., Firth B.G., et al.: Prognostic value of resting and submaximal exercise radionuclide ventriculography after acute myocardial infarction in high-risk patients with single and multivessel disease. *Am. J. Cardiol.* 52:30, 1983.
53. Epstein S.E., Palmeri S.T., Patterson R.E.: Evaluation of patients after acute myocardial infarction. Indications for cardiac catheterization and surgical intervention. *N. Engl. J. Med.* 307:1487, 1982.
54. Meier B., Hollman J., Gruentzig, A.R.: Percutaneous transluminal coronary angioplasty: key references. *Circulation* 676:1155, 1983.
55. Meier B., Gruentzig A.R., Hollman J., et al.: Does length or eccentricity of coronary stenoses influence the outcome of transluminal dilatation? *Circulation* 67:497, 1983.
56. Ischinger T., Gruentzig A.R., Hollman J., et al.: Should coronary arteries with less than 60% diameter stenosis be treated by angioplasty? *Circulation* 68:148, 1983.
57. Kanemoto N., Hor G., Kober G., et al.: Noninvasive assessment of left ventricular performance following transluminal coronary angioplasty. *Int. J. Cardiol.* 3:281, 1983.
58. Bonow R.L.O., Kent K.M., Rosing D.R., et al.: Improved left ventricular

diastolic filling in patients with coronary artery disease after percutaneous transluminal coronary angioplasty. *Circulation* 66:1159, 1982.
59. Manashil G.B., Thunstrom B.S., Thorpe C.D., et al.: Outpatient transluminal angioplasty. *Radiology* 147:7, 1983.
60. Famularo M., Vasilomanolakis E.C., Schrager B., et al.: Percutaneous transluminal angioplasty of aortocoronary saphenous vein graft: morphologic observations. *JAMA* 249:3347, 1983.
61. Murphy D.A., Craver J.M., Jones E.L., et al.: Surgical revascularization following unsuccessful percutaneous transluminal coronary angioplasty. *J. Thorac. Cardiovasc. Surg.* 84:342, 1982.
62. Choy D.S.J., Stertzer S., Rotterdam H.Z., et al.: Transluminal laser catheter angioplasty. *Am. J. Cardiol.* 50:1206, 1982.
63. Lee G., Ikeda R.M., Stobbe D., et al.: Laser irradiation of human atherosclerotic obstructive disease: simultaneous visualization and vaporization achieved by a dual fiberoptic catheter. *Am. Heart J.* 105:163, 1983.
64. Lee G., Ikeda R.M., Herman I., et al.: The qualitative effects of laser irradiation on human arteriosclerotic disease. *Am. Heart J.* 105:885, 1983.
65. Choy D.S.J., Stertzer S.H., Rotterdam H.Z., et al.: Laser coronary angioplasty: experience with 9 cadaver hearts. *Am. J. Cardiol.* 50:1209, 1982.
66. Mehta J., Mehta P., Ostrowski N.: Effects of nitroglycerin on human vascular prostacyclin and thromboxane A_2 generation. *J. Lab. Clin. Med.* 102:116, 1983.
67. Kaplan K., Davison R., Parker M., et al.: Intravenous nitroglycerin for the treatment of angina at rest unresponsive to standard nitrate therapy. *Am. J. Cardiol.* 51:694, 1983.
68. DePace N.L., Herling I.M., Kotler M.N., et al.: Intravenous nitroglycerin for rest angina: potential pathophysiologic mechanisms of action. *Arch. Intern. Med.* 142:1806, 1982.
69. Mandelkorn J.B., Wolf N.M., Singh S., et al.: Intracoronary thrombus in nontransmural myocardial infarction and in unstable angina pectoris. *Am. J. Cardiol.* 52:1, 1983.
70. Hultgren H.N., Shettigar U.R., Miller D.C.: Medical versus surgical treatment of unstable angina. *Am. J. Cardiol.* 50:663, 1982.
71. Braunwald E., Kloner R.A.: The stunned myocardium: prolonged, postischemic ventricular dysfunction. *Circulation* 66:1146, 1982.
72. Cohn P.F., Brown E.J. Jr., Wynne J., et al.: Global and regional left ventricular ejection fraction abnormalities during exercise in patients with silent myocardial ischemia. *J. Am. Coll. Cardiol.* 1:931, 1983.
73. Murphy M.L., Hultgren H.N., Detre K.: Treatment of chronic stable angina: a preliminary report of survival data of the randomized Veterans Administration Cooperative Study. *N. Engl. J. Med.* 297:7, 1977.
74. CASS Principal Investigators. Coronary Artery Surgery Study (CASS): A randomized trial of coronary artery bypass surgery: "quality of life" in randomized subjects. *Circulation* 68:951, 1983.
75. Reeves T.J., Oberman A., Jones W.B., et al.: Natural history of angina pectoris. *Am. J. Cardiol.* 33:423, 1974.
76. Andersen, P.E. Jr., Thayssen P., Haghfelt T.: The effect of coronary bypass surgery on anginal state and left ventricular function. *Dan. Med. Bull.* 90:190, 1983.
77. Gray R.J., Matloff J.M., Conklin C.M., et al.: Perioperative myocardial infarction: late clinical course after coronary artery bypass surgery. *Circulation* 66:1185, 1982.
78. Pfisterer M., Emmenegger H., Schmitt H.E., et al.: Accuracy of serial myocardial perfusion scintigraphy with thallium-201 for prediction of

graft patency early and late after coronary artery bypass surgery: a controlled prospective study. *Circulation* 66:1017, 1982.

79. Frick M.H., Harjola P-T., Valle M.: Persistent improvement after coronary bypass surgery: ergometric and angiographic correlations at 5 years. *Circulation* 67:491, 1983.
80. Gohlke H., Gohlke-Bärwolf C., Samek L., et al.: Serial exercise testing up to 6 years after coronary bypass surgery: behavior of exercise parameters in groups with different degrees of revascularization determined by postoperative angiography. *Am. J. Cardiol.* 51:1301, 1983.
81. Loop F.D., Golding L.R., MacMillan J.P., et al.: Coronary artery surgery in women compared with men: analyses of risks and long-term results. *J. Am. Coll. Cardiol.* 1:383, 1983.
82. Fisher L.D., Kennedy J.W., Davis K.B., et al.: Association of sex, physical size, and operative mortality after coronary artery bypass in the Coronary Artery Surgery Study (CASS). *J. Thorac. Cardiovasc. Surg.* 84:334, 1982.
83. Gersh B.J., Kronmal R., Frye R.L., et al.: Coronary arteriography and coronary artery bypass surgery: morbidity and mortality in patients ages 65 years or older. A report from the Coronary Artery Surgery Study. *Circulation* 67:483, 1983.
84. Smith S.H., Geer J.C.: Morphology of saphenous vein-coronary artery bypass grafts. *Arch. Pathol. Lab. Med.* 107:13, 1983.
85. Pucci J.J., Walesby R.K., Smith E.E.J., et al.: Reoperation for failed aortocoronary bypass grafts. *J. Cardiovasc. Surg.* 23:453, 1982.
86. Hertzer N.R., Loop F.D., Taylor P.C., et al.: Combined myocardial revascularization and carotid endarterectomy. *J. Thorac. Cardiovasc. Surg.* 85:577, 1983.
87. Jenkins C.D., Stanton B.-A., Savageau J.A., et al.: Coronary artery bypass surgery: physical, psychological, social and economic outcomes six months later. *JAMA* 250:782, 1983.
88. Rosenfeldt F.L., Lambert R., Burrows K., et al.: Hospital costs and return to work after coronary bypass surgery. *Med. J. Aust.* 1:260, 1983.
89. Chew C.Y.C., Brown B.G., Singh B.N., et al.: Effects of verapamil on coronary hemodynamic function and vasomobility relative to its mechanism of antianginal action. *Am. J. Cardiol.* 51:699, 1983.
90. Weiner D.A., McCabe C.H., Cutler S.S., et al.: Efficacy and safety of verapamil in patients with angina pectoris after 1 year of continuous, high-dose therapy. *Am. J. Cardiol.* 51:1251, 1983.
91. Frishman W.H., Charlap S.: Verapamil in treatment of chronic stable angina. *Arch. Intern. Med.* 143:1407, 1983.
92. Klein H.O., Ninio R., Oren V., et al.: The acute hemodynamic effects of intravenous verapamil in coronary artery disease: assessment of equilibrium-gated radionuclide ventriculography. *Circulation* 67:101, 1983.

27. Valvular Heart Disease

27–1 **Clinical Clue of Severe Aortic Stenosis: Simultaneous Palpation of the Carotid and Apical Impulses.** In patients with severe aortic stenosis, simultaneous palpation of the carotid and apical impulses yields a palpable lag time between the two. Patrick K. C. Chun and Bruce E. Dunn (Walter Reed Army Med. Center, Washington, D.C.) report that apexcardiograms and carotid pulse tracings were recorded in 66 control subjects and in 30 patients with aortic stenosis.

With the QRS peak used as a reference, the peak appearance time of the carotid pulse tracings and apexcardiograms was measured, and the difference was calculated as a lag time. Twenty-one of the 30 patients had a palpable lag time. Twenty-two patients had aortic valve areas of less than 1 sq cm at catheterization; 21 of these patients had a palpable lag time.

The sensitivity of a palpable lag time for aortic valve areas of less than 1 sq cm was 95%; specificity, 100%; positive predictive value, 100%; negative predictive value, 89%. Measured lag times correlated poorly with aortic valve areas and with the palpable lag times because of several instances of difficulty encountered in recording an accurate waveform. Group means for measured lag times between controls (70 ± 7 msec) and patients with aortic stenosis (133 ± 7 msec) showed a definite difference.

On linear regression analysis, the palpable lag time had a correlation coefficient of .68, third in rank to the aortic valve gradient and ECG for pedicting aortic valve area. Multiple regression analysis showed that the combination of palpable lag time, ECG, syncope, and shudder waves could be used to predict the aortic valve area ($r = .85$), although syncope and shudder waves by themselves had poor correlation coefficients.

▶ [Although it is possible to diagnose the presence of aortic stenosis noninvasively, the critical problem is to identify those patients who have critical aortic stenosis necessitating catheterization and surgical interventions, i.e., those patients whose stenotic aortic valve orifices are less than 1 sq cm. The simple physical sign described in this paper by Chun consists of simultaneous palpation of the carotid and apical impulses and appears to be a useful adjunct in the clinical examination of patients with severe aortic stenosis. In patients with severe aortic stenosis, there is a distinct lag between the initial systolic outward thrust of the apex and the peak of the carotid pulse.

Since reading this article, I have employed the sign a number of times clinically and find it far more easy to elicit than the classical pulsus tardus et parvus. Obviously, many other factors may affect this interval; these include ventricular dyskinesia, tachyarrhythmia, hypertension, and associated valvular disease, but in the absence of these confounding factors, I agree with the authors that the palpable apex to carotid lag time is a useful noninvasive index suggesting the presence of severe aortic stenosis.

(27–1) Arch. Intern. Med. 142:2284–2288, December 1982.

It is important to note that mild valvular aortic stenosis tends to progress. In a study of 26 patients with this condition followed up for an average period of 9 years after the initial evaluation, the gradual progress of the severity of stenosis, averaging 0.1 sq cm/year in 10 of the patients and less in the remaining 16, was observed. Although the rate of progression of valvular aortic stenosis in adults is usually slow, moderate stenosis may become severe within several (3–5) years, and therefore careful follow-up of these patients is required.[1]] ◀

27–2 **Effect of Aortic Valve Replacement on Survival.** The correct timing of valve replacement in patients with chronic left ventricular overload remains a problem. Franz Schwarz, Peter Baumann, Joachim Manthey, Manfred Hoffman, Gerhard Schuler, Helmuth C. Mehmel, Wolfgang Schmitz, and Wolfgang Kübler (Univ. of Heidelberg) compared the survival of 252 patients who were operated on with that of 47 medically managed patients who had symptomatic aortic valve disease. Aortic stenosis predominated in 144 patients, and insufficiency in 155. Initial hemodynamic and angiographic findings were similar in the surgical and medical groups. No patient underwent surgery on an emergent basis. A Björk-Shiley prosthesis was used in 71% of operations. Mean follow-ups were 2 years in the surgical group and 1.9 years in the medical group. The only significant difference in baseline features was that patients with predominant stenosis who were not operated on were older.

Overall operative mortality was 7%. Myocardial failure was the chief cause of death in both treatment groups. Patients with aortic stenosis who were operated on had better long-term survival than those who were not operated on, but actuarial survivals were similar in the two groups with aortic insufficiency. Survival was not influenced by the type of valve prosthesis used. In aortic stenosis, operation improved survival regardless of whether the hemodynamics were normal or abnormal. Survival was poor for patients who were not operated on regardless of the hemodynamic findings. Among patients with aortic insufficiency in functional class III, survivals were similar in those who were operated on and those who were not, but class I patients tended to live longer if operation was performed. Patients with aortic insufficiency who were not operated on lived longer than those with aortic stenosis who were not operated on.

Aortic valve replacement substantially improves the long-term outlook for symptomatic patients with predominant aortic stenosis, even if left ventricular function is normal. Operation is recommended when a severe hemodynamic lesion is established, and it should also be done when left ventricular dysfunction is present. Patients with predominant insufficiency should be operated on only if severe symptoms persist despite medical treatment or if left ventricular dysfunction is documented.

▶ [The correct timing of valve replacement in patients with both aortic stenosis and aortic regurgitation remains a challenging problem. This is an important study in that it compares the long-term survival in surgically and medically treated cohorts with severe aortic valve disease. The major message is that aortic valve replacement improved the prognosis in patients with severe aortic stenosis, regardless of whether they had normal or impaired left ventricular function. Therefore, aortic valve replacement should be

---

(27–2) Circulation 66:1105–1110, November 1982.

carried out in patients with severe aortic stenosis, regardless of the degree of left ventricular dysfunction. On the other hand, in patients with aortic regurgitation, surgery did not improve the prognosis in those with normal left ventricular function.

A related problem is the degree of return of normal myocardial function in patients with aortic regurgitation. Donaldson et al.[2] found that the myocardial biopsy was predictive of outcome in that massive fiber hypertrophy, increased interstitial fibrous tissue, reduced levels of myofibrillar and mitochondrial adenosine triphosphatases and succinate dehydrogenases correlated with persistent dilatation, cardiac failure, and poor survival. Carroll et al.[3] in a study of serial changes after chronic aortic regurgitation reported that dysfunction persisted in those patients with postoperative left ventricular enlargement and persistent left ventricular hypertrophy.

Although the problem of carrying out cardiac valve replacement in patients with aortic regurgitation and good left ventricular function has not yet been settled, there is increasing evidence that as surgical skills improve, patients with severe valve disease, even those with left ventricular dysfunction, should be subjected to corrective operation. Thus, David et al.[4] reported on 41 patients with severely impaired left ventricular function (ejection fractions less than 40% and left ventricular end-diastolic pressure greater than 18 mm Hg.). The 3-year actuarial survival rate, including operative deaths, was 79%. Thus, although it would clearly have been preferable to operate on these patients earlier and achieve a better survival rate, patients with advanced left ventricular dysfunction clearly can tolerate operation. Thus, I believe it is rarely too late to operate on a patient with advanced aortic valve disease.

When both aortic valve disease and coronary artery disease are present one should not hesitate to recommend a combined operation. Nunley et al.[5] reported an operative mortality of 5% and an incidence of perioperative myocardial infarction of 2% for patients subjected to aortic valve replacement and myocardial revascularization.] ◀

27–3 **Open Mitral Valvotomy: Fourteen Years' Experience.** P. H. Kay, P. Belcher, K. Dawkins, and S. C. Lennox (London) reviewed the results of open mitral valvotomy in 157 patients, representing 71% of all patients seen in 1968–1980 with predominant mitral stenosis and severe dyspnea. Female patients predominated in a ratio of 4:1. The average age was 39 years. Systemic embolism had occurred in 17 patients. Eleven patients had undergone one, and 5 patients had undergone two closed mitral valvotomies a mean of 9 years previously. Surgery was done under bypass and, more recently, cold cardioplegic myocardial protection. In 20 patients, thrombus was removed from the left atrium. The left atrial appendage was not excised or excluded. Great care was taken to avoid dividing the chordae. The valve leaflets were decalcified in one fourth of patients.

There was only 1 hospital death. Six of 7 late deaths were due to congestive heart failure. The actuarial 10-year survival rate was 90%. Perioperative embolism occurred in 1 patient who recovered fully. Eight patients required mitral valve replacement for restenosis, 2 of which occurred within 5 years of valvotomy. Six patients required early valve replacement for excessive mitral regurgitation. Five patients had late cerebrovascular accidents; none of them had thrombus present in the left atrium at the time of valvotomy. All surviving patients gained considerable benefit from the operation, and were in New York Heart Association grade 1 or 2 for exercise tolerance at follow-up. Nearly 60% of survivors are taking digoxin for atrial fibrillation. All patients aged 25–70 years who are in atrial fibrillation receive anticoagulant therapy.

(27–3) Br. Heart J. 50:4–7, July 1983.

Valve preservation is desirable in patients with mitral stenosis. More than two thirds of patients with predominant stenosis have undergone open mitral valvotomy, and some have had their native valves salvaged by a combination of open valvotomy and mitral valve annuloplasty. The ability of the leaflets to coapt and their pliability are important determinants of the long-term success of open valvotomy. Where a fixed eccentric orifice is present and extensive plastic surgery on the cusps, chordae, and annulus is necessary, mitral valve replacement is preferable.

▶ [In the past few years surgical treatment of mitral stenosis has become progressively more radical. Thus, in most surgical centers, open mitral valvulotomy has replaced the closed operation, since the risk of cardiopulmonary bypass is small and aortic cross-clamping is relatively safe with the use of cold cardioplegic arrest. Surgeons in the United States are much more likely to replace a deformed stenotic mitral valve with a prosthesis than are those in other countries. Perhaps this difference in practice is related to the cost of prosthetic valves, which can be borne more easily in this country. In any event, this interesting paper documents the effectiveness of open mitral valvulotomy and indicates that there is still a role for this operation. The mortality was low (0.6%), comparing favorably with that of closed mitral valvulotomy and certainly better than that for mitral valve replacement (approximately 5%). The actuarial 10-year survival rate of 90% also compares favorably with that for mitral valve replacement. Recurrent stenosis, requiring mitral valve replacement was 14.8% over a 10-year period.

An obvious advantage of leaving the native valve in situ is that the complications of prosthetic valves, i.e., thromboembolic complications in patients with mechanical prostheses and late breakdown of patients with bioprostheses, can be largely avoided. In the long run, many of the patients who undergo mitral valve replacement, may well require a second operation, but the patient may be expected to benefit from the advances in technology of artificial valves which are certain to occur by that time. Of course, in patients in whom open repair of the stenotic valve is not possible, the surgeon should not hesitate to replace the valve.] ◀

Chapter 27 References

1. Jonasson R., Jonsson B., Nordlander R., et al.: Rate of progression of severity of valvular aortic stenosis. *Acta Med. Scand.* 213:51, 1983.
2. Donaldson R.M., Florio R., Rickards A.F., et al.: Irreversible morphological changes contributing to depressed cardiac function after surgery for chronic aortic regurgitation. *Br. Heart J.* 48:589, 1982.
3. Carroll J.D., Gaasch W.H., Zile M.R., et al.: Serial changes in left ventricular function after correction of chronic aortic regurgitation: dependence on early changes in preload and subsequent regression of hypertrophy. *Am. J. Cardiol.* 51:476, 1983.
4. David T.E., Dunin-Bell O., Orr S., et al.: Cardiac valve surgery in patients with poor left ventricular function. *Can. J. Surg.* 26:157, 1983.
5. Nunley D.L., Grunkemeier G.L., Starr A.: Aortic valve replacement with coronary bypass grafting. *J. Thorac. Cardiovasc. Surg.* 85:705, 1983.

28. Cardiac Arrhythmias

28–1 **Right Bundle Branch Block: Long-Term Prognosis in Apparently Healthy Men.** It is not known whether the presence of right bundle branch block (RBBB) in apparently healthy subjects increases the risk of subsequent cardiac events. Jerome L. Fleg, Dhirendra N. Das, and Edward G. Lakatta (Nat'l Inst. on Aging, Baltimore) reviewed the data on 24 clinically healthy men with complete RBBB who were among 1,142 men in the Baltimore Longitudinal Study on Aging. None of the 24 had evidence of associated cardiac disease at the outset. These subjects were followed up for an average of 8½ years, along with control subjects matched for age.

Mean age at the time of diagnosis of RBBB was 64 years. Antecedent coronary risk factors and obstructive lung disease were comparably frequent in the study and control groups. New cardiac events or abnormalities also were similarly frequent in the two groups. Clinical coronary disease developed in 17% of study subjects and in 13% of controls. Latent coronary heart disease was observed on exercise testing in 20% of the study subjects tested and in 28% of controls tested. Left axis deviation was more frequent in the study group. Prolongation of the PR interval by 40 msec or more also was more frequent than in the control group. No significant differences in blood pressure or heart size were observed between the study and control subjects. Exercise performance was comparable in the two groups.

Cardiovascular morbidity and mortality were not increased in asymptomatic men with RBBB in this study. No increase in the prevalence of coronary risk factors or latent coronary disease was apparent, and there was no impairment of maximal aerobic performance in these subjects. The findings of more prevalent left axis deviation and PR interval prolongation support the view that RBBB is a manifestation of a more general abnormality of the cardiac conduction system in men without other evidence of heart disease.

▶ [Most previous studies of the natural history of right bundle branch block (RBBB) were derived from hospital-based populations which included many patients who had heart disease; as might be anticipated, the long-term cardiovascular morbidity and mortality in these patients were quite high, and this electrocardiographic abnormality got a bad name. The Framingham Study, employing an age-matched control population, found a 2.5-fold increase in coronary disease and a nearly fourfold increase in the rate of development of congestive heart failure in 53 patients with RBBB who were followed during a 6-year period.[1] The incidence of coronary disease and congestive heart failure and the cardiovascular mortality were most marked in patients with RBBB, a QRS duration greater than 130 msec and a QRS axis less than −45 degrees. In other community studies, the combination of RBBB with left axis deviation less than −30 degrees was also associated with a high prevalence of cardiovascular disease, but uncomplicated RBBB was not.[2] No increase in coronary risk

(28–1) J. Am. Coll. Cardiol. 1:887–892, March 1983.

occurred in a large military population with RBBB.[3] The study abstracted above is of great importance, since it focuses on the meaning of RBBB in an apparently normal population. Thus, we can conclude that RBBB is a benign finding when picked up in routine screening of presumably healthy persons and when unaccompanied by left axis deviation, QRS prolongation, or clinical evidence of coronary artery disease.] ◀

28–2 **Long-Term Survival of Patients With Malignant Ventricular Arrhythmia Treated With Antiarrhythmic Drugs.** The protective effect of antiarrhythmic agents for patients with malignant ventricular arrhythmia (defined as noninfarction ventricular fibrillation or sustained hemodynamically compromising ventricular tachycardia) remains uncertain. Thomas B. Graboys, Bernard Lown, Philip J. Podrid, and Regis DeSilva (Boston) analyzed the extent to which survival among 123 such patients (average age, 53.6 years) was dependent on the abolition of salvos of ventricular tachycardia and R-on-T ventricular premature beats (Lown grades 4B and 5) by antiarrhythmic drugs.

During an average follow-up period of 29.6 months, there were 35 deaths (11.2% annual mortality); 23 patients died suddenly (8.2% annual mortality). No statistical difference in mortality was observed among patients on the basis of the type of arrhythmia (ventricular tachycardia or ventricular fibrillation) at entry.

Among 98 patients in whom antiarrhythmic drugs abolished grade 4B and grade 5 ventricular premature beats (group A), only 6 sudden deaths occurred; the overall mortality for this group was 5.5% and the annual rate of sudden death was 2.3% (Fig 28–1). Of 25 patients whose arrhythmia was not controlled (group B), 21 died, 17 of them suddenly (annual mortality, 52.5%; rate of sudden death, 43.6%). The difference in survival between groups A and B was statistically significant.

Of 79 patients who underwent analysis of left ventricular function, 44 (56%) showed left ventricular dysfunction, defined as an ejection fraction of less than 0.50. The presence of left ventricular dysfunction did not correlate with control of arrhythmia. Among patients with

Fig 28–1.—Total cardiac mortality *(left)* and rate of sudden death *(right)* among patients with malignant ventricular arrhythmia, on the basis of control *(crosses)* or lack of control *(closed circles)* of ventricular premature beats. (Courtesy of Graboys, T.B., et al.: Am. J. Cardiol. 50:437–443, September 1982.)

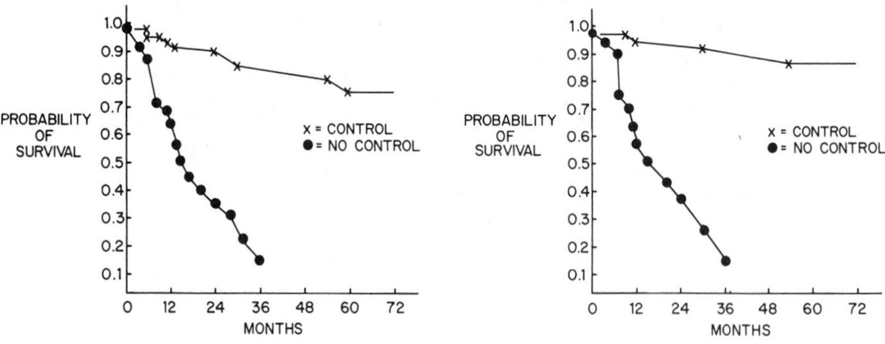

(28–2) Am. J. Cardiol. 50:437–443, September 1982.

left ventricular dysfunction, control of ventricular premature beats was a critical element predicting survival. Of 32 patients whose arrhythmia was controlled, 5 died (7.8% total annual mortality); 2 deaths were sudden arrhythmic events (annual rate of sudden death, 3.1%). Ten of 12 patients without control of arrhythmia died, 7 suddenly (59.4% total mortality, 41.5% rate of sudden death).

Antiarrhythmic drugs can protect against the recurrence of life-threatening arrhythmias in patients with ventricular fibrillation or ventricular tachycardia. Abolition of certain advanced grades of ventricular premature beats is an effective therapeutic objective. The approach necessitates individualized selection of antiarrhythmic drugs and use of multiple antiarrhythmic agents.

▶ [The approach employed by Drs. Graboys and Lown in these patients has two components. During the acute drug testing phase, after a suitable control monitoring period, they administer a single large dose of an antiarrhythmic drug. The dose generally consists of half of the commonly employed daily maintenance dose of the particular agent to be studied. The patient is exercised hourly after the administration of the selected drug, and blood concentrations are obtained. After a 24-hour washout period, the patient undergoes approximately six acute drug tests. Those drugs that prove effective during phase 1 are applied in phase 2, which is continued for 48–96 hours and is designed to determine drug efficacy, which is assessed by means of 24-hour Holter monitoring and maximal exercise stress testing. An effective response requires the elimination of grades 4B and 5 ventricular premature beats and a reduction in the frequency of lower grade premature beats. The best-tolerated, most efficacious drug is selected for maintenance. The average hospital stay to define an effective drug program is 17 days.

The results of this investigation are impressive. Of course, all patients were treated (i.e., there was no placebo-treated control group), which is understandable enough given the severity of the illness. It is not clear whether those patients who survived on drug therapy would or would not have had a recurrent event had they been left untreated. Thus, this study does not prove definitively that those patients in whom high-grade ventricular ectopic activity was eliminated by means of pharmacotherapy were not the same patients who might not have been at risk of a subsequent episode of ventricular tachycardia or fibrillation. Nonetheless, until such a study is done—and this will be very difficult, perhaps impossible considering the very high mortality rate in these patients—the approach to the management of patients with malignant ventricular arrhythmias described above makes a good deal of common sense.] ◀

28–3 **Amiodarone in Refractory Life-Threatening Ventricular Arrhythmias.** Amiodarone, first used as a coronary vasodilator, has been reported to be effective in controlling a majority of life-threatening ventricular tachyarrhythmias in patients refractory to conventional drugs. Koonlawee Nademanee, Bramah N. Singh, Joann Hendrickson, Vanida Intarachot, Becky Lopez, Gregory Feld, David S. Cannom, and James L. Weiss evaluated amiodarone in 96 patients with life-threatening ventricular arrhythmias refractory to 2 or more conventional antiarrhythmic agents. The 83 men and 13 women had a mean age of 56 years. All but 5 patients had organic heart disease, and 68 had coronary artery disease. Most had failed to respond to 3 or more antiarrhythmic agents. All patients were considered to be at a high risk of sudden death. Amiodarone was given in a loading dose of 1,400–1,800 mg daily for 1–4 weeks, followed by maintenance therapy with 200–600 mg daily.

(28–3) Ann. Intern. Med. 98:577–584, May 1983.

MAJOR SIDE EFFECTS OF AMIODARONE THERAPY

Side Effects	Patients
	n
Gastrointestinal disturbances (constipation, anorexia, increased alanine transaminase levels)	17
Insomnia	11
Photosensitivity	5
Central nervous system disturbances (incoordination, tremor, ataxia, impaired memory)	5
Proximal muscle weakness	2
Interstitial pulmonary fibrosis	2
Halovision	3
Symptomatic bradycardia and sinus arrest	3
Weight loss	1
Hypothyroidism*	1

*Confirmed by measurements of thyroid-stimulating hormone in the setting of a compatible clinical presentation. The complication is not specific for the drug. (Courtesy of Nademanee, K., et al.: Ann. Intern. Med. 98:577–584, May 1983.)

Seventy-five patients have continued to take amiodarone and have been without symptoms for a mean of 15 months. Three of 12 deaths were sudden, and 2 may have resulted from inadequate treatment. Amiodarone was ineffective in 4 patients, and 5 others were withdrawn from amiodarone therapy because of limiting side effects. The table lists the major side effects. Amiodarone prevented the induction of ventricular tachycardia during electrophysiologic studies in several instances. Excellent clinical results were usually obtained despite a lack of suppression of inducible ventricular tachycardia or fibrillation.

Amiodarone is highly effective in preventing recurrent life-threatening ventricular arrhythmias in patients refractory to conventional antiarrhythmic agents. The drug lengthens the action-potential duration and, therefore, the effective refractory period in all cardiac tissues. The drug may be clinically effective even if inducible ventricular tachycardia is not suppressed during electrophysiologic study.

▶ [Amiodarone is an interesting drug which is effective in the treatment of recurrent ventricular tachycardia and fibrillation (1982 YEAR BOOK, p. 301). Its fundamental mechanism of action is not clearly understood except that it prolongs the action-potential duration without changing the rate of rise of upstroke of the action potential or the resting-membrane potential. Gloor et al.[4] have demonstrated that the drug also depresses both the sinus node and the atrioventricular junction and that these actions may involve blockade of the slow channels.

Interestingly, maximal antiarrhythmic efficacy with oral administration requires administration for several days or even weeks. Saksena et al.[5] studied the chronic electrophysiologic, systemic, and pharmacologic effects of chronic oral amiodarone therapy in patients with refractory ventricular tachycardia and organic heart disease. The drug prolonged the R-R, Q-Tc, and A-H; H-V and PR intervals, the QRS duration, the corrected sinus node recovery time, the effective refractory period of the atrium, the atrioventricular A-V node, and the ventricle. Programmed electrical stimulation after a month's therapy is highly predictive of long-term beneficial results if suppression of the arrhythmia induction is demonstrated. However, even though the drug may not prevent electrical initiation of ventricular tachyarrhythmias, many patients do not develop recurrence of spontaneous arrhythmias.[6]

Long-term follow-up (as long as 20 months) has demonstrated a marked reduction in clinical symptoms but a significant recurrence of "slow" ventricular tachycardia, which was often well tolerated. Fogoros et al.[7] followd 96 patients with recurrent, drug-refractory tachyarrhythmias who were treated with amiodarone for an average of 8 months. Fourteen of the 96 developed toxicity which limited therapy. The incidence of successful amiodarone therapy in patients with ventricular tachycardia and fibrillation was 52% at 12 months and 65% in patients treated for supraventricular tachyarrhythmias.

Amiodarone is not a safe drug and should only be used if other antiarrhythmic agents have failed. In 80 patients treated for an average of 15 months, McGovern et al.[8] noted adverse reactions to 69 and serious toxicity in 13; 4 patients developed interstitial pneumonitis; 4, incessant ventricular tachycardia; 3, sustained sinus node arrest; 1, hepatitis; and 1, hypercalcemia with renal failure. A rise in serum concentration of digoxin and potentiation of warfarin anticoagulation also occurred. Because of these serious side effects, amiodarone should only be used in patients with life-threatening or seriously disabling arrhythmias in whom longer established drugs have been demonstrated to be ineffective.

Transbronchial lung biopsy on a patient with amiodarone-induced pneumonitis, which usually presents as a fine interstitial pattern and nodularity, showed chronic pneumonitis with C3 deposition by immunofluorescence.[9] If the drug is continued the pulmonary fibrosis may be fatal. Fortunately, it is reversible following cessation of amiodarone and initiation of corticosteroid therapy.

The effects of amiodarone on thyroid function are complex and interesting. It may produce latent or overt hypothyroidism and, more rarely, thyrotoxicosis. Other patients may remain clinically euthyroid but develop free-thyroxine levels above the normal range. Reverse T3 is often elevated, presumably owing to inhibition of peripheral conversion of thyroxine to T3 with diversion to reverse T3. Thyroid function tests should be carried out every 6 months in patients who receive maintenance amiodarone. Laboratory evidence of hypothyroidism is likely to be clinically important, whereas elevated levels of thyroxine are usually not.[10]

Chronic therapy with amiodarone has also been shown to produce a peripheral neuropathy involving both sensory and motor deficits in 10% of patients. Most commonly it manifests itself as parasthesias in the lower extremities with weakness, symmetric sensory loss, gait difficulty and absent reflexes.[11] The drug also causes corneal changes. Ingram et al.[12] made serial observations on 105 patients treated with amiodarone for 3 months to 7 years. Corneal abnormalities were detected by slit-lamp examination in 98%. The corneal microdeposits, whose development and size are dose dependent, do not appear to impair visual acuity. They progressed for several months but then stabilized. The abnormalities regressed and disappeared in those patients in whom treatment was discontinued. Fortunately, these ocular changes are not progressive and are rarely of sufficient significance to require reduction in dosage or discontinuation of the drug. Amiodarone has relatively few cardiovascular side effects other than mild sinus bradycardia. It rarely depresses myocardial function, permitting its use in patients with left ventricular dysfunction.[6]

In my experience, loading doses of amiodarone of approximately 1 gm/day should be given for 10 days followed by 500 mg/day for 10 days and a subsequent reduction to 300 mg/day. This will often achieve a salutary therapeutic response with minimal side effects. As already pointed out, the time required to achieve a full antiarrhythmic effect is prolonged, often to as long as 1 month.] ◀

28–4 **Arrhythmogenic Right Ventricular Dysplasia: Generalized Cardiomyopathy?** There are indications that cardiac regions other than the right ventricle may be involved in arrhythmogenic right ventricular dysplasia (ARVD), but the incidence of anatomical and functional left ventricular (LV) involvement is unknown. Dante E. Manyari, George J. Klein, Sajad Gulamhusein, Derek Boughner, Gerard M. Guiraudon, George Wyse, L. Brent Mitchell, and William J. Kostuk, with the technical assistance of Paul Purves, prospectively

(28–4) Circulation 68:251–257, August 1983.

evaluated cardiac function at rest and during exercise by ECG-gated cardiac scintigraphy and echocardiography in 6 consecutive patients with ARVD. The 4 men and 2 women had a mean age of 41 years. Diagnosis was based on recurrent ventricular tachycardia of left bundle branch block morphology with no evidence of coronary disease or other organic heart disease. Angiography documented right ventricular wall motion abnormality in all cases. Right ventricular (RV) origin of tachycardia was confirmed by electrophysiologic study in 4 patients. Ten asymptomatic control subjects and 5 patients on amiodarone therapy for Wolff-Parkinson-White (WPW) syndrome also were studied.

The mean RV ejection fraction in study patients was 25% at rest and 26% on exercise. Normal subjects had respective values of 51% and 59%. The right ventricular/left ventricular (RV/LV) end-diastolic diameter ratio was 0.60 in study patients and 0.37 in normal subjects. The respective RV/LV end-diastolic volume ratios were 2.41 and 1.16. All patients with ARVD had an abnormal LV ejection fraction on exercise, and 2 had abnormal resting values. The mean LV ejection fraction in study patients was 57% at rest and 55% on exercise. Normal subjects had perspective values of 61% and 72%. All but 1 of the study patients had new LV wall motion abnormalities on exercise. Patients with WPW syndrome at rest and exercise had left and right ventricular ejection fractions similar to those of normal subjects.

Global and segmental right ventricular dysfunction was present in patients with ARVD, and latent left ventricular dysfunction was detected during exercise. It remains unclear whether ARVD represents a generalized cardiomyopathy with predominant right ventricular involvement. A surgical technique known as "right ventricular free wall disconnection" should be effective where arrhythmogenicity is confined to the RV free wall, but the finding of uniform LV involvement raises the possibility of ventricular tachycardia recurring with progression of the disease process.

► [Arrhythmogenic right ventricular dysplasia is an uncommon disorder; it is a cardiomyopathy with a hypokinetic area involving the wall of the right ventricle. It may be related to Uhl's anomaly (parchment-thin right ventricular wall), and in some children and young adults with otherwise normal hearts it can be an important cause of ventricular arrhythmias. Right ventricular failure or asymptomatic right ventricular enlargement may be present. The electrocardiogram during sinus rhythm exhibits complete or incomplete right bundle branch block.

The finding in the study by Manyari et al. abstracted above, i.e., that left ventricular dysfunction may be present in these patients, suggests that arrhythmogenic right ventricular dysplasia represents a generalized cardiomyopathy. One must wonder, in view of these observations, about the possibility of the development of recurrent ventricular tachycardia with progression of the disease to the left ventricle following surgical treatment, which consists of disconnecting the free wall of the right ventricle.] ◄

28–5 **Treatment of Life-Threatening Digitalis Intoxication With Digoxin-Specific Fab Antibody Fragments: Experience in 26 Cases.** Thomas W. Smith, Vincent P. Butler, Jr., Edgar Haber, Harry Fozzard, Frank I. Marcus, W. Fraser Bremner, Ira C. Schulman, and

---

(28–5) N. Engl. J. Med. 307:1357–1362, Nov. 25, 1982.

Anthony Phillips used purified digoxin-specific Fab fragments from sheep to treat 26 patients with advanced digitalis toxicity resistant to conventional measures. Twenty-three patients had life-threatening digoxin toxicity and 3 had digitoxin toxicity. Actually or potentially life-threatening hyperkalemia or arrhythmias were present. After skin testing and administration of an intravenous test dose, patients received Fab fragments intravenously in an isotonic saline-sorbitol vehicle, usually over a period of 15–30 minutes. Nineteen patients had a serum digoxin level above 5 ng/ml at the time of Fab administration. Thirteen patients had taken large overdoses of digoxin accidentally or with suicidal intent.

All patients responded favorably initially to doses calculated to be equivalent on a molar basis to the amount of glycoside in the body. Four patients with prolonged hypotension and low cardiac output died of cerebral or myocardial hypoperfusion. One patient did not receive enough Fab to reverse a massive suicidal ingestion, and died after recurrent ventricular arrhythmias developed. In the remaining 21 patients, arrhythmias and hyperkalemia were rapidly reversed and recovery was complete. No adverse reactions resulted from treatment. Many patients responded dramatically.

Administration of purified digoxin-specific Fab fragments is an effective, safe means of reversing advanced, life-threatening digitalis intoxication. This approach may prove useful in reversing untoward effects of other drugs, toxins, and endogenous hormones.

► [The advantages of using the 50,000-dalton Fab fragments rather than the 150,000-dalton parent IgG molecule (antibody) in the treatment of digitalis intoxication include more rapid distribution and elimination, faster and more reliable reversal of cardiac arrhythmias, and reduced immunogenicity with the former than the latter. Fab fragments of digoxin-specific antibodies have also been used successfully in infants with severe arrhythmias due to digoxin poisoning.[13, 14] The rare complication of digitoxin-induced severe thrombocytopenia can also be reversed with Fab antibody fragments. This is possible because of the cross-reaction between digitoxin and digoxin-specific antibodies.[15]

Other means of treating digoxin intoxication include the use of resins such as colestipol or cholestyramine.[16] A similar effect may be achieved with activated charcoal fiber,[17] but both of these methods are relatively weak in comparison to specific Fab fragments. In patients who are not acutely and severely intoxicated with digitalis, but who may have digitalis-induced arrhythmias associated with prolonged administration of the drug, it is possible that decreased cellular magnesium content (as determined in circulating lymphocytes) with either normal or depressed serum magnesium levels predisposes to digitalis-toxic arrhythmias.[18]] ◄

28–6 **Effect of Whiskey on Atrial Vulnerability and "Holiday Heart."** Cardiomyopathy in persons who chronically ingest ethanol is associated with conduction disorders and arrhythmias such as atrial fibrillation and flutter. The onset of atrial tachyarrhythmias after a bout of alcohol abuse in the absence of overt cardiomyopathy or congestive failure constitutes the "holiday heart" syndrome. Toby R. Engel and Jerry C. Luck (Med. College of Pennsylvania) examined the arrhythmogenic effects of ethanol by assessing vulnerability to atrial tachyarrhythmias with the extrastimulus technique after acute ethanol ingestion. Fourteen men aged 43–75 years underwent right

(28–6) J. Am. Coll. Cardiol. 1:816–818, March 1983.

atrial extrastimulation. Eleven were habitual alcohol abusers. Seven of them, including 5 who had a paroxysm of atrial fibrillation or flutter after a bout of drinking, were studied before and after drinking 60 or 120 ml of 86-proof whiskey in 30 minutes.

Vulnerability to atrial tachyarrhythmia was demonstrated in the basal state in 2 alcohol abusers. In 5 other patients tachyarrhythmia was induced after drinking whiskey. Ethanol levels averaged 72 mg/dl. Pulmonary capillary wedge pressures were normal in all 7 at baseline and did not change after drinking. Refractory periods were shortened by more than 10 msec in 4 of 5 vulnerable patients by drinking whiskey. Vulnerability was apparent at sites with the shortest refractory periods in these patients.

Drinking whiskey facilitates the demonstration of vulnerability to atrial tachyarrhythmia in some alcohol abusers without manifest cardiomyopathy and in some nondrinkers with bradycardia. Holiday heart syndrome can be reproduced by ingestion of a small amount of whiskey. Although the mechanism is not clear, it appears that social amounts of ethanol may be harmful to persons at risk of atrial fibrillation or flutter, such as those with sinus node or valvular disease.

▶ [In the past the holiday heart has been assumed to result from the development of arrhythmias following spree-drinking in patients with frank alcoholic cardiomyopathy. In this study the arrhythmias resulting from ethanol occurred in patients *without* clinical evidence of cardiomyopathy, valvular disease, or congestive heart failure. These arrhythmias may be caused by focal, intramyocardial, or adrenal release of catecholamines, nonuniform autonomic nervous system discharge, or the electrophysiologic effects of the alcohol metabolite acetaldehyde. It is interesting that vulnerability to atrial flutter and fibrillation occurred in some alcohol abusers free of manifest cardiomyopathy and in some nondrinkers with bradycardia. In a related study, Greenspon and Schaal[19] observed that after 90 ml of 80-proof whiskey, 10 of 14 patients with a history of chronic alcohol consumption, some of whom also had cardiomegaly, developed sustained or nonsustained atrial or ventricular tachyarrhythmias during electrophysiologic testing.] ◀

28–7 **Cardiac Arrest in Young, Ostensibly Healthy Patients: Clinical, Hemodynamic, and Electrophysiologic Findings.** Previous studies have suggested that associated cardiac disease is nearly always present in young, ostensibly healthy cardiac arrest victims. D. Woodrow Benson, Jr., David G. Benditt, Robert W. Anderson, Ann Dunnigan, Marc R. Pritzker, Thomas J. Kulik, and James H. Zavoral reviewed the findings in 11 patients, aged 15 months to 29 years, who were successfully resuscitated from out-of-hospital cardiac arrest in 1978–1982. The 8 male and 3 female patients had a mean age of 18 years. All had previously been in good health, and for all patients, cardiac arrest was the first manifestation of cardiac disease. All patients but 1 underwent electrophysiologic studies within a month of cardiac arrest.

Six patients were relatively sedentary at the time of cardiac arrest, 2 were asleep, and the others were engaged in no more than moderate exercise. Six patients received a cardiovascular diagnosis after cardiac arrest. Three patients had dilated cardiomyopathy, and 1 patient each had viral myocarditis, tricuspid valve prolapse, and myocardial

---

(28–7) Am. J. Cardiol. 52:65–69, July 1983.

bridges with restrictive cardiomyopathy. No patient was found to have congenital heart disease, hypertrophic cardiomyopathy, or arrhythmogenic right ventricular dysplasia. Rapid, sustained tachycardia was initiated on electrophysiologic study in 8 patients; the other 3 were studied at a time when the stimulation protocol was limited to 2 extrastimuli. Accessory atrioventricular connections were demonstrated in 2 patients. Three patients had recurrent cardiac arrest, and 3 had symptomatic ventricular tachycardia on follow-up despite antiarrhythmic drug therapy. Autopsy showed dilated cardiomyopathy in 1 of the 2 patients examined and no structural defects in the other.

Careful programmed electrical stimulation may demonstrate life-threatening tachycardia in young, presumably healthy patients who survive cardiac arrest. Treatment is difficult, but electrophysiologic studies may aid the management of these patients.

▶ [In an international cooperative study of 254 cases of sudden unexpected death in patients under the age of 21 years, only 3% had no previous history of cardiovascular disease.[20] Previous reports of young survivors of cardiac arrest have been limited to individual case reports. The study abstracted above is particularly valuable, since it describes a series of 11 such patients. However, only 6 patients in this series had evidence of cardiac disease, and in only 5 of these patients were the associated cardiovascular abnormalities considered to be responsible for the arrhythmia.

The approach to the difficult problem presented by young survivors of cardiac arrest described in this article by Benson et al. is sensible, i.e., carry out detailed electrophysiologic testing as a guide to selection of therapy to prevent recurrences. Occasionally surgical treatment should be carried out; this may involve release of myocardial bridges or ablation of accessory atrioventricular connections.] ◀

28–8 **Neurologic Recovery After Out-of-Hospital Cardiac Arrest.** More persons are resuscitated from out-of-hospital cardiac arrest, and global brain ischemia accompanying cardiac arrest has become a common cause of coma. W. T. Longstreth, Jr., Thomas S. Inui, Leonard A. Cobb, and Michael K. Copass (Univ. of Washington) undertook a retrospective cohort study of the neurologic sequelae of out-of-hospital cardiac arrest in 459 consecutive patients who were resuscitated and admitted to hospital during a 10-year period. Only episodes of ventricular fibrillation or asystole were included. All patients had global brain ischemia with cessation of blood flow to the brain. Awakening was defined as comprehensible speech or the ability to follow commands.

Sixty-one percent (279) of the patients awakened, 91 of whom had persistent neurologic deficits. Fifty-nine patients had only cognitive deficits, and 32 had both motor and cognitive deficits. Patients who never awakened died after a median of 3½ days. The longer a patient survived without awakening, the less chance he had of ever awakening or awakening without deficit. Fourteen patients who awakened after 4 days had some deficit, and 6 who awakened after 14 days had severe deficits.

These findings indicate that neurologic sequelae are common in persons who awaken after being resuscitated from out-of-hospital arrest. The risk of neurologic sequelae will increase as more patients

---

(28–8) Ann. Intern. Med. 98:588–592, May 1983.

are successfully resuscitated, confronting families and society with therapeutic, ethical, and economic problems. Until specific treatment is available, the control of neurologic sequelae resulting from out-of-hospital cardiac arrest will depend on efficient paramedic systems and training the public to initiate cardiopulmonary resuscitation.

▶ [Gulati et al.[21] reported a success rate of 17% in elderly patients subjected to cardiopulmonary resuscitation (CPR) in the hospital, which compares well with rates reported in younger patients. It is interesting that advanced age in itself is not a major determinant of the outcome of attempted CPR. It is the nature of the arrest episode, the underlying disease, and the speed with which resuscitation is instituted that is a far better predictor of outcome than chronological age.

However, the important question remains: Should CPR be attempted in every patient who develops cardiopulmonary arrest in the hospital? If not, under what conditions should it be withheld?[22] There are four potential reasons for limiting treatment: *(1)* the patient declines CPR before the arrest; *(2)* the treatment is deemed to be futile; *(3)* the costs are too great; or *(4)* the quality of life is unacceptable. The latter two are, of course, in a very gray area. Bedell et al.[23] carried out a prospective study of in-hospital CPR in 294 patients. Only 14% were discharged from the hospital, and 11% were alive 6 months later. Predictors of negative outcome included resuscitation lasting more than 15 minutes or the presence of the following conditions before arrest: oliguria, acute stroke, sepsis, metastatic cancer, or pneumonia. In patients with hypotension, renal failure, or left ventricular dysfunction with an S3 gallop and those who were home-bound before hospitalization, survival was less than 5%. However, again, age per se did not affect the outcome.

The problem of when to order "do not resuscitate" also brings up the question of "limited" or "partial" CPR.[24] This usually means that although CPR is initiated, drugs are not administered and intubation is not performed, or resuscitation is stopped after a predetermined period of time. I have found these orders to be very confusing to nurses, house officers, and senior medical staff. These "limited codes" are often improperly intended to reassure the family that "everything was done." It is probable that in the long run sympathetic explanation and active supportive psychological care of the family represent a better solution than a half-hearted therapeutic effort.] ◀

28–9 **Prospective Evaluation and Follow-Up of Patients With Syncope.** A wide spectrum of disorders can result in syncope, but a specific cause is not established in many patients, and information on their prognosis is limited. Wishwa N. Kapoor, Michael Karpf, Sam Wieand, Jacqueline R. Peterson, and Gerald S. Levey (Univ. of Pittsburgh) undertook a prospective follow-up study of 204 patients with syncope, defined as sudden, transient loss of consciousness and inability to maintain postural tone, not compatible with seizure disorder, vertigo, coma, shock, or other states of altered consciousness. Patients requiring cardioversion and those with a postictal state or aura were excluded.

The mean age was 56 years. A single syncopal episode had occurred in 65 patients. The history and physical examination revealed the cause of syncope in 52 of the 204 patients, and prolonged ECG monitoring showed a cause in 29. Electrophysiologic studies indicated inducible ventricular tachycardia in 3 of the 23 patients examined. Cardiac catheterization was done in 25 patients, cerebral angiography in 11, and electroencephalography in 101. Also, 65 patients had computed tomographic scanning, but in no case was a cause of syncope established. A cause was found in a total of 107 patients (table). Sixteen patients died suddenly during a mean follow-up of 10.6 months;

(28–9) N. Engl. J. Med. 309:197–204, July 28, 1983.

CAUSES OF SYNCOPE

CAUSE	NO. OF PATIENTS	CAUSE	NO. OF PATIENTS
Cardiovascular	53	Noncardiovascular	54
Ventricular tachycardia	20	Vasodepressor syncope	9
Sick-sinus syndrome	10	Situational syncope	15
Bradycardia	2	Drug-induced syncope	6
Supraventricular tachycardia	3	Orthostatic hypotension	14
Complete heart block	3	Transient ischemic attacks	3
Mobitz II atrioventricular block	2	Subclavian-steal syndrome	2
		Seizure disorder	3
Pacemaker malfunction	1	Vagal reaction with trigeminal neuralgia	1
Carotid-sinus syncope	1		
Aortic stenosis	5	Conversion reaction	1
Myocardial infarction	2	Unknown	97
Dissecting aortic aneurysm	1		
Pulmonary embolus	1		
Pulmonary hypertension	2		

(Courtesy of Kapoor, W.N., et al.: N. Engl. J. Med. 309:197–204, July 28, 1983; reprinted by permission of The New England Journal of Medicine.

in 11 of these a cardiovascular cause of syncope was identified. The cumulative mortality at 12 months was 14%; it was 30% in patients with a cardiovascular cause of syncope. This causation was an important risk factor even after adjustment for age and previously identified cardiac risk factors.

These findings suggest that the cause of syncope often is not established. Cardiovascular causes were found in about 25% of the present series, and noncardiovascular causes in a similar proportion. Mortality was significantly greater in the former group.

▶ [It is interesting that following a careful history and physical examination, a series of cardiac tests, i.e., electrocardiography, electrocardiographic monitoring, electrophysiologic studies, and cardiac catheterization, most frequently provided a diagnosis of previously unexplained syncope. The electroencephalogram and computed tomographic scan of the head, frequently used in the workup of patients with syncope, provided little useful information. Among the cardiac diagnoses were frequent sinus arrest, recurrent ventricular tachycardia, atrial fibrillation with extremely slow ventricular rates, symptomatic and sustained supraventricular tachycardia, complete heart block, and pacemaker malfunction. The survival of patients with syncope that was proved to be due to a noncardiovascular cause or that remained of unknown origin was good and averaged 90% over a 12-month period.

A common cause of hypotension, and therefore syncope, in the elderly was recently described by Lipsitz et al.[25] They evaluated the effects of a meal on systolic blood pressure and heart rate in elderly subjects with and without a history of syncope. Thirty-five minutes after a meal, systolic blood pressure had declined by an average maximum of 25 mm Hg, presumably as a result of impaired baroreflexes. Thus, postprandial reduction in blood pressure may be responsible for syncope as well as other forms of symptomatic hypotension in the elderly.] ◀

28–10 **Cardiac Sequelae of Acute Stroke.** Acute stroke has been associated with various cardiac abnormalities, and it has been proposed

(28–10) Stroke 13:838–842, Nov./Dec. 1982.

RESULTS OF 24-HOUR HOLTER MONITOR ECG RECORDING

				No. arrhythmia hours					
						Heart block			
	n	V. tach*	Couplet*	VPB* 5+/min	VPB 1–4/min	1°	2°*	3°*	No. Serious arrhythmia hours
Strokes	100	5	33	167	504	95	3	17	225
Controls	50	—	4	48	218	24	—	—	52
Matched strokes	50	1	6	72	280	4	1	2	82

*Serious arrhythmias.

V. tach indicates ventricular tachycardia; *couplet* indicates 2 consecutive ventricular beats; and *VPB* indicates ventricular premature beats.

(Courtesy of Myers, M.G., et al.: Stroke 13:838–842, Nov.–Dec. 1982; by permission of the American Heart Association, Inc.)

that acute stroke may increase sympathetic activity, resulting in ECG abnormalities and myocardial cell necrosis. Martin G. Myers, John W. Norris, Vladimir C. Hachinski, Michael E. Weingert and Michael J. Sole (Toronto) evaluated the cardiac status of 100 stroke patients admitted to an intensive care unit in 1977–1980, and 50 control patients with diagnoses other than stroke or transient ischemic attacks. Patients receiving β-blocking or antiarrhythmic drugs or digitalis were excluded. Continuous ECG recordings were obtained for 24 hours within 48 hours of admission to the stroke unit. Serum cardiac enzyme levels and plasma norepinephrine levels were measured within 48 hours of admission. Sixty-four patients had hemispheric infarction, 26 had brainstem infarction, and 10 had intracerebral hemorrhage.

The stroke patients had more cardiac arrhythmias of all types than the control subjects (table.) Both serious ventricular ectopic activity and heart block were more frequent in the stroke group. In a few patients, the excess of serious arrhythmias could not be attributed to the presence of frequent rhythm disturbances. The excess also was not related to coexisting heart disease. Patients with hemispheric infarction had more serious arrhythmias than those with brainstem infarction. Age also was a significant factor in the occurrence of serious arrhythmias. Plasma norepinephrine levels were elevated in the stroke group. Blood pressure and heart rate were slightly elevated in this group. Patients with high norepinephrine levels did not exhibit an increase in cardiac arrhythmias. Serious arrhythmias were equally prevalent in patients with high and those with normal serum creatine kinase values.

These findings favor an association between cerebral infarction and abnormal cardiac function. The cardiac abnormalities seen in stroke patients may be caused by the cerebral event, rather than simply reflecting coexisting heart disease.

▶ [The results of this study indicate that acute stroke may cause arrhythmias and myocardial necrosis, the latter through stroke-induced increases in sympathetic tone. An important finding is that the cardiac arrhythmias were not related to the presence of the underlying cardiac disease, suggesting that the stroke itself may have been responsible. It is likely that the myocardial damage resulted from increases in sympathetic tone, since elevated plasma norepinephrine values were associated with abnormally high creatine kinase concentrations.

The prognosis in patients with stroke was studied by Miah et al.,[26] who found that it should be based not only on neurological findings but on also the presence or absence of cardiac disease. ST-segment deviation and bundle branch block were markers of a poor prognosis. Thus patients with pathologic ST segments had a mortality of 54%, whereas those with normal ST segments had a mortality of 29%. Patients with bundle branch block had a mortality of 50%, and those without bundle branch block had a mortality of 19%. These simple electrocardiographic findings, as well as the clinical diagnosis of heart failure, were of prognostic importance.] ◀

Chapter 28 References

1. Schneider J.F., Thomas H.E., Kreger B.E., et al.: Newly acquired right bundle branch block: the Framingham Study. *Ann. Intern. Med.* 92:37, 1980.
2. Edmunds R.E.: An epidemiologic assessment of bundle branch block. *Circulation* 34:1081, 1966.
3. Johnson R.L., Averill K.H., Lamb L.E.: Electrocardiographic findings in 67,375 asymptomatic subjects. VI. Right bundle branch block. *Am. J. Cardiol.* 6:143, 1960.
4. Gloor H.O., Urthaler F., James T.N.: Acute effects of amiodarone upon the canine sinus node and atrioventricuar junctional region. *J. Clin. Invest.* 71:1457, 1983.
5. Saksena S., Rothbart S.T., Cappello G.: Chronic effects of amiodarone in patients with refractory ventricular tachycardia. *Int. J. Cardiol.* 3:339, 1983.
6. Rotmensch H.H., Belhassen B., Ferguson R.K.: Amiodarone: benefits and risks in perspective. *Am. Heart J.* 104:1117, 1982.
7. Fogoros R.N., Anderson K.P., Winkle R.A., et al.: Amiodarone: clinical efficacy and toxicity in 96 patients with recurrent, drug-refractory arrhythmias. *Circulation* 68:88, 1983.
8. McGovern B., Garan H., Kelly E., et al.: Adverse reactions during treatment with amiodarone hydrochloride. *Br. Med. J.* 287:175, 1983.
9. Sudrez L.D., Poderoso J.J., Elsner B., et al.: Subacute pneumopathy during amiodarone therapy. *Chest* 83:566, 1983.
10. Jaggarao N.S.V., Grundy E.N., Sheldon J., et al.: The effects of amiodarone on thyroid function. *Postgrad. Med. J.* 58:693, 1982.
11. Martinez-Arizala A., Sobol S.M., McCarty G.E., et al.: Amiodarone neuropathy. *Neurology* 33:643, 1983.
12. Ingram D.V., Jaggarao N.S.V., Chamberlain D.A.: Ocular changes resulting from therapy with amiodarone. *Br. J. Ophthalmol.* 66:676, 1982.
13. Murphy D.J. Jr., Bremner W.F., Haber E., et al.: Massive digoxin poisoning treated with Fab fragments of digoxin-specific antibodies. *Pediatrics* 70:472, 1982.
14. Zucker A.R., Lacina S.J., DasGupta D.S., et al.: Fab fragments of digoxin-specific antibodies used to reverse ventricular fibrillation induced by digoxin ingestion in a child. *Pediatrics* 70:468, 1982.
15. Hess T., Riesen W., Scholtysik G., et al.: Digitoxin intoxication with severe thrombocytopenia: reversal by digoxin-specific antibodies. *Eur. J. Clin. Invest.* 13:159, 1983.
16. Kilgore T.L., Lehmann C.R.: Treatment of digoxin intoxication with colestipol. *South. Med. J.* 75:1259, 1982.
17. Reissell, P., Manninen V.: Effect of administration of activated charcoal and fibre on absorption, excretion and steady state blood levels of digoxin and digitoxin: evidence for intestinal secretion of the glycosides. *Acta Med. Scand.* 668:88, 1982.

18. Cohen L., Kitzes R.: Magnesium sulfate and digitalis-toxic arrhythmias. *JAMA* 249:2808, 1983.
19. Greenspon A.J., Schaal S.F.: The "holiday heart": electrophysiologic studies of alcohol effects in alcoholics. *Ann. Intern. Med.* 98:135, 1983.
20. Lambert E.C., Menon V.A., Wagner H.R., et al.: Sudden unexpected death from cardiovascular disease in children. *Am. J. Cardiol.* 34:89, 1974.
21. Gulati R.S., Bhan G.L., Horan M.A.: Cardiopulmonary resuscitation of old people. *Lancet* 2:267, 1983.
22. Fox M., Lipton H.L.: The decision to perform cardiopulmonary resuscitation. *N. Engl. J. Med.* 309:607, 1983.
23. Bedell S.E., Delbanco T.L., Cook E.F., et al.: Survival after cardiopulmonary resuscitation in the hospital. *N. Engl. J. Med.* 309:501, 1983.
24. Lo B., Steinbrook R.L.: Deciding whether to resuscitate. *Arch. Intern. Med.* 143:1561, 1983.
25. Lipsitz L.A., Nyquist R.P. Jr., Wei J.Y., et al.: Postprandial reduction in blood pressure in the elderly. *N. Engl. J. Med.* 309:81, 1983.
26. Miah K., von Arbin M., Britton M., et al.: Prognosis in acute stroke with special reference to some cardiac factors. *J. Chron. Dis.* 36:279, 1983.

29. Heart Failure

29–1 **Evaluation of New Bipyridine Inotropic Agent, Milrinone, in Patients With Severe Congestive Heart Failure.** Milrinone is a bipyridine derivative having much more inotropic potency than amrinone does on a weight basis; it does not cause fever or thrombocytopenia in animals or in normal persons. Donald S. Baim, Arthur V. McDowell, Joseph Cherniles, Ernest S. Monrad, J. Anthony Parker, Jerome Edelson, Eugene Braunwald, and William Grossman evaluated the intravenous and oral forms of milrinone in 20 patients with severe congestive heart failure who were followed up for as long as 11 months. The 14 men and 6 women had a mean age of 61 years. All had New York Heart Association class III or IV congestive heart failure refractory to standard medical therapy. Thirteen patients had ischemic cardiomyopathy, 5 had idiopathic cardiomyopathy, and 2 had cardiomyopathy combined with valvular heart disease. Catheterization was carried out in conjunction with infusion of 25 μg/kg of milrinone at a rate of 100 μg/second. Some patients received repeat infusions of 50 μg/kg and then a 24-hour infusion of milrinone at a median rate of 0.33 μg/kg/minute. Patients then received the drug orally in doses of 5–7.5 mg every 4–6 hours.

All patients experienced acute hemodynamic improvement in response to milrinone infusion. The left ventricular (LV) end-diastolic pressure fell by a third, and the cardiac index rose by about half after a median infusion of 75 μg/kg. Systemic vascular resistance declined by about a third. Beneficial hemodynamic effects were sustained throughout the 24-hour infusion of milrinone. No adverse effects were noted. The 12 patients who continued with oral treatment continued to experience improvement in the signs and symptoms of heart failure and in exercise tolerance with no serious side effects. Nuclide ventriculography indicated a 27% rise in resting LV ejection fraction in 10 patients studied after 6 months or more of milrinone therapy.

Milrinone is active both intravenously and orally in patients with severe refractory congestive heart failure. It appears to act through a combination of enhanced myocardial contractility and peripheral vasodilation.

▶ [Amrinone, the prototype new bipyridine inotropic agent, was discussed in the 1980 YEAR BOOK (p. 327) as well as in the 1981 YEAR BOOK (p. 298). This remarkable drug, a nonglycoside, nonsympathomimetic agent, was shown to be a potent inotropic agent in normal subjects as well as in patients with severe heart failure and also to be a balanced systemic vasodilator, i.e., one which acts upon both arterioles and veins. It was beneficial in short-term studies in patients with refractory congestive

(29–1) N. Engl. J. Med. 309:748–756, Sept. 29, 1983.

heart failure. however, with chronic oral administration, adverse effects including nausea, vomiting, fever, and thrombocytopenia were frequent, and they have limited use of this drug.[1]

Milrinone is a congener of amrinone. (Locally we refer to it as "son of amrinone.") It has a hemodynamic spectrum indistinguishable from amrinone, i.e., it is a potent inotrope and a balanced vasodilator. However, its half-life is shorter (approximately 2 hours vs. 6 hours). Therefore, treatment given four, or even five, times a day in patients with severe heart failure is necessary. The only major difference is that it is much more potent than amrinone on a per-milligram basis, and hence the side effects, which are probably not related to the hemodynamic effects of the drug, have not been observed.

Maskin et al.[2] have described the hemodynamic benefits of milrinone. They observed no attentuation of the effectiveness with six consecutive doses and reported that maximal oxygen uptake was increased by the drug. They also found that withdrawal of milrinone resulted in rapid clinical and hemodynamic deterioration, which was reversed by reinstitution of the drug.

At the time of this writing, I believe that milrinone, which is under active investigation in our hospitals, is a very promising drug for the treatment of chronic congestive heart failure. I have yet to see a patient with chronic heart failure who did not show a favorable hemodynamic response *initially*. Of course, the drug does not confer immortality, and with progression of the underlying disease, the patient may require at first increasing doses of the drug and may ultimately decompensate even in the presence of large doses of milrinone. In the few instances when patients deteriorated on milrinone and we suspected that it might be caused by the drug and therefore withdrew it, we noted that the patients' deterioration accelerated.

A number of important questions remain. First of all, Does milrinone actually prolong life? I suspect that it does, but one could argue that stimulating a failing heart might actually accelerate deterioration and shorten life! A second important question is, What are the effects of milrinone in patients with less severe heart failure? Perhaps it is in this group that one might expect the greatest prolongation of survival. I think that these important questions can be answered only by means of a prospective randomized study in which milrinone is compared with standard therapy.

In the past few years, a number of other new inotropic agents have been developed. Although their chemical structure bears little resemblance to amrinone or milrinone, they also are nonsympathomimetic, noncardiac glycoside inotropes with concomitant vasodilator actions.[3–6] It has been suggested that the fundamental mechanism of action of these drugs is to inhibit intracellular phosphodiesterase, thereby reducing the breakdown and increasing the intracellular concentration of cyclic AMP, the so-called second messenger, which exerts a positive inotropic action on the heart, presumably by increasing intracellular calcium concentration.] ◄

29–2 **Regression of Myocardial Cellular Hypertrophy With Vasodilator Therapy in Chronic Congestive Heart Failure Associated With Idiopathic Dilated Cardiomyopathy.** Vasodilator therapy is an accepted means of managing patients with heart failure refractory to digitalis and diuretics, but its effects on myocardial morphology are unknown. Donald V. Unverferth, John P. Mehegan, Raymond D. Magorien, Barbara J. Unverferth, and Carl V. Leier (Ohio State Univ.) examined the effects of oral isosorbide dinitrate, hydralazine, and their combination on myocardial cell size in 37 men and 12 women with idiopathic dilated cardiomyopathy (IDC) and chronic, severe congestive heart failure. Average age was 57 years. Three patients were in New York Heart Association functional class II, 34 in class III, and 12 in class IV. Patients received 40 mg of isosorbide dinitrate orally, or hydralazine, 1 mg/kg, or the combined drugs, on successive days to identify adverse reactions. They then received 160

(29–2) Am. J. Cardiol. 51:1392–1398, May 1, 1983.

mg of isosorbide dinitrate or 3 mg/kg of hydralazine daily, or a placebo, or combined treatment for 3 months before endomyocardial biopsy was repeated. Thirty-three patients completed the study.

There were 5 deaths during the study. The echographic percent change in left ventricular diameter and the systolic ratio of preejection period to left ventricular ejection time both improved significantly in the groups given hydralazine and combined treatment. The pulmonary wedge and mean pulmonary artery pressures, as well as pulmonary vascular resistance, decreased significantly in the isosorbide dinitrate and combined treatment groups. Systemic vascular resistance decreased, and cardiac index increased with hydralazine therapy and with combined treatment. Myocardial cell diameter decreased with hydralazine alone and with combined treatment. Changes in cell diameter correlated with cardiac index and systemic vascular resistance, but not with changes in pulmonary capillary wedge pressure or pulmonary vascular resistance.

In patients with IDC, treatment of refractory heart failure with hydralazine or hydralazine combined with isosorbide dinitrate leads to a persistent augmentation of cardiac function and improved myocardial cellular morphology. Regression of myocardial hypertrophy is potentially beneficial through a reduced intercapillary distance and an increase in capillary density, but any long-term effects on myocardial function or mortality remain to be determined.

▶ [In the past, it had been shown that aortic valve replacement in aortic stenosis or treatment of hypertension will cause the regression of hypertrophy, but this study by Unverferth et al. is the first demonstration that vasodilator therapy of congestive cardiomyopathy may also result in the regression of hypertrophy. The hypertrophied ventricle is often less efficient than the normal ventricle; the intercapillary distance increases with potential hypoxia of cells or portions of the cell, and there may be a reduction in the ratio of mitochondria to myofibrils, and the adenosine triphosphate (ATP) concentration may decline. As a consequence, the hypertrophied myocardium is not fully oxygenated, and ATP concentration is reduced, as is the force generated by the myocardium per unit of ATP consumed.] ◀

29–3 **Intermittent, Continuous Outpatient Dobutamine Infusion in the Management of Congestive Heart Failure.** Mark M. Applefeld, Kathryn A. Newman, William R. Grove, Frederick J. Sutton, David S. Roffman, William P. Reed, and Steven E. Linberg (Univ. of Maryland) describe the use of outpatient dobutamine infusions administered with a small, portable infusion pump in 3 patients with intractable congestive heart failure (CHF). Dobutamine was given through an indwelling venous catheter (Hickman) surgically inserted in the external jugular vein and located proximal to the right atrium. The distal end of the catheter exited in the parasternal area. Patients were taught proper catheter care, including techniques for daily irrigation with saline solution and heparin (total of 1,500 units) and aseptic connection of the catheter to the infusion pump. Infusion rates were calibrated to deliver 2 ml/hour. Development of tolerance to dobutamine was avoided by giving 24-hour infusions twice weekly.

With this therapy, left ventricular function improved and CHF re-

---

(29–3) Am. J. Cardiol. 51:455–458, February 1983.

solved in each patient. Except for 3 mild infections around the catheter exit site, there were no complications of this therapy in 58 cumulative patient-weeks. Patient acceptance of the catheter and infusion pump was excellent. Given a willing patient in whom preload and postload reducing agents have been unsuccessful for treatment of chronic CHF, continuous dobutamine infusion should be considered.

▶ [One of the problems with the use of sympathomimetics as inotropic agents for the treatment of chronic congestive heart failure is the development of tolerance, presumably due to "down-regulation" of myocardial β-receptors. Therefore, it has been proposed that *intermittent* treatment with sympathomimetics might be useful in the treatment of advanced heart failure. Of the available sympathomimetics, dobutamine is perhaps the most useful, since it improves ventricular performance and increases cardiac output and decreases left ventricular filling pressure and systemic vascular resistance without causing a significant increase in heart rate.

Unverferth et al.[7] have described a prolonged subjective clinical remission following a 3-day infusion of dobutamine in patients with nonischemic congestive cardiomyopathy. One of the possible mechanisms of action of this drug may be to augment subendocardial blood flow. They observed that it improved myocardial energetics as represented in the adenosine triphosphate–creatine ratio in myocardial biopsies, with decreased swelling of subendocardial myochondria.

A few comments about other drugs in the treatment of heart failure: In patients with left ventricular failure due to acute myocardial infarction, an infusion of nitroglycerin and dobutamine resulted in marked lowering of the left ventricular filling pressure and elevation of the cardiac index with maintenance of arterial pressure. This would appear to be a useful combination for the short-term treatment of acute heart failure.[8] There is continuing interest in the use of vasodilators in the treatment of heart failure. Among the new vasodilators, there is endralazine,[9] a potent drug of the hydralazine class, which causes a substantial increase in cardiac output but which does not appear to result in drug-induced systemic lupus erythematosus. The angiotensin-converting enzyme inhibitors, captopril,[10, 11] and one that is not yet on the market, enalapril,[12] are two important new entries into the vasodilator field. These drugs cause a significant reduction of systemic vascular resistance and pulmonary wedge pressure associated with elevations of cardiac index and a marked reduction of plasma aldosterone. Hemodynamic improvement is maintained with chronic therapy.

At the present time, vasodilator therapy of chronic congestive heart failure is usually begun only when patients have remained or become symptomatic despite treatment by means of salt restriction, diuretics, and cardiac glycosides. There is currently increasing interest in the possibility that vasodilator therapy may be useful earlier in the course of heart failure and may actually prolong life when it is begun before the development of decompensation. See the abstract below.] ◀

29–4 **Left Ventricular End-Systolic Stress-Shortening and Stress-Length Relations in Humans: Normal Values and Sensitivity to Inotropic State.** There is experimental evidence that the extent of left ventricular fiber shortening is determined by both wall stress at end-systole and the contractile state. Kenneth M. Borow, Laurence H. Green, William Grossman, and Eugene Braunwald (Harvard Med. School) examined the relationship between these variables by M-mode echography, phonocardiography, and carotid pulse tracings in 26 healthy subjects, 15 females and 11 males, aged 8–41 years. After premedication with atropine, methoxamine was infused at a rate of 25 μg/kg/minute up to 1 mg/minute to alter afterload. Ten subjects subsequently received dobutamine at a rate of 5 μg/kg/minute to increase contractility.

(29–4) Am. J. Cardiol. 50:1301–1308, December 1982.

The relation between end-systolic stress and percent internal dimension shortening was inversely linear. Dobutamine led to a higher percent fractional shortening for a given end-systolic stress. In individual subjects, dobutamine infusion regularly shifted stress-dimension lines to the right compared with their baseline position, resulting in a smaller end-systolic dimension for any end-systolic wall stress.

Left ventricular end-systolic wall stress and percent fractional shortening are inversely and linearly related. Their relationship can be accurately assessed noninvasively. The end-systolic stress-shortening relation is highly sensitive to alterations in the inotropic state of the left ventricle. The end-systolic stress-dimension relation is a less sensitive value. This approach could be useful in following asymptomatic patients with valvular heart disease, in whom deteriorating contractility often precedes the development of symptoms. It may aid decisions on early operation. The method also could be used to assess potentially cardiotoxic drugs and drugs purported to have positive inotropic effects.

▶ [The assessment of intrinsic left ventricular contractile state, i.e., of myocardial contractility, is challenging when invasive techniques (angiocardiography and cardiac catheterization) are employed. It is even more difficult using noninvasive methods. However, the latter are often required if one is to follow a patient sequentially or to determine a dose-response curve to a drug or other intervention. In particular, it may be important to determine whether a given agent exerts a beneficial or deleterious effect in patients with congestive heart failure.

Contractility can be expressed as left ventricular fiber shortening at any given level of wall stress. It can be determined by the method described above, which is entirely noninvasive and involves only echocardiography and indirect pulse tracings. Wall stress is estimated from the thickness of the ventricular wall (determined echocardiographically) and the intraventricular pressure (estimated from a sphygmomanometric cuff). A range of wall stresses is produced by an infusion of methoxamine and the relation between end-systolic stress and shortening is determined. This relation provides a measure of myocardial contractility.] ◀

Chapter 29 References

1. Dunkman W.B., et al.: Adverse effects of long-term amrinone administration in congestive heart failure. *Am. Heart J.* 105:861, 1983.
2. Maskin C.S., et al.: Sustained hemodynamic and clinical effects of a new cardiotonic agent, WIN 47203, in patients with severe congestive heart failure. *Circulation* 677:1065, 1983.
3. Thormann J., Schlepper M., Kramer W., et al.: Effects of AR-L 115 BS (Sulmazol), a cardiotonic agent, in coronary artery disease: improved ventricular wall motion, increased pump function and abolition of pacing-induced ischemia. *J. Am. Coll. Cardiol.* 2:332, 1983.
4. Solaro R.J., Ruegg J.C.: Stimulation of Ca^{++} binding and ATPase activity of dog cardiac myofibrils by AR-L 115BS, a novel cardiotonic agent. *Circulation Res.* 51:290, 1982.
5. Uretsky B.F., Generalovich T., Reddy P.S., et al.: The acute hemodynamic effects of a new agent, MDL 17,043, in the treatment of congestive heart failure. *Circulation* 67:832, 1983.
6. Kino M., Hirota Y., Yamamoto S., et al.: Cardiovascular effects of a newly synthesized cardiotonic agent (TA-064) on normal and diseased hearts. *Am. J. Cardiol.* 51:802, 1983.

7. Unverferth D.V., et al.: The hemodynamic and metabolic advantages gained by a three-day infusion of dobutamine in patients with congestive cardiomyopathy. *Am. Heart J.* 106:29, 1983.
8. Awan N.A., et al.: Effect of combined nitroglycerin and dobutamine infusion in left ventricular dysfunction. *Am. Heart J.* 106:35, 1983.
9. Quyyumi A.A., et al.: Acute hemodynamic effects of endralazine: a new vasodilator for chronic refractory congestive heart failure. *Am. J. Cardiol.* 51:1353, 1983.
10. Wenting G.J., et al.: Effects of captopril in acute and chronic heart failure: correlations with plasma levels of nonadrenaline, renin, and aldosterone. *Br. Heart J.* 49:65, 1983.
11. Schanzenbacher P., Liebau G.: Effect of captopril on left ventricular dynamics in patients with chronic left ventricular volume overload. *Klin. Wochenschr.* 61:343, 1983.
12. Cody R.J., et al.: Evaluation of a long-acting converting enzyme inhibitor (enalapril) for the treatment of chronic congestive heart failure. *J. Am. Coll. Cardiol.* 1:1154, 1983.

30. Other Topics

30–1 **Evaluation of Right-Heart Catheterization in the Critically Ill Patient Without Acute Myocardial Infarction.** Catheterization of the right side of the heart is now widely used to monitor patients with critical illnesses other than acute myocardial infarction. Alfred F. Connors, Jr., D. Robert McCaffree, and Barry A. Gray (Univ. of Oklahoma) prospectively evaluated 62 right heart catheterizations done in critically ill patients who had no evidence of recent acute myocardial infarction. The patients generally were severely ill and had deteriorated rapidly or had failed to respond to appropriate management. The 56 patients included 33 men and 23 women with an average age of 56 years. The most common disorders were hypotension, respiratory failure, congestive heart failure, sepsis, and pulmonary edema. No patients had had acute infarction in the previous 2 weeks. All had some degree of hemodynamic instability.

The rate of accurate predictions of right atrial, mean pulmonary artery, and capillary wedge pressures and cardiac index, though better than random, was quite low (Fig 30–1). The predictions of attending physicians and critical-care fellows were no more accurate than those of house staff and medical students. Catheterization data led to a change in therapy in about half the cases. Most often a drug was begun or stopped or the rate of fluid administration was altered on the basis of the catheterization findings. Complications related to catheterization were infrequent. Only 1 patient required antiarrhythmic therapy.

Catheterization of the right side of the heart appears indicated for severely ill, hemodynamically unstable patients without acute myocardial infarction if they fail to respond to appropriate treatment after careful clinical evaluation. The information obtained may lead to a more accurate hemodynamic assessment and, frequently, a change in treatment.

▶ [Although flow-directed right heart catheterization with a balloon catheter (Swan-Ganz) is standard practice for the management of complicated patients with acute myocardial infarction, this technique is equally useful in the hemodynamic assessment of critically ill patients without myocardial infarction. The present study makes it clear that in such patients pulmonary capillary wedge pressure and cardiac index could be predicted less accurately than in patients with acute myocardial infarction. Physical findings that correlate reasonably well with hemodynamics in a relatively clear-cut syndrome, i.e., myocardial infarction, may not correlate well in the presence of multiple organ system failure.

An interesting new technique which might be useful in the monitoring of critically ill patients involves the use of a flexible fiber-optic catheter inserted into the pulmo-

(30–1) N. Engl. J. Med. 308:263–267, Feb. 3, 1983.

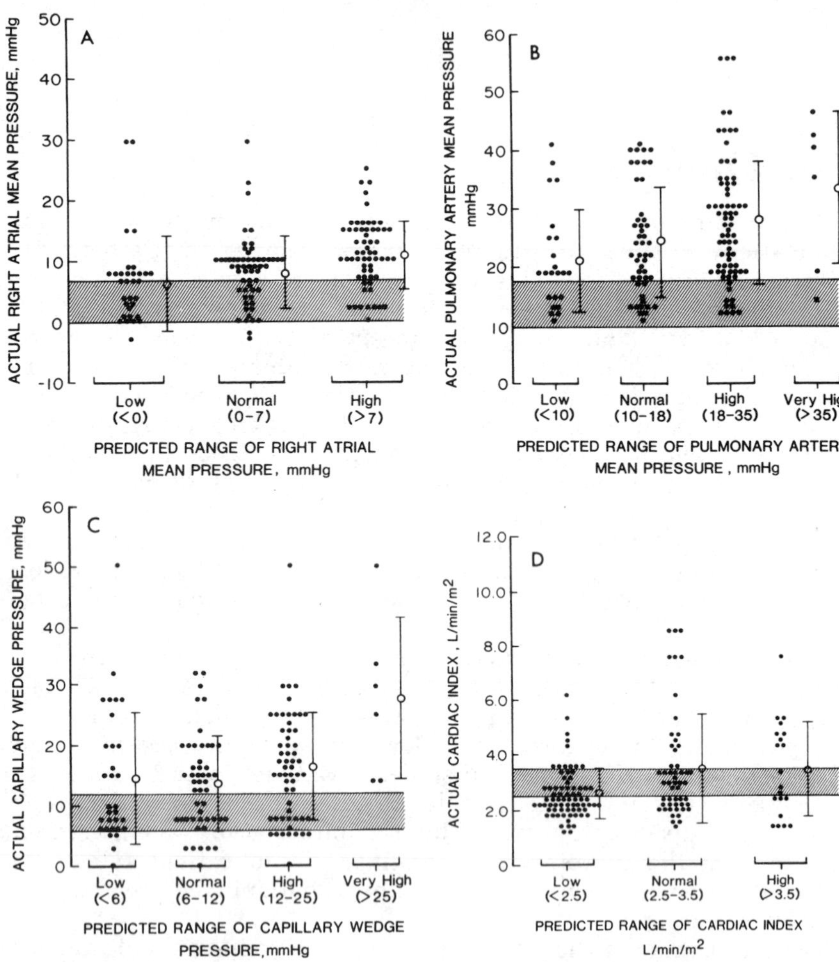

Fig 30–1.—Comparison of actual and predicted values in 56 patients undergoing 62 catheterizations of the right side of the heart. There were 150 sets of predictions. The range predicted for the patient is plotted against the value actually measured for the 4 variables: **A,** right atrial mean pressure; **B,** mean pulmonary artery pressure; **C,** capillary wedge pressure; and **D,** cardiac index. The mean ±SD of the actual measurements is shown for each predicted range. The values defining each predicted range were those provided the clinician on the study form. (Courtesy of Connors, A.F., Jr., et al.: N. Engl. J. Med. 308:263–267, Feb. 3, 1983; reprinted by permission of The New England Journal of Medicine.)

nary artery.[1] This device permits the continuous in vivo measurement of mixed venous oxygen saturation and thereby can be used as an indicator of the adequacy of tissue oxygenation.] ◀

30–2 **Diagnostic Accuracy of Indium-111 Platelet Scintigraphy in Identifying Left Ventricular Thrombi.** Scintigraphy with ^{111}In-labeled platelets has been used to identify intravascular thrombi at various sites. Michael D. Ezekowitz, Robert D. Burrow, Paul W. Heath,

(30–2) Am. J. Cardiol. 51:1712–1716, June 1983.

Terri Streitz, Eileen O. Smith, and Donald E. Parker (Univ. of Oklahoma) attempted to define the optimal imaging-time window after injection of labeled platelets to detect left ventricular (LV) thrombi, and to identify the most useful imaging views. Analysis was made of 662 images obtained from 38 patients with LV aneurysms, 23 with mitral valve disease, and 3 with acute myocardial infarction who later died. Imaging was carried out an average of about a week before surgery or death. A large-field-of-view gamma camera with a medium-energy collimator was used. Imaging was carried out on the day of injection of the platelet suspension and at least on alternate days thereafter for as long as 6 days. Interpretation of the findings is illustrated in Figure 30–2.

Twelve patients were found at operation or autopsy to have left ventricular thrombi. Diagnostic accuracy was highest at 3–4 days in the anterior and left anterior oblique views. Specificity exceeded 95% at all intervals. Sensitivity was highest in the left anterior oblique view at 3–4 days, when it was 54%. A diagnostic accuracy as high as 90% was obtained when patients with inactive thrombi were excluded. Sensitivity also was enhanced. Overall intraobserver agreement was 91%.

Imaging done with ^{111}In-labeled platelets to detect left ventricular thrombi should be carried out on the day of platelet injection and 3 or 4 days later. At both times, left and right anterior oblique, left

Fig 30–2.—Scintiphotos obtained from 4 different patients 72 hours after injection of platelet suspension. Images are oriented with the top of the image cephalad. Activity in the right lower quadrant is from the spleen and that in the left lower quadrant is from the liver. *Arrows* indicate areas of increased activity within the left ventricle corresponding to typical active thrombi within large anteroapical left ventricular aneurysms. *ANT,* anterior; *LAO,,* left anterior oblique. (Courtesy of Ezekowitz, M.D., et al.: Am. J. Cardiol. 51:1712–1716, June 1983.)

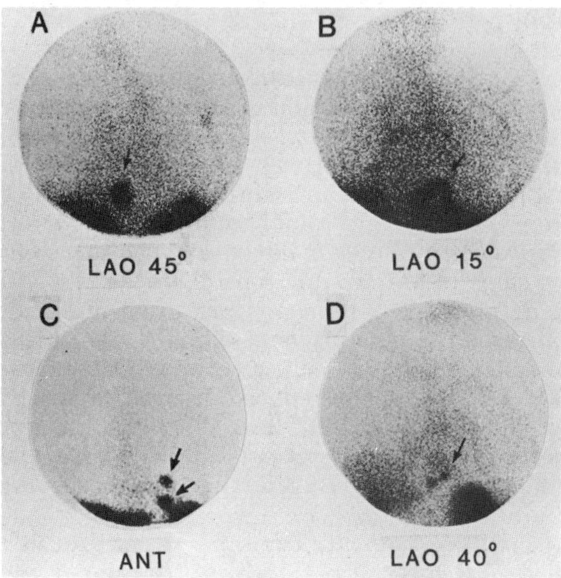

lateral, and anterior views should be obtained, especially following acute myocardial infarction, when multiple sites of thrombosis are a possibility. Images should be interpreted only after a chest roentgenogram has excluded an elevated left hemidiaphragm.

▶ [Bergmann et al.[1] improved on the radioactive indium (^{111}In) platelet method by tagging red blood cells with technetium-99m and using this to correct for activity attributable to circulating platelets. This technique has been utilized for the identification of coronary thrombi produced experimentally[2] and their lysis achieved by means of intracoronary streptokinase.

Besides indium-111 platelet scintigraphy, several other noninvasive techniques have been used to identify left ventricular thrombi. These include two-dimensional echocardiography, which may be used for repeated studies and which has a sensitivity and specificity of 77% and 93%, respectively. Computed tomography has also recently been proposed as a means of identifying left ventricular clot. Visser et al.[3] carried out a prospective study of 96 patients with acute myocardial infarction by means of two-dimensional echocardiography and detected left ventricular thrombi in 18 patients, the majority of which developed within the first four days, despite the fact that the patients had received anticoagulants. All had large anterior wall infarctions complicated by pump failure, but the thrombi did not cause systemic embolization. Thus, left ventricular thrombus is a common, though usually silent, complication of acute anterior wall infarction, even in patients who are treated with anticoagulants.] ◀

30–3 **Marfan Syndrome: Demonstration of Abnormal Elastin in Aorta.** Marfan's syndrome, a prototype of heritable connective tissue disorders, involves aberrations in the extracellular matrix in several organs. The most important complications result from weakness of the aortic structures. Previous biochemical studies suggested collagen aberrations. P. A. Abraham, Andrea J. Perejda, William H. Carnes, and Jouni Uitto examined the biochemical composition of aortic connective tissue from 3 patients who died of vascular complications of Marfan's syndrome. All had a classic form of the disease. Aortae from 8 age-matched controls also were examined.

Abnormal elastic fibers in the aorta of a patient with Marfan's syndrome are shown in Figure 30–3. Values for desmosine and isodesmosine in elastin preparations were reduced in the 3 patients to about 50% of control values. A corresponding increase in lysyl residues was noted. The concentration of elastin per unit dry weight of tissue was reduced in the Marfan's syndrome patients, and the hydroxyproline content of elastin was increased in 2 of them. Alkali treatment solubilized more elastin in Marfan than in control specimens. The concentration and solubility of collagen were unchanged. The genetic types of insoluble collagen and the amino acid composition were the same in Marfan and control aortae.

Cross-linking of aortic elastin appears to be reduced in Marfan's syndrome. A defect in elastin could explain the vascular fragility present in affected patients, which sometimes causes fatal aortic complications. The reasons for the reduced desmosine content and loss of elastin in Marfan aorta are not clear. Marfan's syndrome may develop in a heterogeneous group of patients with different underlying molecular defects affecting collagen, elastin, or other components of the extracellular matrix.

▶ [Marfan's syndrome is characterized by aberrations in the extracellular matrix af-

(30–3) J. Clin. Invest. 70:1245–1252, December 1982.

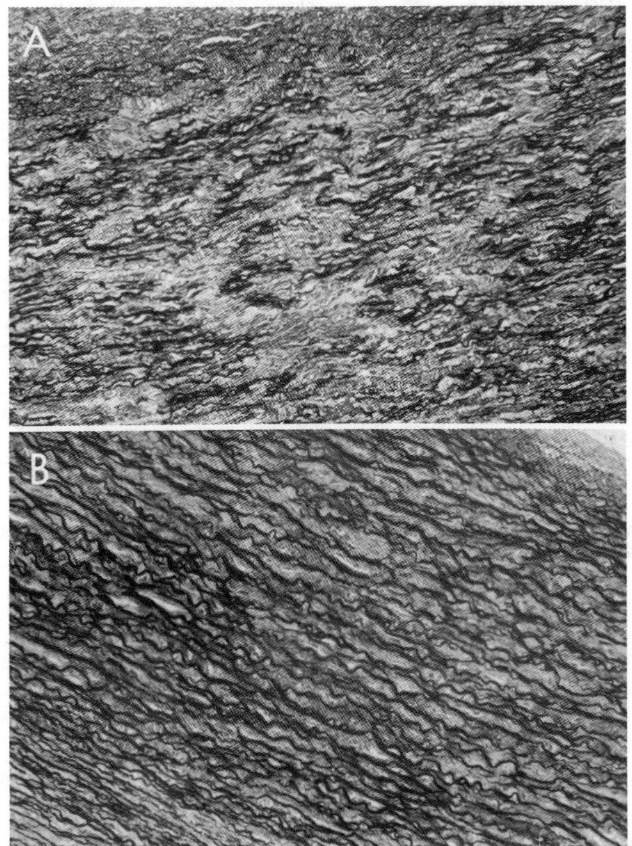

Fig 30–3.—Abnormal elastic fibers in aorta of patient with Marfan's syndrome. **A,** in diseased aorta, fragmentation and patchy loss of elastic fibers can be noted. **B,** normal aorta. Verhoeff-van Gieson; original magnification ×10. (Courtesy of Abraham, P.A., et al.: Reproduced from J. Clin Invest. 70:1245–1252, December 1982, by permission of the American Society for Clinical Investigation.)

fecting several organs, including the ocular, cutaneous, skeletal, and cardiovascular systems. It is transmitted as an autosomal dominant. The most serious complications result from weakness of the aortic wall resulting in aneurysms, dissection, and rupture of the aorta. Previous studies have demonstrated changes in the *collagen* of patients with Marfan's syndrome, i.e., increased solubility suggesting deficient cross-linking, reduced quantities of chemically stable intramolecular cross-links of collagen and an abnormal α_2 chain of type I collagen. The important article abstracted above focuses on abnormal *elastin* in the aorta and demonstrates that the content of elastin in the aorta is reduced and that values for desmosine and isodesmosine are reduced. These biochemical findings can explain the pathologic changes in the aorta, i.e., fragmentation and loss of elastin fibers. Desmosine is a cross-linking compound which is not present in other mammalian proteins and which is derived from the oxidative deamination of lysyl residues; it seems possible that the activity of the enzyme lysyl oxidase is reduced and that this enzymatic defect is one of the fundamental molecular changes in some patients with the Marfan's syndrome.] ◀

Chapter 30 References

1. Bergmann S.R., et al.: Noninvasive detection of coronary thrombi with In-111 platelets: concise communication. *J. Nucl. Med.* 24:130, 1983.
2. Quan S.F.: Mixed venous oxygen. *Am. Fam. Pract.* 27:211, 1983.
3. Visser C.A., et al.: Left ventricular thombus following acute myocardial infarction: a prospective serial echocardiographic study of 96 patients. *Eur. Heart J.* 4:333, 1983.

PART FIVE

THE DIGESTIVE SYSTEM

NORTON J. GREENBERGER, M.D.

31. Esophagus

31–1 **Mechanisms of Gastroesophageal Reflux in Patients With Reflux Esophagitis.** Wylie J. Dodds, John Dent, Walter J. Hogan, James F. Helm, Richard Hauser, Ganesh K. Patel, and Mark S. Egide (Med. College of Wisconsin, Milwaukee) evaluated the mechanisms of gastroesophageal reflux in 10 patients with reflux esophagitis and compared the results with findings from 10 controls.

The patients had more episodes of reflux (35 ± 15 in 12 hours compared with 9 ± 8 in controls, $P < .001$) and a lower pressure of the lower esophageal sphincter (LES; 13 ± 8 mm Hg compared with 29 ± 9 in controls, $P < .001$). There was no significant correlation between mean 12-hour LES pressure and the number of reflux episodes per 12-hour period. The temporal profile of LES pressure in controls and patients showed a significant decrease in pressure lasting for 2 hours after the meal, with a rise above control values during the night (Fig 31–1).

Reflux occurred by 3 different mechanisms: transient complete relaxation of the LES, a transient increase in intraabdominal pressure, or spontaneous free reflux associated with a low resting pressure of the LES. In controls, 94% of reflux episodes were caused by transient sphincter relaxation. By contrast, 65% of reflux episodes in patients

Fig 31–1.—Lower esophageal sphincter *(LES)* pressure during 12 hours of recording in 10 controls and in 10 patients with reflux esophagitis. LES pressure is plotted as mean ±1 S.D. for each hour. Shaded areas represent 1 S.D. For each hour of recording, LES pressure was significantly lower in patients than in controls ($P < 0.05$). For both groups, LES pressure decreased significantly *(asterisks)* below the respective before-meal values for 2 or 3 hours after the meal and increased significantly *(asterisks)* above before-meal values during the night. (Courtesy of Dodds, W.J., et al.: N. Engl. J. Med. 307:1547–1552, Dec. 16, 1982; reprinted by permission of The New England Journal of Medicine.)

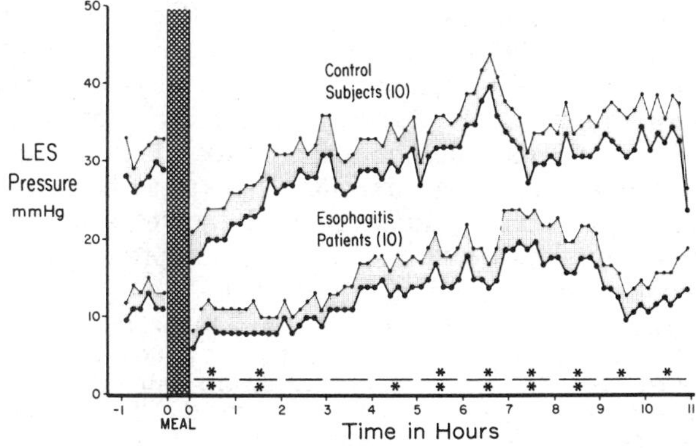

(31–1) N. Engl. J. Med. 307:1547–1552, Dec. 16, 1982.

MECHANISMS RESPONSIBLE FOR EPISODES OF GASTROESOPHAGEAL REFLUX IN 10 CONTROLS AND 10 PATIENTS WITH REFLUX ESOPHAGITIS

	Mechanisms of Gastroesophageal Reflux			Total No. of Reflux Episodes
	Transient LES relaxation	Transient intra-abdominal pressure increase	Spontaneous free reflux	
	number (per cent)			
Controls	84 (94)	4 (5)	1 (1)	89
Patients	228 (65) *	59 (17) *	65 (18) *	352 *

*Significantly different controls ($P < 0.01$).
(Courtesy of Dodds, W.J., et al.: N. Engl. J. Med. 307:1547–1552, Dec. 16, 1982; reprinted by permission of The New England Journal of Medicine.)

accompanied transient LES relaxation, 17% accompanied a transient increase in intraabdominal pressure, and 18% occurred as spontaneous free reflux (table). The predominant reflux mechanism in individual patients varied; some had normal resting LES pressure and reflux that occurred primarily during transient LES relaxation, whereas others with low resting LES pressure had spontaneous free reflux or reflux that occurred during an increase in intraabdominal pressure.

A minimal resting LES pressure in the range of 5–10 mm Hg generally prevented reflux, even during transient increase in intraabdominal pressure, and reflux did not occur during partial LES relaxation. However, many transient complete LES relaxations were not accompanied by detectable acid reflux. Patients had a higher percentage of LES relaxation associated with acid reflux than did controls.

It is concluded that gastroesophageal reflux may occur by any one of several different mechanisms. The common denominator is low sphincter tone, accounted for by either persistently low resting LES pressure or a transient LES relaxation. These findings luminate several troublesome paradoxes, such as how gastroesophageal reflux occurs in normal subjects, why sample values of LES pressure are normal in some patients with reflux esophagitis, why drugs that increase LES pressure do not always decrease reflux, and why it is sometimes impossible to induce gastroesophageal reflux at fluoroscopy.

Although transient LES relaxation appears to be a major mechanism explaining gastroesophageal reflux in some patients with esophagitis, this notion should not be generally accepted until the findings are confirmed in large numbers of patients.

▶ [This study clarifies the mechanisms of gastroesophageal reflux in normal subjects and in patients with reflux esophagitis. It is important to note that reflux occurs frequently in normal subjects and that this is usually due to transient sphincter relaxation. That such reflux infrequently results in symptoms is due to the efficient clearance of esophageal acid in normal subjects.

In this regard, the same group of investigators evaluated factors that affect esophageal acid clearance in normal subjects.[1] A 15-ml bolus of 0.1 N HCl (pH 1.2) was injected into the esophagus, and the subject then swallowed every 30 seconds. Manometric and pH monitoring demonstrated that esophageal acid clearance occurred by a series of step increases in pH, each associated with a swallow-induced peristaltic sequence. Between peristaltic sequences, pH increase was minimal. Saliva stimulation by oral lozenge greatly improved acid clearance, whereas oral aspiration of saliva abolished the step increases in esophageal pH and markedly delayed acid clearance. Similar to the effect of the oral lozenge, bethanechol (5 mg subcutaneously) improved esophageal acid clearance, but this improvement was reversed by oral aspiration of saliva, which markedly delayed acid clearance. A change from the recumbent to the sitting position tended to improve acid clearance slightly, but this improvement was not statistically significant. It is concluded that in normal subjects (1) swallowing carries saliva into the esophagus, and peristalsis empties intraesophageal fluid into the stomach; (2) the neutralization of acid by saliva carried into the esophagus with each swallow accounts for the occurrence of acid clearance by step increases in pH; (3) the improvement in acid clearance with bethanechol is due to saliva stimulation; and (4) gravity contributes little to esophageal acid clearance in the presence of normal peristaltic stripping waves.] ◀

31–2 **Prospective Manometric Evaluation With Pharmacologic Provocation of Patients With Suspected Esophageal Motility Dysfunction.** Patients with suspected esophageal symptoms continue to be a clinical problem, especially when there is major unexplained chest pain. Stanley B. Benjamin, Joel E. Richter, Carmel M. Cordova, Thomas E. Knuff, and Donald O. Castell (Bethesda, Md.) undertook a prospective manometric study of 34 consecutive patients referred with suspected esophageal motility abnormality causing chest pain or dysphagia or both. All patients had clinically noncardiac chest pain, dysphagia without radiographic or endoscopic evidence of obstruction, or both conditions. Manometric studies were carried out in conjunction with hydrogen chloride infusion, edrophonium, pentagastrin, and bethanechol. Criteria for manometric diagnosis are listed in Table 1. Patients were followed up for 18 months.

Eleven patients had normal manometric findings, 10 met criteria for "nutcracker esophagus," and 13 had nonspecific esophageal motility disorders (Table 2). Five of the patients with nonspecific abnormalities had a hypertensive lower esophageal sphincter (LES). Mean baseline LES pressures did not differ significantly in the normal and "nutcracker" groups. Edrophonium reproduced chest pain in 3 of the latter patients; bethanechol, in 1 patient. Achalasia subsequently developed in 2 patients who had a nonspecific abnormality and decreased amplitude of peristalsis. No significant cardiac or neurologic responses occurred with any of the pharmacologic tests.

A large proportion of patients with symptoms of apparent esophageal origin will have abnormal esophageal manometric findings, but the significance of this remains unclear. The "nutcracker" esophagus is the most frequent defect. Although attempts to provoke symptoms with acid or drugs are not generally effective, edrophonium has been the most helpful agent for precipitating motility defects and reproducing the patient's pain pattern. It is suggested as the single best provocative agent for use in symptomatic patients suspected of having abnormal esophageal motility.

▶ [There is considerable debate over the usefulness of this type of classification of

(31–2) Gastroenterology 84:893–901, May 1983.

TABLE 1.—CRITERIA FOR MANOMETRIC DIAGNOSIS*

I. Normal
  1. LES pressure 10–26 mmHg ($\bar{x}$ ± 2 SD) with normal relaxation.
  2. Mean peristaltic amplitude in the distal esophagus 50–110 mmHg ($\bar{x}$ ± 2 SD).
  3. Absence of spontaneous, repetitive, or simultaneous contractions.
  4. Single wave forms (with not more than two peaks).
  5. Mean duration of peristaltic waves in the distal esophagus 1.9 ± 5.5 s ($\bar{x}$ ± 2 SD).

II. Primary motility disorders
  1. Achalasia†
    a) Aperistalsis in esophageal body.
    b) Incomplete LES relaxation.
    c) Elevated LES pressure (≥26 mmHg).
    d) Increased intraesophageal baseline pressures relative to gastric baseline.
  2. Diffuse esophageal spasm (DES)
    a) Simultaneous (nonperistaltic) contractions:
      1) repetitive (at least three peaks) contractions
      2) increased duration (>5.5 s).
    b) Spontaneous contractions.
    c) Periods of normal peristalsis.
    d) Contractions may be of increased amplitude.
  3. "Nutcracker esophagus"
    a) Mean peristaltic amplitude (10 "wet" swallows) in the distal esophagus ≥120 mmHg.
    b) Increased mean duration of contractions (>5.5 s) often found.
    c) Normal peristaltic sequence.
  4. Nonspecific esophageal motility disorders (NEMD)—Abnormal manometry representing primary esophageal motor disorders other than achalasia, DES, or "nutcracker esophagus."
    a) Hypertensive LES.
      1) LES pressure >26 mmHg with normal relaxation.
      2) Normal esophageal peristalsis.
    b) Decreased or absent amplitude of esophageal peristalsis.
      1) Normal LESP.
      2) Normal LES relaxation.
    c) Other abnormalities of peristaltic sequence (including any combination of the following):
      1) Abnormal wave forms.
      2) Isolated simultaneous contractions.
      3) Isolated spontaneous contractions.
      4) Normal peristaltic sequence maintained.
      5) LES normal.

*Abbreviations: *LES,* lower esophageal sphincter; *LESP,* lower esophageal sphincter pressure.

†a and b required; c usually present; d sometimes present.

(Courtesy of Benjamin, S.B., et al.: Reprinted by permission of the publisher from Gastroenterology 84:893–901, May 1983, copyright by the American Gastrological Association.)

esophageal motility disorders. I shall present two opposite points of view. First, the view of the authors: "It is apparent from this study that patients presenting with clinical symptoms felt to be of esophageal origin will have abnormal esophageal manometry in a high percentage of cases. The significance of this finding is not clear at this time; i.e., is the abnormal manometry responsible for the symptoms? Further understanding of esophageal neurohormonal control may provide us with a safe and effective way of clearly proving the esophagus is the inciting organ in the future. Until that time, careful patient evaluation, careful cataloging of abnormalities, and long-term followup may help answer some of the questions relating to the significance of these findings."

Cohen has written a provocative editorial[2] on this subject, and I have excerpted some of his key points: "The etiology of esophageal motility disorders is not known. It is unclear whether these disorders represent a spectrum of disease with a common etiology but with varying degrees of severity, or whether the disorders are caused by multiple etiologic factors. Clinical esophageal physiology has had its major limitation in having only a single measure of esophageal function. We measure the final event, muscle contraction, without knowledge of electrophysiologic changes, neurotransmitter function, or myogenic properties, or chemistry. The present study, again, attempts a uniform classification based on observations in a limited number of patients. The most important measure of the usefulness of this classification of esophageal motility disorders would be in its ability to help in the clinical management of patients with these disorders. Symptoms of chest pain or dysphagia were similar in all of the groups, regardless of whether they were diagnosed as having normal manometry, nutcracker esophagus, or a nonspecific motility disorder. Likewise, manometric classification failed to predict the response to provocative testing or to the subsequent development of achalasia. Thus, the classification of these patients into specific groups offers no practical clinical information to the physician or to the patient."

I feel that the classification in question is useful, and I recognize its limitations. In particular, it calls attention to the patients with "nutcracker esophagus." This problem may well be the most common primary disorder of esophageal motility and more common than diffuse esophageal spasm, achalasia, and nonspecific esophageal motor disorders. Although its etiology and functional significance have not been elucidated, the fact remains that the problem needs to be recognized and treated appropriately.] ◀

31–3 **Esophageal Acid Perfusion in Coronary Artery Disease: Induction of Myocardial Ischemia.** Most studies on esophageal acid perfusion for reproducing pain of esophageal origin have been done on patients with either symptomatic reflux alone or angina alone. Mark H. Mellow, Allan G. Simpson, Linda Watt, Lawrence Schoolmeester, and Oswald L. Haye (Georgetown Univ.) examined cardiovascular responses to esophageal acid perfusion in 37 men, mean age 53, who subsequently underwent coronary angiography for chest pain. Twenty-five patients had coronary disease, and 12 had normal coronary arteries. Nine patients had past infarction. Twenty patients with coronary disease had normal left ventricular function. Tests were done with 0.1 N HCl, and results were considered negative if no pain occurred within 30 minutes.

The heart rate–blood pressure product increased from 10.0 to 15.2 in patients with coronary disease who experienced chest pain during acid perfusion testing. Three of 9 patients had concomitant ECG evidence of myocardial ischemia (Fig 31–2). Two thirds of the patients with coronary disease but infrequent or no symptoms of reflux had positive test results. More than half of the patients with coronary disease who had pain on testing were unable to distinguish it from their usual angina. Ten of 18 such patients thought that they were experiencing their usual ischemic pain during acid perfusion testing.

Acid perfusion, and presumably gastroesophageal reflux, can increase the rate-pressure product and induce myocardial ischemia in

---

(31–3) Gastroenterology 85:306–312, August 1983.

TABLE 2.—MANOMETRIC DATA*

Patients	Mean LES pressure (mmHg)	Mean distal amplitude (mmHg)	Mean distal duration (s)	Pain	Acid Motility change	Amplitude (mmHg)
Normal Manometry						
1. A.S.	8.7	84.0	4.0	–	–	80.6
2. D.J.	7.7	53.7	3.4	–	–	64.1
3. J.A.	18.4	52.1	3.2	–(A)	–	47.2
4. D.S.	11.0	69.0	4.1	–	–	50.0
5. F.W.	11.0	117.0	5.3	–	–	99.0
6. R.M.	15.4	63.0	4.7	–	–	37.0
7. W.B.	11.0	94.0	3.4	–	–	77.0
8. P.S.	23.2	107.6	6.5	–	–	93.9
9. M.D.	23.6	102.6	4.1	–	–	115.6
10. E.P.	13.2	53.8	3.2	–	–	48.8
11. H.M.	11.2	92.5	6.9	–	–	104.7
Mean	14.0	80.9	4.4			74.4
SE	1.7	7.1	0.4			8.1
"Nutcracker esophagus"						
12. V.F.	31.8	139.8	8.2	–	–	57.3
13. L.B.	16.0	187.4	5.4	–(A)	–	48.2
14. V.S.	15.00	144.3	5.5	–	–	135.0
15. L.L.	31.0	232.6	7.2	–	–	203.5
16. G.D.	41.0	122.1	4.8	–	–	152.0
17. M.H.	24.0	158.8	8.6	–	–	210.0
18. E.W.	23.6	120.9	5.3	ND	ND	ND
19. W.M.	12.3	164.8	4.5	–	–	92.6
20. C.B.	8.2	218.5	7.1	–	–	125.5
21. D.W.	6.0	149.8	6.0	–	–	138.7
Mean	20.9	163.9	6.3			129.2
SE	3.6	12.0	0.5			18.9
Nonspecific esophageal motility disorders (NEMD)						
Hypertensive LES						
22. M.F.	35.4	67.3	2.7	–	–	80.2
23. E.A.	31.0	80.0	4.4	–	–	77.0
24. M.H.	30.6	53.8	4.5	+	+(AP)	23.4
25. J.F.	39.0	57.6	3.7	–	–	69.0
26. V.L.	28.8	85.0	3.7	–	–	88.0
Mean	33.0	68.7	3.8			67.5
SE	1.9	6.1	0.3			11.4
Decreased amplitude						
27. A.H.	13.2	44.3	4.9	–	+(SP)	49.7
28. R.D.[a]	30.0	9.2	3.0	–	–	12.2
29. W.L.[a]	19.4	22.0	3.5	–	–	23.0
30. R.N.	15.5	32.0	3.0	–	–	31.4
31. R.M.	6.7	41.9	2.9	+(A)	–	40.0
32. S.S.	8.6	30.6	2.1	–	–	31.1
33. M.D.	11.6	39.0	3.6	–	+(SP)	34.3
Mean	15.0	31.3	3.3			31.7
SE	2.8	4.7	0.3			4.5
Other (Frequent simultaneous contractions)						
34. M.C.	10.2	108.9	4.3	–(A)	+(SP)	152.3

*Abbreviations: *A*, positive acid infusion, burning substernal discomfort; *SP*, spontaneous contractions; *SC*, simultaneous contractions; *AP*, absent peristalsis; *AW*, abnormal single peristaltic wave forms; *ES*, esophageal spasm; ND, not performed.

[a]Developed classic achalasia subsequently.

[b]Uninterpretable.

(Courtesy of Benjamin, S.B., et al.: Reprinted by permission of the publisher from Gastroenterology 84:893–901, May 1983, copyright by the American Gastrological Association.)

Edrophonium			Pentagastrin			Bethanechol		
Pain	Motility change	Amplitude (*mmHg*)	Pain	Motility change	Amplitude (*mmHg*)	Pain	Motility change	Amplitude (*mmHg*)
–	–	104.1	–	–	41.6	–	+(AW)	104.8
+	–	67.0	+	–	41.3	–	–	43.0
–	–	64.0	–	–	77.6	–	+(AW)	97.2
+	+(AP, AW)	83.5	–	–	48.0	–	–	51.0
–	–	121.0	–	–	104.0	–	–	94.0
–	–	97.0	–	+(AW)	74.0	+	–	43.0
–	–	72.8	–	+(AW)	96.2	–	–	103.0
–	+(SC)	117.6	–	–	101.3	–	–	115.1
–	–	172.4	–	–	118.9	–	–	132.6
–	–	95.3	–	–	51.6	–	–	67.8
–	+(AW)	137.6	–	–	114.7	–	+(AW)	141.1
		102.9			79.0			90.2
		9.9			9.0			10.4
+	+(ES)	145.1	–	–	118.4	–	–	78.3
–	–	188.0	–	+(AW)	121.0	–	–	168.0
–	–	176.0	–	–	152.0	–	+(ES)	181.0
–	–	209.5	–	–	249.0	–	–	215.5
–	–	150.0	–	–	101.0	–	–	125.0
–	–	258.0	–	–	73.0	–	–	191.5
+	+(AW)	125.0	+	+(SP)	115.2	–	+(ES)	115.0
+	–	235.5	–	–	205.0	–	–	252.5
+	–	220.5	–	–	203.0	–	–	205.0
+	+(ES)	173.5	–	–	141.5	+	+(SP)	149.6
		188.1			147.9			168.1
		13.5			17.3			16.5
–	–	97.0	–	–	85.4	–	–	76.0
–	+(ES)	155.0	–	–	127.0	–	+(ES)	144.0
+	–	105.7	–	–	94.1	+	–	52.5
–	–	62.0	–	–	114.2	–	–	120.7
–	–	140.0	–	–	104.0	–	+(AW)	106.0
		111.9			104.9			99.8
		16.4			7.3			16.2
–	–	81.0	–	–	76.6	+	–	79.8
–	–	8.8	+	–	12.6	–	–	34.2
–	–	31.0	–	–	25.0	+	–	UNINT[b]
+	+(AW)	131.7	–	+(AW)	52.7	–	+(AW)	115.2
–	+(AW)	79.1	–	+(ES)	64.0	–	+(ES)	71.5
–	–	46.1	–	–	45.0	–	–	29.6
–	+(SP)	43.4	–	+(SP)	25.3	–	+(ES)	61.0
		60.2			43.0			65.2
		15.3			8.8			12.9
+	+(ES)	239.9		-ND-			-ND-	

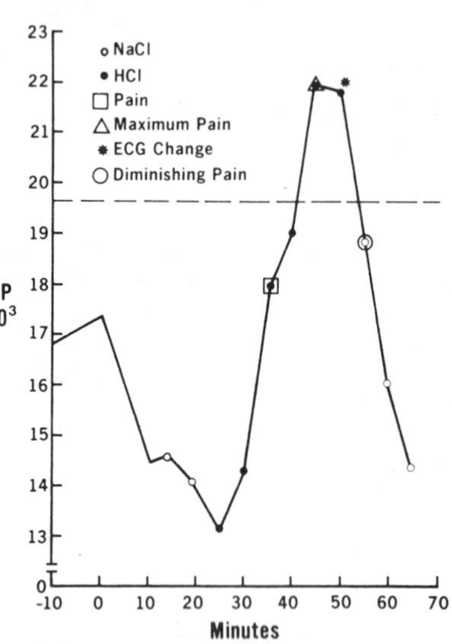

Fig 31–2.—Time-course of rate-pressure product (RPP) during performance of acid perfusion testing in patient with ECG evidence of myocardial ischemia. Time zero = nasogastric tube placement. Dotted line refers to patient's ischemic threshold as determined by exercise ECG testing. (Courtesy of Mellow, M.H., et al.: Reproduced by permission of the publisher from Gastroenterology 85:306–312, August 1983, copyright by the American Gastrological Association.)

patients with coronary artery disease. The presence of esophageal acid sensitivity is not accurately predicted by the clinical history in patients with coronary disease, who frequently confuse pain of esophageal origin with angina. Physicians must be aware of coexisting coronary artery disease and gastroesophageal reflux. Once the coexistence is diagnosed, aggressive treatment is indicated, with the goal of preventing all episodes of pain. Initial use of an H_2-receptor antagonist in addition to standard treatment seems to be indicated.

▶ [The major finding in this study is that patients with known coronary artery disease but infrequent or no symptoms of gastroesophageal reflux experienced chest pain during perfusion of the distal esophagus with dilute acid. Importantly, the patients thought they were experiencing their usual ischemic chest pain during this acid perfusion testing. Since coronary artery disease and gastroesophageal reflux are two common conditions, it should not be surprising that they coexist in certain patients and may actually mimic each other.

Another related problem concerns the patient who has chest pain and angiographically normal coronary arteries and in whom abnormalities in esophageal motility have been demonstrated. In such patients it is often concluded that chest pain is of esophageal origin. However, a recent study by Clause et al.[3] suggests that chest pain and esophageal abnormalities may not be causally related. Nine patients with intermittent chest pain that was thought on the basis of clinical evidence to be secondary to esophageal "spasms" developed typical pain while being studied with an intraluminal transducer probe placed in the distal esophagus. Manometric changes from control periods were examined preceding and during pain episodes. No significant difference in distal esophageal wave duration or amplitude or in frequency of abnormal peristalsis was observed preceding or during pain episodes when compared with nonpain periods during a mean monitoring time of 227 min. No change from the nonpain periods in esophageal baseline pressure occurred during pain episodes, nor was there any other obvious manometric change by gross inspection of the tracings. Clause et al. conclude that patients clinically suspected of having esophageal "spasms" as the source of chest pain frequently do not, regardless of the presence or absence of motility abnormalities on conventional esophageal manometric studies.

For an up-to-date review on chest pain of esophageal origin see the article by Benjamin and Castell.[4]] ◀

31-4 **Double-Blind Comparison of Liquid Antacid and Placebo in Treatment of Symptomatic Reflux Esophagitis.** Most physicians believe that antacids are effective in relieving heartburn, but it is not known whether these agents influence the natural course of reflux esophagitis. David Y. Graham and David J. Patterson (Baylor Coll. of Medicine) undertook a double-blind comparison of liquid antacid and placebo in 32 patients with chronic heartburn, in whom gastroesophageal reflux was confirmed by acid perfusion testing and use of the intraesophageal pH probe. Patients received 15-ml doses of Maalox or a placebo 7 times daily, 1 and 3 hours after meals and at bedtime, for 5 weeks. The antacid had a neutralizing capacity of 5.3 mEq/ml, or 80 mEq per dose. The placebo consisted of sorbitol, lactose, gum guar, and titanium dioxide.

Ten of the 21 patients in the study received the antacid. The two groups were clinically comparable. The average patient initially had severe heartburn 2–5 times a day, and severe friability of the esophageal mucosa was observed on endoscopy. After 4 weeks of treatment the average patient had 1 episode of mild to moderate heartburn daily, and esophagitis was greatly improved. The two groups both improved significantly in terms of the frequency and severity of heartburn during the study period, with no significant differences between them. The time to reproduce heartburn on Bernstein testing increased with both antacid and placebo administration. Endoscopy showed less esophagitis in both groups.

This study asked, Does regular antacid therapy have a favorable influence on the natural history of symptomatic reflux esophagitis, i.e., does therapy heal or otherwise change esophagitis so that painful episodes are either less frequent or less severe or both? It was found that the natural history of symptomatic reflux esophagitis was to improve when patients received either antacid or placebo. No significant clinical differences over the short term were observed between antacid-treated and placebo-treated patients in the present study. It is more difficult to define successful therapy in reflux esophagitis than it is in gastric or duodenal ulcer disease.

▶ [I selected this article because it highlights many of the vexing problems in the treatment of patients with gastroesophageal reflux. First, many patients with severe reflux symptoms have little or no evidence of esophagitis. Thus, in this study of Graham and Patterson, 18 of 32 patients with chronic heartburn had grade 0 or grade 1 esophagitis, and only 3 had grade 3 esophagitis. Second, many patients will respond to placebo, and this response may be maintained over a 4-week study period. There is a tendency for a major syptomatic response to placebo to occur early, but such placebo responses are often short-lived. The reason(s) for sustained improvement remains unclear. It is interesting to note that in the cimetidine trials conducted in the United States in patients with esophagitis, one third achieved a heartburn score of 0 after 1 week of placebo treatment.[5] Third, despite intensive therapy many patients will continue to experience reflux symptoms. Indeed, cimetidine along with metoclopramide is often used in this setting. A recent study, however, suggests that, despite the plausible pharmacologic rationale, there is no clinical advantage in coprescribing cimetidine and metoclopramide for esophageal acid reflux disease.[6]] ◀

(31–4) Dig. Dis. Sci. 28:559–563, June 1983.

Chapter 31 References

1. Helm J.F., Dodds W.J.,Riedel D.R., et al.: Determinants of esophageal acid clearance in normal subjects. *Gastroenterology* 85:607–612, 1983.
2. Cohen S.: Classification of the esophageal motility diseases. *Gastroenterology* 84:1050–1058, 1983.
3. Clause R.E., Staiano A., Landan D.W., et al.: Manometric findings during spontaneous chest pain in patients with presumed esophageal "spasms." *Gastroenterology* 85:395–402, 1983.
4. Benjamin S.B., Castell D.O.: Chest pain of esophageal origin: where are we and where should we go? *Arch. Intern. Med.* 143:772–776, 1983.
5. Behar J., Brand D.L., Brown F.C., et al.: Cimetidine in the treatment of symptomatic gastroesophageal reflux. *Gastroenterology* 74:441–447, 1978.
6. Temple J.G., Bradby G.V.H., O'Connor F.O., et al.: Cimetidine and metoclopramide in oesophageal reflux disease. *Br. Med. J.* 1:1863–1864, 1983.

32. Stomach

2–1 **Association of Adrenocorticosteroid Therapy and Peptic Ulcer Disease.** Early anecdotal reports gave rise to a widely held view that corticosteroids are potentially ulcerogenic, but other studies have failed to confirm such an association. Julio Messer, Dinah Reitman, Henry S. Sacks, Harry Smith, Jr., and Thomas C. Chalmers (Mount Sinai School of Medicine) reexamined this association by pooling data from 71 controlled clinical trials in which patients were randomized to systemic corticosteroid or ACTH therapy or to nonsteroid therapy. Peptic ulcer was diagnosed in 1.8% of 3,064 corticosteroid-treated patients and in 0.8% of 2,897 controls, for a relative risk of 2.3 with 95% confidence limits of 1.4–3.7. Gastrointestinal bleeding occurred in 2.5% of corticosteroid-treated patients and 1.6% of controls, for a relative risk of 1.5 with 95% confidence limits of 1.1–2.2. Similar trends persisted on separate analyses of studies that were double-blind, used only oral or only parenteral corticosteroid therapy, or excluded patients with a history of ulcer. The incidence of ulcers varied directly with the dose of corticosteroid (table).

INCIDENCE OF ULCERS, ACCORDING TO PRESENCE OR ABSENCE OF PREDISPOSING ILLNESS AND DAILY CORTICOSTEROID DOSAGE

CATEGORY	NO. OF PATIENTS	NO. OF TRIALS	INCIDENCE OF ULCERS/ 1000/ 21 DAYS	RELATIVE RISK (95% CONFIDENCE INTERVAL)
With predisposing illness				
Steroid (<20 mg)	273	4	2.6	1.3 (0.2–7.0)
Control	254	4	1.9	
Steroid (20–40 mg)	58	4	85.3	1.5 (1.1–2.2)
Control	67	4	57.3	
Steroid (>40 mg)	260	7	73.3	2.3 (1.5–3.5)
Control	262	7	33.2	
Without predisposing illness				
Steroid (<20 mg)	306	8	1.6	* (0.4–138.3)
Control	311	8	0.0	
Steroid (20–40 mg)	723	14	2.4	2.6 (0.3–22.5)
Control	747	14	0.6	
Steroid (>40 mg)	265	7	6.1	* (0.3–113.3)
Control	287	7	0.0	

*Since value for controls was zero, relative risk cannot be calculated.

(Courtesy of Messer, J., et al.: N. Engl. J. Med. 309:21–24, July 7, 1983; reprinted by permission of The New England Journal of Medicine.)

(32–1) N. Engl. J. Med. 309:21–24, July 7, 1983.

This study strongly suggests that corticosteroids increase the risk of peptic ulcer and gastrointestinal hemorrhage. In the study of Conn and Blitzer, the null hypothesis of no association between corticosteroids and ulcer was accepted simply because there was insufficient evidence to reject it. It remains unclear whether corticosteroid-induced ulceration or hemorrhage is pathologically the same as the naturally occurring states, but this is not critical for clinicians who prescribe or for recipients of corticosteroids. The risk of peptic complications will depend on the underlying disease and on the dose. It will probably be greater in patients with previous ulcer disease, and it may vary with age, sex, nutritional status, and route of corticosteroid administration.

▶ [Spiro has written a provocative editorial entitled "Is the Steroid Ulcer a Myth?," and much of what follows has been abstracted from that editorial.[1]

In 1976 Conn and Blitzer combined the data from 42 randomized controlled trials and concluded that steroids do not cause peptic ulcers unless they are administered for more than 30 days or up to a total dose exceeding the equivalent of 1,000 mg of prednisone.[2] However, in their study, there was an increased relative risk of 1.7 overall for patients taking steroids. Thus, although Conn and Blitzer did not confirm any excess in the number of reported cases of ulcer associated with steroids at the conventional 5% level of statistical significance, their evidence was nonetheless suggestive of such an association and could be interpreted as supporting the idea that steroids do increase the risk of peptic ulcer.

In the study abstracted above, Messer et al. have pooled data from 71 controlled clinical trials. Peptic ulcer was diagnosed in 1.8% of 3,064 corticosteroid-treated patients and in 0.8% of 2,897 controls, for a relative risk of 2.3. Spiro responds to these results as follows: "How does this latest study change what the clinician should think or do? The clinician who before 1976 gave antacids to every patient receiving steroids regardless of diagnosis and who broke that habit in 1977 should not yet reach for the prescription pad to write a prescription for H-2 blockers or sucralfate. Common sense is needed. An ulcer develops in 1 percent of control patients not receiving steroids; the 2 percent figure for patients receiving steroids represents a doubling of the effect. To forestall such a relatively rare complication of steroid therapy, 98 patients will have to take another drug to spare possibly 2 people; the added benefit is really for only 1 person in every 100. The increase from 1 to 2 percent indicates that steroids do modestly increase the incidence of peptic ulcer; that the incidence is doubled is of only secondary interest to the clinician, since it is still only 2 percent. Therefore, one should prescribe steroid with prudence and for good indications, as always. An H-2 blocker should be given along with the steroids only to patients who are taking other medications that make the likelihood of an ulcer greater than in the group studied by Messer and his colleagues."] ◀

32–2 **Healing of Benign Gastric Ulcer With Low-Dose Antacid or Cimetidine: A Double-Blind Randomized, Placebo-Controlled Trial.** There is no clear consensus that either antacid or cimetidine hastens the healing of gastric ulcer, although either agent promotes healing of duodenal ulcer. Jon I. Isenberg, Walter L. Peterson, Janet D. Elashoff, Mary Ann Sandersfeld, Terry J. Reedy, Andrew F. Ippoliti, Gary M. Van Deventer, Harold Frankl, George F. Longstreth, and Daniel S. Anderson conducted a 12-week, double-blind, placebo-controlled study to determine whether cimetidine (300 mg with meals and at bedtime) or a liquid aluminum-magnesium antacid (Maalox, 15 ml 1 hour after meals and at bedtime) expedite healing or relief or symptoms in patients with benign gastric ulcer.

(32–2) N. Engl. J. Med. 308:1319–1324, June 2, 1983.

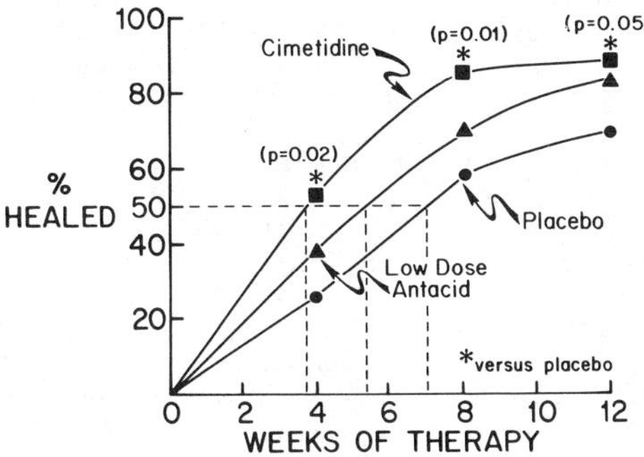

Fig 32–1.—Cumulative proportions of patients with healed gastric ulcer with each regimen at each time period. (Courtesy of Isenberg, J.I., et al.: N. Engl. J. Med. 308:1319–1324, June 2, 1983; reprinted by permission of The New England Journal of Medicine.)

Of 101 patients completing the trial according to protocol, 32 were given the antacid, 36 received cimetidine, and 33 received placebo. At 4, 8, and 12 weeks after the start of the study, the ulcers had healed in 53%, 86%, and 89% of the patients treated with cimetidine, respectively, compared with 26%, 58%, and 70%, respectively, of those who received placebo (*P* = .02, .01, and .05) (Fig 32–1). Healing at these intervals had occurred in, respectively, 38%, 70%, and 84% of those treated with the antacid. During the 12-week period, enlargement of the ulcer was observed in 24% of those receiving placebo, but in only 3% of those receiving cimetidine and 6.3% of those given the antacid. Patients in the group receiving placebo showed less improvement in pain scores than the other patients, but the differences between groups were not significant. At both 4 and 8 weeks, the presence or absence of pain was a relatively poor predictor of the presence or absence of an ulcer crater. No serious side effects occurred and no patient discontinued the trial because of side effects.

The results indicate that cimetidine, compared with placebo, significantly hastens the healing of benign gastric ulcers. By 4 weeks, most patients in each group were asymptomatic, but many still had endoscopic evidence of an ulcer. Thus, the absence of symptoms does not necessarily indicate healing. As healing occurred by 8 weeks in almost all patients treated with cimetidine whose ulcers would eventually heal, it appears that 8 weeks is a logical time for the first endoscopic or radiographic follow-up evaluation.

▶ [This elegant multicenter trial clearly indicates that cimetidine leads to healing of gastric ulcer faster and more frequently than placebo. With regard to the efficacy of antacids, outcomes were intermediate between those with placebo and those with cimetidine, significantly different from neither.

Two additional clinical trials have indicated that cimetidine is effective not only in the initial treatment of gastric ulcer but also in the prevention of relapse. In the study of Hentschel et al., 146 gastric ulcer patients were given open treatment using 1.0 gm cimetidine daily to heal their ulcer.[3] Of 130 who completed the acute treatment period of 8 weeks, 112 (86%) had healed ulcers. Of these 112 patients with healed ulcers, 108 entered a 1-year double-blind study to compare the effect of cimetidine maintenance therapy (400 mg at bedtime) with placebo. Of the 84 patients available for assessment at the end of 1 year, 36 (86%) of 42 in the cimetidine-treated group were in remission compared with 19 (45%) of 42 in the placebo-treated group. Interestingly, 7 (24%) of 29 recurrences in both groups were asymptomatic. These results indicate that cimetidine heals nearly 90% of acute gastric ulcers within 8 weeks and that subsequent low-dose maintenance treatment at night offers a considerable benefit over placebo.

Similar results were obtained by Baer et al.[4] who assessed the effectiveness of cimetidine in a dose of 400 mg twice daily in the prevention of gastric ulcer recurrence during a 2-year period. The trial was double-blind and placebo controlled; 24 patients received cimetidine and 25 received placebo. All had had a gastric ulcer within the preceding 6 weeks, and healing was demonstrated by endoscopy or by barium meal. The patients were contacted at monthly intervals, and if symptoms were present, investigations were performed. Annual barium meal examinations or endoscopy were also performed in all except 7 patients. In the placebo group, there was rapid recurrence within the first 12 months; 12 of the 13 recurrences that occurred in this group during the 2-year period took place within the first 12 months. In the cimetidine-treated group, there were 8 recurrences during the 2-year period, 5 of which occurred in the first year. Log rank comparison showed a significant benefit due to cimetidine at 1 year, but not during the 2-year period.] ◀

32–3 **Recurrent Ulcer After Successful Treatment With Cimetidine or Antacid.** Cimetidine and antacid therapy both produce healing of duodenal ulcers in most patients, but many experience recurrent ulceration within 6–12 months of cessation of therapy. A. Ippoliti, Janet D. Elashoff, J. Valenzuela, R. Cano, H. Frankl, M. Samloff, and R. Koretz (Univ. of California at Los Angeles) compared rates of ulcer healing and recurrence after these treatments in patients seen at 6 centers with duodenal, pyloric channel, or prepyloric ulcers. Eighty-

RELATIONSHIP OF PATIENT VARIABLES TO HEALING AND RELAPSE

		Healing at 6 wk (%)		Recurrence at 6 mo (%)	
		Healed	Not healed	No recurrence	Recurrence
Age	<50 yr	87	13	46	54
	>50 yr	77	23	42	58
Sex	M	80	20	40	60
	F	96	4	65	35
Duration	<48 mo	90	10[a]	57	43[a]
	≥48 mo	75	25	28	72
Comp	none	74	26	38	62
	≥1	87	13	47	53
Bleed	none	81	19	40	60
	yes	85	15	51	49
Fam Hx	neg	84	16	49	51
	pos	79	21	30	70
Pain frequency	≤3	87	13	44	56
	>3	78	22	45	55
Smoking	<0.5 pack/day	88	12[a]	51	49
	≥0.5 pack/day	73	27	30	70
BAO	<4	91	9	51	49
	≥4	79	21	41	59
PAO	<30	94	6[a]	59	41[a]
	≥30	77	23	35	65

[a]Significant at $P < .05$ by χ^2.

(Courtesy of Ippoliti, A., et al.: Reprinted by permission of the publisher from Gastroenterology 85:875–880, October 1983; Copyright by the American Gastrological Association.)

(32–3) Gastroenterology 85:875–880, October 1983.

three patients received 7 oz of Mylanta II daily, and 78 received 1,200 mg of cimetidine daily in divided doses. The two treatment groups were clinically comparable.

Endoscopic healing was similar in both groups. Of 138 patients completing the healing phase of the study, 82% were asymptomatic after 6 weeks. There were no differences in recurrence rates during a 1-year period in patients initially treated with antacid or cimetidine. Several patient variables are related to ulcer healing and relapse in the table. The duration of ulcer disease significantly affected both the incidence of ulcer healing and that of relapse but not the rate of healing. Other variables associated with delayed ulcer healing or ulcer recurrence included sex, pain frequency, smoking, and acid secretion. Smoking was a very important factor in ulcer healing in the present study, delaying healing by about 20% in smokers.

Rates of duodenal ulcer healing and rates of recurrence after discontinuance of therapy appear to be similar in patients initially treated with cimetidine and with an intensive antacid regimen. At 3 and 6 months, the cumulative percentages of patients with recurrence were 29% and 56% after antacid therapy and 35% and 55% after cimetidine therapy.

▶ [Of the many factors associated with delayed healing and relapse of peptic ulcers smoking appears to be especially important. Recently, Boyd et al.[5] have demonstrated that cigarette smoking actually *reversed* the inhibition of nocturnal gastric secretion produced by the H_2-receptor antagonists cimetidine and ranitidine in 9 duodenal ulcer patients. As a consequence of smoking, nocturnal secretion of acid increased by 91.5% and of pepsin by an average of 59% when compared with control studies when the patients did not smoke. Patients with duodenal ulcers secrete abnormally large amounts of gastric juice at night and inhibition of nocturnal secretion is an important therapeutic effect of many antisecretory drugs in promoting ulcer healing and especially in preventing recurrences. The observations of Boyd et al. may therefore have therapeutic implications. Although patients who smoke habitually often do not or cannot heed advice to stop smoking completely, a recommendation to avoid smoking after taking the nighttime antisecretory tablet should be acceptable and may prove to be clinically relevant and useful.

Another factor, often not appreciated in the development of symptomatic peptic ulcer disease, is a stressful life event. Peters and Richardson[6] evaluated two patients with symptomatic gastric ulcer disease who dated the onset of their illnesses to stressful events in their lives. One patient reported that six family members had recently died and that he feared he too would soon die. The other patient was accused of grand theft, was under police surveillance, and had lost his job. Both patients had markedly increased gastric acid secretion rates that decreased to normal after hospitalization and reassurance in the first case and acquittal in the second case. Ulcer symptoms subsided at the same time as the decrease in acid secretion. Although it cannot be proved that severe emotional stress in these patients led to acid hypersecretion and ulcer disease, their courses suggest that stressful life events caused increased acid secretion which in turn led to ulceration and symptoms.] ◀

32–4 **Effect of Daily Oral Omeprazole on 24-Hour Intragastric Acidity.** Omeprazole is a new substituted benzimidazole that inhibits basal and stimulated acid secretion in normal persons and inhibits basal secretion in patients with Zollinger-Ellison syndrome. The acid-inhibitory effect of the drug is of prolonged duration. R. P. Walt, M. de F. A. Gomes, E. C. Wood, L. H. Logan, and R. E.

(32–4) Br. Med. J. 287:12–14, July 2, 1983.

Pounder (London) examined the effects of omeprazole in daily oral doses of 30 mg on 24-hour intragastric acidity in 9 men, mean age 47, with endoscopically diagnosed duodenal ulcers in remission. Antisecretory drugs were not given for 2 weeks before the study. Two studies were carried out a week apart, before and after administration of omeprazole for 1 week.

The studies were well tolerated by all patients, and no laboratory abnormalities were observed. One patient had a lichenoid eruption 11 days after stopping the drug. Treatment led to a marked reduction in intragastric acidity in all patients. The mean 24-hour intragastric hydrogen ion activity fell significantly from 38.5 to 1.95 mmole/L during omeprazole treatment. Cimetidine (1.0 gm/day) and ranitidine (300 μg/day) significantly decreased mean 24-hour intragastric hydrogen ion activity by 48% and 69%, respectively, whereas omeprazole (30 mg/day) caused a 95% decrease. Only 12% of pH measurements before treatment were above 3.0 compared with 86% of measurements during treatment; the respective median pH values were 1.4 and 5.3 (an 8,000-fold decrease in acidity with omeprazole).

Oral omeprazole administered for 1 week virtually eliminated intragastric acidity in these peptic ulcer patients, although it did not produce anacidity. No adverse side effects were observed. This study was done under conditions approximating those of everyday life. Clinical trials of omeprazole are indicated in patients in whom the control of gastric acid secretion is beneficial.

▶ [Recently, substituted benzimidazoles have been shown to be powerful inhibitors of gastric acid secretion in various animal models and in humans. Previous investigators have suggested a target site for this class of compounds within the parietal cell and beyond second-messenger activation of the acid formation process, possibly by a direct interaction with the proposed gastric proton pump, the H^+-K^+-ATPase.[7] Under carefully defined experimental conditions, Wallmark et al. have demonstrated that cimetidine only counteracts histamine-induced acid secretion, consonant with its H_2-receptor antagonism.[8] In contrast, omeprazole not only inhibited histamine-induced secretion but also basal acid formation and acid formation induced by dibutryl cyclic AMP and a high cell-medium concentration of K^+.

Rapid healing of duodenal ulcers with omeprazole also has been demonstrated by Gustavsson et al.[9] In a double-blind, dose-comparative trial, 32 patients with duodenal ulcer were assigned to receive either 20 mg or 60 mg of omeprazole per day for 4 weeks. The 2-week healing frequency of *100%* in the 60-mg/day group was significantly higher than that in the 20-mg/day group (63%). After 4 weeks, all ulcers but 1 in the 20-mg/day group were healed (93% healing frequency). In both groups, transient and mostly slight rises in serum alanine aminotransferase levels were observed (total 10 patients). One patient in the 20-mg/day group was withdrawn because of a pronounced rise in serum alanine aminotransferase on day 8. The reason for these liver reactions is not clear, but exclusion of a causal relation with omeprazole treatment must precede further clinical evaluation of this drug.

These findings of a 100% healing rate after 2 weeks' treatment with 60 mg of omeprazole per day suggest that there is a considerable further clinical benefit to be gained by acid reduction in ulcer therapy in terms of both healing rate and percentage of patients healed, possibly because the inhibition of acid secretion induced by omeprazole lasts longer than that induced by H_2-receptor blockade. In clinical trials within the same population as this study, the same investigators found healing rates with cimetidine treatment (1 gm daily) of 63% and 74% after 3 and 4 weeks, respectively.[8, 9] These results indicate therefore that omeprazole is more effective than other available treatment regimens.] ◀

32–5 **Cimetidine and Tranexamic Acid in Treatment of Acute Upper Gastrointestinal Tract Bleeding.** Claims made for the efficacy of both histamine H_2-receptor antagonists and antifibrinolytic drugs in patients with gastrointestinal tract bleeding have been based on small trials and on clinical assessments of rebleeding rates. David Barer, Alan Ogilvie, David Henry, Michael Dronfield, David Coggon, Shelagh French, Susan Ellis, Michael Atkinson, and Michael Langman (Nottingham, England) undertook a large, controlled, double-blind trial of cimetidine and tranexamic acid, an antifibrinolytic drug, in 775 patients admitted on an emergency basis with a primary diagnosis of hematemesis, melena, or both, between 1980 and 1982. Either cimetidine was given intravenously in a dose of 400 mg every 6 hours for 48 hours, followed by the same dose orally every 6 hours for 5 days, or tranexamic acid was given in an intravenous dose of 1 gm and subsequently orally, or placebo injections and tablets were given.

Rebleeding and operation rates seem not to have been influenced by treatment. Mortality was 7.2% lower with tranexamic acid than with placebo; the reduction in mortality with cimetidine was less marked, and the difference between the two active drugs was slight. The outcome in patients completing the trial is given in the table. Benefit from tranexamic acid was apparent at both hospitals participating in the study. Much of the advantage of this drug was seen in patients who were operated on. Of the 22 deaths resulting directly from continued or recurrent bleeding, 2 were in tranexamic acid-

OUTCOME IN PATIENTS WHO CONTINUED TREATMENT

	CIMETIDINE	TRANEXAMIC ACID	PLACEBO	TOTAL
Total in group	232	225	219	676
Number transfused	149 (64)	140 (62)	133 (61)	422 (62)
Mean transfusion requirement (units)	5.3	5.7	5.7	
Number with evidence of rebleeding	49 (21)	55 (24)	50 (23)	154 (23)
Operations				
Overall	32 (14)	44 (20)	35 (16)	111 (16)
After rebleeding	30	36	29	95
Deaths	18 (8)	8 (4)	23 (11)	49 (7)
Hospital 1	*8*	*5*	*14*	*27*
Hospital 2	*10*	*3*	*9*	*22*
After rebleeding	13	7	18	38
Without rebleeding	5	1	5	11
After operation	7	4	10	21
Without operation	11	4	13	28
Postoperative mortality rate	22%	9%	29%	19%

(Courtesy of Barer, D., et al.: N. Engl. J. Med. 308:1571–1575, June 30, 1983; reprinted by permission of the New England Journal of Medicine.)

(32–5) N. Engl. J. Med. 308:1571–1575, June 30, 1983.

treated patients, 8 in cimetidine-treated patients, and 12 in placebo patients. However, treatment with tranexamic acid was not associated with any decrease in the rate of rebleeding or the need for operation.

In this study there was significantly lower mortality resulting from gastrointestinal tract bleeding in patients given tranexamic acid than in placebo patients. In view of its efficacy, apparent safety, and convenience, tranexamic acid can be recommended for routine use in patients over age 60 years, who are at the greatest risk of dying of upper gastrointestinal tract hemorrhage. The reasons for the low mortality in tranexamic acid–treated patients are unclear.

▶ [This provocative study provides convincing evidence that use of tranexamic acid is associated with significantly reduced mortality in patients with acute upper gastrointestinal bleeding (UGIB). The mechanism for this effect is unknown.

Fleischer has prospectively studied the etiology and prevalence of episodes of acute UGIB that are severe and persistent.[10] During a 12-month study period, 175 patients had 1 or more episodes of UGIB. Thirty-six (20.6%) of the 175 patients had bleeding that was classified as severe and persistent. The criteria for such bleeding included the following: (1) The presence of bright red blood per nasogastric aspirate after 4 hours of initial resuscitation in patients who had received 2 units or more of blood or who had signs of hemodynamic instability; (2) the presence of blood in the NG aspirate after 1 hour of gastric lavage in a patient who rebled in the hospital and required 1 unit or more of blood; and (3) those patients who had clinically persistent bleeding and who were found to have active bleeding at endoscopy were defined as having endoscopically persistent bleeding. Upper gastrointestinal bleeding that occurred more than 24 hours after admission was more apt to persist than bleeding that was a presenting complaint (32.4% vs. 12.8%, $P<.001$). The presence of esophageal varices was the single most common cause of such bleeding. Because most UGIB is self-limited, studies to evaluate new therapeutic modalities should attempt to *exclude* patients whose bleeding will abate spontaneously. Further, in comparative studies, the time of intervention must be controlled. Finally, the return of red or reddish-pink blood per nasogastric tube may not signify active bleeding. Therefore, active bleeding must be demonstrated by endoscopy before various treatment modalities are compared.] ◀

32–6 **Duodenal Prostaglandin Synthesis and Acid Load in Health and in Duodenal Ulcer Disease.** It was suggested that prostaglandins may help prevent duodenal mucosal injury from an acid load. David A. Ahlquist, Roger R. Dozois, Alan R. Zinsmeister, and Juan-R. Malagelada (Mayo Clinic) used a radiometric method to measure prostaglandin synthetic activity in 10 patients with symptomatically inactive duodenal ulcer disease. Ulceration was documented endoscopically or roentgenographically in all 10 patients who were otherwise healthy. Eight normal subjects also were evaluated. Mucosal biopsy specimens, obtained from the duodenal bulb before and after a test meal consisting of an amino acid soup, were incubated in ^{14}C-arachidonic acid.

The mean duodenal acid load was greater in the ulcer patients, but the ranges overlapped. There were no significant qualitative differences between the ulcer patients and the controls with regard to prostanoid synthesis, and mean fasting protaglandin synthesis was greater in the ulcer patients. Prostaglandin synthesis activities tended to increase post cibum in controls but changed little or de-

(32–6) Gastroenterology 85:522–528, September 1982.

creased in patients with duodenal ulcer. However, the two groups were clearly distinguished when both parameters of acid delivery to the duodenum and mucosal synthesis of 6-keto-prostaglandin F1α were considered.

Prostaglandin synthesis in the duodenal mucosa is increased after a meal, and this may represent an important protective mechanism. Adaptive cytoprotection may be defective in duodenal ulcer patients because of either inflammation or an intrinsic mucosal defect. An absolute deficiency of mucosal prostaglandin synthetic capacity does not seem to be responsible for duodenal ulcer disease, and an abnormal profile was not observed. The findings should be confirmed in broader groups and with the use of a variety of technical approaches.

32–7 **Intravenous Infusion of L-Isomers of Phenylalanine and Tryptophan Stimulate Gastric Acid Secretion at Physiologic Plasma Concentrations in Normal Subjects and After Parietal Cell Vagotomy.** Animal studies indicate that individual L-amino acids can increase gastric acid secretion when in direct contact with the oxyntic-gland mucosa by a gastrin-independent mechanism. Katherine E. McArthur, Jon I. Isenberg, Daniel L. Hogen, and Susan J. Dreier (Univ. of California, San Diego) attempted to determine

Fig 32–2.—Mean (± SEM) gastric acid secretory response (expressed in millimoles per hour) to intravenous infusion of graded doses of phenylalanine *(Phe),* tryptophan *(Trp),* glycine *(Gly),* alanine *(Ala),* histidine *(His),* and saline *(NaCl)* control in 9 normal subjects. *B* indicates basal acid secretion. Each dose was infused at rate of 125 ml/hour. Responses to 0.025–0.1 M Phe, 0.01–0.04 M Trp, and 0.025 M and 0.05 M Gly were significantly different from responses to NaCl control. *Indicates significance at level of $P<.05$; **, $P<.01$. Responses to Ala and His were not significantly different from responses to NaCl control. (Courtesy of McArthur, K.E., et al.: Reproduced from J. Clin. Invest. 71:1254–1262, May 1983, by permission of the American Society for Clinical Investigation.)

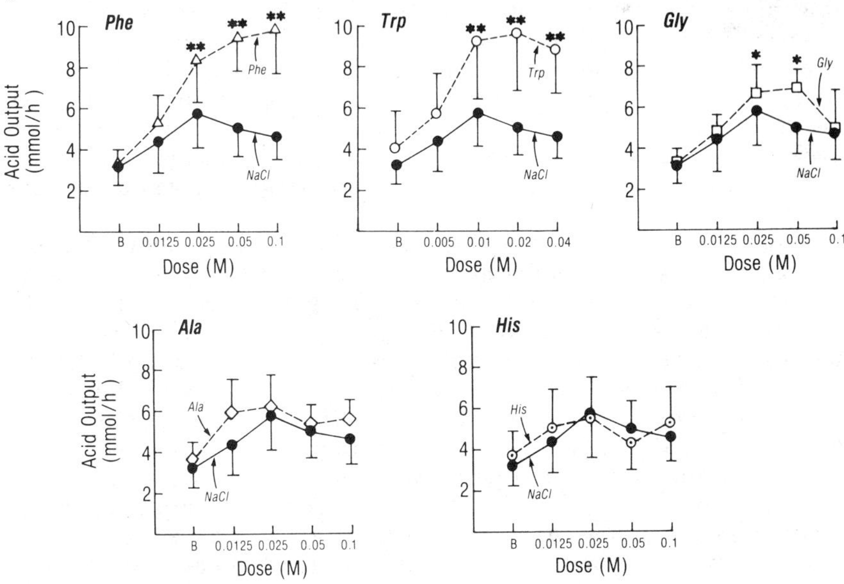

(32–7) J. Clin. Invest. 71:1254–1262, May 1983.

whether the infusion of L-isomers of individual amino acids stimulates gastric acid secretion in man. Nine normal subjects with a mean age of 31 years participated in the study, along with 5 subjects who had had parietal-cell vagotomy a mean of 35 months previously for duodenal ulcer disease. Completeness of vagotomy was documented by testing with insulin. Graded doses of phenylalanine, tryptophan, glycine, alanine, and histidine were infused on separate days. The doses bracketed the amounts of the individual amino acids present in Freamine II, which is a potent gastric secretory stimulus in man.

Both phenylalanine and tryptophan significantly stimulated gastric acid secretion (Fig 32–2). Alanine and histidine were ineffective, and glycine had only a slight effect. Serum gastrin levels did not change significantly except in response to 0.1 M phenylalanine. Plasma amino acid concentrations were comparable with those present after a steak meal or were lower at the time when acid secretion was increased during the infusion of phenylalanine or tryptophan. Phenylalanine and tryptophan also stimulated acid secretion in the vagotomized subjects, whereas histidine had no such effect. Both basal and pentagastrin-induced acid secretory responses were lower in the vagotomized subjects than in normal subjects.

These findings suggest a physiologic role for circulating levels of phenylalanine and tryptophan in gastric acid secretion. The acid secretory responses to these amino acids probably are mediated by a non-gastrin-related, vagally independent mechanism. It appears that these 2 amino acids have either a direct or an indirect effect on or near the parietal cell.

32–8 **Medical and Surgical Options in the Management of Patients With Gastrinoma.** The efficacy of H_2-receptor antagonists in controlling hypersecretion of gastric acid, at least in the short term, has renewed debate regarding the management of patients with Zollinger-Ellison syndrome due to gastrinoma. Juan-R. Malagelada, Anthony J. Edis, Martin A. Adson, Jonathan A. Van Heerden, and Vay Liang W. Go (Mayo Clinic and Found., Rochester, Minn.) reviewed their experience with the surgical and medical management of 53 patients with Zollinger-Ellison syndrome due to gastrinoma seen since 1970.

Abdominal surgery was performed in 44 of the 53 patients (Fig 32–3). Laparotomy did not disclose a tumor in 13 (29.5%) of these 44 patients. In the remaining 31 patients, surgery revealed a tumor; 18 of these tumors were resectable with hope of cure, and 13 were not, because of gross regional extension, liver metastasis, or both. Of the 18 patients in whom resection for cure was attempted, 1 died of an acute myocardial infarction. Tumor resection was unsuccessful in 10 of the 17 remaining patients, with serum gastrin and acid levels essentially remaining at preoperative levels. Thus, a surgical "cure," defined as resection of all identifiable tumor with normalization of serum gastrin and gastric secretory variables, was achieved in 7 (16%) of the 44 patients (Table 1). Five of these 7 patients had duo-

(32–8) Gastroenterology 84:1524–1532, June 1983.

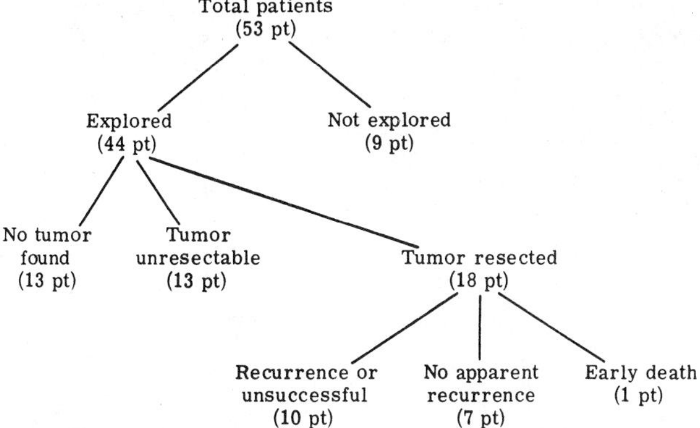

Fig 32–3.—Management decisions and outcomes in 53 patients with gastrinoma (1970–1980). Four of the 9 patients not explored had liver metastasis. Of the 10 patients with recurrence or unsuccessful surgery, 3 had multiple endocrine neoplasia (MEN) type 1, and 2 had duodenal wall tumor; of the 7 patients without apparent recurrence, none had MEN type 1, and 5 had duodenal wall tumor. (Courtesy of Malagelada, J.-R., et al.: Reprinted by permission of the publisher from Gastroenterology 84:1524–1532, June 1983; copyright by the American Gastrological Association.)

denal wall tumors, and none had multiple endocrine neoplasia (MEN) type 1. All 7 of these have remained well and are not receiving therapy, and none has apparent metastatic disease. Gastrectomy was ultimately performed in 18 patients, all before 1976 when H_2-receptor antagonists became available; no patient has since undergone total gastrectomy for management of gastric hypersecretion due to gastrinoma. Since July 1976, 18 patients with symptomatic gastrinoma were treated with cimetidine, 11 of whom were managed with doses of 1.8 gm/day or less, whereas the other 7 required higher doses (Table 2). In 16 of the 18 patients, cimetidine provided adequate control of symptoms and basal acid output without major side effects; follow-up averaged 28.9 months (range, 7–59 months). Of the 18 patients who underwent total gastrectomy, 2 died of carcinomatosis and 5 have stable pancreatic or liver metastasis. Eleven of these patients noted weight loss, and almost all ex-

TABLE 1.—CLINICAL AND LABORATORY STATUS OF 7 PATIENTS WITH APPARENTLY SUCCESSFUL RESECTION OF GASTRINOMA

MEN, type 1	Tumor site	Current status	Follow-up (*mo*)	BAO (*mmol/h*)		Fasting serum gastrin (*pg/ml*)		Gastrin response to secretin, peak (*pg/ml*)			
				Preop	Postop	Preop	Postop	Preop	0–6 mo postop	6 mo–1 yr postop	1–10 yr postop
No	Duodenal wall	Well, no Rx	112	—	1.1[a]	—	20[a]	—	—	—	—
No	Duodenal wall	Well, no Rx	98	19.9	10.0[a]	383	90[a]	493	—	135	141
No	Duodenal wall	Well, no Rx	74	34.2	4.8[a]	586	146[a]	1893	77	—	189
No	Duodenal wall	Well, no Rx	61	49.2	4.6[a]	654	108[a]	2034	84	—	90
No	Peripancreatic	Well, no Rx	48	8.4[b]	2.4[a]	1281	140[a]	9479	352	328	210
No	Duodenal wall	Well, no Rx	41	24.2	7.5[a]	349	100[a]	717	127	92	142
No	Pancreas head	Well, no Rx	39	21.0	0.5[a]	902	168[a]	1327	58	179	130

BAO, basal acid output.
[a]Value at date of latest follow-up.
[b]Prior gastric surgery.
(Courtesy of Malagelada, J.-R., et al.: Reprinted by permission of the publisher from Gastroenterology 84:1524–1532, June 1983; copyright by the American Gastrological Association.)

TABLE 2.—RESULTS OF MEDICAL THERAPY IN 18 PATIENTS WITH GASTRINOMA

		Medical therapy with oral cimetidine							
Prior surgery	Chemotherapy	Duration of treatment (mo)	Average optimal dose (g/day)	Highest dose required (g/day)	Pre-Rx BAO (mmol/h)	Average BAO on Rx (mmol/h)	Average decrease in BAO (%)[a]	Symptoms on therapy	Current status
None	Yes	48	1.8	1.8	32.9	16.8	49	None	Well
Vagotomy and pyloroplasty	Yes	14	1.8	2.4	29.9	9.8	67	None	Well
None	No	36	2.4	2.4	52.8	38.0	28	Occasional diarrhea	Well
None	No	59	1.5	1.5	53.0	22.0	58	Occasional diarrhea	Well
None	No	38	2.4	3.6	18.0	10.1	44	None	Well
Billroth I and vagotomy	No	48	1.5	1.8	8.4	2.4	71	None	Well
None	No	38	1.2	2.4	56.6	36.1	36	None	Well
Billroth II and vagotomy	No	36	2.4	2.4	24.2	5.1	79	Melena	Bleeding ulcer, surgery
Vagotomy and pyloroplasty	No	23	1.8	2.4[b]	9.4	3.6	62	Mild diarrhea	Well
None	No	7	1.2	1.2	21.0	—	—	None	Well
None	No	22	1.5	1.5	61.9	17.8	71	None	Well
None	No	20	2.1	2.4	12.0	—	—	Occasional diarrhea	Well
Vagotomy and pyloroplasty	No	35	1.2	1.2	28.1	6.1	78	None	Well
Billroth II and vagotomy	No	12	1.2	1.2	9.0	2.9	68	None	Well
None	No	32	1.5	1.5	79.5	45.0	43	None	Well
Billroth II and vagotomy	No	28	2.1	2.4[b]	5.8	1.2	79	None	Asymptomatic recurrent ulcer
None	Yes	17	1.8	2.1	26.1	7.8	70	None	Well
None	No	8	2.1	2.4	96.6	30.3	69	None	Well
Mean		28.9	1.8	2.0	34.7	15.9	60.8		

[a]*BAO,* basal acid output. Treatment was dose adjusted to level associated with minimal or no symptoms.
[b]With the addition of propantheline bromide (15 mg orally 4 times daily).
(Courtesy of Malagelada, J.-R., et al.: Reprinted by permission of the publisher from Gastroenterology 84:1524–1532, June 1983; copyright by the American Gastrological Association.)

perienced 1 of several side effects, including esophageal reflux, early satiety, dumping, or diarrhea. Two of these 18 patients developed stenosis of the esophagogastric junction requiring dilatations.

It is concluded that although the probability of a surgical cure is small, patients with Zollinger-Ellison syndrome without MEN type 1 or metastasis should undergo exploratory laparotomy and, possibly resection of identifiable gastrinomas. Chronic therapy with H_2-receptor antagonists can provide satisfactory control in most patients and is preferable to total gastrectomy. The major threat to survival for patients with unresectable gastrinomas, particularly non-Men type 1, is tumor death. An early positive response to secretin is highly suggestive that a surgical cure has not been achieved.

▶ [There are several controversial issues in the management of gastrinomas (Zollinger-Ellison syndrome [ZES]). These include the following: (1) How effective are histamine H_2-receptor antagonists in the control of acid hypersecretion and its attendant sequelae? (2) What are the prospects that some patients can be cured of their gastrinomas? (3) When should laparotomy be performed? (4) What is the place of total gastrectomy in the management of ZES? (5) What is the place of vagotomy in the management of these patients?

Regarding the effectiveness of histamine H_2-receptor blockers, the accumulating evidence suggests that up to one third of ZES patients can be expected to fail treatment with cimetidine. Passaro reviewed 6 reports of gastrinoma patients treated with cimetidine and noted that 33 of 93 patients or 35% failed treatment with histamine H_2-blockers.[11] Thus, the Mayo Clinic experience (2 failures in 18 patients treated with H_2-blockers) may not reflect a broader experience with cimetidine. Finally, it should be emphasized that it is possible that better control of acid hypersecretion will be obtained with new H_2-blockers (ranitidine) and H^+/K^+ ATPase inhibitors.

Regarding the prospects of surgical cure of gastrinoma, several recent reports suggest that successful excision of gastrinoma is feasible in approximately 20% of patients. Most of these patients, however, will have duodenal wall tumors.

Regarding surgical exploration, an attempt should be made to identify patients in whom an operation for cure should be recommended and to exclude patients with metastatic liver disease. This is accomplished by performance of upper gastrointestinal endoscopy, computed tomographic (CT) scanning, angiography, and in selected cases by portal venous sampling. If all of the above tests are negative, a key question arises. Should an exploratory laparotomy be done and if so, when? Most authorities would now recommend that under these circumstances, an exploratory laparotomy should be done as there is a 20% chance of finding a curable lesion. The next question is, When should such surgery be done? I subscribe to Passaro's view that any young, otherwise healthy patient not found to have MEN type 1 or multiple liver metastases preoperatively should be explored after a 6–12-month trial of H_2-receptor antagonist therapy.[11] The evidence suggests that patients who fail medical therapy will do so within 6–12 months. This would permit identification of patients who as treatment failures should undergo more definitive surgical treatment. There is considerable debate as to whether proximal gastric vagotomy (PGV) or total gastrectomy should be done under these circumstances. Preliminary favorable observation on the effectiveness of PGV is based on a small, noncontrolled trial. Prospective randomized trials are now underway, and any role for PGV in the management of gastrinoma should await the results of these studies.

There are now several reports which attest to the effectiveness of total gastrectomy in ZES.[12] If a patient has clearly failed a 6–12 month trial of medical therapy, then I believe a total gastrectomy is indicated. It will be interesting to learn if the newer H_2-blocker and H^+/K^+ ATPase inhibitor can effect better control of acid secretion in ZES and thus obviate the need for total gastrectomy. Preliminary reports with ranitidine are encouraging. Collen et al. evaluated prospectively the effectiveness and safety of ranitidine, a histamine H_2-receptor antagonist that is 5–10 times more potent than cimetidine, in the long-term control of acid secretion in 10 patients with ZES.[13] All patients were given ranitidine with or without an anticholinergic agent in sufficient dose to reduce gastric acid secretion to 10 mEq/hour prior to the next dose of medication. Patients were maintained on this dose of ranitidine, and control of gastric acid secretion and upper gastrointestinal endoscopy were assessed within 6 months. All patients were followed with a complete history, and biochemical and hematologic studies were made at 1, 3, 6, and 12 months. Ranitidine inhibited gastric acid secretion in all patients and ranitidine plus an anticholinergic agent gave greater inhibition than either agent alone. Four patients were maintained on ranitidine alone (mean dose, 1.2 gm/day) and 6 patients on ranitidine (mean dose, 3.2 gm/day) plus an anticholinergic. Ranitidine was 2.5 times more effective than cimetidine (2 gm/day vs. 5.3 gm/day). All patients have been followed for 6 months, 7 patients for 9 months, and 5 patients for at least 12 months; and ranitidine has continued to control gastric acid hypersecretion. On follow-up endoscopy no patient developed peptic ulcer while taking ranitidine, and no patient developed any of the side effects reported with cimetidine (e.g., gynecomastia). Long-term ranitidine therapy did not increase serum creatinine, change serum gastrin, or affect any hematologic values. Ranitidine treatment did not elevate serum transaminases in any patient, and in 4 patients whose pretreatment values were elevated, the transaminases returned to normal during ranitidine therapy. These results indicate that in patients with ZES, ranitidine alone or with an anticholinergic agent can control gastric acid secretion both acutely and on a long-term basis. Furthermore, ranitidine was 2.5 times more potent than cimetidine, did not cause any dose-related toxicity even at high doses (6 gm/day) taken for longer than 1 year, and did not cause any of the side effects that have been reported with cimetidine.] ◀

Chapter 32 References

1. Spiro H.M.: Is the steroid ulcer a myth? *N. Engl. J. Med.* 309:45–47, 1983.
2. Conn H.O., Blitzer B.L.: Nonassociation of adrenocorticosteroid therapy and peptic ulcer. *N. Engl. J. Med.* 294:473–479, 1976.
3. Hentschel E., Schütze K., Weiss W., et al.: Effect of cimetidine treatment in the prevention of gastric ulcer relapse: a one year double blind multicentre study. *Gut* 24:853–856, 1983.
4. Barr G.D., Kang J.Y., Canalise J., et al.: A two year prospective controlled study of maintenance cimetidine and gastric ulcer. *Gastroenterology* 85:100–104, 1983.
5. Boyd E.J.S., Wilson J.A., Wormsley K.G.: Smoking impairs therapeutic gastric inhibition. *Lancet* 1:95–97, 1983.
6. Peters M.N., Richardson C.T.: Stressful life events, acid hypersecretion, and ulcer disease. *Gastroenterology* 84:114–119, 1983.
7. Feldenius E., Berglindh T., Sachs G., et al.: Substituted benzimidazoles inhibit acid secretion by blocking the H^+, K^+-ATPase. *Nature* London 290:159–161, 1981.
8. Wallmark B., Jaresten B.M., Larsson H., et al.: Differentiation among inhibitory actions of omeprazole, cimetidine, and SCH^- on gastric acid secretion. *Am. J. Physiol.* 245:G64–G71, 1983.
9. Gustavsson S., Lööf L., Adami H.O.: Rapid healing of duodenal ulcers with omeprazole: double blind dose-comparative trial. *Lancet* 2:124–125, 1983.
10. Fleischer D.: Etiology and prevalence of severe persistent upper gastrointestinal bleeding. *Gastroenterology* 84:538–543, 1983.
11. Passaro E.: Of gastrinomas and their management. *Gastroenterology* 84:1621–1623, 1984.
12. Thompson J.G., Lewis B.G., Weiner T.: The role of surgery in the Zollinger-Ellison Syndrome. *Ann. Surg.* 197:594–607, 1983.
13. Collen M.J., Howard J.M., McArthur K.E., et al.: Long-term medical therapy with ranitidine in patients with Zollinger-Ellison Syndrome [abstract]. *Gastroenterology* 84:1983.

33. Small Bowel

33–1 **Small-Bowel Enema: An Underutilized Method of Small-Bowel Examination.** Larry Gurian, John Jendrzejewski, Ronald Katon, Marcia Bilbao, Ray Cope, and Clifford Melynk (Oregon Health Sciences Univ., Portland) retrospectively compared the results of 88 consecutive small-bowel enemas (SBE) with the results of 52 routine small-bowel series (SBS) and 50 barium enemas (BE) done in the same patients.

Of the documented diagnoses made by SBE, 96% were correct, as compared with only 65% in the total number of SBS done. The only SBE documented to be incorrect showed a false-negative result in 1 patient with regional enteritis (RE) in the ileum at laparotomy (table). The incorrect SBS studies were mostly false negatives; the abnormalities missed included RE, small-bowel obstruction, intestinal lymphoma, and radiation enteritis. The BE failed to achieve ileal reflux in 26% of patients and had a 23% false negative rate when reflux was achieved; the overall accuracy of the BE when reflux was achieved was 84%.

A technically adequate, routine SBS failed to diagnose RE in a significant number of patients, and the diagnosis was subsequently made by SBE in all but 1 case. Because SBS as done by conventional methods was significantly less accurate than SBE, it is believed SBE should be considered in patients with suspected small-bowel disease when other studies are negative. The Bilbao-Dotter tube allows rapid, predictable intubation of the duodenum.

▶ [Lesions of the small bowel are notoriously difficult to diagnose, many only com-

INDICATIONS AND EFFECTIVENESS OF SMALL-BOWEL ENEMA

	Number of patients	Number with small-bowel disease	Ability of studies to diagnose small-bowel disease (abnormal/number done) SBE	SBS	BE
Suspected regional enteritis	19	11	10/11	0/7	5/10
Activity regional enteritis	20	11	11/11	6/9	5/7
Suspected small-bowel obstruction	12	8	8/8	3/6	1/2
Gastrointestinal bleeding	15	2	2/2		
Abdominal pain	11	0			
Small-bowel fistula	3	0			
Suspected carcinoid	3	0			
Radiation enteritis	2	1	1/1	0/1	
Malabsorption	2	0			
Jejunal ulcers	1	1	1/1	1/1	
Total	88	34	33/34	10/24	11/19

SBE, small-bowel enema; *SBS,* small-bowel series; *BE,* barium enema.
(Courtesy of Gurian, L.: Dig. Dis. Sci. 27:1101–1108, December 1982.)

(33–1) Dig. Dis. Sci. 27:1101–1108, December 1982.

ing to light at laparotomy. In addition to the report abstracted above, Keddie and associates also have documented the clear superiority of the small-bowel enema vs. the routine small-bowel series in the diagnosis of small-bowel lesions.[1] Eighty-two patients had a total of 84 small-bowel enemas. The technique proved to be accurate in more than 90% of cases with only 2% false negative and 1% false positive results. The most common diagnosis was Crohn's disease (found in 25 cases), which can be very accurately assessed by small-bowel enema. Other lesions diagnosed included small-bowel involvement by lymphoma, benign stricture, ileal diverticulum, and adhesions. This technique appears to be the most satisfactory for radiological evaluations of the small bowel, and it should be much more widely available.] ◀

33–2 **Human Cryptosporidiosis in Immunocompetent and Immunodeficient Persons: Studies of an Outbreak and Experimental Transmission.** Human infections with the parasitic protozoa cryptosporidia have been considered to be rare and to be opportunistic. William L. Current, Norman C. Reese, John V. Ernst, Wilford S. Bailey, Melvin B. Heyman, and Wilfred M. Weinstein report an outbreak of cryptosporidiosis in 12 previously healthy, immunocompetent persons who were exposed to infected calves. The patients had direct contact with the feces of the calves during three unrelated outbreaks of calf cryptosporidiosis. Nine of the subjects had diarrhea and abdominal cramps lasting 1–10 days (table). Six other exposed subjects were not affected.

The infection was diagnosed and monitored by detecting oocysts in the feces with the use of a modified Sheather's flotation technique and phase-contrast microscopy. Oocysts of *Cryptosporidium* were isolated from calves but not from other animals with which the patients had

Clinical Features of 12 Immunocompetent Subjects Infected With Calf *Cryptosporidium*

Case No.	Age (yr)/ Sex	Total Days of Illness	Diarrhea	Other Symptoms	Examination of Stool	Observation of Oocysts
			days *		*days* *	
1	19/M	10	2–5	Malaise, fever, abdominal cramps	1–4, 6, 8, 10 12–13	1–4, 6 8, 10
2	45/M	3	2–3	None	4, 7	4
3	50/M	1	1	None	4, 9	4
4	22/M	7	0	Malaise	5, 12	5
5	60/M	0	0	None	7, 10, 11	7
6	24/F	0	0	None	7, 13	7
7	39/M	9	2–3	Malaise, nausea, abdominal cramps	2, 5, 10	2, 5
8	25/M	3	2–3	Headache, malaise	1–6, 8	2, 3
9	21/M	7	2–5	Malaise, fever, abdominal cramps	4, 6, 10	4, 6
10	18/M	2	1–2	Abdominal cramps	3, 8, 15	3, 8
11	20/M	1	1	Abdominal cramps	3, 8, 15	3, 8
12	23/F	10	2–6	Malaise, nausea, abdominal cramps	5–8, 10–14	5–8 10, 11

*No. of days after onset of illness or after contact with infected calves if illness was not present.

(Courtesy of Current, W.L., et al.: N. Engl. J. Med. 308:1252–1257, May 26, 1983; reprinted by permission of The New England Journal of Medicine.)

(33–2) N. Engl. J. Med. 308:1252–1257, May 26, 1983.

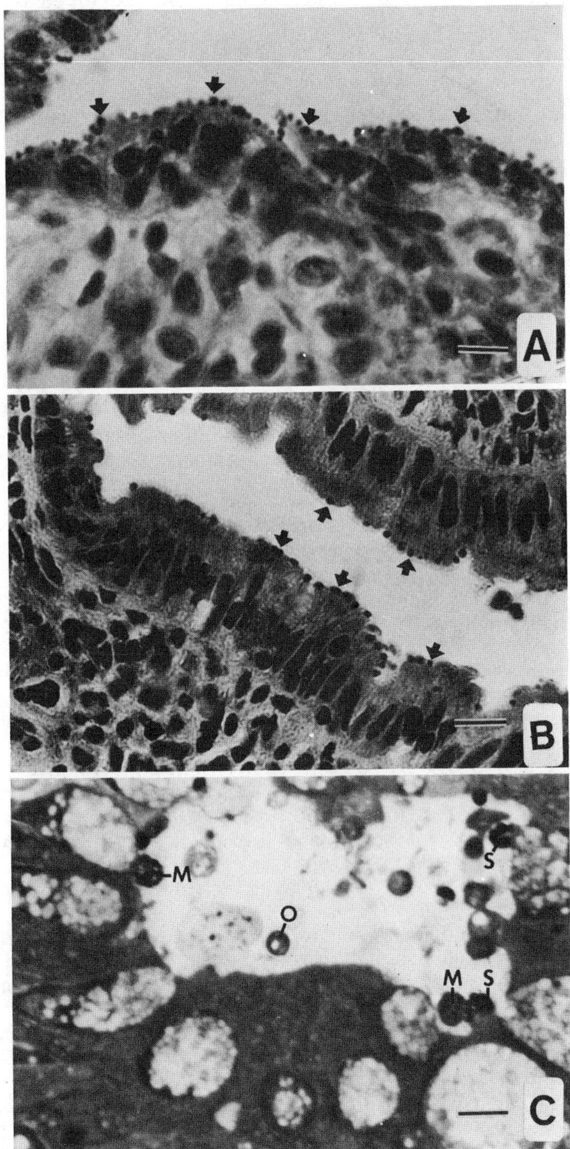

Fig 33–1.—Endogenous stages of *Cryptosporidium* in histologic sections. **A,** ileum of naturally infected calf shows numerous parasites *(arrows)* in microvillous border. Bar represents 25 μm; hematoxylin-eosin. **B,** small-bowel biopsy sample from subject with congenital hypogammaglobulinemia shows numerous parasites *(arrows)* in microvillous border. Bar represents 25 μm; hematoxylin-eosin. **C,** large-bowel biopsy sample from patient with AIDS. Endogenous stages, such as schizonts *(S)*, macrogametes *(M)*, and oocysts *(O)*, can be seen in microvillous border deep within crypt. Bar represents 10 μg; plastic section (0.5 μm); toluidine blue. (Courtesy of Current, W.L., et al.: N. Engl. J. Med. 308:1252–1257, May 26, 1983; reprinted by permission of the New England Journal of Medicine.)

been in contact. They were also detected in the feces of 2 immunodeficient patients with persistent cryptosporidiosis. The infected calves had severe diarrhea, malabsorption, and dehydration. The histologic appearances are shown in Figure 33–1. Apparently identical infection was transmitted to calves and mice by using oocysts from infected calves and human subjects. Oocysts from one of the immunodeficient subjects produced infection in kittens, puppies, and goats.

Immunocompetent persons can develop a self-limited, flulike gastrointestinal illness from *Cryptosporidium*. The disease contrasts with the prolonged, severe diarrhea that develops in exposed immunocompromised subjects. Calves with diarrhea should be considered a potential source of human infection, and immunocompromised persons should avoid contact with such animals. *Cryptosporidium* should be viewed as a possible cause of diarrhea in immunocompromised patients, particularly those with acquired immune deficiency syndrome.

▶ [There are additional recent reports of cryptosporidiosis in immunocompetent persons. Jokipii et al. reviewed data on 1,422 fecal samples sent by general practitioners for routine parasitological examination during a 3-month period.[2] Approximately 10.8% of the specimens were short-listed for special examination for cryptosporidium oocysts; those were fecal concentrates containing abundant small organisms with a diameter less than 10 μm. Fourteen samples (9.1% of those short-listed and 1% of the total) were positive for *cryptosporidium.* Importantly, all 14 patients had symptoms of gastrointestinal infection which seemed to be related to a trip abroad. The incubation period varied between 4 and 12 days. Clinically, cryptosporidiosis could not be distinguished from giardiasis, but its duration was shorter (median, 10 days). Strong abdominal pain and cramps were more common, and bloating, anorexia, and weakness were less common. The diseases can be diagnosed by identification of oocysts in fecal samples that have undergone formalin-ether concentration. There is no specific treatment for it, and recovery is spontaneous in immunocompetent patients.

Cryptosporidium should also be considered in the differential diagnosis of diarrhea in immunocompromised patients, especially those with acquired immunodeficiency syndrome (AIDS). The differential diagnosis of diarrhea in such immunocompromised patients is now very long indeed. It includes all of the following disorders: *Salmonella* and *Shigella* infections, syphilis, amebiasis, gonorrhea, giardiasis, and infections due to herpes-virus cytomegalovirus, *Campylobacter, Chlamydia, cryptosporidium,* and *Isospora belli.*

For an excellent up-to-date review of AIDS, see the article by Gottlieb et al.[3] concerning this devastating illness that has dramatically emerged in the United States, Europe, and Haiti. The syndrome represents an unprecedented epidemic form of immunodeficiency involving prominent defects of the T-lymphocyte arm of the immune system. *Pneumocystis carinni* pneumonia, other opportunistic infections, and the previously rare cancer Kaposi's sarcoma are the most conspicuous illnesses that have this profound state of immune compromise as their underlying basis. Two years after the onset of clinical illness the case-fatality rate may exceed 90%. A steadily growing body of epidemiologic evidence indicates an infectious (probably viral) cause of the immunodeficiency, although the responsible agent(s) remains obscure. Critical issues surrounding the diagnosis, screening of blood products, treatment of complicating infections and cancers, and prognosis for immunologic recovery in affected persons are unresolved. The identification of the cause of AIDS and the institution of effective preventive measures require the urgent attention of the medical and scientific community worldwide.] ◀

33–3 **Jejunal Diverticulosis: Heterogeneous Disorder Caused by a Variety of Abnormalities of Smooth Muscle or Myenteric Plexus.** Shoba Krishnamurthy, Mary M. Kelly, Charles A. Rohr-

(33–3) Gastroenterology 85:538–547, September 1983.

TABLE 1.—CLINICAL FINDINGS*

Patient	Age/sex	Years of symptoms	Obstructive symptoms†	Weight loss (kg)	Raynaud's phenomenon	Esophageal manometry: Peristalsis	Esophageal manometry: LESP (mmHg)	Pathological findings consistent with:
1	63 F	43	+	10	–	Not done	—	PSS
2	62 F	20	+	12	+	Normal	7	PSS
3	52 M	12	+	20	+	Normal	7	PSS
4	59 F	14	+	15	+	Not done	—	PSS
5	59 M	40	+	45	+	Low amplitude (15 mm)	0	Visceral neuropathy
6	69 M	24	+	12	–	Normal	18	Visceral myopathy
7	26 F	5	+	15	–	No contractile activity	6	Visceral myopathy
8	77 M	1	–	10	+	Simultaneous contractions	15	No tissue available
9	65 F	7	+	—	–	Not done	—	No tissue available
10	84 M	16	+	5	–	(a) Spontaneous & simultaneous contractions (b) Partial relaxation of LES	20	No tissue available

*Abbreviations: *LES*, lower esophageal sphincter; *LESP*, LES pressure; *PSS*, progressive systemic sclerosis.

†Obstructive symptoms include intermittent abdominal pain and distention, nausea, and vomiting.

(Courtesy of Krishnamurthy, S., et al.: Reprinted by permission of the publisher from Gastroenterology 85:538–547, September 1983; copyright by the American Gastrological Association.)

TABLE 2.—RADIOGRAPHIC FINDINGS*

Patient	Plain films: Pneumoperitoneum	Plain films: Air-fluid levels	Plain films: Small bowel dilatation	Barium studies: Esophagus	Barium studies: Stomach	Barium studies: Duodenum	Barium studies: Jejunum	Barium studies: Ileum	Barium studies: Colon	Pathologic findings consistent with:
1	−	−	−	N	N	Diverticula	Diverticula	Diverticula	Not done	PSS
2	+ Pneumatosis	+	+	N	N	N	Diverticula ↑ Width	N	Diverticula	PSS
3	+	+	+	↑ Length tertiary contractions	Long Patulous	Diverticula	Diverticula ↑ Width Abnormal folds	Diverticula	Diverticula	PSS
4	−	−	−	Not done	N	↑ Width	↑ Width	N	N	PSS
5	−	−	+	↑ Width	N	Diverticula ↑ Width	Diverticula ↑ Width	Diverticula	Diverticula	Visceral neuropathy
6	+	+	+	N	N	Diverticula ↑ Width	Diverticula ↑ Width Abnormal folds	↑ Width	Elongated	Visceral myopathy
7	−	−	−	N	↑ Size	N	Diverticula Abnormal folds	Abnormal folds	N	Visceral myopathy
8	−	−	−	N	N	Diverticula	Diverticula	N	Diverticula	Not available
9	−	+	+	N	N	Diverticula	Diverticula	Diverticula	N	Not available
10	+	−	+	Not done	N	N	Diverticula	Diverticula	Diverticula	Not available

*Symbols and abbreviations: +, present; −, absent; *N*, normal; ↑, increased; *PSS*, progressive systemic sclerosis.
(Courtesy of Krishnamurthy, S., et al.: Reproduced by permission of the publisher from Gastroenterology 85:538–547, September 1983; copyright by the American Gastrological Association.)

mann, and Michael D. Schuffler (Univ. of Washington) reviewed the findings in 10 patients referred with jejunal diverticulosis during an 8-year period. All but 1 of the 5 men and 5 women were aged 59 or older. Nine patients had had gastrointestinal symptoms for 5 years or longer. The clinical findings are given in Table 1. Eight patients had had a total of 18 operations, most of them for suspected small-bowel obstruction. Most patients had abdominal distention and borborygmi on examination. Air-fluid levels were seen on upright abdominal x-ray films in 6 of 8 cases, and 4 patients had free intraperitoneal air. The findings from barium studies are included in Table 2. Three of the 7 patients who underwent esophageal manometry exhibited spontaneous reflux.

Four of the 7 evaluable patients had histologic findings consistent with progressive systemic sclerosis. Two others had fibrosis associated with degenerated smooth muscle cells, as in visceral myopathy. One patient had findings consistent with visceral neuropathy, including neuronal and axonal degeneration and neuronal intranuclear inclusions. Medical management included intermittent courses of antibiotics, dietary manipulations, and parenteral nutrition. Seven patients stopped having diarrhea and gained weight when given broad-spectrum antibiotics for 10–21 days. Responses to repeated courses were, however, variable. No patient had symptomatic relief after small-bowel resection. One patient died shortly after emergency surgery for volvulus and massive small-bowel infarction. Surgery probably was lifesaving for 2 patients with perforated diverticula and intraabdominal abscesses.

It is concluded that intestinal pseudoobstruction is a major clinical manifestation of jejunal diverticulosis. In contrast to intestinal obstruction without diverticulosis, jejunal diverticulosis less frequently involves the esophagus, stomach, and colon. Jejunal diverticulosis appears to result from abnormal structure of either the intestinal smooth muscle or the myenteric plexus. Some patients probably have progressive systemic sclerosis limited to the gastrointestinal tract or a form of visceral myopathy or neuropathy. The end result is either localized areas of weakness in the muscle, with protrusion of all components of the wall, or uncoordinated activity leading to protrusion of the mucosa and submucosa through thickened muscle at gaps for blood vessels at the mesenteric border.

33–4 **Intestinal Pseudoobstruction as the Presenting Manifestation of Small-Cell Carcinoma of the Lung: Paraneoplastic Neuropathy of the Gastrointestinal Tract.** Ogilvie described a type of intestinal pseudoobstruction associated with metastatic cancer outside the gastrointestinal tract. Michael D. Schuffler, H. Wallace Baird, C. Richard Fleming, C. Elliott Bell, Thomas W. Bouldin, Juan R. Malagelada, Douglas B. McGill, Samuel M. LeBauer, Murray Abrams, and James Love encountered a woman with intestinal pseudoobstruction who later developed severe, diffuse autonomic insufficiency and died 9 months after onset of illness with small-cell lung cancer and a severe neuropathy of the myenteric plexus.

(33–4) Ann. Intern. Med. 98:129–134, February 1983.

Woman, 58, developed midabdominal pain, nausea, and vomiting and was found to have gastric dilatation, delayed marker transit throughout the duodenum, and esophageal spasm. Contrast study showed a high-grade functional obstruction in the third part of the duodenum. Exploration yielded normal findings except for mild duodenal dilatation; a side-to-side duodenojejunostomy was created. The patient did not improve despite cholinergic and metoclopramide therapy, and required continuous nasogastric suction and total parenteral nutrition for the duration of her illness. The barium column stopped abruptly in the midileum on subsequent study, and adequate filling of the ileum took 24 hours. A soft tissue density was found in the left hilar region on computed tomography. Manometric study showed absence of the normal interdigestive motor complex and its replacement by irregular contractile activity of reduced amplitude. Postural dizziness later developed, with gait ataxia, tremulousness, and absent deep tendon reflexes in the lower extremities. Autonomic function studies showed absent sweating in the lower extremities and no change in the pulse rate during the Valsalva maneuver. The patient developed recurrent septicemia, pseudomembranous colitis, and bronchopneumonia and died 9 months after the onset of gastrointestinal symptoms.

Autopsy showed small-cell carcinoma of the lung with metastases in lymph nodes. Widespread degeneration of the myenteric plexus was found with a reduction in the number of neurons and infiltration by plasma cells and lymphocytes. Neuron loss and lymphocytic infiltration were also seen in the dorsal root ganglia. Slight lymphocytic meningitis was present. No immunoglobulin was found in association with myenteric plexus or tumor cells.

A gastrointestinal neuropathy causing intestinal pseudo-obstruction may be the presenting feature of a paraneoplastic syndrome associated with small-cell carcinoma of the lung. Tumor antigens may elicit an immune response that cross-reacts with neural tissue. The myenteric plexus was the site of the putative cross-reaction in this patient, and the result was an intestinal neuropathy and the syndrome of intestinal pseudoobstruction.

▶ [This is truly a remarkable case in which intestinal pseudoobstruction overshadowed all other problems, including a not so obvious 1-cm undifferentiated small-cell carcinoma of the lung which was the primary tumor. Other interesting features included markedly delayed gastric emptying and gastric hypersecretion.

As we learn more about intestinal pseudoobstruction, the number of cases that we term "primary" or "idiopathic" will obviously decrease. Listed below is a classification of this group of disorders that I have found clinically useful.

- I. Primary or idiopathic
- II. Secondary
  - A. Endocrine disorders
    1. diabetes mellitus
    2. hypothyroidism
  - B. Infiltrative disorders
    1. amyloidosis
  - C. Collagen vascular disease
    1. scleroderma
    2. dermatomyositis/polymyositis
    3. systemic lupus erythematosus
  - D. Neurological diseases
    1. Chaga's disease
  - E. Paraneoplastic syndrome
    1. carcinoma lung
  - F. Drugs
    1. tricyclics
    2. clonidine
    3. opiates

G. Miscellaneous
   1. jejunoileal bypass
   2. jejunal diverticulosis

33-5 **Diet for Patients With a Short Bowel: High Fat or High Carbohydrate?** Low-fat, high-carbohydrate diets are commonly prescribed for patients with a short bowel, but previous studies have not been controlled for fluid intake, timing of fluids in relation to meals, or fiber intake. Graham M. Woolf, Cindy Miller, Regina Kurian, and Kursheed N. Jeejeebhoy (Univ. of Toronto) examined the relative merits of fat and carbohydrate in 8 patients with a short bowel resulting from intestinal resection, who had been in clinically stable condition for at least 6 months. A diet containing 60% of calories as fat and 20% as carbohydrate and the reverse diet, both with 20% of total calories as protein, were given for 5 days each in a crossover design. Both diets were lactose free and had low fiber content. Fluid intake was kept constant. A $^{51}CrCl_3$ marker was used to insure completeness of collection. Over 95% of the marker was recovered in the stool or ostomy output within 3 hours of administration. The test diets approximated the usual diet of the patients, insuring good compliance.

No changes in weight or blood pressure occurred during the study. There were no differences in blood chemical values, stool or ostomy volumes, zinc, calcium, or magnesium balances, urine volume, or electrolyte excretion between patients on the two diets. Total calories absorbed (Fig 33–2) and excreted were comparable on the two diets. No significant differences in fecal excretion and net absorption of calcium, magnesium, or zinc were observed (Fig 33–3).

Low-fat diets appear to provide no special benefit in the overall nutrition of patients with bowel disease in remission and a short bowel after resection. Hence, dietary restriction is not recommended for these patients. Dietary fat has a role in providing essential fatty acids and in enhancing the palatability of food, encouraging patients to eat more. Requirements for and losses of fat-soluble vitamins in patients on a high-fat diet require further study.

▶ [The reader is referred to an excellent brief review by Young of diet in short bowel syndrome.[4]

This provocative study raises a number of important questions regarding effective nutritional management of patients with shortened intestine and will stimulate further interest and clinical investigation. A major question to be answered concerns the effects of high fecal fat excretion when on a high fat diet, particularly if such a diet is designed for long-term use. There are data to suggest that such a diet can cause increased loss of divalent cations such as calcium, magnesium, zinc, and copper.[5] Ovesen et al. studied the effect of diet on jejunostomy output of fluid, fat, sodium, potassium, calcium, magnesium, zinc, and copper in 5 metabolically stable, home parenteral nutrition patients. Three isocaloric diets were compared: one low in fat (30% kcal) but high in complex carbohydrate (55% kcal), and two high in fat (60% kcal) but low in carbohydrate (25% kcal). Although increasing the percentage of fat in the diet increased the amount of steatorrhea, altering the polyunsaturated/saturated fatty acid ratio had no clearly beneficial effect on the amount of fat absorbed. Neither the amount of fat nor the type of fat had any consistent influence on jejunostomy volume. The sodium and potassium concentration of the jejunostomy fluid stayed remarkably constant, and hence net monovalent cation losses reflected jeju-

(33–5) Gastroenterology 84:823–828, April 1983.

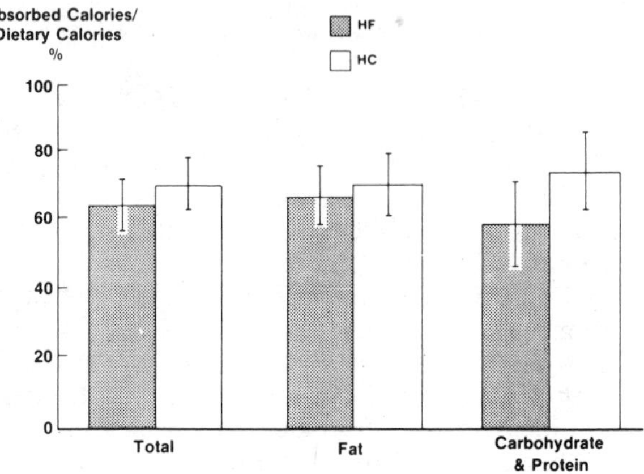

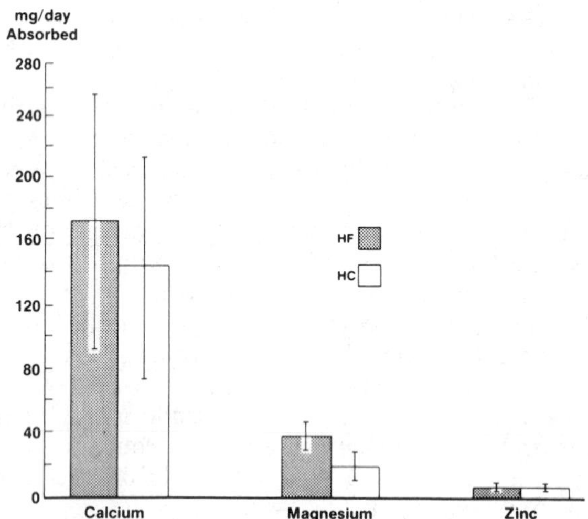

Fig 33–2 (top).—Total calorie absorption. There were no significant differences in mean total calories, fat calories, or protein plus carbohydrate calories absorbed, expressed as percentage of intake between high-fat *(HF)* and high-carbohydrate diets *(HC)*. Mean percentage absorptions of fat and nonfat calories were similar and averaged 65% of intake.

Fig 33–3 (bottom).—Divalent cation absorption. There were no significant differences in absorption of calcium, magnesium, or zinc between high-fat *(HF)* and high-carbohydrate *(HC)* diets.

(Courtesy of Woolf, G.M., et al.: Reproduced by permission of the publisher from Gastroenterology 84:823–828, April 1983; copyright by the American Gastrological Association.)

nostomy volume rather than the fat carbohydrate content of the diet eaten. The most consistent effect of the high fat diet was a marked increase in ostomy losses of divalent cations: calcium, magnesium, zinc, and copper. In conclusion, the proportion of fat vs. carbohydrate calories does not appear to influence ostomy volume or monovalent cation loss in extreme short bowel, and jejunostomy patients; however, a high fat intake causes a significant net secretion of divalent cations.

A high-fat diet contributes significantly to the total caloric needs of these patients, especially when the caloric needs are increased. The present study, as well as several other studies, shows that fecal excretion of fat increases as the dietary fat increases. The percentage of dietary fat that was excreted in the stool on the high-fat diet was similar to that on the high-carbohydrate diet.

The long-term use of a high-fat diet with subsequent high-fat excretion may have significant effects on the absorption of the fat-soluble vitamins. Although the absorption of fat-soluble vitamins was not determined in this study, this should be an important consideration in future investigations. In contrast to the findings of Ovesen et al., Woolf et al. found that the high-fat excretion did not significantly increase total stool weight, osmolality, cations, or urea nitrogen. This is of some importance as several studies have shown that divalent cations may bind to fatty acids in the stool.] ◀

33–6 **Jejunoileal Bypass for Morbid Obesity: Late Follow-up in 100 Cases.** Michael P. Hocking, Margaret C. Duerson, J. Patrick O'Leary, and Edward R. Woodward (Univ. of Florida) reviewed the results of jejunoileal bypass surgery for obesity in 100 consecutive patients with intact bypasses seen an average of more than 5 years postoperatively. An end-to-side anastomosis of jejunum to ileum was made, leaving a blind limb of defunctionalized small bowel. All patients had initially been 100 lb or more over ideal weight and had failed to lose weight with conservative measures for 5 years or longer. All had medical complications of obesity or psychosocial indications for bypass surgery. The mean follow-up period after surgery was 66 months. The mean age at the time of bypass was 34 years.

The mean weight had fallen from 315 to 219 lb 1 year postoperatively and to 212 lb at 5 years. Only 3 patients had inadequate weight loss. Glucose tolerance improved after surgery in all patients with abnormal tolerance initially. Hypertension resolved in 76% of affected patients. Of 8 patients with heart failure before surgery, 7 were asymptomatic without medication postoperatively. Symptoms of ventilatory insufficiency resolved in all 9 affected patients. Of 48 patients with elevated serum triglyceride levels preoperatively, 40 had normal levels after the procedure. Venous stasis ulcers healed in 3 patients. Antidiarrheal medication was used by 18% of patients 5 years postoperatively. One third of patients were hypokalemic at 5 years, and 38% had hypomagnesemia. More than half the patients had decreased B_{12} and folate levels at 5 years. Of 69 patients without evidence of cholelithiasis at the time of bypass, 14 required cholecystectomy afterward. Nephrolithiasis developed in 21 patients after bypass surgery. Nearly one third of patients had progressive hepatic abnormalities, and cirrhosis developed after bypass surgery in 7%.

Nearly half the patients in this series definitely benefited from bypass surgery for obesity, another third had mixed results, and about one fifth were considered surgical failures. The risk-benefit ratio 5 years postoperatively seems to be acceptable, but continued late adverse effects have led to the abandonment of jejunoileal bypass in favor of gastric bypass surgery.

▶ [I selected this article to remind readers that there are a considerable number of patients who have undergone jejunoileal bypass for morbid obesity and who are candidates for the late sequelae described here by Hocking et al. It will be recalled that one third of the patients had mixed results and 20% were surgical failures. Diarrhea persisted in approximately 60%, nephrolithiasis developed in 20%, and cholelithiasis in 20% of the patients. Not surprisingly, the operation has been abandoned in favor of gastric bypass surgery.] ◀

(33–6) N. Engl. J. Med. 308:995–999, Apr. 28, 1983.

33-7 **Purging and Calorie Absorption in Bulimic Patients and Normal Women.** Self-induced purging with laxatives is commonly practiced for weight control by persons with bulimia nervosa, chiefly young women, but its efficacy in reducing calorie absorption has not been documented. Health food stores encourage the practice, compounding the problem. George W. Bo-Linn, Carol A. Santa Ana, Stephen G. Morawski, and John S. Fordtran (Baylor Univ. Med. Center, Dallas) measured calorie absorption during a single day to determine the extent to which phenolphthalein or saline purging reduced calorie absorption. Studies were done in 2 bulimic women meeting DSM-III (*Diagnostic and Statistical Manual of Mental Disorders,* ed. 3) criteria for the diagnosis and 5 normal young women. Both patients had regularly used Correctol (phenolphthalein and dioctyl sodium sulfosuccinate) for weight control for 5 years; both were of normal weight.

Even extreme purging that produced 4–6 L of diarrhea caused calorie absorption to decline by only about 12% of caloric intake. Saline purging caused calorie absorption to decrease by a mean of 75 kcal.

Purging with Correctol can cause acute weight loss with severe volume depletion, but calorie absorption decreases only slightly. Long-term ingestion of excessive amounts of cathartics containing phenolphthalein and bisacodyl has caused mild steatorrhea. It is uncertain whether the knowledge that Correctol or salt solutions are ineffective will dissuade persons from using laxatives for weight control. Most bulimic persons, however, are relatively well adjusted, aware that they have an eating disorder, and are receptive to education and counseling. Both patients in this study have discontinued laxative abuse. The theoretical basis on which laxatives are used for weight control is unsound.

▶ [Bulimia is an abnormal craving for food that results in gorging followed by induced vomiting. The DSM-III diagnostic criteria for bulimia are listed below:

A. Recurrent episodes of binge eating (rapid consumption of a large amount of food in a discrete period of time, usually less than two hours)
B. At least three of the following:
   1. Consumption of high-caloric, easily ingested food during a binge
   2. Inconspicuous eating during a binge
   3. Termination of such eating episodes by abdominal pain, sleep, social interruption or self-induced vomiting
   4. Repeated attempts to lose weight by severely restrictive diets, self-induced vomiting or use of cathartics or diuretics
   5. Frequent weight fluctuations greater than 10 lb due to alternating binges and fasts
C. Awareness that the eating pattern is abnormal and fear of not being able to stop eating voluntarily
D. Depressed mood and self-deprecating thoughts following eating binges
E. The bulimic episodes are not due to anorexia nervosa or any known physical disorder

For an excellent review article on bulimia, see the paper by Gross.[6] He points out that growing numbers of young women and men are resorting to vomiting as a weight control measure. This secretive behavior is becoming popular on college campuses. Indeed, it has been estimated that as much as 13% of college students experience the major symptoms of bulimia; 87% are females. The cost of the habitual excessive food intake can be enormous. Gross[6] estimates costs to be $8–$10 per

---

(33–7) Ann. Intern. Med. 99:14–17, July 1983.

binge and with 4 or 5 such binges a day, minimum costs would be $40–$50 daily. Some bulimics resort to shoplifting, forgery, selling drugs, or prostitution to finance these binges. Frequent episodes of overeating and vomiting can lead to severe weight loss. In women, a loss of more than 25% of body weight usually results in anorexia nervosa. Such anorexia nervosa combined with bulimia is termed bulimia nervosa or bulimarexia. Excessive vomiting also leads to enlargement of the parotid glands, and bulimics may look as if they are suffering from mumps. They often sustain severe destruction of tooth enamel from vomiting as well as from sugar.

Important medical complications of bulimia include pharyngitis, esophagitis, hypokalemia, dehydration, cardiac arrhythmias, irregularities of menstruation including amenorrhea, easy bruisability, and abnormal tests of liver function.

Most people who have bulimia have made repeated attempts to lose weight either by dieting or using cathartics, diuretics, or diet pills. Recent studies suggest that bulimia can be effectively controlled by psychotherapy.[7] Pretreatment indicators of a poorer prognosis include alcohol abuse and a history of anorexia nervosa.] ◀

33–8 **Starch Blockers: Their Effect on Calorie Absorption From a High-Starch Meal.** It is known that certain plant foods, such as kidney beans and wheat, contain a substance that inhibits the activity of salivary and pancreatic amylase. This antiamylase has been purified and marketed for use in weight control under the generic name "starch blockers." Although this approach to weight control is popular, it has never been shown whether starch-blocker tablets actually reduce the absorption of calories from starch in humans.

Using a 1-day, calorie-balance technique and a high-starch (100 gm) meal (spaghetti, tomato sauce, and bread), George W. Bo-Linn, Carol A. Santa Ana, Stephen G. Morawski, and John S. Fordtran (Baylor Univ. Med. Center, Dallas) measured the excretion of fecal calories after normal subjects took placebo or starch-blocker tablets (Carbo-Lite; total dose of the amylase inhibitor phaseolamin was 1,500 mg).

If the starch-blocker tablets had prevented the digestion of starch,

RESULTS IN 5 NORMAL SUBJECTS ON DAYS OF PLACEBO AND STARCH-BLOCKER TESTS

SUBJECT NO.	PLACEBO TEST DAY			STARCH-BLOCKER TEST DAY		
	DUPLICATE TEST MEAL *	RECTAL EFFLUENT	$^{51}CrCl_3$ MARKER RECOVERY	DUPLICATE TEST MEAL *	RECTAL EFFLUENT	$^{51}CrCl_3$ MARKER RECOVERY
	kcal	*kcal*	%	*kcal*	*kcal*	%
1	664	81	97.8	665	76	96.6
2	675	84	95.2	672	84	98.3
3	682	80	97.4	681	73	94.4
4	686	67	95.5	675	75	103.6
5	676	89	96.3	687	83	106.9
Means	677	80	96.4	676	78	100
±S.E.M.	±4	±4	±0.5	±4	±2	±2

*Does not include calories contained in 3 placebo tablets (each tablet, 1.2 ± 0.1 kcal) or in 3 Carbo-Lite tablets (each tablet, 2.8 ± 0.1 kcal) that were ingested with the test meal.

(Courtesy of Bo-Linn, G.W., et al.: N. Engl. J. Med. 307:1413–1416, Dec. 2, 1983; reprinted by permission of The New England Journal of Medicine.)

(33–8) N. Engl. J. Med. 307:1413–1416, Dec. 2, 1982.

fecal calorie excretion should have increased by 400 kcal. However, fecal calorie excretion was the same on the two test days (table). Similar results were obtained in 1 subject studied with another starch-blocker preparation, Amyl-Lite.

It is concluded that starch-blocker tablets do not inhibit the digestion and absorption of starch calories in humans. It is believed that starch blockers most likely failed to prevent starch absorption because the human pancreas probably secretes many more times the amount of amylase after meals than is needed for hydrolysis of the ingested starch, and despite ingestion of the starch blockers, there may still be more than enough unbound, active pancreatic amylase in the intestinal lumen to digest the ingested starch totally.

▶ [The reader is referred to a thoughtful editorial entitled "Starch blockers—still no calorie-free lunch" written by Rosenberg.[8] Much of what follows has been abstracted from that article.

"The report by Bo-Linn et al. showing that one of the leading preparations of "starch blockers" had no demonstrable effect on the absorption of starch calories, raises a number of challenging questions about marketing, consumer response, and the appropriate role of federal regulatory agencies in the volatile field of nutritional products. It is appropriate to note that the long-term effectiveness of all these purported starch blockers—mostly extracts of kidney beans—although doubtful, has not been disproved by this single, carefully designed clinical study. What is clear, however, is that there are no clinical studies that establish the effectiveness or indeed the safety of the more than 200 such products that poured onto the market over a two-year span and were consumed at an estimated rate of 1 million tablets per day, before the Food and Drug Administration ordered their marketing discontinued. As physicians who are accustomed to debate the time required for a drug to be released in this country as safe and effective, we are particularly puzzled by this case history. How do unproved products get on the market? How or why are they being taken off? What generalizations can be made about the checks and balances within our society with respect to the purveying of products that appeal to the public's desire for a "quick fix" for the problem of weight control, not to mention its search for unending youth, vigor, beauty, and sexual prowess through dietary supplements? And finally, where is the medical profession in all this?

How did the checks and balances work in this case? Did the companies that marketed these products behave properly? The companies took advantage of the discretionary gray zone between food and drugs to market the products as foods without tests of effectiveness. The counterweights to an aggressive nutritional-products industry that has every right to pursue the development and marketing of new products under our laws are an informed public, vigilant regulatory agencies, and a diligent, involved medical profession. Many consumers are consistently responsive to overstated or fraudulent claims for tonics and remedies. Are we now seeing a phenomenon of much greater magnitude with more sophisticated marketing? That a very substantial number of the starch-blocker tablets were sold in health-food stores is an observation that might be analyzed by the medical profession. Is this another indication that an increasing proportion of the population has become alienated from standard medical practice, particularly when it comes to the management of obesity and approaches to diet and nutrition? Have the health-food stores become the foci of an alternative health system that claims to focus on health and the prevention of disease while the medical profession is seen in caricature as being concerned only with drugs? One need only enter a health-food store and examine the shelves of products to learn that the health-food "system," too, depends heavily on pills and capsules; however, for regulatory purposes these are foods or dietary supplements. We must ask whether the response of physicians and scientific medical societies to the public's increasing appetite for nutritional information has been adequately informed and sufficiently concerned."] ◀

33–9 **Intrinsic Factor-Mediated Absorption of Cobalamin by Guinea Pig Ileal Cells.** The fate of the intrinsic factor (IF)-cobalamin (Cbl) complex after its attachment to receptors on the ileal absorptive cell surface is uncertain. Cyrus R. Kapadia, Del Serfilippi, Kurt Voloshin, and Robert M. Donaldson, Jr. (Yale Univ.) investigated these events in isolated guinea pig enterocytes and tied-off loops of guinea pig ileum. Both uptake of ^{57}Co-labeled Cbl and cellular uptake of a purified IF preparation biosynthetically labeled with ^{35}S-methionine were examined.

When the labeled IF-Cbl complex was incubated for 30 minutes with isolated guinea pig ileal cells under conditions blocking cellular metabolism, virtually all cellular activity could be removed by washing the cell surface with ethylenediamine tetraacetate (EDTA) or acid. Washing removed only half the radioactivity from cells incubated in oxygen at 37 C. When residual cellular activity was extracted and analyzed by gel filtration, 80%–94% of both ^{35}S and ^{57}Co activities eluted in the same fractions as the original complex. The rest of the activity eluted as free ^{57}Co-Cbl or ^{35}S-methionine. When labeled complex was instilled into tied-off ileal loops of intact animals and nondissociable radioactivity was extracted after 2–4½ hours, the proportion of extracted ^{57}Co eluting as free Cbl increased to 39%–46%, and the proportion eluting as IF-Cbl complex fell to 22%–45%; and 9%–34% eluted as a macromolecule that reacted with antitranscobalamin II antibody but not with anti-IF antibody. Extracted ^{35}S activity eluted in several peaks besides the IF peak.

These findings suggest that (1) an energy-dependent process prevents removal of the IF-Cbl complex from the cell surface by EDTA or acid after its attachment to the ileal cell surface receptor; (2) Cbl dissociates from IF and binds to a molecule antigenically similar to transcobalamin II; and (3) IF is slowly degraded at the same time and forms breakdown products that are detectable in ileal extracts. Further studies are needed to determine the precise paths taken by IF and Cbl during ileal absorption of the vitamin.

Chapter 33 References

1. Keddie N., Watson-Baker R., Saran, M.: The value of the small bowel enema to the general surgeon. *Br. J. Surg.* 69:811–812, 1982.
2. Jokipii L., Pohjola S., Jokippi A.M.M.: Cryptosporidium: a frequent finding in patients with gastrointestinal symptoms. *Lancet* 2:358–361, 1983.
3. Gottlieb M.S., Groopman J.E., Weinstein J.M.: The acquired immunodeficiency syndrome. *Ann. Intern. Med.* 99:208–220, 1983.
4. Young E.A.: Short bowel syndrome: high-fat versus high-carbohydrate diet. *Gastroenterology* 84:872–875, 1983.
5. Ovesen L., Chu R., Howard, L.: The influence of dietary fat on jejunostomy output in patients with severe short bowel syndrome. *Am. J. Clin. Nutr.* 38:270–277, 1983.

(33–9) J. Clin. Invest. 71:440–448, March 1983.

6. Gross M.: Aspects of bulimia. *Cleve. Clin. Q.* 50:19–25, 1983.
7. Lacey J.H.: Bulimia nervosa, binge eating, and psychogenic vomiting: a controlled treatment study and long term outcome. *Br. Med. J.* 1:1609–1613, 1983.
8. Rosenberg I.H.: Starch blockers: still no calorie-free lunch. *N. Engl. J. Med.* 307:1444–1445, 1982.

34. Colon

34–1 **Studies of the Mechanism of the Antidiarrheal Effect of Codeine.** To determine whether the antidiarrheal action of opiate drugs in human beings is the result of enhanced intestinal absorption rates, as recent experiments in animals have suggested, or is the result of altered intestinal motility, as is traditionally believed, Lawrence R. Schiller, Glenn R. Davis, Carol A. Santa Ana, Stephen G. Morawski, and John S. Fordtran (Dallas) investigated the effect of therapeutic doses of intramuscularly injected codeine (30 mg) on experimentally induced diarrhea and on the rate of intestinal absorption of water and electrolytes in normal human subjects.

Injection of codeine promptly reduced cumulative stool volume during experimental diarrhea induced by intragastric infusion of a balanced electrolyte solution, with a decrease in mean volume from 802±50 ml to 499±28 ml for as long as 24 hours after injection ($P<.02$). There was no delayed appearance of diarrhea, which indicates that codeine increased net intestinal absorption of the infused electrolyte solution. Study of stool polyethylene glycol (PEG) marker concentrations when stool volumes were reduced by codeine showed that PEG concentration was the same with or without codeine. Thus, less stool was produced during the first hour after codeine injection because of delayed passage of fluid through the intestine, not because of an increased rate of intestinal absorption by mucosal cells. When a second injection of saline or codeine (30 mg) was given 1 hour after the first, the findings were similar, with codeine delaying the onset of stool passage and resulting in significantly less cumulative stool volume (1048±111 ml with saline vs. 633±126 ml with codeine; $P<.05$) (Fig 34–1). During the time that the difference in stool volumes after saline and codeine injection was greatest, stool PEG concentrations were similar, with or without codeine, again suggesting that less stool was produced after codeine because of delayed passage of fluid through the intestine rather than because of an enhanced rate of intestinal absorption by mucosal cells. However, during steady-state experimental diarrhea induced by continuous total intestinal perfusion, a large therapeutic dose of codeine did not affect either stool output or the rate of intestinal water absorption. To determine whether the colon was the region in which codeine affected fluid passage in the non-steady-state experimental diarrhea studies, a 1,500-ml bolus of balanced electrolyte solution was infused into the colon; codeine had no effect on stool output or on mean PEG concentration in stool and PEG output. Measurement of segmental transit time during steady-

(34–1) J. Clin. Invest. 70:999–1008, November 1982.

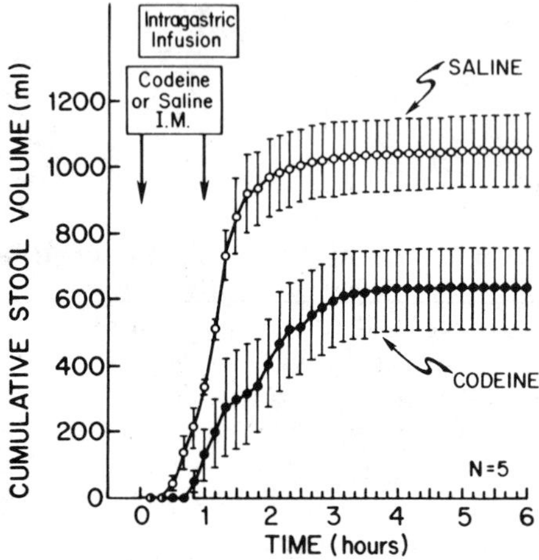

Fig 34–1.—Effect of codeine on cumulative stool volume (mean ± SE) of experimental diarrhea induced by intragastric infusion of 2,700 ml balanced electrolyte solution for a period of 90 minutes after intramuscular injection of saline or 30 mg of codeine. A second injection of saline or 30 mg of codeine followed 1 hour after the first. Significant differences by paired *t* test ($P < .05$) were present at 50 minutes, 70 minutes, and from 1.5 to 6 hours. (Courtesy of Schiller, L.R., et al.: Reproduced from J. Clin. Invest. 70:999–1008, November 1982, by permission of the American Society for Clinical Investigation.)

state intestinal perfusion showed that codeine injection significantly prolonged ($P < .01$) mean transit time through the 30-cm jejunal test segment, but did not affect mean transit times through the ileum and colon (table). Thus, codeine produced fluid retention in the proximal, but not distal, gastrointestinal tract. In another study, it was found

GASTROINTESTINAL EFFECTS OF CODEINE IN STEADY-STATE PERFUSION STUDIES

	Control	Codeine
Jejunum (n = 6)		
Mean transit time, *min*	7.6±1.2	18.8±2.3*
Mean flow rate, *ml/min*†	6.6±0.4	6.7±0.4
Segmental volume, *ml/30 cm*	50.9±8.9	123.2±11.3*
Ileum (n = 6)		
Mean transit time, *min*	7.7±2.2	6.9±1.5
Mean flow rate, *ml/min*†	8.7±0.4	8.7±0.5
Segmental volume, *ml/30 cm*	70.9±25.6	61.8±15.6
Colon (n = 5)		
Mean transit time, *min*	11.3±4.5	8.3±2.0
Mean flow rate, *ml/min*†	16.9±1.4	16.6±1.5
Colonic volume, *ml/total colon*	175.8±61.5	127.4±20.9

*$P < .01$ vs. control.

†Average of the calculated flow rates at the proximal and distal collecting sites.

(Courtesy of Schiller, L.R., et al.: Reproduced from J. Clin. Invest. 70:999–1008, November 1982, by permission of the American Society for Clinical Investigation.)

that naloxone, an opiate antagonist, did not significantly affect water or electrolyte absorption rates in the jejunum or ileum.

It is concluded that therapeutic doses of codeine increase net intestinal absorption, thereby reducing stool volume, by increasing the time luminal fluid is in contact with mucosal cells, not by increasing the rate of absorption by mucosal cells, and that endogenous opiates do not regulate intestinal absorption in human beings.

▶ [This elegant study has clarified the mechanism of the antidiarrheal effect of codeine. To recapitulate briefly, the major findings were as follows: (1) codeine causes a marked slowing of fluid movement through the *jejunum* but has no effect on the movement of fluid through the ileum or colon; (2) theapeutic doses of codeine increase *net* intestinal absorption (and thereby reduce stool volume) by increasing the contact time of luminal fluid with mucosal cells and not by increasing the rate of absorption by the mucosal cells; and (3) the opiate antagonist naloxone did not significantly affect water or electrolyte absorption rates in the jejunum or ileum, suggesting that endogenous opiates do not regulate intestinal absorption in humans.] ◀

34–2 **Corticotropin Versus Hydrocortisone in the Intravenous Treatment of Ulcerative Colitis: Prospective, Randomized, Double-Blind Clinical Trial.** Samuel Meyers, David B. Sachar, Judith D. Goldberg, and Henry D. Janowitz (Mt. Sinai School of Medicine, New York) compared the effect of ACTH and hydrocortisone administered intravenously to 66 patients hospitalized with severe ulcerative colitis between 1977 and 1981. All had evidence of active colitis after 24 hours of observation. The diagnosis was confirmed in all 18 patients operated on within a year of initial evaluation. Thirty-five patients (group A) were given continuous oral steroid therapy, having received at least 5 mg of prednisone or its equivalent daily for 30 days before hospitalization; 31 patients (group B) were not so treated. Patients in both groups were randomized to receive either 40 units of aqueous ACTH or 100 mg of hydrocortisone sodium succinate every 8 hours for 10 days. Group A patients were given 1.5 mg of dexamethasone orally each day throughout the study.

Therapeutic success was achieved in 42% of all patients. Although ACTH seemed to be more effective in inducing remissions in group B patients, the opposite was the case in group A (table). The response was influenced chiefly by the presence or absence of previous steroid therapy. Most patients had minimal adverse effects from parenterally administered corticosteroid therapy, and in no case was treatment stopped because of side effects. Sustained remission occurred most often in patients in whom initial treatment succeeded. Therapeutic success could not be related to serum levels of cortisol or dehydroepiandrosterone sulfate.

Intravenously administered ACTH seems indicated for the treatment of severe ulcerative colitis in patients not previously given steroids, and intravenously administered hydrocortisone appears to be effective in patients receiving steroid therapy at the time of evaluation. The explanation for the opposite trends of the therapeutic superiority of ACTH or hydrocortisone in the two patient groups is not clear. It is entirely possible that subtle, unrecognized clinical differ-

---

(34–2) Gastroenterology 85:351–357, August 1983.

RESULTS OF STUDY THERAPY

Strata	Treatment groups								
	ACTH			Hydrocortisone			Total		
	No. of patients	No. in remission	% in remission	No. of patients	No. in remission	% in remission	No. of patients	No. in remission	% in remission
Prior steroids (group A)	16	4	25	19	10	53[a]	35	14	40
No prior steroids (group B)	16	10	63	15	4	27[b]	31	14	45
Total	32	14	44	34	14	41	66	28	42

[a]Difference between ACTH and hydrocortisone therapy, $.05<P<.10$.
[b]Difference between ACTH and hydrocortisone therapy, $.25<P<.05$.
(Courtesy of Meyers, S., et al.: Reproduced by permission of the publisher from Gastroenterology 85:351–357, August 1983; copyright by the American Gastrological Association.)

ences between these groups account for their differing responses to parenteral therapy.

▶ [The major finding in this study is that the presence or absence of prior steroid therapy appears to be associated with a preferential response to either hydrocortisone or ACTH. Patients who had not been receiving prolonged steroid therapy did better with ACTH. Similar, but not as striking, data have been reported in previous studies.[1, 2]

It bears emphasizing that this was an *acute* study, and disease activity was reassessed at the completion of each patient's 10-day study period. Further, at the completion of the study period, future therapy was at the discretion of the referring physician. Each physician attempted to reduce corticosteroid therapy as quickly as tolerated.

Not surprisingly, the follow-up data showed that when initial therapy was successful, patients were more likely to have a sustained remission than when initial therapy had failed. Twenty (71%) of 28 patients achieving remission during the 10-day study period continued in remission 1 year later.

Lennard-Jones has written a thoughtful editorial on the optimal use of corticosteroids in ulcerative colitis and Crohn's disease, and I have selected two key paragraphs from that review.[3]

"Little is known about the relative therapeutic merits in acute ulcerative colitis and Crohn's disease of corticosteroids given either intermittently to produce short lived high peak drug levels, or near continuously to yield a relatively constant lower level of drug in the blood. This is another appropriate question for study by controlled trial. Intermittent doses may have some advantage in avoidance of side effects and convenience. Thus prednisolone given in one dose of 40 mg daily appears to be as effective as the same total dose spread through the day in the treatment of acute colitis. The same dose of prednisolone on alternate mornings, at a time when the blood cortisol is highest, has given encouraging results in active chronic colitis. Results in other disorders suggest that long term suppression of endogenous corticosteroid secretion is reduced, or absent with such an alternate day regime.

Few attempts have yet been made to establish by prospective trial a relationship between dose and response in acute disease. There is some evidence in ulcerative colitis that prednisolone 40 or 60 mg daily is more effective than 20 mg daily. It seems likely that there is a threshold dose below which no therapeutic activity is detectable, but there is a maximal dose beyond which no further benefit accrues, and graded response between these two extremes. Can we distinguish differences between those patients who respond and those who do not? Are we so constrained by justifiable fear of corticosteroid therapy that we withhold adequate treatment until late in the disease when structural change has supervened? Ought we to investigate the possible benefit of giving a single large dose, or a very few smaller doses of a corticosteroid at the first symptoms of recurrent inflammation, before damage to the mucosa has occurred?"] ◀

34–3 **Absorption of Prednisolone in Patients With Crohn's Disease.** Patients with Crohn's disease have variable responses to steroid therapy, and the development of side effects is unpredictable. J. A. Shaffer, S. E. Williams, L. A. Turnberg, J. B. Houston, and M. Rowland (Univ. of Manchester, England) attempted to determine whether impaired absorption of prednisolone contributes to the variable responsiveness in these patients. Five women and 2 men aged 22–50 years with mild to moderate Crohn's disease were included in the study. Two patients had undergone resectional surgery. All were taking sulfasalazine, and 5 were also taking prednisolone in doses of 10–30 mg. Eight healthy persons served as controls. A dose of 20 mg of prednisolone containing 6,7-^{3}H-prednisolone was administered orally after a 12-hour fast. The same dose was administered intravenously on a different day.

(34–3) Gut 24:182–186, March 1983.

A little more than half of the labeled drug was excreted in the urine by patients after oral dosing, compared with more than 80% in controls. The oral-intravenous availability ratio was 0.61 in the patients and 0.89 in controls. A similar difference was found for the ratios of areas under the plasma concentration-time curves. Fecal excretion of labeled drug after oral ingestion was 19% in the patients and 7% in the controls. No untoward effects occurred.

Absorption of prednisolone from the normal bowel is nearly complete, but absorption is incomplete and extremely variable in patients with Crohn's disease. The reason for apparent malabsorption of steroid in Crohn's disease is not clear, because the steroid is lipid soluble and should be readily absorbed by passive diffusion. Possible factors include a reduced intestinal surface area, rapid transit, dispersion in bulky unabsorbed luminal contents, and changes in mucosal drug-metabolizing enzymes.

▶ [Lennard-Jones has written a timely editorial entitled "Toward Optimal use of Corticosteroids in Ulcerative Colitis and Crohn's Disease."[3] Much of what follows has been abstracted from that article. In the carefully done study abstracted above, Shaffer and his colleagues show that when compared with a normal control group, absorption of prednisolone given by mouth was reduced in 7 patients with Crohn's disease as judged by isotopic measurements in plasma, urine, and feces (3 patients). All but one of the patients had ileal disease of mild to moderate severity, but there was no steatorrhea or excess protein loss from the intestine. These observations differ from those of Tanner et al. who found, by measurement of prednisolone serum levels using a specific radioimmunoassay, that the mean peak levels and areas under the curve were not significantly different from normal in nine patients with Crohn's disease given 20 mg of prednisolone by mouth. The observations of Shaffer et al. cannot therefore be extrapolated to every patient with Crohn's disease. Their work now needs to be extended to compare prednisolone absorption in patients with Crohn's disease having small or large bowel involvement and having slight or severe evidence of inflammation.

Even though drug levels can be measured, the results are difficult to interpret in clinical terms because the biological effects of the drug on endogenous cortisol secretion or on experimentally induced inflammation persist longer than would be predicted from the plasma level. Thus the plasma half-life of prednisolone after intravenous administration is around 3–4 hours, but the biological half-life is 18–36 hours. Furthermore, although antiinflammatory activity appears to be quantitatively related to the concentration of active steroid in the tissue, no clear relation has been observed between plasma level achieved and the therapeutic response in colitis. The situation is further complicated by the fact that therapeutic activity (and the liability to side effects) are related, not to total drug levels, but to levels of drug unbound to protein. The main proteins concerned are transcortin (corticosteroid-binding globulin), which has low capacity and high affinity, and albumin, which has high capacity but low affinity. It can be predicted that at low drug doses a greater proportion of the drug will be bound to protein than at higher doses, and measurements show that with decreasing levels of serum albumin the proportion of free prednisolone rises with an associated increase in drug side effects.] ◀

34–4 **Organic and Functional Disorders in 2,000 Gastroenterology Outpatients.** An estimated 30% to 70% of newly referred patients with abdominal symptoms have functional disorders, but little is known about the relative frequencies of different types of functional and organic disorders. Richard F. Harvey, S. Y. Salih, and Alan E. Read reviewed the findings in 2,000 patients referred over a 5-year

(34–4) Lancet 1:632–634, Mar. 19, 1983.

TABLE 1.—ORGANIC DISORDERS SEEN WITH A FREQUENCY OF > 5/1,000 REFERRED PATIENTS

Disorder	n
Peptic ulcer*	197
Oesophageal reflux and peptic oesophagitis†	188
Inflammatory bowel disease‡	168
Gallstones	48
Carcinoma of colon	28
Coeliac disease	26
Cirrhosis of liver	21
Infective diarrhoea	21
Alcoholism	16
Postgastrectomy or postvagotomy difficulties	14
Carcinoma of stomach	13
Hepatitis	11

*Includes 135 duodenal, 27 gastric, 12 pyloric canal, 23 others.
†Excluding esophageal strictures and tablet-induced ulceration.
‡Includes 57 Crohn's disease, 111 proctitis and proctocolitis.
(Courtesy of Harvey, R.F., et al.: Lancet 1:632–634, Mar. 19, 1983.)

TABLE 2.—NONORGANIC DISORDERS SEEN WITH A FREQUENCY OF > 5/1,000 REFERRED PATIENTS

Disorders	n
Abdominal pain with altered bowel habit (irritable bowel syndrome, spastic colon type)	449
Painless diarrhoea	107
Endoscopy-negative dyspepsia	77
Predominant depression, with abdominal pain	50
Painless constipation	39
Habit disorders (aerophagy, rumination &c)	34
Predominant anxiety, with gut symptoms	24
Mad and incurable (including Munchausen syndrome)	15
Eating problems	10

(Courtesy of Harvey, R.F., et al.: Lancet 1:632–634, Mar. 19, 1983.)

period to a gastroenterology clinic. Organic disorders were diagnosed in 980 patients (Table 1). About half of these patients had peptic ulcer, esophagitis, or inflammatory bowel disease. A total of 888 patients had functional disorders of the gastrointestinal tract without organic disease (Table 2), and about half of these patients had irritable bowel syndrome of the spastic colon type. The next most common nonorganic disorders were painless diarrhea and depression with abdominal pain. The patients designated as "mad and incurable" had bizarre complaints, and some were considered to have Munchausen's syndrome.

Difficulties in terminology complicated the classification of patients with nonorganic disorders of the gastrointestinal tract. Painless constipation and diarrhea are probably only different ends of the spectrum of normal colonic function. Many patients with dyspepsia and negative endoscopic findings also have symptoms of colonic spasm.

Some patients may have the same type of disorder as those who have colonic spasm with involvement of the upper end of the alimentary tract rather than the lower. The data obtained by Manning et al. in a separate study suggested that a simple history can be used to diagnose functional intestinal disorder with 95% certainty. A clinical examination, including sigmoidoscopy, and tests for occult blood and some simple blood tests are then performed, followed by a trial of therapy. Many unnecessary tests can be avoided by this approach.

▶ [The irritable bowel syndrome (IBS) continues to be the commonest of all gastrointestinal disorders, accounting for 50%–70% of all patients with digestive complaints. However, accumulating evidence suggests that IBS is a heterogeneous disorder with multiple causes. In this regard, Cann et al. have provided support for the concept that IBS should be considered a disease of the small intestine as well as the colon.[4] These investigators measured the time taken for a solid meal to pass through the stomach, small intestine, and colon in 61 patients with irritable bowel syndrome, who were subdivided according to their presenting symptoms, and in 53 healthy volunteers. Small bowel transit times were significantly shorter in patients who complained predominantly of diarrhea (3.3 ± 0.3 hours vs. 4.2 ± 0.2 hours; $P = .01$; $n = 21$) and significantly longer in patients who complained predominantly of constipation (5.4 ± 0.3 hours vs. 4.2 ± 0.2 hours; $P<.01$; $n = 23$) or pain and distension (5.4 ± 0.4 hours vs. 4.2 ± 0.2 h; $P<.01$; $n = 17$) compared with controls. Whole gastrointestinal transit times were shorter in patients who complained of diarrhea (35 ± 5 hours vs. 53 ± 4 hours; $P<.01$) and longer in patients with constipation (87 ± 13 hours vs. 53 ± 4 hours; $P<.05$) compared with controls. No significant differences in gastric emptying rates were shown between any of the patient groups and normal controls. Thirty-four patients reported pain, particularly in the right iliac fossa, during the meal-transit test, and in 25 (74%) of these, the onset of the pain was associated with the arrival of residues of the test meal in the cecum.

With regard to treatment, there is increasing evidence that the combination of medical therapy with psychotherapy improves outcome, not only in the short term but also in the long run. Svedlund et al. have carried out a controlled study of psychotherapy on irritable bowel syndrome.[5] One hundred one outpatients with irritable bowel syndrome were randomly allocated to two treatment groups. Both groups received the same medical treatment, but patients in one group also received dynamically oriented individual psychotherapy in 10 hour-long sessions spread over 3 months. After 3 months there was a significantly greater improvement in somatic symptoms in the psychotherapy group. The difference became more pronounced a year later, with the patients given psychotherapy showing further improvement, and the patients who received medical treatment showing some deterioration.] ◀

34–5 **Fructose: Incomplete Intestinal Absorption in Humans.** Fructose is an increasingly important commercial sweetener. Some patients report abdominal symptoms after ingesting fructose-containing foods. William J. Ravich, Theodore M. Bayless, and Miriam Thomas (Johns Hopkins Univ., Baltimore) assessed the completeness of fructose absorption by the small intestine by analysis of breath hydrogen excretion in 16 healthy volunteers; incomplete absorption was defined as a peak rise in breath hydrogen of >20 ppm. Only subjects whose colonic bacteria produced hydrogen after ingestion of lactulose were included in the study.

Fructose, 50 gm as a 10% solution, was incompletely absorbed in 6 of 16 subjects (37.5%). This was associated with symptoms of cramps or diarrhea, or both, in 5 of these subjects. Increasing the concentration of fructose to 50 gm as a 20% solution resulted in an increased frequency

---

(34–5) Gastroenterology 84:26–29, January 1983.

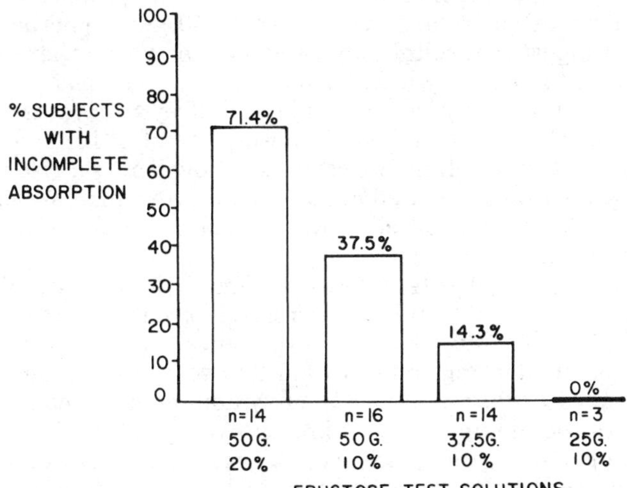

Fig 34–2.—Frequency of incomplete absorption of fructose in normal subjects. Subjects ingested solutions of varying amounts and concentrations of fructose. The 3 subjects tested with the 25-gm fructose solution had incompletely absorbed the 37.5-gm fructose load. (Courtesy of Ravich, W.J., et al.: Reproduced by permission of the publisher from Gastroenterology 84:26–29, January 1983; copyright by the American Gastrological Association.)

of incomplete absorption in 10 (71.4%) of 14 subjects (Fig 34–2). In comparison, all of 15 subjects who were studied after ingestion of sucrose (50 gm as a 10% solution) completely absorbed this sugar load.

Incomplete absorption of fructose should be considered as a possible cause of gastrointestinal symptoms (flatulence, cramps, and diarrhea). A careful dietary history should be obtained to determine whether unusually large amounts of fructose are being consumed.

▶ [This article provides convincing data on three issues that I have discussed repeatedly in the YEAR BOOK during the last five years. First, absorption of carbohydrates in normal human subjects is not complete. Second, as a consequence of such incomplete absorption, carbohydrates pass directly into the colon where they are metabolized by bacteria with the generation of products that can cause flatulence, cramps, and diarrhea. Third, it is important to take a careful dietary history in all patients with irritable bowel symptoms. If the history reveals daily ingestion of excessive amounts of simple sugars and cola beverages (fructose is a frequently used sweetener in such beverages), a sharp reduction of simple sugar intake alone is often successful in ameliorating symptoms of irritable bowel syndrome.

In addition to simple sugars, other carbohydrates are also incompletely absorbed. Recent studies[6] indicate that 2%–20% of dietary starch escapes absorption in the small bowel, confirming the results of other investigators who used breath tests alone. Breath tests, though more convenient than intubation studies, may be a less sensitive index of starch malabsorption. Further, there is evidence that subtle carbohydrate absorption may be more frequent in the aging human subject than in younger individuals.[7]

That other "sugar-free" products can also cause functional gastrointestinal complaints is discussed in the next abstract.] ◀

34–6 **Sorbitol Intolerance: An Unappreciated Cause of Functional Gastrointestinal Complaints.** Sorbitol, a polyalcohol sugar, is the

(34–6) Gastroenterology 84:30–33, January 1983.

sweetener in most "sugar-free" products and may produce an osmotic diarrhea if ingested in large amounts (20–50 gm). Whether smaller amounts of ingested sorbitol may be associated with other symptoms characteristic of carbohydrate malabsorption has not been determined. Using breath hydrogen analysis, Jeffrey S. Hyams (Hartford Hosp., Hartford, Conn.) studied the absorption of 5, 10, and 20 gm of sorbitol in 7 healthy volunteers capable of developing a rise in breath hydrogen after ingestion of 10 gm of lactulose. An increase of 10 ppm hydrogen above fasting baseline was considered diagnostic of carbohydrate malabsorption.

In a majority of subjects, ingestion of as little as 5 gm of sorbitol was associated with a significant increase in breath hydrogen concentration (Fig 34–3). Most subjects experienced mild gastrointestinal distress (gas or bloating) after 10 gm and severe symptoms (cramps or diarrhea) after 20 gm. Severity of symptoms was not always correlated with the maximal rise in breath hydrogen.

The data demonstrated great intersubject variability in the amount of hydrogen production from 10 gm of sorbitol. The data also suggest a large intersubject variability in the percent absorption of 10 gm of sorbitol.

The table lists the sorbitol content of "sugar-free" gums, candies, and several common foods. The results of this study suggest that evaluation of patients with "functional" gastrointestinal complaints should include inquiry into use of commercial and natural products containing sorbitol.

▶ [It is instructive to study the table and appreciate that there is a considerable amount of sorbitol not only in "sugar-free" gum and mints but also in other fruits

Fig 34–3.—Maximum increase in breath hydrogen concentration over fasting baseline in 7 healthy adults after ingestion of 5, 10, and 20 gm of sorbitol. Symptomatic patients experienced gas, bloating, cramps, or diarrhea. (Courtesy of Hyams, J.S.: Reproduced by permission of the publisher from Gastroenterology 84:30–33, January 1983; copyright by the American Gastrological Association.)

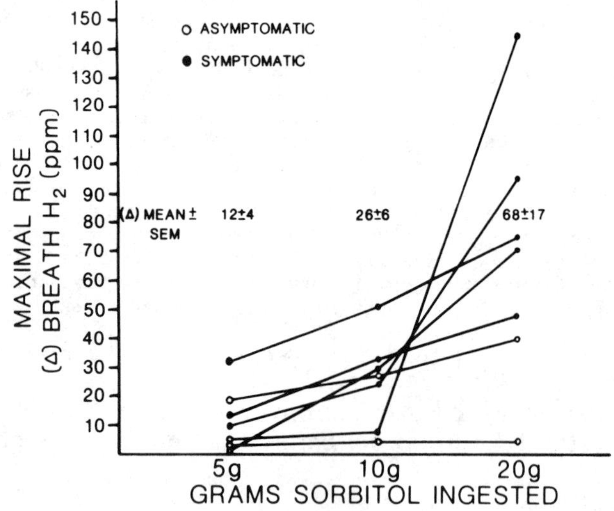

SORBITOL CONTENT OF "SUGAR-FREE" PRODUCTS AND VARIOUS FOODS

"Sugar-free" gum	1.3–2.2 g/piece
"Sugar-free" mints	1.7–2.0 g/piece
Pears	4.6 g[a]
Prunes	2.4 g[a]
Peaches	1.0 g[a]
Apple juice[b]	0.3–0.9 g[a]

[a]Expressed as grams of sorbitol per 100 gm of dry matter or juice. Dry weight equals approximately 15% of fresh weight; based on data from Washuttl, J., et al.: J. Food Sci. 38:1262–1263, 1973.

[b]Based on data from Weiss, J., et al.: Mitt. Klostern. 29:81–84, 1979.

(Courtesy of Hyams, J.S.: Reproduced by permission of the publisher from Gastroenterology 84:30–33, January 1983; copyright by the American Gastrological Association.)

and fruit juices. I have had several patients with irritable bowel symptoms who were using from 5 to 10 "sugar-free" mints per day and who experienced partial or complete resolution of their symptoms when use of these products as well as other simple sugars was discontinued. The fact that fruit juices such as apple juice contain up to 900 mg of sorbitol per 100 ml also has therapeutic implications. Such fruit juices should not be given routinely to patients with chronic diarrheal diseases (inflammatory bowel disease) and especially to patients with short bowel syndrome. Physicians need to be more aware of the sorbitol content of various foods when dealing with patients who have a diarrheal disorder.] ◀

34–7 **Polymicrobial Origin of Intestinal Infections in Homosexual Men.** Anorectal and intestinal infections by a variety of pathogens are common in homosexually active men. Thomas C. Quinn, Walter E. Stamm, Steven E. Goodell, Emanuel Mkrtichian, Jacqueline Benedetti, Lawrence Corey, Michael D. Schuffler, and King K. Holmes reviewed the findings in 119 homosexual or bisexual men presenting with intestinal symptoms. All had been ill for less than 4 weeks and had not used antibiotics in the past 2 weeks. Rectal or intestinal pathogens were identified in 80% of the study group and in 39% of a comparison group without symptoms. Two or more pathogens were present in 22% of the symptomatic group and in 4% of the comparison group.

Neisseria gonorrhoeae was cultured from rectal swabs in 31% of the study group and 23% of the asymptomatic men. Herpes simplex virus infection and *Chlamydia trachomatis* were more frequent in the study group. Eleven study men and 5 controls were seropositive for syphilis. *Campylobacter* organisms were isolated more often from symptomatic men. Definite anoscopic abnormalities were seen in 86% of the study group and in 27% of controls. Sigmoidoscopy showed mucosal abnormalities in all but 2 of 63 men with abnormal anocopic findings. The syndromes of proctitis, proctocolitis, and enteritis were differentiated on the basis of predominant symptoms, and findings and sigmoidoscopy are correlated with the microbiologic findings (table). Oral-anal

(34–7) N. Engl. J. Med. 309:576–582, Sept. 8, 1983.

MICROBIOLOGIC AND SYMPTOMATIC CORRELATES OF PROCTITIS, PROCTOCOLITIS, AND ENTERITIS AMONG 65 HOMOSEXUAL MEN WITH INTESTINAL SYMPTOMS WHO UNDERWENT SIGMOIDOSCOPY TO A DISTANCE ABOVE 15 CM.

	PROCTITIS	PROCTOCOLITIS	ENTERITIS
	SIGMOIDOSCOPIC FINDINGS ABNORMAL ONLY BELOW 15 CM (N = 41)	SIGMOIDOSCOPIC FINDINGS ABNORMAL BEYOND 15 CM (N = 15)	SIGMOIDOSCOPIC FINDINGS NORMAL (N = 9)
Sexually transmitted rectal pathogens			
Neisseria gonorrhoeae	12	0	2
Herpes simplex virus	13	1	0
Chlamydia trachomatis (non-LGV) *	8	1	0
Treponema pallidum	6	0	0
Total with any rectal pathogen	*33* †	*2*	*2*
Infectious causes of colitis			
Campylobacter jejuni/C. fetus fetus	3	4	0
Shigella flexneri	0	2	0
Chlamydia trachomatis (LGV) *	0	3	0
Entamoeba histolytica ‡	5 (26)	4 (11)	1 (8)
Clostridium difficile cytotoxin	1	1	0
Total with any colitis pathogen	*8*	*9* †	*1*
Infectious causes of inflammation limited to small intestine			
Giardia lamblia ‡	2 (26)	2 (11)	4 (8)
Any three of four symptoms present: diarrhea, abdominal pain, bloating, nausea	3	8	9 †
Any three of four symptoms present: constipation, rectal discharge, anorectal pain, tenesmus	38 †	7	0

*LGV denotes lymphogranuloma venereum.
†$P<0.05$, by multiple logistic regression analysis.
‡Figures in parentheses indicate number of patients who submitted stools for examination for ova and parasites.
(Courtesy of Quinn, T.C., et al.: N. Engl. J. Med. 309:576–582, Sept. 8, 1983.)

sexual practices correlated well with infection by *Entamoeba histolytica* and *Giardia lamblia*.

Most homosexual men presenting with anorectal or intestinal symptoms are infected by one or more sexually transmissible anorectal or enteric pathogens. The impact of repeated polymicrobial intestinal and rectal infections in these men may extend beyond that of the individual infections. Treatment without epidemiologic measures will not greatly reduce the occurrence of these infections in a homosexual male population. The onset of symptoms should lead to cessation of sexual contact until a specific diagnosis is made, a treatment given, and a cure documented.

These data demonstrate that intestinal symptoms in homosexual men are attributable to a complex spectrum of microorganisms but that careful clinical classification can serve as a guide to the selection of microbiologic studies and to a rational initial choice of therapy.

▶ [This article provides a useful means of correlating the syndromes of proctitis, proctocolitis, and enteritis with specific pathogens. Thus, *Neisseria gonorrhoeae,* herpes simplex virus (HSV), *Chlamydia trachomatis* (non-lymphomogranuloma-venereum serotypes), and *Treponema pallidum* were associated with 80% of cases with symptomatic proctitis. Known causes of colitis, including *Campylobacter jejuni, Chlamydia trachomatis* (lymphomogranuloma venereum [LGV] serotypes), *Entamoeba histolytica,* and *Clostridium difficile* were identified in 60% of the cases of proctocolitis. *Giardia lamblia* was the only agent significantly correlated with enteritis.

This group of investigators has also described the clinical, sigmoidoscopic, and histopathological features of HSV proctitis in homosexual men.[8] Acute HSV infection was detected in 23 of 102 consecutively examined, sexually active male homosexuals who presented with anorectal pain, discharge, tenesmus, or hematochezia, as compared with 3 of 75 homosexual men without gastrointestinal symptoms ($P<.01$). Findings that were significantly more frequent in men with HSV proctitis than in men with proctitis due to other infectious causes included fever (48%), difficulty in urinating (48%), sacral paresthesia (26%), inguinal lymphadenopathy (57%), severe anorectal pain (100%), tenesmus (100%), constipation (78%), perianal ulcerations (70%), and the presence of diffuse ulcerative or discrete vesicular or pustular lesions in the distal 5 cm of the rectum (50%). Serologic evidence indicated that 85% of the men with symptomatic HSV proctitis were having their first episode of HSV type 2 infection. The diagnosis of HSV proctitis is suggested by the presence of severe anorectal pain, difficulty in urinating, sacral paresthesia, or pain, and diffuse ulceration of the distal rectal mucosa.

That unusual forms of colitis may occur in otherwise healthy individuals is underscored by the report of Riley et al.[9] In this article, which is abstracted in the "Infections" section of the YEAR BOOK (see abstract 1–4), the investigators reported two outbreaks of an unusual gastrointestinal illness that affected at least 47 people in Oregon and Michigan in February through March and May through June 1982. The illness was characterized by severe crampy abdominal pain, initially watery diarrhea followed by grossly bloody diarrhea, and little or no fever.

It was associated with eating at restaurants belonging to the same fast-food restaurant chain in Oregon ($P<.005$) and Michigan ($P=.0005$) and with eating any of three sandwiches containing three ingredients in common (beef patty, rehydrated onions, and pickles).

Stool cultures did not yield previously recognized pathogens. However, a rare *Escherichia coli* serotype, 0157:H7, that was not invasive or toxigenic by standard tests was isolated from 9 of 12 stools collected within 4 days of onset of illness in both outbreaks combined and from a beef patty from a suspected lot of meat in Michigan. The only known previous isolation of this serotype was from a sporadic case of hemorrhagic colitis in 1975. Riley et al. describe a clinically distinctive gastrointestinal illness associated with *E. coli* 0157:H7, apparently transmitted by undercooked meat.] ◀

34–8 **Prevention of Travelers' Diarrhea With Trimethoprim-Sulfamethoxazole and Trimethoprim Alone.** H. L. DuPont, E. Galindo, D. G. Evans, F. J. Cabada, P. Sullivan, and D. J. Evans, Jr. (Univ. of Texas Health Science Center, Houston) report that 145 United States students enrolled in a double-blind study to evaluate the protective effect of trimethoprim-sulfamethoxazole (TMP/SMX), given as 160 mg of TMP and 800 mg of SMX, or TMP alone (200 mg) taken to prevent diarrhea while in Mexico; each preparation was taken orally once daily for 14 days.

Ten (33%) of 30 students taking placebo experienced diarrhea compared with 8 (14%) of 58 taking TMP and 1 (2%) of 57 taking TMP/SMX (Fig 34–4). Differences were significant when occurrence of diarrhea in the TMP/SMX group was compared with that in the TMP

(34–8) Gastroenterology 84:75–80, January 1983.

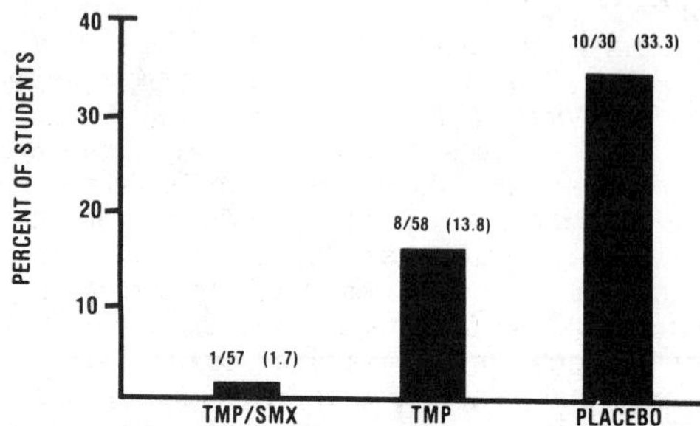

Fig 34–4.—Number of students experiencing diarrhea during a 14-day trial, according to assigned medication. Percentage is given in parentheses. (Courtesy of DuPont, H.L., et al.: Reproduced by permission of the publisher from Gastroenterology 84:75–80, January 1983; copyright by the American Gastrological Association.)

group, when the TMP/SMX group was compared with students receiving placebo, and when the TMP group was compared with students receiving placebo.

An enterotoxigenic *Escherichia coli* (ETEC) was isolated from a diarrheal stool of 3 of 8 students receiving TMP alone and from stool of 5 of 10 students with illness receiving placebo. A *Shigella* strain was detected in specimens from 3 of 10 students, and a *Salmonella* strain was identified in the stool of 1 student receiving placebo. Neither *Shigella* nor *Salmonella* organisms were identified in students who received either active preparation.

Only 1 ETEC strain in a TMP-treated student with diarrhea was found to be resistant to TMP and to TMP/SMX. The remaining enteropathogens identified with diarrhea during the trial or 1 week posttreatment, including 14 ETEC strains, 12 *Shigella* strains, and 2 *Salmonella* strains, were susceptible to TMP/SMX. There did not appear to be a differential effect of TMP/SMX on ETEC strains according to the type of toxin produced.

Development of a generalized cutaneous eruption, occurring in 2% of students receiving TMP/SMX and 3% of TMP-treated subjects, was the major reason for continuing the medication. Illness commonly occurred when the drugs were stopped and the students remained in Mexico, underscoring the need for continuing the drugs as long as the traveler is at risk.

It is advised that travelers receiving TMP/SMX for prophylaxis be given a dose of 160 mg of TMP and 800 mg of SMX once daily. The medication must be continued beyond the period of exposure (1–2 days after returning home) if illness is to be prevented rather than merely postponed.

▶ [In the discussion section of this article, DuPont et al. emphasize several key points. (1) Approximately 40% of travelers from low- to high-risk regions will develop diarrhea unless they take a prophylactic antibiotic. (2) Food is the source of most of the illness in these areas, and where one eats and what one eats will influence diarrhea rates even while taking an effective drug prophylactically. (3) There are three groups of persons to whom drugs might be given to prevent travelers' diarrhea during brief periods of high risk: (a) persons on important business trips; (b) military populations; (c) individuals who may be at greater risk to complications or more susceptible to infection, such as those with achlorhydria, those having had a previous gastric resection, those taking diuretics, those with other underlying illness, and those with previous severe travelers' diarrhea.

In addition, TMP/SMX is highly effective in treating the disorder once it has developed. The usual dose is 160 mg of TMP and 800 mg of SMX taken twice daily for 5 days.

Two other drugs effective in the treatment of travelers' diarrhea are doxycycline and bicozamycin, and recent experience with these agents is summarized below. Freeman et al. conducted a prospective, randomized double-blind trial of doxycycline prophylaxis for travelers' diarrhea on 145 volunteers during a 2.5-day visit to Mexico.[10] Travelers' diarrhea occurred in 15 (21%) of the placebo group and in 3 (4%) of the doxycycline group (P = .002). There was no rebound increase in the incidence of acute diarrhea after departure from the high-risk area in the doxycycline-treated group. A variety of bacterial pathogens was isolated from individuals symptomatic with travelers' diarrhea. Nausea alone (8%) or nausea with vomiting (4%) occurred in the doxycycline-treated group only and were the only side effects observed (P = .003). It is concluded that doxycycline is safe and efficacious for the prophylaxis of travelers' diarrhea for short-term exposure in a high-risk area.

Ericsson et al. assessed the efficacy of bicozamycin, a poorly absorbed antibiotic, in the treatment of acute diarrhea in a prospective, double-blind study of 140 adults from the United States visiting Guadalajara, Mexico.[11] Patients randomly received bicozamycin (500 mg orally 4 times daily) or placebo for 3 days. The mean duration of illness was shorter in the bicozamycin than the placebo treatment groups for patients with diarrhea due to *Shigella* (37 vs. 90 hours; P = .01), toxigenic *Escherichia coli* (31 vs. 60 hours; P = .003), and unknown pathogens (18 vs. 41 hours; P = .02). Cramps were significantly relieved by bicozamycin in all patients. Treatment failed in significantly fewer patients treated with bicozamycin than in those treated with placebo when diarrhea was associated with *Shigella, Salmonella,* or toxigenic *E. coli.* Bicozamycin was well tolerated and appears to be effective therapy for acute travelers' diarrhea of diverse causes. These data show the value of an antibiotic in the therapy of toxigenic *E. coli* infection and indicate a need to reevaluate the clinical dictum that nonabsorbable antibiotics are ineffective against invasive enteropathogens.] ◀

Chapter 34 References

1. Kaplan H.P., Partnoy B., Bender H.J.: A controlled evaluation of intravenous adrenocorticotropic hormone and hydrocortisone in the treatment of acute colitis. *Gastroenterology* 69:91–95, 1975.
2. Powell-Tuck J., Bucknell N.A., Lennard-Jones J.E.: A controlled comparison of corticotropin and hydrocortisone in the treatment of severe proctocolitis. *Scand. J. Gastroenterol.* 12:971–975, 1977.
3. Lennard-Jones J.E.: Optimal use of corticosteroids in ulcerative colitis and Crohn's disease. *Gut* 24:177–181, 1983.
4. Cann P.A., Read N.W., Brown C., et al.: Irritable bowel syndrome: relationship of disorders in the transit of a single solid meal to symptom patterns. *Gut* 24:405–411, 1983.
5. Svedlund J., Ottosson J.O., Sjöden J., et al.: Controlled study of psychotherapy in irritable bowel syndrome. *Lancet* 2:589–591, 1983.
6. Stephen A.M., Hoddod A.C., Phillips, S.F.: Passage of carbohydrate into the colon: direct measurements in humans. *Gastroenterology* 85:589–595, 1983.
7. Feibusch J.M., Holt P.R.: Impaired absorptive capacity for carbohydrate in the aging human. *Dig. Dis. Sci.* 27:1095–1100, 1982.
8. Goodell S.E., Quinn T.C., Mkrtichian E., et al.: Herpes simplex proctitis in homosexual men. *N. Engl. J. Med.* 308:868–871, 1983.
9. Riley L.W., Remis R.S., Helgerson S.D., et al.: Hemorrhagic colitis associated with a rare *Escherichia coli* serotype. *N. Engl. J. Med.* 308:681–685, 1983.

10. Freeman L.D., Hooper D.R., Lathen D.F., et al.: Brief prophylaxis with doxycycline for the prevention of traveler's diarrhea. *Gastroenterology* 84:276–280, 1983.
11. Ericsson C.D., Dupont H.L., Sullivan P.: Bicozamycin, a poorly absorbable antibiotic, effectively treats traveler's diarrhea. *Ann. Intern. Med.* 98:20–25, 1983.

35. Liver

35–1 **Clinical Importance of Protein-Bound Fraction of Serum Bilirubin in Patients With Hyperbilirubinemia.** Apart from unconjugated bilirubin and the monoglucuronide and diglucuronide forms, an albumin-bound bilirubin fraction was recently identified by a new reversed-phase, high-performance liquid-chromatography procedure. Janet S. Weiss, Anil Gautam, John J. Lauff, Michael W. Sundberg, Peter Jatlow, James L. Boyer, and David Seligson attempted to define the clinical importance of albumin-bound bilirubin in studies of healthy subjects and hyperbilirubinemic patients. The study group included 200 patients with hyperbilirubinemia of various causes, whose bilirubin levels ranged from 0.3 to 65 mg/dl.

The albumin-bound fraction was not present in appreciable amounts in sera of normal adults or patients with disorders characterized chiefly by unconjugated hyperbilirubinemia. In patients with hepatocellular and cholestatic jaundice and in those with Dubin-Johnson syndrome, albumin-bound bilirubin constituted 8%–90% of total bilirubin (Fig 35–1). Albumin-bound bilirubin constituted a higher proportion of total bilirubin during clinical recovery than when jaundice was worsening (Fig 35–2). The percentage of albumin-

Fig 35–1.—Albumin-bound bilirubin as percentage of total bilirubin *(T BILI)* in normal controls and patients. Number of subjects is indicated for each diagnostic category. Solid circles represent serum samples from patients with clinical worsening and increasing total bilirubin value. Open circles represent samples from patients with clinical improvement and falling total serum bilirubin levels. Range bars indicate means ± SD. (Courtesy of Weiss, J.S., et al.: N. Engl. J. Med. 309:147–150, July 21, 1983; reprinted by permission of The New England Journal of Medicine.)

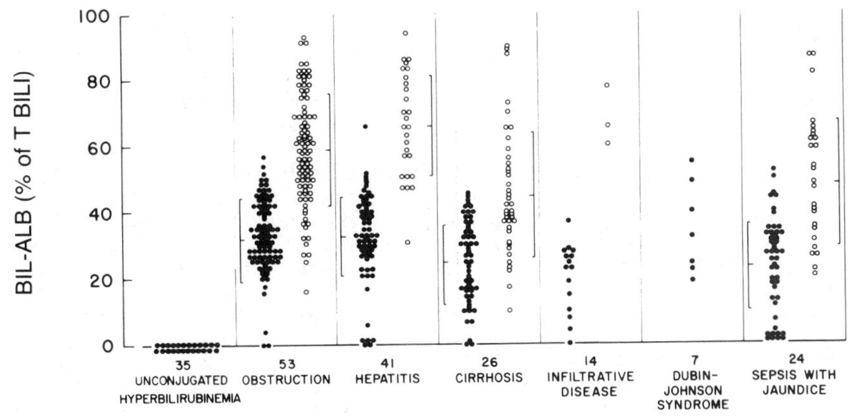

(35–1) N. Engl. J. Med. 309:147–150, July 21, 1983.

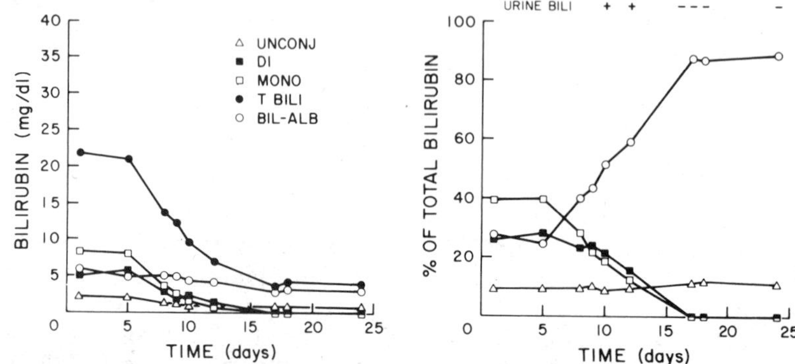

Fig 35–2.—Total bilirubin level and subfractions in patient recovering from postoperative jaundice and sepsis. **Left,** absolute amounts; **right,** bilirubin fractions expressed as percentages of total bilirubin. Presence (+) or absence (−) of bilirubin in the urine was determined with Ictotest tablets. UNCONJ = Unconjugated bilirubin; DI = diconjugated bilirubin; MONO = monoconjugated bilirubin; T BILI = total bilirubin; BIL-ALB = albumin-bound bilirubin. (Courtesy of Weiss, J.S., et al.: N. Engl. J. Med. 309:147–150, July 21, 1983; reprinted by permission of The New England Journal of Medicine.)

bound bilirubin was not related to the serum albumin level. Patients with physiologic jaundice did not have albumin-bound bilirubin before or after phototherapy.

Albumin-bound bilirubin appears in the serum when the hepatic excretion of conjugated bilirubin is impaired. It becomes a larger component of the total serum bilirubin level as jaundice subsides, delaying resolution of the disorder and causing bilirubin to persist in the plasma after it has disappeared from the urine. Prolonged turnover of albumin-bound bilirubin may be a factor in the slow resolution of jaundice in some patients whose hepatobiliary function has otherwise returned to normal.

▶ [Bilirubin is generally thought to exist in three major forms in serum: as unconjugated bilirubin, as the monoglucuronide, or as the diglucuronide. The latter two subfractions give a "direct" reaction with standard diazo reagent, whereas unconjugated bilirubin gives an "indirect" reaction. A fourth fraction, albumin-bound bilirubin, has now been identified by use of a new reversed-phase high-performance liquid-chromatography procedure. The studies of Weiss et al. provide important new information on the clinical applications of this new protein-bound fraction of serum bilirubin. It was not detected in normal volunteers, neonates with physiologic jaundice, or patients with Gilbert's disease or hemolysis. Albumin-bound bilirubin appears in the serum when the hepatic excretion of conjugated bilirubin is impaired.

The formation of albumin-bound bilirubin provides an explanation for two previously unexplained clinical phenomena in hyperbilirubinemic states. First, during recovery from jaundice, bilirubin often disappears from the urine, whereas the plasma remains icteric. The findings in this study indicate that this phenomenon occurs when monoconjugated and diconjugated bilirubin have disappeared from the serum and only the albumin-bound bilirubin remains. The albumin-bilirubin complex is not filtered at the glomerulus and therefore does not appear in the urine. Second, it is known that jaundice resolves slowly after resolution of active hepatobiliary disease and that the resolution time for bilirubin in serum is dependent on the day when recovery begins and may be retarded in the later phases of recovery. The prolonged turnover of albumin-bound bilirubin may contribute to this slow resolution of jaundice in some patients whose hepatobiliary function has otherwise appeared to return to normal.] ◀

35–2 **Blinded Prospective Study Comparing Four Current Noninvasive Approaches in the Differential Diagnosis of Medical Versus Surgical Jaundice.** In distinguishing intrahepatic obstruction from extrahepatic obstruction, the extent to which the physician should rely on the clinical impression or the results of the various noninvasive diagnostic tests remains poorly defined. Katherine W. O'Connor, Philip J. Snodgrass, James E. Swonder, Stephen Mahoney, Robert Burt, Edward M. Cockerill, and Lawrence Lumeng (Indianapolis) prospectively compared the diagnostic accuracy of clinical evaluation, ultrasonography (US), computed tomography (CT), and technetium-99m nuclear medicine biliary scans (NMBS) using iminodiacetic acid derivatives (HIDA/PIPIDA) in distinguishing intrahepatic jaundice from extrahepatic jaundice in 50 patients.

A final diagnosis was established and anatomically confirmed in all 50 patients. Jaundice due to intrahepatic (hepatocellular) disease was present in 29 patients and extrahepatic obstruction was present in 21. Alcoholic liver disease accounted for 14 of the 29 cases of hepatocellular disease confirmed by liver biopsy. Clinical evaluation was the most sensitive (95%) single approach in the diagnosis of extrahepatic obstruction, followed by CT (63%), US (55%), and NMBS (41%) (Table 1). However, clinical evaluation was also the least specific (76%) single approach, with the specificities for CT, US, and NMBS being 93%, 93%, and 88%, respectively (see Table 1). The overall accuracies for clinical evaluation, CT, US, and NMBS were, respectively, 84%, 81%, 78%, and 68% (see Table 1). As none of the noninvasive approaches was both highly sensitive and specific, the combined utility of any two diagnostic modalities was evaluated. A combined sensitivity of 98% was achieved when either clinical evaluation or US was positive for obstruction or when clinical evaluation or CT was positive for obstruction (Table 2). Combined specificities of 98%–99% were found when a positive result was redefined as one requiring that both clinical evaluation and US be positive, that both clinical evaluation and CT be positive, or that both US and CT be positive.

TABLE 1.—COMPARISON OF CLINICAL EVALUATION (CE), ULTRASOUND (US), COMPUTED TOMOGRAPHY (CT) AND NUCLEAR MEDICINE BILIARY SCANS (NMBS) IN THE DIAGNOSIS OF EXTRAHEPATIC CHOLESTASIS

	False positive (%)	False negative (%)	Sensitivity (%)	Specificity (%)	Overall accuracy (%)
CE (n = 50)	24	5	95	76	84
US (n = 49)	7	45	55	93	78
CT (n = 47)	7	37	63	93	81
NMBS (n = 41)	12	59	41	88	68

(Courtesy of O'Connor, K.W., et al.: Reproduced by permission of the publisher from Gastroenterology 84:1498–1504, June 1983; copyright 1983 by the American Gastrological Association.)

(35–2) Gastroenterology 84:1498–1504, June 1983.

TABLE 2.—SENSITIVITIES AND SPECIFICITIES IN COMBINED USE OF CLINICAL EVALUATION (CE), ULTRASOUND (US), AND COMPUTED TOMOGRAPHY (CT) IN THE DIAGNOSIS OF EXTRAHEPATIC CHOLESTASIS

	Combined sensitivity	Combined specificity
CE or US positive*	98%	71%
CE and US positive†	52%	98%
CE or CT positive	98%	71%
CE and CT positive	60%	98%
US or CT positive	83%	86%
US and CT positive	35%	99%

*If a positive result is defined as a positive result in either test A or B, then (1) the % of combined sensitivity = % sensitivity of A + ([100% − % sensitivity of A] × % sensitivity of B); (2) the % combined specificity = % specificity of A × % specificity of B.

†If a positive result requires that both tests, A and B, be positive, then (1) the % combined sensitivity = % sensitivity of A × % sensitivity of B; (2) the % combined specificity of A + ([100% − % specificity of A] × % specificity B).

(Courtesy of O'Connor, K.W., et al.: Reproduced by permission of the publisher from Gastroenterology 84:1498–1504, June 1983; copyright by the American Gastrological Association.)

The results support the contention that carefully performed clinical evaluation is the single most effective noninvasive means of detecting extrahepatic biliary obstruction in a jaundiced patient. Although US, CT, and NMBS are less sensitive than clinical evaluation, they are highly reliable if positive for extrahepatic obstruction. An algorithm for the evaluation of the jaundiced patient based on the combined use of clinical evaluation, invasive, and noninvasive tests is presented (Fig 35–3).

▶ [In studies done over 20 years ago, Schenker et al. demonstrated that the clinical differential diagnosis of jaundice based upon history, physical examination, and liver tests can be correct in approximately 85% of cases.[1] During the subsequent 20 years,

Fig 35–3.—Algorithm for evaluation of the jaundiced patient based on the combined use of clinical evaluation, noninvasive, and invasive tests. (Courtesy of O'Connor, K.W., et al.: Reproduced by permission of the publisher from Gastroenterology 84:1498–1504, June 1983; copyright by the American Gastrological Association.)

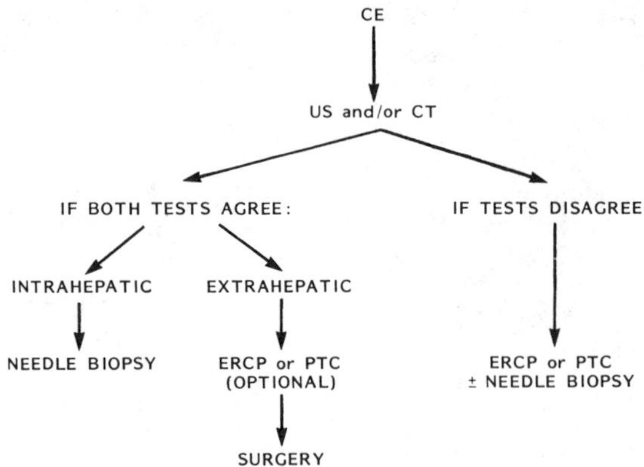

a genuine diagnostic revolution has occurred with the availability of ultrasound (US), computed tomography (CT), percutaneous transhepatic-cholangiography (PTC), endoscopic retrograde cholangiopancreatography (ERCP), and nuclear medicine hepatobiliary scans (NMHS). The clinician must now decide how best to make a specific diagnosis as efficiently and safely as possible by the selective use of these procedures.

The studies of O'Connor et al. confirm the high sensitivity of the clinical evaluation. Clinicians do well diagnostically but tend to overcall extrahepatic obstruction. The lower specificity of the clinical evaluation (76%) vs. US, CT, or NMHS indicate that about 25% of patients with suspected obstruction actually have hepatocellular disease.

Vennes and Bond have written a thoughtful editorial on the approach to the jaundiced patient, and I have excerpted a key paragraph from that article.[2] "The first question is whether diagnostic precision is necessary for successful management of the jaundiced patient. The answer clearly is yes. The causes of jaundice tend to be progressive and require specific management for their control or cure. Clear separation of intrahepatic from extrahepatic origins is the crucial first stage of the investigative process. We should first insist on very high diagnostic sensitivity to avoid missing important disease, although this may cause us to occasionally suggest disease that is not present. When extrahepatic or large ductal causes of jaundice are present, the second diagnostic phase is the accurate determination of the site and etiology of obstruction. Surgical management may be facilitated and shortened by knowing these specific details; but more importantly, the possible selection of new 'nonsurgical' alternatives makes precise diagnosis essential. These therapeutic options include transhepatic or endoscopic dilatation of narrowed ducts and the placement of stents across benign or malignant strictures, and endoscopic retrograde sphincterotomy for removing common duct calculi. Also, a diagnosis of pancreatic or biliary malignancy can be confirmed with guided transabdominal fine needle cytology. So while surgical therapy is frequently chosen for the management of biliary tract disease, the term 'surgical' jaundice no longer generally applies. But to make the right decision, we must first be diagnostically exact."] ◀

35–3 **Ultrasonography, Computed Tomography, and Cholescintigraphy in Suspected Obstructive Jaundice: A Prospective Comparative Study.** Peter Matzen, Axel Malchow-Møller, Birgitte Brun, Sven Grønvall, Aksel Haubek, Jens H. Henriksen, Kirsten Laursen, Jørgen Lejerstofte, Poul Stage, Kjeld Winkler, and Erik Juhl (Univ. of Copenhagen) prospectively compared the diagnostic accuracy of ultrasonography (US), computed tomography (CT), and cholescintigraphy (HIDA) in 56 consecutive jaundiced patients in whom extrahepatic cholestasis was suspected clinically. Predictions as to the patency of the large bile ducts were compared with the findings at direct cholangiography and confirmed by autopsy, biopsy, operation, and the clinical course. A simple scoring scale was used to assess the possible clinical impact of the predictions: 2+, correct prediction of definitely obstructed or definitely normal bile ducts; 1+, correct prediction, but the diagnosis required direct cholangiography; 0, no result; −1, wrong prediction, and the diagnosis required direct cholangiography for clarification; and −2, wrong prediction of definitely obstructed or definitely normal bile ducts.

The final diagnoses were obstruction of the large bile duct in 39 patients (70%) and bile duct patency in 17 (30%). Out of a possible total prediction score of 112 points, US had 72 points, CT 56 points, and HIDA 37 points (table). The difference in scores between US and

(35–3) Gastroenterology 84:1492–1497, June 1983.

PREDICTIONS OF PRESENCE OR ABSENCE OF BILE DUCT OBSTRUCTION*

Predicted state of bile ducts	Ultrasonography			Computed tomography			Cholescintigraphy		
	True diagnosis			True diagnosis			True diagnosis		
	obstruct-ed	not ob-structed	Total	obstruct-ed	not ob-structed	Total	obstruct-ed	not ob-structed	Total
Definitely obstructed	25 (+50)	2 (−4)	27 (+46)	22 (+44)	0 (—)	22 (+44)	24 (+48)	6 (−12)	30 (+36)
Possibly obstructed	10 (+10)	1 (−1)	11 (+9)	8 (+8)	4 (−4)	12 (+4)	5 (+5)	2 (−2)	7 (+3)
Inconclusive	0 (—)	0 (—)	0 (—)	1 (0)	0 (—)	1 (0)	0 (—)	0 (—)	0 (—)
Possibly normal	3 (−3)	6 (+6)	9 (+3)	2 (−2)	4 (+4)	6 (+2)	6 (−6)	6 (+6)	12 (0)
Definitely normal	1 (−2)	8 (+16)	9 (+14)	6 (−12)	9 (+18)	15 (+6)	4 (−8)	3 (+6)	7 (−2)
Total	39 (+55)	17 (+17)	56 (+72)	39 (+38)	17 (+18)	56 (+56)	39 (+39)	17 (−2)	56 (+37)

*Total prediction scores are given in parentheses (scoring scale: true "definite" prediction, +2; true "possible," +1; inconclusive, 0; false "possible," −1; false "definite," −2). Ultrasonography vs. cholescintigraphy: McNemar $.025<p<.01$; Wilcoxon $P=.007$. Other comparisons were not statistically significant. (Courtesy of Matzen, P., et al.: Reproduced by permission of the publisher from Gastroenterology 84:1492–1497, June 1983; copyright by the American Gastrological Association.)

HIDA was statistically significant ($P = .01$). The only trend in the false US predictions was that 2 of the 3 patients predicted to have "possibly normal bile ducts" had stones in nondilated common bile ducts. No specific trend was observed regarding the false CT predictions. Four of 5 patients with drug hepatitis of the cholestatic type were misdiagnosed by HIDA.

Ultrasonography with a dynamic scanner is the noninvasive imaging procedure of choice in jaundiced patients suspected to have bile duct obstruction. Although CT is a possible alternative to US, its high cost and the large number of secondary direct cholangiographies implicit in its use make direct cholangiography preferable to CT screening. HIDA is not recommended for the differentiation of obstructive and hepatic jaundice.

► [Richter et al. used a clinical decision analysis and a computer model to evaluate 10 diagnostic strategies for the diagnosis of extrahepatic obstructive jaundice.[3] The sensitivity, specificity, complications, and costs of currently used individual tests were used to determine the overall sensitivity, specificity, complications, and costs of each strategy at different disease prevalences. In patients with a low probability of extrahepatic obstructive jaundice (20% or less), the optimal strategy begins with ultrasonography, followed by a cholangiogram when dilated ducts are present. When dilated ducts are not present, patients may be observed clinically, and endoscopic retrograde cholangiopancreatography is done if the jaundice does not resolve. In patients with a higher probability of extrahepatic obstructive jaundice, a cholangiogram is needed for an accurate diagnosis. In patients with a low probability of extrahepatic obstructive jaundice, the optimal strategy has an overall sensitivity of 92% and a specificity of 99%. About 40% of patients need a cholangiogram at an average cost of $1,000 per patient. In patients with a higher probability of extrahepatic obstructive jaundice, the optimal strategy has an overall sensitivity of 97%, specificity of 98%, and cost of $1,000–$1,200 per patient.] ◄

35–4 **Prognostic Importance of Clinical and Histologic Features in Asymptomatic and Symptomatic Primary Biliary Cirrhosis.** To determine the life expectancy of patients with primary biliary cirrhosis, Joseph Roll, James L. Boyer, Daniel Barry, and Gerald Klatskin (Yale Univ.) analyzed survival data from 280 patients with symptomatic (243) or asymptomatic (37) disease. Nearly all asymptomatic patients were identified on the basis of a raised serum level of alkaline phosphatase or aspartate aminotransferase detected during a routine physical examination. Patients were followed for a mean of 6.9 years.

Findings for the two groups of patients at the time of diagnosis are compared in the table. Pruritus, the most frequent symptom, was the presenting complaint in 58% of cases. Hepatomegaly was the only abnormal physical finding in many asymptomatic patients.

The estimated mean length of survival from the onset of symptoms in symptomatic patients was 11.9 years—nearly twice that reported in other studies. In contrast, during a 12-year period the survival of asymptomatic patients after diagnosis did not differ from that of a control population matched for age and sex.

Jaundice, weight loss, hepatomegaly, splenomegaly, ascites, a serum albumin level lower than 3.0 gm/dl, and a total immunoglob-

(35–4) N. Engl. J. Med. 308:1–7, Jan. 6, 1983.

FREQUENCY OF VARIOUS FINDINGS AT DIAGNOSIS IN SYMPTOMATIC AND ASYMPTOMATIC PATIENTS WITH PRIMARY BILIARY CIRRHOSIS

FINDING	SYMPTOMATIC PATIENTS (N = 243)	ASYMPTOMATIC PATIENTS (N = 37)	P VALUE †
	per cent		
Physical examination			
Jaundice	59	5	<0.01
Hepatomegaly	74	46	<0.01
Splenomegaly	48	11	<0.01
Ascites	6	0	<0.01
Hyperpigmentation	41	11	<0.01
Xanthomas/xanthelasma	30	11	<0.05
Laboratory values			
Mitochondrial antibody positive	81	81	N.S.
Mitochondrial antibody titer >1:500	47	23	<0.01
Alkaline phosphatase > twice upper limit of normal	97	92	N.S.
Serum IgG >2.0 g/dl	53	32	N.S.
Serum bilirubin >1.5 mg/dl	61	13	<0.01
Serum cholesterol >300 mg/dl	66	29	<0.01
Serum albumin <3.0 g/dl	30	3	<0.01
Histologic features of liver			
Degree of fibrosis	(N = 190 *)	(N = 35 *)	
1+	20	49	<0.01
2+	25	40	N.S.
3+	55	11	<0.01
Portal granulomas	33	49	N.S.
Periportal cholestasis	42	0	<0.01
Erosion of limiting plate			
Absent	1	7	<0.05
Segmental	59	90	<0.01
Complete	40	3	<0.01

*Number for whom adequate records of histology were available.
†Significance was tested by the Z statistic. *NS,* not significant.
(Courtesy of Roll, J. et al.: N. Engl. J. Med. 308:1–7, Jan 6, 1983; reprinted by permission of The New England Journal of Medicine.)

ulin level higher than 2.0 gm/dl were each associated with a poor prognosis. Prognosis correlated, also, with the histologic stages of hepatic fibrosis, cholestasis, and periportal cell necrosis. A multivariate analysis of clinical features showed that at the onset of disease, older age, hepatomegaly, and elevated serum bilirubin levels were independent discriminators of a poor prognosis. A histologic finding of fibrosis limited to portal areas and without bridging or cirrhosis improved this discrimination, correlating with prolonged survival. No other factors enhanced the prediction of risk.

The average age of the asymptomatic patients in this study and in

2 other studies was the same as or higher than that of the symptomatic group, suggesting that early detection is not the explanation for longer survival. Rather, it seems likely that some patients in the asymptomatic group had nonprogressive or very slowly progressive disease.

▶ [This same group of investigators has extended the median follow-up of 36 of the 37 asymptomatic patients from 6.9 to 11.4 years.[4] Despite an additional 5 years of follow-up (range of observation, 0.5–20.5 years), 22 patients (61.1%) continued to be asymptomatic. Only 14 (38.8%) developed symptoms, and 8 of these died, 6 from liver disease. Survival data were analyzed by the Kaplan-Meier life-table method. Over this period, survival of this group of 36 patients did not differ from that of an age- and sex-matched control group drawn from the general population. The investigators confirmed that, assuming that deaths occurred in a Poisson distribution, the survival of this cohort was normal. In addition, clinical features that might correlate with either a continuing asymptomatic condition or disease progression were assessed. The association of an autoimmune disorder (thyroiditis, sicca syndrome, Raynaud's phenomenon) correlated with decreased survival ($P = .02$). Interestingly, the presence of granulomas on initial biopsy correlated with a continued asymptomatic state ($P = .02$). No other clinical features, including hepatomegaly, antimitochondrial antibody titer, jaundice, and hepatic fibrosis, correlated with survival or the development of symptoms. *In this group of 36 patients with asymptomatic primary biliary cirrhosis, 60% did not develop symptoms or manifestations of "disease" for up to 20 years after presentation.* Although a subgroup with associated autoimmune disorders had a poorer prognosis, the survival of patients with asymptomatic primary biliary cirrhosis was the same as that of the normal population.] ◀

35–5 **Role of Fat-Storing Cells in Disse Space Fibrogenesis in Alcoholic Liver Disease.** In Japan, chronic liver injury from alcohol abuse progresses to cirrhosis without demonstrable Mallory bodies. The fibrosis is characterized by collagen deposition in the Disse space, where fat-storing cells are abundant. Yukihito Minato, Yasushi Hasumura, and Jugoro Takeuchi (Tokyo) examined the relationship between collagen deposition in the Disse space and ultrastructural changes in fat-storing cells in the livers of 40 chronic alcoholics who ingested more than 80 gm of ethanol daily for more than 10 years.

Nine liver biopsy specimens showed minimal changes, 6 had mild hepatic fibrosis, 14 had moderate fibrosis (Fig 35–4), and 11 had severe fibrosis (cirrhosis). Collagen in the Disse space increased as hepatic fibrosis progressed, and the gradual development of rough endoplasmic reticulum (RER) in fat-storing cells also was observed. In patients with cirrhosis, collagen scores were high owing to formation of a basement membrane–like structure in the Disse space, but only a small number of fat-storing cells, whose RER was well developed, were noted. An increased rate of in vitro collagen synthesis, assessed in 17 samples, correlated significantly with the presence of well-developed RER in fat-storing cells.

The development of RER in the fat-storing cells of the liver appears to be a morphological correlate of their activated fibrogenesis and transformation into fibroblasts. The findings suggest that, in alcoholic liver injury, the fat-storing cells may have an important role in fibrogenesis in the Disse space of the liver cells. The progression of hepatic fibrosis without Mallory bodies, as seen both in Japanese patients and

---

(35–5) Hepatology 3:559–566, July/August 1983.

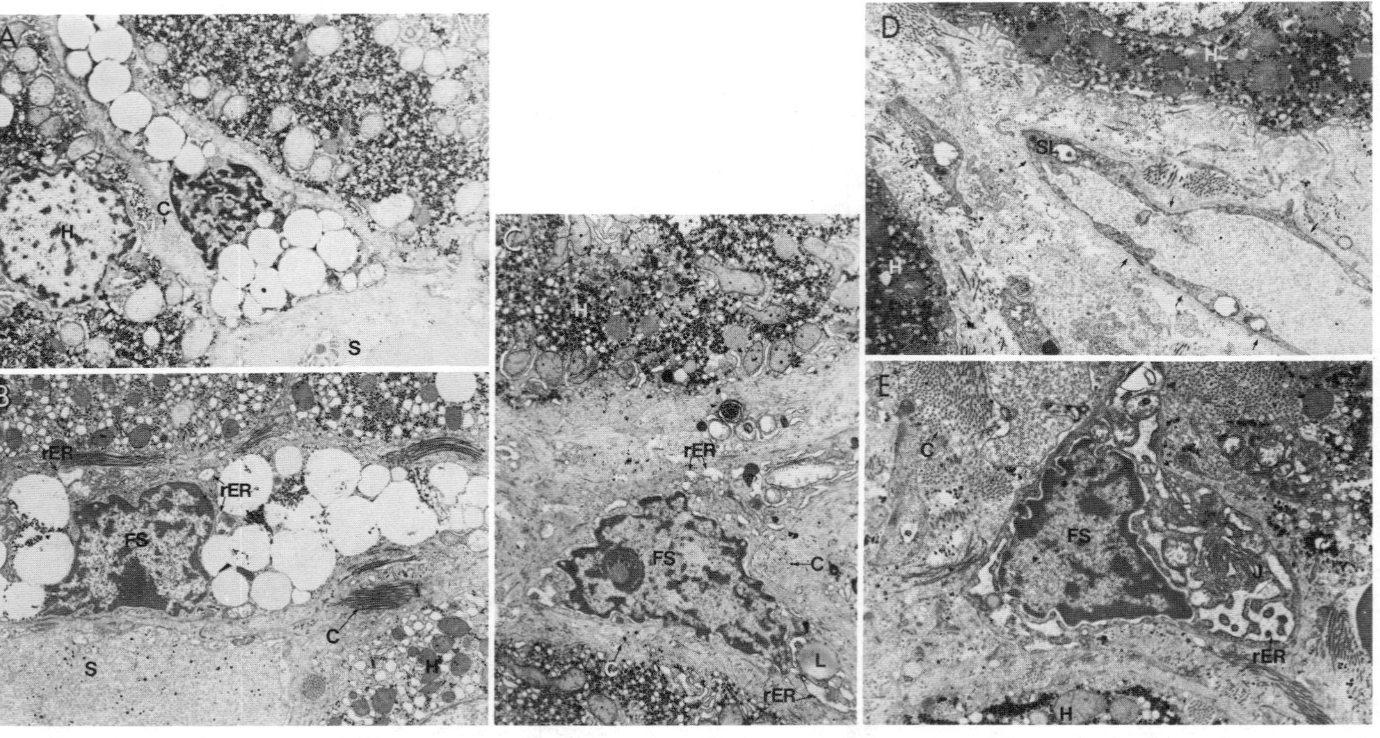

Fig 35–4.—A, electron micrograph of liver shows nonspecific changes (grade 0+). Small amounts of collagen fibrils *(C)* are seen (grade 0+), and rough endoplasmic reticulum *(RER)* in fat-storing cells *(FS)* is inconspicuous (grade 1+). H = hepatocyte; S = sinusoid. Original magnification, ×8,500. **B,** electron micrograph of liver shows mild fibrosis (grade 1+). Collagen bundles *(C)* are seen in the Disse space (grade 1+). Well-developed RER is seen in an FS cell (grade 2+). Original magnification, ×8,500. **C,** electron micrograph of the liver shows moderate fibrosis (grade 2+). Collagen fiber bundles *(C)* are increased and are seen in the intercellular space (grade 2+). An FS cell contains RER with dilated cisternae (grade 3+). A few small lipid droplets *(L)* can be seen. Original magnification, ×8,500. **D,** electron micrograph of liver shows severe fibrosis (grade 3+). Basement membrane–like material *(arrows)* is seen (grade 3+) between the sinusoidal lining cell *(SL)* and hepatocytes *(H)*. Original magnification, ×11,000. **E,** electron micrograph of the liver shows severe fibrosis (grade 3+). An FS cell is conspicuous with abundant and well-developed RER (grade 3+). The Disse space is widened, and many collagen bundles *(C)* exist around the FS cell. Original magnification, ×8,500. (Courtesy of Minato, Y., et al.: Hepatology 3:559–566, July/August 1983.)

in baboons given an alcoholic diet, suggests the possibility of a direct effect of alcohol on collagen synthesis by the fat-storing cells.

▶ [These studies provide an important link between steatosis and fat-storing cells and fibrogenesis in alcoholic liver disease and help explain the transition from fatty liver to cirrhosis.

Uchida et al. have described a newly recognized clinical and morphological pattern of acute alcoholic liver disease.[5] Twenty-one patients, having the hepatic morphologic features of alcoholic foamy degeneration, were retrospectively analyzed. All patients had a significant history of chronic alcoholism. Jaundice and hepatomegaly were usually present. Hepatic encephalopathy, ascites, bleeding esophageal varices, or functional renal failure occurred in less than 10%. Usually this was the first episode of decompensation. Laboratory studies revealed a pattern of very transient marked elevation of serum aminotransferase and more prolonged elevation of alkaline phosphatase activity and bilirubin levels. In the majority of cases, leukocytosis was absent, and serum cholesterol was elevated. The laboratory profile differed significantly from that of acute sclerosing hyaline necrosis. Serologic markers of acute viral hepatitis A and B were absent. Needle biopsy specimens of the liver revealed intact lobular architecture except for 1 case of cirrhosis. *The perivenular hepatocytes revealed foamy fatty change characterized by striking cell swelling with massive accumulation of microvesicular fat, i.e., tiny fat droplets in the swollen cytoplasm with shrunken central nuclei.* Megamitochondria were frequently identified. Multiple foci of hepatocyte dropout without significant parenchymal neutrophilic exudation and delicate intrasinusoidal collagen fibers were present in the perivenular area. Macrovesicular fatty change coexisted to a variable degree. The affected hepatocytes had extensive disorganization of the organelles by electron microscopy and decreased or absent functional activity by enzyme histochemical staining. These changes appear to be a purely degenerative process without inflammatory reaction. All patients in the present series showed a rapid recovery upon abstaining from alcohol.] ◀

35–6 **Grade I Reye's Syndrome: Frequent Cause of Vomiting and Liver Dysfunction After Varicella and Upper Respiratory Tract Infection.** Philip K. Lichtenstein, James E. Heubi, Cynthia C. Daugherty, Michael K. Farrell, Ronald J. Sokol, Robert J. Rothbaum, Frederick J. Suchy, and William F. Balistreri (Cincinnati) undertook a 1-year prospective study to determine whether vomiting and elevated serum aspartate or alanine aminotransferase levels, occurring after a viral upper respiratory tract infection or varicella, are manifestations of mild Reye's syndrome. The study group included 25 children who had prodromal upper respiratory infection or varicella, acute onset of recurrent vomiting, and enzyme levels at least threefold above normal. None was jaundiced, and lumbar puncture excluded cerebrospinal fluid infection. Nineteen patients had liver biopsies yielding adequate samples for diagnosis. The patients were treated with fluid and electrolytes and, when indicated, intracranial pressure monitoring, intubation with controlled ventilation, and administration of intravenous mannitol or pentobarbital.

The 19 patients with grade 1 (mild) disease had an average age of 6½ years. Fourteen had biopsy findings diagnostic of Reye's syndrome (Fig 35–5). No biopsy showed changes of viral or toxic hepatitis. One biopsy from a child with Reye's syndrome had features suggestive of α-antitrypsin deficiency; this patient had an SZ phenotype. Ultrastructural studies showed considerable variation. Five patients had marked mitochondrial changes, and 4 others had moderate changes.

(35–6) N. Engl. J. Med. 309:133–139, July 21, 1983.

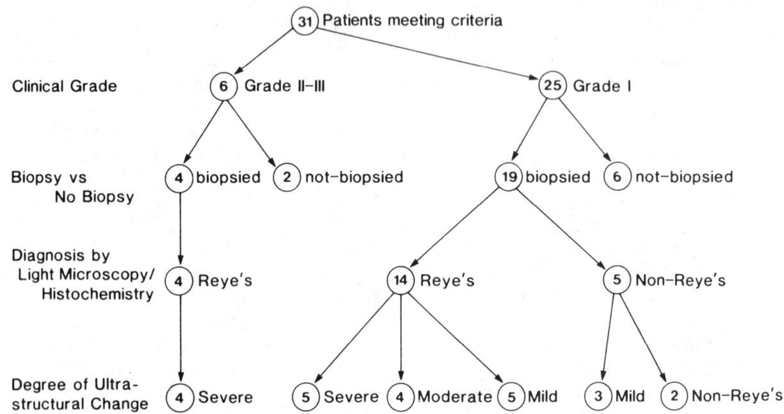

Fig 35–5.—Findings on light and electron microscopy in biopsy specimens from children with the clinical diagnosis of Reye's syndrome. (Courtesy of Lichtenstein, P.K., et al.: N. Engl. J. Med. 309:133–139, July 21, 1983; reprinted by permission of The New England Journal of Medicine.)

The severity of the ultrastructural findings could not be related to the duration of illness or to enzyme levels at admission.

The estimated minimum incidence of Reye's syndrome in metropolitan Cincinnati, based on biopsy-proved cases only, was 3.5 cases per 100,000 children per year. The findings in this study suggest that the clinical complex of vomiting, hepatic dysfunction, and minimal neurologic impairment developing after varicella or upper respiratory tract infection usually represents Reye's syndrome. This syndrome is more frequent than previously recognized. It is possible that children with transient elevations of transaminase levels to more than twice normal values also have Reye's syndrome.

▶ [There are only a few disorders characterized by microvesicular fat deposition. These include (1) Reye's syndrome, (2) acute fatty liver of pregnancy, (3) Jamaican vomiting sickness, (4) congenital defects of urea cycle enzymes, and (5) sodium valproate hepatotoxicity. The hepatic findings include centrizonal intrahepatocytic microvesiculation shown by specific staining to be fat, glycogen depletion, and lack of significant necrosis, inflammation, bile stasis, and bile duct proliferation. They all share the same clinical features. The onset is marked by fatigue, nausea, and vomiting, often severe and persistent, with variable jaundice, impairment of consciousness, and coma. Seizures may occur. Renal failure and disseminated intravascular coagulation of varying severity may be complications. Bleeding is caused by disseminated intravascular coagulation rather than by failure of the liver to synthesize clotting factors. The liver is not the only organ involved, and triglyceride accumulations may be found in the renal tubules and occasionally in myocardium and pancreas. Liver failure does not seem to be the usual cause of death. Coma may be related to increases in blood ammonia levels or to cerebral edema.

For an excellent review of the microvesicular fat diseases, see the article by Sherlock.[6]

There is evidence that salicylate may be a causal or contributory factor in Reye's syndrome. To determine whether pathology findings could be used to differentiate these illnesses, Starko and Mullick[7] characterized the hepatic and cerebral findings in salicylate-induced deaths. They studied two groups of children whose records were on file with the Armed Forces Institute of Pathology: those with accidental salicylate intoxication and those with therapeutically induced salicylate intoxication. Histology or necropsy records of 13 children were examined for the presence of hepatic and cerebral pathology findings characteristic of Reye's syndrome. Liver sections stained with hematoxylin and eosin showed intrahepatocytic microvesiculation (10 of 12 children) and absence of significant inflammation or necrosis (10 of 12 children). All 6 specimens of liver tissue stained with oil red O showed intrahepatocytic microvesicular fat with central hepatocytic nuclei distributed either diffusely throughout the lobule or more prominently in the lobular periphery. Liver tissue stained with the periodic acid–Schiff method showed complete absence of stainable glycogen in 5 of 6 children. Nine of 12 children for whom information was available had cerebral edema.

It was concluded that the *light-microscopy hepatic findings and the gross cerebral findings* for the majority of these children with salicylate intoxication were the same as those for children with Reye's syndrome. However, while the hepatic injury of Reye's syndrome and salicylate may be similar by light microscopy, examination by more sophisticated means such as electron microscopy might demonstrate significant differences. Nevertheless, the scant electron-microscopic evidence available on salicylate intoxication shows many similarities with that on Reye's syndrome. Starko and Mullick point out that salicylate may cause the structural damage in children with Reye's syndrome as well as that which occurs during salicylate intoxication. Nevertheless, a major difference in these disorders is that patients with Reye's syndrome apparently take "therapeutic" doses of salicylate and have "low" salicylate levels when admitted to hospital. The relation between the salicylate level and toxic tissue effects is complex, however, as exemplified by the finding that the levels in 5 of the subjects before death were less than or equal to 33 mg/100 ml. Conceivably either the prodromal illness or a pharmacogenetic factor may increase sensitivity to salicylate at therapeutic doses.] ◀

35–7 **Is Intravenous Administration of Branched Chain Amino Acids Effective in the Treatment of Hepatic Encephalopathy? Multicenter Study.** It has been proposed that the administration of branched-chain amino acids (BCAAs) may benefit patients with hepatic cirrhosis and encephalopathy through correction of an imbalance in neurotransmitter synthesis produced by an increase in aromatic amino acids in the brain. John Wahren, Jacques Denis, Philippe Desurmont, Ljusk S. Eriksson, Jean-Marc Escoffier, André P. Gauthier, Lars Hagenfeldt, Henri Michel, Pierre Opolon, Jean-

Fig 35–6.—Changes in EEG grading in branched-chain amino acid (BCAA) and placebo groups before and during therapy. (Courtesy of Wahren, J., et al.: Hepatology 3:475–480, May/June 1983.)

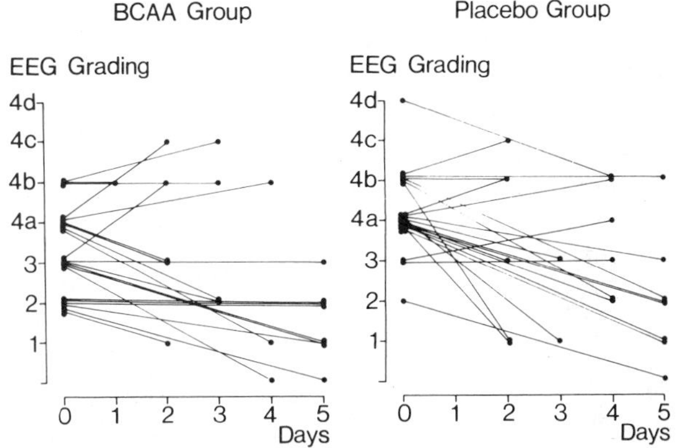

(35–7) Hepatology 3:475–480, May/June 1983.

Claude Paris, and Michel Veyrac examined the effects of infused BCAAs on brain function in a double-blind study of 50 patients with acute hepatic encephalopathy and evidence of cirrhosis. Half the patients received 20 or 40 gm of BCAAs in 5% glucose daily for up to 5 days or for 1 day after encephalopathy had improved to grade 0 or 1. The others received glucose only. The control patients received no caloric compensation for the amino acids given the BCAA recipients. The two groups were clinically comparable. The mean duration of coma was about 24 hours in both groups at the onset of treatment.

Fourteen BCAA-treated patients and 12 control patients woke up. Three patients in each group deteriorated during the study. Changes in EEG patterns during treatment were similar in the two groups (Fig 35–6). Significant reductions in plasma phenylalanine, tyrosine, and methionine levels occurred during BCAA administration, and the ratio of BCAAs to aromatic amino acids increased consistently. Laboratory findings are given in the table. About a third of both groups survived 25 days after the end of the trial. Twice as many patients in the BCAA group as in the placebo group died of encephalopathy.

It appears that the administration of BCAAs orally or intravenously does not ameliorate either chronic or acute hepatic encepha-

LABORATORY DATA*

		Before therapy	Last day of therapy†
Ammonia	BCAA	219 ± 30	225 ± 46
	Placebo	256 ± 29	283 ± 58
Urea	BCAA	101 ± 16	122 ± 16‡
	Placebo	101 ± 14	92 ± 16
Creatinine	BCAA	105 ± 15	140 ± 34
	Placebo	112 ± 14	120 ± 21
Albumin	BCAA	73.1 ± 2.8	63.4 ± 4.5§
	Placebo	76.2 ± 3.7	67.9 ± 5.0
Sodium	BCAA	94.8 ± 1.0	91.4 ± 1.5‡
	Placebo	96.6 ± 0.7	90.0 ± 1.0¶
Bilirubin	BCAA	334 ± 62	334 ± 60
	Placebo	380 ± 52	419 ± 65
SGOT	BCAA	527 ± 114	—
	Placebo	311 ± 87	—
SGPT	BCAA	331 ± 86	—
	Placebo	190 ± 31	—
Prothrombin index	BCAA	49 ± 3	—
	Placebo	45 ± 4	—

*All data presented as means ± SE, expressed as percentage of corresponding normal value.

†Symbols denote probability that differences between values before and during therapy were caused by random factors: ‡, $P<.05$; §, $P<.01$; ¶, $P<.001$.

(Courtesy of Wahren, J., et al.: Hepatology 3:475–480, May/June 1983.)

lopathy. The failure of apparent normalization of the amino acid pattern to improve encephalopathy raises doubt as to the pathogenetic significance of deranged plasma amino acid levels and the validity of the "false neurotransmitter" hypothesis.

It is concluded that BCAA administration, in the dose and composition employed in the present study, neither improves cerebral function nor decreases mortality in patients with hepatic encephalopathy.

▶ [There continues to be considerable controversy over the indications for use of and the efficacy of branched-chain amino acids (BCAAs) in the treatment of hepatic encephalopathy. The conflicting results are due, at least in part, to the different types of patients being evaluated and to different therapeutic regimens. Thus, BCAAs have been studied in patients with chronic stable portal systemic encephalopathy, acute decompensation in previously stable cirrhotic patients, and acute hepatic encephalopathy. Further, both oral and intravenous preparations have been utilized. Acute encephalopathy, often precipitated by bleeding, constipation, dehydration, or infection, is hard to evaluate because of the unpredictable changes associated with the precipitating factor. Encephalopathy is difficult to quantitate and at present has no universal definition. Clinical assessment may be notoriously inaccurate, but addition of quantitative psychometric measurements and EEG analysis offers the best methods available for measuring encephalopathy at this time.

In a carefully done study, McGhee et al. evaluated Hepatic-Aid® by comparing a 50-gm casein diet with an identical diet of 20 gm of casein/30 gm of Hepatic-Aid per day in a crossover study.[8] Four patients with biopsy-proved stable cirrhosis, encephalopathy, and undernutrition were studied. Each study period included 3 days of equilibration and 8 days of metabolic balance, with the following measured at baseline and on balance days 5 and 8: routine biochemistry, fasting ammonia, psychometric tests, EEG, and plasma amino acid profiles. There was no significant change in clinical status, routine biochemistry, fasting ammonia, psychometrics, or EEG between the two study periods. Mean nitrogen balance on the casein diet at 1.5 $\pm$ 1.5 ($\pm$15.0) gm/day was not significantly different from that on the Hepatic-Aid diet at 1.5 $\pm$ 1.2 gm/day. Plasma amino acid profiles showed a significant fall in fasting and intraprandial tyrosine (tyr) and phenylalanine (phe) on Hepatic-Aid, but only intraprandial leucine (leu), isoleucine (ile), and valine (val) were significantly increased on Hepatic-Aid. The ratio of leu + ile + val to tyr + phe was significantly increased on Hepatic-Aid. It is concluded that Hepatic-Aid, as given in this study, maintains N balance similar to casein and alters the amino acid profile towards normal but does not ameliorate encephalopathy.

McCullough et al. have written a thoughtful editorial on BCAA therapy in liver disease, and much of what follows has been abstracted from that article. "Whether BCAA are superior nitrogen sources to standard amino acid mixtures administered by the same route remains to be answered. This is particularly relevant because of evidence that, in alcoholic hepatitis, *standard amino acid solutions* are well tolerated and increase survival. Therefore, justification for supplementation with BCAA should be based upon their selective effect on protein degradation and amino acid oxidation. Precautions are required with any BCAA preparation used for nutritional purposes in patients with liver disease to ensure that deficiencies of other amino acids do not develop. Administration of total parenteral nutrition solutions devoid of the nonessential amino acids tyrosine and cysteine may prevent achievement of positive nitrogen balance in cirrhosis despite provision of adequate essential amino acid precursors. This emphasizes that intrinsic liver functions may be rate-limiting in cirrhosis, such as ability to synthesize adequately cysteine from methionine and tyrosine from phenylalanine. Therefore, the routine use of currently available BCAA solutions may be capricious, expensive, and harmful, especially if, as in several standard mixtures, the formulations are nutritionally incomplete or contain other amino acids (e.g., glycine, proline, lysine, threonine, and arginine) in amounts which may not be cleared normally by a liver with reduced ureagenic capacity.

Since mechanisms for the proposed benefit of BCAA in liver disease remain ill-defined, guidelines for patient selection and endpoints of therapy remain in doubt. It seems reasonable, although expensive and still unproved, to employ BCAA-enriched solutions for nutritional purposes in cirrhotics who otherwise require protein restriction to control hepatic encephalopathy. However, most patients with chronic liver disease tolerate standard high protein diets and probably benefit from them in terms of protein turnover, nitrogen balance, and improved survival.

In summary, the use of BCAA solutions for nutritional purposes offers considerable potential benefit to patients with a wide spectrum of liver diseases. However, more work is required to quantify the benefits and define indications for BCAA therapy lest scientific rationale be preempted by commercial availability."] ◀

35–8 **Potential Role of Increased Sympathetic Activity in Impaired Sodium and Water Excretion in Cirrhosis.** Daniel G. Bichet, Vicki J. Van Putten, and Robert W. Schrier (Univ. of Colorado Health Sciences Center, Denver) studied 26 patients with cirrhosis to examine the potential role of increased sympathetic discharge, as assessed by the radioenzymatic determination of plasma norepinephrine, in the renal impairment of water and sodium excretion.

The plasma norepinephrine concentration in 7 cirrhotic patients with normal excretion did not differ significantly from that in normal volunteers. However, norepinephrine concentrations were significantly higher in 19 cirrhotic patients who abnormally excreted an acute water load than in the 7 who excreted the load normally (table). There was also a significant positive correlation between plasma levels of norepinephrine and arginine vasopressin after the water load, as well as a negative correlation between plasma norepinephrine and the percentage of the load excreted. The patients with impaired water excretion had a lower plasma osmolality and lower plasma levels of sodium and albumin but significantly higher pulse rates and higher levels of plasma renin activity, plasma aldosterone, and plasma arginine vasopressin (see the table).

A positive correlation between plasma norepinephrine and plasma renin activity, as well as between norepinephrine and aldosterone, was observed. In addition, there was a negative correlation between plasma norepinephrine and urinary sodium excretion (Fig 35–7). No correlation was noted between the plasma level of norepinephrine and creatinine clearance. Clinically detectable ascites was present in all 19 patients with impaired water excretion and in 2 of the 7 with normal water excretion.

The findings indicate that increased sympathetic activity, as assessed by plasma levels of norepinephrine, correlates closely with sodium and water retention in cirrhotic patients and thus may be of pathogenetic importance. It is hypothesized that a decrease in "effective" blood volume in cirrhotic patients secondary to peripheral vasodilatation, hypoalbuminemia, and splanchnic venous pooling would be expected to stimulate baroreceptors in the left atrium and carotid sinus. This stimulation would cause a decrease in vagal and glossopharyngeal afferent-nerve traffic to the midbrain and hypothalamus, with resultant release of arginine vasopressin, and an increase in sympathetic efferent-nerve activity. The associated increase in renal sympathetic tone may then activate the renin-angiotensin-aldosterone axis and thereby enhance distal sodium reabsorption. In addi-

(35–8) N. Engl. J. Med. 307:1552–1557, Dec. 16, 1982.

BIOCHEMICAL CHARACTERISTICS OF 26 PATIENTS WITH CIRRHOSIS, ACCORDING TO DEGREE OF WATER EXCRETION

CHARACTERISTIC	PATIENT GROUP *		P VALUE †
	IMPAIRED EXCRETION (n = 19)	NORMAL EXCRETION (n = 7)	
Norepinephrine (pg/ml)	834±116	306±33	<0.001
Epinephrine (pg/ml)	73±8	47±19	NS
Urinary sodium excretion (mmol/5 hr)	2.5±0.7	17.1±2.8	<0.001
Plasma renin activity (ng/ml/hr)	7.7±1.0	1.55±0.21	<0.001
Aldosterone (ng/dl)	67.0±14.0	20.4±2.0	<0.005
Arginine vasopressin (pg/ml)	2.06±0.46	0.68±0.09	<0.01
Pulse (beats/min)	90.0±3.0	74.0±2.3	<0.001
Per cent water excretion	29.0±3.4	82.4±0.8	‡
Minimum urinary osmolality (mOsm/kg water)	243.0±37.0	71.8±6.8	<0.001
Albumin (g/dl) §	2.6±0.1	3.3±0.2	<0.02
Plasma osmolality (mOsm/kg water)	277.0±2.3	282.0±1.6	<0.05
Plasma sodium (mmol/liter)	132.6±1.4	140.0±0.6	<0.001
Creatinine clearance (ml/min/1.73 m^2)	70.0±7.3	107.0±11.7	<0.01
Inulin clearance (ml/min/1.73 m^2)	58.4±7.3	92.0±15.0	NS
Para-aminohippurate clearance (ml/min/1.73 m^2)	333.0±30.5	507.0±87.0	NS

*Values are presented as means ± S.E.
†*NS,* not significant.
‡The values for this characteristic were the prospective criteria for classifying patients into groups.
§To convert to gm/L, multiply by 10.
(Courtesy of Bichet, D.G., et al.: N. Engl. J. Med. 307:1552–1557, Dec. 16, 1982; reprinted by permission of The New England Journal of Medicine.)

tion, renal-nerve stimulation may directly enhance sodium reabsorption in the proximal tubule. The results provide support for the traditional view that effective blood volume in cirrhosis with ascites is contracted.

▶ [Other investigators have also observed that sympathetic nervous activity, as assessed by the plasma norepinephrine concentration, is dramatically increased in decompensated cirrhosis.[10] Since the kidney releases norepinephrine into the peripheral circulation in this condition, it has been suggested that increased sympathetic nervous activity may be of importance in the renal cortical vasoconstriction in decompensated cirrhosis.[11]

The data in the table indicate that the patients with impaired water excretion, who had significantly elevated plasma concentrations of aldosterone, also had significantly lower urinary sodium excretion and a much higher incidence of ascites. A major question therefore is, Why do patients with cirrhosis not "escape" from the

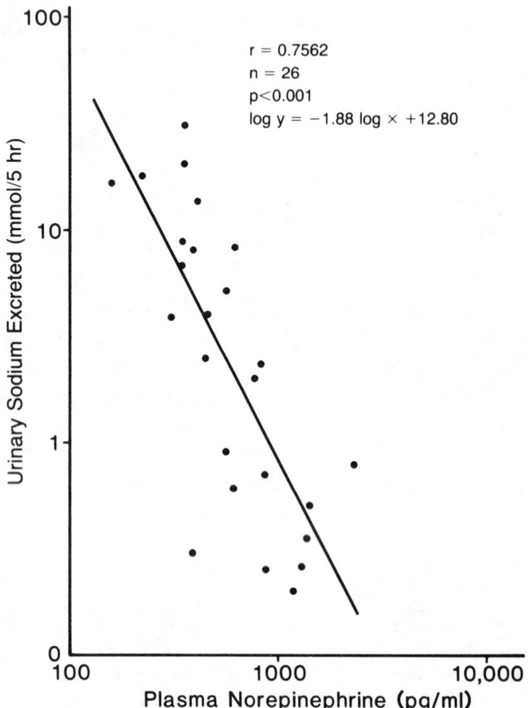

Fig 35–7.—Plasma norepinephrine concentration and sodium excretion after water loading. The log-log regression line is shown. Each symbol represents the mean of determinations made for 5 hours after acute water loading. (Courtesy of Bichet, D.G., et al.: N. Engl. J. Med. 307:1552–1557, Dec. 16, 1982; reprinted by permission of The New England Journal of Medicine.)

sodium retaining effect of aldosterone? Bichet et al. in the discussion section of the article abstracted above provide a rational explanation and it is as follows: "It is known that the process of aldosterone "escape" involves expansion of the extracellular-fluid volume and decreased reabsorption of sodium in the proximal tubule. The resultant increased distal sodium delivery may therefore exceed the distal sodium reabsorptive capacity, including that mediated by continued excess plasma concentrations of aldosterone. Since micropuncture studies in rats have shown that renal-nerve stimulation increases sodium reabsorption in the proximal tubule, increased renal sympathetic activity in patients with cirrhosis and normal excretion may cause diminished distal sodium delivery and thereby be an important factor in the ability of cirrhotic patients to escape from the sodium-retaining effect of aldosterone. Such a renal nerve–mediated decrease in distal sodium and fluid delivery in these patients may also contribute to the impairment of water excretion, in addition to any effect mediated by the nonosmotic release of arginine vasopressin."] ◀

35–9 **Randomized Comparative Study of Efficacy of Furosemide Versus Spironolactone in Nonazotemic Cirrhosis With Ascites: Relationship Between the Diuretic Response and the Activity of the Renin-Aldosterone System.** R. M. Pérez-Ayuso, V. Arroyo, R. Planas, J. Gaya, F. Bory, A. Rimola, F. Rivera, and J. Rodés (Univ. of Barcelona, Spain) compared furosemide and spironolactone in 40 nonazotemic cirrhotic patients with ascites and avid sodium reten-

(35–9) Gastroenterology 84:961–968, May 1983.

BASELINE LABORATORY VALUES IN PATIENTS TREATED WITH FUROSEMIDE OR SPIRONOLACTONE

	Glomerular filtration rate (*ml/min*)	Urine volume (*ml/day*)	Sodium excretion (*mEq/day*)	Total bilirubin (*mg/dl*)	Plasma albumin (*g/L*)	Prothrombin time (%)	Plasma renin activity (*ng/ml · h*)	Aldosterone (*ng/dl*)
Patients treated with furosemide								
Positive response (11 cases)	112.7 ± 19.4	686. ± 53.	11.0 ± 2.5	1.55 ± 0.22	27.3 ± 1.6	70.0 ± 5.6	2.77 ± 0.83	32.51 ± 10.04
Negative response (10 cases)	95.08 ± 7.51	839. ± 80.	3.4 ± 0.9	1.64 ± 0.35	27.1 ± 2.4	65.6 ± 5.7	10.42 ± 6.92	118.9 ± 21.4
			$p < 0.02$				$p < 0.001$	$p < 0.001$
Patients treated with spironolactone								
150 mg/day (14 cases)	83.8 ± 6.9	864. ± 80.07	9.1 ± 2.2	1.81 ± 0.23	25.5 ± 1.4	59.3 ± 6.6	2.67 ± 0.62	33.5 ± 6.1
300 mg/day (13 cases)	101.5 ± 9.6	863 ± 79.71	1.8 ± 0.3	1.46 ± 0.25	27.4 ± 1.9	64.0 ± 6.3	11.93 ± 1.79	114.3 ± 15.6
			$p < 0.01$				$p < 0.001$	$p < 0.001$

(Courtesy of Pérez-Ayuso, R.M., et al.: Reprinted by permission of the publisher from Gastroenterology 84:961–968, May 1983; copyright by the American Gastrological Association.)

tion. All had a urinary sodium excretion of less than 30 mEq daily after 5 days on a diet with 50 mEq of sodium per day. Cirrhosis was alcoholic in most cases. Twenty-one patients received furosemide in an initial dose of 80 mg daily, increased to 160 mg as needed, and 19 received spironolactone in an initial dose of 150 mg daily, increased to 300 mg daily as needed. Response criteria consisted of a mean body weight loss of at least 200 mg daily and urinary sodium excretion of at least 50 mEq daily. The two groups were clinically comparable. All but 8 of the 40 patients had elevated plasma aldosterone levels.

Eleven of 21 patients responded to furosemide, 8 of them to 80 mg daily. All but 1 of 19 patients responded to spironolactone, 13 to a dose of 150 mg daily. Nine of the 10 furosemide-treated patients who failed to respond did well when given spironolactone. The spironolactone-resistant patient also failed to respond to furosemide. Eight patients given furosemide required potassium supplementation. The serum potassium level rose in most patients given spironolactone. Factors influencing the responses are shown in the table. Importantly, patients with higher plasma renin and aldosterone levels were the most resistant to both treatments. Moderate renal failure developed in 3 patients during treatment. All patients who were discharged from the hospital eventually lost their ascites. Only 1 was satisfactorily treated with furosemide alone, and most received both drugs.

These results indicate that at the dosages used in the study, spironolactone is more effective than furosemide in patients with nonazotemic cirrhosis and ascites. Further, the activity of the renin-aldosterone system influences the diuretic response to furosemide and spironolactone. Increased tubular sensitivity to aldosterone could explain why patients without hyperaldosteronism respond to spironolactone. Loop diuretics not only fail to increase urinary sodium excretion in many cases but also can cause serious hypokalemia.

▶ [To briefly summarize the major findings in this study, spironolactone (150–300 mg daily) caused a diuresis in 18 of the 19 patients studied, whereas furosemide (80–160 mg daily) was effective in only 11 of 21 patients. In addition, 9 of the 10 patients who failed to diurese with furosemide responded to subsequent therapy with spironolactone.

Several recent studies have demonstrated that spironolactone, when used as the only drug in the treatment of cirrhotic ascites, is effective in causing a satisfactory diuresis in 50%–85% of patients.[12–14] It is usually necessary to give spironolactone in doses of 300–600 mg daily.

The effects of furosemide in cirrhotic ascites are receiving increasing attention. Fogel et al. have observed that modest doses of furosemide (40–120 mg daily) will initiate a diuresis in patients with ascites. Interestingly, however, a continued increase in dosage to levels as high as 400 mg daily is often necessary to maintain a diuresis.[14]

Boyer and Warnock have written a thoughtful editorial on the use of diuretics in the treatment of cirrhotic ascites.[15] They have raised the question of why the "potent" loop diuretics are unable to cause a natriuresis and diuresis in many patients with cirrhosis. They point out that the failure to obtain a natriuresis with furosemide may not be indicative of a failure of the diuretic to cause an increase in the distal delivery of sodium. The diuretic may be effective in reducing sodium reabsorption in the proximal nephron; however, an aldosterone-mediated increase in reabsorption of sodium and secretion of potassium by the distal nephron results in a kaliuresis without a natriuresis. This dissociation between the natriuretic and kaliuretic effects of loop diuretics was observed by Pérez-Ayuso et al. in those patients who failed to respond to furosemide and by other investigators as well.] ◀

35–10 **Hyponatremia and Arginine Vasopressin Secretion in Patients With Refractory Hepatic Ascites Undergoing Peritoneovenous Shunting.** Hyponatremia in cirrhotic patients with ascites

(35–10) Gastroenterology 84:713–718, April, 1983.

that is not due to diuretic therapy may be related to a persistent elevation of the antidiuretic hormone arginine vasopressin (ADH). R. K. Reznick, B. Langer, B. R. Taylor, S. Seif, and L. M. Blendis examined ADH changes after peritoneovenous shunting in 7 patients with persistent hyponatremia, normal or elevated serum arginine vasopressin concentrations, and refractory ascites related to proved hepatic cirrhosis. The ascites had not responded to long-term treatment with maximal diuresis and sodium and fluid restriction in the hospital. The serum bilirubin concentration was below 4 mg/dl, and the prothrombin time was no more than minimally elevated. Patients were given a 20-mEq sodium, 1,200-ml diet preoperatively; diuretics were stopped; and studies were done after 3–8 days of equilibration (phase 1). Studies were repeated in intensive care postoperatively (phase 2), 24–72 hours postoperatively (phase 3), and after about 2 weeks (phase 4), when patients were receiving the 20-mEq sodium, 1,200 ml diet without diuretics.

No significant changes in liver function followed shunting. Urine output rose markedly as urine osmolality fell (Fig 35–8). Sodium excretion increased significantly within 24 hours of shunt implantation and remained elevated in the subsequent phases. Creatinine clearance increased significantly within 6 hours of shunting but subsequently fell. Renal blood flow and cardiac output both increased but

Fig. 35–8.—Changes in urine volume, urine osmolarity, osmolar clearance, and sodium excretion during four phases of study. Single asterisks indicate $P < .05$; double asterisks, $P < .01$. (Courtesy of Reznick, R.K., et al.: Reprinted by permission of the publisher from Gastroenterology 84:713–718, April 1983; copyright by the American Gastrological Association.)

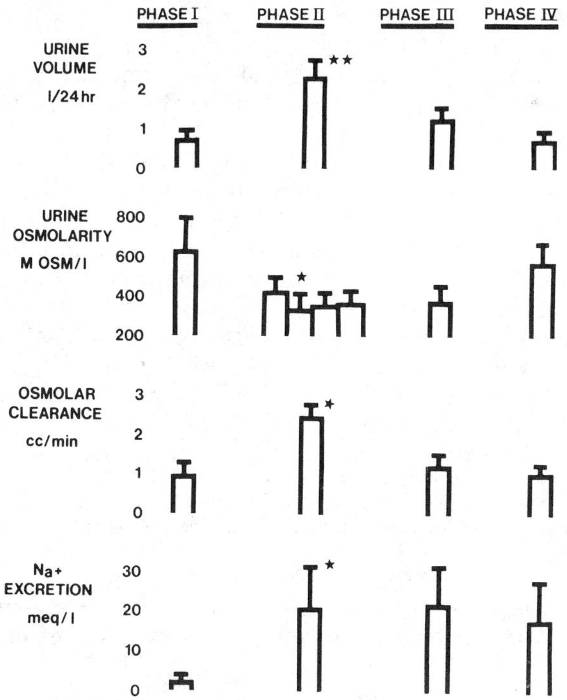

PHASE I PHASE II PHASE III PHASE IV

URINE VOLUME l/24hr

URINE OSMOLARITY M OSM/l

OSMOLAR CLEARANCE cc/min

Na+ EXCRETION meq/l

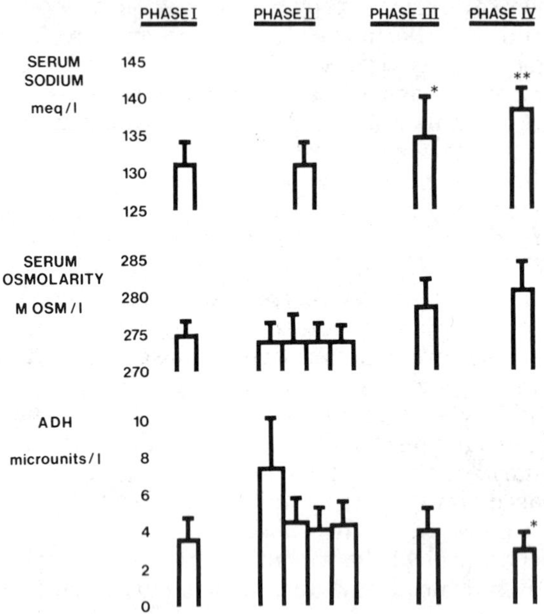

Fig. 35–9.—Changes in serum sodium concentrations, serum osmolarity, and serum ADH concentrations during four phases of study. Single asterisks denote $P < .05$; double asterisks, $P < .01$. (Courtesy of Reznick, R.K., et al. Reprinted by permission of the publisher from Gastroenterology 84:713–718, April 1983; copyright by the American Gastrological Association.)

not significantly. Plasma renin activity fell significantly after shunting, as did the serum aldosterone concentration. Changes in serum sodium concentration, osmolarity, and ADH concentration are shown in Figure 35–9. The ADH values fell significantly by phase 4, but remained above the upper limit of normal.

Hyponatremia in patients with cirrhotic ascites is initially reversed by increased water excretion from intravascular volume expansion and increased delivery of filtrate to the distal segment after peritoneovenous shunting. The changes are eventually associated with a decrease in ADH, although ADH concentrations remain inappropriately elevated.

These results indicate that in this group of cirrhotic patients with refractory ascites, intrarenal factors, such as decreased delivery of filtrate to the distal nephron as well as elevated inappropriate levels of arginine vasopressin, are important in the pathogenesis of hyponatremia.

▶ [For a timely brief review of mechanisms of disturbed renal water excretion in cirrhosis, see the editorial by Schrier.[16]

The recent experimental availability of a specific antagonist to the hydroosmotic action of ADH is of considerable interest.[17] This antagonist is being used to further investigate the role of ADH in the water retention observed in experimental cirrhosis. Its use in clinical trials is eagerly anticipated.] ◀

35–11 **Effect of Inhibitors of Prostaglandin Synthesis on Induced Diuresis in Cirrhosis.** Active renal vasoconstriction tends to occur

(35–11) Hepatology 3:50–55, Jan./Feb. 1983.

in patients with cirrhosis and ascites, and increased renal production of the E prostaglandins, which function to counteract strong renal vasoconstricting influences, has been proposed. Daniel Mirouze, Robert D. Zipser, and Telfer B. Reynolds examined the role of renal prostaglandins in the maintenance of renal function in patients with cirrhosis. Patients with alcoholic liver disease and ascites were given a daily diet containing 20 mEq of sodium, and they also received diuretics. The natriuretic response to 80 mg of furosemide given intravenously was monitored in conjunction with pretreatment with indomethacin, naproxen, or aspirin. Other patients received spironolactone in a dose of 300 mg daily for a week before the study. Three doses of anti-inflammatory drug were given; the individual doses were 50 mg of indomethacin, 250 mg of naproxen, and 900 mg of aspirin.

Pretreatment with indomethacin reduced natriuresis by more than 80%, whereas creatinine clearance was reduced by only 16%. The urinary prostaglandin E_2 level declined. Natriuresis was also reduced by naproxen treatment. Spironolactone-induced natriuresis was reduced by indomethacin, naproxen, and aspirin, in decreasing order of potency. In normal persons indomethacin reduced furosemide-induced diuresis by 14% and did not influence the creatinine clearance.

These drug interactions appear to involve renal hemodynamics that are significantly influenced by renal prostaglandins in patients with hepatic disease and ascites. Possible explanations include (1) sodium retention by prostaglandin synthetase inhibitors themselves; (2) increased synthesis of vasodilatory prostaglandins by the diuretics; and (3) impairment of renal blood flow and glomerular filtration by indomethacin and related drugs. The findings indicate that drugs that inhibit prostaglandin synthetase should be avoided during diuretic therapy in patients with sodium retention caused by liver disease.

▶ [For a current brief review of renal prostaglandins in cirrhosis, see the editorial by Levine.[18] Much of what follows has been abstracted from that article.

Although prostaglandin synthesis inhibitors rarely lead to clinically significant renal dysfunction when given to persons with normal systemic and renal hemodynamics, they frequently lead to marked oliguria and diminished glomerular filtration rate in patients with salt-retaining states such as hemorrhage, congestive heart failure, and cirrhosis, and in patients in whom renal function is even modestly decreased by diabetes mellitus, hypertension, old age, or collagen-vascular disease. In these patients, maintenance of glomerular filtration and renal blood flow depends upon the ability of endogenous vasodilator prostaglandins to block the effects of neural and hormonal renal vasoconstrictors.

In studies similar to those carried out by Mirouze et al., Zipser et al.[19] demonstrated that indomethacin decreased creatinine clearance by more than 50% in a group of salt-retaining cirrhotic patients, all of whom had intense ascites and urinary sodium excretion rates less than 10 mEq/day. The patients who were the most avid salt retainers (sodium excretion rate less than 1 mEq/day) developed the largest decreases in glomerular filtration rate after indomethacin, although it was difficult to assess the diminution of salt excretion because the basal rates were so low. Renal plasma flow measurements were not performed. Urinary prostaglandin E levels were elevated in all of the patients and decreased after indomethacin. Pressor sensitivity to exogenous angiotensin II was increased by indomethacin as well, although the effects of angiotensin II on renal function were not examined. Both studies support a major role for hemodynamic changes in mediating the antinatriuretic effects of prostaglandin synthesis inhibitors.] ◀

35–12 **Recovery of Sexual Function in Abstinent Alcoholic Men.** Hypogonadism is common in chronically alcoholic men and is due to alcohol toxicity at both the testicular level and the hypothalamic-pituitary level. David H. Van Thiel, Judith S. Gavaler, and Ajit Sanghvi (Univ. of Pittsburgh) examined the reversibility of alcohol-induced hypogonadism in 60 alcohol-abstinent chronically alcoholic men followed up prospectively for 4 years. All had been abstinent for at least 3 months; most, for 6 months or more. All had a history of impotence or loss of libido or both. The mean patient age was 36 years. The patients had taken at least the equivalent of a pint of whiskey daily for an average of 12 years. Forty-five patients did not improve spontaneously in 2 years of observation. They were then given clomiphene in increasing doses for 1 year, followed by injections of human chorionic gonadotropin, if necessary, and then by treatment with fluoxymesterone in doses increasing to 80 mg daily.

The characteristics of the study group are given in the table. One fourth of the men had spontaneous recovery of adequate sexual functioning in the first 2 years of observation. Recovery tended to occur early (Fig 35–10). The duration of alcohol abuse was related to both testicular atrophy and cirrhosis. All men who recovered spontaneously had had normal testicular volumes at entry to the study. Normal gonadotropin responses to LRF and to clomiphene were closely associated with spontaneous recovery of sexual function. All 13 men with normal sperm concentrations at the outset had spontaneous recovery, compared with only 2 of the 47 with reduced concentrations. No men had a return to adequate sexual function with clo-

Characteristics of 60 Men Studied

	No.	Percent
Age = 36 ± 4 yr[a]		
Liver histology		
cirrhosis	11	(18%)
portal fibrosis	24	(40%)
nonspecific changes	12	(20%)
normal	13	(22%)
Testicular atrophy[b]		
present	38	(63%)
absent	22	(37%)
Years of alcohol abuse = 12 ± 2 yr[a]		
Period of abstinence before entry = 5.3 ± 0.1 mo[a]		
Marital status[c]	33	(55%)

[a]$\bar{X}$ ± SEM

[b]Largest diameter <2.5 cm

[c]Married and living with wife or living with woman but not married

(Courtesy of Van Thiel, D.H., et al.: Reprinted by permission of the publisher from Gastroenterology 84:677–682, April 1983; copyright by the American Gastrological Society.)

(35–12) Gastroenterology 84:677–682, April 1983.

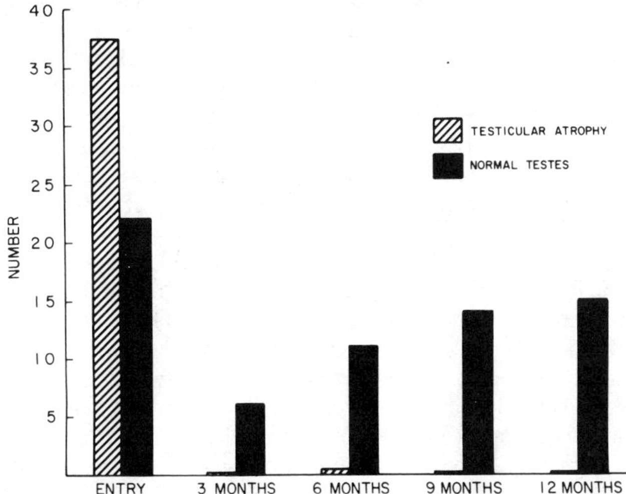

Fig 35–10.—Distribution and cumulative rate of spontaneous recovery of normal sexual functioning of abstinent alcoholics. Ordinate shows number of men achieving normal sexual functioning. Abscissa shows duration of alcoholic abstinence before return of normal sexual functioning. (Courtesy of Van Thiel, D.H., et al.: Reprinted by permission of the publisher from Gastroenterology 84:677–682, April 1983; copyright by the American Gastrological Association.)

miphene therapy, and none responded to chorionic gonadotropin therapy. Eight men became potent with a fluoxymesterone dose of 40 mg daily, 21 with a dose of 60 mg daily, and 3 with a dose of 80 mg daily. No men with testicular atrophy responded to a dose of less than 60 mg daily.

About one fourth of alcoholic men who are abstinent for 6 months or longer can be expected to have a spontaneous return of adequate sexual function if gonadal atrophy is absent. In men with testicular atrophy, treatment with nonaromatizable androgen in high dosage can lead to a return of potency, although a loss of fertility also occurs.

▶ [These carefully done studies have shown that alcohol-induced gonadal dysfunction is spontaneously reversible in some chronically alcoholic men who achieve sobriety, but only if they do not have gonadal atrophy. Adequate sexual functioning in such men with testicular atrophy was achieved only with very large doses of exogenous androgen. It is quite possible that chronically alcoholic men may be androgen-receptor deficient. In support of such a conclusion is the finding that despite very large doses of exogenous androgen, the more common untoward effects of androgen therapy such as prostatic hypertrophy, gynecomastia, acne, hirsutism, priaprism, hypercalcemia, and jaundice were not observed in these patients.] ◀

35–13 **Endoscopic Sclerotherapy for Bleeding Esophageal Varices: Effects and Complications.** Poorer than expected results from portacaval shunt surgery have led to the increased use of endoscopic esophageal vein sclerosis. However, Steven J. Ayres, John S. Goff, and George H. Warren (Univ. of Colorado) obtained evidence that the procedure leads to severe necrotizing inflammation of the esophageal wall rather than to benign thrombosis. Ten patients who had rigid or

(35–13) Ann. Intern. Med. 98:900–903, June 1983.

flexible fiber-optic esophageal vein sclerosis between 1977 and 1982 came to autopsy. They represented all autopsied patients in a treatment population of 55 persons. All patients had at least 1 documented hemorrhage from varices before sclerosis, and all were in general Child's class C. About half of the patients had persistent variceal bleeding despite vasopressin therapy or use of a Sengstaken-Blakemore tube. All procedures except 1 were done with 5% sodium morrhuate, 3% sodium tetradecyl sulfate being used in the 1 instance.

The acute injury from sclerotherapy was characterized by variceal thrombosis, ulceration of the esophageal wall, and acute inflammation. Six patients had esophageal ulcers, most of which were limited to the submucosa or inner muscularis propria. The 6 chronic reactions were characterized by a progression from granulation tissue to mature collagen. The accompanying chronic inflammatory cell infiltrate became less prominent over time. Three patients were free of superimposed acute changes from sclerosis in the last month of life. Three deaths were attributed directly to complications of sclerotherapy. Two patients died of bleeding from esophageal ulcers, and 1 of mediastinitis and empyema secondary to perforation of an esophageal ulcer. All fatal complications occurred during acute reactions.

Esophageal wall necrosis and fibrous repair can follow the injection of sclerosing agents to thrombose esophageal varices, and serious complications such as hemorrhage, abscess formation, ulceration, stricture, and perforation can result. The result of sclerosis is dependent on the balance struck between thrombosis, necrosis, and fibrosis. Good long-term results may reflect necrotizing destruction of varices with esophageal wall fibrosis rather than organized thrombotic occlusion of varices. Further studies are needed before esophageal vein sclerosis can be recommended for preventing variceal bleeding.

▶ [The two key questions regarding endoscopic sclerotherapy for bleeding varices (ESBV) are (1) Is endoscopic sclerotherapy of established value in the treatment of acutely bleeding varices where bleeding does not stop after less invasive procedures? and (2) Does endoscopic sclerotherapy prevent recurrent bleeding and alter the natural history of bleeding esophageal varices? With regard to the first question, Galambos[20] has reviewed the literature on ESBV and noted that in 7 reported series, one or more variceal sclerotherapy procedures effectively controlled almost 90% of 584 acute variceal hemorrhages. However, despite the cessation of hemorrhage, the overall mortality rates were still about 28%. Both survival and bleeding-free intervals appear to be related to the severity of the underlying liver disease. DiMagno et al. have determined mortality and rebleeding in 145 patients with bleeding esophageal varices sclerosed 423 times and in 92 patients who also had bleeding esophageal varices but who were not sclerosed.[21] The overall 1-year survival was similar in the sclerosis and nonsclerosis groups, i.e., 67% and 68%, respectively. However, the 1-year survival in the sclerosis group was 84%, 63%, and 0 for patients classified as Child's grade A, B, and C, respectively. Similarly, the 6-month bleeding-free interval in the sclerosis group was 63%, 44%, and 21% for patients classified as Child's group A, B, and C, respectively. Thus, both survival and bleeding-free intervals are clearly related to the severity of the underlying liver disease and this obtains both for patients undergoing endoscopic sclerotherapy and for patients not sclerosed. The role of prophylactic endoscopic sclerotherapy, therefore, remained incompletely defined.

With regard to complications of ESBV, Galambos[20] has noted that the same sclerosing solutions injected on 103 occasions in the same manner in 41 jaundiced or ascitic or otherwise decompensated (Child's class C) cirrhotic patients produced esophageal ulcerations more frequently ($P<.01$) than did 133 sets of injections in 64 patients whose clinical state was better (Child's class A or B).

Finally, acute respiratory failure developed in 2 of 30 patients within 8–24 hours after sodium morrhuate esophageal sclerotherapy.[22] From additional experiments in animals it was found that sodium morrhuate injection in sheep causes marked but transient pulmonary hypertension associated with an increased flow of relatively protein-poor lymph. Thus, sodium morrhuate esophageal sclerotherapy may affect pulmonary hemodynamics and contribute to respiratory difficulties in patients.] ◀

–14 **Relapse Following Treatment Withdrawal in Patients With Autoimmune Chronic Active Hepatitis.** The optimal duration of steroid therapy for chronic active hepatitis (CAH) and the factors involved in determining the outcome after withdrawal of treatment remain undefined. John E. Hegarty, Kayhan T. Nouri Aria, Bernard Portmann, Adrian L. W. F. Eddleston, and Roger Williams (London) undertook a prospective study of the effects of treatment withdrawal in 30 patients with the "autoimmune" type of CA with evidence of remission for 1½ to 9 years while receiving maintenance steroid and azathioprine therapy. Remission was defined as an absence of symptoms, a serum glutamic oxaloacetic transaminase level below 40 IU/L for at least 18 months, and only mild inflammation in the portal and fibrous areas on liver biopsy. The 20 females and 10 males were aged 16–67 years. Of these, 28 received azathioprine as well as prednisolone for maintenance. In 3 patients, previous attempts to withdraw treatment led to biochemical relapse. Azathioprine was withdrawn at the outset, and steroids were reduced by 2 mg every 2 weeks thereafter.

Reactivation of disease occurred in all but 4 patients within a year of starting withdrawal of treatment (Fig 35–11); the median interval was 9 weeks. Reactivation was confirmed histologically by the presence of piecemeal necrosis in 20 patients. Some patients relapsed before prednisolone therapy was completely withdrawn. Symptoms were frequent and severe. Symptoms resolved and biochemical abnormalities were reversed within a median of 6 weeks after reinstitution of treatment except in 1 patient who died in cardiac arrest with extensive recent confluent hepatic necrosis. All biopsies in surviving pa-

Fig 35–11.—Percentage of patients (30 total) with chronic active hepatitis remaining in remission after withdrawal of corticosteroid and azathioprine therapy. (Courtesy of Hegarty, J.E., et al.: Hepatology 3:685–689, September/October 1983.)

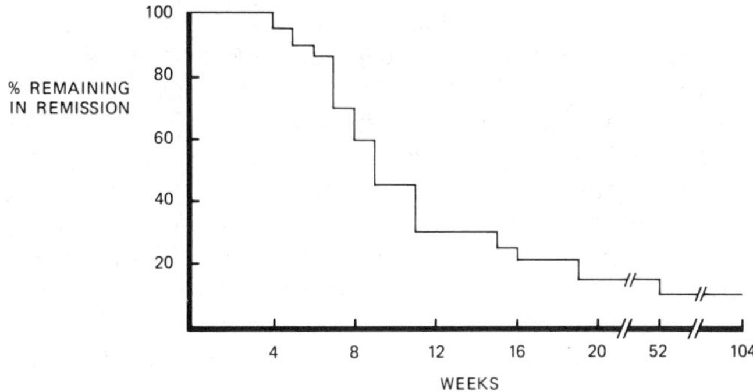

(35–14) Hepatology 3:685–689, September/October 1983.

tients showed changes similar to those present before treatment withdrawal. No clinical features were found that predicted relapse after withdrawal of treatment.

Only 13% of the present patients with "autoimmune" CAH whose disease was well controlled for prolonged periods remained in remission after withdrawal of steroids and azathioprine. Withdrawal of treatment can have disastrous results. It is arguable whether treatment should ever be discontinued in this group of patients, since the dose of steroids needed for adequate maintenance therapy often is as low as 5–10 mg daily.

▶ [There are rather marked differences in the relapse rates in this series of patients with chronic active liver disease (CALD) and other series when corticosteroid therapy was withdrawn. In a Mayo Clinic series, only 48% relapsed when corticosteroid therapy was withdrawn.[23] However, only 54% of the patients in the Mayo Clinic series had severe disease as evidenced by the presence of bridging or multilobular necrosis. Moreover, since chronicity of disease was defined by the presence of clinical and biochemical abnormalities of a 10-week or longer duration, compared with a 6-month duration in the study of Hegarty et al. abstracted above, it is possible that some of the patients in the Mayo Clinic series may have had a self-limiting illness which would not require long-term maintenance corticosteroid therapy. In the Royal Free Hospital series, prednisolone had been discontinued after 6–108 months in 15 (75%) of 20 patients with CALD, apparently without ill effect; none of these patients required reintroduction of therapy during a follow-up period of at least 30 months.[24] The suggestion from other studies that disappearance of autoantibodies (antinuclear antibody) during treatment predicted a satisfactory outcome to treatment withdrawal was not substantiated by the results of the study of Hegarty et al.] ◀

35–15 **Effect of Immunosuppressive Therapy on HBsAg-Positive Chronic Active Hepatitis in Relation to Presence or Absence of HBeAg and Anti-HBe.** Evangelista Sagnelli, Felice Piccinino, Giuseppe Manzillo, Francesca M. Felaco, Pietro Filippini, Giuseppe Maio, Giuseppe Pasquale, and Crescenzo M. Izzo reviewed the results of immunosuppressive therapy in a prospective study of 204 patients with chronic active hepatitis (CAH) who were positive for hepatitis B surface antigen (HBsAg). Azathioprine or prednisolone or both were given to 153 patients; 51 were untreated. Patients were followed up for at least 2 years. Groups of 51 patients received 100 mg of azathioprine daily, 20 mg of prednisolone daily, or 50 mg of azathioprine plus 20 mg of prednisolone daily. A total of 178 patients had a second liver biopsy after 2 years, and 30% had a third biopsy after 5–7 years.

Initially, hepatitis B **e** antigen (HBeAg) was present in 26% of patients, antibody to HBeAg (anti-HBe) in 58%, and antibody to hepatitis B core antigen (anti-HBc) in 100%. Neither prednisolone therapy nor combination therapy modified the course of CAH in HBeAg-positive patients, and azathioprine may have had adverse effects. In the HBeAg-negative group, patients deteriorated or died more often when untreated than when given combined azathioprine-prednisolone therapy. Prednisolone therapy alone was moderately effective, but azathioprine alone did not modify the outcome. The prevalence of cirrhosis increased during the study in all groups, but progression to cirrhosis was less frequent in patients given combined therapy than

---

(35–15) Hepatology 3:690–695, September/October 1983.

in the other groups, whether they were HBeAg-positive or negative. Six of the 7 patients who died during the study were untreated; 1 received azathioprine therapy. All of these patients had cirrhosis at the start of the study. Eight patients withdrew from the study because of side effects.

The findings are consistent with the suggestion that azathioprine and prednisolone therapy may favor the replication of hepatitis B virus. Immunosuppressive therapy should be used quite cautiously in HBsAg-positive CAH. Patients infrequently recover, and relapses are frequent when treatment is stopped. Side effects are frequent. Immunosuppressive therapy may be considered in HBsAg-positive and HBeAg-negative patients until more effective treatment becomes available.

▶ [I selected this article for publication in the 1984 YEAR BOOK because it provides some interesting and difficult-to-find data on the natural history of HBsAg-positive chronic active hepatitis (CAH) and the effect of various treatment regimens. Fifty-three of 178 patients improved during a 2-year period. In the subgroups, 22 of 47 improved with combination therapy, 13 of 41 with prednisolone alone, 8 of 30 with no treatment, and 0 of 41 with azathioprine alone. Thus, improvement was comparable in patients receiving corticosteroids alone and in controls (13 of 41 vs. 8 of 30 patients). The most evident improvement occurred in the anti-HBe–positive patients suggesting that immunosuppressive therapy might be helpful when viral replication is suppressed or inactive in patients with chronic B virus–related CAH. However, because there is convincing evidence that immunosuppressive doses actually enhance viral replication in patients with chronic type B hepatitis, such therapy is potentially dangerous and should be considered only if there is obvious evidence of clinical deterioration (increasing serum bilirubin, prolonged prothrombin time, falling serum albumin, ascites, etc.) and there is no evidence of superimposed δ infection.

A recent study has clarified the clinical and histological events preceding hepatitis B **e** antigen (HBeAg) seroconversion in chronic type B hepatitis.[25] A 60-month longitudinal study has been undertaken in 99 HBeAg-positive patients with clinicopathologically verified chronic hepatitis. Clearance of HBeAg occurred in 30 patients at a rate of approximately 17% per year. A phenomenon of abrupt elevation of serum glutamic pyruvic transaminase (more than 300 IU/L) with histological changes compatible with chronic lobular hepatitis was observed in 13 (65%) of 20 patients preceding spontaneous HBeAg clearance. In contrast, 8 of 10 patients on immunosuppressive or antiviral therapy or both had uneventful HBeAg clearance. It was concluded that HBeAg clearance can occur in patients with varying immunologic status. The mechanism responsible for HBeAg clearance awaits further study.] ◀

5–16 **Serodiagnosis of Recent Hepatitis B Infection by IgM Class Anti-HBc.** Virus-specific IgM-class antibodies represent a prominent early immune response in many viral infections and usually are short-lived, making them potentially useful markers for acute illness. Kurt H. Chau, Martha P. Hargie, Richard H. Decker, Isa K. Mushahwar, and Lacy R. Overby (North Chicago, Ill.) examined the temporal course of antibody to hepatitis B core antigen (anti-HBc) IgM in patients with hepatitis who were positive for hepatitis B surface antigen (HBsAg). A solid-phase radioimmunoassay was developed using the IgM capture procedure with polystyrene beads coated with goat antibody to human IgM. Hepatitis B core antigen (HBcAg) was purified from serum Dane particles and used as a probe with ^{125}I-labeled anti-

(35–16) Hepatology 3:142–149, March–April 1983.

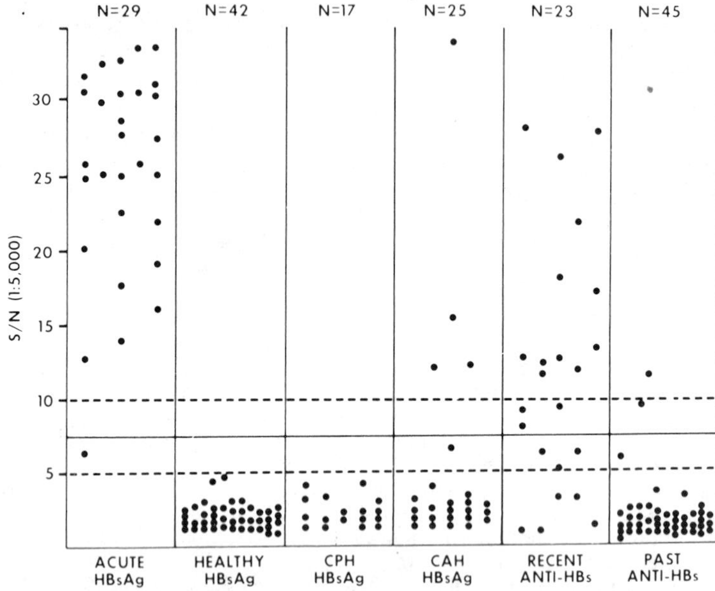

Fig 35–12.—Anti-HBc IgM levels in patients with varying consequences of hepatitis B virus infection. Testing was performed on single serum samples from patients with indicated clinical diagnoses: *CPH,* chronic persistent hepatitis; *CAH,* chronic active hepatitis; *recent anti-HBs,* seroconversion within 9 months of date of serum collection; *past anti-HBs,* healthy blood donor positive for anti-HBs and anti-HBc. (Courtesy of Chau, K.H., et al.: Hepatology 3:142–149, March/April 1983.)

HBc IgG. Serum specimens were obtained serially from normal subjects and hemodialysis patients being monitored for hepatitis B exposure during an 8-year period.

A marked prozoning phenomenon was noted; relative serum titers differed widely with the serum dilution tested. When all serum specimens were tested at a dilution of 1:5,000, comparable results were obtained in different patient groups. Detectable levels of anti-HBc IgM persisted for as long as 2 years. The results are shown in Figure 35–12. All serum samples from patients with HBsAg-positive acute

Serodiagnosis of Acute Viral Hepatitis: Patterns of Reactivity

IgM Anti-HAV	HBsAg	IgM Anti-HBc	Interpretation
Positive	Negative	Negative	Acute type A hepatitis
Positive	Positive	Negative	Acute type A hepatitis in a chronic HBsAg carrier
Negative	Negative	Positive	Acute type B hepatitis
Negative	Positive	Positive	Acute type B hepatitis
Negative	Positive	Negative	Chronic HBsAg carrier with a superimposed hepatitis (non-A, non-B, delta, drug-related, etc.)

(Courtesy of Hoofnagle J.: Hepatology 1:386–391, 1981.)

hepatitis yielded assay ratio values greater than 10 when tested at a 1:5,000 dilution. Chronic HBsAg carriers without evidence of liver injury and patients with chronic persistent HBsAg-positive hepatitis had assay ratios of 5 or below. By contrast, ratio values above 10 were mostly found in samples from patients with "recent" active hepatitis (onset of antigenemia within the preceding 9 months). Only 4 of 25 patients with chronic active hepatitis who had acquired infection more than 6 months previously had assay ratios above 10.

These studies suggest that determinations of anti-HBc IgM may be helpful in distinguishing recent and current hepatitis B virus (HBV) infections from remote infections; in eliminating HBV as the agent for non-A, non-B hepatitis in asymptomatic HBsAg carriers; and in detecting HBV as the causative agent during silent (HBsAg-negative) infections.

▶ [Hoofnagle has written a timely editorial on serodiagnosis of acute viral hepatitis.[26] The key points follow: "Chau and coworkers report that testing serum at a dilution of 1:5,000 by radioimmunoassay for IgM anti-HBc separates acute from chronic hepatitis B virus infection. Patients with acute type B hepatitis have high titers of IgM anti-HBc that persist for only a few months. Patients with chronic type B hepatitis may have IgM anti-HBc, but at lower titers than those found during acute infection. Thus, application of IgM anti-HBc testing may be helpful in the diagnosis of acute type B hepatitis by correcting both false negative and false positive results obtained from HBsAg testing alone.

Other authors have not been as successful in separating acute from chronic type B hepatitis by IgM anti-HBc testing. Indeed, the presence of IgM anti-HBc was reported to correlate with persistence of high levels of viral replication, activity of the underlying chronic hepatitis, and the presence of hepatocellular carcinoma. In chronic type B hepatitis, however, titers of IgM anti-HBc are usually low. Chau and coworkers deliberately chose a high dilution for IgM anti-HBc testing so that chronic HBsAg carriers would test negative. Among 84 serum specimens from persons with various forms of chronic type B hepatitis (i.e., "healthy" carriers, chronic persistent hepatitis, and chronic active hepatitis), IgM anti-HBc was present at a titer of 1:5,000 in only 5%. Furthermore, the presence of high titers of IgM anti-HBc appeared to correlate with the duration of the chronic HBeAg carrier state rather than with the outcome or activity of chronic hepatitis. Thus IgM anti-HBc testing appears to provide helpful and accurate information in the serodiagnosis of acute viral hepatitis.

These difficulties in the serodiagnosis of acute type B hepatitis may appear trivial. Unfortunately, they are not. In most studies, 5 to 10% of patients with acute type B hepatitis are missed when serum is tested for HBsAg alone. Furthermore, 10 to 30% of patients with suspected type B hepatitis, based on HBsAg testing alone, may have other forms of acute liver injury superimposed on the chronic HBeAg carrier state.

The table shows Hoofnagle's useful scheme summarizing the serodiagnosis.[26]

35–17 **Hepatitis B Viral DNA in Liver and Serum of Asymptomatic Carriers.** Carriers of hepatitis B virus (HBV), who usually are asymptomatic, represent a major reservoir of HBV infection. Wing Kam, Leslie B. Rall, Edward A. Smuckler, Rudi Schmid, and William J. Rutter (Univ. of California, San Francisco) used closed HBV DNA to probe for viral DNA in liver tissue and serum from 14 asymptomatic carriers of hepatitis B surface antigen (HBsAg) and 2 former carriers. Three groups of carriers were distinguished (table). In group I, HBV DNA was found in both liver and serum, and hepatitis B **e** antigen (HBeAg) was consistently present in the serum. In 1 case, viral DNA was integrated into liver genomic DNA. In group II, lower

(35–17) Proc. Natl. Acad. Sci. USA 79:7522–7526, December 1982.

RESULTS OF HEPATITIS B VIRUS ANTIGEN, ANTIBODY, AND DNA TESTS*

				Serological markers					HBV DNA		
										Liver	
Subject	Age, yr	Sex	Race	HBsAg†	HBeAg	Anti-HBe	Anti-HBs	Anti-HBc	Serum	Non-integrated	Integrated
Group I											
A	18	M	Asian	400	+	–	–	+	+	++	+
B	21	M	Asian	400	+	–	–	+	+	++	–
C	19	M	Caucasian	400	+	–	–	+	+	++	–
D	36	M	Caucasian	400	+	–	–	+	+	++	–
Group II											
E	33	F	Asian	100	–	–	–	+	–	+	+
F	28	M	Black	100	–	+	–	+	–	+	+
G	36	M	Asian	100	–	+	–	+	–	+	+
H	35	F	Asian	70	–	+	–	+	–	+	+
I	30	M	Black	100	–	+	–	+	–	–	+
Group III											
J	27	M	Asian	15	–	+	–	+	–	–	–
K	37	M	Asian	4	–	+	–	+	–	–	–
L	31	F	Asian	3	–	+	–	+	–	–	+
M	31	M	Asian	3	–	+	–	+	–	–	–
N	33	M	Asian	2	–	+	–	+	–	–	–
Former carriers											
O	21	M	Black	–	–	–	+	–	–	–	–
P	22	M	Black	–	–	–	–	–	–	–	–

*Abbreviations used: *HBV*, hepatitis B virus; *HBsAg*, hepatitis B surface antigen; *HBeAg*, hepatitis B e antigen; *anti-HBe*, *anti-HBs*, and *anti-HBc*, antibodies to HBeAg, HBsAg, and hepatitis B core antigen, respectively.

†HBsAg titers $\times 10^{-3}$.

(Courtesy of Kam, W., et al.: Proc. Natl. Acad. Sci. USA 79:7522–7526, December 1982.)

levels of nonintegrated HBV DNA were present in the liver, and none was found in the serum. Tests for HBeAg were negative in this group, and integrated viral DNA was present in all cases. In group III, there was no nonintegrated viral DNA in liver or serum, but 1 patient had integrated sequences. All carriers lacked antibody to HBsAg and had antibody to hepatitis B core antigen. All had nonspecific histologic abnormalities in the liver.

These findings indicate significant quantitative and qualitative differences among asymptomatic HBsAg carriers and suggest that their infectivity may be highly variable. The consequences of integration of HBV DNA into genomic DNA are incompletely understood. Integrated viral sequences could serve as a source of recurrent viral infection, but this seems unlikely. Integration should not, however, be considered of no significance. The presence of integrated HBV copies in a large proportion of hepatomas is consistent with a primary or secondary role for HBV integration in oncogenesis. It also is possible that integration of viral sequences and persistent production of surface antigen contribute to progressive liver disease and cirrhosis in asymptomatic carriers.

▶ [These results confirm and extend previous studies which demonstrated that HBV DNA is present in the serum of patients who are HBsAg-positive ($HBsAg^{+}$) or anti-HBe–positive ($anti\text{-}HBe^{+}$).[27] The serum HBV DNA therefore represents a more sensitive marker of viral replication than does HBeAg.

Hadziyannis et al. have analyzed the type of liver disease, nuclear HBcAg, viral replication, and HBV DNA in liver and serum of $HBeAg^{+}$ vs. $anti\text{-}HBc^{+}$ carriers of HBV.[28] Nine $HBeAg^{+}$ and 24 $anti\text{-}HBe^{+}$ subjects with chronic HBV infection were studied for HBV DNA in the serum by molecular hybridization, for HBcAg in the liver by immunofluorescence, and for histologic evidence of liver disease. All $HBeAg^{+}$ patients had underlying chronic liver disease (chronic persistent hepatitis, chronic active hepatitis, or cirrhosis with or without hepatocellular carcinoma), and all were found to be positive for both HBV DNA in the serum and HBcAg in the nucleus of hepatocytes. Of the 24 anti-HBe$^+$ individuals, 18 had various forms of chronic liver disease. Six HBsAg$^+$–anti-HBe$^+$ patients had normal liver histology except for numerous "ground-glass" hepatocytes with abundant cytoplasmic HBsAg. All six were negative for nuclear HBcAg and serum HBV DNA, but three showed HBV DNA which appeared to be integrated into unique sites in host liver DNA by hybridization analysis. In contrast, 14 (78%) of 18 HBsAg$^+$–anti-HBe$^+$ patients with chronic liver disease were positive for nuclear HBcAg, serum HBV DNA, or both of these markers of HBV replication. These findings suggest that in long-term HBsAg carriers with serum anti-HBe and normal liver histology, viral replication is suppressed or inactive and HBV potential infectivity is presumably very low or absent. However, when viral replication is present in HBsAg$^+$–anti-BHe$^+$ carriers (as demonstrated by serum HBV DNA or nuclear HBcAg or both), active liver disease is often found. In these individuals, active chronic liver disease appears to be related to continued replication and secretion of HBV and may occur in a much higher porportion of HBsAg$^+$–anti-HBe$^+$ patients than was previously suspected.] ◀

35–18 **Value of Screening for Markers of Hepatitis in Dialysis Units.** Serum enzyme determinations recently have been supplemented by assays for antibodies to the core (anti-HBc) and surface (anti-HBs) components of hepatitis B virus (HBV) and for antibodies to hepatitis A virus for use in screening. Athol J. Ware, Nancy L. Gorder, Lawrence E. Gurian, Clark Douglas, James W. Shorey, and Thomas Parker (Univ. of Texas, Dallas) examined the role of these assays in the control of viral hepatitis in dialysis patients in 2 dialysis units. Serum samples were examined monthly for serum glutamic oxaloacetic transaminase (SGOT) and hepatitis B surface antigen (HBsAg) in 406 patients and 170 staff members during a 4-year period. Stored serum samples were examined for anti-HBc, anti-HBs, and antibodies to hepatitis A. The dialysis patients were followed up for a mean of 24 months; the staff members, for a mean of 19 months.

Only 30% of patients had consistently normal SGOT values, but most abnormal values were less than 100 units/ml. Viral hepatitis

HEPATITIS B VIRUS INFECTIONS ACQUIRED IN DIALYSIS UNIT*

	Patients (n = 316)	Staff (n = 150)
HBsAg detected	21 (6.6%)	6 (4.0%)
+ anti-HBc	*9*	*0*
+ anti-HBc + anti-HBs	*12*	*6*
HBsAg not detected	11 (3.5%)	6 (4.0%)
Anti-HBc alone	*2*	*0*
Anti-HBs alone	*3*	*1*
Anti-HBc + anti-HBs	*6*	*5*
Total	32 (10.1%)	12 (8.0%)

*Abbreviations used: *HBsAg,* hepatitis B surface antigen; *anti-HBc,* antibody to core component of hepatitis B virus; *anti-HBs,* antibody to surface component of hepatitis B virus.

(Courtesy of Ware, A.J., et al.: Hepatology 3:513–518, May/June 1983.)

(35–18) Hepatology 3:513–518, May/June 1983.

was a reasonable explanation for only half of the instances in which SGOT values were higher than 100 units/ml. Hepatitis A virus did not appear to contribute to dialysis-associated liver disease in this population. The acquisition of HBV infection in the dialysis units is outlined in the table. Testing for HBsAg alone missed about 40% of the HBV infections acquired in the dialysis units, but only 2 episodes were epidemiologically significant. There were high rates of potentially "false-positive" reactions with all the antibody assays. The positive predictive value of these assays was only about 50%.

Screening of dialysis patients for SGOT activity or serum glutamic pyruvic transaminase activity or both seems reasonable, but minor abnormalities must be interpreted cautiously; isolation is not indicated for a single abnormal result. All dialysis patients who remain vulnerable to HBV infection should be screened regularly for HBsAg. Initial screening with anti-HBc and anti-HBs is also suggested. The availability of HBV vaccine should minimize the number of patients at risk. Antibody findings must be interpreted in light of the actual counts obtained, and "weak" positive reactions should be interpreted very cautiously.

▶ [Recent studies indicate that the hepatitis B vaccine should substantially reduce the incidence of clinical and subclinical hepatitis B among renal dialysis staff members as well as prevent secondary cases among their families, and it should nearly eliminate the need for past-exposure prophylaxis with hepatitis B immune globulin.

Szmuness et al. evaluated the efficacy of hepatitis B vaccine (Heptavax-B) containing only the ad subtype in a randomized, placebo-controlled, double-blind trial among 865 staff members of 43 hemodialysis units in the United States (29). Surface antibody developed in 92.6% of the subjects after two doses of vaccine and in 96% after the 6-month booster. The incidence of infections with hepatitis B virus (HBV) (with or without hepatitis) was 9.9% in placebo recipients and 2.2% in vaccine recipients ($P<.01$). The 2 cases of hepatitis B among vaccine recipients did not occur in subjects in whom antibody had developed. In 81% of the hepatitis events, the virus was of the ay subtype. The incidence of ay virus was 8.2% among placebo recipients and 1.2% among vaccine recipients ($P<.005$). These data confirm the efficacy of the vaccine and demonstrate subtype cross-protection.

The natural history of HBV infection in renal transplant patients has also been assessed.[30] Markers for HBV were measured in 83 renal transplant patients who were followed for 2–15 years. Sixty nine patients were negative for HBsAg before transplantation. It was found that reactivation of HBV replication or continued hepatitis B virion replication occurs as commonly or more commonly than de novo infection in renal transplant recipients. The presence of HBeAg in serum predisposes to long-term Dane particle expression in immunosuppressed patients, whereas anti-HBe–positive carriers may not always be susceptible to reactivation of HBV replication despite immunosuppression.] ◀

35–19 **Synthesis of Antibodies to Hepatitis B Virus by Cultured Lymphocytes From Chronic Hepatitis B Surface Antigen Carriers.** It has been proposed that host immune defects may be responsible for the development and persistence of the hepatitis B surface antigen (HBsAg) carrier state. The nature of these defects is unknown, but the absence of a readily detected antibody response to HBsAg (anti-Hbs) may be important. Geoffrey M. Dusheiko, Jay H. Hoofnagle, W. Graham Cooksley, Stephen P. James, and E. Anthony Jones (Bethesda) measured the synthesis of both anti-HBs and antibody to hepatitis B core antigen (anti-HBc) in cultures of peripheral

---

(35–19) J. Clin. Invest. 71:1104–1113, May 1983.

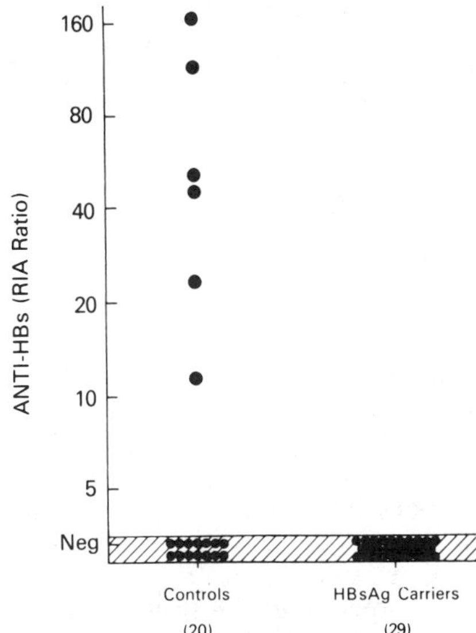

Fig 35–13.—Levels of antibody to hepatitis B surface antigen (HBsAg) *(anti-Hbs)* in supernatants of pokeweed mitogen–stimulated peripheral blood mononuclear cells from 20 controls and 29 chronic carriers of HBsAg. The anti-HBs levels are expressed as a ratio of the test sample to negative control counts per minute by radioimmunoassay (greater than 2.1 is positive). (Courtesy of Dusheiko, G.M., et al.: J. Clin. Invest. 71:1104–1113, May 1983; by copyright of the American Society of Clinical Investigation.)

blood mononuclear cells in the presence of pokeweed mitogen using lymphocytes from 46 chronic HBsAg carriers and 28 controls. Most of the carriers also had positive findings for hepatitis B **e** antigen, and most had hepatitis B virus–specific DNA polymerase.

Similar amounts of polyclonal IgG and IgM were synthesized by cultures containing lymphocytes from carriers and controls. In 21 carriers and 2 controls, anti-HBc was detected in lymphocyte supernatants, and anti-HBs was found in samples from 6 controls but no HBsAg carriers (Fig 35–13). When B lymphocytes from carriers were cocultured with allogeneic irradiated T lymphocytes from controls, they synthesized normal amounts of immunoglobulins and anti-HBc but not anti-HBs. When B lymphocytes from controls were cocultured with irradiated T lymphocytes from carriers, the T lymphocytes from 16 of 24 carriers augmented anti-HBs production by control B cells normally. When mixtures of control B cells and irradiated T lymphocytes were cocultured with T lymphocytes from chronic HBsAg carriers, 5 of 12 carriers showed active suppression of anti-HBs production, and in 3 the suppression was specific.

Chronic HBsAg carriers appear to have a specific B lymphocyte defect in anti-HBs production. Defects in the function of regulatory T lymphocytes may contribute to the absence of anti-HBs synthesis in some HBsAg carriers. It is possible that anti-HBs–producing lymphocytes are held in an inactive state, perhaps rendered tolerant by the presence of excess circulating HBsAg.

35–20 **Prevalence of Delta-Antibody Among Chronic Hepatitis B Virus Infected Patients in the Los Angeles Area: Its Correlation With Liver Biopsy Diagnosis.** It has been suggested that the δ-

(35–20) Gastroenterology 85:160–162, July 1983.

COMPARISON OF PREVALENCE OF ANTI-δ IN CHRONIC HEPATITIS B VIRUS–INFECTED PATIENTS REPORTED SINCE 1977*

Author	Year	PH	CAH	Geographic region
Rizzetto et al.	1977	6/31 (19.3%)	7/32 (21.8%)	Italy, France
Rizzetto et al.	1979	6/83 (7.2%)	42/144 (29.2%)	Italy
Rizzetto et al.	1979	1/18 (5.6%)	7/17 (41.2%)	New Jersey
Rizzetto et al.	1979	0/33 (0.0%)	2/56 (3.6%)	Japan
Stocklin et al.	1981	1/137 (0.7%)	9/175 (5.1%)	Switzerland
Current study	1982	1/23 (4.3%)	18/57 (31.5%)	Los Angeles, Calif.

*No. of patients with δ-antibody/total no. of patients; % of patients with δ-antibody is given in parentheses.

(Courtesy of Govindarajan, S., et al.: Reproduced by permission of the publisher from Gastroenterology 85:160–162, July 1983; copyright by the American Gastrological Association.)

agent that concomitantly infects some persons with chronic hepatitis B virus (HBV) disease is important in the progression of chronic liver disease. Sugantha Govindarajan, Gary C. Kanel, and Robert L. Peters (Univ. of Southern California, Downey) determined the prevalence of δ-antibody in 80 patients with chronic HBV infection and its relation to the severity of liver disease. Fifty-seven patients had a biopsy diagnosis of chronic active hepatitis (CAH) and 23 a diagnosis of persistent hepatitis (PH). All were hepatitis B antigen positive by serologic study. δ-Antibody was estimated by a blocking solid-phase radioimmunoassay.

Eighteen patients with CAH (31.5%) and 1 with PH (4.3%) had serums containing δ-antibody, a significant difference. Anti-δ was present in 9 of 32 CAH patients with cirrhosis and in 9 of the 25 without. More than 80% of parenteral drug abusers were anti-δ positive, as was only 1 of the other patients, a sexually active male homosexual. The correlation between parenteral drug use and the presence of serum anti-δ was highly significant. The presence of anti-δ also correlated significantly with lack of the "e" antigen. Anti-δ was not significantly correlated with hepatitis B surface antigen subtypes.

The prevalence of anti-δ in chronic HBV-infected patients in various reports is given in the table. The overall incidence of δ-antibody in such patients in the Los Angeles area is 24%. It is present in nearly a third of patients with CAH. Intravenous drug abuse appears to be the nearly exclusive means of δ-agent transmission among HBV-infected patients in this area. Drug abusers are repeatedly exposed to HBV agents and can acquire the δ-agent after HBV infection is established. Simultaneous infection with both agents via the parenteral route is equally possible.

▶ [The δ-antigen-antibody system was first reported in 1977 in Italian carriers of hepatitis B surface antigen (HBsAg). The unique feature of the δ-antigen is its dependence on a replicating hepatitis B virus (HBV). Tissue δ-antigen has not been found without an established HBV infection. The δ-antigen is a protein with a molecular weight of approximately 68,000. In serum, δ-antigen has been shown to be an internal component of a 35–37-mm particle coated with HBsAg. Unlike the HBV virion that contains DNA, the internal component of δ-antigen is a low molecular weight RNA. The seroconversion to δ-antibody secures the diagnosis of acute δ-infection. Both

HEPATITIS ALGEBRA IN PATIENTS WITH HEPATITIS B VIRUS INFECTION

Changes	Interpretations
1. Detection of hepatitis A antibody	
a. IgG antibody positive	Remote hepatitis A infection
b. IgM antibody positive	Acute hepatitis A infection
2. Detection of delta antibody	
a. IgM antibody positive	Acute delta infection
3. Detection of high titer HBcAg IgM antibody and HBeAg	Reactivation of hepatitis B viral infection; active viral replication
4. Detection of CMV* antibody, IgM fraction	Acute CMV infection
5. None of the above in a patient with acute changes in liver tests	Consider non-A, non-B hepatitis

*CMV = cytomegalovirus.

IgM and IgG antibodies are in current use. Acute δ-infection may occur with HBV, during the late resolution phase of recent acute HBV, or as an acute infection superimposed on a chronic HBV infection.

Epidemiologic surveys have shown that δ-infection has a worldwide distribution, yet is predominant in the Mediterranean area and among drug addicts in Western countries.

In patients with known chronic HBV disease, a deterioration in liver tests raises several questions. In such settings, an understanding of hepatitis algebra (table) is essential. (I am indebted to Telfer B. Reynolds for coining the term.) For a timely brief review of δ-agent, see the editorial by Redeker.[31]] ◀

35–21 **Chronic Hepatitis in Carriers of Hepatitis B Surface Antigen, With Intrahepatic Expression of the Delta Antigen: Active and Progressive Disease Unresponsive to Immunosuppressive Treatment.** The expression of δ-antigen results from infection with a hepatitis agent apparently distinct from hepatitis B virus, which has a putative RNA genome enclosed in particles coated with hepatitis B surface antigen (HBsAg). Mario Rizzetto, Giorgio Verme, Serafino Recchia, Ferruccio Bonino, Patrizia Farci, Sarino Aricò, Renata Calzia, Antonio Picciotto, Massimo Colombo, and Hans Popper reviewed the findings in 137 patients with intrahepatic δ-antigen who were seen at 5 centers in Italy since 1976, and they followed up 101 of the patients for 2–6 years. Fifty patients had been treated with prednisone or azathioprine or both, usually for 1½ years or longer.

Chronic hepatitis was seen in all subjects, usually in the form of chronic active hepatitis. Cirrhosis was present in 32 cases, and 1 patient had hepatocellular carcinoma. In most cases, δ-antigen was present only in hepatocytic nuclei. Hepatitis B core antigen (HBcAg) was identified in 9 specimens, 7 of them from drug addicts. Antibody to hepatitis B **e** antigen (anti-HBe) was found in a large majority of the patients assessed. Eight patients with cirrhosis died of liver failure or variceal bleeding during follow-up. Three others required portacaval shunting for hematemesis, and 3 had recurrent ascites. Cirrhosis developed in 31 of the 75 patients without nodular regeneration on initial biopsy: 5 of these patients died. Treatment

(35–21) Ann. Intern. Med. 98:437–441, April 1983.

Histologic Findings and Effect of Treatment in 75 Patients With δ-Antigen–Positive Chronic Hepatitis

Patients	Histologic Diagnosis at Presentation	Period of Follow-up	Treatment with Azathioprine	Prednisone	Azathioprine plus Prednisone	Untreated	Histologic Features at End of Follow-up Period
n		*yrs*	←	— *n* —		→	
26	CAH*	3.9†	1	3	15	7	CAH with cirrhosis‡
29	CAH	4.1†	...	6	15	8	CAH
8	CAH	3.4†	...	3	3	2	Mild CAH or CPH
1	CAH	6	...	...	1		Portal scarring
3	CPH	2,4,6	...	...	...	3	CAH with cirrhosis§
1	CPH	5	...	...	...	1	CAH
2	CPH	2,4	...	...	...	2	CPH
2	CLH	2,2	...	...	...	2	CAH with cirrhosis
2	CLH	3,4	...	...	2	...	CAH
1	CLH	3	...	1	...	...	CPH

*CAH, chronic active hepatitis; CPH, chronic persistent hepatitis; CLH, chronic lobular hepatitis.
†Mean.
‡Three patients died of liver failure.
§Two patients died of liver failure.
(Courtesy of Rizzetto, M., et al.: Ann. Intern. Med. 98:437–441, April 1983.)

with prednisone or azathioprine did not lead to amelioration of hepatitis or prevent cirrhosis in either adults or children (table).

Chronic HBsAg-positive hepatitis with intrahepatic expression of the δ-antigen is an active, progressive disease that fails to respond to conventional immunosuppressive therapy. The mechanism by which the δ-agent induces disease is not clear. The genome appears to be an RNA that inhibits the synthesis of hepatitis B products, and synthesis of the δ-agent may be enhanced by the reduction in hepatitis B virus replication.

▶ [The key observations in this study can be summarized as follows: First, 137 of 568 HBsAg carriers were positive for intrahepatic δ-antigen. Second, chronic hepatitis was seen at histologic examination in all 137 carriers with intrahepatic δ-antigen; 93 (70%) had chronic active hepatitis, 30 (20%) had chronic hepatitis with cirrhosis, and 12 (8%) had either chronic persistent hepatitis (CPH) or chronic lobular hepatitis (CLH). Third, 8 of the 12 patients with CPH or CLH developed chronic active hepatitis, 5 with cirrhosis. Fourth, a fatal outcome due to liver disease occurred in 13 patients (12.8%) during a 2–6-year follow-up period. These observations suggest that the chronic δ-infection worsened the histologic lesion and accelerated the clinical course.

Two other studies have also demonstrated that HBsAg-positive patients with δ-antibody had more severe and progressive chronic liver disease.[32, 33] Since the great majority of these patients lacked the IgM antibody to hepatitis B core antigen, it is quite possible that the δ-infection and not hepatitis B viral disease per se was responsible for progression of chronic liver disease.

Finally, I should mention that δ-infection can enhance the likelihood that fulminant hepatitis will develop in patients with hepatitis B. In this regard, the prevalence of serum markers of primary δ-infection was determined in 532 patients with acute benign hepatitis B seen in Italy and in 111 patients with fulminant hepatitis B seen in Italy, France, and England.[34] Patients with fulminant hepatitis had a significantly higher prevalence of δ-infection markers (43 [39%] of 111) than did those with benign hepatitis (101 [19%] of 532). In 25 of the 43 patients with δ-positive fulminant hepatitis, serum markers indicated a primary hepatitis B infection; but in the remaining 18, IgM antibody to hepatitis B core antigen was absent, indicating that hepatitis B preceded superinfection with the δ-agent. The increased morbidity of HBsAg hepatitis with δ-infection may result from the cumulative simultaneous exposure to hepatitis B virus and δ-agent or from superinfection of HBsAg carriers with δ-agent.] ◀

Chapter 35 References

1. Schenker S., Balint J.: Differential diagnosis of jaundice: report of a retrospective study of 61 proved cases. *Dig. Dis. Sci.* 7:449–463, 1962.
2. Vennes J.A., Bond J.H.: Approach to the jaundiced patient. *Gastroenterology* 84:1615–1618, 1983.
3. Richter J.M., Silverstein J.D., Schapiro, R.: Suspected obstructive jaundice: a decision analysis of diagnostic strategies. *Ann. Intern. Med.* 99:46–51, 1983.
4. Beswick D.R., Klatskin G., Boyer J.L.: Prognostic determinants in asymptomatic primary biliary cirrhosis (PBC): a heterogeneous disorder with normal survival [abstract]. *Gastroenterology* 84:1104, 1983.
5. Uchida T., Kap H., Quispe-Sjogren M., et al.: Alcoholic foamy degeneration: a pattern of acute alcoholic injury of the liver. *Gastroenterology* 84:683–692, 1983.
6. Sherlock S.: Acute fatty liver of pregnancy and the microvesicular fat diseases. *Gut* 24:265–269, 1983.
7. Starko K.M., Mullick F.G.: Hepatic and cerebral pathology findings in children with fatal salicylate intoxication: further evidence for a causal relation between salicylate and Reye's syndrome. *Lancet* 1:326–329, 1983.
8. McGhee A., Henderson J.M., Millican W.J. Jr., et al.: Comparison of the effects of hepatic aid and a casein modular diet on encephalopathy, plasma amino acids and nitrogen balance in cirrhotic patients. *Ann. Surg.* 197:288–293, 1983.

9. McCullough A.J., Mullen K.D., Tavill A.S.: Branched chain amino acid therapy in liver disease: dearth or surfeit? *Hepatology* 3:269–271, 1983.
10. Henriksen J.H., Cristensen N.J., Ring-Larsen H.: Noradrenaline and adrenaline concentrations in vascular beds in patients with cirrhosis: relation to hemodynamics. *Clin. Physiol.* 1:293–304, 1981.
11. Ring-Larsen H., Hesse B., Henriksen J.H., et al.: Sympathetic nervous activity and renal and systemic hemodynamics in cirrhosis: plasma norepinephrine concentration, hepatic extraction, and renal release. *Hepatology* 2:304–310, 1982.
12. Gregory P.B., Broekelschen P.H., Hill M.D.: Complication of diuresis in the alcoholic patient with ascites: a controlled trial. *Gastroenterology* 73:534–538, 1977.
13. Campra J.L., Reynolds T.B.: Effectiveness of high dose spironolactone therapy in patients with chronic liver disease and relatively refractory ascites. *Dig. Dis. Sci.* 23:1025–1030, 1978.
14. Fogel M.R., Sawhney V.K., Neal E.A., et al.: Diuresis in the ascitic patient: a randomized controlled trial of three regimens. J. Clin. Gastroenterol. (Suppl. 1) 3:73–80, 1981.
15. Boyer T.D., Warnock D.G.: Use of diuretics in the treatment of cirrhotic ascites. *Gastroenterology* 84:1051–1054, 1983.
16. Schrier R.W.: Mechanism of disturbed renal water excretion in cirrhosis. Gastroenterology 84:870–872, 1983.
17. Manning M., Lemmek B., Kolodzicjczyic A.M., et al.: Synthetic antagonists of in vivo antidiuretic and vasopressor responses to arginine vasopressin. *J. Med. Chem.* 24:701–706, 1981.
18. Levine S.D.: Renal prostaglandins in cirrhosis. *Hepatology* 3:457–459, 1983.
19. Zipser R.D., Hoefs J.C., Speckhart R.F., et al.: Prostaglandins: modulation of renal function and pressor resistance in chronic liver disease. *J. Clin. Endocrinol. Metab.* 48:895–900, 1979.
20. Galambos J.T.: Endoscopic sclerotherapy. *Ann. Intern. Med.* 98:1009–1011, 1983.
21. DiMagno E.P., Laughlin B., Hughes R.W., et al.: Does sclerotherapy alter the natural history of bleeding esophageal varices? [abstract]. *Gastroenterology* 84:1137, 1983.
22. Monroe P., Morrow C.F., Millen J.E., et al.: Acute respiratory failure after sodium moribuate esophageal sclerotherapy. *Gastroenterology* 85:693–699, 1983.
23. Czaja A.J., Luding J., Baggenstoss A.H., et al.: Corticosteroid-treated chronic active hepatitis in remission. *N. Engl. J. Med.* 304:5–9, 1981.
24. Kirk A.P., Jain S., Pocock S., et al.: Late results of the Royal Free Hospital prospective controlled trial of prednisolone therapy in hepatitis B surface antigen negative chronic active hepatitis. *Gut* 21:78–83, 1980.
25. Liaw Y.F., Chu C., Su I.: Clinical and histological events preceding hepatitis B e antigen seroconversion in chronic type B hepatitis. *Gastroenterology* 84:216–219, 1983.
26. Hoofnagle J.: Serodiagnosis of acute viral hepatitis. *Hepatology* 3:267–268, 1983.
27. Bonino F., Hoyer B., Nelson J., et al.: Hepatitis B virus DNA in the sera of HBsAg carriers: a marker of active hepatitis B virus replication in the liver. *Hepatology* 1:386–391, 1981.
28. Hadziyannis S., Lieberman H.M., Karvountzis G.G., et al.: Analysis of liver disease, nuclear HBcAg, viral replication, and hepatitis B virus DNA in liver and serum of HBeAg vs. anti-HBc positive carriers of hepatitis B virus. *Hepatology* 3:656–662, 1983.

29. Szmuness W., Stevens C.E., Harley E.J., et al.: Hepatitis B vaccine in medical staff of hemodialysis units. *N. Engl. J. Med.* 307:1481–1486, 1982.
30. Dusheiko G., Song E., Bowyer S.: Natural history of hepatitis B virus infection in renal transplant patients: a fifteen year followup. *Hepatology* 3:330–336, 1983.
31. Redeker A.G.: Delta agent and hepatitis B. *Ann. Intern. Med.* 98:542–543, 1983.
32. Farci P., Sinedile A., Lavarini C., et al.: Delta hepatitis in apparent carriers of hepatitis B surface antigen. *Gastroenterology* 85:699–673, 1983.
33. Colombo M., Carnbieri R., Rumi M.G., et al.: Long term delta superinfection in hepatitis B surface antigen carriers and its relationship to the course of chronic hepatitis. *Gastroenterology* 85:235–239, 1983.
34. Sinedile A., Verme G., Cargnel A., et al.: Influence of delta infection on severity of hepatitis B. *Lancet* 2:945–947, 1982.

36. Gallbladder

36–1 **Does Total Parenteral Nutrition Induce Gallbladder Sludge Formation and Lithiasis?** Some anecdotal reports have suggested that acalculous cholecystitis or cholelithiasis can occur as a result of total parenteral nutrition (TPN). To assess the prevalence of gallbladder sludge and lithiasis in patients during TPN, Bernard Messing, Christian Bories, Francis Kuntslinger, and Jean-Jacques Bernier used serial biliary ultrasonography to evaluate 23 selected adult gastroenterologic patients during and after TPN. All patients were without evidence of hepatobiliary disease before TPN.

In 19 patients, initial sonograms obtained on day 12±2 of TPN were normal. In the remaining 4 patients, the initial sonograms, which were not obtained until day 39±10 of TPN were positive for sludging, but did not reveal gallstones (P<.001). Ten initially sludge-negative patients were later found to be sludge-positive on sonograms taken on day 42±5 of TPN. Overall, 6% of the patients were sludge-positive during the first 3 weeks of TPN, 50% became sludge-positive after 4–6 weeks of TPN, and *all* patients who received TPN for 6 weeks or more exhibited signs of sludge formation. Serial studies of 8 initially sludge-negative patients showed that once sludge had formed, it persisted throughout TPN. During the post-TPN period, sludge positivity decreased from 88% during the first 3 weeks of oral feeding to 0 after the fourth week. Six patients, all sludge-positive, developed gallstones during or just after TPN, and 3 of them required cholecystectomy between days 35 and 55 of TPN because of complications secondary to cholelithiasis. Analysis of bile from these patients showed thick bile-containing cholesterol crystals and small stones of mixed bilirubin-cholesterol type.

The results strongly suggest that bowel rest and bile stasis during TPN lead to sludge production, which can eventually result in gallstone formation. It is recommended that in patients receiving TPN for more than 1 month, gallbladder stasis should be palliated to prevent cholelithiasis formation. Theoretically this would be achieved by stimulating gallbladder contractions with intermittent oral administration of fat or protein or by intravenous administration of cholecystokinin or cerulein when oral nutrients cannot be given.

▶ [Several recent reports suggest that both children and adults maintained on prolonged TPN are at increased risk for gallstone formation. Roslyn et al. assessed the incidence of gallbladder disease among patients 15 years and older who had received a minimum of 3 months of TPN.[1] Of the patients meeting these criteria, 128 were on TPN a mean of 13.5 months. Nineteen had gallbladder disease before receiving TPN, leaving 109 patients at risk. Of these patients, 25 (23%) developed gallbladder disease after the initiation of TPN. Because of their known propensity for cholelithiasis, 94 of

(36–1) Gastroenterology 84:1012–1019, May 1983.

the patients with ileal disorders (Crohn's disease or ileal resection or both) were considered separately. The 40% incidence of gallbladder disease in these 94 patients was significantly higher than expected from a series of similarly defined patients with ileal disorders not receiving TPN ($P<.05$). Further, in patients less than 30 years of age, the incidence of gallbladder disease in patients with ileal disease receiving TPN was 31%. By contrast, the incidence in patients with ileal disease not receiving TPN was only 14%. The enhanced risk of gallbladder disease among patients on long-term TPN appears to result from multiple factors, including prolonged stasis of bile within the gallbladder and a previous ileal resection.

The same investigators have extended these studies and analyzed the gallstones of 12 patients who developed cholelithiasis during a prolonged course of TPN.[2] Gallstones were obtained from 6 children (mean age, 29 months; 1 female and 5 males) and 6 adults (mean age, 46 years; 5 females and 1 male). All of the children and 4 of the 6 adults had previously undergone an ileal resection. When cholecystectomy was performed, children and adults had received TPN a mean of 25 and 14 months, respectively. Evidence that none of these patients had gallstones at the initiation of TPN was available by gallbladder ultrasonography (4 children, 6 adults) or by virtue of age (2 children). Gallstone composition was determined by infrared spectroscopy and confirmed by direct analysis of cholesterol content. Infrared spectroscopy showed that calcium bilirubinate was the main constituent of the stones in 11 (92%) of the 12 patients. This analysis suggests that, despite factors which may increase cholesterol saturation index, the majority of gallstones developing during long-term TPN consists mainly of calcium bilirubinate. It is concluded that gallbladder stasis and altered bilirubin metabolism are important factors in the pathogenesis of TPN-induced gallstones.] ◀

36–2 **Mucin Glycoprotein Content of Human Pigment Gallstones.** Gallbladder mucus is a potentially important unmeasured constituent of gallstones. Mucus glycoproteins are secreted in increased amounts in patients with lithogenic bile. They can bind calcium and lipids and appear to form a matrix or nidus in human pigment gallstones. J. Thomas LaMont, Allen S. Ventola, Bruce W. Trotman, and Roger D. Soloway analyzed the glycoprotein content of human black pigment gallbladder stones obtained from cholecystectomy specimens. The mucin glycoproteins were isolated by gel chromatography and density gradient ultracentrifugation and were further analyzed by alkaline hydrolysis and oligosaccharide analysis.

The mean glycoprotein content of eight black pigment stones containing 18%–65% calcium bilirubinate was 12.4%. The stones contained two glycoprotein fractions on Sepharose 4B column chromatography, a high-molecular-weight glycoprotein in the void volume and a lower weight fraction in the included volume. On density gradient ultracentrifugation in cesium chloride, three separate mucin fractions had an average buoyant density of 1.48 gm/ml. Bile pigment was associated with high-molecular-weight mucin even after extensive dialysis, gel filtration, and density gradient ultracentrifugation.

Mucin glycoproteins are present in significant concentration in human black pigment stones. The association of bile pigment with gallbladder mucin even after extensive purification is consistent with the view that mucin contributes to the matrix of pigment gallstones. A number of experimental and clinical observations suggest that gallbladder mucin can contribute to gallstone formation through providing a matrix for the precipitation of lipid components.

(36–2) Hepatology 3:377–382, May–June, 1983.

▶ [There is also solid evidence for a potent nucleating factor in the gallbladder bile of patients with cholesterol gallstones. Burnstein et al. determined whether the rapid nucleation time of gallbladder bile obtained from patients with cholesterol gallstones was due to the addition of a nucleating agent or the removal of an antinucleating agent by the gallbladder.[3] Isotropic phases of gallbladder bile from normal controls (control bile) and from patients with gallstones (abnormal bile) were mixed and the nucleation times of the mixtures and parent biles were determined. The mixtures had rapid nucleation times, similar to those of the gallbladder bile from gallstone patients, indicating that a nucleating factor was present in the abnormal bile. Experiments were then performed using mixtures in which the proportion of abnormal bile was reduced. These studies showed that the nucleating agent was potent. The results were not due to changes in cholesterol saturation or total lipid concentration. The conclusions reached in the first study were supported in a second set of similar experiments in which hepatic bile from gallstone patients was mixed with their own gallbladder bile. It was also found that filtration of abnormal bile did not eliminate its nucleating potency, indicating that the results could not be explained by the presence of residual microcrystals in the abnormal bile.] ◀

36–3 **Prophylactic Cholecystectomy or Expectant Management for Silent Gallstones: Decision Analysis to Assess Survival.** Silent gallstones may be treated by either prophylactic cholecystectomy or expectant management. As many as 7% of cholecystectomies may be done in subjects without symptoms. David F. Ransohoff, William A. Gracie, Lewis B. Wolfenson, and Duncan Neuhauser undertook a decision analysis to compare the consequences of these 2 approaches under the assumption that cholecystectomy would be done if either

Fig 36–1.—Results for patients who choose prophylactic cholecystectomy (solid bar) compared with those for patients who choose expectant management (shaded area). Operative deaths from prophylactic cholecystectomy occur immediately; those after expectant management occur in later years, as patients age, have pain or complications, or have cholecystectomies. (Courtesy of Ransohoff, D.F., et al.: Ann. Intern. Med. 99:199–204, August 1983.)

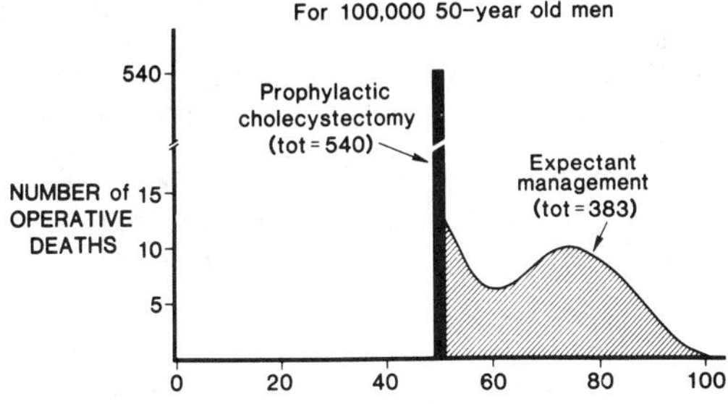

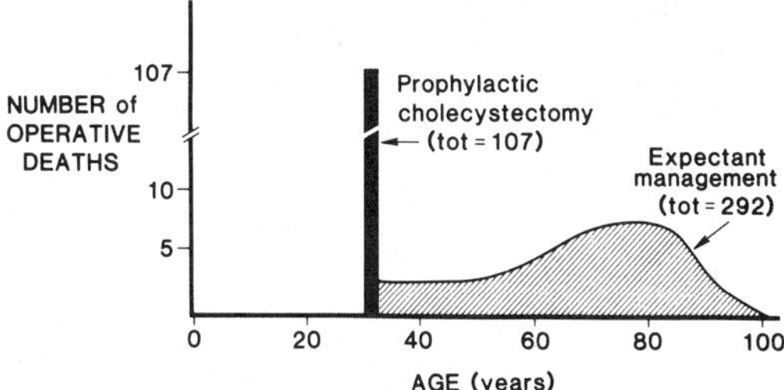

(36–3) Ann. Intern. Med. 99:199–204, August 1983.

biliary pain or a biliary complication developed. Probability values were derived from a study of the natural course of silent gallstone disease, reported cholecystectomy mortality, and life tables. The cumulative numbers of person-years lost for hypothetical cohorts of men and women were calculated. The natural history study involved 123 subjects with asymptomatic gallstones.

Prophylactic cholecystectomy was found to slightly reduce overall survival. More operative deaths occur with the prophylactic procedure than with expectant management in men aged 50 years; for men aged 30, there are more operative deaths with expectant management (Fig 36–1). A man aged 30 who chose prophylactic cholecystectomy would lose 4 days of life on average, whereas a man aged 50 would lose 18 days. Cost considerations favor expectant management.

The differences between prophylactic cholecystectomy and expectant management for patients with silent gallstone disease remain small over a broad range of probability values for both men and women. A policy of prophylactic cholecystectomy does not increase survival and is substantially more expensive than a policy of expectant management. Therefore, prophylactic cholecystectomy should not be routinely recommended for persons with silent gallstones. Patients at increased risk for biliary complications or gallbladder cancer may be considered for the prophylactic procedure, as may patients for whom operative mortality rates increase at an exceptionally high rate with advancing age.

► [The data of Ransohoff et al. suggest that a policy of prophylactic cholecystectomy does not increase survival for persons with silent gallstones and is substantially more expensive than a policy of expectant management. These investigators believe that prophylactic cholecystectomy should not be routinely recommended for persons with silent gallstones.

It bears emphasizing that these data were derived from asymptomatic or hyposymptomatic men. There may be some groups of persons with silent gallstones who should be considered for prophylactic cholecystectomy because of risks that are greater than those considered in the analysis of Ransohoff et al. Such groups might include diabetics, patients with calcification of the gallbladder, and patients with ileal resection. Predictors of such high risk, however, are controversial.] ◄

Chapter 36 References

1. Roslyn J.J., Pitt H.A., Mann L.L., et al.: Gallbladder disease in patients on long-term parenteral nutrition. *Gastroenterology* 84:148–154, 1983.
2. Pitt H.A., Berquist W.E., Mann L.L.: Parenteral nutrition induces calcium bilirubinate gallstones [abstract]. *Gastroenterology* 84:1274, 1983.
3. Burnstein M.J., Ilson R.G., Petronica C.N., et al.: Evidence for a potent nucleating factor in the gallbladder bile of patients with cholesterol gallstones. *Gastroenterology* 85:801–807, 1983.

37. Pancreas

37–1 **Potentiation Effect of Cholecystokinin-Octapeptide on Pancreatic Bicarbonate Secretion Stimulated by a Physiologic Dose of Secretin in Humans.** Little secretin is released after eating, and other factors probably are involved in pancreatic bicarbonate secretion in the postprandial period. Chul H. You, John M. Rominger, and William Y. Chey (Univ. of Rochester) examined the effect of cholecystokinin on secretin-stimulated pancreatic secretion in 5 healthy subjects aged 24–39 years. Pancreatic bicarbonate and trypsin outputs were determined with the use of a triple-lumen duodenal tube and the indicator dilution technique, with complete aspiration of gastric juice. Secretin was infused intravenously at a physiologic rate of 0.03 clinical units/kg of body weight/hour, and cholecystokinin-octapeptide was added in doses of 2.6–109.4 pmole/kg/hour.

The course of pancreatic bicarbonate output is shown in Figure 37–1. The output of bicarbonate with combined infusion of secretin and cholecystokinin was significantly greater than with either alone and was also greater than the sum of the outputs produced by each

Fig 37–1.—Pancreatic bicarbonate output after intravenous infusion of secretin in a dose of 0.03 clinical units *(cu)*/kg of body weight/hour and of graded doses of cholecystokinin-octapeptide *(CCK-OP)* and after simultaneous intravenous infusion of secretin and CCK-OP in same doses. Each bar represents mean ± SE for 5 subjects. (Courtesy of You, C.H., et al.: Reprinted by permission of the publisher from Gastroenterology 85:40–45, July 1983; copyright by the American Gastrological Association.)

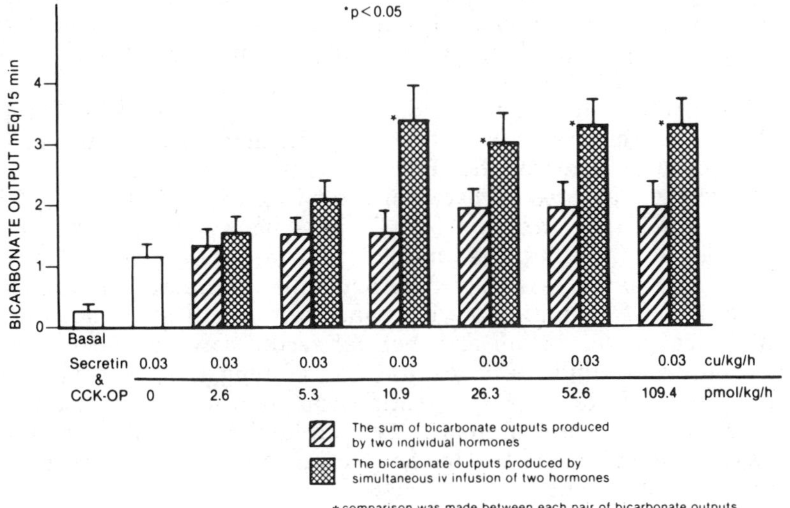

(37–1) Gastroenterology 85:40–45, July 1983.

hormone. A potentiating effect of cholecystokinin-octapeptide was evident at an infusion rate of 10.9 pmole/kg/hour, and no further augmenting effect was evident at higher dose rates. Administration of the 2 hormones together had no potentiating effect on trypsin output.

Cholecystokinin-octapeptide, in a relatively low dose range, potentiates the pancreatic bicarbonate secretion stimulated by secretin in physiologic dosage in normal humans. Pancreatic enzyme secretion, in contrast, is not potentiated by administration of the two hormones together.

▶ [These findings extend our understanding of normal pancreatic physiology in humans. The major observation is that the secretin and cerulein (cholecystokinin octapeptide) potentiate pancreatic bicarbonate secretion but not enzyme secretion in man. This finding has now been confirmed by other investigators.[1]

There has been considerable interest in the effect of calcium channel blockers on pancreatic exocrine function. Two preliminary reports suggest that verapamil inhibits pancreatic volume, bicarbonate secretion, and amylase secretion.[2, 3] It is possible that treatment with calcium channel blockers could unmask latent pancreatic exocrine insufficiency in patients with advanced but subclinical chronic pancreatitis.] ◀

37–2 **Bentiromide as a Test of Exocrine Pancreatic Function in Adult Patients With Pancreatic Exocrine Insufficiency: Determination of Appropriate Dose and Urinary Collection Interval.** The bentiromide test is a reliable means of diagnosing exocrine pancreatic insufficiency. Orally administered bentiromide is split by chymotrypsin; free para-aminobenzoic acid is absorbed from the small bowel and partially conjugated by the liver, and its metabolites are excreted in the urine. Phillip P. Toskes (Univ. of Florida) attempted to determine the optimal dose of bentiromide and the best urinary collection interval. A dose-ranging crossover study was carried out in 47 patients with chronic pancreatic disease who had pancreatic calcification, increased stool fat excretion with a low secretin test result, or a low secretin test result and a low serum carotene level. Sixty-one healthy subjects also were assessed. The 2 groups had mean ages of 50 and 33 years, respectively. Bentiromide was given in doses of 100 mg, 500 mg, 1 gm, and 5 gm, with postdosing urine collection periods of 3, 6, 12, and 24 hours.

Urinary arylamine excretion data are given in the table. The patient and control groups were best distinguished with the use of the 500-mg dose of bentiromide and a 6-hour urine collection period. Some overlap was present between the two groups in the 50%–75% range of arylamine recovery (Fig 37–2). With a cutoff point of 57% there were 5% false-positive and 20% false-negative results. No control patient showed less than 50% arylamine excretion for the 0–6-hour period. Of 10 patients with pancreatic calcification but either normal fecal fat excretion or a normal serum carotene level, 7 had abnormal bentiromide test results. The 500-mg dose was virtually without side effects. Repeated testing was followed by a serum glutamic oxaloacetic transaminase elevation lasting 3 months or longer in 4 asymptomatic subjects. One patient had respiratory distress after 2 doses of bentiromide.

(37–2) Gastroenterology 85:565–569, September 1983.

CUMULATIVE URINARY ARYLAMINE EXCRETION*

Subjects	100-mg dose		500-mg dose		1-g dose		5-g dose	
	0–3 h	0–6 h	0–3 h	0–6 h	0–3 h	0–6 h	0–3 h	0–6 h
Abnormal pancreatic function								
(*mean* ± *SD*)	25 ± 16	47 ± 18	18 ± 13	42 ± 17	21 ± 12	45 ± 16	11 ± 7	25 ± 12
n†	45	45	46	45	47	47	45	45
Normal pancreatic function								
(*mean* ± *SD*)	52 ± 13	73 ± 11	45 ± 12	71 ± 7	39 ± 13	65 ± 11	16 ± 7	37 ± 12
n†	59	59	59	59	61	61	59	59
Wilcoxon test								
(normal approximation)	6.87	6.95	7.42	7.97	6.25	6.37	3.92	4.76
p	<0.001	<0.001	<0.001	<0.001	<0.001	<0.001	<0.001	<0.001
Cutoff point								
(*mean* ± 2 *SD*)	26	51	21	57	13	43	2	13
False positives (%)	3	2	0	5	5	5	2	0
False negatives (%)	45	44	37	20	66	60	91	87

*Expressed as percentages.
†Indicates number of samples. Sample sizes vary owing to missing data from some dose and collection-interval combinations.
(Courtesy of Toskes, P.P.: Reprinted by permission of the publisher from Gastroenterology 85:565–569, September 1983; copyright by the American Gastrological Association.)

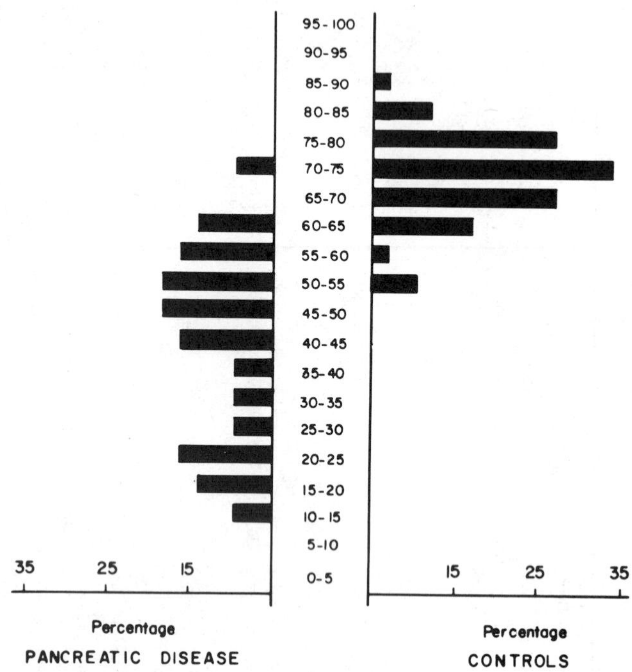

Fig 37–2.—Relative frequency distributions of urinary arylamines (0–6 hours, 500 mg of bentiromide) for patients in chronic pancreatic disease group and for control subjects. (Courtesy of Toskes, P.P.: Reprinted by permission of the publisher from Gastroenterology 85:565–569, September 1983; copyright 1983 by the American Gastrological Association.)

The bentiromide test is a simple and reliable means of evaluating exocrine pancreatic disease. Optimal conditions appear to include a dose of 500 mg and a 6-hour postdosing urine collection period.

▶ [Reports from several centers have indicated that the bentiromide test is a simple and reliable *screening test* for evaluating pancreatic exocrine disease.[4–7] It is not quite as sensitive as the secretin-cholecystokinin-pancreozymin test or Lundh test meal, but its overall sensitivity (65%) is quite acceptable. Importantly, it is an easy test to do and does not require duodenal intubation, fluoroscopy, intravenous injection(s), or analysis of intraduodenal contents. It should be emphasized, however, that for optimal specificity (approximately 90%) the bentiromide test should be done along with a D-xylose test. This is especially so in patients with diarrhea and suspected malabsorption. If a D-xylose test is not done in such patients, the false-positive rate can be as high as 25%–30%.

It should also be noted that the bentiromide test is an excellent means of assessing exocrine pancreatic function in patients with cystic fibrosis.[8] Moreover, serial tests have proved useful in assessing the adequacy of pancreatic enzyme replacement therapy.] ◀

Chapter 37 References

1. Beglinger C., Gyr K., Freed M., et al.: Potentiating interaction between secretin and caerulein for pancreatic bicarbonate but not enzyme secretion in man [abstract]. *Gastroenterology* 84:1102, 1983.
2. Newman J., Lewis B.G., Swicrczek J.S., et al.: The effect of graded doses of verapamil on pancreatic exocrine secretion in awake dogs [abstract]. *Gastroenterology* 84:1259, 1983.

3. Ckersten M., Bank J., Burns G., et al.: The effect of verapamil on pancreatic exocrine secretion [abstract]. *Gastroenterology* 84:1163, 1983.
4. Arvanatakis C., Taskes P., Greenberger, N.J.: Tripeptide pancreatic function test: multicenter evaluation of patients with pancreatic and nonpancreatic disease [abstract]. *Gastroenterology* 74:1004, 1978.
5. Toskes P., Greenberger N.J.: Acute and chronic pancreatitis. *D.M.* 29:1–79, 1983.
6. Imamura K., Nakamura T., Miyazawa T., et al.: Oral administration of a chymotrypsin labile peptide for a new test of exocrine pancreatic function (PFT) in comparison with pan-reazymin-secretion test. *Am. J. Gastroenterol.* 65:572–578, 1978.
7. Lang C., Gyr K., Stolder G., et al.: Assessment of exocrine pancreatic function by oral administration of *N*-benzoyl-L-tyrosyl-*p*-aminobenzoic acid (bentiromide): 5 years clinical experience. *Br. J. Surg.* 68:771, 1981.
8. Nousia-Arvanitakis S., Arvanitakis C., Desai N., et al.: Diagnosis of exocrine pancreatic insufficiency in cystic fibrosis by the synthetic peptide *N*-benzoyl-L-tyrosyl-*p*-aminobenzoic acid. *J. Pediatr.* 92:734–737, 1978.

PART SIX

METABOLISM

PHILIP K. BONDY, M.D.

Introduction

During the past few years, a large number of polypeptide factors have been isolated from brain, skin, salivary glands, and many other organs, which have some of the characteristics of hormones. They modulate growth and differentiation; they stimulate the secretory activity of cells in the traditional endocrine system and are involved in feedback control of the endocrine glands. Indeed, today the endocrine system can no longer be thought of as a few glands, such as the pituitary, adrenal, thyroid, gonads, etc., but rather must be seen as an integrative system with both secretory and receptor components in all cells of the body. Moreover, there is evidence that the system is a phylogenetically ancient one, since polypeptide compounds similar to mammalian hormones and their receptors are found in phyla other than mammals and, indeed, in unicellular organisms. For example, the pathogenic gram-negative organism, *Yersinia enterocolitica* has receptor sites for thyrotropin.[1] Evidence for the interaction of the nontraditional polypeptide hormones with the established system is developing on many fronts. A human pituitary tumor producing proopiomelanocortin, the precursor of ACTH, was stimulated by arginine vasopressin, vasoactive intestinal polypeptide, met-enkephalin, thyrotropin-releasing hormone, and oxytocin. Somatostatin-14, somatostatin-28 and leu-enkephalin suppressed secretion.[2] Similar results were obtained in a mouse pituitary tumor with vasoactive intestinal polypeptide (VIP).[3] The integration of these regulatory effects is facilitated by the fact that several of the controlling polypeptides are found in a single neuron. Corticotropin-releasing factor, a VIP-like polypeptide and enkephalin are all demonstrable by immunofluorescence in the same neuron in the parvocellular portion of the paraventricular nucleus.[4] Polypeptide hormones may also antagonize other types of effects which are mediated by hormone-like mechanisms. For example, the analgesic effect of morphine, believed to reflect its ability to interact with endorphin receptors in nervous tissue, is antagonized by cholecystokinin, which is now recognized as a neuropeptide as well as a gastrointestinal hormone.[5]

Epidermal growth factor (EGF) is a polypeptide with powerful ability to stimulate growth in general, to increase cellular uptake of nutrients and to promote the synthesis of RNA and proteins. Its effects on the synthesis of the specific protein prolactin are exerted by increasing transcription of the prolactin gene.[6] EGF also acts as a growth hormone in vivo. Excision of the submandibular salivary glands of mice—a potent source of both EGF and nerve growth factor—results in stunted growth and a shift away from carbohydrate in the metabolic mix of the operated mice.[7] Polypeptides closely related to EGF, called "polypeptide transforming growth factors" and also isolated from kidneys and salivary glands, promote wound healing.[8]

Many of these relationships and effects have been reviewed in succinct form by Polak and Bloom.[9]

In addition to the ability of newly recognized polypeptide hormones to affect the metabolism of many different kinds of cells, it is also becoming apparent that hormones previously recognized for specific actions have functions in the brain and therefore can be considered as neuropeptide hormones. I have discussed some of these, notably ACTH, in this space in previous years. The presence of insulin as a normal constituent of the brain, at least of rats, suggests that it should be added to the list of peripheral hormones with neural activities.[10]

References

1. Weiss M., Ingbar S.H., Winblad S. et al.: Demonstration of a saturable binding site for thyrotropin in *Yersinia enterocolitica*. *Science* 219:1331–1333, 1983.
2. Shibasaki T., Masui H.: Effects of various neuropeptides on the secretion of

proopiomelanocortin-derived peptides by a cultured pituitary adenoma causing Nelson's syndrome. *J. Clin. Endocrinol. Metab.* 55:872–876, 1982.

3. Westendorf J.M., Phillips M.A., Schonbrunn A.: Vasoactive intestinal polypeptide stimulates hormone release from corticotropic cells in culture. *Endocrinology* 112:550–557, 1983.
4. Hökfelt T., Fahrenkrug J., Tatemoto K., et al.: The PHI(PHI27)/corticotropin-releasing factor/enkephalin immunoreactive hypothalamic neuron: possible morphological basis for integrated control of prolactin, corticotropin, and growth hormone secretion. *Proc. Natl. Acad. Sci. USA* 80:895–898, 1983.
5. Faris P.L., Komisaruk B.R., Watkins L.R. et al.: Evidence for the neuropeptide cholecystokinin as an antagonist of opiate analgesia. *Science* 219:310–312, 1983.
6. Murdoch G.H., Potter E., Nicolaisen A.K., et al.: Epidermal growth factor rapidly stimulates prolactin gene transcription. *Nature* 300:192–194, 1982.
7. Li A.K.C., Schattenkerk M.E., DeVries J.E., et al.: Growth and metabolic alterations after submandibular sialadenectomy in male mice. *Am. J. Physiol.* 244:R41–R44, 1983.
8. Sporn M.B., Roberts A.B., Shull J.H., et al.: Polypeptide transforming growth factors isolated from bovine sources and used for wound healing in vivo. *Science* 219:1329–1331, 1983.
9. Polak J.M., Bloom S.R.: Regulatory peptides: key factors in the control of bodily functions. *Br. Med. J.* 286:1461–1466, 1983.
10. Baskin D.G., et al.: Regional concentrations of insulin in the rat brain. *Endocrinology* 112:898–903, 1983.

38. Pituitary Gland

No single development has had a greater impact on the diagnosis of pituitary tumors than the introduction of computed tomographic (CT) scanning. With modern high-resolution equipment, it is possible to make "cuts" of only 1.5 mm and to recognize with some security lesions 2 or 3 mm in diameter. The increased accuracy with which the gland can be studied has resulted in modified standards for normal. For example, the dimensions of the pituitary in adult women with a normal menstrual history who are not taking contraceptives are 5.4–9.7 mm in height and 9.5–16.7 mm in width in the coronal plane, which is somewhat larger than the limits commonly used. Focal defects are also common.[1] The CT scan makes it possible to recognize lesions that are missed by ordinary radiography. For example, in a group of 16 young women with hyperprolactinemia whose sella radiograms were considered normal even with lateral polytome hypocycloidal tomography with 3-mm cuts, CT scanning recognized 9 of 10 with tumors.[2] The increased accuracy of CT scanning as compared with other methods of diagnosis should make it possible to evaluate patients more rapidly and to reach therapeutic decisions more economically than by earlier methods. But is this actually the case? When three cohorts of patients with pituitary adenomas studied in 1976, 1978, and 1980 were compared, it was found that the average preoperative stay decreased from 6.8 to 1.9 days, the charge for diagnostic radiology (in constant dollars) decreased from $1,747 to $585, and the cost of radiologic diagnosis as a percentage of the entire hospital bill dropped from 17.3% to 11.9%. These changes in cost coincided with the introduction of CT scanning and the virtual elimination of angiography and pneumoencephalography.[3] Thus one of the major advantages of the CT scan is that it permits elimination of most of the other neuroradiologic methods that were previously necessary. This reduces cost and trauma to the patient, since the methods used previously were painfully invasive. But the situation is not entirely simple. In some instances, the CT scan can be misleading, as in the following case report.

38–1 **Bilateral Intracavernous Carotid Aneurysms Mimicking a Prolactin-Secreting Pituitary Tumor.** The abnormalities of the sella turcica that are seen on radiologic study and associated with ophthalmoplegia and hyperprolactinemia usually indicate a pituitary tumor, but intracavernous aneurysms can produce the same findings. Joel S. Mindel, Ved P. Sachdev, Lanning B. Kline, Mark A. Sivak, Donald A. Bergman, Wen C. Yang, In S. Choi, and Yun P. Huang report data on 2 patients with bilateral intracavernous carotid aneurysms who presented with hyperprolactinemia, abnormalities of the sella turcica seen at radiologic study, and ophthalmoplegia. The patients were elderly women with serum prolactin levels of 71 and 32 ng/ml, respectively. One patient had a high-resolution computed tomography (CT) study after injection of contrast medium; the results were incorrectly interpreted as showing a pituitary tumor, but cerebral angiography showed bilateral aneurysms. The other patient had bilateral aneurysms demonstrated by contrast CT and confirmed by radionuclide angiography.

These patients were correctly diagnosed before potentially lethal attempts to perform a biopsy or to remove the lesions. The aneurysms

---

(38–1) Surg. Neurol. 19:163–167, February 1983.

presumably produced hyperprolactinemia and ophthalmoplegia by compression or ischemia, or both, of the pituitary stalk–hypothalamus and the intracavernous cranial nerves. Either compression or ischemia could interfere with the dopaminergic pathway to the anterior pituitary gland and result in release of the prolactin-secreting cells from inhibition. It also is possible that the patients had small incidental prolactin-secreting pituitary microadenomas. Compression or ischemia of the cranial nerves could explain the ocular muscle fatigue noted in 1 of the patients. Close follow-up of these patients will be necessary to make sure that they do not develop panhypopituitarism.

▶ [It is not clear what causes prolactinomas to develop. In addition to thyrotropin-releasing hormone, which stimulates prolactin secretion, it now appears that epidermal growth factor can increase the transcription of the gene for prolactin synthesis.[4] Whether it can also increase the rate of growth and thus potentially cause tumors is uncertain. The fact that estrogens can stimulate prolactin secretion has raised a question of whether prolonged administration of oral contraceptives could be a factor in the development of prolactinomas. This question is discussed in the next abstract.] ◀

38–2 **Pituitary Adenomas and Oral Contraceptives: A Multicenter Case-Control Study.** There is evidence for a causal relationship between endogenous estrogen levels and the development of pituitary adenomas, and it is possible that exogenous estrogens, as in oral contraceptives, have a role in causing these tumors. The Pituitary Adenoma Study Group undertook a case-control study of the possible association between the use of oral contraceptives and an increased risk of developing prolactin-secreting pituitary adenomas. A total of 212 women aged 18–39 years with adenomas, 140 of them surgically confirmed, were recruited from 4 centers and matched for age and race with neighborhood control subjects. Study was also made of 119 hyperprolactinemic women with amenorrhea or galactorrhea or both, but normal or equivocal tomograms and 205 normoprolactinemic women with amenorrhea-galactorrhea, all matched with neighborhood control subjects.

There was no increased relative risk for the use of oral contraceptives in any patient group. A history of infertility, menstrual problems, or amenorrhea-galactorrhea was associated with a significantly increased risk of pituitary adenoma, as was nulliparity. The use of oral contraceptives by women with a history of menstrual disorder or infertility was not associated with an increased risk of pituitary adenoma.

These results and those of other studies indicate no relation between the use of oral contraceptives and the risk of developing pituitary adenoma, but it remains possible that exposure to estrogens can exacerbate a preexisting adenoma. There is in vitro evidence for a modulating role of estrogen in prolactin production and secretion, but it is not known whether this takes place in vivo and in pituitary adenomas. Further studies are needed to identify any influence of oral contraceptives on existing pituitary adenomas.

▶ [The same conclusions were reached by a Swedish Group who studied 70 women

(38–2) Fertil. Steril. 39:753–760, June 1983.

with prolactinomas in a group ranging from 19 to 38 years of age. Although the percentage of patients with prolactinomas who were using oral contraception was the same as that in the general population, the duration of symptoms was shorter, the serum prolactin levels were lower and the sella turcica was less severely enlarged in the group using contraceptives than in that which did not. The authors conclude that oral contraceptives probably lead to earlier manifestations of clinically latent prolactin-producing tumors.[5] Similar results were obtained in a study in the state of Washington. The authors of that study point out, however, that if oral contraceptives are used to regulate the menstrual cycle, the incidence of prolactinomas is seven times higher than for the general population.[6] To me this suggests that oral contraceptives are not prone to promote prolactinomas but rather that patients with menstrual abnormalities resulting from prolactinomas are likely to resort to oral contraceptives in an attempt to regulate their menses.

In addition to its effects on the mammary glands, the reproductive organs and (at least in some species) the electrolyte balance, it now appears that prolactin and growth hormone (which is closely related in its amino acid sequence) suppress antibody formation and the development of cell-mediated immunity.[7] I am not aware that there has been a systematic study of the immune mechanisms of patients with prolactinomas, but it might be a worthwhile project. And is it possible that this effect is related in some way to the acquired immunodeficiency syndrome? Seems a remote possibility, but perhaps worth considering.] ◀

38–3 **Coexistent Primary Empty Sella Syndrome and Hyperprolactinemia: Report of 11 Cases.** The term *primary empty sella syndrome* refers to an intrasellar extension of the subarachnoid space that results in flattening of the pituitary. The syndrome occurs most often in obese, hypertensive, middle-aged women and is usually accompanied by normal pituitary function and an enlarged sella turcica. Coexistence of an empty sella and hyperprolactinemia may cause diagnostic difficulty when the presence of a prolactinoma is to be excluded. Hossein Gharib, Harald M. Frey, Edward R. Laws, Jr., Raymond V. Randall, and Bernd W. Scheithauer (Mayo Clinic and Found., Rochester, Minn.) describe the findings in 11 normotensive women, aged 23–76 years, with hyperprolactinemia and primary empty sella syndrome.

Eight patients had amenorrhea, 2 had oligomenorrhea, and 1 was postmenopausal. Six patients had galactorrhea and 3 had both amenorrhea and galactorrhea. All patients had hyperprolactinemia and their basal serum concentrations of PRL ranged from 33 to 498 ng/ml (normal, 23 ng/ml or less). One patient had primary hypothyroidism. Polytomography in 8 patients demonstrated an enlarged sella in each. Bone erosion, asymmetric sellar floor, or demineralization of the sella was present in 4 patients. Computed tomographic scanning of the head was performed on 8 patients, bilateral carotid angiography on 6, and pneumoencephalography on 3.

Of 8 patients undergoing transsphenoidal sellar exploration, only 1 had a pituitary microadenoma and an empty sella; the other 7 had only an empty sella with a flattened pituitary. Conventional histologic methods and immunocytologic studies of the gland showed no abnormalities.

When an enlarged sella or sellar bony erosions are found by roentgenography in the presence of high serum PRL concentrations and

(38–3) Arch. Intern. Med. 143:1383–1386, July 1983.

blunting PRL increase stimulated by thyrotropin-releasing hormone, PRL-producing adenoma must be strongly suspected. If roentgenographic and endocrinologic studies show no pituitary microadenoma, operation on the sella should be deferred in preference to periodic reassessment and long-term follow-up, for hyperprolactinemia, with or without galactorrhea-amenorrhea, may occur in association with an empty sella in the absence of an associated pituitary tumor.

▶ [I don't entirely understand what is so special about that last statement. There is no indication for pituitary surgery in a hyperprolactinemic patient even if a microadenoma is present—and certainly if no tumor is found—as long as the patient responds appropriately to bromocriptine or an equivalent medication.

Other studies of patients with the hyperprolactinemia syndrome in association with the empty sella syndrome have been reported.[8, 9, 10] One of these patients also had acromegaly!

Is it possible to distinguish hyperprolactinemia caused by a prolactinoma from that caused by hypothalamic dysfunction? Ferrari and colleagues[11] found that patients with prolactinomas respond both to thyrotropin-releasing hormone (TRH) and the dopamine agonist sulpiride, whereas patients with organic hypothalamic lesions failed to respond to sulpiride. It is not uncommon for women to be infertile although no evidence is present for a prolactinoma, and random serum prolactin measurements are normal. In some such patients, repeated measurements of serum prolactin reveal transient hyperprolactinemia, which may help explain their infertility. Treatment with bromocriptine is often useful.[12]] ◀

38–4 **Natural History of Microprolactinomas: Six-Year Follow-up.** Rational management of microprolactinomas requires an understanding of the natural history. Martin H. Weiss, James Teal, Peggy Gott, Robert Wycoff, Richard Yadley, Michael L. J. Apuzzo, Steven L. Giannotta, Oscar Kletzky, and Charles March undertook a prospective study of 27 female patients who harbored microprolactinomas. They were followed up for 6 years without therapeutic intervention. The patients ranged in age from 18 to 47 years. At the outset all had serum prolactin levels exceeding 50 ng/ml, and all had been amenorrheic for at least a year. Polytomography showed distortion of the floor of the sella turcica without gross erosion or invasion of the sphenoid sinus. Visual field examination showed no abnormality, and computed tomography showed no evidence of a tumor more than 1 cm in diameter. Most patients had symptomatic galactorrhea. There was no evidence of other endocrinopathy.

Seven patients received bromocriptine in an attempt to conceive, and 6 have done so. The remaining women were untreated during observation. Three women in all showed growth of their tumor on radiographic evaluation. The increase in tumor size occurred about 4 years after the onset of symptoms in 2 instances and after about 8½ years in 1 case. Six patients have had a progressive fall in prolactin levels without specific treatment. Three had a decrease to below 30 ng/ml and resumed having normal menses; 2 of the others also resumed menstruating, although irregularly. The results of thyroid-releasing hormone stimulation tests remained abnormal. These patients had been symptomatic for 38 to 66 months before the decline in their prolactin levels.

(38–4) Neurosurgery 12:180–183, February 1983.

The authors generally follow up patients with microprolactinoma for at least a year in the absence of such factors as psychological stress or a wish to become pregnant. Surgery has been recommended for patients aged 15–30 years with radiographically verifiable tumors. Patients older than age 45 years are usually managed nonoperatively. The management of patients aged 30–45 years who show no change in status after 12–18 months of follow-up is individualized but weighted toward surgical removal of the tumor.

▶ [It is useful to have information about the natural history of the untreated prolactinoma, but 7 of these patients also received bromocriptine, so they should be deleted from the statistics. Bromocriptine usually controls both the hypersecretion of prolactin and the growth of the tumor. Indeed, even large tumors may shrink to the point where previously impaired visual fields may return to normal.[13] The amount of bromocriptine required for adequate treatment may sometimes be quite small, and administration of a single nocturnal dose of 2.5 mg may be adequate to return ovarian function to normal.[14] Some patients who cannot tolerate bromocriptine can be controlled with pergolide mesylate, a dopamine agonist with effects similar to those of bromocriptine.[15]

In spite of the well-documented ability of dopamine agonists to cause prolactinomas to shrink, the mechanism by which they reduce tumor bulk has been obscure. Tindall and colleagues studied 6 macroadenomas associated with hyperprolactinemia. Two were removed without preoperative treatment. Two were treated with bromocriptine until the time of surgery; these shrank as anticipated. And two others responded to treatment and then were allowed to escape from bromocriptine for one and two weeks before operation; these showed regrowth after the drug was discontinued. The treated tumors showed no vascular damage or tumor cell necrosis, but there was a reduction in total cell size, which reflected reduced size of cytoplasmic, nuclear, and secretory granules. The authors conclude that the reduced size of the tumors produced by bromocriptine is not a result of a reduction in the total number of cells but rather in the size of individual cells.[16] Thus it is not entirely inappropriate for Weiss and colleagues to worry about whether bromocriptine-suppressed tumors will grow beyond the size that will permit satisfactory results from operation. This is a possible but rare phenomenon; however, it is one that justifies careful review of patients during medical treatment.] ◀

38–5 **Transsphenoidal Microsurgical Treatment of Prolactin-Producing Pituitary Adenomas: Results in 100 Patients.** Raymond V. Randall, Edward R. Laws, Jr., Charles F. Abboud, Michael J. Ebersold, Pai Chih Kao, and Bernd W. Scheithauer (Mayo Clinic and Found., Rochester, Minn.) reviewed the results of transsphenoidal microsurgery in 84 women and 16 men with prolactinoma seen in 1974–1979. Follow-up ranged from 3 to 5 years. The median age at the time of surgery was 26 years for the women compared with 45 years for the men. All the women had some type of menstrual abnormality at presentation, most often secondary amenorrhea, and nearly 90% had galactorrhea. Fourteen women reported infertility as a presenting complaint. Nine men presented with gonadal dysfunction, usually decreased or absent libido. About two thirds of patients had skull roentgenographic findings consistent with intrasellar tumor. Forty-five patients had basal serum PRL values below 100 ng/ml. Nine patients had visual field defects.

Nine patients had transient diabetes insipidus postoperatively, and 1 had cerebrospinal rhinorrhea that was repaired surgically. One pa-

(38–5) Mayo Clin. Proc. 58:108–121, February 1983.

tient with empty sella syndrome had a second operation for correction of visual field defects. Forty-nine women had normal PRL levels after surgery. The best results were in those with a microadenoma and a preoperative PRL value below 100 ng/ml. The men had less favorable results. Only 1 patient failed to have any reduction in PRL concentration after surgery. Eighteen women conceived after surgery, 2 of them twice. Two of the 8 men who had been receiving thyroid replacement therapy preoperatively were able to discontinue it after surgery.

Transsphenoidal surgery for prolactinoma carries minimal risks. The best results are obtained in patients with small adenomas. The lower the initial serum PRL level, the greater the chance for a surgical cure. Mass effects of large prolactinomas are reversed by surgery in the great majority of cases. When transsphenoidal microsurgery is used judiciously to treat prolactinomas, in conjunction with medical treatment and radiation therapy, satisfactory control of the disease and its manifestations can be obtained in most cases.

▶ [What is the long-term result of surgical removal of prolactin-secreting microadenomas? The plasma prolactin levels were restored to normal in all of 27 women operated on by Barbarino and colleagues in Rome, and normal menses returned. Within a month, normal responses to thyrotropin-releasing hormone (TRH) and metoclopramide returned in 16; but in 9 the prolactin levels were low and failed to respond to stimulation. Normal control mechanisms returned over a period of several months. The two remaining patients, whose plasma prolactin concentrations remained a bit elevated, failed to respond to stimulation, and evidence of return of tumor activity gradually developed. Thus several months are required before a final decision can be made about the success of surgery in restoring normal endocrine control to patients with microprolactinomas.[17] In contrast, 20% of large chromophobe adenomas removed surgically recurred in significant form, even though they had been irradiated postoperatively. The recurrence rate for prolactinomas was 30%. It should be noted that none of these patients were treated with bromocriptine.[18] Similar results were observed in 44 patients operated on by the neurosurgical group at the University of Montreal. Normal function resumed in 85% of the microadenomas, and the recurrence rate was 50%, whereas restoration of function occurred in only 50% of the macroadenomas, and the recurrence rate was 80% after 2–3 years. Poor postoperative prognosis could not be predicted preoperatively, but the level of serum prolactin immediately after operation was significantly lower in the group with good prognosis than in those whose disease recurred.[19] All of these data suggest that surgery is not the ideal choice for treatment of prolactinomas, since it apparently does not remove the cause of the tumor (which is probably hypothalamic) and since bromocriptine and other dopaminergic drugs usually provide a better prognosis with less unpleasant side effects. It must, nevertheless, be recognized that some adenomas (especially the large ones) may not be controlled by bromocriptine.[20]

As I mentioned in an earlier comment, a single daily dose of bromocriptine may suffice to control hypersecretion of microprolactinomas.[14] Pergolide appears to have an even longer duration of effectiveness, since a single dose usually controls prolactin levels for 48 hours or more.[21] Although this is still an experimental drug, its longer duration of action may make treatment with it much easier than bromocriptine.] ◀

38-6 **Impaired Pituitary Response to Bromocriptine Suppression: Reversal After Bromocriptine Plus Tamoxifen.** Dopamine agonists such as bromocriptine reduce the volume of some PRL-secreting pituitary adenomas, but suppression is poor in some instances. Wernfrid Völker, Werner G. Gehring, Renate Berning, Rüdiger C. Schmidt, Jörg Schneider, and Alexander von zur Mühlen (Hannover,

---

(38–6) Acta Endocrinol. (Copenh.) 101:491–500, December 1982.

West Germany) evaluated combined treatment with bromocriptine and tamoxifen, which enhances the sensitivity of dispersed PRL-secreting tumor cells to bromocriptine, in 12 female patients aged 15–54 years. Ten hyperprolactinemic patients with pituitary tumors who had failed to respond to daily administration of 2.5–10 mg of bromocriptine were given 10–20 mg of tamoxifen as well. Two had had incomplete resections of chromophobe adenomas; the others had refused surgery or irradiation. Two women who had had side effects from bromocriptine also received combined treatment. Eight patients had a substantial fall in serum PRL concentration. Two were the patients who had had side effects from bromocriptine and who tolerated the drug when used in conjunction with tamoxifen. The other 6 patients had clinical improvement. Amenorrhea resolved in 4 of 5 women; galactorrhea, in 4 patients. One woman conceived after 12 years of infertility. Two patients had elevated gonadotropin levels during antiestrogen therapy, and 1 of them had an elevated serum estradiol level. Benefit from combined treatment was evident after the first week; further improvement occurred after 4 weeks.

In most cases of hyperprolactinemia caused by pituitary tumor, the suppressive effect of bromocriptine on PRL secretion can be enhanced by adding tamoxifen. Side effects from bromocriptine may be considerably ameliorated by adding tamoxifen. Antiestrogens are competitive inhibitors of estradiol binding to receptors, and it appears that tamoxifen competes for greater or lesser concentrations of receptor sites in prolactinomas.

▶ [However, four patients failed to respond to combined treatment, so it is not universally useful. It is probably worth a try in nonresponders.

Three different dopaminergic drugs were studied as treatment for 191 prolactinomas of various sizes. Bromocriptine, metergoline, and lisuride all were highly effective in most patients. Patients who failed to respond usually were controlled by increasing the drug dosage. Mild side effects occurred frequently as treatment was started, but they usually subsided with continued treatment. In the 12 who failed to respond even to large doses of one drug, response occurred in 11 when one of the other drugs was tried. Thus the combination of bromcriptine and tamoxifen is only one of several possible approaches to initial failure of treatment.[22]] ◀

38–7 **Human Pancreatic Growth-Hormone-Releasing Factor Selectively Stimulates Growth-Hormone Secretion in Man.** Michael O. Thorner, Jean Rivier, Joachim Spiess, Joao L. Borges, Mary Lee Vance, Stephen R. Bloom, Alan D. Rogol, Michael J. Cronin, Donald L. Kaiser, William S. Evans, Joan D. Webster, Robert M. MacLeod, and Wylie Vale have characterized a GHRF isolated from a pancreatic tumor in a woman, aged 21 years, who had acromegaly and pituitary somatotroph hyperplasia. This human pancreatic GHRF is a linear peptide of 40 amino acids with a free carboxyl terminal and is designated hpGHRF-40. A dose of 1 μg/kg of body weight was administered intravenously as a bolus to 6 healthy men with a mean age of 25 years. All were within 15% of ideal body weight.

The serum GH concentration increased within 5 minutes of injection of the factor in 4 subjects, peaked at 30–60 minutes (Fig 38–1),

(38–7) Lancet 1:24–28, Jan. 1–8, 1983.

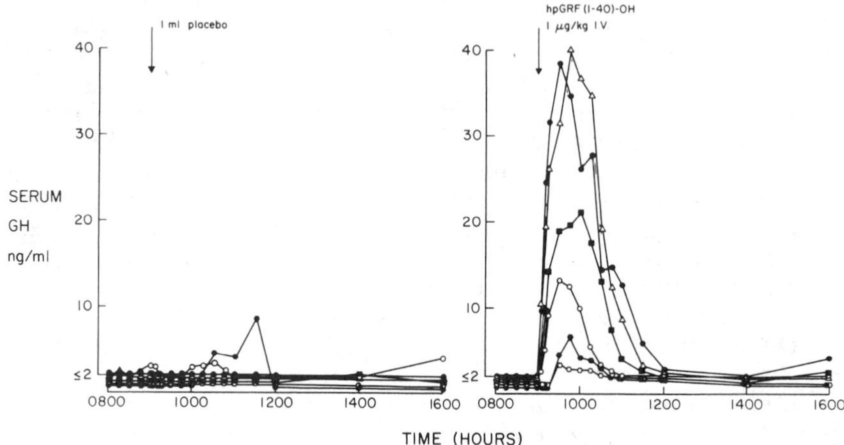

Fig 38–1.—Serum GH level before and after placebo *(left panel)* and before and after hpGRF *(right panel)* in 6 normal men. (Courtesy of Thorner, M.O., et al.: Lancet 1:24–28, Jan. 1–8, 1983.)

and returned to control levels within another 90 minutes. No changes occurred in serum PRL, thyrotropin, LH, or corticotropin levels. Blood glucose, pancreatic glucagon, and plasma insulin, gastrin, motilin, and somatostatin levels were unchanged by hpGHRF-40 injection. No side effects were observed, and there were no changes in pulse rate, blood pressure, blood cell counts, serum electrolyte values, or liver function. In 2 subjects, peak serum GH was less than 5 ng/ml, and one of these responded normally to an insulin test.

The characteristics of hpGHRF-40 fulfill many of the criteria for a hypophysiotropic GHRF. Because it is highly specific in stimulating GH secretion and is without side effects, it offers promise in both diagnostic and therapeutic applications. Development of a radioimmunoassay for hpGHRF-40 may allow patients with ectopic GHRF secretion to be identified before pituitary surgery and may allow tumors secreting hpGHRF to be identified and removed as initial treatment of acromegaly. The peptide may also be used to treat idiopathic GH deficiency.

▶ [This paper is one of the first to attempt to work out the dynamics of the response to the releasing factor as a clinical test. The fact that 2 of 6 subjects tested failed to respond raises a question of the reliability of a negative response.

The discovery of a GH-releasing hormone from pancreatic tumor was mentioned in the discussion of endocrinology in last year's YEAR BOOK (PP. 477–478). The hormone was identified simultaneously by Roger Guillemin's group as well.[23] The patient is described in detail by Thorner et al.[24] Her serum GH level averaged 95 ng/ml, and her somatomedin C concentration was 11 units/ml. After administration of glucose, her GH level rose rather than falling in the normal fashion. Pituitary tissue removed by transsphenoidal hypophysectomy showed hyperplasia of the somatotrophs without tumor. Moreover, removal of pituitary tissue did not improve her acromegaly. Her physicians interpreted this as evidence that she had a tumor producing GH-releasing factor. The tumor, which was in the pancreas, was the source from which Vale's group isolated GHRF, as described in the abstract above. Antibodies raised against GHRF isolated from the pancreatic islet tumor by Guillemin's team have made it possible to demonstrate that the material is present neuronal cells of the arcuate nucleus of the primate hypothalamus, with fibers projecting into the median eminence and ending in close contact with portal vessels. The synthetic material has characteristics indistinguishable from those of the ectopic islet hormone,[25] and stimulates rat pituitary cells in culture to release GH. It appears to be identical to rat hypothalamic GHRF. The stimulating effect is blocked by somatostatin.[26]

The secretion of GH is stimulated by GHRF, but other hormones also play a part. Both glucocorticoids and thyroid hormones stimulate accumulation of the messenger RNA for GH by increasing gene transcription. The effects of the two hormones, although parallel, are independent.[27] The group that studied RNA synthesis also achieved a well-publicized breakthrough when they managed to make giant mice by inducing genes for GH isolated from rats to fuse functionally with the DNA of mouse ova. This produced mice that grew larger than normal.[28] The gene for GH was fused to that governing the liver protein metallothioneine-I, and the GH formed under the influence of the rat was made largely in the liver, the normal site of metallothioneine production. The amount of hormone produced was small, but the somatic effect was probably amplified because it was produced in the liver, where it had maximal concentration near the hepatic cells which produce somatostatin. Thus, although production of a foreign species of GH was achieved, the mechanisms of control and the site of production were not normal. The experiment represents a step toward reproducing the normal pattern with a foreign protein but is not yet there. We will have to wait a while before we can make pygmies into normal-sized people—if, indeed, we want to do so. The authors suggest, however, that the artificial gigantism thus produced might have economic utility in making animals raised for meat grow more rapidly and economically.] ◀

38–8 **Abnormalities of Growth Hormone Release in Response to Human Pancreatic Growth Hormone Releasing Factor (GRF[1-44]) in Acromegaly and Hypopituitarism.** Human pancreatic GH releasing factor (GRF[1-44]) is the parent molecule of several peptides recently extracted from pancreatic tumors associated with acromegaly. S. M. Wood, J. L. C. Ch'ng, E. F. Adams, J. D. Webster, G. F. Joplin, K. Mashiter, and S. R. Bloom (Hammersmith Hosp., London) investigated the effects of GRF(1-44) on GH release in 11 healthy male volunteers and in 8 patients with hypopituitarism and 6 with acromegaly. The 3 men and 3 women, aged 28–65, with acromegaly had an enlarged pituitary fossa on roentgenographic examination; computed tomography showed 3 of these patients to have a partially empty sella. The 6 men and 2 women, aged 26–63, with hypopituitarism had impaired GH responses to insulin-induced hypoglycemia, but other anterior pituitary dysfunction was variable. Hypothalamic-pitutary function was assessed as for the patients with acromegaly. No blood was sampled for 30 minutes after an intravenous catheter was placed; basal blood samples were then taken during the subsequent 45 minutes. A bolus intravenous injection of 100 μg of GRF(1-44) was then given over 30 seconds, and blood samples were taken 12 times within 2 hours.

Figure 38–2 illustrates the variability in the normal response of GH to 100 μg of GRF(1-44). In all 11 normal subjects, onset of the response was rapid, and there was a measurable rise in concentration within 5 minutes of injection of GRF(1-44). The peak value was reached between 12 and 50 minutes; it occurred in 9 subjects by 30 minutes. The mean GH concentrations had returned almost to basal values within 2 hours. Pulse rate and blood pressure were unaffected; the only mild side effect was warmth of the face in 1 subject.

Patients with pituitary adenomas secreting GH fell into two groups

(38–8) Br. Med. J. 286:1687–1691, May 28, 1983.

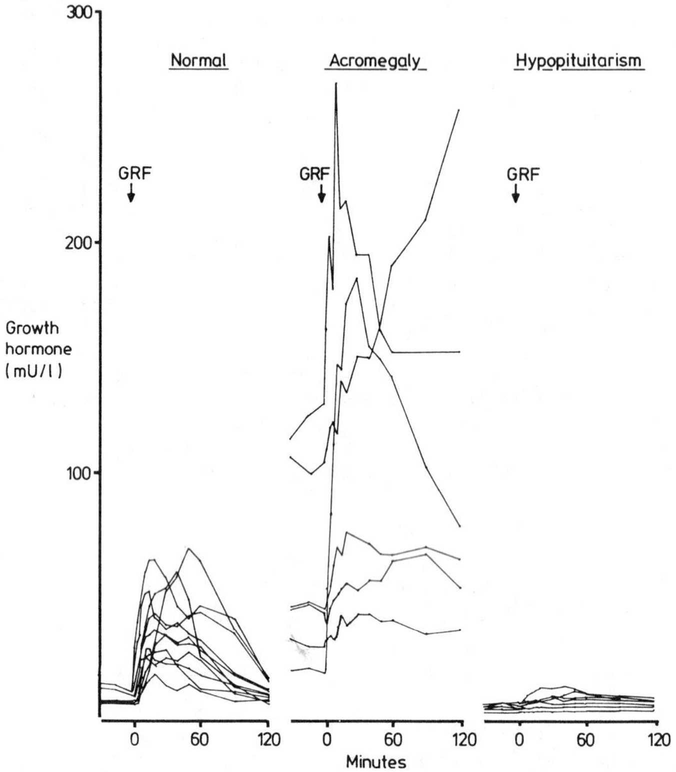

Fig 38–2.—Growth hormone values in response to GRF(1-44), 100 μg given intravenously at time zero, in 11 normal volunteers, 6 patients with acromegaly, and 8 patients with hypopituitarism. (Courtesy of Wood, S.M., et al.: Br. Med. J. 286:1687–1691, May 28, 1983.)

as regards response to GRF(1-44). One group had an absolute rise in GH values within the same range as normal subjects and exhibited at least a 20% suppression of GH in response to oral glucose ingestion. The other group had a large rise in GH values in response to GRF(1-44) and showed only a small suppression or a paradoxical rise in GH concentrations in response to glucose. A more active disease seemed to be suggested by an exaggerated response.

In patients with hypopituitarism, GRF(1-44) was at least as potent in releasing GH as insulin-induced hypoglycemia. The response to GRF was of more rapid onset, providing the basis for a shorter stimulation test.

Avoidance of the dangers of hypoglycemia and the lack of side effects of GRF(1-44) favor strongly the use of this peptide instead of insulin as a routine GH stimulation test.

▶ [This article presents further information about the response of human subjects to GH-releasing material. The preparation tested here is not quite the same as that used in the previous abstract, since that material consisted of a 40–amino acid polypeptide whereas this one is a 44–amino acid peptide. The two materials are, however, quite similar, so probably the clinical results reported by this group in their early calibration of GHRF as a clinical test modality will foreshadow what can be expected with other slightly smaller preparations. Further information concerning the 40-residue preparation in patients with hypopituitarism is reported later in this section.

The clinician will naturally be interested in substances that inhibit the secretion of GH as well as in those that stimulate it. Insulin-like growth factors (IGFs) can inhibit GH secretion, a finding that is not totally unexpected. IGFs are closely related or identical to the somatomedins which are peripheral effectors of GH. When IGFs were injected intracerebrally into rats, both plasma GH levels and food intake were suppressed. Insulin and saline had no such effect.[29] This effect of IGF is therefore similar to that for somatomedin and separate from the effects of insulin itself.] ◀

38–9 **Size and Erosive Features of the Sella Turcica in Acromegaly as Predictors of Therapeutic Response to Supervoltage Irradiation.** Robert F. Dons, Kenneth G. Rieth, Phillip Gorden, and Jesse Roth (Nat'l. Inst. of Health) compared the results of supervoltage radiation therapy in patients with acromegaly with the volume of the sella turcica and its Hardy classification at the time of treatment. Sixty-two patients received conventional supervoltage irradiation to the pituitary in 1964–1981. Fifty-seven patients had follow-up GH levels estimated prospectively for up to 16 years after treatment.

Growth hormone levels were reduced by 50% at 2 years and by 77% after 5–10 years. About 80% of patients had levels of 10 ng/ml or below by 10 years after treatment. A positive linear relationship was found between basal GH levels and sellar volume and also between GH levels and the sella grade according to the classification system developed by Hardy and Somma. The percentage drop in GH level over time was not related to sellar grade.

Plasma GH levels in patients with acromegaly correlate with the mass of the pituitary tumor, but the response to pituitary irradiation is not related to sellar grade. Further study of specific clinical parameters may in time provide a more objective guide to the selection of treatment in acromegaly. Computed tomographic scanning of the sella with current-generation scanners may make it possible to measure the size of pituitary adenomas directly rather than merely approximating their size by indirect measurement methods.

▶ [The usual method of treating acromegaly is by surgical removal of the pituitary tumor. The slow response after irradiation and the belief that microsurgery can cure the disease whereas irradiation merely controls it has tended to downgrade the advantages of radiation in the minds of many clinicians. Yet it is unusual for the secretory pattern of GH to be restored entirely to normal after microsurgery for acromegaly, although the mean serum level of GH was reduced 71% in a group of 34 patients, 14 of whom had concomitant hyperprolactinemia. The percentage reduction of serum GH was the same regardless of the initial GH concentration, so only those patients starting with moderate GH elevations achieved normal levels after surgery. Of 15 patients whose GH levels were normalized by surgery, only four had normal postoperative GH responses to TRH and DOPA.[30] The probability of a successful result after microsurgery can thus be predicted by the original concentration of GH, but the change of GH concentration during the early hours after operation may also be helpful. When GH levels fall to 5 ng/ml or less within 3 hours after operation, the long-term prognosis is usually good.[31]

Hyperprolactinemia has been reported in patients with acromegaly, as mentioned in the previous paragraph. This abnormality seems to be inherent in the disease rather than a result of therapy. In some patients, however, treatment augments the prolactin level. After irradiation, for example, the serum prolactin level rose in all 12 patients treated by Clark and colleagues, and it reached the clinical hyperprolacti-

---

(38–9) Am. J. Med. 74:69–72, January 1983.

nemic range in 5. Probably both the tumor and the treatment increase prolactin secretion by interfering with secretion of dopamine, the prolactin inhibiting factor.[32]

It is generally agreed that the major physiologic effects of hypersecretion of GH are mediated by increased production of somatomedin. When patients with acromegaly are treated with bromocriptine, about a third have no clinical improvement, only a slight decline in serum somatomedin C and usually no change of serum GH levels. When clinical improvement occurs, the serum somatomedin C level falls by 30% or more, but in many such patients the GH level is not reduced. Thus there is a closer correlation between changes of the clinical condition and somatomedin C than with the GH level.[33]] ◀

38–10 **Effects of Human Pancreatic Tumor Growth Hormone Releasing Factor on Growth Hormone and Somatomedin C Levels in Patients With Idiopathic Growth Hormone Deficiency.** The effects of human pancreatic tumor growth hormone releasing factor (hpGRF-40) administration in 11 patients with idiopathic GH deficiency and 1 with GH deficiency presumably resulting from hypothalamic infiltration by Hand-Schüller-Christian disease are reported by João L. C. Borges, Robert M. Blizzard, Marie C. Gelato, Richard Furlanetto, Alan D. Rogol, William S. Evans, Mary Lee Vance, Donald L. Kaiser, Robert M. MacLeod, George R. Merriam, D. Lynn Loriaux, Joachim Spiess, Jean Rivier, Wylie Vale, and Michael O. Thorner. Subjects were tested on 2 consecutive days; on the first day hpGRF-40 (10 μg/kg) was administered intravenously, and on the second day a combined test of pituitary function was performed by intravenous administration of soluble insulin, thyrotropin-releasing hormone, and gonadotropin releasing hormone. Blood samples were drawn for measurement of serum GH every 15 minutes between 8 and 10 A.M. and every ½ hour thereafter until 11:30. Serum concentrations of GH, PRL, cortisol, TSH, LH, thyroxine, testosterone (men), and estradiol (women) were measured by standard radioimmunoassays; triiodothyronine resin uptake was also determined.

Administration of hpGRF-40 caused an increase in serum GH concentrations in all 6 normal subjects. Eight of the 12 GH-deficient patients showed no significant response; in the other 4, serum GH concentrations increased to more than 1.5 ng/ml. Mean serum somatomedin C concentrations in patients with idiopathic GH deficiency before and 24 hours after 10 μg of hpGRF-40 per kg were 0.19 and 0.23 U/ml, respectively.

In patient 2, who had isolated GH deficiency, with a minimal GH response to hpGRF-40 and hypoglycemia, serum GH concentrations increased to a peak of 2.0 ng/ml after 5 days of repetitive hpGRF-40 administration (Fig 38–3), and serum somatomedin C concentrations rose (Fig 38–4).

Idiopathic GH deficiency is characterized by short stature, growth failure, and GH deficiency, which is either isolated or accompanied by multiple anterior pituitary hormone deficits and may well be due to hypothalamic dysfunction. Since the patients in the study group grew at normal or accelerated rates in response to exogenous GH administration, their poor growth must have been the result of GH deficiency.

(38–10) Lancet 2:119–124, July 16, 1983.

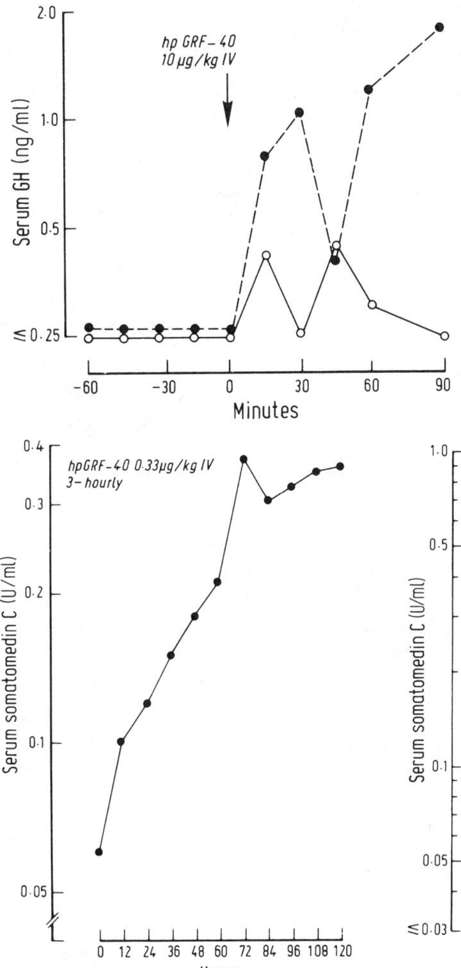

Fig 38–3 (top).—Serum GH concentrations in Patient 2 with isolated GH deficiency in response to hpGRF-40 before *(open circles)* and after *(solid circles)* 5 days of hpGRF-40 (0.33 µg/kg) administration every 3 hours for 5 days.

Fig 38–4 (bottom).—Serum somatomedin concentrations in Patient 2 with isolated GH deficiency during 5 days of treatment with hpGRF-40. Logarithmic scale. (Courtesy of Borges, J.L.C., et al.: Lancet 2:119–124, July 16, 1983.)

The deficiency may have been caused either by a somatotroph abnormality, which resulted in reduced or abnormal synthesis or release of GH or both, or by abnormal hypothalamic regulation of the somatotroph by gonadotropin releasing hormone or somatostatin.

▶ [The dose of GHRF used in this study was about 10 times that recommended as a test dose in earlier studies described in this section (abstract 38–7). The high dose led to flushing but had no other unpleasant effects. Other authors in Britain, using a dose of 200 µg of synthetic 40–amino acid GHRF, tested 4 patients with hypothalamic tumors and deficient secretion of GH who responded to 200 µg of the test substance with a clear rise of the circulating level of GH.[34] Thus the use of GHRF permits the clinician to recognize a group of patients with deficient secretion of GH because of hypothalamic rather than pituitary disease. Measurements of the response of somatomedin may prove to be more reliable than that of GH; but since some patients appear to secrete GH but not to produce somatomedin, it is probably useful to measure both hormones. One might also explore the response to multiple doses of GHRF, which may be more sensitive as a test than the response to a single dose. Ultimately, it may prove possible to identify patients with solitary GH deficiency whose growth can be restored by chronic administration of GHRF rather than GH. This would be especially important in the group of patients whose initial response to exogenous GH is rapidly terminated by development of blocking antibodies to the hormone.] ◀

38–11 **Human Growth Hormone Treatment of Children With Growth Failure and Normal Growth Hormone Levels by Immunoassay: Lack of Correlation With Somatomedin Generation.** Children with growth failure and normal GH responses to stimulation testing but with low somatomedin levels are being increasingly recognized. Leslie P. Plotnick, Quentin L. Van Meter, and A. Avinoam Kowarski (Baltimore) studied 16 such children to determine the value of somatomedin generation in predicting growth responses to exogenous human GH (hGH). All but 1 of the patients were boys. Age range was 3–17 years. All but 2 were prepubertal, and all were more than 2 SD below the mean height for their age. Most patients had growth velocities at or below the third percentile for chronologic age. Patients who had an increase in somatomedin C after a trial of 3 units of hGH given intramuscularly twice daily for 5 days were placed on 0.07–0.15 units/kg on alternate days. Two patients received 0.18 units/kg on alternate days.

All patients had an increase in somatomedin C level to normal range after receiving exogenous hGH. Mean growth velocity increased significantly from 3.6 to 8.6 cm/year after 4 months of treatment and to 7.1 cm/year at 12 months; however, the short-term somatomedin response to hGH did not predict the growth response at 8 months. There was no correlation between the responses to somatomedin and growth.

Variable growth responses to hGH therapy are evident in children with low somatomedin levels but normal GH responses to stimulation testing. The growth response is not predicted by the short-term increase in serum somatomedin level after injection of hGH. Better means of predicting the growth response are needed to properly select patients who will potentially benefit from hGH treatment.

▶ [The syndrome of growth deficiency in pygmies has been recognized as a reflection of failure to produce somatomedin C (also called insulin-like growth factor [IGF] I), although they produce normal amounts of IGF II. Two dwarfed adult patients were described recently in the United States who also had failure to respond to GH by producing somatomedin C. Like pygmies, these patients had normal serum levels of IGF II.[35]

Most physicians using GH in the treatment of dwarfism give it intramuscularly. There is no loss of activity, and the patients seem to tolerate treatment better if the hormone is given subcutaneously.[36]] ◀

38–12 **Five Cases of Somatostatinoma: Clinical Heterogeneity and Diagnostic Usefulness of Basal and Tolbutamide-Induced Hypersomatostatinemia.** Daniël Pipeleers, Etienne Couturier, Willy

(38–11) Pediatrics 71:324–327, March 1983.
(38–12) J. Clin. Endocrinol. Metab. 56:1236–1242, June 1983.

Gepts, Jean Reynders, and Guido Somers (Brussels) report data on 5 cases of somatostatinoma, 4 located primarily in the pancreas and 1 in the duodenum. The clinical features were quite heterogeneous. Two patients had severe hypoglycemic attacks; 2 had obstructive jaundice; and 1 had gallstones, steatorrhea, and diabetes. Somatostatin-immunoreactive cells were the chief cell type seen on immunocytochemical study of 2 of the 4 evaluable tumors. All the tumors evaluated contained more than 1 pancreatic hormone, but somatostatin immunoreactivity was most prominent. The 2 metastases that were examined contained only somatostatin activity. Three patients had increased basal plasma somatostatin levels; the 2 with normal levels had increases on intravenous tolbutamide testing. The level of peripheral insulin did not increase after tolbutamide injection in 1 patient.

The clinical presentation of somatostatinoma was quite variable in these cases, but all patients had increased basal or tolbutamide-induced somatostatin levels or both. Estimates of plasma somatostatin immunoreactivity might lead to the more frequent detection of this endocrine tumor. Increased peripheral somatostatin levels may be found more often in the presence of hepatic metastases. The absence of decreased levels of plasma insulin, glucagon, or pancreatic polypeptide does not rule out a pancreatic somatostatinoma. The circulating levels of these hormones are dependent not only on their release from normal pancreatic tissue and possible inhibition by tumoral somatostatin, but also on their potential tumoral origin, in concert with somatostatin.

► [It may seem inappropriate to place a discussion of somatostatinoma of the pancreas in the pituitary portion of this section; but since somatostatin was originally described in relation to the pituitary and hypothalamus, I feel it is about as appropriate here as anywhere. The importance of this article is the fact that 4 of these 5 patients failed to present the "typical" clinical picture of somatostatinoma (diabetes mellitus, cholelithiasis, and steatorrhea). In the initial evaluation, 2 were considered to have insulinomas and the other 2 to have nonendocrine pancreatic islet cell tumors. The article discusses mechanisms that might explain this clinical heterogeneity and emphasizes the usefulness of peripheral somatostatin levels in diagnosis. Tolbutamide-induced hypersecretion of somatostatin is especially useful diagnostically. The polymorphic nature of somatostatinomas was also mentioned by Stacpoole and colleagues,[37] who reported 2 patients, 1 with symptoms dominated by diarrhea and flushing and the other quite asymptomatic.] ◄

38–13 **Effect of Synthetic Ovine Corticotropin-Releasing Factor: Dose Response of Plasma Adrenocorticotropin and Cortisol.** To establish the dose-response relationship between synthetic ovine corticotropin-releasing factor (CRF) and the release of pituitary ACTH, David N. Orth, Richard V. Jackson, G. Stephen DeCherney, C. Rowan DeBold, A. Nancye Alexander, Donald P. Island, Jean Rivier, Catherine Rivier, Joachim Spiess, and Wylie Vale conducted a double-blind study on 29 healthy men, aged 20–46 years. Corticotropin-releasing factor was administered as an intravenous bolus, and ACTH was assessed by measuring concentrations of immunoreactive (IR)-ACTH and IR-cortisol in peripheral plasma. Doses of CRF ranged from 0.001 to 30 μg/kg body weight. The threshold dose appeared to

(38–13) J. Clin. Invest. 71:587–595, March 1983.

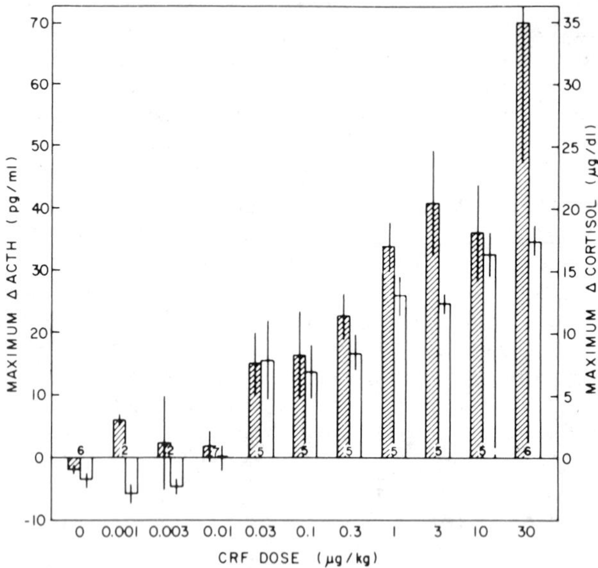

Fig 38–5.—Maximum changes in concentrations of plasma immunoreactive ACTH *(hatched bars)* and immunoreactive-cortisol *(open bars)* after intravenous administration of synthetic ovine CRF to normal male volunteers. Maximum change in concentrations (either decrement or increment, whichever was greater) during 120 minutes after CRF injection from concentration measured at zero time, immediately before CRF injection, was calculated for each subject. Height of bar represents mean of individual values and bracket represents SEM. Number of subjects in each group is indicated at base of each pair of bars. (Courtesy of Orth, D.N., et al.: J. Clin. Invest. 71:587–595, March 1983 by copyright of the American Society for Clinical Investigation.)

be 0.01–0.03 μg/kg. As the dose of CRF was increased by threefold increments, there were progressive increases in the plasma IR-ACTH and IR-cortisol concentrations, expressed either as a function of time after injection or of maximum deviation from the zero minute basal value (Fig 38–5).

The concentrations of IR-ACTH rose as early as 2 minutes after CRF injection, reached peak values in 10–15 minutes, and declined slowly thereafter. The IR-cortisol concentrations rose at 10 minutes or later and reached peak levels in 30–60 minutes. At a dose of 30 μg/kg, neither IR-ACTH nor IR-cortisol fell from peak mean concentrations of 82 pg/ml and 23 μg/dl, respectively, indicating that CRF has a sustained effect on ACTH release, prolonged circulating plasma half-life, or both. There was little or no increase in concentrations of other anterior pituitary hormones. At doses of CRF of 1 μ/kg and higher, facial flushing, tachycardia, and, in some subjects, 15–29 mm Hg declines in systemic arterial blood pressure occurred.

In man, synthetic ovine CRF seems to be a potent and specific ACTH secretagogue. It appears to have a prolonged half-life in circulating plasma and a sustained stimulatory effect on ACTH secretion. Administered with proper precautions in view of the demonstrated vasomotor effect of higher doses, CRF promises to be a safe and useful investigative, diagnostic, and, possibly, therapeutic agent.

▶ [At the clinical level, the discovery of CRF has already proved itself useful. It is apparently a much safer method of testing the ability of the pituitary to release ACTH than the previous best method, insulin-induced hypoglycemia. The recent characterization of the nature of CRF (1983 YEAR BOOK) has also begun to bear fruit in physiologic and clinical studies. Corticotropin-releasing hormone itself causes a rise of blood glucose concentration when injected into the brains of rats. This effect occurs even when the pituitary and adrenal have been removed. Although discharge of adrenal medullary epinephrine plays a part in this effect, it is chiefly a result of discharge of catecholamines by the sympathetic nervous system. In this respect it differs from bombesin, TRF, or endorphins, whose effect is mediated largely or entirely by release of epinephrine from the adrenal medulla.[38] This intracerebral effect may be of physiologic importance, since CRF-like immunoreactivity can be demonstrated in the brain, especially the median emminence. Smaller amounts are also found in the frontal, parietal, occipital, and temporal areas of the cortex. The limbic system, basal ganglia, and brain stem contain much smaller amounts.[39]

The distribution of CRF in the brain is reminiscent of that of somatostatin, so it is, perhaps, not surprising that CRF-like immunoreactivity is also demonstrable in the vertebrate endocrine pancreas.[40]

The impact of surgery on pituitary function has elicited a good deal of interest during the past year. It has also raised several interesting questions; for example, How often does pituitary surgery cause hypopituitarism? In a series of 11 patients with large nonfunctioning pituitary adenomas, 8 had hypopituitarism preoperatively and 5 had partial recovery after operation. All of the 3 with normal function preoperatively retained normal function after surgery.[41] Thus surgery is more likely to restore function than to reduce it further. Another question is, How often do pituitary adenomas recur after transcranial pituitary surgery? In a series of 289 pituitary adenomas operated upon by this technique, 13 (4.8%) histologically proved recurrences were demonstrated, and 6 more had computed tomographic scan or pneumoencephalographic evidence of recurrence, for a total recurrence rate of 7.4%. Most appeared within 10 years of the first operation, and the rest before 20 years. Two patients had frankly malignant tumors at the time of second operation. Postoperative radiation after surgical resection appears to reduce the recurrence rate.[42]] ◀

Chapter 38 References

1. Swartz J.D., et al.: High-resolution computed tomographic appearance of the intrasellar contents in women of childbearing age. *Radiology* 147:115–117, 1983.
2. Jung R.T., et al.: CT abnormalities of the pituitary in hyperprolactinaemic women with normal or equivocal sellae radiologically. *Br. Med. J.* 285:1078–1081, 1982.
3. Newton D.R., et al.: Economic impact of CT scanning on the evaluation of pituitary adenomas. *American Journal of Radiology* 140:573–576, 1983.
4. Murdoch G.H., et al.: Epidermal growth factor rapidly stimulates prolactin gene transcription. *Nature* 300:192–194, 1982.
5. Hulting A.-L., et al.: Oral contraceptive steroids do not promote the development of growth of prolactinomas. *Contraception* 27:69–73, 1983.
6. Shy K.K., et al.: Oral contraceptive use and the occurrence of pituitary prolactinoma. *JAMA* 249:2204–2207, 1983.
7. Nagy E., et al.: Regulation of immunity in rats by lactogenic and growth hormones. *Acta Endocrinol.* 102:351–357, 1983.
8. Brismar K.: Prolactin secretion in the empty sella syndrome in prolactinomas and in acromegaly. *Acta Med. Scand.* 209:397–405, 1981.
9. Futterweit W.: Galactorrhea, amenorrhea, hyperprolactinemia and pseudotumor cerebri in a patient with primary empty sella syndrome: case report with review of the literature. *M. Sinai J. Med. (NY)* 49:514–518, 1982.

10. Stacpoole P.W., et al.: Primary empty sella, hyperprolactinemia and isolated ACTH deficiency after postpartum hemorrhage. *Am. J. Med.* 74:905–908, 1983.
11. Ferrari C., et al.: Functional characterization of hypothalamic hyperprolactinemia. *J. Clin. Endocrinol. Metab.* 55:897–901, 1982.
12. Ben-David M., Schenker J.G.; Transient hyperprolactinemia: a correctable cause of idiopathic female infertility. *J. Clin. Endocrinol. Metab.* 57:442–444, 1983.
13. Kahn S.E., Miller J.L.: Rapid resolution of visual field defects and reduction in macroprolactinoma size with bromocriptine therapy: a case report. *S. Afr. Med. J.* 62:696–699, 1982.
14. de Bernal M., de Villamizar M.: Restoration of ovarian function by low nocturnal single daily doses of bromocriptine in patients with the galactorrhea-amenorrhea syndrome. *Fertil. Steril.* 37:392–396, 1982.
15. Franks S., et al.: Effectiveness of pergolide mesyulate in long term treatment of hyperprolactinemia. *Br. Med. J.* 286:1177–1179, 1983.
16. Tindall G.T., et al.: Human prolactin-producing adenomas and bromocriptine: a histological, immunocytochemical, ultrastructural and morphometric study. *J. Clin. Endocrinol. Metab.* 55:1178–1183, 1982.
17. Barbarino A., et al.: Dopaminergic mechanisms regulating prolactin secretion in patients with prolactin-secreting pituitary adenoma: long-term studies after selective transsphenoidal surgery. *Metabolism* 31:1100, 1982.
18. Salmi J., et al.: Recurrence of chromophobe pituitary adenomas after operation and postoperative radiotherapy. *Acta Neurol. Scand.* 66:681–689, 1982.
19. Serri O., et al.: Recurrence of hyperprolactinemia after selective transsphenoidal adenomectomy in women with prolactinoma. *N. Engl. J. Med.* 309:280–283, 1983.
20. Breidahl H.D., et al.: Failure of bromocriptine to maintain reduction in size of a macroprolactinoma. *Br. Med. J.* 287:451–452, 1983.
21. L'Hermite M., Debusschere P.: Potent 48 hours inhibition of prolactin secretion by pergolide in hyperprolactinaemic women. *Acta Endocrinol. (Copenh.)* 101:481–483, 1982.
22. Crosignani P.G., et al.: Treatment of hyperprolactinemic states with different drugs: a study with bromocriptine, metergoline and lisuride. *Fertil. Steril.* 37:61–67, 1982.
23. Guillemin R., Brazeau P., Bohlen P., et al.: Growth hormone-releasing factor from a human pancreatic tumor that caused acromegaly. *Science* 281:585–587, 1982.
24. Thorner M.O., Perryman R.L., Cronin M.J., et al.: Somatotroph hyperplasia: successful treatment of acromegaly by removal of a pancreatic islet tumor secreting a growth hormone-releasing factor. *J. Clin. Invest.* 70:965–977, 1982.
25. Bloch B., Brazeau P., Ling N., et al.: Immunohistochemical detection of growth hormone-releasing factor in brain. *Nature* 301:607–608, 1983.
26. Brazeau P., Ling N., Bohlen P., et al.: Growth hormone releasing factor, somatocrinin, releases pituitary growth hormone in vitro. *Proc. Natl. Acad. Sci. USA* 79:7909–7913, 1982.
27. Evans R.M., Birnberg N.C., Rosenfeld M.G.: Glucocorticoid and thyroid hormones transcriptionally regulate growth hormone gene expression. *Proc. Natl. Acad. Sci. USA* 79:7659–7663, 1982.
28. Palmiter R.D., Brinster R.L., Hammer R.E., et al.: Dramatic growth of mice that develop from eggs microinjected with metallothionein-growth hormone fusion genes. *Nature* 300:611–615, 1982.

29. Tannenbaum G.S., Guyda H.J., Posner B.I.: Insulin-like growth factors: a role in growth hormone negative feedback and body weight regulation via brain. *Science* 220:77–79, 1983.
30. Hulting A.-L., Werner S., Wersäll J., et al.: Normal growth hormone secretion is rare after microsurgical normalization of growth hormone levels in acromegaly. *Acta Med. Scand.* 212:401–405, 1982.
31. Bynke O., Karlberg B.E., Kagedal B., et al.: Early post-operative growth hormone levels predict the result of transsphenoidal tumor removal in acromegaly. *Acta Endocrinol. (Copenh.)* 103:158–162, 1983.
32. Clark A.J.L., Mashiter K., Goolden A.W., et al.: Hyperprolactinaemia after external irradiation for acromegaly. *Clin. Endocrinol.* 17:291–295, 1982.
33. Wass J.A.H., Clemmons D.R., Underwood L.E., et al.: Changes in circulating somatomedin-C levels in bromocriptine-treated acromegaly. *Clin. Endocrinol.* 17:369–377, 1982.
34. Grossman A., Savage M.O., Wass J.A.H., et al.: Growth-hormone-releasing factor in growth hormone deficiency: demonstration of a hypothalamic defect in growth hormone release. *Lancet* 2:137–138, 1983.
35. Merimee T.J., Zapf J., Froesch E.R., Insulin-like growth factors (IGFs) in pygmies and subjects with the pygmy trait: characterization of the metabolic actions of IGF I and IGF II in man. *J. Clin. Endocrinol. Metab.* 55:1081–1088, 1982.
36. Russo L., Moore W.V.: A comparison of subcutaneous and intramuscular administration of human growth hormone in the therapy of growth hormone deficiency. *J. Clin. Endocrinol. Metab.* 55:1003–1006, 1982.
37. Stacpoole P.W., Kasselberg A.G., Berelowitz M., et al.: Somatostatinoma syndrome: does a clinical entity exist? *Acta Endocrinol. (Copenh.)* 102:80–87, 1983.
38. Brown M.R., Fischer L.A., Speiss J., et al.: Corticotropin-releasing factor: actions on the sympathetic nervous system and metabolism. *Endocrinology* 111:928–921, 1982.
39. Côté J., Lefèvre G., Labrie F., et al.: Distribution of corticotropin-releasing factor in ovine brain determined by radioimmunoassay. *Regul. Pept.* 5:189–195, 1983.
40. Petrusz P., Merchenthaler I., Maderdrut J.L., et al.: Corticotropin-releasing factor (CRF)-like immunoreactivity in the vertebrate endocrine pancreas. *Proc. Natl. Acad. Sci. USA* 80:1721–1725, 1983.
41. Arafah B.M., Brodkey J.S., Manni A., et al.: Recovery of pituitary function following surgical removal of large nonfunctioning pituitary adenomas. *Clin. Endocrinol. (Oxf.)* 17:213–222, 1982.
42. Symon L., Logue V., Mohanty S.: Recurrence of pituitary adenoma after transcranial operation. *J. Neurol. Neurosurg. Psychiatry* 45:780–785, 1983.

39. Adrenal Glands

▶ [Improvements in diagnostic tests for adrenal function can take at least two forms: extension of the technology that permits expansion of diagnostic horizons and changes in the methods that simplify the tests for the patients. The discovery of corticotropin-releasing factor and the application of computed tomographic (CT) scanning of the pituitary are examples of new approaches which expand the basic approach to the diagnosis of adrenal and pituitary disease. These techniques have been discussed in chapter 38. A much simpler modification, which involves measuring cortisol in the saliva rather than the blood or urine, does not provide a new insight into function, but it is a good deal easier on the patient than multiple venipunctures. Cortisol concentrations in the saliva follow the pattern of plasma cortisol but reflect free rather than total cortisol, which is measured in the ordinary assays of plasma steroids. Thus they give information more pertinent to physiologic levels than does the usual plasma determination, and they do this on the basis of a body fluid which is easier to collect than blood or 24-hour urine specimens.[1] The contribution of CT scanning of the adrenal region is discussed in the next abstract.] ◀

39–1 **Computed Tomography in Adrenal Disease.** J. E. Adams, R. J. Johnson, D. Rickards, and I. Isherwood (Univ. of Manchester) report the computed tomography (CT) findings in 98 patients with suspected adrenal disease who were evaluated in 1977–1980. The 74 female and 24 male patients were aged 19 months to 77 years. Seventy-three patients were ultimately found to have an adrenal lesion. Sixty-six patients with adrenal disease had abnormal adrenal function. Four were studied for recurrence after removal of a functioning adrenal tumor. Seven patients had nonfunctioning adrenal tumors. Computed tomography scans were obtained with an EMI 5005 scanner using a 320 × 320 matrix. Patients received Gastrografin 30 minutes before scanning. Bowel paralysis was produced with hyoscine butylbromide or propantheline. In 52 patients sections through the adrenals were repeated after intravenous sodium iothalamate injection.

All but 4% of the adrenals were identified by CT. All but 1 of 39 mass lesions were correctly identified and localized. Adenomas were seen as well-defined round lesions in the suprarenal region. Failure to identify some adrenals and one adrenal tumor was due to a paucity of intraabdominal fat. The appearance of adrenal hyperplasia is shown in Figure 39–1. Residual adrenal tissue in a patient with post-adrenalectomy Cushing's syndrome is shown in Figure 39–2. The appearance of a pheochromocytoma is shown in Figure 39–3. Two ectopic abdominal pheochromocytomas were not identified. Several patients with adrenal carcinoma had obvious node involvement or hepatic metastases or both at initial CT examination. The patients without proved adrenal disease had normal CT findings.

Computed tomography is an accurate means of demonstrating normal adrenal glands and adrenals enlarged by tumor. A paucity of

(39–1) Clin. Radiol. 34:39–49, January 1983.

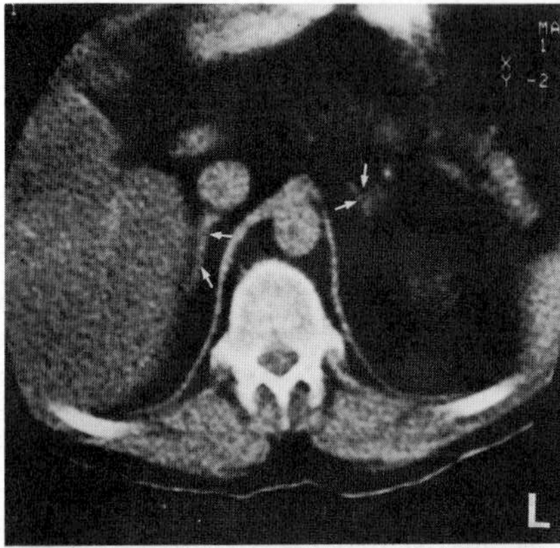

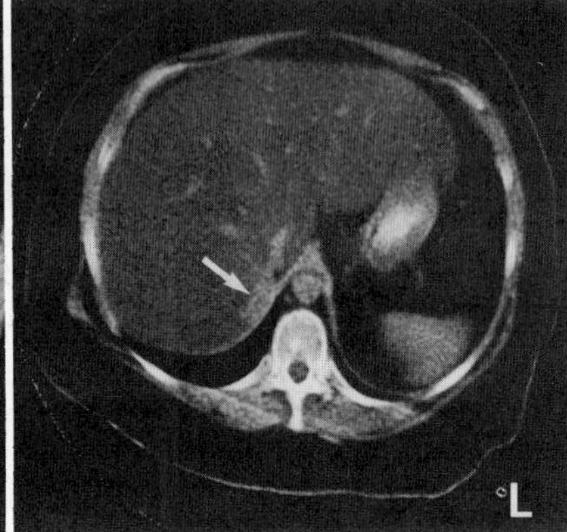

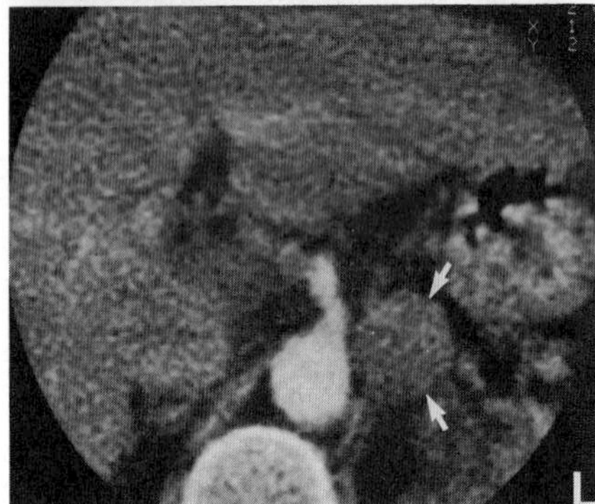

Fig 39–1 (above left).—Adrenal hyperplasia (Cushing's syndrome). The adrenals *(arrows)* are normal in size and shape and are well demonstrated because of an abundance of intraabdominal fat (L+0025, W0250).

Fig 39–2 (above).—Residual right adrenal tissue *(arrow)* in a patient with postadrenalectomy, recurrent, pituitary-dependent Cushing's syndrome. The liver is reduced in attenuation, indicating fatty infiltration (L+0025, W0250).

Fig 39–3 (left).—Left adrenal phaeochromocytoma *(arrows)* adjacent to the aorta (postcontrast). The tumor is round and smooth in outline homogeneous in density, and shows no enhancement, features indicative of a benign lesion (L+0040, W0400).

(Courtesy of Adams, J.E., et al.: Clin. Radiol. 34:39–49, January 1983.)

abdominal fat may limit the usefulness of CT in a few patients, usually children, but it is the best method of localizing adrenal tumors now available. Computed tomography distinguishes between adrenal hyperplasia and functioning adrenal tumors and between benign and malignant lesions with considerable certainty. Some hyperplastic adrenals, however, appear normal on CT, precluding its use in screening for biochemically unproved adrenal disease.

▶ [Most observers now feel that CT scanning of the adrenal is the most specific method for diagnosing adrenal tumors and is much superior to the functional tests which have been popular in the past. Of course, retroperitoneal gas studies should be totally rejected nowadays; and conventional tomographic studies are not of much use, either. For other purposes than the diagnosis of tumors, however, functional tests continue to be important. The next abstract discusses a modification of considerable practical value, both for its specificity and its convenience.] ◀

39–2 **Superiority of the Metyrapone Test Versus the High-Dose Dexamethasone Test in the Differential Diagnosis of Cushing's Syndrome.** Specific treatment directed at the cause of Cushing's syndrome is important because of the high mortality in untreated pa-

---

(39–2) Am. J. Med. 74:657–662, April 1983.

tients. Bruce H. Sindler, George T. Griffing, and James C. Melby (Boston Univ.) compared the serum 11-deoxycortisol response to metyrapone with the urinary free cortisol response to high-dose dexamethasone in distinguishing between the various causes of Cushing's syndrome. Studies were done in 14 patients with Cushing's disease, 10 with adrenocortical neoplasm, and 1 with ectopic ACTH syndrome associated with renal carcinoma. Seven patients with Cushing's disease had a pituitary tumor. All but 2 of those with adrenocortical neoplasia had carcinomas. Metyrapone was given orally in a dose of 750 mg every 4 hours for 6 doses. Dexamethasone was given orally in a dose of 1 mg, followed by 2 mg every 6 hours for 8 doses over a 2-day period.

Suppression of urinary free cortisol by dexamethasone was significantly greater in patients with Cushing's disease than in those with adrenocortical neoplasms; 7 of the former patients and 1 of the latter had a greater than 50% suppression. The patient with ectopic Cushing's syndrome also had more than 50% suppression of urinary cortisol. The diagnostic accuracy of the test in distinguishing Cushing's disease from adrenocortical neoplasm was 81%. All patients with Cushing's disease had a postmetyrapone 11-deoxycortisol level of more than 10 μg/dl, whereas all of those with adrenocortical neoplasia had a level below 10 μg/dl, as did the patient with ectopic Cushing's syndrome.

The 11-deoxycortisol response to metyrapone is more useful than the high-dose dexamethasone test in determining the cause of Cushing's syndrome. Also, in addition to being more accurate, the meytrapone test is more convenient than the high-dose dexamethasone test. Neither test appears to help in differentiating ectopic ACTH syndrome from Cushing's disease or adrenocortical neoplasm.

▶ [I have never been happy with the standard dexamethasone suppression test, which is clumsy, prolonged, and very often confusing. This form of the metyrapone test appears to be easier to use and may prove more accurate. However, it certainly needs further testing, and one patient with the ectopic ACTH syndrome does not provide enough experience to permit a statement about its usefulness in this disease.

One of the most useful diagnostic tools in distinguishing pituitary hyperadrenocorticism from that caused by tumors of either the adrenal cortex itself or some other source producing ectopic ACTH is measurement of the plasma ACTH concentration. Unfortunately, this level fluctuates widely during the day, so standardization of the method is essential. If plasma is drawn for ACTH determination between 9:00 and 9:30 AM, highly consistent results are reported. In seven patients with Cushing's disease caused by pituitary tumor, the plasma ACTH level ranged from 39 to 109 pg/ml. In 58 normal subjects, plasma drawn at the same time ranged from 9 to 24 pg/ml. Thus excellent discrimination was provided if plasma was obtained within this narrow time range.[2] The test was much less useful if less rigid time limits were observed.

Another type of test, suitable for detecting the early approach of autoimmune adrenocortical failure, is the demonstration of serum antibodies against the adrenal, which appears to provide strong evidence of the likelihood that Addison's disease will develop within the next few years.[3]

While we are discussing Addison's disease, I might mention an excellent review of the nature of cardiac failure in patients with adrenal insufficiency.[4] Seven patients were discussed, who had been under treatment for 10–41 years and were aged 59–87 years. Congestive heart failure was not related to treatment of adrenocortical insufficiency and was treated in the same way as other forms of failure, but with some caution because the patients tended to be fragile when diuresed too actively. The authors recommend that in these patients one should discontinue the salt supplement they use in treatment; but since I have not used sodium supplements for many years, I don't consider this a real change.

Ketoconazole, a useful antimycotic agent, blocks biosynthesis of adrenal corticosteroids by inhibiting the activity of enzymes dependent on cytochrome P_{450}. Patients receiving ketoconazole should therefore be watched for evidence of failure to produce adequate amounts of steroids of all types, including those of the adrenal cortex.[5]] ◀

39–3 **Cushing's Disease Treated by Total Adrenalectomy: Long-Term Observations of 43 Patients.** Many alternative treatments are advocated for Cushing's syndrome. William F. Kelly, Ian A. MacFarlane, Donald Longson, Derek Davies, and Howard Sutcliffe (Manchester, England) report data on 43 patients, among 56 with Cushing's disease, who were treated by bilateral adrenalectomy. Clinical and biochemical evidence of Cushing's disease was available. Histologic study showed diffuse bilateral hyperplasia or nodular hyperplasia. Preoperative observation was for at least 1 year. There were 2 early postoperative deaths, 1 due to pancreatitis and pneumonia and 1 to subphrenic abscess, pneumonia, and pulmonary embolus. Three patients were not cured and subsequently underwent pituitary irradiation.

Thirty-eight patients (88%) had lasting clinical remissions that were biochemically confirmed. Six (group A) had normal skin pigmentation, 21 (group B) developed increased pigmentation, and 11 (group C) developed increased pigmentation and further pituitary expansion (Nelson's syndrome). Five patients in group C had suprasellar extensions, 2 with visual field defects. Seven patients in this group underwent nine operative attempts to remove pituitary tumors, and 6 also received pituitary irradiation. The interval between adrenalectomy and detection of further expansion of the pituitary fossa ranged from 3 to 13 years.

As the primary abnormality in Cushing's disease does not occur in the adrenal, alternative treatments have been sought. Metyrapone can restore cortisol concentrations but has a number of undesirable side effects. Mitotane combined with pituitary irradiation is said to have brought about sustained remission in some patients.

In favor of total adrenalectomy is the prospect of rapid cure, against which must be weighed the immediate surgical morbidity, the need for replacement therapy, and the risks of later pituitary expansion. Pituitary operations have lower early morbidity and mortality, but they have a slightly lower cure rate and the risk of partial or total pituitary failure.

▶ [This is a very useful summary, but total adrenalectomy is no longer generally recommended as treatment for hyperadrenocorticism caused by hypersecretion of pituitary ACTH. Pituitary Cushing's syndrome is usually a result of a corticotropin-secreting microadenoma. This has resulted in general agreement that the first line of therapy should be transsphenoidal resection of the tumor. An informal survey of the results of such treatment[6] showed that the cure rate varied from an estimated 100% with no recurrences to 10% with 100% recurrences. In large clinics, which claimed to operate on more than 10 patients annually, the cure rate was about 70% and recurrences around 5%. Many clinics indicated that they had "not yet" seen recurrences, suggesting a proper attitude of conservatism. I was most struck, however, by the large number of eminent clinics that reported only 5 or fewer cases a year. It is hard

(39–3) Q. J. Med. 52:224–231, Spring 1983.

for me to see how such a small experience could lead to the best possible technical skill in treatment. It might be advantageous to set up regional centers where surgical and diagnostic experience could be accumulated. Advantageous, but impractical, since our method of distributing medical care makes such cooperative arrangements financially disadvantageous to the surgeons and physicians.

A major advantage of treating Cushing's disease by resection of the pituitary tumor is the frequency with which the pituitary remnant resumes normal function. In one series of 4 patients (2 each with macroadenomas and microadenomas) all returned to normal ACTH and steroid secretory patterns within a few months after surgery.[7]

For some years I have suspected that Cushing's disease associated with a pituitary corticotropin-secreting tumor might reflect the long-term effects of excessive secretion of hypothalamic corticotropin-releasing factor (CRF). My idea received no support whatever in a study presented at the May meetings of the Association of American Physicians, where Hollander and colleagues reported that the level of CRF in cerebrospinal fluid (CSF) was not increased in 3 patients with Cushing's disease as compared with 6 normal subjects. Indeed, the mean level was somewhat lower than normal. One might question whether CSF hormone levels are a good indicator of the concentrations in the blood bathing the pituitary, and one might wonder whether the stress of lumbar puncture affects the concentration of CRF in CSF, but these questions do not permit me to set aside this interesting and unexpected finding.[8]

The medical treatment of prolactinomas has been so successful that it has naturally produced continuing interest in the possibility of finding a medical treatment for Cushing's disease. The proposal by Krieger some years ago that cyproheptidine might control the disease was not generally accepted, both because only a small fraction of patients responded to this medication and because relapse occurred almost immediately after it was discontinued. Now, however, the same group has reported that at least one patient had a sustained remission lasting more than 3 years after cyproheptidine therapy.[9] While this is an encouraging result, it must be remembered that some patients with Cushing's disease have a spontaneous remission.

It is unusual for patients with Cushing's syndrome to become pregnant, and when they do, the results are not favorable. Twenty-six cases have been reported in the literature. Of these, 30% aborted spontaneously and 25% had premature delivery. Fetal loss was randomly distributed in all three trimesters. However, there were no congenital abnormalities in surviving babies. In the patient reported by Liu and others,[10] no treatment was offered for the mother's hyperadrenocorticism, but I feel it might have been justified to consider pituitary exploration after the end of the first trimester.] ◀

39–4 **Carcinoma of Adrenal Cortex Causing Primary Hyperaldosteronism: Case Report and Review of the Literature.** Adrenocortical carcinoma is a rare tumor; most patients with primary hyperaldosteronism have benign lesions. Peter H. Th. J. Slee, Aart Schaberg, and Peter Van Brummelen (Univ. Hosp., Leiden, The Netherlands) report data on a patient in whom primary hyperaldosteronism was the initial manifestation of adrenocortical carcinoma.

Man, 41, with insulin-dependent diabetes, developed hypokalemia and subsequently polyuria despite adequate diabetic control. Blood pressure was 160/110 mm Hg. Serum potassium level was 2.6 mmole/L and urinary potassium excretion was above 80 mmole/L daily. Metabolic alkalosis was identified. Blood pressure and serum potassium level became normal when spironolactone was given in a daily dose of 100 mg. Further studies 3 years later revealed a tender mass in the left upper abdomen, which on arteriography was seen to be hypovascular. Ultrasonography showed a solid mass measuring 10 × 7 × 5 cm. Plasma renin activity was very low during free sodium intake and after a week of sodium restriction. Plasma aldosterone level was elevated and increased further on ambulation. Insulin requirements increased, and

(39–4) Cancer 51:2341–2345, June 15, 1983.

the patient had increasing pain in the lumbar region. A large left suprarenal tumor involving the tail of the pancreas was removed along with the kidney and spleen and was found to be an adrenocortical carcinoma with fairly numerous mitoses and moderate nuclear polymorphism. Blood pressure and serum potassium level were normal after operation, as was plasma renin activity. Subphrenic abscess necessitated a second laparotomy. Subsequently, liver metastases were diagnosed, and the patient died after failing to respond to treatment with 1,1-dichloro-2-(O-chlorophenyl)-2-(p-chlorophenyl)-ethane.

This patient fulfilled all criteria for primary aldosteronism, and this was the only endocrine manifestation of the adrenocortical carcinoma. The plasma cortisol level was normal, and there was no excess urinary excretion of any steroid. So-called "hybrid" cells were present in the tumor, and these may be characteristic of aldosterone-producing tumors. The tumor also contained cells that resembled zona fasciculata cells and cells of the zona glomerulosa type.

▶ [Increased aldosterone secretion is quite common in adrenocortical carcinomas in which the major symptom complex is that of Cushing's syndrome, but isolated hyperaldosteronism is very rare in carcinoma. Nevertheless, two other patients with this disease pattern have been reported recently from Paris.[11] Although aldosteromas are usually discussed in Dr. Epstein's section of the YEAR BOOK, I included this case in the endocrine section because of its malignant character. It also illustrates the risk of treating aldosteroma with spironolactone; but the danger of overlooking malignancy in this disease is certainly less than the risk of the operation, which is low.] ◀

39–5 **An ACTH-Secreting Pituitary Tumor Arising in a Patient With Congenital Adrenal Hyperplasia.** Pituitary tumors are known to develop when there is failure of a target endocrine gland. P. M. Horrocks, S. Franks, A. D. Hockley, E. B. Rolfe, Susan Van Noorden, and D. R. London report the case of a patient with congenital adrenal hyperplasia in whom an ACTH-secreting pituitary tumor developed, which is a previously unreported association. The feedback tumor did not respond to conventional doses of steroids.

Woman, 46, had undergone laparotomy at age 11 because of an ambiguous sexual phenotype, and was found to have a uterus and ovaries. Cyclic estrogens were given at age 23. At age 32, the patient was seen with amenorrhea, hirsutism, and infertility; congenital adrenal hyperplasia was diagnosed. She menstruated while receiving dexamethasone but remained infertile despite clomiphene therapy. Dexamethasone was continued, most recently in daily doses of 0.25–0.5 mg. Severe frontal headache, vomiting, and amenorrhea developed, followed by thirst and polyuria that lasted 3 months. An abnormal pituitary fossa and an elevated serum PRL level were found. Computed tomography (CT) showed a pituitary tumor with suprasellar extension. The serum PRL level fell on bromocriptine therapy, but the plasma ACTH concentration remained elevated at 271–314 ng/L. A year later, the patient presented with blurred vision in the left eye and diplopia; further extension of the pituitary tumor was evident on CT. A basophil adenoma was removed, and a repeat CT scan showed improvement.

An eluate from the tumor contained high levels of ACTH as well as β-endorphin-like immunoreactivity, but no PRL. The plasma ACTH concentration during the day is compared with that of other patients with congenital adrenal hyperplasia in Figure 39–4. Immunocytochemical study of the pa-

---

(39–5) Clin. Endocrinol. (Oxf.) 17:457–468, November 1982.

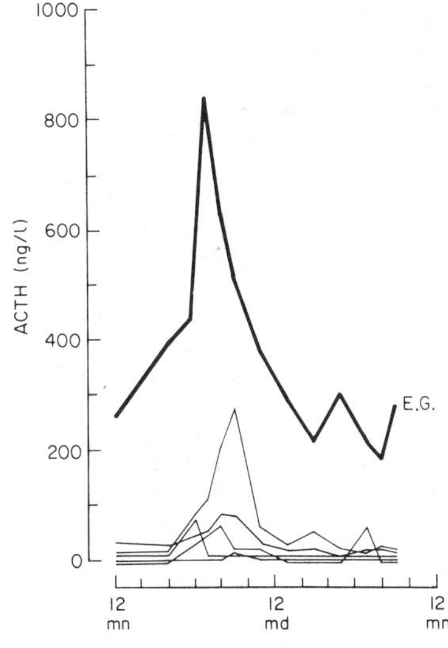

Fig 39–4.—Comparison of 24-hour ACTH profiles in patient *(E.G.)* and in 5 other patients who had congenital adrenal hyperplasia but did not have pituitary tumors. All 6 patients received 0.75 mg of dexamethasone daily. (Courtesy of Horrocks, P.M., et al.: Clin. Endocrinol. (Oxf.) 17:457–468, November 1982.

tient's tumor showed positive staining with antisera to ACTH and β-endorphin. Preabsorption of the antibody to ACTH prevented the positive staining.

This patient had both congenital adrenal hyperplasia and an ACTH-secreting pituitary tumor, which apparently was an autonomous feedback tumor. Craniotomy cured the local complications of the tumor but did not produce a biochemical cure. The possibility of this complication is another reason to obtain good control in patients with congenital adrenal hyperplasia.

▶ [The patient probably suffered from a 21-hydroxylase defect, since the level of urinary pregnanetriol was greatly elevated, but more specific studies were not reported. This patient is unusual in modern practice because one would not expect a period of 32 years to have elapsed before appropriate treatment was begun. Would the tumor have been prevented if corticosteroids had been administered earlier? One never could be sure; but this type of tumor is not a common complication of congenital adrenal hyperplasia. One must also wonder whether the administration of estrogens contributed to the development of the tumor. Since the tumor did not contain prolactin, the high concentration of that hormone in the serum (about 3 times normal) may have reflected interference by the tumor with normal hypothalamic constraints on prolactin secretion.

The secretion of aldosterone and associated precursor steroids in patients with congenital adrenal hyperplasia follows different patterns according to the type of defect. In patients with the 21-hydroxylase defect, levels of aldosterone and 18-hydroxycorticosterone are elevated while the 18-hydroxydeoxycorticosterone concentration is normal. In the presence of the 17-α-hydroxylase defect the 18-hydroxylated compounds are elevated and aldosterone is below normal. The 11-β-hydroxylase defect is associated with depressed levels of all three steroids.[12] The enzyme 3-β-hydroxysteroid dehydrogenase is required for aldosterone biosynthesis, so one would expect a defect to interfere with production of that hormone; but this does not occur, because the enzyme in the zona glomerulosa, where aldosterone is synthesized, is under different genetic control from that of the zonae fasciculata and reticularis, where the corticosteroids and androgens are synthesized. Although the gonads lack the enzyme in these patients, enough activity is present in peripheral tissues to maintain normal conversion of the androgen precursor, dehydroepiandrosterone, to testosterone and androstenedione.[13]

Deficiency of 17,20-desmolase, the enzymes responsible for cleaving the side chain from 17-hydroxypregnenolone or 17-hydroxyprogesterone to produce a 17-ketosteroid, can manifest itself in two different ways. When the defect partially blocks the pathway from both progesterone and pregnenolone, sexual development is ambiguous, and some degree of male development occurs at puberty because the patient can form small amounts of both testosterone and dehydroepiandrosterone. When only the 17-hydroxyprogesterone pathway is blocked, the patient has a female sexual phenotype; dehydroepiandrosterone is formed but testosterone is lacking, so no masculinization occurs at puberty.[14] This observation is interesting for two reasons. The first is that it indicates that two different enzymes are probably involved, one capable of utilizing both the delta-4 and delta-5 steroid as a substrate, and the other capable only of using the delta-4 (i.e., 17-hydroxyprogesterone) configuration as a substrate. The other point of interest is that even though generous amounts of dehydroepiandrosterone are formed in the second type, masculinization does not occur. This shows that dehydroepiandrosterone is not androgenic, although it may be a precursor of other androgenic steroids.

Tumors producing hyperaldosteronism do not ordinarily cause changes in the sexual habitus; but when a woman with an aldosteroma became pregnant, her daughter was born with enlargement of the clitoris and hyperkalemia. The latter probably reflected potassium given to the mother during labor. The electrolyte abnormality resolved in a few hours after birth. Studies of the daughter showed no evidence of a defect in the adrenal corticosteroid biosynthetic pathways. Presumably the maternal hyperaldosteronism caused a high level of aldosterone in the fetus, and this may have altered the pattern of androgen production. The child developed normally, except for clitoral enlargement. The mother had an exacerbation of hypertension and hyperaldosteronism after delivery, which led to removal of the aldosteroma. This tumor did not contain or produce androgenic substances.[15]] ◀

Chapter 39 References

1. Peters J.R., Walker R.F., Riad-Fahmy D. et al.: Salivary cortisol assays for assessing pituitary adrenal reserve. *Clin. Endocrinol.* 17:583–592, 1982.
2. Horrocks P.M., London D.R.: Diagnostic value of 9 AM plasma adrenocorticotrophic hormone concentrations in Cushing's disease. *Br. Med. J.* 285:1302–1303, 1982.
3. Betterle C., Zanette F., Zanchetta R., et al.: Complement-fixing adrenal autoantibodies as a marker for predicting onset of idiopathic Addison's disease. *Lancet* 1:1238–1241, 1983.
4. Knowlton A.I., Baer L.: Cardiac failure in Addison's disease. *Am. J. Med.* 74:829–836, 1983.
5. Loose D.S., Kan P.B., Hirst M.A., et al.: Ketoconazole blocks adrenal steroidogenesis by inhibiting cytochrome P_{450}-dependent enzymes. *J. Clin. Invest.* 71:1495–1499, 1983.
6. Burch W.: A survey of results with transsphenoidal surgery of Cushing's disease. *N. Engl. J. Med.* 308:103–104, 1983.
7. Trost B.N., Landolt A.M.: Morbus Cushing: bleiben Patienten nach mikrochirurgischer Hypophysendenoma-Extirpation substitutionsabhangig? *Schweiz. Med. Wochenschr.* 113:298–301, 1983.
8. Hollander C.S., Audhay T., Frey A., et al.: Distribution, biosynthesis and physiological role of ovine corticotropin releasing factor in man. *Clin. Res.* 31:528A, 1983.
9. Wiesen M., Ross F., Krieger D.T.: Prolonged remission of a case of Cushing's disease following cessation of cyproheptidine therapy. *Acta. Endocrinol.* 102:436–438, 1983.
10. Liu L., Jaffe R., Borowski G.D., et al.: Exacerbation of Cushing's disease during pregnancy. *Am. J. Obstet. Gynecol.* 145:110–111, 1983.
11. Alexandre J.H., Fraioli J.P., Regnard J.F., et al.: Corticosurrénalomes malins responsables d'un hyperaldostéronisme primaire et d'un hypercor-

ticisme biologique: reflexions à propos de 2 cas opérés. *J. Chir. (Paris)* 120:311–313, 1983.

12. Kater C.E., Biglieri E.G.: Distinctive plasma aldosterone, 18-hydroxycorticosterone and 18-hydroxydeoxycorticosterone profile in the 21-, 17α-, and 11β-hydroxylase deficiency types of congenital adrenal hyperplasia. *Am. J. Med.* 75:43–48, 1983.
13. Nonsalt-losing congenital adrenal hyperplasia due to 3β-hydroxysteroid dehydrogenase deficiency with normal glomerulosa function. *J. Clin. Endocrinol. Metab.* 56:808–818, 1983.
14. Zachmann M., Werder E.A., Prader A.: Two types of male pseudohermaphroditism due to 17,20-desmolase deficiency. *J. Clin. Endocrinol. Metab.* 55:487–490, 1982.
15. Elterman J.J., Hagen G.A.: Aldosteronism in pregnancy: association with virilization of female offspring. *South. Med. J.* 76:514–516, 1983.

40. Thyroid Gland

40–1 **Fine Needle Aspiration Biopsy of Thyroid Nodules.** Thyroid nodules are present in as much as 7% of the population of the United States and cause concern because they may indicate the presence of thyroid cancer. Richard A. Prinz, Patricia J. O'Morchoe, Anthony L. Barbato, Susan S. Braithwaite, Marion H. Brooks, Mary Ann Emanuele, Ann M. Lawrence, and Edward Paloyan evaluated fine needle aspiration biopsy of thyroid nodules in 109 patients seen in a 2-year period with a palpable nodule that was hypofunctioning on thyroid scintiscanning. All patients subsequently had thyroidectomy. Biopsies were obtained with a 20- or 22-gauge needle in an outpatient department. No complications resulted from the procedure.

Thirty-one patients had inadequate cellular material for diagnosis. Twenty-seven had a cytologic diagnosis of benign goiter, 22 of follicular neoplasm, and 12 of thyroiditis. Nine patients had findings suggestive of papillary cancer, and 5 had a diagnosis of Hürthle-cell tumor. There was 1 cytologic diagnosis of medullary carcinoma, 1 of lymphoma, and 1 of metastatic adenocarcinoma. Overall sensitivity of aspiration biopsy in diagnosing thyroid neoplasms was 88%, and specificity was 80%. Thyroiditis was confirmed in all 12 patients given this diagnosis after aspiration biopsy. One patient diagnosed as having benign goiter was found at operation to have carcinoma. Three of the 5 patients with a biopsy diagnosis of Hürthle-cell tumor were found to have carcinoma, and another had an adenoma.

Fine needle aspiration biopsy is useful in selecting patients with nodular thyroid disease for thyroidectomy. It is a safe procedure. No implantation of tumor along the biopsy tract with use of a fine needle has been described. The technique may provide diagnostic information that mandates earlier operation. Three of the present patients, who had little clinical evidence that suggested malignancy, probably would have been placed on thyrotropin suppression for extended periods if a cytologic diagnosis of carcinoma had not been made.

▶ [It is useful to recognize the presence of thyroid tumor in nodules, but it is a serious question whether the prognosis of patients operated on for follicular tumors is improved by operation. At the Mayo Clinic, the introduction of fine needle biopsy clarified the diagnosis in patients with nodules and permitted a reduction of thyroid operations from 67% before biopsy was available to 43% thereafter. In spite of this, the "yield" of carcinomas increased from 14% to 29%. As a result, the mean cost of medical care per patient was reduced by 25%.[1] The procedure is most useful for ruling in thyroiditis and least useful for ruling out cancer. The effectiveness of the procedure depends greatly on the experience of the cytologist, so the record will probably improve still further when more biopsies have been studied.

While we are discussing diagnostic methods, I'd like to recommend a brief review

(40–1) Ann. Surg. 198:70–73, July 1983.

of the status of ultrasound in the diagnosis of thyroid disease. The technique is commonly used for evaluating solitary nodules. It is especially useful in defining cystic lesions, but it also has value in detecting multiple nodules (a finding which significantly reduces the likelihood that the original large nodule was malignant). Thyroid cancer, when present, appears as a solid mass or a complex combination of solid and small cystic lesions. The tumor is usually less echo-genic than normal tissue, so its density is somewhere between those of normal thyroid and a cyst. Solid follicular tumors may be impossible to distinguish from a benign adenoma.[2] But this distinction is also often difficult even when the biopsy is examined by a microscopist!] ◀

40–2 **Aging and the Thyroid: Decreased Requirement for Thyroid Hormone in Older Hypothyroid Patients.** There is indirect evidence that thyroid hormone secretion declines with advancing age in euthyroid persons, and if this is so, older patients with hypothyroidism may require less thyroid hormone than younger ones. Clark T. Sawin, Talia Herman, Mark E. Molitch, Maria H. London, and Sybil M. Kramer (Boston) determined the daily dose of thyroxine (T_4) needed to lower the serum level of thyrotropin (TSH) to the normal range in a series of 84 patients with primary hypothyroidism, confirmed by a serum TSH level above 10 μU/ml. The 40 men and 44 women were aged 23–84 years; 40 patients were older than age 60. Twenty-seven patients had become hypothyroid after treatment for hyperthyroidism. Oral T_4 was begun in a dose of 50 μg daily, or 25 μg daily for many patients older than age 60 years, and the dose was increased at intervals of at least 1 month until the basal serum TSH level was below 5 μU/ml.

Overall mean dose of T_4 was 126 μg, daily. The daily dose correlated negatively with age to a significant degree. This relationship held for both men and women. The necessary dose was significantly lower in patients aged 40–60 years than in younger patients. The range of doses was quite broad at all ages, but a daily requirement of 100 μg or less was common in patients older than age 40 years. All 5 patients who required 50 μg daily or less were older than age 60 years. The initial presence of hyperthyroidism did not influence the dose requirement.

Older hypothyroid patients require less T_4 than younger patients. The reason for this is not clear, but there is a sound physiologic basis for the common practice of giving low doses of T_4, such as 25 μg daily, to older hypothyroid patients at the outset of treatment. It may be reasonable to reassess the T_4 dose requirement after several years in older patients.

▶ [Overdosage with thyroid hormones is especially dangerous in the elderly because of the high likelihood that their circulatory systems may be impaired, so this is excellent advice. A similar study, involving 23 patients older than 65 years is in agreement with Sawin's results. In the elderly group, averaging 75.7 years of age, the mean daily requirement was 118 μg/day, whereas in the younger group of 44 patients, averaging 48.1 years of age, the mean daily requirement was 158 μg/day.[3]] ◀

40–3 **Fasting Decreases Thyrotropin Responsiveness to Thyrotropin-Releasing Hormone: Potential Cause of Misinterpretation of Thyroid Function Tests in the Critically Ill.** To determine

(40–2) Am. J. Med. 75:206–209, August 1983.
(40–3) J. Clin. Endocrinol. Metab. 57:380–383, August 1983.

whether caloric deprivation inhibits thyroxine (T_4) metabolism and blunts the thyrotropin (TSH) response to TSH-releasing hormone (TRH) in hypothyroid subjects, George C. Borst, Robert C. Osburne, John T. O'Brian, Leon P. Georges, and Kenneth D. Burman studied 7 hypothyroid patients (4 women), aged 30–60 years. They were within 20% of ideal body weight. Each had an initial serum T_4 concentration of less than 5 μg/dl, a basal TSH concentration greater than 5 μU/ml, and a peak TSH concentration after TRH administration greater than 50 μU/ml. Each had idiopathic primary hypothyroidism and malaise, lethargy, and cold intolerance. Serum was obtained for T_4, free T_4, triiodothyronine (T_3), and reverse T_3 measurements before and after a 60-hour fast. Thyrotropin releasing hormone tests were performed before and after the fast by intravenous administration of a 500-μg TRH bolus, with TSH determinations 0, 20, 40, 60, and 80 minutes thereafter.

Short-term fasting reduced the maximum serum TSH increment by 29% and the integrated TSH response to TRH by 32% ($P < .01$). The percent reduction in the integrated TSH response was greatest (42.3% and 67.5%) in the 2 patients with the lowest integrated responses (Fig 40–1). In these 2 patients with mild hypothyroidism, the basal TSH concentration and the response to TRH were reduced to values within the normal range by 60 hours of fasting. Specifically, the basal TSH concentration decreased from 11.0 to 4.1 μU/ml in patient 3 and from 7.6 to 3.5 μU/ml in patient 6. The peak TSH response to TRH, which was greater than 50.0 μU/ml in each of these 2 patients initially, fell to less than 30.0 μU/ml after fasting.

Fasting-induced alterations in thyroid hormone concentrations are similar to, but not identical with, those observed in ill patients. Insofar as direct comparisons between critically ill and fasting subjects may apply, the data suggest that basal TSH concentrations would

Fig 40–1.—Response of TSH to TRH stimulation in 2 patients. Thyrotropin releasing hormone stimulation tests were performed before and after 60-hour fast. Patients 3 and 6 were the 2 subjects studied who had fasting-induced normalization of their basal and TRH-stimulated TSH concentrations. (Courtesy of Borst, G.C., et al.: J. Clin. Endocrinol. Metab. 57:380–383, August 1983.)

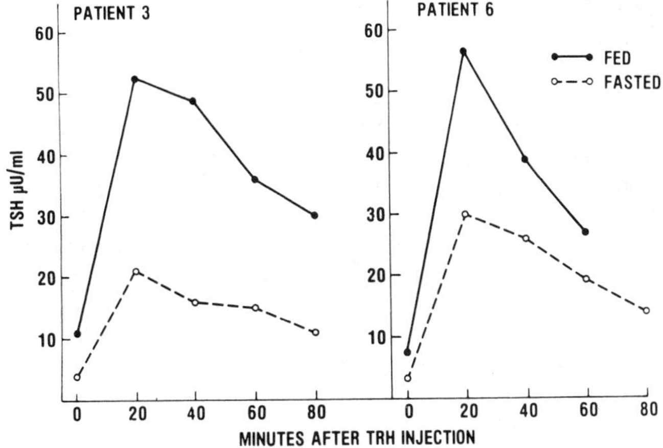

accurately identify critically ill subjects who are moderately or severely hypothyroid. Mild degrees of hypothyroidism (patients 3 and 6) might be overlooked because of suppressant effect of fasting or poor caloric intake on basal TSH concentrations and on TRH responsiveness.

▶ [The "sick thyroid" syndrome continues to draw a great deal of attention. Jack Oppenheimer has written an excellent editorial concerned with the difficulties of interpreting thyroid function tests in patients with nonthyroidal disease.[4] The concentration of total T_4 is usually reduced, but so is the level of thyroxine-binding globulin, so the free T_4 is generally normal. On the other hand, the conversion of T_4 to T_3 may be inhibited, so the normal free T_4 level may be misleading. The TSH concentration in this group of euthyroid patients is usually normal. Oppenheimer suggests that the diagnosis of abnormal thyroid function be discarded if the TSH level is not higher than 15 μU/ml. Good advice, but since it takes some days to get back the results of a TSH determination—at least in our hospital—and since the patients are often desperately sick, a decision may have to be made before the TSH results are available. The response of TSH to TRH is usually low or normal—never elevated—as one would expect if the patient were truly hypothyroid.[5] Indeed, it has been suggested that one factor in the development of the syndrome is reduced secretion of TSH in critically ill patients.[6] Unfortunately, it usually takes too long for this test to be reported to make it useful, except in retrospect. Patients with the sick thyroid syndrome have a very bad prognosis.[5]

Of course, in evaluating patients who are seriously ill, one must remember to check the influence of their medications on thyroid function tests. It is generally accepted that dilantin alters the binding of thyroid hormones to plasma protein carrier proteins and that this accounts for the reduced concentration of hormone found in the plasma of patients treated with the medication. Another mechanism for reducing the serum T_4 concentration, at least in a patient with dilantin toxicity, is reduced TSH secretion, even in response to stimulation with TRH.[7] Release of prolactin, LH, and FSH was responsive to the usual stimuli in this group of patients, so the difficulty did not reflect a global suppression of pituitary responsiveness.] ◀

40–4 **Hyperthyroidism Due to Thyrotropin-Secreting Pituitary Tumors: Diagnostic and Therapeutic Considerations.** Robert C. Smallridge and Charles E. Smith (Walter Reed Army Inst. of Res., Washington, D.C.) reviewed the salient clinical features of 33 patients (17 women) who had hyperthyroidism with elevated serum concentrations of thyroxine (T_4) or triiodothyronine (T_3), documented inappropriate thyrotropin (TSH) secretion, and evidence of a pituitary tumor.

A measurable serum TSH concentration despite elevated serum concentrations of T_4 or T_3 or both is the most important diagnostic feature. If it is uncertain whether the thyroid hormone concentrations are elevated, a serum free T_4 test by dialysis should be done. Values for TSH obtained from a commercial kit assay should be confirmed in a research radioimmunoassay that is specific for TSH. Ancillary data supporting the diagnosis include a molar ratio of α-subunit to TSH greater than 1.0, an absent TSH response to TSH-releasing hormone, suppression of serum TSH by glucocorticoids, and lack of suppression of serum TSH by dopaminergic agonists. It is important that roentgenographic evaluation be done early, since all patients in this study had pituitary tumors (macroadenomas) larger than 10 mm that were visible on plain films; tumors that are less than 10 mm may require tomograms or computed tomographics scans.

(40–4) Arch. Intern. Med. 143:503–507, March 1983.

The only successful treatment of patients with TSH-secreting pituitary tumors has been pituitary operation, irradiation, or both. Pituitary operations cured 8 of 16 patients of hyperthyroidism, although 1 patient required two operations. Radiation therapy as the initial treatment of the pituitary tumor cured only 1 of 4 patients. Pharmacologic management must be viewed with reservation until there is better understanding of the biologic behavior of these tumors. Unlike prolactin- and GH-secreting pituitary tumors, which may regress with bromocriptine, no regression of TSH-secreting tumors has been reported.

▶ [Several additional reports have been published,[8–10] presenting a total of 7 more patients. Clearly the disease is much less common than true Graves' disease, which is associated with a thyroid-stimulating antibody, and in which the concentration of pituitary TSH in serum is below 0.8 μU/ml. In most patients with TSH-secreting tumor, TRH fails to raise the serum TSH level, although 2 patients had a response early in their course.[8, 10] For the 1 patient in whom it was measured,[9] the α-subunit of TSH was also elevated and, like TSH itself, failed to respond to TRH.

An unusual situation was reported in a clinically euthyroid newborn girl, who had an elevated level of TSH on neonatal screening. The mother also had elevated TSH, and it was believed that the infant's elevated concentration was caused by transplacental delivery of maternal hormone. The mother's elevated TSH level was explained by the presence of a TSH-blocking antibody in her serum. The mother's serum blocked the activity of TSH in vitro. After delivery, the infant's elevated TSH rapidly fell to normal levels.[11]] ◀

40–5 **Single Daily Dose Short-Term Carbimazole Therapy for Hyperthyroid Graves' Disease.** Initial treatment for patients younger than age 40–50 years with hyperthyroid Graves' disease is traditionally carbimazole, 10–15 mg three or four times daily. To predict how quickly a given patient will respond to a given dose of carbimazole and thus to plan follow-up treatment, I. A. MacFarlane, D. Davies, D. Longson, S. M. Shalet, and C. G. Beardwell (Manchester, England) studied 21 hyperthyroid patients during a 24-month period. The criteria for inclusion in the group (median age, 33 years) were no previous antithyroid drug treatment or thyroid surgery and age younger than 50 years. All patients had elevated 2-hour ^{132}I uptake, and none had a nodular goiter.

Carbimazole, 30 mg, was prescribed as 1 dose each morning. Propranolol, 40 mg 3 times daily, was also given for the first 3 weeks. Serum triiodothyronine (T_3) and thyroxine (T_4) concentrations, clinical score, and 20-minute response to intravenous injection of 200 μg of thyrotropin (TSH) releasing hormone (TRH) were measured every 3 weeks. Carbimazole was stopped soon after a normal TSH response was obtained.

The data before and during 9 weeks of treatment are shown in Figure 40–2. In 19 patients the serum T_4 concentration became normal in a median of 3 weeks (range, 0–18 weeks), the T_3 concentration became normal in a median of 6 weeks (range, 3–18 weeks), and a detectable TSH response to TRH (greater than 2 mU/L) was found after a median of 18 weeks (range, 6–39 weeks). The time taken for the serum T_3 concentration to become normal was highly corre-

(40–5) Clin. Endocrinol. (Oxf.) 18:557–561, June 1983.

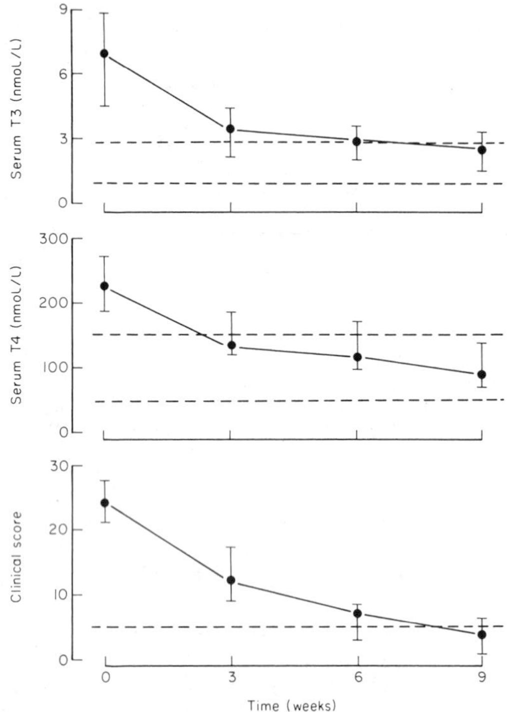

Fig 40–2.—Alterations in serum triiodothyronine *(T_3)* and thyroxine *(T_4)* concentrations and clinical score in 21 thyrotoxic patients after 30 mg of carbimazole once daily. Propranolol, 40 mg three times daily, was also given for the first 3 weeks. Solid circles and vertical bars indicate median and interquartile range; broken lines show normal range. (Courtesy of MacFarlane I.A., et al.: Clin. Endocrinol. (Oxf.) 18:557–561, June 1983.)

lated with the time taken for the TSH response to appear ($P < .0001$).

Carbimazole, 30 mg once daily, is a convenient and effective treatment for hyperthyroid Graves' disease. Prolonged remissions will be achieved in many patients if treatment is stopped when serum T_3 and T_4 concentrations are in the low normal range, usually 2–4 months after clinical euthyroidism has been reached.

▶ [Carbimazole is commonly used in the United Kingdom in preference to propylthiouracil (PTU), but the results of this study can probably be applied to PTU and methimazole as well. In my experience, there are a few patients who do not respond to single-dose schedules, but I have not made a systematic study of the relative success rates of multiple vs. single doses. Obviously, the single-dose schedule is much more convenient and probably more likely to be followed than the multiple-dose regimen.

Progressive exophthalmos is one of the most unfortunate accompaniments of Graves' disease, but its relationship to the disease is not clear. When an ophthalmologist studied 194 patients with "Graves' ophthalmopathy" in whom orbital decompression was under consideration, he found that 29 had never been clinically hyperthyroid. In the others, the onset of ophthalmopathy was symmetrically distributed within 18 months before or after onset of hyperthyroidism. These observations suggest that the eye complication is neither induced nor prevented by the type of treatment undertaken for the thyroid disease. They do not support the common contention that radioiodine treatment or surgical intervention initiates the process.[12]] ◀

40–6 **Agranulocytosis Associated With Antithyroid Drugs: Effects of Patient Age and Drug Dose.** Treatment with potent antithyroid drugs may be complicated by toxic reactions, and agranulocytosis is an infrequent but potentially fatal side effect seen in about 0.3–6% of patients taking propylthiouracil and methimazole. David S. Cooper, David Goldminz, Ann A. Levin, Paul W. Ladenson, Gilbert H. Daniels, Mark E. Molitch, and E. Chester Ridgway (Boston) sought risk factors for antithyroid drug–related agranulocytosis in 14 patients seen at two Boston hospitals and in 36 reported patients with the syndrome. All had a total leukocyte count of 1,000/cu mm or less and a granulocyte count of 250/cu mm or less. Fifty comparison hyperthyroid patients were selected. Two of the authors' patients, 10 reported patients, and 15 controls had received more than one course of antithyroid drugs.

The patients with agranulocytosis were significantly older than the comparison patients. The risk of agranulocytosis developing in patients older than age 40 years was 6.4 times that in younger patients. Mean doses of methimazole in both study groups were significantly higher than in the comparison group, and the risk of agranulocytosis occurring with doses above 40 mg daily was 8.6 times that with smaller doses. Mean doses of propylthiouracil did not differ among the three groups. Previous allergic reactions to antithyroid drugs did not differ significantly in frequency in the authors' patients and the comparison group. One of the authors' patients died and was found to have polyarteritis nodosa; he had received propylthiouracil.

Antithyroid drugs should be given cautiously to patients older than 40 years of age. Methimazole in doses below 30 mg daily may be safer than higher doses or treatment with conventional doses of propylthiouracil. Warnings about symptoms of agranulocytosis are especially important in the earliest phase of treatment, since agranulocytosis usually is seen within 2 months of the start of therapy.

▶ [The fact that older patients are more likely to develop agranulocytosis after exposure to antithyroid drugs gives additional support to the idea that Graves' disease in patients over the age of 40 should ordinarily be treated with ^{131}I. Of course, radioiodine treatment is not without its drawbacks. Cunnien and colleagues reviewed their experience with hypothyroidism developing in patients with Graves' disease after treatment with ^{131}I and found that the incidence of thyroid failure has increased in recent years. They relate this to an increase in the mean dose from 8.1 mCi when ^{131}I was first introduced to 13.8 mCi in the most recent group of patients. The increased dose probably reflects a tendency to estimate the thyroid weight as larger in the recent than in the first group.[13]

How should one treat toxic nodular goiter (Plummer's disease)? Subtotal thyroidectomy has often been recommended, and claims have been made that permanent cure is more likely with this type of treatment than with radioiodine. A recent review of experience in Amsterdam, however, indicates that local autonomous function persists in at least 20% of patients treated with surgery. Since autonomy of the nodules is the basic cause of hypersecretion, it seems only a matter of time before most of these patients will manifest hyperthyroidism. Perhaps ^{131}I is a preferable form of treatment.[14]] ◀

40–7 **Hyperthyroxinemia Due to Decreased Peripheral Triiodothyronine Production.** Hyperthyroxinemia usually is due to hyperfunc-

---

(40–6) Ann. Intern. Med. 98:26–29, January 1983.
(40–7) Lancet 2:849–851, Oct. 16, 1982.

tion of the thyroid gland. It can occur in the presence of euthyroidism, as in familial euthyroid thyroxine (T_4) excess. M. Jansen, E. P. Krenning, W. Oostdijk, R. Docter, B. E. Kingma, J. V. L. van den Brande, and G. Hennemann report a previously unrecognized syndrome of hyperthyroxinemia in 2 euthyroid patients in whom an elevated serum free T_4 level is necessary to produce adequate triiodothyronine (T_3) peripherally.

Woman, 60, underwent subtotal thyroidectomy for Graves' disease at age 43 years. She had an apparent relapse 4 years later, and carbimazole was given. Carbimazole therapy was stopped the following year. The serum T_4 and T_3 levels remained normal until a second relapse 4 years later, with definite symptoms and high levels of T_4 and an elevated free T_4 index. Carbimazole and thyroid hormone were given, followed by radioiodine. The serum thyrotropin (TSH) concentration rose slightly within 1½ years, despite an elevated T_4 level and free T_4 index. Another dose of radioiodine was given, and the patient became clinically hypothyroid. She then received L-T_4 in increasing doses; the serum T_4 levels rose to above normal, and the TSH concentration remained slightly elevated. Throughout her course, serum T_3 levels remained within normal limits except on one occasion. Binding capacities were within normal ranges. No serum antibodies to thyroid hormones were identified. The patient's daughter and 4 sisters had normal serum thyroid hormone levels.

The other patient, a boy aged 8 years, had a similar abnormal pattern of T_4 levels. The patients had elevated free T_4 levels but were not clinically hyperthyroid. It appears that a high extracellular free T_4 level is necessary to insure normal intracellular availability of biologically active thyroid hormone in these cases. The basic defect may be inhibition of T_4 transport into tissue cells or reduced intracellular 5′-deiodinase activity catalyzing T_4 to T_3. The prevalence of the syndrome is uncertain, and it is not yet clear whether the disorder is hereditary.

► [This syndrome should be distinguished from Refetoff's syndrome, in which the level of plasma T_3 is also elevated. Thus in this type of disease the problem is probably failure to convert T_4 to its active form, T_3, whereas in Refetoff's syndrome there is, apparently, resistance to the effects of thyroid hormones in general, as discussed in the next abstract.] ◄

40–8 **Resistance to Thyroid Hormones: Disorder Frequently Confused With Graves' Disease.** In 1967, there was a report of 3 siblings with goiter, increased protein-bound iodine levels and thyroidal radioiodine uptakes, deaf-mutism, and stippled epiphyses. It was proposed that end-organ resistance to thyroid hormones might be responsible. There were no symptoms or signs of hyperthyroidism. John P. Bantle, Steven Seeling, Cary N. Mariash, Robert A. Ulstrom, and Jack H. Oppenheimer (Univ. of Minnesota) report the data on 5 patients from 2 unrelated families who appeared to have general resistance to thyroid hormones.

Boy, 34 months, the second son of another patient, was born after 36 weeks' gestation to a mother who, because of suspected hyperthyroidism, took methimazole in a dose in the final month of pregnancy of 15 mg 3 times daily. A small goiter was noted in the child at birth. At age 1 week, the child's

---

(40–8) Arch. Intern. Med. 142:1867–1871, October 1982.

serum thyroxine (T_4) concentration was 40 μg/dl, the triiodothyronine (T_3) level was more than 500 ng/dl, and the thyrotropin (TSH) level was 9 μU/ml, but the infant fed well and gained weight normally. The goiter was smaller when the child was 1 month old, but the resting heart rate was 160 beats per minute, and the serum T_3 concentration was 644 ng/ml. Propylthiouracil was given for much of the next 2 years, but the serum T_4 and T_3 levels remained elevated. Growth and development were normal. The TSH concentration rose to 40 μU/ml after injection of thyrotropin-releasing hormone (TRH) at age 2 years, and propylthiouracil was discontinued. When last seen, the boy was in the 65th percentile for height and the 55th percentile for weight. The thyroid was twice normal size. The serum T_4 concentration was 21 μg/dl; the T_3, 482 ng/dl; the TSH, 4 μU/ml. The boy has continued to be healthy and to grow normally without any treatment.

All 5 patients had measurable levels of TSH, and the 4 who were tested had a rise in thyrotropin after TRH injection. Study of nuclear T_3 receptors from cultured fibroblasts of 1 patient showed a normal equilibrium association constant and a maximal binding capacity above control values, suggesting that thyroid hormone resistance in this case was not attributable to a decrease in either the affinity or the number of specific nuclear T_3 receptors.

These patients presumably have general resistance to the effects of thyroid hormones and require elevated levels of T_4 and T_3 to maintain a eumetabolic state. The disorder can easily be mistaken for Graves' disease, leading to inappropriate treatment for hyperthyroidism, as in 3 of the present patients. The key to making a correct diagnosis is the TRH stimulation test, which should be done in all patients with elevated hormone levels but no clinical signs of hyperthyroidism. The mechanism of resistance to thyroid hormones is still uncertain.

▶ [The original description of unresponsiveness to thyroid hormones by Refetoff and colleagues[15] included deaf-mutism and stippled epiphyses as part of the syndrome; but many authors include under the term *Refetoff's syndrome* all patients with reduced sensitivity to thyroid hormone manifested by an abnormally high level of thyroid hormones in serum combined with an elevated plasma TSH level but without clinical evidence of hyperthyroidism. The TSH response can be used to differentiate this syndrome from that of hyperthyroidism, because in the latter there is a negligible response to TRH, whereas the response is, if anything, exaggerated in patients with Refetoff's syndrome. It should not be necessary to do a TRH test on every patient—only on those whose clinical picture of euthyroidism contradicts the evidence of the laboratory that the T_4 level is elevated. Patients with hyperthyroidism caused by a pituitary tumor that secretes TSH can best be differentiated by demonstration of a pituitary tumor on computed tomographic scanning. Also, as mentioned previously, the TRH response is usually absent in patients with hyperthyroidism of pituitary origin. Failure to recognize the syndrome can be detrimental to the patient's welfare, because if inappropriate treatment is prescribed, the patient may become hypothyroid, goiter may develop, and mental activity may be impaired—an especially unfortunate effect in children.[16] When the correct diagnosis is recognized, it may be wise to treat the patient for a while with T_3 to shrink the goiter and minimize the time to resumption of normal brain function.

What is the explanation of the defective response to thyroid hormones? The previous abstract discussed failure to convert T_4 to T_3. Other possibilities are the presence of an abnormal thyroid hormone–binding protein in plasma,[17] a situation which is normal in pregnancy—a sort of physiological Refetoff's syndrome. Other possible causes include reduced transport of the hormone across the cell membrane[18] and reduced nuclear binding of the hormone.[19] In addition, certain acute illness and medications may produce a syndrome reminiscent of Refetoff's disease.[20] Thus, although hyperthyroidism is a common disease, and the misleading hyperthyroxinemic euthyroid syndrome(s) is rare, the clinician must be alert to detect them.] ◀

40–9 **Hypothyroidism Masquerading as Polymyositis.** Muscle involvement in hypothyroidism usually is mild, but in rare instances severe myopathy develops, which may be misdiagnosed and mistreated as polymyositis. Shaltiel Cabili, Amos Pines, Naomi Kaplinsky, and Otto Frankl (Tel Aviv Univ.) report the cases of three patients who presented with proximal muscle weakness and elevated muscle enzyme levels. They initially were thought to have polymyositis but were subsequently found to have hypothyroidism. They responded well to thyroid hormone replacement.

Woman, 49, presented with muscle weakness, arthritis, and eyelid swelling a year after pain, swelling, and stiffness developed in the wrist, metacarpophalangeal joints, ankles, and knees. On physical examination, the patient was found to have coarse skin, a hoarse voice, proximal muscle tenderness, weak upper and lower extremities, and swollen eyelids. The sedimentation rate was 20 mm/hour. The serum creatine kinase (isoenzyme MM) concentration was 128–190 units/dl. The serum glutamic oxaloacetic transaminase and lactic dehydrogenase levels were also elevated. Slowed Achilles tendon relaxation was noted, and the patient admitted to cold sensitivity, constipation, and weight gain. Primary hypothyroidism then was documented, with a thyroxine concentration of 0.3 μg/dl and an elevated thyrotropin level. The 2-hour radioactive iodine uptake was 4%. Treatment with L-thyroxine in doses increasing to 150 μg/day led to gradual improvement. Muscle strength and serum muscle enzyme levels returned to normal; facial puffiness resolved, and the patient lost weight.

Hypothyroid myopathy can simulate all features of polymyositis, including elevated serum muscle enzyme levels and myopathic EMG abnormalities. There may even be muscle biopsy changes compatible with polymyositis. The hallmark of hypothyroid myopathy is complete clinical recovery and resolution of the laboratory abnormalities after thyroid replacement. Thyroid function should be assessed in all patients with unexplained myopathy, because hypothyroidism with muscle involvement is a treatable condition with a good prognosis.

▶ [I was caught off base in discussing a patient with this syndrome some years ago in a Clinical Pathological Conference. It is easy to forget that polymyositis can be the presenting symptom of hypothyroidism and may, in a few patients, be the major clinical problem.

Prompt treatment of hypothyroidism is important, but never more so than in infancy. In a study from Finland, it was demonstrated that infants whose deficiency was under treatment within the first month of life ultimately had a level of intellectual function similar to that of their siblings; but if treatment was delayed beyond 3 months after birth, detectable defects persist. The longer treatment is delayed, the more serious the intellectual deficit.[21]] ◀

40–10 **Pituitary Enlargement and Primary Hypothyroidism: A Report of Two Cases With Sharply Contrasting Outcomes.** An association between primary hypothyroidism and pituitary hyperplasia or adenoma has long been recognized, and symptomatic pituitary enlargement has been successfully managed by thyroid hormone replacement. Other patients, however, have had progressive pituitary

---

(40–9) Postgrad. Med. J. 58:545–547, September 1982.
(40–10) Neurosurgery 11:792–794, December 1982.

symptoms despite medical treatment. Ronald S. Gup, Leslie R. Sheeler, Michael C. Maeder, and John M. Tew, Jr. report data on 2 adults with pituitary enlargement and primary hypothyroidism, both of whom were treated with L-thyroxine. In one patient a prompt decrease in size of the enlarged pituitary was seen on computed tomography scanning after replacement doses of L-thyroxine. The other patient had progressive pituitary enlargement during L-thyroxine therapy and underwent removal of a pituitary adenoma more than 2 years after the start of treatment. Normal serum thyrotropin levels were documented in this patient during L-thyroxine administration.

Repeat evaluation of all patients with pituitary enlargement thought to be due to primary hypothyroidism is recommended to document regression of the pituitary after administration of L-thyroxine. One of the two present patients had progressive pituitary enlargement despite such treatment and had neurologic sequelae. The histologic results were consistent with a nonsecreting adenoma. The tumor in this patient probably developed independently of the hypothyroidism, but this is not certain. A substantial reduction in pituitary size can be expected after 8–10 weeks of L-thyroxine therapy. If this does not occur, the patient should be approached as if a pituitary tumor were present.

▶ [The reader will recognize an obvious parallel between this situation and that discussed in abstract 35–9 as a result of untreated congenital adrenal hyperplasia. Since hypothyroidism results in an increased secretion of TRH and since TRH stimulates secretion of prolactin, it is not surprising that patients with hypothyroidism may have hyperprolactinemia and all of the symptoms associated with that disease. If the patient also has pituitary enlargement, the unwary clinician may make a diagnosis of a prolactin-secreting pituitary adenoma rather than of hypothyroidism.[22, 23] After patients with this type of pituitary tumor are treated with thyroid hormone, the tumor regresses and the symptoms of hyperprolactinemia disappear.[23]

Hypothyroidism may be secondary to failure of the pituitary to secrete TSH, either because of global pituitary failure or because of solitary failure to secrete the hormone. In some instances, such isolated failure reflects inadequate production of hypothalamic TRH; but in others it apparently is a result of secretion of a form of hormone which is relatively impotent. Five patients with this pattern were studied by Faglia and colleagues.[24] The basal levels of α-subunit of TSH were normal, but the concentration of the β-subunit was higher than normal, though lower than that of patients with primary hypothyroidism. After administration of TRH, the response was also intermediate for both α- and β-subunits. Since the response to TRH was increased and the pattern returned to normal when TRH was given chronically by mouth for 4 weeks, the authors conclude that the abnormal TSH reflects subnormal stimulation by TRH in this syndrome as well.] ◀

40–11 **Visual Field Defects and Pituitary Enlargement in Primary Hypothyroidism.** The incidence of visual failure in primary hypothyroidism was studied by Kunihiro Yamamoto, Koshi Saito, Takaji Takai, Makoto Naito, and Sho Yoshida (Jichi Med. School, Tochigi, Japan) in 14 patients who had overt hypothyroidism with undetectable thyroxine (T_4) and high thyrotropin (TSH) concentrations.

An unexpectedly high incidence (10 patients, 71.4%) of visual field defects was found. The extent of visual field change varied over a wide range, from early chiasmatic compression to apparent bitem-

---

(40–11) J. Clin. Endocrinol. Metab. 57:283–287, August 1983.

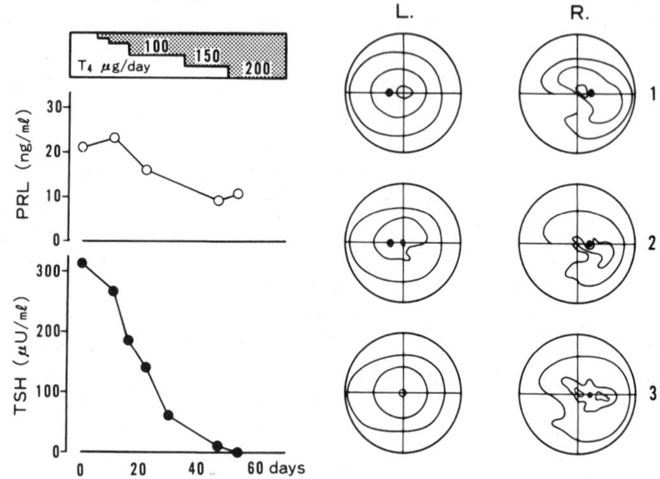

Fig 40–3.—Time course of visual field changes during thyroxine (T_4) replacement therapy in woman, 39, who had had primary hypothyroidism for 13 years. Before treatment *(1)*; 36th day of treatment *(2)*; and 56th day of treatment *(3)*. (Courtesy of Yamamoto, K., et al.: J. Clin. Endocrinol. Metab. 57:283–287, August 1983.)

poral hemianopia. The abnormality was characteristically a restriction in the central visual field. The sella turcica was significantly enlarged in these patients, compared with controls. Roentgenographic measurements of the volume of the sella turcica were performed in the 14 patients and in 24 normal subjects. The sella turcica was significantly ($P < .01$) enlarged in the patients with primary hypothyroidism as compared with controls. Both basal serum TSH concentration and total pituitary TSH reserve correlated significantly with volume of the sella turcica ($P < .001$).

Replacement with T_4 was started at a dose of 25 µg/day for 2 weeks and then increased by increments of 25 or 50 µg daily every 2 weeks up to a maintenance dose of 100 µg/day. In 8 patients, the restricted visual field improved after 1–4 months of replacement therapy. In 2 patients, however, the visual defects became worse during replacement. Figure 40–3 shows the time course of the changes in visual fields in 1 patient. The paradoxical course of visual failure during T_4 replacement may be due to an imbalance between TSH synthesis in the pituitary and TSH release, which may induce an increase in pituitary size.

It is appropriate to treat the patient with primary hypothyroidism who has visual failure with thyroid hormone replacement therapy and careful follow-up studies of vision. Improvement in the visual field defect during thyroid hormone replacement suggests that the visual failure is caused by pituitary hypertrophy rather than by pituitary tumor.

▶ [In some respects these patients resemble the one described in the previous abstract. Most of the patients responded to treatment with T_4 by shrinking their pituitaries, but 2 did not, and these proved to have true tumors which were removed surgically. In this article the emphasis was on the impairment of visual fields, which suggests that even without an actual tumor, pituitary enlargement in hypothyroidism may be sufficiently severe to produce pressure effects on the optic chiasm.] ◀

40–12 **Correlation of Thyroid Antibodies and Cytologic Features in Suspected Autoimmune Thyroid Disease.** Although techniques for the detection of antibodies are numerous, the most commonly measured antibodies in patients with autoimmune thyroid disease are antithyroglobulin and antimicrosomal antibodies. Barbara A. Baker, Hossein Gharib, and Harold Markowitz (Mayo Clinic and Found., Rochester, Minn.) evaluated the correlation between the results of antithyroid antibody determination and a diagnosis of Hashimoto's thyroiditis made clinically and cytologically. Charts of 643 patients were reviewed. Antithyroglobulin antibodies were present in 101 and antimicrosomal antibodies in 338. Among 122 patients on whom fine needle biopsy was performed, satisfactory aspirate was obtained from 108.

Of patients with high titers of antithyroglobulin antibody, 49.1% (28 of 57) were considered clinically to have Hashimoto's thyroiditis; however, 36.9% (198 of 537) of patients without detectable antibody had physical findings suggestive of autoimmune thyroiditis. Of 65 patients with cytologically proved Hashimoto's thyroiditis, only 15 had positive antithyroglobulin antibody tests (11 titers or 17.5% of the total were 1:1,600 or higher), whereas 61 had positive antimicrosomal antibody tests (50 titers or 76.9% of the total were 1:1,600 or higher).

The results seem to indicate that measurement of antithyroglobulin antibody gives no information that is more useful in the diagnosis of Hashimoto's thyroiditis than that which can be obtained by clinical evaluation and measurement of antimicrosomal antibody, since there is no single laboratory test of decisive value. If the antimicrosomal antibody test is negative, but a strong clinical suspicion of Hashimoto's thyroiditis remains, fine needle aspiration biopsy of the thyroid for cytologic confirmation is useful in establishing the diagnosis.

▶ [This article is especially useful because it helps plan a diagnostic program that minimizes laboratory expense. In the new era of diagnosis-related groups, the hero is the physician who comes to a correct decision using the least possible resources.

A number of contributions have recently appeared that are related to the immunologic changes in patients with autoimmune thyroid disease. A symposium providing a comprehensive review of the influence of immune processes on thyroid function has recently been published. It includes discussions of thyroid-stimulating antibodies, autoimmune thyroiditis, and effects of thyroid disease on immune function.[25] There are many different populations of thyroid-stimulating autoantibodies, some of which promote cell growth, whereas others increase thyroid activity, and still others do both. Most of these also compete with thyroid-stimulating hormone (TSH) for binding sites and block the activity of TSH. The antibodies all have activities per mole of protein that are manyfold less than that of TSH.[26] In addition, T cells probably also play a role, since the suppressor T lymphocytes are defective in patients with Graves' disease.[27]

In spite of the frequency with which patients with Graves' disease show abnormalities of the immune system, the finding of such abnormalities is not universal. For example, a familial pattern of Graves' disease has been reported in which the patients had no evidence of autoimmune processes, and the thyroid glands showed no evidence of lymphocytic infiltration.[28]] ◀

(40–12) Am. J. Med. 74:941–944, June 1983.

40–13 **Treatment of Lymphocytic Thyroiditis With Spontaneously Resolving Hyperthyroidism (Silent Thyroiditis).** Lymphocytic thyroiditis (LT) with spontaneously resolving hyperthyroidism (SRH) continues to be a common entity, accounting for more than 10% of cases of hyperthyroidism. About half the patients eventually have persistent thyroid disease. Thomas F. Nikolai, Guerdon J. Coombs, Alan K. McKenzie, Richard W. Miller, and G. John Weir, Jr. (Marshfield, Wis.) monitored the course of hyperthyroidism in 34 patients with LT and SRH. In 22 cases, LT was confirmed histologically. Eleven patients were not treated. Four patients were treated with propylthiouracil, 3 with both propylthiouracil and propranolol, 6 with propranolol, and 14 with prednisone. Propylthiouracil was given in daily doses of 300–800 mg. Propranolol was given in a dose of 20–40 mg 4 times daily. Prednisone was given in decreasing doses during a period of 4 weeks, starting with 50 mg daily.

The untreated patients had resolution of hyperthyroidism within a mean of 57 days. Those given propylthiouracil or propranolol or both had resolution in a mean of 45 days, whereas hyperthyroidism resolved in 15 days in the prednisone-treated patients. Four patients had a recurrence of SRH more than a year after the episode studied. Three had permanent hypothyroidism. After recovery, nearly one fourth of all patients had episodes of transient hypothyroidism, usually lasting 2–4 weeks. In another study group, 16 patients received thyroid suppression therapy with levothyroxine because of persistent thyromegaly or further growth of a goiter. Three of them had episodes of SRH while receiving suppressive therapy. Two other patients with chronic LT who were receiving thyroid suppression therapy had SRH. Recovery from SRH took 4–8 weeks after thyroid hormone therapy was stopped.

A dramatic response to prednisone therapy is evident in patients with LT and SRH. Thyroid suppression with thyroid hormone may not prevent the condition. Thyroid hormone suppression still is recommended, since it is the logical treatment for a persistent or enlarging goiter. Whether prednisone therapy will prevent permanent thyroid disease is not clear. Removal of the thyroid seems to be indicated in patients with disabling or recurrent episodes of LT and SRH.

▶ [It is difficult for me to accept the recommendation that the thyroid be removed in patients with recurring hyperthyroidism caused by thyroiditis. Since prednisone controls the attacks so successfully, why not give an additional course of steroids?

Although hyperthyroidism is a complication of acute thyroiditis during its active phase, reduced thyroid function occasionally occurs after subacute thyroiditis. Permanent thyroid failure was found in 2 of 32 patients followed for as long as 13 years after an attack. A characteristic feature in these patients was persistence of circulating thyroid antibodies in high titers from the onset of the attack of thyroiditis, indicating that autoimmune processes were persisting. The presence of low titers of antibodies was not associated with thyroid failure.[29]] ◀

40–14 **Impact of Therapy for Differentiated Carcinoma of the Thyroid: An Analysis of 706 Cases.** N. A. Samaan, Y. K. Maheshwari, S. Nader, C. S. Hill, Jr., P. N. Schultz, T. P. Haynie, R. C. Hickey, R.

(40–13) Arch. Intern. Med. 142:2281–2283, December 1982.
(40–14) J. Clin. Endocrinol. Metab. 56:1131–1138, June 1983.

L. Clark, H. Goepfert, M. L. Ibanez, and C. E. Litton (Univ. of Texas, Houston) reviewed data on 514 female and 192 male patients treated for differentiated thyroid carcinoma in 1951–1975 and followed up until 1981. Ages ranged from 5 to 84 years, but more than one third of the patients presented at 33–50 years of age. Two thirds of the lesions were of the mixed type. Only 3% of patients had Hürthle cell carcinoma. All patients had thyroid surgery; nearly 70% had total thyroidectomy. Radioactive iodine was given to 34% of patients. Sixty-four patients had a past history of head and neck irradiation for nonthyroidal disease.

Postoperative disease was present in 21% of patients, and 18.7% had recurrences. At last follow-up, 188 patients had died, 78 of thyroid cancer. Nearly one half of the deaths occurred within 5 years after diagnosis, and nearly two thirds occurred within 10 years after diagnosis. Patients whose carcinoma was diagnosed before age 40 lived significantly longer than older patients, and female patients lived longer than male. Papillary lesions appeared to be the least aggressive type, followed by mixed, follicular, and Hürthle cell tumors. Total thyroidectomy was associated with longer disease-free periods and fewer recurrences. Patients given ablative doses of radioactive iodine after operation had fewer recurrences than others, but no differences in disease-free intervals or survival rates were noted. Patients with follicular and mixed tumors benefited from radioactive iodine therapy, as did those who had total thyroidectomy. Other malignancies were present in many patients, most often affecting the breast, larynx, uterine cervix, endometrium, lungs, and colon.

Differentiated thyroid carcinoma is a relatively benign disease, usually compatible with long survival. Female patients, those younger than age 40 years at diagnosis, and those with papillary carcinoma have the best prognosis. Total thyroidectomy is recommended, followed by ablative radioactive iodine therapy, at least in patients with follicular and mixed tumors.

▶ [The presence of hyperthyroidism in a patient with a mass in the thyroid is usually taken as strong evidence that the process is benign; but this interpretation is sometimes incorrect. In a series of 720 patients with proved hyperthyroidism operated on at the Singapore General Hospital, 3 had clinically malignant thyroid tumors. In one of these, the disease presented as triiodothyronine toxicosis. In an additional 6 patients there was histologic evidence of malignancy but no clinical evidence of the disease. Two tumors were follicular; all the rest were papillary.[30]] ◀

Chapter 40 References

1. Hamberger B., Gharib H., Melton L.J. III, et al.: Fine-needle aspiration biopsy of thyroid nodules: impact on thyroid practice and cost of care. *Am. J. Med.* 73:381–384, 1982.
2. Cole-Beuglet C., Goldberg, B.B.: New high-resolution ultrasound evaluation of diseases of the thyroid gland: a review article. *JAMA* 249:2941–2944, 1983.
3. Rosenbaum R.L., Barzel U.S.: Levothyroxine replacement dose for primary hypothyroidism decreases with age. *Ann. Intern. Med.* 96:53–55, 1982.
4. Oppenheimer J.H.: Thyroid function tests in nonthyroidal disease. *J. Chron. Dis.* 35:697–701, 1982.

5. Bratusch-Marrain P., Vierhapper H., Grubeck-Loebenstein B., et al.: Pituitary-thyroid dysfunction in severe non-thyroidal disease: "low-T_4 syndrome." *Endokrinologie* 80:207–212, 1982.
6. Vierhapper H., Laggner A., Waldhausl W., et al.: Impaired secretion of TSH in critically ill patients with "low T_4-syndrome." *Acta Endocrinol.* 101:542–549, 1982.
7. Surks M.I., Ordene K.W., Mann D.N., et al.: Diphenylhydantoin inhibits the thyrotropin response to thyrotropin-releasing hormone in man and rat. *J. Clin. Endocrinol. Metab.* 56:940–945, 1983.
8. Gharib H., Carpenter P.C., Scheithauer B.W., et al.: The spectrum of inappropriate pituitary thyrotropin secretion associated with hyperthyroidism. *Mayo Clin. Proc.* 57:556–563, 1982.
9. Smith C.E., Smallridge R.C., Dimond R.C., et al.: Hyperthyroidism due to a thyrotropin-secreting pituitary adenoma: studies of thyrotropin and subunit secretion. *Arch. Intern. Med.* 142:1709–1711, 1982.
10. Hill S.A., Falko J. M., Wilson C.B., et al.: Thyrotrophin-producing pituitary adenomas. *J. Neurosurg.* 57:515–519, 1982.
11. Lazarus J.H., John R., Ginsberg J., et al.: Transient neonatal hyperthyrophinaemia: a serum abnormality due to transplacentally acquired antibody to thyroid stimulating hormone. *Br. Med. J.* 286:592–594, 1983.
12. Gorman C.A.: Temporal relationship between onset of Graves' ophthalmopathy and diagnosis of thyrotoxicosis. *Mayo Clin. Proc.* 58:515–519, 1983.
13. Cunnien A.J., Hay I.D., Gorman C.A., et al.: Radioiodine-induced hypothyroidism in Graves' disease: factors associated with the increased incidence. *J. Nucl. Med.* 23:978–983, 1982.
14. Weiner J.D.: Is partial thyroidectomy definitive treatment for Plummer's disease (autonomous goiter)? *Clin. Nucl. Med.* 8:78–82, 1983.
15. Refetoff S., DeWind T., DeGroot, L.J.: Familial syndrome combining deafmutism, stippled epiphyses, goiter and abnormally high PBI: possible target organ refractoriness to thyroid hormone. *J. Clin. Endocrinol. Metab.* 27:279–294, 1967.
16. Refetoff S., Salazar A., Smith T.J., et al.: The consequences of inappropriate treatment because of failure to recognize the syndrome of pituitary and peripheral tissue resistance to thyroid hormones. *Metabolism* 32:822–834, 1983.
17. Borst G.C., Premachandra B.N., Burman K.D., et al.: Euthyroid familial hyperthyroxinemia due to abnormal thyroid hormone-binding protein. *Am. J. Med.* 73:283–289, 1982.
18. Wortsman J., Premachandra B.N., Williams K., et al.: Familial resistance to thyroid hormone associated with decreased transport across the plasma membrane. *Ann. Intern. Med.* 98:904–909, 1983.
19. Kvetny J.: Nuclear binding and cellular metabolism of thyroxine in a euthyroid patient with hyperthyroxinaemia. *Clin. Endocrinol.* 18:251–257, 1983.
20. Borst G.C., Eil C., Burman K.D.: Euthyroid hyperthyroxinemia. *Ann. Intern. Med.* 98:366–378, 1983.
21. Virtanen M., Mäenpää J., Santavuori P., et al.: Congenital hypothyroidism: age at start of treatment versus outcome. *Acta Paediatr. Scand.* 72:197–201, 1983.
22. Semple C.G., Beastall G.H., Teasdale G., et al.: Hypothyroidism presenting with hyperprolactinaemia. *Br. Med. J.* 286:1200–1201, 1983.
23. Guerrero L.A., Carnovale R.: Regression of pituitary tumor after thyroid replacement in primary hypothyroidism. *South. Med. J.* 76:529–531, 1983.

24. Faglia G., Beck-Peccoz P., Ballabio M., et al.: Excess of β-subunit of thyrotropin (TSH) in patients with idiopathic central hypothyroidism due to the secretion of TSH with reduced biological activity. *J. Clin. Endocrinol. Metab.* 56:908–914, 1983.
25. Werner S.C., Von Westarp C.: The thyroid and immunology. *Life Sci.* 32:1–163, 1983.
26. Valente W.A., Vitti P., Yavin Z., et al.: Monoclonal antibodies to the thyrotropin receptor: stimulating and blocking antibodies derived from the lymphocytes of patients with Graves disease. *Proc. Natl. Acad. Sci. USA* 79:6680–6684, 1982.
27. Hallengren B., Forsgren A.: Suppressor T-lymphocytes in Graves' disease. *Acta Endocrinol.* 101:354–358, 1982.
28. Thomas J.-L., Leclere J., Hartemann P., et al.: Familial hyperthyroidism without evidence of autoimmunity. *Acta Endocrinol.* 100:512–518, 1982.
29. Tikkanen M.J., Lamberg B.-A.: Hypothyroidism following subacute thyroiditis. *Acta Endocrinol.* 101:348–353, 1982.
30. Yeo P.P.B., Wang K.W., Sinniah R., et al.: Thyrotoxicosis and thyroid cancer. *Aust. N.Z. J. Med.* 12:589–593, 1982.

41. Gonads

Two excellent issues of *Seminars in Reproductive Endocrinology* have appeared. One, edited by Leon Speroff, is concerned with the menopause,[1] and the other, edited by Caroline B. Coulam, discusses premature gonadal failure.[2]

Two articles in *The Lancet* concerned with an alleged relationship between the use of oral contraceptives and breast or cervical cancer have generated a great deal of discussion this year. The study of mammary cancer[3] reports retrospective evaluation of contraceptive usage by 314 patients compared with a matched equal series of women not having known breast cancer. I use this phraseology rather than "not having breast cancer" because the tumor can be present for some years before it becomes large enough to diagnose. The authors concluded that long-term use of oral contraceptives before the age of 25 increases the risk of cancer, that the relative risk increases with more prolonged use of contraceptive pills before the age of 25, and that preparations containing relatively high amounts of progestogen are much more dangerous than those with low levels. I have some problems with these data, because matching the patients and subjects did not result in a close match of the time the two groups were taking the various preparations, because the effect might have been to unmask the tumor earlier rather than to induce it, and because retrospective studies always carry some risk of hidden bias. The British Committee on Safety of Medicine (roughly the equivalent of the American Food and Drug Administration) responded to this article by reminding the public and physicians that oral contraceptives with the lowest effective concentrations of hormones should be preferred to those with high levels and by advising that patients ask their physicians to consider changing them to low-progestogen pills. I guess this is sensible. It should be remembered that there are many studies of very much larger populations, including one by the Centers for Disease Control, in which 1,000 women with cancer were compared with 4,000 matched controls, and no relationship was discovered between oral contraceptives and breast cancer.

The second article,[4] concerned with biopsy-proved carcinoma of the cervix, compared 6,838 parous women receiving oral contraceptives with 3,154 using an intrauterine contraceptive device. All were followed prospectively by the same family planning clinic in Oxford, England. Only 13 patients developed invasive cancer, and all were in the oral contraceptive group. Nine had used the pill more than 6 years. The incidence of carcinoma in situ and cervical dysplasia was also higher in the group using oral contraceptives, but the differences were not statistically significant. The study is seriously flawed by absence of any information about the number of sexual partners or the age of onset of sexual activity in the two groups. Since high levels of activity with multiple partners is associated with an increased incidence of cervical cancer, and since young girls just beginning their sexual lives without the benefit of clerical or familial sanction are probably more likely to use pills than intrauterine devices, I don't think that the relationship between oral contraceptives can be considered proved. The Committee on Safety of Medicines responded to this article simply by recommending that young women on contraceptive pills have a Papanicolaou smear at least every five years. This also sounds sensible to me.

41–1 **The Prolactin Response to Thyrotropin-Releasing Hormone Differentiates Isolated Gonadotropin Deficiency From Delayed Puberty.** It has been difficult to distinguish hypogonadotropic hypogonadism, believed to be due to lack of delivery of endogenous LRF to the pituitary gonadotropes, from delayed puberty, which is related to retarded activation of pituitary gonadotropin secretion. Irving M.

(41–1) N. Engl. J. Med. 308:575–579, Mar. 10, 1983.

Spitz, Harry J. Hirsch, and Stefan Trestian found that an impaired PRL response to thyrotropin-releasing hormone (TRH) can be used to identify isolated gonadotropin deficiency. Ten male patients with this condition and 15 with constitutional delayed puberty were assessed. A bolus of 100 μg of LRF was followed by a maximum of 200 μg of TRH; the subjects with gonadotropin deficiency received the maximum dose. Twenty-six normal men were tested for comparison.

Basal serum testosterone levels were similar in the two study groups and were lower in both than in normal men. Most patients in both groups had undetectable levels of estradiol. Mean basal levels of LH were lower than normal in both study groups. Basal FSH and PRL levels were lower in patients with gonadotropin deficiency than in the boys with delayed puberty or in normal men, but much overlap

Fig 41–1.—Response to releasing hormones in normal adult men, boys with delayed puberty, and patients with isolated gonadotropin deficiency. Upper panels show basal hormone levels. Lower panels show peak gonadotropin responses to LRF and PRL responses to thyrotropin-releasing hormone. Means (± SEM) are indicated by horizontal lines; symbols indicate individual responses. (Courtesy of Spitz, I.M., et al.: N. Engl. J. Med. 308:575–579, Mar. 10, 1983; reprinted by permission of The New England Journal of Medicine.)

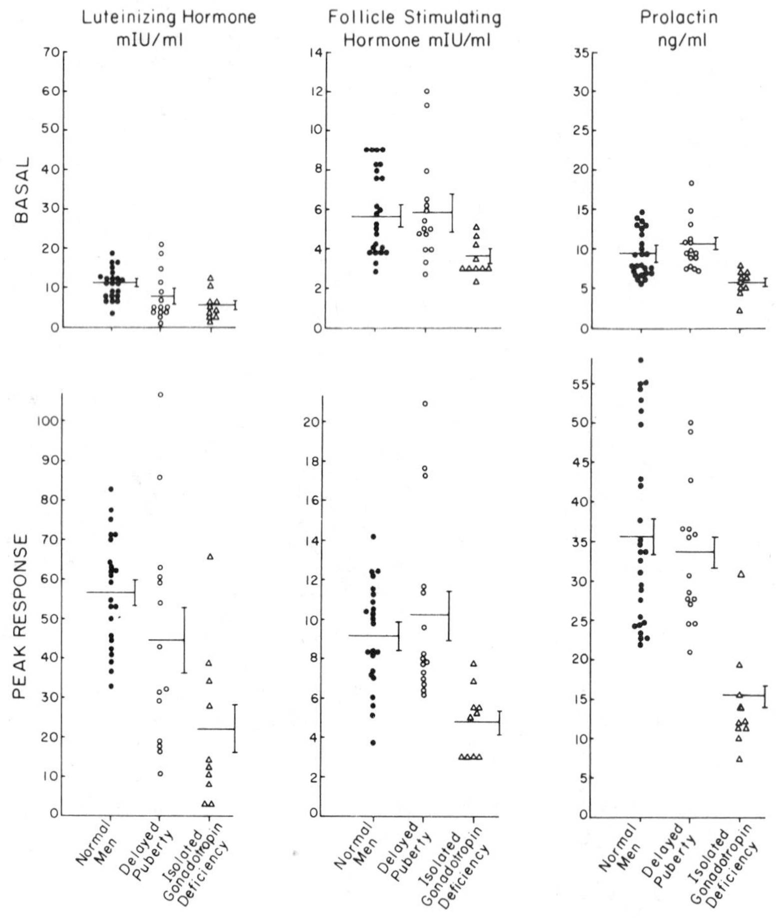

was present. Responses to the releasing hormones are shown in Figure 41–1. Increases in LH and FSH concentrations after injection of LRF were comparable in the two groups, but 9 of 10 patients with gonadotropin deficiency had a PRL level of less than 22 ng/ml after TRH injection. The 4 boys with delayed puberty who had low peak LH responses were clearly distinguished by their normal PRL responses. The 4 patients with gonadotropin deficiency who had the highest LH peaks had low PRL responses to TRH.

An impaired PRL response to TRH is a feature of isolated gonadotropin deficiency and facilitates its differentiation from delayed puberty. The precise mechanism underlying the difference in response is unclear. A subtle difference in estradiol levels is a possible explanation. Alternatively, a degree of estrogen insensitivity may characterize isolated gonadotropin deficiency.

▶ [This sounds like a useful technique, but the numbers of patients studied are very small, and a good deal of experience will be needed before its value is established.

Note: GnRH, LRH, and LRF all refer to the same hormone, gonadotropin-releasing hormone.] ◀

41–2 **Critical Illness and Low Testosterone: Effects of Human Serum of Testosterone Transport Into Rat Brain and Liver.** Acutely ill patients tend to have a marked decrease in plasma testosterone level, which resolves when the insult is eliminated. Nonthyroidal illness has been associated with the inhibition of thyroid hormone–binding plasma proteins. Onoufrios S. Goussis, William M. Pardridge, and Howard L. Judd (Univ. of California, Los Angeles) have now examined the effects of acute illness on testosterone–binding plasma proteins in 10 male patients in an intensive care unit and 9 control subjects. Respective mean ages were 43 and 31 years. Most patients were hospitalized for acute respiratory failure, ventricular arrhythmia, or congestive heart failure. Mean serum thyroxine concentration was 2.6 μg/dl. None of the patients had received hormonal therapy or had a history of pituitary or gonadal disease.

Total plasma testosterone level was 66% lower in patients than in control subjects. Serum sex hormone–binding globulin (SHBG) was increased 35%, and albumin was reduced 24%. The free testosterone fraction was not significantly altered, but the non-SHBG–bound fraction was reduced 35%. Studies in rats showed the unidirectional extraction of testosterone H^3 by rat brain and liver to be significantly reduced by patient serum. The exchangeable fraction was reduced 24% in brain and 35% in liver.

The pathogenesis of low serum testosterone levels in acute illness differs from that of low serum thyroid hormone levels. The increase in serum binding of testosterone by SHBG may be due in part to the greater age of patients in this study. If testosterone clearance is abnormal in acutely ill patients, clearance is likely to be reduced, and the low serum testosterone concentration would appear to be chiefly due to decreased testicular secretion.

▶ [As the authors point out, this observation suggests superficially a pattern reminiscent of the "sick thyroid" syndrome, and indeed the patients had low serum T_4 levels.

(41–2) J. Clin. Endocrinol. Metab. 56:710–714, April 1983.

In fact it is quite different. The sex hormone–binding globulin level is high rather than low, and the entry of testosterone into the tissues is reduced. In both situations, however, the concentration of free hormone in the plasma is normal.

The impact of a specific form of stress on testicular function—exposure to irradiation during treatment of acute lymphoblastic leukemia—is discussed in an interesting article. It is impossible to avoid this type of irradiation in some children, but it imposes a penalty. Ten of 12 boys irradiated 1–8 years previously had low Leydig cell response to chorionic gonadotropin or an increase of plasma luteinizing hormone or both. All pubertal patients had diminished testicular volume, implying tubular atrophy.[5]] ◀

41–3 **Induction of Puberty in Men by Long-Term Pulsatile Administration of Low-Dose Gonadotropin-Releasing Hormone.** Episodic discharge of hypothalamic gonadotropin-releasing hormone (GnRH) appears to be the central event in the initiation of puberty, and faulty secretion appears to be the primary defect in idiopathic hypogonadotropic hypogonadism. Andrew R. Hoffman and William F. Crowley, Jr. (Massachusetts Genl. Hosp., Boston) evaluated episodic administration of GnRH, delivered with a portable infusion pump, in a long-term study of 6 men with idiopathic hypogonadotropic hypogonadism. Each had failed to undergo puberty spontaneously by age 18 years and had low circulating gonadotropin and testosterone levels but no evidence of other hypothalamic-pituitary abnormalities. Initially, a dose of 25 ng of GnRH per kilogram of body weight was administered subcutaneously every 2 hours.

Levels of gonadotropins and testosterone rose in all patients with short-term GnRH therapy (Fig 41–2). Four patients achieved serum testosterone levels in the adult range within the first week of treatment. All patients noted increased spontaneous erections, nocturnal emissions, and androgen-induced skin changes. Somatic growth oc-

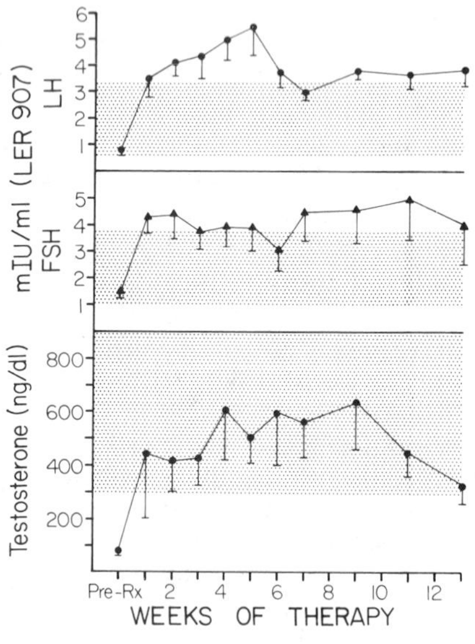

Fig 41–2.—Mean levels (± SE) of LH, FSH, and testosterone in 6 men with idiopathic hypogonadotropic hypogonadism. Shaded areas represent range of normal values in men; values for weeks 6 and 9 are those in 5 patients; values in week 13 are those of 4 patients. (Courtesy of Hoffman, A.R., and Crowley, W.F., Jr.: N. Engl. J. Med. 307:1237–1241, Nov. 11, 1982; reprinted by permission of The New England Journal of Medicine.)

(41–3) N. Engl. J. Med. 307:1237–1241, Nov. 11, 1982.

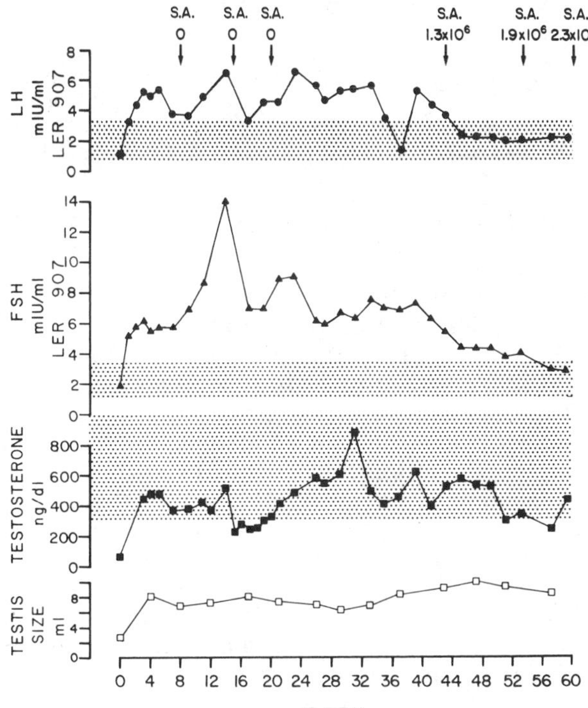

Fig 41–3.—Course of long-term therapy in 1 patient. Dose of gonadotropin-releasing hormone (GnRH) was 25 ng/kg of body weight in weeks 1–38, 10 ng in weeks 39–50, and 5 ng in weeks 51–59. Drug was delivered every 2 hours except during weeks 23–27, when it was administered every hour, and during weeks 28–33, when it was administered every 90 minutes. Results of semen analysis *(S.A.)* are expressed as number of sperm per milliliter of seminal fluid; shaded area represents range of normal values for adult men. Each measurement of LH, FSH, and testosterone represents value determined for pool of 25 specimens obtained every 20 minutes during 8-hour period. Testis size is expressed as average value for patient's testes, as measured with Prader orchidometer. (Courtesy of Hoffman, A.R., and Crowley, W.F., Jr.: N. Engl. J. Med. 307:1237–1241, Nov. 11, 1982; reprinted by permission of The New England Journal of Medicine.)

curred in 5 patients whose epiphyses were unfused. Transient mild breast discomfort was universal, and 3 patients had mild persistent gynecomastia. Maturation of spermatogenesis was achieved in 3 patients after 4, 11, and 43 weeks of treatment, respectively. The course of long-term therapy in 1 of these patients is shown in Figure 41–3. The wife of 1 patient conceived after the 26th week of his treatment. Serum estradiol levels remained normal in all patients throughout treatment.

Long-term episodic GnRH administration apparently can reverse idiopathic hypogonadotropic hypogonadism. The ability to stimulate gonadotropin secretion in this way should permit studies of the normal dynamics of hypothalamic-pituitary interactions.

▶ [One hopes that it would also restore normal sociosexual interactions as well.

There has been a good deal of interest in the ability of analogues of gonadotropin-releasing hormone (GnRH) to inhibit fertility. The fact that these polypeptides can inhibit steroidogenesis in rat ovarian granulosal and luteal cells and testicular Leydig cells suggests that they may have the ability to block receptors for tropic factors such as LH or FSH. If such is the case, it should be possible to demonstrate receptors in these tissues. In fact, such receptors have been demonstrated in rodent cells, but apparently no receptor activity can be demonstrated in human corpus luteum or monkey testis. In contrast, receptors can be found in adult and fetal human anterior pituitary tissue. Thus it seems unlikely that there is a direct inhibitory effect of GnRH on primate gonadal tissue.[6] It will be interesting to see whether this fact will alter the future usefulness of GnRH and its derivatives as contraceptives in man.

Precocious puberty is rare in humans, and so are gonadotropin-secreting pituitary tumors. The demonstration of sexual precocity in a 4-year-old boy as a result of an LH-secreting tumor is therefore a real rarity. Removal of the tumor resulted within 10 days in restoration of serum LH, testosterone, and prolactin levels to normal from their preoperative elevated state.[7]] ◀

41–4 **Episodic Luteinizing Hormone (LH) Secretion and the Response of LH and Follicle-Stimulating Hormone to LH-Releasing Hormone in Aged Men: Evidence for Coexistent Primary Testicular Insufficiency and an Impairment in Gonadotropin Secretion.** The defect in testicular function that accompanies aging appears to be intrinsic to the testis, since levels of circulating gonadotropins are elevated. However, it is not clear whether differing gonadotropin secretory patterns have a role in the gonadotropin elevation. Stephen J. Winters and Philip Troen (Univ. of Pittsburgh) examined the effects of aging on episodic LH secretion and on gonadotropin release after LRF administration in 14 healthy men aged 65–80 years. All were fathers except 1 who had married an older woman. Most were not using medications. Ten normal young men and 8 men aged 20–35 years with primary gonadal failure also were assessed.

Mean morning serum testosterone levels were 16% lower in the elderly men than in the young men. Mean serum gonadotropin concentrations were increased 2- to 3-fold in the older group. The circulating testosterone-binding globulin concentration was increased, but estrone and estradiol levels were unchanged in the elderly men. Both normal groups had comparably frequent LH pulses, but a slower rate of decline from peak occurred in the older men. A 2-fold increment in LH pulse height was noted in the men with primary gonadal failure, and the mean LH level was increased 4-fold. Peak LH levels after LRF administration were similar in the normal groups, but the median peak response occurred later in the older men. The rate of disapperance of LH from serum was slower in the elderly men. No difference in the apparent molecular size of LH was found between the normal groups.

These findings indicate that Leydig cell function declines in healthy elderly men as a result of primary testicular insufficiency. Episodic LH secretion appears to take place normally in older men, but LH responses to administered LRF are abnormal, indicating an additional hypothalamic-pituitary disorder of gonadotropin secretion associated with aging.

▶ [Aging is certainly a common cause of mild progressive hypogonadism (in spite of tales of potency and fertility in some men at advanced ages). Hypogonadism is also often associated with obesity, another common metabolic problem. In a group of 21

(41–4) J. Clin. Endocrinol. Metab. 55:560–565, September 1982.

otherwise healthy obese men (52%–332% above desirable weight) aged 18–50 years, the total and free testosterone and the FSH all were about 30% depressed as compared with those of 24 age-matched nonobese men. Levels of LH were also mildly depressed, which is especially abnormal in view of the low levels of testosterone. On the other hand, dihydrotestosterone levels, libido, potency, and spermatogenesis were all essentially normal in the obese group. The pattern is one of mildly suppressed pituitary gonadotropic function consistent with the mild hyperestrogenemia which can also be demonstrated in obese individuals.[8] However, I interpret the normal dihydrotestosterone and functional levels as evidence that the defect in testosterone secretion is compensated by adequate conversion in peripheral tissues of testosterone to its active form, dihydrotestosterone.] ◀

Chapter 41 References

1. Speroff L. (ed.): Menopause. *Seminars in Reproductive Endocrinology* 1:1–77, 1983.
2. Coulam C.B. (ed.): Premature gonadal failure. *Seminars in Reproductive Endocrinology* 1:79–178, 1983.
3. Pike M.C., Henderson B.E., Krailo M.D., et al.: Breast cancer in young women and use of oral contraceptives: possible modifying effect of formulation and age at use. *Lancet* 2:926–929, 1983.
4. Vessey M.P., Lawless M., McPherson K., et al.: Neoplasia of the cervix uteri and contraception: a possible adverse effect of the pill. *Lancet* 2:930–934, 1983.
5. Brauner R., Czernichow P., Cramer P., et al.: Leydig-cell function in children after direct testicular irradiation for acute lymphoblastic leukemia. *N. Engl. J. Med.* 309:25–28, 1983.
6. Clayton R.N., Huhtaniemi I.T.: Absence of gonadotropin-releasing hormone receptors in human gonadal tissue. *Nature* 299:56–59, 1982.
7. Faggiano M., Criscuolo T., Perrone L., et al.: Sexual precocity in a boy due to hypersecretion of LH and prolactin by a pituitary adenoma. *Acta Endocrinol.* 102:167–172, 1983.
8. Strain G.W., Zumoff B., Kream J., et al.: Mild hypogonadotropic hypogonadism in obese men. *Metabolism* 31:871–875, 1982.

42. Ectopic Hormones

42-1 **Glycoprotein-Hormone α-Chain Production by Pancreatic Endocrine Tumors: Specific Marker for Malignancy: Immunocytochemical Analysis of Tumors of 155 Patients.** It is difficult to document malignant pancreatic endocrine tumors early in their course. Philipp U. Heitz, Marlis Kasper (Univ. of Basel), Günter Klöppel (Univ. of Hamburg), Julia M. Polak (Univ. of London), and Judith L. Vaitukaitis (Boston Univ.) tested 157 pancreatic endocrine tumors from 155 patients for the presence of α- or β-subunits of human chorionic gonadotropin (hCG) by means of the immunocytochemical technique. The series included 83 female and 72 male patients, aged 12–78 years. The presence of α-reactive hCG cells was detected in 75% of 56 functioning malignant pancreatic endocrine tumors, in only 1 of 67 functioning benign tumors (a possibly benign glucagonoma), in 1 of 17 nonfunctioning malignant tumors, and in none of 17 nonfunctioning benign tumors. No β-hCG immunoreactivity was localized in any of the tumors. The distribution of cells showing α-hCG immunoreactivity was very irregular: there often were large clusters of stained cells in one section but not in another of the same tumor.

The α-subunit of hCG appears to be a reliable marker for malignancy in functioning pancreatic endocrine tumors. Its detection by immunocytochemical study is a useful qualitative marker, since it apparently is produced virtually exclusively by functioning and malignant pancreatic endocrine tumors. It also is a useful quantitative marker. Occasionally, this glycoprotein is the only detectable secretion product of pancreatic endocrine tumors. Systematic study of the production and secretion of hCG subunits may permit the detection of small, potentially curable tumor foci.

▶ [This study confirms, in a histological context, the clinical observations of Kahn et al., who demonstrated the value of measuring plasma hCG concentrations in differentiating malignant islet cell tumors of the pancreas from benign adenomas.[1]

The concept of amine-precursor uptake decarboxylation (APUD) tumors continues to generate a lot of conflict. An excellent brief summary (entitled "Dogma Disputed") was published in *The Lancet.*[2] It reviews the evidence that alleges that secreting argyrophilic cells ("APUD" cells) are derived from a single source and that most tumors secreting polypeptide hormones are derived from this single line of cells originating embryologically in the neural crest and migrating into the somatic organs. However, when the neural crest is excised in the embryo, pancreatic β cells (alleged to be of APUD—i.e., neuroendocrine—origin) still develop; the alleged migration of neural crest cells into the somatic organs during embryonic development has been disproved by studies of chimeras in which the neural crest from quails was implanted into chick embryos, but the "APUD" cells were derived from chick rather than quail cells; the ultrastructural details of tumors generally agreed to be of neuroendocrine origin, such as medullary carcinoma of the thyroid, carotid body tumors, and pheo-

---

(42–1) Cancer 51:277–282, Jan. 15, 1983.

chromocytomas, differ fundamentally from other "APUD" tumors such as small-cell undifferentiated carcinomas of the lung, appendix, and kidney. Many of these tumors contain areas which differentiate into mucus-secreting or squamous cells, which would be unexpected if the APUD hypothesis were correct. In addition, there are numerous instances of tumors that produce hormonal polypeptides although they are clearly carcinomas. For example, ACTH has reported as a product of myeloblastic leukemia; renal adenocarcinomas can produce insulin and glucagon in massive amounts; and squamous cell carcinoma of the cervix uteri can release enough insulin to cause hypoglycemia. Moreover, as discussed previously in the section on the pituitary in this volume, hormonal polypeptides are produced by almost all cells of the body and by some lower organisms including unicellular entities. For example, normal lung and thyroid tissue contain ACTH, endorphin, and lipotropin.[3] For all of these reasons, the "APUD" concept seems unnecessary and confusing and should be abandoned.

Nevertheless, there is probably a relationship among the various types of tumors that secrete small polypeptides. It has recently proved possible to isolate a monoclonal antibody that reacts with normal and neoplastic tissues containing secretory granules. The tissues include normal adrenal medulla, gastrointestinal endocrine glands, endocrine pancreas, parathyroid, anterior pituitary, and thyroid C cells. Other glandular tissues, which are not considered to be of APUD origin, do not stain. Those not staining include the adrenal cortex, exocrine pancreas, posterior pituitary and thyroid follicular cells. The findings are consistent with the presence of a common protein in a wide variety of endocrine cells with secretory granules. The new antibody offers a tool both for clinical diagnosis and for dissecting the relationships among these related tissues and tumors.[4] Still, the specificity of the new antibody for APUD tumors is not entirely proved. One could also interpret these findings as evidence that all secretory granules, whatever their origin, contain a single protein, perhaps as part of their secretory "machinery."

It has been suggested that the syndrome of multiple endocrine adenomatosis type I (MEA-I) can be recognized by the presence of elevated concentrations of serum gastrin and pancreatic polypeptide.[5] The statement is based on a study of 51 members of 3 families carrying the MEA-I trait, of whom 25 had clinical evidence of tumors. Among the group with proved or probable pancreatic tumors, 78% had high gastrin levels and 67% had high pancreatic polypeptide concentrations.

What is the mechanism of the hypoglycemia produced by extrapancreatic tumors? An easy answer in the past has been that the tumors secrete an insulin-like growth factor, IGF-II. However, the serum concentration of IGF-II in 22 such patients was not elevated in 30 specimens which were analysed by radioimmunoassay or radioreceptor assay, even when special steps were taken to dissociate the polypeptide from its carrier protein.[6]

There is increasing indirect evidence that the hypercalcemia associated with certain types of nonparathyroid tumors in the absence of extensive bony metastasis is caused by some factor other than parathyroid hormone. This position is bolstered by the demonstration that tumors causing this humoral hypercalcemia of malignancy do not contain the messenger RNA for parathyroid hormone.[7] They don't contain parathyroid hormone either, of course.

Everyone who has had to deal with a patient with the ectopic ACTH syndrome has probably considered whether a surgical approach would be beneficial. The experience of the Hammersmith Hospital group in dealing with this question has recently been summarized.[8] Two approaches are discussed: removal of the primary tumor and adrenalectomy. Most patients have metastatic disease before diagnosis and die of the tumor causing the syndrome, but a few tumors are indolent enough that the patient can benefit from their surgical extirpation. These include carcinoids of the bronchus or appendix which are believed to be benign. In these patients, removal of the tumor produced a rapid remission of the syndrome, although subsequent recurrences sometimes limited the duration of relief. Bilateral total adrenalectomy was undertaken in patients in whom the primary cause of the syndrome could not be identified. (One later proved to have a benign bronchial adenoma.) In this group, remission was prompt and persistent. In the group of 8 patients treated either by removal of the primary benign tumor or the adrenals, and without visceral metastases, 7 are in remission 1 to 15 years after operation. Thus the surgical approach is valuable in this limited group of patients.] ◀

Chapter 42 References

1. Kahn C.R., Rosen S.W., Weintraub B.D., et al.: Ectopic production of chorionic gonadotropin and its subunits by islet cell tumors. *N. Engl. J. Med.* 297:565–569, 1977.
2. Stevens R.E., Moore G.E.: Inadequacy of APUD concept in explaining production of peptide hormones by tumors. *Lancet* 1:118–119, 1983.
3. Clements J.A., Funder J.W., Tracy K., et al.: Adrenocorticotropin, endorphin, and -lipotropin in normal thyroid and lung: possible implications for ectopic hormone secretion. *Endocrinology* 111:2097–2102, 1982.
4. Lloyd R.V., Wilson B.S.: Specific endocrine tissue marker defined by a monoclonal antibody. *Science* 222:628–630, 1983.
5. Öberg K., Wälinder O., Boström H., et al.: Peptide hormone markers in screening for endocrine tumors in multiple endocrine adenomatosis type I. *Am. J. Med.* 73:619–630, 1982.
6. Widmer U., Zapf J., Froesch E.R.: Is extrapancreatic tumor hypoglycemia associated with elevated levels of insulin-like growth factor II? *J. Clin. Endocrinol. Metab.* 55:833–839, 1982.
7. Simpson E.L., Mundy G.R., D'Souza S.M., et al.: Absence of parathyroid hormone messenger RNA in nonparathyroid tumors associated with hypercalcemia. *N. Engl. J. Med.* 309:325–330, 1982.
8. Davies C.J., Joplin G.F., Welbourn R.B.: Surgical management of the ectopic ACTH syndrome. *Ann. Surg.* 196:246–257, 1982.

43. Carbohydrate Metabolism

INTRODUCTION

New factors influencing the secretion of the hormones that control carbohydrate metabolism continue to be found. Bombesin causes a sharp and prompt rise of plasma insulin concentration when given intravenously. Pancreatic glucagon level also rises, but intestinal glucagon responds much more slowly. It appears therefore that the effect is primarily on the pancreatic islet cells, since the response is too rapid to be secondary to changes in blood glucose concentration.[1] β-Endorphin also causes a prompt increase of plasma glucagon level and, following this, of glucose concentration. Insulin concentration also rises in normal, but not in diabetic, individuals; and the insulin response precedes that of glucagon. The dosage of endorphin required to demonstrate the effect is very small—only 5 μg—but this is sufficient to raise the plasma concentration 40-fold.[2]

Johnson has recently reviewed the history of the introduction into the therapeutic armamentarium of human insulin synthesized through recombinant DNA technology.[3] The big advantage is almost unlimited availability of insulin. It may sometimes have a therapeutic advantage over hog or bovine insulin. For example, in a patient with Arthus's phenomenon after injection of purified bovine or porcine insulin, switching to human recombinant insulin eliminated the skin rashes. Curiously, antibodies to human insulin were present before it was administered.[4] On the other hand, in a double-blind crossover study no evidence could be found for superiority of recombinant human insulin over porcine or bovine insulin in respect to the fasting blood glucose level, mean diurnal glucose concentrations, or insulin requirement. Indeed, it appears that human insulin may be slightly inferior to porcine hormone—perhaps because of a difference in the pharmacokinetics of the two preparations.[5] In addition, human insulin appears to have no advantage over purified porcine or bovine insulins in reducing the titer of circulating antibodies to insulin.[6]

Among the several factors that have been proposed as causes of inheritable diabetes, abnormality of the control mechanisms for insulin synthesis is of special interest. This control is exerted in part by the sequences of DNA adjacent to the insulin genome. Consequently, it is intriguing that variations have been found in the DNA sequence flanking the 5′ end of the insulin gene. Polymorphism is present both in normal and in type II diabetics, but it is very much more common in the diabetics than in the normal population ($P = .01$). Thus polymorphism of this type might be a marker for the genetic tendency to develop type II diabetes.[7] Three patients have now been described, in addition, who have abnormal insulin genomes. In each instance, the patient has diabetes with high levels of plasma insulin but with normal sensitivity to exogenous insulin; presumably the abnormal insulin has reduced effectiveness and—even when present in high concentrations—fails to maintain normal blood glucose levels.[8]

Progress has been made in defining the nature of the insulin receptor found on the cell membranes. Highly purified preparations of receptor protein have tyrosine-specific protein phosphokinase activity.[9, 10] Antibodies to the receptor protein block insulin binding and inhibit insulin activity.[11] But the ability of insulin to bind to the receptor is not in itself enough to produce an effect. The receptors of a patient with the extreme insulin resistance of leprechaunism had an abnormally high binding affinity for insulin.[12] Presumably some abnormality of the structure of the receptor increases its ability to bind the hormone while interfering with the next step in the action of insulin—probably the induction of protein kinase activity. Improved understanding of the nature and action of the insulin receptor should ultimately lead to useful increases in our ability to evaluate and treat diabetic patients; but at present information about the receptors in health and disease has not had any appreciable impact on clinical practice.[13]

It is well established that increasing age is associated with reduced sensitivity to insulin and consequent deterioration of glucose tolerance and a shift toward the development of a sort of diabetes. The explanation apparently lies in alterations in insulin activity at some point within the cell after the interaction with the receptor, since receptor activity does not change with age.[14, 15]

43–1 **Postprandial Glucose and Insulin Responses to Meals Containing Different Carbohydrates in Normal and Diabetic Subjects.** The glucose and insulin responses to five meals, each containing a different form of carbohydrate but all with nearly identical amounts of total carbohydrate, protein, and fat, were studied by John P. Bantle, Dawn C. Laine, Gay W. Castle, J. William Thomas, Byron J. Hoogwerf, and Frederick C. Goetz (Univ. of Minnesota) to determine whether the form of dietary carbohydrate influences these responses. The study population consisted of 10 healthy subjects (7 women) with a mean age of 39 years, all within 10% of desirable body weight; 12 patients who had type I diabetes (8 women), whose mean age was 26 years and all of whom were within 10% of desirable body weight; and 10 patients with type II diabetes (3 women), whose mean age was 62 years and 7 of whom were within 10% of desirable body weight. All patients with type I diabetes took insulin injections once or twice daily. None of the type II patients took insulin or oral hypoglycemic agents. The meals contained fructose, sucrose, potato, wheat, or glucose.

The mean peak increment in plasma glucose concentration was smallest in the 10 healthy subjects after the meal containing fructose and largest after the meal containing glucose. In both groups of diabetics, the fructose meal again produced the smallest mean peak increment and the smallest mean area increment in plasma concentration of glucose (Fig 43–1). The glucose meal also produced the largest increase in both. The sucrose, potato, and wheat meals produced peak increments in plasma concentrations of glucose and increments in

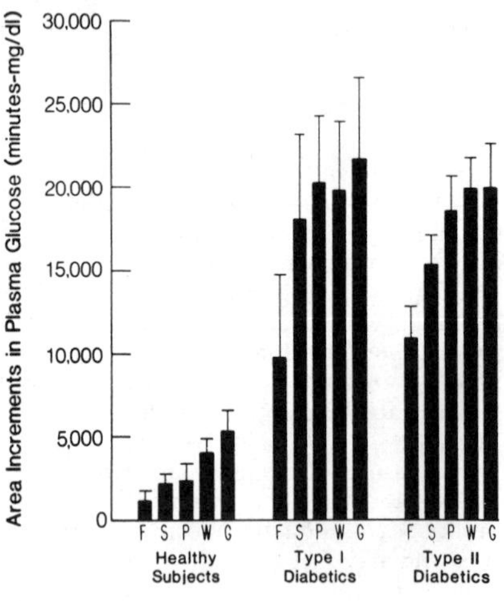

Fig 43–1.—Area increments in plasma concentrations of glucose (mean ± SEM). Test meals are indicated as follows: *F,* fructose; *S,* sucrose; *P,* potato; *W,* wheat; and *G,* glucose. (Courtesy of Bantle, J.P., et al.: N. Engl. J. Med. 309:7–12, July 7, 1983; reprinted by permission of the New England Journal of Medicine.)

(43–1) N. Engl. J. Med. 309:7–12, July 7, 1983.

area under the plasma glucose–response curves that were not significantly different within subject groups. In healthy subjects and patients with type II diabetes, peak serum insulin concentrations were not significantly different in response to the five test carbohydrates.

The data do not support the assumption that dietary sucrose aggravates hyperglycemia in diabetics, as in both type I and type II diabetics, sucrose, when consumed in a mixed meal that also contained protein and fat, did not produce a more rapid rise, a greater peak increment, or a greater area increment in plasma glucose concentration than did comparable amounts of potato or wheat starch. The data support the conclusion that fructose produces less postprandial hyperglycemia than do other common types of carbohydrate.

▶ [This observation has been foreshadowed by previous studies over the past 50 years, but it is much better documented than most earlier reports, and it comes at a time when clinicians' minds are better prepared than previously. There is a touching and ill-founded faith in the kind of "diabetes diet" that is based only on the total amount of carbohydrate in the diet. This approach has previously been disowned by the American Diabetes Association. Yet many practitioners and most dieticians continue to act as though quantitative control of the dietary composition (as differentiated from the total caloric intake) were an important therapeutic tool. Old habits and prejudices are almost impervious to new information.

In contrast to the poor correlation between the amount of carbohydrate in the diet and the blood glucose level, there is an important relationship between the qualitative nature of the diet and the blood glucose level, as indicated in the abstract. Other substances such as fiber ingested along with carbohydrate affect its rate of absorption, as has been discussed in these pages previously. A recent article emphasizes the value of adding a small amount (7 gm) of apple pectin to the diet in reducing the postprandial insulin requirement.[16] In addition, it is well established that depletion of the body potassium stores can exaggerate carbohydrate intolerance. Thiazide diuretics, for example, can inhibit the pancreatic β-cell response to hyperglycemia and reduce glucose tolerance.[17] In patients with reduced glucose tolerance this could induce or exacerbate the clinical manifestations of diabetes mellitus.] ◀

43–2 **Insulin Resistance Is a Prominent Feature of Insulin-Dependent Diabetes.** Insulin resistance is a well-known feature of non-insulin-dependent type II diabetes, but it is not clear whether it also is present in insulin-dependent type I diabetes. Ralph A. DeFronzo, Rosa Hendler, and Donald Simonson (Yale Univ.) used the insulin-clamp technique to assess tissue sensitivity to insulin in 19 insulin-dependent diabetics, who had a mean age of 33 years and ideal body weight, and in 36 healthy subjects aged 21–49 years. The mean duration of diabetes was 12 years, and the mean daily insulin dose was 35 units of NPH or the equivalent. The plasma insulin concentration was acutely raised by about 100 μU/ml above the fasting level. Eleven patients were assessed at their fasting hyperglycemic level; 8, after the plasma glucose concentration had been reduced to the euglycemic level.

Insulin-mediated glucose metabolism was reduced by 32% in the diabetics assessed at hyperglycemic levels (Fig 43–2). Controls who were clamped at hyperglycemic levels comparable to those in the diabetics had glucose metabolism that was more than 250% above that of the diabetics. Diabetics studied at euglycemic levels showed an

---

(43–2) Diabetes 31:795–801, September 1982.

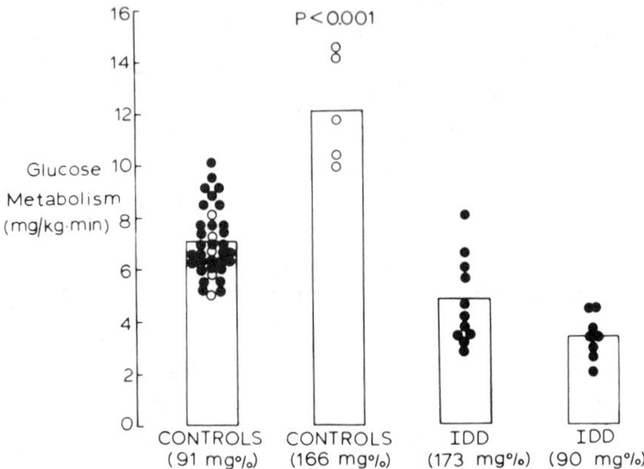

Fig 43–2.—Insulin-mediated glucose uptake in insulin-dependent diabetics (IDD) and control subjects assessed at euglycemic and hyperglycemic levels. Steady-state plasma glucose level at which insulin-clamp study was performed is shown in parentheses. Height of bar represents mean ± SEM for each group; filled circles represent individual data points for each subject; open circles represent 5 control subjects reassessed at hyperglycemic levels. (Courtesy of DeFronzo, R.A., et al.: Diabetes 31:795–801, September 1982.)

even greater reduction in insulin-mediated glucose metabolism. The metabolic clearance rate was reduced by more than half in the diabetics compared with control subjects. Basal hepatic glucose production was 26% greater in the diabetic group, and correlated closely with the fasting plasma glucose concentration. Hepatic glucose production was suppressed by about 95% after induction of hyperinsulinemia in both the diabetics and the control subjects.

Impaired insulin action appears to be a common feature of insulin-dependent diabetes, despite daily insulin requirements that would not indicate insulin resistance. The insulin resistance seen in these patients was marked and appeared to reside in peripheral tissues. The cellular mechanism of the resistance remains to be clarified. Both an increase and a decrease in insulin receptor number have been described in insulin-dependent diabetics.

▶ [Thus both type I and type II diabetes are characterized by reduced responsiveness to insulin. The relationship of insulin resistance to type II diabetes was the subject of a symposium, which has been published in the *American Journal of Medicine.*[18]] ◀

43–3 **Identification of Type I Diabetic Patients at Increased Risk for Hypoglycemia During Intensive Therapy.** Type I diabetics have deficient glucagon responses and are dependent on epinephrine to promote glucose recovery from hypoglycemia. Epinephrine secretion is reduced in diabetic autonomic neuropathy, and the combination of defects would increase the risk of recurrent severe hypoglycemia in insulin-treated patients. Neil H. White, Donald A. Skor, Philip E. Cryer, Lucy A. Levandoski, Dennis M. Bier, and Julio V. Santiago (St. Louis) attempted to find a way of prospectively identifying such patients. Twenty-two patients with insulin-dependent diabetes participated in the study. The mean duration of diabetes was 12 years.

(43–3) N. Engl. J. Med. 308:485–491, Mar. 3, 1983.

Seven patients had evidence of peripheral diabetic polyneuropathy, and 3 had overt autonomic neuropathy. Three patients had proliferative retinopathy, but all had normal renal function. All patients had had symptomatic hypoglycemia, which in 9 cases had been severe. Ten nondiabetic controls also were assessed. After overnight fasting, studies were performed with insulin and 6,6-$^2H_2$-glucose.

Glucose counterregulation was inadequate in 9 of the 22 study patients. The study had to be ended prematurely in 3 of these patients. The presence of peripheral or autonomic neuropathy and a history of severe hypoglycemic episodes were poor predictors of failure of response to hypoglycemia in the insulin-infusion test. No increment in plasma glucagon concentration occurred in response to hypoglycemia in either group of patients with type I diabetes (Fig 43–3). The epinephrine response to hypoglycemia was markedly reduced in the patients with inadequate glucose counterregulation but was normal or exaggerated in those with adequate counterregulation. Plasma free insulin levels rose comparably in the two groups of diabetics. On follow-up, episodes of severe hypoglycemia occurred in all but 1 of the patients with inadequate glucose counterregulation but in only 1 of the other patients.

Intravenous insulin-infusion testing can identify patients with type I diabetes who are at an increased risk for recurrent severe hypogly-

Fig 43–3.—Plasma concentrations (mean ± SE) of glucagon, epinephrine, norepinephrine, and cortisol during infusions of regular insulin (40 mU/kg of body weight/hour; infusion period is indicated *(arrows)* in 10 normal controls *(stippled areas)*, in 13 insulin-dependent patients with diabetes mellitus who had adequate glucose counterregulation (●), and in 9 insulin-dependent patients who had inadequate glucose counterregulation (○). (Courtesy of White, N.H., et al.: N. Engl. J. Med. 308:485–491, Mar. 3, 1983; reprinted by permission of The New England Journal of Medicine.)

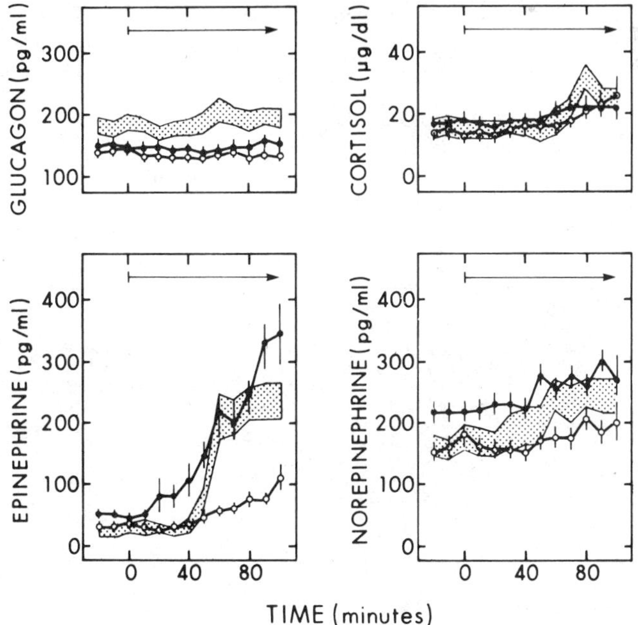

cemia during intensive treatment for diabetes. Patients at risk can be advised to maintain a prebreakfast plasma glucose concentration of at least 140 mg/dl and to periodically check the glucose level at 3 A.M. to make sure it exceeds 60 mg/dl.

▶ [The distinguishing characteristic is failure of epinephrine to respond normally to hypoglycemia, since norepinephrine and glucagon failed to respond in both hypoglycemia-prone and hypoglycemia-resistant patients. The main value of this test would be to predict which patients may get in trouble with tight control, especially on the insulin pump or on a regimen of multiple injections. Obviously demonstration of the tendency does not mean that tight control should not be attempted—only that great care should be exercised in designing the therapeutic regimen. The effects of hypoglycemic reactions and the disruption of normal biochemical control produced by low blood glucose in type I diabetics have been reviewed recently.[19]] ◀

43–4 **Can Future Type I Diabetes Be Predicted? Study in Families of Affected Children.** A. N. Gorsuch, K. M. Spencer, J. Lister, E. Wolf, G. F. Bottazzo, and A. G. Cudworth (St. Bartholomew's Hosp. Med. College, London) examined the risk of type I (insulin-dependent) diabetes in siblings of affected children in relation to HLA genotypes. The standard microlymphocytotoxicity technique was used. The 288 available siblings of 160 diabetic probands were grouped according to number of HLA haplotypes in common with their probands (Table 1).

Eleven (3.5%) of the parents and 14 (5%) of the siblings had type I diabetes. The prevalence in the siblings (grouped according to HLA-ABC genotype identity with their probands) is shown in Table 2, which also gives the relative risks (RR) for diabetes calculated by comparing the frequencies in the siblings with the age-adjusted frequencies derived from a British study and a Danish study as low and high estimates of general population frequency. Whichever set of control figures is used, the RR for HLA-identical siblings is significantly higher than that for haploidentical siblings (P = 11 and P = .008, respectively). Genetic susceptibility is mainly HLA linked, in that prevalence in siblings is significantly associated with increasing HLA haplotype concordance with probands. These results reinforce

TABLE 1.—SIBLINGS GROUPED ACCORDING TO HLA-A, -B, AND -C HAPLOTYPE CONCORDANCE WITH PROBAND

Number of haplotypes in common with proband*	2	2/1†	1	1/0	0	Total
Number of siblings‡	50	8	151	8	71	288
Number diabetic at entry	5	0	4	0	1§	10
(%)	(10)		(3)		(1)	(3)

*Intra-HLA recombinants are grouped according to B locus identity with proband because not all families have been HLA-DR genotyped.

†Either two or one haplotype in common with proband, but ambiguous because the two haplotypes in one parent are indistinguishable (10 families).

‡Distribution of 272 siblings among the three unambiguous groups, compared with the 68, 136, and 68 "expected"; χ^2 = 6.55; P = .038.

§This child has an HLA/DR recombinant haplotype and is thus identical with her proband for the DR region of that haplotype.

(Courtesy of Gorsuch, A.N., et al.: Diabetes 31:862–866, October 1982.)

(43–4) Diabetes 31:862–866, October 1982.

TABLE 2.—CURRENT PREVALENCE OF DIABETES IN SIBLINGS GROUPED BY HLA GENOTYPE IDENTITY WITH PROBAND

Group	HLA-identical	Haplo-identical	Non-identical	All siblings*
Number of siblings	50	151	71	288
Number diabetic	7	6	1	14†
Prevalence (%)	14	4	1	5
Compared with N:‡ relative risk (95% confidence limits)	118 (52–265)	31 (13–69)	NS	36 (20–64)
P	$<10^{-10}$	$<10^{-10}$	0.09§	$<10^{-10}$
Compared with D:‡ relative risk (95% confidence limits)	76 (35–164)	20 (9–43)	NS	23 (14–39)
P	$<10^{-10}$	$<10^{-10}$	0.15§	$<10^{-10}$

*Including those with ambiguous HLA genotypes.
†Distribution among nonambiguous groups compared with that expected if no linkage between HLA and diabetes: $P = .0053$. Analysis for quadratic trend: $P < .005$.
‡Age-corrected frequencies of diabetes in general population samples: *N*, Northampton, 1964: 66/45,500 (0.15%); *D*, Denmark, 1977: 1,629/716,285 (0.23%).
§One-tailed binomial test.
(Courtesy of Gorsuch, A.N., et al.: Diabetes 31:862–866, October 1983.)

other evidence that HLA-linked susceptibility to type I diabetes is not determined by a single dominant gene and are compatible with hypotheses involving recessive or intermediate inheritance or interaction of two or more genes.

Siblings who are HLA identical (both haplotypes in common) have a risk of developing type I diabetes that is approximately 100 times greater than that of the general population; this risk is significantly higher than that in haploidentical siblings (1 haplotype in common). Some 30% of these siblings would be diabetic by age 30 in the North European population. The risk in nonidentical siblings (neither haplotype in common) is not significantly increased. These findings are of considerable importance for genetic counseling.

▶ [If prevention of type I diabetes is ever to be practicable, it will be essential to identify the individuals at risk *before* the disease is evident. This article provides one tool for recognizing high risk patients. Additional information about the genetic component involved in the pathogenesis of type I diabetes is provided by other work of the group at St. Bartholomew's Hospital, London, which has examined 123 patients and their families. Ninety-eight percent of probands possessed either DR3 or DR4 HLA types. The relative risk for DR3 was 5 times that of controls; for DR4 6.8 times; and both antigens together, 14.3 times. Half of the patients were DR3-DR4 heterozygotes. In the families of the diabetic patients DR3 and DR4 were common, but homozygosity was not increased. In contrast, DR7 and DR2 were rare and carried only about 10% of the normal risk of diabetes.[20]

There is also apparently an infectious element in the pathogenesis of the disease. For example, the presence of infection with coxsackievirus type B and islet cell antibodies can often be demonstrated as much as three years before overt diabetes develops.[21]

The evidence that there is an autoimmune component to the pathogenesis of insulin-deficiency diabetes is constantly being reinforced. For example, it has now been possible, in BB/W rats, to transfer diabetes passively by injecting lymphocytes from rats of the same strain with active diabetes into nondiabetic animals.[22] Moreover, the ratio of helper to suppressor T cells is abnormally increased in patients with type I diabetes.[23] The fact that cyclosporine prevents the development of diabetes in Wistar BB rats, 75% of which develop a spontaneous diabetes similar to type I in humans,[24] suggests that one might consider immunosuppressive treatment in humans at high risk. In a very small group of patients with recent onset of type I diabetes, immune suppression with antithymocyte globulin together with prednisone dramatically reduced the insulin requirement, whereas prednisone alone had no significant effect.[25] Cyclosporine would probably be safer than this approach, although solid data derived from long-term follow-up are not yet available. All of these considerations suggest that we are approaching the time when trials of immunosuppression might be justified, although some people feel that we are not quite ready for that step.[26]] ◀

43–5 **Long-Term Correction of Hyperglycemia and Progression of Renal Failure in Insulin-Dependent Diabetes.** Strict control of glycemia with insulin reverses some of the renal changes caused by experimental diabetes in rats; however, this model is inadequate because clinical nephropathy and renal failure do not develop in animals. G. C. Viberti, R. W. Bilous, D. Mackintosh, J. J. Bending, and H. Keen (Guy's Hosp. Med. School, London) examined the effect of long-term strict glycemic control on the rate of deterioration of renal function in 6 insulin-dependent diabetics with established clinical diabetic nephropathy. In all cases, proteinuria had appeared more than 10 years after the diagnosis of diabetes and had persisted for at least 1 year. Renal biopsy specimens from 2 patients showed diabetic changes only. After a baseline period of 10–24 months, the patients were changed from conventional injection therapy to continuous subcutaneous insulin infusion for a mean of 20.5 months. Six similar patients continued to receive conventional treatment and were followed up for a mean of 18 months.

A significant, sustained fall in glycosylated hemoglobin levels occurred in the study group, and plasma glucose profiles were greatly improved. Elevated blood pressure was treated equally effectively in the two groups. No significant difference was found between the slopes of regression lines for glomerular filtration rate over time before and after starting infusion treatment. The mean rate of fall in filtration rate did not differ significantly in the two groups initially or during the experimental period. The plasma creatinine concentration rose in all but 1 of the study patients. Plasma β_2-microglobulin levels also increased during the study, as did the mean fractional clearance of albumin and IgG.

The process that ends in renal failure apparently becomes self-perpetuating by the time glomerular function has begun to decline in patients with diabetic nephropathy and is little influenced by the degree of metabolic control. Patients with urinary albumin excretion of 50–200 mg/24 hours may be viewed as being at risk, and should be treated vigorously in an attempt to prevent clinical diabetic nephropathy.

▶ [For years, the most pressing question in the treatment of diabetes has been whether or not physiologic control would reverse or prevent the progression of the vascular and neurologic complications of the disease. With the advent of the open circuit insulin infusion pump it became possible to achieve something approaching physiologic control, but long-term follow-up of the use of this type of treatment is

(43–5) Br. Med. J. 286:598–602, February 19, 1983.

only now beginning to be possible. Viberti's report is important both because of its depressing information and because it indicates that there is still more to the problem of complications than good control of carbohydrate metabolism. These observations have been confirmed, in a group followed for only a year, by Cataland and O'Dorisio.[27] Moreover, diabetic nephropathy can appear for the first time during a period of improved glycemic control.[28] Cataland and O'Dorisio also point out that progression was closely associated with hypertension. Carrying this point further, Mogensen emphasizes that control of hypertension by the usual medical methods slows the decline of renal functions over a period of 6 years or more.[29] Thus more is involved in controlling this aspect of diabetic complications than mere improvement in metabolic control. Since thiazide diuretics often play a significant role in the medical treatment of hypertension, it is important to remember that they interfere with normal carbohydrate metabolism.[30] The effect is probably a result, at least in part, of potassium depletion.

It is generally agreed that it is important to keep the diabetic condition under tight control during pregnancy. How useful is the pump in this situation? Undoubtedly it works, but probably no better than careful control imposed by multiple injections of insulin and control of diet.[31] Tight control with the insulin pump or multiple injections of insulin improves the growth rate of young diabetic patients, even when their rate of growth during "ordinary" treatment is within normal limits.[32] This suggests that some juvenile diabetics benefit from tight control even though growth appears to be unimpaired.

The electroretinogram is often abnormally low even in newly diagnosed diabetic patients. It may improve significantly after only a week or so of intensive treatment.[33] I don't know what this implies about the prognosis for developing retinopathy or other neural abnormalities often seen some years after the onset of diabetes.

In extremely brittle diabetes, the Biostator, a closed circuit pump system, can bring metabolism under control.[34] This approach would be necessary only in very rare instances. The Biostator is too large to be portable. Yet the advantage of a closed circuit feedback-controlled insulin pump is obvious. Slow progress continues to be made in the direction of developing a portable machine of this type. A recent report describes a needle-type glucose sensor which would be an essential component of the system. Unfortunately, it has not yet demonstrated reliability over a period of more than about a week.[35]

An impressive symposium concerned with diabetic microangiopathy was held in May 1982. Its proceedings have recently been published.[36]] ◀

43–6 **Prevention of Deterioration of Renal and Sensory Nerve Function by More Intensive Management of Insulin-Dependent Diabetic Patients: A Two-Year Randomized Prospective Study.** Current management of insulin-dependent diabetes does not prevent the development of complications. R. R. Holman, T. L. Dornan, V. Mayon-White, J. Howard-Williams, C. Orde-Peckar, L. Jenkins, J. Steemson, R. Rolfe, B. Smith, D. Barbour, K. McPherson, Pyw Poon, C. Rizza, J. I. Mann, A. H. Knight, A. J. Bron, and R. C. Turner undertook a prospective study of insulin-dependent diabetic patients with background retinopathy to determine the degree to which near normal glycemia can be achieved by two daily insulin injections and whether the progress of diabetic complications can be retarded. Seventy-four patients were randomized to receive either a continuation of usual care or ultralente insulin as basal cover and soluble insulin at mealtime. The latter patients received closer dietary supervision and were taught to monitor blood glucose at home. They were seen at least every 6 weeks at a special clinic.

Mean insulin doses were not changed during the study in either group. Study patients maintained significantly lower glycosylated he-

(43–6) Lancet 1:204–208, Jan. 29, 1983.

moglobin levels during the study than controls, although the mean level also declined in the control group after nearly 2 years of study. Both renal and sensory nerve functions were significantly better maintained in the study patients. The plasma creatinine level increased in control patients, and the fall in creatinine clearance was significantly less in study patients. The rate of progression of retinopathy was similar in the two groups. Significant improvement in low-density lipoprotein cholesterol and in whole blood low-shear viscosity was noted in study patients.

It would appear that deterioration in neural and renal functions can be retarded by more intensive diabetic control. A more physiologic insulin regimen and capillary blood glucose monitoring at home can improve glycemic control, and this may reduce morbidity from complications of insulin-dependent diabetes. The course of retinopathy was not influenced by better glycemic control in the present study.

▶ [Here is another relatively long-term study. The authors believe that there is some protection of renal function by careful regulation but no effect on retinal disease. The effect on nerve function appears to be beneficial, as measured by improvement of nerve conduction—an effect also reported from Sweden.[37] Perhaps the most important consideration is that good control, approaching the physiologic, could be achieved by carefully adjusted multiple doses of insulin. The pump is not necessary to achieve this level of metabolic adjustment. The cornerstone of this improved control appears to me to be the availability of simple methods for measuring the capillary blood glucose concentration in the home. Thus I was surprised to find that in a controlled trial diabetics achieving excellent metabolic adjustment by following urine glucose while under close clinical supervision failed to improve the level of control when they were given the added information obtained from monitoring their capillary blood glucose concentrations.[38] Another study which confirms that careful metabolic control has little effect on retinal disease was reported from Denmark.[39] Pregnancy has sometimes been blamed for progression of retinal disease; but this appears not to be the case. In patients whose retinal disease was well controlled by photocoagulation, pregnancy was not associated with advance of retinopathy; indeed, it appeared to become somewhat better![40]

One of the most distressing aspects of diabetes is neuropathic pain. In many instances, this can be controlled by amitriptyline or fluphenazine; but there is some hesitation to use these medications in patients with concomitant renal failure. With care, however, the medications can be used safely and usually with good effect even in the presence of progressive renal failure.[41]

Chronic ulcers of the foot may be difficult to heal, but sometimes intensified efforts to improve diabetic control may lead to healing. In two such cases, reported from the Bronx VA Medical Center, use of the open circuit subcutaneous insulin pump produced rapid healing.[42]] ◀

43–7 **Test for Chlorpropamide-Alcohol Flush Becomes Positive After Prolonged Chlorpropamide Treatment in Insulin-Dependent and Non-Insulin-Dependent Diabetics.** Some diabetics treated with chlorpropamide have facial flushing after ingesting alcoholic drinks. A previous study indicated that non-insulin-dependent (type II) diabetics who are receiving chlorpropamide regularly respond to the flush test much more often than those given other types of treatment, but prolonged exposure to the drug rather than a genetically determined mechanism may be responsible. Serge Ng Tang Fui,

---

(43–7) N. Engl. J. Med. 309:93–96, July 14, 1983.

Harry Keen, John Jarrett, Ved Gossain, and Philip Marsden (London) examined the effects of multiple doses of chlorpropamide on flushing in 10 patients with type II diabetes and 10 with insulin-dependent (type I) diabetes, all of whom responded negatively to a single challenge test for chlorpropamide-alcohol flushing. No patient had been treated with chlorpropamide. Either 250 mg of chlorpropamide or a placebo was taken each morning for 1 week, followed by a crossover after a 3-week interval.

No patient flushed when challenged with sherry after receiving placebo for 7 days, but after receiving chlorpropamide 8 with type II and 7 with type I diabetes reported definite flushing. Mean plasma concentration of chlorpropamide was 62 mg/L after 7 doses of the drug, compared with 22.5 mg/L after a single dose. Responders and nonresponders had similar mean plasma levels after 7 doses, and also similar mean plasma alcohol concentrations. Two of the negative responders also had no flushing on challenge after taking 500 mg of chlorpropamide daily for another week, despite a rise in mean plasma drug level to 172 mg/L.

These findings cast doubt on suggestions of a genetic association between the inheritance of diabetes and the chlorpropamide-alcohol flush phenomenon. The phenomenon is not a reliable marker for a major subtype of non-insulin-dependent diabetes.

▶ [This chlorpropamide-alcohol flush business continues to occupy a good deal of space in the literature. Many observers believe that the effect reflects the dose or plasma concentration of chlorpropamide rather than a genetic difference in the type of diabetes. The proposed correlation between the flush and reduced risk of coronary heart disease has not held up in one study of 36 subjects,[43] and a close correlation has been found between the plasma chlorpropamide level and the presence of the flush reaction.[44, 45] It has been proposed that the mechanism of the flush is the ability of chlorpropamide, above a certain critical plasma level, to inhibit the oxidation of acetaldehyde generated from oxidation of ethanol. In support of this hypothesis, the authors have found a correlation between plasma acetaldehyde levels and the intensity of the flush.[44] However, decreased ability to oxidize acetaldehyde has also been noted in vitro in the erythrocytes of patients with flushing, even when no chlorpropamide is present. This observation supports the idea that there is a specific metabolic difference between flushers and nonflushers.[46] Moreover, the insulin secretory response after a glucose load is lower and the plasma glycerol concentration is higher in patients who flush than in those who do not, again supporting a metabolic difference between the two groups.[47] There is still room for doubt about the significance of the phenomenon. The idea that type II diabetes represents more than one basic type of disease is neither new nor difficult to accept. It will be an important contribution if the chlorpropamide flush phenomenon identifies one of the subgroups with a specific clinical pattern. Further evidence will be worth waiting for.

There is a good deal of evidence that type II diabetics suffer from insulin resistance resulting from a postreceptor defect in insulin response. Evidence for insulin resistance is well established by studies of the intact patient; but most of the evidence to support the postreceptor localization of the defect is based on studies of the adipocyte or other cells freshly isolated and studied in vitro. Such fresh cells may still be under the influence of endogenous factors to which they were subjected in vivo before isolation. When fibroblasts cultured from normal persons and type II diabetics are studied in vitro, no difference can be demonstrated in insulin sensitivity.[48] I don't know whether this means that the fibroblast is different from the adipocyte or lymphocyte or whether it means that culture has permitted the cells to escape from the putative endogenous antiinsulin influence; but in either case, it suggests caution in accepting the usual theories about the nature of the metabolic defect.

It would be useful to have an animal model of the thickening of capillary basement membranes which occurs in diabetes mellitus. One explanation of this thickening has been that the aldose pathway permits accumulation of polyhydric alcoholic derivatives of glucose within the cells. A similar pattern is described in rat retinas when the animals are given a high intake of galactose, which produces a form of dietary galactosemia. Perhaps the most interesting point is that thickening of the capillary basement membrane can be prevented by feeding a blocker of aldose reductase, called sorbinil. Does this mean that sorbinil might also reduce the microvascular side effects of hyperglycemia in human diabetics? It is a consideration worth exploring.[49] In fact, improvement of nerve conduction velocity has been reported in diabetic patients after administration of sorbinil, so it may prove of practical value.[50]] ◀

43–8 **Treatment of Non-Insulin-Dependent Diabetes Mellitus With Enzyme Inducers.** To determine the role of hepatic enzyme induction on carbohydrate and drug metabolism in diabetics with non-insulin-dependent diabetes mellitus (NIDDM), Eero A. Sotaniemi, Arno J. Arranto, Seppo Sutinen, Jari H. Stengård, and Sirkka Sutinen, (Univ. of Oulu, Finland) studied 7 women and 3 men with NIDDM who had never been treated with drugs known to induce the hepatic microsomal enzyme system. Ten age- and sex-matched subjects with normal liver histologic findings served as controls.

In NIDDM, hepatic microsomal enzyme activity is reduced, and since postreceptor glucose metabolism is influenced by these enzymes, the patients were treated with the enzyme-inducing drugs phenobarbital and medroxyprogesterone acetate (MPA). Blood glucose and plasma immunoreactive insulin (IRI) determinations were used to re-

Fig 43–4.—Increase in blood glucose concentration during phenformin and glibenclamide treatment; poor response to glipzide, insulin, and chlorpropamide; and marked blood glucose decrease and antipyrine metabolism increase after addition of phenobarbital in patient with NIDDM. (Courtesy of Sotaniemi, E.A., et al.: Clin. Pharmacol. Ther. 33:826–835, June 1983.)

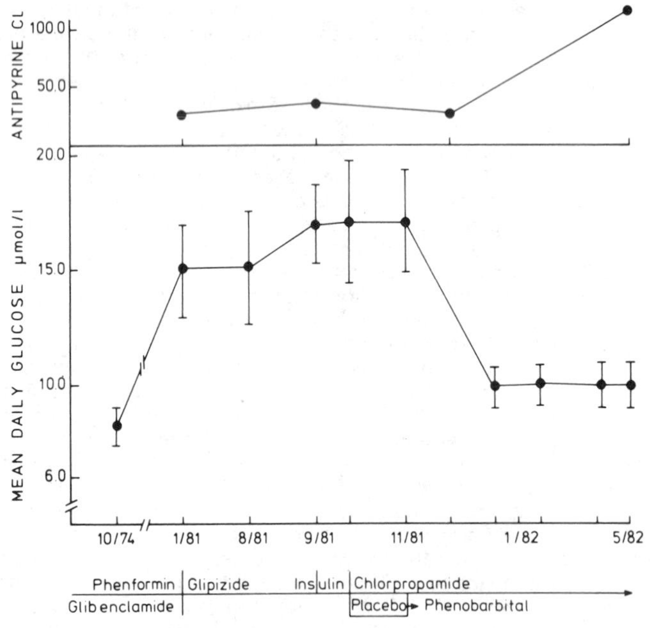

(43–8) Clin. Pharmacol. Ther. 33:826–835, June 1983.

flect carbohydrate metabolism, and results of conventional liver function tests and plasma antipyrine clearance rate were used to assess hepatic function.

Phenobarbital and MPA, when added to a glipzide or chlorpropamide regimen, reduced blood glucose and plasma IRI concentrations and increased hepatic microsomal enzyme activity as indicated by increased antipyrine metabolism. Placebo did not alter blood glucose concentrations. Inducer administration decreased serum aminotransferase activities, which had been high. Body weight fell, and liver fat content decreased. Figure 43–4 shows the marked response to phenobarbital in a patient with NIDDM.

Enzyme inducers may be a useful adjuvant to treatment of patients with NIDDM who have reduced microsomal enzyme activity without insulin deficiency. This treatment is not curative, but it leads to better control of diabetes. More than 200 drugs with inducing properties are available. Activation of the liver enzyme system suggests a new approach to NIDDM.

▶ [This is an interesting example of a method of stimulating mitochondrial enzymes in a nonspecific way, coupled with a treatment directed toward a specific disease. It is uncertain at present whether it will be of practical value in the clinic. Will it stabilize the carbohydrate metabolism as well as the blood glucose?

Other manipulations of enzymes have also been suggested as worthy of study for practical usefulness. The most widely discussed is a blocker of amylase derived from kidney beans. The idea is that if the blocker were administered along with starch it would inhibit digestion of the carbohydrate and therefore make it unabsorbable. The sale of these inhibitors over the counter has been tremendous until recently when it was blocked by the FDA. One reason that it has been ruled illegal is that it doesn't work. Addition of the blocker to the diet failed to alter the response of blood glucose, plasma insulin, or breath hydrogen (an indicator of the rate of glucose metabolism) to a test meal.[51]

The final report of the University Group Diabetes Program has appeared.[52] It evaluates the effects of insulin on prevention of complications and on mortality of patients with type II diabetes, and it concludes that insulin treatment does not prevent or delay either complications or mortality as compared with untreated patients and those treated with other modalities. This finding is contrary to the expectations and hopes of those who advocate close control of diabetes to prevent complications; but the design of the study did not result in the type of physiologic control attempted in modern therapy. Undoubtedly the report will generate a good deal of comment.] ◀

43–9 **Prospective Survey for Insulinomas in a Neurology Department.** Most insulinomas producing symptomatic hypoglycemia are benign adenomas of the pancreas. M. G. Harrington, A. P. McGeorge, J. P. Ballantyne, and G. Beastall (Glasgow, Scotland) report data on 25 consecutive patients (16 women) with intermittent episodes of deranged CNS function, which might include a combination of sensory, motor, and autonomic disturbances and changes in behavior, personality, and intellect. Other features included a relation between attacks and exercise or lack of food and a long history of ill-documented seizures with a poor response to anticonvulsant therapy and normal EEG and computed tomographic (CT) findings.

Clinical assessment, EEG, skull roentgenography, brain CT, liver function tests, syphilis serology tests, erythrocyte sedimentation rate

---

(43–9) Lancet 1:1094–1095, May 14, 1983.

measurement, and serum urea, electrolyte, calcium, and phosphate determinations were performed. Only water was permitted after 11 A.M. During the fast, fluid balance, body temperature, blood pressure, pulse rate, respiratory rate, and body weight were determined, and the urine was checked for protein and ketones. Plasma glucose and insulin concentrations were measured at the start of the fast and 24, 28, 48, 52, and 72 hours thereafter. At the end of the fast, a second EEG was made and a meal was given.

Urinary ketones were detected in every patient within the first 24 hours of the start of the fast. Body temperature, pulse rate, blood pressure, and fluid balance were normal throughout the study. The EEG was abnormal in 16 patients, with no significant changes between prefasting and late-fasting results. No diagnostic abnormalities were associated with the EEGs of the patients proved later to have insulinomas.

Clinical attacks occurred during the fast in 8 patients. Plasma glucose and insulin concentrations and amended insulin-glucose ratios were normal (Fig 43–5), except in 3 patients. Hypoglycemia was significant in 2 patients with inappropriately high insulin concentrations; insulin-secreting adenomas were subsequently found. No further symptoms followed surgical section of the tumors. The third patient had slight hypoglycemia, and long-term telemetry showed focal temporal lobe discharges coinciding with 50% of the clinical attacks, indicating an epileptic cause.

The excellent response to surgical treatment of insulinomas emphasizes the importance of intensive evaluation of patients with the symptoms described.

Fig 43–5.—Insulin to glucose *(I/G)* ratios of 22 patients during 72-hour fast (means and ranges). Broken horizontal lines are authors' laboratory normal upper limits for nonobese and obese patients and lower limit for insulinoma patients. Solid circles represent 2 patients who had hypoglycemia and hyperinsulinemia. Dotted line joins values of patient (nonobese) who had normal plasma glucose but high plasma insulin concentrations. (Courtesy of Harrington, M.G., et al.: Lancet 1:1094–1095, May 14, 1983.)

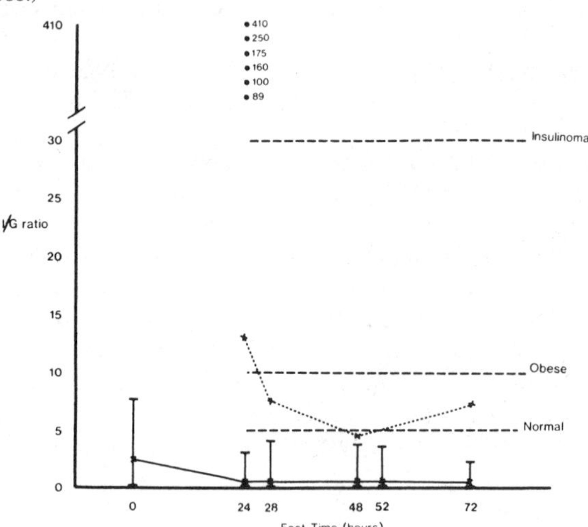

▶ [A yield of 8% may not seem very high, but over the entire population of patients with intermittent neuropsychological complaints, it adds up to a lot of potentially curable disease.

Nesidioblastosis is generally considered to be a disease of infants; but recently this pattern of islet cell hyperplasia associated with symptomatic hypoglycemia has been reported in 6 adult patients.[53, 54] In patients with this disease, no tumor can be demonstrated clinically, but the plasma insulin is inappropriately elevated in the presence of demonstrated hypoglycemia.

Another unusual cause of hypoglycemia is the presence of antibodies to the insulin receptor. The situation here is comparable to that in hyperthyroidism, in which the antibody binds to the receptor and imitates the effect of the polypeptide that the receptor normally recognizes.[55]] ◀

Chapter 43 References

1. Bruzzone R., Tamburrano G., Lala A., et al.: Effect of bombesin on plasma insulin, pancreatic glucagon and gut glucagon in man. *J. Clin. Endocrinol. Metab.* 56:643–647, 1983.
2. Feldman M., Kiser R.S., Unger R.H., et al.: Beta-endorphin and the endocrine pancreas: studies in healthy and diabetic human beings. *N. Engl. J. Med.* 308:349–353, 1983.
3. Johnson I.S.: Human insulin from recombinant technology. *Science* 219:632–637, 1983.
4. Mirouze J., Monnier L., Rodier M., et al.: Urticaire insulinique chronique: efficacité thérapeutique et bonne tolérance des insulines humaines. *Nouv. Presse Med.* 11:3121–3124, 1982.
5. Clark A.J.L., Adeniyi-Jones R.O., Knight G., et al.: Biosynthetic human insulin in the treatment of diabetes: a double-blind crossover trial in established diabetic patients. *Lancet* 2:354–357, 1983.
6. Peacock I., Tattersall R.B., Taylor A., et al.: Effects of new insulins on insulin and C-peptide antibodies, insulin dose, and diabetic control. *Lancet* 1:149–152, 1983.
7. Rotwein P.S., Chirgwin J., Province M., et al.: Polymorphism in the 5′ flanking region of the human insulin gene: a genetic marker for non-insulin-dependent diabetes. *N. Engl. J. Med.* 308:65–71, 1983.
8. Shoelson S., Haneda M., Blix P., et al.: Three mutant insulins in man. *Nature* 302:540–543, 1983.
9. Roth R.A., Cassell D.J.: Insulin receptor: evidence that it is a protein kinase. *Science* 219:299–301, 1983.
10. Kasuga M., Fujita-Yamaguchi Y., Blithe D.L., et al.: Tyrosine-specific protein kinase activity is associated with the purified insulin receptor. *Proc. Natl. Acad. Sci. USA* 80:2137–2141, 1983.
11. Roth R.A., Cassell D.J., Wong K.Y., et al.: Monoclonal antibodies to the human insulin receptor block insulin binding and inhibit insulin action. *Proc. Natl. Acad. Sci. USA* 79:7312–7316, 1982.
12. Taylor S.I., Hedo J.A., Underhill L.H., et al.: Extreme insulin resistance in association with abnormally high binding affinity of insulin receptors from a patient with leprechaunism: evidence for a defect intrinsic to the receptor. *J. Clin. Endocrinol. Metab.* 55:1108–1113, 1982.
13. Seltzer H.S.: Are insulin receptors clinically significant? *J. Lab. Clin. Med.* 100:815–821, 1982.
14. Fink R.J., Kolterman O.G., Griffin J., et al.: Mechanisms of insulin resistance in aging. *J. Clin. Invest.* 71:1523–1535, 1983.
15. Rowe J.W., Minaker K.L., Palotta J.A., et al.: Characterization of the insulin resistance of aging. *J. Clin. Invest.* 71:1581–1587, 1983.

16. Poynard T., Slama G., Tchobroutsky G.: Reduction of post-prandial insulin needs by pectin as assessed by the artificial pancreas in insulin-dependent diabetics. *Diabete. Metab.* 8:187–189, 1982.
17. Helderman J.H., Elahi D., Andersen D.K., et al.: Prevention of the glucose intolerance of thiazide diuretics by maintenance of body potassium. *Diabetes* 32:106–111, 1983.
18. Reaven G.M. (ed.): The role of insulin resistance in the pathogenesis and treatment of noninsulin-dependent diabetes mellitus: a symposium. *Am. J. Med.* 74:1–112, 1983.
19. Wilson D.E.: Excessive insulin therapy: biochemical effects and clinical repercussions. Current concepts of counterregulation in type I diabetes. *Ann. Intern. Med.* 98:219–277, 1983.
20. Wolf E., Spencer K.M., Cudworth A.G.: The genetic susceptibility to type 1 (insulin-dependent) diabetes: analysis of HLA-DR association. *Diabetologia* 24:224–230, 1983.
21. Asplin C.M., Cooney M.K., Crossley J.R., et al.: Coxsackie B-4 infection and islet cell antibodies three years before overt diabetes. *J. Pediatr.* 101:398–400, 1982.
22. Koevary S., Rossini A., Stoller W., et al.: Passive transfer of diabetes in the BB/W rat. *Science* 220:727–728, 1983.
23. Horita M., Suzuki H., Onodera T., et al.: Abnormalities of immunoregulatory T cell subsets in patients with insulin-dependent diabetes mellitus. *J. Immunol.* 129:1426–1429, 1982.
24. Laupacis A., Stiller C.S., Gardell C., et al.: Cyclosporin prevents diabetes in BB Wistar rats. *Lancet* 1:10–11, 1983.
25. Eisenbarth G.S.M., Srikanta S., Jackson R., et al.: Immunotherapy of recent onset type I diabetes mellitus. *Clinical Research* 31:500A, 1983.
26. Prevention of insulin-dependent diabetes, editorial. *Lancet* 1:104–105, 1983.
27. Cataland S., O'Dorisio T.M.: Diabetic nephropathy: clinical course in patients treated with the subcutaneous insulin pump. *JAMA* 249:2059–2061, 1983.
28. Ellis D., Avner E.D., Transue D., et al.: Diabetic nephropathy in adolescence: appearance during improved glycemic control. *Pediatrics* 71:824–829, 1983.
29. Mogensen C.E.: Long-term antihypertensive treatment inhibiting progression of diabetic nephropathy. *Br. Med. J.* 285:685–688, 1982.
30. Murphy M.B., Lewis P.J., Kohner E., et al.: Glucose intolerance in hypertensive patients treated with diuretics: a fourteen-year follow-up. *Lancet* 2:1293–1295, 1982.
31. Cohen A.W., Liston R.M., Mennuti M.T., et al.: Glycemic control in pregnant diabetic women using a continuous subcutaneous insulin infusion pump. *J. Reprod. Med.* 27:651–654, 1982.
32. Rudolf M.C.J., Sherwin R.S., Markowitz R., et al.: Effect of intensive insulin treatment on linear growth in the young diabetic. *J. Pediatr.* 101:333–339, 1982.
33. Frost-Larsen K., Christiansen J.S., Parving H.-H.: The effect of strict short-term metabolic control on retinal nervous system abnormalities in newly diagnosed type 1 (insulin-dependent) diabetic patients. *Diabetologia* 24:207–209, 1983.
34. Connor H., Atkin G., Attwood E.: Short-term control of brittle diabetes using a Biostator. *Br. J. Med.* 285:1316–1317, 1982.
35. Schichiri M., Kawamori R., Yamasaki Y., et al.: Wearable artificial endocrine pancreas with needle-type glucose sensor. *Lancet* 2:1129–1131, 1982.

36. McMillan D.E., Ditzel J. (eds.): Proceedings of a conference on diabetic microangiopathy. *Diabetes* 32(Suppl. 2):1–104, 1983.
37. Agardh C.-D., Rosén I., Scherstén B.: Improvement of peripheral nerve function after institution of insulin treatment in diabetes mellitus: a case-control study. *Acta Med. Scand.* 213:283–287, 1983.
38. Worth R., Home P.D., Johnston D.G., et al.: Intensive attention improves glycaemic control in insulin-dependent diabetes without further advantage from home blood glucose monitoring: results of a controlled trial. *Br. Med. J.* 285:1233–1240, 1982.
39. Lauritzen T., Frost-Larsen K., Larsen H.-W., et al.: Effect of 1 year of near-normal blood glucose levels on retinopathy in insulin-dependent diabetics. *Lancet* 1:200–203, 1983.
40. Gerke E., Meyer-Schwickerath G.: Proliferativ diabetische Retinopathie und Schwangerschaft. *Klin. Monatsbl. Augenheilkd.* 181:170–173, 1982.
41. Mitas J.A. II, Moseley C.A. Jr., Drager A.M.: Diabetic neuropathic pain: control by amitriptyline and fluphenazine in renal insufficiency. *South. Med. J.* 76:462–467, 1983.
42. Rubinstein A., Pierce C.E. Jr., Bloomgarden Z.: Rapid healing of diabetic foot ulcers with continuous subcutaneous insulin infusion. *Am. J. Med.* 75:161–163, 1983.
43. Laakso M., Nuorva K., Aro A., et al.: Chlorpropamide-alcohol flushing and coronary heart disease in non-insulin dependent diabetics. *Br. Med. J.* 286:1317–1318, 1983.
44. Jerntorp P., Almér L.-O., Öhlin H., et al.: Plasma chlorpropamide: a critical factor in chlorpropamide-alcohol flush. *Eur. J. Clin. Pharmacol.* 24:237–242, 1983.
45. Hillson R.M., Smith R.F., Dhar H., et al.: Chlorpropamide-alcohol flushing and plasma chlorpropamide concentrations in diabetic patients on maintenance chlorpropamide therapy. *Diabetologia* 24:210–212, 1983.
46. Öhlin H., Jerntorp P., Bergström B., et al.: Chlorpropamide-alcohol flushing, aldehyde dehydrogenase activity, and diabetic complications. *Br. Med. J.* 285:838–840, 1982.
47. Barnett A.H., Spiliopoulos A.J., Pyke D.A., et al.: Metabolic studies in chlorpropamide-alcohol flush positive and negative type 2 (non-insulin dependent) diabetic patients with and without retinopathy. *Diabetologia* 24:213–215, 1983.
48. Bernhau P., Tsai P., Olefsky J.M.: Insulin-stimulated glucose transport in cultured fibroblasts from normal and noninsulin-dependent (type II) diabetic human subjects. *J. Clin. Endocrinol. Metab.* 55:1226–1230, 1982.
49. Robison W.G. Jr., et al.: Retinal capillaries: basement membrane thickening by galactosemia prevented with aldose reductase inhibitor. *Science* 221:1177–1179, 1983.
50. Judzewitsch R.G., Jaspan J.B., Polonsky K.S., et al.: Aldose reductase inhibition improves nerve conduction velocity in diabetic patients. *N. Engl. J. Med.* 308:119–125, 1983.
51. Carlson G.L., Li B.U.K., Bass P., et al.: A bean alpha-amylase inhibitor formulation (starch blocker) is ineffective in man. *Science* 219:393–395, 1983.
52. Knatterud G.L., Klimt C.R., Goldner M.G., et al.: Effects of hypoglycemic agents on vascular complications in patients with adult-onset diabetes. VIII. Evaluation of insulin therapy: final report. *Diabetes* 31(Suppl. 5):1–81, 1982.
53. Keller A., Stone A.M., Valderrame E., et al.: Pancreatic nesidioblastosis in adults: report of a patient with hyperinsulinemic hypoglycemia. *Am. J. Surg.* 145:412–416, 1983.

54. Weidenheim K.M., Hinchey W.W., Campbell W.G. Jr.: Hyperinsulinemic hypoglycemia in adults with islet-cell hyperplasia and degranulation of exocrine cells of the pancreas. *Am. J. Clin. Pathol.* 79:14–24, 1983.
55. Taylor S.I., Grunberger G., Marcus-Samuels B., et al.: Hypoglycemia associated with antibodies to the insulin receptor. *N. Engl. J. Med.* 307:1422–1426, 1982.

44. Inborn Errors of Metabolism

44–1 **Effect of Estrogen-Progestin Potency on Lipid-Lipoprotein Cholesterol.** Changes in lipid metabolism may underlie the increased risk of vascular disorders ascribed to oral contraceptive use. Patricia Wahl, Carolyn Walden, Robert Knopp, Joanne Hoover, Robert Wallace, Gerardo Heiss, and Basil Rifkind examined the effects of 10 hormone preparations with varying estrogen-progestin potencies on plasma concentrations of lipid and lipoprotein cholesterol in women in the Lipid Research Clinics Program. The findings in 374 women who were using oral contraceptives were compared with those in 284 women who were receiving estrogen preparations after the menopause and in 1,086 women not using hormones.

Data adjusted for age, obesity, and smoking and drinking habits indicated higher plasma cholesterol levels in younger women who are using oral contraceptives or equine estrogens than in nonusers. Plasma triglyceride levels were higher in most user groups. Levels of high-density lipoprotein cholesterol tended to be highest in users of estrogen-dominant preparations and lowest in women using progestin-dominant preparations. Low-density lipoprotein cholesterol levels generally were highest in women using low-dose estrogen preparations. Levels of very low density lipoprotein cholesterol were elevated in all oral contraceptive users and in younger menopausal women using equine estrogens.

Estrogen and progestin potency and the type of progestin present in hormonal preparations are important influences on lipoprotein lipid levels in women and may be associated with an increased risk of arteriosclerotic disease in oral contraceptive users. Caution is indicated in prescribing progestin-dominant oral contraceptives to women with known risk factors for cardiovascular disease. The prolonged use of progestin-dominant oral contraceptives may be undesirable, as may their use by older women of child-bearing age, for whom age itself is a risk factor. An attempt should be made to achieve a physiologic balance between progestin and estrogen potencies in oral contraceptive preparations in order to minimize changes in low-density and high-density lipoprotein cholesterol levels.

▶ [Add to this disadvantage of high progestin the widely publicized study that alleges an increase of cervical cancer in patients receiving progestin-containing contraceptive medications (which was discussed in the introduction to chapter 41 in this Year Book), and one might begin to worry about the use of this type of oral contraceptive medication in young women. Apparently the problem is largely related to progestins; estrogens are much less important, since no effect is seen on cholesterol content of the plasma when estrogens are given to castrated women. The proportion of high-density lipoproteins is increased and that of low-density lipoproteins (LDL) is

(44–1) N. Engl. J. Med. 308:862–867, Apr. 14, 1983.

reduced, but very low density lipoprotein levels are unaffected by estrogens.[1]

The relationship between dietary cholesterol, plasma cholesterol concentrations, and atherosclerosis has been confusing for at least 35 years. The demonstration that cholesterol biosynthesis is controlled through a biofeedback loop which requires the presence of cell surface receptors for LDL was helpful but incomplete. In animals that cannot control cholesterol biosynthesis, feeding the sterol causes increased cholesterol deposition in many locations, whereas for most humans excessive cholesterol deposits appear chiefly in the coronary arteries and aorta. Thus cholesterol feeding experiments may not be directly related to the human disease. Additional light has now been shed on this relationship by studies of the strain of rabbits isolated by Watanabe in 1973, which has a genetically determined form of hypercholesterolemia similar to that observed in human patients with familial hypercholesterolemia. Like humans with the disease, the rabbits lack the cell surface receptor for LDL. In addition, they produce excessive amounts of LDL. This abnormality appears to be a result of failure of the liver to clear very low density lipoprotein fragments after peripheral processing to remove part of their triglyceride content, leaving chiefly cholesterol in the LDL fragment. The fragment, which is the sole source of LDL, accumulates because normal methods for its removal are lacking. In rabbits and humans, the process can be partially reversed by cholestyramine (which binds cholesterol in the gastrointestinal tract and depletes the liver of the sterol), but the effect is insufficient to provide a normal plasma cholesterol level in most patients. Newly discovered products of molds (compactin and mevinolin) have an additional effect of blocking cholesterol synthesis. The mechanism is not yet clear. This subject has been reviewed recently by Kolata.[2] A symposium has recently been published which brings up to date the status of the relationship between diet, coronary heart disease, lipoprotein abnormalities, and treatment.[3]

In 1980, a great deal of attention was focused on an article by De Luise and colleagues which claimed that the sodium pump was defective and that the intracellular Na^+ level was increased in obese patients. This observation has been reexamined, and unfortunately, none of the observations of De Luise et al. could be confirmed. Thus the question of whether an abnormality of the Na-K adenosine triphosphatase pump is responsible for some aspect of obesity remains unanswered.[4]] ◀

44–2 **Reduction of Serum Cholesterol in Heterozygous Patients With Familial Hypercholesterolemia: Additive Effects of Compactin and Cholestyramine.** Familial hypercholesterolemia is an autosomal dominant disorder characterized by increased low-density lipoprotein (LDL) cholesterol concentrations, tendon xanthomas, and premature coronary atherosclerosis. The disorder results from a defect of the LDL receptor that normally controls the degradation of LDL; LDL cholesterol concentrations in affected persons are 2.5 times normal. Hiroshi Mabuchi, Takeshi Sakai, Yasuyuki Sakai, Akira Yoshimura, Akira Watanabe, Takanobu Wakasugi, Junji Koizumi, and Ryoyu Takeda (Kanazawa Univ., Japan) studied the effect of cholestyramine alone and combined with the experimental agent compactin on serum lipoprotein concentrations in 10 Japanese patients with heterozygous familial hypercholesterolemia. All patients were on a diet low in cholesterol and saturated fat. After 4 to 8 weeks of an optimal dietary regimen, cholestyramine was started (4 gm 3 times daily), and after 2–16 months, compactin (30 mg 3 times daily) was added for 12 weeks.

The mean serum cholesterol concentration fell by 20%, from 356 to 285 mg/dl during cholestyramine treatment ($P < .001$). With the addition of compactin, the mean serum cholesterol concentration fell by

---

(44–2) N. Engl. J. Med. 308:609–613, Mar. 17, 1983.

a further 24% to 217 mg/dl ($P < .001$). Serum cholesterol concentrations returned to those present during diet-cholestyramine 4 weeks after withdrawal of compactin. Mean serum triglyceride concentration decreased from 150 mg/dl during diet alone to 99 mg/dl during diet, cholestyramine, and compactin treatment. Compared with diet alone, cholestyramine reduced mean LDL cholesterol concentrations by 28%, from 263 to 190 mg/dl ($P < .001$). When compactin was added, LDL cholesterol concentrations fell by a further 34% at the 12th week. The total reduction from values during diet alone was 53% ($P < .001$). Mean high-density lipoprotein (HDL) cholesterol increased significantly, to 50 mg/dl with cholestyramine compared with 36 mg/dl with diet alone. This increased concentration of HDL cholesterol persisted after compactin treatment was added.

For the treatment of heterozygous hypercholesterolemia, cholestyramine, cholestipol, nicotinic acid, clofibrate, and probucol are effective in lowering serum cholesterol concentrations. Compactin belongs to a new class of cholesterol synthesis inhibitors that lower the plasma concentration of LDL cholesterol. If long-term safety can be demonstrated, the compactin-cholestyramine regimen described here may be useful in heterozygous familial hypercholesterolemia.

► [In familial hypercholesterolemia, measures that reduce the plasma cholesterol concentration may be lifesaving. But how does one approach a patient like the one described by Vega and colleagues in whom typical tendinous xanthomas with high cholesterol content were associated with a *normal* plasma cholesterol concentration? The lipoprotein patterns showed mainly a reduction in the level of very low density lipoprotein (VLDL) apo-B. (The level of LDL apo-B was normal.) The synthesis of VLDL apo-B was also increased. There was no evidence of atherosclerotic disease. The authors interpret this peculiar picture as consistent with an abnormality of VLDL apo-B synthesis, resulting in a defect in the metabolism of the lipoproteins containing this chain; but the mechanism by which xanthomas would be produced is unclear (at least to me).[5]] ◄

44–3 **Effect of Metabolic Control on Lipid, Lipoprotein, and Apolipoprotein Levels in 55 Insulin-Dependent Diabetic Patients: Longitudinal Study.** Improved diabetic control is thought to lead to a fall in plasma lipid concentrations, but the effects on lipoprotein levels are unclear. Maria F. Lopes-Virella, Hulda J. Wohltmann, Ronald K. Mayfield, C. B. Loadholt, and John A. Colwell (Med. Univ. of South Carolina, Charleston) examined the effects of 2–3 weeks of intensive insulin therapy on plasma lipid, lipoprotein, and apolipoprotein values in 55 insulin-dependent diabetics, 35 female and 20 male patients with a mean age of 17 years. The mean duration of diabetes was 7 years. Twelve patients had retinopathy, 3 had proteinuria, and 2 had nephropathy. Twenty-two patients were treated wih a closed-loop insulin delivery system for 2 days and then with continuous subcutaneous insulin infusion, and 33 patients received conventional treatment. The overall mean daily dose of insulin was 1.03 units/kg of body weight.

Levels of total, low-density lipoprotein, and very low density lipoprotein (VLDL) cholesterol and triglycerides, VLDL triglycerides, and apolipoprotein B were significantly reduced at discharge from the

---

(44–3) Diabetes 32:20–25, January 1983.

metabolic unit. Levels of high-density lipoprotein (HDL) cholesterol and apolipoprotein (Apo A_1) were significantly increased. The changes were most marked in patients admitted in poor glycemic control. Male patients had significant increases in both HDL cholesterol and Apo A_1 levels after glycemic control, but no significant change in Apo A_1 concentration occurred in those admitted in fair control. A small but significant increase in HDL cholesterol level occurred in female patients admitted in poor control. No significant change in Apo A_1 concentration occurred regardless of the degree of glycemic control at the outset.

Normalization of plasma lipid, lipoprotein, and apolipoprotein levels was observed in insulin-dependent diabetics given intensive insulin therapy. Improved glycemic control appears to have favorable effects on some changes in diabetics that are associated with coronary heart disease, but long-term studies are needed to determine whether the atherosclerotic process is actually delayed.

▶ [This is a preliminary report, since 2–3 weeks is clearly not enough time to permit a sound judgment. Nevertheless, it raises questions worth further study. The reported increase in HDL with treatment is especially interesting in view of the generally accepted association of high levels of this complex with protection against atherosclerosis. The relationship between low levels of HDL and diabetes has been somewhat uncertain because of conflicting data in previous reports. A very well controlled study from San Diego confirms the presence of reduced concentrations of HDL in 97 type II diabetics who were compared with 194 age- and sex-matched controls who were also matched for comorbid variables such as obesity, smoking, alcohol intake, exercise, and estrogen treatment.[6] In type II diabetics, abnormalities of HDL and apolipoprotein A_1 were the same in groups of diabetics studied at the time of diagnosis and in others who had been treated with diet alone or with chlorpropamide and diet. Thus these forms of treatment did not affect lipoprotein patterns. Although this group was not so well controlled as the San Diego group, the direction of the abnormalities was the same.[7] Of course, one cannot compare the absence of effect of treatment in type II diabetics with the good (if early) results reported in the abstract in type I diabetics. For one thing, the type II diabetics did not receive insulin. This may be a critical difference because an abnormality of cholesterol transport in this group is normalized by insulin. The critical parameter in these studies may not have been the addition of insulin but the ability of the physicians to control hyperglycemia with insulin whereas they could not control it with diet and oral hypoglycemic agents.[8] It is well known that insulin deficiency alters triglyceride levels because the hormone is needed for activation of lipoprotein lipase. But, in addition to hypoinsulinemia (which is usually not present in patients with type II diabetes) hyperglycemia itself may alter lipoprotein patterns by increasing nonenzymatic glucosylation of apolipoproteins. This effect is comparable to the glycosylation of hemoglobin which results in a high level of hemoglobin A_{1c} in poorly controlled diabetic patients. In guinea pigs, increased nonenzymatic glucosylation of HDL is associated with more rapid clearance of the protein from the plasma. Most of the glucose is incorporated in apoprotein A_1, but other apoproteins are glucosylated as well.[9] If this mechanism can be confirmed in human patients, it may help to explain the reduced HDL concentrations in the plasma of poorly controlled diabetic patients discussed above.] ◀

44–4 **An Adult Case of Type Ib Glycogen-Storage Disease: Enzymatic and Histochemical Studies.** Patients with type Ib glycogen-storage disease are clinically similar to those with typical von Gierke's disease but have nearly normal hepatic glucose-6-phosphatase activity. A deficiency in the glucose-6-phosphate transport sys-

---

(44–4) N. Engl. J. Med. 308:566–569, Mar. 10, 1983.

tem at the membrane of the endoplasmic reticulum may be responsible. Takeshi Kuzuya, Ayako Matsuda, Sho Yoshida, Kuniaki Narisawa, Keiya Tada, Takuma Saito, and Masaya Matsushita report the case of an adult with type Ib glycogen-storage disease in whom such a defect was suggested by enzymatic studies.

Woman, 25, had grown slowly in infancy and was noted at age 4 years to have short stature and hepatomegaly. Yellow-red spots on the legs and hypertension were noted at age 18. Subsequently, hyperlipidemia and proteinuria were discovered. Examination at age 20 showed eruptive xanthomas on the legs and hands and 3^+ proteinuria. Gross hyperlipidemia was present, with a markedly increased pre-β-lipoprotein level. Liver biopsy and enzyme assay findings led to a diagnosis of type Ib glycogen-storage disease. The findings were unchanged at age 25. The fasting blood glucose concentration was still about 50–80 mg/dl. Clofibrate therapy led to resolution of the xanthomas, but the hyperlipidemia recurred. Allopurinol and antihypertensive drugs were also given.

Glucose-6-phosphatase activity was decreased in the absence of taurocholate. When taurocholate was added, the latency of the activity was 83%, compared with 30%–38% in control biopsy specimens. Enzyme activity was clearly evident histochemically in the liver but was hardly detectable in a patient who had type Ia glycogen-storage disease.

This patient had typical clinical features of von Gierke's disease and a laboratory diagnosis of type Ib glycogen-storage disease. Adults with type Ia glycogen-storage disease often have liver adenomas. Adenomas were suspected in the present patient because of findings on isotopic, ultrasonic, and computed tomographic scans of the liver. This suggests that they probably can occur in type Ib glycogen-storage disease as well.

▶ [The ability of taurocholate to increase the level of glucose-6-phosphatase suggests that a lipid abnormality (of the membrane?) is restored to normal by the detergent effect of the bile acid.

Idiopathic hemochromatosis is often associated with diabetes mellitus. But how about the presence of other types of abnormality as well. The endocrine status of a series of 12 patients with hemochromatosis was compared with age-matched controls (12 with diabetes and 5 with hepatic cirrhosis). Gonadotropin deficiency was demonstrable in 7 patients, of whom 6 had clinical evidence of deficiency. Testosterone levels were depressed in 5 of the 8 men and, on average, in the women as well. Estradiol levels were normal in both sexes. Sex hormone binding protein concentrations were normal in the men and elevated in the women as compared with controls. Basal prolactin levels were depressed slightly though significantly. Thyroid and adrenal function were normal. Nine patients had a subnormal response of prolactin to TRH. Thus, in idiopathic hemochromatosis there was selective depression of prolactin and gonadotropin secretion but other pituitary function appeared to be normal. Hypogonadisim in this group of patients appears to be of gonadotropic origin.[10]] ◀

Chapter 44 References

1. Notelovitz M., Gudat J.C., Ware M.D., et al.: Lipids and lipoproteins in women after oophorectomy and the response to oestrogen therapy. *Br. J. Obstet. Gynaecol.* 90:171–177, 1983.
2. Kolata G.: Cholesterol-heart disease link illuminated. *Science* 221:1164–1166, 1983.
3. Levy R.I. (ed.): Hyperlipoproteinemia: dietary and pharmacologic inter-

vention. Proceedings of a symposium. *Am. J. Med.* 74(Suppl. 5A):1–28, 1983.
4. Simat B.M., Mayrand R.R., From A.H.L., et al.: Is the erythrocyte sodium pump altered in human obesity? *J. Clin Endocrinol. Metab.* 56:925–929, 1983.
5. Vega G.L., Illingworth D.R., Grundy S.M., et al.: Normocholesterolemic tendon xanthomatosis with overproduction of apolipoprotein B. *Metabolism* 32:118, 1983.
6. Barrett-Connor E., Witztum J.L., Holdbrook M.: A community study of high density lipoproteins in adult noninsulin-dependent diabetics. *Am. J. Epidemiol.* 117:186–192, 1983.
7. Billingham M.S., Leatherdale B.A., Hall R.A., et al.: High density lipoprotein cholesterol and apolipoprotein A-I concentrations in non-insulin dependent diabetics treated by diet and chlorpropamide. *Diabete. Metab.* 8:229–233, 1982.
8. Fielding C.J.H., Reaven G.M., Fielding P.E.: Human noninsulin-dependent diabetes: identification of a defect in plasma cholesterol transport normalized in vivo by insulin and in vitro by selective immunoadsorption of apolipoprotein E. *Proc. Natl. Acad. Sci. USA* 79:6365–6369, 1982.
9. Witztum J.L., Fisher M., Pietro T., et al.: Nonenzymatic glucosylation of high-density lipoprotein accelerates its catabolism in guinea pigs. *Diabetes* 31:1029–1032, 1982.
10. Walton C., Kelly W.F., Laing I., et al.: Endocrine abnormalities in idiopathic haemochromatosis. *Q. J. Med.* 52:99–110, 1983.

PART SEVEN

KIDNEY, WATER, AND ELECTROLYTES

FRANKLIN H. EPSTEIN, M.D.

45. Glomerular Diseases

45–1 **Role for Intrarenal Mechanisms in Impaired Salt Excretion of Experimental Nephrotic Syndrome.** It remains unclear whether salt retention in nephrotic syndrome is caused chiefly by an intrinsic inability of the kidneys to excrete salt and water normally, or whether it represents a normal response to a stimulus extrinsic to the kidneys, presumably geared to volume regulation. I. Ichikawa, H. G. Rennke, J. R. Hoyer, K. F. Badr, N. Schor, J. L. Troy, C. P. Lechene, and B. M. Brenner (Boston) attempted to distinguish between these mechanisms in a unilateral form of puromycin aminonucleoside (PAN) glomerulopathy, induced in Munich-Wistar rats by the in vivo perfusion of a single kidney with PAN. Micropuncture studies of salt and water reabsorption were made at varying sides along accessible superficial nephrons in the perfused and nonperfused kidneys. Saralasin was infused in some rats for whole-kidney clearance studies.

Albumin excretion was increased and sodium excretion reduced in PAN-perfused kidneys but not in nonperfused kidneys. The systemic plasma protein concentration remained at baseline. The total-kidney glomerular filtration rate (GFR) and superficial single-nephron GFR were reduced in PAN-perfused kidneys by an average of about 30%, the result largely of a marked fall in the glomerular capillary ultrafiltration coefficient. A depression of absolute proximal reabsorption was associated with a decrease in peritubular capillary oncotic pressure in the PAN-perfused kidneys. Sodium reabsorption was suppressed in both the proximal convoluted tubules and short loops of Henle in PAN-perfused kidneys. Saralasin infusion led to a substantial increase in total-kidney and single-nephron GFR values in PAN-perfused kidneys, but urinary sodium excretion remained far below that of nonperfused kidneys. Ultrastructural study of PAN-perfused kidneys showed effacement of the glomerular epithelial cell cytoplasm, increased numbers of lysosomes, and obliteration of slit pores. The basement membrane was of normal thickness.

The reduced amounts of fluid and sodium reaching the end of the proximal convoluted tubules in PAN-treated rats (Fig 45–1) are the result of both a reduced filtered load and reduced rates of reabsorption along the proximal convoluted tubule segments. The changes indicate a mechanism intrinsic to the proteinuric kidney. The renin-angiotensin system may have an important role in the origin of the fall in GFR in PAN-perfused kidneys, but it is not very impor-

(45–1) J. Clin. Invest. 71:91–103, January 1983.

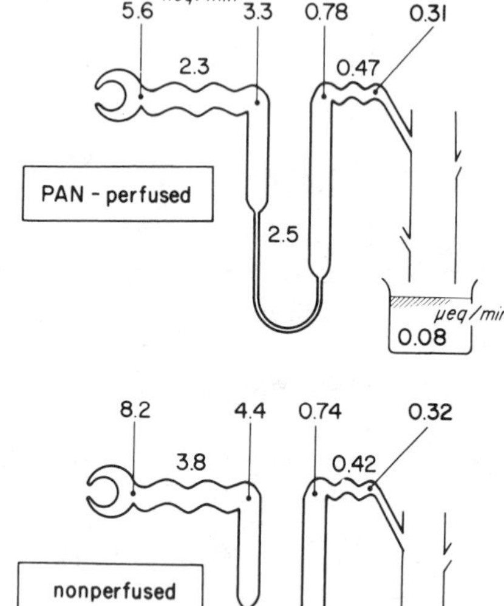

Fig 45–1.—Sodium delivery and reabsorption along superficial nephron segments in puromycin aminonucleoside (PAN)-perfused and nonperfused kidneys. Absolute mean values are shown. (Courtesy of Ichikawa, I., et al.: Reproduced from J. Clin. Invest. 71:91–103, January 1983 by copyright of the American Society for Clinical Investigation.)

tant in mediating the overall salt retention of the proteinuric kidney.

▶ [Why does the kidney retain sodium in the nephrotic syndrome? The conventional answer is that when plasma volume contracts because of a lowered oncotic pressure, the kidney responds to signals of a diminished effective circulating blood volume, transmitted via renin, aldosterone, and perhaps other messengers. In certain patients with nephrosis, however, plasma volume, renin, and aldosterone appear to be normal even when edema is forming.[1] In such cases of "nephritic edema," glomerular filtration rate is reduced, presumably because of a reduction in the capillary area available for glomerular filtration, and the usual explanation for sodium retention involves a decrease in the amount of sodium that is both filtered and delivered to distal nephron sites.

In the ingenious experiments in rats summarized above, systemic hypoalbuminemia was avoided, since only one kidney was rendered nephrotic; so any reduction in urinary sodium seen in the affected kidney must have had an intrarenal rather than a systemic cause. As anticipated, single-nephron GFR was depressed by puromycin, owing to a reduction in the ultrafiltration coefficient (reflecting glomerular capillary area). The urinary sodium concentration was low. Unexpectedly, however, as you can see in Figure 45–1, the amount of sodium delivered to the distal tubule appeared to be normal, so the renal retention of sodium that was observed must have reflected enhanced reabsorption in the collecting ducts. Thus, an intrinsic glomerular lesion localized to one kidney produced accelerated sodium reabsorption in the distal nephron. How the message gets from the glomerulus to the collecting duct is still a mystery.] ◀

45–2 **Controlled Studies of Oral Immunosuppressive Drugs in Lupus Nephritis: Long-Term Follow-Up.** The role of immunosuppressive drug therapy in the management of patients with systemic lupus and renal involvement remains unclear. Simon Carette, John H. Klippel, John L. Decker, Howard A. Austin, Paul H. Plotz, Alfred D. Steinberg, and James E. Balow (Nat'l Insts. of Health, Bethesda, Md.) reviewed the results of treatment with oral azathioprine, oral cyclophosphamide

(45–2) Ann. Intern. Med. 99:1–8, July 1983.

combined with low-dose prednisone, or prednisone alone in 53 patients seen from 1969 to 1975 with lupus nephritis. The mean follow-up period was 85 months. Immunosuppressive drug doses were maintained at as high a level as possible (not to exceed 4 mg/kg/day) without the development of leukopenia below 2,500/cu mm. Immunosuppressive therapy was continued indefinitely unless serious complications developed. Prednisone was given in short high-dose courses not exceeding 1 mg/kg daily for 4–6 weeks for exacerbations of nephritis. The maintenance steroid dose was adjusted to control extrarenal disease activity.

Renal function deteriorated in 17 patients during follow-up, and in

Fig 45–2.—A, probability of maintaining stable renal function by number of months after entry into the study for patients receiving cyclophosphamide *(CY)*, azathioprine *(AZ)*, or prednisone *(PR)*. **B,** probability of avoiding end-stage renal failure in the months after study entry for all 3 therapeutic groups. (Courtesy of Carette, S., et al.: Ann. Intern. Med. 99:1–8, July 1983.)

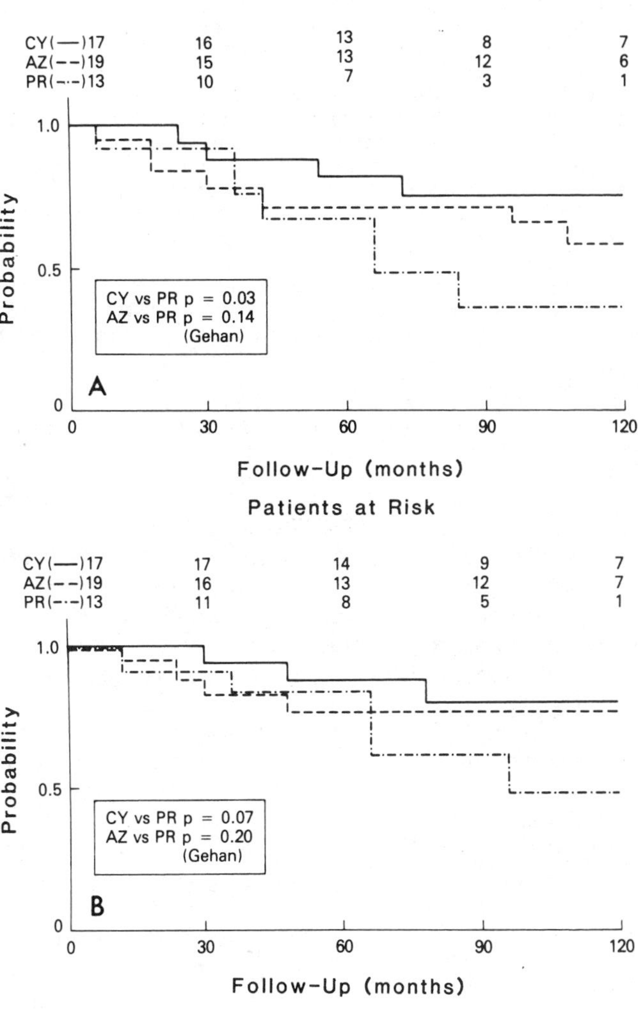

12 of these end-stage renal failure developed. The course of renal function is compared in the various treatment groups in Figure 45–2. Cyclophosphamide appears to be marginally superior to prednisone in maintaining renal function and preventing end-stage renal failure. Renal function tended to deteriorate more in patients with chronic changes noted on renal biopsy. Among patients with changes of intermediate chronicity, all 3 treated with prednisone have progressed to end-stage renal failure.

Patients in this study who had minimal chronic changes of lupus nephritis had excellent outcomes whether treated with prednisone alone or with immunosuppressive drugs. Most of those with a high degree of chronic change progressed to end-stage renal failure. Progression to dialysis did not depend on treatment. Patients with biopsy findings of intermediate chronicity appeared to benefit from the addition of azathioprine or cyclophosphamide to low-dose prednisone therapy, but drug toxicity may be substantial with this treatment.

▶ [This prospective controlled study provides pretty strong evidence in favor of cyclophosphamide or Imuran over prednisone alone when renal disease has become well established in lupus erythematosus. The most helpful prognosticator and aid in assigning treatment turned out to be the renal biopsy. If few or no fibrotic changes were seen, the outlook (over the average 85 months of follow-up) was good, regardless of the choice of treatment. If scarring was widespread, fairly rapid deterioration was the rule. However, in the 14 patients with "intermediate" changes of chronicity (mostly sclerotic glomeruli, fibrous crescents, tubular atrophy, and interstitial scarring), the selection of treatment seemed to make a big difference: end-stage renal failure developed in all 3 patients treated with prednisone but in none of the 6 given azathioprine or the 5 given cyclophosphamide. Note that (as others have noted) the biopsy changes were not reliably predicted from the usual measures of renal function (e.g., serum creatinine). In chronic lupus nephritis, immunosuppressive treatment has another virtue in that it minimizes the necessity for toxic doses of prednisone that produce the distressing symptoms of Cushing's syndrome.

In a comparative study of the natural history of 15 patients with focal proliferative lupus nephritis and 15 with diffuse proliferative lupus nephritis, the focal form tended to follow a course similar to that of the diffuse type.[2] About the same number had hypertension and, surprisingly, but perhaps accidentally, more patients (6 of 15) with focal disease had central nervous system involvement. One third of the patients with focal nephritis had the nephrotic syndrome. Two of the 15 progressed to diffuse glomerulonephritis with deterioration of renal function.] ◀

45–3 **Long-Term Clinical Course of Systemic Lupus Erythematosus in End-Stage Renal Disease.** Long-term hemodialysis with a reduction in immunosuppressive therapy may be associated with a favorable short-term course in patients with systemic lupus erythematosus. Norman S. Coplon, Charles J. Diskin, Jeffrey Petersen, and Robert S. Swenson (Stanford Univ.) reviewed a 12-year experience at a center in which patients with end-stage renal disease due to systemic lupus erythematosus are managed by dialysis and transplantation. Findings in 28 consecutive patients with lupus nephritis, seen between 1969 and 1980, were reviewed. The diagnosis was confirmed histologically in 25 patients. Dialysis was begun on the same indications as are used for patients with nonlupus renal failure.

The clinical activity of nonrenal manifestations decreased markedly within months of onset of end-stage renal disease (Fig 45–3),

(45–3) N. Engl. J. Med. 308:186–190, Jan. 27, 1983.

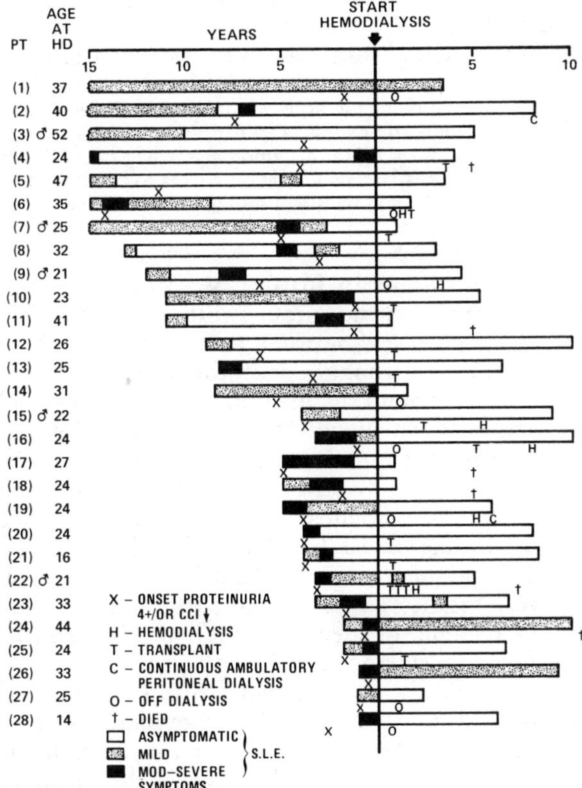

Fig 45–3.—Clinical course in patients with systemic lupus erythematosus, lupus nephritis, and end-stage renal disease. Outcome in the 28 patients is represented by horizontal bars arranged in order of decreasing duration of symptoms before initial hemodialysis. Systemic lupus erythematosus was categorized clinically as asymptomatic, inducing mild symptoms (arthralgias only), or inducing moderate or severe symptoms (arthritis and multiple organ symptoms). (Courtesy of Coplon, N.S., et al.: N. Engl. J. Med. 308:186–190, Jan. 27, 1983); reprinted by permission of The New England Journal of Medicine.

despite administration of lower doses of immunosuppressive agents. Transplant patients received immunosuppressive therapy in the same doses as those given to transplant recipients without lupus. No clinical recurrence of lupus nephritis was noted in 12 patients with transplants, whose cumulative graft survival at the end of follow-up was 501 months. Serologic markers of lupus tended to decline in parallel with the nonrenal activity of the disease after the start of hemodialysis. Overall patient surivival was 79%. Eight patients had spontaneous remission of end-stage renal disease for reasons that were not clear. Dialysis was discontinued after a mean of about 4 months in these cases. All but 2 of the 22 surviving patients presently maintain a normal level of physical activity.

Patients with lupus nephritis who receive long-term hemodialysis and, when indicated, undergo renal transplantation, have a favorable long-term prognosis. Such patients can be expected to lead fully active, productive lives. The treatment is associated with relatively low morbidity and mortality. Minimizing immunosuppressive drug therapy may reduce the risk of fatal sepsis in these patients.

▶ [The surprising finding here, confirmed in similar reports from other centers, is that extrarenal and systemic manifestations of lupus tend to become quiescent with the appearance of azotemia. Perhaps this is an expression of the immunosuppressive influence of the uremic state; long-term hemodialysis has been shown to increase the number of suppressor cells.[3] Transplantation seems to be well tolerated. In lupus patients who have developed renal failure, steroids and immunosuppressives should be reduced to the lowest dose tolerated in order to reduce the risk of death from sepsis and morbidity from things like femoral neck necrosis.] ◀

45–4 **Renal Vein Thrombosis in Idiopathic Membranous Glomerulopathy and Nephrotic Syndrome: Incidence and Significance.** An association of nephrotic syndrome and renal vein thrombosis has long been recognized. Although sporadic reports have implicated traumatic renal vein thrombosis as a possible cause of nephrotic syndrome, serial studies have shown renal vein thrombosis to be a complication of nephrotic syndrome rather than its cause. Richard D. Wagoner, Anthony W. Stanson, Keith E. Holley, and Christine S. Winter (Mayo Clinic and Found., Rochester, Minn.) undertook a prospective study of 33 patients seen in 1976–1979 with a diagnosis of idiopathic membranous glomerulopathy and nephrotic syndrome. The 27 evaluable patients were monitored for changes in renal function, degree of proteinuria, and evidence of thromboembolism. Those with renal vein thrombosis received warfarin for at least 1 year.

Thirteen of the 27 study patients were initially found to have renal vein thrombosis, and another patient had evidence of thrombosis at autopsy 2 months later. Ten patients had involvement of the main renal vein, and 4 had bilateral involvement. All 3 patients restudied after a year of anticoagulant therapy for bilateral main renal vein thrombosis had normal findings. No significant morphologic differences were found in renal biopsy specimens from patients with and those without renal vein thrombosis. Initial clinical parameters also were similar in these 2 groups. Coagulation studies showed a significantly prolonged thrombin time in several patients but did not distinguish between patients with or without renal vein thrombosis. Changes in proteinuria during follow-up for an average of 28 months were similar in the two patient groups. The rate of renal functional deterioration also was similar in the two groups. No patient had thromboembolic complications during follow-up.

Renal vein thrombosis is frequent in patients with idiopathic membranous glomerulopathy with nephrosis. Its influence on renal function and proteinuria is questionable. Coagulation abnormalities may be responsible for renal vein thrombosis in this setting. Anticoagulation therapy may be warranted for patients who do not have a nephrotic remission, but prophylactic anticoagulation treatment does not seem warranted.

▶ [The bad news is that a full 50% of all patients with membranous glomerulonephritis have renal vein thrombosis as a complication. The good news is that it doesn't

(45–4) Kidney Int. 23:368–374, February 1983.

matter! Since the influence of renal vein thrombosis on renal function and clinical course appears to be negligible (with the exception of those few cases with pulmonary emboli), it doesn't seem worthwhile to go to the trouble of doing the extensive radiologic studies necessary to make the diagnosis.] ◀

45–5 **Macroscopic Hematuria in Mesangial IgA Nephropathy: Correlation With Glomerular Crescents and Renal Dysfunction.** William M. Bennett and Priscilla Kincaid-Smith (Univ. of Melbourne) reviewed the renal biopsy findings in 186 specimens from 79 adults with mesangial IgA nephropathy and correlated them with the clinical findings at the time of biopsy. No patient had evidence of systemic disease associated with glomerular IgA deposition. The appearance of focal and segmental proliferative glomerulonephritis is shown in Figure 45–4. Forty patients (group 1) had a documented history of macroscopic hematuria, whereas 39 (group 2) did not.

The clinical and histologic findings in patients with and without a history of gross hematuria are compared in the table. Focal and segmental proliferation was associated in a high proportion of patients with gross hematuria and focal crescent formation. Both patients without gross hematuria who had renal failure had heavy microscopic hematuria. No significant differences were noted between the groups in extent of proteinuria. The proportions of patients with hypertension also did not differ significantly. There were no group differences in types of immunoglobulin deposition in renal biopsy specimens. The serum IgA level was elevated in comparable proportions of group 1 and 2 patients.

Fig 45–4.—Biopsy specimen at time of macroscopic hematuria with numerous red blood cells in Bowman's space and renal tubules. This glomerular hemorrhage could result from a break in continuity of a glomerular capillary *(arrow)*. Masson trichrome; original magnification, ×360. (Courtesy of Bennett, W.M., and Kincaid-Smith, P.: Kidney Int. 23:393–400, February 1983.)

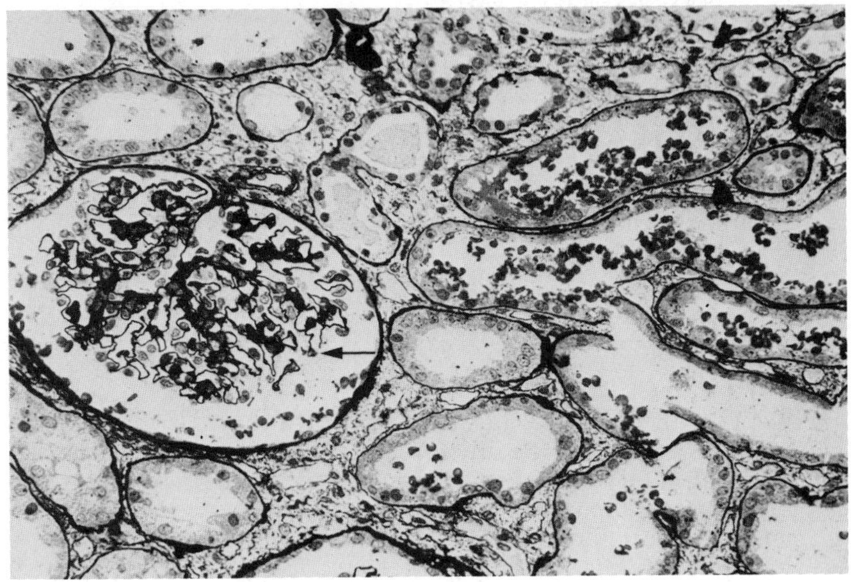

(45–5) Kidney Int. 23:393–400, February 1983.

COMPARISON OF PATIENTS WITH OR WITHOUT HISTORY OF MACROSCOPIC HEMATURIA[a]

	Group 1	Group 2
Number of patients	40	39
Number of biopsies	116	70
Serum creatinine at presentation, *μmoles/liter* *normal < 110 μmoles/liter*	240 ± 20	140 ± 14[b]
Creatinine clearance at presentation, *ml/min;* normal, *90 to 130 ml/min*	69 ± 36	87 ± 30[c]
Daily protein excretion, *normal < 0.1 g/day*	1.4 ± 1.1	1.0 ± 1.2
% Patients with blood pressure > 150/100	36	28
Serum IgA > 4 mg/ml	12 of 39 biopsies	4 of 22 biopsies
C1 binding > 4%	7 of 24 biopsies	8 of 16 biopsies
% Biopsy specimens with crescents	36.2	18.6[b]
% Biopsy specimens with focal and segmental proliferation	35.9	24.3
% Biopsy specimens with focal and segmental hyalinosis/ sclerosis	35.4	40
% Patients presenting with renal failure *serum creatinine > 300 μmoles/liter* or *< 45 ml/min*	22.5	5.1[c]

[a]Values listed are means ± SD or percentages. The extent of statistical significance is noted by footnotes *b* and *c*. When no footnote is present, differences between groups 1 and 2 were not significant at $P < .05$.

[b]$P < .01$.

[c]$P < .05$.

(Courtesy of Bennett, W.M., and Kincaid-Smith, P.: Kidney Int. 23:393–400, February 1983.)

Patients with mesangial IgA nephropathy and either recent gross hematuria or more than 1 million red blood cells per ml of urine are likely to have focal and segmental proliferative changes with crescent formation on renal biopsy. In other patients, the presence of focal and segmental sclerosis and hyalinosis probably represents healing of a previous proliferative lesion. Episodes of gross hematuria often are associated with renal dysfunction that may be reversible.

▶ [The percentage of patients with gross hematuria who had glomerular crescents in their kidney biopsy specimen (36%) is much higher in this series than in other reports of IgA nephritis. An explanation offered by the authors is that they performed biopsies immediately after the episode of bleeding in most patients, rather than later, and that "crescents and proliferation may disappear within a matter of weeks leaving hyalinotic and sclerotic lesions as their only residue."[4] They postulate that focal breaks in the glomerular basement membrane as a result of segmental proliferation lead to both hematuria and crescent formation. Since glomerular crescents are thought to heal by scarring, the repeated episodes of urinary bleeding following respiratory infections or exercise that characterize the course of many patients with IgA nephropathy may not be as benign as once thought. However, the experience of most nephrologists is that it is persistent proteinuria, rather than recurrent hematuria, that predicts progression to renal failure, as discussed in the next article.

IgA nephropathy is significantly associated with certain HLA types, e.g., HLA-DR4 and BW35.[5] Circulating IgA-containing immune complexes have been identified in the serum of patients with IgA nephritis and may play a role in the pathogenesis of the renal lesion.[6] Dermatitis herpetiformis, which is characterized by IgA deposits in skin and gastrointestinal tract, may in rare instances also be associated with IgA glomerulonephritis.[7]] ◀

45–6 **IgA Nephropathy: Prognostic Significance of Proteinuria and Histologic Alterations.** Yutaka Kobayashi, Sumio Tateno, Yoshiyuki Hiki, and Hidekazu Shigematsu undertook a retrospective review of findings in 166 patients seen between 1972 and 1980 with IgA nephropathy. All were followed up for at least a year after initial renal biopsy. The diagnosis was based on the finding of predominantly IgA deposits in the mesangium and along peripheral loop segments in a granular pattern. Most patients received no specific treatment.

Sixty-one patients had a creatinine clearance below 90 ml/minute at the time of initial renal biopsy. When last assessed after a mean of 34 months, 82 patients had impaired renal function. In 12 patients, terminal renal failure developed requiring hemodialysis. Proteinuria exceeding 1 gm daily correlated closely with impaired renal function both at the outset and at final follow-up. None of 39 patients in whom mild or moderate initial proteinuria resolved during follow-up had deterioration in renal function. The outcome was not related to the presence of microscopic hematuria, gross hematuria, or elevated serum IgA levels. Renal functional impairment was associated with sclerotic lesions, interstitial fibrosis, and tubular atrophy and with certain active changes, e.g., mesangial hypercellularity and tuft adhesion. The same patients tended to have prominent localization of IgA and C3 in the mesangium as well as in capillary loops.

These observations indicate that IgA nephropathy may progress slowly in about 50% of affected patients. Both marked proteinuria and severe histologic changes seem to correlate closely with an unfavorable clinical course, although further follow-up data are needed to relate these factors more precisely to the ultimate prognosis of IgA nephropathy. It is not known whether a decrease in marked proteinuria and resolution of active glomerular lesions will prevent subsequent progression of the disease.

▶ [Hypertension and vascular sclerosis, signifying progressive renal disease, were present in one quarter to one third of 43 patients with IgA nephropathy in a series collected at New York University.[8] In only 2 of 12 children in Sweden who had IgA

(45–6) Nephron 34:146–153, July 1983.

nephropathy and who were followed for 9 years did renal function remain undiminished with normal blood pressure.[9] Thus IgA nephritis, though benign in many instances, is a major cause of progressive renal scarring.] ◀

45–7 **Plasma Exchange in Goodpasture's Syndrome.** Ian J. Simpson, Peter B. Doak, Laurie C. Williams, Hilary A. Blacklock, Roger S. Hill, Clinton A. Teague, Peter B. Herdson, and Curtis B. Wilson monitored levels of antibody to glomerular basement membrane (GBM) in 20 patients with Goodpasture's syndrome managed by plasma exchange and immunosuppression in 8, immunosuppression alone in 4, and no specific measures in 8. Patients given immunosuppression alone received azathioprine (2–3 mg/kg) and 60 mg of prednisone daily for 2 weeks and then lower doses. Those who had plasma exchange received cyclophosphamide (1.5 mg/kg) and prednisone (60 mg) daily for 1 or 2 weeks, followed by lower doses of prednisone. Usually, 3 L of patient plasma was exchanged for cryoprecipitate-depleted plasma. The goal was a minimum of 10 plasma exchanges in the first 2 weeks. Levels of antibody to GBM were measured by radioimmunoassay.

All patients had active glomerulonephritis at the outset with linear deposits of IgG along the GBM. Also, IgM was detected in 8 biopsies and IgA in 4. Most biopsies disclosed C3 deposits. Levels of GBM antibody fell more rapidly in patients treated by plasma exchange and immunosuppression; pulmonary hemorrhage was less protracted in this group. One patient with severe renal failure improved markedly, and disease in 4 with milder renal involvement did not progress. Normal renal function persisted in 2 of the 4 patients given immunosuppressive therapy only, as well as in 2 of the 8 given no specific treatment. One of the 6 patients in the latter group in whom renal failure developed had only mild renal involvement initially. The baseline level of GBM antibody correlated with the severity of the renal biopsy changes but not with the degree of lung hemorrhage. Seven patients subsequently received cadaver allografts, and in 4 the graft was still functioning after 6–30 months.

Patients having plasma exchange and immunosuppressive therapy had the most favorable course in this study. A controlled trial of this treatment in comparison with immunosuppression alone is underway. The rapid removal of GBM antibody may lead to a better long-term outcome in patients with Goodpasture's syndrome.

▶ [The proper place for plasma exchange in Goodpasture's syndrome is still not entirely clear and awaits a good prospective study. Professor D.K. Peters of Hammersmith Hospital, London, who pioneered the technique, thinks that it is valuable in management and that it conserves renal function although the prognosis remains dismal in patients who are oliguric.[10] Plasma exchange is also reported to be helpful in the diffuse proliferative glomerulonephritis of systemic lupus erythematosus,[11] and the acute renal failure associated with multiple myeloma.[12] Plasma exchange is also said to be beneficial in hemolytic-uremic syndrome, but the benefit may well arise from the plasma factors that are given to the patient, rather than those that are removed (see the next article).] ◀

45–8 **Hemolytic Uremic Syndrome: Therapeutic Effect of Plasma Infusion.** Intravascular platelet aggregation appears to be important

(45–7) Am. J. Nephrol. 2:301–311, Nov.–Dec. 1982.
(45–8) Br. Med. J. 285:1304–1306, Nov, 6, 1982.

in the pathogenesis of hemolytic uremic syndrome, which has many similarities to thrombotic thrombocytopenic purpura. Plasma infusion has produced remissions of the latter disorder. Rocco Misiani, Aldo Claris Appiani, Alberto Edefonti, Eliana Gotti, Alberto Bettinelli, Marisa Giani, Edoardo Rossi, Giuseppe Remuzzi, and Giuliano Mecca evaluated plasma infusion therapy in 10 children and 7 adults with hemolytic uremic syndrome seen in a 2-year period. The diagnosis was based on the presence of microangiopathic hemolytic anemia, thrombocytopenia, and renal failure. A loading dose of 30–40 ml/kg of fresh frozen plasma was given over 8 hours or during the first hemodialysis session, followed by a daily infusion of 15–20 ml/kg until hematologic remission occurred. Plasmapheresis was used in 1 patient who did not benefit from plasma infusion. Early relapses and recurrent episodes were treated by the same schedule.

Eleven patients were anuric initially, and 4 other were oliguric. All patients but 1 had a hematologic response within 3 days of the start of plasma infusion therapy, and the exceptional patient responded later. Platelet counts returned to normal in a mean of 3 days. A renal response occurred in 1–6 weeks in 14 patients. Nine patients, including 7 of the 10 children, experienced complete remission after the initial course of plasma infusion. The effectiveness of plasma infusion was particularly evident in 1 patient who relapsed when infusion was stopped and responded when it was restarted (Fig 45–5). All 4 early relapses in 2 patients responded to further treatment. The only nonresponder did well after plasmapheresis. Seven patients had chronic renal failure after recovering from hemolytic uremic syndrome, but only 2 required long-term hemodialysis. Three patients experienced hypersensitivity reactions during plasma infusion therapy, and 2 others had hepatitis temporally related to plasma infusion. No patient had evidence of volume overload.

Plasma infusion is a promising approach to treatment of the hemolytic uremic syndrome and warrants further clinical evaluation.

Fig 45–5.—Temporal relation between infusions of plasma and changes in platelet count and haptoglobin and serum creatinine concentrations in a patient treated for hemolytic uremic syndrome. (Courtesy of Misiani, R. et al.: Br. Med. J. 285:1304–1306, Nov. 6, 1982.)

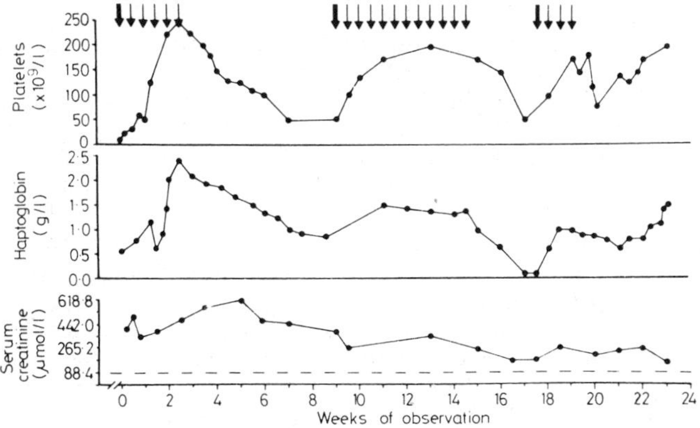

Some deficiency of a normal plasma component may have a role in development of the microangiopathy. The missing factor may be the physiologic stimulator of vascular prostacyclin. In patients who fail to respond promptly, plasma exchange can remove certain etiologic factors and material such as damaged red blood cell membranes from the circulation.

▶ [Plasma infusions were first tried in patients with the hemolytic-uremic syndrome because of the benefit reported from plasma *exchange,* in which, of course, plasma infusion is part of the treatment. The authors postulate that the plasma of patients with this syndrome lacks a factor that normally stimulates the release of the antiplatelet-aggregating factor, prostacyclin, from vascular endothelium. It's not easy to evaluate the efficacy of treatment in hemolytic uremic syndrome because of the high rate of spontaneous improvement; however, the prompt rise in platelet count that followed plasma infusions, especially in patients who relapsed when the infusions were discontinued (as shown in Figure 45–5) looks impressive.

We still don't know the cause of this disease. Almost all cases begin with severe diarrhea, either of viral or bacterial origin, and the pathological changes of fibrin thrombi in small blood vessels are so reminiscent of Shwartzman's phenomenon that endotoxin shock has been strongly implicated.[13] A soluble cytotoxin produced by certain strains of *Escherichia coli* has recently been suggested as a possible etiology.[14]] ◀

Chapter 45 References

1. Meltzer J.I., et al.: Nephrotic syndrome: vasoconstriction and hypervolemic types indicated by renin-sodium profiling. *Ann. Intern. Med.* 91:688–696, 1979.
2 Magil A.B., Bollon H.S., Rae A.: Focal proliferative lupus nephritis: a clinicopathologic study using the W.H.O. classification. *Am. J. Med.* 72:620–630, 1982.
3. Ilfeld D., Weil S., Kuperman O.: Correction of a suppressor cell deficiency and amelioration of familial Mediterranean fever by hemodialysis. *Arthritis Rheum.* 25:38–41, 1982.
4. Whitworth J.A., Tuener D.R., Leibowitz S., et al.: Focal segmental sclerosis or scarred focal proliferative glomerulonephritis. *Clin. Nephrol.* 9:229–234, 1981.
5. Hibi Y., Kobayashi Y., Tateno S., et al.: Strong association of HLA-DR4 with benign IgA nephropathy. *Nephron* 32:222–226, 1982.
6. Hall R.P., Stachura I., Cason J., et al.: IgA circulating immune complexes in patients with IgA nephropathy. *Am. J. Med.* 74:56–63, 1983.
7. Bartol E., Bosincu L., Costanzi G., et al.: IgA pseudolinear deposits in glomerular basement membranes in dermatitis herpetiformis. *Am. J. Clin. Pathol.* 78:377–380, 1982.
8. Feiner H.D., Cabili S., Baldwin D.S., et al.: Intrarenal vascular sclerosis in IgA nephropathy. *Clin. Nephrol.* 18:183–192, 1982.
9. Linne T., Aperia A., Broberger O., et al.: Course of renal function in IgA glomerulonephritis in children and adolescents. *Acta Paediatr. Scand.* 71:735–743, 1982.
10. Pusey C.D.: Glomerulonephritis due to autoantibodies to the glomerular basement membrane: treatment with plasma exchange. *Medical Grand Rounds* 1:67–74, 1982.
11. Clark W.F., Williams W., Cottran D.C., et al.: A controlled trial of chronic plasma exchange therapy in S.L.E. nephritis, abstract. American Society of Nephrology, 16th Annual Meeting, p. 24A, 1983.
12. Dancik J., Heyka R. Shapiro H.: Plasmapheresis in acute renal failure

associated with multiple myeloma, abstract. American Society of Nephrology. 16th Annual Meeting, p. 25A, 1983.

13. Koster F., Levin J., Walker L., et al.: Hemolytic-uremic syndrome after Shigellosis: relation to endotoxemia and circulating immune complexes. *N. Engl. J. Med.* 298:927–933, 1978.
14. Karmali M.A., Petric M., Steele B.T., et al.: Sporadic cases of hemolytic-uraemic syndrome associated with faecal cytotoxin and cytotoxin-producing *Escherichia coli* in stools. *Lancet* 1:619–620, 1983.

46. Other Diseases of the Kidney

46–1 **Predominantly Vascular Amyloid Deposition in Kidney in Patients With Minimal or No Proteinuria.** Proteinuria is considered the most common clinical feature of renal amyloidosis and is claimed to always be present at some stage. H. M. Falck, T. Törnroth, and O. Wegelius (Helsinki) report data on 9 patients who had renal amyloidosis but little or no proteinuria found among 72 seen from 1966 to 1980 with amyloidosis secondary to rheumatic disorders. The patients had proteinuria of less than 0.5 gm/24 hours. All had rheumatoid arthritis, and 4 were seropositive. The mean age at onset of arthritis was 38.5 years, and the mean interval before the first sign of amyloidosis was 15 years.

The mean protein excretion was 0.06 gm/24 hours. The mean serum creatinine level was 181 μmoles/L. All patients but 1 had received gold therapy. Seven patients had a serum creatinine elevation or reduced creatinine clearance. Protein excretion remained very low during follow-up in all patients but 1, in whom the nephrotic syndrome developed after 2½ years. Renal function deteriorated to some degree in all patients except 1, and 2 died of uremia. The glomeruli lacked amyloid in 3 patients; the others had only slight glomerular deposits. The blood vessels, however, were moderately or severely involved in all patients, and all but 1 of the biopsies showed glomerular hyalinization. Tubular atrophy roughly paralleled the degree of interstitial fibrosis. The amyloid deposits were of the secondary (AA) type in all 6 patients studied.

These patients with renal amyloidosis but minimal or no proteinuria had considerably more amyloid in their renal vessels than in the glomeruli. In other respects, they were clinically similar to patients who had the usual pattern of renal amyloid deposition. The degree of renal functional impairment appeared to correlate with the degree of glomerular hyalinization and interstitial fibrosis. Other types of systemic amyloidosis were ruled out.

▶ [These 9 patients developed signs of renal insufficiency in the course of severe rheumatoid arthritis. Before reading this article I would not have ventured to diagnose amyloid disease, because of the absence of proteinuria. The message is that secondary amyloidoses can involve the kidneys heavily without producing proteinuria, by infiltrating the vessels and causing a special kind of renal vascular sclerosis. Interestingly, hypertension is often absent. Unfortunately, there is no note in this paper about the size of the kidneys.

These findings would not have surprised Virchow, who noted that "lardaceous kidneys" (with amyloid disease) were difficult to perfuse because of the heavy infiltration of the vessels with amyloid material.] ◀

46–2 **Urinary Red Cell Morphology During Exercise.** Both proteinuria and hematuria have been associated with exercise. Recent stud-

---

(46–1) Clin. Nephrol. 19:137–142, March 1983.
(46–2) Br. Med. J. 285:1455–1457, Nov. 20, 1982.

ies suggest that the hematuria arises from the lower urinary tract rather than being of glomerular origin. Robert G. Fassett, Julie E. Owen, Jacinth Fairley, Douglas F. Birch, and Kenneth F. Fairley (Melbourne) examined midstream urine samples obtained from 47 males and 1 female before and just after a long-distance run. The mean age was 31.4 years. Forty-one subjects ran 9 km and 7 ran 14 km. The samples were examined by phase-contrast microscopy.

All of the runners had urinary red blood cell counts below 10,000 cells/ml before exercise, but an appreciable increase was noted after exercise in all but 4 persons (Fig 46–1); in 19 the count more than doubled. Seven runners had counts exceeding 50,000/ml. Postexercise hematuria was clearly related to proteinuria. All but 4 of the 18 with + or + + proteinuria had red blood cell counts of more than 20,000/ml. The urinary red blood cells were dysmorphic both before and after exercise. Only 2 of 8 persons with more than 100 casts/ml before exercise had hematuria after running. Most of the runners had increased urinary nucleated cell counts after exercise. There was little change in urinary pH after exercise, and no significant change in urine osmolality was noted.

Fig 46–1.—Urinary red blood cell counts before and after exercise in 48 runners. Significance of rise after exercise, $P < .0005$. (Courtesy of Fassett, R.G., et al.: Br. Med. J. 285:1455–1457, Nov. 20, 1982.)

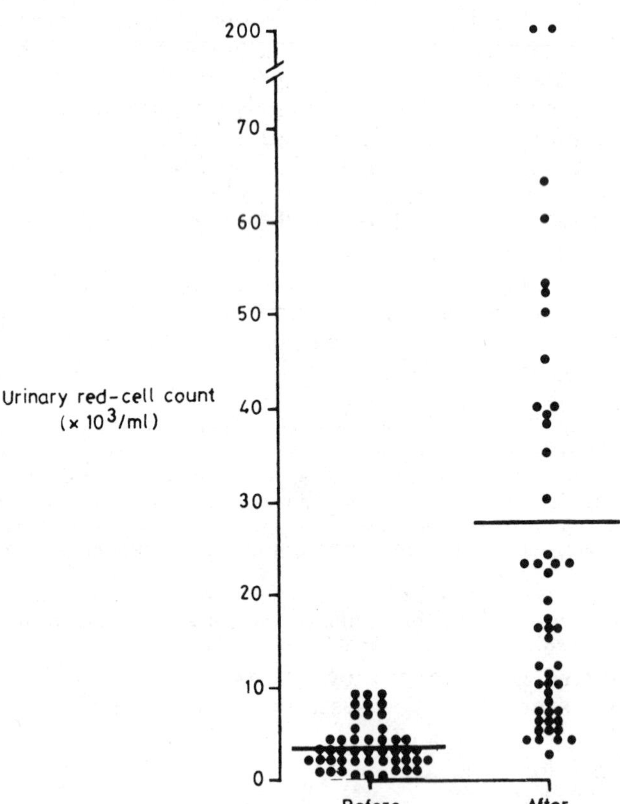

The presence of red blood cell casts in some subjects after exercise and the dysmorphic appearance of urinary red blood cells indicate that postexercise hematuria is of glomerular origin. Most persons appear to have increased glomerular bleeding after long-distance running. The hematuria may be substantial and may be accompanied by proteinuria and the presence of red blood cell casts.

▶ [Exercise hematuria has been known for years, but what is not so well known is that red blood cell casts, leukocytes, and tubular cells can also appear in the urine after strenuous exercise so that the urinary sediment may resemble that of glomerulonephritis. Severe renal vasoconstriction of exercise is probably the cause. If the serious jogger or marathon runner has been taking nonsteroidal antiinflammatory agents for orthopedic aches and pains, the fall in renal blood flow is likely to be intensified, leading to transient rises in BUN and serum creatinine levels that together with blood urine may further suggest the diagnosis of nephritis. The diagnostic dilemma is compounded by the fact that urinary abnormalities in a patient with mild underlying glomerulonephritis, e.g., IgA nephritis, may regularly be exacerbated by exercise. So, if you see red blood cells and erythrocyte casts in the urine of a runner, ask him (or her) to stop back and leave a specimen after a few days of rest.] ◀

46–3 **Prospective Trial of Operative Versus Nonoperative Treatment of Severe Vesicoureteric Reflux: Two Years' Observation in 96 Children** is reported by the Birmingham Reflux Study Group. The relationship between vesicoureteral reflux and renal parenchymal scarring is recognized, but possible benefit from reimplanting the ureters must be weighed against the tendency toward spontaneous resolution of reflux. A prospective trial was undertaken to compare surgery and medical management in 96 children without urinary tract anomalies or previous operative treatment. Children under age 1 year, aged 1–5 years, and more than age 6 were allocated to either reimplantation or chemoprophylaxis only. All of the children received chemoprophylaxis throughout the 2-year study period.

There were no significant differences between the two treatment groups in the incidence of breakthrough urinary tract infections, renal length, new scar formation, or progression of existing scars. The slope clearance of ^{51}Cr-edetic acid was similar in the two groups. Reimplantation was technically successful in all but 3% of the children, but 74% of ureters in medically managed patients still exhibited significant reflux after 2 years.

Neither ureteral reimplantation nor chemoprophylaxis alone had significant advantages over the short term in children with severe vesicoureteral reflux. Further study of the long-term effects of severe, persistent reflux is needed. It is likely that vesicoureteral reflux must be identified before the development of urinary tract infection in order to prevent reflux nephropathy, but this is not feasible with present invasive methods. A noninvasive technique of cystourethrography would be useful. Screening by conventional methods may be warranted in younger siblings of children with known reflux.

▶ [Although the authors emphasize that a period of follow-up longer than 2 years is certainly necessary, it is already apparent from their results that once the scarring process is initiated, neither chemotherapy nor surgical intervention is likely to dimin-

(46–3) Br. Med. J. 287:171–174, July 16, 1983.

ish it. That is also the general experience in adults—repair of refluxing ureters in patients with proteinuria and renal insufficiency doesn't seem to alter the downhill course.] ◀

46–4 **Controlled Comparison of Gentamicin and Tobramycin Nephrotoxicity.** The aminoglycoside antibiotics are cornerstones of treatment for gram-negative bacterial infections, but their use is often limited by the development of nephrotoxicity or ototoxicity. Gary R. Matzke, Richard L. Lucarotti, and Howard S. Shapiro compared the nephrotoxic potential of gentamicin and tobramycin in a series of 317 adults with suspected or documented infections other than cystitis. They were chiefly older, compromised patients with chronic disease. Many underwent surgery during their hospitalization, and most received multiple other drugs, including antibiotics. Dosing was by either the Sawchuk-Zaske method, with a loading dose of 1.5–2 mg/kg and maintenance dosing based on 3 serum concentrations; or a modification of the McHenry method, with administration of a maintenance dose of 1 mg/kg at a frequency dependent on the serum creatinine level.

There were 196 patients completing 6 days of aminoglycoside therapy who could be evaluated for nephrotoxicity. The patients in each dosing group were clinically comparable and had similar trough serum aminoglycoside levels. Nephrotoxicity, defined as a rise in the serum creatinine level of 0.5 mg/dl (or more if the initial level was below 2 mg/dl) or a rise of 30% (or more if initially 2 mg/dl or above), developed in 10% of patients given gentamicin by the modified McHenry method and in 18% of those given tobramycin by this method. In the Sawchuk-Zaske dosing group, 8% of gentamicin-treated patients and 17% of those given tobramycin experienced nephrotoxicity. The difference in toxicity frequency between the 2 drugs was not significant in either dosing group. Nephrotoxicity developed in 34% of the patients having elevated trough serum aminoglycoside levels and in 4% of others.

This prospective study found no significant difference in the nephrotoxic potential of gentamicin and tobramycin when the results were adjusted for the dosing regimen. There would appear to be no marked clinical difference between these drugs. The need for an aminoglycoside should be carefully considered, and the serum creatinine and aminoglycoside concentrations should be monitored regularly during treatment.

▶ [Far more important than any minor differences in nephrotoxicity that may or may not exist between one or another aminoglycoside is the impact of associated drugs and the condition of the patient on the capacity of the antibiotic to injure the kidney. Dehydration, hypotension, or renal ischemia from any other cause will potentiate aminoglycoside nephrotoxicity.[1] Aminoglycosides, in turn, increase renal susceptibility to an acute ischemic insult.[2] Metabolic acidosis also potentiates gentamicin toxicity.[3] Furosemide[4] and cephalosporins[5] seem to enhance the risk. Finally, of course, the serum level of the drug, both at its peak and lowest point, are critically important in determining nephrotoxicity. Here, the most common error is to overestimate the patient's capacity for renal excretion of the antibiotic (and thus to overestimate dosage requirement) by relying on the serum creatinine level, which may be misleadingly low in elderly patients with diminished muscle mass.] ◀

(46–4) Am. J. Nephrol. 3:11–17, January–February 1983.

46-5 **Identification of Risk for Renal Insufficiency From Nonsteroidal Antiinflammatory Drugs.** Reversible depression of renal function has been associated with the use of nonsteroidal antiinflammatory drugs (NSAIDs). Patients at risk have been described as those having an ineffective circulatory volume or active vasoconstriction. It has been proposed that renal function may decline in settings where the maintenance of renal function is dependent on synthesis of local prostaglandins. Joseph L. Blackshear, Morris Davidman, and M. Thomas Stillman (Minneapolis) report data on 7 cases of reversible depression of renal function by NSAIDs. Age range of these patients was 61–86 years; mean age was 76 years. All had evidence of atherosclerotic cardiovascular disease. Six were receiving a diuretic. Mean rise in serum urea nitrogen level was 44 mg/dl and in serum creatinine level, 2.2 mg/dl (Fig 46–2). In 3 cases the fractional excretion of

Fig 46–2.—Changes in serum urea nitrogen, serum creatinine, and serum potassium levels and in body weight before initiation of nonsteroidal antinflammatory drug (NSAID) (value to left of day 0), on day of last dose of NSAID (values at day 0), and after recovery from NSAID (values to right of day 0). Body weight given as plus or minus kilograms from weight before NSAID therapy. Serum potassium level unavailable in patient 7; weights are unavailable in patients 5 and 7. (Courtesy of Blackshear, J.L., et al.: Arch. Intern. Med. 143:1130–1134, June 1983.)

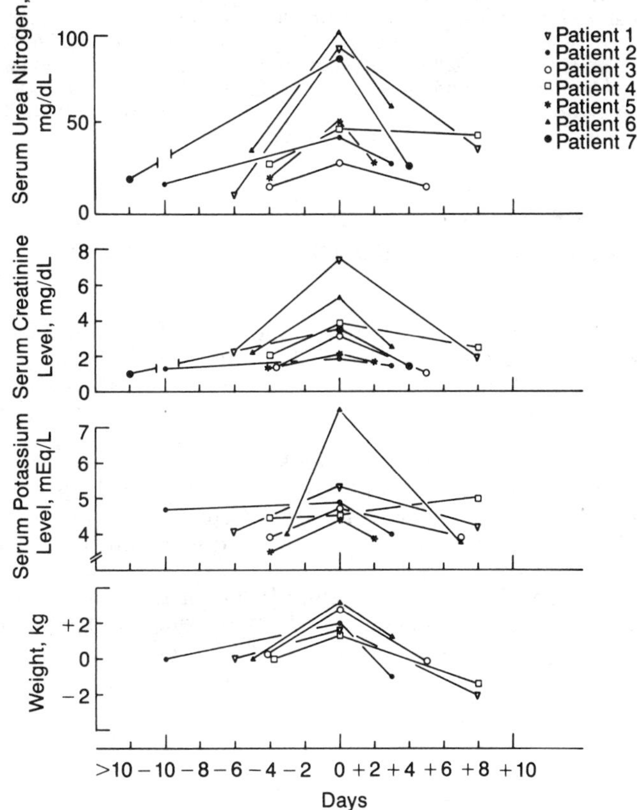

(46–5) Arch. Intern. Med. 143:1130–1134, June 1983.

sodium at the time of maximal weight gain was less than 1%. Treatment for acute gouty arthritis was the most common precipitating event in this series.

Previous reports of NSAID-related renal insufficiency also have shown the importance of advanced age, use of diuretic drugs, and chronic renal vascular disease. Evolving renal insufficiency in this setting is characterized by increasing serum urea nitrogen, serum creatinine, and potassium levels; gain in body weight; and low fractional excretion of sodium. All the patients in this study had rapidly reversible renal insufficiency. The inhibitory effects of NSAIDs on renal cyclo-oxygenase lessened during a period of 8–24 hours. Other proposed risk factors for NSAID-related renal insufficiency include cirrhosis and ascites, decompensated congestive heart failure, nephrotic syndrome, and acute and chronic renal failure. Patients at risk of NSAID-related renal insufficiency should be monitored for abnormality in renal function. If renal function deteriorates progressively, NSAID therapy should be discontinued.

▶ [With the widespread use of nonsteroidal antiinflammatory agents that inhibit prostaglandin formation, we're seeing more and more examples of this kind of initially alarming but usually reversible drug-induced renal insufficiency. Those patients most at risk are the elderly and those in whom the renal circulation is impaired so that the local vasodilating action of prostaglandins within the kidney assumes increased importance. In addition to weight gain and rising BUN, patients may also have hyperkalemia, hypertension, and hyponatremia. The reason for the latter is that prostaglandin inhibition interferes with water diuresis. Because prostaglandins are important intermediates in stimulating renin secretion, prostaglandin inhibitors can mimic the syndrome of hyporeninemic hypoaldosteronism.[6]] ◀

Chapter 46 References

1. Browning M.C., Hsu C.Y., Wang P.L., et al.: Interaction of ischemic and antibiotic-induced injury in the rabbit kidney. *J. Infect. Dis.* 147:341–351, 1983.
2. Zager R.A., Sharma H.M.: Gentamicin increases renal susceptibility to an acute ischemic insult. *J. Lab. Clin. Med.* 101:670–678, 1983.
3. Hsu C.H., Kurtz T.W., Easterling R.E., et al.: Potentiation of gentamicin toxicity by metabolic acidosis. *Proc. Soc. Exp. Biol. Med.* 146:894–897, 1974.
4. Adelman R.D., Spangler W.L., Beason F., et al.: Furosemide enhancement of gentamicin nephrotoxicity. *J. Infect. Dis.* 140:342–352, 1979.
5. Wade J.C., Smith C.R. Petty B.G., et al.: Cephalothin plus an aminoglycoside is more nephrotoxic than methicillin plus an aminoglycoside. *Lancet* 2:604–606, 1978.
6. Tan S.Y., Shapiro R., Franco R., et al.: Indomethacin-induced prostaglandin inhibition with hyperkalemia: a reversible cause of hyporeninemic hypoaldosteronism. *Ann. Intern. Med.* 90:783–785, 1979.

47. Chronic Renal Insufficiency

47–1 **Hemodynamically Mediated Glomerular Injury and the Progressive Nature of Kidney Disease** are discussed by Barry M. Brenner (Harvard Med. School). Surviving patients with massive peripartum hemorrhage and acute renal cortical necrosis may have deteriorating renal function. Progression to end-stage renal disease in these patients may represent a predictable consequence of the initial loss of nephron mass induced by widespread, irreversible ischemic renal injury. Such hemodynamically mediated progression may be a final common pathway in many renal disorders involving an irreversible reduction in the number of functioning nephron units. There is increasing evidence from animal studies that single-nephron hyperfiltration, as occurs after a reduction in renal mass, may eventually prove injurious to the integrity of the remaining glomeruli. Increments in glomerular transcapillary pressures and flows may be responsible for eventual functional deterioration. An increased mean glomerular transcapillary hydraulic pressure difference may harm the capillary network through a process analogous to the effects of systemic hypertension on arterioles. Any loss of glomerular units imposes a further hemodynamic burden on less affected glomeruli, eventually leading to their destruction (Fig 47–1). Both clinical and experimental evidence shows that renal hemodynamics may be important in the initiation and progression of diabetic glomerulopathy.

It remains unknown whether there is a critical number of function-

Fig 47–1.—Role of sustained increments in glomerular pressure and flow in start and progression of glomerular sclerosis. (Courtesy of Brenner, B.M.: Kidney Int. 23:647–655, April 1983.)

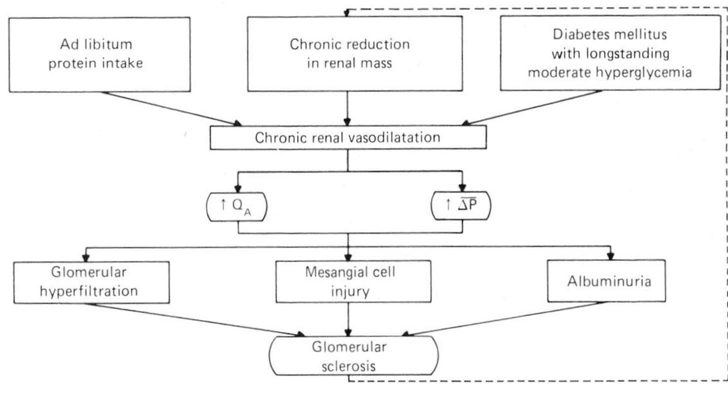

(47–1) Kidney Int. 23:647–655, April 1983.

ing nephrons below which hemodynamically mediated glomerular injury is inevitable. The remaining glomeruli do undergo functional and structural hypertrophy when the number of nephrons is reduced by more than half, and glomerular sclerosis and progressive renal failure ensue. There also is evidence that unilateral renal agenesis in man predisposes to focal and segmental glomerular sclerosis and even to end-stage renal failure. An unrestricted protein diet could exaggerate the increments in glomerular pressures and flows associated with nephron loss and could accelerate the development of glomerular sclerosis and the loss of renal function. Current management of chronic renal insufficiency does little to interrupt the hemodynamic mechanisms of progressive renal failure. A reduction in protein intake may be effective. The early institution of rigid metabolic control may help prevent glomerulopathy in patients with juvenile-onset diabetes.

▶ [The hyperfiltration theory (discussed in the 1981 YEAR BOOK OF MEDICINE, pp. 599–601) is so powerful and attractive as an explanation of progressive renal disease that it may be well to mention some caveats. First of all, the rat seems to be the ideal model to demonstrate the evils of glomerular hyperfiltration. High protein diets or partial renal ablation cause marked increases in glomerular blood flow associated with glomerular injury and scarring in this species. But the same phenomenon is not seen (or is not nearly as marked) in dogs.[1] Whether it is reasonable to extrapolate the results in rats to humans is still uncertain. Secondly, the case for hyperfiltration as an *exacerbator* of underlying renal disease is better than the case for it as a *cause* of renal scarring per se and de novo. (It may be no accident that most strains of laboratory rats have a mild form of endemic nephritis.)

The implications for therapy are profound but also perplexing. Measures that reduce glomerular filtration rate in patients with renal insufficiency (inhibitors of prostaglandin synthesis, reduction of blood pressure, low-protein diet) all have their short-term dangers—but those might be worth enduring if long-term benefit were really assured. Careful, controlled, unprejudiced observation of human patients is likely to give us the answer.] ◀

47–2 **Clinical Results of Long-Term Treatment With Low Protein Diet and New Amino Acid Preparation in Patients With Chronic Uremia.** A. Alvestrand, M. Ahlberg, P. Fürst, and J. Bergström evaluated an unselected protein-restricted diet and a new amino acid preparation containing altered proportions of essential amino acids plus added tyrosine and histidine in 15 severely uremic patients. The diet contained 16–20 gm of protein daily. The 10 women and 5 men aged 36–68 years had a mean serum creatinine level of 965 μmoles/L. They received the diet for an average of 225 days, and compliance with the dietary regimen was good.

The plasma urea concentration decreased, as did serum creatinine levels (Fig 47–2), and uremic symptoms resolved during dietary treatment. Patients remained free of symptoms for as long as several months. Seven patients were able to work full time, and all were able to perform housework. Nitrogen balance studies, done in 6 patients after a mean of 151 days on the diet, showed a mean corrected nitrogen balance of +0.4 gm/day. A small, insignificant fall in the serum albumin concentration was noted during dietary therapy. Serum total protein levels were unchanged.

(47–2) Clin. Nephrol. 19:67–73, February 1983.

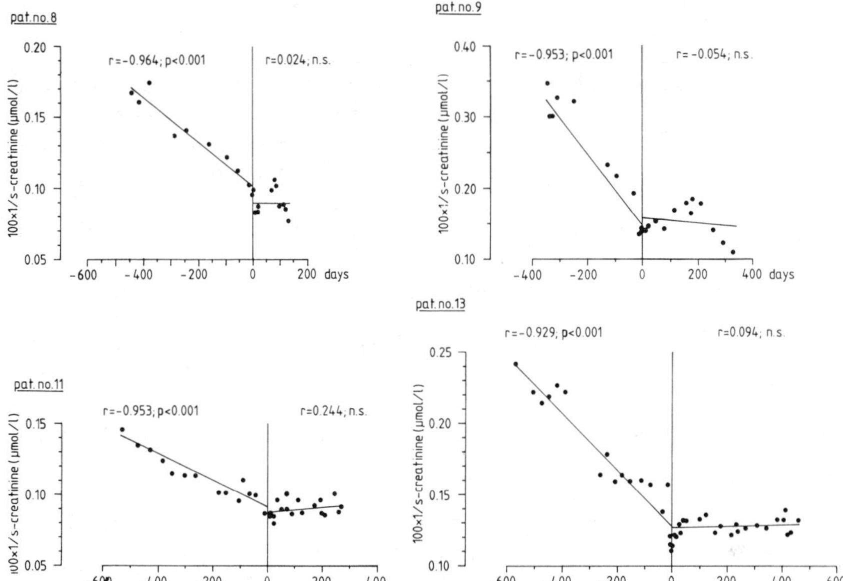

Fig 47–2.—Plots of reciprocal serum creatinine levels vs. time in 4 patients with chronic uremia before and after treatment with a low-protein diet incorporating an amino acid formula (instituted at 0 time). (Courtesy of Alvestrand, A., et al.: Clin. Nephrol. 19:67–73, February 1983.)

Nitrogen equilibrium can be maintained during long-term treatment with this new low-protein diet incorporating a new amino acid formula, in which the proportions differed from those previously considered optimal for normal human beings. The progression of renal insufficiency may be slowed by use of this dietary regimen.

▶ [Since the turn of the century it has been known that low-protein diets could temporarily ameliorate uremic symptoms in some patients with renal failure. At one time, low-protein diets were advocated as treatment for all patients with nephritis, but this was later discouraged by clinicians who emphasized the frequent occurrence of protein malnutrition, especially when accompanied by large urinary losses of albumin. Because protein feeding increases renal blood flow and glomerular filtration rate, thus inducing glomerular hyperperfusion that might act over the long term to injure the kidney, there has been a resurgence of interest in the possibility of altering the inexorable progression of renal disease by instituting low-protein diets early in the course of the disease process. Two excellent reviews of the influence of dietary factors on chronic renal disease were published during the past year.[2, 3]

Unpublished work by Drs. W. Mitch and T. Steinman on our own service at Beth Israel and at Brigham and Women's Hospitals suggests that in about half of patients with chronic renal insufficiency there is a significant improvement in the rate of decline of the reciprocal of the serum creatinine, when a low-protein diet supplemented with keto-acid analogues of essential amino acids is prescribed. It is not yet clear, however, whether this reflects a real improvement in glomerular filtration or merely a change in the amount of creatinine-claiming excretion. The most constant feature of the treatment is an initial early fall in the serum creatinine, implying a *rise* in glomerular filtration rate, and this is difficult to reconcile with the notion that the diet's mode of action is to *decrease* glomerular perfusion. An exciting recent experimental development is the discovery that in rats, high-protein diets enhance the production of thromboxane, a potent glomerular vasoconstrictor, by the kidney.[4] So it is possible that the beneficial effect of low-protein feeding in renal disease may be related to endogenous vasoactive or inflammation-enhancing substances produced by the kidney.] ◀

47–3 **Uremic Bleeding: Role of Anemia and Beneficial Effect of Red Cell Transfusions.** The bleeding tendency seen in uremic patients is not well understood; however, these patients often are anemic. Earlier studies found that the bleeding time is prolonged in anemic patients and is restored to normal by transfusing washed red blood cells. Manuela Livio, Eliana Gotti, Donatella Marchesi, Giuliano Mecca, Giuseppe Remuzzi, and Giovanni de Gaetano studied 65 chronically uremic patients, most of them in good clinical condition, just before routine hemodialysis. Two uremic patients with symptomatic anemia and very long bleeding times were studied in conjunction with washed, packed red blood cell transfusions. Six other patients with packed cell volumes (PCVs) of 16%–21% were infused with washed, filtered red blood cells. Sixty-five normal persons, matched with the uremic patients for age and sex, and 15 patients with anemia unrelated to uremia also were studied.

A significant negative correlation between bleeding time and PCV was found in evaluable uremic patients (Fig 47–3), 13 of whom had bleeding times exceeding 15 minutes. No such correlation was evident in normal persons, but there was a negative correlation in patients with anemia unrelated to uremia. In 15 randomized uremic patients with PCVs comparable to those of the anemic patients, bleeding times were significantly longer. The 2 uremic patients who required transfusions had a progressive increase in PCVs but no shortening of the bleeding time until the PCV exceeded 30%. Five of 6 patients with hemorrhagic complications had a considerable reduction in bleeding time after washed red blood cell transfusion. Platelet retention on glass beads was markedly improved in 3 of these 6 patients. After 3 months the PCV and bleeding time were at pretransfusion levels in all cases.

The prolonged bleeding time in uremic patients is strongly influenced by anemia, which adds to the other hemostatic defects (e.g.,

Fig 47–3.—Correlation between bleeding time and packed cell volume in 65 patients with chronic uremia examined before hemodialysis. (Courtesy of Livio, M., et al.: Lancet 2:1013–1015, Nov. 6, 1982.)

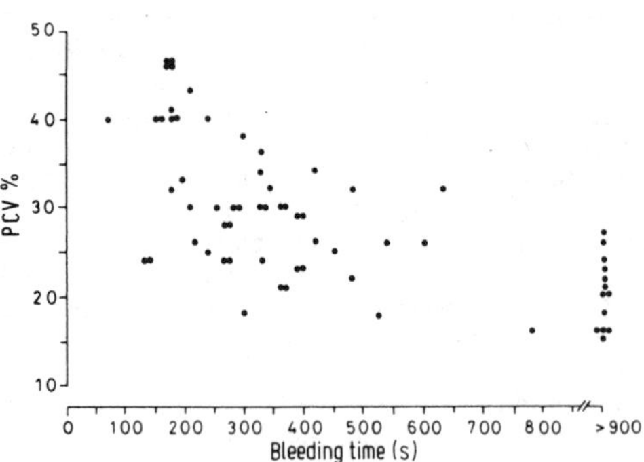

(47–3) Lancet 2:1013–1015, Nov. 6, 1982.

platelet abnormalities) that often are associated with renal failure. Improvement in bleeding times with red blood cell transfusion suggests that red blood cells enhance hemostasis through an effect on the platelet-vessel wall interaction in vivo. Red blood cell transfusions may be an appropriate prophylactic measure in patients with platelet-mediated hemostatic defects.

▶ [There is an interesting explanation for the beneficial effect of transfusion on uremic bleeding tendency demonstrated here. The motion of red cells flowing through vessels causes platelets to diffuse radially, so each platelet collides more often with the vessel wall, favoring hemostasis and thrombus formation. So transfusion of packed erythrocytes alone may be expected to improve the situation in uremic bleeding. The same group of investigators report that 1-desamino-8-D-arginine-vasopressin shortens the bleeding time in uremia (see abstract 25-2) because of its action to release factor VIII coagulant activity from vascular endothelium.[5]] ◀

–4 **Effect of Hemodialysis on Left Ventricular Function: Dissociation of Changes in Filling Volume and in Contractile State.** The occurrence of a uremic cardiomyopathy remains an unsettled issue. Previous studies of the effects of hemodialysis on left ventricular function (LVR) have failed to distinguish between the removal of uremic toxins and altered cardiac filling volume. J. V. Nixon, Jere H. Mitchell, John J. McPhaul, Jr., and William L. Henrich (Dallas) attempted to separate these effects by examining LVR by serial echocardiography in 5 stable male hemodialysis patients in conjunction with hemodialysis with volume loss; ultrafiltration, involving volume loss only; and hemodialysis without volume loss. Mean age of the patients was 53 years. All 5 had chronic renal failure. Studies were repeated after 90 minutes of 5-degree head-down tilting and after the application of lower-body negative pressure to lower the cardiac filling volume.

Both end-diastolic and end-systolic volumes decreased significantly after dialysis with volume loss, with no change in stroke volume. Ejection fraction rose from 42% to 52%, and mean velocity of circumferential fiber shortening (VCF) increased significantly. After ultrafiltration, end-diastolic volume decreased with stroke volume without significant changes in end-systolic volume or VCF. After hemodialysis without volume loss, end-systolic volume decreased and stroke volume increased, without change in end-diastolic volume. Ejection fraction rose from 44% to 59%, and VCF increased significantly. Ventricular function curves indicated that ultrafiltration produced a pure Frank-Starling effect, but hemodialysis, with or without volume loss, led to a shift in the curve, reflecting an increased contractile state of the left ventricle.

It is concluded that the changes in LVR produced by regular hemodialysis are the combined results of a decrease in end-diastolic volume and an increase in the contractile state of the left ventricle. Studies of the effects of calcium or bicarbonate changes during dialysis may help determine the mechanisms responsible for improved LVR with hemodialysis.

▶ [It has been known, of course, that the signs of left ventricular failure could be

---

(47–4) J. Clin. Invest. 71:377–384, February 1983.

improved and pulmonary congestion rapidly relieved by hemodialysis in patients with renal failure, but it was not clear whether the effect was entirely the result of removing fluid (like that of a diuretic) or in part of improved contractility of the heart muscle itself. This article shows that cardiac contractility does indeed improve after dialysis. The most likely reason for the beneficial inotropic effect is that dialysis increases the concentration of ionized calcium in plasma.] ◀

47–5 **Effect of Oral Zinc Therapy on Gonadal Function in Hemodialysis Patients: A Double-Blind Study.** Abnormal sexual function is not uncommon in patients in chronic renal failure, and uremic patients may be deficient in zinc. Zinc deficiency can cause testicular atrophy in growing animals. Sudesh K. Mahajan, Ali A. Abbasi, Ananda S. Prasad, Parviz Rabbani, William A. Briggs, and Franklin D. McDonald (Detroit) undertook a double-blind study of oral zinc and a placebo to evaluate the possibility that zinc deficiency is a reversible cause of gonadal dysfunction in uremic patients.

Twenty stable male patients with end-stage renal disease who had been on hemodialysis 3 times a week for more than 6 months were studied. Most had renal disease due to hypertensive nephrosclerosis. All 20 had been sexually active before the onset of renal failure, and 14 had fathered children. The patients received either 50 mg of elemental zinc as zinc acetate or a placebo orally each day. Capsules were taken twice daily, 1–2 hours before meals.

The patients had lower mean baseline plasma zinc and serum testosterone levels and lower mean sperm counts than age-matched normal men. Patients also had higher serum gonadotropin levels. Only 2 patients had normal plasma zinc levels; 2 had normal serum testosterone levels. All the patients were oligospermic. Levels of both zinc and testosterone increased significantly in patients given oral zinc, and all but 1 had normal levels within 6 months. Mean sperm count increased but remained significantly below normal. Gonadotropin levels decreased in all patients who received zinc supplements. No such changes were seen in the placebo group. Seven of 8 patients with sexual dysfunction who received zinc supplements noted definite improvement in sexual potency; the other patient had low zinc and testosterone levels during treatment. None of 7 symptomatic patients in the placebo group had increased sexual potency. Sexual satisfaction, libido, and frequency of intercourse all increased in zinc-treated patients. Potency could not be related to zinc or testosterone levels before or after the study period.

Impotence in uremic patients on hemodialysis appears to be due to gonadal dysfunction. Supplementation with oral zinc was associated with improved sexual function in the present patients, but caution is indicated because the long-term effects of zinc therapy and its possible interaction with other drugs are unknown. Zinc is recommended only for patients known to be deficient and only when other causes of impotence are excluded.

▶ [The conjunction of a low level of testosterone and a high level of gonadotropic hormone in the plasma of a patient with chronic renal failure would be compatible with primary testicular failure and, if these authors are correct, might therefore sug-

(47–5) Ann. Intern. Med. 97:357–361, September 1982.

gest a trial of oral zinc therapy. Remember, however, that there are other causes of impotence in patients on dialysis. One of these is persistently high levels of prolactin—in fact, many complex peptide hormones tend to be elevated in chronic renal failure because they are normally disposed of by the kidney. Malnutrition, anemia, drug treatment for hypertension, and psychic depression, all cause sexual dysfunction in women as well as men.

Zinc deficiency has also been implicated in the disturbances of taste and smell that are regularly encountered in uremia.[6]] ◀

Chapter 47 References

1. Robertson J.L., Bovee K.C., Hill G.S., et al.: Effects on glomerular morphology in partially nephrectomized dogs fed 56, 27 or 19% protein, abstract. American Society of Nephrology, 16th Annual Meeting, p. 115A, 1983.
2. Klahr S., Buerkert J., Purkerson M.L.: Role of dietary factors in the progression of chronic renal disease. *Kidney Int.* 24:579–587, 1983.
3. Mitch W.E., Steinman T.I.: Can the course of chronic renal failure be altered by diet? *The Kidney* 16:31–35, 1983.
4. Ichikawa I., Purkerson M., Yates J., et al.: High protein diet augments renal vasoconstriction induced by bilateral ureteral obstruction (BUO), abstracts. American Society of Nephrology, 16th Annual Meeting, p. 94A, 1983.
5. Manucci P.M., Remuzzi G., Pusineri F., et al.: Deamino-8-D-arginine vasopressin shortens the bleeding time in uremia. *N. Engl. J. Med.* 308:8–12, 1983.
6. Mahajan S.K., Prasad A.S., Lambujon J., et al.: Improvement of uremic hypogeusia by zinc: a double blind study. *Am. J. Clin. Nutr.* 33:1517–1521, 1980.

48. Hypertension

48–1 **Long-Term Antihypertensive Treatment Inhibiting Progression of Diabetic Nephropathy.** It remains unclear why diabetic nephropathy develops in some patients but not in others despite a long duration of diabetes. C. E. Mogensen (Aarhus, Denmark) determined renal function serially in conjunction with long-term antihypertensive therapy in 6 juvenile-onset diabetics with established nephropathy. The patients, all men aged 26–35 years with insulin-dependent diabetes, had a mean blood pressure of 162/103 mm Hg and persistent proteinuria. All but 1 had proliferative retinopathy; none had evidence of hypertrophy. The mean daily dose of insulin was 57 IU. The patients were followed for a mean of 73 months. A constant infusion clearance method was applied, using ^{125}I-iothalamate as a marker of filtration and ^{131}I-hippuran to measure renal plasma flow. Most patients were treated with propranolol and later with metoprolol.

Significant decreases in systolic and diastolic blood pressures occurred during antihypertensive therapy. Changes in the glomerular filtration rate (GFR) are shown in Figure 48–1. The mean monthly decline in the GFR fell from 1.23 ml/min to 0.49 ml/min. The decline in renal plasma flow appeared to be reduced by antihypertensive therapy, but the effect was not significant. Albumin clearance was virtually stabilized during the study. The fall in the GFR correlated significantly with changes in arterial pressure. No significant changes in fasting plasma glucose levels or insulin requirements were noted. Retinopathy became slightly worse in 3 patients and was unchanged in 2.

In this study, antihypertensive therapy reduced the decline in GFR in patients who had juvenile-onset diabetes with nephropathy. The results of ongoing studies of treatment starting in the incipient phase of diabetic nephropathy will help define the best management. Apart from the effect on systemic blood pressure, modification of glomerular hemodynamics through blockade of local receptors may be operative.

▶ [Although the *average* rate of decline in GFR seemed to improve after treatment for hypertension was started, a more realistic picture is obtained from inspection of Figure 48–1. Patients 1 and 3 seemed to benefit, but 2 and 4 didn't, and patient 5 wouldn't, if the line were drawn through the last point. In a similar study by Parving et al., reported from Copenhagen, 10 hypertensive diabetics with nephropathy were treated.[1] In half there was a significant slowing of the rate of decline in GFR after treatment for hypertension was begun, but in half there was no improvement. In neither study, disappointingly, was retinopathy improved. Control of hypertension diminished proteinuria in early diabetic nephrop-

(48–1) Br. Med. J. 285:685–688, Sept. 11, 1982.

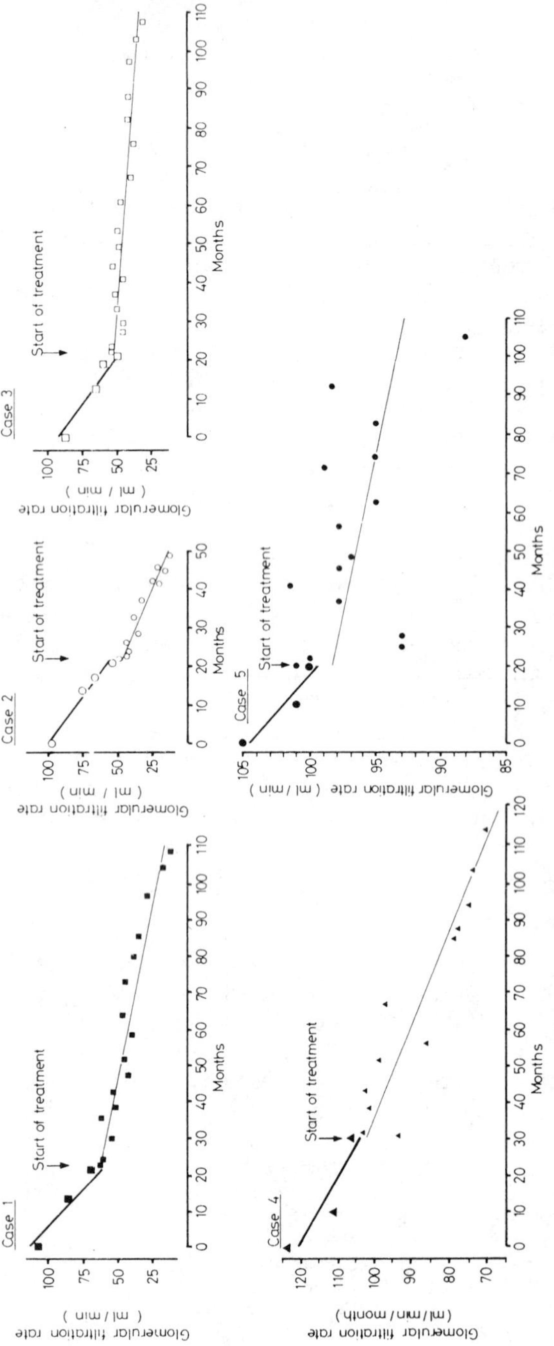

Fig 48–1.—Glomerular filtration rates in 5 patients with juvenile-onset diabetes before and during treatment with antihypertensive agents. (Courtesy of Mogensen, C.E.: Br. Med. J. 285:685–688, Sept. 11, 1982.)

athy, but it remains to be seen whether it can reliably retard the progression of renal disease.] ◀

48–2 **Reductions in Plasma Catecholamines and Blood Pressure During Weight Loss in Obese Subjects.** Changes in sympathetic nervous system activity have been described during feeding and starvation. Michael L. Tuck, James R. Sowers, Leslie Dornfeld, Larry Whitfield, and Morton Maxwell examined blood pressure and plasma catecholamine changes serially in obese patients during 8 weeks of weight reduction with a supplemented fast containing normal or low levels of sodium. Ten patients of each sex, aged 23–62 years, participated. All initially weighed more than 25% above ideal body weight. None had cardiovascular disease, insulin-dependent diabetes, or severe hypertension. A 320-calorie diet containing either 40 or 120 mmoles of sodium was given daily. The 2 dietary groups were comparable in age, body weight, arterial pressure, and baseline urinary sodium excretion.

Initial upright plasma norepinephrine levels were higher in the patients than in normal subjects and correlated with the mean arterial pressure. Weight loss in both diet groups was accompanied by a fall in the norepinephrine concentration, the mean level at 8 weeks being 42% below baseline. Significant but less marked declines in upright epinephrine levels also were noted. The fall in body weight correlated with both the reduction in the norepinephrine level and the decrease in upright plasma renin activity.

Weight loss in obese patients is accompanied by significant reductions in upright catecholamine levels, which may contribute to the accompanying reduction in blood pressure. The fall in upright plasma renin activity with weight loss could result from depressed sympathetic nervous system activity; also, decreased production of angiotensin II may contribute to the fall in blood pressure.

▶ [Clinicians have known for many years that weight reduction was good treatment for high blood pressure in obese patients, but the precise reasons were not clear. Suggested explanations varied from a reduction in the thickness of the arm around which the blood pressure cuff was wrapped to a diminution in salt intake that would usually accompany a decrease in the amount of food eaten. This article indicates that a depression in activity of the sympathetic nervous system, as reflected in circulating levels of norepinephrine, is responsible for the salutary effects of a reducing diet. The idea is consistent with the important experimental finding that the sympathetic nervous system is turned on by feeding and turned off by starvation.[2]

48–3 **Mild Hypertension: When and How To Treat** are discussed by Norman M. Kaplan (Univ. of Texas at Dallas). Mild hypertension, with diastolic blood pressures of 90–104 mm Hg, is present in an estimated 40 million Americans. Most of them will receive drugs if prevalent recommendations are followed, but the results of large-scale studies do not in themselves justify routine drug therapy for mild hypertension. Most patients with mild hypertension do not have adverse consequences, at least in a period of a few years, although a risk of cardiovascular disease is increased in this population. Most patients at risk can be identified clinically and given appropriate an-

---

(48–2) Acta Endocrinol. (Copenh.) 102:252–257, February 1983.
(48–3) Arch. Intern. Med. 143:255–259, February 1983.

tihypertensive drug therapy. Also, most of those with mild hypertension can be managed safely by a period of 6–12 months of careful monitoring and appropriate nondrug measures.

Nondrug treatment often results in a fall of 5–10 mm Hg in blood pressure, and it should not be expected to produce more marked reductions. Both restricted sodium intake and weight reduction are effective measures. These therapies do not require much physician time. Properly designed patient education, especially when directed toward behavioral change, has generally proved effective in the management of hypertension and other chronic disorders. The author believes that, if the diastolic pressure can be kept below 100 mm Hg without the use of drugs, patients are at least as well off as those whose hypertension is controlled with drugs, and probably are better off.

If drug treatment is necessary, the stepped-care approach is generally used by American physicians today, starting with a diuretic and proceeding to β-blockers. β-Blockers may be preferable because they reduce the risk of recurrent myocardial infarction and also because diuretics may lead to hypokalemia. A single daily dose of either a long-acting diuretic or a β-blocker should control the blood pressure in most mildly hypertensive patients. A diuretic probably is better to use in elderly patients and in blacks, and a β-blocker in younger patients and whites.

▶ [Support for this conservative view (to which I subscribe) comes from the Australian therapeutic trial.[3] In that study, for patients with diastolic blood pressure of 100 mm Hg or below, hypertensive and cardiovascular complications were consistently *less* frequent in those given a placebo than in those taking drugs. Weight reduction for patients who are obese is probably the most efficacious nondrug therapy; salt restriction and muscle relaxation training may also be effective. All drugs have some side effects. β-blockers tend to raise serum lipids, whereas diuretics lower serum potassium and probably increase the incidence of cardiac arrhythmias.[4, 5] Diuretics are usually given in too high a dosage; 25 mg per day of hydrodiuril will produce most of the antihypertensive effect of a dose 2–4 times as large.

You should be aware that there are claims that calcium supplements[6] and potassium administration[7] lower blood pressure slightly in *normal* young people, but the relevance of this to hypertension is not known.] ◀

48–4 **Captopril-Induced Functional Renal Insufficiency in Patients With Bilateral Renal Artery Stenoses or Renal Artery Stenosis in a Solitary Kidney.** The acute renal failure occasionally seen in conjunction with captopril therapy has been ascribed to a direct nephrotoxic effect of the drug, hypersensitivity, and renal ischemia resulting from a fall in systemic blood pressure. Donald E. Hricik, Philip J. Browning, Richard Kopelman, Warren E. Goorno, Nicolaos E. Madias, and Victor J. Dzau (Boston) report data on 11 patients who developed acute renal insufficiency while receiving captopril for severe hypertension associated with bilateral renal artery stenoses (7 patients) or renal artery stenosis in a solitary kidney (4 patients). The 7 women and 4 men were aged 36–81 years. All had long-standing hypertension. Captopril was given in a maximum daily dose of 75–225 mg. All patients also were taking a diuretic.

(48–4) N. Engl. J. Med. 308:373–376, Feb. 17, 1983.

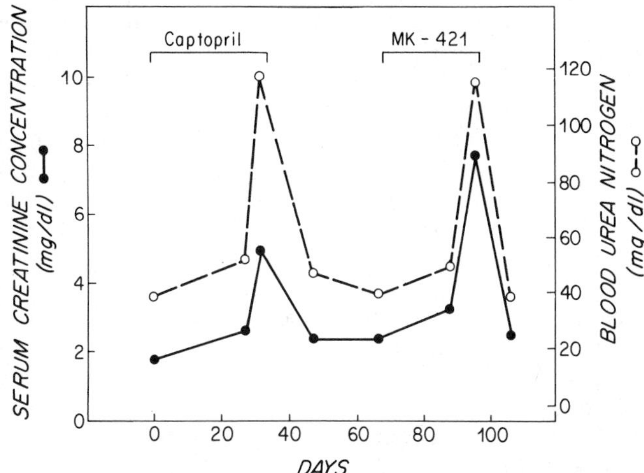

Fig 48–2.—Responses of serum creatinine and blood urea nitrogen to the converting-enzyme inhibitors captopril and MK421 in patient 2. To convert blood urea nitrogen values to millimoles per liter, multiply by 0.357. (Courtesy of Hricik, D., et al.: N. Engl. J. Med. 308:373–376, Feb. 17, 1983; reprinted by permission of The New England Journal of Medicine.)

The systemic blood pressure was reduced during captopril therapy except in 2 patients. Seven patients had some degree of renal insufficiency before receiving captopril. After captopril was discontinued and other antihypertensive medications were given, all patients had substantial reductions in systemic blood pressure and also improved renal function. Renal function consistently improved within a week of cessation of captopril therapy (Fig 48–2).

These cases may represent a functional disturbance of autoregulation of glomerular filtration caused by captopril in the presence of a markedly reduced renal arterial perfusion pressure. The renin-angiotensin system appears to be important in the autoregulation of renal blood flow and glomerular filtration when renal arterial perfusion pressure is substantially reduced. A direct nephrotoxic effect of captopril cannot be entirely excluded.

If captopril must be used in a patient with bilateral renal artery stenoses or renal artery stenosis in a solitary kidney, diuretics should be used cautiously and renal function monitored closely. Development of acute renal insufficiency during captopril therapy should raise a suspicion of renal artery stenosis.

▶ [When renal arterial pressure is low, the renin-angiotensin system plays a crucial role in regulating glomerular filtration rate. With a decrease in arterial pressure, increased secretion of renin and production of angiotensin II results in constriction of the efferent glomerular arteriole, thus maintaining effective glomerular filtration pressure.[8] Of all the hypotensive drugs we have in our armamentarium, converting enzyme inhibitors like captopril are uniquely designed to interfere with this protection. Renal function is therefore at special risk when any converting enzyme inhibitor is given to a patient with hypertension who has a preglomerular obstruction to renal blood flow. These include patients with a single kidney and renal artery stenosis, bilateral renal arterial stenosis, and renal artery stenosis in a transplanted kidney.[9] Although some decrease in renal function often accompanies treatment of hypertension with a variety of agents, the decline is more abrupt and more marked when captopril is given to such patients, and in fact this phenomenon may sometimes be useful in suggesting the diagnosis of an obstructed renal artery.] ◀

48–5 **Changing Clinical Spectrum of Primary Aldosteronism.** Emmanuel L. Bravo, Robert C. Tarazi, Harriet P. Dustan, Fetnat M. Fouad, Stephen C. Textor, Ray W. Gifford, and Donald G. Vidt (Cleveland Clinic) undertook a prospective study of 80 patients seen in a 10-year period with primary aldosteronism. Seventy had adrenal adenomas and 10 had adrenal hyperplasia. The 44 male and 36 female patients were aged 20–67 years at diagnosis; most were in the third to fifth decades of life. The diagnosis was suspected in 32 patients because of spontaneous hypokalemia and in 43 because of moderately severe hypokalemia induced by conventional doses of potassium-wasting diuretics. All medications were withheld for at least 2 weeks before evaluation.

The fasting serum potassium level was 3.5 mEq/L or higher during a normal dietary intake of sodium in 22 patients (Fig 48–3); 10 patients remained normokalemic during a high-sodium intake (Fig 48–4). Nearly one half of the patients were normovolemic. More than two thirds had suppressed supine plasma renin activity values. An aldosterone excretion rate higher than 14 μg/24 hours after 3 days of salt loading identified all but 3 patients with primary aldosteronism and was the most sensitive and specific diagnostic measure. Spontaneous hypokalemia (serum potassium level below 3 mEq/L) was seen only in patients with adenoma. Catheterization of the adrenal vein frequently failed on the left side. The smallest tumor shown by adrenal venography was 1.5 cm in greatest diameter; computed tomography (CT) identified tumors as small as 0.8 cm in diameter.

Fig 48–3.—Serum potassium values during normal dietary sodium intake. Each point represents the mean of at least 3 determinations. For patients with primary aldosteronism, *solid circles* represent adenomas (n = 70) and *open circles with dotted centers* represent hyperplasia (n = 10). The cross-hatched area represents 95% confidence limits (3.5–4.6 mEq/L) of values obtained from 60 healthy subjects. (Courtesy of Bravo, E.L., et al.: Am. J. Med. 74:641–651, April 1983.)

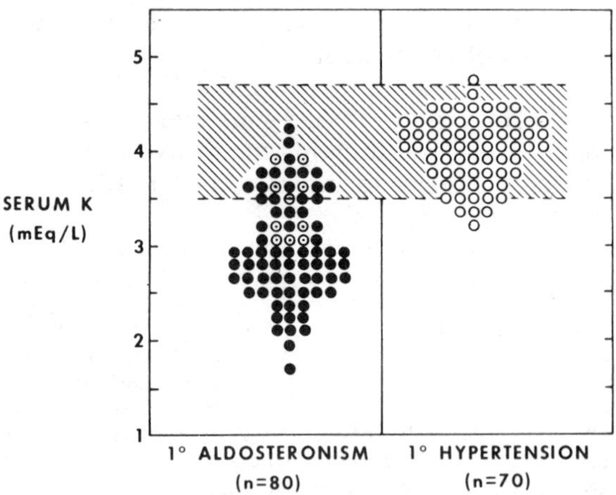

(48–5) Am. J. Med. 74:641–651, April 1983.

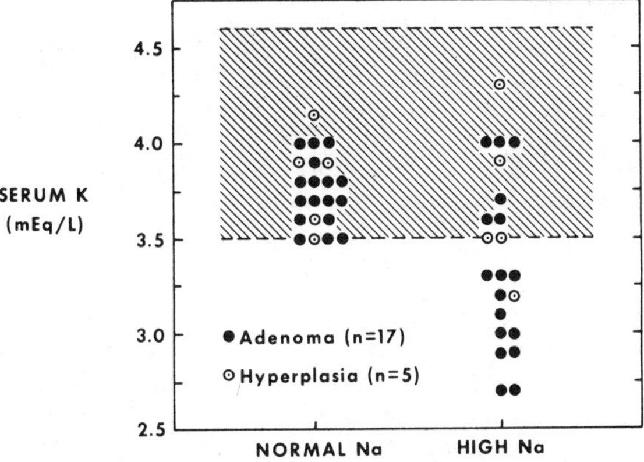

Fig 48–4.—The effect of 3 days of salt loading on serum potassium values in 22 patients with normal basal values. For patients with primary aldosteronism, *solid circles* represent adenomas (n = 70) and *open circles with dotted centers* represent hyperplasia (n = 10). The cross-hatched area represents 95% confidence limits (3.5–4.6 mEq/L) of values from 60 healthy subjects. (Courtesy of Bravo, E.L., et al.: Am. J. Med. 74:641–651, April 1983.)

Primary aldosteronism appears not to be uncommon. The clinical spectrum is wider than previously recognized. Nonsuppressible aldosterone production is the chief diagnostic hallmark of the condition and is the basis for the best screening procedure. The most precise means of identifying and localizing tumors remains adrenal venous sampling for aldosterone estimation. Adrenal CT may be the logical first step in localizing an adrenal adenoma.

▶ [An anomalous postural decrease in plasma aldosterone has been described as a way to distinguish adrenal adenoma from adrenal hyperplasia. This is an important distinction because surgical intervention is likely to result in cure of hypertension in patients with adenoma whereas in hyperplasia it is seldom helpful. However, in this large series of patients the test was unreliable. More than a third of patients with adrenal adenoma had a rise in plasma aldosterone when standing, and 1 of 10 patients with hyperplasia had an anomalous fall.

The most common presenting sign of hyperaldosteronism in this era of diuretic therapy was unexpectedly severe hypokalemia following the use of diuretics. It's noteworthy that in 1 out of 8 patients the serum potassium remained normal despite taking a high-sodium diet for 3 days—a standard test that I used to think reliable. The lesson of this excellent review is best summed up in the words of the authors:

"In view of the absence of hypokalemia in a large number of patients and the number of false-positive and false-negative results with plasma renin activity measurements, we recommend that patients suspected of having primary aldosteronism should have as the initial screening test the determination of urinary aldosterone levels obtained during prolonged salt loading. This evaluation can be accomplished readily as an outpatient by simply adding 10 to 12 grams of salt to the patient's daily intake and determining the values of serum potassium and 24-hour urinary excretion of sodium, potassium and aldosterone after 5 to 7 days. A 24-hour urinary sodium of at least 250 mEq would give some assurance of adequate salt repletion. Priority of examination should be given to patients with a history of spontaneous hypokalemia, marked sensitivity to potassium-wasting diuretic agents, or those with "refractory" hypertension. Patients who demonstrate non-suppressible aldosterone production (i.e., an aldosterone excretion rate greater than 14.0 μg/24 hours when the urinary sodium value is equal to or greater than 250 mEq/24 hours) should undergo additional studies to rule out primary aldosteronism. The presence of hypokalemia and/or suppressed plasma renin activity values provides corroborative evidence, but their absence does not preclude the diagnosis."] ◀

Chapter 48 References

1. Parving H.-H., Smidt U.M., Andersen A.R., et al.: Early aggressive antihypertensive treatment reduces rate of decline in kidney function in diabetic nephropathy. *Lancet* 1:1175–1179, 1983.
2. Landsberg L., Young J.B.: Fasting, feeding and regulation of sympathetic nervous system. *N. Engl. J. Med.* 298:1295–1300, 1978.
3. Management Committee: Untreated mild hypertension. *Lancet* 1:185–191, 1982.
4. Johansson B.W. (ed.): Electrolytes and cardiac arrhythmias. *Acta Med. Scand.* [*Suppl.*] 647:1–71, 1980.
5. Holland O.B., Nixon J.V., Kuhnert L.: Diuretic-induced ventricular ectopic activity. *Am. J. Med.* 70:762–768, 1981.
6. Belizan J.M., Villar J., Pineda O., et al.: Reduction of blood pressure with calcium supplementation in young adults. *JAMA* 249:1161–1165, 1983.
7. Khaw K.T., Thom S.: Randomised double-blind cross-over trial of potassium on blood pressure in normal subjects. *Lancet* 2:1127–1129, 1982.
8. Curtis J.J., Luke R.G., Whelchel J.D., et al.: Inhibition of angiotensin-converting enzyme in renal transplant recipients with hypertension. *N. Engl. J. Med.* 308:377–381, 1983.
9. Blythe W.B.: Captopril and renal autoregulation. *N. Engl. J. Med.* 308:390–391, 1983.

49. Transplantation

▶ I am grateful to Dr. Terry Strom for his assistance in selecting the articles for this chapter and for his comments. ◀

49–1 **Improving Success Rates of Kidney Transplantation.** Paul I. Terasaki, Sondra T. Perdue, Nori Sasaki, M. R. Mickey, and Lesley Whitby (Univ. of California, Los Angeles) discuss the current improvement in the success of renal transplantation, which contrasts with the decline seen in North America between 1968 and 1975. Data from more than 100 centers in North America indicate steady improvement in the average results, largely attributable to a policy of pretransplantation transfusion. One-year patient survival improved from 84% in 1968 to 97% in 1980 for recipients of parental donor grafts and from 65% to 90% for recipients of cadaver grafts. Graft survival has improved since 1975 at rates of 2.4%/year for parent donor grafts and 2.7%/year for cadaver kidneys. The rate of pretransplantation transfusion exposure rose from 52% in 1977 to 91% by 1981. About one fourth of patients in 1977 received more than 5 transfusions, compared with 50% in 1981. Graft success rates were nearly always higher in subsets of patients given more than 5 pretransplantation transfusions than in those given none.

It appears that renal transplantation has achieved a new level of acceptance as a clinical treatment and that blood transfusion has substantially improved graft survival. Renal transplantation should be made available to more patients maintained on dialysis. Presently only 10% of patients undergoing dialysis in the United States are on transplant waiting lists. Recognition by the medical community at large of recent improvements in the outcome of transplantation might lead to better use of this treatment option.

▶ [Dr. Terasaki and his colleagues have documented in this report and previous publications the dramatic improvements in the rate of engraftment for cadaver donor renal transplants that are obtained by use of pretransplant blood transfusion. Although the survival of patients following transplantation has shown steady improvement since the late 1960s, the period from 1968 to 1975 was marked by a period of diminished use of pretransplant blood transfusions and a poor rate of engraftment. As Dr. Terasaki's message is being heard with increasing clarity throughout the transplant community, pretransplant blood transfusions have been used to good advantage, and graft survival rates are now sharply increasing. The improved rate of engraftment was also noted in another important publication that appeared this year in which Krakauer et al.[1] reported on the data obtained from the federally funded end-stage renal failure program. In this study Krakauer et al. also recognized a steady rise in the rate of engraftment in each of the calendar years from January 1977 to December 1981. Despite these dramatic improvements, the rate at which patients who have end-stage renal failure are transplanted remains rather low, i.e., 10%. It will be interesting in years to come to note whether blood transfusions synergize with the

(49–1) JAMA 250:1065–1068, Aug. 26, 1983.

effects of cyclosporine. The next article, from the Brigham and Women's Hospital, notes that among long-term transplant recipients the leading cause of mortality is liver failure, suggesting that blood transfusions are not totally without adverse effect.] ◀

49–2 **Late Mortality and Morbidity in Recipients of Long-Term Renal Allografts.** The late results of renal transplantation and the effects of long-term immunosuppression are incompletely understood. Robert L. Kirkman, Terry B. Strom, Matthew R. Weir, and Nicholas L. Tilney (Boston) reviewed experience with 217 renal allografts that functioned for more than 5 years during the period 1951–1976 in which 535 patients received a total of 589 renal allografts at the authors' institution. Follow-up data through 1981 were available for all but 5 patients. Grafts continued to function for 5 years in 52% of living-related-donor cases and in 24% of cadaver- or living-unrelated-donor cases. Patient survivals were 88% at 10 years and 66% at 15 years. The respective graft survival rates were 85% and 75%.

There were no differences in patient or graft survival between the living-related and cadaver-donor cases. The most common causes of deaths occurring more than 5 years after transplantation were chronic liver failure and sepsis. Grafts were lost by 32 patients after 5 years, most commonly as a result of chronic rejection. Another 33 patients had evidence of graft dysfunction due to chronic rejection, recurrent glomerulonephritis, ureteral obstruction, or renal artery stenosis. Chronic rejection generally failed to respond to intensified immunosuppressive therapy. Over 90% of patients had complications; the most common were hypertension, cataract, avascular necrosis, malignancy, urinary tract infection, and pneumonia. Malignancy developed in 14% of patients. Arteriosclerotic complications were relatively uncommon.

A renal allograft that has functioned for 5 years can be expected to survive as long as the patient. Recipients of long-term renal allografts have significant mortality and morbidity, but this does not detract from the impressive rehabilitative potential of a majority of patients, most of whom have led and continue to lead productive lives. The patients require continued close care at centers experienced in transplantation.

▶ [Although medical and surgical complications arising in the early posttransplant period have received deserved attention, the health problems of the long-term renal allograft recipient have not been assiduously defined. The high incidence of medical problems found by the authors among long-term recipients is noteworthy, although many of these problems caused little morbidity. Half of the patients had hypertension and one fourth had cataracts. One patient of every 7 died at times ranging from 5½ to 20½ years after transplantation. Unexpectedly, the most common cause of death in these long-term transplant recipients was chronic liver disease. That chronic liver disease would prove to be a major cause of mortality had not been anticipated, although some other units have noted a high incidence of liver failure within the first several years following transplantation in hepatitis B carriers. We were surprised by this finding for several reasons. First, the rate of hepatitis B infection is low in the Brigham's end-stage renal failure program. Secondly, because azathioprine is a hepatotoxin in experimental animals, and acute rejection episodes are uncommon in renal graft recipients with liver dysfunction, this unit has routinely curtailed or

(49–2) Transplantation 34:347–351, December 1982.

stopped azathioprine therapy in the presence of liver dysfunction despite the fact that clinical evidence of pure azathioprine-induced hepatotoxicity is exceedingly rare in man. Finally, in contrast to the experience of many other units, the incidence of liver disease at the Brigham in the early posttransplant period is low.[2] This report serves notice that although pretransplant blood transfusions are of extraordinary value in achieving a high rate of renal engraftment, that particular form of pretransplant immunologic conditioning probably exacts a stiff price in the form of a slowly progressive non-A, non-B hepatitis. We may anticipate that as recent improvements in assuring renal engraftment foster a higher rate of transplantation in patients with end-stage renal failure, we will see increased numbers of long-term transplant patients who will have significant medical problems and will need medical surveillance.] ◀

49–3 **Localization of Major Histocompatibility Complex (HLA-ABC and DR) Antigens in 46 Kidneys: Differences in HLA-DR Staining of Tubules Among Kidneys.** The HLA system is important in the outcome of renal transplantation, but it is not known whether DR antigens in the kidney act as target antigens for antibody-mediated graft destruction in the presence of donor-specific antibodies. S. V. Fuggle, P. Errasti, A. S. Daar, J. W. Fabre, A. Ting, and P. J. Morris (Oxford, England) used monoclonal antibodies and the peroxidase-antiperoxidase method to study the distribution of HLA-ABC and DR antigens in biopsy specimens from 46 kidneys subsequently used in transplantation.

The HLA-ABC antigen was present on all renal parenchymal cells, and the HLA-DR antigen was consistently found on the glomerular endothelium and in intertubular capillaries, but not significantly on the endothelium of large vessels. The HLA-DR antigen was absent from the proximal renal tubular cells in 23% of kidneys, and probably absent or only very weakly expressed in another 17%. Donors of tubular R-negative kidneys tended to be HLA-DR3 positive. The survival of tubular DR-negative kidneys at 1 year was 70% compared with 57% for positive organs, not a significant difference. The tubular DR-positive kidneys may have had a higher rate of delayed function in patients with a donor-specific positive B-cell cross-match.

Graft survival tends to be better when DR is not expressed on the tubules of the donor kidney. A high proportion of kidneys with tubular DR fail to function immediately in the presence of a positive B-cell cross-match. Larger studies are needed to confirm these findings.

▶ [Several recent studies of cadaver-donor renal transplantation have indicated that matching of donor and recipient pairs for HLA molecules of the DR locus is of greater importance than matching for HLA molecules of the A, B, or C locus. The special significance of HLA-DR matching is almost certainly attributable to the capacity of class II HLA molecules (e.g., DR) but not class I HLA molecules (HLA-A, -B, and -C), to stimulate helper T cells,[3,4] because helper T cells initiate almost all immune responses. In support of this concept, several laboratories have noted the transcendent importance of helper T cells for reconstituting transplant immunity in immunodeficient animal models of transplantation.[5,6] Since the distribution of HLA-DR is known to be more restricted than that of HLA-A, -B, and -C, the distribution of HLA-DR antigens in kidneys destined for transplantation is of great interest. The marked variation found in the expression of HLA-DR among kidneys is a surprise. It will be important as such studies are expanded to ascertain whether "DR-poor" kidneys are indeed more likely to become successfully engrafted than "DR-rich" kidneys. As kidneys obtained from individuals with the HLA-DR3 phenotype are more likely to be "DR poor,"

(49–3) Transplantation 35:385–390, April 1983.

the variation in tissue expression of HLA-DR may be under genetic influence. It is also of interest to note that the expression of HLA-DR upon the plasma membranes of cells from several tissues,[7] including endothelial cells,[8] can be induced by the release of γ-interferon from activated T cells. Hence the rejection process may contain a vicious cycle. Alloimmune T cells are incited to elaborate γ-interferon which in turn causes DR negative cells within the graft to express HLA-DR which in turn heightens the immunogenicity of the graft. This article points out that prior to the event of rejection some hosts may be at a disadvantage because they were grafted with kidneys laden with HLA-DR.] ◀

49–4 **Fractionated Total Lymphoid Irradiation as Preparative Immunosuppression in High Risk Renal Transplantation: Clinical and Immunologic Studies.** Patients in renal failure who have rapidly rejected previous grafts are at high risk of graft loss after retransplantation. John S. Najarian, Ronald M. Ferguson, David E. R. Sutherland, Shimon Slavin, Tae Kim, John Kersey, and Richard L. Simmons (Univ. of Minnesota) treated 22 such patients with fractionated total lymphoid irradiation (FTLI) before transplantation between 1979 and 1981. Two patients received primary, 16, secondary, and 4 tertiary renal allografts. All the retransplant patients had rapidly rejected previous grafts; mean survival of all previous grafts was 4.5 months. The 2 first-transplant recipients were given kidneys from two-haplotype-mismatched living donors. All patients but 1 underwent splenectomy before irradiation. Mantle and inverted-Y fields were irradiated simultaneously with a 10-meV or a 4-meV accelerator to total doses of 3,200–4,050 rad in the initial group of patients. Subsequently a total dose of 2,500 rad was administered. Three patients received maintenance irradiation while waiting for a compatible cadaver kidney. Posttransplant immunosuppression was with azathioprine and prednisone. Five patients received low-dose marrow from their donors at transplantation.

The rate of graft function at 2 years was 72% compared with 38% for a historical control group of patients given second or third grafts and conventional immunosuppression. Results were best when 2,500 rad were delivered in 100-rad fractions, followed by transplantation within 2 weeks, maintenance azathioprine therapy, and tapered prednisone therapy. Most patients had complications of FTLI requiring temporary interruption of treatment. One patient developed pneumonitis and a drug reaction and died in cardiorespiratory arrest before transplantation. Studies of immune function showed marked T-cell depletion and loss of in vitro responsiveness to mitogens after FTLI. Administration of donor marrow did not result in chimerism.

The findings indicate that FTLI can result in improved graft survival in patients receiving retransplants after rapidly rejecting previous renal allografts. Posttransplant immunosuppression is best carried out with maintenance azathioprine and a tapering schedule of prednisone. The interval from radiotherapy to transplantation should be minimized.

▶ [Patients who rapidly reject a renal transplant are known to be at high risk for graft failure upon retransplantation. A group of patients who had rapidly rejected a primary transplant were subjected to experimental immunotherapy involving total lymphoid

---

(49–4) Ann. Surg. 196:442–452, October 1982.

irradiation as well as traditional maintenance posttransplant immunosuppressive therapy. The experimental protocol is derived from human and experimental studies conducted at Stanford University. It was first noted that patients treated with fractionated total lymphoid irradiation for Hodgkin's disease evidenced impairment of cell-mediated immune functions persisting for at least 6 months. These human studies led to experimental studies in a variety of animal models which demonstrated the profound salutary effect of fractionated total lymphoid irradiation upon experimental transplant models. Remarkably, indefinite survival of skin or other tissue grafts was obtained in rodents that were treated with fractionated total lymphoid irradiation and given donor bone marrow simultaneously with the tissue graft. These animals became chimeric and lacked evidence of graft-vs.-host disease. Thus, it is of extreme interest to note the influence of fractionated total lymphoid irradiation upon a population of patients likely to reject a renal transplant. In this series of patients an admirably high rate of engraftment was achieved; however, these patients were also susceptible to numerous complications. Seventeen patients required interruption of drug therapy; 6 patients experienced profound leukopenia; 7 patients had severe gastrointestinal symptoms; 1 patient died as a consequence of bilateral pneumonitis after receiving 3,000 rad of radiation; and 2 patients eventually succumbed to complications resulting from disseminated lymphoma. Thus, although fractionated total lymphoid irradiation plus traditional immunosuppressive therapy results in a high rate of engraftment, it also results in formidable complications. It will be of interest in the future to note whether the high rate of complications can be reduced by the use of less intense adjunctive immunosuppression.] ◀

49–5 **Cyclosporine in Treatment of Acute Cadaveric Kidney Graft Rejection Refractory to High-Dose Methylprednisolone.** Use of cyclosporine is established as an effective means of preventing allograft rejection, but its value in treatment of rejection is unclear. Raimund Margreiter, Christoph Huber, Martin Spielberger, and Paul König (Univ. of Innsbruck) evaluated cyclosporine in the treatment of renal graft rejection resistant to high-dose methylprednisolone therapy. Cyclosporine was used as maintenance therapy in 75 of 152 cadaver-kidney recipients treated in 1980–1982, whereas azathioprine was used in the remaining 77 recipients. Graft loss occurred in all cases of steroid-resistant rejection in the azathioprine-treated group that were managed with bolus methylprednisolone injections. Subsequent cases were therefore managed with cyclosporine in an oral dose of 17 mg/kg and 20 mg of prednisone daily. Cyclosporine was reduced to 15 mg/kg daily after 2 weeks and then tapered by 2 mg/kg/day every month to a maintenance dose of 7 mg/kg daily. The maintenance dose of prednisone was 7.5 mg daily.

All 6 patients treated with high-dose methylprednisolone lost their grafts. All patients treated with cyclosporine and prednisone responded to this regimen. Eight had renal transplants and 1 had a liver transplant. None of these grafts was lost during an average observation period of 97 days. Fever resolved soon after the first oral dose of cyclosporine, and the patients' general condition improved rapidly. No patient has had another rejection episode. One lethal fungal pneumonia occurred after 3 months of cyclosporine therapy. Some patients had increased creatinine concentrations until the dose of cyclosporine was reduced to less than 9 mg/kg daily.

Treatment with cyclosporine and prednisone appears to be effective in patients with graft rejection refractory to high-dose methylpredni-

(49–5) Transplantation 36:203–204, August 1983.

solone therapy. A controlled clinical trial of cyclosporine as a treatment for allograft rejection appears to be warranted.

► [Studies in experimental animal models suggest that although cyclosporine is a remarkable drug for use in preventing rejection, it has not been of great value in animal models as an antirejection drug per se; i.e., it does not reverse ongoing rejection episodes. Apparently, cyclosporine may well be an effective antirejection drug in the clinic, since reversal of rejection episodes was universal in this small trial. If subsequent trials confirm the experience of Margreiter et al., a profound impact on clinical practice may result. More than 20 years of experience with azathioprine therapy have demonstrated the utility and relative safety of this drug for long-term therapy. Recent controlled studies, however, indicate that cyclosporine is a superior immunosuppressive for use in cadaver-donor transplantation in terms of achieving successful engraftment at 1 year. Nonetheless, the high incidence of nephrotoxicity, the uncertain long-term side effects, and the high cost reduce the attractiveness of this agent. Several ongoing trials are aimed at reducing the incidence of nephrotoxicity observed in patients treated with cyclosporine. Low-dose cyclosporine protocols may prove serviceable, although the objections of high cost and the uncertainty as to long-term safety will not be obviated. If most kidneys can be engrafted by use of azathioprine maintenance therapy and the remainder salvaged by cyclosporine "rescue therapy" with the occurrence of rejection episodes, an attractive protocol will be in sight.] ◄

Chapter 49 References

1. Krakauer H., Grauman J.S., McMullan M.R., et al.: The recent U.S. experience in the treatment of end-stage renal disease by dialysis and transplantation. *N. Engl. J. Med.* 308:1558–1563, 1983.
2. Strom T.B.: Editorial retrospective: hepatitis B, transfusions, and renal transplantation—five years later. *N. Engl. J. Med.* 307:1141–1142, 1982.
3. Biddison W.E., Rao P.E., Talle M.A., et al.: Possible involvement of the T4 molecule in T cell recognition of class II HLA antigens: evidence from studies of proliferative responses to SB antigens. *J. Immunol.* 131:152–157, 1983.
4. Engleman E.G., Beinke C.J., Grumet F.G., et al.: Activation of human T lymphocyte subsets: helper and suppressor/cytotoxic T cells recognize and respond to distinct histocompatibility antigens. *J. Immunol.* 127:2124–2129, 1981.
5. Tilney N.L., Kupiec-Weglinski J.W., Heidecke C.D., et al.: Mechanisms of rejection and prolongation of vascularized organ allografts. *Immunol. Rev.* 77:1984 (in press).
6. Dallman M.J., Mason D.W.: Role of thymus-derived and thymus-independent cells in murine skin allograft rejection. *Transplantation* 33:221–223, 1982.
7. Kelley V.E., Fiers W., Strom T.B.: Cloned human gamma-interferon, but not beta-or alpha-interferon induced expression of HLA-DR determinants by fetal monocytes and myeloid leukemic cell lines. *J. Immunol.* 132:240–245, 1983.
8. Pober J.S., Gimbrone M.S., Cotran R.S., et al.: Ia expression by vascular endothelium is inducible by activated T cells and by human gamma-interferon. *J. Exp. Med.* 157:1339–1353, 1983.

50. Dialysis

▶ I am grateful to Dr. Robert Brown for helping to select these papers and for his comments. ◀

50–1 **Regional Citrate Anticoagulation for Hemodialysis in Patients at High Risk for Bleeding.** Hemodialysis frequently causes bleeding in patients at risk because of systemic anticoagulation. Robert V. Pinnick, Thomas B. Wiegmann, and Dennis A. Diederich developed a method of regional anticoagulation in which the hemodialysis assembly alone is anticoagulated by infusing sodium citrate into blood being withdrawn from the patient. Anticoagulation is reversed by removing the citrate by hemodialysis against a calcium-free bath and subsequently restoring ionized calcium in blood returned to the patient. A sterile solution of 102 mM trisodium citrate is infused by a pump; final concentrations of citrate anion of 2.5–7.5 mM are produced.

Fifteen hemodialyses using citrate anticoagulation performed in 4 patients with acute renal failure and active bleeding. Six other dialyses were done in 4 stable patients with chronic renal failure. The efficacy of citrate was compared with that of high-dose heparin in 3 of these instances and with low-dose heparin in the other 3. No side effects occurred in the actively bleeding patients. The leukopenia and thrombocytopenia known to be induced by dialysis were blunted by citrate anticoagulation of the dialyzer. Serum calcium levels remained stable with replacement of 7 mg/minute. In the stable patients, citrate anticoagulation appeared equal to heparinization in maintaining hemodialyzer efficiency.

Regional citrate anticoagulation provides an effective, safe method of performing hemodialysis in patients who are actively bleeding or are at high risk for bleeding during dialysis. The method may be useful in patients who require dialysis within 3 days of surgery or severe trauma, as well as in those with coagulopathy, intracranial disease, or mucosal ulcerations. Regional citrate anticoagulation also may be considered for use in patients with active diabetic retinopathy, polycystic kidney disease, or malignant hypertension.

▶ [The use of sodium citrate infusion during hemodialysis provides a new kind of "regional heparinization." We have utilized the method described by the authors with confirmation of its safety and efficacy. However, care must be taken to avoid causing hypercalcemia, which we noted after dialysis in 1 patient who was normocalcemic predialysis in contrast to the patients reported above in whom the serum calcium was low before dialysis.

Two other methods of performing hemodialysis without heparin have undergone further investigation. Ivanovich and co-workers[1] have shown that the use of a cellulose acetate membrane dialyzer together with periodic flushing of the blood tubing

(50–1) N. Engl. J. Med. 308:258–261, Feb. 3, 1983.

with physiologic saline could prevent clotting and maintain coagulation parameters without causing defibrination in 9 patients who were poor risks for heparin anticoagulation. A potential disadvantage of both the citrate and saline-flush-dialysis methods is the large volume of fluid infused, up to 600 ml/hour, necessitating high-performance hemodialyzers for adequate ultrafiltration. Smith et al.[2] have confirmed that prostacyclin is an effective substitute for heparin during hemodialysis, but hypotension, particularly when an acetate dialysate was used, remained as the most serious side effect. Moreover, these authors have shown that prostacyclin inhibited platelet aggregation significantly, whereas heparin did not, raising the question of whether prostacyclin would actually provide any safer anticoagulation than heparin in actively bleeding patients.] ◀

50–2 **Peritoneal Access and Related Complications in Continuous Ambulatory Peritoneal Dialysis.** Hans J. Gloor, Walter K. Nichols, Michael I. Sorkin, Barbara F. Prowant, Juanita M. Kennedy, Betty Baker, and Karl D. Nolph (Columbia, Mo.) reviewed experience with 50 patients receiving continuous ambulatory peritoneal dialysis during a 4-year period (1977–1980). A double-cuff, Silastic, Tenckhoff catheter was inserted in each case. All but 2 procedures were done electively. Most patients began receiving automated exchanges of 1 L immediately after catheter insertion, followed by exchanges of 2 L for 1–2 weeks until a regular schedule of continuous treatment was adopted. The mean patient age was 53 years. Twenty-eight percent of the patients had glomerulopathies, 18% had diabetic nephopathy, and 12% had vascular nephropathy.

The total period of continuous ambulatory peritoneal dialysis was about 60 patient-years, and the average time on continuous dialysis was 14.3 months. The average number of patient-days in the hospital was 48 per treatment year, including the initial admission for catheter surgery and the break-in and training periods. At the last follow-up (in June 1981) 40% of the patients remained on continuous ambulatory dialysis. Four patients died of myocardial infarction; 3 deaths resulted from peritonitis with sepsis and 2 from a perforated colon with sepsis. Overall, 20% of the patients withdrew from the program because of recurrent, refractory, or fungal peritonitis. Patient survival at 2 years was 77%, and the probability of continuing in the program was 48% at 2 years. Since the adoption of solutions in plastic bags, the 2-year survival has been 85%, and 63% of patients have continued in the program at 2 years. The overall incidence of peritonitis was 2.4 episodes per patient-year but only 1.3 episodes per patient-year after use of solutions in plastic bags. The chief reasons for removing catheters were infection and mechanical dysfunction. One-fourth of the patients required surgery for hernia repair.

Continuous ambulatory peritoneal dialysis is a valuable method of managing patients with end-stage renal disease, regardless of age. Most problems are of a technical nature and related to peritoneal access and drainage, as well as maintenance of sterility. It is hoped that these problems will be decreased by improvements in catheter design, in methods, and in patient training procedures.

▶ [There has been a steady growth in the number of patients receiving continuous ambulatory peritoneal dialysis (CAPD) in the United States, Europe, and Australia.[3]

(50–2) Am. J. Med. 74:593–598, April 1983.

The frequency of peritonitis and the high patient-dropout rate with CAPD in other parts of the world appear to be quite similar to those reported by Gloor et al. above. Although the simplicity and short training period of CAPD have made it initially preferable to home dialysis for many patients with chronic renal failure, the higher mortality rate, hospitalization rate, and dropout rate of CAPD suggest that hemodialysis is still a preferable treatment for most patients who can perform either type of dialysis at home.[4]

On the positive side, the complications of CAPD have been decreasing with technical improvements, and CAPD offers several advantages over hemodialysis, including better control of hypertension, improved steady-state chemistries with less hyperphosphatemia, and higher hematocrits.[4] In diabetic patients, CAPD with the use of intraperitoneal insulin may be the treatment of choice.[5] Although concern has been raised that peritoneal clearance rates will fall, a long-term prospective study has shown no change in peritoneal clearance of urea, creatinine, and inulin and no increase in peritoneal protein losses during periods as long as 6 years.[6]] ◀

50–3 **Erythrocytosis in Patients on Long-Term Hemodialysis.** Erythrocytosis can complicate various renal diseases and may occur after renal transplantation. Robert J. Shalhoub, Uma Rajan, Vo V. Kim, Eugene Goldwasser, John A. Kark, and Lucy D. Antoniou describe findings in 2 patients in whom erythrocytosis developed while they were undergoing maintenance hemodialysis for chronic glomerulonephritis, a state usually associated with anemia. Each patient had acquired cystic disease of end-stage kidneys.

Man, 47, with onset of hematuria at age 22, had undergone hemodialysis for 15 years for end-stage renal disease secondary to apparent chronic glomerulonephritis. The patient had been totally anuric for more than 7 years. The hematocrit rose gradually in the course of hemodialysis to levels as high as 54%. Periodic declines were associated with episodes of iron deficiency and accidental dialyzer blood loss. Sonography had recently disclosed renal cystic changes, and abdominal computed tomography (CT) showed diffuse cystic changes (Fig 50–1) as well as diffuse vascular and renal calcifications. A ^{51}Cr

Fig 50–1.—Computed tomographic scan of the abdomen with contrast medium shows both kidneys, which contain many cysts. (Courtesy of Shalhoub, R.J., et al.: Ann. Intern. Med. 97:686–690, November 1982.)

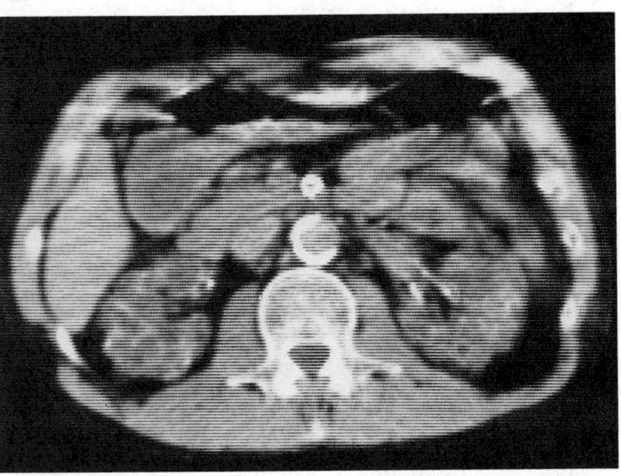

(50–3) Ann. Intern. Med. 97:686–690, November 1982.

study showed an elevated erythrocyte mass. The serum erythropoietin concentration was found by radioimmunoassay to be 36 mU/ml (normal mean ± SD, 21 ± 6 mU/ml). Leukocyte and platelet counts were consistently normal.

The second patient, a 61-year-old man with membranoproliferative glomerulonephritis by renal biopsy, developed progressive erythrocytosis (hematocrit level as high as 54%) during a 6-year period on hemodialysis. The erythrocyte mass and serum erythropoietin (70mU/ml) were elevated. Abdominal CT showed diffuse cystic changes of the kidneys consistent with acquired cystic disease.

These 2 patients had normal hematocrits 3–4 years after the start of dialysis; erythrocytosis developed 2–3 years later in association with acquired cystic disease of end-stage kidneys. A search for nonrenal causes of erythrocytosis was not helpful. Both patients had high serum erythropoietin levels, the origin of which was unclear. Dialysis, by mitigating the adverse effects of uremia on erythrocyte production and survival, may have unmasked a preexisting tendency toward erythrocytosis related to the original parenchymal renal disease.

▶ [Although the development of erythrocytosis is quite rare in patients receiving maintenance hemodialysis, a rise of the hematocrit to levels as high as 50% is quite common in patients treated with continuous ambulatory peritoneal dialysis (CAPD), particularly those with polycystic kidney disease and high erythropoietin levels.[7] An attractive hypothesis might propose that acquired or hereditary renal cystic disease is associated with increased erythropoietin and erythrocytosis if factors favoring anemia are controlled. This may explain some of the erythrocytosis observed in almost 20% of patients who have received successful renal transplants.[2] However, about one fifth of such patients with posttransplant erythrocytosis had undergone pretransplant bilateral nephrectomy,[8] and we have observed high hematocrits (48%–54%) in two patients who were anephric receiving CAPD. Thus, it seems likely that an alternative extrarenal erythropoietic mechanism may play a role in some patients with chronic renal failure and erythrocytosis.] ◀

50–4 **Review of Significant Findings From the National Cooperative Dialysis Study and Recommendations.** Herschel R. Harter (Washington Univ.), with the other principal investigators and section heads of the National Cooperative Dialysis Study, reviewed the chief findings in an investigation designed to evaluate means of individualizing dialysis and keeping patients as free as possible from the adverse clinical sequelae of renal failure. Four different groups of patients who underwent dialysis for periods of 2½–3½ hours or 4½–5 hours had time-averaged blood urea nitrogen (BUN) levels of either 50 or 100 mg/dl. Data were collected from 9 dialysis units in the United States having patient populations ranging from 28 to 325 patients.

An increased BUN value was associated with lower protein intake in the first 3 months of the study. Patients undergoing shorter dialyses had lower Minnesota Multiphasic Personality Inventory scores for hysteria than the others had. Early findings of deterioration on EEG were more frequent in the groups with high BUN levels. Transfusion requirements were greater in these groups. Changes in the serum potassium level correlated positively with changes in the BUN value. The plasma phosphate and parathormone levels both increased

(50–4) Kidney Int. 23(Suppl. 13):S107–S112, April 1983.

in the groups with high BUN values despite increased aluminum hydroxide therapy. Osteopenia and vascular calcification were not prominent findings despite an average treatment time of about 4 years. Cardiovascular morbidity appeared to be more prevalent in the higher time-averaged urea groups, and hospitalizations were more numerous.

Several factors appear to be associated with morbidity in dialysis patients. It is recommended that dialysis be designed to produce a time-averaged BUN level in the range of 50 mg/dl. The dietary prescription should be individualized and should contain adequate amounts of nutrients to produce an optimal nutritional status. Monitoring of variables such as the serum potassium and phosphorus levels, and the EEG, may help identify patients at an increased risk of morbidity. Very short dialysis times should be used cautiously in patients likely to have cardiovascular complications, especially if the BUN is high.

▶ [The findings of the National Cooperative Dialysis Study have emphasized the importance of measuring the BUN as an indicator of clinical manifestations of uremia in patients undergoing hemodialysis three times a week with standard cellulosic membranes, provided that their intake of protein and calories is adequate. The dialysis prescription should seek to maintain predialysis BUN levels at 60–80 mg/dl (consistent with time-averaged BUN levels of about 50 mg/dl) in most patients. Although the study results emphasize the need to individualize the dialysis prescription, the group data would suggest that when the predialysis BUN is as high as 110–130 mg/dl (consistent with a time-averaged BUN level of 100 mg/dl), dialysis should be made more effective. Either the dialysis time should be lengthened (if it is short), or else the dialyzer area and efficiency should be increased, or blood flow through the dialyzer should be increased (if there is not significant blood recirculation at high flows) in order to minimize the risk of uremic complications.] ◀

50–5 **Hepatitis B Vaccine in Medical Staff of Hemodialysis Units: Efficacy and Subtype Cross Protection.** Plasma-derived vaccines against hepatitis B have proved highly effective in several recent trials in high-risk populations. Wolf Szmuness, Cladd E. Stevens, Edward J. Harley, Edith A. Zang, Harvey J. Alter, Patricia E. Taylor, Anita DeVera, George T. S. Chen, Aaron Kellner, and the Dialysis Vaccine Trial Study Group report data on a multicenter double blind, placebo-controlled trial of the *ad* subtype hepatitis B vaccine (Heptavax-B, Merck Sharp and Dohme) in the medical staff at hemodialysis centers. A total of 865 staff members of 43 units in the eastern United States were included in the trial. All were initially serologically negative for hepatitis B surface antigen, antibody to hepatitis B surface antigen, and antibody to hepatitis B core antigen. Vaccine was administered to 442 subjects.

Side effects were not more prominent in vaccine recipients, and vaccination did not appear to influence the outcome of pregnancies. Surface antibody developed in 92.6% after the 6-month booster. The incidence of hepatitis B virus (HBV) infection was 2.2% in vaccine recipients and 9.9% in placebo recipients. Two affected vaccine recipients had not developed antibody. The incidence of infection by virus of the *ay* subtype was 1.2% in vaccine recipients and 8.2% in placebo

---

(50–5) N. Engl. J. Med. 307:1481–1486, Dec. 9, 1982.

recipients. There were 4 cases of non-A, non-B hepatitis in the vaccine group and 2 in the placebo group.

This trial confirmed the efficacy of the Merck hepatitis B vaccine in a population in which HBV infection is acquired chiefly by a parenteral route. Staff members at most dialysis units should be considered to be at risk, regardless of recent experience with HBV in their units. Routine use of this vaccine should substantially reduce the occurrence of clinical and subclinical hepatitis B in health professionals, prevent secondary cases in their families, and nearly eliminate the need for postexposure prophylaxis with hepatitis B immune globulin.

▶ [Although screening of donated blood for hepatitis B antigen and more stringent infection control techniques have decreased the incidence of hepatitis B in dialysis unit patients and staff, this trend should not promote complacency. This study not only documents the presence of a small, but significant, risk of hepatitis B infection and clinical hepatitis in dialysis unit staff, but shows the effectiveness of Heptavax-B vaccine in prevention of most cases. With minimal side effects, vaccination of dialysis personnel should now be advised routinely.] ◀

50–6 **Dialysis Encephalopathy: Clinical, Electroencephalographic, and Interventional Aspects.** Dialysis encephalopathy, or dialysis dementia, is a progressive, potentially fatal condition occurring in patients undergoing chronic hemodialysis. James A. O'Hare, Noel M. Callaghan, and Dermont J. Murnaghan (Cork, Ireland) reviewed the findings in 14 patients aged 9–61 years with a variety of end-stage renal diseases who were dialyzed for periods of 22–93 months. Measurements of the aluminum content in the water used for dialysis, which were started near the end of the study period, showed levels as high as 450 μg/L. Dialysate was prepared by mixing tap water with Nephrolyte, and all patients received aluminum hydroxide.

In all of the patients, a distinct speech disorder ultimately developed characterized by speech arrest, as did myoclonic epilepsy and abnormal EEG findings typically paroxysmal high-voltage delta activity. Twelve patients had other forms of epilepsy as well. Symptoms developed a mean of about 4 years after the start of dialysis, and their rate of progression varied widely. Three patients had visual hallucinations, and 7 eventually were globally demented. Five patients underwent renal transplantation. The other 3 survivors were transferred to a dialysis center where the water for dialysis was prepared by deionization. Osteomalacia usually preceded the onset of encephalopathy in these patients. Severe anemia of a microcytic, hypochromic type was present in most. The water and serum aluminum concentrations correlated closely, and serum aluminum levels declined in patients transferred to the unit in which deionized water was used in the dialysate.

No new reports of dialysis encephalopathy or associated osteomalacia appeared after 3 years in the new dialysis unit. Two of 3 patients with encephalopathy improved markedly when transferred. In contrast, 3 of the 5 patients who received renal transplants died after

(50–6) Medicine (Baltimore) 62:129–141, May 1983.

acceleration of the disorder, and 2 survived with a mild residual seizure disorder.

▶ [The association of dialysis encephalopathy with renal osteodystrophy, predominantly osteomalacia[9]—and of both these dialysis complications with high dialysate water and serum aluminum levels—is becoming increasingly well accepted. The recent finding of aluminum deposition along the fronts of bony mineralization in patients with uremic osteomalacia[10] add to the many reports of high levels of aluminum in the brains of patients dying with dialysis encephalopathy. The improvement of some patients with dialysis encephalopathy who were switched to low-aluminum deionized water for dialysis or received a renal transplant is consistent with the benefit reported for dialysis encephalopathy[11] or fracturing renal osteodystrophy[12] with intravenous desferrioxamine, an alternative way of accelerating aluminum removal from the body.] ◀

Chapter 50 References

1. Ivanovich P., Xu C.G., Kwaan H.C., et al.: Studies of coagulation and platelet functions in heparin-free hemodialysis. *Nephron* 33:116–120, 1983.
2. Smith M.C., Danviriyasup K., Crow J.W., et al.: Prostacyclin substitution for heparin in long-term hemodialysis. *Am. J. Med.* 73:669–678, 1982.
3. Nolph K.D., Boen F.S.T., Farrell P.C., et al.: Continuous ambulatory peritoneal dialysis in Australia, Europe, and the United States: 1981. *Kidney Int.* 23:3–8, 1983.
4. Rubin J., Barnes T., Burns P., et al.: Comparison of home hemodialysis to continuous ambulatory peritoneal dialysis. *Kidney Int.* 23:51–56, 1983.
5. Rottembourg J., el Shahat Y., Agrafiotis A., et al.: Continuous ambulatory peritoneal dialysis in insulin-dependent diabetic patients: a 40-month experience. *Kidney Int.* 23:40–45, 1983.
6. Diaz-Buxo J.A., Chandler J.T., Farmer C.D., et al.: Long-term observations of peritoneal clearances in patients undergoing peritoneal dialysis. *American Society of Artificial Organs Journal* 6:21–25, 1983.
7. Zappacosta A.R., Caro J., Erslev A.: Normalization of hematocrit in patients with end-stage renal disease on continuous ambulatory peritoneal dialysis. *Am. J. Med.* 72:53–57, 1982.
8. Wickre C.G., Norman D.J., Bennison A., et al.: Postrenal transplant erythrocytosis: a review of 53 patients. *Kidney Int.* 23:731–737, 1983.
9. Prior J.C., Cameron E.C., Knickerbocker W.J., et al.: Dialysis encephalopathy and osteomalacic bone disease. *Am. J. Med.* 72:33–42, 1982.
10. Cournot-Witmer G., Zingraff J., Plachot J.J., et al.: Aluminum localization in bone from hemodialyzed patients: relationship to matrix mineralization. *Kidney Int.* 20:375–385, 1981.
11. Ackrill P., Ralston A.J., Day J.P., et al.: Successful removal of aluminum from patient with dialysis encephalopathy. *Lancet* 2:692–693, 1980.
12. Brown D.J., Ham K.N., Dawborn J.K., et al.: Treatment of dialysis osteomalacia with desferrioxamine. *Lancet* 2:343–345, 1982.

51. Water, Sodium, and Potassium

51–1 **Hypodipsia in Geriatric Patients.** Paul D. Miller, Richard A. Krebs, Billy J. Neal, and Donald O. McIntyre (Denver) studied 6 elderly patients who had hypodipsia in the absence of apparent hypothalamic or pituitary disease. The patients, aged 68–91 years, were hospitalized because of dehydration and hypernatremia detected on routine monthly biochemical screening in a nursing home. All were hospitalized on previous occasions for the same problem. Strokes had occurred but did not appear to involve hypothalamic or pituitary function. The patients had normal serum sodium and creatinine levels before their strokes.

The mean plasma osmolality was 363 mOsm/L, and volume depletion was present; but none of the patients were thirsty. Their mental status seemed normal. Moderate orthostatic hypotension was present with intact baroreceptor function. The mean urine osmolality was 718 mOsm/L and did not change when 5 units of vasopressin were given subcutaneously. Hyperosmolality and azotemia resolved after hydration, with a mean weight gain of 5 kg. The subsequent mean spontaneous water intake was 765 ml daily, less than the mean insensible loss of 817 ml daily. Hypernatremia recurred. The euosmolar state could not be maintained by encouraging fluid intake, and it was necessary to prescribe 800–1,000 ml of fluid every 8 hours as a medication order.

These elderly persons were not thirsty despite the presence of both hyperosmolality and hypovolemia, stimuli that increase thirst sensation. The defect in thirst recognition probably was caused by a cortical lesion. Recognition of hypodipsia in elderly patients may avoid hospitalization for dehydration. Also, hypernatremia is associated with increased mortality. Fluid intake must be mandated as a pharmacologic order; it is not adequate merely to encourage water intake.

▶ [This good short article calls attention to the importance of an impaired sense of thirst in generating the vicious circle of hypernatremia in elderly nursing home patients. What happens is that the diminished intake of fluids engenders hypernatremia, which itself depresses central nervous system acuity, reducing further the sense of thirst, and so on until the patient lapses into coma. A prior stroke is not necessary to reduce thirst to an abnormal degree (though it helps)—diminution in thirst can be detected in many "normal" elderly persons, apparently as a consequence of aging.

Loss of thirst is not limited to the aged; it can cause chronic hypernatremia in infants as well.[1] The subject of thirst and vasopressin function is updated in a nice review by Gary Robertson in the March 1983 issue of the *Journal of Laboratory and Clinical Medicine.*[2]

Paradoxically, the elderly are susceptible to hyponatremia, as well as to hypernatremia, as the next article illustrates.] ◀

(51–1) Am. J. Med. 73:354–356, September 1982.

51–2 **Idiopathic Syndrome of Inappropriate Antidiuretic Hormone Secretion Possibly Related to Advanced Age.** Patients with the syndrome of inappropriate secretion of antidiuretic hormone (SIADH) typically have underlying psychiatric disorder or other medical problems. Carl S. Goldstein, Seth Braunstein, and Stanley Goldfarb (Univ. of Pennsylvania) describe findings in a patient whose hypotonic hyponatremia was caused by SIADH in the absence of other abnormal findings.

Man, 88, was in excellent health when a serum sodium level of 128 mEq/L was discovered incidentally. Prostatectomy had been done 30 years before, and subsequent urinary infections were readily treated with short courses of oral antibiotics. There were no specific complaints or abnormal physical findings. The serum sodium level at hospital admission was 120 mEq/L. The endogenous creatinine clearance was 70 ml/minute. The ECG showed right bundle branch block with left anterior hemiblock. The blood urea nitrogen and uric acid levels were low, supporting a diagnosis of SIADH; this was confirmed by water loading. The pattern of antidiuretic hormone (ADH) release on testing was consistent with the "vasopressin leak" form of inappropriate antidiuresis. Fluid restriction was successful. When hospitalized 4 months later with pneumonia, the patient had a serum sodium level of 130 mEq/L. Findings on bronchoscopy were normal. The patient was doing well after 17 months, with no evidence of underlying disease.

A review of 10 reported patients with "idiopathic" SIADH showed that, in each, SIADH was associated with neuropsychiatric or other medical disorders. The present findings suggest that idiopathic inappropriate antidiuresis does exist and represents a discrete category of SIADH. Advanced age may be a risk factor for this condition. The syndrome may account for the increased susceptibility to hyponatremia observed in older persons.

▶ [Older men and women apparently have an increase in "osmoreceptor sensitivity," as judged by an exaggerated response of plasma antidiuretic hormone to the infusion of hypertonic saline.[3] It is also more difficult in the elderly to suppress antidiuretic hormone secretion by infusing ethanol, which turns off antidiuretic hormone in younger subjects. Thus, aging seems to be characterized by a more exuberant, less easily inhibited propensity to secrete antidiuretic hormone. This may explain the frequency of low serum sodium in elderly patients and the extreme susceptibility of some old persons to hyponatremia after small doses of thiazide diuretics or nonsteroidal antiinflammatory agents.] ◀

51–3 **Micropuncture Studies of the Renal Effects of Atrial Natriuretic Substance.** Studies by de Bold et al. have shown that injection of atrial muscle extract produces diuresis and natriuresis in rats, and it was proposed that the effect is due to a naturally occurring substance, possibly a peptide, in secretory granules in the atrial myocytes. Josephine P. Briggs, Boris Steipe, Gisela Schubert, and Jürgen Schnermann (Munich, Federal Republic of Germany) undertook micropuncture studies to identify the site of action of this substance and to determine whether changes in filtration rate may contribute to the increase in sodium excretion. The effects of both bolus injections and infusions of atrial extracts were examined in Sprague-Dawley rats.

(51–2) Ann. Intern. Med. 99:185–188, August 1983.
(51–3) Pflügers Arch. 395:271–276, December 1982.

Extracts were prepared from both atrial and ventricular tissue by boiling and centrifugation.

Injection of atrial extract from one rat heart led to a 10-fold rise in urine flow and a 30-fold increase in sodium excretion. Ventricle extracts had no such effects. During infusion at a rate of 3 atria per hour, mean urine flow and sodium excretion both increased without significant changes in glomerular filtration rate, single nephron filtration rate, or fluid absorption at the level of the proximal tubule or the loop of Henle. Filtration rate did increase with infusion of 6 atria per hour when measured for both the whole kidney and the single nephron. Delivery of fluid and chloride to the distal tubule increased significantly as a result.

These findings suggest that the natriuresis produced by atrial extracts in the rat is, to a major degree, caused by transport inhibition along the collecting tubules and collecting ducts. A rise in filtration rate contributes to the natriuretic effect at higher dose levels. Changes in the rates of synthesis and release of a sodium-wasting agent in atrial tissue could underlie a number of poorly understood alterations in excretion of sodium chloride.

▶ [You'll be learning much more about atrial natriuretic substances in months to come. They are peptides present in secretory granules in the right atrium of human as well as rat hearts.[4] Furthermore, they appear to have a physiologic role in enhancing natriuresis, since rats with amputation of the atrial appendage have a diminished sodium diuresis in response to saline infusion.[5] Two of the atrial peptides, both potent vascular relaxants and diuretics, have already been isolated and characterized by Philip Needleman and his coworkers.[6] A major endocrine regulatory system seems about to be uncovered.] ◀

51–4 **Association of Hypotension With Hyperreninemic Hyperaldosteronism in Critically Ill Patient.** A paradoxical suppression of the plasma aldosterone level may occur in critically ill patients with elevated plasma renin activity (PRA). Mark W. Davenport and Robert D. Zipser (Univ. of Southern California) investigated this phenomenon in a series of 100 consecutive patients admitted to a medical intensive care unit. Control samples were obtained from 98 patients having increased PRA, usually the result of sodium restriction or diuretic administration.

The PRA and aldosterone concentration correlated closely in the control group, but 22 study patients had hyperreninemia and inappropriately reduced levels of plasma aldosterone. Their aldosterone-PRA ratio was below the 98th percentile of the control population. The patients did not differ from the others with respect to electrolyte levels, nutritional status, medications used, or survival; but persistent hypotension was present in 91% of them compared with 53% of the patients with normal aldosterone levels.

An impaired aldosterone response to hyperreninemia is not infrequent in critically ill patients. It may be related to adrenal damage from persistent hypotension. Necrosis of the zona glomerulosa has been described. Because some patients with an appropriate aldosterone response have comparable hypotension, other factors also may

---

(51–4) Arch. Intern. Med. 143:735–737, April 1983.

be involved. Hypotension in the present patients was related to such conditions as sepsis, heart failure, and hypovolemia. The effects of impaired aldosterone secretion during acute and convalescent illness remain to be determined.

▶ [Some patients in shock tend to have a plasma aldosterone that is unexpectedly low, but the significance of that finding is not yet clear. The authors of this article were careful to exclude known iatrogenic suppressors of aldosterone secretion like heparin[7] or infusions of dopamine.[8] They leave open the possibility that endogenous dopamine (either neural or humoral) might be responsible, since dopamine is known to reduce the output of aldosterone from the adrenal's zona glomerulosa. Since the most important action of aldosterone is on the kidney rather than the circulation, it is unlikely that administration of aldosterone would help these desperately ill patients, but I'm surprised that no one has tried it.] ◀

51–5 **Prior Thiazide Diuretic Treatment Increases Adrenaline-Induced Hypokalemia.** Transient hypokalemia is a feature of many acute disorders in patients with a variety of underlying diseases. A. D. Struthers, R. Whitesmith, and J. L. Reid (Glasgow, Scotland) attempted to determine whether thiazide therapy leads to more marked hypokalemia at times of increased sympathoadrenal activity. Studies were done in 6 healthy persons aged 25–30 years, each studied twice at least 2 months apart. Either 5 mg of bendrofluazide daily or a placebo was given in a single-blind design for 1 week before assessment. An infusion of *l*-epinephrine was given in increasing doses of 0.01–

Fig 51–1.—Serum potassium level (mean ± SD) during infusion of 5% dextrose; epinephrine, 0.06 μg/kg/minute; and 5% dextrose again in 6 patients after pretreatment with placebo or bendrofluazide (5 mg) for 7 days. (Courtesy of Struthers, A.D., et al.: Lancet 1:1358–1360, June 18, 1983.)

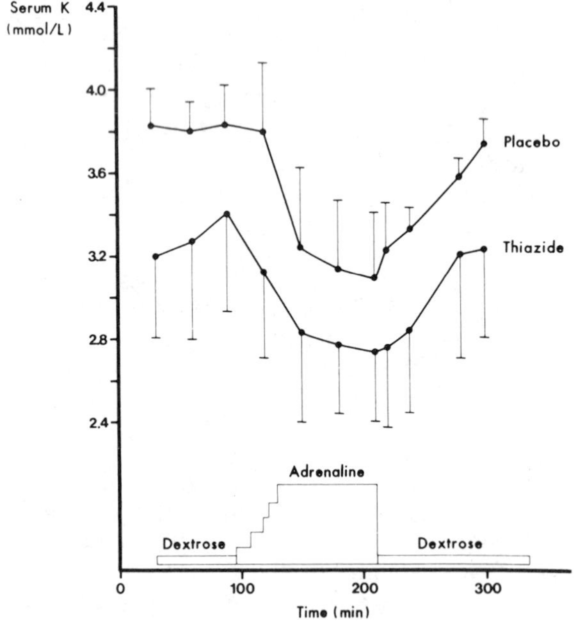

(51–5) Lancet 1:1358–1360, June 18, 1983.

0.06 μg/kg/minute, and the peak dose rate was continued for 90 minutes.

Bendrofluazide administration did not significantly alter baseline blood pressure or heart rate, and hemodynamic responses to epinephrine were similar in the thiazide and placebo studies. Changes in the serum potassium level are shown in Figure 51–1. The baseline serum potassium level was lower after thiazide administration than after placebo was given, and the serum potassium level was significantly lower during epinephrine infusion after thiazide pretreatment. The ECG changes noted during epinephrine infusion were not influenced by thiazide administration. Plasma epinephrine levels were not altered by thiazide pretreatment.

These findings suggest that transient profound hypokalemia may increase the risk of ventricular arrhythmias in diuretic-treated patients. Routine monitoring of the baseline serum potassium level may underestimate this risk. This effect may explain the recent finding of higher coronary mortality in hypertensive patients given thiazide therapy than in controls, despite better reduction of blood pressure in the treated group.

▶ [The fall in serum potassium level produced by epinephrine (0.6–0.8 mEq/L) in these experiments is of particular interest to clinicians because the plasma level of epinephrine attained was within the range actually measured in other patients with acute myocardial infarction. The frequency of ventricular arrhythmias during myocardial infarction is greatly increased in hypokalemic patients[9]; thus, catecholamine-induced hypokalemia may conceivably predispose to arrhythmias in stressed persons, particularly those susceptible because of digitalis treatment or depletion of potassium by diuretics. The decline in serum potassium produced by epinephrine is mediated by β_2-adrenergic receptors (like those in bronchial muscles), rather than β_1-receptors (as in the heart).[10] A "nonselective" inhibitor of both β_1- and β_2-receptors (like propranolol) might therefore be expected to be more efficacious than a cardioselective β-blocker in preventing epinephrine-induced hypokalemia.

Other examples of the influence of catecholamines on potassium levels come to mind. The hypokalemia commonly seen in delirium tremens may result partly from increased sympathetic tone and circulating epinephrine. Hypokalemia may complicate the treatment of asthma with salbutamol or the treatment of premature labor with terbutaline (both are selective β_2-agonists). On the other hand, nonselective β-blockers prescribed for hypertension or angina may predispose to an elevation of serum potassium levels, particularly in the presence of diabetes mellitus or renal failure.] ◀

Chapter 51 References

1. Schaff-Blass E., Robertson G.L., Rosenfield R.: Chronic hypernatremia from a congenital defect in osmoregulation of thirst and vasopressin. *J. Pediatr.* 102:703–708, 1983.
2. Robertson G.L.: Thirst and vasopressin function in normal and disordered states of water balance. *J. Lab. Clin. Med.* 101:351–371, 1983.
3. Helderman J.H., Vestal R.E., Rowe J.W., et al.: The response of arginine vasopressin to intravenous ethanol and hypertonic saline in man: the impact of aging. *J. Gerontol.* 33:39–47, 1978.
4. Kifor I., Levenson D.J., Ohuoha D.C., et al.: Purification and characterization of human atrial natriuretic factor, abstract. American Society of Nephrology, 16th Annual Meeting, p. 167A, 1983.
5. Sonnenberg H., Veressa A.T.: Atrial natriuretic factor mediates the renal

response to acute hypervolemia abstract. American Society of Nephrology, 16th Annual Meeting, p. 180A, 1983.
6. Currie M.G., Geller D.M., Cole B.R., et al.: Purification and sequence analysis of bioactive atrial peptides (atriopeptins). *Science* 223:67–69, 1984.
7. O'Kelly R., Magee F., McKenna T.J.: Routine heparin therapy inhibits adrenal aldosterone production. *J. Clin. Endocrinol. Metab.* 56:108–112, 1983.
8. Carey R.M., Thorner M.O., Ortt E.M.: Effect of metaclopramide and bromocryptine on the renin-angiotensin-aldosterone system in man. *J. Clin. Invest.* 63:727–735, 1979.
9. Solomon R.J., Cole A.G.: Importance of potassium in patients with acute myocardial infarction. *Acta Med. Scand.* [*Suppl.*] 647:87–93, 1981.
10. Brown M.J., Brown D.C., Murphy M.B.: Hypokalemia from beta$_2$-receptor stimulation by circulating epinephrine. *N. Engl. J. Med.* 309:1414–1419, 1983.

52. Acid-Base

52–1 **Metabolic Alkalosis due to Absorption of "Nonabsorbable" Antacids.** Nicolaos E. Madias and Andrew S. Levey (Boston) report data on a patient with end-stage renal disease on long-term maintenance hemodialysis in whom moderately severe metabolic alkalosis developed without vomiting or gastric drainage, apparently in relation to the administration of "nonabsorbable" antacids (aluminum hydroxide and magnesium hydroxide), neutral phosphate, and a cation-exchange resin.

Man, 52, had been on hemodialysis for 6 years because of end-stage renal disease due to chronic glomerulonephritis. A vasculitic syndrome had been treated 2 years earlier by prednisone and cyclophosphamide and was complicated by *Listeria* monocytogenes meningitis and *Candida* endophthalmitis. Postmeningitic communicating hydrocephalus had led to seizures, gait impairment, and intermittent hypoventilation. The patient was receiving phenytoin, ketoconazole, prednisone, total parenteral nutrition, and nonabsorbable antacids (consisting of hourly administration of aluminum and magnesium hydroxide suspensions [30 ml of Mylanta II and 15 ml of ALternaGEL]) for upper gastrointestinal bleeding. Neutral phosphate was given for hypophosphatemia.

Twenty-four hours after dialysis, arterial pH was 7.45, Pa_{CO_2} was 38 mm Hg, and serum total CO_2 was 26 mEq/L. Over the course of the next 48 hours, during which the patient had a grand mal seizure and was given 25 gm of sodium polystyrene sulfonate (Kayexalate), the serum bicarbonate rose, first to 30 and then to 34 mEq/L, while serum chloride fell from 92 to 85 mEq/L. During this time there was no gastric drainage or vomiting. After a 4-hour hemodialysis, arterial pH was 7.56, Pa_{CO_2} was 38 mm Hg, and serum total CO_2 was 33 mEq/L. Because of concern that the alkalemia might contribute to neuromuscular irritability, dilute hydrochloric acid was administered. No further alkalemia was observed (table).

Moderately severe metabolic alkalosis in this patient probably resulted from the coadministration of magnesium and aluminum hy-

ACID-BASE COMPOSITION AND SERUM POTASSIUM VALUES

Treatment	Time from Last Hemodialysis (hr)	pH	$PaCO_2$ (mm Hg)	Total CO_2 (meq/liter)	Potassium (meq/liter)
Hourly aluminum and magnesium hydroxide suspensions; neutral phosphate (0.75 g phosphorus)	24	7.40	46	28	5.5
Hourly aluminum and magnesium hydroxide suspensions; neutral phosphate (1.5 g phosphorus)	48	7.45	38	26	4.5
Grand-mal seizure; hourly aluminum and magnesium hydroxide suspensions; sodium polystyrene sulfonate 25 g and neutral phosphate (1.0 g phosphorus)	60	7.49	40	30	6.3
Hourly aluminum and magnesium hydroxide suspensions; neutral phosphate (1.25 g phosphorus)	72	7.34	65	34	5.0

(Courtesy of Madias, N.E., and Levey, A.S.: Am. J. Med. 74:155–158, January 1983.)

(52–1) Am. J. Med. 74:155–158, January 1983.

droxides, sodium polystyrene sulfonate and neutral phosphate in the absence of renal function. Neutral phosphate has not previously been implicated in this syndrome, but it might contribute to alkalosis if given with aluminum hydroxide, owing to the precipitation of insoluble aluminum phosphate and the consequent formation of sodium hydroxide. Substantial risks are associated with metabolic alkalosis, and severe alkalosis can develop after the combined ingestion of nonabsorbable antacids, cation-exchange resins, and, possibly, neutral phosphate in patients with renal insufficiency. The authors strongly recommend that the use of nonabsorbable antacids be separated from administration of the other agents by several hours when coadministration is necessary.

▶ ["Nonabsorbable" antacids ($Mg[OH]_2$ and $Al[OH]_3$) fail to make the body alkaline because the Mg^{++} or Al^{+++} are excreted in the stool as insoluble carbonates, withdrawing carbonate from the body and leaving hydrogen ions which combine with leftover hydroxide to form water. However, when these antacids are given in conjunction with sodium polystyrene sulfonate resin or sodium phosphate, an alkalinizing reaction occurs (predictable by any high school chemistry student) in which the cationic moiety of the antacid combines with the anion of the resin or with phosphate to form an insoluble residue. Sodium hydroxide (or sodium bicarbonate) is left over to be absorbed. Incidentally, you should be aware that "Kayexalate" resin is prepared in the sodium form, and it gives up 1 mEq of Na^+ (which is absorbed) for every 1 mEq of K^+ it withdraws from the body. Since most of the K^+ removed in this way comes from cells and is replaced by hydrogen ions, resin treatment of hyperkalemia can be alkalinizing all by itself.] ◀

52–2 **Renal Tubular Acidosis: New Look at Treatment of Musculoskeletal and Renal Disease.** Musculoskeletal symptoms and renal stone formation are well-recognized manifestations of renal tubular acidosis. Thomas M. Harrington, Thomas W. Bunch, and Christian J. Van Den Berg (Mayo Clinic) reviewed the findings in 31 female and 17 male patients, with a mean age of 38 years, seen in 1970–1980 with renal tubular acidosis. The diagnosis was based on a bicarbonate level below 20 mEq/L with a urinary pH above 5.5. The onset was spontaneous in 23 patients; in 25 patients diagnosis was confirmed after challenge with oral ammonium chloride. Forty-four patients had type I (distal) renal tubular acidosis, and 4 had type II (proximal) involvement. Twenty-five patients presented with musculoskeletal symptoms, and 23 had symptoms reflecting nephrolithiasis.

A total of 33 patients had musculoskeletal complaints. Mean duration of these symptoms before diagnosis was 29 months. Twelve of the 33 patients had associated connective tissue disease. Arthralgia was the most common rheumatic complaint; the hip and ankle were most often affected. Five patients had monarticular arthralgia of the hip joint. Twelve patients had diffuse myalgias, and 12 had muscle weakness. Low back pain not related to trauma was predominant in 9 cases. Nine patients had metabolic bone disease; 4 had osteomalacia, and 5 had osteoporosis. Most musculoskeletal complaints resolved with systemic base replacement.

Thirty-four patients had evidence of renal lithiasis. Of 15 patients who received oral base treatment with sodium bicarbonate or sodium

(52–2) Mayo Clin. Proc. 58:354–360, June 1983.

and potassium citrate solutions, 13 had metabolically inactive renal lithiasis at follow-up. Three of 4 other patients who received a phosphate supplement continued to have active renal lithiasis.

Both musculoskeletal complaints and renal lithiasis are common presentations of renal tubular acidosis, and both frequently subside with treatment of the renal tubular acidosis. Early diagnosis will minimize morbidity from renal lithiasis and its complications. The condition should be suspected if hyperchloremia or hypokalemia is present, if there is muscle weakness with a normal creatine kinase level, or if unexplained metabolic bone disease is discovered.

▶ [The most interesting clinical message here is that almost three fourths of these 48 patients with renal tubular acidosis had severe rheumatic complaints that improved when their electrolyte abnormalities (hypokalemia or acidosis) were corrected. Not all of the muscular weakness, aches, and pains could be attributed to potassium depletion, since hypokalemia was present in many but not all patients. Acidosis itself may therefore be responsible for some of these symptoms. It would be interesting to see if low 1,25-dihydroxyvitamin D levels could be correlated with musculoskeletal complaints in this group of acidotic patients, since the symptoms resemble the muscular aches and weakness of adult osteomalacia.] ◀

52–3 **Diuresis or Urinary Alkalinization for Salicylate Poisoning?** Acute salicylate poisoning is a common medical emergency associated with high mortality. Forced alkaline diuresis reduces the plasma salicylate level, but recovery of salicylate from the urine is disappointing, and the procedure is not without risk. The unnecessary administration of large amounts of fluid is undesirable in this setting. L. F. Prescott, M. Balali-Mood, J. A. J. H. Critchley, A. F. Johnstone, and A. T. Proudfoot (Edinburgh) compared the effects of oral fluids alone, standard forced alkaline diuresis, forced diuresis alone, and sodium bicarbonate alone in 44 otherwise healthy adults with uncomplicated aspirin overdosage. Sixteen patients with plasma salicylate levels of 250–400 mg/L received oral fluids only. Sixteen others received standard forced alkaline diuresis, and 6 had forced diuresis alone; 6 received sodium bicarbonate (alkali) without diuresis. No patient had a plasma salicylate level above 700 mg/L. Gastric lavage was done on patients hospitalized within 12 hours of taking aspirin. The three active treatment groups were clinically comparable.

The plasma salicylate level fell rapidly in all active treatment groups. At 4–16 hours, the mean plasma salicylate half-life was 9 hours with alkali treatment, 12 hours with forced alkaline diuresis, and 39 hours with forced diuresis. In control patients it was 29 hours. Urinary recovery of unaltered salicylate was greatest with alkali treatment alone and least in the forced diuresis and control groups. Positive fluid balance and weight gain were noted at 4 hours in the groups given forced diuresis and forced alkaline diuresis, and fluid retention persisted at 16 hours in these groups. Renal salicylate excretion appeared to depend much more on the urinary pH than on the flow rate. Hyponatremia and hypokalemia occurred frequently in the patients having forced diuresis and forced alkaline diuresis, but not in patients treated with alkali only.

(52–3) Br. Med. J. 285:1383–1386, Nov. 13, 1982.

In this study, treatment with sodium bicarbonate alone was at least as effective as, and possibly more effective than, forced alkaline diuresis in enhancing salicylate elimination; it did not lead to fluid retention or to biochemical abnormalities. Forced diuresis without alkali had very little useful effect. Salicylate can be removed effectively and safely from the body simply by administering sodium bicarbonate.

▶ [Most textbooks recommend caution in the administration of sodium bicarbonate in salicylate poisoning because of the danger in exacerbating alkalosis due to overbreathing. Actually, respiratory alkalosis is an early phenomenon in salicylate intoxication and is rapidly succeeded by metabolic acidosis. The key to accelerating the urinary excretion of salicylate is to maintain the pH of urine at a level more alkaline than the pH of plasma. Repletion of body fluids is necessary to accomplish this, and expansion of fluid volume makes it easier, since it is hard for the kidneys to excrete an alkaline urine when they are retaining sodium. Thus, generous infusion of isotonic sodium bicarbonate until the urine pH reaches about 8.0 is probably the best treatment.] ◀

53. Calcium, Magnesium, Stones, and Bones

53–1 **Comparative Study of Available Medical Therapy for Hypercalcemia of Malignancy.** Hypercalcemia is a frequent complication of malignant disease and occasionally threatens life. Many different drugs have been tried in this setting. Gregory R. Mundy, Robert Wilkinson, and David A. Heath examined the relative efficacy of oral phosphate, mithramycin, glucocorticoids, indomethacin, and ethane-1-hydroxy-1, 1-diphosphonate (EHDP) in a randomized study of 25 adults with neoplastic hypercalcemia, all of whom had known metastatic disease. Nine nonrandomized patients with malignancy were treated with amino-hydroxypropane diphosphonate (APD) and 5 with glucocorticoids. Eight patients with primary hyperparathyroidism were treated with oral phosphate or APD. Hypercalcemia was defined as an albumin-corrected calcium level above 11.2 mg/dl. Dehydration was corrected before drug treatment was undertaken.

No single agent was consistently effective in treating hypercalcemia of malignancy, but oral phosphate and mithramycin were the most effective agents. Some patients did not tolerate phosphate therapy because of diarrhea. A rapid rebound in the calcium level sometimes followed initially successful treatment with mithramycin. Corticoids were effective in 2 of 5 randomized patients and in 3 of the 5 nonrandomized patients. Indomethacin and EHDP were effective in 1 patient each. Treatment with ADP significantly reduced the serum calcium level within 72 hours in 9 of 12 patients. Six of 8 patients who completed a 10-day course of APD therapy had a fall in the serum calcium level to normal. No serious adverse effects resulted from APD treatment.

There is no universally effective agent for use in treating hypercalcemia due to malignancy. Combined treatment may prove to be more effective than single-agent therapy. Treatment with calcitonin and glucocorticoids may be tried, and calcitonin with phosphate also may be useful. The newer diphosphonates such as APD may prove to be more effective than present agents when used either alone or in combination with other agents such as calcitonin or oral phosphate.

▶ [In the initial treatment of patients with hypercalcemia of malignancy, rehydration with saline is often effective in lowering serum calcium, sometimes to normal. However, once extracellular volume has been repleted and a copious urinary flow established, it is usually a mistake, in my view, to rely exclusively on enormous volumes of saline infusion coupled with furosemide diuresis to keep the serum calcium level down. Much less traumatic and more efficacious is the use of mithramycin intravenously, 20 mg/kg. Mithramycin will usually produce at least a temporary fall of cal-

(53–1) Am. J. Med. 74:421–432, March 1983.

cium to normal levels, a decrease that often lasts several days. Oral agents such as inorganic phosphorus and diphosphonates can then be started.

In addition to malignancy, a variety of disseminated granulomatous diseases, of which Boeck's sarcoid is the prime example, can occasionally cause hypercalcemia. Disseminated candidiasis can now be added to that list,[1] which also includes histoplasmosis and coccidioidomycosis. Excessive production of 1,25-dihyroxyvitamin D seems to be the cause.] ◀

53–2 **Diuretic-Associated Hypomagnesemia.** Diuretics can cause magnesium depletion, and ventricular arrhythmias and sudden deaths have been reported in hypomagnesemic patients. John Sheehan and Aideen White (Dublin) examined the magnitude of the problem by measuring serum magnesium levels in patients exposed to either short-term intensive diuretic treatment or long-term, moderate-dose therapy in the presence of such factors as general depression and lethargy, muscle weakness with depressed tendon reflexes, hypokalemia, atrial fibrillation, or a high alcohol intake. Treatment was with intramuscular boluses of 4–8 mmole of magnesium sulfate, followed by administration of oral magnesium sulfate salts. Dietary supplementation was attempted, using bananas.

Of the 40 patients studied, 21 had appreciable hypomagnesemia of 0.7 mmole/L or less. The mean serum magnesium level was 0.54 mmole/L (1.3 mg/dl). The mean patient age was 67 years. The chief clinical diagnosis was congestive heart failure, and more than half of the patients had atrial fibrillation. Furosemide was the most commonly used diuretic and often was given intravenously in high dosage. Nine patients were hypokalemic. Five experienced digitalis toxicity. Symptoms improved promptly after administration of intramuscular magnesium. Atrial fibrillation remained under control during continued treatment. Spironolactone, used in 6 patients, had magnesium-sparing properties.

Chronic low-grade magnesium deficiency from diuretic treatment appears to be more frequent than has been recognized. Risk factors include old age, residence in a soft water area, excessive alcohol consumption, and a diet low in magnesium. Patients have done well after systemic and then oral administration of magnesium, although magnesium salts are poorly absorbed and can cause diarrhea. Bananas are a useful source of magnesium.

▶ [Because magnesium is preferentially absorbed by the thick limb of Henle's loop, the "loop diuretics" like furosemide, bumetanide, and ethacrynic acid are particularly likely to cause hypomagnesemia and magnesium depletion. As these authors point out, the troublesome effects of low serum magnesium levels in cardiac patients are likely to be resistant atrial and ventricular arrhythmias, often associated with hyokalemia. The latter is caused by renal wasting of potassium, which stops when magnesium is repleted. Hypomagnesemia can also predispose to convulsions. For unknown reasons, alcohol accelerates renal excretion of magnesium, and alcoholics are therefore especially susceptible to hypomagnesemia.] ◀

53–3 **Sodium-Dependent Idiopathic Hypercalciuria in Renal-Stone Formers.** Most calcium-stone formers with a normal serum calcium have idiopathic hypercalciuria. Some patients with very high urinary

(53–2) Br. Med. J. 285:1157–1159, Oct. 23, 1982.
(53–3) Lancet 2:484–486, Aug. 27, 1983.

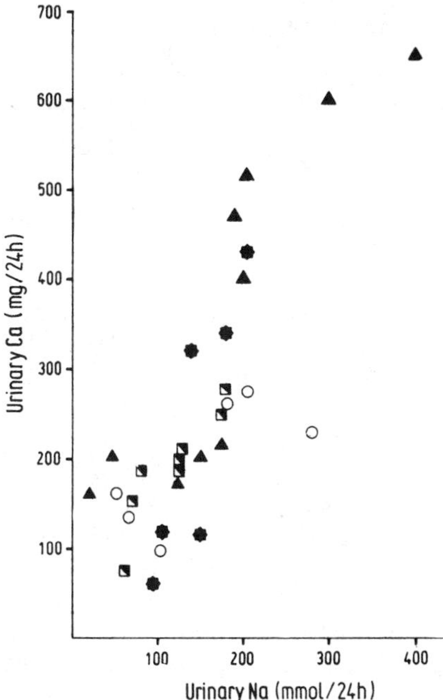

Fig 53–1.—Effect of variations in dietary sodium on urinary calcium in four patients. (Courtesy of Silver, J., et al.: Lancet 2:484–486, Aug. 27, 1983.)

calcium excretion have been found to have high urinary sodium levels as well. Justin Silver, Dvora Rubinger, M. M. Friedlaender, and M. M. Popovtzer (Jerusalem) report on 4 patients with renal stones whose hypercalciuria was induced by a high-salt diet and effectively corrected by a low-salt diet.

Man, 30, had had bilateral renal stones with colic and urinary tract infections for 3 years and had undergone partial right nephrectomy. Serum calcium was 10 mg/dl with normal electrolytes. Urinary calcium was 700 mg/24 hours on a 1-gm calcium diet. The nephrogenous cyclic AMP was 1,800 pmole/dl glomerular filtrate. Urinary calcium was 160 mg/24 hours on a 400-mg calcium diet, and the urinary sodium was 130 mmole/24 hours. On a 1-gm calcium diet in hospital the patient excreted 225 mg calcium and 180 mmole of sodium in 24 hours. The urinary calcium fell to 200 mg daily on a 50-mmole sodium diet and rose to 600 mg daily on a 300-mmole sodium diet. On 30 mmole of sodium daily he excreted 200 mg of calcium per 24 hours.

Hypercalciuria was remarkably dependent on sodium intake in these patients (Fig 53–1). All became normocalciuric when their sodium excretion was below 150 mmole/24 hours. Sodium restriction may be important in the management of idiopathic hypercalciuria. Many patients who were thought to have primary renal hypercalciuria may actually have sodium-dependent hypercalciuria. Urinary sodium excretion should be determined in all hypercalciuric patients with renal stone disease.

▶ [Urinary excretion of calcium is not fixed and immutable—it's conditioned normally by a variety of factors that also operate in disease states—so that "hypercalciuria" must always be defined with respect to the background. For example, calcium excretion normally increases in proportion to the amount of sodium in the diet and the urine, and it is reduced to very low levels when salt is restricted. On a high-sodium diet (300–400 mEq/day), most young men will fit the usual definition of hypercalciuria (more than 250–300 mg of urinary calcium per day). Ingestion of carbohydrate or protein also increases calcium excretion,[2] as does acidosis and, of course, the intake of calcium itself. All of these hypercalciuric influences probably have an exaggerated effect in individuals with "idiopathic hypercalciuria" and contribute to their propensity to form stones.[3]] ◀

53–4 **Aluminum Is Associated With Low Bone Formation in Patients Receiving Chronic Parenteral Nutrition.** In some patients who have lost small bowel function and are maintained with chronic total parenteral nutrition, metabolic bone disease develops at a time when other signs of malnutrition are improving. Susan M. Ott, Norma A. Maloney, Gordon L. Klein, Allen C. Alfrey, Marvin E. Ament, Jack W. Coburn, and Donald J. Sherrard quantitated the histologic findings on bone biopsy in 16 patients with bone pain or pathologic fracture who were receiving chronic total parenteral nutrition. They also determined bone aluminum levels because aluminum has been implicated as a bone toxin in animals and in patients with renal failure. The average patient age was 51 years. Fourteen patients received casein hydrolysate, and 2 were given free amino acids. Five patients had biopsy repeated after 6–54 months. Biopsy specimens were also obtained from the iliac crest in normal persons matched with the patients by age and sex.

Mean total bone area was reduced in the patient group, whereas the mean osteoid area was more than twice as great as in controls. There was little difference from control values when only the patients given casein hydrolysate were considered. Stainable aluminum was detected in all patients receiving casein hydrolysate but not in those receiving amino acids. The bone formation rate was reduced in patients with positive findings for aluminum on staining. No significant histologic changes were noted in repeat biopsies.

These findings resemble those obtained in aluminum-intoxicated patients undergoing hemodialysis. Both dialysis patients and those given chronic total parenteral nutrition also have low parathyroid hormone levels. Aluminum appears to be an important factor in the pathogenesis of osteodystrophy in patients receiving total parenteral nutrition or dialysis. A low rate of bone formation in these patients may lead to bone pain and to fractures. Solutions used for total parenteral nutrition should be carefully monitored to avoid contamination by aluminum.

▶ [The resemblance between this syndrome of resistant osteomalacia in patients receiving total parenteral nutrition and that seen in chronic dialysis patients is striking. In patients given parenteral nutrition, the source of the aluminum was presumably the intravenous supplements themselves, some of which have been shown to contain large amounts of aluminum.[4] I have seen no reports of neurologic deterioration in such patients that might suggest "dialysis dementia."

Aluminum intoxication is increasingly recognized as the cause of renal osteodystrophy with normal or only slightly elevated serum levels of alkaline phosphatase and immunoreactive parathyroid hormone.[5] It is not well appreciated that such patients

(53–4) Ann. Intern. Med. 98:910–914, June 1983.

may be hypercalcemic, especially if they are receiving vitamin D and being dialyzed against a high-calcium bath. Unless aluminum intoxication is suspected and looked for by bone biopsy, subtotal parathyroidectomy may be wrongly advised for patients in whom the best treatment is withdrawal of vitamin D, lowering of bath calcium, and perhaps chelation of excess aluminum with desferrioxamine.[6]] ◀

53–5 **Chronic Acidosis With Metabolic Bone Disease: Effect of Alkali on Bone Morphology and Vitamin D Metabolism.** Osteomalacia is a potential complication of the chronic hyperchloremic acidosis resulting from renal tubular disorders or operations placing a bowel segment in continuity with the urinary tract. Some patients fail to respond well to alkali therapy. John Cunningham, Lawrence J. Fraher, Thomas L. Clemens, Peter A. Revell, and Socrates E. Papapoulos (London) examined the effects of alkali therapy in two patients in whom hyperchloremic acidosis and osteomalacia developed after urinary diversion with a bowel segment. Control data were obtained from 20 subjects aged 46–83 years who died suddenly. Both patients had good clinical, histologic, and biochemical responses to treatment with alkali alone, despite the presence of markedly impaired glomerular filtration in one. Vitamin D metabolite levels were low initially in one patient and became normal during alkali therapy. In one patient, two episodes of acidosis responded favorably to alkali therapy, but there was no change in 1,25-dihydroxyvitamin D levels. No vitamin D treatment was given.

Successful treatment of the osteomalacia of chronic acidosis is not necessarily accompanied by changes in plasma vitamin D metabolite levels. Treatment with alkali alone may be more appropriate than administration of vitamin D analogues, even when acidosis and osteomalacia are accompanied by marked glomerular dysfunction. Although impaired 1,25-dihydroxyvitamin D metabolism has been demonstrated in experimental acidosis, further studies are needed in vitamin D–replete animals and in man before acidosis-induced changes in vitamin D metabolism can be clearly implicated in the development of this form of bone disease. Many factors may contribute to the development of osteomalacia in patients with chronic metabolic acidosis.

▶ [It is well known that chronic metabolic acidosis can cause thin bones, but the mechanism is still uncertain. Several factors are involved. Acidosis depresses appetite and therefore reduces the intake of nutrients necessary for bone growth.[7] Bone mineral tends to dissolve in acid, and in addition, acidosis has a direct effect on the kidney to increase calcium excretion in the urine to produce a negative calcium balance. Acidosis may also affect vitamin D metabolism. In experimental animals, metabolic acidosis impairs renal hydroxylation of 1,25-dihydroxyvitamin D, producing a kind of functional renal rickets,[8] but there is some question as to whether this is the case in humans.

The two patients of this report illustrate clearly that treatment of acidosis heals osteomalacic bone, but not that it necessarily does so by a single mechanism. In one patient, vitamin D levels, initially low, rose to normal. In the other, however, osteomalacia improved with treatment of acidosis, even though the plasma level of 1,25-dihydroxyvitamin D remained at the lower limits of normal. The important inference is that in patients with renal disease and real or potential bone problems, prevention of acidosis may be as important as treatment with vitamin D.] ◀

(53–5) Am. J. Med. 73:199–204, August 1982.

Chapter 53 References

1. Kantarjian H.M., Saad M.F., Estey E.H., et al.: Hypercalcemia in disseminated candidiasis. *Am. J. Med.* 74:721–724, 1983.
2. Epstein F.H.: Calcium and the kidney. *Am. J. Med.* 45:700–714, 1968.
3. Hypercalciuria—dietary pressure or metabolic quirk?, editorial. *Lancet* 2:495–496, 1983.
4. Klein G.L., Alfrey A.C., Miller N.L., et al.: Aluminum loading during total parenteral nutrition. *Am. J. Clin. Nutr.* 35:1425–1429, 1982.
5. Boyce B.F., Elder H.Y., Elliot H.L., et al.: Hypercalcaemic osteomalacia due to aluminum toxicity. *Lancet* 2:1009–1012, 1982.
6. Brown O.J., Dawborn J.K., Mann K.N., et al.: Treatment of dialysis osteomalacia with desferrioxamine. *Lancet* 2:343–345, 1982.
7. McSherry E., Morris R.C.: Attainment and maintenance of normal stature with alkali therapy in infants and children with classic renal tubular acidosis. *J. Clin. Invest.* 61:509–527, 1978.
8. Lee S.W., Russell J., Avioli L.V.: 25-hydroxycholecalciferol to 1,25 dihydroxycholecalciferol: conversion impaired by systemic metabolic acidosis. *Science* 195:994–996, 1977.
9. Weber H.P., Gray R.W., Dominguez J.H., et al.: The lack of effect of chronic metabolic acidosis on 25-hydroxyvitamin D metabolism and serum parathyroid hormone in humans. *J. Clin. Endocrinol. Metab.* 1047–1055, 1976.

PART EIGHT

RHEUMATOLOGY

STEPHEN E. MALAWISTA, M.D.

54. Rheumatoid Arthritis

54–1 **Intractable Rheumatoid Arthritis: Treatment With Combined Cyclophosphamide, Azathioprine, and Hydroxychloroquine.** Daniel J. McCarty and Guillermo F. Carrera (Med. College of Wisconsin) have used relatively small doses of three drugs to control rheumatoid disease in patients with severe, progressive involvement. Seventeen patients seen between 1974 and 1981 with definite or classic rheumatoid arthritis had progressive erosive, seropositive disease refractory to conventional therapy. The 15 women and 2 men completed an average of 27 months of combined drug therapy. All but 1 of the patients had previously received gold therapy. Current doses of hydroxychloroquine and salicylate were maintained during the trial. The morning blood salicylate concentration was maintained at 20–35 mg/dl. Cyclophosphamide or azathioprine was given in an initial daily dose of 25 mg, and after 2–3 weeks the third drug was added, and the drug doses were increased alternately at 2–3-week intervals until a modest leukopenia of 3,000–4,000 white blood cells per cu mm was reached.

Three patients, 1 of them noncompliant, failed to respond. The duration of morning stiffness decreased to 16% of baseline, and stiffness resolved completely in 9 patients. Mean grip strength increased by more than half over baseline. The mean proximal interphalangeal joint circumference decreased, as did the sedimentation rate and, often, the rheumatoid factor titer. The mean American Rheumatism Association functional class fell from 2.8 to 2.1. Five patients achieved a complete remission with no clinical evidence of disease activity. All medications were stopped in 2 of these patients, 1 of whom now uses only aspirin. Evidence of vasculitis resolved in all 6 patients affected. Saliva returned in 2 of 7 patients with Sjögren's syndrome. Definite disease progression was seen roentgenographically in 3 patients and definite recortication of lesions in 9. Side effects were frequent, but most were transient, tolerable, or both. Two patients had episodes of herpes zoster, and 1 had marked symptoms of cystitis. No retinal degeneration was seen.

Several of these refractory patients had striking suppression of disease on combined treatment with cyclophosphamide, azathioprine, and hydroxychloroquine. Until a controlled study is perfomed, however, this treatment should be regarded as experimental.

▶ [Let's start with the authors' conclusions: The study was uncontrolled, and the regimen is experimental and not recommended for general use. Having said that, one is still impressed by what appears to be potent disease suppression in many severely afflicted patients who were receiving doses of cyclophosphamide and azathioprine

---

(54–1) JAMA 248:1718–1723, Oct. 8, 1982.

that were lower than those reported to be effective when either drug is used separately. These patients, whose relentless disease was treated with conservative therapy for an average of 2 years before combination chemotherapy was begun, are not likely to have remitted on their own; the usual course in such individuals is one of continuous joint inflammation with progressive anatomic deformities and functional loss. And placebo effects, to which patients with rheumatoid arthritis are extremely susceptible (see abstract 54–3), are not likely to be markedly delayed in onset. (Improvement was not established for an average of 7 months [range, 3–16 months.]) Nor are they likely to be endless. (Reevaluation took place after 27 months [range, 5–60].) In those with less than complete remission, inflammatory flares seemed to follow attempts to taper any of the 3 drugs from their optimal established doses.

Although these points suggest that the combined regimen was working, we do not know how the same patients would have done on single immunosuppressive drugs (or, for that matter, on penicillamine alone). And triple therapy, even in small doses, may in the long term increase accordingly the toxicities that may accrue, e.g., damage to the eye (hydroxychloroquine), damage to the bladder (cyclophosphamide), and perhaps malignancy (cyclophosphamide and azathioprine). Even in this preliminary study, 5 patients had symptoms of cystitis, and the 2 premenopausal women developed amenorrhea. So I share the authors' hopes, and echo their caution. (*JAMA* may not have been the best vehicle for an experimental therapy of a difficult-to-treat illness, that seems promising but is not recommended for general use ["but don't go near the water"]).] ◀

54–2 **Case-Control Study of Rheumatoid Arthritis and Prior Use of Oral Contraceptives.** A negative association has been described between rheumatoid arthritis and oral contraceptive use. Athena Linos, J. W. Worthington, W. M. O'Fallon, and L. T. Kurland (Mayo Clinic and Found.) undertook a case-control study to determine whether the decrease in incidence of rheumatoid arthritis in women noted in Rochester, Minn. after the introduction of oral contraceptives in the late 1950s was due to a protective effect of oral contraception. Review was made of the data on 229 women with probable or definite rheumatoid arthritis seen in 1960–1974 and 458 control subjects matched for age with the cases. No association was found between rheumatoid arthritis and oral contraceptive use or the use of estrogens for menopausal or postmenopausal symptoms.

These findings fail to support previous suggestions that use of oral contraceptives may help prevent rheumatoid arthritis. Estrogen use in the perimenopausal period also does not appear to prevent the development of rheumatoid arthritis.

▶ [Sex-related host factors seem to play a role in susceptibility to rheumatoid arthritis. Although the overall sex ratio among patients with rheumatoid arthritis is almost 3 women to 1 man, it is 5 to 1 in adults under age 60 and moves toward equality in later years. In a case-control study by the Royal College of General Practitioners in the United Kingdom,[1] a halving of the incidence of rheumatoid arthritis was found among users of oral contraceptives. The current authors[2] have previously noted a decrease in the incidence of rheumatoid arthritis in Rochester, Minn. after 1960 and wondered whether the introduction of oral contraceptives was responsible. Meanwhile, a group[3] in The Netherlands seemed to confirm the British study.

Now the Rochester group has carried out its own study and found no association. For each case, they selected two controls of the same age and same city of residence who had registered in the same year in the same medical facility as that in which the case was first diagnosed. Cases and controls had the same numbers of medical contacts in the preceding 3 years and did not differ significantly with respect to age at menarche, age at menopause, or numbers of pregnancies, miscarriages, or live-born

---

(54–2) Lancet 1:1299–1300, June 11, 1983.

children. With duration of use as the risk factor for the development of rheumatoid arthritis, there was no indication of either protective or causal association at 3 different levels.

In the backs of all these workers' minds was the well-known tendency of rheumatoid arthritis to remit during pregnancy and to be exacerbated postpartum. The mechanism of that phenomenon is unclear and may have more to do with the 9-month tolerance of a "fetal homograft"[4] than with more direct hormonal effects. At any rate, the current study does not indicate a protective effect of oral contraceptives on rheumatoid arthritis.] ◀

54–3 **Plasmapheresis Therapy in Rheumatoid Arthritis: Controlled, Double-Blind, Crossover Trial.** Altered immune mechanisms have been implicated in rheumatoid arthritis. Isaac L. Dwosh, Alan R. Giles, Peter M. Ford, Joseph L. Pater, Tassos P. Anastassiades, and the Queen's University Plasmapheresis Study Group

Fig 54–1.—Changes in clinical measures during trial of plasmapheresis. Each lettered point represents specific clinical assessment for which data were available. *A* denotes group A (9 patients who received true apheresis first); *B*, group B (11 patients who received sham apheresis first). Standard errors of mean were omitted for clarity; none of observed differences was significant at level of $P = .05$. (Courtesy of Dwosh, I.L., et al.: N. Engl. J. Med. 308:1124–1129, May 12, 1983; reprinted by permission of The New England Journal of Medicine.)

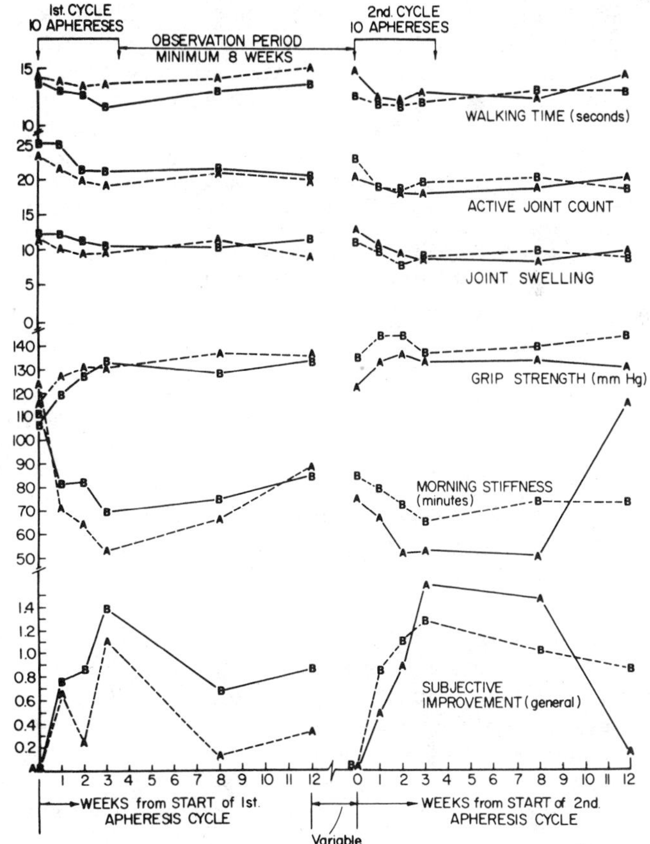

(54–3) N. Engl. J. Med. 308:1124–1129, May 12, 1983.

(Kingston, Ontario, Canada) undertook a controlled double-blind crossover trial of plasmapheresis therapy in 20 patients with chronic rheumatoid arthritis who were managed solely as outpatients. All had had classic or definite disease for at least a year and had evidence of active joint disease at the time of study. The patients had failed to respond to or had been intolerant of, nonsteroidal antiinflammatory therapy and standard second-line drugs. True and sham procedures were carried out with the use of a continuous-flow cell separator. An average of 3 L of plasma was discarded; the volume infused was adjusted to provide fluid balance at the end of the procedure.

Improvement of 15%–20% occurred in both groups in most measures (Fig 54–1). Analysis of various clinical measures failed to show significant differences between the true and sham procedures. There were, however, significant reductions in the sedimentation rate, rheumatoid factor titer, and levels of hemoglobin, IgM, and C3 with true plasmapheresis only. Side effects occurred in a minority of the 430 completed apheresis procedures.

These findings clearly indicate that there is no substantial clinical benefit from plasmapheresis in patients with chronic rheumatoid arthritis, despite the occurrence of favorable laboratory changes. Plasmapheresis does not seem indicated in this setting as either primary or adjunctive therapy, even in patients receiving slow-acting antirheumatic drugs concurrently. The observed changes in laboratory values cannot be equated with improvement in the disease.

▶ [As pointed out in the accompanying editorial,[5] this well-executed study is another example of the importance of controlled therapeutic trials in rheumatoid arthritis, a disease in which so many of the variables used in evaluation—duration of morning stiffness, degree of tenderness in 30 or 40 joints or joint groups, grip strength, and time to walk a measured distance (see Fig 54–1)—are subjective in nature. New treatments tend to "work," at least for awhile, and especially if they are elaborate and well publicized.

The initial hope was that plasmapheresis would benefit rheumatoid arthritis in some way by unloading circulating rheumatoid factor and immune complexes. However, it has become increasingly clear that, rather than going to the synovium and making trouble there, these components are produced primarily in the inflamed joint and escape into the circulation. A better case for plasmapheresis can be made for severely ill patients with such problems as hyperviscosity, cryoglobulinemia, vasculitis, or Felty's syndrome or in those who have large amounts of circulating immune complexes. Even so, the future would seem to lie in the removal of specific components rather than of large, indiscriminate volumes of plasma.] ◀

54–4 **Long-Term Outcome in Felty's Syndrome.** Felty's syndrome of rheumatoid arthritis, leukopenia, and splenomegaly is now generally considered to be a unique variant of rheumatoid disease characterized by both prominent extraarticular features and destructive joint disease. Carter Thorne and Murray B. Urowitz (Univ. of Toronto) report a prospective study of 25 patients with classic or definite rheumatoid arthritis, splenomegaly, and white blood cell counts of less than 4×10^9/L or platelet counts of less than 100×10^9/L. There was no other apparent cause for cytopenia or splenomegaly in these patients. The 17 women and 8 men were followed up for a mean of 5 years and had

(54–4) Ann. Rheum. Dis. 41:486–489, October 1982.

a mean age at follow-up of 62.5 years. Mean duration of rheumatoid disease at last follow-up was 23.5 years and that of Felty's syndrome, 7.5 years.

About half the evaluable patients showed substantial improvement in arthritis at follow-up. Some extraarticular abnormalities resolved. Spleen size had become normal in 6 patients. Fifteen had a history of infection. Five of the 9 deaths were related to sepsis. Five of 7 patients who underwent splenectomy for infection continued to have infection despite normal white blood cell counts, and 3 of them died of infection. Nine of 10 patients followed after splenectomy had white blood cell counts exceeding 5×10^9/L.

Felty's syndrome is characterized by severe joint involvement, many extraarticular abnormalities, and a high incidence of infection. Splenectomy appears not to protect against infections in these patients, and it may contribute to infection. Mortality in Felty's syndrome is high; infection is the chief cause of death. The mechanism of leukopenia in Felty's syndrome is unclear. Patients in this series who died were 5 years older on average than those who survived. There was no difference in duration of disease or frequency of extraarticular features between survivors and patients who died.

▶ [Recurrent infection is a primary concern in Felty's syndrome, a rare and generally late complication of rheumatoid arthritis. In addition to rheumatoid factor, two thirds of these patients have antinuclear antibodies which are often granulocyte specific. The cause(s) of the neutropenia is not simple; almost every known mechanism of undersupply or excess removal has been invoked. Treatments have included remission-inducing antiinflammatory drugs, low-dose corticosteroids, and when severe infections develop, splenectomy.

Most reviews of Felty's syndrome have been retrospective; this one is a prospective study of 25 patients available from a group of 34 first described in 1977. A few points are of special interest. The arthritis need not progress; in the majority of patients it improved. Some extraarticular features—subcutaneous nodules, hepatomegaly, Sjögren's syndrome, episcleritis, vasculitis, Raynaud's phenomenon, myopathy—did increase, a finding that emphasizes the systemic nature of this syndrome.

A persistent normalization of the white blood cell count—hematologic remission—can occur; here it happened in 16 of 24 patients, including 7 of 14 who had *not* undergone splenectomy. Moreover, splenectomy did not appear to protect patients against recurrent infections; 5 of 10 splenectomized patients continued to have them despite white blood cell counts above 5×10^6/ml. (Skin ulcers did improve.) There was a 36% 5-year mortality: 9 of 25 patients died, 5 of them from sepsis. The wisest course in this illness may be to treat conservatively and hope for a hematologic remission. Although splenectomy may sometimes be lifesaving, there is no clear guideline for who might respond in the long term.] ◀

54–5 **Calf Hematoma Following Anticoagulants in Synovial Rupture.** Synovial rupture at the knee can closely simulate deep vein thrombosis, and an incorrect diagnosis of thrombosis can lead to inappropriate anticoagulant therapy. Richard A. D. Wigley and Donald E. Paterson report 4 cases of calf hematoma in patients with rupture of the knee synovium in whom deep vein thrombosis was incorrectly diagnosed.

Woman, 68, with osteoarthritis of the knees, hands, and shoulders, had aching and tiredness in the right leg that suddenly worsened and prevented walking. The calf was tender and swollen. Deep venous thrombosis was di-

(54–5) N.Z. Med. J. 95:630–632, Sept. 8, 1982.

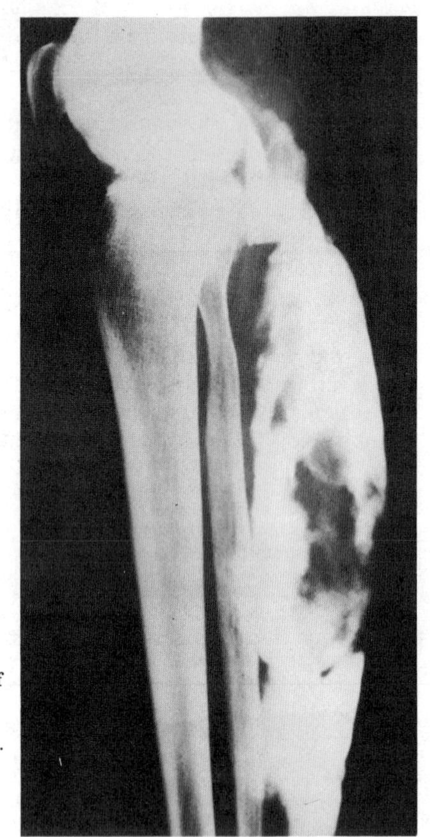

Fig 54–2.—Arthrogram showing extension of contrast medium from popliteal cyst into hematoma extending to ankle. (Courtesy of Wigley, R.A.D., and Paterson, D.A.: N.Z. Med. J. 95:630–632, Sept. 8, 1982.)

agnosed and heparin therapy was begun, but the calf became more swollen and bruising was noted. A venogram failed to fill the deep veins above the ankle, but no thrombus was seen. Soft tissue radiography showed a rounded opacity and loss of anatomical detail in the calf, and an arthrogram showed a popliteal cyst communicating with a massive cyst extending to the ankle (Fig 54–2). Symptoms resolved rapidly when anticoagulation therapy was stopped. No disability was present 9 months later.

There have been a number of reports of calf hematoma after anticoagulation therapy in cases of synovial rupture. If hemorrhage is initiated by synovial rupture, anticoagulation would increase the bleeding. Synovial rupture was not excluded in some cases of calf hematoma simulating deep venous thrombosis. Careful clinical study with aspiration often will permit a confident diagnosis of synovial rupture. When doubt remains, venography, with or without simultaneous arthrography, should be done before deciding on anticoagulant therapy. Most patients with synovial rupture can be managed at home with rest after aspiration of the knee joint fluid and intraarticular steroid instillation.

▶ [This article addresses a common error: synovial rupture at the knee is mistaken for deep vein thrombosis; the patient is anticoagulated; and the condition is made worse. Of the 4 patients presented, 1 had rheumatoid arthritis, 2 osteoarthritis, and 1 trauma. There is often a history of the knee having been swollen, from whatever cause, and sometimes of popliteal swelling (Baker's cyst). Rupture tends to be posterior, down, and deep—hence the confusion. When a calf becomes tender and swollen, mischief may often be prevented by inquiry into the knee.] ◀

Chapter 54 References

1. Wingrave S., Kay C.R.: Reduction in incidence of rheumatoid arthritis associated with oral contraceptives. *Lancet* 1:569–571, 1978.
2. Linos A., Worthington J.W., O'Fallon W.M., Kurland L.T.: The epidemiology of rheumatoid arthritis in Rochester, Minnesota: a study of incidence, prevalence, and mortality. *Am. J. Epidemiol.* 111:87–98, 1980.
3. Vandenbrouke J.P., Valkenburg H.A., Boersma J.W., Cats A., Festen J.J.M., Huber-Bruning O., Rasker O.: Oral contraceptives and rheumatoid arthritis: further evidence for a preventive effect. *Lancet* 2:839–842, 1982.
4. Denman A.M.: Pregnancy and immunological disorders, editorial. *Br. Med. J.* 284:999–1000, 1982.
5. Decker J.L.: Apheresis and rheumatoid arthritis, editioral. *Ann. Intern. Med.* 98:666–667, 1983.

55. Systemic Lupus Erythematosus

55–1 **Polyspecificity of Monoclonal Lupus Autoantibodies Produced by Human-Human Hybridomas.** In patients who have systemic lupus erythematosus (SLE), cross-reactions of the monoclonal antibodies to DNA and other antibodies may help elucidate the origin of antibodies to DNA. Yehuda Shoenfeld, Joyce Rauch, Hélene Massicotte, Syamal K. Datta, Janine André-Schwartz, B. David Stollar, and Robert S. Schwartz examined the serologic properties of 30 monoclonal human lupus antibodies produced by hybridomas derived from lymphocytes of patients with SLE. These hybridomas were made by fusing a human lymphoblastoid cell line, derived from a patient with multiple myeloma, with peripheral blood or splenic lymphocytes from 6 patients with SLE. The monoclonal autoantibodies were selected for their ability to react with denatured DNA.

Eighteen of the 30 monoclonal autoantibodies reacted with three or more additional polynucleotides, including native DNA, left-handed double-helical DNA, poly(I), and poly(dT). Ten autoantibodies reacted with both nucleic acids and the phospholipid cardiolipin.

It appears that monoclonal lupus autoantibodies can bind to a variety of antigens, presumably because of the presence of appropriately spaced phosphodiester groups in both the polynucleotides and the phospholipid. The sharing of antigenic groups by polymers of differing nature may contribute to the apparent diversity of serologic reactions in SLE.

Probably DNA itself need not be the immunogenic stimulus for autoantibody formation in this disease. Diester phosphate groups may constitute a family of important autoantigens in SLE. Lupus "anti-DNA" autoantibodies that react with cardiolipin can explain the biologically false-positive serologic tests for syphilis obtained in patients with SLE.

▶ [The authors developed human-human hybridomas (1983 YEAR BOOK OF MEDICINE, p. 623) for the production of monoclonal human lupus autoantibodies. Many of the antibodies to DNA also reacted with other polynucleotides, and some reacted with cardiolipin (hence, VDRL positivity). These findings indicate that lupus autoantibodies can have diverse serologic reactions by binding to antigenic determinants that recur on different molecules. Thus, the autoreactivity that characterizes patients with lupus may not represent a general loss of immune regulation. Rather, it may, for a given patient, represent a fairly narrow and highly specific pattern of response to antigenically similar tissue components. Anti-DNA antibodies might then arise from an antigenic stimulus that leads to the production of antibodies that cross-react with native DNA, from initiation by native DNA itself of a perpetuated immune response in genetically susceptible individuals, or from a highly specific lapse in immune regulation.] ◀

55–2 **Fetal Survival After Prednisone Suppression of Maternal Lupus Anticoagulant.** Intrauterine deaths are common in pregnant

(55–1) N. Engl J. Med. 308:414–420, Feb. 24, 1983.
(55–2) Lancet 1:1361–1363, June 18, 1983.

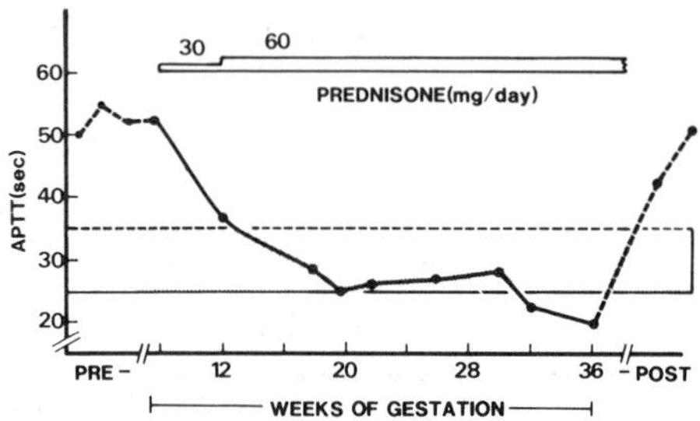

Fig 55–1.—Activated partial thromboplastin times (APTTs) in 1 patient before, during, and after third pregnancy. Pregnancy terminated successfully at 36 weeks. Boxed zone indicates limits for normal values of APTT. (Courtesy of Lubbe, W.F., et al.: Lancet 1:1361–1363, June 18, 1983.)

women with circulating lupus anticoagulant, an acquired immunoglobulin that is associated with reduced prostacyclin release from vessel walls and that interacts with the phospholipid fraction of platelets to predispose to thrombosis. W. F. Lubbe, W. S. Butler, S. J. Palmer, and G. C. Liggins (Auckland, New Zealand) administered prednisone and aspirin to 6 pregnant women with lupus anticoagulant. They had prolonged activated partial thromboplastin times (APTTs) and kaolin clotting times not correctable by dilution with normal plasma. All 14 previous pregnancies in the 5 multigravida patients had ended in intrauterine death. Three women had had thrombotic episodes during pregnancy. Systemic lupus erythematosus was diagnosed in 4 patients. Antinuclear antibody was identified in all 6 patients.

The patients received 40–60 mg of prednisone and 75 mg of aspirin daily. Lupus anticoagulant activity was suppressed in 5 patients, all of whom gave birth to live infants. The course of the APTT in 1 patient is shown in Figure 55–1. One intrauterine death occurred when the APTT was only partly corrected. The APTT had previously been corrected by prednisone treatment between pregnancies in this patient. All the surviving infants are doing well. Steroid therapy was gradually withdrawn except in a patient with arthritic symptoms.

All women with systemic lupus erythematosus, thrombotic episodes, recurrent intrauterine deaths, or a biologically false-positive VDRL test result should be screened for presence of the lupus anticoagulant, since prednisone and aspirin therapy can suppress the anticoagulant and lead to successful pregnancy. Five of 6 patients in this study has a good outcome of pregnancy after treatment with prednisone and aspirin.

▶ [The lupus anticoagulant is an acquired immunoglobulin inhibitor of blood coagulation that interferes with the phospholipid portion of the prothrombin activator complex (factors Xa and V, calcium, and phospholipid). Patients generally have a prolonged activated partial thromboplastin time (APTT), but rarely bleed unless a second hemostatic defect is present. Instead, thrombotic episodes predominate, and thromboses in the placenta lead to fetal death. Carreras et al.[1] showed that the serum IgG fraction (containing a lupus anticoagulant) of a young woman with a history of recurrent arterial thrombosis and repeated intrauterine death, inhibited the release of prostacyclin (PGI_2) from rat aorta rings and pregnant human myometrium. Prostacyclin is a major natural defense mechanism against intravascular platelet aggregation.[2] They proposed that this antiphospholipid antibody may interfere with the release of arachidonic acid (substrate for PGI_2 production) from cell membrane phospholipids and thereby predispose the tissue to thrombosis.

The current authors took the bull by the horns: they mapped out a reasonable therapeutic regimen and used it. High-dose corticosteroid therapy is known to suppress the activity of the lupus anticoagulant. To this they added low-dose aspirin in an attempt to prevent platelet-mediated thrombosis. The regimen worked. Their 6 patients had had among them 14 pregnancies lost, 7 beyond 20 weeks of gestation, and no live births. Three patients had had major thrombotic episodes. With therapy, 5 infants survived pregnancy and are thriving. One intrauterine death occurred at 16 weeks, before the APTT had become normal. (It takes several weeks of treatment [see Fig 55–1].)

Note that the authors' observations were made over a 3-year period when 15,000 pregnancies were handled at their hospital. Screening for the lupus anticoagulant was done *only* in women in whom it was suspected—those with histories of unexplained fetal losses, thrombotic episodes, or clinical evidence of systemic lupus erythematosus. The true frequency of the lupus anticoagulant, and the risk to the fetus of an asymptomatic woman who has it, are still to be determined.] ◀

55–3 **Connective Tissue Disease, Antibodies to Ribonucleoprotein, and Congenital Heart Block.** A strong association has been found between congenital complete heart block and maternal connective tissue disease, and it has been proposed that anti-Ro(SS-A) and anti-La(SS-B) antibodies may be related to congenital heart block as well as to neonatal skin lesions in children born to women with sys-

TABLE 1.—Serologic Findings in 41 Mothers of Infants With Isolated Congenital Complete Heart Block

	Total	Immunodiffusion			Immunofluorescence	
		Anti-Ro	Anti-La	Other antibodies	Antinuclear antibody	Anti-DNA
		no. of mothers			*no. of mothers*	
Mothers with connective-tissue disease	17	16	11	1 *	11	1
Asymptomatic mothers	24	18	6	2 †	5	0
Totals	*41*	*34*	*17*	*3*	*16*	*1*

*Sm.
†Identical, unidentified.
(Courtesy of Scott, J.S., et al.: N. Engl. J. Med. 309:209–212, July 28, 1983; reprinted by permission of The New England Journal of Medicine.)

TABLE 2.—Serologic Findings in 21 Children With Isolated Congenital Complete Heart Block

Age at Time of Serum Collection	No. of Children				No. of Mothers
	Total	With Anti-Ro	With Anti-La	With Antinuclear Antibody	With Anti-Ro
<3 mo	8	7	6	2	7
>6 mo	13	0	0	0	11

(Courtesy of Scott, J.S., et al.: N. Engl. J. Med. 309:209–212, July 28, 1983; reprinted by permission of The New England Journal of Medicine.)

(55–3) N. Engl. J. Med. 309:209–212, July 28, 1983.

temic lupus erythematosus. James S. Scott, Peter J. Maddison, Pamela V. Taylor, Eva Esscher, Olive Scott, and R. Paul Skinner examined the relation between congenital heart block and maternal connective tissue disease by antibody screening of serum samples from 45 patients with isolated congenital complete heart block. Samples were obtained from 41 mothers, 17 of whom had connective tissue disease, most often systemic lupus erythematosus, and from 21 children.

Positive serologic findings were obtained in the subjects with congenital complete heart block but not in those with other types of heart block. The serologic findings in the mothers of study infants are given in Table 1, and the findings in the children are given in Table 2. Most mothers had antibody to the soluble tissue ribonucleoprotein antigen Ro on immunodiffusion testing, and anti-Ro was found in 7 of 8 serum samples from infants younger than age 3 months but not in 13 samples from older children.

These findings indicate very close correlation between isolated congenital complete heart block and the presence of anti-Ro in maternal serum. The maternal antibody presumably crosses the placenta and is a marker for the risk of congenital complete heart block. The absence of anti-Ro from maternal serum indicates that an infant is unlikely to be affected. Probably anti-Ro or a related antibody is involved in the pathogenesis of congenital complete heart block.

▶ [It has been known for some time that IgG can cross the placenta as early as 12 weeks of gestation and that appropriate antibodies can bring the mother's problems transiently to the fetus in such disorders as Graves disease, myasthenia gravis, and thrombocytopenic purpura. It was also known that in connective tissue diseases, newborn infants sometimes had transient features of the mother's illness, and marker IgG antibodies, e.g., lupus erythematosus factor or antinuclear antibody, could be found in their circulation; but for a long time matters were no more precise than that. More recently, a strong association has been established between congenital complete heart block and maternal connective tissue disease,[3] and it has been suggested that anti-Ro—also called SS-A (the SS standing for Sjögren's syndrome)—and anti-La(SS-B) may be related to skin lesions seen in some neonates whose mothers have systemic lupus erythematosus (SLE) and to congenital heart block.[4] Approximate prevalences of anti-Ro are thought to be more than 40% in Sjögren's syndrome, 25%–30% in SLE, 5% in rheumatoid arthritis, and only 6 per 5,000 in persons without connective tissue disease.

The current authors found a very high correlation between isolated congenital complete heart block and anti-Ro antibody in maternal serum, whether or not the mothers had symptoms. The association is so high (see Table 1) that the presence of maternal anti-Ro antibodies should help to establish a suspected diagnosis of heart block in a fetus during pregnancy. Their absence in relation to a newborn child with heart block might suggest that the disorder is due to cardiac malformation or is familial. Note that testing the infant's serum after 6 months of age is likely to be futile; the evidence (maternal anti-Ro antibody) will be gone.

Global screening of pregnant women is not indicated because the returns will be extremely small; the presence of the antibody by no means indicates that heart block will occur in the child; and preventative methods are not currently available. In pregnant women with connective tissue disease, a negative test might be reassuring. Asymptomatic mothers of affected children should clearly be screened for the presence of anti-Ro antibody and followed with regard to its persistence and to the possible eventual development of disease.] ◀

55–4 **Serologic and HLA Associations in Subacute Cutaneous Lupus Erythematosus, a Clinical Subset of Lupus Erythematosus.** Lupus erythematosus is a very heterogeneous disorder. Richard D. Sontheimer, Peter J. Maddison, Morris Reichlin, Robert E. Jordon, Peter Stastny, and James N. Gilliam reviewed the serologic findings in 27 patients with a widespread, nonscarring, often photosensitive form of cutaneous lupus erythematosus, termed subacute cutaneous lupus erythematosus. All had active skin disease at the time of study. The 22 women and 5 men had a mean age of 42 years. The eruption (Fig 55–2) occurred predominantly on the shoulders, arms, upper back, and V area of the neck. Gray-white hypopigmentation persisted after subsidence of the erythema of active lesions. Both papulosquamous and annular lesions were observed.

If cutaneous criteria are excluded, only 5 patients had systemic lupus erythematosus as defined by the American Rheumatism Association criteria. Antinuclear and anticytoplasmic antibodies and circulating immune complexes are frequently identified. Rheumatoid factor and antilymphocyte, anti-DNA, anti-nRNP, and anti-Sm antibodies were found less frequently. Abnormal levels of circulating immune complexes were found in 13 of the 22 patients studied. Patients with annular skin lesions showed a striking concordance of anti-Ro antibodies and the HLA-DR3 histocompatibility phenotype.

Patients with subacute cutaneous lupus erythematosus usually do not have the same frequency of serious systemic involvement as patients with systemic lupus erythematosus, but they have more fre-

Fig 55–2.—Lesions of subacute cutaneous lupus erythematosus. **A,** patient in annular subgroup. **B,** patient in papulosquamous subgroup. (Courtesy of Sontheimer, R.D., et al.: Ann. Intern. Med. 97:664–671, November 1982.)

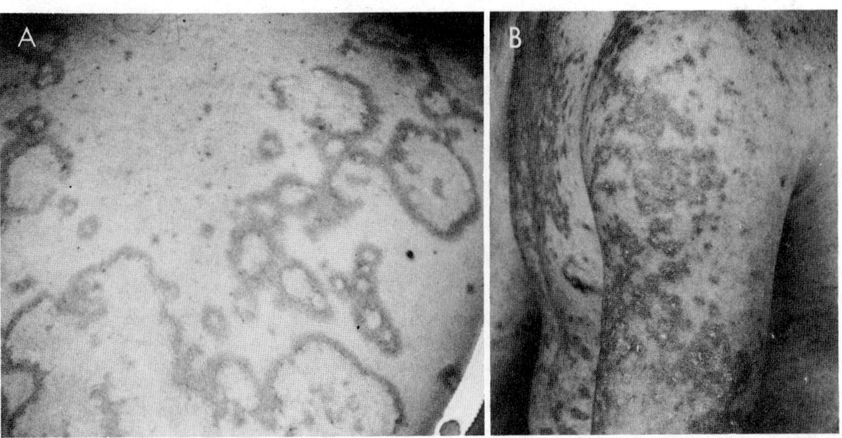

(55–4) Ann. Intern. Med. 97:664–671, November 1982.

quent clinical and serologic evidence of disease activity beyond the skin than patients with discoid lupus erythematosus.

▶ [The hallmark of subacute cutaneous lupus erythematosus is a widespread, nonscarring, often light-induced skin lesion, which may be annular or papulosquamous. Clinically these patients have predominantly skin and joint involvement and therefore an excellent prognosis; they rarely have significant serosal, renal, or CNS disease. The current study deals with serologic and HLA associations. Fifteen of 27 patients (63%) had antibodies to the primarily cytoplasmic RNA-protein particle, Ro (with or without anti-La activity, which almost always has concomitant anti-Ro). In contrast, anti-Ro occurred in only 26% of a large general unselected population with systemic lupus erythematosus (SLE) ($P = .001$). Other serologic findings do not separate this subgroup from SLE in general but help distinguish it from the subgroup with discoid lupus erythematosus (discoid LE; see below), which rarely has them. The B-cell alloantigen HLA-DR3 was found in 20 of 26 patients vs. 22 of 100 controls ($P < .00008$), including all 12 of the patients with annular lesions. Here then is another example of an immunogenetic marker possibly influencing the variety of immune response and, perhaps, thereby the clinical expression of disease.

In the past, this syndrome has been called by such names as "subacute disseminated lupus erythematosus" or "disseminated discoid lupus erythematosus." "Disseminated" sometimes referred to the extent of skin involvement. (Discoid LE can also be extensive.) And it sometimes referred to involvement of other systems (rare in discoid LE). The current term seems better. Other features that distinguish subacute cutaneous lupus erythematosus from discoid LE include the lack of true atrophic scarring associated with the residual hypopigmentation (although I find it hard to believe that these lesions cannot eventually atrophy and scar, given repeated attacks and enough time) and the frequency of serologic abnormalities (for example, only about 3% of patients with discoid LE have anti-Ro antibodies).

Patients with subacute cutaneous lupus erythematosus closely resemble clinically those with so-called "antinuclear antibody negative" SLE, and 62% of the latter have anti-Ro antibodies.[5, 6] The two syndromes may be the same, the chief apparent difference having been the lack of antinuclear antibody in the latter. However, those serum samples had been tested against mouse liver cell nuclei, which in retrospect lack certain relevant antigens. When the samples were retested against a human KB tumor cell substrate (which was used in the current studies), 66% had antinuclear antibodies.[6] Moral: Give your syndrome a clinical name; a serologic one can turn around and bite you.] ◀

55–5 **Randomized Trial of Plasma Exchange in Mild Systemic Lupus Erythematosus.** Plasma exchange or apheresis can benefit patients with diseases that are influenced by the presence of abnormal proteins. All the presumed pathogenic factors in systemic lupus erythematosus (SLE) may be removed in this way. Nathan Wei, John H. Klippel, David P. Huston, Russell P. Hall, Thomas J. Lawley, James E. Balow, Alfred D. Steinberg, and John L. Decker (Natl. Inst. of Health, Bethesda, Md.) undertook a double-blind trial of brief, intensive plasma exchange in 20 patients, aged 18–60 years, with mildly active SLE. All satisfied at least four preliminary criteria of the American Rheumatism Association and had a creatinine clearance rate higher than 20 ml/minute.

The patients were randomized to receive six 4-liter plasma exchanges or to undergo a similar control procedure during a 2-week period. Exchanges were with 5% albumin in normal saline, supplemented with potassium chloride and calcium gluconate. Most patients were receiving steroids or nonsteroidal antiinflammatory drugs at the outset; none were receiving cytotoxic drugs.

(55–5) Lancet 1:17–21, Jan. 1/8, 1983.

Two patients were withdrawn as treatment failures before completing the trial. Plasma exchange led to significant reductions in serum immunoglobulin levels and in circulating immune complexes, estimated by ^{125}I-C1q binding assay. The serologic measures returned to baseline within a month after plasma exchange with no rebound effect. Antibody to DNA was reduced immediately after plasma exchange but often returned to baseline before the next exchange. Clinical activity remained stable or improved in all but 2 of the 18 patients who completed the trial. The degree of improvement was comparable in the study and control groups. No side effects resulted from plasma exchange therapy.

This controlled study failed to show significant improvement in the clinical manifestations of mild, acute SLE with brief but intensive plasma exchange therapy, compared with a sham exchange procedure. It would seem that plasma exchange in SLE, especially in mild cases, should continue to be an investigational procedure. It is possible that a longer study period would have shown some benefit from plasma exchange, although extended observations of some patients have been negative.

▶ [Immunoglobulins and immune complexes are thought to be important in the pathogenesis of SLE. Six 4-liter plasma exchanges over a 2-week period reduced significantly the concentrations of these materials for almost 4 weeks (immunoglobulins) or more (immune complexes). No such changes were produced by a sham procedure, yet clinical improvement was no greater with plasma exchange than without it. Why not?

The authors cite a number of possible reasons. The numbers were small: 10 plasma exchange patients and 10 controls. However, the authors calculate that for the largest measured difference, assuming it is representative, to become significant (two-sided test, $\alpha = 0.05$, $\beta = 0.20$), 146 subjects would be required—an impractically large number. Sicker patients might have done better, although this procedure has not been uniformly successful for severe SLE either. They note that DNA-binding capacity was not substantially reduced in several patients; it or some critical unknown substance may still have been operative. One can only say that the volumes they removed were reasonable for a practical and economically feasible form of treatment. And if simply running blood through the centrifuge somehow produced the modest clinical improvement seen in controls, it did not show in serologic measurements.

Perhaps the unloading of circulating inflammogens takes more than 6 weeks to be expressed as decreased inflammation in tissues. Against this hypothesis is the fact that the authors did not see such effects in patients followed beyond the end of the study. Finally, these patients were not also receiving cytotoxic drugs, a combination advocated for a sustained clinical and serologic response to plasma exchange.[7] That would have required a much larger study of 4 groups of patients (real or sham apheresis; cytotoxic drug or placebo).

In sum, the authors of this thoughtful article address possible design problems that could have prevented them from detecting the benefits of plasma exchange; alternatively, the sought-for benefits may simply not be there.] ◀

Chapter 55 References

1. Carreras L.O., Defreyn G., Machin S.J., Vermylen J., Deman R., Spitz B., Van Assche A.: Arterial thrombosis, intrauterine death and "lupus" anticoagulant detection of immunoglobulin interfering with possible prostacyclin formation. *Lancet* 1:244–246, 1981.
2. Moncada S., Higgs E.A., Vane J.R.: Human arterial and venous tissues generate prostacyclin (prostaglandin X), a potent inhibitor of platelet aggregation. *Lancet* 1:18–20, 1977.

3. Chameides L., Truex R.C., Vetter V., Rashkind W.J., Galioto F.M. Jr., Noonan J.A.: Association of maternal systemic lupus erythematosus with congenital complete heart block. *N. Engl. J. Med.* 297:1204–1207, 1977.
4. Kephart D.C., Hood A.F., Provost T.T.: Neonatal lupus erythematosus: new serologic findings. *J. Invest. Dermatol.* 77:331–333, 1981.
5. Provost T.T., Ahmed A.R., Maddison P.J., Reichlin M.: Antibodies to cytoplasmic antigens in lupus erythematosus: serologic marker for systemic disease. *Arthritis Rheum.* 20:1457–1463, 1977.
6. Maddison P.J., Provost T.T., Reichlin M.: Serological findings in patients with "ANA-negative" systemic lupus erythematosus. *Medicine (Baltimore)* 60:87–94, 1981.
7. Verrier Jones J., Robinson M.F., Parciany P.K., Layfer L.F., McCloud B.: Therapeutic plasmapheresis in systemic lupus erythematosus: effect on immune complexes and antibodies to DNA. *Arthritis Rheum.* 24:1113–1120, 1981.

56. Spondyloarthropathy and Reactive Arthritis

56–1 **Natural Disease Course of Ankylosing Spondylitis.** Simon Carette, Donald Graham, Hugh Little, Joel Rubenstein, and Philip Rosen (Univ. of Toronto) reviewed data on 150 World War II veterans with anklyosing spondylitis (AS) who were entered into a prospective study in 1947 to delineate the natural history of this disease. In 1957, 142 were traced, and they have been restudied periodically. Eighty-one patients were living in 1980, and 51 of them were reexamined. Another 16 patients completed a questionnaire. Mean age at onset of symptoms in the 51 patients who were reexamined was 24 years. Mean duration of symptoms was 38 years.

Thirty-two percent of patients reviewed denied having pain, and only 4% reported severe pain. Seventy-two percent of patients reported no change in symptoms in the past 10 years. Fifty-four percent of patients were employed; 42% had retired for reasons unrelated to AS. Three patients were in functional class III (American Rheumatism Association), and 1 was in class IV because of a cervical fracture and resultant paraplegia. Severe spinal restriction was observed in 41% of patients. Moderate to severe deformity was present in one third of patients. Thirty-six percent had peripheral joint involvement. Nearly 90% of patients tested were positive for HLA-B27.

In all, 5 patients had deteriorated after 1947, whereas 14 had improved after this time, according to mobility ratings. Early peripheral joint involvement was a good predictor of disease severity. Iritis also was associated with more severe involvement. Eight of 61 deaths were thought to be due to disease-related events, excluding treatment effects.

► [Ankylosing spondylitis can have a benign course. After 38 years, 92% (47 of 51) of patients were functioning well, 68% continued to have symptoms, and only 41% had progressed to having severe spinal restriction. On x-ray films, even at this late date, 6 (of 48) patients had evidence of sacroiliac, but not spinal, involvement. Only 8 of the 61 deaths were thought to be disease-related: 2 with cervical subluxations, 3 with aortic insufficiency, 2 with respiratory failures associated with severe spinal abnormality, and 1 with amyloid nephropathy. A 30-year follow-up[1] of 76 patients from Finland confirms this generally good long-term prognosis.

In most patients a predictable pattern of disease emerged within the first 10 years. The disease did not progress in 74% of those whose restriction in 1947 was mild, and 81% of those with severe disease in 1980 were already severely restricted in 1947. Early peripheral joint involvement was a bad prognostic sign; but again, if hip disease had not developed within the first 10 years of illness, it was not likely to do so later.

We have all seen patients with functionally debilitating, severe, fixed-flexion deformities of the spine in this disorder. I would emphasize that loss of mobility need

(56–1) Arthritis Rheum. 26:186–190, February 1983.

not be associated with deformity. In this study 13 patients (25%) with moderate or severe loss of mobility had little or no deformity. When the disease is active, nonsteroidal antiinflammatory agents help patients resist the drift toward flexion that pain engenders and allow them to perform extension exercises whose purpose is to maintain and possibly improve the range of motion. The hope is that if a patient's spine is destined to fuse, it will do so in a good functional position.] ◀

56–2 ***Klebsiella*-Related Antigens in Ankylosing Spondylitis.** It has been suggested that *Klebsiella pneumoniae* may have a role in the pathogenesis of HLA-B27–positive ankylosing spondylitis (AS). André D. Beaulieu, François Rousseau, Evelyne Israël-Assayag, and Raynald Roy (Laval, Univ.) examined the cytotoxic potential of 98 antiserums to various *Klebsiella* strains, including antiserums to two strains, K_{21} and K_{43}, which are reported to give rise to lymphocytotoxicity in HLA-B27–positive AS patients. Antiserums to the *Klebsiella* strains isolated from the feces of AS patients and to the K_{21} and K_{43} strains were raised in rabbits. Both a hemagglutination assay and a lymphocytotoxicity assay were used. None of the antiserums tested was found to be lymphocytotoxic. They included four antiserums raised against strains of *Klebsiella* isolated from AS patients. Rabbit K_{21} and K_{43} antiserums with high hemagglutinating titers exhibited no significant cytotoxic activity in 12 HLA-B27–positive AS patients.

Klebsiella pneumoniae antiserums were found not to have significant cytotoxic activity against lymphocytes of patients with AS in this study. The inability to find a single active antiserum despite extensive efforts indicates the complexity of seeking *Klebsiella*-related antigens in AS.

▶ [The strong association of ankylosing spondylitis with the presence of the human histocompatibility leukocyte antigen HLA-B27—close to 100% of white patients have it—suggests that immune mechanisms are somehow involved in the pathogenesis of this disorder. Other B27-associated diseases such as Reiter's syndrome and the so-called reactive spondyloarthropathies are known to be triggered by infections due to *Yersinia, Shigella flexneri, Chlamydia,* or *Salmonella.* In the issue containing the article abstracted above, an editorial[2] entitled "Ankylosing Spondylitis, a Disease in Search of Microbes," reviews the evidence for a "*Klebsiella* connection" to ankylosing spondylitis. It hinges on two interrelated sets of observations. The first was of a preferential colonization of the intestine by *Klebsiella* species in ankylosing spondylitis. This finding has been convincingly disputed; the apparent increase seems more a characteristic of both healthy and diseased subjects who frequent health care facilities. The second set of observations suggested that certain *Klebsiella strains* (notably K43 and K21) may possess antigenic cross-reactivity with HLA-B27. It is the relevant findings from those studies that the current workers (and others as well) have been unable to confirm. Until such confirmation is forthcoming, the "*Klebsiella* connection" will remain an attractive possibility, but no more than that.] ◀

56–3 **Spondyloarthropathy Associated With Hidradenitis Suppurativa and Acne Conglobata.** Arthropathy has been described in association with acne conglobata but not with hidradenitis suppurativa, a related cicatricial cutaneous disorder. Itzhak A. Rosner, David E. Richter, Timothy L. Huettner, George H. Kuffner, Jeffrey J. Wis-

(56–2) J. Rheumatol. 10:102–105, 1983.
(56–3) Ann. Intern. Med. 97:520–525, October 1982.

nieski, and Carol G. Burg (Case Western Reserve Univ.) studied 10 patients with hidradenitis suppurativa, acne conglobata, or both, who developed arthritis. The 6 men and 4 women were aged 22–46 years. Nine were black and 1 was Japanese. Eight patients had hidradenitis suppurativa, 9 had acne conglobata, 7 had both, and 3 also had dissecting cellulitis of the scalp. No patient had a history of acne fulminans.

Nine patients had evidence of peripheral arthritis with episodic oligoarthritis affecting mainly larger joints. Eight also had involvement of hand and foot joints. Both symmetric and asymmetric involvement were seen. Symptoms tended to persist in involved peripheral joints between flares. Nine patients had evidence of axial arthritis including lumbosacral involvement. Six patients had sacroiliac tenderness. One patient required prednisone besides nonsteroidal antiinflammatory agents to control symptoms. Three others required corticosteroids to control the skin disorder. One patient received D-penicillamine for progressive erosive arthritis. Three patients had pyoderma gangrenosum, and 2 had a history of erythema nodosum. Two patients had xerophthalmia. Two had a history of conjunctivitis and urethral symptoms. All patients but 1 had an elevated sedimentation rate. None had a positive rheumatoid factor test.

This is the first report of arthropathy associated with hidradenitis suppurativa. The pathogenetic significance of the relation between arthritis and these skin disorders is unclear, but it appears that the arthropathy may be a reaction to chronic cutaneous infection. In 8 of the 9 evaluable patients the skin disease preceded the onset of joint symptoms by 1–20 years, and in 1 patient symptoms of arthritis preceded skin disease by 1 month.

▶ [This abstract relates spondyloarthropathy to three chronic, suppurative, and cicatricial cutaneous disorders that may occur alone or together: hidradenitis suppurativa, acne conglobata, and dissecting cellulitis of the scalp. The authors believe that most earlier connections between acne and arthritis were in patients with acne fulminans,[3] a disorder primarily of white male adolescents in which acute arthritis or arthralgias of peripheral joints may occur in the setting of a febrile, toxic illness. In contrast, acne conglobata consists of comedones, cysts, abscesses, discharging sinuses, and scarring, predominantly of the back, chest, and buttocks, usually with few constitutional symptoms. Hidradenitis suppurativa refers to chronic, suppurative, cicatrizing lesions of apocrine gland–bearing areas of the skin, principally in the axillary and anogenital region.

Moreover, all 10 current patients were mature adults, all but one were black (possibly because of the clinic population under study), four were women, and axial joint involvement was prominent. And these patients had many features familiar to students of the previously known seronegative spondyloarthropathies, including ocular and genitourinary inflammation (2 patients), mucosal ulceration (1), pyoderma gangrenosum (3), erythema nodusum (2), and a lack of subcutaneous nodules or IgM rheumatoid factors. (None had psoriasis or inflammatory bowel disease.) No increase in HLA-B27 positivity was found (1 patient had it), but the series is small, and black patients with ankylosing spondylitis are much less likely to have this antigen (frequency, about 50%) than are white patients (nearly 100%). Of possible pathogenetic significance are the observations that 3 patients thought the exacerbations of arthritis accompanied flares of skin disease, and conversely, improvement of arthritis followed surgical therapy for scalp cellulitis and hydradenitis suppurativa in 2 patients. In sum, we seem to have here another variety of reactive arthritis, but we need more cases and further analysis of histocompatibility antigens.] ◀

56–4 **Retinoid Hyperostosis: Skeletal Toxicity Associated With Long-Term Administration of 13-*cis*-Retinoic Acid for Refractory Ichthyosis.** The synthetic vitamin A derivative 13-*cis*-retinoic acid (isotretinoin) controls a wide variety of dermatoses, including keratinizing states such as lamellar ichthyosis. Richard A. Pittsley (Michigan State Univ.) and Frank W. Yoder (Ohio State Univ.) observed disorder of ossification resembling diffuse idiopathic skeletal hyperostosis in 4 of 9 consecutive patients given long-term 13-*cis*-retinoic acid therapy for ichthyosis.

Woman, 33, received 13-*cis*-retinoic acid in a dose of 3 mg/kg of body weight daily for 2 years for lamellar ichthyosis. Arthralgias developed but resolved when the drug was stopped. Disabling musculoskeletal pain developed when the drug was continued because of marked improvement in the dermatosis. Motion at several joints was painful, and the cartilaginous parts of the rib cage were tender. X-ray films showed striking ossification in the region of the anterior longitudinal ligament of the cervical spine (Fig 56–1). Focal asymmetric flowing ossification was seen in the thoracic spine. Beak-like ossifications were noted superior to the carpometacarpal articulations. Iliolumbar ligament ossification and extraspinal hyperostosis at the elbows, ankles, hips and calcaneal regions also were noted. The costal cartilages were diffusely calcified. The patient has continued to use low doses of 13-*cis*-retinoic acid and has had less pain, but hyperostotic lesions have continued to increase in size and number.

Fig 56–1.—Hyperostosis in 33-year-old woman after 4 years of treatment with 13-*cis*-retinoic acid. Disk spaces and facet joints appear to be intact. (Courtesy of Pittsley, R.A., and Yoder, F.W.: N. Engl. J. Med. 308:1012–1014, Apr. 28, 1983; reprinted by permission of The New England Journal of Medicine.)

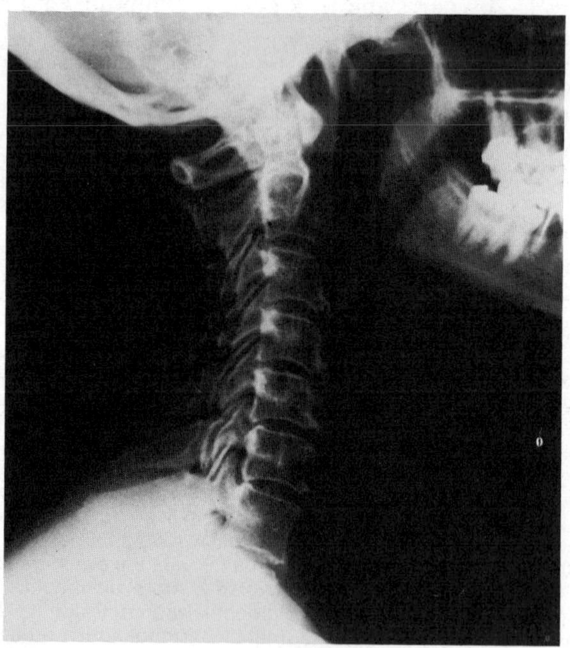

(56–4) N. Engl. J. Med. 308:1012–1014, Apr. 28, 1983.

Patients with ichthyosis may be particularly vulnerable to this complication of 13-*cis*-retinoic acid therapy because of their need for high daily doses over a long period. The drug-induced lesions are thinner and more sclerotic than those typically seen in diffuse idiopathic skeletal hyperostosis. Retinoid hyperostosis appears to be a distinct rheumatic disorder. Caution is needed in the intensive use of retinoids, especially in view of the fact that reports of benefit in treating severe acne and in preventing cancer have been widely disseminated to the public.

▶ [13-*Cis*-retinoic acid (isotretinoin, Accutane), 2–3 mg/kg/day for 2 years or more, can produce a disorder of ossification that resembles diffuse idiopathic skeletal hyperostosis (DISH syndrome; Forestier's disease). The latter, a disease of unknown cause, features anterolateral spinal ligament calcification involving (by definition) at least four contiguous vertebral bodies with large flowing osteophytes; posterior elements are spared, and disk height is maintained. The lesions associated with the synthetic retinoid are thinner and more sclerotic, and they progress more rapidly. When the treatment was stopped, musculoskeletal symptoms subsided, but deformities and diminished motion persisted.

Although x-ray changes are not known after the lower doses (1–2 mg/kg/day) and shorter periods (4–5 months) of treatment with this substance for severe nodulocystic acne, 80% of those patients develop dry skin, pruritis, epistaxis, dry nose and mouth, sore lips and/or conjunctivitis. Pseudotumor cerebri and major fetal abnormalities can occur. About 15% of patients have mild-to-moderate musculoskeletal symptoms. These symptoms are reversible, and remission is generally both complete and long-lasting. Nevertheless, this group of patients receiving lower doses is now being watched more closely for skeletal changes (which may precede symptoms). For the nonacne disorders of keratinization in which long-term, higher-dose isotretinoin has been employed, Pochi[4] now recommends its use only in severe disease, with additional measures to limit the total dosage—decreased daily intake when possible, intermittent courses, and intensive concomitant topical therapy. Periodic skeletal x-rays may pick up cases early.] ◀

56–5 **Effect of Revision of Intestinal Bypass on Postintestinal Bypass Arthritis.** Arthritis occurs in as many as 30% of patients after jejunoileal bypass for obesity. Its cause is unknown, but circulating immune complexes have been found in patients after intestinal bypass. Robert D. Leff, Marlene A. Aldo-Benson, and James A. Madura (Indiana Univ.) examined the effects of revision in 50 patients who had end-to-end jejunoileal bypass for morbid obesity since 1972 and who required either revision of the length of bypassed bowel or complete anastomosis because of metabolic problems or arthritis. Initially the blind loop was drained into the distal part of the ileum just above the cecum. Eight patients had total revision of the bypass; the other 42 had partial revision with reinsertion of an average of 19 cm of bowel. Twelve patients had postintestinal bypass arthritis. The 11 evaluable patients developed musculoskeletal symptoms 3 to 55 months after operation. The arthritis was usually polyarticular, asymmetric, and migratory. Nine patients failed to respond to nonsteroidal antiinflammatory drugs.

Five patients with arthritis had total anastomosis of the bypass, and 6 had partial revision. All 5 of the former had complete relief from arthritis within several weeks of operation. Remissions have been sustained for up to 14 months. Four of the 6 patients who had

---

(56–5) Arthritis Rheum. 26:678–681, May 1983.

partial revision had clinical arthritis at the time, and in 3 the arthritis persisted after operation. One patient had complete remission of arthritic symptoms. Another had a recurrence of arthritis after partial remission.

Arthritis and dermatitis occurring after jejunoileal bypass may result from bacterial overgrowth in the blind loop and formation of immune complexes by antibody to bacterial antigens. Total revision could then be expected to lead to remission, and this has been observed. Several patients who have undergone only partial revision have continued to have arthritis. Total bypass revision appears to be an effective treatment for patients with debilitating postintestinal bypass arthritis that has failed to respond to other treatments.

▶ [Jejunoileal bypass for morbid obesity is no longer a popular procedure because of the extent and persistence of late postoperative complications. They may include diarrhea, electrolyte disturbances, diminished levels of vitamin B_{12} and folate, calcium oxalate nephrolithiasis, gallstones, and progressive hepatic structural changes or cirrhosis.[5,6] The associated arthritis is thought to stem from the absorption of intestinal bacterial antigens from the blind loop created at surgery, their incorporation into circulating immune complexes, and immune-complex-mediated tissue injury. Supporting this mechanism is the occasional reported improvement in joints after reanastomosis of bowel.

From the point of view of pathogenesis, the most impressive finding in the current study is that the 5 patients who underwent total revision did not simply improve; every one of them was in complete joint remission within several weeks of surgery and remained there throughout the period of follow-up (4–14 months). This finding rules out true autoimmunity, i.e., a self-perpetuating immune attack by the host on his or her own tissues, perhaps triggered initially by a cross-reacting exogenous antigen. It rules out persistence in the joint of some antigenic, nonbiodegradable bacterial product. Instead, it says that, whatever the mechanistic details, this variety of "reactive" arthritis depends on the persistence of the situation that produced it in the first place. There are not many rheumatic diseases in which we can choose definitively among these pathogenetic possibilities.] ◀

56–6 **Bowel-Bypass Syndrome Without Bowel Bypass: Bowel-Associated Dermatosis-Arthritis Syndrome.** The bowel-bypass syndrome of inflammatory skin lesions resembling those of acute febrile neutrophilic dermatosis, polyarthritis, and other systemic features occurs in as many as a fifth of patients who have ileojejunal bypass surgery for morbid obesity. The syndrome might result from circulating immune complexes arising from bacterial overgrowth in the blind bowel loop. Joseph L. Jorizzo, Prapand Apisarnthanarax, Paul Subrt, Adelaide A. Hebert, John C. Henry, Sharon S. Raimer, Scott M. Dinehart, and James A. Reinarz (Univ. of Texas, Galveston) report the cases of 4 patients with an identical syndrome who did not have bowel-bypass surgery but who had other bowel disorders.

Woman, 46, had had episodes of fever, myalgias, arthralgias, occasional frank arthritis, and a vesiculopustular eruption (Fig 56–2) for about 4 years. The symptoms had recently increased in frequency and severity, and abdominal pain developed; a pyloric ulcer had previously been demonstrated. A skin biopsy specimen showed changes of Sweet syndrome (neutrophilic dermatosis), and serum cryoglobulins were detected. Nearly complete duodenal obstruction was seen on radiography. Symptomatic improvement occurred on treatment with 60 mg of prednisone daily; however, melena developed, and a

---

(56–6) Arch. Intern. Med. 143:457–461, March 1983.

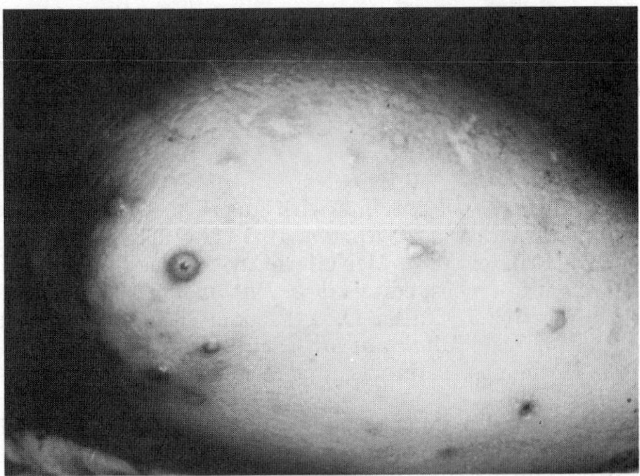

Fig 56–2.—Pustular lesions on purpuric bases on right elbow and forearm. (Courtesy of Jorizzo, J.L., et al.: Arch. Intern. Med. 143:457–461, March 1983.)

choledochoduodenal fistula was found. A cholecystectomy had been done many years earlier. Laparotomy showed a large duodenal diverticulum entering the fistula, and a Billroth II gastrojejunostomy was done with truncal vagotomy. Symptoms of the dermatosis-arthritis syndrome recurred, along with symptoms of dumping. The symptoms were relieved by tetracycline therapy; sulfamethoxazole-trimethoprim therapy also was effective. Findings from a repeat skin biopsy were again consistent with Sweet syndrome.

All 4 patients had gastrointestinal disorders that presumably predisposed them to the syndrome, possibly via circulating immune complexes with bowel-associated antigens. Apart from the presence of bowel disease rather than bypass surgery, the syndrome seems identical to the bowel-bypass syndrome. The term *bowel-associated dermatosis-arthritis syndrome* is proposed to include both medical and surgical cases. The term *bowel-associated circulating immune complex disease* might be adopted if future studies document a pathogenesis mediated by immune complexes.

▶ [Among patients with arthritis associated with intestinal bypass, two thirds have a cutaneous vasculitis whose manifestations vary from macules, urticarial papules, and nodular plaques, to typical vesiculopustular lesions.[7] Like the arthritis, this problem is thought to be due to immune complex deposition (see abstract 56–5), and an "intestinal bypass arthritis-dermatitis syndrome" has been promulgated. The current authors would replace *intestinal bypass* by *bowel-associated,* having found 4 patients without bypasses—2 with gastrointestinal tract diverticula and 2 with inflammatory colitis—all of whom had skin lesions and 2 of whom had arthralgias and arthritis. The syndrome seemed to wax and wane with exacerbations and remissions of the bowel disease.

Their argument hinges on the identity between the skin lesions seen in their 4 patients and those seen in the bypass syndrome. The lesions did seem identical in character, progression, distribution, and histopathologic features. They appear primarily on the upper extremities and upper trunk, develop their typical vesiculopustular character over a day or two, last for several days, and recur perhaps every few weeks. Histologically, they may have all the features of allergic venulitis (leukocytoclastic angiitis and palpable purpura) except for fibrinoid necrosis (and of course palpable purpura favors dependent areas). These lesions are identical histologically to those seen in Sweet's syndrome (acute febrile neutrophilic dermatosis), a clinically different disorder.

I think the authors have made their case, with the result that, long after bowel bypass is a thing of the past, the syndrome first associated with it will still be popping up.] ◀

Chapter 56 References

1. Lehtinen K.: Seventy-six patients with ankylosing spondylitis seen after 30 years of disease. *Scand. J. Rheum.* 12:5–11, 1983.
2. Kinsella T.D., Fritzler M.J., McNeil D.C.: Ankylosing spondylitis: a disease in search of microbes, editorial. *J. Rheumatol.* 10:2–4, 1983.
3. Davis D.E., Viozzi F.J., Miller O.F., Blodgett R.C.: The musculoskeletal manifestations of acne fulminans. *J. Rheumatol.* 8:317–320, 1981.
4. Pochi P.E.: Hormones, retinoids, and acne, editorial. *N. Engl. J. Med.* 308:1024–1025, 1983.
5. Hocking M.P., Duerson M.C., O'Leary J.P., Woodward E.R.: Jejunoileal bypass for morbid obesity: late follow-up in 100 cases. *N. Engl. J. Med.* 308:995–999, 1983.
6. Alpers D.H.: Surgical therapy for morbid obesity, editorial. *N. Engl. J. Med.* 308:1026–1027, 1983.
7. Stein H.B., Schlappner O.L.A., Boyko W., Courlay R.H., Reeve C.E.: The intestinal bypass arthritis-dermatitis syndrome. *Arthritis Rheum.* 24:684–690, 1981.

57. Sclerosing Syndromes

57–1 **Controlled Double-Blind Trial of Nifedipine in Treatment of Raynaud's Phenomenon.** The slow calcium-channel antagonist nifedipine relieves arterial vasospasm and increases cutaneous blood flow in normal subjects. Richard J. Rodeheffer, James A. Rommer, Fredrick Wigley, and Craig R. Smith (Johns Hopkins Univ.) undertook a 7-week, prospective, double-blind, crossover trial of nifedipine in 15 patients with symptomatic Raynaud's phenomenon related to cold or stress. The 12 women and 3 men had a mean age of 34 years. Nine patients had systemic sclerosis, and 1 patient had systemic lupus erythematosus with cryoglobulinemia. Mean duration of Raynaud's symptoms was about 6 years. Seven patients had had digital ulcers. Nifedipine was given in an initial dose of 10 mg 3 times daily and then in a dose of 20 mg 3 times daily if no severe side effects developed.

Moderate to marked improvement was reported by 9 patients while they were taking nifedipine and by 2 taking placebo capsules. The respective mean attack rates of Raynaud's phenomenon were 11 and 15 per 2 weeks during administration of nifedipine and placebo. The fall in digital artery systolic pressure on cold exposure was attenuated by nifedipine in 4 of 9 patients, and digital pallor was ameliorated by nifedipine in 5 of 11. Personal responses to both nifedipine and placebo were variable. The most common side effect was mild, transient headache. Light-headedness was more frequent in nifedipine-treated patients. No significant changes in electrolyte values or blood cell counts were observed.

This study and two other double-blind, controlled, clinical trials have shown nifedipine to be effective in the management of Raynaud's phenomenon. About two thirds of patients appear to respond to this treatment. Nifedipine is conveniently administered and well tolerated. Further study is needed to determine the long-term efficacy of nifedipine therapy for Raynaud's phenomenon and to identify predictors of clinical responsiveness.

▶ [The treatment of Raynaud's phenomenon by any number of manuevers has been marked by high hopes in the short term and disappointment in the long. Numerous vasodilators, sympatholytics, and surgical sympathectomy have eventually come a cropper, but the search for effective and lasting treatment goes on. Some of the more interesting reports in recent years have concerned induced vasodilation,[1] biofeedback,[2] topical glyceryl trinitrate,[3] captopril,[4] prostacyclin,[5] and the calcium-channel blockers.[6] The current study is the third independent double-blind controlled clinical trial to suggest that nifedipine, of the last group of agents, works in certain patients, at least initially.

If one separates the patients with Raynaud's phenomenon into two groups accord-

---

(57–1) N. Engl. J. Med. 308:880–883, Apr. 14, 1983.

ing to whether they had demonstrable systemic disease, some interesting differences appear. Among those with only Raynaud's phenomenon (such patients are said to have Raynaud's *disease*), 4 of 5 responded to nifedipine, vs. 4 of 10 who had associated systemic illness. The attack rate for the 5 patients without systemic disease fell from a mean of 10.0 attacks per 2 weeks with placebo to 2.6 with nifedipine. The mean attack rate for the 9 patients with systemic sclerosis was 15.0 per 2 weeks with placebo and 13.1 with nifedipine. The mean decrease in attack rate per two weeks was 7.8 for patients without systemic disease and 3.1 for patients with systemic sclerosis ($P < .05$). Similarly, the authors of the first controlled study of nifedipine[6] found the drug somewhat useful for Raynaud's phenomenon associated with connective tissue diseases but still more effective in Raynaud's disease.

The difference may lie in the pathophysiology of the two groups. The diameter of digital arteries in Raynaud's disease depends primarily on vasomotor tone; their anatomy is usually normal. In contrast, patients with secondary Raynaud's phenomenon may have additional problems—e.g., endarteritic occlusive disease, platelet activation, blood hyperviscosity—that thwart even the best of dilators. And again, the ultimate test of nifedipine in either primary or secondary Raynaud's phenomenon will be its long-term usefulness.] ◀

57–2 **D-Penicillamine Therapy in Progressive Systemic Sclerosis (Scleroderma): Retrospective Analysis.** Varying results have been reported with the use of D-penicillamine to treat scleroderma. Virginia D. Steen, Thomas A. Medsger, Jr., and Gerald P. Rodnan (Univ. of Pittsburgh) reviewed the results of D-penicillamine therapy in 73 patients with diffuse scleroderma who had had symptoms for less than 3 years and who received the drug for at least 6 consecutive months. Forty-five comparable patients who were not given D-penicillamine also were reviewed (Fig 57–1). D-Penicillamine was prescribed for an average of 2 years in a median daily dose of 750 mg. The mean follow-up period was 38 months. Most of the patients given D-penicillamine did not receive other drugs.

Skin thickness decreased considerably more in the patients treated

Fig 57–1.—Origin of patients for study of D-penicillamine (DPA) in progressive systemic sclerosis (PSS). (Courtesy of Steen, V.D., et al.: Ann. Intern. Med. 97:652–659, November 1982.)

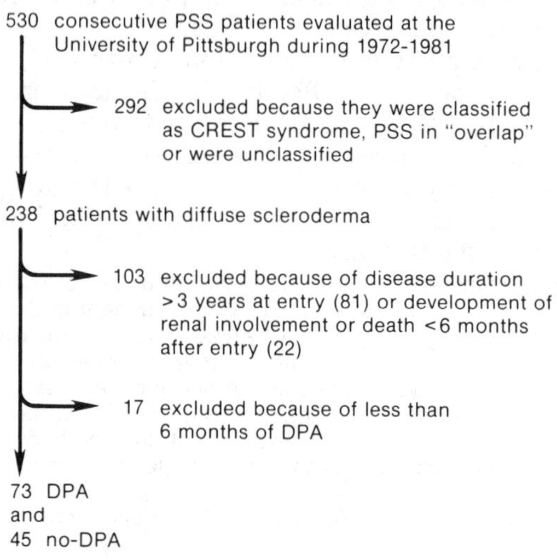

(57–2) Ann. Intern. Med. 97:652–659, November 1982.

with D-penicillamine than in control patients during follow-up. Forearm skin scores and biopsy specimen weights correlated closely. Finger-to-palm distances tended to decrease in study patients and increase in controls. The rate of new visceral organ involvement, especially for the kidneys, was reduced in patients given D-penicillamine. Renal disease developed in only 3 study patients compared with 9 controls. Cumulative survival at 5 years was 88% in the D-penicillamine group and 66% in the control group. Survival was not significantly influenced by treatment with colchicine or immunosuppressive agents. Twelve study patients discontinued D-penicillamine therapy after 6 months or more because of side effects; 2, because of lack of improvement; 1, because of pregnancy.

Despite the many limitations of this study, enough evidence for the usefulness of D-penicillamine was obtained to warrant a prospective controlled study in patients with progressive systemic sclerosis. Patients should be classified as having diffuse scleroderma or the CREST syndrome (calcinosis, Raynaud's phenomenon, esophageal dysmotility, sclerodactyly, and telangiectasia). Objective methods of assessing both cutaneous and visceral involvement are needed.

▶ [This retrospective study represents a 10-year experience with D-penicillamine in the treatment of progressive systemic sclerosis (scleroderma) at a major referral center for this disease. Working within the limits of any retrospective clinical trial, the authors have made a superb case for the initiation of a prospective controlled study of a therapy that, because it is by no means innocuous, should remain experimental until its efficacy is established.

This is a particularly difficult illness in which to evaluate therapy. In the CREST subgroup (see abstract below) skin involvement may be limited, and the lower rates of visceral involvement lead to increased survival. In addition to variations in severity and in progression, many patients with scleroderma have spontaneous lessening of dermal sclerosis. Moreover, psychophysiologic factors can affect symptomatology (e.g., in Raynaud's phenomenon and dysphagia), and changes in internal organ involvement are difficult to measure objectively.

The authors handled these problems by choosing their patient population carefully (see Fig 57–1) and by reporting only quantifiable measures. Thus, they considered only patients with progressive systemic sclerosis and diffuse scleroderma. This form of disease is associated with extensive and at times rapidly progressive skin and visceral involvement. The 3-year restriction on duration of illness excluded patients who were more likely to have irreversible fibrosis of skin and viscera. Because penicillamine seemed to take at least 6 months to begin working, they excluded patients treated for shorter periods, as well as those who developed renal involvement (because of their extremely poor prognosis) or died in the interim. To allow for spontaneous regression in dermal sclerosis, they established an untreated group for comparison. They studied a large number of patients, examined them frequently, and followed them for prolonged periods. Finally, they used objective measurements: total skin score, weight of biopsy specimens from similar skin sites, standard measurements of contracture, and survival data. A first-rate job from the group of Dr. Rodnan, one of our premier rheumatologic scholars, who died this past year.] ◀

57–3 **Anticentromere Antibody: Clinical Correlations and Association With Favorable Prognosis in Patients With Scleroderma Variants.** The presence of antibody to the chromosomal centromere (anticentromere antibody, ACA) appears to be associated with a subset of patients with the limited CREST form of scleroderma, which is

(57–3) Arthritis Rheum. 26:1–7, January 1983.

characterized by calcinosis, Raynaud's phenomenon, esophageal dysmotility, sclerodactyly, and telangiectasia. Gale Anne McCarty, John R. Rice, Mary L. Bembe, and Franc A. Barada, Jr. (Duke Univ.), attempted to define the prognostic value of ACA by following up 27 patients identified as having ACA by screening antinuclear antibody testing with human epithelial cell substrates for 2 years. Twenty-five patients with diffuse scleroderma also were followed up. Antinuclear antibody screening was by the indirect immunofluorescence technique. Autoantibodies were identified by immunodiffusion and counterimmunoelectrophoresis.

No patient with isolated Raynaund's phenomenon or the CREST variant had diffuse scleroderma or features of other connective tissue disease on follow-up, nor did 6 patients with secondary Raynaud's phenomenon have features of diffuse scleroderma. Major organ system involvement was infrequent in patients who had ACA initially (discrete speckled pattern) compared with those who had the speckled or nucleolar patterns. Renal disease was present in large majorities of the latter patients at the end of the study, but not in the 9 patients with ACA and the CREST variant or the 11 with secondary Raynaud's phenomenon. Titers of ACA did not correlate with carbon monoxide diffusion or the activity of Raynaud's phenomenon in study patients.

This study confirms the primary association of ACA with the CREST variant of scleroderma. Major organ system involvement is less frequent in patients with ACA than in those with speckled or nucleolar antinuclear antibody patterns. Screening of patients with isolated Raynaud's phenomenon for ACA may be prognostically useful. Attempts are being made to develop a solid-phase quantitative assay for ACA.

▶ [The introduction of tissue culture substrates for detecting antinuclear antibodies (ANA) in patients with progressive systemic sclerosis has increased the frequency of positivity for these antibodies from 30%–60% to close to 90% and allowed a diversity of specificities to appear. The antigenic targets of these antibodies were less apparent in organ slices (mouse kidney and rat liver) than they are in actively dividing tissue culture cells. The ANA patterns in progressive systemic sclerosis are usually nucleolar or speckled, occasionally homogeneous. Anticentromere antibody produces a subset of the speckled pattern that has been called "discrete speckled." One sees distinctive, uniformly fluorescing dots in mitotic cells, and nuclear speckles in interphase cells. If one uses lysed cells that have been arrested at metaphase (by colcemid), it is clear that this antibody is directed against determinants in the chromosomal centromere, also called the kinetochore; this is the region on each chromosome from which mitotic spindle fibers originate. Although there is as yet no rationale linking anticentromere antibody to pathogenesis, the antibody appears to be an excellent marker for general benignity within a class of illness that can be relentless and lethal.] ◀

57–4 **Eosinophilic Fasciitis Responsive to Cimetidine.** Diffuse fasciitis with eosinophilia is emerging as a distinct clinicopathologic entity, although some still consider it to be a variant of progressive systemic sclerosis. Gary Solomon, Peter Barland, and Harold Rifkin (Albert Einstein College of Medicine) encountered a patient with eo-

(57–4) Ann. Intern. Med. 97:547–549, October 1982.

sinophilic fasciitis whose disease was completely suppressed on two occasions with the specific histamine H_2 receptor antagonist cimetidine.

Man, 53, had developed diffuse arthralgias and myalgias, and during indomethacin therapy, edema of the legs developed and progressed to involve the arms and abdomen. Edema persisted despite loss of 21 kg of body weight on a low-sodium diet over 3 months. Brawny, nontender, nonpitting edema was observed, with no impairment of joint motion and no sclerodactyly. Eosinophils constituted as much as 12% of white blood cells. Biopsies showed marked fascial thickening and hyalinization and infiltration of the fascia by plasma cells, lymphocytes, and rare eosinophils. The edema decreased dramatically on treatment with 20 mg of prednisone daily, and the peripheral eosinophilia resolved. Epigastric pain developed a year later, and brawny edema recurred when the dose of prednisone was reduced. Induration resolved on treatment with 400 mg of cimetidine every 6 hours, as did the epigastric pain, and prednisone therapy was stopped without recurrence of the fasciitis during 1 year. Maintenance therapy was with 400 mg of cimetidine twice daily. Symptoms recurred when cimetidine was stopped, and they again resolved when cimetidine was reinstituted. The patient remains in complete remission with cimetidine therapy.

This patient, with well-documented eosinophilic fasciitis, responded completely on two occasions to cimetidine therapy. Prednisone must still be considered to be the preferred treatment of uncomplicated eosinophilic fasciitis, but in patients who do not tolerate corticosteroid therapy or who have unacceptable side effects from high doses, cimetidine may be a valuable adjunct or, in some instances, an alternative primary treatment.

► [When a "proper" study of cause and effect eventually gets done, the initial, uncontrolled observations on which it was based may be referred to as anecdotes, sometimes patronizingly (as in "mere anecdotes") and always imprecisely (the word derives from the Greek for *un*published items). Yet it is these odd, apparent connections that quicken the blood, stir the imagination, and provide the starting points for most of our progress.

The above abstract concerns a corticosteroid-dependent patient with eosinophilic fasciitis who was given cimetidine for epigastric pain, had a complete remission of the fasciitis that lasted for 1 year on cimetidine (without steroid), stopped cimetidine and developed evidence of fasciitis again, restarted it and returned promptly to complete remission. Eosinophilic fasciitis is characterized by symmetrical, often widespread inflammation and sclerosis of the deep fascia, subcutis, and dermis. It usually resolves eventually (2–5 years) without complications. It differs from progressive systemic sclerosis by the usual sparing of fingers, absence of Raynaud's phenomenon and visceral involvement; frequent onset after intense physical exercise (not in this case); acute onset; laboratory findings of elevated erythrocyte sedimentation rate, (early) peripheral eosinophilia, increase in serum eosinophil chemotactic activity, and hypergammaglobulinemia; and dramatic response to (often low-dose) corticosteroids. Large numbers of lymphocytes and plasma cells in affected tissues, as well as humoral suppression of erythropoiesis in some patients, support an immune-mediated pathogenesis. Toward a possible explanation of the apparent therapeutic effect of cimetidine in this condition, the authors cite studies of a subpopulation of lymphocytes containing H_2 receptors, which when stimulated with histamine suppress several types of immune responses and whose suppressor T-cell function may be inhibited by H_2 receptor antagonists such as cimetidine.

Will the apparent therapeutic effect of cimetidine in eosinophilic fasciitis turn out to be sheer post hoc-ery? It is too early to say; at least one subsequent patient did not improve, but another patient apparently did.[7] Meanwhile, the chase is on, and that's good.] ◄

Chapter 57 References

1. Jobe J.B., Sampson J.B., Roberts D.E., Beetham W.P. Jr.: Induced vasodilation as treatment for Raynaud's disease. *Ann. Intern. Med.* 97:706–709, 1982.
2. National Institutes of Health: Biofeedback for patients with Raynaud's phenomenon. *JAMA* 242:509–510, 1979.
3. Franks A.G. Jr.: Topical glyceryl trinitrate as adjunctive treatment in Raynaud's disease. *Lancet* 1:76–77, 1982.
4. Miyazaki S., Miura K., Kasai Y., Abe K., Yoshinaga K.: Relief from digital vasospasm by treatment with captopril and its complete inhibition by serine proteinase inhibitors in Raynaud's phenomenon. *Br. Med. J.* 284:310–311, 1982.
5. Belch J.J.F., Drury J.K., Capell H., Forbes C.D., Newman P., McKenzie F., Leiberman P., Prentice C.R.M.: Intermittent epoprostenol (prostacyclin) infusion in patients with Raynaud's syndrome. *Lancet* 1:313–314, 1983.
6. Kahan A., Weber S., Amor B., Saporta L., Hodara M., Degeorges M.: Etude controlée de la nifedipine dans le traitement du phénomène de Raynaud. *Revue Rhum. Mal. Osteoartic.* 49:337–343, 1982.
7. Laso F.J., Pastor I., de Castro S.: Cimetidine and eosinophilic fasciitis [letter]. *Ann. Intern. Med.* 98:1026, 1983.

58. Crystal-Associated Arthritis

58–1 **Acute Polyarticular Gout** continues to occur despite the availability of effective hypouricemic therapy. Donald A. Raddatz, Maren L. Mahowald, and Paul J. Bilka reviewed the findings in 41 men seen at the Minneapolis VA Medical Center in a 3-year period with acute polyarticular gout. Diagnosis was based on the presence of acute arthritis in two or more joints and the finding of urate crystals in synovial fluid by polarizing microscopy. These patients represented 28% of cases of gout seen during the review period. Mean patient age was 59 years. Patients generally had complex medical histories and often had one or more serious medical illnesses. More than one half of the patients were hypertensive and nearly one half were obese. Chronic alcoholism, heart disease, and chronic renal disease were other frequent findings. Six patients had malignant disease; 5 were diabetic.

Joint pain and swelling were present for as long as 2 weeks before acute gout was diagnosed. Nearly one half of the patients were febrile, and constitutional symptoms were frequent. Nine patients had severe medical illness. Five patients developed acute gout 2–4 days after surgery. A change in medication in the past 2 weeks was noted in 11 cases. A mean of about 4 joints per patient was involved. Serum uric acid levels were elevated in 20 patients at the time of the acute attack, and all but 1 of the 17 patients studied were hyperuricemic at some time. Synovial fluids appeared inflammatory or contained crystals in all but 2 of 41 cases.

Indomethacin was the most commonly used drug. All patients responded within 48 hours, and most of them within 24 hours of the start of treatment. Acute gout recurred during a mean follow-up of 14 months in 20 of 33 patients. Nine serious drug reactions occurred in 8 patients given nonsteroidal antiinflammatory drugs. Two patients died of gastrointestinal hemorrhage, and 1 died after perforation of a duodenal ulcer.

Gout should be kept in mind in patients presenting with acute polyarthritis. Patients with acute polyarticular gout respond promptly to antiinflammatory therapy, but serious drug reactions have occurred and have caused deaths and prolonged hospitalizations. The risk of serious drug toxicity necessitates careful continued monitoring of these patients.

▶ [Classic monoarticular acute gouty arthritis—onset sudden, intensity severe, resolution complete—is difficult to misdiagnose, particularly if it involves the bunion joint (first metatarsophalangeal joint; podagra). When multiple joints are affected in a complex medical setting, as was often the case here, the diagnosis is often missed. And yet in retrospect there were frequent clues that might have led sooner to the

(58–1) Ann. Rheum. Dis. 42:117–122, April 1983.

search for urate crystals in synovial fluid. There was a history of intermittent acute arthritis highly suggestive of gout in 85% of these 41 patients. Sixty-one percent had prior polyarticular attacks, but the first attack was polyarticular in only 12% (lower than the 27%–44% in previous reports). Fifty-six percent had documented hyperuricemia, and 39%, tophi. One or more of these clues were present in all 19 cases not recognized initially as gout. The key to diagnosis is a lower threshold of suspicion for gout in patients with acute polyarthritis.] ◀

58–2 **Leukotriene B_4, an Inflammatory Mediator in Gout.** Leukotriene B_4 (LTB_4) is an arachidonic acid metabolite and a potent cytotoxin that is generated by human polymorphonuclear leukocytes (PMNs) exposed to inflammatory stimuli. It enhances the ability of leukocytes to penetrate the vascular endothelium, stimulates their movement toward inflammatory foci, causes release of lysosomal enzymes, and interacts with vasodilatory prostaglandins to produce increased vascular permeability. S. A. Rae, E. M. Davidson, and M. J. H. Smith (King's College Hosp. Med. School, London) sought LTB_4 in gouty effusions obtained from the knee joints of 6 men with gout; they also studied specimens from 12 patients with rheumatoid arthritis and 9 with osteoarthritis. In addition, the release of LTB_4 from human PMNs exposed to monosodium urate (MSU) crystals was measured.

TABLE 1.—LEUKOTRIENE B_4 CONTENT OF SYNOVIAL FLUID

Group	No. of patients	LTB_4 (means and ranges) In whole specimen (ng)	Concentration (ng ml^{-1})
Osteoarthritis	9	1·2 (0– 5·2)	0·10 (0–0·4)
Rheumatoid arthritis	12	5·0 (0–17·2)	0·34 (0–1·5)
Gout	6	28·4 (2·5–88·3)*	2·70 (0·2–7·4)*

*Results significantly different from those of either osteoarthritis or rheumatoid arthritis groups.
(Courtesy of Rae, S.A., et al.: Lancet 2:1122–1123, Nov. 20, 1982.)

TABLE 2.—METABOLISM OF EXOGENOUS LEUKOTRIENE B_4 BY HUMAN PERIPHERAL BLOOD POLYMORPHONUCLEAR NEUTROPHILS IN EITHER ABSENCE OR PRESENCE OF MONOSODIUM URATE

Exp. no.	Unchanged LTB_4 (ng) PMNs alone	PMNs+MSU*
1	30	88
2	42	86
3	13	21
4	42	100
5	54	79
6	44	64
Mean±SD	37·5±14·2†	73·0±28·1†

*Results corrected by subtraction of 11 ng to allow for effect of MSU on biosynthesis of LTB_4.
†Significantly different.
(Courtesy of Rae, S.A., et al.: Lancet 2:1122–1123, Nov. 20, 1982.)

(58–2) Lancet 2:1122–1123, Nov. 20, 1982.

Synovial fluid specimens from the patients with gout contained significantly higher concentrations of LTB_4 than specimens from patients with other rheumatic conditions (Table 1). When the results were corrected to allow for biosynthesis of the leukotriene induced by the inflammatory stimulus, preincubation with MSU crystals was seen to cause PMN suspensions to convert significantly less added LTB_4 to its biologically inactive metabolites (Table 2).

These findings suggest that LTB_4 is an important chemical mediator of acute gouty attacks. Monosodium urate crystals may not only act as an inflammatory stimulus for the production of LTB_4 by PMNs in gouty effusions, but may also hinder disposal of the leukotriene, causing it to persist. The leukotriene consequently may function as an important cytotactic mediator in acute gouty attacks, being both produced by and acting on the inflammatory leukocytes.

▶ [Once acute gouty arthritis (or any acute inflammation, for that matter) gets underway, it should be no surprise to find evidence for participation of a variety of inflammatory mediators (kinins, complement components, clotting factors, and so forth)—a rounding up of "the usual suspects," so to speak. For a proper pathogenetic analysis, however, we need to know how things get started, before general recruitment of mediators has begun. And any initiator worthy of the name will have to work within the uniqueness of gouty inflammation, a process that seems driven by the interaction of urate crystal and polymorphonuclear leukocyte, and which responds, especially early, to colchicine, a generally weak antiinflammatory agent.

There is already one favored candidate for early mediator of gouty inflammation, an 8,400-dalton glycoprotein chemotactic factor generated by the addition of urate crystals to PMNs and exquisitely sensitive to inhibition by colchicine.[1] Thus colchicine would break a vicious cycle of phagocytosis of crystals, generation of chemotactic activity, and further infiltration of leukocytes. Now we have a second candidate, LTB_4, a product of the lipoxygenase pathway of arachidonic acid metabolism. Not only do urate crystals appear to generate this material from PMN membrane phospholipid, they also seem to inhibit its breakdown. For me, a major test of the relevance of LTB_4 in acute gouty arthritis will be the effect of colchicine on its generation or function.] ◀

58–3 **Ethanol-Induced Hyperuricemia: Evidence for Increased Urate Production by Activation of Adenine Nucleotide Turnover.** Alcohol consumption long has been associated with hyperuricemia and the precipitation of acute gouty arthritis. Jason Faller and Irving H. Fox (Univ. of Michigan) attempted to determine whether ethanol increases the serum urate level by reducing uric acid excretion, by increasing its production, or by both mechanisms. Six patients with gouty arthritis and normal renal function received ethanol orally in a dose of 1.8 gm/kg of body weight every 24 hours for 8 days, or intravenously at a rate of 0.25–0.35 gm/kg/hour for 2 hours. Drugs that alter uric acid metabolism were discontinued 2 weeks before the study, and 5 patients received an isocaloric, purine-free diet. Ethanol infusion studies were begun 3 days after the infusion of 8-^{14}C-adenine.

The mean serum urate concentration increased from 8.4 to 10.1 mg/dl during oral ethanol intake; the whole-blood lactate, from 1.3 to 3.1 mmole. Urinary oxypurine levels increased markedly. Urate clearance rose to 145% of the baseline value. The daily uric acid turnover

(58–3) N. Engl. J. Med. 307:1598–1602, Dec. 23, 1982.

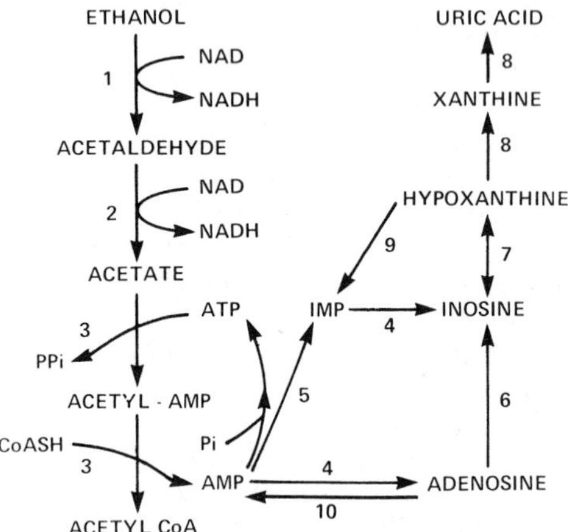

Fig 58–1.—Proposed mechanism for accelerated turnover of adenosine triphosphate (ATP) during ethanol administration. Ethanol is converted to acetate. Formation of acetylcoenzyme A (acetyl CoA) consumes ATP. If the small portion of adenosine monophosphate (AMP) that is formed is not salvaged back to ATP, AMP may be degraded, leading to increased production of oxypurines (hypoxanthine and xanthine) and uric acid. Adenosine could stimulate ATP production by being converted to AMP. Number *1* denotes alcohol dehydrogenase; *2*, aldehyde dehydrogenase; *3*, acetyl-CoA synthase; *4*, 5′-nucleotidase; *5*, AMP deaminase; *6*, adenosine deaminase; *7*, purine nucleoside phosphorylase; *8*, xanthine oxidase; *9*, hypoxanthine-guanine phosphoribosyltransferase; *10*, adenosine kinase; *IMP*, inosine monophosphate; *NAD*, nicotinamide adenine dinucleotide; *NADH*, reduced NAD; *Pi*, inorganic phosphate; *PPi*, inorganic pyrophosphate. (Courtesy of Faller, J., and Fox, I.H.: N. Engl. J. Med. 307:1598–1602, Dec. 23, 1982; reprinted by permission of The New England Journal of Medicine.)

increased to 170% of baseline during the long-term oral ethanol study. The uric acid pool size showed only a small increase. In the ethanol infusion study, the serum urate concentration, urate clearance, and urinary uric acid excretion were not markedly changed. Urinary activity from the adenine nucleotide pool increased to 127%–149% of baseline. Urinary oxypurine levels increased as much as 415% over baseline. The mean peak blood ethanol level during the infusion was 105 mg/dl.

Ethanol appears to increase urate synthesis by enhancing the turnover of adenine nucleotides, as shown in Figure 58–1. Accelerated turnover of adenosine triphosphate may contribute to the hepatotoxicity associated with ethanol ingestion. Adenosine and allopurinol prevent the development of ethanol-induced fatty liver in rats, presumably through enlargement of the adenine nucleotide pool. The conversion of reducing equivalents of reduced nicotinamide adenine dinucleotide to adenosine triphosphate by oxidative phosphorylation is facilitated. Pharmacologic manipulation of adenine nucleotide metabolism may open new approaches to the treatment of ethanol-induced liver disease.

▶ [Ethanol-induced hyperuricemia has been attributed to ethanol-induced hyperlacticacidemia[2] and the competition between these weak organic acids for renal tubular clearance. In the current study, hyperuricemia is attributed to increased urate production by activation of adenine nucleotide turnover, and not to decreased excretion. Both mechanisms may operate at appropriate ethanol levels. In the study summarized above, patients had blood ethanol levels of 150 mg/dl, vs. over 200 mg/dl in earlier studies. Thus binge drinking superimposed on chronic consumption of alcohol may add decreased excretion to increased production.] ◀

Chapter 58 References

1. Spilberg, I., Mandell B., Mehta J., Simchowitz L., Rosenberg D.: Mechanism of action of colchicine in acute urate crystal-induced arthritis. *J. Clin. Invest.* 64:775–780, 1979.
2. Lieber C.S., Jones D.P., Lowsowsky M.S., Davidson C.S.: Interrelation of uric acid and ethanol metabolism in man. *J. Clin. Invest.* 41:1863–1870, 1962.

59. Vasculitis

59–1 **Polymyalgia Rheumatica: A Ten-Year Epidemiologic and Clinical Study.** Tsu-Yi Chuang, Gene G. Hunder, Duane M. Ilstrup, and Leonard T. Kurland (Mayo Clinic and Found.) have reviewed the data on 67 women and 29 men from Olmsted County, Minnesota, seen with polymyalgia rheumatica in 1970–1979. Only those aged 50 years and older were included in the study. All had bilateral, moderately severe to severe aching and stiffness for one month or longer that involved at least two of the following: neck or torso, shoulders or proximal regions of the arms, and hips or proximal aspects of the thighs. Sedimentation rate was above 40 mm/per hour. Average annual incidence in the study population increased from about 20 per 100,000 in persons aged 50–59 years to a maximum of 112 per 100,000 in those aged 70–79.

Giant cell arteritis was identified in 15 patients. Seventeen patients had findings consistent with rheumatoid arthritis. The clinical features are given in the table. Shoulder involvement was a nearly constant finding. Proximal symptoms were most prominent, but many

CLINICAL FINDINGS IN 96 PATIENTS WITH POLYMYALGIA RHEUMATICA

Findings	Patients	
	n	%
Pain and morning stiffness	96	100
Shoulder	92	96
Hip	74	77
Neck	63	66
Upper arms	60	63
Thighs	52	54
Torso	43	45
Peripheral pain and stiffness	80	83
Lower extremities (knee to toe)	70	73
Upper extremities (elbow to finger)	54	56
Systemic symptoms and signs	52	54
Fever (> 38 °C)	12	13
Malaise, fatigue	29	30
Depression	14	15
Weight loss	14	15
Anorexia	13	14
Tenderness	37	39
Shoulder	25	26
Upper arms	23	24
Bicipital tendon-groove	16	17
Synovitis (concurrent)	11	12

(Courtesy of Chuang, T.-Y., et al.: Ann. Intern. Med. 97:672–680, November 1982.)

(59–1) Ann. Intern. Med. 97:672–680, November 1982.

patients had peripheral aching. Levels of α_2-globulin and serum albumin were altered less than the sedimentation rate in response to the inflammatory process. Fluorescent antinuclear antibody tests were positive in 11 of the 57 patients studied.

Corticosteroids were given to 54 patients. Eighty-three patients (86%) recovered by the end of the study. Median duration of disease was 11 months. Most patients improved within 3 months of the onset of disease. Recurrences were uncommon. The disease did not affect survival.

Polymyalgia rheumatica is a relatively common disorder in middle-aged and older persons. It generally follows a self-limited course. Patients given steroid therapy have responded most rapidly, but nonsteroidal antiinflammatory drugs have been used successfully, particularly in milder cases, and adverse reactions are less frequent than in steroid-treated patients.

▶ [There is great interest in the literature in the syndrome of polymyalgia rheumatica, its proper management, and its relationship to giant cell (temporal; cranial) arteritis. The current authors used a centralized diagnostic index for Olmsted County, Minnesota, to study the epidemiology of polymyalgia rheumatica seen in that population during a 10-year period. That retrieval system has been shown previously to identify practically everyone from the county who has any significant illness. The advantages of reviewing unselected cases, uninfluenced by referral patterns, are clear.

Polymyalgia rheumatica is not rare. The average annual incidence of 53.7 cases per 100,000 persons approaches that of cases in the same age range (over 50 years) presenting with definite or classic rheumatoid arthritis (77 per 100,000 in Olmsted County); rheumatoid arthritis is the most common chronic inflammatory rheumatic disease.

Forty-two of the 96 patients were treated without corticosteroids, most of them with aspirin alone (8–24 300-mg tablets per day). However, of the 54 patients who did get corticosteroids (median initially, 20 mg/day; range, 5–100 mg/day), 37 had begun with aspirin or other nonsteroidal antiinflammatory drugs without a satisfactory response. The response to corticosteroid was quicker than to nonsteroidal agents in the first month of therapy, but by the end of 3 months of treatment, disease control as reflected in the erythrocyte sedimentation rate was similar in the two groups.

In this unselected population the incidence of giant cell arteritis was only 16%, lower than in some other studies. (In contrast, given giant cell arteritis, about 40% of patients at the same institution had the syndrome of polymyalgia rheumatica.[1]) Of temporal artery biopsies in 40 patients, 14 were positive; 13 of these 14 patients had signs or symptoms suggestive of an underlying arteritis. (The classic presentation is scalp pain or tenderness, headache or visual symptoms; sudden blindness is of primary concern.) Given the relative paucity of cases with apparent arteritis, the inclusion of polymyalgic rheumatica in a chapter on vasculitis is arguable.

The prognosis of polymyalgia rheumatica is generally good. Eighty-three of the 96 patients (86%) had recovered by the end of the study; they did so in a median of 11 months but with a big range (2–54 months). For patients given corticosteroids or nonsteroidal drugs other than aspirin, the end of the disease was defined as remission of symptoms and findings without treatment. For patients given aspirin, it was defined as complete or nearly complete remission of symptoms and normal laboratory findings, with patients on 6 or fewer aspirin daily. Recurrence was uncommon, and survival unaffected by the disease.] ◀

59–2 **Takayasu's Arteritis: A Hospital-Region-Based Study on Occurrence, Treatment, and Prognosis.** Takayasu's arteritis (TA) is an arteritis of autoimmune origin that affects the aorta and its main branches and occasionally the pulmonary artery. A. Urban Waern, P.

(59–2) Angiology 34:311–320, May 1983.

Andersson, and A. Hemmingsson (University Hosp., Uppsala, Sweden) examined the occurrence of TA on the basis of hospital-treated cases seen in a defined area of Sweden during an 8-year period. Only cases of idiopathic TA confirmed by aortography were included. (Estimated yearly prevalence of TA in this region was 0.64 per 100,000 patients in 1969–1976. The study area consists of 1.25 million residents.)

Fifteen cases of TA were diagnosed, all in women. Mean age at diagnosis was 42 years. The sedimentation rate was elevated in all but 2 patients. Lesions were most frequent in the subclavian arteries; only 2 patients had aortic involvement. Most patients presented with fatigue and fever. Initially, steroid therapy equivalent to 30 mg of prednisolone daily was given to 6 subjects, with a mean maintenance dose of 5 mg daily. Four patients also received azathioprine in a maintenance dose of 100 mg daily. Two subjects had a good and 2 had a fair response. One patient had a Dacron graft placed between the aorta and left subclavian artery.

Six patients died a mean of 11 years after diagnosis. All but 1 of them had angina, and all but 1 had intermittent claudication. Death was sudden for 4 of the 6. At autopsy, 2 patients had pathologic changes of the great vessels that were consistent with TA.

Total aortography is necessary to properly evaluate patients with TA. Six of the present 15 patients have died. Those who died were more likely to have been hypertensive and hypercholesterolemic and were more likely to have smoked than those who survived. Treatment with steroids and azathioprine appear to improve the prognosis.

▶ [Takayasu's arteritis (pulseless disease) is a chronic obliterative large-vessel disorder distinguished by ischemic features that relate to the site of obstruction, e.g., diminished or weak arterial pulsations, low blood pressure, and muscular weakness in the arms (hence the term "reversed coarctation of the aorta") in the aortic arch syndrome. However, there are early or overlapping constitutional or rheumatic complaints that include fever, fatigue, polyarthralgia, and myalgia, as well as nonspecific laboratory findings typical of inflammatory disease: elevated erythrocyte sedimentation rate, leukocytosis, and hypergammaglobulinemia with elevation of IgA and IgM. Women with the disease far outnumber men. The peak age of onset is in the twenties. Although giant cells may be seen histologically, this disorder is usually easily separated from giant cell (cranial or temporal) arteritis, primarily a disease of the elderly, by age and by target vessels.

But "cranial" arteritis need not be limited to vessels of the head, and as older patients with aortic arch involvement are reported we can expect to see cases in which the distinction begins to blur. An unusual aspect of the 15 cases of Takayasu's arteritis reported here is that the mean age at diagnosis (42 years) was substantially higher than in other series; 3 patients were over 60 years of age. Of these 3, all had either occlusive or stenotic lesions of both right and left subclavian arteries; the eldest (age 66) also had stenosis (not examined histologically) of the right common carotid artery.] ◀

59–3 **Cellular Sensitivity to Collagen in Thromboangiitis Obliterans.** Thromboangiitis obliterans, or Buerger's disease, is an occlusive arterial disease that affects the medium and small arteries of young male smokers and often causes severe disability or necessitates amputation. The cause of the disease is unknown, but its association

---

(59–3) N. Engl. J. Med. 308:1113–1116, May 12, 1983.

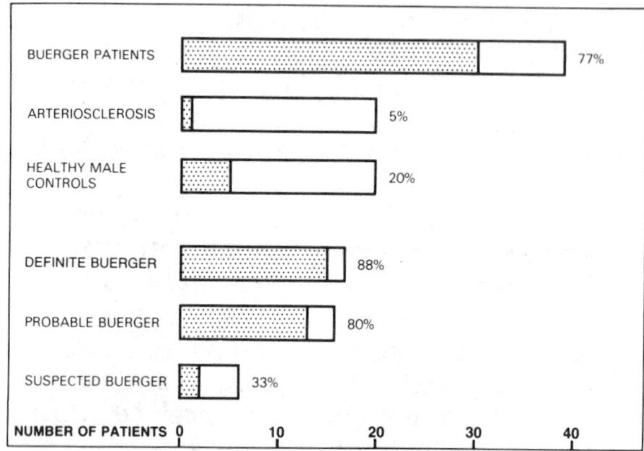

Fig 59–1.—Responses to type I or type III collagen (or both) in 3 groups studied *(upper part)* and according to clinical severity of Buerger's disease *(lower part)*. Stippled areas represent percentages of positive responses. (Courtesy of Adar, R.: N. Engl. J. Med. 308:1113–1116, May 12, 1983; reprinted by permission of The New England Journal of Medicine.)

with certain histocompatibility antigens suggests that it may be a distinct immunogenetic entity. Raphael Adar, Moshe Z. Papa, Zamir Halpern, Mark Mozes, Shmuel Shoshan, Batya Sofer, Heidy Zinger, Molly Dayan, and Edna Mozes (Israel) examined the cellular and humoral immune responses to native human collagen types I and III, which are constituents of blood vessels, in 39 patients with Buerger's disease. Twenty men with arteriosclerosis obliterans and 20 healthy men also were studied. Cell-mediated sensitivity to the collagens was measured with an antigen-sensitive thymidine-incorporation assay. Serum samples were tested for anticollagen activity with a solid-phase binding assay.

The ratio of thymidine incorporation in the presence of antigen to that in its absence with both type I and type III collagens was significantly higher in the patients with Buerger's disease than in either control group. Positive responses were more frequent as the clinical picture of Buerger's disease became more typical (Fig 59–1). Nearly half the serum samples from patients with Buerger's disease had low but significant antibody activity. No antibody activity was detected in either control group.

There appears to be a distinct etiologic factor in thromboangiitis obliterans. The findings suggest that it may be possible to distinguish immunologically between thromboangiitis obliterans and arteriosclerosis obliterans. Further studies are needed to establish the role of the immune system in Buerger's disease and its relation to cigarette smoking.

▶ [As is pointed out in an accompanying editorial,[2] no other occlusive peripheral arterial disease has the same predisposition for young (heavy-smoking) men, affects the small and medium-sized arteries of the wrist and hand with almost the same frequency as those of the leg and foot, and is accompanied so often by superficial thrombophlebitis (about 40% of cases). Diagnosis is more difficult when a patient is over 40 years of age or a woman, especially without a history of phlebitis, and a specific noninvasive diagnostic test would be welcome.

In the present series, a positive test response (77%; see Fig 59–1) seemed helpful for differentiation of these patients from those with arteriosclerosis (only 5% positive). Specificity is another matter. One in five healthy male controls had positive responses, and no control group with other vasculitides was offered. Still more problematic is the relationship of cell-mediated sensitivity to collagen, to the *initiation* of the vascular abnormality in thromboangiitis obliterans; the immune reactivity may be secondary and may contribute late or not at all to the inflammatory process. One might pursue this question by looking for immune reactivity early in the illness[3]; most of those in the current study had had the disease for several years. HLA associations of those with and without immune reactivity would also be of interest.

59–4 **Wegener's Granulomatosis: Prospective Clinical and Therapeutic Experience With 85 Patients for 21 Years.**

This article—which is summarized in Part Two, "The Chest," (see abstract 15–2)—provides an excellent record of long-term complete remissions in patients with Wegener's granulomatosis given cyclophosphamide and prednisone. I hope the good results do not discourage randomized trials that include less toxic medications; cyclophosphamide alone is associated with bone marrow suppression, hemorrhagic cystitis, hair loss, gonadal dysfunction, and neoplasia (each acknowledged and discussed by the authors). Without such trials the therapeutic community will be "locked in" to this regimen, for better or for worse. (This point was stressed in a subsequent letter to the journal.[4])

59–5 **Monoclonal Cryoglobulinemia With High Thermal Insolubility.** Although patients with monoclonal cryoglobulinemia often are asymptomatic, they may have Raynaud's phenomenon, purpura, cold urticaria, ulceration, or gangrene of the extremities on exposure to cold. Louis Letendre and Robert A. Kyle (Mayo Clinic and Found., Rochester, Minn.) report data on 2 patients with cryoprotein levels of 1–2 gm/dl who had purpura, ulceration, and sloughing of the skin because their cryoproteins precipitated at temperatures above 25 C. One is described below.

Woman, 43, developed a pruritic, erythematous rash of the lower extremities. After a walk in the snow, the lesions became purpuric and ulcerated. Small necrotic lesions were noted on the legs, cheeks, and forearms at admission. A monoclonal IgG κ cryoprotein that precipitated in vitro at 26 C was present in a concentration of 1.7 gm/dl. The cryocrit value was 21%. A marrow aspirate showed 60% myeloma cells. The patient was given melphalan and prednisone; but after exposure to the draft of an air conditioner, full-thickness skin necrosis of large areas of the legs and gangrene of the right calf and all digits of the right foot (Fig 59–2) developed, despite plasma-pheresis. Extensive plastic and orthopedic surgery failed, and the right leg was amputated. Histologic study showed no evidence of vasculitis. Subsequently, room temperatures in the patient's home were kept at 80 F. Melphalan and prednisone were given at 3-month intervals. An episode of leg weakness later was found to be due to a complete spinal block, and focal radiation therapy was delivered.

The 2 patients had severe hypersensitivity to cold exposure despite low amounts of monoclonal cryoproteins in the blood, presumably because of the high thermal insolubility of the cryoproteins. Seven similar patients have previously been described. The patients were younger at presentation than those with multiple myeloma or monoclonal gammopathy of unknown significance. Great care is needed to provide a warm environment for these patients, because even a slight draft

(59–4) Ann. Intern. Med. 98:76–85, January 1983.
(59–5) Mayo Clin. Proc. 57:629–633, October 1982.

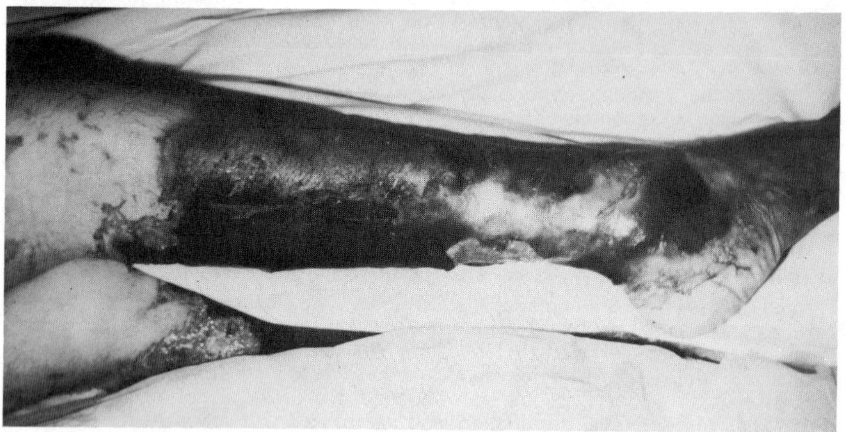

Fig 59–2.—Full-thickness skin necrosis of large areas of thigh and calf in patient with monoclonal cryoglobulinemia. (Courtesy of Letendre, L., and Kyle, R.A.: Mayo Clin. Proc. 57:629–633, October 1982.)

can lead to disastrous complications. Alkylating agents have given equivocal results in these cases.

▶ [On being cooled, each monoclonal cryoglobulin has a particular temperature at which it begins to precipitate, and there is a wide range of thermal insolubility among the cryoproteins that turn up in man. This property of the protein seems more important than its concentration. Thus, patients with 4–5 gm/dl of IgG or IgM monoclonal cryoproteins may be asymptomatic, whereas others, like the two reported here, may have 1–2 gm/dl, with catastrophic results. (Although the concentration is lower, this latter range is hardly insignificant; it approximates the total amount of IgG found in normal serum.)

Paradoxically, the patients most at risk—i.e., those with high thermal insolubility—are the ones whose cryoglobulins are most likely to be reported as lower than they actually are, unless the simple test for cryoprecipitates is done correctly, as it often is not. Properly, the blood is drawn into a warmed syringe and transferred directly to a water bath at 37 C, where it is allowed to clot. Only then is its serum placed at 4 C for 72 hours to encourage cryoprecipitation. If, instead, the blood is drawn and allowed to clot at room temperature, proteins of high thermal insolubility may precipitate and end up in the clot rather than in the serum to be tested.] ◀

Chapter 59 References

1. Calamia K.T., Hunder G.G.: Clinical manifestations of giant cell (temporal) arteritis. *Clin. Rheum. Dis.* 6:389–403, 1980.
2. Spittell J.A.: Thromboangiitis obliterans: an autoimmune disorder?, editorial. *N. Engl. J. Med.* 308:1157–1158, 1983.
3. Smolen J.S., Weidinger P., Menzel E.J.: Sensitivity to collagen in thromboangiitis obliterans, letter. *N. Engl. J. Med.* 309:857–859, 1983.
4. Steinberg A.D.: Assessing treatments with cyclophosphamide, letter. *Ann. Intern. Med.* 98:1026–1027, 1983.

60. Infectious Arthritis

► ↓ An article about Lyme disease[1] that appears in Part One, "Infectious Diseases," of this book (see abstract 10–1)—together with the article summarized below—illustrates the close relationship between infectious disease and the inflammatory side of rheumatology. In fact, the lines that separate them are sometimes mainly managerial. We tend to share disorders in which the infecting organism is immunogenic, but sufficiently unaggressive—at least initially—to allow the host's immune response to become a significant determinant of disease expression. Some examples of frankly infectious disorders that may turn up first in a rheumatologist's office are hepatitis B, rubella in adults, subacute bacterial endocarditis, and disseminated gonococcal disease. And one may suspect that a number of disorders are presently viewed as strictly rheumatologic only because an agent lurking somewhere in the tissues has not yet been identified. With these two articles we begin to share Lyme disease with Dr. Rogers and his colleagues in infectious diseases. This complex immune-mediated multisystem disorder, inflammatory or "rheumatic" in expression, is now shown to be caused by a spirochete.[1] ◄

60–1 **Treatment of the Early Manifestations of Lyme Disease.** Lyme disease, now known to be caused by a spirochete, is characterized by erythema chronicum migrans, which may be followed by inflammatory involvement of the nervous system, heart, or joints. Allen C. Steere, Gordon J. Hutchinson, Daniel W. Rahn, Leonard H. Sigal, Joseph E. Craft, Elise T. DeSanna, and Stephen E. Malawista (Yale Univ.) compared the efficacy of 3 different antibiotics in treating 108 adults with early Lyme disease who were seen in the preceding 3 summers. All patients were managed out of hospital. Each patient received 250 mg of phenoxymethyl penicillin or erythromycin or tetracycline 4 times daily for 10 days.

An increase in symptoms (Herxheimer-like reaction) in the first 24 hours of treatment was most frequent in patients given penicillin and tetracycline. Erythema chronicum migrans resolved more rapidly in patients given these antibiotics than in erythromycin-treated patients, and fewer of the former patients required retreatment. No patient treated with tetracycline developed major late manifestations (table). Late minor complications were frequent in all the treatment groups. Of 27 children treated with phenoxymethyl penicillin in 1980 to 1982, only 1 required retreatment because of persistent symptoms. Three children had major late complications.

All patients with severe illness were likelier than others to develop late symptoms. These patients more often had multiple skin lesions, marked arthralgias, and increased serum IgM levels at the onset of illness.

Tetracycline appears to be the most effective antibiotic for use in treating patients with early Lyme disease. Penicillin is the next most effective agent. Children may be given phenoxymethyl penicillin or (if they are allergic to penicillin) erythromycin. Currently, higher

(60–1) Ann. Intern. Med. 99:22–26, July 1983.

OUTCOME OF TREATMENT IN PATIENTS WITH ERYTHEMA CHRONICUM MIGRANS

	Children		Adults				
	1980-1982, Penicillin			1980-1981		1982, Tetracycline	
	Age 2-7 (n = 15)	Age 8-15 (n = 12)	Penicillin (n = 40)	Erythromycin (n = 29)	Tetracycline (n = 39)	10 Days (n = 25)	20 Days (n = 24)
				n			
No late disease	10	7	16	14	22	17	16
Minor late disease							
Facial palsy	0	1	1	1	0	1	0
Supraventricular tachycardia	0	0	0	0	1	0	0
Brief arthritis (< 2 weeks)	0	1	1	2	2	0	1
Musculoskeletal pain	3	2	20	11	14	8	7
Total*	3	4	20	11	17	8	8
Major late disease							
Myocarditis	0	0	0	0	0	0	0
Meningoencephalitis	1	0	1	2	0	0	0
Recurrent arthritis	1	1	2	3	0	0	0
Total*	2	1	3†	4†	0†	0	0

*Some patients had more than one later manifestation; thus, total number of patients may be less than total number of manifestations.

†None of 39 patients given tetracycline developed major late complications compared with 3 of 40 penicillin-treated patients and 4 of 29 given erythromycin (χ^2 with 2 degrees of freedom = 5.33, P = .07.)

(Courtesy of Steere, A.C., et al.: Ann. Intern. Med. 99:22–26, July 1983.)

dose parenteral penicillin regimens are under evaluation for late complications of Lyme disease. Minor late complications are very frequent in patients with Lyme disease; the pathogenesis of these symptoms is unclear.

▶ [For the early treatment of Lyme disease—i.e., at the time of the skin lesion (erythema chronicum migrans) which is the best marker of clinical onset—oral tetracycline has become the drug of choice for adults, because no one who received it developed major late manifestations of disease: myocarditis, meningoencephalitis, or recurrent attacks of arthritis (see table). However, only 3 of 40 patients given oral penicillin developed such complications, and patients who received any of the 3 oral antibiotics did much better than untreated patients studied earlier. It may be that higher doses of penicillin are indicated in early treatment; high-dose parenteral penicillin is currently being evaluated for late manifestations of Lyme disease, when oral regimens have not worked.

Late manifestations designated as minor, were less dramatic than the major ones and generally without associated signs. Nevertheless, such late symptoms could be debilitating. They included recurrent headache or pain in joints, tendons, bursae, or muscle—often accompanied by lethargy—or simply fatigue. These late problems were well represented in all 3 treatment groups and occurred especially in the patients who were sickest at disease onset. In 2 patients, symptoms did not respond to high-dose intravenous penicillin. The subsequent course of this group will be of interest; their symptoms could result from a sequestered or altered causative agent, from retained antigen that is difficult to degrade, or from autoimmunity.] ◀

60–2 **Concentrations of Some Antibiotics in Synovial Fluid After Oral Administration, With Special Reference to Antistaphylococcal Activity.** Septic arthritis is an important complication of joint disease, especially rheumatoid arthritis, and *Staphylococcus aureus* is by far the most common cause of septic arthritis. It is often resistant to penicillin. M. A. Sattar, S. P. Barrett, and M. I. D. Cawley (Southampton, England) examined the penetration of several antibiotics into synovial fluid after oral administration in 20 patients, aged 24–80 years, with knee effusions requiring diagnostic or therapeutic aspiration. Twelve effusions were due to rheumatoid arthritis or other

(60–2) Ann. Rheum. Dis. 42:67–74, February 1983.

inflammatory arthropathies. Sodium fusidate, flucloxacillin, amoxicillin, and cephradine were given in conventional oral dosages for 1 day. Seven patients received 250 mg of amoxicillin every 8 hours; 6 received 500 mg of cephradine every 6 hours; 6 received 250 mg of flucloxacillin every 6 hours; and 6 received 500 mg of sodium fusidate every 8 hours. Synovial fluid was sampled serially over 36 hours through an indwelling cannula.

Satisfactory antistaphylococcal concentrations were achieved in synovial fluid with sodium fusidate and amoxicillin, but cephradine often failed to reach the minimal inhibitory concentration for *S. aureus,* and the penetration of flucloxacillin was unpredictable. There was wide interpatient variation in both serum and synovial fluid concentrations of the antibiotics. The variation appeared to be independent of the underlying disease and the severity of inflammation. Synovial fluid antibiotic concentrations could not be related to clinical or laboratory indices of inflammation.

Sodium fusidate given orally appears to be appropriate in the initial treatment of nonresistant staphylococcal joint infections, although resistance may develop during treatment. Penicillin G may be appropriate in infections due to a penicillin-sensitive *Staphylococcus.* Amoxicillin and ampicillin can serve as second antistaphylococcal agents, or as first-line drugs if the nature of infection is unknown. Synovial fluid antibiotic concentrations should be estimated if possible to insure that there is adequate penetration into the joint. It is probably best to give antibiotics parenterally in the early stages of infection or orally in dosages greater than those usually recommended.

▶ [In my opinion oral antibiotics as initial therapy for staphylococcal arthritis are a prescription for disaster. Staphylococci and other nongonococcal infections can tear up a joint in short order. On x-ray, only soft tissue swelling is likely to be seen during the first week, but evidence of loss of articular cartilage and erosion of bone may appear rather soon thereafter in patients treated inappropriately. Successful management depends primarily on early institution of appropriate antimicrobial therapy and effective drainage of the joint space. To this end, when bacterial arthritis is suspected, prompt joint aspiration and both Gram stain and culture of synovial fluid are imperative; most nongonococcal bacteria will be recovered. When gram-positive grape-like bacterial clusters are seen, one assumes infection with penicillin-resistant staphylococci and treats accordingly, until the sensitivities are back.

Where delay in effective management can lead rapidly to permanent structural damage, oral therapy, with the attendant problems of compliance, absorption, and widely variable eventual concentrations in the joint, seems strongly ill-advised. (Gonococcal arthritis is different; the milder course and the usual rapid response to therapy make oral regimens acceptable, especially before significant effusion has developed.[2]) For nongonococcal arthritis, antibiotics should continue to be given parenterally,[3] often in high doses, for 2–4 weeks depending on the clinical situation and the response.] ◀

Chapter 60 References

1. Steere A.C., Grodzicki R.L., Kornblatt A.N., Craft J.E., Barbour A.G., Burgdorfer W., Schmid G.P., Johnson E., Malawista S.E.: Spirochetal etiology of Lyme disease. *N. Engl. J. Med.* 308:733–740, 1983.
2. Masi A.T., Eisenstein B.I.: Disseminated gonococcal infection (DGI) and gonococcal arthritis (GCA): clinical manifestations, diagnosis, complica-

tions, treatment, and prevention. *Semin. Arthritis Rheum.* 10:173–197, 1981.

3. Rosenthal J., Bole G., Robinson W.D.: Acute non-gonococcal infectious arthritis: evaluation of risk factors, therapy, and outcome. *Arthritis Rheum.* 23:889–897, 1980.

61. Other Topics

61–1 **Pancreatitis With Arthropathy and Subcutaneous Fat Necrosis: Evidence for Pathogenicity of Lipolytic Enzymes.** The occurrence of peripheral fat necrosis in occasional cases of pancreatic disease is not understood. H. Alexander Wilson, Ali D. Askari, Dewey H. Neiderhiser, A. Myron Johnson, Brian S. Andrews, and Lansing C. Hoskins attempted to clarify the relation of lipolytic enzymes to peripheral tissue injury in a patient with pancreatitis and disseminated fat necrosis.

Man, 48, was admitted to the Cleveland VA Medical Center 6 weeks after developing pain and erythema of the right foot and painful swelling of both ankles, followed by intermittent fever and polyarthralgia. Nontender erythematous nodules appeared on the chest and legs, and a biopsy showed fat cell ghosts characteristic of pancreatitis-induced fat necrosis. Serum amylase level was 1,260 Somogyi units/dl; serum lipase level was 34 Sigma-Tietz units/ml. Fat globules were identified in an aspirate from a knee effusion. No specific pancreatic lesion was identified. New crops of subcutaneous nodules developed despite treatment for pancreatitis that included tetracycline, a lipase inhibitor. The patient died in respiratory insufficiency. At autopsy a pancreatic pseudocyst was found along with extensive fat necrosis involving the peripancreatic, renal pelvic, and retroperitoneal fat tissue. Bilateral bronchopneumonia also was observed.

A marked increase in lipids was found in the synovial fluid of this patient, due entirely to elevation of the nonesterified fatty acid (NEFA) fraction. Lipids in the aspirate of a subcutaneous nodule also were chiefly nonesterified. Serum fatty acid values and NEFA fractions were basically normal. Activity of serum lipolytic and proteolytic enzymes was persistently elevated. No proteinase inhibitor was detected, and there were no significant immunologic abnormalities.

Selective necrosis of fat cells is the pathologic hallmark of this syndrome. A relatively unique lipid array in the fat cell membranes may permit enzyme adsorption, or a connection between the fat cells and vascular lumens provided by a continuous membrane leaflet may be responsible for the selective fat cell necrosis. The best approach is to identify a remediable pancreatic lesion. Once extensive fat necrosis is present, infection even by relatively drug-sensitive bacteria becomes difficult to treat.

▶ [Pancreatic disorders of various kinds—especially pancreatitis (often with pseudocyst) and acinar cell (exocrine) carcinoma—are in rare cases associated with a syndrome of fever, subcutaneous fat necrosis (nodular panniculitis), periarticular and articular inflammation, and sometimes visceral effusions and osseous intramedullary fat necrosis. Selective necrosis of fat cells is the pathologic hallmark of this syndrome. The patient described here had not only persistent serum elevations of phos-

(61–1) Arthritis Rheum. 26:121–126, February 1983.

pholipase A, trypsin, and, as previously reported, lipase, but also high levels of hydrolyzed fatty acids in synovial fluid and in a subcutaneous nodule, i.e., evidence of lipolytic activity in involved tissues. Two additional patients with this syndrome and with markedly elevated synovial fluid concentrations of free fatty acids were reported in the same issue.[1] That article emphasized the known phlogisitic potential of free fatty acids in concentrations that exceed the binding capacity of albumin. (Recall for example acne, in which resident bacteria *(Propionibacterium acne)* provide the lipases that break down triglycerides in sebum to form irritating free fatty acids.) Like Trousseau's migratory thrombophlebitis, this unusual syndrome serves as a signpost pointing to pancreatic disease that is often occult.] ◀

61–2 **Lines of T Lymphocytes Induce or Vaccinate Against Autoimmune Arthritis.** Adjuvant arthritis (AA) is a model of human rheumatoid arthritis induced in rats by a single intradermal injection of killed *Mycobacterium tuberculosis* in complete Freund's adjuvant. An autoimmune process involving T lymphocytes appears to be responsible for the development of AA. Joseph Holoshitz, Yaakov Naparstek, Avraham Ben-Nun, and Irun R. Cohen examined the pathophysiologic nature of autoimmune arthritis by isolating lines of effector T lymphocytes from rats in which AA was induced with *M. tuberculosis* in adjuvant. Lines of T cells reactive to the purified protein derivative of *M. tuberculosis* and to the whole bacterium and a line reactive to type II collagen were isolated.

Irradiated rats inoculated intravenously with the cell line reactive to *M. tuberculosis* developed arthritis. Unirradiated recipients did not develop arthritis, but these rats were resistant to subsequent attempts to induce AA, as were rats recovering from cell-mediated arthritis. Lines of T lymphocytes selected for responsiveness to other antigens had no effect.

A line of T lymphocytes responsive to bacteria or to type II collagen can both induce autoimmune arthritis and serve as a vaccinating agent. That irradiated rats acquired resistance to active AA suggests that the mechanism responsible for vaccination may be resistant to irradiation. Rheumatoid arthritis, although apparently arising spontaneously, may be triggered by an environmental agent, possibly infective, that initiates a self-perpetuating autoimmune process.

▶ [In an earlier study, some of the same workers isolated and propagated in culture a T lymphocyte that reacts against myelin basic protein and which, injected into syngeneic animals, causes the disease associated with that material: experimental autoimmune encephalomyelitis. When they attenuated the lymphocyte's virulence (with irradiation or with mitomycin C) the resultant "vaccine" no longer produced the disease, and it protected animals against its virulent counterpart (1983 YEAR BOOK OF MEDICINE, p. 667). Thus they prevented an autoimmune disease by treating a specific aggressor cell as though it were an infectious agent.

With some differences, they have now applied this procedure to adjuvant arthritis in rats, a transient inflammatory disorder induced by complete Freund's adjuvant (CFA). This time they used a T-lymphocyte cell line from rats immunized with CFA, a line with proliferative reactivity to the tubercle bacillus (which is what imparts "completeness" to incomplete [i.e., oil alone] Freund's adjuvant). This cell line did not produce the disease in rats unless the latter were first irradiated. (Irradiation is not necessary in CFA-induced disease, but it does increase host susceptibility.) Conclusion: specific T lymphocytes reactive against *M. tuberculosis* can induce autoimmune

(61–2) Science 219:56–58, Jan. 7, 1983.

arthritis, and suppressor mechanisms sensitive to radiation can participate in the regulation of arthritis.

In the study abstracted above, they looked for a vaccination effect by challenging rats with CFA 35 days after inoculation of the cell line. They found 100% protection, independent of previous irradiation of the animals. Given the intense current interest in the triggering of rheumatic conditions by known or unknown infectious agents, their second conclusion is worthy of special note: autoimmune effector T lymphocytes can be isolated by their response to bacterial antigens, and such cells can vaccinate against experimental arthritis.] ◀

61–3 **Simian Stance: Sign of Spinal Stenosis.** Lumbar spinal stenosis can be difficult to diagnose if severe lumbar pain is not associated with the classic radicular radiation and with discrete neurologic deficits. Peter A. Simkin (Univ. of Washington) found that affected patients may attempt to relieve compression on the nerve roots by adopting a stooped posture with flexion of the hips, knees, and lower back. The resultant stance resembles the bipedal posture of anthropoid apes (Fig 61–1).

Fig 61–1.—A, standing chimpanzee. Lumbar lordotic curve is absent, and hips and knees remain flexed, with center of gravity *(dashed line)* falling in front of hips and behind knees. **B,** patient with severe spinal stenosis also stands with hips, knees, and lumbar spine in flexion. Bowed head is important in maintenance of balance. (Courtesy of Simkin, P.A.: Lancet 2:652–653, Sept. 18, 1982.)

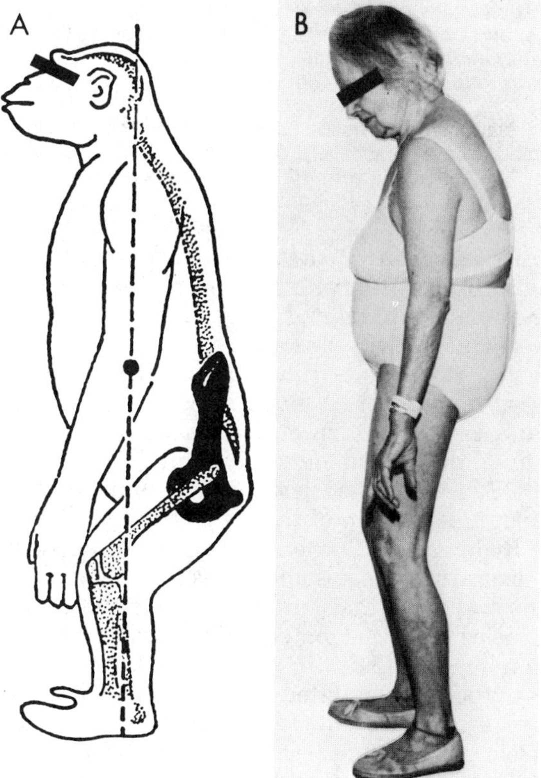

(61–3) Lancet 2:652–653, Sept. 18, 1982.

Woman, 80, presented with low back and buttock pain that was greatly worsened by standing and walking. The only neurologic abnormality was bilaterally absent Achilles tendon reflexes. Computed tomography showed severe spinal stenosis, with hypertrophied laminae and facet joints impinging on the subarachnoid space at many levels. Myelography showed a nearly complete block at the L4–5 level. Decompressive laminotomies restored the patient's ability to stand and walk erect.

Basal neural function may be preserved in patients with spinal stenosis who gradually alter their pattern of activities and posture to relieve pressure on the lumbar spinal nerve roots. Postural adaptations may prove inadequate when the patient is active. Downhill walking may make the symptoms worse, while uphill walking provides relief. The patient may seek relief by leaning forward and resting with the hands on the knees in a "leapfrog" position or by adopting the simian stance. The latter may be an early manifestation of spinal stenosis. Any patient with a simian stance should be thoroughly examined for lumbar spinal stenosis if disability progresses.

▶ [There is increasing awareness of lumbar spinal stenosis, an important and often surgically correctable cause of chronic disability; the term refers to any type of narrowing of the lumbosacral canal, nerve tunnels, or intervertebral foramina.[2] Compression may result from any number of factors, alone or in combination: central prolapse of a disk, hypertrophic changes within a narrowed spinal canal, angulation from loss of disk height, degenerative disk disease, Paget's disease of bone, spondylolysis and spondylolisthesis, and bony and ligamentous compression at the exit foramina. Patients present with lumbago, (sometimes bizarre) radicular symptoms, or neurogenic claudication that is often confused with the intermittent claudication of peripheral vascular disease.

The key to the relationship between posture and symptoms lies in further compression of the affected area by maneuvers that produce lumbar extension, and the reverse for flexion. Thus someone with difficulty walking downhill, or walking upright on the flat, may be comfortable walking uphill or exercising on a racing bicycle. The simian stance is a particularly graphic sign and reminder of this syndrome.] ◀

61–4 **Stimulation of Muscle Protein Degradation and Prostaglandin E_2 Release by Leukocytic Pyrogen (Interleukin-1): Mechanism for the Increased Degradation of Muscle Proteins During Fever.** Marked loss of body protein characteristically occurs in patients with fever, sepsis, and traumatic or burn injury, and a severe loss of body mass or temporary impairment of growth can result. Fever induced in rats by injection of *Escherichia coli* endotoxin accelerates protein breakdown and increases muscle production of prostaglandin E_2 (PGE_2), which is known to stimulate protein breakdown in muscle through activation of the lysosomal pathway. Vickie Baracos, H. Peter Rodemann, Charles A. Dinarello, and Alfred L. Goldberg (Boston) examined the possible role of leukocytic pyrogen, which signals the onset of fever and induces prostaglandin synthesis in the brain. Rat muscles were incubated with highly purified human leukocytic pyrogen, or interleukin-1.

Leukocytic pyrogen stimulated net protein degradation of 62%–118% in muscles incubated at 37 C. Proteolysis was increased, but the rat of muscle protein synthesis was unchanged. Muscle synthesis of PGE_2 was markedly stimulated by the pyrogen. Addition of indo-

---

(61–4) N. Engl. J. Med. 308:553–558, Mar. 10, 1983.

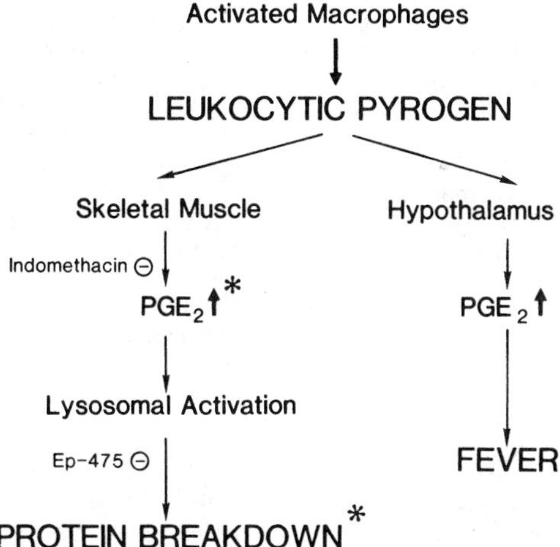

Fig 61–2.—Proposed mechanism for effects of leukocytic pyrogen in inducing fever and muscle protein breakdown. Asterisk indicates augmented response at febrile temperatures; *Ep-475,* inhibitor of lysosomal thiol proteases; *PGE₂*, prostaglandin E_2. (Courtesy of Baracos, V., et al.: N. Engl. J. Med. 308:553–558, Mar. 10, 1983; reprinted by permission of The New England Journal of Medicine.)

methacin prevented PGE_2 synthesis and eliminated the increase in proteolysis induced by leukocytic pyrogen. Accelerated protein breakdown also was blocked by an inhibitor of lysosomal thiol proteases. In muscles incubated at 39 C to simulate fever, protein breakdown increased, but addition of the pyrogen led to further marked increases in proteolysis and PGE_2 production.

Human leukocytic pyrogen can stimulate intralysosomal proteolysis in skeletal muscle by increasing PGE_2 production. It is possible that the marked increase in PGE_2 production, especially at higher temperatures, can explain the myalgia that accompanies many infections and that responds to cyclooxygenase-inhibiting drugs. A proposed scheme is illustrated in Figure 61–2. Cyclooxygenase inhibitors may be useful in treating febrile patients in negative nitrogen balance.

▶ [Grandmother used cyclooxygenase inhibitors—her favorite was aspirin—to lower body temperature and to eliminate discomfort. Hippocrates knew that fever and wasting go hand in hand. Now we learn that fever and muscle protein degradation share a common mediator, interleukin-1.

Interleukin-1 refers to a protein (or closely related group of proteins) that is produced by the monocyte/macrophage (and probably by certain other cell types) in response to such stimuli as microbial agents, bacterial endotoxin, and immune complexes. Its elucidation recalls the story of the blind men and the elephant; workers in different systems were describing different properties of this multipotent mediator, each with its own name. For example, leukocytic or endogenous pyrogen, lymphocyte activating factor, and leukocyte endogenous mediator, reflect the ability of what we now call interleukin-1 to promote fever, lymphocyte proliferation, and synthesis of acute-phase proteins in the liver, respectively.

Fever and wasting sound bad, but within limits, they may have survival value for the host. Skeletal muscle provides a metabolically dynamic protein bank and potential source of free amino acids, which are needed during stress for the synthesis of proteins required for both immunologic and nonimmunologic host defense mechanisms.[3] Branched-chain amino acids can be used by muscle as direct sources of energy. Others may travel to the liver and become substrates for acute-phase proteins or for gluconeogenesis. The additional glucose may then be used to initiate and sustain the increased oxygen consumption that accompanies fever. Fever meanwhile potentiates not only the breakdown of muscle protein (see abstract above) but also the production of immune reactants.[4] Both interleukin-1–induced T-cell proliferation and antibody production increase up to 20-fold when the cells are cultured at febrile (39 C), rather than at normal (37 C), temperatures. In short, interleukin-1 is a stress hormone with multiple, highly integrated effects which include the unique ability to provide an optimal body temperature for its activities.

Should we then give up aspirin, which blocks or dampens some of these apparently important functions? Not at all; aspirin is one of the great blessings of mankind. We must simply continue to use what grandmother, with less information, was using: clinical judgment.] ◀

Chapter 61 References

1. Simkin P.A., Brunzell J.D., Wiener D., Fiechtner J.J., Carlin J.S., Wilkens R.F.: Free fatty acids in the pancreatitic arthritis syndrome. *Arthritis Rheum.* 26:127–132, 1983.
2. Critchley E.M.R.: Lumbar spinal stenosis, editorial. *Br. Med. J.* 284:1588–1589, 1982.
3. Beisel W.R.: Mediators of fever and muscle proteolysis, editorial. *N. Engl. J. Med.* 308:586–588, 1983.
4. Atkins E.: Fever—new perspectives on an old phenomenon, editorial. *N. Engl. J. Med.* 308:958–960, 1983.

Cumulative Subject Index 1980–1984

This cumulative index gives the volume (year) and page locations of subjects included in the five most recent annual editions of the YEAR BOOK. It will accumulate with each subsequent edition by deletion of the earliest year's references. The volumes (years) appear in *italic* type, preceding the page numbers and separated from them by a colon.

A

B

C

D

F

G

H

I

M

Q

R

S

U

V

Z

Index to Authors

C

D

E

F

N

O

P

T

Z